SUSSEX SCHOOLS
IN THE
18th CENTURY

Schooling Provision,
Schoolteachers
and Scholars

by

JOHN CAFFYN

SUSSEX RECORD SOCIETY
Volume 81

Issued to members of the Society
for the years 1995 and 1996

Published 1998 by
Sussex Record Society,
Barbican House,
High Street,
Lewes,
East Sussex, BN7 1YE

ISBN 085445 042 4

Printed by Hobbs the Printers Ltd., Totton, Hampshire.

SUSSEX RECORD SOCIETY

VOLUMES ISSUED BY THE SOCIETY

Volumes marked with an asterisk can be obtained from the Hon. Secretary, Sussex Record Society, Barbican House, Lewes, East Sussex, BN7 1YE.

Volumes 1-68 are available on microfiche from Messrs. Chadwyck-Healey Ltd., The Quorum, Barnwell Road, Cambridge, CB5 8SW.

CONTENTS

ILLUSTRATIONS

The dustjacket design is based on an example of the penmanship of Charles New, a pupil at Tarring Academy, from his school workbook dated 1803. (WSRO Add MS 36773)

PRESTON near Brighthelmston

Preston near Brighthelmston by James Lambert, 1763.
The building in front of the church is Preston Manor, where Mrs Norton opened her girls' boarding school in 1796.   James Lambert (1725-88), a celebrated artist, taught music and painting at Lewes.   *(Royal Pavilion, Art Gallery, Brighton (Preston Manor))*

INTRODUCTION

The purpose of this volume is to provide a topographical guide to education in Sussex in the 18th century, and a comprehensive reference source for local, social and other historians. It brings together all the information we have about schooling in Sussex in the 18th century and, in doing so, it can contribute also to the wider field of the history of education, where the 18th century appears to have been much neglected and perhaps misunderstood.

The volume draws on a rich array of sources (see 'Note on Sources', pages 20-24). For the endowed grammar and charity schools, it draws on reports of the charity commissioners published 1819-40. For charity schools set up in the first quarter of the century, on the SPCK archives (which need to be used with care). For the development of private schools in the second half of the century, on numerous advertisements in surviving local papers. It draws also on invaluable contemporary records of particular schools - the managers' register of Mayfield charity school, 183 loose school lists of boys at Saunders' charity school at Rye, the Brighthelmston school book begun in 1701, the financial accounts of the Grey Coat and Oliver Whitby charity schools at Chichester, notebooks concerned with the charity schools at Sedlescombe and Petworth and with Rev Thankful Frewen's small private school at Northiam. Nevertheless, there are no comprehensive central records of 18th-century schools or schoolteachers,[1] and much of our knowledge derives from casual references in a great diversity of sources. For example, we know that there was a school at Chiddingly in the 1760s, but only from the printer's preface to a book of poems published by the schoolmaster. We know that Mr Wood kept a school at Newick in the early 1780s, but only because William Kenward in his journal, written when he was a Chelsea Pensioner and preserved in the family, gives an account of his schooling there. We know that James Sayer was a schoolmaster at Petworth from his probate inventory taken after his death in January 1726; that Thomas Waters of Houghton was a schoolmaster in 1762 from a property deed; that Mary Cornwell of Lewes was a schoolmistress from her will of 1800. We know from many parish records that the overseers paid for the schooling of individual pauper children on occasion throughout the century. We can glean details from diocesan subscription books and schoolmasters' licences, from personal and solicitors' accounts, from deeds and documents, diaries and letters. Clearly, the present volume will inevitably have missed some schooling references from such indirect sources; and omissions will necessarily arise from 'lost data'. There are two kinds of lost data - those concerning schools or teachers which were never entered in any record, and those once recorded in documents which have since been lost. (For an example of the latter, see the last paragraph in 'Note on Visitation Returns' on page 26.)

For ease of reference, the records in this volume have been arranged in three schedules:

Schedule 1   lists all schools and provisions for schooling in chronological order of reference under parishes or towns, listed in alphabetical order. (Towns comprising two or more parishes are here treated as a single centre.) After each school are listed: (a) all known teachers at the school (to permit cross-reference to Schedule 2); (b) notes giving the documentary source of all items relating to the school. To provide a frame of reference, the size of each parish/town is indicated by the number of families in 1717 or 1724 (where known)[2] and by the population in 1801.[3] It will be noted how small were the towns and villages in Sussex in the 18th century. At the end of the parishes/towns are listed, under 'Unplaced Schools', a few schools whose locations are at present unknown, and brief notes on 'Some schools outside Sussex that advertised in Sussex', which were directly competitive to the Sussex private schools.

This schedule includes almost 200 charity schools (of all types, including provision of charity schooling) and 400-500 private schools (depending on definitions).[4] It covers all the endowed grammar and charity schools and most, though perhaps not quite all, of the subscription and sponsored charity schools. It includes most of the Sunday schools set up in the last 15 years of the century. It will include all the principal private schools in the county, and a great many of the smaller private schools, including dame schools. It necessarily omits a large number of dame and petty schools that did not find a place in any surviving record, and probably one or two Sunday schools and workhouse schools, and a few small private schools kept by clergymen.

Schedule 2 lists, in alphabetical order, all known 18th-century school-masters and schoolmistresses, including specialist teachers, and summarises such biographical details as we have.

This schedule covers 700 schoolmasters and schoolmistresses. It will include all the masters and mistresses of the principal 18th-century schools in the county, and a great many teachers at lesser schools. It will omit a number of ushers and lesser teaching staff, and the dames and petty schoolmasters of schools for which there is no surviving record.

Schedule 3 lists, in alphabetical order, nearly 2,000 Sussex scholars of the 18th century. It therefore only covers a minority of the children who would have attended school in the course of the century. Most of the records derive from charity school lists. Nevertheless, the schedule does span the range of scholars, from paupers to aristocracy, and provides an important quantified base for the study of a number of educational issues (see page 14 below).

*   *   *   *   *   *   *   *

These 18th-century records must be read against the context of their times. There were a number of social factors that determined the ethos of the schools and set the parameters for any educational developments.

There were many fewer people about. The population of the whole county was only 160,000 by the end of the century - it was much smaller at the beginning. The larger towns were the size of our villages, villages were tiny. When we consider the number of schools operating in the course of the century against the size of the population, the educational effort becomes apparent.

The great divide of the 18th century was between rich and poor. It is probable that by the end of the century between 50% and 60% of the families in the county were poor.[5] In 1793 it was calculated that an honest labouring family in rural Sussex could not earn enough to keep them even at subsistence level.[6] The poor were dependent, to some extent always and in the hard winters and the inflationary years very much so, on the charity of the affluent. During the century this division between rich and poor was an accepted fact of life. Schooling was not seen as a means of achieving upward social mobility (though many feared that schooling the poor would lead to social unrest). As M.G.Jones has written: 'the conception of a liberal education found little place in the minds of the men and women who were responsible for the charity school movement. They envisaged, in accordance with the social philosophy of the age, a stratified society, based upon a rigid class system.'[7] At the beginning of the century the SPCK promoted schools where: 'Children are made tractable and submissive by being early accustomed to Awe and Punishment and Dutiful Subjection. From such timely Discipline the Publick may expect Honest and Industrious Servants.'[8] At the model girls' charity school at Newick, set up in 1771, the girls were to be taught reading, writing and needlework, and such other work as would 'make them useful servants'. We should be careful not to react wrongly to the word 'condescend': this now carries a pejorative meaning, it did not do so in the 18th century. When the *Sussex Weekly Advertiser* reported (5 January 1789), 'The attention shown to the poor children of the Brighthelmston Sunday-School, by the ladies who condescended to dine at their table on Christmas-day, was truly laudable', the action was indeed truly laudable.

With more than half the county impoverished, and almost a quarter in receipt of poor relief,[9] it is perhaps surprising that 'There was virtually no support in Sussex for the French Revolution when it broke out in 1789'.[10] The Lewes schoolmistress Hannah Adams held radical views, as did her protégé and later schoolmistress Elizabeth Hitchener, and presumably Elizabeth Ollive, a young schoolmistress who at 21 married the republican Thomas Paine (who later wrote *The Rights of Man*, with its blueprint for a welfare society 150 years ahead of its time). Radical Lewes schoolmasters included Paul Dunvan, sometime usher at the grammar school, who was named as a 'riotous' Radical at a town meeting in 1792, and whose anonymous *History of Lewes and Brighthelmston* (1795) was aggressively radical; John Button, a Philosophical Radical, who was allegedly listed in Pitt's own Black Book as a 'dangerous demagogue', but who denied being a

Leveller or a Republican; Edward Pugh, who supported the Advanced Radical William Green at the 1796 election. But throughout the century, notwithstanding compassion and philanthropy and a radical minority, the fundamental separation of rich and poor was an unchanging reality. This meant that all education had to be paid for, more or less directly, by the affluent. It was the motives of the rich that determined the education - if any - of the poor majority.

Almost all the charity schools and most of the private schools were Church of England schools. But there was a greater toleration of dissent in Sussex than in some other places. In the 1670s about a third of the population of Lewes were dissenters, and in the early 18th century probably more than a third of the population of Horsham.[11] The Brighton charity school (1701) was promoted by the bishop, was clearly an 'SPCK' school, and was under the control of the vicar, but from 1702 for almost 50 years the master was John Grover, an active Quaker all his life. One of the largest educational benefactions made in Sussex in the 18th century was by a Baptist, James Saunders, who endowed four charity schools; when the school at Rye was opened in 1721, the corporation, as governors, ruled:

> That the founder of the said school being a dissenter, and no persons either of the Church of England or of the Protestant dissenters being excluded by the founder's will from the same privilege with those of his own persuasion, no schooler or schoolers shall be required by the master to goe to any place of worship or to learn any catechism without the consent and approbation of his or their parents or guardians, soe as they goe to some place of worship on every Lord's Day.

In 1724 the Steyning churchwardens reported of the dissenting families in the parish, 'Many of the Children of these come to Church'. Dissenters were accepted in Church of England charity schools (eg. Brighton, Mayfield) and Sunday schools. At least 17 schoolmasters and mistresses were Baptists, and there were three other schools (at Rusper, Horsham and Ditchling) that were almost certainly Baptist. There were at least seven other nonconformist schools (including two Methodist and one (apart from a Sunday school) Countess of Huntingdon's Connexion). There were also three Roman Catholic schools, plus two others kept by Roman Catholics, and two Jewish schools.

The law was harsh. Under the 'Bloody Code', by 1765 about 160 offences carried the death penalty - though judges often mitigated death sentences before leaving the assizes.[12] In 1796 Thomas Johnston, a boy of 16, was sentenced to death at East Grinstead assizes for stealing a pony from a stable at Hailsham; he was reprieved before the judge left the town; then later received his Majesty's pardon, on condition of his being confined two years in Lewes's 'House of Correction'.[13] Nevertheless many were judicially killed. And when in January 1749 six ringleaders of a gang of smugglers were hanged at Chichester for torturing and murdering a revenue officer and his informer, their bodies were gibbeted in chains around the county for all to see - including the children.[14] In 1800 three men were hanged at Horsham, 'in the presence of upwards of a thousand spectators', for raping Miriam Bennet:[15] children would have been among the crowd. For theft of property, punishment was severe. In 1790 Thomas Peckham received over 300 lashes at Lewes for stealing a bushel of wheat.[16] In 1791 William Stevens, a servant lad at Wilbar's school in Brighton, stole two watches and sundry articles of wearing apparel and ran away; he was caught (at Chichester) and sentenced to transportation for seven years. In January 1801 Charles Field received the same sentence for stealing a quantity of wet linen from George Waller, a Horsham schoolmaster.

Frank McLynn has written: 'The level of routine physical violence in the eighteenth century was very high. Children were beaten in schools and within the family. There was great tolerance of cruelty, especially in spectator sports like prize-fighting, or in 'recreations' involving animals, like bear-baiting, goose-riding, or cock-fighting.'[17] (The young Collier boys of Hastings appear to have had their own cocks.)   To this list we can add bull-baiting (it is typical of the century that John Burgess of Ditchling, who recorded in his diary for 1788 a 'Bull Bait at Fryers Oake' when his dog took part and 'was Call'd the best', was a deeply religious man and a Baptist preacher);[18] and the vicious Shrove Tuesday 'sport' of 'cock scailing'. In his memoirs, James Spershott, a Baptist of Chichester and one time pastor there, gives a detailed description of this last 'unmanly and cruel' pastime, when tethered cocks were stoned to death ('... And thus their Legs are Broken and their Bodies Bruised in a shocking manner, and often when they appear to be dead, they put their Heads under Ground and bring them to and set them up again.')   But he added (he died in 1789):

> But Thanks be to Heaven, men of late are grown wiser, and have
> learnt to be more Mercifull, and this Cruel Practice is almost over
> in these parts ... [19]

As McLynn noted: '... there is much evidence that attitudes to violence began to change in the later eighteenth century.'[20] And in this violent age young children could walk several miles to school, often on their own, along the lanes and across lonely commons, without being molested.

Corporal punishment of children may have been an accepted part of life, but there is no evidence in the small Sussex schools of the tyrannies of the great public schools or the large boarding charity schools such as Christ's Hospital in London. Of the many thousand records in this volume there are only three that refer to boys being beaten: in 1759 Walter Gale at Mayfield recorded that the father of one of his boys (a private pupil) had quarrelled with him for correcting the boy 'for some enormous crimes', but in the end 'he confessed everything that the boy was beat for'; in a public petition against Steyning grammar school in 1816 one witness swore that he had been obliged to leave around 1780 because of harsh treatment, but this was the only such allegation and went back 36 years before the enquiry; at the end of the century, John Wooll at Midhurst grammar school banished the cane and introduced 'the more classical birch'. An unsubstantiated report (not included in the present Schedules because neither school nor master nor boy were identified) appeared in a local paper in 1789: 'We learn from Steyning, that one day last week a school-master at that place, beat one of his pupils so unmercifully with a stick, that the child's life was some time in the most imminent danger. The master, fearing the consequence of his cruelty, absconded soon after the affair. The child, our correspondent informs us, is now thought out of danger.'[21] It will be noted that the master was reported to have absconded: there were inhibitions against too harsh discipline. As far as Sussex schools went, a problem for charity day schools was ensuring attendance of the scholars, and with harsh or unjust treatment parents would have taken them away, while at the small private schools, as we shall see, parents expected gentle treatment of their children. Moreover, in the 18th century children sought the approbation of their parents and teachers; at his dame school, William Hersee was encouraged by the schooldame's smile for good work so that 'none to learn more cheerful toil'd', and later by promotion to head boy; prizes were beginning to be awarded for school work (as at Parrott's school at Petworth, and Midhurst grammar school) - rewards as well as punishments. For 525 children of Mayfield charity school we know the reasons why they left: only one was dismissed for misbehaviour.

Roy Porter has written of the century: 'What we have above all lost from the world we have lost is the stench.'[22] 'People almost never bathed';[23] dung and excrement were everywhere; sanitation was appalling. The opening of the Grey Coat charity school at Lewes in 1711 had been delayed 'by reason of the Small Pox wch 1000. people there have had, and of wch about 120. are dead'. In March 1715, at Oliver Whitby's charity boarding school at Chichester, eight of the 12 boys had the smallpox. One of the rules of Storrington charity school (c.1763) was that a child was to be 'forbidden the School' if 'found to have a Scald Head, or Vermin therein more than Common, or to be infected with the Itch': the phrase 'more than Common' is revealing. At Robertsbridge charity school (1796), every child was to be sent to school 'perfectly free from Vermin, their Hands and Face washed clean; and as neat in apparel as the Circumstances of their Parents will admit.' In the last quarter of the century the private boarding schools were much concerned to promote their healthy location, and to insist that the most careful attention would be paid to the health of their pupils.

The 18th century was harsh, but there was a lighter side. 'Georgian life bears witness to an infectious gaiety and sense of fun self-censored in certain ages.'[24] Dancing came into its own. Professor Plumb has written:

> [Dancing] trained both boys and girls in deportment, and the way one moved in the eighteenth century was a badge of one's social class...

> On nights of the full moon coaches and horses clattered towards the inns and assembly rooms of towns great and small, where attorneys, prosperous farmers and shopkeepers who had subscribed for the balls danced the night away. A new world of sound and song and dancing had come into being.[25]

Throughout the century dancing was available, as an optional extra, at virtually every boarding school, both for boys and girls (25 dancing masters are included in Schedule 2). Of a more modest pastime, the Lewes paper reported in 1799: 'The exercise of *skipping over a rope*, has lately become very fashionable with the

Boarding school Misses and other young Ladies of this town and neighbourhood.'[26]

* * * * * * * *

Against this background, we can consider the different types of school that were operating in the 18th century.

Charity schools
M.G. Jones drew attention to the 'charity school movement' of the early years of the 18th century, largely attributable to the activities of the SPCK.[27] Some later historians, such as J.Simon, have queried the significance of this;[28] and recent histories of education seem to have followed her revisionist approach. But in Sussex at least there was very definitely a 'charity school movement', and it was largely influenced by the SPCK. John Williams, bishop of Chichester 1696-1709, was a member of the SPCK. Bishop Thomas Manningham, who followed him, was also an SPCK supporter; before coming to Chichester he had promoted two schools at Windsor, and at his death in 1722 he left £100 to the boys' and girls' charity schools in Chichester. William Hayley, dean of Chichester, was another early SPCK subscriber, and had promoted a charity school in his previous parish in London.[28a] When the century began, there were in Sussex - apart from the free grammar schools - seven elementary charity schools, plus one provision for some charity schooling. In the first 25 years of the century, 32 charity schools were set up in the county, and eight provisions for charity schooling, or 40 new educational facilities in total. Some of these were small, some may not have lasted very long, but the momentum of the first quarter-century affected the whole of the rest of the century. The number of charity schools and provisions for charity schooling operating at some point in each quarter-century increased steadily throughout the century - from 48, to 60, to 72, to 85.[29]

There were three main types of charity school. (1) Subscription schools, where a number of people undertook to subscribe a certain amount each year; variants included the charity school at Mayfield, where the original subscriptions provided capital, the interest of which financed the school, and that at Robertsbridge, where subscribers could nominate one poor child to the school for each guinea subscribed. (2) Endowed schools, which were the most stable, but which could suffer problems: Edward Lightmaker's first trustees mismanaged or misappropriated the capital he had provided for his school at Horsted Keynes, so that after about 30 years nothing remained but the schoolhouse itself; and a number of trustees were taken to the court of Chancery for abusing their trusts, the corporations of Rye and Hastings among them. (3) Sponsored schools, financed by a single individual, often no doubt for evangelical or philanthropic motives but also sometimes for political motives.

But such categories were not always distinct: some subscription schools were later endowed; some endowed schools benefited also from subscriptions; subscription schools could become sponsored schools; sponsored schools could be later endowed by their benefactors. One characteristic of charity schools in Sussex

An ACCOUNT of the METHODS

Whereby the

CHARITY-SCHOOLS

HAVE BEEN

Erected and Managed,

And of the Encouragement given to them:

Together with

A PROPOSAL of Enlarging their Number, and Adding some WORK *to the Childrens Learning, thereby to render their Education more ufeful to the* Publick.

IT is manifeft, That a Chriftian and Ufeful Education of the Children of the POOR, is abfolutely neceffary to their Piety, Virtue, and honeft Livelihood.

'Tis alfo as plain and evident, That Piety, Virtue, and an honeft Way of Living, are not only of abfolute Neceffity to their Happinefs both *Here* and *Hereafter* ; but are neceffary alfo to the Eafe and Security of all other People whatfoever: In as much as there is no Body but may ftand in Need of their Help, or be liable to receive Injuries from them.

But that which ought more efpecially to be the Beginning, and End of Chriftian Charity, is the Glory of God, and the Good of Mankind.   And thefe great and moft defirable Ends cannot be by private Perfons more univerfally and effectually fecured, than by Contributing to the Chriftian Education and ufeful Bringing-up of the Poor.

Therefore there having of late been feveral Schools, called *Cha-rity-Schools,* Erected for that Purpofe,' namely, *For the Education of Poor Children in the Knowledge and Practice of the Chriftian Religion, as Profefs'd and Taught in the Church of* England ; *and for Teaching them*

A 2   *fuch*

---

1.   Opening of the SPCK annual *Account of the Charity-Schools* for 1707. The Society's initiative in promoting charity schools was supported by the senior clergy of the Chichester diocese.

in the 18th century was that few were *only* charity schools. Most were small, the master's salary meagre, and it was expedient to allow the master to increase his income by taking paying scholars in addition to the charity children.

Motives for setting up charity schools were mixed. The SPCK initiative had an evangelical purpose: children were to be taught to read (so they could read the Bible) and taught their catechism, and thereby, it was hoped, would become good Christians; 'It is manifest, That a Christian and Useful Education of the Children of the POOR, is absolutely necessary to their Piety, Virtue, and honest Livelihood.' But the SPCK added: 'Tis also as plain and evident, That Piety, Virtue and an honest Way of Living, are not only of absolute Necessity to their Happiness both *Here* and *Hereafter*; but are necessary also to the Life and Security of all other People whatsoever.' The SPCK went on to recommend 'Adding some WORK to the Childrens Learning, thereby to render their Education more useful to the Publick.'[30] The composite motive - the inculcation of Christian principles, leading to a stable social order (through the subservience, obedience and occupation of the poor) - dominated all educational charities through the 18th century. It should be noted, however, that among the ruling class many strongly held the view that to educate the poor would make them dissatisfied with their lot and invite social disruption. Also, no charity school could survive if the parents of poor children decided not to send their children to it. And why should they? The rural poor had little incentive to become literate, and children's earnings were often important to the family. In March 1711 it was reported that there were 10 children at the Buxted charity school set up by Anthony Saunders, 'and he would increase ye Number if ye poor would send 'em.' Throughout most of the 18th century the promoters of charity schools were faced not only with resistance from those classes whose financial support was necessary, but also with apathy from those whom they set out to help. The very real advance made during the century should be evaluated against these difficulties.

In the 18th century there was a clear demarcation between learning to read and learning to write. A child first learnt to spell and to read (the methods of teaching were uninspiring and based essentially on rote learning); only when he or she was a proficient reader - and provided they stayed at school long enough - did they move on to learning to write and cipher. Of the Sussex charity schools in the 18th century, all taught reading, but only about 60% taught writing and only about 40% taught 'the three Rs'. Girls were also taught to knit and sew; and at six of the boys' charity schools along the coast more advanced mathematics and navigation were taught.[31]

Grammar schools
As elsewhere,[32] in Sussex the free grammar schools decayed in the 18th century. A classical education had become increasingly irrelevant to poor parents. The value of some endowments fell and it was difficult to attract qualified masters. Salaries paid to masters of the Sussex free grammar schools in the 18th century ranged from about £17 a year at Cuckfield to £60 a year at Lewes, plus a house; this was clearly inadequate, and masters were obliged to take private pupils or combine

schoolmastering with clerical appointments - or both.   But problems can be distinguished from abuses. Some clergy took their salaries as masters but did not teach at all. Trustees were often lax and ineffective. During the century all the endowed free grammar schools appear to have abused their trusts, some more so than others. The grammar schools that flourished were *private* schools that widened their curricula beyond Latin and Greek and that in most cases appropriated to themselves the buildings and income of charitable trusts intended for the benefit of poor boys.

Of the nine endowed grammar schools at the beginning of the 18th century, one recently established (Petworth) failed early in the century.   By the early 19th century three other foundations (Horsham, Hastings, Rye) had ceased to be grammar schools and had become elementary charity schools; and when these moribund free grammar schools were turned into elementary schools, all the free places were immediately taken up - 60 at Horsham, 90 at Hastings, 50 at Rye. All the remaining five foundations (Chichester, Cuckfield, Lewes, Steyning, Midhurst) had by that time become essentially private grammar schools, with either no or very few free scholars.

There was still a demand for a classically-based education. Throughout the century, many clergy kept small schools where they prepared boys for the public schools or for university. Towards the end of the century some private schools were promoted as 'grammar schools' - Mossop's 'Grammar School, Brighthelmstone', Neale's 'Arundel Grammar School', Edward's 'Hurst Grammar School'.

Workhouse schools/parish schools/parish schooling
The problem of coping with the increasing numbers of poor was never solved in the 18th century. Workhouses, a 17th-century development, spread through the county in the course of the century and, in one form or another, were common to most parishes by 1800. There are references to workhouse schools in Sussex from the 1730s. In the last quarter of the century, ten workhouse schools are known to have been operating, and probably 13; there were almost certainly others. Children were supposed to be taught to read and to work (spin, &c.). With some exceptions, the 'education' given was minimal, but workhouse schools were significant on two counts. The first was acceptance of the idea that it was expedient for schooling to be provided out of the rates (there was no question of altruism: the demands on the poor rate were extreme, and by the end of the century the county had the highest poor rates in England[33]). The second was that the 'scholars' at workhouse schools were not mainly from the deserving or respectable poor, but from the paupers at the very bottom of the heap. These ideas prefigured, not the expansion of elementary education that occurred in the early decades of the 19th century, which was based on charitable contributions, but, the better part of a century later, Foster's Education Act of 1870, which promoted (but did not compel) primary education for all children, largely paid for out of local rates.

In this connection we should also note a number of parish schools supported by the poor rate (see for example Bexhill, Billingshurst, Icklesham); and that in some parishes (eg Warnham) 'the parish Children'/'the workhouse Children' were put out to respectable petty or dame schools; and that throughout the century there is evidence that in many parishes the schooling of individual children was paid for out of the poor rate.

Sunday schools

Although parish clergy were supposed to teach the children in their parish the catechism (and some did so, and there are indications that one or two may have operated an early form of Sunday school - see Edburton, Mayfield, Steyning), the 'Sunday school movement' as such did not gather momentum until in 1784 Robert Raikes published an account of four small Sunday schools he had started in Gloucester.[34]   There were Sunday schools at Pulborough and Waldron by the beginning of 1786, and at least 18 were set up in Sussex between 1785 and 1797. There were undoubtedly others, but as with other types of school we are often dependent on casual references for evidence of their existence.

As was the case with charity schools, motives for setting up Sunday schools were mixed, but it would seem that in Sussex the principal purpose of those who funded the schools was 'to instil morality into the minds of youth',[35] to preserve the social order: a Christian indoctrination of children of the poor was seen as a means to this end. At the Quarter Sessions held in Lewes in October 1792, 'the Chairman in his charge to the Grand Jury observed and lamented, that of late felonies had much increased in this division of our County; and as a means of preventing them in future, he recommended attention to *Sunday* Schools.'[36]

Sunday schools were one-day-a-week charity schools; although a good deal of time was spent at church services, there was also time for teaching to read. At Brighton the children wore uniforms. (For an account of a successful Sunday school, see Waldron; for the rules of a Sunday school, see Glynde; for administrative structures and financing, see Brighton and Lewes; for examples of the low costs of teaching Sunday school, see Pulborough and Bishopstone.)

The significance of the Sunday schools lay in the large number of children that they taught. The Sunday school at Brighton was in 1789 by far the largest school of any kind in Sussex. That at Waldron was even more remarkable: by 1801 the total population was only 752, but in 1788, two years after its beginning, the Sunday school had 134 children, aged from 7 to 16, both boys and girls, of whom 100+ would be present on any one Sunday - an unprecedented number for any type of school at any Sussex village prior to that date. At Horsham Sunday school in 1787 there were 'upwards of sixty poor children, of both sexes'; at Arundel in 1792 there were 30 boys and 30 girls; at the small village of East Dean (West Sussex) in 1795 there were 40 children. By 1819 there were 91 Sunday schools in Sussex, and 6,750 children were enrolled in them.[37]

Private schools

Schedule 1 lists 400-500 18th-century private schools in Sussex (depending on definitions)[38] and illustrates the great diversity of such schools. Many dame and petty schools are now 'lost', but it is clear that there was a significant expansion of private schools in the course of the century.

(a)

(b)

(c)

2. ADVERTISEMENTS FOR PRIVATE BOARDING SCHOOLS.

(a) Thornton's school, Horsham, 1783. Thornton was an innovator, and his school (later 'Horsham Academy') was successful. (*SWA* 14.4.1783)

(b) Mr and Mrs Dubbins school, Horsham, 1791. This advertisement is notable for its reasoned claim of gentle treatment of pupils as opposed to harsh discipline, and for evidence of the widening curriculum offered in girls' schools towards the end of the century. (*SWA* 24.1.1791)

(c) Mrs Norton's school at Preston, 1791. Note the detailed list of fees (eg extra charges for 'Tea, twice in the day' and 'A Single Bed'). As here, all Sussex boarding schools promoted their healthy location. (*SWA* 16.5.1796)

Numerous dame schools taught very young children to read for 2d a week. Some of the dames were poor old women, and we have the example of John Dudeney who was taken away from Dame Mascall after a few weeks because 'I learnt nothing there but to drive the ducks into the moat'; but many and probably most were competent within their limited range. (For contemporary accounts of dame schools, see Coldwaltham, and the brief details of Dame Willard's school at Warnham.) There were also several small village schools, often taught by the parish clerk. Many clergy kept small schools, usually boarding a few boys (often the sons of local gentry), teaching them the classics and preparing them for the public schools or university - or for 'business'. One of the major developments in the 18th century was the increase in the number of schools educating boys for 'business'. Seeking pupils from the middle and lower-middle classes, their basic subjects were reading, writing and 'merchants' accounts', but a surprising number (at least 37) also offered the higher mathematics necessary for 'mensuration', land-surveying and navigation. Two other important developments in the 18th century were the widening of the curricula of the boarding schools (discussed below), and the marked increase in the number of boarding schools. The number of boarding schools known to have been operating in each quarter-century rose from 5 in the first quarter-century and 6 in the second, to 30 in the third and 101 in the fourth. (Of these, for girls' boarding schools the numbers were 0, 2,14, and 38.) We have here a pattern of dynamic growth, that was well under way in the third quarter of the century and accelerated greatly in the fourth. One school of special interest is the Allfrees' coeducational school at Herstmonceux. The Allfrees boarded both boys and girls, and provided a full education for both sexes (and laid on balls, to which parents were invited); it must have been one of the earliest of its kind in the country - it preceded by 30 years the interest aroused by Pestalozzi's experimental coeducational schools on the continent, and by 125 years the opening in a country house near Lindfield, of Bedales, which developed into what has been claimed as 'the first fully coeducational boarding school'.[39] It is important to note that, back in the 18th century, the Allfrees' school was successful.

Home instruction
Very little is known about the incidence of this primary educational resource, but without it - and the contribution of the dame and petty schools - it is not possible to account for the relatively high levels of literacy that were achieved in the 18th century. (Of adults - of all classes - who married in East Sussex, 1754-1810, over half could write, at least to the extent of signing their names (53%: 65% of males, 42% of females)[40] and a considerably higher proportion would have been able to read - probably 75% or more.) John Dudeney, the shepherd boy, records: 'My mother taught me to read and my father taught me to write a little in the winter evenings and to do addition and subtraction (all he knew of arithmetic).' This experience must have been repeated in many homes across the county. The potential for home instruction is indicated by the fact that in almost three-quarters of all families (73%, 1754-90) either the husband or wife (or both) could sign their names,[41] and in a higher proportion of families at least one parent could read.

There are also a number of examples in Schedule 2 of self-instruction - of later schoolmasters who, having been taught to read and perhaps write a little, taught themselves further from books.

                    *   *   *   *   *   *   *   *

The information in this volume can be used in two ways. Firstly, it is sufficiently comprehensive to provide a quantified basis for answering many questions concerning educational developments during the 18th century. Secondly, it provides anecdotal examples of individual persons and particular events, to help our understanding of schooling in Sussex in this period. For this latter function, the volume retains as much detail and as much contemporary quotation as it has been practical to include. Thus -

Schedule 3 records almost 2,000 Sussex scholars of the 18th century. Here we can find brief accounts of the schooling of pauper children (such as Winefred Banks, or the Head children of Playden); of the charity schooling at Rye in the first half of the century of boys from French Protestant refugee families (Adrien, Espenet, Foshier, Merion); of the schooling of a radical schoolmistress (Elizabeth Hitchener) and of an almost entirely self-taught schoolmaster - and the help he received along the way (John Dudeney); of future poets (Daniel Foote, William Hay, William Hersee, Elizabeth Hitchener, James Hurdis, Charlotte Turner, Percy Bysshe Shelley); we can read how John Inskip, son of a poor currier but heir to Sir John Lade, was schooled to become a gentleman, and of the education of the Duke of Richmond's illegitimate daughter at Goodwood House (Henriette Le Clerc). Here are incidents such as the drowning of a schoolboy while bathing in the sea (James Lord), or the two boys who ran away from school and were lost for several days (Christopher and Henry White). We can obtain insights from many details: the difference between free and private scholars at grammar school, from Nicholas Gilbert who, when a private pupil at Lewes grammar school for five years early in the century, had his head shaved and wore a wig; the reading and pastimes of a gentleman's sons at preparatory school, from the correspondence of the Collier family of Hastings; the education of the sons of Henry Manning, surgeon-apothecary of Lewes, and the costs involved; the subjects a boy at a private school was taught in the 1770s, from the exercise books of William Gorringe. But of greater value historically than such details is the fact that the schedule provides a quantified basis for analyses of a number of educational issues. It has been possible to trace the births or baptisms of about 800 charity school children. After allowance for the birth/baptism interval, and with the details given in a very large number of school lists, it is possible to arrive at reasonably reliable estimates of the ages of children at Sussex charity schools in the 18th century, and how long they were at school. Moreover, the data are sufficiently extensive to permit examination of the different patterns at different schools, and the different patterns for boys and girls. For Mayfield school we can, with care, estimate how long it took the children to learn to read, and what proportion went on to join the writing class; for over 500 Mayfield scholars we know the reasons why they left school. Such records are, for the 18th century, extremely rare.

Similarly for Schedule 2, which records 700 schoolmasters and schoolmistresses. About many of these we know little. But there are a large number of vignettes from which we can gain insights into the lives of 18th-century teachers. For example: Elizabeth Burt, a poor woman of Icklesham, who for 28 years was paid by the parish for schooling poor children; the gentry daughters of Lancelot Harison Esq of Folkington Place, who for a time kept a school for all the poor children of their parish; Philadelphia Russell, schoolmistress at Chichester for more than half a century (who at one time owned the playhouse); Hannah Adams, a radical, caught in Paris by the war and detained there for three years through the height of the Terror; Elizabeth Allfree, who married at 17, had 13 children, and with her husband ran a successful coeducational school, and died aged 84; Jane Beard, wife of a bankrupt, who kept girls' boarding schools successively at Hailsham, Brighton and Seaford (an advertisement for the last being addressed to 'the Nobility and Gentry'); Mary Blesard, at one time paid for schooling children, who became the mistress of a duke, had three daughters by him, and £450 a year under his will; Benjamin Martin, essentially self-taught, author of successful text-books, who became a celebrated lecturer and instrument maker - and a bankrupt and attempted suicide; the gentle James Capper, vicar and schoolmaster of Wilmington; John Curteis of Uckfield, who was swept away and died in a flash flood; the self-taught William Dine, schoolmaster, parish clerk and poet of Chiddingly; dancing masters such as the very different Stephen Philpot and John Thring of Lewes and Laurent Xavier Martin de Lambilly of Chichester, and music masters, such as William Prince of Brighton, who was also a composer (and wrote an opera performed many times). For a few we have more extensive details: Walter Gale of Mayfield, transcript excerpts from whose diary have survived, and whose life has been well researched; Cater Rand junior of Lewes, whose scientific interests led him to become an imaginative surveyor and civil engineer; John Mossop, curate of Brighton, a young schoolmaster with many interests and achievements; and the very remarkable Dr Thomas Hooker of Rottingdean.

Apart from these individual histories, by bringing together all the information we have, we can arrive at certain conclusions. Schoolmasters were in general poorly paid; many or most of them took on additional occupations to augment their income. For more than half the schoolmasters we do not yet know whether or not they had other occupations. Of the 181 we know about, 176 did have some other occupation. Nearly half of these also held one or more church appointments. Of the others, at least 30 were also surveyors (most of these were masters of schools that educated boys for 'business'), at least 15 were also parish clerks, 15 also published books of one kind or another.[42] Others were also shopkeepers or tradesmen, booksellers, public lecturers, insurance agents, postmasters. Several had a number of supplementary activities. Of the just under 200 schoolmistresses recorded in the schedule, for all but 13 we know the type of school they taught at: about 40% taught dame schools or other private day schools with weekly or quarterly fees, about 35% kept private boarding schools, about 20% taught at charity schools and 5% at Sunday schools or workhouse schools. Of the 165 schoolmistresses whose marital status we know, 30% were single women, 57% married women, 13% widows.[43]

Schedule 1 records all we know at present about schooling in the 18th century in every town and parish in the county. The cumulated data provide a quantified basis for a number of important analyses and conclusions: identification of the charity school movement at the beginning of the century, which has been mentioned above, the equally important evidence of growth in the number of charity schools throughout the century, details of the Sunday school movement towards the end of the century. We can analyse the salaries paid to charity school masters and masters of the free grammar schools, and the range of fees charged by the private schools, how they increased towards the end of the century, what were charged as extras and how much was charged for them - writing, dancing, music, drawing, &c., and the less obvious 'breakings-up and servants', the increasingly common provision of tea, and, revealingly, at Mrs Norton's girls' school at Preston, 'A Single Bed will be an extra charge of Two Guineas per Anum'. We can examine the length and timing of school holidays (they were relatively short) and the different patterns for charity schools and private schools; for the latter, we can see how holidays increased towards the end of the century, and trace the change of the summer holiday from Whitsuntide to midsummer from about 1780. We can track the widening curricula of the private schools, subject by subject - for example, the remarkable growth in the provision of French (in the last quarter-century 23 boys' boarding schools are known to have offered French, and 20 girls' boarding schools; in 1787 Raymond opened his successful boys' boarding school at Lewes where 'French is the only Language allowed to be spoken among the Scholars, in and out of school hours; Sundays only excepted'; Elizabeth Phillips at Arundel, whose girls' school had been established in 1780, noted in 1788 that 'French is the general language of her School', and French was the only language allowed to be spoken among the scholars of Miss Rockett's girls' school at Hastings in 1793; as the Allfrees at Herstmonceux noted in 1793, the French language 'is now become almost a necessary part of education'). Among the more occasional references, we find for the first time 'the Sciences' being taught to girls (notably by the Dubbins at Horsham, from 1791; the 'sciences' covered history, chronology, geography, astronomy and natural history); Mrs Gell at Lewes taught her girls 'a Knowledge of Domestic Œconomy' (1798); at Jenkins' boys' boarding school at Seaford chemistry was included among the subjects taught (1790) and at Barwick's at Lindfield shorthand was among the subjects covered by the basic fee (1793).

Among the more important developments in the second half of the century, the private schools almost without exception claimed, with increasing emphasis, that great attention would be paid to the health of their scholars, and that children would be treated, not with severity, but with tenderness (the word 'tenderness' entered the vocabulary of school advertisements around 1770). As the Dubbins put it in 1791: the pupils of their girls' school 'will be treated with great kindness, not only from principles of humanity, but from a thorough conviction, founded on observation and experience, that more beneficial effects will ever be wrought in juvenile minds by mild persuasion and rational argument, than by the cruel severity of harsh discipline'. New ideas were creeping in - that children could like their preceptors, that children could actually enjoy their schooling. There are occasional references to the 'pleasure' and 'happiness' of pupils. The Sussex boarding schools were small by later standards, and personal care of the children was practical. They were highly competitive, and however stereotyped such claims in advertisements may have become, it is clear that what those who could afford to send their children to private boarding schools wanted for their children, was care given to their health and gentleness used towards them. Among the lesser 18th-century developments were the introduction of school plays (from about 1770 in Sussex) and the involvement of schoolchildren in charitable activities in the last decade of the century (Miss Ryall's and Miss Adams's girls' schools at Lewes, Mossop's boys' school at Brighton, Capper's at Wilmington, Thornton's at Horsham).

*   *   *   *   *   *   *   *

What can we conclude from the records presented in this volume?

There is clear evidence that the 18th century was not stagnant in terms of educational activity, and that such activity involved change and innovation. While the free grammar schools became moribund (Latin and Greek had become irrelevant to the poor) at the same time private grammar schools widened their curricula and flourished. There was accelerating expansion in the number of private schools of all types, especially those that educated boys for trade or 'business', and boarding schools, both for girls and boys. Such schools reflected changing social mores: they expanded the range of subjects that they taught, and those parents and guardians who paid for their children's schooling required that proper attention be given to their children's health, and that their children be treated with gentleness. (It was in many ways a rough age and corporal punishment was a part of life, but there is no evidence of draconian discipline in the Sussex schools of the 18th century.)

The most important overall conclusion is the extent to which the developments of the 18th century determined the structure of schooling for many years to come. The expansion of elementary education that occurred in the early decades of the 19th century followed the pattern set in the 18th. This had begun with the remarkable 'charity school movement' at the beginning of the century, the influence of which persisted, so that the number of operative charity schools steadily increased as the century progressed. Towards the end of the century the charity schools were supplemented by Sunday schools, which introduced the idea of schooling, to some extent at least, large numbers of local children. The education of the poor was essentially based - and continued to be based for a further three-quarters of a century - on personal charity.

Finally, there were intimations of the future in the funding of workhouse and parish schools out of the local poor rate, and in such innovations as a successful coeducational boarding school, prize days, the introduction of newspapers into school libraries, the first 'cadet corps', school involvement in charitable activities, and extra-curricular school plays.[44]

INTRODUCTION : NOTES

Documentary sources for the references to particular schools, schoolmasters, schoolmistresses and scholars are given in the appropriate Schedules.

1. Stephens, W.B., and Unwin, R.W. *Materials for the Local and Regional Study of Schooling 1700-1900* (British Records Association, Archives and the User, No.7, 1987).

2. From West Sussex Record Office, Ep.I/26/3. (The alternative parish names are from this same source.) For some parishes for which 1724 figures are not available, figures for 1717 have been taken from *Sussex Record Society* **78**, 227-30. The figure from this source for West Tarring relates to 1720. For five parishes for which no 1717 or 1724 figures are available, details c1760 have been taken from Gregory, J. *The Speculum of Archbishop Thomas Secker* (*Church of England Record Society,* vol. 2, 1995).

3. Despite errors, the 1801 census can be regarded as reasonably accurate: qv Wrigley, E.A., and Schofield, R.S. *The Population History of England 1541-1871* (1981), 122-6.

4. Analysis of data in Schedule 1. In the counts of private schools given here and below, numbers include private schools grafted onto charity or free grammar schools. Since private schools were small, their identity determined by their proprietor and by their location, when a school changed hands it is treated as a separate school. But where a school had a clear continuing identity (eg private school grafted onto a free grammar school or charity school, or a school continued by a family such as the Rands at Lewes) it is counted only once. Where a school changed its location in the same town, this is ignored; but where the same master or mistress ran different schools at different times in widely different locations, each is treated as a separate school. On the basis of these definitions, over 400 private schools have been traced (including dame schools), with a further 100 probably operating within the century. Some subjectivity has been necessary when classifying the schools.

5. In 1803 23% of the population of Sussex received relief out of the poor rate [*Abstract of Returns relative to the Expence and Maintenance of the Poor, 1803* (1804)]. But there were many others who were poor, who may not have received relief but did not pay the poor rate (the criterion for eligibility to the Oliver Whitby charity school, for example). An analysis of the number of families in 1801 and the number paying the poor rate, based on 15 East Sussex parishes, suggests an overall estimate for these parishes of just over 50% poor, ranging from about 40% in towns with a population over 2,000 to as high as 70% in parishes with a population of 300 or less. [Caffyn, J .M., MS, 1990]

6. Young, Rev A. *A General View of the Agriculture of the County of Sussex* (for the Board of Agriculture, 1813), 438-42.

7. Jones, M.G. *The Charity School Movement* (1938), 73.

8. ibid, citing SPCK *An Account of the Charity Schools lately erected* (1708).

9. See note 5.

10. Lowerson, J. *A Short History of Sussex* (1980), 132.

11. Brent, C., 'Lewes Dissenters outside the Law, 1663-86', *Sussex Archaeological Collections,***123**, 196; West Sussex Record Office, Ep.I/26/3.

12. McLynn, F. *Crime and Punishment in Eighteenth-century England* (1989), xi.

13. *County Mirror And Chichester Magazine,* Apr 1796, 171; *Sussex Weekly Advertiser,* 9 May 1796, and earlier reports.

14. Lowerson, J., op. cit., 130.

15. *Sussex Weekly Advertiser*, 25 Aug 1800.

16. Brent, C. *Georgian Lewes* (1993), 70.

17. McLynn, F., op. cit., 306.

18. Burgess, D.S. and P. N., Maguire, L.J., ed. *The Journal and Correspondence of John Burgess from 1785 to 1819* (priv. pub., 1982), 54.

19. *Sussex Archaeological Collections*, **29**, 229.

20. McLynn, F., op. cit., 307.

21. *The Lewes and Brighthelmston Pacquet* 1 Oct 1789.

22. Porter, R. *English Society in the Eighteenth Century* (1982), p/b edn. 33.

23. ibid.

24. ibid, 275.

25. Plumb, J.H. *Georgian Delights* (1980), 82.

26. *Sussex Weekly Advertiser*, 15 Apr 1799.

27. Jones, M.G., op. cit..

28. Simon, J., 'Was there a Charity School Movement? The Leicestershire Evidence', *Education in Leicestershire 1540-1940* (1968). On this issue see also Unwin, B., 'The Established Church and the Schooling of the Poor: the Role of the SPCK 1699-1720', *The Churches and Education* (History of Education Society, 1984).

28a. Unwin, op. cit., 16,17.

29. Analysis of data in Schedule 1.

30. SPCK, *An Account of the Methods Whereby the Charity-Schools have been Erected and Managed, &c.*, (1707), 3.

31. Analysis of data in Schedule 1.

32. See for example: Vincent, W.A.L. *The Grammar Schools: Their Continuing Tradition 1660-1714* (1969), 3, 106-7, 115, 226-7; Lawson, J., and Silver, H. *A Social History of Education in England* (1973), 195-6; O'Day, R. *Education and Society 1500-1800* (1982), 199.

33. Lowerson, J., op. cit., 134.

34. Dick, M., 'Religion and the origins of mass schooling: the English Sunday School c.1780-1840', *The Churches and Education* (History of Education Society, 1984), 34, 48.

35. *Sussex Weekly Advertiser*, 26 Apr 1790, reporting the resolutions of a meeting at East Grinstead setting up a Sunday school.

36. *Sussex Weekly Advertiser*, 8 Oct 1792.

37. *A Digest of Parochial Returns made to the Select Committee appointed to inquire into the Education of the Poor, 1818* (1820), Vol.III, 1171, 1494.

38. See note 4.

39. Perkin, L.B. *Coeducation in its historical and theoretical setting* (1939), 75-6, 92.

40. Based on an analysis of the marriage registers of 18 parishes in East Sussex, 1754-1810: no. of marriages, 5,230; no. of adults, 10,460. The parishes were, by 1801 population size of parish or town embracing more than one parish: (over 2,000) Lewes St Michael, Lewes St John sub Castro, Battle; (1,001-2,000) Mayfield, Wadhurst, Fletching; (601-1,000) Ewhurst, Seaford, Chiddingly; (301-600) Westham, Brightling, Hooe, Newick; (0-300) Ripe, Patcham, Falmer, Bodiam, Pevensey. [Caffyn, J.M., MS 1990]. See also Smith, D.E., 'Eighteenth Century Literacy Levels in West Sussex', *Sussex Archaeological Collections*, **128**, 177-86. This study was based on 2,736 marriages, 1754-99. Reworking the data gives 57% who could sign their names (67% male, 47% female). These figures are slightly higher than the East Sussex data cited, but 70% of the sample married in the city of Chichester ('literacy' was in general higher in the towns than rural parishes).

41. From the East Sussex study; see note 40.

42. Analysis of data in Schedule 2.

43. ibid: five schoolmistresses taught, at different times, at two different types of school; eight are entered in two of the marital status categories.

44. Coeducational boarding school - Alfree, Herstmonceux. Prize days - Midhurst GS. Newspapers in schools - Thornton, Horsham; Goldring, Petworth; Williams, Burwash; (and by 1804, Adams girls' school, Lewes). 'Cadet corps' - Mossop, Brighton; (and in 1801, Frant school). Charitable activities - Ryall, Lewes; Adams, Lewes; Mossop, Brighton; Capper, Wilmington; Thornton, Horsham. School plays - Joel, Chichester; Clowes, Chichester; Thornton, Horsham; Brook, Brighton (other kinds of public performances included 'public examinations' or recitations, which sometimes featured short plays - Neale, Arundel; Button, Lewes; Hackman, Chichester; Midhurst GS - and the singing of hymns by Sunday school children, as at Brighton; the earliest public performance so far traced was in 1769 at Joel's school, Chichester, which included pastoral duets).

NOTE ON SOURCES

<u>Main sources</u>

Reports of the Commissioners on the Education of the Poor (1819-40)

SPCK: 'Abstract Letter Books' and annual *Account of the Charity- Schools* to 1740; selected use also made of other archives. [These sources should be used with care: see for example comments under 'LEWES, <u>Charity school</u>' and 'BATTLE, <u>Charity schools</u>'.]

The Sussex Weekly Advertiser or Lewes Journal [MF at (eg) Eastbourne and Brighton Public Libraries. The British Library Newspaper Library does not hold any other 18th-century Sussex newspapers.]

Annotated visitation question sheets [see note on page 25] (WSRO Ep.I/22/1)

'The free-School Book of Brighthelmston Anno Domini 1701' (Brighton Reference Library, SB 379 FRE)

Chichester Grey Coat boys' Charity School (and references to Chichester Blue Coat girls' Charity School): accounts and school lists (WSRO Cap.V/1/1); sacrament money accounts (WSRO Cap.I/24/5)

Chichester Oliver Whitby Charity School accounts (WSRO E35D/3/1); rules set by trustees (WSRO E35D/8/12)

Rye, Saunders' Charity School: 183 loose 18th-century school lists c.1722-85 [nine undated, several gaps in sequence, most signed by the master] (ESRO RYE 114/10); records relating to the school (ESRO RYE 112/49-61, 114/1, 114/13)

'Sedlescomb School 1748'; memorandum book relating to the Charity School (ESRO ESC 148/1/1)

'A Register of the Transactions of the Managers & Trustees of the Charity School at Mayfield in the County of Sussex founded in the year of our Lord 1750' (ESRO AMS 5601/1)

School histories: Baines, J.M., and Conisbee, L.R. *The History of Hastings Grammar School 1619-1956* (1956, rev. edn, with Bygate, N., 1967); Hackworth, J. *Sir Henry Fermor C of E School 1744-1994* (1994); Row, E.P. *A History of Midhurst Grammar School* (1913); Sleight, J.M. *A Very Exceptional Circumstance* (1981) [Steyning Grammar School] : Vidler, L.A. *History of Rye Grammar School 1639-1939* (1939); Willson, A.N. *A History of Collyer's School 1532-1964* (1965) [Horsham Grammar School]

Sussex Archaeological Collections, including *Sussex Notes and Queries*

Other documentary sources

Subscription books (WSRO Ep.I/3/3; Ep.I/3/4; Ep.I/3/5; Ep.I/3/7; Ep.I/39/21; Ep.II/1/1)

Schoolmasters licences (WSRO Ep.I/1/10; Ep.I/1/11)

Bishop Bower's visitation 1724 (WSRO Ep.I/26/3; now published in *Chichester Diocesan Surveys 1686 and 1724*, ed. W.K. Ford, *Sussex Record Society* **78**)

Wills, Lewes [ESRO index lists testators' occupations]

Church Court Detections [extracts; sources not searched] (Arundel, WSRO Ep.I/17/36); Seaford, WSRO Ep.II/15/10)

Rev Thankful Frewen's school memorandum book (ESRO FRE 533)

Papers relating to Lightmaker's Charity School, Horsted Keynes (ESRO GLY 3466)

Petworth Charity School, notebook (WSRO Petworth House Archives 1763)

Woolgar, T., 'Spicilegia', MS (SAS Library)

Frewen archives (ESRO FRE 1284-7, 1294, 8181-3, 8182/31)

John Fuller's accounts, letter books (ESRO SAS/RF 15/21, 15/25-8)

Pelham/Newcastle papers: BL Add MSS 32,688; 32,689; 33,058; 33,059; 33,139; 33,157; 33,161; 33,338; 33,341; 33,617 [extracts sent by correspondents]. Pelham account books (ESRO AMS 2132, 2133; SAS/FB 112). Pelham Charity School list (ESRO AMS 6005)

Accounts: Accounts of the trustees of Nicholas Gilbert (ESRO ACC 2462/1);Stapley
family   account book (ESRO HIC 472); Manning household expenses (ESRO SAS/I 302); Henry Campion's accounts (ESRO DAN 2198) ; Goodwood steward's accounts (WSRO Goodwood MS 244, 245, 247); 3rd Viscount Gage's personal account book (ESRO SAS/G/ACC 741); accounts of Charles Gilbert, as agent for George Medley (ESRO SAS/GT/1/3/3-5), as agent for Rev D'Oyly (ESRO SAS/GT/1/2/1-3); Simon Grover's accounts (ESRO AMS 634)

Deeds and records: Chatsworth, Devonshire Collections [excerpts from Compton Place accounts sent by correspondent]; papers relating to Cater Rand's bankruptcy and property ownership (ESRO SAS/LEW 33, 34; AMS 2133); Balneath Manor Court Book (1753, re Philpot) (ESRO AMS 4599) ; property deeds, re Richard Jarrett, Henry Jarrett, Sarah Wybourn (ESRO AMS 4635, WMD Box 14, Box 18), re Smallfield (ESRO SAS Box 11 [temp. ref.]), re Sedlescombe (ESRO AMS 1582); Apprentices register, Guildhall Museum, Rochester (RCA/02/19) [extract sent by correspondent]

School books: School exercise book of William Killick, 1763 (WSRO MP 2671);

school exercise books of William Gorringe, 1773-6 (WSRO MP 2972, Add MS 39,850-3); paper with poem by Francis Woodhatch, 1783 (WSRO E102K/19/89); writing book of Charles New, 1803 (WSRO Add MS 36,773); workbook of Richard Lambe, 1822, with map of the Allfree estate at Herstmonceux (ESRO AMS 5879/1)

Personal records: Collier family of Hastings correspondence (ESRO SAY); 'The Journal of William Kenward' (MS in private possession); 'Frank Evershed's Notebooks' (MS in private possession) [extracts sent by correspondent]; 'Reminiscences of Mary Sybella Peckham' (W.D.Peckham collection, MSP 4, in private possession)

Numerous source references to maps by schoolmasters are given in Schedule 2.

Contemporary published sources include [selectively used]:

The Gentleman's Magazine; *The Topographer* (1791); *The County Mirror and Chichester Magazine* (June 1796, at SAS Library)

Magna Britannia (Cox, T., 1730); *A Description of England and Wales* (Newberry and Carnan, 1770); Mossop, J. *A Description of Brighthelmstone and Its Vicinity* (Crawford, 1793); *Brighthelmston New Guide* (Fisher, 1800, 1804); *The Chichester Guide* (c.1804)

The Lewes and Brighthelmston Pacquet [this short-lived weekly ran from 30 July 1789 to 21 January 1790: copies in private possession]; *The Portsmouth Gazette*; *The Hampshire Chronicle* [extracts sent by correspondent]

Directories: *Bailey* 1784; *Universal* 1791, 92, 93, 94; *Cobby* 1799, 1800; *Baxter* 1805; *Holden* 1805, 1811

Poll books: 1768, 82, 91, 93, 96, 1802

Abstract of the Returns of Charitable Donations for the Benefit of Poor Persons 1786-88 (1816)

Burr, T. *History of Tunbridge Wells* (1766); Dine, W. *Poems on Several Occasions* (1771); Dunvan, P. *History of Lewes and Brighthelmston* (1795); Hay, A. *History of Chichester* (1804); Hersee, W. *Poems, Rural and Domestic* (1810); Horsfield, T.W. *The History and Antiquities of Lewes and its Vicinity* (I, 1824; II, 1827); Horsfield T.W. *The History, Antiquities, and Topography of the County of Sussex* (1835); Walesby, A., 'Memoir of John Ellman', *The Library of Agricultural and Horticultural Knowledge* (3rd edn 1834)

Extensive use has been made of the following sources:

Parish registers, parish accounts and other parish records. Also nonconformist, Quaker, Roman Catholic and Freemason registers and documents [as recorded in the Schedules]

Clergy Index at SAS Library

Foster, J. *Alumni Oxonienses* (1887-92) [a few dates queried]

Venn, J.A. *Alumni Cantabrigienses* (1922-54) [a few dates queried]

Land Tax returns

Budgen, W., MS notebooks at SAS Library [include t/s of many documents now at Chatsworth]

Other 19th and 20th century sources. A: Manuscripts

Burchall, M.J., 'Educating the Poor, Mayfield School 1750-71', BA dissertation, West Sussex Institute of Higher Education (1982); Cobau, J., 'Stephen Philpot: A Gentleman Dancing-Master' (MS in private possession); Cutten, M.J., t/s of Chichester census 1784 (WSRO MP 414) and notes on same (WSRO MP 417); Kinoulty, M.K., 'A Social Study of Roman Catholicism in West Sussex in the Eighteenth Century', MA thesis, University of Wales (1982) (WSRO Add MS 34,673); Matthews, H.M., 'The Papers of John Collier of Hastings. A Catalogue' (with introduction, 1966) (ESRO SAY)

School records at ESRO and WSRO [limited 18th-century references]

Probate inventories: indexed by occupation (East Sussex, ESRO card index; West Sussex, WSRO microfiche, from Ep.I/29)

Monumental Inscriptions [selectively used] by Bax, Cockayne, Dunkin, Slyfield (SAS Library)

Other 19th and 20th century sources. B : Journals &c [selectively used]

Chichester Papers ; *Ringmer History/Ringmer History Newsletter* ; *SAS Newsletter*; *Sussex County Magazine*; *Sussex Family Historian*; *Sussex Genealogist and Local Historian*; *Sussex History*; *Sussex Industrial History*; *West Sussex History*.

East Grinstead Observer (7.11.1896, 25.9.1909); *The Observer and West Sussex Recorder* (24.11.1909); *Sussex Daily News* (29.9.1913).

Other 19th and 20th century sources. C : Printed books include [selectively used]

Sussex Record Society volumes, including Marriage Licences **6, 9, 12, 25, 26, 32, 35**; and **78**, the last for 'Extracts from Archbishop Wake's Primary Visitation, 1717' (Lambeth MS 1115)

Gregory, J. *The Speculum of Archbishop Thomas Secker* (*Church of England Record Society*, vol. 2, 1995)

The Victoria History of the County of Sussex [some entries in early volumes queried]

Cowdray Archives (1964); *Danny Archives* (1966); *Goodwood Estate Archives* (1970); *Glynde Archives* (1964); *Wiston Archives* (1975, 1982)

Sussex Militia List 1803 Pevensey Rape Northern Division, and *Southern Division* (1988, PBN Publications)

Dictionary of Land Surveyors (draft 2nd edn, c.1994); *Dictionary of National Biography*; *Encyclopaedia Britannica* (13th edn)

Albery, W. *A Parliamentary History of Horsham 1295-1885* (1927); Albery, W. *A Millennium of Facts in the History of Horsham and Sussex 947-1947* (1947); Andrews, F., ed. *The Torrington Diaries* (1954 edn); Austen, E. 'John Wesley, the 'Pikes' and early Methodism in Robertsbridge...', *The Proceedings of the Wesley Historical Society* (1926); Austen, E. *Brede, the Story of a Sussex Parish* (1946); Bishop, J.G. *A Peep into the Past: Brighton in the Olden Time* (1892); Bishop, J.H. *Singleton and East Dean Guide* (1961); Bishop, J.H. *A Sussex Pot-Pourri* (1986); Brent, C. *Historic Lewes and Its Buildings* (1985); Brent, C. *Georgian Lewes* (1993); Budgen, W. *Old Eastbourne* (c.1912); Burchall, M.J., ed. *Eastern Sussex Settlement Certificates 1670-1832* (1979); Cameron, K.N. *The Young Shelley* (1951); Chambers, R.F. *The Strict Baptist Chapels of England: Sussex* (1954); Cheal, H. *History of Ditchling* (1901); Comber, J. *Sussex Genealogies* (1931-3); Cooper, W.V. *History of the Parish of Cuckfield* (1912); Curwen, E.C., ed. *The Journal of Gideon Mantell* (1940); Dale, A. *Brighton Town and Brighton People* (1976); Davey, L.S. *The Street Names of Lewes* (1970); Davis, W.L. *0 Rare Norgam* (1965); De Candole, H. *The Story of Henfield* (1976); Egerton, J.C. *Sussex Folk and Sussex Ways* (3rd edn, 1924); Firmin, B. *An Account of Sir Henry Fermor's Endowment at Crowborough* (1891) (ESRO AMS 5818); Frewen, A.L. *History of Brickwall in Sussex and of the Parishes of Northiam and Brede* (1909); Geering, T. *Our Sussex Parish* (19c; 1925 edn); Godfrey, W.H. *At the Sign of the Bull* (1924); Goodwin, J. *Burwash and the Sussex Weald* (nd but c.1958); Gordon, H.D. *History of Harting* (1877); Harrison, F., and North, J.S. *Old Brighton, Old Preston, Old Hove* (1937); Hills, W.H. *History of East Grinstead* (1906); Holloway, W. *History of the Town and Port of Rye* (1847); Holmes, R. *Shelley: the Pursuit* (1974); Jennings, G.H., ed. *Thomas Turner - the Diary of a Georgian Shopkeeper* (1979); Jones, F.L. *The Letters of Percy Bysshe Shelley* (1964); Kelch, R.A. *Newcastle: A duke without money: Thomas Pelham-Holles 1693-1768* (1974); Kensett, E. *History of the Free Christian Church Horsham* (1921); Lindsey, J. *The Story of a Sussex Village* (1983); Lower, M.A. *The Worthies of Sussex* (1865); Lucas, E.V. *Highways and Byways in Sussex* (2nd edn, 1935); Lucy, B. *Twenty Centuries in Sedlescombe* (1978); Maguire, L.J., ed. *The Journal and Correspondence of John Burgess 1785-1819* (pub. priv. 1982); Meade-Fetherstonhaugh, M., and Warner, O. *Uppark and its People* (1964); Millburn, J.R. *Benjamin Martin* (1976); Millburn, J.R. *Benjamin Martin Supplement* (1986); Plumley, N., and Lees, J. *The Organs and Organists of Chichester Cathedral* (1988); Reese, M.M. *Goodwood's Oak* (1987); Spokes, S. *Gideon Algernon Mantell* (1927); Stewart, B., and Cutten, M.J. *Chichester Artists 1530-1900* (1987); Vaisey, D., ed. *The diary of Thomas Turner* (1984); Valentine, C.H. *The Story of the Beginnings of Nonconformity in Arundel* (nd, but 1920s); Vidler, L.A. *New History of Rye* (1934); Wace, A.A., ed. *The Story of Wadhurst* (by Mrs Rhys Davids, 1894) (1924); Williamson, A. *Thomas Paine* (1973); Willis, T.G. *Records of Chichester* (1928); Worcester, D.K. *The Life and Times of Thomas Turner of East Hoathly* (1948); Wright, J.C. *Bygone Eastbourne* (1902); Yorke, P.C. *The Diary of John Baker* (1931)

A NOTE ON VISITATION RETURNS

In some years of the 18th century the diocese sent out, prior to the visitations, a printed list of questions, some of which related to schools and teachers. In some cases the churchwardens made notes in the margins of the question sheet, though in many cases there are no such annotations. The years for which such question sheets survive and (in brackets) the number of returns with annotations against the schooling questions or against the section heading under which the schooling questions were listed (which heading also covered other concerns - see below) were as follows: 1726 (39), 1729 (14), 1733 (58), 1737 (47), 1742 (83) 1745 (1), 1755 (26), 1758 (108), 1762 (100), 1765 (38), 1769 (57), 1772 (23), 1775 (90), 1779 (27). Valuable as these 711 annotated returns are, in the great majority of cases the value lies in 'negative' information, the churchwardens noting 'no' or 'None' against the section heading or the schooling questions. Moreover, the annotations are often ambiguous - as indeed are some of the questions to which they relate. With 'School-Masters' (only) in the heading and mentioned specifically in some of the questions, many churc wardens appear to have been uncertain whether or not they should answer at all in respect oi school-dames. In some cases the annotations are incompatible with information we have about the parish from other sources. While this source therefore has to be treated with ition, it is of real value when unambiguous annotations identify that there was no school a parish at a particular time, or where there was indeed a schoolmaster, or where there were one or more school-dames.

The printed questions were as follows (abbreviated references to them are made in Schedule 1):

For 1726 and 1729:

Concerning School-masters, Schools, and Hospitals, Physicians, Surgeons, and Midwives

1. What School-master, private or publick, is there in your Parish? Is he of a sober Life, and licensed by the Bishop? Doth he teach his Scholars the Church Catechism? Doth he cause them orderly to repair to the Church or Chapel on Sundays and Holidays?
2. What Hospital, Alms-House, or Free-School hath been founded in your Parish? Are they so ordered in their Revenue or Use as the Founders appointed, and the Law of the Land allows?

From 1733 (for which year only a separate printed sheet for answers was sent with the questions):

Concerning Hospitals, School-Masters, Physicians, Chirurgeons, and Midwives

I.   Is there in your Parish any Hospital, Alms-house, or Free-School?
II. What Revenue belongs to each of them?
III. Are they Governed, and the Revenue employed according to the Will of the Donors?
IV. Doth any one in your Parish teach School publickly or privately without Licence from the Ordinary?
V.   Is your School-master of good Life and Sober Conversation; and is he diligent in the Business of his Station?
VI. Doth the School-master come to Church himself, and cause his Scholars

also to come duly at the Times of Divine Service?

VII.   Doth he diligently instruct his Scholars in the Church Catechism?

VIII.   Is there any Charity-School in your Parish? When was it set up? How is it supported?   By Endowment, Subscription, or accidental Contributions?

IX.   What number of Children are taught at it? What are they taught? What Work are they employed in?   And what Business are they generally put out to?   Husbandry, Trade, or Service?

X.   Do any in your Parish practise Physick or Chirurgery, or undertake the Office of a Midwife without Licence?

All the surviving annotated returns above relate to the archdeaconry of Chichester [WSRO Ep.I/22/1]. For the archdeaconry of Lewes only the first page (which does not include the schooling questions) of one list of questions (for Streat 1785) has survived [WSRO Ep.II/14/1].

ACKNOWLEDGEMENTS

In the preparation of this volume I have drawn on many books and published articles, all of which are acknowledged in the text. I have made extensive use of the libraries at the Sussex Archaeological Society and the University of Sussex, and the Public Libraries at Brighton, Eastbourne and Lewes, and of the resources and archives of the East Sussex and West Sussex Record Offices, and the SPCK. I have greatly appreciated the help I have received from the librarians and archivists of these institutions. I have also received help from many people who have made available to me details of their own research or of papers in their private possession, or have given me the benefit of their knowledge or drawn my attention to sources that I would otherwise have missed. In some cases this help has concerned a single source or reference; in others it has resulted in a considerable correspondence across the years. My grateful thanks, then, to the following, all of whom have contributed material included in this volume: Leslie Baker, M.E.Benham, John Bleach, Pat Bracher, Colin Brent, Judith Brent, Angela Bromley-Martin, Philip Bye,Eric Byford, Elizabeth Doff, Peter Evershed, John Farrant, Sibylla Jane Flower, Richard Goulden, John Hackworth, Annabelle Hughes, John Kay, Denis Kenward, Elise Knapp, Michael Leppard, Wendy Lines, Timothy McCann, Claire McGill, Leonard Maguire, T.F.Pettitt, Norma Pilbeam, Hylda Rawlings, Henry Smith, Emlyn Thomas, the late Ron Tibble, Kenneth Twinn, Christopher Whittick, Peter Wilkinson, Sandra Williams. I also wish to record my thanks to the Sussex Record Society for making this volume possible, and for editorial advice and help from Andrew Foster and Peter Wilkinson. And to Peter Wilkinson (again) and his production team - Philip Bye, Fred Horne, Graham and Rosie Ritchie - for their laborious and painstaking work in preparing the text for printing.

For permission to use illustrations I gratefully acknowledge the courtesy of the following: The Royal Pavilion, Art Gallery and Museums, (Preston Manor),Brighton (frontispiece); the County Archivist of East Sussex, copyright reserved, (Nos. 6, 7, 9 and 12); the Society for Promoting Christian Knowledge (No. 1); the Sussex Archaeological Society (No.8); the County Archivist of West Sussex (for permission to use the base map for Nos. 3 and 4, and for Nos. 5, 11 and 13, and dustjacket.)

* * * * * * *

The Sussex Record Society has been given most valuable help by generous grants towards publication from the East Sussex Record Office, the West Sussex Archives Society, the West Sussex County Council and the West Sussex Record Office. The Council would like to record its gratitude for this assistance, without which publication would have been almost impossible. The Council would also like to add its sincere thanks to the three members, Philip Bye, Fred Horne and Peter Wilkinson, who undertook the complex task of typesetting and preparing the text for publication - an exercise on a scale never before attempted.

EDITORIAL NOTE

To accord with the usual style of Sussex Record Society publications editorial references to place names have normally adopted the modern conventional form (e.g. "Brighton" for "Brighthelmston"). References to the Lewes parish of St Peter and St Mary Westout have been rationalised to the more usual 18th century title of St Anne.

For 1700-99 dates expressed wholly in numbers, the century, '17', has been omitted; thus '12.10.75' (but '3.9.1697' and '21.6.1805').

The following convention has been adopted for the dating of Old Style years (pre 1752), which began on 25 March. For dates between 1 January and 24 March the year shown is that beginning on 25 March next. That is, the contemporary '14 February 1715' or '14 February 1715/6' is shown as '14 February 1716'.

ABBREVIATIONS

Account   SPCK *Account of the Charity-schools*

Add MS(S)Additional Manuscript(s) (BL and WSRO)

ALB   SPCK 'Abstract Letter Book'

Al. Cant.   Venn, J.A. *Alumni Cantabrigienses* (1922-54)

Al. Oxon.   Foster, J. *Alumni Oxonienses* (1887-92)

AMS   Additional Manuscript (ESRO)

Arch.   Archives

B   born

Bishop   Bishop, J.G. *A Peep into the Past: Brighton in the Olden Time* (1892)

BL   British Library

bp   baptised, baptism

BSB   'The free-School Book of Brighthelmston Anno Domini 1701', at Brighton Reference Library: SB 379 FRE

BT   bishop's transcript

B'ton   Brighthelmston, Brighton

bur   burial, buried

Chic   Chichester

chw   churchwarden(s)

CI   Clergy Index at the Sussex Archaeological Society Library

Comber   Comber, J. *Sussex*
Sussex   *Genealogies* (Horsham Centre,
Gen.   1931; Ardingly Centre, 1932;

Lewes Centre, 1933)

cur   curate

D   death, died

DLS   *Dictionary of Land Surveyors* (2nd edn, c.1994)

Enc. Brit.   *The Encyclopaedia Britannica* (13th edn, 1926)

EP   *Report of the Commissioners on the Education of the Poor,* followed by the number and date of the report; 32 reports were issued, 1819-40, the later reports being concerned with all charities, not just educational charities

ESRO   East Sussex Record Office

ev   evening

exhib   exhibitioner

f   father, folio (pl. ff), following page (ff pages)

F   founded

Harrison   Harrison, F. and North, J.S.
& North   *Old Brighton, Old Preston, Old Hove* (1937)

HCS   Willson, A.N. *A History of Collyer's School 1532-1964* (1965)

HHGS   Baines, J.M., Conisbee, L.R. *The History of Hastings Grammar School 1619-1956* (1956, rev. edn, with Bygate, N., 1967)

HM   Hastings Museum

HMGS   Row, E.F. *A History of Midhurst Grammar School*

(1913)

| | | | RSB | 183 loose 18th-century school lists, c.1722-1785, of boys at Saunders' charity school, Rye; nine undated, several gaps in the sequence, most signed by the master: ESRO RYE 114/10 |

Horsfield Lewes — Horsfield, T.W. *The History and Antiquities of Lewes and its Vicinity* (I, 1824; II, 1827)

Horsfield Sussex — Horsfield, T. W. *The History, Antiquities, and Topography of the County of Sussex* (1835)

HRGS — Vidler, L.A. *History of Rye Grammar School, 1639-1939* (1939)

illeg — illegitimate

inst — instituted

LD — Lady Day (25 March)

lic — licensed

Lower Worthies — Lower, M.A. *The Worthies of Sussex* (1865)

marr — marriage, married

MI — memorial inscription

Mich — Michaelmas

mids — midsummer

ML — marriage licence

MSB — 'A Register of the Transactions of the Managers & Trustees of the Charity School at Mayfield in the County of Sussex founded in the year of our Lord 1750': ESRO AMS 5601/1

par — parish

ped — pedigree

pers. comm. — personal communication

pr — proved (of wills)

PR — parish register

R — reference, register

s — son

SAC — *Sussex Archaeological Collections*

SAS — Sussex Archaeological Society (Library)

SCM — *Sussex County Magazine*

Secker — Gregory, J. *The Speculum of Archbishop Thomas Secker* (*Church of England Record Society*, vol. 2, 1995)

SFH — *Sussex Family Historian*

SFHG — Sussex Family History Group

SGLH — *Sussex Genealogist & Local Historian*

SNQ — *Sussex Notes & Queries*

SPCK — Society for Promoting Christian Knowledge

SRS — *Sussex Record Society* volume

SSB — 'Sedlescomb School 1748', a memorandum book relating to the charity school: ESRO ESC/148/1/1

survg — surviving

SWA — *The Sussex Weekly Advertiser or Lewes Journal*

t/s — transcript

VCH — (Victoria County History) *The Victoria History of the County of Sussex*

Woolgar — Woolgar, T. 'Spicilegia': MS, late 18c-early 19c, at Sussex

Archaeological Society Library

WSRO   West Sussex Record Office

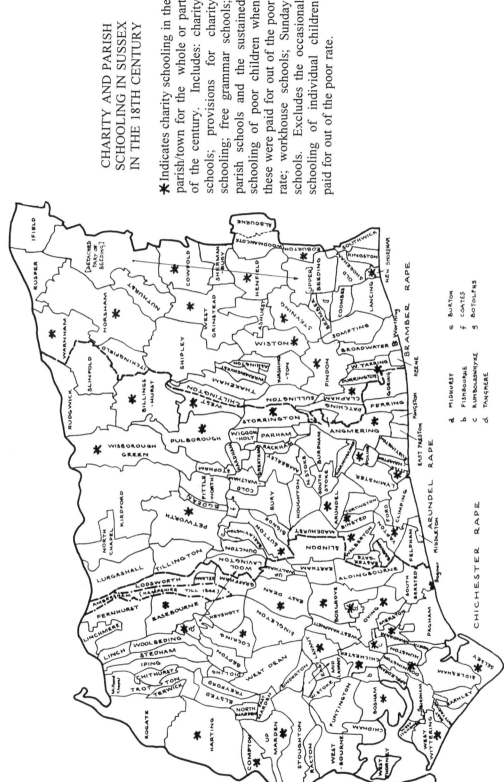

CHARITY AND PARISH
SCHOOLING IN SUSSEX
IN THE 18TH CENTURY

✱ Indicates charity schooling in the parish/town for the whole or part of the century. Includes: charity schools; provisions for charity schooling; free grammar schools; parish schools and the sustained schooling of poor children when these were paid for out of the poor rate; workhouse schools; Sunday schools. Excludes the occasional schooling of individual children paid for out of the poor rate.

a MIDHURST
b FISHBOURNE
c RUMBOLDSWHYKE
d TANGMERE
e BURTON
f COATES
g BOTOLPHS

CHICHESTER RAPE
ARUNDEL RAPE
BRAMBER RAPE

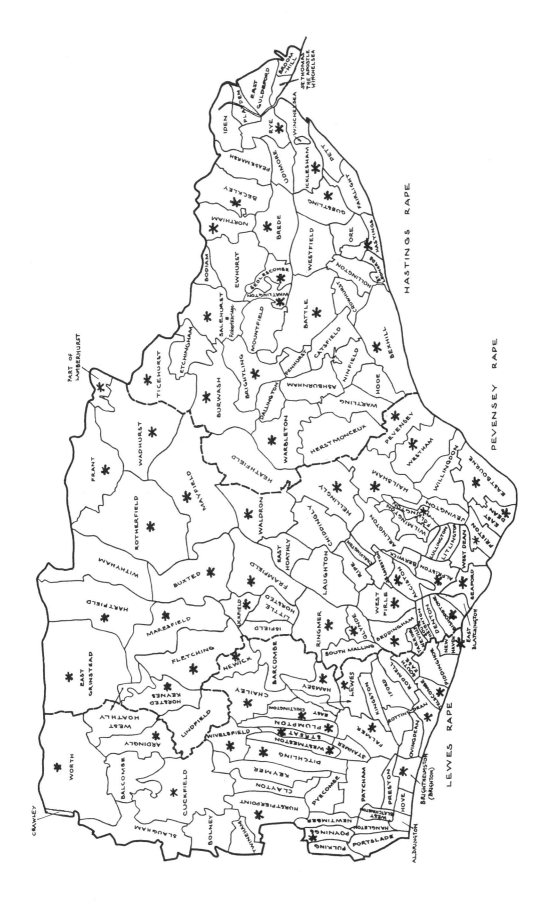

SCHEDULE 1

SCHOOLS AND SCHOOLING PROVISION IN SUSSEX
IN THE 18TH CENTURY

Schools and schooling provision are arranged in chronological sequence of reference under each parish or town, which are listed alphabetically.

Towns comprising more than one parish are here treated as a single centre.

At the end of each school or schooling provision are listed:

> 1. All known masters/mistresses teaching at that school/schooling provision (to provide a cross-reference to Schedule 2, where known biographical details about them are summarised).

> 2. The source references relating to that school/schooling provision.

Source references relating to masters/mistresses which are given in Schedule 2 are not in general repeated here.

After the records of all the parishes/towns there are listed:

> 1. A number of 'unplaced schools', the locations of which are uncertain.

> 2. Brief notes on some schools outside Sussex that advertised in Sussex and were thus actively competitive with the Sussex private schools.

Schools in square brackets indicate schools likely to have been operating in the 18th century but for which documentary evidence of the fact has not yet been traced.

Where 'op. cit.' is used the full reference will be found earlier under the same parish or town.

ALBOURNE   1724: 25 families   1801: pop. 253

No 18th-century schooling traced.

ALCISTON (AASON)   1724: 21 families   1801: pop. 186

Parish schooling   (Rs: 1747-59)
The parish paid small sums to women to 'school' individual children in the Easter-to-Easter years 1747-8, 1749-50, 1750-1, 1753-4, 1754-5, 1757-8, 1758-9. The most paid in any one year appears to have been £1 2s 5d (to Dame Richardson in 1757-8 for schooling two children). The parish accounts often do not specify what payments were for and further payments to dames for schooling may have been made in 1752-3, and from 1762-3 to 1773-4.[1] [*Elizabeth Richardson, Dame Burges, Sarah Roffe?*]
1. ESRO PAR 227/31/1.

Charity schooling   (Rs: 1792, 1793)
The 3rd Viscount Gage's personal account book includes the following entries:

		£. s. d.
1792 Dec 31 Mr. Ridge for Flour given to the poor		
Alciston £1.2.0 Schooling Children £2.0.0		3. 2. -
1793 Dec 31 Mr. Ridge Wheat to poor at Alciston £1.10.0		
Mrs. Stiff Schooling Children £5.0.0		6.10. -

The composite nature of these entries makes it almost certain that the schooling payments related to Alciston. (A separate payment 31 December 1793 relates to schooling at West Firle).[1]   [*Mrs Stiff*]
1. ESRO SAS/G/ACC 741.

Sunday school?   (R: 1800?)
A further entry in Viscount Gage's account book gives the following:
          1800 Dec 31...4 Bush'l of Wheat by Mr. Ridge to the Poor
                    Alciston £2.8.0   Prayer Book Children 36/-   4. 4. 0
The 'Prayer Book Children' may have been Sunday school children.

ALDINGBOURNE   1724: 73 families   1801: pop. 725

No 18th-century schooling traced.

ALDRINGTON   1724: no house in parish 1801: pop. 0

Not surprisingly, no 18th-century schooling traced.

ALFRISTON (AASON TOWN) 1724: 53 families   1801: pop. 576

Parish schooling   (Rs: 1768-72)
Two pages in the parish register contain accounts for sacrament collections made on the first Sunday after Michaelmas, Christmas Day, the Sunday after Easter, and Whit-sunday, beginning with the collection on the Sunday after Michaelmas 1766. The first four such collections totalled £1 12s of which £1 10s 6d was 'given away' on 8 June 1767. Thereafter, until the account ends at March 1772, all the disbursements were for schooling. The amounts received from the collections varied; in 1770 they totalled £1 18s. All but two of the 17 payments recorded were made to Mr Cooper or Mrs French: Cooper was paid 3d per week per child, and French probably the same (all the payments to her are divisible by 3d). The Cooper payments were from 1768 to 1771, the French payments payments from 1769 to 1771.[1] [*Mr Cooper, Mrs French*]

1. ESRO PAR 230/1/1/1.

Private schools?
It is probable that both Cooper and French had small schools, to which the parish sent a few
poor children.

AMBERLEY   1724: 63 families   1801: pop.346

School   (R: 1740)
Thomas Halsey was admitted to Peterhouse, Camb., from 'Amberley School', 27 March
1740[1]. (Bell Carleton was vicar of Amberley, 1721-46, and perhaps Halsey's master.[2])
[*Bell Carleton?*]
1. *Al. Cant.*   2. CI.

Dame schools   (R: 1742)
In the visitation return for 1742 there was no free or charity school, but 'some women' kept
school. 'The Mistresses' were of 'good Life' and 'diligent', and 'come to Church'.[1] So more
than one dame school then.
1. WSRO Ep.I/22/1.

ANGMERING   1724: 64 families   1801: pop. 708

Charity school   (F: c1679. Rs through 18c)
William Older by will, 16 March 1679, gave £100 to Thomas Oliver in trust to purchase
land, on which a house might be built for a schoolmaster to teach poor children within the
parishes of East and West Angmering, and, after the death of Older's wife, the schoolmaster
was to receive all the rents and profits of all his lands. A schoolhouse was built soon after
Older's death.[1]
1714   Marriage Licence for Adrian Nichols, schoolmaster of Angmering.[2]
1724   Value of endowment £25 pa, for teaching 25 poor children; 'there is built a good
        dwelling house & School house' for the master and his successors.[3]
1742   Value of endowment £27 pa; 24 or 26 children taught. A schoolmaster of 'good
        Life' and 'diligent', who comes to Church and causes his scholars to come.[4]
1758   Schoolmaster as at 1742.[5]
1772   Revenue now £30 pa; schoolmaster as at 1742.[6]
1781   Churchwardens present that some of the buildings belonging to the free school are
        falling down.[7]
[About 1815, William Oliver, heir of Thomas mentioned in Older's 1679 will, built
additions to the school. By 1819 the income was £104 10s, all paid to the schoolmaster,
who taught about 60 children of both sexes.[8]]
[*Adrian Nichols, Henry Walmsley, Richard Cunningham, Samuel Akerman*]
1. *EP*2 (1819), 147.   2. *SRS* **12**, 147.   3. WSRO Ep.I/26/3.   4. WSRO Ep.I/22/1.   5. ibid.   6. ibid.
7. SAS Wadey index.   8. *EP*2 (1819), 147.

APPLEDRAM   1724: 8 families   1801: pop. 136

No 18th-century schooling traced.

ARDINGLY   1724: 40 families   1801: pop.506

Workhouse school   (R: 1778)
In an advertisement by the parish for a governor to manage the workhouse, February 1778,
he was also required to keep the parish accounts and to teach the children in the workhouse
to read. A footnote added: 'N.B. If qualified to teach Writing and Arithmetic, he will meet

with good Encouragement, a School being for his own Advantage. There is a convenient Room in The Workhouse for a School.'[1]

1. *SWA* 2.2.78.

Private school?
The above advertisement encouraged the setting up of a private school in the parish, but it is not known if this developed.

ARLINGTON (ERLINGTON)   1724: 65 families   1801: pop. 472

No 18th-century schooling traced.

ARUNDEL   1724: 188 families   1801: pop. 1,855

Catholic dame school   (R: 1714)
In 1714 Elizabeth Girle of Arundel was prosecuted by the ecclesiastical court in Chichester, it being alleged 'that she being a reputed Papist teacheth schoole within ye said parish.'[1] The case was dismissed when she pleaded that 'she only teacheth some Children to worke at their needle & sometimes hears them read in the Bible or new Testament in our own translation and no other'.[2] Apparently she did not deny that she was a papist.   [*Elizabeth Girle*]

1. Kinoulty, M.K. 'A Social Study of Roman Catholicism in West Sussex in the Eighteenth Century', MA thesis, University of Wales (1982), WSRO Add MSS 34,673, 179, citing WSRO Ep.I/17/36, 75.   2. ibid, citing WSRO Ep.I/17/36, 85.

Evan's school   (F: c1721. Rs: 1721-6)
Hugh Evans, vicar of Arundel from 21 September 1720 to his death in 1732, subscribed and was licensed 5 September 1721 to instruct children in a school in Arundel.[1] At the 1726 visitation, 'Mr. Evans has a private school & licensed, & every way regular.'[2]   [*Hugh Evans*]

1. WSRO Ep.I/1/10; Ep.I/3/5.   2. WSRO Ep.I/22/1.

Charity school   (R: 1726)
At the 1726 visitation, 'Thomas Thorncomb has a Charity School'.[1] [*Thomas Thorncomb*]
1. WSRO Ep.I/22/1.

Dissenting private school   (R: 1726)
At the 1726 visitation, 'The dissenting preacher teaches a private school.'[1]
1. WSRO Ep.I/22/1.

Green's boys' school   (R: 1730)
On 1 July 1730 Thomas Green was licensed to teach boys in the parish of Arundel.[1] [*Thomas Green*]
1. WSRO Ep.I/1/11.

School   (R: 1758)
At the 1758 visitation there was a schoolmaster in the parish, of 'good Life' and 'diligent', who came to church and caused his scholars to come, and taught them the catechism.[1]
1. WSRO Ep.I/22/1.

Grammar School   (R: 1766)
Charles Caraccioli was 'Master of the Grammar School' when he published in 1766 *Antiquities of Arundel.*[1]
1. Butler, G. Slade in *SAC* **18**, 97.

School (R: 1769 - perhaps the same school as at 1758)
At the 1769 visitation there was a schoolmaster in the parish.[1]
1. WSRO Ep.I/22/1.

<u>Mrs Phillips' girls' boarding school</u>   (Rs: 1780-93)

In January 1780 Mrs Phillips advertised for a writing and arithmetic master to attend her boarding school in the High-Street.[1]   In June 1781 she advertised for a person to teach music and drawing.[2]   In June 1788 she denied a report that she was intending to give up her school: she took boarders at 18 guineas a year, and 2 guineas entrance; or 20 guineas a year without entrance 'or any other extra Charge, except what is paid to the different Masters, with Tea twice a Day included'; parlour boarders, 25 guineas a year. 'French is the general Language of her School', and both French and English were taught 'with grammatical Accuracy'; and all sorts of useful and ornamental needle-work.[3]   Also, 'Italian taught on reasonable Terms; a Person residing in the House who is perfect Mistress of the Language.'[4]   Advertised in *SWA* Jan 1780; Jun, Jul 81; Jun (4) 88. In Univ.Dir 1793.   *[Elizabeth Phillips]*

1. *SWA* 17.1.80.   2. *SWA* 25.6.81, with erratum in editorial 2.7.81 ('for a Person qualified to teach Music and DANCING, read Music and DRAWING').   3. *SWA* 9.6.88.   4. *SWA* 30.6.88.

<u>Catholic school</u>   (R: 1780)

In 1780 there was a Catholic school at Arundel, which included 20 Protestants among its pupils.[1]   The inclusion of Protestant children indicates a self-supporting Catholic teacher who needed their fees, and perhaps the absence of a comparable Protestant school at that time.

1. Kinoulty, M.K. op. cit. 179, citing Papist Census, 1788, House of Lords Record Office, Main Papers 5 March 1781 (Diocese of Chichester).

<u>Priest's boys' boarding school</u>   (F: 1783. Rs: 1783-93)

Announced opening of his boarding school September 1783. Offered board, washing, mending, and English, writing and arithmetic for 13 guineas pa, 1 guinea entrance; with, as extras, geometry, geography, drawing (at 10s 6d per qr each, 10s 6d entrance); dancing (at 15s per qr, 15s entrance); merchants accounts, music (at 1 guinea per qr each, 1 guinea entrance). 'A Diligence to and from London, three Times a Week.'[1] Advertised for an assistant July, September 1783.[2]   Advertisement January 1787 by 'Priest and Davis'; now offers, for 15 guineas pa, 1 guinea entrance, board, washing, mending, and English, writing, arithmetic, Latin, mensuration, geography, with the use of the globes, merchants' accompts ('after the true Italian method'), with drawing, dancing and music as separate charges.[3]   In January 1789 Priest was advertising on his own again: terms still 15 guineas but no entrance required; geography had become an extra again (at 10s 6d per qr).[4]   In September 1791 the terms were down to 14 guineas pa. Advertised in *SWA* Sep (3) 1783; Jun, Jul (2), Sep 84; Jan (2) 87; Jan, Jun 89; Jan 90; Sep 91; Jul 92; Jan 93. In *Univ. Directory* 1793. *[Henry Priest, Davis]*

1. *SWA* 8.9.83.   2. *SWA* 28.6.84.   3. *SWA* 1.1.87.   4. *SWA* 5.1.89.   *SWA* 16.9.91.

<u>Barclay's boarding academy for boys</u>   (F: 1787. Rs: 1787-90)

Rev William Barclay opened his academy 23 July 1787, and advertised this every week from 11 June to 27 August 1787. Offered instruction 'in the various Branches of useful and polite LITERATURE', at 18 guineas pa, and 1 guinea entrance.[1]   In December 1789, denied that he was about to leave Arundel, and announced the reopening of his academy (after the Christmas vacation) on 18 January 1790.[2]   Advertised in *SWA* Jun (3), Jul (5), Aug (4) 1787; Jul 88; Dec 89. (Not in *Univ. Directory* 1793: perhaps his school taken over by Neale in 1790, [qv].) *[William Barclay]*

1. *SWA* 11.6.87.   2. *SWA* 28.12.89.

<u>The Miss Blanches' girls' boarding school</u>   (F: 1788. Rs: 1788-99)

Mary and Martha Blanch opened their girls' boarding school at Michaelmas 1788, offering, for 18 guineas pa, board, French, English, geography, and all sorts of plain and ornamental needle-work. 'No entrance required, or any extra Charges whatsoever, except Writing, Dancing, Drawing, and Music, which are on the usual Terms.' Parlour boarders, 22 guineas pa; half-boarders, 12 guineas and 1 guinea entrance. 'A large airy House is provided for the School.'[1] In *Univ. Directory* 1793, under Blanch, Mary & Martha. On 9 March 1799, a large piece of concealed timber adjoining a chimney of the school caught fire, but was discovered before any material damage had been done.[2] Advertised in *SWA* Jun, Jul (2) 1788. [*Martha Blanch, Mary Blanch*]

1. *SWA* 30.6.88.   2. *SWA* 11.3.99.

Rev Neale's private grammar school for boys   (Rs: 1790-3)
Advertised June 1790 under the heading 'Arundel Grammar School'. Offered Latin and Greek, 'the most useful Branches of Science, and Polite Literature', including mathematics (arithmetic, book-keeping, navigation, &c.), geography, morals, composition, and elocution. 'And the principles of composition and elocution, will not be confined to the learned languages, but will extend to Public Exercises, in writing and speaking the English tongue with elegance and propriety.' The pupils were taught by Mr Neale and 'proper Assistants'; 'and those whom he receives into his house, are treated as part of his family; even those hours which are not appropriated to study, he will endeavour to improve to their advantage, by particularly attending to their manners and dispositions.' French taught by a native of France, resident in the seminary (in January 1791, 'by a native of Paris, and a Graduate of that University'[1]). Music, dancing, and drawing, by proper masters. 'The terms... are moderate; and all incidental expenses kept as low as possible, and avoided, unless absolutely necessary.'[2] In January 1792, the curriculum was more briefly expressed as instruction in 'English, Latin, Greek, French, Mathematical, Commercial, Naval, and Philosophical Literature... A Dancing and Drawing Master attends.'[3] In *Univ. Directory* 1793, under Neale, Rev Robert. Advertised in *SWA* Jun (2), Jul 1790; Jan 91; Jan (2) 92. He had previously kept a school at Littlehampton. [*Robert Neale*]

1. *SWA* 10.1.91.   2. *SWA* 21.6.90.   3. *SWA* 9.1.92.

Sunday school   (F: 1792. Rs: 1792-4)
In March 1792 a Sunday school was instituted 'for the Benefit of 30 Boys and 30 Girls... and Mr. Bushby, Mayor of that Town [Arundel], and Mr. Thomas Coote, have the credit of the Institution. Yesterday the young objects of this judicious charity walked together to Church for the first time.'[1] In March 1794, 30 boys and 30 girls were being 'attentively educated', and every Sunday, 'the clergyman and committee, or at least two of them, attend regularly to hear them read the lessons of the day, &c. &c.'[2]

1. *SWA* 19.3.92.   2. *SWA* 10.3.94.

[Prior's school]   (R: between 1797-1805)
James Prior, minister of Arundel Free Church c1797-1805, opened a private day school to supplement his small stipend.[1] [*James Prior (Pryer)*]

1. Valentine, C.H. *The Story of the Beginnings of Nonconformity in Arundel* (nd but 1920s), 21.

Other master

Simon Clement, schoolmaster of Arundel 1787/8. Later at Shoreham [qv]. Also surveyor. (*DLS*)

ASHBURNHAM   1724: 45 families   1801: pop. 473

No 18th-century schooling traced.

ASHINGTON   1724: 20 families   1801: pop. 173

Dame schools   (R: 1737)
At the 1737 visitation: 'There are only School-Dames in our Parish'.[1] So more than one
dame school then.
1. WSRO Ep.I/22/1.

ASHURST   1724: about 50 families 1801: pop. 385

Dame schools   (Rs: 1733, 1762, 1775)
At the 1733 visitation: 'some women teach small children to spell, read & say their
Catechism'. So more than one dame school then. At the 1762 visitation: 'We have a little
School for small children', where 'very small children taught to read & nit'; 'We know of
no licence the Schoolmistress has'. At the 1775 visitation: 'A few children are taught by
some Women in the Parish, who are capable of Teaching to read... but have no Licence
from the Ordinary for that Purpose'. [Re coming to Church]: 'The Scholars are left to the
Care of their Parents in this Respect'. [Re instructing the scholars in the catechism]: 'We
believe the School Dames do thus instruct their Scholars'. 'The Children taught are chiefly
those of Farmers & Labourers'. So more than one dame school then.[1]
1. WSRO Ep.I/22/1.

Williams' school   (R: 1758)
At the 1758 visitation: 'The Curate teaches & we do not know yt he has a licence'.[1] The
curate was then Miles Williams.[2] [*Miles Williams*]
1. WSRO Ep.I/22/1.   2. Townsend, J.D.R. *Eatons School Ashurst* (1996).

BALCOMBE   1724: about 50 families 1801: pop. 451

No 18th-century schooling traced.

BARCOMBE   1724: about 90 families 1801: pop. 615

No 18th-century schooling traced.

BARLAVINGTON (BARLTON) 1724: 9 families   1801: pop. 78

No 18th-century schooling traced.

BARNHAM   1724: 16 families   1801: pop. 124

No 18th-century schooling traced.

BATTLE   1801: pop. 2,040

Lord's school   (R: 1702)
George Luxford was put to school at Battle with Mr Lord, at 40s a year, boarding
with John Page for £10 pa.[1] [*Mr Lord*]
1. *SNQ* **12**, 170.

Charity schools   (Rs: 1707-45; c1793- into 19c)
The SPCK annual *Account of the Charity-Schools* first records a charity school at Battle in
1707: 'Here is a School wherein about 40 poor Children are taught to Read, to say the
Catechism, and those who desire it, to Write.' George Barnsley, rector of Sedlescomb,
confirmed the continuance of the school for 40 children at Battle, in letters to the SPCK in
January 1712, February 1713 ('Supported by Subscriptions but ye contributions are not

sufficient to Cloath ym.') and February 1714. But in October 1719 he reported: 'That the School at Battel is sunk since Christmas, the Master then leaving it, and the chief Persons in the Town being not willing to admit a Stranger in his Room. however means will be used, if possible, to set it up again.'[1] The SPCK annual reports continued to list Battle, specifically in 1724, and continuously, by implication from the county summary totals, from 1719 to at least 1740; though, since the lists recorded not a single change in the number of charity schools or children taught in Sussex from 1730, these later lists must be treated as suspect. However, John Fuller of Brightling paid £2 pa, due on 2 February each year, to the charity school at Battle, from at least 1733 to 1745. Payments were made variously to Thomas and John Vigorwaite, both of whom, at different times, are described as schoolmaster.[2]

Elizabeth Langton, widow, who was buried at Battle 16 May 1793, by will dated 8 December 1791, left in trust to the dean, churchwardens and overseers of Battle, £1,500 4% consols, the full interest from which (£60 pa) was to be paid to a man and his wife for instructing 15 boys 'in the Art and Science of Reading' and 15 girls 'in the Art and Mystery and Science of Reading Sowing and Knitting'. They were to instruct the children 'in Way and Manner of Sunday School as now practised at Brighthelmstone or Lewes', as the dean, churchwardens and overseers should think best. The master and mistress were 'not to follow any other Vocation or Calling whatsoever nor any night School' and were 'to devote themselves altogether for the good Lord'. The children's lessons 'shall be entirely out of the holy Scriptures'; and they were to go off after three years schooling. She also left £200 4% consols, the interest from which (£8 pa) was to be spent on spelling books, bibles, testaments and common prayer books, and other religious books; each child was to carry home their respective books on leaving school. She also left to the master and mistress her own copy of Birkett on the Testament (14th edition), 'for the better admonition of all the Scholars'.[3] An undated plan of Battle church, probably late 18th century, shows a school in the NE corner of the church, against the vestry and chancel. This is probably where the Elizabeth Langton school was kept.[4] By 1819, the number of children was kept up, the children being selected by the dean, churchwardens and overseers (trustees under the will) from the most deserving in the Sunday school at Battle. The children were then taught in the schoolmaster's house, the boys reading (as directed by the will) and also writing and arithmetic, the girls the same plus plain work.[5]

[*John Vigorwaite, Thomas Vigorwaite*, probably *William King* (see Ticehurst's school below)]

1. SPCK ALB v.3, 2949; v.4, 3453; v.5, 3905; v.10, 6229.   2. ESRO SAS/RF 15/28.
3. ESRO PAR 236/1/1/5, f5, f78.   4. ESRO PAR 236/4/1.   5. *EP1* (1819), 222.

Mrs Thorpe's boys'and girls' boarding school   (Rs: 1728-c1753)

Mrs Thorpe, probably assisted by her daughters, kept a boarding school for boys and girls, to which were sent in turn the seven children (who survived infancy) of John and Mary Collier of Hastings - two boys and five girls. The boys went out to a master, and their subjects included Latin (they could both read and write before going to Mrs Thorpe). Dancing was available. The Collier boys went on to Westminster school when they were 12 and 11 respectively; the girls went on to Mrs Russell's school at Hampstead. The first surviving letter addressed to the eldest boy at Mrs Thorpe's (he was then 8) was dated November 1728; from their ages, Collier children would have attended the school until about 1753.[1] [*Mrs Thorpe*]

1. ESRO SAY: Matthews, H.M. 'The Papers of John Collier of Hastings. A Catalogue' (1966), introduction; and SAY MSS, Collier family correspondence.

Gridley and Cripps' girls' boarding school   (F: 1771)
Opened on 8 July 1771 by Charlotte Gridley and Elizabeth Cripps.[1] By 1781 Gridley had married and, as Mrs Betts, had opened her own school (see below); she then claimed to have been educating young ladies for many years, so presumably the Gridley and Cripps school continued for some time.[2] Advertised in *SWA* May, Jun, Jul 1771. [*Charlotte Gridley, Elizabeth Cripps*]
1. *SWA* 20.5.71.   2. *SWA* 9.4.81.

Mrs Betts' girls' boarding school   (F: 1781. Rs: 1781-97)
In April 1781 Mrs Betts (late Miss Gridley) announced that she had opened a boarding school for young ladies; she offered every kind of needle-work ('viz. Plain Work, Childbed Linen, Embroidery, &c. &c.'); writing, dancing, music and French 'will be taught if required' (ie as extras); full boarders, £14 pa, entrance 1 guinea; half-boarders, £10 pa, entrance 1 guinea. 'BATTLE is remarkable for its healthy Situation, is 56 Miles from London, in the Turnpike Road to Hastings; from whence a Diligence goes to and from, in the Winter twice a week, in the Summer three Times.'[1] By 1787 she had 'proper Assistants'.[2] In December 1796 she denied a report that she had given up the school. The terms for board and education were now up to £20 pa, and 1 guinea entrance; 'Mrs. BETTS does not intend having more than ten at a time. - Two Parlour-Boarders may be genteely accomodated at 30 l. per annum.'[3] Advertised in *SWA* Apr (4) 1781; Jan 87; Dec 96; Jan 97. [Mrs Betts, see *Charlotte Gridley*]
1. *SWA* 9.4.81.   2. *SWA* 8.1.87.   3. *SWA* 26.12.96.

Ticehurst's school?   (R: 1793)
Univ. Directory 1793 listed two schoolmasters at Battle, William King and William Tycehurst (Ticehurst elsewhere). One was probably master of the Elizabeth Langton charity school, the other probably had a private school. Ticehurst was also a surveyor,[1] and since Langton had specified that the master of her charity school should have no other occupation, it was probably Ticehurst who had his own school. [*William Ticehurst*]
1. *SWA* 7.1.93 (ad for 'The New British Tontine')

[Mrs Weekes' girls' boarding school] . (R: 1801)
Mrs Weekes had a girls' boarding school at Battle by 1801,[1] but it is not known when the school started. [*Mrs Weekes*]
1. *SWA* 11.1.1802.

BECKLEY   1724: about 70 families   1801: pop. 742

Charity school   (F: c1770?)
Odiarne Hooper,vicar of Hailsham at his death in 1769 left a charity which, in 1835, was being used, with other subscriptions, to support two national schools in Beckley, for boys and girls. It seems probable that the charity was for educating poor children and that it became operative in the 18th century.[1] Early in the 19th century, the Frewen family of neighbouring Northiam were benefactors of the charity school in Beckley, and paid bills for building a schoolhouse 1808-9.[2]
1. Horsfield *Sussex* I, 510.   2. ESRO FRE 8181-8183.

Parsons' boys' boarding school   (Rs: 1792, 1797)
J. Parsons had a boys' boarding school by 1792. He offered board, writing, arithmetic, practical geometry, mensuration of superficies and solids, algebra and book-keeping, at 14 guineas pa, money for entrance, breaking-up and servants included.[1] (He was also a surveyor.) On 13 November 1797 he advertised for information about two boys, Christopher and Henry White, who had run away. They had gone to their father-in-law, Benjamin

Linghams, at Crowhurst; on 23 October Linghams had ordered them to return to school, but they had not been heard of since. 'Had on when they went away blue coats; the oldest boy is aged twelve years, a short stout lad, has dark hair; the youngest boy is eight years old, pale complexion, and light hair.' Anyone giving information to any of a number of named persons at Beckley, Icklesham and Ticehurst, 'shall be satisfied for their trouble and all reasonable expences paid.'[2] The following week the paper reported that the missing boys had been found and 'returned to their friends'.[3] Advertised in *SWA* Jun, Jul 1792; Nov 97. [*J. Parsons*]

1. *SWA* 25.6.92.   2. *SWA* 13.11.97.   3. *SWA* 20.11.97.

BEDDINGHAM   1724: 45 families   1801: pop. 219

Charity school   (R: 1766-7)
William Hodgson, steward to Richard Trevor, Bishop of Durham (who inherited the Glynde estates in 1743), paid £9 4s 1d for teaching the poor children of Beddingham for the year ending 10 October 1767.[1]

1. ESRO GLY 2937.

BEPTON   1724: 13 families   1801: pop. 129

Thomas Nepiker, rector of Bepton from 1667 to 1706, took pupils (apparently gentlemen's sons): there are references to pupils in his accounts for 1685,[1] but no 18th-century references have been traced.

1. *SAC* **36**, 103-5.

BERWICK   1724: 21 families   1801: pop. 170

No 18th-century schooling traced.

BEXHILL   1724: about 100 families 1801: pop. 1,091

Parish free school   (Rs: 1754-1800)
Surviving overseers' accounts running from Easter 1753 to Easter 1800 show that the parish supported a small school.[1] Payments of £6 pa, plus c10s 'for firing for the free Scholars', were made to schoolmasters from Easter 1754 to Easter 1756, from Easter 1769 to Easter 1771, almost certainly from Easter 1772 to Easter 1776 (the payments during these years not being specifically identified as for schooling), and continuously from that date to Easter 1800. During the apparent gap, from Easter 1756 to Easter 1769, payments may have been made through another account; in March 1767 the overseers paid 1s 9½d 'for a Testament, 2 Catichisms, 1 Hornbook', suggesting that the parish still had responsibility for a school. On occasion the school is referred to as 'the Free School' (1777, 1781) and the pupils as 'the free Scholars' (1784-8); in April 1784 they are specifically described as 'the 10 free Scholars', and this number was probably maintained throughout. In this event, the parish paid 3d per week per child for a 48-week year, or 12s pa per child.

The precise amounts paid for schooling are not always clear, since the schoolmasters were also paid for other parish services and entries of payments to them do not always show details of their bills. The first schoolmaster we know of, William Smith, was also the clerk, for which he was paid £2 pa; and he was paid a further £1 pa for keeping the overseers' accounts. He was often paid 2s 6d 'for a Knell and Grave' at pauper burials; in September 1763 he was paid 6s 'one half for Making of Benj. Godwin Indentures', and there are other small payments for clerical work. In May 1770 the parish gave him 5s 'to pay his Nurse'. From April 1776 he gave up his parish duties, and John

Dann was paid as schoolmaster. From April 1782 Dann was also paid £1 a year for 'Book keeping for Overseers'; and in 1784, 1785, 1786 (twice) and 1787 he was paid 'for writing the Militia List', at 2s a time. From April 1789 the schooling was taken over by Evenden Cruttenden (referred to initially in the accounts as 'Edmun'); he was then aged 47, and died in 1824. In the years from 1796 his bills to the parish totalled considerably more than the £6 for schooling plus c10s for firing: £10 3s 8¼d, £7 13s 3d, £8 7s 1d, £13 2s 6d; so he may also have been paid for other services, or possibly for goods for the workhouse; or perhaps more children were then being put out to school.
[*William Smith, John Dann, Everenden (Evenden) Cruttenden*]
1. ESRO PAR 240/30/1, PAR 240/30/2.

Private schools?   (Rs: 1754?-1800?)
Masters of the 'Free School', with its 10 scholars paid for by the parish at £6 pa (see above), very probably took private pupils as well. The frequent reference in the overseers' accounts to 'the free Scholars' suggests that there were other scholars who were not free. [*William Smith?, John Dann?, Everenden Cruttenden?*]

Barwick's boys' boarding school   (R: 1781)
In 1781 the curate of Bexhill kept a private boys' boarding school. James Lord, son of William Lord, rector of Northiam, then aged 14, was buried at Northiam, 4 September 1781, the register entry noting: 'drowned August 31 having been permitted by his schoolmaster the Curate of Bexhill with several other less boys to bathe in the sea on a flowing tide, they escaped.'[2] The curate was Henry Barwick, who carried out marriages at Bexhill as curate from February 1780 to February 1792.[2] He had opened a school at Hastings at Easter 1779 - possibly this school - for 12 young gentlemen, to qualify them for business, the public schools, or university, at 20 guineas a year, 2 guineas entrance [qv]. In January 1793 he opened a similar school at Lindfield [qv]. [*Henry Barwick*]
1. Northiam PR.   2. Bexhill PR.

BIGNOR   1724: 19 families   1801: pop. 95
No 18th-century schooling traced. At the 1775 visitation, 'None teach'.[1]
1. WSRO Ep.I/22/1.

BILLINGSHURST   1724: about 140 families 1801: pop. 1,164
Parish schooling   (Rs: 1731, 1732, 1775- into 19c)
Parish expenses for the workhouse in 1731 included, at 2 October:
    one horn Book 1d: Two large Combes & one primmer 7d   0. 0. 8
A workhouse contract made in 1732 with Richard Greenfield includes 'that he the said Richard Greenfield shall and will during the time aforesaid teach and instruct or cause to be tought & instructed the poor children in the said workhouse that are or shall be capable of being tought & instructed in the reading of the Primer the New Testament and Bible...'[1]

        The surviving overseers' accounts run from 1776 to the end of the century.[2] In October 1776 the parish paid William Puttock £2 5s for 'a yrs Schooling 6 Charity Children', and similar payments may have been made earlier. Except for the church year 1777-8, when a different arrangement seems to have been made (see below), this payment, for six charity children, was continued to the end of the century, the amount paid increasing to £2 12s pa from Michaelmas 1796. William Puttock at his burial was described as 'schoolmaster', which implies that he taught more than the six charity children. It is probable that he and his successors ran private schools, to which the parish sent the six charity children. (The fact that six children were consistently schooled in this way through such a long period, within which there were severe pressures on the poor rate, suggests that the payments may have arisen from a bequest for the purpose, although there is no record of any such receipt.) William Puttock was also the vestry clerk, receiving £2 2s (eg 1783) or £2 (eg 1785) pa for that role; and he was also paid smaller amounts for other clerical work. From the beginning of May 1787 the payments for schooling the six charity children were made to Robert Parsons, who, like William Puttock, was also parish clerk, sharing the annual fee of £2 2s with John Clare, who had been clerk for the 1786-7 year, following Puttock's death. He died in July 1794, when the schooling of the six charity children was taken over by John Lander. The payment for the half-year from Michaelmas 1795 was shared between Lander and John Jones, curate of the parish. For the following year, Jones was paid for the schooling (now £2 12s pa), but he had left the parish by November 1798. Lander took over the schooling of the six charity children again from Michaelmas 1797, and continued to do so for the remainder of the century.

The churchwardens' accounts for 1789 show a payment of 13s 8d for 'Car'g bricks to the School Chimney & lime';[3] so there was a school then for which the parish was responsible. It is probable that this was the school at which the six charity children were taught, though it could have been one at the workhouse (see below).

From April 1777 to April 1778 weekly payments were made by the overseers to Dame Booker for schooling the parish children. For most weeks the number of children is noted: these ranged from 14 to 17, with 19 in the first week. The average weekly payment per child was about 2½d. There were no payments to Dame Booker for a number of weeks during the year, but the total amount paid to her during the church year 1777-8 (including a last payment on 3 May 1778) was £7 8s 5½d. In the previous year, 1776-7, the overseers had paid £2 5s for the schooling of six charity children (see above); it may be that in 1777-8 the parish tried a different approach, schooling not just six but all the poor children in the parish; but that this proved too costly to sustain. Later, however, they paid for some schooling of the workhouse children, apart from the six charity children mentioned above.

In September 1779 there was a further payment for schooling to Dame Booker (3s 11d). From Michaelmas 1784 until Easter 1788, William Jenner was paid 6d a week to school the children in the workhouse. He was also paid 5s a week for 'looking after the Workhouse', and his accounts are complicated by other expenses he incurred on behalf of the parish, including paying the workhouse people for work done, and by money he received for work done by them. In the 1787-8 year, the last for which he was paid, he received 'his pay' (5s a week) but not payment for schooling for two weeks in June (probably the Whitsun holiday - Whitsunday was 27 May), one week at Christmas and one week at Easter. From the end of May 1788 until the end of June 1789, Dame Hawkins was paid 6d a week for schooling - presumably taking over from Jenner the schooling of the workhouse children. (She later received 'relief' payments from the parish, and from 1796 regular weekly poor pay of 1s, plus occasional extra relief.) In July 1790, a payment to Mr Peskett for various workhouse expenses he had paid for, included 'School'g'; but in the late 1780s and early 1790s there were longer and longer lists of poor people receiving weekly pay, and the strain on the poor rate appears to have inhibited workhouse schooling until 1797. The governor of the workhouse was then getting £83 a month. In July 1797 there was a 2s payment to James Wensley for schooling. (On 1 July 1798 the parish gave Wensley 10s 6d 'to help Burying his Son', and on 3 November 1799 7s 'for Cloaths for his Girl'.) From Michaelmas 1800 and into 1801 he was paid 1s a week for 'Schooling the Children in the House'.[4]

[*William Puttock, Dame Booker, William Jenner, Robert Parsons, Mary Hawkins, John Lander, John Jones, James Wensley*]

1. Newnham, J.M., transcript of vestry minutes, WSRO MP 248 [missing 1989].   2. WSRO Par 21/31/l,
Par 21/31/2.   3. Newnham, J.M., transcript of churchwardens' accounts 1732-1839, WSRO MP 247.   4. WSRO
Par 21/31/1, Par 21/31/2.

Bullis's school   (R: 1733)
John Bullis was vicar 1706-37, and in 1733 was keeping a school.[1] He was buried 22
December 1737, aged 56, and the school probably continued until then. His inventory
included 'A Library of Books' valued at £30. [*John Bullis*]
1. WSRO Ep.I/22/1.

Dame schools   (Rs: 1733, 1737, 1742)
Visitation returns give the following:[1]
1733 'there are some Dame-schools'
1737 'We have a Little School or two', but apparently no schoolmaster.
1742 One or more unlicensed teachers, one of whom - according to the return - appears to
have been a schoolmaster (but this may have been a form-filling error).
See also Parish schooling above for references to dames 1777-9, 1788-9.
1. WSRO Ep.I/22/1.

Private school   (R: 1762)
In 1762 there was a schoolmaster in the parish, but no free or charity school.[1] He was of
'good Life' and 'diligent', came to church and caused his scholars to come, and instructed
them in the catechism. This may well have been William Puttock (see his school below).
1. WSRO Ep.I/22/1.

Puttock's school   (Rs: 1775-86)
From at least Michaelmas 1775 the parish paid William Puttock £2 5s pa to school six
charity children, and - with the exception of the 1777-8 year - these payments continued
until his death in 1786 (see Parish schooling above). He is described as 'schoolmaster' at his
burial, and since no schoolmaster could manage on £2 5s pa, he would have taught private
pupils as well as the six charity children; the 1779 visitation return records that there was
in the parish a school for reading, writing and arithmetic (but no free school),[1] and this was
almost certainly Puttock's school. [*William Puttock*]
1. WSRO Ep.I/22/1.

[Parsons' school]   (Rs: 1787-94)
Following the death of William Puttock (see his school above), Robert Parsons was paid by
the parish £2 5s pa to school six charity children, and these payments continued until his
death in 1794 (see Parish schooling above). It is very probable that he taught private pupils
as well as the six charity children, as Puttock appears to have done. [*Robert Parsons*]

[Evershed's school]   (R: 1788)
The will of John Dean of Shipley, yeoman, dated 26 June 1788, mentions 'William Evershed
of Billingshurst, Schoolmaster'.[1] Evershed was a General Baptist. In the later 1790s he had
a day school, with a few boarders, in Steyning [qv]. [*William Evershed*]
1. Evershed, P.B., pers. comm.

Lander's school   (Rs: 1794- into 19c)
Following the death of Robert Parsons (see his school above), John Lander was paid by the
parish, from August 1794 until Michaelmas 1795, for teaching six charity children, at the
rate of £2 5s pa. For the six months to Lady Day 1796 the payment of £1 2s 6d was paid
jointly to Lander and John Jones, the curate. From Lady Day 1796 to Michaelmas 1797 the
payment - increased to £2 12s pa - was made to Jones. From Michaelmas 1797, and into
the 19th century, the payments were again made to Lander.[1] It is very probable that he
taught private pupils as well as the six charity children, and that he continued his school

during the period when the curate was teaching the six charity children. [*John Lander*]

1. WSRO Par 21/31/1, Par 21/31/2.

[Jones' school]   (Rs: 1795-7)

John Jones, curate of the parish, shared with John Lander (see his school above) £1 2s 6d paid by the parish for schooling six charity children for six months from Michaelmas 1795. For the period from Lady Day 1796 to Michaelmas 1797, Jones received the full payment for teaching the six charity children, now increased to £2 12s pa.[1] (He had left the parish by November 1798, and probably at Michaelmas 1797.)   He may well have taught private pupils as well as the six charity children. [*John Jones*]

1. WSRO Par 21/31/2.

BINDERTON   1801: pop. 53

No 18th-century schooling traced.

BINSTED   1724: 20 families   1801: pop. 100

Charity schooling   (F: 1733   Rs: 1733- into 19c)

Under the will of John Nash, dated 24 May 1732, Binsted had the right to one sixth of the accomodation of the schoolhouse at Walberton,[1] for which Nash bequeathed a newly built house, together with provision for its repair and maintenance, and an annuity of £12 to be spent on the education of poor children.[2] The school was operating by 1733.[3] (In 1819, in return for the annuity and accomodation - now a different house - the schoolmaster and his wife were teaching 18 boys and girls reading, writing and arithmetic; Binsted's entitlement was presumably three places.[4])

1. WSRO School Records Catalogue   2. *EP2* (1819), 185.   3. WSRO Ep.I/22/1, Walberton.
4. *EP2* (1819), 185.

[Private school]   (R: 1758?)

At the 1758 visitation, there was apparently a schoolmaster in the parish (of 'good Life' and 'diligent'):[1] if so, he is likely to have had a private petty school, unless the churchwardens were thinking of the schoolmaster at Walberton, to whom a few of the Binsted children were sent.

1. WSRO Ep.I/22/1.

BIRDHAM   1724: about 30 families   1801: pop. 100

Dame schools   (R: 1737)

At the 1737 visitation, 'some Women who teach children to read & their Catechism':[1] so two or more dame schools then.

1. WSRO Ep.I/22/1.

BISHOPSTONE   1724: 19 families   1801: pop. 188

Sunday school   (F: 1793?   Rs: 1793- into 19c)

The 'Parish Book', dated 11 October 1792, records payments to Mrs Clark for Sunday school, the first being for the year starting 8 April 1793, which probably indicates the foundation date of the school. She received £2 12s a year (presumably 1s per week) until 1798-9 and 1799-1800, when it was £2 10s; in 1800-1 she was paid £2 14s 9d. The school is referred to variously as 'Sunday School', 'ye Charity School', 'ye School', 'the Childrens Schooling'.[1] [*Mrs Clark*]

1. ESRO PAR 247/31/1.

BODIAM   1724: 21 families   1801: pop. 228

No 18th-century schooling traced.

BOGNOR REGIS - see SOUTH BERSTED

BOLNEY   1724: 88 families   1801: pop. 497

West's school   (R: 1791)
John West, schoolmaster, and his wife Susannah owned two buildings in the parish in 1791, living in one and renting out the other.[1] [*John West*]
1. From legal documents in the possession of S. Williams.

BOSHAM   1801: pop. 880

Charity schooling/charity school   (Rs: 1734- into 19c)
Elizabeth Nash of Halnaker, in the parish of Boxgrove, by indenture dated 10 November 1716, gave to trustees a house and several parcels of land in Sidlesham, and, after deduction of £1 for the poor of Walberton, one third of the residual rents were to be given to the minister of Bosham and the occupier of Nash's farmhouse in Bosham, in trust, to distribute amongst the needy poor of Bosham.[1] Accounts of the charity from June 1734 to March 1769, during Richard Lawson's incumbency, were kept in the churchwardens' account book.[2] For most years, the income from the charity was £4 13s 4d; in addition to gifts to the poor of money, cloth, clothing, shoes, and occasionally food, small sums were paid each year for schooling poor children. In most years, three children were paid for; in four years, two; in four years, four. The sums paid out ranged from 13s 10d (1747) to £1 12s 2d (1735). The entry for 1768 reads: 'in schooling 2 children, 61 weeks each - £1 0s 4d', showing that then 2d a week was paid for each child.

George Parker, the elder, by will dated 15 November 1722, bequeathed £70, to be laid out 'for the keeping or schooling and teaching' of poor children of the parish. His son, George Parker, did not lay out his father's bequest in his lifetime, but by his will dated 24 November 1733 he gave a further sum of £70 to be laid out in the same way and for the same purposes as mentioned in his father's will. Following a Chancery case, a rent charge of £4 pa was obtained for the charity, from these two bequests.[3] The charity was operating by 1737, when the visitation return reported 'twelve children taught by charity only to read'.[4] In 1758 there was a free school for ten children, with a revenue of £4 a year; replies to the visitation questions suggest there was a schoolmaster of 'good Life' and 'diligent', who came to church and caused his scholars to come, and taught them the catechism.[5] In 1762 the income of the free school was reported as 4 guineas; to the visitation question, 'Is your School-master of a good Life...[&c]?' the churchwardens answered, 'for ought we know'; and to 'Doth the Schoolmaster come to Church...[&c]?', 'not duly'.[6] In 1765 there was a 'small free school' where children were taught to read; in reply to the questions about their schoolmaster, the churchwardens noted, 'Here is only a schoole mistress'.[7] In 1775 they reported 'Something of a free School', where eleven poor children were taught to read.[8] The charity was still in effect in 1819.[9]

1. *EP*2 (1819), 149; *EP*30 (1837), 637 [under Boxgrove].   2. WSRO Par 25/9/1.   3. *EP*2 (1819), 148-9.
4. WSRO Ep.I/22/1.   5. ibid.   6. ibid.   7. ibid.   8. ibid.   9. *EP*2 (1819), 148-9.

Dame and petty schools   (Rs: 1735, 1761-3, and 1734?- into 19c?)
The schooling of 2-4 poor children each year under the Nash charity (see above), at least from 1734 to 1769, suggests that during this period there were dame or petty schools to which children could be sent. The Nash charity accounts specifically refer to 'the School

dame' in 1735, and to payments 'for schooling from March 16: 1761 to April 25th 1763: to Wm Miles 0:18:2 to widow Oakshot, 0 7 10'.[1] These schools, or one of them, may have been the 'free school' under the Parker bequests, but it is likely that the Parker provision for schooling 10 or 11 children used the same schools as the Nash charity, and that these schools took paying pupils. [*William Miles, Widow Oakshot*]

1. WSRO Par 25/9/1, ff 21, 43.

Gregory's school   (R: 1775)
At the 1775 visitation, 'The Curate teaches by Licence'.[1] The curate at the time was John Gregory (curate from 1772 until 1778).[2] [*John Gregory*]

1. WSRO Ep.I/22/1.   2. WSRO Par 25/9/1; Mrs Bromley-Martin, pers. comm.

BOTOLPHS (BUTTOLPHS) - see BRAMBER

BOXGROVE   1801: pop. 682

Charity school   (Rs: 1716- into 19c)
Mrs Elizabeth Nash, by indenture dated 10 November 1716, gave lands in trust from which one-third of the rents and profits were to be used for the clothing and schooling of two poor children of the honest inhabitants of Boxgrove; they were to be clothed in blue, as the children were clothed in the charity schools then lately erected in Chichester. By 1819 the income from this charity was £8 11s 9d, of which £1 4s was paid to the schoolmaster and the same sum to the schoolmistress of the school then established, and the remaining £6 3s 9d spent on clothing one boy and two girls.[1]

The charity school proper 'was set up in ye year 1741'.[2] By indenture dated 2 January 1741, enrolled the following month, Mary Countess Dowager of Derby (the daughter of Sir William Morley, she had married James, Earl of Derby; she died in 1752, aged 85[3]) granted lands to be sold for certain charitable purposes, including the building of almshouses and a pension of £8 pa plus £1 pa for fuel for each of the poor widows or maidens in them, and provision for a charity school for clothing and teaching twelve poor boys and girls in reading, writing and arithmetic. The schoolmaster was to receive £15 pa plus £1 for fuel, plus his house. If any of the widows or maidens in the almshouses were qualified to teach reading and needlework, they were to get £10 pa (that is, £2 pa more than the pension they would otherwise receive). £12 pa was to be used for clothing the 12 children. Six of the poor boys or girls were to be from Boxgrove, four from East Lavant, two from Tangmere. However, the income of £140 pa had to accumulate to allow for the erection of a competent building for the schoolmaster and 12 poor women; this was completed towards the end of 1750 (in the Countess's lifetime), but a schoolmaster was not appointed until Michaelmas 1752. In 1787 the trustees agreed to educate, but not to clothe, a further six boys of the same parishes in like proportions. By 1819 the income from this charity, for schooling, was £39 19s: £20 was paid to the schoolmaster, for 12 boys; £2 8s to the schoolmistress, for six girls; £17 11s for clothing six boys and six girls.[4]

By indenture dated 20 December 1752, arising from the will of Barnard Frederick dated 6 March 1740, and following a life interest of a Mary Mears, lands of yearly value of £6 were devised for putting out yearly two or more poor children, either boys or girls, of the parish of Boxgrove, to school, to be instructed in reading, writing and needlework, and clothing them in the manner charity children were clothed. The income was found insufficient to clothe the two children, and until 1819 all the income was paid to the schoolmaster.[5]

In visitation returns there are references to the charity school and to a schoolmaster (of 'good Life' and 'diligent', who came to church and caused his scholars to come, and

taught them the catechism) in 1755, 1758, 1762, 1765, 1775. The number of children is consistently given as 12, except in 1758 when the churchwardens noted 'We cannot exactly tell'; in 1775 they were described as '12 boys - writing, reading'.[6] In 1819 23 children were being educated under the combined charities, 15 boys and 8 girls, of whom 15 were completely clothed (7 boys and 8 girls). The proportions from the three parishes were as Lady Derby had stipulated, but those from East Lavant were being sent to Chichester, 'that city being more convenient to them in point of distance.'[7]
[*John Tapner?*]

1. *EP2* (1819), 149-50.   2. WSRO Ep.I/22/1.   3. Horsfield *Sussex* II, 60.   4. *EP2* (1819),149-50; *Abstract of the Returns of Charitable Donations for the Benefit of Poor Persons 1786-88* (1816), 1266.   5. *EP2* (1819),149-50; *VCH* ii, 439.   6. WSRO Ep.I/22/1.   7. *EP2* (1819), 149-50 (this source gives 8 boys and 7 girls as being clothed, which, from the details given, appears to be a transposition error).

[Tapner's school]   (R: 1761)
John Tapner (also a surveyor) was a schoolmaster of Boxgrove in 1761.[1] Probably master of the charity school (see above) but - in view of his qualifications - probably took private pupils as well. [*John Tapner*]
1. *DLS.*

[See also WESTHAMPNETT for possible Goodwood estate schooling.]

BRAMBER cum BUTTOLPHS 1724: 24 families   1801: pop. 127
(Bramber, 91; Buttolphs, 36)

No 18th-century schooling traced.

BREDE   1724: 83 families   1801: pop. 801
Charity school   (F: 1777. Rs: 1777- into 19c)
In July 1777 the parish advertised for a schoolmaster, to start at Michaelmas, the inhabitants having subscribed a salary of £25 pa. A room in the church was available for the school. Since this was a subscription school, advertised by the churchwardens and accomodated in the church, it was clearly a charity school; but the advertisement also included, 'According to his Merits, so may he expect Encouragement', which implies that he was free to take on private pupils.[1] On 11 June 1794 Edward Wood, schoolmaster, was buried.[2] At a vestry on 20 June 1794 it was agreed, 'That Thomas Noakes for the parish of Brede should have the school in the Church for instructing of children.' A gallery was erected for their use. The school was discontinued six years later owing to a complaint made by chancellor Hollinbery to the bishop that the school and gallery were a nuisance. On 30 March 1800 the vestry agreed 'to the removal of the school and the taking down of the gallery.'[3] However, in 1802 Mr Smallfield was a schoolmaster at Brede, occupying a house on Brede Hill, which suggests that the school continued in the parish .[4] [*Edward Wood, Thomas Noakes, Smallfield*]
1. *SWA* 14.7.77.   2. Brede PR.   3. Austen, E., *Brede, the Story of a Sussex Parish*(1946), 83.
4. ESRO SAS/unaccessioned box 11

BRIGHTHELMSTON - see BRIGHTON

BRIGHTLING   1724: about 50 families   1801: pop. 507
Mary Herbert's charity school for girls   (F: 1732 or 33. Rs: 1733- into 19c)
Mary Herbert, a widow, of St Andrew's, Holborn, Middlesex, who had been born at Brightling, by will dated 4 April 1728, gave to the minister and churchwardens of Brightling, £200, to be used to purchase land, the rent thereof to be applied for the teaching of as many

poor girls of Brightling as it conveniently could, in writing, reading, casting accounts and plain work. Each girl, at the age of 15, was to have a prayer book, a bible, and *The Whole Duty of Man* 'of a Good Print'. By indenture dated 24 June 1732, land in Chiddingly was purchased, at a cost of £227 6s.[1]

The school was operating by the summer of 1733. The schoolmistress, Sarah Cruttenden, received payment for teaching from the end of June that year (assuming there was, as later, no school in August).[2] In 1734 or 1735, John Fuller's accounts (he was a churchwarden, and thus one of the trustees) show that he purchased a book for the school, for 2s 6d, and on 13 February 1737 paid John Hassell 13s 6d for a map of the school land.[3] The school continued into the 19th century. In 1814 the rent of the school's land was raised to £16 pa; in 1819 11 girls were being taught, the schoolmistress received 8 guineas pa, about £2 was spent each year on books, and the land tax paid was £1 16s - total expenditure of £12 4s. Before 1814, income only slightly exceeded expenditure; but by 1815 a fund of £160 had accumulated, which was reserved for building a school. In 1819 another Mr Fuller was supplying the schoolhouse at a very low rent, and he proposed to settle a tenement in Brightling for the use of the school; it was anticipated that the interest on the accumulated fund would then be used to educate a larger number of girls.[4]

An unbound notebook has survived which gives details of the early years of the school.[5] It records the terms of 'Mary Harbart's' will, and the rules for the school agreed on 2 April 1735 by the trustees - William Burrell, the rector, and John Fuller and Lawrence Noakes, the churchwardens. Amendments were subsequently made to some of the rules, and some are incomplete (for example, in the rule setting out the school hours for summer and winter, the actual hours are not entered). The notebook records admissions of girls and payments made to the schoolmistress; it runs from April 1735 to December 1761, with brief references to December 1763. Originally, the schoolmistress was paid 3s a week, except for August when there was no school, 'by reason the Children are all of then employed in Gleaning and Hopping'; she received £7 4s pa for 48 weeks teaching - though there were additional holidays on Holy Days, with two weeks at Christmas. In April 1738, however, the trustees agreed that, because the trust income could not support this salary, considering the debt due upon the land, 'And also considering the many Holy dayes, And the great Neglects of the Parents in Sending their Children, So that half their time is lost, And the Children not taught, tho' the Mistress is paid', therefore in future the schoolmistress would be paid 'One penny a day for each child that Shall come, without Any Allowance For Holy Dayes.' With the usual dame school or petty school charge at 2d or 3d a week, the potential 6d a week for a fully attending child was fair; but Sarah Cruttenden's salary fell to £4 9s 4d for the year to 1 May 1739, and to £4 2s 4d for the following year. For the year ending 30 April 1742, it had risen to £5 10s 8d. Payments to her were erratic, often covering more than a year - one payment covered 3½ years (though the rules stated that the teacher's salary was to be paid half-yearly) - and although the school-book accounts name each child and give the number of days in the period that she attended, it is difficult, in view of irregularities of attendance, to determine how many girls were at the school at any one time. It is clear from the 'Minister and Churchwardens' Account' in John Fuller's personal account book, in which he recorded the cash he paid (as trustee) to Sarah Cruttenden, that the establishment was six girls from the start of the school until at least May 1738 (eg, 7 August 1733: 'To Sarah Cruttenden school mistress for Teaching 6 Children 1 year att 3 sh p week...'; the number six was specified also with payments made on 15 April 1735, 5 May 1737, 21 April 1738, 6 February 1739).[6] In the year to 30 April 1741 10 different girls were taught, but four of them on only 21 days; these were probably replacing leavers, and for the year to 30 April 1742 only six different girls were taught. The maximum number of days any child attended school in any one year would seem to have been about 265. On average, a girl attended the school on 681 school days in total, but the range was wide, from 53 to at least 1,416 days. Girls appear to have started at the school when they were about 11, but only a minority stayed until they were 15, as the founder had envisaged.

One of the difficulties charity school trustees sometimes experienced was collecting the rents of lands owned by the charity; in April 1751 John Fuller wrote to 'Master Elphick':

> You Owe for your Farm to the Charity School at Brightling five Years and a halfe Rent at Lady day last Which is 55 pounds   I have sent to you, call'd upon you, wrote to you, and all to no Purpose, and when you have promised to come you never keep your word, I have told you often tis no Farm of mine but I am Intrusted with it & my own Credit & Reputation is concern'd as a Trustee and Parish Officer to see it paid   I am now to tell you that this is the last Letter, you will have from me for if forty pounds of it is not paid forthwith, you have Brought this Trouble on your Selfe & the Law shall take its Course   I am sorry for it...[7]

[*Sarah Cruttenden, Elizabeth Venes*]

1. *EP*2 (1819), 153; ESRO PAR 254/25/1.   2. ESRO PAR 254/25/1.   3. ESRO SAS/RF 15/27
4. *EP*2 (1819), 153.   5. ESRO PAR 254/25/1.   6. ESRO SAS/RF 15/27, dates cross-checked with SAS/RF 15/28, ff 29, 48, 71, 82, 93.   7. ESRO SAS/RF 15/25.

Dame schools

Sarah French   (Rs: 1732-45)
John Fuller's '1731 Cash Booke' shows 10 payments to Sarah French, wife of Edward French, for 'schooling' between 1732 and 1745. Two of the payments were made to her husband, one to 'Widd French' (perhaps her mother-in-law?); sometimes the children taught are named - never more than two, but she probably had pupils from other sources. She was paid 3d a week for teaching 'Lusteds Girl', 2d a week each for 'Sanders boy' and 'Crouchs'; Isaac Venice and Richard Relf were other named pupils.[1] [*Sarah French*]

1. ESRO SAS/RF 15/28, ff 15, 27, 38, 48, 59, 82, 110, 143, 155, 174.

Sarah Cruttenden   (Rs: 1736-43)
In addition to teaching the Mary Herbert charity girls, Sarah Cruttenden was also paid by John Fuller for schooling other children: on 1 June 1736, 'for Teaching Wm Perry 41 weeks ending the 5th May Last att 2d - 6.10'; 17 October 1740, for teaching 'Richard and Mary Axel 71 weeks ending 11th Instant - 11.10' (ie at 2d a week); and 31 January 1743, £1 13s 8d for the same children.[1] She probably kept her own school in addition to the girls' charity school. In 1747 she had her own house, and in a window tax assessment was assessed for 2s tax under 'Houses that have not Ten Lights'.[2] [*Sarah Cruttenden*]

1. ESRO SAS/RF 15/28, ff 61, 116, 151.   2. ESRO SAS/RF 15/21.

[It is noted that John Cooper, by will dated 27 July 1691, directed that if his children died without issue, then his estates, after his wife's death, were to be let or disposed of to pay £20 a year to a suitable woman, in the town of Robertsbridge, to teach poor children from the parishes of Salehurst, Etchingham, Ewhurst, Mountfield or Brightling. But no such school was ever established, or money paid for that purpose. (*VCH* ix, 224; *EP*1 (1819), 239-40)]

BRIGHTON (BRIGHTHELMSTON) 1724: about 500 families   1801: pop. 7,339

Other population estimates:[1]   1724:   2,375
                                                                1744:   2,380
                                                                1761:   2,035
                                                                1786:   3,620
                                                                1794:   5,669

1. Farrant, J. and S. *Aspects of Brighton, 1650-1800* (1978), 4: 1724 and 1761 based on reports of the number of families in the parish; 1744, on the number of houses; 1786 and 1794, on counts made in connection with mass inoculation against smallpox.

Charity school for boys   (F: 1701. Rs: 1701- into 19c)
There are references to schoolmasters in Brighton in 1581, the 1650s and 1660s, and in 1681; and to 'the reeding house', which may mean a schoolhouse, in 1660, and to 'the Free-scoole' in a rental of 1665.[1] (The latter was in 'the Hempshares', and in 1722 Martha Lewes of Bermondsey released to Thomas Wood alias Din of Brighton a tenement in the Hempshares, called the Schoolhouse, containing five low rooms with an entry, two chambers and a garret, and having a garden and two parcels of land.[2]) 'The free-School Book of Brighthelmston Anno Domini 1701', which has survived, contains a list of 26 boys headed 'Writers January.12th 1702' [internal evidence suggests the year is 1701/2, ie 1702 NS] (in another part of the book there is a list of 27 boys headed 'Readers', who were almost certainly the readers at January 1702): the fact that there were so many writers at January 1702, who would have earlier been taught to read, suggests that the school was started at the beginning of 1701, or earlier. The school book above was begun in that year; and at an SPCK meeting in December 1702 the bishop of Chichester reported that 'at his late visitation... he has procur'd the erecting of a Charity School at Lewes' - 'Lewes' being an error in the minute book for 'Brighthelmstone' (see LEWES Charity School).[3]

In 1701 the school was in a house towards the southern end of the east side of Black Lion Street, which was rented for £2 10s a year. It was there until 1725, when Anthony Springett and his brother William bought a house and garden in Meeting House Lane (facing down Union Street), which the school occupied from January 1726 until 1828. William Springett died in 1732 and Anthony in 1735; the latter, at his death, transferred the property to his executors as trustees.[4]

Until 1735 the school was financially dependent on subscriptions; these were administered by the vicar, and often paid to him. No list of subscribers has been found, but some have been identified through their private account books; none of these had any direct connection with Brighton. It is probable that they were influenced by the needs of the poor in Brighton (Sussex gentry outside Brighton made a number of other charitable donations to the poor of the town, and in the early years of the century several neighbouring parishes were required to contribute to the relief of Brighton[5]); and by the exhortations of the SPCK, which from 1699 was encouraging the teaching of reading as a preparation for learning the catechism, and as a way of bringing children into the Church. The school was in correspondence with the SPCK by 1704, if not before, when the Society's *Account of the Charity-Schools* recorded annual subscriptions of about £47. In 1710 they had fallen to £40, and in 1713 to £30.[6] Richard Springett, another of the Springett brothers of Plumpton, who became an apothecary in the City of London, was a subscriber, and at his death without issue in 1718 left £200 to be applied by his executors for the benefit of the school; and the interest was paid regularly until 1735. In 1735 this bequest was subsumed within the greater bequest of Anthony Springett who, like his three brothers who predeceased him, died without issue; he left an exchequer annuity running to 1806, of which £25 a year was to be given to the school (four further village schools received £23 a year between them). He thus provided the school with a house and an income. Born in 1662 into a gentry family, he went to Cambridge, apparently without graduating, and many years later, in 1716, at the age of 54, was ordained and presented to the living of Westmeston, which he retained until his death in 1735.[7] He was involved with the school from the beginning of the century. In July 1702 he paid for 20 boys' coats: these were supplied by William Sanders, tailor, whose bill totalled £5 0s 2d - £3 13s 6d for the materials and £1 6s 8d for making them up. (At the same time, the vicar, George Hay, paid for 20 boys' hats and hatbands, supplied by Thomas Gatford for £1 5s.) He ordered the opening of a girls' school in 1702 (see below), and paid the mistress in 1703 and 1705. He wrote, in 1713 and 1716, letters to the SPCK on the state of the Brighton school.[8] Other benefactors were George Beach, a mariner, of Southwark but formerly of Brighton, who by will, proved 3 June 1735, left interest on a small sum which yielded £1 pa or less; and Lady Mary Countess Dowager Gower, who in 1771 left annuities yielding £7 0s 9d pa to the school.[9]

The school was very much a Church of England school. The 'Orders for the Scholars', given in the school book of 1701, were:

> On Sunday morning they shall meet at the Schoolhouse before ten, answer to their names, and goe to Church in order.
> As also in the afternoon.
> And if any of them make noise or disturbance when at Church: the Monitors are on monday to return their names.
> Each day of the week, (after morning prayer,) the Catalogue to be recited, the absents marked.
> Evrie writer is to read in the morning a chapter in course before he beginn to write. [Presumably a chapter from the Bible]
> Evry reader haveing first conn'd his lesson is to be heard twice in the morning by the Usher, & as often in the afternoon.
> Evrie Monday's night and evrie Wednesday the readers are to be heard of ye Catechism by the Usher.
> And the writers by the Master.

Control of the school was in the hands of the vicar. Springett's endowment of 1735 stipulated that while benefiting from the school the children were to resort only to the services of the Church of England.[10] It is therefore surprising that in 1702 John Grover was appointed master, for he was a Quaker, and remained so all his life. Such an appointment would not have been approved by the SPCK, but George Hay, vicar in 1702, and William Colbron who succeeded him in 1705, and Anthony Springett, whose contribution to the school during Grover's time was such that he could surely have removed him had he wished, were clergy of greater toleration. Grover remained master for almost 50 years. His salary, like that of his predecessor, John Scras, was only £8 pa - well below that usually offered to charity school masters. There were 50 boys in the school, and although he had the assistance of an usher, it is hard to understand why the master was paid so little, in the light of the subscriptions raised for the school. Moreover, he does not appear to have lived in the schoolhouse at any time. To augment his salary he engrossed legal documents, and for the church (though a Quaker) he made out the annual transcripts of the parish register for submission to the bishop for many years from 1702, and was even appointed as the bishop's attorney in the lease of the rectory in 1741. And he took paying pupils. This was a common arrangement in charity schools and there are two pieces of evidence that it occurred at Brighton. In the school book there is the indicative statement, probably made in 1706, that Francis Cook had been 'taken off from the free School... his parents now being Able continue him at schoole at their own Charge'. And on 8 October 1730, Anthony Stapley, son of John of Hickstead, 'went to board and school at Brighthelmstone. He boards at Thomas

Brown's, at 4s.6d. per week; and goes to school to John Grover, to learn to read and write, and cast accounts'; £7 6s 10d was paid to Grover and Brown on 8 April 1731 for his board and schooling (he was not there long: in May 1731 he was sent to Thomas Pointin's school).[11]

After the death of Grover in 1752, and of Colbron in 1750 (he was vicar only until 1744, but continued as minister until his death) the school may have become more strictly Anglican. In 1752, over 300 books and pamphlets were ordered from the SPCK.[12]

From the school book, there appear to have been 53 boys at the school in January 1702, and 50 at December 1705. The SPCK annual *Account* for 1704 notes: 'Fifty boys taught to Read, Write, Cast Account, and the Art of Navigation.' In the early 1720s, a writer stated that 'Gentlemen of the Neighbouring Parts' had augmented the vicar's maintenance by £50 pa, on the condition 'that he shall instruct 50 poor Boys of the Town in Reading and Writing'.[13] With half the boys in the writing class, the level of education was above that of many charity schools. Grover acquired a considerable reputation as a mathematician. Navigation was an important subject in this seafaring town. Of the boys who left between 1702 and (probably) 1706, over three-quarters went to sea (we can also note that as many as a quarter of all leavers were put out as apprentices);[14] in April 1716 Anthony Springett reported that since 1701, 122 boys had gone from the school, 'of wch 90 to sea, the rest to trades and Service'.[15] Among the books and pamphlets obtained from the SPCK in 1752 were 100 copies of the *Seaman's Monitor* (at a cost of 8s 6d).[16]

Analysis of the school book and baptismal registers indicates that in 1702 and 1705 the boys' ages ranged from 5 to 16, and that their average age was just over 11.[17]

Stephen Buckoll, schoolmaster at Brighton in 1791, stated in 1793 that he had 'had the care of a large Day-School upwards of forty years.' This was probably the charity school, and Buckoll may have followed Grover as master.[18]

[*John Scras, John Grover, William Grover*?, and see Other schoolmasters below]

1. Farrant, J.H., 'The Brighton Charity School in the early 18th century', *SAC* **122**, 139 (Farrant hereafter). 2. *VCH* vii, 247. 3. 'The free-School Book of Brighthelmston Anno Domini 1701' (BSB hereafter); held by Brighton Library, SB 379 FRE. 4. Farrant, 142; BSB. 5. Farrant, S. and J.H., in *SAC* **118**, 341. 6. Farrant, 141. 7. ibid, 142 (as corrected by J.F., pers. comm.). 8. BSB; SPCK ALB v.4, 3480 & v.6, 4772. 9. Farrant, 142; *EP*1 (1819), 224. 10. Farrant, 141. 11. ESRO HIC 472. 12. BSB. 13. Farrant, 141, citing Mr Haylor in Cox, T. *Magna Britannia*, 5 (1730), 511. 14. BSB: the list covers 56 boys; of these, no trades are given for 11 (of whom three died - one 'Drownded at Sea' - two left the town, one was 'taken off' because his parents could afford to pay for his schooling). 15. SPCK ALB v.6, 4772. 16. BSB. 17. Based on estimated ages of 83 of the 103 boys. 18. *Univ. Directory* 1791; *SWA* 14.1.93.

Charity school for girls   (F: 1702.   Rs: 1702-5, 1725, 1770)
The school opened on 30 September 1702, 'by Mr. Springetts order', and was presumably financed by the same subscriptions that supported the boys' charity school (see above); details relating to both schools are included in 'The free-School Book of Brighthelmston Anno Domini 1701'. Its fortunes were, however, different from those of the boys' school, and it is treated here as a separate school.

The school opened with 20 scholars; a list of their names in the school book is headed: 'List of the poor Girles who are taught to read, by Mrs. Gamon & are to be instructed in their Catechism & to come constantly to Church on the Lord's day'. And below the list is the note: 'Memorand: that the Girles are to come constantly to school, otherwise their names to be struck out and others to be taken in their room.' One of the salary receipts signed by the teacher, Margaret Gamon, shows that she taught them 'to read and knit'. The SPCK annual *Accounts* confirm the number of girls as 20, and the 'Account' for 1710 notes that they were taught 'to Read and Knit and Sew and the Catechism'.[1]

At some point in the 18th century the school failed, to be revived again between 1805 and 1818.[2]   The first mistress, Margaret Gamon, was paid by Mr Springett from the

opening of the school at Michaelmas 1702 to Lady day 1705, in April 1703 at the rate of £6 10s pa and in June 1705, 'for teaching twenty Girles to read & knitt', at the rate of £8 pa - the same salary as was paid to John Grover, master of the boys' school.[3] John Grover's daughter, Elizabeth, entered in her memorandum book: 'Began first to Teach in the new Schooll house in ye 11th mo. 1725/6'; she was then 19 years old and it is probable that she was teaching girls at the school at that date.[4] The school may well have survived to at least 1770, when there was in the town a charity school for 20 girls.[5]
[*Margaret Gamon, Elizabeth Grover*]

1. The school book (BSB), held by Brighton Library, SB 379 FRE. 2. Farrant, J.H., in *SAC* **122**, 145.
3. BSB. 4. Clayton, C.E., in *SAC*, **36**, 88. 5. *A Description of England and Wales* (printed for Newberry and Carnan) (1770), IX, 158.

Marchant's boys' boarding school (F: 1757)
Opened in 1757 by Richard Marchant (late of Truely, in Edburton), who offered: 'Writing, Arithmetic, Algebra, Geometry in its several Branches of Planimetry, Altimetry, Long-imetry, Stereometry,Trigonometry, and Navigation; Heraldry, or the Art of Armoury and Blazoning; Book-keeping and Merchants' Accompts; Surveying, and making Draughts and Maps of Land, &c. with proper Decorations and Coats of Arms; Chronological or Ecclesiatical Calculations of Time, &c.'[1] [*Richard Marchant*]
1. Bishop, 16.

Grimmett's charity school for boys (F: 1768. R: 1768- into 19c)
William Grimmett, who had been taught by Grover at the Brighton charity school, and became a mariner and later a wealthy London merchant, by will dated 14 March 1749 left a bequest for establishing a charity school in Brighton. After his death his affairs were in the court of Chancery, and it was not until 1768 that the bequest was determined and invested in £2,231 stock in old South Sea annuities, which yielded an income of £70 a year. In his will Grimmett stipulated that his bequest was to be applied in clothing and educating 20 poor boys, sons of parishioners of Brighton, in the principles of the Protestant religion, agreeable to the present national and established Church of England, and in reading, writing, arithmetic, merchants accounts and navigation; none to be admitted under 8, nor to continue after 15 years of age; and he appointed the minister and churchwardens for the time being, and 12 other principal inhabitants of the parish (to be chosen at a public vestry) trustees and governors of his charity school.[1]

By 1779 the school was established on a site in Cragg's Lane (now Duke Street), on the south side near the west end.[2] (Between 1801 and 1818 the older charity school, known as Springett's, and Grimmett's were combined under one master at the former's premises in Meeting House Lane. They were separated in 1818, but in 1828 both were subsumed into the Central National school newly built in Church Street.[3]) At the end of the century E. Thorp was master; he also had his own private school. In April 1801 he announced that he had given up Grimmett's and in consequence could increase the number of his private pupils.[4]

In 1819: 'The number is always kept full. The master's salary is £34 14s 8d a year, and the remainder of the income is applied in clothing and books, for which it is barely sufficient. There is no school-house belonging to the charity. The master is therefore obliged to rent one, in consideration of which he is allowed to take not exceeding 20 private pupils...'[5]
[*E.Thorp*; and see Other schoolmasters below]

1. Harrison and North, 150; *EP1* (1819), 223. 2. Yeakell & Gardner map, pub by Richard Thomas, Brighton, 1 June 1779. 3. Farrant, J.H., in *SAC* **122**, 145. 4. *SWA* 20.4.1801. 5. *EP1* (1819), 223.

Russell and Rickword's girls' boarding school   (F: 1769. Rs: 1769-75)
Miss Russell and Miss Rickword opened their boarding school for young ladies in January 1769. With 'proper Assistants', they offered board and schooling at £16 pa, with 1 guinea entrance. French was an extra, at 2 guineas pa. Writing, music and dancing, also extras, were 'by proper MASTERS attending'.[1]
The partnership broke up in May 1775, when Mrs Jane Beard announced in *SWA* that she had 'taken Miss RUSSELL's established BOARDING SCHOOL, at BRIGHTHELMSTON'; and in the same issue Miss Mary Rickword announced 'that she continues to take young Ladies at her BOARDING-SCHOOL, LITTLE-EAST-STREET, BRIGHTHELMSTON.'[2]   For these two schools, see below.
Advertised in *SWA* Jan (2), Feb 1769.
[*Miss Russell, Mary Rickword*]
1. *SWA* 23.1.69.   2. *SWA* 22.5.75.

Thomas Hadleston, French, dancing, and fencing master   (R: 1772)
In July 1772 he opened a school in Chichester for teaching French, dancing, and fencing with the small sword. He attended at Brighton every Thursday, at the *New Ship* inn.[1] (For details of what he offered and his charges, see under CHICHESTER.) [*Thomas Hadleston*]
1. *SWA* 20.7.72.

Mrs Beard's girls' boarding school   (F: 1775. Rs: 1775-84)
In May 1775 Mrs Jane Beard, who had previously had a girls' boarding school at Hailsham, announced that she had taken Miss Russell's established boarding school at Brighton (Miss Russell's partner, Mary Rickword, continued to run her own boarding school in the town).[1] In 1778, she, 'with proper Assistants, continues to instruct YOUNG LADIES in every useful Accomplishment. A Musick, Dancing, and Writing Master attends.'[2] In 1784 she had both boarders and day scholars, and took an advertisement to deny that she intended to give up teaching (her husband had lately died).[3] At Michaelmas 1784, 'at the Desire of her Friends' (that is, the parents of her girls) she moved her school from her house opposite the parsonage in Brighton, to Seaford. In an advertisement addressed to 'the Nobility and Gentry', she extolled the virtues of Seaford over Brighton - 'many insuperable Objections having been made to a Place of public Resort and Amusement for Female Tuition.'[4] [*Jane Beard*]
1. *SWA* 22.5.75.   2. *SWA* 16.3.78.   3. *SWA* 2.2.84.   4. *SWA* 31.5.84.

The Misses Rickword's girls' boarding school   (F: 1775. Rs: 1775- into 19c)
With Miss Russell, Mary Rickword opened a girls' boarding school in 1769. In May 1775 Mrs Beard took over 'Miss Russell's established boarding school', and Mary Rickword set up her own boarding school for young ladies in Little-East-street.[1] In *Bailey's Directory* 1784 as 'Rickwards, Miss schoolmistress'. In *Univ. Directory* for both 1791 and 1793 the school appears as the Misses Rickwords. By 1785 'Miss Rickward' was in West Street, and in 1793, Mossop, in his *Description of Brighthelmstone*, noted: 'There are also, for the instruction of young ladies, in every useful and polite accomplishment, three different Boarding Schools, all of deserved eminence', one of them being kept 'by Miss Rickword, in West-street'.[2] *Cobby's Directory* of 1799 lists Barbara Rickword, schoolmistress, at 48 West-street. *Fisher's New Guide* of 1800, and 1804, refers to Miss Rickword's boarding school in West-street, among others, adding: 'It gives us great pleasure to inform our readers, that the ladies, by whom these different schools are conducted, are extremely well qualified for the situations they are in, and are deserving of every success. The health, morals, and improvement of the young ladies committed to their care, we believe to be most conscientiously attended to.'[3] [*Mary Rickword, Barbara Rickword*]

1. *SWA* 22.5.75.   2. Land Tax; Mossop, J. *A description of Brighthelmstone & Its Vicinity* (Crawford, 1793), 36.   3. op. cit. (1800), 26; (1804), 37.

Mrs Harrington's school for ladies   (R: 1775)

A portrait artist ('sole artist, by the King's special appointment'), she taught, in 1775, '(to Ladies only) the Sciences and Languages as usual.' She published, for the benefit of her pupils, *A New Introduction to Geography, with the Knowledge and Use of Maps*, price 3s, illustrated with maps and copper plates.[1] [*Mrs Harrington*]

1. *SWA* 24.7.75.

Paine's boys' boarding school   (F: 1777. Rs: 1777- into 19c)

Cornelius Paine opened his boarding school for young gentlemen on 7 April 1777, offering English, writing, arithmetic, merchants accompts, mensuration, geometry, trigonometry, navigation, &c.[1] A year later he had assistants and Latin was included in the curriculum; merchants' accounts were now described as 'the common and Italian Methods of Book Keeping'.[2] In December 1778 his advertisements first drew attention to the benefit of being beside the sea: '... the Situation of the Place is undoubtedly the most healthful, being adjacent to the Sea, and consequently will save the great Expence, which Parents and Guardians are unavoidably obliged to be at, when the Indisposition, or Health of Young Gentlemen render it necessary.'[3] In June 1781 he noted that his pupils 'have an Opportunity of Bathing in the Sea, with proper Attendance'.[4] By 1781, Greek, French, geography and the use of the globes, had been added to the curriculum.[5] In 1782 he was advertising as 'Brighthelmston School' and referring to it as 'Paine's Academy': offered board and education in reading, writing and arithmetic at 16 guineas pa, with 1 guinea entrance; the other subjects were 2 guineas pa extra, and dancing was to be paid for separately; those who remained at the school 'during the usual Vacations of Christmas and Midsummer, to pay a Guinea for the Holidays.'[6] In the summer of that year he recruited a young Welshman from Oxford, William Thomas, as an assistant, who, on 28 July, 'was seized with a violent fit of coughing, as he was coming out of church, and expired in about ten minutes afterwards.'[7] In 1792 the school was advertised under 'Mr. Paine's Academy' and was located in North Street: the curriculum was now English, Latin, Greek and French, writing, arithmetic, merchants' accompts, mensuration, land surveying, navigation, geography and the use of the globes, taught by himself and assistants, with music, dancing and drawing 'by able Masters'.[8] Despite the inclusion of the classics, *A Description of Brighthelmstone* (1793) by John Mossop (who himself had a private grammar school in Brighton) refers to Mr Paine's Academy as 'principally to qualify youth for business';[9] and this comment was copied by *Fisher's New Guide* of 1800 and 1804.[10] In the summer of 1798, Paine moved his school from 79 North Street to a larger house in the same street ('lately occupied by Sir Richard Heron, Bart.'), which enabled him to increase the number of his pupils. ('The former House to be lett, unfurnished.')[11] In *Button's Directory* of 1805, besides the academy in North Street, there was additionally 'Payne's Preparatory Academy' in Great East Street. In 1800 Paine was High Constable of Brighton. [12]

Advertised in *SWA* Mar (2) 1777; Jun (3), Dec (2) 78; Jun, Jul 81; Jul 82; Jan (2), Jul, Aug 92; Jun (2), Jul 94; Jun, Jul 98; Jul (2) 99. In *Bailey's Directory* 1784; *Univ. Directory* 1791, 1793; Mossop's *Description* 1793; *Cobby's Directory* 1799; *Fisher's New Guide* 1800, 1804; *Button's Directory* 1805.
[*Cornelius Paine, William Humphrey Thomas*]

1. *SWA* 24.3.77.   2. *SWA* 1.6.78.   3. *SWA* 21.12.78.   4. *SWA* 25.6.81.   5. ibid.   6. *SWA* 15.7.82.   7. *SWA* 5.8.82.   8. *SWA* 9.1.92.   9. op. cit., 35.   10. op.cit., (1800), 26; (1804), 36.   11. *SWA* 18.6.98.   12. *SWA* 26.5.1800.

Owen and Hudson's boys' day and boarding school, later Hudson's (F: 1778. Rs: 1778-87)
Hugh Owen and Thomas Hudson opened their boarding school in Middle Street on 25
March 1778.[1] The house ('late in the Possession of Capt. WHICHELO') was 'in every Way
calculated for the Purpose, with an extensive Garden, Play-Yard, Lawns, &c. and withall,
for the Conveniency of Bathing, if thought necessary.' They were 'late of the Rev. Mr.
GILPIN's ACADEMY, at CHEAM': this was a celebrated school in Surrey where William
Gilpin after 1752 practised new methods of teaching and moral training through
self-government.[2] Thomas Hudson was curate of Brighton from at least April 1779 until
November 1789, when he became vicar there.[3] Later in 1778 they referred to their school
as 'the Academy in Brighthelmston'. With 'able Assistants', they offered, 'on reasonable
Terms', Latin, Greek, French, English, writing and arithmetic, merchants accounts, the
practical parts of mathematics, history, chronology, geography and the use of the globes,
drawing, dancing, music, fencing, &c. &c. They were willing to take day-scholars as well
as boarders: 'Young Gentlemen coming here for the Benefit of their Health, will be carefully
attended, boarded, and educated; or educated only, on the most reasonable Terms.'[4] The
partnership was dissolved, by mutual consent, on 24 June 1782.[5] Owen was later in
partnership with John Dulot, who had a circulating library on the Steine (which partnership
was dissolved on 29 December 1791).[6] Hudson apparently continued with the school. He
was at New Buildings in January 1784.[7] John Mossop, another curate at Brighton, took over
Hudson's school from January 1787, and promoted it as the 'Grammar School,
Brighthelmstone' [qv].[8]
     Advertised in *SWA* Apr (2), Jun, Aug 1778; Aug (2) 82.
[*Hugh Owen, Thomas Hudson*]
1. *SWA* 6.4.78.   2. Lawson, J. and Silver, H. *A Social History of Education in England* (1973), 204.   3. St
Nicholas PR, marriage banns.   4. *SWA* 15.6.78, 24.8.78.   5. *SWA* 19.8.82.   6. *SWA* 16.4.92.   7. Reference
in Pullen & Widgett ad, *SWA* 12.1.84.   8. *SWA* 29.1.87.

Rawlins' academy of dancing   (F: 1783. Rs: 1783-93)
In November 1783 James Henry Rawlins ('Mr. Rawlins, Jun.') announced the opening of his
academy of dancing at his house, 61 East Street. 'Half a Guinea Entrance, and a Guinea per
Quarter, for two Lessons per Week; or Fifteen Shillings for One lesson per Week.' He also
attended boarding schools, and taught ladies and gentlemen privately at their homes or at
his own house, and taught music.[1] By July 1788 he had moved to 9 North-Row, and 'begs
Leave to acquaint the Nobility and Gentry, as also the Governesses and Masters of Schools,
that he instructs Ladies and Gentlemen in all fashionable Dances, viz. Minuet, with the
much-admired Minuet de Hygeia, Minuet de la Cour and Gavot, Devonshire Minuet, and
Rondau, Allemandes, the favourite Scotch Reel as danced at the Opera-House, Codrils,
Cotillons, Country Dances, &c. &c. - Mr. RAWLINS, in Justice to himself, must observe,
that he attends, twice a Year, the best Masters in London, in order to be able to teach every
Thing that is, or may be new and fashionable. N.B. MUSIC TAUGHT; private Instructions
given every Saturday at Mr. Rawlins's House.'[2] In July 1793 there was advertised 'Mr.
RAWLIN'S NIGHT. CONCERT AND BALL, WITH CATCHES AND GLEES', at the
White Horse Tavern, East Street, on 9 July; included in the programme was 'Figure dancing
by Mr. RAWLIN's Pupils.'[3] Perhaps this was a finale, for in September of that same year
advertisements by another dancing master began: 'MR. DENNIS, being engaged to succeed
Mr. RAWLINS, as DANCING MASTER, in the several different Boarding-Schools, in
Brighton...'[4] For Rawlins' other musical activities, see Schedule 2. Advertised in *SWA* Nov
(3) 1783; Jul (2) 88; Jan (2), Jul (2) 93. In *Univ. Directory* 1791 and 1793, as 'Dancing &
Music-master'. [*James Henry Rawlins*]
1. *SWA* 3.11.83.   2. *SWA* 14.7.88.   3. *SWA* 1.7.93.   4. *SWA* 2.9.93.

Pullen and Widgett's girls' boarding school, later Pullen's   (F: 1784. Rs: 1784-1800)
Mrs Isabella Pullen ('late Governess of the Boarding School at CAMBERWELL') and Miss
Widgett opened their boarding school for young ladies in North Row at Lady-tide 1784.
Announcing this in January, enquirers were referred to Miss Widgett at the Rev. Mr.
Hudson's, New Buildings [qv his school above: for Widgett's probable connection with
Hudson, see Schedule 2].[1] By 1788 Miss Widgett had left, to join up with Miss Wayte [qv
below].[2] In 1793 Mrs Pullen's school, now in East Street, was one of three girls' boarding
schools described by Mossop in his *Description of Brighthelmstone* as 'of deserved
eminence... The flourishing state of all these schools and seminaries, need not be wondered
at, from the healthiness of the situation, and the care and attention shown towards the
pupils.'[3] By 1799 she had moved to 5 New Steyne, at the east side of the town (*Cobby's
Directory*). Cobby has her at the same address in his directory for 1800, but *Fisher's New
Guide* for 1800 gives her school as in Great East Street. *Fisher's New Guide* for 1804 omits
the school, so Mrs Pullen may have given it up between 1800 and 1804. In *Bailey's
Directory* 1784; *Univ. Directory* 1791, 1793; *Cobby's Directory* 1799, 1800; *Fisher's New
Guide* 1800.
[*Isabella Pullen, Miss Widgett*]
1. *SWA* 12.1.84.   2. *SWA* 21.7.88.   3. op. cit., 36.

Wilbar's boys' boarding school   (F: 1787. Rs: 1787-92)
In December 1786 Henry Wilbar advertised that, at the request of his friends, he had 'taken
an elegant House, situate in MIDDLE-STREET, with an extensive Play-Ground, and erected
a large SCHOOL, for the Reception of YOUNG GENTLEMEN'. He offered board and
English, Latin, Greek, writing, arithmetic, merchants' accounts, geography, the use of the
globes, geometry, trigonometry, mensuration, and the other parts of the mathematics, for 13
guineas pa for those under 10, 15 guineas for those aged from 11 to 15 [sic], and 16 guineas
for those aged 15 and upwards. Dancing would be an extra charge; 'those who bathe in the
Sea, will be attended by the Assistants, gratis.' The opening words of his advertisement
were, apart from the name, copied word for word from an advertisement by Mr and Mrs
Allfree of Herstmonceux that had appeared the month before, viz.: 'HENRY WILBAR,
being impressed with a deep Sense of Gratitude, for the many distinguished Marks of
Approbation he has repeatedly received from his Friends...'[1] In July 1787 he was advertising
for an assistant to teach Latin, who was also capable of translating French into English.[2]
In June 1789, ' At the ACADEMY, MIDDLE-STREET, BRIGHTHELMSTON, YOUNG
GENTLEMEN are commodiously Boarded, and expeditiously taught every Branch of
USEFUL and POLITE LITERATURE, necessary to fit them for the UNIVERSITY,
COMMERCE, MECHANICAL or RURAL LIFE;   By H.WILBAR, and qualified
ASSISTANTS.' Music and French had been added to the optional extras; 'but those who
bathe in the Sea are attended gratis.' The age bands for fees had been modified: now under
10, 10 to 14, and 14 and upwards. There was now 1 guinea entrance. He announced that he
had annexed the adjoining house and ground, 'which has made his Play Ground very
spacious, and will enable him to increase his Number from Twenty to Thirty.'[3] But by April
1790 he had moved his school from Middle Street to the Steine.[4] This was almost certainly
Steyne-House Academy, 'a well established Academy in which there are 20 Boarders',
disposal of the unexpired lease of which was advertised in 1792, the year Wilbar died, by
the same lawyer as dealt with his personal estate.[5]

　　　For accounts of a theft by Wilbar's servant lad and the latter's sentence of transportation for seven years; of Wilbar's winning £20 damages for defamation; of a man and
woman committed on a charge of stealing clothing from him; see WILBAR, Henry, in
Schedule 2.

Advertised in *SWA* Dec (3) 1786; Jan (3), Jul (2), Aug 87; Jun (2), Dec 89; Jan, Feb, Apr, Sep, Oct 90; Jun 91. In *Univ. Directory* 1791 and 1793 (although he died in 1792).
[*Henry Wilbar*]
1. *SWA* 4.12.86.   2. *SWA* 23.7.87.   3. *SWA* 15.6.89.   4. *SWA* 5.4.90.   5. *SWA* 6.8.92.

Mossop's private boarding grammar school for boys   (F: 1787. Rs: 1787-94)
John Mossop was a curate at Brighton when he started his boys' boarding school in January 1787, taking over the school of Thomas Hudson, another Brighton curate. He styled it the 'GRAMMAR SCHOOL, BRIGHTHELMSTONE', and offered board, Latin, Greek, French, English, writing, arithmetic, geography, and the different branches of the mathematics. He promoted Brighton's healthy situation, 'which is the grand Object in all Schools', claiming that it was acknowledged that Brighton had 'a preference to any other in Sussex'. He also advertised for a writing master, 'against Shrove-Tide'.[1] In July that year, he was the first school to refer to sea-bathing in the headline of an advertisement - 'SEA-BATHING AND EDUCATION'. (The Rev Davies copied this idea for his school at Eastbourne later that year.) There was in fact no further mention of sea-bathing in the advertisement that followed; in it, Mossop announced the date of the reopening of the school after the midsummer vacation, and apologised for an unsatisfactory usher: 'Mr. Mossop further begs Leave to add, that he has engaged an Assistant upon whose Care and Attention he can with Confidence rely, and hopes he will give that Satisfaction, which he is sorry to find, his late Usher has not done.' He also noted that: 'A French Master, of liberal Education, resides in the House.'[2] (He was not the first to claim a resident French master - Thornton, at Horsham, had done so in 1784.)   In 1788 the summer vacation was 4½ weeks, typical of the time, from Wednesday 18 June to Monday 21 July;[3] and the Christmas vacation 4½ weeks, from Wednesday 17 December to Monday 19 January.[4] The same pattern followed in later years.

In 1789, 'the young gentlemen of the Rev. Mr. Mossop's School' were commended in *SWA* for 'their proficiency in military manoeuvres', which they had performed in public on Church Hill on 27 May; Mr. Serjeant-Major Alexander, of Lord Heathfield's Light Dragoons, had been their instructor.[5] There was a similar commendation the following year, when the young gentlemen (whom the paper styled 'The Brightonian Academic Volunteers') had their 'annual review' on 31 March.[6] This is the only Sussex school known to have engaged in such military involvement at that time, which is of special interest in view of Mossop's public support for Dr Knox, a visitor who in 1793 had preached a sermon at Brighton church on 'perpetual and universal peace to be established on the principles of Christian philantrophy', which had been violently resented by officers of the Surrey Militia, quartered in the town. When in November 1793 a public subscription was raised to provide the army abroad with winter clothing, 'The Rev. Mr. Mossop's School supplied 50 pair of worsted Hose'.[7]

In November 1789 Thomas Hudson succeeded Henry Michell as vicar of Brighton, and when he moved into the vicarage, his house in West Street was taken on by Mossop for his school.[8] This was on the corner of West Street and North Street, fronting onto the east side of West Street, with a yard and piece of land extending down North Street.[9] In December 1791 Mossop announced that he had made 'a considerable addition to his House' enabling him to increase the number of his pupils.[10]

In an advertisement at the beginning of 1790, Mossop gave details of the academic methods used in the school: 'The LATIN and GREEK CLASSICS after the ETON method; FRENCH by a GRADUATE of the UNIVERSITY of ORLEANS; WRITING in the most approved manner, and ARITHMETIC, MATHEMATICS, &c. after Dr. HUTTON.' The

French master was almost certainly Baschet [qv below]. In the same advertisement, Mossop wanted 'a MAN or STOUT BOY, of good character, to wait on the YOUNG GENTLEMEN, and, in short, to do the necessary work of a SERVANT in a BOARDING SCHOOL.'[11]

Mossop died on 7 April 1794, at the age of 38. His assistant, Rev R. Briggs, ran the school until June 1794, when the grammar school (but not the house) was taken on by William Brook.[12] Briggs then set up his own boarding school in Brighton.

Although it continued for only seven years, Mossop's school achieved considerable esteem. According to J.G.Bishop: 'It was the school of the period, and among the scholars were the Tuppens, the Lashmars, and Attrees, and others, the sons of the then principal local tradesmen.'[13]

For details of Mossop's life, his roles as a freemason, his publications and several interests, see Schedule 2.

Advertised in *SWA* Jan, Feb, Jul (2) 1787; Jan, Jun, Dec 88; Jun, Dec 89; Jan, Jun, Jul, Dec 90; Jul, Dec (2) 91; Jan, Jul (2), Aug (3), Sep, Dec 92. Mossop also advertised his book *Mathurini Corderii Colloquia Selecta*, for the use of schools, Sep (3), Nov, Dec 1791. In *Univ. Directory* 1791 and 1793, as 'Master of the Grammar School'. In his own *Description of Brighthelmstone* 1793.

[*John Mossop, Mr. Serjeant-Major Alexander, Serjeant Perry, Nicholas Baschet, R.Briggs*]
1. *SWA* 29.1.87.   2. *SWA* 16.7.87.   3. *SWA* 16.6.88.   4. *SWA* 8.12.88.   5. *SWA* 1.6.89.   6. *SWA* 5.4.90.
7. *SWA* 2.12.93.   8. St Nicholas PR (Hudson signs as curate 8.11.89, as vicar 15.11.89); Bishop, 325.
9. Bishop, 325.   10. *SWA* 12.12.91.   11. *SWA* 11.1.90.   12. *SWA* 23.6.94, ad by Briggs; Bishop, 326; *SWA* 30.6.94, ad by Brook; *Cobby's Directory* 1799.   13. Bishop, 325.

Morling and Breen's boys' boarding French and English school and evening school
(Reinstated: 1788)
Morling and Breen announced that, on Monday, 7 January 1788, they were reinstating the French and English Academy in Little East Street, 'late J. Morling's, deceased'. 'YOUTH are boarded and educated in the several Branches of Learning, and with the greatest Assiduity forwarded for the different Branches for which they are designed, and on the most reasonable Terms.' They also advertised 'An Evening School from Six till Eight.'[1] By October 1790, Breen was running a day school [qv below]. Advertised in *SWA* Dec 1787; Jan 88. [*J.Morling, Morling jun., William Breen*]
1. *SWA* 31.12.87.

Wayte and Widgett's girls' boarding school   (R: 1788)   Later Wayte and Harben's girls' boarding school   (Rs: 1791- into 19c)
In July 1788 'Miss Wayte and Widgett' advertised that they had moved their school from 20 West Street 'to a large, commodious House in New Street'. At the end of the advert-isement they added: 'A good LAUNDRY MAID, in the above School, is wanted'; confirming that it was then a boarding school.[1] (Miss Widgett had earlier been with Mrs Pullen see Pullen and Widgett above.) In July 1791, Miss Wayte and Miss Harben announced that they had taken German Place House, 'THAT LARGE and COMMODIOUS HOUSE, near the Sea' (it was a little to the east of the Steine) 'for the purpose of educating young Ladies, where every attention to their health, morals, and improvement, will be observed. - They have engaged, in the different branches of Education, the best Masters, and their terms in every respect are reasonable.' They added: 'The very convenient, pleasant, and healthy situation of German Place House, induces them to offer accomodation to Ladies for lodging and board, and to young Ladies as Parlour Boarders.' The school was styled 'GERMAN-PLACE BOARDING-SCHOOL'.[2] In *Cobby's Directory* 1799 the address is given as 6, German Place. In *Univ. Directory* 1791 ('Waite and Harben, Ladies'

Boarding-school'), and 1793. One of three girls' boarding schools mentioned in Mossop's *Description of Brighthelmstone* (1793) as being in a 'flourishing state... from the healthiness of the situation, and the care and attention shewn towards the pupils.'[3] Commended in *Fisher's New Guide* 1800 (Miss Wayte and Harben, still in German Place), and 1804 (Mrs Wayte, in German Street; no mention of Harben).[4] [*Miss Wayte, Miss Widgett, Miss Harben*]

1. *SWA* 21.7.88. 2. *SWA* 18.7.91. 3. op. cit., 26. 4. op. cit., (1800), 26; (1804), 37.

Sunday school (F: 1788. Rs: 1788- into 19c)
A subscription for a Sunday school in Brighton was begun in January 1788.[1] An address, circulated to every house-keeper in Brighton, began: 'The intended objects of this institution are infant children of either sex, or of any denomination, whose necessities require this assistance.'[2] Before the school opened, 'near 200 children' had applied for admission.[3] At a committee of subscribers held in the town hall on Tuesday, 12 February, two mistresses and one master were engaged, and 128 children - 54 boys and 74 girls - were admitted (there were two free schools for boys in the town at that time). The school opened on Sunday, 17 February 1788.[4] Nathaniel Kemp was credited as principally responsible for its establishment[5] (he was of Preston Manor, and later Ovingdean Hall; a gentleman of Brighton, he was a town commissioner from at least 1799.[6] His wife was the principal patron of the girls' school of industry, also established in 1788 [qv below].)

The initial subscription was sufficient for the charity to open also a school of industry, and to provide the Sunday school children with uniforms, as the following newspaper report indicates (the occasion was the first anniversary of the school, on 1 March 1789):

> Yesterday se'nnight, being the anniversary of the Brighthelmston Sunday School Institution, the Children appeared in their little uniforms, with the addition of a blue favour, worn in commemoration of the day. - They were in number near two hundred, and walking in procession, made a very neat and respectable appearance... [7]

The institution was fortunate in having the public patronage of 'His Royal Highness the PRINCE of Wales',[8] and later of 'their Royal Highnesses, the PRINCE and PRINCESS of WALES'.[9] At the beginning of September 1788, 'a memorial was presented by the inhabitants of Brighthelmston to his Royal Highness the Prince of Wales, in behalf of the Sunday School and School of Industry, lately established in that town. His Royal Highness we understand, received the memorial with that gracious condescension so peculiar to his character.'[10] Support from the inhabitants sometimes involved more than providing money: at the school's first Christmas - 'The attention shown to the poor children of the Brighthelmston Sunday-School, by the ladies who condescended to dine at their table on Christmas-day, was truly laudable, and affords an example for the imitation of others, whereby these useful seminaries may be rendered as permanent as they are promising to the cause of Religion and Virtue.'[11]

Others contributed both money and services at fund-raising events. For despite the annual subscriptions and royal patronage, the institution was dependent on concerts, charity sermons, and even charity plays given by the theatre. The following notes give some idea of such support:

March 1788: concert and ball, assisted by the band of 11th Regiment Dragoons. Tickets 3s.6d. (Tea included).[12]

September 1788: charity sermon at the parish church; 'The collection, we hear, exceeded sixty pounds.'[13]

September 1789: charity sermon at the parish church. 'In the course of the service, which will begin at eleven o'clock, the occasional HYMNS, by Mrs. CHARLOTTE SMITH, and WM. HAYLEY, Esq; will be sung by the CHILDREN.' [Charlotte Smith (1749-1806), novelist and poet, was at school at Chichester, and lived for some time at Woolbeding and Brighton; her first publication, *Elegaic Sonnets and other Essays* (1784) was dedicated to William Hayley. 'Charlotte Smith is best remembered by her charming poems for children.' William Hayley (1745-1820), celebrated poet in his day, was born at Chichester, lived at Eartham and later Felpham; friend of William Blake, who illustrated his works; in 1790 he was offered the laureateship, which he declined.[14] The sermon was preached by Rev J.F.Fearon, rector of Fittleworth (and master of Cuckfield grammar school) and the collection raised £46. 'The respectable appearance of the children of the Sunday school and school of industry... reflected no small share of credit on Miss Paine, under whose care and tuition they are.'[15]

1789: the idea of the theatre at Brighton playing for the benefit of the Sunday school originated with Lord Eardley.[16]

August 1790: morning and afternoon charity sermons at the parish church; hymns sung by the children; Mrs Barthelemon sang Handel's 'I know that my Redeemer liveth', accompanied by Mr Barthelemon; collection raised £66.[17]

September 1791: charity sermon at Brighton church by Hon. and Rev George Pelham; solo by Mrs Barthelemon; 'The children performed their hymn, "Tis thee, my Saviour, &c.' in a manner that did great credit to Miss Paine, under whose care and instruction they are placed.'[18]

August 1792: charity sermon at the parish church by Dr Taylor, Chaplain in Ordinary to his Majesty; Mrs Barthelemon sang from the Messiah, accompanied by Mr Barthelemon on the violin; 'a very liberal collection'.[19]

August 1794: two charity sermons at the parish church; 'Master Welsh, who sung divinely';'collection amounted to upwards of fifty pounds'. [20]

August 1795: at the opening of the Chapel Royal for divine service, on 3 August, a charity sermon for the children of the Sunday school and school of industry was preached by Dr Langford, canon of Windsor; 'Their Royal Hignesses the PRINCE and PRINCESS of WALES were present'. [21]

August 1797: charity sermon at the parish church; 'Hymns to be sung by the Children'.[22]

October 1797: charity sermon at the Chapel Royal, by the bishop of Rochester; collection 'more than 601.' [23]

September 1798: charity sermon at the Chapel Royal. ' ☞ Hymns to be sung by the Children.'[24]

The dependence of the Sunday school on the collections at charity sermons is clear from the following report on that preached by the bishop of Rochester on 1 October 1797:

> The good Prelate, added example to precept, by a very liberal donation to the charity; and the Committee who superintend the school, are indebted to his Lordship for a continuance of the institution, which without his pious exertions in its behalf, must have sunk under its almost exhausted funds.[25]

The committee could not have anticipated a contribution that had come to them in 1792. At Brighton races on 3 August, Lord Egremont's horse Felix won the £50 plate. Immediately after the race he asked some gentlemen who stood near him whether there was a Sunday school at Brighton. He was told there were two, and desired that the plate might be equally divided between them.[26]

The Sunday school was referred to in 1813.[27]

[*Miss Paine*]

1. *SWA* 4.2.88.   2. *SWA* 25.2.88.   3. *SWA* 4.2.88.   4. *SWA* 18.2.88.   5. Michell, J.C., in his dedication

of the 1829 edn (re-edited by him) of Pelham, A. *Short History of Brighthelmston*, p v.   6. Dale, A. *Brighton Town and Brighton People* (1976), 15, 104.   7. *SWA* 9.3.89.   8. Eg *SWA* 21.9.89.   9. Eg *SWA* 25.9.97.   10. *SWA* 8.9.88.   11. *SWA* 5.1.89.   12. *SWA* 17.3.88.   13. *SWA* 29.9.88.   14. Lucas, E.V. *Highways and Byways in Sussex* (2nd edn 1935), 52, 72, 127; *Enc. Brit.* (13th edn).   15. *SWA* 21.9.89, 28.9.89, 5.10.89; *The Lewes and Brighthelmston Pacquet* 1.10.89.   16. *SWA* 21.12.89.   17. *SWA* 26.7.90, 2.8.90.   18. *SWA* 3.10.91.   19. *SWA* 20.8.92.   20. *SWA* 1.9.94, 8.9.94.   21. *SWA* 3.8.95.   22. *SWA* 21.8.97.   23. *SWA* 25.9.97, 9.10.97.   24. *SWA* 3.9.98.   25. *SWA* 9.10.97.   26. *SWA* 6.8.92.   27. Shoberl, F. *The Beauties of England and Wales* (1813), 113.

School of industry   (F: 1788. Rs: 1788- into 19c)

Founded in 1788, in conjunction with the Sunday school, probably after March (when a fund-raising concert was advertised for the benefit of just the Sunday school[1]) and certainly before 8 September, when the Prince of Wales received a memorial 'in behalf of the Sunday School and School of Industry, lately established'.[2] According to C. Wright, writing in 1818, the school of industry for girls was established in 1788 in the town hall, under the patronage of Mrs Nathaniel Kemp and other ladies. (Nathaniel Kemp was primarily responsible for the establishment of the Sunday school in the same year (see above); he had married Martha Feilde at St Margaret, Westminster, in February 1785; she died in 1821.) By 1813 the school had moved to Church-street and was then educating 46 poor girls. By 1818 it consisted of 150 girls, 70 of whom were clothed (in green, according to J.Erredge), educated, 'and carefully initiated in the sentiments and practice of religion and industry'.[3]

The Sunday school and school of industry were run as a single charity, at least until September 1798, when a charity sermon was preached on their joint behalf.[4] For details of other charity sermons, all of which were on behalf of the two schools, see Sunday school above. In 1789 and 1791 Miss Paine was responsible for the 'care and tuition' of the children of both schools.[5] The joint responsibility is made clear from advertisements for mistresses placed by the charity, which also suggest that the school of industry was concerned to teach girls to read, sew, knit and spin. In April 1792, under 'WANTED IMMEDIATELY', the charity advertised for a mistress 'to instruct a part of the children of the Brighton Sunday School and School of Industry, in plain-work, spinning and knitting. She must be a steady, industrious, middle-aged woman, and one who can be recommended for her good character and morals.'[6] (In May of that year, Miss Paine announced that she would open both a 'child bed warehouse' and a school.) In October 1797 they wanted, for the Sunday school and school of industry, 'A WOMAN, who has been used to a School, who can teach reading, plain sewing, knitting and spinning.' The salary was described as 'considerable'.[7]

[*Miss Paine*]

1. *SWA* 3.3.88.   2. *SWA* 8.9.88.   3. Wright, C. *Brighton Ambulator* (1818), 111-2; *SNQ* **10**, 80; Erredge, J. *History of Brighton* (1862), 355; Shoberl, F. *The Beauties of England and Wales* (1813), 113.   4. *SWA* 3.9.98.   5. *SWA* 5.10.89, 3.10.91.   6. *SWA* 16.4.92.   7. *SWA* 23.10.97.

Countess of Huntingdon's Sunday school   (F: 1788. Rs 1788: into 19c)

The Countess of Huntingdon, Selina Hastings (1707-91) founded a sect of calvinistic methodists, known as the Countess of Huntingdon's Connexion. Up to 1770, she and her chaplains continued as members of the Church of England, but in that year, following a dispute in London, they became a dissenting sect. At her death they had 64 chapels and a college. She built a chapel in Brighton in 1761, just off the south side of North Street.[1] On 28 September 1913 they celebrated there, in North Street, the 125th anniversary of the founding of their Sunday school.[2]

[Humber and Hunter's school attended at the chapel - see below.]

1. *Enc. Brit.* (13th edn).   2. *Sussex Daily News*, 29.9.1913, 6.

Baschet's French evening school   (F: 1788. Rs: 1788-93)
In an advertisement in July 1788 Nicholas Baschet, from the university of Orleans, offered to teach the French language to ladies and gentlemen who intended to spend the season at Brighton. He claimed that he attended 'the principal Schools in Brighthelmston and its Neighbourhood.'[1] Later that year, in November, he opened an evening school, from six to eight on Mondays, Thursdays and Saturdays, at 2 New West Buildings.[2] By inference (from reference to the university of Orleans) he was French master at Mossop's school in 1790, and possibly resident there in 1787. In *Univ. Directory* 1791 and 1793, as French Master. (Not in *Cobby's Directory* 1799 or 1800.) [*Nicholas Baschet*]
1. *SWA* 28.7.88.   2. *SWA* 10.11.88.

Sanders' day school   (F: 1789);
later boys' boarding school   (F: 1793. Rs: 1793- into 19c)
In January 1793 Samuel Sanders opened a boys' boarding school at 44 West Street. Advertising this, he referred to the fact that he had kept a day school for four years, and asked for a continuance of his 'Friends' support in the new undertaking. He now offered board, and instruction in the most useful branches of the mathematics, mensuration, geometry, trigonometry, land-surveying, 'Italian method of Book-keeping', &c. &c. for 12 guineas pa for boys aged 10 and under, 13 guineas for 11-year-olds, 14 guineas for 12-year-olds, and 15 guineas for 13-year-olds. 'Particular attention paid to the religious and moral rectitude, as well as education of his pupils.' And:

> Sea-bathing being the principal motive of many persons who place their children at Brighthelmston; he shall attend those committed to his care to the water, every morning, if requested, without any extra charge, unless they use a machine, which is Sixpence.[1]

In *Cobby's Directory* 1799, at 45 West Street. Presumably the same as 'Saunders, Writing Master, West-street' in *Button's Directory* 1805, and the Samuel Farncombe Sanders, schoolmaster of Brighton, exr of Richard Humber in his will of 4 August 1830. [*Samuel Sanders*]
1. *SWA* 7.1.93.

Watson and Rowe's day school   (F: 1790)
Mrs Watson and Miss Rowe opened, in the first week of August 1790, a day school for teaching children English, useful needle-work, and geography, at North Buildings, north end of New Street. They offered English and plain needle-work at 8s a quarter (or 3s a month), and geography at 8s a quarter.[1] [*Mrs Watson, Miss Rowe*]
1. *SWA* 19.7.90

Breen's day school   (Rs: 1790-1807)
William Breen (formerly of Morling and Breen - see above) advertised in October 1790 for an assistant 'in a reputable Day School'.[1] In *Univ. Directory* 1791 and 1793. Schoolmaster of Brighton in his will of 1807.[2] [*William Breen*]
1. *SWA* 25.10.90.   2. ESRO W/A 70.312.

Cohen's Jewish school   (Rs: 1780s?, 1790s?)
Emanuel Hyam Cohen, a native of Northern Bavaria, arrived in Brighton in 1782, and has been called the real founder of the Brighton Jewish community; he died in 1823. He kept a boys' school in Artillery Place (on the front at the west side of the town), and among other subjects taught Hebrew and German.[1] (Artillery Place not shown on Yeakell and Gardner's map of 1779, but shown on Cobby's map of 1799.) [*Emmanuel Hyam Cohen*]
1. Spector, D., 'Jewry in Sussex', *SGLH* v.3, no.3, 83.

Measor and Hunter's day and evening schools (R: 1791)
later **Humber and Hunter's boys' boarding school** (F: 1792. Rs: 1792-3)
later **Humber's boys'(boarding) school** (Rs: 1799- into 19c)
In June 1791 Measor and Hunter advertised to deny 'a malevolent report' that they were giving up their day school at 38 Middle Street, where they taught writing, arithmetic, geometry, trigonometry, mensuration, and other practical parts of the mathematics. They offered writing and arithmetic at 7d per week; geometry, trigonometry, &c. &c. at 1s per week. They also kept an evening school, from 6 o'clock till 8. That their school had been going for some time is suggested by their comment: 'As an unremitted attention has, and ever will be paid to the business, they still hope to merit that distinguished approbation the Inhabitants of Brighton have so singularly been pleased to honour them with.'[1]

A year later Humber and Hunter opened their boys' boarding school, on 23 July 1792, at the same address - 38 Middle Street. They offered board, writing 'in the most fashionable hands', arithmetic and mathematics, 'in their various and useful branches.'[2] An advertisement of theirs in January 1793 included the following: ('Messrs. Humber and Hunter...')

> Think it proper to inform our friends, that the Chapel the late Lady Huntingdon's being our place of public-worship, shall constantly bring those committed to our care thither also.[3]

By 1799 Humber and his wife, still in Middle Street (but not, apparently, at 38), were on their own. Mrs Humber had been involved in boarding boys since Humber and Hunter opened their school in 1792; she now advertised, from 39 Middle Street, 'that, she has for upwards of seven years been in the habit of rearing children with peculiar care and tenderness. Those Parents or Guardians who have weakly children, whom they wish to enjoy the benefit of sea-bathing, may be assured of every attention being paid to them while under Mrs. HUMBER's care. Reference can be given to many very respectable Ladies, both in Town and Country, whose Children have experienced the happiest effects from sea-bathing, and proper attention.' In the same advertisement, Mr Humber 'continues to teach after the best methods Reading, Writing, Arithmetic, and the useful branches of the Mathematics, Book-keeping, Use of the Globes, Orrery, &c.' His scientific bias is apparent when he adds: 'Youth who have left School taught the rational and pleasing lessons on the Globes, of all spheres of learning the most entertaining and instructive... An excellent pair of modern 12-inch Globes, and Orrery, to lett.'[4] In February 1799 Humber had advertised from 39 Middle Street as a bookseller and bookbinder.[5] In December 1800, from 41 Middle Street, at the end of a long advertisement listing books and periodicals that he had for sale, he confirmed that he 'continues to teach'; and to the basic subjects are added: '... together with pleasing and instructive lessons on the Globes. - Mensuration, and Book-keeping by single and double entry, according to Hutton. - Navigation, after Robertson and Moore, and the pupil will have an opportunity of taking observations with a capital tangent-screw Quadrant, accurately adjusted by J.H.Moore, Esq.'[6] Humber was a founder and first president of the Brighton Scientific Society, instituted 6 October 1800; this involved a small weekly subscription towards the society's 'Instruments, Books, &c.'; the society's first advertisement was issued from 41 Middle Street, and ended: 'And 'tis particularly recommended to the notice of Youth to embrace so favourable an opportunity, on such <u>liberal terms.</u>'[7]

Advertised in *SWA* (under the various names) Jun 1791; Jul 92; Jan (2) 93; Apr (2) 99; Dec (2) 1800. Humber in *Cobby's Directory*, at 41 Middle Street, 1799 and 1800; and in *Button's Directory* 1805 (Humber's Academy, Middle Street).
[*Measor, Hunter, Richard Humber*]

1. *SWA* 20.6.91; gives 'MRASOR', clearly a misprint; there were several Measor families in Brighton (some in Middle Street) at this period. 2. *SWA* 2.7.92. 3. *SWA* 7.1.93. 4. *SWA* 1.4.99. 5. *SWA* 11.2.99.

6. *SWA* 8.12.1800.   7. *SWA* 22.12.1800.

The Misses Pickering's girls' boarding school   (Rs: 1791-1800)
The Misses Pickering had a girls' boarding school by 1791 (*Univ. Directory* 1791 and 1793); at 41 West Street in 1799 (*Cobby's Directory* erroneously gives 'Well-street') and 1800 (*Cobby's Directory*). Possibly the expensive school next but one mentioned, but not one of the three girls' boarding schools referred to in Mossop's *Description of Brighthelmstone* (1793); nor is it among the four girls' boarding schools commended in *Fisher's New Guide* 1800. [*The Misses Pickering*]

Miss Paine's day school   (F: 1792)
Miss Paine - almost certainly the same as the Miss Paine who had the 'care and instruction' of the children of the Sunday school and school of industry in 1789 and 1791[1] - opened, on 4 June 1792, at 9 Little East Street, a 'child bed warehouse' ('where she will make and sell all manner of child-bed linen...'), and at the same time, 'a SCHOOL for the Instruction of Children, in English, and every kind of useful Needle Work, at EIGHT SHILLINGS per Quarter. - Day Boarders, TEN SHILLINGS and SIXPENCE per Month.'[2] [*Miss Paine*]
1. *SWA* 5.10.89; 3.10.91.   2. *SWA* 21.5.92.

Girls' boarding school   (R: 1792)
In September 1792 an advertisement appeared for an unidentified school, notable for being the most expensive girls' school in Sussex in the 18th century:

> *BRIGHTHELMSTON*
>   YOUNG LADIES, to the number of EIGHT, edu-
> cated in   English,   French,   Arithmetic,   Geography   and
> Music.
>   Particular attention will be paid not only to every part of
> their Education and Morals, but also to their health, by every
> proper indulgence in air and exercise.
>   The Terms are FIFTY GUINEAS a year, to the age of four-
> teen years, washing included.
>   Writing Masters, or any others required, will be procured;
> these, as also books, are not included in the above terms.
>   For further particulars enquire at Mrs. LAY's Print Shop,
> on the Steine.[1]

No other references to this school have been traced (unless it was the Misses Pickering's - see above); perhaps it never became established.
1. *SWA* 10.9.92

Jewish school   (F: 1792)
The first Brighton synagogue was established, together with a school, in Jew Street (off Church Street, to the north of the town), in 1792.[1]
1. Spector, D., 'Jewry in Sussex', *SGLH* v.3, no.3, 84.

Buckoll's day school (perhaps the charity school)   (Rs: c1750-93)
later Buckoll's boys' boarding school   (F:1793. Rs: 1793-7)
In January 1793 Stephen Buckoll and Son opened a boys' boarding school 'in a large commodious House, with suitable accomodations', in West Street. Advertising this, Buckoll sen. stated that 'he has had the care of a large Day-School upwards of forty years.' He owned and occupied a house, schoolhouse and garden in West Street in 1785,[1] and was in *Univ. Directory* 1791. The boarding school offered reading, writing, arithmetic, navigation, the use of the globes, &c. at 16 guineas pa, and 1 guinea entrance.

........Those who shall think proper to favour him with the tuition of their children may rely on the most unremitting assiduity to forward their improvement, the tenderest treatment, and the most circumspect attention to the preservation of their health and morals.

N.B. Sea-Bathing carefully superintended gratis, unless Machines are used.

Tea, is an exclusive article, One Guinea per annum.

Residence at the School during each vacation, One Guinea. The vacations are Midsummer and Christmas, one month each.[2]

In June 1794 the school advertised under 'S. BUCKOLL and SONS', at 42 West Street: Greek and Latin had been added to the curriculum, and parlour boarders were now accepted at 20 guineas pa.[3] In January 1795 Stephen Buckoll advertised on his own - no son or sons are mentioned in this or later advertisements. By January 1795 Buckoll had taken 'a large and more commodious House, situated at the Upper End of North Street, with an extensive Play-ground'. The curriculum remained the same, except that French, dancing, music and drawing were now offered as extras, at 1 guinea per quarter each; and the cost for parlour boarders was increased to 25 guineas pa.[4] In January 1797 fees were raised to 18 guineas pa, with 1 guinea entrance; parlour boarders remained at 25 guineas pa, but now with 2 guineas entrance.[5]

Advertised in *SWA* Jan (2) 1793; Jan, Jun (2) 94; Jan (2), Jul (2) 95; Jan (2), Jul (2) 96; Jan (3), Jul (3) 97. In *Univ. Directory* 1791 and 1793.
[*Stephen Buckoll, two of his sons*]

1. Davey, R. *East Sussex Land Tax 1785, SRS* 77, 41.   2. *SWA* 14.1.93.   3. *SWA* 16.6.94.   4. *SWA* 5.1.95.
5. *SWA* 9.1.97.

Cropley's boys' school   (F: 1794)
In May 1794 Rev William Heaton Cropley, then aged 23, proposed to give private tuition to a limited number of young gentlemen, at his appartments at 4 Golden Lion Lane, in mathematics, natural philosophy, classics, history, chronology and geography, to prepare them for university.[1] [*William Heaton Cropley*]
1. *SWA* 12.5.94

Briggs' boys' boarding school   (F: 1794)
Rev R.Briggs was assistant at Mossop's private grammar school when Mossop died on 7 April 1794. Briggs continued to run the school until June 1794, when it was taken over by William Brook. Briggs then engaged 'a large and commodious house' at 2 New Street, and on 21 July opened a boarding school for not more than 12 boys, offering 'the strictest attention to their health and morals, as well as improvement in the sundry branches of literature' (ie education).[1] [*R.Briggs*]
1. *SWA* 23.6.94.

Brook's boys' boarding school   (F: 1794. Rs: 1794- into 19c)
From 21 July 1794, William Brook, 'late of HERSTMONCEUX', took over Mossop's grammar school [qv above], the latter having died on 7 April 1794. Brook's school is treated here as separate from Mossop's because both the master changed and, almost certainly, the location: by December that year Brook was operating from 31 West Street.[1] The same curriculum was followed, but, apart from his opening advertisement, Brook does not seem to have referred to it as 'the grammar school'. He offered board, Greek, Latin, and accompts, history, geography, &c. at 25 guineas pa; no entrance money was required; French ('taught by a native of Orleans' - almost certainly Nicholas Baschet; see above), dancing, drawing and music, were extras.[2] (In advertisements that December, writing was also specifically mentioned as part of the main course .[3]) *Cobby's Directory* 1799 and 1800 gives Brook's

address as 30 West Street. In *Fisher's New Guide*, 1800 and 1804, two boys'academies are mentioned and commended, one being 'that in West-street, of which Mr. Brooke is proprietor, where young gentlemen are boarded and educated both in Classics, according to the Eton plan, and also the Sciences, after the most approved methods.' (The other academy was Mr.Paine's, in North Street, 'principally to qualify youth for business.')[4]

In December 1799 there was a highly favourable report in *SWA* of a play performed by the boys, one 15-year-old boy, Frederick Choppino, being especially commended for the prologue he had written, and spoken, which was printed in full; from the report it is clear that a play was an annual event.[5]

Advertised in *SWA* Jun, Dec (2) 1794; Jan (2) 95.
[*William Brook*]
1. *SWA* 22.12.94.   2. *SWA* 30.6.94.   3. *SWA* 22.12.94.   4. op.cit.,(1800), 25,(1804), 36.
5. *SWA* 23.12.99

Holloway's dancing and music academy   (F: 1796)
In 1793 the young ladies of Mr and Mrs Dubbins' girls' boarding school at Horsham were being taught dancing and music 'by the eminent Mr. HOLLOWAY, of Newington'.[1] By the beginning of 1796 he had moved to Brighton, and by 1 February 1796 had opened an academy at his house in North Street. He offered instruction 'in all the most fashionable Dances, and Music, viz. Minuet, Minuet de la Cour and Gavett, Devonshire Minuet, and Rondo, Slingsby's Allemande, and others. The Scotch Minuet, Reels, Scotch Step, Dutch Step, Hornpipes, Cotillons, &c. &c.'[2] Later that year he additionally opened an academy at Lewes; he continued to attend at his academy in Brighton on Mondays, Thursdays and Saturdays. He also attended schools, procured bands for private and public balls, and tuned piano fortes.[3] [*Holloway*]
1. *SWA* 30.12.93.   2. *SWA* 1.2.96.   3. *SWA* 19.9.96.

Townley and Adeane's girls' boarding school   (Rs: 1799-1800)
Mrs Townley and Mrs Adeane advertised their girls' boarding school in North Street in January 1799. They offered 'Boarding and Instruction in English, French, and every fashionable and useful Needle-work' for 20 guineas pa, parlour boarders 30 guineas; music, dancing, geography, &c. were extra charges.[1] Six months later, in June 1799, they announced that, owing to 'the very rapid success' they had experienced, it had been necessary for them 'to take a much larger House in West-street, within a hundred yards of the Sea, extremely open and airy, with proper Play-ground for the Children'; this was 62 West Street.[2] They were one of four girls' boarding schools commended in *Fisher's New Guide* 1800: '... the ladies, by whom these different schools are conducted, are extremely well qualified for the situations they are in, and are deserving of every success. The health, morals, and improvement of the young ladies committed to their care, we believe to be most conscientiously attended to.'[3] The school was not mentioned in *Fisher's New Guide* for 1804. [*Mrs Townley, Mrs Adeane*]
1. *SWA* 7.1.99.   2. *SWA* 24.6.99.   3. op. cit., 26.

Thorp's school   (R: 1801, and earlier)
In April 1801 E.Thorp announced that he had given up 'Grimmett's well instituted Charity' [qv] and in consequence could increase the number of his private pupils.[1] Then at Duke Street, and there in 1805 as 'Writing master' (*Button's Directory*). Advertised in *SWA* Apr 1801; Jan (2) 1802. [*E.Thorp*]
1. *SWA* 20.4.1801.

Other schoolmasters/mistresses, who would have had their own schools, or have run one of the charity schools, or have been assistant teachers, or perhaps have been a specialist teacher attending a number of schools.

William Grover, schoolmaster in 1735 (Quaker deed) and at marr 1738; perhaps at the charity school, where his father was master [qv].[1]

1. ESRO SOF 9/1; Quaker Brighthelmston R, t/s at SFHG.

English, schoolmistress in 1791 and 1793 (*Univ. Directory*).

Oliver, schoolmaster in 1791 and 1793 (*Univ. Directory*).

James Kennedy, schoolmaster at 17 Duke Street in 1799 and 1800 (*Cobby's Directory*).

John Marchant, schoolmaster at 2 Brighton Place in 1799 and 1800 (*Cobby's Directory*); 'schoolmaster' and 'writing master' at Brighton Place in 1805 (*Button's Directory*).

Dancing and music masters

Thomas Hadleston - see above.   (R: 1772)

James Henry Rawlins - see above.   (Rs: 1783-93)

Mr Dennis   (R: 1793) Announced, September 1793, that he had been engaged to succeed Mr Rawlins as dancing master 'in the several different Boarding-Schools, in Brighton'; and advertised to 'the Nobility and Gentry, and Masters and Mistresses of other Boarding-Schools, at a convenient distance from Brighton'. Offered 'the *Minuet de la Cour*, and other Minuets of the present time, together with *Cotillons, Country-dances*, and the so much admired and fashionable *Scotch-steps*, &c. in a stile, he flatters himself, superior to what they have hitherto been taught in, in the neighbourhood of Brighton.'   He was then at 31 West Street.[1] Advertised in *SWA* Sep (2), Oct (2) 1793.

1. *SWA* 2.9.93.

Mr Holloway - see above.   (R, at Brighton: 1796)

Mr Corbyn sen. and Mr Corbyn jun.   (Rs: 1798-1800) In September 1798 *SWA* reported: 'Mr. Corbyn's Ball on Wednesday, at Hick's Rooms, Brighthelmston, was attended by a great number of fashionable families, all of whom expressed their pleasure at the easy deportment and elegant dancing of Mr Corbyn's pupils. A very little boy, (son of Mr. Paine) danced a hornpipe admirably; and Miss Corbyn, daughter of the dancing-master, displayed abilities which surprised every beholder.'[1] The 'Messieurs Corbyn', dancing masters, were at 35 New Street in 1799 (*Cobby's Directory*). For a very favourable report in *SWA* on Corbyn's 'public night' at Lewes in December 1800 (and a controversy that arose from the report), see under LEWES; Corbyn was, inter alia, dancing master to Mrs Gell's school at Lewes, and to 'a School near Brighton' (presumably Mrs Norton's school at Preston).[2]

1. *SWA* 10.9.98.   2. *SWA* 15.12.1800; 22.12.1800.

William Prince   (Rs: 1799- into 19c) Organist of the Chapel Royal, and music master at 4 Prince's Place 1799 (*Cobby's Directory*). He was music master to Mrs Gell's school at Lewes in 1799, no doubt among others.[1] In 1805, music master at East Street (*Button's Directory*). Also a composer (see Schedule 2).

1. Gell's ad in *SWA* 30.9.99.

Drawing masters and mistress

[Mrs Harrington - see above]   (R: 1775?)   An established portrait artist, it seems probable that, in addition to the sciences and languages that she taught, she also instructed pupils in drawing.

Richard Paine   (Rs: 1791-1800)   In *Univ. Directory* 1791 and 1793. In *Cobby's Directory* 1799 and 1800, as drawing master and stationer, of 8 North Street.

William Austin   (Rs: 1797- into 19c)   An established drawing master in London, he moved to Brighton in 1797,[1] and in January 1798 offered his services to 'the Masters and Governesses of Schools, and Parents and Guardians of Youth, of both sexes, in the neighbourhood.'[2]   He was then at 23 Great Russell Street; from 1799, at 20 Great Russell Street.[3]   He offered instruction in drawing, painting, and etching; figures, heads, landscapes, ruins, caricatures, birds, fruit, flowers, either in oil, water colours, chalks, tints, or body colours, 'all which he studied under the best Italian, French, Flemish and English Masters.'[4]   From another advertisement in 1800, 'Mr. A. may be heard of at all the principal Schools at Brighton, Lewes, and Preston.'[5]   For other details, see Schedule 2.
Advertised in *SWA* Sep 1797; Jan 98; Mar (2), Jun, Jul (3), Aug 1800. In *Cobby's Directory* 1799 and 1800, and *Button's Directory* 1804.
1. *SWA* 11.9.97.   2. *SWA* 29.1.98.   3. *Cobby's Directory* 1799; *SWA* 18.3.1800.   4. *SWA* 18.3.1800. 5. *SWA* 23.6.1800.

Edmund Scott   (Rs: 1799- into 19c)   'Portrait Painter & Drawing Master' 1805 (*Button's Directory*), he had been established in Brighton by 1799.[1]   Freemason.
1. ESRO QDS/1/EW1.

Fencing master

Thomas Hadleston - see above.   (R: 1772)

French masters

Thomas Hadleston - see above.   (R: 1772)

Nicholas Baschet - see above.   (Rs: 1788-93)

[Ringard]   (R: 1794?)   A French Royalist refugee, Doctor of the University of Paris, and Rector of the Royal Parish St Germain L'Auxerrois, being 'desirous of supporting himself by teaching the French Language', advertised in September and December 1794.[1]   It is not known if he taught children.
1. *SWA* 8.9.94.

[Note: By 1811 Brighton's population had jumped to 12,012; by 1821 to 24,429; by 1831 to 40,634. *Baxter's Directory* of 1824 lists 40 Boarding Academies and 39 Day Academies. By 1835, for the children of the poor there were 3 National Schools, with between 1,100 and 1,200 children; a Union School; British and Infant Schools and a School of Industry, with about 300 children; another school for girls; 3 Church of England Sunday schools, and Sunday schools at most of the dissenting chapels; a school for fishermen's children; a blue coat school for boys; an orphan school; Swan Downer's School for girls, with 65 girls; and an infant school for children of tradesmen; there were also an adult school for poor females and an adult school for young men (Horsfield, *Sussex*, I, 147).]

BROADWATER   1724: about 60 families   1801: pop. 1,018

School   (R: 1779)
At the 1779 visitation, there was a schoolmaster in the parish who 'Teacheth Publickly'; he
was of 'good Life' and 'diligent', came to Church and caused his scholars to come, and
taught them the catechism.[1] (There was no free school, and no schoolmaster, in the parish
in 1775.[2])
1. WSRO Ep.I/22/1.   2. ibid.

[Sunday school]
By 1805 the rector and his wife had established a Sunday school for poor children. (The
then rector, Peter Wood, had been instituted in 1797.)[1]
1. *VCH* vi, I, 80, citing Evans *Worthing* (1805), 42-3; CI.

BURPHAM   1724: 41 families   1801: pop. 201

Dame school   (R: 1742)
At the 1742 visitation, the answer to the question, any teachers without licence in the
parish?, was, 'Only a woman'.[1]
1. WSRO Ep.I/22/1. The parish is not identified on the document, but the churchwardens signing it were the same
as those who signed the Burpham bishop's transcript for 1742.

BURTON (BODECTON) **cum COATES** 1724: 6 families 1801: pop. 44
                                                          (Burton 14; Coates 30)

No 18th-century schooling traced. (At the 1726 visitation, beside questions relating to the
schoolmaster, if any, and his behaviour, is written, 'Well', which may possibly imply that
there was a schoolmaster in the parish.[1])
1. WSRO Ep.I/22/1.

BURWASH   1724: about 200 families 1801: pop. 1,524

School/charity school   (Rs: 1724- into 19c)
At the 1724 visitation: '... There is a School House or Vestry adjoyning to it [the chancel]
which belongs to ye Parishioners'.[1] George Barnsley, rector of Sedlescomb and sometime
of Burwash, by will dated 1723, left £500 for the education of poor children in three
parishes, of which Burwash was one, to whom the executors allocated £100.[2] By 1729 there
was a charity school supported by this legacy and other contributions.[3] In 1731, a farm in
Wadhurst (a barn and 22 acres) was purchased for £220, from Barnsley's legacy and
subscriptions; Horsfield cites the Duke of Newcastle, George Jordan, vicar, Thomas Hussey,
gent., Henry Pelham, Esq, as contributors. The rents were to be used to pay for a person to
teach the poor children of Burwash to read, and in the knowledge of the Christian religion,
as professed in the Church of England. In 1818 the rent was raised from £11 to £18.[4] [By
1819, with £350 from the sale of timber on the estate and a legacy of £50, the total income
was £35 10s. This was used to support a national school recently established, which then
had 74 boys and 84 girls. A schoolhouse had been built at the expense of the then rector.
The schoolmaster was paid £30 pa, the mistress £25 pa, the deficiency being made up by
subscriptions.[5]]
1. WSRO Ep.I/26/3, 24-5.   2. *EP*1 (1819), 225; Lucey, B. *Twenty Centuries in Sedlescombe* (1978), 282.
3. SPCK ALB, v.14, 10083.   4. *EP*1 (1819), 225; Horsfield *Sussex* I, 580.   5. *EP*1 (1819), 225.

Parish schooling   (R: 1736)
A loose receipt in the overseers' ledger, 1737-44, records the following:
          Rich Jenner Bill for Schooling

	£. s. d.
Begune the 25 day of March 1736 and Ending the 29 day of Sep'tr for Halfe a year	0 - 4 - 0
and shaveing his head Twice	0 - 0 - 6
	0 - 4 - 6
For shaveing Sam Jenner head } Twise }	0 - 0 - 6

Rec'd in full Content of
this Bill by me   Tho; Alderton [signs]

Richard and Samuel Jenner were poor boys supported by the parish, and the receipt indicates that, apart from the charity school, the overseers paid for the schooling of poor children, at least on occasion. On 2 July 1740 the parish paid Thomas Alderton's bill of £1 5s 3d, for which he signed a receipt, but this may not have been for schooling.[1] *[Thomas Alderton]*
1. ESRO PAR 284/31/1/1.

Edwards' boys' school   (F: 1761)
In 1761 Richard Swinfen Edwards, then aged 29, curate of Burwash, opened a school there 'for the Instruction of Youth in the Latin and Greek Languages, Writing, and Arithmetic'. He added that 'a Conveniency of boarding may be had in a sober Family, not far distant.'[1] He died in 1772, and was buried at Burwash. *[Richard Swinfen Edwards]*
1. *SWA* 30.3.61.

Williams' boys' boarding school   (Rs: 1784-93)
For three weeks in October 1783, the following advertisement appeared: 'WANTED, at BURWASH, in Sussex; A BOARDING SCHOOL for young Gentlemen, or for Gentlemen and Ladies. Any Gentleman, or Persons well qualified for, and inclined to, such an Undertaking, will soon find it the general Wish of the Inhabitants, and that BURWASH is a remarkably good Situation, there being the several surrounding Parishes of Etchingham, Salehurst, Brightling, Dallington, Warbleton, Heathfield, Waldron, Mayfield, Wadhurst, and Ticehurst, from which Pupils may with good Reason be expected, most of them, as well as Burwash, being totally unprovided. There is also to be sold, on the 4th of November next, an exceedingly commodious and well situated House for this Purpose.'[1] Perhaps as a consequence of this, William Williams of Burwash announced in April 1784 that he had removed his school 'into a very large and commodious House', adding that there was 'three Quarters of an Acre of exceeding fine Play Ground adjoining the same for the Recreation of Youth after a Relaxation from their Studies.' It would seem that he had previously had a school, perhaps in Burwash, for his advertisement includes: '... he continues to instruct Youth in the several Branches of Literature hereunder mentioned, i.e. English grammatically, the Rudiments of the Latin Tongue, Vulgar and Decimal Arithmetic, Mensuration of all Kinds of Superficies and Solids, Algebra, Geometry, Trigonometry, Geography, Navigation, Land Surveying, and the Rudiments of Astronomy.' He noted that: 'A Library is kept for the Use of the School. - The News-papers are often introduced into the same.' His terms were £13 pa, with ½ guinea entrance.[2] Like all schools, he stressed the healthy situation: in 1786 - 'BURWASH, is allowed by all those who are acquainted with its Situation, to be particularly eligible for the Salubrity of the Air; and as Proof of which, Mr. WILLIAMS has never had a Pupil the least indisposed, except from the natural Causes of a Cold.' Dancing was then available at 10s 6d per quarter; and tea, if required, at 1 guinea extra.[3] In 1789 accounts were included in the curriculum.[4] In 1792 fees were increased to 13 guineas pa, with 2 guineas entrance.[5]   Williams was also a land surveyor.
Advertised in *SWA* Apr (2) 1784; Nov (2) 86; Jun 89; Dec (2) 92. In *Univ. Directory* 1793. *[William Williams]*
1. *SWA* 13.10.83.   2. *SWA* 5.4.84.   3. *SWA* 13.11.86.   4. *SWA* 8.6.89.   5. *SWA* 24.12.92.

Other masters

> John Lawrence, singing master, subscribed 5s towards a new gallery in the church, 1720. (Egerton, J.C. *Sussex Folk & Sussex Ways* (3rd edn 1924), 153)
>
> [Price] Taught reading & writing, and ABC to young children, 1804 & probably earlier. (Goodwin, J. *Burwash and the Sussex Weald* (nd but c1958), 85)
>
> [Wheeler] Taught reading and writing, and ABC to young children, 1804 and probably earlier. (Goodwin, op. cit., 85)

BURY   1724: 59 families   1801: pop. 361

Dame schools   (Rs: 1742, 1758)
At the 1742 visitation, at the question asking if there were any unlicensed teachers: 'only one woman'. At the 1758 visitation, at the same question: 'only a poor woman'.[1]
1. WSRO Ep.I/22/1.

BUXTED   1717: 120 families   1801: pop. 1,063

Charity school   (R: 1710)
In a letter to the SPCK dated 12 March 1711, Edward Sawyer of Mayfield reported: 'That a Ch: School for 10 Children has been set up at Bucksted in Sussex for a Year past, at ye Charge of ye Revd Dr Saunders Rector of ye Parish, and he would increase ye Number if ye poor would send 'em.'[1] It probably continued until Saunders' death in January 1720: in his will, he left a schoolhouse and provision for setting up a boys' charity school (see below) and for charity schooling for girls (see below).
1. SPCK ALB , v.2, 2511.

Saunders' charity (later private) school for boys   (F: c1720. Rs: c1720- into 19c)
By will dated 31 October 1718, Dr Anthony Saunders, rector of Buxted, who was buried 13 January 1720, left a schoolhouse in the parish of Uckfield, and divers property and lands, the income from which was to maintain the premises and be used to instruct 12 poor boys - six from Buxted, six from Uckfield - to read and write the English language and be taught the church catechism, with £10 going to the master, and the remainder of the income being applied to putting poor boys of Buxted apprentices. He also bequeathed his library of about 200 volumes to the school, for the use of the master and scholars. The school was probably operating by 1718 (when Saunders left the schoolhouse), if not before (see Charity school above). In 1729 William Clarke of Buxted wrote to the SPCK, noting that the charity schools at Buxted had not been 'exactly reported, as appears by the printed Account 1724.' He reported the income for the boys' school as 'abt 30 l. p. Ann left by Dr Saunders.'[1] John Lloyd, clerk of Buxted in 1710, when he married there, and later apparently curate at Uckfield and buried there 1738, was the first master of the school. He took private pupils, as did Robert Gerison who followed him (see UCKFIELD). In 1800, William Rose, lately curate of Little Horsted, moved the private school he had there to Uckfield and engrafted it onto Saunders' school, laying out nearly £1,000 in improvement of the premises. He continued to receive the £10 pa from the Saunders' endowment, and in 1819, with the sanction of the trustees, was paying £20 pa to the master of the National School for the education of the 12 boys provided for under Saunders' will. Rose was curate of Uckfield, signing the register pages from 1799 as such.[2] [*John Lloyd, Robert Gerison, William Rose*]
1. SPCK ALB, v.15, 10384.   2. *EP2* (1819), 184-5; Buxted PR; Uckfield PR.

Saunders' charity school/schooling for girls   (F: before 1718. Rs: before 1718- into 19c)
Before his death, Anthony Saunders had started a school in the northern part of Buxted for

the girls of that parish. By his will dated 31 October 1718, he left the Red-tyled House, Buxted, in which the school had previously been conducted, with 3½ acres, in trust to the minister and churchwardens of Buxted for the time being, the income to be used to teach poor girls of Buxted to read and learn the Church of England catechism. The charity was probably operating by 1724, if not before, and certainly by 1729, when William Clark wrote to the SPCK (see Saunders charity school for boys above); he reported that the income for teaching the poor girls was £7 pa. In 1819 the income of £7 10s was being paid to three schoolmistresses, £2 10s to each, each of whom instructed 5 young children - both boys and girls - in reading and spelling. (The children being very young and the parish being very extensive, three schoolmistresses, in different parts of the parish, were appointed.) [1]

1. Lower *Worthies* (1865), 63; *EP2* (1819), 153; SPCK ALB, v.15, 10384.

Haslewood school   (Rs: 1738, 1739)
The parish register contains a note (perhaps relating to seating in the church) listing by name, under the heading 'Scholars at Haslewood School in 1738', two girls and a boy; with below, '1739', listing two (different) girls and 'either Dray's or Skinner's child'.[1] These may well have been poor children taught by a dame under Saunders' charity schooling for girls (see above). (See also Buxted Wood school below.)

1. ESRO PAR 286/1/1/1, f119.

Buxted Wood school   (R: 1739)
The parish register contains a note (perhaps relating to seating in the church) listing by name, under the heading 'Scholars on Buxted Woo[ ] Side', 1739, six girls.[1] These may well have been poor children taught under Saunders' charity schooling for girls (see above). (See also Haslewood school above.)

1. ESRO PAR 286/1/1/1, f119.

Fermor's charity school   (F: 1744. Rs: 1744- into 19c)
Sir Henry Fermor, by will dated 21 January 1733, left substantial estate to be applied for the benefit of various charities, one of which was a charity school, to be built in or near Crowborough, for the benefit of poor children of the parishes of Rotherfield and Buxted. Provision was made for the maintenance of the schoolhouse, the salary of the schoolmaster, and for clothing the children, who were not to exceed 40 in number, and providing books for them. No child was to be admitted under 7 years old, nor to continue more than 4 years. They were to be taught to read, write, and cast accounts. Sir Henry Fermor died in 1734, but the affairs of his charities were before the court of Chancery from the time of his death until 1796.[1]   Nevertheless, the school was operating long before this date and the schoolhouse was built by 1744. In 1771, a Rotherfield vestry empowered the churchwardens to provide clothing for the children of the charity school, and agreed to indemnify them should the trustees of the Fermor charities fail to pay.[2]   The minister and freeholders of Rotherfield had the residual right to appoint the schoolmaster and children, and it was agreed between the parishes that 30 children, boys or girls, should be sent to the school from Rotherfield and 10 from Buxted (Buxted was further from the school than Rotherfield, and that part of Buxted nearest to the school was less populous than the adjoining part of Rotherfield; some of the Buxted children came nearly four miles to the school). This ratio was first recorded in 1819, but had long been established; the relative proportions are reflected in lists of appointments to the school noted in the Rotherfield vestry minute book from 1792 to 1799.[3] In 1819 it was noted that 'the school is always full, and there are many applications for every vacancy.'[4] (For further details of the school, see ROTHERFIELD.) [*William Okill, David Dadswell, Edward Okill Dadswell*]

1. *EP3* (1820), 440.   2. ESRO PAR 465/4/1, 15 December 1771.   3. *EP3* (1820), 442; ESRO PAR 465/4/1. 4. *EP3* (1820), 442.

Workhouse school   (Rs: 1782-90)
From November 1782 to April 1785, and March 1789 to May 1790, the parish paid 2s or 2s 6d per month 'for Teaching the Children in the workhouse their Books'/'for Teaching School'. The payments were made to women, at least two of whom were poor women supported by the parish.[1] [*Ann Miller, Mary Skinner, Dame Brinkhurst, Dame Burchfield*]
1. ESRO PAR 286/31/1.

CATSFIELD   1724: about 40 families   1801: pop. 464
No 18th-century schooling traced.

CHAILEY   1724: about 130 families 1801: pop. 738
Charity schooling   (F: 1770.   Rs: 1770- into 19c)
Thomas Thompsett, by will dated 8 February 1769, gave £40 to the rector and churchwardens, the interest of which was to be used for putting four poor children of the parish of Chailey to school, to learn to read English. The will was proved 14 April 1770, when the rector and churchwardens accepted from the executor, in lieu of the legacy, a small copyhold estate in Chailey, consisting of a cottage and garden, which yielded £4 pa. By 1819 the rent had risen to £7, and four, and occasionally six children, were being put to school.[1] It seems likely that there were, in the 18th century, a school or schools in the village to which the charity children were sent.
1. *EP3* (1820), 437-8.

CHALVINGTON (CHALTON, CHAUNTON) 1724: 23 families   1801: pop.143
No 18th-century schooling traced.

CHICHESTER   1801: pop. (all parishes) 4,744
Prebendal grammar school   (F: 1497   Rs: through 18c)
There are references to a grammar school at Chichester from as early as 1075. In 1497 Bishop Edward Storey endowed the school with the prebend of Highley (which included the great and some of the small tithes of the parish of Sidlesham), his motive in setting up a free grammar school being to reduce the ignorance of the clergy by providing an education for poor scholars destined for the clergy. He ordained that no gratuity should be offered to the master by the parents of the children: the master was to be fined 10s for each offence. The school continued in the same building in West Street, near the close, from long before the 18th century until the 20th - a stone building with a great cellar and above it the schoolhouse, with a 14th-century arch in it, situated at the corner of the bishop's garden.[1] However, in January 1795 David Davis, the master, advertised that it had been 'Completely rebuilt on a very improved plan'. By that time the grammar school appears to have been primarily a private school, and Davis noted that 'There are at present a few Vacancies'.[2] Horsfield, writing in 1835, noted: 'The institution is no use to the inhabitants of Chichester, though called a free school. The master, it is said, is not bound by the statutes to teach his scholars anything beyond the Latin tongue, and no parent will confine the education of his child to such an attainment; hence that which by the good bishop was intended for the advantage of the city, is by this defect rendered nugatory.'[3] In the latter part of the 18th century, private pupils at least were not restricted in this way. In December 1784, just a month after being appointed 'Master of the Free Grammar School',[4] Davis advertised under 'CHICHESTER GRAMMAR SCHOOL',
        Where young Gentlemen are duly instructed in the Classics, or in any other

Part of SCHOOL LEARNING most agreeable to their intended
Appointments in Life.
BOARD and TUITION, TWENTY GUINEAS a Year.
Entrance, ONE GUINEA.
DAY SCHOLARS, FOUR GUINEAS.
Entrance, HALF-A-GUINEA.
VACATIONS, at MIDSUMMER and CHRISTMAS.
DANCING, &c. by proper Masters.[5]

In December 1786 Davis advertised for an assistant: 'he must be a good PENMAN and
ARITHMETICIAN, and must have some knowledge of the LATIN GRAMMAR.'[6] In
another advertisement for an assistant at this time there was no requirement regarding the
classics ('... a single man, qualified to teach Writing, Arithmetic and Book-keeping'[7]); nor
was there when in May 1789 he was again advertising for an assistant: 'To prevent improper
Applications, he must be a single Man, qualified to teach Writing, Arithmetic, and Book-
keeping, well recommended, and able to bear Confinement.'[8] (He was advertising yet again
for such an assistant in 1794.[9]) In 1818 there were 40 boys at the school, boarders and day
boys combined, the former at 60 guineas a year, the latter at 8 guineas.[10] In 1823 Bishop
Carr (though not empowered to do so) made a statute limiting the number of free scholars
to 10.[11]

[*Robert Top, Thomas Baker, William Wade, Richard Tireman, John Atkinson, David Davis,
John Stevens*]

1. *VCH* ii, 399-403; Horsfield *Sussex* II, 25; Hay, A. *History of Chichester* (1804), 391.   2. *SWA* 12.1.95;
Portsmouth Gazette 19.1.95.   3. Horsfield *Sussex* II, 25-6.   4. *SWA* 1.11.84.   5. *SWA* 6.12.84.
6. *SWA* 18.12.86.   7. *Hampshire Chronicle* 18.12.86.   8. *SWA* 25.5.89.   9. *Portsmouth Gazette* 6.1.94.
10. *VCH* ii, 409.   11. ibid.

Grey Coat boys' charity school   (F: 1710.   Rs: 1710- into 19c)
This subscription charity school opened at Lady Day 1710; at Lady Day 1711 there were
27 boys; at Lady Day 1712, 1713 and 1714, in each case 28.[1] According to the supplement
to the SPCK *Account of the Charity-Schools* for 1710, the subscriptions were 'about 60 1.
per ann.', and 30 boys were being clothed and 'taught to read, write, cast Accompt, and to
repeat the Catechism.' In a letter to the SPCK, dated 24 June 1710, William Barcroft of
Chichester, after also reporting the girls' charity school (see below), noted 'That ye Bp, the
Church, some private Gentlem'n & particularly the Ladies have distinguished themselves in
this Charity. But the Corporation are as yet unconcerned.'[2] For the first five years the
school's income averaged £60 pa (the range was £53-71). For the five years from
Michaelmas 1720, it averaged £51 pa (the range was £30-70). For the five years from
Michaelmas 1730, the average income had fallen to £44 pa (the range was £35-65: the £65
year, 1730-1, included a legacy of £25 from Mrs Reason). Later in the century, income
increased to an average of £56 pa for the five years from Michaelmas 1780; and £55 pa for
the three years from Michaelmas 1790 (the surviving accounts end in 1793).[3]

The Blue Coat girls' charity school was started by subscription also in 1710, but
the subscriptions were separate; however, the benefit of legacies of £100 from Bishop
Manningham, who died in 1722, and of £100 from George Sedgwick, the interest on which
was received from 1 April 1771, were divided equally between the two schools. The proceeds of charity sermons, charity performances of plays, and church collections, were also
divided between them: for the early years the division was roughly 60% to the boys, 40%
to the girls (probably in proportion to their subscription incomes), but later in the century
the division was 50:50.[4] Usually, the money was paid into the boys' school accounts and
then the girls' school share was passed to them. In 1714-5, 'Received for the Boys Share

of Five pounds given to all the Children by Mr. Sheppard the Master of the Players and of Four Pounds Fifteen shillings & 3d. the Collecc'on at a Charity Sermon preached by the Rever'nd Mr. Hayley - 05.10. 9' (so the girls' share was 42%). In 1717-8, of charity sermon money, the girls received £4 of £10 (40%) and £2 16s of £7 2s (39%). In 1723, 'Received at a Play for the benefit of the Charity School charges deducted - 9.10.7'; of which the girls were paid £4 15s (48%); in the same year, of the receipts from two charity sermons totalling £12, the girls were paid £5 (42%). One link between the two schools was that each year from 1715-6 to 1718-9 the boys' school paid 5s to the girls' school 'for the Girles makeing the Boys Shirts'.

For each year from 1741-2 to 1792-3 (when the surviving account book ends), the bishop was the largest subscriber to the boys' school, at £5 5s a year. The Goodwood steward's quarterly accounts for 1775-1800 show the Duke of Richmond subscribing £2 2s every year; the subscription was paid to Dean Harwood in 1775, 'for Charity School', thereafter to the masters - to I.Kilwick from 1776 to 1778, William Ingram from 1779 to 1789, Phillip Wright from 1790 to 1800. Subscriptions, however, were only part of the income: the school was very dependent on the receipts from charity sermons, church collections and legacies; in 1770-1, for example, of the total income of £60 15s 8½d only £24 12s 6d (41%) was attributable to subscriptions.[5]

Robert Clarke was the first master; from 1712, he was also master of the Oliver Whitby charity school (see below). He was initially paid £20 pa for teaching the boys. This was later reduced, and the number of boys varied, presumably according to the financial resources available. On 7 October 1723 the managers agreed: 'That Mr. Clark have 15 l. p. Annum allow'd him for the Teaching the 20 Boys, & finding the Fire when necessary'. In the year from Michaelmas 1739 he only received £11 5s. In the year 1740-1 he was paid £7 10s 'for a years Teaching the Ten Boys'; but the next year, 1741-2, his payment was back to £15, 'for teaching the Twenty Boys'. Later payments to masters show that from that time 20 was the regular number of boys, the master being paid proportionately more whenever the number exceeded 20. The agreement with Kilwick in 1762-3 was:

> That he is to receive Seventeen Pounds, yearly, for teaching Twenty Boys (Firing included), & to make no Demands on the Parents of the children at Breakings-up. [Presumably the previous master, Tupper, had done so.]
> That he be allowed One Pound, a Year, for Pen, Ink and Paper -
> That if the Number of the Children be above Twenty, he Shall be paid for One or More in the Proportion above mentioned.

In 1781-2 and 1782-3 the master, Ingram, was paid £21 5s for teaching 25 boys; in 1787-8 there were 23, in the following year 22.[6]

From the 1750-1 year until 1780-1, boys leaving were given 10s 6d. In the first year the payment is described as 'towards clothing', later as just 'on leaving'. The boys may have got their charity clothes as well as the 10s 6d: in 1754-5 Bryant, 'leaving the school without Cloths', got £1 1s, while two other leavers just got the 10s 6d. The charity also financed the putting out of a number of boys as apprentices; in 1714-5, for example, the trustees paid for the placing of three apprentices, and clothes for them.[7]

In the first four years of the school the average age of admission (given in the accounts for 14 boys) was just under 8; the average age of the boys at the school during this early period was just under 10.[8] In October 1723 the managers agreed, 'That no Boy be admitted into the School till he be full of the Age of 8 Years, & that he continue but 4 years in the School, without the particular Approbation of the Stewards for the Time being.'

In the year Lady Day 1712 to Lady Day 1713, five boys were 'Expel'd' (four of them had been at the school since its foundation in 1710); in the same year two boys were removed 'Into ye other School' - presumably the Oliver Whitby school, which opened in 1712 and shared the same master from 1712 to 1748.[10] The two schools were again under one master from Lady Day 1763 until Michaelmas 1778, Ishmael Kilwick, then master of the Oliver Whitby school, being appointed also master of the Grey Coat school at the former date. Ingram was appointed master of the Grey Coat school in 1778, but Kilwick continued as master of the Oliver Whitby school until 1792.

In 1761 there was published a *Collection of Psalms and Hymns, Chichester,* 'sung by the Charity Children of the City'.[11]

By 1819, the total receipts of the school, from the legacies, subscriptions and collections, was about £70, which was applied to the education and clothing of twenty poor boys at the Chichester National school.[12]

[*Robert Clarke, Tupper, Burnet (singing master), Ishmael Kilwick, William Moon Ingram, Phillip Wright*]

1. WSRO Cap.V/1/1.   2. SPCK ALB, v.2, 2128.   3. WSRO Cap.V/1/1.   4. ibid.; WSRO Cap.I/24/5.
5. WSRO Cap.V/1/1; WSRO Goodwood MS 244, 245, 247.   6. WSRO Cap.V/1/1.   7. ibid.   8. ibid.
9. ibid. (reversed ff).   10. ibid.   11. *SNQ* **13**, 276.   12. *EP*2 (1819), 156.

<u>Blue Coat girls' charity school</u>   (F: 1710. Rs: 1710- into 19c)

Established in 1710 by private subscription.[1]   According to the supplement to the SPCK *Account of the Charity-Schools* for 1710, the subscription was 'about 40 1. per ann.', and 20 girls were clothed, and 'taught to read, write and work with the Needle.'   This number appears to have been maintained: according to the churchwardens of the Subdeanery, there were 20 girls in the school in 1769.[2]   In a letter to the SPCK, dated 24 June 1710, William Barcroft of Chichester, after also reporting the boys' charity school (see above), noted 'That ye Bp, the Church, some private Gentlem'n & particularly the Ladies have distinguished themselves in the Charity.'[3]   Later in the century the Duchess of Richmond, at Goodwood, subscribed £2 2s pa (the Duke subscribed the same amount to the boys' charity school): she died in 1796, the Goodwood steward's accounts recording in 1798 a payment to 'Mrs. Newland her late Graces Sub blue Girl School £2.2.0'; from 1799 to 1801 the subscription was paid to Mrs Newland by the Duke.[4]

Elizabeth Peirce by will dated 13 August 1722, proved 2 February 1723, left £50 for the use and benefit of the charity school for girls.[5]   The school shared equally with the boys' Grey Coat school (see above) in the benefit from legacies of £100 from Bishop Manningham, who died in 1722, and of £100 from George Sedgwick, the interest on which was received from 1 April 1771; and shared the money raised by charity sermons, charity performances of plays, and church collections, initially receiving about 40%, later 50%. With these last items, the money raised was usually paid to the master of the boys' school and entered into the boys' school accounts, a proportion then being paid to the girls' school. The person receiving the money on behalf of the girls' school, when named, was always a woman, and until 1727 it was customary for her to sign the account book by way of receipt. It is assumed that, in most cases, the ladies receiving these items through the 18th century were the mistresses of the girls' school.[6]

The boys' school accounts for the year from Lady Day 1715 to Lady Day 1716 include the following item:

Pd Mrs Holney for the Girles)
makeing the Boys Shirts   )   00. 5. 0

The same payment for making the boys' shirts was received in 1717-8 and 1718-9.[7]

By 1819 the Blue Coat girls' school, from legacies, occasional donations and savings, had realised a fund of £865, yielding £34 12s pa, which with the dividends from the Manningham and Sedgwick charities, provided a total income of £40 pa. This was doubled by subscriptions and collections at church, and about £80 pa was being expended on the education of 22 poor girls at the National School for girls.[8]

[*Mrs Minshull, Eleanor Holney, Mary Goater, Anne Bouchier, Mary Page?, Mary Peckham?, Ann Richardson, Mrs Walter, Mrs Newland*]

1. *EP2* (1819), 157.   2. Bishop, J.H. *A Sussex Pot-Pourri* (1986), 15.   3. SPCK ALB, v.2, 2128.
4. WSRO Goodwood MS 247.   5. SAS, Wadey's Index, citing Deans pec. wills 1704-31, 161.
6. WSRO Cap.V/1/1; Cap.I/24/5.   7. WSRO Cap.V/1/1.   8. *EP2* (1819), 157.

Oliver Whitby's boys' charity school   (known as the 'Blue Boys' or Blue Coat school[1])
(F: 1712.   Rs: 1712- into 19c)
Oliver Whitby was baptised at Chichester 15 July 1664 and buried there 22 February 1703. His father, also Oliver, archdeacon and canon-residentiary at Chichester cathedral, had been a loyalist in the Civil War, and a fugitive in hiding until the Restoration. The family occupied a large house next but one to the bishop's palace in the cathedral close. Young Oliver went to Trinity College, Oxford, at 16, graduating BA in 1684 and BCL in 1687. Later, described as a 'private gentleman of Chichester', he lived partly at Chichester and partly at Harting, on an estate his mother had inherited from a previous marriage. He died aged 39. By will dated 16 February 1702, he left lands in West Wittering, together with the rectory and prebendary lease of that parish, to trustees, to be used to establish a charity school in Chichester. A schoolhouse was to be provided to accomodate the master and 12 poor boys, whose parents were not dissenters and were, by reason of their poverty, exempt from the poor tax. (The will also provided that 'no Parliament man or Dissenter' should ever be a trustee.) Four of the poor boys were to be from Chichester, four from Harting, and four from West Wittering. The master, who had to be 'one of the Communion of the Church of England', was to have his board and lodging, and £20 pa clear, and the boys were to be 'carefully educated in the Principles of Religion as Established in the Church of England, and to be diligently instructed in Reading, Writing, Arithmetic, and so far in Mathematical Learning, as may fit them for honest and useful employments, with a particular Regard to Navigation.' (According to the Subdeanery churchwardens in 1745, referring to the 'Blue Boys', 'nine boys taught navigation - at proper age go to sea or are apprenticed out'.) The boys were to be provided with board and lodging, and an allowance of £1 a year for each, to provide a blue gown, with a crest of the Whitby coat of arms as a metal badge, a blue quilt cap, and such other apparel as shoes and stockings as the £1 would extend to. (By the end of the century, and perhaps throughout, the blue gown was lined with yellow.)[2]

Rules agreed by the trustees add further detail. To be admitted, boys had to be 'Healthy, & strong, Free from distemper, as ye Evill, Scald heads, Itch, Falling Sickness & ye like. to which end, ye Trustees shall carefully view & examin them before their Admission'. In selecting among qualifying boys, 'regard be First & principally had to Orphans, and in ye next place to such as have most Children, & least to Maintain them with'. Boys from Chichester had leave to visit their 'Friends' (parents or guardians) once a week or more often, 'but not suffer'd to stay one night with them'. Religious observance was marked, and notable for the active participation of the boys, and the public nature of their observances at supper on Sunday evenings: 'That every Morning before Breakfast, & in ye Evening before Supper, a Chapter be read, and a Prayer which is compos'd for them be said in ye publick school, by one of ye Boys, (each to take his day in Turn) with a Grace said before & after Breakfast, Dinner, & Supper. And after Supper, ye Boys to Sing a Psalm, & on Sunday nights, their Supper & Exercise to be publick, that any of ye Town, or Strangers may be present, and to conclude with one of the Boys, makeing a publick Thanksgiving for the Benefaction bestowed upon Them.' (A box was to be set up in the hall, 'with a Blew Coat Boy painted over it, to receive the Benevolence of Strangers, and

5.   Oliver Whitby (1664-1703), founder of the Chichester boarding charity school - the only boarding charity school in 18th century Sussex. (WSRO PD 1642)

Visitors'.) Additionally, the boys were 'to goe to ye Morning Prayers at the Subdeanery, and in ye Evening to ye Choir', and were to be catechised every Tuesday and Friday in the evening.[3]

The trustees 18th-century accounts have survived.[4] Although Oliver Whitby died in February 1703, the trustees could not establish the school immediately - 'for want of a Stock to begin, Work has been delayed till 1712 when there was about 1000 l. in Bank.'; the income was then reported to be £150 pa.[5] The school was first established in 1712 at 16 West Street, opposite the cathedral, which was initially rented for £15 pa; the trustees purchased the freehold in 1720 for £300. In his will of 17 November 1727 Henry May, Recorder of Chichester, left £50 to the trustees of Oliver Whitby's 'Mathematicall School', to be employed in putting out boys as apprentices, to sea, or for the general support of the school. The first master, Robert Clarke - who was at the same time also master of the Grey Coat charity school (see above) - was paid from Michaelmas 1712, receiving £24 a quarter for boarding the 12 boys, and £5 a quarter for teaching them. From October 1727 Clarke's teaching payment was increased to £6 10s a quarter, 'in lieu of board', and the board allowance was reduced by the same amount, to £22 10s a quarter. By the end of the century similar amounts were being paid: James McDonald, who was appointed in 1792, was to receive £108 pa for the board of the boys, and £20 for the teaching, to be paid quarterly. Masters were also paid for various incidental expenses; for example, on 1 March 1715, Clarke was paid £6 6s 11½d for expenses incurred by him when 8 of the 12 'charity boys' had the small pox. At the same time, a further £1 11s was paid for 'physik' for the 8 boys.

When Robert Clarke resigned at Christmas 1748, 'upon Account of his great Age and Infirmities', the trustees agreed that he 'for his former Services and on Account of his great Age be allow'd out of the Charity afores'd during his Life an Annuity of Ten pounds...' Clarke had been master for 36 years. Clarke's successor, Ishmael Kilwick, served even longer - for 44 years. He was not initially also master of the Grey Coat school, but from Lady Day 1763 until Michaelmas 1778 he was master of both schools; from Michaelmas 1778 until midsummer 1792 he continued just as master of the Oliver Whitby school.[6] When the trustees advertised for a master in May 1792, 'He will be required to board and instruct twelve poor Boys in Reading, Writing, and the Mathematics. A Person who has a practical knowledge, and is capable of instructing them in Navigation, will be preferred.'[7] (James McDonald was appointed.) Thomas Hackman, who was master from midsummer 1797 until 1808, ran at the same time his own private boarding academy in West Street, from at least January 1799 [qv].[8] This was presumably grafted onto the Oliver Whitby school.

[In 1826 the Court of Chancery authorised the trustees to increase the number of boys, as funds permitted, and the number rose to 20 in 1826, and to 52 in 1878. In the 20th century the income declined, and the trustees were forced to close the school in 1949. The income was thereafter used to provide scholarships at Christ's Hospital, Horsham, for boys from Chichester, Harting and West Wittering.[9]]

[Robert Clarke, Ishmael Kilwick, James McDonald, Thomas Hackman]

1. Eg: the 'Blue Boys' referred to by the Subdeanery churchwardens in 1745 (Bishop, J.H. *A Sussex Pot-Pourri* (1986), 15); 'Blue Coat Boy' by the Trustees in 1702 (WSRO E35D/8/12); 'Blue-Coat Charity School' in ad by school for master 1792 (*SWA* 7.5.92). 2. Subdeanery PR; Tibble, R., 'The Oliver Whitby School, Chichester', *West Sussex History* no.34 (1986), 18; *EP2* (1819), 153-6; Willis, T.G. *Records of Chichester* (1928), 278; Bishop, J.H., op cit., 15; *SNQ* **13**, 37; Hay, A. *Hisory of Chichester* (1804), 392. 3. WSRO E35D/8/12. 4. WSRO E35D/3/1. 5. SPCK *Account of the Charity-Schools*, 1713. 6. WSRO E35D/3/1, Cap.V/1/1; Steer, F.W, & Venables, J.E, ed *The Goodwood Estate Archives* (1970), v.1, 60. 7. *SWA* 7.5.92. 8. WSRO E35D/8/3, E35D/3/1. 9. *SNQ* **13**, 37-8; Tibble, op cit.

Lover's school   (Rs: 1721, 1727)

Joshua Lover kept a school in the 1720s, and probably earlier. According to a contemporary, he was 'a noted School Master'.[1] He is referred to as a schoolmaster in a marriage licence of 1721.[2] In 1727, the year he died, one of his scholars was Patty (Martha) Smith, so he taught both boys and girls.[3] Patty's uncle William was a Baptist minister, and she married James Spershott, who later became joint Baptist minister at Chichester. Lover's daughter, Mary, married Benjamin Martin, schoolmaster [qv], and they were almost certainly the 'Benjamin Martin and his wife' listed in the Chichester Baptist church book. Richard Smith, cooper, brother to the late Baptist minister, William, was surety for the marriage licence for Lover's second marriage in 1727. Lover's school was clearly acceptable to Baptists, and may well have been primarily a dissenting school. (For details of his life and death, see Schedule 2.)

[*Joshua Lover*]

1. *SAC* **30**, 150.   2. *SRS* **9**, 249.   3. *SAC* **30**, 150.

Martin's boys' boarding school   (Rs: 1734-c1741)

Benjamin Martin's book, *The Young Trigonometer's Compleat Guide* (1736), was signed 'From my School in Chichester, April 8, 1734'. Both this book and *The Philosophical Grammar* (1735) carried advertisements for his school, from which its mathematical/ scientific bias is clear:

By the author in Chichester are taught,

I	Writing, in all the common and useful hands.
II	Arithmetic, of every kind.
III	Algebra and fluxions.
IV	Logarithms, with their construction and use.
V	Geometry, in theory and practice.
VI	Trigonometry, both plain and spherical.
VII	Navigation, in every kind.
VIII	Dialling in all its parts.
IX	Astronomy and geography.
X	Surveying of land.
XI	Mensuration of plain superficies and solids.
XII	Gauging, in all the best methods.
XIII	Mechanicks.
XIV	The use of both the globes.
XV	The projection of the spheres in plano.
XVI	The use and construction of all the most useful mathematical instruments.

The theory and practice of all the mathematical arts are very much expedited and facilitated by ocular demonstration, and actual practice by the learner himself; on very large instruments, as globes, spheres, sectors, scales, sliding-rules, maps, charts, diagrams, and other contrivances for the purpose of spherical geometry and trigonometry.

N.B. Youth are boarded very reasonably by the author, Benjamin Martin.[1]

Apart from being taught to read and write at a village school, Martin was entirely self-educated; yet at his death, he was described as 'one of the most eminent mathematicians of the age...'   He married Mary Lover, daughter of the Chichester schoolmaster, Joshua Lover [qv], soon after the latter's death. Martin and his wife were almost certainly General

Baptists, and the Chichester Baptist community were strong subscribers to one of his books published in 1737; and it is probable that his school was supported by the Baptists.

His most successful book, *The Philosophical Grammar* (1735) ('Experimental Physiology, or Natural Philosophy', ie.science), which was translated into Dutch, French, Italian, Greek and Russian, was dedicated to 'British youth of both sexes'.

Early in 1742 the Martins moved to Reading, where he advertised the opening of a boarding academy. It was, however, not as a schoolmaster, but as author, lecturer, and scientific instrument maker, that he won a national reputation (see Schedule 2).
[Benjamin Martin]
1. Millburn, J.R., *Benjamin Martin* (1976), 12.

The Misses Russell's later <u>Philadelphia Russell's girls' day and boarding school</u>
(Rs: c1750- into 19c)
Three Russell sisters kept a girls' boarding school, where the poet William Hayley (1745-1820) was taught 'his Letters'. The youngest of the sisters was Philadelphia, and Hayley wrote: '... while He was a Child in Petticoats He had received from this Lady a bright silver Penny for reading well'. When she died in 1815, Hayley wrote an epitaph for her.[1] The eldest of the three sisters was Mary, who married Richard Shenton, vicar choral at the cathedral, in 1754.[2] She was half-sister to Philadelphia, and to Bridget and Elizabeth, one of whom was almost certainly the third sister.[3]

By August 1776, 'Miss Russell' had bought Sir John Miller's house for £1,100, for her boarding school; which suggests that the school was successful.[4] In 1784, Philadelphia, still a spinster, was shown in the Land Tax returns as owner of the house in South Street where she lived, with five maidservants - presumably the school (she was also owner of the Playhouse in South Street).[5] In 1785 the fees were as follows:

	Per Ann.		Entrance		
Board and Education (Breakfast tea included)	£19	7	£2	2	0
Parlour Boarders	26	5	2	0	0
Music	5	5	1	1	0
Dancing	3	0	0	10	6
French	2	2	0	10	6
Drawing	2	2	0	10	6
Writing and Arithmetic	1	12	0	10	6

☞Every lady to bring with her a silver table spoon and tea spoon, and to pay the full quarter's board tho' taken away before the quarter expires.
Vacations at Midsummer and Christmas.
'Mrs' Russell was then advertising for a French teacher, who 'must be a Protestant, well recommended for her moral character, correct in the pronunciation of the French language, and qualified to speak it grammatically; she will likewise be required to understand Needlework, so as to assist in the school in that department.'[6]

By 1793 the school was listed as Philadelphia Russell's 'Ladies Boarding School', as it was in 1797-8;[7] and again c1804 and in 1811, as 'Mrs. Russell, ladies' boarding-school'.[8]

Eliza Florance, who was sent to the school as a day-boarder in 1800, when she was about 7, and stayed till she was 16, has left an account of it. The school, at the end of South-street, was 'said to be a first-class school, where the children of the "County gentry" were educated... The house was a large red-brick mansion, with spacious airy rooms and wide entrance-hall and staircase... large garden at the rear; extensive buildings for domestic use, laundry, stabling, out-houses; with dining-room and school-room built off to receive

the large number of pupils. These were presided over by seven teachers, and the old lady, Miss R[ussell], made her appearance in the school-room for an hour in the morning and afternoon. She had a class of juveniles to herself, of which class I made one. She was a venerable grey-haired lady, held in high esteem by the leading people in the city and county... There were as many as 50 pupils and 10 lady boarders, or rather parlour boarders. These attended classes with the young ladies, and they had the privilege, by paying £10 10s. per annum extra, of being in the drawing-rooms of an evening, and sharing in the society of visitors when Miss R- received company ... when it was so desired by their friends [ie parents or guardians], young ladies of the school might, under the protection of the governess, attend public balls, concerts, and lectures... The theatre when I was young stood within a hundred yards of the school-house. The company performed three or four months in each year... As a school-girl I was often allowed an evening at the theatre... ... many of [the leading people in the city and county] visited the dancing-class, on dress occasions, to witness the graceful movements of the pupils in the *Minuet de la Cour*, and the "Garland Dance," which was considered a wonderful display of graceful action: twelve damsels with garlands performed various evolutions prescribed by the master. This dance was greatly admired by the visitors, and the girls liked the twisting and twining, and the picturesque attitudes it evolved. My father had a notion that to have a good carriage the dancing-master must be called in to instruct the limbs how to move and the body how to comport itself. The consequence was that I took dancing lessons the whole number of years that I was at school, nine or ten years... The school made a goodly appearance on a Sunday in the Cathedral. There was a large range of seats in the choir over the "Corporation Seat," appropriated to the young ladies... Many of the ladies, or parlour boarders, were handsome young women. At this period Sussex was remarkable for the beauty of its damsels - fair Saxon complexions, blue eyes, and graceful forms. Chichester, especially, was celebrated for beautiful girls. The gay bevy of laughing bright eyes from the Corporation pew attracted many a side glance from the gentlemen, and many a signal was given and exchanged unknown to the matronly gouvernante in attendance, which was followed by "stolen walks through moonlight shades," or promises to meet at public ball or concert, and once upon a time an elopement, to the scandal of Miss R-'s "well-regulated" establishment, occurred.'[9] (For further details of Eliza Florance's education, see Schedule 3.)
[*Mary Russell, (Bridget or Elizabeth) Russell, Philadelphia Russell, Fisher (dancing master)?*]

1. *Chichester Papers* **49**, 14.   2. McCann, A. *The History of the Church and Parish of St. Andrew Oxmarket Chichester* (1978), 11; *SRS* **32**, 130.   3. St Olave PR; St Peter the Great PR.   4. Yorke, P.C. *The Diary of John Baker* (1931), 363.   5. WSRO MP 417.   6. *Hampshire Chronicle* 18.7.85.   7. *Univ. Directory* 1793, 1797/8.   8. *The Chichester Guide*, c1804; *Holden's Directory* 1811.   9. *A Memoir of Mrs Eliza Fox* (1869), BL 10826 BBB 11, 9-12.

Workhouse school   (Rs: 1754, 1756, 1799)
Regulations issued by the Guardians of the workhouse include the following:

1754:   Ordered that a Master & Mistress have the care and management of the poor, keep the Accounts, learn the family to Read, Card, Knitt and Spin, and all other Branches relating to the Woolen Manufactory.. [1] [The occupants of the workhouse were referred to as 'the family'.]

1756:   That all small children above two and under five be washed and cleansed and their heads combed by 8 o'clock in the morning in Summer, and by 10 in the winter and taught to read according to their several capacities.[2]

1756:   That a man be appointed to teach the boys and a woman the girls to read, to write and to take care of the education, manner, and behaviour of the children, that every day in the summer and two hours in the winter [sic] and catechised twice a week, with a liberty for the Master or Mistress to change their hours of work and learning at their Discretion.[3]

1799: At this Court it was agreed on that the children in this House be learnt to Read and Write from four to seven in the afternoon from Michaelmas to Lady Day and that a Master be appointed for that at a future Court.[4]

1. 'Chichester Workhouse', *SAC* **79**, 143.   2. ibid. 149.   3. ibid. 150.   4. ibid. 150.

Blagden's school   (R: 1761)

Rev Bragg Blagden had a small school in All Saints parish in 1761.[1] (Son of an alehouse-keeper, born and schooled in Chichester, then aged 46, he had a large and increasing family, and was described by Archbishop Secker as 'A worthy man'. He held a number of livings near Chichester, was chaplain to the Duke of Richmond, and died in 1781.)
[*Bragg Blagden*]

1. *Secker*, 214.

Joel's boys' boarding school   (Rs: 1769-74)

In February 1770 there was published an elegy on the death of a boy 'at the Rev. Mr. JOEL's Boarding-School, *at* Chichester', written by another pupil of the school.[1] The boy who died, J.Richards, had sung two pastoral duets, in the character of Damon, at a performance given on 18 December 1769. In 1773 the school performed *The Tragedy of Cyrus* at 'the new theatre in this city'; one of the boys, Master Oldfield, who took the lead part, 'gave such proof of a theatrical genius as was scarce ever known'; there was 'a numerous and polite audience'.[2] (This was the earliest school play so far traced in Sussex.) Thomas Joel published *An Easy Introduction to the English Grammar* (Chichester, 1770), composed for the convenience of children under seven, and printed for the use of his school (preface dated 'Chichester, 16 December 1769'). Joel was a General Baptist; he came to Chichester in 1760 as assistant to Mr Preddon, pastor of the General Baptist chapel, and shortly after the latter's death in January 1761, he was elected pastor in Preddon's place, a post he held until July 1762.[3] At East Grinstead assizes in March 1774, Joel was awarded £20 against J.White for 'scandalous injurious words' (Joel claimed the slander had destroyed his school, but the court found that he did not lose any scholar on this account).[4] [*Thomas Joel*]

1. *SWA* 26.2.70.   2. Thomas, E., 'The Original Theatres of Chichester', *Chichester 1991* (1991), 48, citing (pers. comm.) *Salisbury Journal* 3.4.73.   3. McCann, T.J., in *SAC* **130**, 190.   4. *SAC* **52**, 65; Yorke, P.C., ed *The Diary of John Baker* (1931), 277.

Hadleston's French, dancing and fencing school   (F: 1772)

In July 1722 Thomas Hadleston advertised that he had taken the house in North-Street 'in which the late Mr.Greenfield lived', and had opened 'a SCHOOL for Teaching FRENCH, DANCING, and FENCING with the SMALL SWORD'. He claimed to have resided in Paris several years, to have been a pupil of the most celebrated masters, and to have been tutor 'to some Persons of the first Consequence there, in the several Branches he professes.'

He offered French at 1 guinea per quarter, and ½ guinea entrance: 'Ladies at the same Time have an Opportunity of learning or improving in the Italian Writing Hand.' Dancing at ½ guinea per quarter, and ½ guinea entrance: 'In three Weeks time he teaches the Minuet, upon moderate Terms, to any Person from Twelve to Thirty Years of Age and upwards, fit to appear in any Company.' He also composed and taught 'all Sorts of French, Allemande, and English Dances.' Fencing, 'by the true Rules of that noble Art', at 1 guinea per quarter, and 1 guinea entrance.[1]

(He also attended at Lewes every Monday, and at Brighton, at the *New Ship* Inn, every Tuesday.)
[*Thomas Hadleston*]

1. *SWA* 20.7.72.

Clowes' boys' boarding school   (Rs: 1774-8)
In the summer of 1774 William Clowes advertised his school, where 'YOUTH are genteelly boarded, and methodically educated'. For 14 guineas pa, entrance 10s 6d, he offered English, French, &c. writing, in all its various and ornamental hands; arithmetic, vulgar and decimal; merchants accompts, in the Italian method; duodecimals, or cross multiplication; the extraction of the square and cube roots; geometry; trigonometry, both plane and spherical; mensuration of superficies and solids; conic sections; drawing; land surveying; planning and embellishing; gauging; stereometry; stereography; algebra; fortification; gunnery; projection of the sphere; the use of the globes in geography, astronomy, and navigation, and various other mathematical instruments. He noted that, 'as the Number of his Pupils is within a few Months very much encreased, he has engaged an able Assistant'.[1] Six months later, 'the Classicks' were included in the curriculum; the entrance fee was increased to 1 guinea; dancing was available as an extra; it was noted that there was 'A convenient private Yard for the young Gentlemens Exercise', and that 'the greatest Care will be taken of their Health, Learning, and Morals, and every gentle and emulative Method made use of to excite and encourage Diligence.'[2] In a long advertisement in June 1775, the list of mathematical and related subjects was repeated, but in January 1776 the curriculum was summarised as: 'ENGLISH, the CLASSICKS, WRITING, the MATHEMATICS, and MERCHANTS ACCOMPTS, in the Italian method.' French was now an extra, along with 'DANCING, &c.' There is an interesting additional emphasis in the statement about the gentle methods used, viz: '... and every gentle and emulative Method made use of, to excite and encourage Diligence.'[3] In January 1777 the following advertisement appeared:[4]

> CHICHESTER, January 21, 1777.
> WHEREAS a Report has been circulated in several Parts of the Country, that a Malignant and Contagious FEVER prevails in this City, and particularly in the Family of Mr. CLOWES, Master of the BOARDING SCHOOL here, to the Prejudice of Mr. CLOWES, and of other Persons: We the underwritten hereby certify, that, to the best of our Knowledge, and as far as we can learn by a strict Enquiry, no such Fever exists in the Family of Mr. CLOWES, or in the City in general, and that consequently the above Report is totally without Foundation.
> J. BAYLY, M.D.
> T. SANDEN, M.D.

In May 1778, 'by desire of the young Gentlemen of Mr. Clowes Boarding School', they performed the comedy *The Wonder, a Woman keeps a Secret*, with the burletta *The Two Misers*.[5]
      William Clowes died when his son, another William, born in 1779, was still an infant.[6]
      Advertised in *SWA* May, Jun (3) 1774; Jan (4), Jun (2) 75; Jan (3) 76; Jan, Feb 77. Also in *Hampshire Chronicle*, eg Jan 1775, Jun 78.
[*William Clowes*]
1. *SWA* 30.5.74.   2. *SWA* 2.1.75.   3. *SWA* 8.1.76.   4. *SWA* 27.1.77.   5. *Hampshire Chronicle* 11.5.78. 6. Willis, T.G. *Records of Chichester* (1928), 319.

Elizabeth Clowes' school   (R: 1780s)
When William Clowes, schoolmaster, died (see his school above), his widow, Elizabeth, was left with straitened means, to rear and support two children; to which end, she kept a small school.[1]   [*Elizabeth Clowes*]

1. Willis, T.G. *Records of Chichester* (1928), 319; *VCH* ii, 408; St Olave PR.

Hay's school   (Rs: c1780s?- into 19c)

Alexander Hay, chaplain of St Mary's Chapel, Chichester, and non-resident vicar of Wisborough Green from 1785 to his death in 1806, in the introduction to his *History of Chichester*, published in 1804, written when he was 'on the verge of seventy years', referred to '... the very irksome and laborious employment of teaching school, which my circumstances have rendered, and still render necessary.'[1] In 1784 he was living in West Lane, Chapel Street, with his wife, three sons, one daughter, one maidservant and one male lodger, in a house owned by William Ridge. He presumably kept his school there. He died in November 1806 'at his home in the West Lane'.[2] James Florance [qv] was tutor at Hay's school in 1793.   [*Alexander Hay, James Florance*]

1. *Chichester Papers* **20**, 2, 5, 6.   2. WSRO MP 414 and 417.

Moorey's school   (Rs: 1782, 1784)

William Moorey, schoolmaster, in poll book, March 1782.[1] In 1784 he was in a house in St Martin's, with his wife, three sons and two daughters. He owned the house in which he lived, and probably kept his own school there.   [*William Moorey* (Moorry)]

1. WSRO Add MS 2133.   2. WSRO MP 414 and 417.

Mrs Smart's girls' boarding school   (Rs 1783-5)

later Richardson and Smart's girls' boarding school   (Rs: 1785-98)

and later the Misses Richardson's girls' boarding school   (Rs: 1804, 1811)

In March 1783 the following report appeared in *SWA*: 'The next evening [Sunday, 9 March], between seven and eight o'clock, [a] fire broke out at Mrs. Smart's boarding-school, in the West-street, in Chichester, which being timely discovered, was happily got under without doing any further damage than burning the closet where it broke out, and the ceiling of the room adjoining. It was occasioned by one of the young ladies going into the said closet for a book, wherein was some linen that received a spark from the candle, and caught fire, and communicated the flames as above.'[1] In 1785 Mrs Smart resigned the school to her daughter and Miss Richardson. The fees were then £16 pa for board, washing, and all kinds of useful and ornamental needlework, with one guinea entrance; writing, arithmetic, music and dancing, 'by proper masters', were extras, 'on reasonable terms'.[2] 'Richardson & Smart Ladies Boarding School' was listed in *Univ. Directory* 1793 and 1797-8. Richardson was presumably one of the Misses Richardson who had a girls' boarding school in West-Street c1804 (*The Chichester Guide*) and either E.M. or F. Richardson, who had a girls' boarding school in Chichester in 1811 (*Holden's Directory*).

In the spring of 1800 Eliza Florance, then aged about 7, went as a day-girl to Miss Richardson's school in West-street; she has left some account of it. It 'was kept by two ladies held in high repute on account of the very exemplary manners of the young ladies under their care; and the senior was said to be a woman of superior education... She seemed very formal and precise.' On her first day, in the schoolroom were two teachers (apart from Miss Richardson) and about 30 girls, some intent on their on their lessons, others reading aloud, some standing in classes answering questions. Eliza was placed on a form with the smaller children, who were sewing, learning the use of the needle; each in turn was had up to the mistress's table 'to "say their lessons" and to read some portion of Scripture or Bible stories, in the morning; in the afternoon miscellaneous subjects, selected from history, poetry, or biography. The elder girls had their special lessons for each day in the week: for a Monday, History (Magnall's Questions); Tuesday, Geography (Goldsmith's); Wednesday, Grammar (Lindley Murray); Thursday, Spelling (Mavor's Dictionary); Friday, Writing and Ciphering, with a master; Saturday, Repetition, Catechism and Collect, as in use in the Church of England for the following Sunday.' Coming from a dissenting family,

Eliza had difficulty with the collect, which she could not understand, and the catechism - "Please, ma'am, I never say catechism!" - which the school insisted upon. 'The children of the school looked askance at me, and asked questions', and after a very brief time at the school Eliza was moved to Miss Russell's school [qv above], 'where a greater freedom of opinion was tolerated'.[3]

[*Mrs Smart, Miss Smart, Miss (E.M.?) Richardson, Miss (F.) Richardson?*]

1. *SWA* 17.3.63.   2. *Hampshire Chronicle* 18.4.85.   3. *A Memoir of Mrs Eliza Fox* (1869), BL 10826 BBB 11, 6-9.

Walond's singing school   (R: 1784)
In 1784 William Walond had a singing school in a house in the Close, which he owned.[1] He had been appointed deputy organist of the cathedral in 1775 and organist in 1776. He gave up the duties of Master of the Choristers in 1794, paying out of his own salary a lay clerk, Thomas Barber, to take on this responsibility. He retired as organist in 1801.[2]

[*William Walond, Thomas Barber*]

1. Land tax return, in WSRO MP 417.   2. Plumley, N. and Lees, J. *The Organs and Organists of Chichester Cathedral* (1988), 48.

Richard's school   (R: 1792)
John Marsh left 'Mr. Richard's School' 4 June 1792.[1]

1. *'John Marsh Diary'*, vol 14, 175, Huntington Library, USA, MF at WSRO.

Sunday schools   (R: 1789)
'We hear from Chichester, that two Sunday Schools have lately been opened in that city, under the patronage of many respectable Ladies.' (1789)[1] By June 1796, however, there was no Sunday school at Chichester.[2]

1. *SWA* 1.6.89.   2. *The County Mirror And Chichester Magazine*, June 1796, 226, 228.

Florance, private tuition   (R: 1793)
James Florance, later a barrister of Chichester, was as the time of his marriage in 1793 not only tutor at Hay's school (see above) but 'he also received pupils at home, with whom he read the classics and mathematics.' 'Schoolmaster' in 1793 poll book. His wife's family were Quakers; his eldest daughter, born 1793, was baptised aged 6 at the Unitarian chapel, Baffin's Lane, and later married William Johnson Fox, for many years minister at Baffin's Lane and later preacher and politician. Florance belonged to a debating society, which often met at his house and whose members appear to have been mostly nonconformists. He was also co-founder of the Chichester 'Library Society' in 1792, one of the rooms in his house being given over to its use.[1]   [*James Florance*]

1. *A Memoir of Mrs. Eliza Fox* (1869), BL 10826 BBB 11, 1, 4, 5, 15, 16, 19; WSRO Add MS 2135.

Michell's boys' boarding school   (Rs: 1788- into 19c)
Mark Michell, who had been for eight years assistant to Richard Fagg, master of Churcher's College, Petersfield, opened his own boys' boarding school in North-street, Chichester. In 1788 he advertised for an assistant, 'who is a good Penman and Accountant'.[1] In 1792 he offered board, and instruction in the classics, English, writing, arithmetic and merchants accompts, 'on reasonable Terms'.[2] 'Mitchell, school master' in North-street, c.1804 (*Chichester Guide*).   [*Mark Michell*]

1. *Hampshire Chronicle* 14.4.88.   2. *SWA* 9.7.92.

Stevens' boys' boarding and day school   (F: 1796)
Rev John Stevens, then aged 28, fellow of New College, Oxford, proposed opening a boarding school in Chichester on 25 July 1796. His terms were £25 pa, with 1 guinea entrance; day scholars, 4 guineas, or with dinners, 12 guineas, with ½ guinea entrance. 'Dancing, Writing, French, &c. by proper Masters' - presumably as extras.[1]

Stevens was appointed master of the prebendal grammar school in 1797, and continued as such until 1802. If his private school had become established, he would have integrated it with the grammar school; his predecessor, David Davis, had operated the grammar school as both a private and free school.

[*John Stevens*]

1. *SWA* 23.5.96.

Hackman's boys' boarding school   (Rs: 1799- into 19c)

Thomas Hackman, master of the Oliver Whitby school 1797-1808, also ran his own boys' boarding school in West Street (presumably at the Oliver Whitby premises). He advertised in December 1798, under 'HACKMAN's ACADEMY', offering board, and reading, writing, geography, arithmetic, vulgar and decimal fractions, mensuration of planes and solids, and all the useful branches of mathematics, for 18 guineas pa, with 1 guinea entrance. 'And to accomodate those who may be designed for superior stations, the French language is here taught on an improved plan, and Dancing by a complete Master of that elegant accomplishment.' French and dancing were extra charges. 'N.B. A strict attention is paid to the morals and religious principles of the Pupils educated at this Academy.'[1] By January 1800, Latin was included in the curriculum, and drawing as an extra; and accomodation was available for parlour boarders.[2]

In January 1800 *SWA* reported: 'At the commencement of the Christmas Vacation at Mr. Hackman's Boarding-School in Chichester, the young gentlemen underwent a public examination, and recited several essays in verse and prose, much to the credit of themselves and their master. Among other popular pieces they performed the Tragedy of Cato; the characters in which were sustained with great feeling and elegance.'[3]

The school closed in 1804 and its contents were sold at the *Wheatsheaf*; these included 23 beds with their bolsters, coverlids, blankets and sheets.[4]   (But *Holden's Directory* of 1811 still includes 'Hackman Thomas, academy'.)

[*Thomas Hackman*]

1. *SWA* 31.12.98 (also *Portsmouth Gazette* 31.12.98).   2. *SWA* 13.1.1800 (also *Portsmouth Gazette* 13.1.1800). 3. *SWA* 13.1.1800 (also *Portsmouth Gazette* 30.12.99).   4. Thomas, E., MS, citing *Hampshire Telegraph* 21.7.1804, 21.1.1805.

[Miss Bailey's girls' boarding school]   (R: c1804)

Miss Bailey had a girls' boarding school in North-Street by c1804. She was probably the Miss Bailey who rented a house in St Olave's parish from 1799.[1]   [*Miss Bailey*]

1. *The Chichester Guide*, c1804; WSRO Land Tax, St Olave.

Other schoolmasters/schoolmistress

William Lewis, licensed to teach boys in the diocese of Chichester, 21 September 1721. He was vicar of Donnington, and also warden of the Hospital of St James, Chichester.   (WSRO Ep.I/1/10)

John Dixon (1704-74), 'schoolmaster' at his burial.   (*SAC* **50**, 55; St Martin PR)

William Martin, schoolmaster in poll book 1782.   (WSRO Add MS 2133)

John Foocks, schoolmaster in 1784, living in a rented house in Little London, with one maidservant.   (WSRO MP 414 and 417)

William Cooper, schoolmaster in St Andrew parish 1791.   (Poll book, WSRO Add MS 2134)

William Moon Ingram: master of the Grey Coat charity school 1778-94 (see above), from 1797 to 1802 he was paid by the Duke of Richmond as writing master to the Lennox boys at Goodwood House. He was paid £4 1s in the

Christmas 1797 quarter, £32 4s 3d in 1798, £37 13s in 1799, £28 7s in 1800, £7 0s 2d in 1801, £6 12s in 1802. (WSRO Goodwood MS 247)

[Samuel Allen], had an academy in South Street c1804 (*The Chichester Guide*) and in 1805 (*Holden's Directory*).

[Mrs Cathery], had a preparatory school for young gentlemen c1804 (*The Chichester Guide*) and in 1805 and 1811 (*Holden's Directories*).

[Lewis, sen and jun], schoolmasters in Westgate c1804 (*The Chichester Guide*).

[Phillips], schoolmaster in the Pallants c1804 (*The Chichester Guide*).

Dancing masters

Sharpe (-1775)   In 1775, 'Mr. Sharpe (many years a dancing master in this neighbourhood [Chichester] but had retired from business) cut his throat.' (*Hampshire Chronicle* 30.1.75)

Thomas Hadleston - see above.   (R: 1772)

Gosnold (R: 1775) dancing master (who taught also at Petersfield, Havant, Alton, Basingstoke, Kingsworthy, &c), denied in 1775 that he was going to leave Chichester. That year he published his *Cotilion and Country Dance Book*, 'chiefly for the Advantage, Delight and Ease it will give his young Pupils, and those he may hereafter be honour'd with.   The Music collected from the best and most approv'd authors, and the Figures composed by Mr. Gosnold.'   (*Hampshire Chronicle* 17.7.75)

Fisher (Rs: 1776-86), dancing master of Portsmouth who, in 1786, had taught children in Sussex & Hampshire 'for these ten years past'. He announced in June 1786 that his Public Day at Chichester was put off to the last week in October '(by desire of several of the Ladies' friends,) on account of the heat of the weather, and the Fever which is so prevalent in many parts of the country.'   Inviting them to his ball at the New Assembly-Room, he offered 'those of his late Scholars who are desirous to dance that night, if they will please to call on Mr. Fisher, he will give them some lessons with great pleasure.' 'Tickets may be had, free of all expence, at Mr. Fisher's, No. 22, St. Nicholas street, Portsmouth, and at Mrs. Russell's, Southgate-House, Chichester' - so he was presumably dancing master to Philadelphia Russell's school.   (*Hampshire Chronicle* 19.6.86)

Thomas Stretton, dancing master 1782 (poll book 1782).   (WSRO Add MS 2133)

M. Henry   In 1786 he was paid £2 2s by the Duke of Richmond for teaching Henriette Le Clerc (then aged 13 or 14) at Goodwood House. He was probably based in Chichester.   (WSRO Goodwood MS 244)

Monsieur Oliviers: he was paid £4 4s in 1786 and £2 12s 6d in 1787 by the Duke of Richmond for teaching Henriette Le Clerc (then aged about 14) at Goodwood House. He was probably based in Chichester.   (WSRO Goodwood MS 244)

William Stevenson: he was paid £4 4s 2d in 1787 and £2 12s 6d in 1788 by the Duke of Richmond for teaching Henriette Le Clerc (aged 14 or 15 in 1787) at Goodwood House. He was probably based in Chichester.   (WSRO Goodwood MS 244, 245)

Laurent Xavier Martin de Lambilly   (Rs: 1800- into 19c)
Described in *The Chichester Guide* (c1804) as dancing and fencing master and

French teacher in North-Street, he gave dancing lessons to the Lennox boys at Goodwood House in 1800. In the midsummer quarter 1801 he was paid £28 7s for 54 lessons; in the midsummer quarter 1802, £29 18s 6d; and in the Lady day quarter 1803 £4 14s 6d.[1]

He married a Chichester girl, Mary Fifield, eight children being born between 1805 and 1817. In 1807 he was occupying a house in St Bartholomew's owned by himself.

The following account of de Lambilly in action early in the 19th century was recorded by Mary Sybella Peckham whose father, Charles Peckham Peckham (1801-73), was one of de Lambilly's pupils:

> Chichester at that time boasted an aristocratic dancing master in Count de Lambellier. He came to England during the Revolution, with other of the noblesse who abandoned their country, & used to tell his pupils with theatrical gestures how "he stood on the shores of Britannia & said Whither shall I go, shall I turn to the Tanneries or the Potteries?" However he did neither, but settled in Chichester, & had dancing classes for the young elite of both sexes, of whom my Father was one. One of his favourite pupils was Miss Sarah Douglas & when she had to perform some elaborate "pas seule" he used to beat time to his fiddle nodding his head, with a running encouragement in broken English crescendo "Very well Sallee now Miss Do-glass, very well Sallee, now Miss Do-glass, very well, very well, now jomp, jomp jomp" & when the breathless Sally failed to leap the required height, down ran the fiddle in a diminuendo & the Count reproached her with "Mais, ma foi, but why fore you do not jomp?"[2]

(See also Schedule 2.)

1. WSRO Goodwood MS 247.   2. 'Reminiscences of Mary Sybella Peckham (1830-1920)', MSP 4, 59-60, from the collection of the late W.D.Peckham.

Drawing masters

George Smith   (R: c1755-7)   Charlotte Turner (born May 1749) was sent to school at Chichester at the age of six, remaining there about two years, and while there by her father's desire took lessons in drawing from George Smith (Lower, *Worthies*, 16). Smith, a celebrated artist (see Schedule 2) almost certainly took other pupils.

Taylor   (R: 1780)   Advertised 'To the NOBILITY and GENTRY &c. near CHICHESTER' in 1780. 'MR. TAYLOR, Drawing Master and Engraver from London, at the Golden Head, opposite the Lower Church, North Street, Chichester, Teaches Ladies and Gentlemen the art of DRAWING in all its various branches, at their own residence, by the lesson or per quarter. Likewise draws patterns on all sorts of silk or stuffs for needle work, in the most fashionable taste. - Engraves coats of arms on gold, silver or copper, &c. as reasonable as in London.' (*Hampshire Chronicle* 7.8.80)

Fencing masters

Thomas Hadleston - see above.   (R: 1772)

Laurent Xavier Martin de Lambilly - see under Dancing masters above. Described as fencing master in *The Chichester Guide* c1804.

French masters

> Thomas Hadleston - see above.   (R: 1772)

> Laurent Xavier Martin de Lambilly - see under Dancing masters above. Described as French teacher in *The Chichester Guide* c1804.

Italian master

> P.Molini: was paid £4 1s 9d in 1787, £7 12s in 1788, £3 8s 3d in 1789, and £4 4s for 1790 and 1791, by the Duke of Richmond for teaching Henriette Le Clerc Italian at Goodwood House. (She was aged 14 or 15 in 1787.) He was probably based in Chichester. (WSRO Goodwood MS 244, 245)

Music masters

> Dr Arnold: was paid £7 2s 6d in 1786, £11 9s 6d in 1787, £19 18s 7d in 1788, £18 18s 9d in 1789, and £4 14s 6d in 1790, by the Duke of Richmond for music lessons for Henriette Le Clerc at Goodwood House. (She was aged 13 or 14 in 1786.)   He was probably based in Chichester. (WSRO Goodwood MS 244, 245)

> [Bennett], teacher of music (organist), in Westgate c1804 (*The Chichester Guide*).

Singing masters

> Mr Burnet: was paid £1 1s in the year Michaelmas 1760 to Michaelmas 1761 for teaching the boys of the Grey Coat charity school to sing. (WSRO Cap.V/1/1)

> William Walond - see his singing school above.   (R: 1784)

> Thomas Barber, master of the choristers - see Walond's singing school above. (R: 1794)

> William Parsons: was paid £10 10s 9d in 1786, £8 9s 6d in 1787, £12 7s 3d in 1788, and £3 15s 6d in 1789, by the Duke of Richmond for singing lessons for Henriette Le Clerc at Goodwood House. (She was aged 13 or 14 in 1786.) He was probably based in Chichester.   (WSRO Goodwood MS 244, 245)

[Note: The population of Chichester - 4,744 in 1801 - had increased to 6,425 by 1811; 7,362 by 1821; 8,270 by 1831.]

CHIDDINGLY (CHITTINGLY) 1724: about 15 families   1801: pop. 673

Dine's school   (R: 1760s, 1770s)

William Dine had kept a little school in the parish 'for some Time past' when, in 1771, he published *Poems on Several Occasions*. He was then also the parish clerk, and was aged between 40 and 50; prior to becoming a schoolmaster he had been an agricultural labourer, and for a few seasons had been in the hop excise. He was self-taught, and had never been to any school.[1]   [*William Dine*]

1. Preface ('The PRINTER to the READER') to Dine, W. *Poems on Several Occasions* (1771).

[In 1803, Richard Lower, then aged 21, set up school at Muddles Green in Chiddingly, and taught there for 62 years (Lucas, E.V. *Highways & Byways in Sussex* (1935 edn), 346, 349).]

CHIDHAM   1801: pop. 209

No 18th-century schooling traced. At the 1775 visitation, 'no School'.[1]

1. WSRO Ep.I/22/1.

CHILTINGTON - see EAST CHILTINGTON and WEST CHILTINGTON (both parishes were known as 'Chiltington' in their neighbourhoods)

CHITHURST   1724: about 16 families   1801: pop. 94
No 18th-century schooling traced.

CLAPHAM   1724: 21 families   1801: pop. 197
Charity dame school   (Rs: 1769, 1772)
At the 1769 visitation there was a charity dame school, supported by 'contributions'[1]. John Tomkins, estate agent to the Shelleys of Michelgrove, recorded in his diary for 20 June 1772 the names of six children 'at School at Widow Page's at Clapham' - presumably paid for by the estate.[2] (According to the visitation return for 1772, there was no free or charity school, as such, in the parish.[3])   [*Widow Page*]
1. WSRO Ep.I/22/1.   2. *SAC* **71**, 33.   3. WSRO Ep.I/22/1.

CLAYTON   1724: with Keymer, 50 families   1801: pop. (Clayton) 337
No 18th-century schooling traced.

CLIMPING   1724: 20 families   1801: pop. 197
School   (R: 1742)
At the 1742 visitation, there was a schoolmaster, of 'good Life' and 'diligent', who came to church and caused his scholars to come, and taught them the catechism.[1]
1. WSRO Ep.I/22/1.

Dame school   (R: 1772)
At the 1772 visitation, there was no schoolmaster, 'only a old Woman'.[1]
1. WSRO Ep.I/22/1.

COATES - see BURTON

COCKING   1724: about 29 or 30 families   1801: pop. 300
Charity schools/schooling   (Rs: 1726, 1732- into 19c)
In 1726 there was 'A School-Dame where 6 poor Children are taught gratis.'[1]
        Stephen Challen, of Shopwick, yeoman, by will dated 1730, left property in Chichester, half the rents of which were to be used by the minister and churchwardens of Cocking 'for the schooling and teaching of ten poor children... to read.'[2] The parish received £7 17s 6d, being the rent due to them for one and a half years ending Michaelmas 1732, of which £1 4s 7½d was spent on Kings Tax and repairs to the property, £2 18s 5d was paid 'for ye Teaching ten poor children', £2 7s 6d was given as alms 'according to the will of Mr. St Challen', and, after minor expenses, £1 4s 5½d was left in hand. At 9 January 1732 there is a list of the 'poor Parish Children to be taught to read, & to learn ye Church Catechism'. In 1733 13 children were being taught (7 boys and 6 girls) and the accounts include the note: 'The Charge of Teaching thirteen Children at 2d pe. week per head by the year amounts to £5-12-8. The rent of ye houses at Chichester by the year is 5-5-0. So that ye charge of teaching so great a number will exceed ye income - 0.7.8.' The writer was assuming a 52-week teaching year, however, and in the 1733-4 church year only £4 12s 3d was paid out for schooling; and for the six months to Michaelmas 1734, £2 2s 5d.[3]
        Visitation returns suggest that the income available for schooling fell in the 1760s:[4]
1762:   A charity school.   'Ten to read'.

1769:   An endowed free school, with a revenue of £2. '6 children of poor familys'. A schoolmaster of 'good Life' and 'diligent', who came to church and caused his scholars to come, and taught them the catechism.

1775:   A charity school, with 'forty shillings a year to teach four or five children'. 'no schoolmaster But mistress', who came to church and caused the children to come, and taught them the catechism. 'four or five children learn to read & work at their Needle'.

By 1819, the income was still £2 pa, which was paid to a schoolmistress for teaching four children, boys and girls, to read.[5]

[*Sarah Wallis, Ann Heward*]

1. WSRO Ep.I/22/1.   2. *EP2* (1819), 159.   3. WSRO Par 53/12/1.   4. WSRO Ep.I/22/1.
5. *EP2* (1819), 159.

COLDWALTHAM   1724: 26 families   1801: pop. 237

Dame schools   (Rs: 1742, 1769, early 1790s)
Visitation returns give the following:[1]
1742:   [Any unlicensed teachers?] 'one woman only'.
1769:   'two poor women only keep school'.

William Hersee (1786-1854), 'the ploughboy poet', had no formal education other than that 'by the village matron'. He later wrote a poem, 'The Village School-mistress', which gives details of the Coldwaltham dame school he attended. The dame lived in an isolated cottage, with mossy thatch, and pinks and daisies beside the entrance path. The door, 'worm-eaten and decay'd', 'Bespoke the tenant's low estate'; but she was neat and clean, and respected in the village for her learning - 'For well she knew to guide the pin / Across the Primer's mottled page; / And she had read, and could explain, / The Scripture through, with aspect sage.' She kept discipline with the threat of a birch, or, as Hersee often experienced, 'First lectur'd sharp; then was I doom'd / Beneath her chast'ning hand to bow', or he was pinned to her blue apron while the others went out to play; but when she was pleased and 'on me kindly smil'd', 'none to learn more cheerful toil'd.' Hersee became 'head student', helped less able children and 'On ev'ry busy washing day / To regency I made my claim; / Exalted on her brown rush throne, / While foaming suds half hid the dame.'[2]

1. WSRO Ep.I/22/1.   2. Hersee, W. *Poems, Rural and Domestic* (1811 edn; the 1st edn published at Chichester, 1810), preface & 111.

COMPTON   1724: 34 families   1801: pop. 199

Charity schooling   (Rs: c1742?- into 19c?)
In the return to Parliament concerning charities, 1786, it was stated that Rev Dr Cox gave £100 by will for teaching poor children of Compton and Up-Marden, the sum being vested in George Farrell and yielding £3 10s pa. Cox was formerly rector of the parishes of Compton and Up-Marden, and died c1741. Neither the will nor any relevant document relating to the charity has been traced, but in the 1790s, and into the 19th century, £3 10s pa was being paid by the heirs of George Farrell or Farhill to a schoolmaster at Up-Marden.[1] At Compton in 1765 there was 'No... Scool nor Schoolmaster', but perhaps some of the poor children were being taught at Up-Marden, where there was in that year an endowed 'free school' (presumably arising from the Cox bequest).[2]

1. *EP2* (1819), 160.   2. WSRO Ep.I/22/1.

COOMBES   1724: 5 families   1801: pop. 47

School   (R: 1737)
There was no free or charity school but in 1737, although it was such a small parish, there
was a schoolmaster, of 'good Life' and 'diligent', who came to church and caused his
scholars to come, and taught them the catechism.   [Perhaps the minister kept a school?]
No school was being kept in the parish in 1762 or 1775.[1]
1. WSRO Ep.I/22/1.

COWFOLD   1724: about 60 families   1801: pop. 601

Parish schooling   (Rs: 1784-91, 1796- into 19c)
The 'Cowfold Poor Book 1779' and 'Cowfold Account Book' from 1796,[1] show that the
parish paid for schooling poor children from 1784 to 1791 and from 1796 into the 19th
century. (The 'poor Book' also shows summary payments to the overseers, which may
subsume earlier and other schooling payments; the first recorded payment specifically for
schooling was 10 October 1784.) For the first year or so the precise payments for schooling
are not always identified (eg. 19 June 1785, 'Dm Attree Schooling & weaving - 1.14.-') but
from at least Michaelmas 1786, 1s a week was being regularly paid. In June 1786 the
parish paid £13 1s 7½d, a large sum, for 'Cloathing thehildren [sic]'. By April 1790 the
amount paid seems to have increased (with a reduced amount for the July/August harvest
period) reaching c6s 6d a month for September to November that year. In 1791-2 the poor
were being 'put out' (in April 1792 Thos. Knowles was paid £245 4s 2d for one year) and
there are no schooling payments shown 1791-4.   In 1795 Wm. Attree kept the poor, being
paid c£10 a month for keeping c16 people, and other poor were being paid direct; and in
1796 specific schooling payments resume. Two women were now being paid: Dame Attree
at 6d a week and Mrs Vinal at c2s a week:
          11 Dec 1796:   Pd Dame Attree for Scooling 5 weeks -   0. 2. 6
                              Pd. Mrs Vinal 5 weeks Scooling -   -. 9.10
In the church year 1797-8 the parish paid out £3 14s 1d for schooling (one payment, of 6s
8d, was 'for Scooling Et Mending reels'); in 1798-9 identifiable schooling payments totalled
only £1 18s 7d, and in 1799-1800 £2 4s.   All the above payments were probably for
teaching the pauper children.
[*Dame Attree, Ann Vinal, Dame Geere*]
1. WSRO Par 59/31/3, Par 59/31/4.

CRAWLEY   1724: about 20 families   1801: pop. 210

No 18th-century schooling traced, but:

[School?]   (R: 1695?)
The probate inventory of Henry Snashell, late of Crawley, taken in July 1695, refers to the
'Schoole roome' in his house, in which were one old table, 'seven and twenty boards' and
a parcel of wood, all valued at £2. He owned one pair of bellows in the 'Shoppe' and other
implements that suggest he may have been a blacksmith.[1] He may well have let the room
for a schoolroom (cf East Hoathly, where the village school was kept, variously, in a loft
over a barn, in a room over the butcher's shop, and in the attic of a private house).   The
school may possibly have continued into the 18th century.
1. PRO PROB 4/12674, communicated by P.Bracher.

CROWHURST   1724: 35 families   1801: pop. 321

No 18th-century schooling traced.

CUCKFIELD   1724: about 270 families 1801: pop. 1,693

Free/private grammar school   (F: early 16c.   Rs: through 18c)
In his will of 11 July 1521, Edward Flower, 'citizen and marchaunt tailor' of London, noted: 'I for certeine years past at my costs and charge have caused a free Gramer Scole to be mainteined and kepte at Cukfelde for the erudicion and lernyng of pore Scolers...' The school was endowed by his will, proved 1521, enabling the purchase of lands, which in 1589 were let at £6 13s 4d; in that year, by indenture, Thomas Pelham gave £80 to the school and took over the lands, £20 pa being payable to the school; and this £20 continued to be paid into the 19th century.   William Spicer, who died in 1728, also endowed the school, to make up the schoolmaster's salary to £10 (from the £6 10s provided by Flower). The original rules for the school survive, including a detailed curriculum. By 1819 the income was £28, and the master was additionally renting off part of the premises owned by the charity for c£12 pa. By that time the school had, for all practical purposes, ceased to be a free school and was a private boarding school. 'The master keeps a boarding school, in which he has about 45 pupils, and is ready to instruct in the classics any of the parishioners' children who apply to him. He has sometimes received a few boys, and taught them English and accounts; but, excepting these few, he has never had any applications even for such instruction, nor any at all for instructions in the classics.' In fact, the masters - although using the school premises and taking the endowed charity - actively discouraged poor scholars, certainly in the early 19th century and probably before. In 1837, the charity commissioners were scathing: 'The present master, the Rev. J.C.T.Dunn, A.B., ever since his appointment, which was in the year 1830, has made a charge of £8 8s. a-year to each foundation scholar. It is obvious that so high a charge would operate upon the poorer inhabitants as a prohibition, and as far as the instruction of their children went the object of the endowment was frustrated. But even this charge was less exorbitant than that of the former schoolmaster, who exacted the sum of £16 16s., and this at a time when the English schools in the neighbourhood were no more than £3 or at most £4 a-year. But the cause of this difference has been that the present schoolmaster, as well as the former, takes private boarders into the house to be instructed in the higher branches of education at a high price, and is therefore desirous of excluding as much as possible the children of the poor, whose homely apparel might give his school a less respectable appearance, and thus operate as a bar to his readily obtaining that class of private boarders from which his chief income is supplied.'[1]

        All the 18th-century masters also had concurrent church appointments. Thomas Bysshe was also rector of Tarring. Philip Shore was also vicar of Wartling. John Willis was also curate of Cuckfield. John Tattersall was also rector of Hangleton. James Ingram was also curate of Cuckfield and chaplain to Viscount Irwin, and vicar of Oving. William Hopkins was also vicar of Bolney. Joseph Francis Fearon, while master of the school, was also prebendary of Chichester, vicar of Fittleworth, and rector of Selsey; and also at different times rector of Clapham (1786-8), sequestrator of Bury (1789-95?), Prebendary of Hove, vicar of Preston cum Hove (1789-90), sequestrator of Stoughton (from 1790), joint registrar of the archdeaconry of Lewes (from 1793); he became also vicar of Cuckfield in 1801, having given up the school in 1800.
[*Thomas Bysshe, Philip Shore, John Willis, John Tattersall, James Ingram, William Hopkins, Joseph Francis Fearon, Thomas Spencer*]
1. *VCH* ii, 416-21; *EP*2 (1819), 161; *EP*30 (1837), 696; Newcastle estate payments of £20 pa are recorded in BL

Add MS 33,157 (1734) and 33,338, ff 63-4 (1765-8).

Charity schooling   (Rs: c1713- into 19c)

Robert Middleton, vicar of Cuckfield, who died in 1712, left £30 to Timothy Burrell, in trust, the interest of which was to be applied to the putting to school, under a good schoolmaster, poor children of the parish, to be taught to read and write, and to be instructed in the church catechism. Timothy Burrell died in December 1717, and by will left a further £20, to be added to Middleton's bequest and used in the same way.[1] The £50 was initially invested in one of the government lotteries, in the name of the vicar, Daniel Walter, yielding £2 10s interest pa. Later, when the £50 order was paid in, each of five trustees took £10 and paid interest on the same, which was used 'for the putting out poor children to read as is above directed'. In 1738 the trustees used the £50, together with £100 which Timothy Burrell had also bequeathed (to be invested in lands, to yield income to provide bread for six poor parishioners), to purchase a property commonly called the Bull Inn but then rented by the parish as a workhouse; and in 1739 the trustees granted to the parish a 21-year lease of the property, to be used as a workhouse.[2] Thereafter, the application of the Middleton and Burrell charity for schooling is lost, but it appears that the parish did (at least in the early 19th century) pay a woman for teaching some poor children to read, 'which was considered to be on account of Middleton's and Burrell's gifts, and the occupation of the premises by the parish'; and from before 1812 (and up to at least 1819) a school was kept in the workhouse for pauper children, for which 1s a week was paid to the schoolmaster out of the parish rates.[3] At his burial, 3 November 1789, Richard Cook was described as 'schoolmaster, & Governor of the Workhouse ';[4] perhaps he taught the poor children there. [*Richard Cook?*]

1. *SAC* 3, 156, 172.   2. *SAC* 50, 17-18.   3. *EP2* (1819), 163.   4. Cuckfield PR.

Morley schools   (Rs: 1752, 1792-1800)

Richard Morley was described a schoolmaster of Cuckfield in his will dated 7 December 1752.[1] William Morley was described as schoolmaster at the baptisms of his sons in December 1792 and January 1798, in *Univ. Directory* 1793, and at his burial, 17 September 1800, aged 38.[2] He almost certainly kept a private school.   [*Richard Morley, William Morley*]

1. ESRO W/A 58.707.   2. Cuckfield PR.

[Sunday school?]

No record of a Sunday school in the 18th century has yet been found, but Rev J.F.Fearon, master of the grammar school 1786-1800, preached a charity sermon at Brighton, 27 September 1789, on behalf of the Sunday school and school of industry there, which resulted in a 'very considerable' collection;[1] and he was also rector of Selsey from 1790, where a Sunday school had been established by his predecessor in 1788.[2] His influence could well have led to the establishment of a Sunday school at Cuckfield before the end of the century (when he became vicar there).

1. *SWA* 28.9.89.   2. *SWA* 6.10.88.

Other schoolmasters/ mistresses[1]

> Drury Bird (Rs: c1714-34). The tithe book (1714-34) pf Rev Drury Bird, vicar of Bolney, shows that he taught children in Cuckfield, receiving payments 'for Schooling Books and Ink'. (WSRO Par 252/6/8)

> Richard Cook (1757?-89), described as schoolmaster and governor of the workhouse at his burial, 3 November 1789. He may have taught pauper children at the workhouse (see above) but it seems probable that he also had his own private school. Son of John below.

John Cook (-1792), described as schoolmaster and vestry clerk at his burial, 20 May 1792. Father of Richard above.

Mary Brown (1715-91), described as schoolmistress at her burial, 23 October 1791, aged 76. Perhaps kept a school with Mary Wood (see below).

Mary Wood (1716-99), described as schoolmistress at her burial, 24 September 1799, aged 83. Perhaps kept a school with Mary Brown (see above).

[Samuel Picknell], described as vestry clerk and schoolmaster at baptisms of his sons in 1808 and 1812. Possibly succeeded John Cook, who died in 1792, as vestry clerk and schoolmaster (see above).

1. Cuckfield PR (except for Drury Bird).

DALLINGTON   1724: about 60 families   1801: pop. 401

No 18th-century schooling traced.

DENTON   1724: 9 families   1801: pop. 54

No 18th-century schooling traced.

DIDLING   1724: 12 families   1801: pop. 83

No 18th-century schooling traced.

DITCHLING (DYCHENING)   1724: about 80 families   1801: pop. 706

Charity school   (F: by 1722)
In a letter to the SPCK dated 2 June 1722, Anthony Springett reported that a charity school 'is lately set up' at Ditchling, for 20 boys and girls, supported by subscriptions.[1]
1. SPCK ALB v.11, 7081.

Ford's school   (R: 1733)
Thomas Ford was a teacher of mathematics at Ditchling in 1733, and probably kept a small private school there. He was also a surveyor.   [*Thomas Ford*]
1. From a map of Oldland Farm in Keymer, WSRO Add MS 41,248.

Village school   (Rs: 1760, 1770-96)
Henry Dudeney, born 3 November 1753, was sent by his father to school at Ditchling for a while.[1] This suggests that the father probably paid for his son's schooling there.

The will of Joseph Lambert (1701-64), dated 11 May 1760, directed that 'my bene-faction of 40s. a year to the school at Ditchling nr Lewes for teaching poor boys to read... be continued for seven years from my decease.'[2] So some boys were taught free at the school at that time.

James Feldwick, who died in December 1796, had been the village schoolmaster 'for upwards of 26 years' - that is, from c1770 to 1796.[3]
[*James Feldwick*]
1. *SFH* v.7, no.3, 97, citing biographical writings of John Dudeney (1782-1852) at SAS.   2. *SAC* **90**, 115.
3. *SWA* 26.12.96; Ditchling PR.

Workhouse school   (Rs: 1781, (1801))
In the parish overseers' accounts for 1781 there is the following entry:[1]
22 July Speling Book for the use of the parish Children at School 1.-
'The parish Children' almost certainly refers to the children in the workhouse. (There are references to the workhouse in the accounts from 1776 onwards.[2]) In 1801 the parish paid

Mrs Hallet 10s 9d for schooling,[3] so the parish was schooling poor children at this date, unless the payment related to the Sunday school (see below). *[Mrs Hallet?]*

1. ESRO PAR 308/31/1/3.   2. ESRO PAR 308/31/1/2.   3. Benham, M.E. 'School-days in Ditchling' (MS c1984).

Sunday school   (F: c1788.   R: 1789)
John Burgess noted in his diary for January 1789:

> I paid Mr Attree four Shillings What I Subscribed toward the Sunday School at Ditchling this is the first year of its been Established.[1]

John Burgess was a Baptist, but he is clearly referring to a Sunday school at the parish church: there were no Baptist Attrees at the time,[2] and the BTs of the parish registers for the church years 1785-6 and 1786-7 were signed by John Attree as churchwarden (the BTs for 1788-9 and 1789-90 were not signed by the churchwardens).[3]

1. Maguire, L.J., ed. *The Journal & Correspondence of John Burgess 1785-1819* (1982), 69.
2. Twinn, K., pers.comm.   3. BTs at WSRO.

Court Gardens school   (R: 1795)
On 6 May 1795, Mary Browne, who later had her own school in Ditchling (see below), wrote to her sister Ann Billinghurst in America: 'I went to Court gardens yesterday & was very much pleased with the School   the children larn to spell rapidly.'[1]   The school was probably a Baptist school: in 1794, Court Gardens, a substantial property, was owned and occupied by the Baptist, Michael Chatfield; he died in 1795, when it came into the possession of his brother Robert; Robert and another brother John, Baptists, built schools next to the meeting house (open to all denominations) early in the 19th century.[2]

1. Maguire, L.J., pers comm. citing Haydon, R., transcript of a letter (copy, with others, to be deposited at WSRO).   2. ESRO Land Tax; Maguire, L.J., pers comm.; Benham, op cit.

Other schoolmistresses

> Jane Hubbard, described as schoolmistress at her burial, 11 April 1784 (Ditchling PR).

> [Mary Browne] Miss Mary Browne (1758-1845), known in the village as 'Aunt Molly', was a Baptist, and lived with James Browne's family. In a room with a long window overlooking the Baptist church, she kept a small school.[1] Although she may well have taught in the 18th century, no documentary evidence of this has yet been traced. Her deep interest in teaching is evidenced in a letter, 6 May 1795, that she wrote to her sister Ann Billinghurst in America: 'improving Children is my delight   I should like to go into all good Schools I could reach to learn every method they Use to teach & at the same time I should like to be helping.'[2]

> 1. Cheal, H. *History of Ditchling* (1901), 124.   2. See Court Gardens school above, note 1.

DONNINGTON   1724: about 2 houses   1801: pop. 183

[School?]   (R: 1721?)
Thomas Cowley 'was the founder of an educational charity in Donnington'. He died aged 96, bachelor, in 1721.[1] On 21 September 1721 William Lewis signed the subscription book, being now admitted 'to instruct Children in ye School at Donnington' with 'School at Donnington' crossed through and 'Diocese of Chichester' overwritten.[2] (William Lewis was vicar of Donnington, and also warden of the Hospital of St James, Chichester.)   *[William Lewis]*

1. Bayley, T.D.S., in *SAC* **107**, 4.   2. WSRO Ep.I/3/5.

Dame school   (R: 1775)
At the 1775 visitation, 'a poor old woman instructs a few children'.[1]

1. WSRO Ep.I/22/1.

DUNCTON   1724: 30 families   1801: pop. 205

No 18th-century schooling traced. (At the 1758 visitation: 'We have no one that teaches school'.[1]) The rector of Duncton for the time being was one of the trustees of Taylor's charity school, Petworth, under the will of John Taylor (a codicil to which was dated 1775); perhaps children of Duncton were eligible for this school (see PETWORTH).

1. WSRO Ep.I/22/1.

DURRINGTON   1801: pop. 140

No 18th-century schooling traced.

EARNLEY   1724: 11 families   1801: pop.115

No 18th-century schooling traced.

EARTHAM   1801: pop. 114

Dame school   (R: 1737)

At the 1737 visitation, 'We have only a Petty Schoole taught by a widow w'o is of a good character and frequents the Church', and instructs her scholars in the church catechism. But in 1762, 'none are taught'; and in 1765, 'We have no School'.[1]

1. WSRO Ep.I/22/1.

EASEBOURNE   1724: about 100 families 1801: pop. 764

Charity school   (F: 17c.   Rs: through 18c)

John Lock, by will dated 13 June 1674, left £5 pa, arising out of lands, 'to the use of the parish of Easebourne for ever, to be employed towards the putting of poor children of the parish aforesaid, to school.' Five shillings of the £5 was allowed to a trustee, who was required to give an annual account 'to the next justice of the peace within the county of Sussex'. If the nominated trustee refused, the JP was to appoint; and appointments by a JP took place from 1692 to 1784 (the last continuing to 1819). In the time of the last of these trustees, £1 was deducted out of the rent of £5 for land tax.[1]

In 1724 the churchwardens reported: 'Free school wherein 13 Children taught to read for which £5 p An'm to be paid out of A Farme near Petersfield in Hamshire.'[2] In 1742: 'The Scholars are taught by a Woman. 12 poor Children are taught to Read.'; and the school was reported as operational (with a woman teacher) at the visitations of 1762, 1769 and 1775.[3] It continued into the 19th century.[4]

1. *EP2* (1819), 163.   2. WSRO Ep.I/26/3, 76-77.   3. WSRO Ep.I/22/1.   4. *EP2* (1819), 163.

EAST BLATCHINGTON   1724: 22 families   1801: pop. 154

No 18th-century schooling traced.

EASTBOURNE (BOURNE)   1724: 140 families   1801: pop. 1,668

Parish school   (Rs: (1638), 1709, 1769, (1811))

There was a parish school in the 17th century; the schoolhouse was built against the church tower, between the buttresses on the north side. In 1638, small payments were made for repairs to the school, including 6s for 'glazeing the school house'.[1]

On 31 July 1709 a vestry agreed, 'That there should be paid for out of the parsonage, in lieu of breakfasting, the sum of £6, in manner and form following, viz. :- £4, part thereof, to be given to a schoolmaster to instruct 8 of the parishioners' sons in the Latin ['Lattain' in the original[2]] tongue, and £2, the residue thereof, to be given to a schoolmaster to teach 4 children, whose parents are not able to pay, to read and write.'[3]

In 1769 the schoolhouse was put into thorough repair again, and Thomas Chapman was by the vestry 'authorized and empowered to take possession of the school house belonging to the parish, and teach school therein during the pleasure of the said parish.'[4] He probably had his own private pupils, as well as any parish charity children. The repairs authorised by the vestry in 1769 give some idea of the schoolhouse: the churchwardens and overseers were to clean and inspect the roof, and report back to the vestry in a week; they were to lay a new brick floor, to seal [the walls] with reed and loam and 'make good with Plaster and white wash, and to new Glaze the windows as far as they shall think necessary.'[5]

In November 1811 the vestry decided 'that the present school house adjoining the church is a very great nuisance'; and it was subsequently pulled down.[6]

[*Thomas Chapman*]

1. Budgen, W. *Old Eastbourne* (c1912), 210.   2. ibid.   3. *SAC* **14**, 133.   4. Budgen, op. cit., 211.
5. Wright, J.C. *Bygone Eastbourne* (1902), 117.   6. Budgen, op. cit., 211.

Patterson's school   (R: 1714)
In July 1714 Mr Patterson was paid £1 10s for schooling Nicholas Gilbert for ¾ year.[1] Gilbert's home was in Eastbourne, and he was then aged 7:[2] Patterson therefore almost certainly had a petty school in the town.   [*Patterson*]

1. ESRO ACC 2462/1.   2. Budgen, W. *Old Eastbourne* (c1912).

Charity school   (Rs: 1734-47, 1779- into 19c)
In 1729 a subscription was put in hand 'for the Schoolmaster att Bourne to teach the Poore Children', and in January 1735 the Earl of Wilmington's steward, Thomas Worge, drew up a 'Memorial', signed by several parishioners, which began: 'Whereas my Lord Wilmington has been so good to give £15 a year for the Encouragement of a School now carried on by John Akehurst, the School house belonging to the town...'. The charity school in East Bourne for 15 children was supported by the Cavendish family from at least Lady day 1734 - the Compton Place accounts show, on 22 October 1734, a receipt by John Akhurst for £7 10s for the use of the Free School for ½ yrs salary.[1] Akhurst was paid regularly, at the rate of £15 pa, until the relevant account book ends in 1741.[2] According to Horsfield, Lord Wilmington, who died in 1743, left £15 pa for the education of 15 poor children in writing, and Compton estate accounts show the Earl of Northampton paying John Akhurst's salary of £15 pa 'as Master of the Charity Schoole at East Bourn' in 1744, 1745 and 1747.[3] An account book relating to the Sussex estates of Lady Elizabeth Compton and Lord George Cavendish[4] shows the £15 a year payments being made to different masters from 1784 into the 19th century. (For the first nine months of 1784, Thomas Hook was paid at the rate of £10 pa for teaching 10 poor children; otherwise the £15 pa for 15 children was consistent.) *Univ. Directory* 1792 states: 'Here is a free school for 15 boys supported by Lord George Cavendish.' At least two of the masters, Rev Davies and Rev Myers, also ran their own private schools alongside the charity school (see below). *Univ. Directory* 1792 describes Myers as 'Curate of Willingdon, and Master of the Free and Boarding Schools'; his boarding school was in Church Street (at a house later called 'The Gables'); Walter Budgen concludes that the free school was also carried on under the same roof, and was thus distinct from the parish school in the churchyard (see above).[5]

A 'List of Boys at the Free School of East Bourn', 1734-5, in fact gives 14 boys and one girl; but two other lists that have survived, 1738-9 and April 1741, show all boys.[6] However, a list survives for Christmas 1779, in which 7 children are identified only by

surname, while of the other 8, two are girls.[7] In 1795 there was a payment of £4 10s to
Sarah Worger, apparently for teaching poor children at Eastbourne, in addition to the £15
paid to the master, Rev Myers.[8] (For a controversy over the first master, John Akhurst, see
Another (charity?) school below.)
[*John Akhurst, Thomas Palmer?, Morgan Davies, Thomas Hook, John Myers, Sarah Worger,
William Knight?*]

1. SAS Budgen, v.88, ff 12, 51; v.129, 29.   2. ibid. v.129, 41; v.125, 40.   3. Horsfield *Sussex* I, 298;
SAS Budgen, v.89, ff 37, 41, 43.   4. SAS Budgen, v.119.   5. Budgen, W. *Old Eastbourne* (c1912), 211.
6. SAS Budgen, v.129, 29, 39, 43.   7. ibid. v.105, 36; v.117, f30.   8. ibid. v.119, f15.

Another (charity?) school/ Mason's school   (Rs: 1735, 1736)
John Akhurst, the first master of the charity school supported largely, if not entirely, by the
Cavendish family (see above), was opposed by a faction in the parish who tried to remove
him in 1734 - the year he appears to have started there. A petition to the Earl of
Wilmington, signed by 17, proposed that Akhurst be replaced by 'one Mr Mason... we are
informed he is a person every way capable to be a Master, and Quallify'd to teach all the
most usefull branches in the Mathematics, and well assured of his Knowledge in Measuring
and Mapping of Land &c.' A churchwarden who supported Akhurst was threatened with
eviction from his farm (in the event, this did not happen). The Earl of Wilmington's
steward, Thomas Worge, another Akhurst supporter, referring to him as 'old master
Akehurst', reported in January 1735 that he 'is very much amended in his writing and perfect
in Accts to the Rule of three, the man is both diligent and sober.' Although in fact Akhurst
continued as schoolmaster to at least 1747, in January 1735 the opposition had brought into
the parish their candidate, Christopher Mason, who had surveyed land for Sir Walter Parker
two or three years before: Worge wrote, 'the Schoolmaster is come... and John Denman that
uses Sr Walters Park farm at Willingdon is to subscribe £5 a year, there's something afoot...'
In June 1736 Worge reported of a copyhold property, Duards: 'The other part is a
Schoolhouse hired by Mr. Auger [one of the anti-Akhurst faction] as I apprehended & let
by him to the Schoolmaster wch Sr W.P. set up.' So another school had been established
by then, and since it was at least partly supported by subscription, it is likely to have taught
a number of charity children.[1]   [*Christopher Mason*]

1. Chatsworth, Devonshire Collections, Compton Place Papers, Box P, file 28; SAS Budgen, v.88, ff 51, 52, 58,
and v.87, f7.

[Palmer's school]   (R: 1774)
Thomas Palmer was schoolmaster at (probably) Eastbourne, perhaps master of the Charity
School [qv]. Also writing master to a girls' school where Elizabeth Anstie was a mistress,
whom he married in 1774. He was appointed master of East Grinstead charity school
c1775.   [*Thomas Palmer*]

[Girls' school]   (R: 1774)
Elizabeth Anstie was mistress at a girls' school at (probably) Eastbourne; she married in
1774 the visiting writing master, Thomas Palmer.   [*Elizabeth Anstie*]

Davies' school   (F: 1775)
later boys' boarding school   (F: 1787.   Rs: 1791, 1793)
In November 1775 Rev Morgan Davies announced that he had taken the Free School at
Eastbourne, 'where he proposes teaching READING, WRITING, ARITHMETIC in all its
different Branches, and the CLASSICS.'[1] Cavendish estate accounts show a payment of £3
15s to him for teaching 15 poor children at Eastbourne 'Writing & Accompts' for 1 quarter,
up to Christmas 1783, 'when he quitted the School'[2] (see Charity school above). In
December 1787 he advertised under the heading 'PRIVATE EDUCATION and SEA-
BATHING', that he 'proposes to instruct a few young Gentlemen, in the various branches

of Learning suitable to the Line of Life which they are intended to fill.'[3] (Earlier that year John Mossop had used 'SEA-BATHING AND EDUCATION' as a heading in an advertisement for his school at Brighton.) In August 1791 Davies advertised that he 'boards and educates young Gentlemen, in Reading, Writing, Arithmetic, Mensuration, Merchants' Accompts, Latin and Greek' for 20 guineas a year.[4] In *Univ. Directory* 1792 and 1793 as 'Rector of Littlington & Master of a Boarding School'. He was rector of Litlington 1792 to his death in 1799; also perpetual curate of Udimore, 1792-6, and sometime curate of Brede, to 1795. Advertised in *SWA* Nov 1775; Dec (3) 87; Aug, Sep, Dec (2) 91. [*Morgan Davies*]

1. *SWA* 13.11.75.   2. SAS Budgen, v.119, f 9.   3. *SWA* 17.12.87.   4. *SWA* 29.8.91.

Cambridge's girls' boarding school   (F: 1776)
Mary Cambridge announced the opening on Lady day 1776 of her boarding school for young ladies, 'wherein will be taught all Sorts of Needle-work, as likewise Tambour. Board and Schooling FOURTEEN POUNDS, and Breakings-up Ten Shillings a Year, and One Guinea Entrance.' Dancing and music, if required, were extras.[1] Advertised in *SWA* Mar (2), May 1776.   [*Mary Cambridge*]
1. *SWA* 4.3.76.

Bonar's charity school   (R: 1790s)
SWA reported, in September 1799, that 'Mrs. Bonar has for many years, not only fed and clothed many of the poor [at Eastbourne], but has, at her own expence instituted a school for instructing twenty poor girls and boys, in reading and religion; which will be a lasting monument of charity and morality, as it may be a means of teaching the poor their duty to God, as well as to their neightbour.'[1] (Sarah Taylor, schoolmistress in 1792 and 1793 (*Univ. Directory*), may have been a teacher at this school.)   [*Sarah Taylor?*]
1. *SWA* 2.9.99.

Myers' boys' boarding school   (F: 1791.   Rs: 1791-3, (1801))
Payments were made by the Cavendish estates to Rev John Myers, certainly from Michaelmas 1794 to 1798, and almost certainly earlier and later, at £15 pa for teaching 15 poor children at Bourne (see Charity school above).[1] In September 1791 he announced that he had opened a boarding school at Eastbourne...

.... for the reception of a limited number of young Gentlemen, to be educated in the different branches of useful and polite literature.

His Terms for Board, Washing, and Instructions in the Classics, Geography, and the Use of the Globes, Writing, Arithmetic, and Merchants' Accompts, are TWENTY GUINEAS per Annum, and ONE GUINEA entrance.

French, Dancing, &c. are extra charges, as usual.

His House, School-room, and Playground, are in a pleasant and airy situation, commanding an extensive and delightful view of the Sea.[2]

He was in *Univ. Directory* 1792 and 1793 as 'Curate of Willingdon, and Master of the Free and Boarding Schools.' He was also curate of Eastbourne. His school was in a house and half an acre of land in Church Street, afterwards called 'The Gables', which he occupied for 10 years, transferring the school premises in 1801 to Rev Thomas Broome who, like his predecessor, was curate of Eastbourne.[3] Myers was also vicar of Rye from 1793 until his death in 1834, and perpetual curate of Udimore from 1799. He was also a mayor of Rye.

Advertised in *SWA* Sep, Oct, Nov, Dec (2) 1791.
[*John Myers*]
1. SAS Budgen, v.119, ff 15, 16.   2. *SWA* 26.9.91.   3. Budgen, W. *Old Eastbourne* (c1912), 211, 214.

Baker's girls' (boarding) school   (Rs: 1798, 1799)
Miss M. Baker announced the reopening of her school on 23 July 1798, after the
midsummer vacation. She refers to 'the young Ladies intrusted to her care' and 'diligent
attention to their health and morals', and it was almost certainly a boarding school.[1]
Advertised in *SWA* Jul (2) 1798; Jul (2) 99.   [*Miss M.Baker*]
1. *SWA* 16.7.98.

Other schoolmistress/[masters]

> Sarah Taylor, schoolmistress 1792 and 1793 (*Univ. Directory*).
>
> [William Knight (-1809)]   Master of the charity school from at least midsummer
> 1801, and probably had his own school earlier. Owned properties in Eastbourne.
> (See Schedule 2)
>
> [Alexander Hils Debarde]   Schoolmaster in 1803 census of male inhabitants aged
> 17-55; he was aged 17-30, unmarried, and had no children under 10. (*Sussex
> Militia List 1803, Pevensey Rape Southern Division* (PBN Pub 1988))
>
> [Rev Thomas Broom]   Schoolmaster in 1803 census of male inhabitants, and then
> aged 17-30, unmarried. (*Sussex Militia List 1803, Pevensey Rape Southern
> Division* (PBN Pub 1988))   In 1801 he acquired the premises of John Myers
> boarding school (see above).

EAST CHILTINGTON - see WESTMESTON

EASTDEAN (East Sussex)   1724: 29 families   1801: pop. 284
Charity schooling   (Rs: 1775-95)
Three surviving account books of the solicitor, Charles Gilbert, who acted as agent for the
estates of George Medley, that run from January 1776 to January 1796, show that during
the whole of this period Medley paid £5 pa for the schooling of 12 children. From
Michaelmas 1775 to Michaelmas 1779 the children are described as 'of Eastdean and
Friston'; thereafter as '12 Children in Eastdean.'[1]   [*Elizabeth Simpson, Elizabeth Shorter*]
1. ESRO SAS/GT 1/3/3-5.

Michell's boys' boarding school   (Rs: 1783-90?)
Richard Michell, curate of Eastdean, advertised in January 1783 that, as he was now
occupying the whole of the vicarage house, he could accomodate two or three more pupils,
at 20 guineas pa.[1] In January 1787 he announced that he was now provided 'with a careful,
steady PERSON, To serve him in the Capacity of HOUSEKEEPER'.[2] His curriculum can
be inferred from an advertisement he placed in June 1777, as 'Late Curate of
ROTHERFIELD' and before he had settled on a place of residence; he proposed 'to
undertake the Instruction of FIVE or SIX PUPILS, of competent Age, in the *GREEK* and
LATIN-LANGUAGES, as well as other Branches of useful and polite Learning.'[3] Michell
was an author, and frequent contributor to *SWA*. He died on 26 January 1790, leaving three
young children, John, Sarah and Philadelphia, 'and never were poor orphans left more
destitute.'[4] A public subscription was put in hand for them, which raised over £350; among
the subscribers were the 'Young Ladies at Miss Ryal's Boarding School [Lewes], 1.1.0' and
the 'Young Ladies at Miss Adam's Boarding School [Lewes], 2.2.0'.[5] Advertised in *SWA*
June (4) 1777; Jan (3) 83; Jan (3) 87.   [*Richard Michell*]
1. *SWA* 6.1.83.   2. *SWA* 1.1.87.   3. *SWA* 2.6.77.   4. *SWA* 1.2.90.   5. *SWA* 15.2.90, 22.2.90, 1.3.90,
25.10.90.

EAST DEAN (West Sussex)   1801: pop. 305

School   (R: 1782)
The (former) school building carries the date 1782, with the arms of the Duke of Richmond.[1]

1. Bishop, J.H. *Singleton and East Dean Guide* (1961), 8.

Sunday school   (F: 1795)
A Sunday school, with 40 children, was opened in 1795.[1]

1. *Portsmouth Gazette* 31.8.95.

[See also WESTHAMPNETT for possible Goodwood estate schooling.]

EASTERGATE (GATES)   1724: 17 families   1801: pop. 163

School   (R: 1742)
At the 1742 visitation: 'thare is a school master - not very diligent - he cums [to church] but very seldum - I beleve he doeth [instruct his scholars in the catechism].'[1]

1. WSRO Ep.I/22/1.

Dame school   (R: 1758)
At the 1758 visitation: 'There is a person teaches school but whether she has a Licence I don't know'. 'The Mistres does [come to church]' - 'as far as I know She does [teach her scholars the catechism]'.[1]

1. WSRO Ep.I/22/1.

EAST GRINSTEAD   1724: about 310 families 1801: pop. 2,659

Charity schools   (Rs: c1706- into 19c)
Sir Thomas Dyke of Waldron, by will dated 1706, placed a charge of £5 pa out of lands and tenements in East Grinstead, to be paid to some skilful person nominated by the burgage holders of East Grinstead, to teach 10 poor children to read and write.[1]

Robert Payne of Newick, of an old East Grinstead family, died 7 December 1708; in his will dated 16 August 1708 he stated his intention of founding a free grammar school in East Grinstead, to which end he left Serryes Farm in the parish, consisting of 69 acres with a house and farm buildings, the rent from which was to be used to pay a schoolmaster to instruct the youth of the parish, in the schoolhouse then built in the parish. The trustees were to appoint the number of scholars to be taught.[2] In 1724 the rent of the farm was £20,[3] as it was in 1775, when 10 boys were being taught.[4] (By 1819 the income was £41 pa and there were 25 boys at the school on the foundation; there were also 40 further boys at the school, whose parents paid a weekly fee of 6d to 1s.[5]) In 1772 the school was closed for a time, as the trustees could not procure a master to teach Latin in addition to other subjects.[6] In July 1775 they advertised for a schoolmaster in the following terms: 'He must be capable of teaching to read, write, and cast Account. If he understands Grammar, so much the better... The Salary annexed to the School, is TWENTY POUNDS a YEAR... The School may be entered upon immediately.'[7] In 1724 Robert Staples was admitted to Trinity, Cambridge, from 'East Grinstead school' under Gurnett, so the classics were apparently taught then; but Latin and Greek ceased to be taught at the school after 1772.[8]

The original schoolhouse adjoined the church.[9] On 12 November 1785 the church tower fell down: 'The master and scholars had only just left. The school-room, which adjoins the church, was also destroyed.'[10] The school was then kept in the master's (Thomas Palmer's) room adjoining the churchyard.[11] After the rebuilding of the church, 'the vestry was reported to be ready for re-occupation by the school on September 24th, 1808.'[12]

Following the advertisement for a schoolmaster in 1775 (see above), Thomas

Palmer, of Eastbourne, was appointed.[13] In 1793 he was still 'Master of the Free School' - and also bookseller, stationer (he invented a new pen), printer, postmaster, and agent to the Phoenix Fire Office;[14] and in 1784 he had additionally opened his own private boarding school (see below). He gave up the school in 1816, when it was taken over by his son, Thomas, who moved it to Sackville College (almshouse) of which he had been warden from 1813.[15]

[*Thomas Winterbottom, George Gurnett, Thomas Palmer*]

1. *SNQ* **14**, 274.   2. *EP2* (1819), 165.   3. WSRO Ep.I/26/3, 40-41.   4. *EP2* (1819), 165.
5. ibid.; *VCH* ii, 430.   6. Hills, W.H. *History of East Grinstead* (1906), 128; (a transcript of the section of Robert Payne's will relating to the school is given in full, 126-7).   7. *SWA* 24.7.75.   8. *Al. Cant.*; *VCH* ii, 430.
9. Payne's will - Hills, op. cit., 127.   10. *SAC* **20**, 148.   11. Leppard, M.J., pers. comm.
12. Hills, op. cit., 128.   13. ibid.   14. *Univ. Directory* 1793.   15. Leppard, M.J., pers. comm.

Felbridge charity school   (F: 1783.   Rs: 1783- into 19c)

This school was founded by James Evelyn (1718-93), of Felbridge, by indenture dated 4 November 1783. He gave a house and a piece of land on Felbridge Heath, and £21 pa (charged on Stocklands House and 48 acres of land in Bletchingley) for the benefit of the schoolmaster, who was to teach the children reading, writing, arithmetic and to repeat the catechism. Eight boys and four girls were to be admitted free of charge (suggesting that the master could take additional paying pupils) and the master was to find them in quills and ink, but to teach them to make their own pens. The boys were to be between the ages of six and 10, the girls between six and 13, all were to reside within 2½ miles of the school, and to be drawn from the neighbouring parishes - three boys and one girl from Godstone, two boys and one girl from each of Horne and Worth, and one boy and one girl from East Grinstead. (A 1793 codicil to Evelyn's will of 1783, relating to another charity, makes it clear that there was a schoolmistress at the school as well as a master.) After the death of James Evelyn, his wife, and their direct heirs, the scholars were to be chosen by the vicars of the respective parishes, who jointly were to appoint the schoolmaster. This arrangement continued in force until 1864.[1]

1. Hills, W.H. *History of East Grinstead* (1906), 136-7, 139.

Palmer's boys' boarding school   (R: 1784)

In January 1784, under the heading 'THOMAS PALMER, MASTER of the FREE SCHOOL, At EAST GRINSTEAD', Palmer advertised that 'having taken a larger House, he intends to BOARD, as well as EDUCATE Youth in READING, WRITING, ARITHMETIC and several other Branches of useful Learning.'[1]   [*Thomas Palmer*]

1. *SWA* 12.1.84.

Sunday school   (R: 1790)

On 23 April 1790, on the occasion of East Grinstead's celebration of the anniversary of the king's recovery, the inhabitants of the town agreed the following resolutions:

> 1. That the happiness and prosperity of the kingdom depend upon the morality of its people.

> 2. That the meeting considered it a duty incumbent on them, to instil morality into the minds of the youth of the said parish: they therefore agreed to establish a Sunday School, and immediately entered into an annual subscription for that purpose, when upwards of £16 were collected.

> Mr. William Tooth, one of the gentlemen present, exclusive of his subscription, generously offered to supply a house, worth at least £8 a year, for the purpose of keeping the school in.[1]

It seems very likely that the Sunday school was then established.

1. *SWA* 26.4.90.

Mrs and Miss Baldock's girls' boarding school   (Rs: 1792, 1793)
Mrs Baldock and her daughter were keeping a girls' boarding school at East Grinstead in January 1792. Their terms were 14 guineas pa, no entrance required.[1]   *Univ. Directory* 1793 shows 'Baldock, Miss   Ladies Boarding School'.   [*Mrs Baldock, Miss Baldock*]

1. *SWA* 2.1.92.

Mr and Mrs Holman's day school   (Rs: 1793- into 19c)
Mr and Mrs James Holman, of Yew Tree Cottage, Quaybrook, kept a day school for the children living on the Forest. One fact about it that was remembered is that when a boy was naughty he was suspended by the waist to an iron hook nailed on to one of the beams of the ceiling.[1]

James Holman senior, who occupied the cottage, was buried at East Grinstead in April 1790.[2] In 1791 his son, also James, was admitted tenant; he died c1840.[3] Mrs Holman is listed as schoolmistress in *Univ. Directory* 1793, and 'Holman' is in *Palmer's Rhyming Directory* of 1799:

> Holman, Hall, both cheap agree,
> To teach young children A.B.C.[4]

Thomas and Richard Card, the uncle and father respectively of James Card, who was at Broadstone Farm in 1909, were pupils of Holman,[5] so the school almost certainly continued into the 19th century.

[*James Holman, Ann Holman*]

1. Miss Molloy, in *East Grinstead Observer* 25.6.1909.   2. East Grinstead PR.   3. Molloy, op. cit.
4. Reprinted in *East Grinstead Observer* 7.11.1896.   5. Molloy, op. cit.

Swaysland's school   (Rs: 1793- into 19c)
Stephen Swaysland was a schoolmaster at East Grinstead in 1793,[1]   and in *Palmer's Rhyming Directory* of 1799:

> Palmer & Swaysland, if you need,
> Youth instruct to write & read.[2]

He was still there in 1803,[3] but was appointed master of Mayfield charity school from Michaelmas 1807.[4]   [*Stephen Swaysland*]

1. *Univ. Directory* 1793.   2. Reprinted in *East Grinstead Observer* 7.11.1896.   3. See Schedule 2.
4. ESRO AMS 5601/1.

Hall's day school   (Rs: 1793- into 19c)
Elizabeth Hall, schoolmistress 1793 (*Univ. Directory*), kept a school referred to in *Palmer's Rhyming Directory* of 1799:

> Holman, Hall, both cheap agree,
> To teach young children A.B.C.[1]

She was still teaching in 1814.[2]   [*Elizabeth Hall*]

1. Reprinted in *East Grinstead Observer* 7.11.1896.   2. See Schedule 2.

Smith's school   (Rs: 1793, 1799)
Elizabeth Smith, schoolmistress 1793 (*Univ. Directory*), kept a school referred to in *Palmer's Rhyming Directory* of 1799:

> Smith & Ellis each impart
> To misses young, the needles art.[1]

[*Elizabeth Smith*]

1. Reprinted in *East Grinstead Observer* 7.11.1896.

<u>Ellis's school</u>   (R: 1799)
Ellis had a school for young girls in 1799 (see reference under <u>Smith's school</u> above).
[*Ellis*]

<u>Walker's boys' boarding school</u>   (F: 1799.   Rs: 1799, 1800)
On 22 July 1799 Thomas Walker, curate of East Grinstead, opened an academy for young
gentlemen. 'The mode of Education will be adapted to the profession or vocation in life for
which the Pupil is intended.' His terms were 25 guineas a year.[1] In January 1800 he
advertised that he, 'having five young Gentlemen intrusted to his care, wishes to extend it
over ten.' He had increased his terms to 30 guineas a year.[2]   [*Thomas Walker*]
1. *SWA* 24.6.99.   2. *SWA* 13.1.1800.

<u>Other schoolmaster</u>
        <u>Robert Morphew</u>, schoolmaster in 1793 (*Univ. Directory*).

EAST GULDEFORD   1724: 8 families   1801: pop. 59
No 18th-century schooling traced.

EAST HOATHLY   1724: about 40 families   1801: pop. 395
<u>Village school</u>   (Rs: 1755-64)
In April 1755 Thomas Turner, then aged 26, shopkeeper, took over the village school,
following the death of the previous master, Thomas Tomsett. A year later, in May 1756,
Francis Elless became the master, keeping the school until he moved to Alfriston in 1759.
(Turner and Elless were friends; Turner taught Elless decimals and the use of the slide-rule,
and they learnt surveying together.) Elless was followed briefly by Alexander Whitfield,
and he by John Long, another friend of Turner's, who kept the school from January 1760
until 1764.[1]
        Thomas Turner only kept the school for a year, but recorded some details relating
to it in his diary. For one boy, Henry Miller, his father had paid Tomsett 3d a week for
his schooling. For Rippington's boys, Turner received 6d for one week's schooling
(presumably there were two boys). Turner paid Tomsett's brothers-in-law £4 12s for all
his books, paper, forms, &c. On 20 June 1755: 'This day being my birthday, I treated my
scholars with about 5 quarts of strong beer.' (So he must have had a reasonable number
of scholars.) On 23 March 1756: 'This day I entertained my scholars with the sight of a
show which was at Jones's; the man performed in my schoolroom... He performed several
very curious balances, ate fire and red hot tobacco-pipes, brimstone, &c. I gave him 12d.'[2]
        During Turner's and Elless's time, the school was kept variously in a loft over a
barn, a room over the butcher's shop, and in the attic of an old house.[3]
[*Thomas Tomsett, Thomas Turner, Francis Elless, Alexander Whitfield, John Long*]
1. Vaisey, D., ed. *The Diary of Thomas Turner* (1984), passim   2. ibid.   3. Worcester, D.K. *The Life and
Times of Thomas Turner of East Hoathly* (1948), 18.

EAST LAVANT   1717:40 families   1801: pop. 274
<u>Charity schooling</u>   (Rs: 1741- into 19c)
When Mary Countess Dowager of Derby established, in 1741, a charity school at Boxgrove
for clothing and teaching 12 children in reading, writing and arithmetic (see BOXGROVE
for details), she stipulated that four of the boys or girls were to be from East Lavant. In
1787 the trustees agreed to educate, but not to clothe, a further six boys, two of them to be
from East Lavant. In 1819 the six children from East Lavant were being sent to
Chichester, 'that city being more convenient to them in point of distance.'

EAST MARDEN   1724: about 9 families   1801: pop. 46

Dame school   (R: 1758)
At the 1758 visitation: 'we have a dame's School'.[1]
1. WSRO Ep.I/22/1.

EAST PRESTON   1724: 20 families   1801: pop. 170

Dame school   (R: 1758)
At the 1758 visitation, there was no schoolmaster, but one or more dame schools.[1]
1. WSRO Ep.I/22/1.

EAST WITTERING   1724: about 25 families   1801: pop. 202

No 18th-century schooling traced. (In 1733: 'No one teacheth school in the Parish'.[1])
1. WSRO Ep.I/22/1.

EDBURTON   1717: 20 families   1801: pop. 258

Charity schooling   (Rs: 1709, 1758)
George Keith, rector 1705-16, in 1709 advised the SPCK that, although there was no charity school, most of the children could read and say their catechism[1] (almost certainly as a result of his own teaching). In 1758 the parish paid 2s a week from the offertory money to the keeper of a dame school, to teach poor children.[2]   [*George Keith*]
1. SPCK ALB, v.1B, 1830.   2. *VCH* 6 iii, 52; *Secker*, 222.

Dame school   (R: 1758)
There was a dame school in 1758, to which the parish sent a number of poor children (see Charity schooling above).

EGDEAN (EGGIDEN)   1724: 7 families   1801: pop. 72

No 18th-century schooling traced. (At the 1726 visitation, the question asking if there was a schoolmaster, and how he behaved, was answered 'very well', which may imply a schoolmaster there. In 1775: 'None teaches'.[1])
1. WSRO Ep.I/22/1.

ELSTED   1724: 16 families   1801: pop. 121

No 18th-century schooling traced. (At the 1775 visitation: 'No schoolmaster. No scholars. No school. no children taught.'[1])
1. WSRO Ep.I/22/1.

ETCHINGHAM   1724: about 40 families   1801: pop. 114

No 18th-century schooling traced. (For details of the Cooper charity, with provision for teaching poor children of this parish, which did not however come into effect, see SALEHURST.)

EWHURST   1724: about 60 families   1801: pop. 847

Howard's boys' boarding school   (R: 1775)
In April 1775 Jonathan Howard advertised his boys' boarding school, where he taught reading, writing, and arithmetic, for £12 a year, washing and mending included. His advertisement is notable for the following declaration:
        SCHOOLMASTERS, like other Advertisers, in order to catch the Attention

of the Public, are apt to make great Promises, and to undertake more than
they either design, or indeed are capable of making good; - a Species of
Artifice this, that, one would think, could answer to no great Purpose,
because, in the Event, it must always betray itself. The Person who now
advertises, makes no other Professions or Engagements, than what he
hopes to fulfil, to the Satisfaction of all reasonable People; nor does he ask
any further Encouragement than what he shall be found, upon a fair Trial,
to deserve. - Such Parents as shall chuse to entrust him with the Instruction
of their Children, may depend upon their being treated with Tenderness,
and taught with Care, and that without the Neglect of that very important
Object, - their Morals.[1]

[*Jonathan Howard*]

1. *SWA* 24.4.75.

(For details of the Cooper charity, with provision for teaching poor children of this parish,
which did not however come into effect, see SALEHURST.)

FAIRLIGHT (FAIRLY)   1724: about 30 families   1801: pop. 414.

No 18th-century schooling traced.

FALMER   1724: 26 families   1801: pop. 255

Charity school   (Rs: c1735- into 19c)
Anthony Springett (1652-1735) left by will an Exchequer annuity of £10 pa, running to
1806, to Falmer school.[1] Springett was a corresponding member of the SPCK. A
confirmatory receipt survives, made c1752 but confirming receipt in January 1738, and
signed by Edward Bland, for £20 'being the proportion payable to the Charity School at
Falmer... pursuant to the Last Will and Testament of Mr Anthony Springett deceased',
covering two years annuities.[2]

1. Farrant, J.H., in *SAC* **122**, 143.   2. 'The free-School Book of Brighthelmston', at Brighton Library, SB 379
FRE.

FELPHAM   1724: 50 families   1801: pop. 306

[Schooling?]   (R: 1769?)
At the 1769 visitation, 'Yes' to 'Doth he [your School-master] diligently instruct his scholars
in the Church Catechism?';[1] perhaps a reference to the minister catechising children. The
earliest direct reference to a school does not occur until 1810.[2]

1. WSRO Ep.I/22/1.   2. Hudson, T. and A., ed. *Felpham by the Sea* (1985), 51.

FERNHURST (FARNHURST)   1724: near 70 families   1801: pop. 383

School   (R: 1775)
At the 1775 visitation there was a schoolmaster in the parish, of 'good Life' and 'diligent',
who came to church and caused his scholars to come; and 'as far as I know' taught them
the catechism. No free or charity school in the parish, so presumably his was a private
school.[1]

1. WSRO Ep.I/22/1.

FERRING   1724: 37 families   1801: pop. 238

No 18th-century schooling traced.

FINDON   1724: about 40 families   1801: pop. 381

Dame schools   (Rs: 1733, 1762)
Visitation returns give the following[1] - 1733, 'We have only two School Dames'; 1762, 'No school only for Reading'.
1. WSRO Ep.I/22/1.

Parish schooling   (R: 1779?)
At the 1779 visitation, there was at least one of a hospital, almshouse or free-school in the parish, probably the last, as the reply to what number of children were taught at the charity school was 'as many as can' - the parish was probably supporting the schooling of some children.[1]
1. WSRO Ep.I/22/1.

FITTLEWORTH   1724: 70 families   1801: pop. 564

Petty and dame schools   (Rs: 1726, 1733, 1742, 1762, 1769, 1775)
Ambiguous answers to visitation questions in 1726 may indicate that there was then a school in the parish; there was certainly one there in 1733 (but no free or charity school) - 'We have a Person in the Parish that teaches school viz a few Boys to read and write, but know not whether he has a Licence so to do from the Ordinary. He is a Person of a good Life and sober Conversation, and very diligent &c. He does come to Church himself and cause his Scholars also to come duly at the times of divine Service. He diligently instructs his Scholars in the Church Catechism.' There was similarly a schoolmaster there in 1742; and in 1762, when the answer to the question asking if there were any unlicensed teachers was 'only some poor people', there was again a schoolmaster in the parish, as there was in 1769. In 1775, 'two or three teach school one man & two women'.[1]
1. WSRO Ep.I/22/1.

[Sunday school?]
At the charity service for the Brighton Sunday school in September 1789, the sermon was preached by Rev J.F.Fearon. He was then vicar of Fittleworth, and it seems probable, from his being asked to preach on the subject, that there was such a school in his own parish.[1]
1. *SWA* 28.9.89; CI.

FLETCHING   1801: pop. 1,279

[Best's school?]   (R: 1747)
A window tax assessment dated 15 June 1747 lists 'Hen. Best for School rooms', which had 7 lights or windows, but for which no tax was assessed. There is a further entry for Henry Best's house, which had 14 lights - a relatively large number - and was assessed at 9s.[1] It seems probable that Best had a fairly large house and also separate rooms where he kept a school. From at least 1747 until 1753 he appears to have occupied the same house, with a field. He died in December 1755.[2] Perhaps the schoolrooms were used by Thomas Hall (see below).   [*Henry Best?*]
1. ESRO ACC 472 (Land Tax Misc.).   2. ESRO XA 42 (Fletching Poor Book 1742, 1747/8-50/1); Land tax returns 1750-61; Fletching PR.

Hall's school   (R: 1747)
Thomas Hall of Fletching was a schoolmaster in his will of 23 June 1747.[1] (Perhaps he used Henry Best's 'School rooms' - see above.) He died in 1747.   [*Thomas Hall*]
1. ESRO W/A 57.657.

<u>Relfe's school</u>   (Rs: 1763-9)

A bill has survived, addressed to Robert Kenward by John Relfe, the parish clerk of Fletching, for Robert Kenward's schooling, covering a period from Michaelmas 1763 to 1769. He charged initially 3d a week for reading, then from June 1765, 6d a week for writing; from 24 October 1768 the charge was 1d a day, and attendance was somewhat erratic. (The bill does not appear to be completed, and from the time-span, may have been Relfe's own account; it was tucked into the parish overseers account book, which Relfe wrote up.) Included in the account are charges for 'Fireing', at 1s a year, which suggest that there was a schoolroom where Relfe kept school. Relfe received a fee of £3 pa as clerk, and also £2 2s pa for 'writeing', from 1770 to at least the 1777-8 year, when the surviving overseers accounts end. He died in 1797.[1]   [*John Relfe*]

1. ESRO SPK/P 1

<u>Parish schooling</u>   (Rs: 1776, 1777)

The parish paid Elizabeth Gillham 6s 1½d on 17 March 1776, and 4s 11½d on 23 March 1777, 'for Eliz: Smiths Schooling'.[1]

1. ESRO SPK/P 1

<u>Charity schooling</u>   (R: 1800)

At the beginning of January 1801 *SWA* reported: '... Lord Sheffield... has established a bakehouse in Fletching [there was distress among the poor at that time, and a shortage of food that they could afford]... Lady Sheffield, the goodness of whose heart outdoeth all description, employs her leisure hours in visiting the poor, and distributing amongst them money and clothes. Her Ladyship also sends the children to schools, and desires them to be regular at church, where they appear neat and clean in the dresses she provides for them.'[1] By implication, the children were sent to existing private schools.

1. *SWA* 12.1.1801.

<u>Other schoolmaster</u>

>   [<u>Hugh Mitchell</u>], schoolmaster at Fletching in 1803, married there in 1786 (then described as a gardener from Epsom, Surrey) and was probably teaching before the end of the century. (See Schedule 2)

FOLKINGTON (FOINTON)   1724: 13 families   1801: pop. 119

<u>Charity schooling/school</u>   (Rs: c1706- into 19c)

Sir William Thomas, who was buried at Folkington in November 1706,[1] left a sum of money for a school in Folkington, producing £5 pa. In 1724 the churchwardens reported: 'Item 5 pounds P ann given by ye same Gentleman [Sir Wm Thomas] to A School Dame for ye Instruction of ye Poor Children of ye sd Parish.'[2] The £5 pa was regularly paid into the 19th century, and later in the 18th century was supplemented by the Harison family (who were then in possession of the late Sir William Thomas's estate), 'for teaching young children of the parish to read and write'.[3]

The Harison family also provided a rare example of gentry ladies taking an active part in teaching poor children. In March 1797 *SWA* reported: 'The daughters of Lancelot Harison, Esq: of Folkington, have undertaken the education and tuition of all the poor children of the parish in which they reside. A large room in Folkington-place house has been fitted up for the reception of the little rustics, where they are daily instructed by these amiable ladies, in reading, plain needle-work, and knitting stockings. It has been observed, by the neighbouring villagers, that the Miss Harisons were never heard to express a wish, for <u>elegant amusements</u> to DESTROY TIME!!'[4] (This arrangement may not have lasted long: Sally Harison and Mary Harison, daughters of Lancelot Harison, Esq., of Folkington-

Place, married on the same day, 10 August, later that same year.[5])
[*Sally Harison, Mary Harison*]

1. Folkington PR.   2. WSRO Ep.I/26/3, 64-5.   3. *EP1* (1819), 226.   4. *SWA* 6.3.97.
5. *SWA* 14.8.97; Folkington PR.

FORD   1724: 5 families   1801: pop. 70

No 18th-century schooling traced. (Specifically 'No School' at the 1758 and 1772 visitations.[1])

1. WSRO Ep.I/22/1.

FRAMFIELD   1717:102 families   1801: pop. 969

Charity schooling   (F: c1720.   Rs: c1720- into 19c)
Robert Smith, who was buried at Framfield 5 October 1719, by will dated 20 August 1719, bequeathed in trust to the vicar and churchwardens of Framfield the interest of £100, 'toward the schooling and educating the poor children of the said parish' (and the interest of a further £100 for an annual charity sermon (£1) and Christmas doles for the poor). Thomas Wharton, vicar, by will dated 7 December 1764, left £10 and all his right in the Pound Farm (to which farm Smith's legacy was tied), 'to be disposed in the same manner as Mr. Smith's money was.'[1] (According to Horsfield, Wharton gave £50.[2])

From 1792 to the end of the century, the rent from Pound Farm was £12 pa, of which £4 was regularly paid to two men for schooling 10 poor children.[3] (The teachers may have been poor men in the parish: of the three named in a surviving account book, part of the payment in 1794 was paid to 'Dickensons Creditors', and another, Cottington, may have been related to the pauper James Cottington (bachelor) who was buried in 1794.)
[*Dickenson, Tyler, Cottington*]

1. *EP2* (1819), 164; Framfield PR.   2. Horsfield *Sussex* I, 364.   3. ESRO PAR 343/11/2

Parish schooling   (Rs: 1789-99)
The overseers' accounts show regular monthly payments from July 1789 to August 1794 to Henry Pain for schooling children, the payments often being described as 'Pence Money for Schooling Children'. For many of the months 1789-90 the number of children involved is given: these ranged from 16 to 30, and were probably the workhouse children. Pain (or Payne) seems to have been paid only one third of a penny per child per week, so the amount of schooling given is likely to have been minimal. The total paid to him in 1790 was £1 14s, in 1791 £1 12s 6½d, in 1792 £1 6s 3½d, in 1793 18s 11½d. Pain was an elderly pauper; he died in August 1794, aged 71. After a gap of two months, the schooling was taken over by Nicholas Divall: back in 1789 he had been 'allow'd' 5s, presumably by way of relief in need. He ceased to teach school after June 1797; in 1798 and 1799 very occasional payments were made to Mary Axcell, two being specifically identified as for schooling (she died in 1811, a singlewoman, aged 78).[1]   [*Henry Pain, Nicholas Divall, Mary Axcell*]

1. ESRO PAR 343/31/1/4; Framfield PR.

FRANT (FANT)   1724: about 80 families   1801: pop. 1,090

Workhouse school   (R: 1778)
In an agreement dated 1 April 1778 between the parish and William Latter of Frant, farmer, and John Ashdowne of Tonbridge, cider merchant, for the keeping of the poor in the workhouse, the two latter 'shall and will teach and Instruct the Children both Boys and Girls to read and shall and will give all possible attention and diligence to Instruct them in their

Duty to God as Christians...'[1] The poorhouse inventory of 27 December 1798 included 'Sixteen books'.[2]

1. ESRO PAR 344/10/1-8 (misc. papers).   2. ESRO PAR 344/30/IA.

[Boys' boarding school]   (R: 1801)
['The Frant School' was opened on 13 July 1801 for the reception of 12 young gentlemen. 'The terms are FIFTY GUINEAS a year, and Three Guineas entrance: in which, Books and all other Expences are included, except music, dancing, drawing, and military exercise'. 'Military exercise' as an optional extra is notable, as is the following bid for £105 pa fees: 'Two or three gentlemen who may wish to improve themselves in some of the above acquirements; or one or two Foreign gentlemen of respectability, who may be desirous of becoming acquainted with the language, manners, and constitution of this country, may have an apartment to themselves, receive every instruction they may require, and live in the family at the rate of One Hundred Guineas per annum. There is a coach house and stables belonging to the house...'[1]   [*John Watkins?*]]

1. *SWA* 13.7.1801.

Other schoolmaster

> [John Watkins], schoolmaster at Frant in 1803.   Then enrolled in voluntary infantry, and perhaps master of Frant school, where 'military exercise' was an optional extra. (See Schedule 2)

FRISTON   1724: 4 families   1801: pop. 35

Charity schooling   (Rs: 1775-79, 1780?-95?)
Three surviving account books of the solicitor, Charles Gilbert, who acted as agent for the estates of George Medley, that run from January 1776 to January 1796, show that from at least 21 August 1775 to 21 August 1779, George Medley paid Elizabeth Simpson £5 pa for schooling '12 Children of Eastdean and Friston'. When she died in February 1780, the schooling was carried on by her daughter, Elizabeth Shorter, who received the same amount for schooling '12 Children in Eastdean' from 25 March 1780 until at least Michaelmas 1795.[1] Friston and Eastdean were united vicarages.[2]   [*Elizabeth Simpson, Elizabeth Shorter?*]

1. ESRO SAS/GT 1/3/3-5.   2. WSRO Ep.I/26/3, 64-5.

FUNTINGTON   1724: 85 families   1801: pop. 681

Petty and dame schools   (Rs: 1737, 1755, 1758, 1762)
There was no free or charity school in the village, but visitation returns give the following:[1]
1737:   'one teaches small children to read & write. He doth [come to church and cause his scholars to come]. He doth [instruct his scholars in the catechism].'
1755:   'we have only little small schools. ['Is your School-master of good Life... and... diligent?'] 'we believe our Schoolmaster to be so.' 'He does' [come to church and cause his scholars to come]. 'he does' [teach them the catechism].
1758:   'We have several Schools but don't know whether ye teachers have any Licence: one a Master & he of good Character. he does [come to church], but whether he causes his scholars to come we don't know. he does [teach them the catechism].'
1762:   'Our schoolmaster behaves well', and comes to church and causes his scholars to come, and teaches them the catechism.

1. WSRO Ep.I/22/1.

GLYNDE 1717: 22 families 1801: pop. 216

Charity school (Rs: 1765- into 19c)
On 4 February 1765 Thomas Davies, vicar of Glynde, wrote to William Hodgson, steward to Richard Trevor, bishop of Durham, who inherited the Glynde estates in 1743: 'I have got all the little Children to School. There is at present near a score but as Spring comes on many boys will be taken off, to tend Crows, Hogs &c. Dame Burgess is to have 3 pence for the Girls that learn to sow, there is about 5 of them: the rest are 2d per week.'[1] William Hodgson's day book records under 12 January 1767: 'Pd. Mr Davies for educating the Poor Child'n in in Glynde & Beddingham to 10 October 1766 - £7.17s.11d.'[2] In Hodgson's rentals and disbursements book there is the entry: 'Teaching the Poor Children one year ending 10th Oct. 1767. viz. of Glynde besides Mrs Trevors Money 2s.5d; Beddingham £9.4s.1d: Total £9.6.6d.'[3] Mrs Mary Trevor bequeathed £100, the interest of which was to be applied for the better instruction of the poor children of Glynde in the principles of the Christian religion: the money was invested in Glynd Bridge Trust, and the interest of £5 pa was regularly received into the 19th century (the Glynd Bridge Trust became insolvent c1816).[4] [In December 1818 John Ellman, who had been appointed steward of the Glynde estates in 1792, and was a prosperous farmer and celebrated sheep breeder, reported that 'I have paid annually for the last fifteen years £4 to the clerk of the parish, who keeps a Sunday School in the Church, and takes all the boys and girls... who offer themselves, and to a schoolmistress 3d. a week for boys and 4d. a week for girls, 16 or 18 altogether: she teaches the boys reading and the girls reading and needlework. I have paid the same for the last two years although I have received no interest [ie. from the Trevor bequest]. I pay the excess on £5 from my own pocket.'[5] [*Dame Burgess*]

1. Lusted, A. 'Two hundred years of education in Glynde, 1765-1965', *Ringmer History* No.3, citing ESRO GLY 2770. 2. Lusted, op cit., citing ESRO GLY 2938. 3. Lusted, op cit., citing ESRO GLY 2937.
4. *EP*1 (1819), 226. 5. ibid. Appendix, 384-5

Sunday school (F: before August 1789. Rs: into 19c)
The rules for a Sunday school at Glynde survive; included was a list of the managers, one of whom was the vicar, Rev Davies, who died August 1789.[1]

The managers were to meet once every month, 'to make such alterations as shall be thought proper & give directions for the better management of the school and also that the Parents may have an opportunity of having their children admitted into the said School, by making proper application.'

'The children are to be in the School by nine o Clock every Sunday morning and stop till Eleven and at two in the afternoon & stay till four, except when the Evening service begins at two, then to be at school at one o Clock and stop one hour before service and one hour after.' Attendance at the church services may be assumed, although this is not mentioned in the rules; but it is clear that there was time for teaching the children to read. One rule, later deleted, required the master to begin and conclude with a prayer, 'the Children all kneeling'.

Discipline was maintained by the threat of expulsion: 'If any of the scholars are guilty of lying swearing or talking in any indecent manner, or otherwise misbehaving themselves, the teacher shall point out the evil of such conduct, and if after repeated reproof the scholar shall not be reformed, he or she shall be excluded the said school.'

The children were required to be clean and neatly dressed, but the rules show an understanding of the difficulties of poor parents: 'The Parents are desired to send their Children regularly to school clean in their persons and as decently clothed as their circumstances will permit.'

Another rule, that was later deleted, was that the following admonition was to be

6.   Richard Trevor (1710-71), Bishop of Durham, who inherited the Glynde estates in 1743. He provided charity schooling for the poor children of Glynde and Beddingham and was a benefactor of Mayfield charity school. (ESRO *Catalogue of the Glynde Place Archives*; from a portrait at Glynde Place, artist unknown).

read to the children before they left the school: 'Your benefactors require you to refrain (during the remainder of this day) from Hallowing or making any noise - but those who chuse to amuse themselves behave quietly and soberly, thus will recommend yourselves to the favor of your betters and incline them to do you many Acts of kindness, which noisy and Illnatured Children will be excluded.'

From at least 1803, the Sunday school was kept by the parish clerk.[2]

1. ESRO PAR 347/25/1; *SRS* **30**, 72.   2. *EP1* (1819), Appendix 384-5

Farm school   (Rs: 1790s)
John Ellman, tenant of the Great Farm at Glynde, a prosperous sheep farmer of national reputation, engaged a literate and very successful shepherd, Charles Payne, who was accustomed to carry a book with him on the Downs to read while tending his flock, as schoolmaster, to teach the men and maidservants in his house to read and write.[1] While this was properly a form of adult education, it is likely that several of the pupils were boys and girls. Payne married, in 1796, a dairymaid whom he had thus instructed, Lucy Salvage (but she signed the register by mark).[2]   [*Charles Payne*]

1. Walesby, A., 'Memoir of John Ellman', *The Library of Agricultural and Horticultural Knowledge* (4th edn), lviii.   2. ibid.; Glynde PR.

GORING   1724: about 40 families   1801: pop. 419

Dame schools   (Rs: 1733, 1779)
In 1733, 'A poor woman teaches a few small children'; and at the 1779 visitation, in answer to the question asking if there were any unlicensed teachers in the parish, 'An old woman or two'; so more than one dame school then.[1]

1. WSRO Ep.I/22/1.

Smither's preparatory boarding school   (F: 1800)
'Mrs and Misses Smither' announced the opening, on 21 January 1800, of 'a preparatory School for ten Children, under twelve years of age. - Terms, Eighteen Guineas per annum... N.B. Parlour Boarders, Thirty-five Guineas.' They noted that 'their place of abode, Goring, is situate only half a mile from the Sea, two miles from Worthing, fourteen from Brighton, and fifty from London.'[1] Advertised in *SWA* Dec (3) 1799; Jan (3) 1800.   [*Mrs Smither, the Misses Smither*]

1. *SWA* 16.12.99.

GRAFFHAM   1724: about 20 families   1801: pop. 260

Dame school   (Rs: 1758, 1762)
At the 1758 visitation: 'a Woman keeps School - one of good Morals - and comes to Church', and teaches her scholars the catechism. In 1762, in answer to the question asking if there were any unlicensed teachers: 'Yes a very good Woman.'[1]

1. WSRO Ep.I/22/1.

GREATHAM   1724: 11 or 12 families   1801: pop. 79

No 18th-century schooling traced.

GUESTLING   1724: about 33 families   1801: pop. 496

School   (R: 1726)
On 24 June 1726 Stephen Wicking was licensed to teach boys in the parish of Guestling.[1] (In 1721, he had signed the subscription book, 'before his Admission to Teach School in Hasting'.) Perhaps this was a charity school maintained in his lifetime by the rector, Robert

Bradshaw (see <u>Charity school</u> below).   [*Stephen Wicking*]
1. WSRO Ep.I/1/11.

<u>Charity school</u>   (Rs: c1737- into 19c)
Robert Bradshaw, rector of Guestling, who was buried there 24 July 1736, by will dated 20
November 1734, required his executors, during the life of his wife, to pay out of the rents
and profits of his estate, £15 pa, free of all taxes and deductions, to a fit and able person
(to be appointed by Sir William Ashburnham and his heirs and the rector of Guestling for
the time being) to teach 20 poor children of Guestling, aged under 14, to read and, if
desired by their parents or guardians, to write. And after the death of his wife, his executors
were to sell his estate, and to lay out £500 of the proceeds in land and property, to be
settled for the maintenance of a schoolmaster, to reside at Guestling and teach 20 poor
children of the parish, as above. The money raised in due course by the sale of the estate
was greater than that needed to meet the specific bequests in Bradshaw's will, and the matter
was long before the court of Chancery. Under an order of the court dated 30 July 1774, the
fund for the schoolmaster was increased to £1,000 3% consols; but it was not until 1835 that
a scheme was finally settled. In January 1772 R. and S. Everest, schoolmaster and mistress
of Guestling, announced that they had taken 'the Free-School at Guestling', and advertised
for boarders. A different schoolmaster was appointed in 1776; he was still there in 1819,
but 'very old and infirm, in consequence of which and of a preference given by the
inhabitants of Guestling to a private day school in the parish, there are now few and
sometimes no children in the free school'. [As a result of the 1835 settlement, mentioned
above, schools for boys and girls were to be built by the charity, and a schoolmaster and
schoolmistress appointed. By 1867 there were about 60 boys and girls at the schools.][1]
[*R.Everest, S.Everest*]
1. ESRO PAR 350/24/1; Guestling PR; *EP*1 (1819), 226-7; *VCH* ii, 439; *SWA* 27.1.72.

<u>Everests' boys' and girls' boarding school</u>   (F: 1772)
In January 1772, R. and S. Everest, schoolmaster and mistress of Guestling, announced,
under the heading 'WRITING, ARITHMETIC, and NEEDLE-WORK TAUGHT', that 'they
have taken the Free-School at Guestling aforesaid, with a large and elegant Building for the
Reception of Boarders; distant from the Sea about two Miles, and from Hastings four, being
situated very pleasantly, in a healthy Air. Those who shall please to entrust them with the
Tuition of their Sons or Daughters, may depend on their utmost Endeavour and Diligence
to accomplish their Designs, &c.'[1] The school was unusual in being a boarding school for
both boys and girls (the Allfrees, at Hertsmonceux, had established such a school by May
1771). In 1776 a different schoolmaster appears to have been appointed to the free school.[2]
[*R.Everest, S.Everest*]
1. *SWA* 27.1.72.   2. *EP*1 (1819), 226-7.

HAILSHAM (HALISHAM, HAYSHAM) 1724: 52 families 1801: pop. 897

<u>Beard's girls' boarding school</u>   (F: 1774.   Rs: 1774-5)
In June 1774 Mrs Beard, from Rottingdean, having hired a house at Hailsham, announced
the opening of her girls' boarding school. 'She also intends taking Ladies of any Age, as
Parlour Boarders. - A Dancing Master will attend, if desired.'[1] She only kept the school
there for a year. In May 1775 she announced, as 'SCHOOLMISTRESS, from HAILSHAM',
that 'she has hired a House in LEWES, and will open a BOARDING-SCHOOL for YOUNG
LADIES, after Whitsuntide';[2] but later the same month she announced 'that she has declined
all Thoughts of opening a School at LEWES, having taken Miss RUSSELL's established
BOARDING SCHOOL, at BRIGHTHELMSTON.'[3]   [*Jane Beard*]
1. *SWA* 13.6.74.   2. *SWA* 8.5.75.   3. *SWA* 22.5.75.

Evening school   (R: 1777)
In an advertisement in April 1777 for a schoolmaster, the parish officers included the note: 'There is an Evening School all the Winter Season...' This would have been a private school, and the implication is that it had been operative prior to the advertisement.[1]
1. *SWA* 14.4.77.

Charity/private parish school   (Rs: 1777- into 19c)
For three weeks in April 1777, the parish officers inserted in *SWA* the following advertisement (the reference to the milch ass only appeared in the first):

> WANTED, immediately
> A Middle-aged Person, with proper Recommendations, as a Man duly qualified to undertake the Care of a SCHOOL. According to his Merits, so he may expect Encouragement; and that proper Attention may be given, the principal of the Inhabitants have subscribed to the Amount of TWENTY POUNDS per Annum towards supporting the same, so that no one need to apply, but such whose good Morals, as well as good English Learning, (without Enthusiasm,) will sufficiently recommend him.
> ☞There is an Evening School all the Winter Season, exclusive of the above.
> For further Satisfaction apply to the Parish Officers of the Town of HAILSHAM, in Sussex.
> N.B. A fresh MILCH ASS is wanted directly, by Mr. HURDIS, Surgeon, at Hailsham, for which a good reasonable Premium will be allowed.[1]

The school was clearly a charity school (and was held, until 1827, in the old vestry in the parish church[2]); but the references to the 'encouragement' the master could expect, and to the evening school, indicate that he was free to take private pupils as well.

The grave-board in the churchyard of Francis Howlett, who was buried 12 June 1831, aged 80, describes him as 'the First Parish Schoolmaster'.[3] He had arrived in the parish as one of a party of strolling players; he married a local girl; in addition to schoolmaster, he was also postmaster, tax-collector, vestry clerk, printer and travelling librarian.[4]
[*Francis Howlett*]
1. *SWA* 14.4.77.   2. *SGLH* v.3, no.2, 68.   3. ibid.   4. Geering, T. *Our Sussex Parish* (1925 edn), 58, 60.

Box's school   (R: c1790-5?)
Mary Box kept a school in the town. She was a Strict and Particular Baptist, and every Sunday, in all weathers, would walk the 9 miles to Heathfield to hear the preacher, George Gilbert. At her persuasion, Gilbert preached at Hailsham in 1792, and this led to the formation of a little Strict and Particular Baptist church there in April 1795. Francis Brown was invited to be pastor. Mary Box and Francis Brown were married 24 August 1795, but Mary died in December that same year, aged 34.[1]   [*Mary Box*]
1. Chambers, R.F. *The Strict Baptist Chapels of England: Sussex* Vol.II, 73-6.

HAMSEY   1724: 52 families   1801: pop. 367

Charity schooling   (R: 1773)
On 16 August 1773 the following report appeared in *SWA*:

> Thursday morning last died the Rev. Mr. Wenham, of Ham[s]ey, near Lewes, greatly regretted by all who had the pleasure of his acquaintance. The poor of that parish have sustained a loss, we fear, that will not hastily

be retrieved; he was their constant benefactor, distributing among them, 30 three-penny loaves every Sunday throughout the year, and paying for the schooling of all their children, amounting to between 30 and 40.

John Wenham was rector of Hamsey from 1766 until his death on 12 August 1773.[1]

1. CI; *SAC* **71**, 145.

HANGLETON   1724: 5 families   1801: pop. 36

No 18th-century schooling traced.

HARDHAM (HERRINGHAM) 1724: 9 families   1801: pop. 85

No 18th-century schooling traced.

HARTFIELD   1724: about 120 families 1801: pop. 1,050

Charity school   (F: c1640.   Rs: through 18c)

Richard Rands, rector of Hartfield, by will dated 30 June 1640, devised all his lands in Hartfield to trustees, 'to appoint a schoolmaster, being a graduate of one of the Universities, to teach all such children of the parish of Hartfield as should repair unto the said schoolmaster freely, so as all children should be able to read English before they should come to the said schoolmaster'; the master was to be paid £20 pa.[1] There was an inquisition in 1667, after the trustees had, inter alia, installed a non-graduate and paid him less than £20; and from that time the school was purely elementary.[2] In 1724 the churchwardens reported: 'The Revd Mr Rich'd Rands formerly Rector left 20 pound P An'm for A free School but ye Rents are much sunk, now about Fourteen pounds P An'm ... '[3] By indenture dated 11 November 1725, Thomas Earl of Thanet augmented the master's salary by a rent-charge of £10, out of Bolbrook Farm in Hartfield, on condition that the master was appointed by the owner of Hothfield Place, in Kent.[4] John Kelton, who died in May 1777, was for many years master of the school; he had signed the subscription book in 1733. In 1797 and 1801 William Morphew was a schoolmaster at Hartfield, probably of the charity school.[5] A schoolroom was built by subscription about 1812; by 1819 the master was receiving c£27 pa from Rands' endowment, plus £10 pa out of Bolbrook Farm; all the children of the parish who applied were taught reading, writing and arithmetic, the number varying between 80 and 120.[6]   [*John Kelton, William Morphew?*]

1. *EP*2 (1819), 166.   2. *VCH* ii, 427.   3. WSRO Ep.I/26/3, 64-5.   4. *EP*2 (1819), 166.
5. See Schedule 2 for references.   6. *EP*2 (1819), 167.

HARTING   1801: pop. 863

Petty and dame schools   (Rs: 1705, 1726, 1742, 1750, 1758, 1762)

On 6 January 1705, James Ellis subscribed, '... to instruct Children in a School att Harting and to have a Lycence therefore'.[1]

In 1726 there was in the parish 'a sober unlicensed schoomaster yt teaches only to write & reade': there was no free school.[2]

In 1742, 'there is only a Petty School'.[3]

In 1750 John Exall, a Roman Catholic, was a schoolmaster in the parish, and wrote to Caryll asking not to be turned out of the 'great house at Harting', 'I being between 60 and 70 years of age, and my eyes dim.' 'I remember, Sir, the last time I saw you at Lady Holt you was pleased to ask me what school I had. I answered but small...' The room was furnished with 'a Table and Forms made for the Children to sett on they are made out of Old Plank &c.' The school was apparently discontinued in 1749, following an accident in which the schoolmaster had broken his leg.[4]

In 1758 there was no free or charity school but there was apparently a schoolmaster in the parish, of 'good Life' and 'diligent', who came to church and caused his scholars to come, and taught them the catechism.[5]

In 1762, 'several teach school but we believe they have no Licence'. These were probably all or mostly dames, and in 1769, 'We have no School-master'.[6]
[*James Ellis, John Exall*]

1. WSRO Ep.I/3/5.   2. WSRO Ep.I/22/1.   3. ibid.   4. Gordon, H.D. *History of Harting* (1877), 203-4; Kinoulty, M.K., 'A Social Study of Roman Catholicism in West Sussex in the Eighteenth Century', M.A. thesis, University of Wales (1982), WSRO Add MS 34,673, 180, citing BL Add MS 28,231 ff 54-5.
5. WSRO Ep.I/22/1.   6. ibid.

Oliver Whitby's boys' boarding charity school   (F: 1712.   Rs: 1712- into 19c)

Four of the twelve places at Oliver Whitby's school at Chichester [qv], founded under his will of 16 February 1702 and established in 1712, were reserved for poor boys from Harting, whose parents were exempt from the poor tax and were not dissenters. The boys were clothed, provided with board and lodging, and taught writing, arithmetic and the mathematics.

[Charity schooling?]   (Rs: 1750?, 1790s?)

A letter dated 25 February 1750, that the schoolmaster John Exall wrote to Caryll, includes the following: 'I remember, Sir, the last time I saw you at Lady Holt you was pleased to ask me what school I had. I answered but small, and that one of yr Tenants opposed me. You said you would speak to him yourself, which I find you was so good as to do the next day, but I think had not the desired effect, for a little while after Sr Matthew Fetherstone and his Lady came, and their two Brothers, and the 2 latter vewed the Room in order to allow me £15 p.annum to teach a certain number of Poore Children, but the same Farmer tould the Lady I was Idle, &c., shee excused it by saying "Poverty makes some people worse: it may be for want of Incorrigment;" another reported he doughted I was to much Romishly inclined. One was for this man to be Schoolmaster, another was for that man, the Gent. said he thought they troubled themselves with what they had not to do with. So the desire dropt, and it was not done.' H.D.Gordon, in his history of Harting, cites this incident as showing 'the early interest taken by the family of Fetherstonhaugh in the improvement of the Harting poor by means of schools.' (Sir Matthew Fetherstonhaugh had purchased Uppark two years before.) It seems likely that the family did support charity schooling in the parish. After the building of Lady Holt, the old manor house, Harting Place, before it was taken down at some time before 1800, was used for a parish school, and afterwards as a workhouse.[1]

1. Gordon, op. cit., 202-4.

Dr Durnford   (R: early 1760s)

Dr Thomas Durnford, vicar of Harting from 1744 until his death in 1792, taught Harry Fetherstonhaugh (son of Sir Matthew of Uppark) before he was sent to Eton, and probably taught the sons of other local gentry. (Durnford's daughter married Sir Matthew's brother, Ulrick, who succeeded to the rectorship of Harting in 1757.)[1]   [*Thomas Durnford*]

1. Meade-Fetherstonhaugh, M. and Warner, O. *Uppark and its People* (1964), 36-7; CI.

HASTINGS   1724: about 500 families 1801: pop. 3,155
                                  (All Saints, about 200
                                  St Clement, about 300)

Grammar school   (F: 1639.   Rs: through 18c)
Hastings had an ancient collegiate church, and early in the 14th century Henry, count of Eu, specifically referred to a grammar school and a singing school there, naming his grandfather, Robert, count of Eu, as founder of the church at Hastings. After the dissolution, there is a reference in 1607 to a chamber appointed 'for a common school house for this town'. But the foundation of the modern grammar school is attributed to William Parker, rector of All Saints, who, by will dated 15 November 1619, left, after the death of his wife, Judith, 113 acres of lands in Ore to the corporation of Hastings, 'towards the maintenance of a religious and godlie Schoolmaster in the Towne which shall instruct and teach the youth of the Inhabitants of Hastings in Learning, manners and other Virtuous education to gett their living.' Parker died in 1619, but his widow lived until October 1638, and it was not until 1 March 1639 that the first master was appointed. It is of interest, in view of what happened to the other grammar schools in Sussex in the 18th century, that Parker's will included the following: '... I doe peremportily ordaine that neither the Rector of the parish of All Saints aforesaid nor the Rector of the Parish of St.Clement in Hasting, nor their Curats, shall ever be permitted to be Schoolmaster, because noe man is able to p'forme bothe those offices.'[1]

In 1713 there were 20 boys on the foundation.[2] In the 18th century the grammar school was combined with Saunders' charity school [qv below]: this union probably applied from the beginning of Saunders' school, c1719.[3] In 1722 James Cranston, rector of St Clement's, wrote to the SPCK, implying that the charities were then merged: '... Will'm Parker of that Town [Hastings] gave 20.l P an. & James Saunders 30.l p an. for ever towards instructing Young People, so yt the Master there has 50.l p an. who is oblig'd to teach plain Sailing to the Child'n beside reading Writing and Arithmetic, and the Number of Child'n generally under his care is about 60. or 70.'[4] Saunders, in his will, specifically included Latin amongst the subjects to be taught at his school, so there was no conflict with a grammar school curriculum; but there does not appear to be any evidence that Latin was in fact taught through the 18th century. In 1800, when Joseph Hannay was appointed master of the combined schools, he was to receive 2 guineas pa for each child,[5] and was bound to take 40 boys and girls only, who received a purely elementary education, while the master had to pay for the hire of a schoolroom.[6] [In 1806 the number was increased to 55,[7] and from 1809 the master received £3 per head.[8]]

In 1809 and 1810 informations were filed against the corporation in respect of the charities, and the court of Chancery found against the corporation, for abusing the trusts and letting the lands belonging to the charities at too low rents to favoured tenants. Saunder's school was closed from 1812 to November 1818, from which time the two schools were separated - by 1819 there were 90 children in Parker's school and 70 boys in Saunder's, or 160 in all, compared to 55 in total before the Chancery case.[9]

John Goldsworthy Shorter, master of the joint schools 1781-91, who succeeded his father as master at the latter's death, was admitted to the freedom of Hastings in 1783, and was elected jurat in 1791, when he resigned as schoolmaster to devote himself to public work; he was eight times mayor.[10] In 1792 he built a new schoolroom on land adjoining Waterloo Passage, which remained in his possession until 1800.[11]

[*Stephen Wicking?, Samuel Cant, John Shorter, John Goldsworthy Shorter, Joseph Hannay*]

1. *VCH* ii, 409-10; Manwaring Baines, J., and Conisbee, L.R. *History of Hastings Grammar School 1619-1956* (1956), 4-8.   2. SPCK ALB v.4, 3509.   3. *EP3* (1820), 445.   4. SPCK ALB v.11, 7035.
5. Baines et al., 20.   6. *VCH* ii, 411.   7. ibid.   8. Baines et al., 20.   9. *EP1* (1819), 232.

10. Baines et al., 17.　11. ibid, 18.

Charity schooling　(Rs: from 1713)
James Cranston, rector of St Clement's, wrote to the SPCK on 24 March 1713: '... That there are in his Parish near 5000. Souls, and not above 10. Dissenters who also come occasionally to the Church　That he seldom has a Congregation of less than 2000. People on a Sunday. That he catechises abt 2 or 300. Children every Wednesday and Friday.　That they are all taught to read, and the Boys also to write.　And when they are able the Girls are employ'd in making of Nett, and the Boys goe to Sea to be Employ'd either in the Fishing or ye Coasting Trade　That some few are put out to Trades in ye Town　But none to Husbandry or Services in Familys The Neighbouring Country for ye most part　Supplying with Husbandmen and Maid Servants　That as to ye Charity Schools Mr Wm Parker late minister of the Town left 20. pounds p Ann'm for Instructing of 20 Boys That for Joseph Martin a Member of Parliam't allows 5 li p Ann'm for teaching 5 Boys...' (Cranston also rehearsed the details of Saunders' bequest, although that charity was not in fact operating in Hastings at that time.)[1]

Although Cranston's number of 2-300 children being taught may have been an exaggeration, it is clear that there was a large provision for charity schooling at this time. The SPCK annual *Account* for 1713 records this number, and Parker's £20 a year, adding: 'the rest of the charge is made up by Subscription'.

One of the subscribers is likely to have been Richard Ellsworth, who died in August 1714. By will dated 11 July 1714 he left a bequest 'towards the teaching the poorest children of that parish [Hastings] to read and say their catechism, and buying them spelling books, bibles and the whole duty of man.' Ellsworth's bequest comprised all his part of the dissolved priory of Hastings, after paying a tenth to the minister of the parish, whom he appointed to take care that that part of his will should be duly executed.　But the charity commissioners, investigating in 1819, found no record that this bequest had ever been paid, and it was then still subject of a legal case.[2]

In the SPCK annual *Accounts* of charity schools, the number of children being taught in 1715 is given as 200, some of them clothed, in two schools; and this record is continued without change through the years, at least to 1740 (from 1725, by implication from the summary county total, which was all that was then reported).　Since there is no change whatsoever in the county totals from 1730 to 1740, the reports for these years must be treated with caution.

(See also below Saunders' charity schools, and Millward's charity schooling.)

1. SPCK ALB v.4, 3509.　2. *EP1* (1819), 229; *VCH* ix, 28.

Saunders' charity schools　(F: c1719.　Rs: c1719- into 19c)
James Saunders, of Winchelsea at his death, yeoman, with lands at Wittersham in Kent, a Baptist, born at Hastings and buried there 27 January 1709, 'a great benefactor to the Town', by will dated 7 January 1709, left all his estate to set up educational charities in Rye and Hastings.　His was one of the largest educational endowments made in Sussex in the 18th century and, in terms of the number of children eventually taught, by far the most effective. The income from his estate was to be accumulated for 10 years from his death and the resulting sum used to establish a school at Rye [qv]; the estate was then bequeathed to the corporation of Hastings, who were required to apply, out of the rents, £20 pa in placing out as apprentices two poor boys of the town of Hastings, one of the parish of St Clement and the other of the parish of All Saints; £10 pa each to two schooldames, one of St Clement and the other of All Saints, who should teach free of charge all the poor children of both sexes as should come to them, not exceeding 30 in number in each parish, in spelling and reading English; and £40 pa to a sober and discreet master, well qualified to teach Latin,

who should teach all the poor boys of the town of Hastings, not exceeding the number of 70, in reading English, writing, and casting accounts, the mathematics and navigation, and the Latin tongue. He thus provided for the education of up to 130 poor children of Hastings.[1]

In the event, the income from Saunders' estate does not seem to have quite covered the £80 pa disposals specified in his will. The SPCK annual *Account* for 1716, referring to the bequest, gives the income as 'about 70 1 per Annum'; and in 1719, ten years after Saunders' death, £720 was laid out in lands, in trust, for the corporation of Rye to maintain a school there, under the terms of his will.[2] The boys' school at Hastings appears to have been merged with Parker's school (see above) from its beginning: it could not have been begun before 1719, until which time the income was willed to Rye, and James Cranston, rector of St Clement's (who in letters to the SPCK in 1709 and 1713 had detailed the Saunders' bequests totalling £80 pa, as given above[3]) in a letter to the SPCK of 19 April 1722, advised 'That Will'm Parker of that Town gave 20.1 P an. & James Saunders 30.1 p an. for ever... so yt the Master there has 50.1 p an. who is oblig'd to teach plain Sailing to the Child'n beside reading Writing and Arithmetic, and the Number of Child'n generally under his care is about 60. or 70. That 2. School Dames have 9.1 p an. each by Mr Saunders' Charity for teaching 30. Girls, and the same Benefactor has given 18.1 p an. for ever towards putting out 2. Young Men Apprentices to some Honest Employm't.'[4] So the boys' schools were then merged, and the annual payments from Saunders' bequest were reduced to £66. Apparently the dames were now teaching girls only, rather than 'children of both sexes'. At the 1724 visitation of St Clement it was reported: 'Given an Estate of about 70 1 p. An: by James Saunders an Anabaptist to teach poor Children and put out Apprentices.' Interestingly, both St Clement (about 300 families) and All Saints (about 200 families) then reported 'No Papists or Dissenters'.[5]

In 1800 the two schools were still combined, the master being bound to take 40 boys and girls only, who received a purely elementary education; the corporation's income from the charities was then £49 16s from Parker's and £75 10s from Saunders'.[6] In 1809 an information was filed against the corporation for mismanaging the charity, and for letting the lands belonging to the charity for too low rents to favoured tenants; and the court of Chancery found against the corporation. The schools were separated. Saunders' was discontinued from 1812 to 1818, its affairs then being in Chancery; it reopened in November 1818. The new regulations ordered £50 pa instead of £20 for putting out apprentices; £25 instead of £10 for each of the two schooldames; and the residue, after necessary expenses, of about £100 (instead of £40) for the schoolmaster. Seventy boys were immediately admitted to the boys' school, and each of the dames had their full number of 30 children of either sex.[7] So the maximum numbers specified in Saunders' will were then realised.
[*Stephen Wicking?, Samuel Cant, John Shorter, John Goldsworthy Shorter, Joseph Hannay*]

1. Baines et al., op. cit., 13; WSRO Ep.I/26/3, 22-3; St Clement, Hastings, PR; *EP1* (1819), 232.
2. *EP3* (1820), 445.   3. SPCK ALB v.1, 1634, and v.4, 3509.   4. ibid. v.11, 7035.
5. WSRO Ep.I/26/3, 22-3.   6. *VCH* ii, 411.   7. *EP1* (1819), 232.

Millward's charity schooling   (F: 1760.   Rs: 1760- into 19c)
J. Spencer Millward died in 1760 intestate, but recommended to his brother Edward that his estate should pay for the schooling of some poor children; and Edward Millward paid £10 a year to a schoolmistress until his death in 1811 (when J. Spencer Millward's nephew continued to pay a larger sum).[1]
1. *EP1* (1819), 230; *VCH* ix, 28.

Barwick's boys' boarding school   (F: 1779)
Rev Henry Barwick announced the opening of a boarding school, after the Easter holidays,

1779, for 12 young gentlemen only, to qualify them for business, the public schools, or university. His terms were 20 guineas a year, and 2 guineas entrance. He noted that 'HASTING is 63 Miles from LONDON, is situated on one of the finest Shores in the Kingdom, and is an exceedingly dry, healthy Town, accomodated with a Diligence, Waggons, &c. and of late much resorted to for Sea-bathing.'[1] When he opened a similar school at Lindfield in 1793 [qv], he claimed that he had educated 'several of the Nobility, Gentry, &c. of this Kingdom, during a period of upwards of twenty years.'[2] Barwick was curate of St Clement's, Hastings, officiating at marriages there from 3 January to 19 September 1779. He was curate of Bexhill from February 1780 to February 1792, and appears to have moved his school there [qv]. Advertised in *SWA* Mar (4) 1779. [*Henry Barwick*]

1. *SWA* 8.3.79.   2. *SWA* 14.1.93.

Rockett's girls' boarding school   (F: 1793.   Rs: 1793, 1794)
In November 1793 Miss Rockett announced that she had opened a French and English boarding school for young ladies, in the parish of All Saints.[1] In January 1794 the school was advertised as 'Hastings French Boarding School'; the emphasis was on French and needlework - 'young Ladies are carefully taught the French language in all its purity, as French is the only language that is allowed to be spoken among the Scholars; they are likewise taught the very best of plain, and all kinds of the most fashionable needle work of the present age, that is to say, the best of plain work, embroidery, print work, cloth work, fillagree, ribbon work, bottle labels in gold or silver, knitting purses in silk, gold or silver, fringe making in ditto. floss work, Dresden carpeting, artificial fruit and flower making, by Miss ROCKETT, and Assistants, at 13 Guineas per annum. No Entrance. A Half-boarder is wanted. N.B. Writing, Arithmetic, Drawing, Music, and Dancing, by the most approved Masters.'[2] Advertised in *SWA* Nov (2), Dec 1793; Jan 94. [*Miss Rockett*]

1. *SWA* 18.11.93.   2. *SWA* 6.1.94.

Other master

Stephen Wicking, subscribed 9 November 1721, 'before his Admission to Teach School in Hasting'.[1] He may well have been master of the grammar school (see above). In 1726 he was licensed to teach in Guestling.

1. WSRO Ep.II/1/1.

[Note: With c500 families, and therefore a population of c2,300 in 1724 (in 1713 James Cranston of St Clement claimed 'near 5000' souls in his parish), and a population of 3,155 in 1801, Hastings did not grow greatly during the 18th century; but at the beginning of the 19th century expansion was rapid - to 4,025 in 1811, 6,300 in 1821, 10,097 in 1831.]

HEATHFIELD   1724: about 100 families 1801: pop. 1,226

Village school   (Rs: 1710, 1724, 1740, 1750, 1775, 1776)
There are references to a schoolhouse adjoining the church in bills of detection in 1674, 1684 and 1687;[1] the south chapel or south chancel was walled off from the rest of the building and used as a schoolhouse for at least most of the 18th century - it was so used in 1776.[2] In 1710 it was reported that some of the tiles had been blown off the schoolhouse, 'being part of the church'.[3] In 1724 the visitation report noted: '... The Vestry or School House adjoyning belongs to the Parishioners & is in good Repair.'[4] Nicholas Weston, schoolmaster, was buried 14 May 1740.[5] In 1750 John Vine was schoolmaster; at one point he had 40 scholars.[6] In 1775 Thomas Weller, advertising for survey work, described himself as 'Schoolmaster, at Heathfield'.[7] [*Nicholas Weston, John Vine, Thomas Weller*]

1. Doff, E., pers. comm., citing BL Add MS 39,445, ff 61,73,83.   2. *SNQ* **14**, 275, citing BL Add MS 39,357.
3. Doff, E., pers. comm., citing BL Add MS 39,446, f 54.   4. WSRO Ep.I/26/3, 26-7.   5. Heathfield PR.
6. *SAC* **9**, 194 (corrected dating).   7. *SWA* 11.9.75.

<u>Weller's boys' boarding school</u>   (F: 1776.   Rs: 1776-81)
Thomas Weller was schoolmaster at Heathfield, certainly by September 1775, when he
described himself as such in an advertisement for surveying and mapping work.[1] In May
1776 he announced that he had opened a house and school, 'wherein Youth are genteelly
boarded, and carefully instructed in the true Knowledge of English, Writing, Arithmetic,
Algebra, and all the most useful Parts of the Mathematics; with the Practice and Use of
various Sorts of optical and Mathematical Instruments, Merchants Accompts, Drawing,
Mapping, Astronomy, Geography, the Description and Use of the Globes, &c. together with
the Knowledge of Religion, Morality, and History.' His terms were £13 pa, with only 5s
entrance.   Dancing was an extra.   The advertisement ended: 'N.B.   Estates or Lands
surveyed, mapped, divided, or inclosed. Also Plans for Houses, or other Buildings, drawn,
measured, and estimated, for Gentlemen or Artificers, on the most reasonable Terms...'[2]
By December 1777 a dancing master was attending once a week.[3] In January 1780 he
described his school as 'HEATHFIELD BOARDING SCHOOL... WHERE YOUTH find
a kind Reception, and are properly taught the true Knowledge of...[etc].' The advertisement
ended: 'Any one staying the Holidays to pay 5s. a week, or 15s. for each Vacation, viz.
Christmas, and Midsummer, three Weeks each.'[4] In advertisements in 1781, after listing the
subjects taught, Weller added: 'Also Lectures on the Rules and Subjects of useful Learning,
Morality and good Behaviour, are duly read, explained, and delivered to the Pupils every
Evening, by the said THOMAS WELLER, (and proper Teachers)...'[5]
       On 5 December 1783 Weller was appointed master of Mayfield school, from
'Christmas Day next', where he continued to his death in 1807.[6] (His salary there was £24
pa, plus a house, for which he was required to teach 39 poor children; he was not allowed
to take any boys as boarders.[7])
       Advertised in *SWA* Sep 1775; May 76; May (2), Dec (2) 77; Sep (2), Dec 78; Jan,
May (2) 79; Jan (2), Jun, Jul, Dec 80; Jun, Jul, Dec 81.
[*Thomas Weller*]

1. *SWA* 11.9.75.   2. *SWA* 13.5.76.   3. *SWA* 15.12.77.   4. *SWA* 10.1.80.   5. *SWA* 25.6.81.
6. ESRO AMS 5601/1.   7. *SWA* 17.11.83.

HEENE   1801: pop. 101

No 18th-century schooling traced.

HELLINGLY   1724: 113 families   1801: pop. 936

<u>Village school</u>   (Rs: 1744, 1786, 1797)
James Davies, appointed vicar in 1742, had gained the approbation of the vestry by
announcing that he intended to build a school.[1] The churchwardens' accounts for the year
from Easter 1744 include the following:[2]
            for Diging & Carring three Loads of San for the Scool House 0. 5. 6.
            for Diging and Carring 7 Loads of Gravel and for getting
                  it into the Scool house and Ramming   0. 3. 0
There is a further reference to the school in the accounts for 1797:
            April 14   Mending the Church windows and for a
                        tin Cow for the School Chimney   1. 4. 6½
That the parish supported the teaching of poor children at the school, at least towards the
end of the century, is indicated by a note, dated 1786, on the inside front cover of the parish

register:[3]

Sacrament administer'd eight ['four' crossed through and 'eight' superscribed] Times in ye Year, id est Xst'ms, Easterday, Trinity Sunday, The Sunday subsequent to Michaelmas [and later inserted:] & the Sunday before or Sunday after each ....

The Sacrament Money is applied to ye School & ye Residue to old & indigent People of good Lives & Conversation. This is disposed off as the Curate may think most consistent wth the Institution.   1786

[*Samuel Gower?, John Parris?*]

1. Doff, E., pers. comm., citing BL Add MS 33,058, f 449; CI.   2. ESRO PAR 375/9/1.
3. ESRO PAR 375/1/1/3.

Other schoolmasters?

[Samuel Gower], schoolmaster at Hellingly 1803 (see Schedule 2).

[John Parris], schoolmaster at Hellingly 1813, and 'of Hellingly' at marriage January 1802, so perhaps schoolmaster there in 1800 (Hellingly PR).

HENFIELD   1724: about 100 families 1801: pop. 1,037

[Rothwell's boys' school]   (R: 1687)
John Rothwell, vicar of Henfield from 1686 to his death in 1705, was licensed in 1687 'to teach boys grammar in Latin or English, reading and writing in English, and arithmetic, in Henfield.'[1] It is very possible that he continued his school into the 18th century, though no specific reference of this has yet been traced.

1. De Candole, H. *The Story of Henfield* (1976), 184; CI.

[Woollgar's boys' school]   (R: 1692)
On 9 November 1692 William Woollgar was licensed to teach boys within the parish of Henfield in the rudiments of grammar, arithmetic, &c.[1] He may well have continued to teach at Henfield into the 18th century, though no specific reference of this has yet been traced.

1. WSRO Ep.I/1/10.

Dod's school   (R: 1707)
Henry Dod was identified as a schoolmaster of Henfield in an indenture of 1707.[1]

1. De Candole, op cit., 185.

Parish schooling   (Rs: 1786, 1788)
There was a schoolroom in the workhouse or almshouse in 1786, and in 1788 the master of the workhouse was specifically required to teach the pauper children to read, viz: 'Inventory of the Alms-house in the parish of Henfield 15 May 1786' includes:

In the School room
3 woolen wheels; 10 Spinning wheels; 2 Skain winders;
7 Chairs; 1 pair of Stock cards; 2 pair of Hand cards;
2 Stools; 1 Form.[1]

In an agreement dated 22 April 1788, between the churchwardens and overseers of Henfield, with 'Several others of the Principle Inhabitants', and Thos. Fillmer, whereby Fillmer was to take the poor of the parish, from 5 May 1788 to 13 April 1789, at 2s 3d per head per week, he agreed: '... to use his utmost endeavours to Instruct them in all Sorts of Spinning of Linen & Woollen Yarn; in picking & Combing and Sorting of Wooll; in knitting of hose and in teaching the Children to read; in Sending them to Church; in making them say prayers at Night & morning...'[2]

1. WSRO Par 100/37/2.   2. ibid.

Phillips' boys' boarding school   (F: 1785.   Rs: 1785- into 19c)
In December 1786 William Phillips, who had been master of the free school at Storrington
for 14 years, announced that he had opened a school at Henfield 'for the Board and
Education of Youth, in ENGLISH, WRITING in all its various Hands, ARITHMETIC,
GEOMETRY, the ITALIAN METHOD of BOOK KEEPING, &c. by W. PHILLIPS, and
proper Assistants, at TWELVE GUINEAS per Annum - Entrance, HALF-A-GUINEA. As
rendering Youth capable of transacting Business is the most beneficial Accomplishment, the
greatest Attention will be paid to Qualify every Pupil for such Stations of Life they are
likely to move in; and that a studious Attention will be paid to the Preservation of Health,
and the Advancement of Morals.'[1] In August 1787 he noted that his school had been opened
'for more than two Years since'. The terms given above now applied 'from 4 to 12 Years
of Age'; 'from 12 Years of Age and upwards, the Advance will be in Proportion.'[2] In June
1788 he noted that 'near his House there is a new School-Room erected, which is large,
light, and convenient, with a free Circulation of Air, &c.'[3] (In 1783, Thornton, at Horsham,
had announced a newly built schoolroom 'constructed upon such a Principle as to admit a
free Circulation of the Air'.[4]) Later in 1788, he stressed that: 'He has followed that Business
[schoolmastering] without any Variation or other Employment nearly Twenty Years.'[5]
(Parrott, at Petworth, had promoted a similar claim in 1784.[6]) In December 1789 the basic
fee of 12 guineas pa was limited to those aged from 4 to 11.[7] In December 1792 he
announced that 'he has lately taken (adjoining his House and School) an extensive PLAY
GROUND,   containing nearly an Acre and a Half of dry, healthy land, entirely for that
purpose'; and he referred to 'the great accomodations he has lately made in his House'.[8] In
December 1793 he announced that 'he has engaged a native of France, as an Assistant in his
School'; for the first time Latin and French were included in the curriculum (at additional
charges of 2 guineas a year), as were 'all Kinds of Mensuration' and land surveying. The
basic fee was up to 14 guineas pa.[9] (No sliding scale for fees was mentioned, but the fees
were clarified a year later: 14 guineas pa for those under 12; 'above twelve years, in
proportion to their ages'; residence at school at each vacation was 1 guinea.[10])
          On several occasions in his advertisements, Phillips announced both the
commencing and ending dates of holidays, which provides a good record of their actual
length (on other occasions, only the reopening date was given):[11]

		Commences	School reopens	
Midsummer:	1792	Thurs. 21 June	Mon. 23 July	(4½ weeks)
	1793	Thurs. 20 June	Mon. 22 July	(")
	1795	Thurs. 18 June	Mon. 20 July	(")
	1796	Thurs. 23 June	Mon. 25 July	(")
Christmas:	1792	Thurs. 20 December	Mon. 21 January	(")
	1793	Thurs. 19 December	Mon. 20 January	(")
	1794	Thurs. 18 December	Mon. 19 January	(")

          In June 1796 a short advertisement for the school (announcing the midsummer
holiday) ended: 'N.B. Orders for Land-surveying are requested to be sent a short time
previous to the Vacations, at which times Estates will be accurately surveyed and planned'.[12]
In August 1797 William Phillips' son Matthew, at Henfield, and James Phillips, at Horsham,
advertised 'that they purpose, jointly, carrying on the business of surveying and mapping
Estates'. They offered to show plans of estates, 'and the most satisfactory recommendations
obtained from many Gentlemen of respectability'; and ended: 'Young Gentlemen who are
to be instructed in any of the above branches [the different aspects of surveying], will have

an opportunity of much practical experience at Mr. Phillips' Boarding-School, Henfield, for which purpose a complete apparatus of mathematical instruments is kept.'[13] Advertisements for the school in 1798 and 1799 included a paragraph referring to 'M.Phillips, jun.' giving practical instruction in surveying to young gentlemen; and that in July 1799 announced 'The Business of LAND SURVEYING will as usual be attended to...'[14] An advertisement by M.Phillips in April 1800, under 'LAND SURVEYING', requested 'Gentlemen who entrust him with the survey of their Estates to give early notice of their commands, his scholastic employ preventing immediate attention to their favours' (he included a price list for surveying, by acreage).[15] In January 1802 the school was advertised by Messrs. Phillips and Son, under 'ACADEMY, HENFIELD'.[16] When William Phillips retired in 1802, Matthew ran the school until 1806.[17]

A 'wanted' advertisement in January 1800 required 'An Assistant, or Half Boarder, to take the third place in the School.'[18]

William Phillips' advertisement in July 1800 included a detailed account of the claim to adapt the teaching to each boy's needs:[19]

> Particular attention will be paid to the grammatical construction of the English and Latin Languages, and the method of instruction adapted to qualify each Pupil for whatever profession or situation he is designed. Such as are intended for a naval life, will be well instructed in Navigation; others in the business of farming, may have an opportunity of much practical experience in Surveying; and those appointed for the counting house, shop, or any commercial line, will be instructed, as if in actual employ, in Merchants Accompts, and such branches of Arithmetic, best calculated to form the ready accomptant and man of business.

Advertised in *SWA* Dec 1786; Apr, Aug 87; Jun, Dec 88; Dec 89; Jun, Dec 92; Jun, Dec 93; Dec 94; Jun 95; Jan, Jun 96; Aug 97; Jul 98; Jan, Jul (2), Dec 99; Jan, Jul 1800. [*William Phillips, Matthew Phillips*]

1. *SWA* 11.12.86.   2. *SWA* 27.8.87.   3. *SWA* 30.6.88.   4. *SWA* 14.4.83   5. *SWA* 29.12.88.
6. *SWA* 12.1.84.   7. *SWA* 28.12.89.   8. *SWA* 17.12.92.   9. *SWA* 16.12.93.   10. *SWA* 15.12.94.
11. *SWA* 11.6.92; 17.6.93; 15.6.95; 20.6.96; 17.12.92; 16.12.93; 15.12.94.   12. *SWA* 20.6.96.
13. *SWA* 14.8.97.   14. *SWA* 9.7.98; 14.1.99; 8.7.99.   15. *SWA* 7.4.1800.   16. *SWA* 4.1.1802.
17. De Candole, op cit., 184.   18. *SWA* 27.1.1800.   19. *SWA* 7.7.1800.

Burt's boys' boarding naval academy   (F: 1787)
Under the heading 'NAVAL ACADEMY, From LONDON', N. Burt announced that he proposed opening his academy at Henfield on 14 May 1787, 'for the instructing of Youth, in Reading, Writing, Arithmetic, and the Mathematics; as also to survey Coasts, Bays, Harbours, take the Appearance of Land, &c. and delineate the same; having served in the Royal Navy, on Board the famous Ship under the Command of the present first Lord of the Admiralty, therefore knows the Practice as well as the Theory of Navigation.' Perhaps because of his naval experience, he added: 'Those that please to Favour him with Boarders, may depend on their being tenderly treated, and full Allowance of good Provisions.' Terms were, for those that learn the mathematics, £20 pa and 1 guinea entrance; those that do not, £16 and the same entrance; 'Weekly, or Quarterly Scholars, at the usual Country Prices.'[1] [*N.Burt*]
1. *SWA* 30.4.87.

[Hunter and Taylor's girls' school]   (R: 1801)
By 1801 Mrs Hunter and Taylor had a girls' school at Henfield, but it is not known when this first opened.   [*Mrs Hunter, Mrs Taylor*]
1. *SWA* 11.1.1802.

Other schoolmaster

    Thomas Pointin, of Henfield, on 16 January 1722, began teaching Thomas
Marchant's son, William, at Hurstpierpoint, arithmetic three times a week for 2s 6d
a week. In April that year, he began teaching Bett, Marchant's daughter, arithmetic
for an additional 2s 6d a week; 'also M. Balcombe upon the same terms.'[1] (He was
also a surveyor, and later an excise officer.)
    1. *SAC* **25**, 191.

HERSTMONCEUX   1724: 93 families   1801: pop. 961

Allfrees' boys' and girls' boarding school   (F: c1766-8?.   Rs: 1771- into 19c)
The Allfrees' school is notable for being the earliest known boarding school in Sussex
offering a full education for both boys and girls. Edward Allfree and his wife Ann appear
to have first advertised the school in May 1771, but an advertisement in 1786 began: 'Mr.
and Mrs. ALLFREE, being impressed with a deep sense of Gratitude for the many
distinguished Marks of Approbation they have repeatedly received from their Friends,
through the considerable Space of twenty Years, for the eligible System of Education they
have adopted...'[1] And in 1793 they referred to the encouragement 'which their Schools have
received during the space of twenty-five years.'[2] The 1771 advertisement began: 'At a
convenient House, pleasantly situated, and a healthy Air, adjoining to the Turnpike road
from Lewes to Battle, is kept a BOARDING-SCHOOL, for YOUTH of both SEX, for
WRITING in all the most useful Hands; ARITHMETIC, both in whole Numbers and
Fractions, Vulgar and Decimal; GAUGING, &c. Likewise NEEDLE-WORK, in all its
Branches, by EDWARD and ANN ALLFREE...' At the end was noted: 'N.B. Land
accurately measured and beautifully mapp'd, with proper Decorations, and Coats of Arms;
also Timber and Buildings of any Sort.'[3] By May 1772 a dancing and music master was
attending 'constantly every week'.[4] In advertisements in 1777, after stressing 'their utmost
Care and Attention being paid to the Morals, as well as Education, of those young Ladies
and Gentlemen they may be honoured with', the educational arrangement was described:

    Mrs. ALLFREE, in her Department, teaches all the various Sorts of
    Needle-Work now made use of; and also the Tambour, and real Embroidery
    in Colours, as practised at the Schools in France.
    The young Gentlemen are taught by Mr. ALLFREE, in his
    Department, every Branch of Writing and Arithmetic, Timber Measuring,
    Land Surveying, Drawing Plans and Designs for Buildings, Measuring and
    Estimating the same, &c.

The terms were, for girls, 14 guineas pa, 'Writing, Tea and Sugar included' (writing and tea
were usually extras at girls' schools); entrance, half a guinea. For boys, 13 guineas pa;
entrance, half a guinea. Dancing was 15s per quarter, half a guinea entrance; music £1 10s
per quarter, half a guinea entrance.[5] In 1778 the boys' fees were increased to 16 guineas,[6]
but were back to 13 guineas in 1779.[7] By June 1780 the girls fees were, as before, 14
guineas, 'Tea, Sugar, Writing, and Accounts included' - it is interesting to see accounts in
their curriculum, and not as an extra. There were then two fees for boys: 'GENTLEMEN
are properly qualified for the University, at SIXTEEN GUINEAS per Annum, and ONE
GUINEA and a HALF Entrance. - Likewise English, Writing, the Mathematics, Use of the
Globes, &c. at THIRTEEN GUINEAS per Annum, and HALF a GUINEA Entrance.'[8] It
is not known if Edward Allfree went to university, but his son Edward Mott certainly went
to Oxford (and became a Minor Canon of Rochester and two of his sons went to
Cambridge); and another of Edward senior's sons, Henry Francis, also went to Oxford (he
died aged 24).[9]

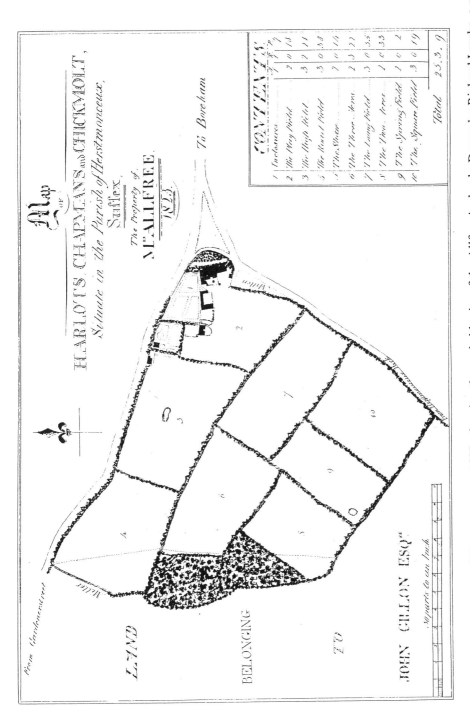

7.   Detail of an estate map of Herstmonceux, 1823, showing the probable site of the Allfrees' school. Drawn by Richard Lambe, a pupil at the school. (ESRO AMS 5879/1 p.11)

Ann Allfree died in 1780. In 1783 Edward Allfree, then aged 39, married Elizabeth Simmons, daughter of a Seaford blacksmith. She was only 17 when she married: in addition to running the girls' school, she had 13 children by Edward, seven sons and six daughters, none of whom appear to have died in infancy (three died as children), the first being baptised a little over a year after her marriage. Edward died in 1808, aged 64. Elizabeth apparently continued to own the school, at least to 1839. She died in 1850, aged 84.[10]

An advertisement for the school in 1786 contains the only known request of the time for advance notice of the removal of pupils, suggesting that the school was kept full: 'The several Apartments being established upon the exactest Regularity, Mr. and Mrs. ALLFREE hope their Friends will grant them the Indulgence of previous Information at each Vacation, of their intended Favours, in order to preclude every Inconveniency which may arise; and at the same Time the Period when they propose, from their Progression in Learning, to leave the School.'[11]

Advertisements in the summer of 1790 announced that Mr Allfree had 'lately compleated a spacious School-room', and also highlighted French [later than many schools]: 'As the FRENCH LANGUAGE has obtained a general admission into the more polite circles of conversation, Mrs. Allfree means, after the present vacation, to introduce into her school a French Teacher.'[12] In April 1793 [France had declared war in February], they noted: 'As the French language is now become almost a necessary part of education, they take this opportunity of informing the public that they have engaged a gentleman, who has taken his degrees in the University of Paris, to superintend that branch of literature.' They added: 'The Classics are taught by a Clergyman of the University of Cambridge; and Writing, Accompts, Surveying, Drawing and Designs for Buildings, &c. by Mr. ALLFREE, and proper assistants.'[13]

Advertisements for the school in May 1793 included an announcement of the date of Mr Thring's Ball, presumably at the school, and Mr and Mrs Allfree invited all their 'Friends' [ie. the parents] 'to favour them with their company'.[14] John Thring was a dancing and music master based at Lewes. In May 1797, under the heading 'HERSTMONCEUX ACADEMY', was announced 'MR. RICHARD's BALL for the young Ladies and Gentlemen under his tuition', and 'Mr. ALLFREE will be happy to see as many of his Friends as shall be pleased to honour him with their company. N.B. The Ball will open between five and six o'clock.'[15]

In 1798 Mrs Allfree advertised for an additional (lady) teacher: 'No one need apply who is not well acquainted with the French language, and is not a good English Scholar.'[16]

A workbook of Richard Lambe, a pupil at the school, has survived; dated 1822 and 1823 (when he was 15/16), it features excellent penmanship, maps, architectural drawings, and includes an estate map of 'Harlots, Chapmans and Chickmolt / Situate in the Parish of Herstmonceux, / Sussex, / The Property of / MRS. ALLFREE / 1823.'[17]

In view of the success of the Allfrees' boys' and girls' boarding school, it is interesting that two of Edward and Elizabeth's children - John, then aged 31, and Mary Ann, then aged 24 - had, by 1822, established adjacent boarding schools for boys and girls in Gloucester Place, Brighton.[18]

Advertised in *SWA* May (2) 1771; May 72; May(2), June 77; Oct, Nov, Dec 78; Jan (2), May (2) 79; Jun, Jul 80; Jan 82; Nov, Dec 86; Jul (3) 90; Apr (3), May (2), Jul (3) 93; Jun (2) Jul 94; Jan 95; May 97; Aug (2) 98; Jan (2) 1800.

[*Edward Allfree, Ann Allfree, Elizabeth Allfree, John Thring* (dancing master), *Richards* (dancing master)]

1. *SWA* 20.11.86.   2. *SWA* 8.4.93.   3. *SWA* 13.5.71.   4. *SWA* 11.5.72.   5. *SWA* 19.5.77.
6. *SWA* 12.10.78.   7. *SWA* 24.5.79.   8. *SWA* 19.6.80.   9. *Al.Oxon.; Al.Cant.*; Herstmonceux PR.

10. Herstmonceux PR; *SRS* **25**, 7; ESRO TD/E 89 - Herstmonceux.   11. *SWA* 20.11.86.
12. *SWA* 5.7.90.   13. *SWA* 8.4.93.   14. *SWA* 20.5.93.   15. *SWA* 8.5.97.   16. *SWA* 20.8.98.
17. ESRO AMS 5879/1.   18. At 11 and 14 Gloucester Place respectively, *Baxter's Directory* 1822, 1824;
identified by christian names in *Pigot's Directory* 1828 (and Herstmonceux PR), Mary Ann then having moved her
school to King's Rd.; by 1832, *Swaysland's Directory*, her school was at 15 Cannon Place, John's at 10 Gloucester
Place.

HEYSHOTT   1724: 25 families   1801: pop. 275
(HEIGHSHOT, HEDSHOT, HIGHLISHOT)

No 18th-century schooling traced.

HOLLINGTON   1724: about 30 families   1801: pop. 208

No 18th-century schooling traced.

HOOE   1724: between 40 and 50 families 1801: pop. 424

Croft's girls' boarding school   (F: 1793)
In September 1793 'Mrs. Croft and Co.' announced 'that they have opened a French and
English Boarding School, for young Ladies, in the village of HOOE... where they teach the
best of plain and all sorts of fashionable works, drawing, in its various branches, writing and
arithmetic, at the terms as follows: Young Ladies from four to ten years of age, Ten
Guineas per annum; all above ten years, Twelve Guineas. No Entrance. N.B. The strictest
care and attention will be paid to the morals of the young Ladies.'[1]   [*Mrs Croft*]
1. *SWA* 30.9.93.

HORSHAM   1724: (parish) about 130 families 1801: pop. (borough & parish) 3,204

Collyer's grammar school[1]   (F: 1541.   Rs: through 18c)
The school was founded under the will of Richard Collyer, who died 1533, though, for
testamentary reasons, the school was not set up until 1541. It was to be a free school, for
60 scholars, who were to be at no charge for their schooling, with preference given when
selecting the scholars to the poor of Horsham and its neighbouring parishes. The master
was to have £10 a year and the usher 10 marks [£6 13s 4d]. The Mercers Company were
trustees; they paid the salaries, repaired the school, and had the right to confirm the master
and usher in office.   The master and scholars were to be chosen by the vicar and
churchwardens of Horsham parish church, together with eight 'of the moost honest men of
the said p'ishe' for choosing the master and two such honest men for choosing the scholars.
The school flourished in the 17th century, the number of boys (not all of them poor men's
sons) reaching 'neare an hundred' in 1666. During the 18th century the school suffered a
decline, to the point of being 'entirely deserted by scholars, the Master and Usher alone
remaining.'
          Collyer's will gave no details of what was to be taught in his free school, but he
clearly intended it to be a grammar school; his intention was so described in a court case
in the 16th century, and it was operated as such in the 17th; visitation returns for 1737 and
1742 state that Latin was taught at the school.[2] This led to difficulties in the 18th century:
the salary available was considered too meagre to attract a master of sufficient education,
and the appointment was usually given to beneficed clergymen, to whom it was an
additional emolument; moreover, as schoolmasters, they could gain more from private
pupils, letting the number of free scholars decline with the connivance or apathy of the
trustees and the parish. As an additional factor, a grammar school education became, during
this century, increasingly less attractive to poor men for their sons, or indeed to tradesmen.

Alexander Hay, vicar of Itchingfield, was appointed master in 1700. (He involved the school in litigation with the powerful Michell family, as a result of which the school lost the bulk of its orchard and a slice of the schoolhouse.) Hay resigned in 1706 and Thomas Pittis, rector of Warnham, was appointed. He died in 1712; Rev Peter Stockar, a young man, was the next master, but he was 'tempted from us' by a better preferment after only a few months. Next was John Reynell, vicar of Horsham, who died in 1722. He was followed, after a contested election, by Francis Osgood, at one time curate of Westmeston, who had come to Horsham as assistant to Reynell and had married one of the latter's daughters; he was master for 51 years. From 1722 to 1744 he was also rector of Saltfleet by St Peter in Lincolnshire; at his death he had farms at Nuthurst, Hurstpierpoint and Twineham. William Jameson, curate of Horsham, was appointed master in 1773; he was also rector of Clapham from 1788, and vicar of Horsham from 1796; he resigned as master in 1806.

In 1733 there were about 50 boys at the school, 'Taught ye Grammar, Writing and Accompts';[3] but the school was moribund by the middle of the century. Referring to the period of a Chancery case between the parish, led by the vicar, and the Company (concerning the Company's liability, if any, to use the surplus from the charity for the upkeep of local Horsham roads) which lasted from 1749 to 1758, which the parish eventually lost, the Company later recorded (in 1869) that at that time the school had been 'entirely deserted by scholars, the Master and Usher alone remaining.' In 1793 there was, in a national directory, an unusual public condemnation: 'Here is likewise a free-school, and other charitable gifts, which are most shamefully abused.'[4] In 1807 the school was referred to as 'a school wholly without scholars'. But in 1807-8 the Company and parish combined to revive the school. Throughout the 18th century the master's salary had been £30; in 1808 it was increased to £110.[5] It is interesting to note that in 1817 the master, Rev Thomas Williams, told Carlisle: 'I take pupils but never more than two at once whom I fit for the Universities, my terms being Two Hundred Guineas for each per annum';[6] there were then 60 free scholars, so a single private pupil brought in to the master nearly twice as much as all 60 free scholars. The usher's salary had been £20 through the 18th century; in 1808 it was increased to £66 13s 4d.[7] And from 1809 the school was filled again with its 60 children of poor parents, who were given an elementary education, 'and competition for places was so intense that the wardens even had to exclude brothers, on the grounds that a family could not expect to be favoured more than once.'[8]

In 1813, by the Lord Chancellor's decree, the foundation school formally ceased to be a grammar school: it was to be for the education of 60 local poor boys, aged 8-14, who were to be taught reading, writing and arithmetic, and the principles of religion, and sent to be catechised in the church - though the decree added, 'Also that any number of boys at the discretion of the Schoolwardens, be also taught the Latin language.' [In 1819, only four boys were learning Latin, 'the boys being selected chiefly from the lower orders'.[9]]

[*Richard Hunt, Alexander Hay, Thomas Pittis, Peter Stockar, John Reynell, Francis Osgood, Charles Hunt sen., William Jameson, Charles Hunt jun., Richard Collins*]

1. Except where otherwise noted, all the facts in this summary (but not necessarily the interpretation) are from Willson, A.N. *History of Collyer's School 1532-1964* (1965).   2. WSRO Ep.I/22/1.   3. ibid.
4. *Univ. Brit. Directory* 1793.   5. *EP2* (1819), 169.   6. Willson, op cit., 124, citing Carlyle II, 601.
7. *EP2* (1819) 169.   8. Willson, op cit., 122.   9. *EP2* (1819), 169.

School   (R: 1714)
John Knight, yeoman of Horsham, died in May 1714. His probate inventory shows that there was a schoolroom in his house (with 2 tables, 3 forms and 1 chair). One of the bedrooms in the house was identified as 'the Schoole Chamber', which suggests that the

school was well established there. From Knight's circumstances as shown in his will and inventory, it is unlikely that he was also a schoolmaster: he probably made the schoolroom available for schooling Baptist children - the leading Horsham General Baptists were beneficiaries under or overseers of his will. One beneficiary was John Tasker, blacksmith (qv Schedule 2); he was a Baptist and was described a few years later as a schoolmaster, and perhaps taught at the school in Knight's house as a young man (he was 26 when Knight died).[1] [*John Tasker?*]

1. WSRO Ep.I/29/106/347, STC I/31 f501; Caffyn, J.M. *Sussex Believers* (1988).

Charity schooling   (Rs: 1716, 1718)

In a letter of 13 November 1716, John Reynell, vicar of Horsham and also master of Collyer's school, advised the SPCK 'That he has been very desirous of erecting a Charity School there [Horsham], But the Misshap is, most of the Inhabitants are but in a mean Condic'on. That however at present there are several poor Children maintained at School on Private Charitys, and by the help of some of the Comunion money. That in a few yrs he hopes to advance to a publick Establishment.'[1] He wrote again on 15 April 1718 to similar effect: 'That notwithstanding all his Endeavours he can't get a Cha: School settled there, tho' a great Market Town, but there are many poor Children kept to School and to Work by the Charity of some private Persons, & by the Assistance of some of the Comunion Money.'[2] On the basis of the first of these letters, the SPCK rather optimistically listed one charity school at Horsham from 1717, identifying the foundation date, in the *Account* for 1724, as '1716'.

1. SPCK ALB v.7, 5001.   2. SPCK ALB v.8, 5572.

Workhouse school   (Rs: 1734, 1773, 1774)

An inventory of the workhouse, made on 4 June 1734, included:[1]

In the School Room marked No.7

Four Formes.   1 pair of Iron Grafted to the Chimney.   1 Table

In the overseers' accounts for 1774 there is the following entry:[2]

Mar 6   Pd for Books for the School at
             Workhouse   -. 13. 4

John Baker, a solicitor of the Inner Temple who, in 1773, was then 61 and living at Horsham, included in his diary for 20 May 1773 the following entry:

> I walked down after noon to Church Walk and after Church Yard, where all the workhouse children came about me in so free a manner as I never saw in children, pulling the seals of my watch. One little Nancy Taylor, daughter of the man who keeps it, the very picture of Nancy Bannister at Mrs. Bellnott's. She said she went to Mrs. Hunt's school, being a little above the rest... one Nanny Offard (or so pronounced it) the most comical free little thing I ever saw... one Churchman, of 10 or 11 years old, the ugliest hard-faced Devil my eyes ever beheld - about 15 or 16 of them in all, playing, sprawling and tumbling about like little puppies.[3]

1. WSRO Par 106/31/1, f[166].   2. WSRO Par 106/31/3, f[10 - '8' old pag.].   3. Yorke, P.C. *The Diary of John Baker* (1931), 259; Blunt, W.S., 'Extracts from Mr. John Baker's Horsham Diary', *SAC* **52**, 54.

Thornton's boys' boarding school   (F: c1765.   Rs: c1765- into 19c)

In December 1786 Richard Thornton claimed that his school had 'flourished above Twenty years',[1] and in January 1793 that it had been 'established near Thirty Years',[2] giving an opening date around 1765. (He was of Mickleham, Surrey, schoolmaster, when he married in Horsham in 1763.)

Richard Thornton was an entrepreneur, with energy and imagination, was later involved in politics, and became Bailiff of the Borough (see Schedule 2). His school was very successful. Although his local opposition was only the moribund grammar school, he was a notable innovator - his ideas and promotional gambits were copied by other schools throughout the county - and his flair for profitable response to the educational market of the time makes the development of his school of considerable interest.

He made extensive use of advertisements in *SWA*. From 1775 to 1778 these were modest:

At HORSHAM in SUSSEX

YOUNG Gentlemen are Boarded and Educated in English, Writing, Arithmetic, and Mathematics, together with the Elements of Natural and Experimental Philosophy, the Italian Method of Book-keeping, Geography, with the Construction and Use of Maps, Charts, &c. the Use of the Globes, and the Rudiments of Astronomy,

By RICHARD THORNTON.

To which he added a specific pitch for the sons of tradesmen and the like:

As Writing, with a due Knowledge of Accounts, and the Practical Parts of the Mathematics, are the most eligible Accomplishments that a Person in Business can be Master of, therefore the greatest Attention will be paid to qualify every Pupil for that Station in Life for which he is designed.[3]

Benjamin Hearnden in 1769 and Cater Rand in 1773, both at Lewes, had specifically promoted their schools for qualifying boys for business; but Phillips at Henfield, advertising in 1786, appears to have copied closely from Thornton: 'As rendering Youth capable of transacting Business is the most beneficial Accomplishment, the greatest Attention will be paid to Qualify every Pupil for such Stations of Life they are likely to move in.'

Thornton's terms were, in 1777, as follows:

The Terms from Four Years of Age to Fourteen for Board, Education, Washing, &c. are TWELVE GUINEAS per Annum, and ONE GUINEA Entrance. - From Fourteen Years or upwards, in Proportion to their Ages.
☞ Any one continuing at the School either of the Vacations, which are Christmas and Whitsuntide, a Fortnight each Time, to pay Half a Guinea at each Vacation.[4]

This is the first reference we have to differential fees by age, later adopted by several schools, including Wilbar at Brighton (1786), Mercer at Ninfield (1792), Sanders at Brighton (1793), Mrs Croft at Hooe (1793), Mrs Norton at Preston (1796). This is also the first reference we have in Sussex to accomodating, for a fee, children left at the school during the holidays, which became a common practice in private schools.

The holidays, of a fortnight each, were short: by 1783 Thornton had increased them to three weeks, still at Christmas and Whitsuntide; and by 1790 to 'a month each time', at Christmas and - like the other schools - midsummer.[6] The vacation charge was, by 1783, increased to 15s, and by 1790, to 1 guinea.[7]

Thornton was, in Sussex, the first to promote the boys' access to a general library, and to daily newspapers. In April 1783 he noted -

In this School are introduced the best ENGLISH Authors, the Daily Papers, History, &c. and the greatest Care will be taken that they are read with Propriety... A select Library is kept for the Use of the School.[8]

This idea was taken up by Goldring at Petworth later that year (the best authors and newspapers: December 1783) and by Williams at Burwash the following year (library and newspapers: 1784).

Thornton was, in 1783, the first to make a special claim for geography:

A proper Attention will also be paid to GEOGRAPHY, as without its Assistance, we cannot read any History with Profit, nor so much as understand the common News-Papers.[9]

And in 1783, Thornton's was the first boys' school so far traced in Sussex to offer tea as an optional extra: 'Such as have Tea for Breakfast, to pay ONE GUINEA per Ann. extraordinary.' By the 1790s five other boys' schools were offering tea as an extra. (As early as 1777, at the Allfrees' school at Herstmonceux, 'Tea and Sugar' for the girls had been included under the basic fee.)

In this same advertisement Thornton noted - as all schools did - the healthy location and accessibility to London:

> The House is very large, commodious and elegant, and the Situation is in the most open and pleasant Part of the Town of HORSHAM, commanding an extensive, pleasing Prospect, and is allowed to be one of the healthiest Places in the Kingdom.
>
> Next to the House is an extensive Play-Ground; adjoining to which is an elegant School Room, 48 feet by 28, (newly built) and constructed upon such a Principle as to admit of a free Circulation of the Air.

(The claim of a 'free Circulation of Air' in a newly-built schoolroom was also made later by Phillips at Henfield, in 1788.)

> HORSHAM is situated on a pleasant Turnpike Road, from LONDON to BRIGHTHELMSTON, 36 miles from the former, and 20 from the latter; and is well accomodated with Stage Coaches, and other Conveniences.

The advertisement included an unusual offer:

> Gentlemen who chuse a separate Apartment may be genteely accomodated.

A music and dancing-master was then in attendance, and by the end of the year, 'A FENCING, MUSIC and DANCING MASTER'.[10]

About this time Thornton obtained for his school the old gaol, fronting on the Carfax. The new gaol came into use in 1779; it was decided in 1782 that the old gaol, which had been condemned by John Howard, should be sold by auction and Lady Irwin bought it for £620, mainly because it carried a burgage vote - though because the remaining trustees had not the power to convey it, a special act of parliament had to be passed, which was not done until January 1787.[11] It is not known when Thornton occupied the old gaol. At the general election in 1790, he was 'of the Scarfox, schoolmaster'.[12]

By September 1786 French and Latin were available as extras, at 2 guineas pa each; 'and to establish a pure and elegant Method of speaking the French Language, a Native of France constantly resides in the House to superintend the Conversation of the Pupils.'[13] Thornton's was the first school in Sussex to announce a resident French teacher. Similar claims were made by Mossop at Brighton in 1787, and Phillips at Henfield in 1793 (in 1787 Raymond opened his French academy at Lewes where 'French is the only Language allowed to be spoken among the Scholars' (except on Sundays), and - among the girls' schools - at Mrs Phillips at Arundel in 1788, 'French is the general Language of her School', and at Miss Rockett's at Hastings in 1793, 'French is the only language that is allowed to be spoken among the Scholars'.)

In 1786, 'Such as have Tea for Breakfast, or an extra Change of Linen, to pay One Guinea a Year extraordinary.'[14]

By the end of 1786 the school was advertised as 'Mr. Thornton's Academy' (later as 'Horsham Academy') and, in addition to Latin and French, Greek had been added to the curriculum.[15]

A paper sheet with printed illustrated frame and heading, 'The Five Senses', with a handwritten 4-line verse, subscribed 'Francis Woodhatch - 1794 - Horsham Academy', has survived (WSRO E102K/19/89).

From about 1790 the school performed an annual play at Christmas: a report in

SWA in December 1800 begins: 'In the course of last week the young gentlemen of Horsham Academy (as they have been accustomed to do for about ten years past) performed a play and a farce.'[16] This is the only record of a school performing regularly each year, but there are records of earlier school plays - by Joel's school at Chichester in 1773 and Clowes' school at Chichester in 1778. In October 1794 the boys of a Brighton boarding school performed, as their first attempt in public, *George Barnwell* and *The Miller of Mansfield*;[17] the same tragedy and farce were performed by Thornton's boys the following year.[18] The *SWA* of 5 January 1795 reviewed the Thornton play for that year as follows:

> On Saturday last was performed by the young gentlemen of Messrs. Thornton's academy, the first part of King Henry the Fourth; the character of Falstaff, by Master Cornelys, - Prince Henry, by Master Challen, - Hotspur, by Master Hitchener, - and Douglas, by Master Lucas, - were supported with great propriety; and the other characters acquitted themselves very much to the satisfaction of the Gentry and Inhabitants of the town of Horsham, at whose particular request it was performed again the Monday following.

The review of the plays given at Christmas 1800 (the tragedy of *The Distressed Mother*, and *The village Lawyer*) included mention of what must be yet another Thornton first - the school raising money for local charities:

> The admission to these little theatricals have been heretofore gratuitous; but the present year's admission was by tickets at one shilling each. And the gross receipt, amounting to nearly twenty pounds, was distributed amongst the debtors in Horsham gaol [a well-supported Christmas charity of the time], and a select number of the most deserving objects of charity in the parish of Horsham.[19]

So - unless some of those attending donated more than the 1s entrance - nearly 400 tickets were sold.

By the beginning of 1792 Thornton had been joined by his son, James,[20] and in 1793 the school was described as 'Messrs. Thornton and Son's Academy'.[21] In 1801 James Thornton was appointed usher of Collyer's school, but as that school had no pupils, he was able to draw the usher's salary and still continue to assist his father at the Thornton academy. He also had the usher's house at Collyer's, and for some years early in the 19th century was involved in a legal conflict with that school over the validity of his appointment as usher (and therefore of his salary) and continued occupancy of the usher's house.

Thornton would only take boarders, at least by 1790,[22] and in 1795 announced, 'The number of young Gentlemen is now limited to Sixty.'[23] The terms for boys aged four to 14 were then 14 guineas pa, 2 guineas more than in the early days of the school; and parlour boarders were now accomodated at 20 guineas pa.[24] Dancing and music were extras at 15s per quarter each.[25]

> Navigation was in the curriculum, at least by 1790, and was emphasised in 1799:[26]
> ... Navigation, the use of the Octant and Sextant, with the new method of finding the Latitude by double Altitudes of the Sun, and by the Meridian Altitude of the Moon, or fixed Stars; also the method of determining the Longitude at Sea, by the Moon's distance from the Sun, or a fixed Star, according to the latest and most approved methods...

The price of food had greatly increased in recent years; in 1796 one Horsham school had increased its fees by 2 guineas pa, 'In consideration of the great advance in price of almost every article of daily consumption'.[27] In 1799 Thornton's basic fee had increased by a guinea, to 15 guineas pa (though only 1 guinea pa extra was now charged for French or Latin),[28] and in January 1800 he announced: 'If the present high price of provisions should continue, an extra charge of One Guinea will be made for the ensuing half year';[29] and the surcharge was confirmed that July.[30]

Some of Thornton's advertisements were long - that for 1799 ran to 44 lines - and tended to cumulate the various items discussed separately above. His success would appear to be due to his offering, at very reasonable prices, the kind of schooling for which there was a demand, and to his imaginative attention to detail and to promotion.

The school was extensively advertised in *SWA*, viz: Dec (2) 1775; Mar (2), May, Jun, Dec (2) 76; Mar (2), May (2), Nov (2) 77; Apr (2), Oct (2), Dec 78; Jan, Dec 79; Jan, May (2) 80; Apr, Oct (2), Dec 83; Jan 84; Sep, Dec (2) 86; Jan (2) 87; Mar (2), Jul (2), Sep, Dec 89; Jan, Jun, Jul 90; Jan (3), Jul (2) 91; Jan, Jul 92; Jan 93; Jan (2) 94; Jan, Jul (2), Dec 95; Jan 96; Jul (2) 97; Jan (2) 98; Jan (2), Jul 99; Jan, Mar, Jun, Jul 1800. Also in *The Lewes & Brighthelmston Pacquet* Jan 1790.

[*Richard Thornton, James Thornton*]

1. *SWA* 18.12.86. 2. *SWA* 14.1.93. 3. *SWA* 18.12.75. 4. *SWA* 10.11.77. 5. *SWA* 14.4.83.
6. *SWA* 14.4.83; *Lewes & Brighthelmston Pacquet* 7.1.90 (*Pacquet* hereafter). 7. ibid. 8. *SWA* 14.4.83.
9. ibid. 10. *SWA* 29.12.83. 11. Willson, op cit. 107; Albery, W. *A Millenium of Facts in the History of Horsham and Sussex 947-1947* (1947), 395-6. 12. Albery, W. *A Parliamentary History of Horsham 1295-1885* (1927), 159. 13. *SWA* 25.9.86. 14. ibid. 15. *SWA* 18.12.86. 16. *SWA* 22.12.1800.
17. *SWA* 20.10.94. 18. *SWA* 21.12.95. 19. *SWA* 22.12.1800. 20. *SWA* 16.1.92. 21. *SWA* 14.1.93.
22. *Pacquet*. 23. *SWA* 5.1.95. 24. ibid. 25. *SWA* 28.12.95. 26. *Pacquet*; *SWA* 7.1.99.
27. Mr & Mrs Dubbins' school: *SWA* 4.1.96. 28. *SWA* 7.1.99. 29. *SWA* 13.1.1800.
30. *SWA* 14.7.1800.

Mrs Hunt's school   (R: 1773)

Referred to by John Baker in his diary, 20 May 1773.[1] Nancy Taylor, daughter of the workhouse governor, went there. (For a transcript of the entry, see <u>Workhouse school</u> above.)

1. Yorke, op cit., 259.

Morfoot's school   (R: 1778)

According to a report in *SWA* (4.1.79), the following is an exact copy of an advertisement that had been nailed to a tree near Horsham:

> Shaving's Dun here for a Penny, Each Pursson
> Likewise Children carefully Edicated in Reading
> Righting, & Account at this House by me
>   JAMES MORFOOT.
> To begin One Monday the 12th Octr. 1778.

[*James Morfoot*]

Mrs Waller's girls' boarding school   (F: 1781.   Rs: 1781-95)

Mrs Waller announced that she would open her girls' boarding school on Monday, 15 January 1781, 'where YOUNG LADIES will be taught Embroidery, Point, and every Kind of Needle Work, Netting, &c. and to read English with Propriety.' Her terms were 12 guineas a year, with 1 guinea entrance. Writing and arithmetic were included. Dancing was an optional extra.[1]

By 1784 she had 'proper Assistants', and the curriculum now included French ('... to educate them in the true Reading and Pronunciation of the ENGLISH and FRENCH LANGUAGES...'). Needle-work (now including clothwork), English, French, writing and arithmetic, were all covered by the basic fee of 12 guineas pa. Parlour boarders were 2 guineas a year extra.[2] In 1786, dancing and music were 15s a quarter each.[3]

By 1789, board and education, writing and arithmetic were covered by the basic fee of 12 guineas (with 1 guinea entrance), but French had become an extra, at 2 guineas pa. Parlour boarders were 14 guineas pa, as before (with 1 guinea entrance), and dancing and music 15s a quarter each (with no entrance). 'Horsham is an airy and healthy Situation, with Stages to and from London every day.'[4]

By January 1794 she had taken a new house, 'in an airy and pleasant situation, in the same town, and every way convenient, and calculated for a BOARDING SCHOOL... Stage Coaches pass the door, from London to Brighton, every day, it being 36 miles from the former, and 20 miles from the latter.' Geography was now included in the basic curriculum, and it was noted that French (2 guineas extra) was taught by an assistant 'who received her education in France'. Music was up to 1 guinea a quarter, with 1 guinea entrance.[5]

The last advertisement by Mrs Waller to appear in *SWA* was in January 1795. (See also George Waller's school below, who was almost certainly her husband. He was at marriage an innholder, and was bankrupt April 1778, shortly before Mrs Waller started her school.) Advertised in *SWA* Dec 1780; Sep 84; Dec 86; Jan (2), Jul 87; Jan 88; Jun 89; Jan 91; Jan, Mar, Jul 94; Jan 95.
[*Ann Waller*]
1. *SWA* 25.12.80.   2. *SWA* 27.9.84.   3. *SWA* 25.12.86.   4. *SWA* 29.6.89.   5. *SWA* 13.1.94.

Mrs Jones' girls' boarding school   (Rs: 1782-4)
Under the heading 'A BOARDING SCHOOL for Young LADIES, at HORSHAM, in SUSSEX', Mrs Jones, widow of the Rev Mr Jones, late of Slinfold (he was curate at his death there in 1776), announced in July 1782 'That she opens her School, after the Vacation, on Monday 23d of July, in a new commodious House...' - suggesting that she had kept a school before. '... and with the Assistance of proper Masters, will board, and teach Young Ladies ENGLISH, FRENCH, Tambour, Embroidery, and all Sorts of Needle-Work, at SIXTEEN GUINEAS per YEAR, and ONE GUINEA Entrance. - Writing and Dancing to be paid for separate.'[1] In 1783 geography, music and arithmetic were added to the optional extras.[2] In 1784 she noted that 'Parlour Boarders may be accomodated with a private Apartment.'[3] [*Mrs Jones*]
1. *SWA* 22.7.82.   2. *SWA* 21.7.83.   3. *SWA* 19.1.84.

Mrs (later Mr and Mrs) Dubbins' girls' boarding and day school   (Rs: 1786- into 19c)
In October 1786 Mrs Dubbins advertised her boarding school as follows:
> YOUNG LADIES are genteelly boarded and carefully instructed in every Kind of NEEDLE-WORK, the ENGLISH and FRENCH LANGUAGES, WRITING, and ARITHMETIC, at FOURTEEN GUINEAS per Annum. - Parlour Boarders, SIXTEEN GUINEAS. - Entrance, ONE GUINEA.
> No Boys are admitted; nor any DAY SCHOLARS under TWELVE SHILLINGS per Quarter.
> The House is very large and commodious, being erected purposely for a School, in a pleasant, airy Situation, with a good Garden and Play Ground behind; the whole unconnected with any other Premises, and in all Respects calculated for Health as well as Pleasure.
> Parents and others, who shall place Young Ladies under Mrs. DUBBINS's Tuition, may depend on the utmost Assiduity being exerted, to improve them in all the above Branches of useful and polite Education; and that a studious Attention will be paid to the Preservation of Health, and the Advancement of Morals.
> MUSIC and DANCING to be paid for separately.
> The Vacations are MIDSUMMER and CHRISTMAS.[1]

It is interesting that the house had been built 'purposely for a School', and rare to find 'Pleasure' referred to in such an advertisement.

In 1788 Mrs Dubbins advertised for a teacher of the French language, 'Who must be a Person of strict Morals, steady Disposition, and affable Behaviour; and will be more eligible if not very young.'[2] By 1789, 'Each Lady is expected to bring half a Dozen Towels.'[3]

From December 1790 Mr Dubbins was joined with his wife in advertisements for their girls' boarding school.[4] In January 1791 they strongly advocated the gentle approach to teaching -

> The Pupils will be treated with great kindness, not only from principles of humanity, but from a thorough conviction, founded on observation and experience, that more beneficial effects will ever be wrought in juvenile minds by mild persuasion and rational argument, than by the cruel severity of harsh discipline. - Great care will be taken to regulate their sentiments respecting religion and morality; and the preservation of health will be ever studiously attended to.[5]

The same advertisement advocated a broader approach to girls' education (perhaps made practical at this school by Mr Dubbins' participation) than was usual in the 18th century, and appears to have been unique in Sussex at that time:

> Exclusive of the customary instructions in Needle-Work, Writing, and Arithmetic, and an accurate attention to the grammatical construction and correct pronunciation of the English and French Languages, the Outlines of the Sciences of HISTORY, CHRONOLOGY, GEOGRAPHY, ASTRONOMY, and NATURAL HISTORY, will be taught in the School. For, though it be the commonly received opinion, that a complete knowledge of the above Sciences is unnecessary for the Female Sex in general; yet it must be acknowledged that most People will deem it an advantage not to be wholly ignorant of them.

Drawing was now included among the optional extras. By the end of 1793 French had become an extra: 'For instruction in the French Language, One Guinea extra per Annum is charged to Boarders, and Half a Guinea per Annum to Day Scholars... Dancing, Music, and Drawing, are taught by approved Masters; Dancing and Music by the eminent Mr. HOLLOWAY, of Newington.'[6]

In January 1796 fees were raised because of inflation:

> In consideration of the great advance in price of almost every article of daily consumption, it is hoped and presumed, that every intelligent Friend will think it reasonable that the terms of Schools should be raised, so as to afford a proper compensation to the Instructors, and enable them to treat their Pupils equitably, without injury to themselves.[7]

The fees were now as follows:

> Entrance, One Guinea.
> Board and Education, exclusive of the French Language, 16 Guineas per annum. [Up 2 guineas.]
> Instruction in the French Language, 2 Guineas per annum. [Up 1 guinea.]
> Tea, One Guinea per annum. [Not previously mentioned.]
> Residence at the School, during either of the Vacations, 2 Guineas. [Not previously mentioned.]
> Music, One Guinea per quarter, and One Guinea Entrance. [Terms not previously given.]
> Dancing, and Drawing, each 15s. per Quarter, and 10s.6d. Entrance. [Terms not previously given.]
> Each lady is desired to bring 6 napkins.

Day-Scholars, 12s. per Quarter, exclusive of the French Language, which
is an extra charge of 10s.6d. per Quarter. [Basic fee, no change;
French up 1½ guineas.]
The vacations are at Midsummer and Christmas, one Month each.
In July 1800 'Writing and Arithmetic' became an extra, at 2 guineas pa. And notice was
given of extra charges that would have to be made for food (see Thornton's school above
for the increase made by Thornton for the same reason at this same time):

The late unprecedented high price of provisions, &c. having prevented
the Managers of Schools from being even indemnified, during the last half-
year, it is humbly presented that no friend will, without a specific demand,
object to making an extra allowance, proportionate to extra expences, till
the prices shall be again reduced to a moderate standard.[8]

And in January 1801 Mr and Mrs Dubbins were charging an extra half a guinea per quarter
(the same as Thornton) owing to the high cost of provisions.[9]

Although from 1790 the school was advertised by 'Mr. and Mrs. Dubbins', the
Univ. Directory for 1793 listed it under 'Mrs. Dubbins'. The school was advertised
extensively in *SWA*, viz: Oct 1786; Jan (3), Jul (2) 87; Jan, Jun, Jul 88; Jan, Jun, Jul, Dec
89; Jan, Jul (2), Dec 90; Jan, Jul (2) 91; Jan (2), Jul (2) 92; Jan (2), Jul (2), Dec 93; Jan,
Jun, Jul, Dec 94; Jan, Jun, Jul 95; Jan (2), Jul (2) 96; Jan (2), Jul (2) 97; Jan (2), Jul 98;
Jan, Jul 99; Jan, Jul 1800; (Jan 1801).
[*Mrs Dubbins, Mr Dubbins, Mr Holloway* (dancing and music master)]
1. *SWA* 16.10.86.   2. *SWA* 30.6.88.   3. *SWA* 29.6.89.   4. *SWA* 27.12.90.   5. *SWA* 24.1.91.
6. *SWA* 30.12.93.   7. *SWA* 4.1.96.   8. *SWA* 7.7.1800.   9. *SWA* 12.1.1801.

Sunday school   (F: 1787.   R: 1788)
A Sunday school was started in Horsham in 1787, and by February 1788 60 poor children,
of both sexes, were being taught reading, 'and a proper observance of the Lord's day'.[1]
1. *SWA* 4.2.88.

Phillip's boys' boarding school   (Rs: 1789, 1793, (1797))
James Phillips had a boys' boarding school in 1789 where, with a 'proper assistant', he taught
Latin, French, English, writing, arithmetic, geometry, merchants' accounts, &c. His terms
were 12 guineas pa, with 1 guinea entrance, and French or Latin were 4 guineas extra. In
Univ. Directory 1793.
In August 1797 he set up a joint surveying business with Matthew Phillips, who
was based at Henfield, where his father, William, had a boys' boarding school [qv]; James
was based at Horsham, where he presumably continued with his school. They offered plans
of estates for inspection, and 'the most satisfactory recommendations from many Gentlemen
of respectability'.[2]
[*James Phillips*]
1. *SWA* 2.3.89.   2. *SWA* 14.8.97.

Waller's school   (Rs: 1793, 1800)
George Waller is listed as a schoolmaster in *Univ. Directory* 1793, and probably had his
own school. He was almost certainly the husband of Mrs Waller, whose girls' boarding
school was advertised 1781-95 [qv] but was not listed in *Univ. Directory* 1793; her school
and George Waller's were possibly the same.
In the early part of 1800 a quantity of wet linen was stolen from the house of 'Mr.
Waller, schoolmaster, at Horsham' (in a later report identified as George Waller). The thief,
Charles Field, was arrested, but escaped; he was rearrested, near Fulham, on 1 January 1801,
and that same month was convicted at the quarter sessions at Chichester, and sentenced to
transportation for 7 years.[1]

George Waller (1742-1815) was an innholder at his marriage in 1770, and was almost certainly the George Waller, innholder, bankrupt in 1778 (Mrs Waller started her school January 1781).

[*George Waller*]

1. *SWA* 5.1.1801, 19.1.1801.

Other masters and mistress

> John Tasker, referred to as a schoolmaster of Horsham in the 1724 will of Elizabeth Furlonger.[1] He was originally a blacksmith. He was a Baptist, and secretary to the Horsham meeting, and elder there 1733-68; he was frequently 'scribe' to the Baptist General Assembly in London, and published Baptist pamphlets (see Schedule 2).
>
> 1. Evershed, P.R., pers. comm.

> Robert Blunt, schoolmaster at Horsham in 1772. From John Baker's diary for 30 May 1772: 'Afternoon Sir John [Blois], Mr. Dyer and I out on common, saw boys play at cricket, among them oldest master, Robert Blunt.'[1]
>
> 1. *SAC* **52**, 43-4.

> Richard Collins, schoolmaster of South Street at the 1790 general election.[1] He was the parish clerk, and had been appointed usher of Collyer's school in 1789,[2] but as there appear to have been no foundation pupils at the grammar school, he probably kept his own private school in addition. He died in 1801.
>
> 1. Albery, W. *A Parliamentary History of Horsham 1295-1885* (1927), 160.   2. Willson, op cit., 111.

> Maggs Burges, schoolmaster in 1793 (*Univ. Directory*). (In South Street 1787.[1])
>
> 1. Hughes, A.F., pers. comm. citing churchwardens' rates.

> Mrs Stanford, schoolmistress in 1793 (*Univ. Directory*).

HORSTED KEYNES   1724: about 45 families   1801: pop. 591

Lightmaker's charity school   (F: by 1707.   Rs: 1707-38, (1744-77), 1777- into 19c)

Edward Lightmaker, of Broadhurst in Horsted Keynes, by will dated 2 April 1708,[1] left a house and brewhouse called Mote Croft, that he had built near the church, together with £400 to purchase lands to provide an annuity of £20 pa, 'for the yearly Maintenance and perpetuating my Free School'. At the date of the will the house was occupied by Jenkyn Jones, schoolmaster, and Lightmaker had already set up his school: the SPCK annual *Account of the Charity-Schools* for 1707 included a school at Horsted Keynes - 'A Gentleman has built an House and settled it with 20 l. per Annum Tax-free...' Lightmaker was almost certainly influenced by the SPCK, and he was in receipt of packets of tracts from the society; Joseph Grave, who had received 10 packets from the society for distribution, wrote to the society from Lewes, 21 September 1708, to the effect 'That Mr. Lightmaker being dead, he desires leave to present the Packet designed for him to Mr. Sawyer of Mayfield.'[2] Lightmaker died on 7 April 1708, five days after signing his will, 'and was buried on the 10th in the evening in his own Chancel'.[3] The will is long and not wholly coherent, and Lightmaker's pious exhortations and his practical instructions are sometimes muddled.

Under the will the master was to have the £20 pa and was to teach 20 poor children of the parish, chosen by the trustees (and from adjacent parishes should there not be 20 to be had from Horsted Keynes). At two points in the will - where he gives the rules for catechising the children and for their attendance at church on Sundays - the children are described as 'the Boys'; but when providing bibles for leavers he refers to 'his or her going away'. The master was to be allowed to take in, for his benefit, 21 further paying scholars (later in the same sentence referred to as the 'twenty'). The master was to be a practising member of the Church of England, but not the holder of any cure or church living; and he should be 'chosen out of the universitys not that I hereby enjoin him to fitt his Charity Scholars for the same only that I find that without the understanding of the Latin Tongue they cannot be Masters of the English either to read or spell'. He should have been a 'Servitor' at college, who would have constantly attended the divinity lecturers, 'for my chief end and design is to have these poor Children Instructed in the happy Rudiments of Christian Knowledge that may make them wise unto Salvation as being the more fitted to find it amongst those that are Students in these things than to make choice upon any that accidentally break into it such as those who have been Tradesmen and sometimes broken & decayed Tradesmen thinking that after all their inabilities to be fit enough for this'.

School was to begin at 8 o'clock with morning prayers; the children were to have a two-hour break between 11 and 1 o'clock. References in the will imply that Lightmaker assumed that reading, writing, arithmetic and casting accounts would be taught at his school. The master was also 'to teach them all to Sing by notes the Psalms of David'; and on Wednesdays and Fridays was to hear their catechism and explain it 'suitable to their Capacities'. As to teaching methods, 'every Reader is first to con his Lesson and then in his turn to come forth and read thereafter return to his Seat and Prepare for a second Reading the same to be done in the afternoon'; the writers and cypherers 'shall first of all read a Chapter [ie. of the bible] Morning and Evening and then set about writing or cyphering and shall always present his writing or arithmetick to be veiwed & Examined'. The master was to take the boys to church on Sundays, both morning and evening, and was to sit as near to them as possible and to have 'a White Wand' in his hand or by him, 'the frequent aspect of the Master Eye upon them keeping them in good order'. Despite the master's 'wand', he was to instruct them 'in the words of the Scripture' 'by all kind Methods of persuasions... forbearing Threatining rather and all inordinate ways of Passion and anger... as they are the budding and blossoms of the year so they must be treated with the gentler Dews and Distillac'ons of Heavenly Country'.

In addition to providing the schoolhouse and the master's salary, Lightmaker left a further £100 to his trustees, to be invested in land and the rents applied to maintaining the clock he had erected at Horsted Keynes (10s pa to the parish clerk to wind the clock, and 5s pa to a clocksmith to clean and maintain it), the residue to be used to repair the charity school and schoolhouse, and when not needed for this, to provide the charity scholars with bibles, prayer books and primers; and the surplus, if any, for finding bibles, 'of five Shillings price', for the most deserving children on leaving school; and if anything remained after that, it should be used to buy a cord of wood for winter firing, and to provide a 'Plumb Cake' at every 'Breaking up', to be equally divided amongst the charity scholars, 'after they have first paid their Homage at Gods House in the Morning of the said Festivals'; and if any money was left over it was to be spent on clothes for the poor children. The provision for 'Plumb Cake' was a compassionate idea, and most unusual, but it is hard to see how the rent, probably between £3 and £4, could often cover this (or clothing) after the prior commitments on it.

By codicil, Lightmaker left 40 books 'which I have lately bought and had marked on the Cover with the Letters of Horstead Keyns', as a library for his school, for the use of the master (he had clearly bought the books for this purpose); he required an 'exact Catalogue' of them to be made, to be signed by the master and held by the trustees; the books were to remain at the school 'for all times coming never to be lent out... at the request or desire of any person or persons whatsoever'. Thirteen of the books survived in 1979 -

four at Horsted Keynes church and nine on loan to Chichester Cathedral Library.[4] Lightmaker also provided books for the use of the scholars - 10 bibles to be used by them at church only; 20 prayer books to be used at church; 20 Dr Patricks Psalms books for daily use; 20 singing books (not marked); and 10 primers.[5]

Lightmaker's first trustees were his niece, Elizabeth, and her husband Thomas Osborne of Newtimber; after their deaths (he died in 1727, she in 1735[6]) the trusteeship was to devolve on the owners of Broadhurst manor. No trace of Lightmaker's legacies of £400 and £100 has ever been found; they were apparently never invested in lands, as the will required, though the capital may have been used to pay the schoolmaster for a time.[7] In 1724 the churchwardens reported that: 'Edward Lightmaker Gent founded a Free School for Twenty poor Children and endowed it with A Good House & Twenty pounds P Ann'; so it was then continuing.[8] The following receipt of 1738, when Thomas Pigott owned the manor of Broadhurst, has survived; it shows that the master's salary was then four years in arrears: 'These are to certifie, yt I have rec'd of ye hands of Thos Pigott Esqr ye sum of Eighty five Pounds in full for four Years and a quarters salary as Schoolmaster of the Free School at Horsted kains & also ye sum of four pounds fourteen Shillings I laid out in Repairs about ye house, which in all Amounts to eighty nine Pounds fourteen Shillings, being the whole due to me save ten Shillings and tenpence halfpenny wch had there been Money in hand I believe I should have likewise rec'd as Witness my hand this 28 day of Jan'ry 1737. - Charles Baker'.[9]

Charles Baker is believed to have then given up the school and to have left the parish. The endowment had vanished, only the schoolhouse, with its brewhouse and garden, remained. The parish later took this over, and rented it out for about £10 pa (one of the tenants was Thomas Pigott's widow, there in 1758). The rent was given as alms to poor persons in the parish, except for £2 a year paid to Widow Mitchell, 'for teaching a few poor children'. (From 1744 to 1771 small payments for schooling individual children, and for wood for the poor children at school, and for books for them, were made from the offertory money - see Parish schooling below.) About 1777 the parish appointed John Newnham as master, at a salary of £8 pa to teach eight poor children; Widow Mitchell was still receiving £2 pa to teach four. John Stone succeeded Newnham as master c1780, and when Widow Mitchell died in December 1781, he was paid £12 pa to teach 12. Stone, who had obtained a copy of Lightmaker's will, was formally reappointed master in 1800 by Viscount Hampden, then owner of Broadhurst manor and so trustee under the will, with the authority to appoint the master. It was not until 1806, when the schoolhouse became vacant and no other tenant could be found, that the school moved back there: Stone occupied the house and garden in lieu of salary, and Hampden took on responsibility for repairs to the buildings.[10]

Stone was still schoolmaster in 1833, when he reported to the charity commissioners that he had been master for 50 years and had 'constantly Instructed in Reading Writing and Arithmetic Twelve poor Children (Eight Boys and four Girls whose Age when they enter is about five or six Years And they generally leave School at ten or twelve)'. The girls were also taught needlework 'by the schoolmaster's wife (Stone's third wife, 'Phillydelphia'). Stone also took other children, for whom their parents paid.[11]

[*Jenkyn Jones, George Shillito?, Charles Baker, Widow Mitchell, John Newnham, John Stone*]

1. ESRO GLY 3466: this archive comprises a bundle of papers relating to the school, undoubtedly prepared by John Stone, then master, for the charity commissioners' enquiries of 1819 and 1833; included is an abstract from Lightmaker's PCC will, dated 2 April 1708, probate 15 May 1708.   2. SPCK ALB v.1, 1400.
3. Horsted Keynes PR.   4. Bird, R. 'The Lightmaker Free School', *Sussex History* v.2, no.7, 13.
5. ESRO GLY 3466: includes a copy, made by John Stone on 3 March 1799, of the catalogue of Lightmaker's books given to the Free School, certified as correct by William Lucas.   6. Bird, op cit., 13.
7. *EP3* (1820), 438.   8. WSRO Ep.I/26/3, 66-7.   9. ESRO GLY 3466: includes a copy of the receipt, taken

from the Parish Book, made by John Stone on 3 March 1799 and certified as correct by William Lucas.
10. ESRO GLY 3466: includes a draft and fair copy of 'particulars' relating to the school, dated 26 May 1819, and an account of repairs to the schoolhouse by John Stone, from July 1806 to March 1809, totalling £61 13s 2d, submitted to John Ellman as agent for Viscount Hampden; Bird, op cit., 13-14.   11. ESRO GLY 3466: includes a list of poor children at the school in 1819; Bird, op cit., 14; *EP3* (1820), 439.

Parish schooling   (Rs: 1744-71)
The offertory money collected on 'Whitsunday, Trinity Sunday, Michaelmas Day, Xmas Day, Sunday after Xmas, Easter Sunday, Sunday after Easter', was for many years distributed 'for ye poor', and disbursements included three kinds of schooling payments - for teaching individual poor children, 'for wood for ye Poor Children at School', and for books for them.[1] Teaching payments appear to have been at the rate of 2d a week per child, and those for 1744 were:

> I paid Dame Holford for teaching Care's boy   0 - 1 - 6
> I pd Wm Botting for teaching John Upton's Boy   0 - 2 - 6
> I pd for a Spelling-Book for Michael Michell   0 - 1 - 0
> I pd James Holford's Wife for teaching Care's Boy
>   from Whitsuntide till Xmas   0 - 4 - 8
> Paid James Holford's Wife for
>   teaching Care's Boy from Xmas to Easter   0 - 2 - 0

The teachers were probably themselves poor - James Holford, whose wife, Joan, is mentioned above, received charity cash payments from the offertory money. In 1745 and 46 Joan Holford was paid small sums for teaching Henry Care's boy; but it would seem that she was probably paid, from another source, for teaching other poor children, almost certainly at the workhouse:

> 1747 I paid for half a Cord of Wood
>   which Joan Holford had on ye acct
>   of ye poor Children   0 - 6 - 0

For 21 of the 27 years from 1744 to 1771 offertory money was used to pay for wood 'for ye Poor Children at School'/'for ye School-Children'/'for ye School'. From 1744 to 1750 such payments ranged from 5s to 7s; from 1751 to 1760 the range was 5s to 12s 5¼d; from 1761 to 1771, 11s 3d to 13s (for each of the last 5 years, 13s was paid). It is clear that the parish was here supporting, with the offertory money, the village school (see Lightmaker's charity school above), for which some teaching of poor children was probably paid for out of the rent, received by the parish, for Lightmaker's schoolhouse. The village school was then probably kept at the workhouse, and John Stone, the master from c1780, was paying land tax as occupier of Steadman's Workhouse from 1785 to 1808.[2]

Offertory money was also used to buy books for the school. Apart from Michael Michell's spelling book (1s), noted above, and a similar book for Edward Newman in 1746 (1s), in 1748 10s was paid for 'Books bought for ye Poor Children', and in 1760 2s for 'Books for ye School-Children'.

[*Joan Holford, William Botting*]
1. WSRO Par 384/12/1.   2. Bird, op cit., 14.

Osborne's charity schooling   (Rs: 1774-8)
Rev John Osborne, second son of Lightmaker's first trustees, Thomas and Elizabeth Osborne, purchased Westland in Horsted Keynes for £160 in 1752. By will dated 8 November 1770, he directed his executrix, his niece Mrs Ann Dennett, and his heirs, to pay 16s pa towards the Christian education of poor children of Horsted Keynes. He died in May 1774: his executrix renounced probate, but for some time during her life made payments for teaching poor children of the parish; but no payments were made for this purpose by her or under Osborne's will after 1778.[1]

1. *EP3* (1820), 440.

HOUGHTON   1724: 23 families   1801: pop. 144

School   (Rs: 1742, 1758, 1762)
In 1742, and again in 1758, there was a schoolmaster in the parish, of 'good Life' and
'diligent', who came to church and caused his scholars to come, and taught them the
catechism. There was no free or charity school in the parish, so presumably his was a
private school.[1]
    In August 1762 a property in Washington was conveyed to Thomas Waters of
Houghton, schoolmaster.[2]
[*Thomas Waters*]
1. WSRO Ep.I/22/1.   2. *Wiston Arch.*, 224: 3372-3379

Dame school   (R: 1772)
At the 1772 visitation, 'we have only a school kept by one woman who is diligent and
sober'.[1]
1. WSRO Ep.I/22/1.

HOVE (HOVA)   1801: pop. 101

No 18th-century schooling traced.

HUNSTON   1724: 11 families   1801: pop. 123

No 18th-century schooling traced.

HURSTPIERPOINT (HURSTPERPOUND) 1724: 100 families 1801: pop. 1,104

Charity school (Hart's school/Muzzell's school)   (Rs: 1714-33, 1751- into 19c)
On 24 May 1714 John Hart subscribed, before being admitted to teach in a school in
Hurstpierpoint.[1] Thomas Marchant, a yeoman of Hurstpierpoint, recorded in his diary for
Sunday, 3 October 1714: 'Mr. Hart received the Sacrament to qualify himself for a
certificate from the Sessions.' And on 8 October, at the sessions at Lewes, 'Mr. Hart was
sworn, and had a Certificate. Mr. Norden, Mr. Whitpaine, John Lindfield, Mr. Hart, and
I came home together, and drank four pints of wine at John Smith's.'[2]
    On 2 March 1719 Marchant records: 'Mr. Hart, who had been sent for to teach
school at Deptford, concluded to stay with us to teach our school, and Mr. Whitpaine
promised to contribute £7 per annum, Mr. Scutt £7, and myself £3, and to be answerable
for £1 for my mother if she should object to continue it.'[3] This indicates that the school was
a charity school supported by local subscriptions. The subscriptions were apparently now
being increased to a minimum of £18 pa as recorded here, but the last phrase suggests that
there had been earlier subscriptions.
    On Sunday 29 November 1719 Hart preached at the parish church.[4]
    In 1727 and 1728 Henry Campion of Danny was subscribing £6 pa to the school,
and also paying Hart for boarding a boy. His personal accounts show:[5]
        3 October 1727, paid Mr Hart for three-quarters of a year for the
        free school and boarding Jacky Shore, £15.
        4 April 1728, paid Mr John Hart for Jack Shore's board due Lady
        Day £7, and for half a year for the free school £3.
The payments to Hart for the school continued and he was there until Michaelmas 1731.
In 1732 Henry Campion was paying £4 pa to Abraham Muzzal (Muzzel) for the school, and
in 1733 £6 pa to Muzzell on behalf of himself and his son. John Hart had almost certainly

moved on to be master of Steyning grammar school.

The charity school was endowed in 1751, when by indenture dated 16 February 1751, Henry Campion gave a yearly rent of £5 as an endowment for a school to teach 20 children of the parish to read. The schoolmaster was to be nominated by himself during his life, and afterwards by the rector, churchwardens and overseers; and Campion nominated Abraham Muzzell (who had been master as far back as 1732). Although this seems a very small endowment for the purpose, the school survived, and by 1819, with the support of later bequests from others, 100 boys and girls were being sent to different schools in the parish.[6]

[*John Hart, Abraham Muzzell*]

1. WSRO Ep.II/1/1.   2. *SAC* **25**, 167.   3. ibid. 184.   4. ibid. 185.   5. ESRO DAN 2198.
6. *EP2* (1819), 170.

Muzzell's school   (R: 1719)

In 1719 Abraham Muzzell was paid 7s 6d by Thomas Marchant, yeoman, for the schooling of William Balcombe. (See also Charity school above.)   [*Abraham Muzzell*]
1. *SAC* **25**, 185.

Edwards' private boys' boarding and day grammar school   (Rs: 1796, 1797)

Under the heading 'GRAMMAR SCHOOL', in July 1796 Rev E.Edwards advertised his school where, with 'an able and respectable Assistant', he taught boys the classics, writing, arithmetic, mensuration, merchants' accounts, algebra, geometry 'and other Branches of Mathematical Learning'. Terms for boarders, who were limited to eight, were 18 guineas pa; for day scholars, 1 guinea per quarter. French, taught 'by an eminent Master', was an extra at 1 guinea per quarter. A dancing master attended once a week.[1] In 1797 the school was styled 'Hurst Grammar School'.[2]   [*E.Edwards*]
1. *SWA* 11.7.96.   2. *SWA* 16.1.97.

Other masters

> Mr Pointin, of Henfield, in January 1722 began to teach Thomas Marchant's son, William, arithmetic: 'he is to come three times a week, and to have 2s.6d. per week for teaching'. William was then aged 21. From April 1722 he was also to teach Marchant's daughter, Bett, arithmetic for an additional 2s.6d. per week, 'also M. Balcombe upon the same terms.' Later, in 1731, he appears to have kept a school, and this may have been in Hurstpierpoint. In 1740 he was 'of Hurstpierpoint'. Also surveyor, and excise officer. (*SAC* **25**, 191; Hurstpierpoint PR; ESRO HIC 472)

> John Pilbeam (1724-91): Rs 1774, 1779, but was at Hurstpierpoint c1748 to death. (WSRO Par 400/34/4/12; *SRS* **26**; see also Schedule 2)

Dancing master

> Mr Lun   Thomas Marchant recorded in his diary for 14 May 1718: 'Mr.Lun, the dancing master, began to teach at Kester's.' Lun was also then dancing master at Lewes grammar school. (*SAC* **25**, 183)

ICKLESHAM   1724: about 30 families   1801: pop. 384

Parish schooling and free school   (Rs: 1724?, 1744-86, 1793)

The churchwardens' accounts for 1724 include a payment of 10d on 2 November 'for Worsted and a Hornebooke for Widow Wickens Children';[1] which may suggest that the parish was supporting the education of some poor children at that time. But the first specific reference to schooling so far traced does not occur until December 1744, when the overseers paid 7s 8d 'for the poor childrens schooling'.[2] On 15 April 1745 they paid Dame Burt 5s 'for Teaching School', and from the church year 1745-6 to 1756-7 Dame Burt was regularly paid 8s a quarter or £1 12s a year. These entries suggest that from at least Michaelmas 1744 the parish was paying for the education of poor children. From the beginning of 1758 the payments to Dame Burt were doubled, to 16s per quarter or £3 4s a year, for which she was schooling eight parish children. From midsummer 1760 she was teaching nine children and her pay was increased to 18s per quarter; and from midsummer 1761 10 children for £1 a quarter. She was thus paid 2d a week per child for a 48-week year. This rate of £4 pa continued until the last schooling payment to her, on 2 January 1773. She had then been teaching poor children for 28 years. She was first referred to as 'Widow' on 7 May 1769. She was a poor woman: from 1739 to 1741 she was paid small sums from the offertory collections on certain Sundays, disbursed to the poor,[3] and she received 'poor pay', at 2s 6d a week, at least from 1764 to 1769. She also received payments from the overseers for other services - for boarding poor folk, knitting, mending clothes.

In the church year 1773-4 the schooling was taken on by Widow Stone. Towards the end of that year the parish had to deal with a problem common to charity schools - the casual attendance of the free scholars. The following minute of a vestry on 6 March 1774 has survived, on a loose sheet, somewhat worm-eaten (it will be noted that the number of children then being taught had increased to 14):

Whereas the intention of a charitable contribution for putting to school fourteen poor children of this parish has been & thro' the negligence & indirection of their Parents or Guardians continues to be much abused [as] well to [reme]dy this, as to provide against the Evils;

At a Vestry held this 6th day of March 1774 by the Minister, Churchwardens & other principal Inhabitants,

O r d e r ' d   That [the] hours of School be throughout the year from 8 to 11 beforenoon & from 1 to 4 afternoon, during which times the mistress shall hear them three lessons, & catechize them once. -

That the mistress be paid 2 pence p. week for each child, & an additional penny by those for whom they work.

That no holidays be kept, but a fortnight at Christmas, & at Easter & Whitsuntide a week each. -

That those Children who are absent one whole day or two half days in any one week shall be immediately discharged from the said school, unless a good reason be assigned on the following Sunday.

That those children who are half an hour behind the time prefix'd, shall be deem'd absent.

That the Mistress do lay a faithful account of each child absent or behind the time prefix'd upon the table in the Vestry every Sunday immediately before Church

That the Mistress be paid 4 shillings & 6 pence a year for the Vestry account, as above. -

That those persons whose children have made themselves liable to be discharged for want of a proper attendance, do by themselves or a neighbour give their reasons to the Vestry on the sunday following for such neglect: their silence to be understood as having none to give. -

That the Mistre[ss] [to/do] take care to bring all her Scholars to [be] catechized at church every sunday in the afternoon between Lady=day & Michaelmas.[4]

Despite these resolutions, from Easter 1775 the payments by the overseers for schooling reverted to £4 pa, which they paid regularly until Michaelmas 1786. In 1778 the school is first referred to as the 'Free School'. From Easter 1776 (and possibly for the previous year) the schoolmistress was Dame Amon. When she died in 1779, the school was continued by her husband, Joseph Amon. They were poor folk: at her death, the parish paid for the 'laying forth' and burying of Joseph Amon's wife, and he was on several occasions in receipt of 'poor pay' from 1780 to 1787 (when the poor were put out).

After November 1786 there are no further payments for schooling in the overseers' accounts, but at a vestry meeting in 1793, it was agreed that the overseers should 'have a Room in the House lately Occupy'd as a Poor-House' repaired and fitted out as a schoolroom; and that 'from Lady day next' £16 pa should be paid 'to a Proper Person for Instructing therein Twenty Poor Children; to Learn their Books so as to Spell and Read well; and in Religious Principles, Conformable to, and Agreeable with the Church of England: - The said Sum to be paid by the Overseers for the time being, out of the Money collected for the use of the Poor: - as it is the Opinion of this Meeting that the Money thus expended will prove to be equal, if not more future benefit to the Poor off, and the said Parish; than by any other means the said Money cou'd be expended or Apply'd...' The schoolmaster was ordered to request the parents of the children to direct them to attend divine service in the parish church 'every Sunday, & Prayer Days' - all the boys were to sit together in one pew, and all the girls in another. Three trustees were appointed, to choose the schoolmaster and nominate, 'without favour or Affection', the 20 poor children most in need of such instruction. If the schoolmaster, in their opinion, failed to do his duty, they had power to dismiss him at the end of any one year ending at Lady day, and to appoint another. The trustees, or at least two of them, were asked to meet in the schoolroom once each month, during school hours, 'to hear the Children say their Books, and also the Church Catechism.'[5]

But there are no payments in the overseers' accounts specifically for the school or schooling from that date to the end of the century; and by 1835, according to Horsfield, the only school in the parish was a Sunday school, supervised and paid for by the vicar.[6]
[*Widow Wicken?, Dame Burt, Widow Stone, Mary Amon, Joseph Amon*]

1. *SAC* **32**, 114.   2. ESRO PAR 401/30/1: the references to overseers' accounts that follow are from this for 1736-68; PAR 401/30/2 for 1768-86; PAR 401/30/3 for 1786-98; PAR 401/30/4 for 1798-1801.   3. Icklesham PR.   4. ESRO PAR 401/25/1.   5. *SAC* **32**, 117.   6. Horsfield *Sussex* I, 477.

IDEN   1724: about 36 families   1801: pop. 289
No 18th-century schooling traced.

IFIELD   1724: about 70 families   1801: pop. 637
No 18th-century schooling traced.

IFORD   1724: 21 families   1801: pop. 140
No 18th-century schooling traced.

IPING   1724: about 19 families   1801: pop. 209
School   (R: 1765)
At the 1765 visitation, there was a schoolmaster in the parish, of 'good Life' and 'diligent', who came to church and caused his scholars to come, and taught them the catechism.[1] There was no charity school, so his was presumably a private school.
1. WSRO Ep.I/22/1.

ISFIELD   c1760: 39 houses   1801: pop. 334

No 18th-century schooling traced.

ITCHINGFIELD   1724: about 42 families   1801: pop. 249

No 18th-century schooling traced. In 1762, 'No Charity School and no other School'.[1]
1. WSRO Ep.I/22/1.

JEVINGTON   1724: 32 families   1801: pop. 229

No 18th-century schooling traced.

KEYMER   1724: with Clayton, 50 families   1801: pop. (Keymer) 465

No 18th-century schooling traced.

KINGSTON, near Lewes   1724: about 30 families   1801: pop. 124

No 18th-century schooling traced.

KINGSTON, Arundel rape   1801: pop. 53

No 18th-century schooling traced.

KINGSTON-BY-SEA   1724: 6 families   1801: pop. 77
near Shoreham (KINGSTON BOWSEY)

No 18th-century schooling traced.

KIRDFORD   1724: 160 families   1801: pop. 1,340

Petty and dame schools   (Rs: 1726, 1742, 1765, 1775)
From visitation returns:[1]

1726   'we have no schoolmaster in our parish only a person who sometimes teaches
        children to write'
1742   an unlicensed teacher, probably a schoolmaster, of 'good Life' and 'diligent', who
        came to church and caused his scholars to come, and taught them the catechism.
(1762) ('We have no School Master. We have no Charity-School.')
1765   'We have a Schoolmaster', of 'good Life' &c as in 1742.
1775   'two or three small schools by women for reading'
1. WSRO Ep.I/22/1.

LAMBERHURST [in diocese of Rochester]   (1801: pop. in Sussex part of parish, 569)

Charity schooling   (F: c1713.   Rs: c1713- into 19c)
By will dated 15 December 1712, Dame Elizabeth Hamby left an annuity or rent charge of
£6, issuing out of the manor of Lamberhurst, to the minister of Lamberhurst and other
trustees, to be used for teaching little children of Lamberhurst to read English. This sum
continued to be paid regularly into the 19th century; by 1819 the then lord of the manor was
in fact paying more than the rent charge, and 14 boys and girls were being sent to a
schoolmaster and schoolmistress.[1]
1. *EP1* (1819), 234.

LANCING (LAUNCING)   1724: about 30 families   1801: pop. 451

Dame school   (R: 1733)
At the 1733 visitation: 'we know only of a little School where a woman Teaches a few
Children to Read and Work.'[1]
1. WSRO Ep.I/22/1.

LAUGHTON   1801: pop. 539

Parish schooling   (Rs: 1723?, 1738-9, 1751-2, 1755?)
The overseers' accounts for the period 1723-59 show very occasional payments for the
schooling of poor children.[1] In July 1723 they paid 5s 'for wood for ye Children' - a phrase
that may imply that the parish children were being taught in a schoolroom, perhaps at the
workhouse. In the church year 1738-9 they made two payments, totalling 7s, 'for John
Easons Schooling'. (They paid 6s a month for keeping him, and bought clothes for him to
1741.) In 1751-2 they paid 4s 'for a Book & Schooling for Edw Marten's Child', and paid
1s 'for thred & tape & for altering her Coat' (and they paid 6s a month for her keep). In
the same year they paid 5s 7d for Lucy Page's schooling (and paid various sums for her
keep up to 1759-60). In 1755 they paid 2d 'for a horning Book for John Merchant's boy'.
Other schooling payments may possibly have been subsumed in paid bills where goods or
services are not specified, or in larger items as (1754-5) 'Mr. Curtis' Charitable Use Money
£7 13s 2d'; (1756)'the Churchwardens bills £25 4s 4d'; (1759) 'A great many Small
Expences £10 6s 5d'.
1. ESRO PAR 409/31/1/2.

[Sunday school?]
In September 1791 the Hon and Rev George Pelham preached the annual charity sermon
at Brighton on behalf of the Sunday school and school of industry there. He was then vicar
of Laughton. It seems probable, from his being asked to preach on the subject, that there
was a Sunday school in his own parish.[1]
1. *SWA* 3.10.91; CI.

LEWES (all parishes)	1724 (no. of families)		1801: pop.
All Saints		54	1,196
St Anne	about	50	590
St John sub Castro	about	56	737
St John the Baptist, Southover		64	487
St Michael	about	100	786
	about	324	
St Thomas in the Cliffe (1717)		101	1,113
South Malling (1717)		22	348
	about	447	5,257

Grammar school   (F: 1512.   Rs: through 18c)
A school at Lewes is mentioned as early as 1248 (when the monks of the Cluniac priory
chose their 'beloved clerk, Lucas, schoolmaster of Lewes', to represent them at Rome in a
case before the papal auditor),[1] but the modern school was founded under a bequest by
Agnes Morley, widow, whose will was proved in October 1512.[2] She left an annuity of
£20, together with a house and garden in Southover, for the endowment of a free grammar
school. Of the £20 pa, £10 pa was to go to the schoolmaster, £5 pa to the usher, and the
rest used for repairs. The master was to be a priest, but not to have any cure of souls. The
house and garden were for the benefit of the schoolmaster and usher, and were used as the

schoolhouse and playground for 200 years. There was a further bequest of £3 pa from Thomas Blunt, given under his will of 1611.[3]

In 1709 Mrs Mary Jenkins, of Chelsea, willed a house, stable and garden in the parish of St Anne, formerly the Chantry House, 'to be inhabited and enjoyed by the schoolmaster for the time being of the Free Grammar School, in Southover juxta Lewes, for ever'. (The premises had been purchased by Mrs Jenkins the preceding year for £194.) She also left £1,534, to be used 'in making provision for the free instructing and teaching at the said Free Grammar School' of as many children as her trustees should nominate. They could spend up to £15 pa on books for the free scholars, the residue of the income going to the schoolmaster, usher and writing master, whose appointments and dismissals were at the trustees' discretion. In 1714 the school moved from Southover to the premises given by Mrs Jenkins.[4] The cash book of Henry Pelham of Stanmer for 1715 shows payments totalling £100 to Mr Peirce [master of the grammar school] 'by order of Mrs Jenkins... for building the schoolroom'.[5]

In 1775, Robert Austen, then master of the school, wrote to Mr Shelley giving details of the master's remuneration: he reported it as £57 16s 8d pa - £20 less a fee farm rent of 13s 4d from the Morley bequest; an annuity of £3; £35 10s from the Jenkins' bequest. The master also had the 'commodious house for the purpose of taking boarders with a Stable and Garden'. (Although not mentioned by Austen, the Jenkins' charity paid a further £17 5s pa towards a writing master.) Austen noted that for the salary from the Jenkins' charity the master was supposed to teach '12 to 20 Boys', but 'The general Number is about 12.'[6] Thus, no boys at all were being taught on account of the Morley and Blunt charities (as the charity commissioners noted in 1819); and by the later years of the 18th century the charities were being further abused - when William Gwynne was master, for most of the time not more than six boys were on the foundation. Additionally, the commissioners in 1819 criticised the school for charging the free boys on the Jenkins' foundation for books and stationery, which they should have had free as Mrs Jenkins had provided £15 pa for that purpose.[7]

Contrary to Agnes Morley's stipulation, a number of the 18th-century masters had 'cure of souls'. Thomas Peirce, licensed to teach boys in the grammar school in 1706, subscribed as curate of St Anne's in 1706, and signed the bishop's transcripts at Hamsey in 1715, 1717, 1718, and was probably curate there; he was rector of St Thomas-at-Cliffe from July 1718, and also rector of St Anne's from May 1720, both until his death in 1725. It is interesting that when Josiah Welby was then appointed master 'the Trustees obliged me to promise not to take Orders... because... my Predecessor was negligent in his teaching School; because he had his hands full in the cure of his Parishes'. (Welby was eventually ordained, but not until 1743, shortly before his death in January 1745.) John Bristed followed him as master, 1745-c50; in 1749 he was instituted to the rectory of Slaugham (and at his death in 1783 also had the livings of St Anne and St Michael in Lewes). Robert Austen, master at 1753 and until he resigned at Michaelmas 1775, signed the bishop's transcripts at Hamsey in 1752, 1756 and 1770, and was probably curate there, and signed the St Anne's register as curate by March 1753, and probably kept the register from 1750 (he unsuccessfully sought clerical preferment for many years - he tried for Firle and Beddingham (1752), Isfield or Hangleton (1755), Eastdean and Friston (1764), Heathfield (1764), Catsfield (1765) - but it was not until 1778 that Lord Pelham presented him to the vicarage of Laughton; he died in 1786). James Castley, master 1775-78, signed the bishop's transcripts at Hamsey in 1773 and 1779 and was probably curate there, and signed the St Anne's register as curate by June 1773 (and probably, from the handwriting, kept the register from June 1772) and until April 1778. He was succeeded as master at Michaelmas 1778 by William Gwynne, who was curate of Hamsey from 1780 and rector there from 1784; in

1779 he appears as curate of St Anne (from the burial register) and in 1784 he was, additionally to Hamsey, appointed rector of that parish, and also one of the Earl of Abergavenny's domestic chaplains; in 1801 he was appointed vicar of South Malling; he resigned as master in 1807.[8]

The big perquisite for the masters was the ability to graft their private boarding school onto the free grammar school, using for it (from 1714) the house given to the free school by Mary Jenkins. In 1713, Joseph Grave in a letter to the SPCK recommended Thomas Peirce, master of the free school at Lewes 'which Flourishes under his Conduct', as a corresponding member of the society, noting that: 'The Sons of Considerable Gentlemen boarding with him in ye Town gives him an opportunity of an Enlarged Conversation by which he may be useful to promote ye designs of ye Society.'[9] Advertising the mastership in 1775, the trustees gave the income as £60, adding that this was 'exclusive of a large House... very convenient for the Purpose of taking Boarders.'[10] Nicholas Gilbert (1706-74), whose father, Nicholas Gilbert, gentleman of Eastbourne, had died in May 1713, was sent to Thomas Peirce at Lewes grammar school at Michaelmas 1714. His guardians kept detailed accounts of the money expended on his behalf,[11] from which it appears that Peirce charged 1 guinea entrance and £16 pa - though his annual bills totalled £20-£24. Additionally, £1 pa was paid separately to a writing master there (Keeler) and two payments of 10s to Mr Lun, the dancing master. Gilbert was at the school until midsummer 1718, that is from the age of just under eight to just under 12. During the whole of this period his guardians paid for his head to be shaved, and for wigs for him (which cost between 17s and £1 5s each). Private pupils at the school, then, wore wigs, which would have distinguished them from the free scholars. There were also private day boys. In the 1740s and 50s Henry Manning, surgeon-apothecary of Lewes, sent his sons there. Schooling cost £2 2s pa, plus extras for books, 'firing', 'breaking-up', and the writing master - Halstead, Rand - who appear to have taught the grammar school boys at their own schools (for details, see MANNING entries in Schedule 3). Manning also gave generous 'perquisites' - in both 1753 and 1754 £2 2s to the master, Austen, and 10s 6d to the usher.[12] It is not unlikely that some masters (and Gwynne in particular) discouraged the free scholars, whose appearance might tend to put off the parents of potential paying pupils - as certainly happened at Cuckfield grammar school [qv]. In 1790 Gwynne had 30 people living in his house,[13] presumably most of them private boarders. [In 1819, the then master had 12 free boys and 15 private pupils.[14]]

In January 1779 Gwynne offered 'the Greek and Latin Classics' for £25 pa and 3 guineas entrance,[15] but later that year, in May, the basic fee was down to 20 guineas ('Mr. GWYNNE takes this Opportunity of informing the PUBLIC, that he is prevailed upon by his Friends, to take BOARDERS, for the future, at the Terms of TWENTY GUINEAS per Annum, and THREE GUINEAS Admission.')[16] In 1781, the curriculum, taught by 'The Rev. Mr. GWYNNE, and proper ASSISTANTS', was given in a little more detail:

> Though the Knowledge of the GREEK and LATIN Classics is professedly the more immediate Object of Pursuit, in the above School; yet particular Care is taken that the Scholars read the ENGLISH Language with Taste, and write it with Accuracy and Elegance... The Articles of WRITING and DANCING are charged separately as usual.[17]

Gwynne was perhaps under pressure of competition from other schools, for in May the following year the subjects taught were further extended:

> In the above SCHOOL are taught the Greek, Latin, and English Languages; Writing and Arithmetic. After this Recess, will be taught also French and Geography.[18]

In 1800 William Austin was drawing master to the school.[19]

In 1779 there was a confrontation between Gwynne and Cater Rand (see <u>Rand family boys' school</u> below) over the timing of the summer holidays. In May Gwynne announced:

> ... instead of the usual Recess at WHITSUNTIDE, his next Vacation will commence on the 6th of AUGUST, and continue till the 6th of SEPTEMBER.[20]

Cater Rand immediately announced that 'having consulted with many of the Parents and Guardians of those young Gentlemen under his care, respecting the Alteration Mr. GWYNNE... hath made, in Breaking-up his School on the 6th of August, instead of the customary Time, at WHITSUNTIDE, which they by no Means approve of his coming into (as it happens at a Season of the Year when they can neither conveniently send for their Children, nor enjoy the Pleasure of their Company when at Home) begs Leave to inform those whom he hath not had the Opportunity of consulting, and the Public, that his Vacation will commence, as usual, on the <u>Thursday next before Whit-Sunday, viz. the 20th Instant.</u>'[21] But the Whitsuntide holiday tradition was broken then in Lewes: the following week Cater Rand announced:

> MR. RAND would be very sorry for any Person to understand from his Advertisement, that he means to insinuate any Thing slighting, or, in the least Degree, prejudicial to Mr. GWYNNE's Character. There was a Difference between them respecting the Summer Vacation, they have talk'd the Matter over, and have agreed, after this Summer, to break up their Schools together, at Midsummer.[22]

(By 1787, Gwynne's summer vacation stretched to 5½ weeks, longer than others, from Thursday 28 June to Monday 6 August.[23])

One of Gwynne's pupils, William Tilt (son of Mr Tilt of Brighton, presumably the Mr Tilt who had the Public Subscription Rooms there), who later went on to Eton and then to Trinity College, Cambridge, and was ordained, won at the latter the Middle Bachelors' prize in 1796 and the Senior Bachelors' prize in 1797, for Latin essays (see Schedule 3).

Paul Dunvan, whose *History of Lewes and Brighthelmston* was published in 1795, was sometime usher at the school.[24]

Robert Austen, in his letter of 1775 referred to above, giving details of the master's remuneration, noted that 'there is an exhibition in Lewes of £10 pr ann or more not appropriated to the School but easily to be obtained by the Master.'[25] This was the charity of George Steere, who by will dated 1 November 1661 left four houses in Lewes to the town to finance one poor scholar ('the sonne of godly poore parents in or neare to the sayd Towne of Lewes, especially the sonne of a godly poore minister') at Cambridge or Oxford, 'by and during the terme of foure yeares'. For the last two decades of the 18th century, the exhibition was worth £15 pa, or £60 for the four years; and William Gwynne acquired this for two of his sons - in 1795 for William Gwynne junior (£60) and in 1800 for his fifth son, Frederick (£72).[26]

[*Reading?, Thomas Peirce, Bland* (usher), *Stephen Keeler* (writing master), *(James?) Lun* (dancing master), *Josiah Welby, James Halstead* (writing master), *Cater Rand sen.* (writing master), *John Bristed, Robert Austen, Charles Rand* (writing master), *James Castley, William Gwynne, Paul Dunvan* (usher), *William Austin* (drawing master)]

1. *VCH* ii, 411.   2. *SAC* **46**, 134-44.   3. *EP1* (1819), 234.   4. Horsfield, *Lewes*, 309-10.
5. Farrant, J., pers.comm., citing BL Add MS 33,341.   6. Woolgar *Spicilegia* I, 275, MS at SAS.
7. Horsfield *Lewes*, 310; *EP1* (1819), 235-6.   8. CI; and (re Welby) Knapp, E.F., pers. comm. citing BL Add MS 4,321; (re Bristed) *SWA* 3.2.83; (re Austen) Brent, C., pers. comm. citing Newcastle correspondence and St Anne's register; (re Castley) Brent, C., pers.comm. citing St Anne's register; (re Gwynne) *SWA* 31.8.78, 10.5.84, 1.11.84: Woolgar, op. cit., I, 318; ibid. II, 474; *SAC* **26**, 83.   9. SPCK ALB v.4, 3716.
10. *SWA* 24.7.75.   11. ESRO ACC 2462/1.   12. ESRO SAS/I 302.   13. Woolgar, op. cit., I, 525-44.

14. *EP*1 (1819), 235.   15. *SWA* 4.1.79.   16. *SWA* 3.5.79.   17. *SWA* 24.12.81.   18. *SWA* 27.5.82.
19. *SWA* 24.3.1800 (Austin ad).   20. *SWA* 3.5.79.   21. *SWA* 10.5.79.   22. *SWA* 17.5.79.
23. *SWA* 25.6.87.   24. Lower, *Worthies*.   25. Woolgar, op cit., I, 275.   26. Horsfield, *Lewes*, 310-12; *SRS*
48, 87.

Charity school   (F: 1711.   Rs: 1711-24 (and probably later))

The SPCK annual *Account of the Charity-Schools* for 1704 included under Lewes: 'A School
for 50 Boys, they are all Cloath'd, and another is there setting up for Girls.'   The entry
derived from minute 16 of an SPCK meeting on 10 December 1702: 'The Ld Bp. of
Chichester reported at his late Visitation of his Diocess he has procur'd the erecting of a
Charity School at Lewes in Sussex, wherein are now 50 Boys clothed, & that he is in hopes
of setting up another School for girls there.'   But in another copy of the minutes 'Lewes' is
scored out and 'Brighthelmston' substituted.[1] The correction is correct: (i) there was indeed
a charity school for 50 boys at Brighton at that time; (ii) a charity school for girls was
indeed set up there - it opened 30 September 1702; (iii) the entry under Lewes was removed
in the next annual *Account* (1705); (iv) in a codicil to his will dated 19 January 1708,
Thomas Lord Pelham left 'To the Charity School in the said County [Sussex] Fifty pounds',
implying that there was only one such school, and there was certainly one at Brighton.[2]
Similarly, the SPCK *Account* for 1707 gave, under Lewes, as set up since the previous
year's *Account*: 'In the Neighbourhood of this Town, are two Charity-Schools. In one the
Master teaches gratis about 30 Children.   In the other, about 25 Children are taught gratis,
besides 12 whose Schooling is paid for.'   These schools have not been identified, but the
entry is almost certainly an error insofar as Lewes is concerned.   Again, the entry was
deleted in the next SPCK list (1709 - there was no list published in 1708).

        The charity school at Lewes, later known as the Grey Coat school, was opened in
May 1711 (and the SPCK *Accounts* from 1712 onwards give this as the opening date of the
charity school at Lewes). In July 1710 Mr Pelham (almost certainly Henry Pelham, 'of
Lewes' until he bought Stanmer in 1713[3]) promised £20 pa towards settling a charity school
at Lewes, but 'the opening of Mr Pelham's Charity School in that Town [Lewes] had been
delay'd by reason of the Small Pox wch 1000. people there have had, and of wch about 120.
are dead', and it did not open until 28 May 1711 - 'for 20. Boys cloath'd at the charge of
Mr Pelham who finds them Books & gives the Master 20. pounds P An. to teach them to
Read, Write, Cast Accounts, the Catechism, and to Sing Psalms.'[4] By August that year
another gentleman had added four children to Pelham's 20 (but not clothed them); by
October another had been added; by February 1713 the additional children numbered eight.[5]
In February 1713 Joseph Grave, writing to the SPCK from Lewes, noted 'That one of the
Children of ye Charity School in his Parish, by reason of his Extraordinary parts is removed
to ye Gramar School which flourishes under a very worthy master'.[6] In March 1713 the
school was reported to be in 'a flourishing Condic'on', and the founder had given them
'Lewis's Exposic'on of ye Ch'h Catechism and C: Pray'r Books &c.'[7] By April 1716, 13
children had been put out to trades and other employments.[8] Henry Pelham's cash account
book contains references to 'the Ch. Boyes' in 1719 and 1720.[9] He died in 1721 and was
succeeded by his eldest son, Henry, who continued the cash book and included the following
entries:[10]

		£ s. d.
1721	18 July, to Mr. Michell for clothing the Grey coats	18. 9. 0
1721	13 June, to Mr. Head for teaching the Grey Coat boys	20.10.0
1722	19 May, paid John Michell for the charity boys clothes	18. 9. 4

1723	10 Jan, to Mr. Head for half a year's teaching the Greycoat boys due 28th Sept.	10. 0. 0
1724	2 Sept., to Mr. Rigg for cloathing the boys	20. 0. 0

In 1726 and 1728 Head was also writing master to two daughters of Henry Farncombe, charging for each 6s 3d per qr, plus 1s per qr for pens, 'books' at 6d each, and 1s for breaking up at Whitsuntide.[11]

John Head was apparently still master of the charity school in 1733.[12] That year he switched his allegiance from the Pelhams to their political opponents and was installed as master of a rival charity school [qv <u>Another charity school</u> below]. Cater Rand was receiving payments from Pelham and the Duke of Newcastle for schooling from 1732, and from at least 1737 was being paid £20 a year. It would appear that the Pelham charity school was continued through the century through the Rand family school [qv below]. [*John Head*]

1. McClure, E. *The Minutes of the [SPCK]...* (1888), 207. 2. ESRO CHR 14/1. 3. Farrant, J., pers. comm. citing *VCH* 7, 239. 4. SPCK *Misc. Abstracts to 1772*, 'Charity Schools reported to be Erecting'; SPCK ALB v.3, 2618. 5. SPCK ALB v.3, 2680, v.3, 2814, v.4, 3479. 6. SPCK ALB v.4, 3479. 7. SPCK ALB v.4, 3480. 8. SPCK ALB v.6, 4772. 9. Farrant, J., pers. comm. citing BL Add MS 33,341, ff 23, 26. 10. ibid. ff 29, 30; BL Add MS 33,617, ff 3, 13, 24. 11. *SAC* **40**, 275. 12. Brent, C., pers. comm., citing BL Add MS 32,688, f 526.

<u>Stephen Philpot, dancing and music master</u> (Rs: 1729-70?)
and <u>Philpot's girls' boarding school</u> (F: by 1757. Rs: 1757-72)
Stephen Philpot started his career as a dancing master c1727, having studied under teachers in London.[1] He was also a musician (and described as such in the 1768 poll book, shortly before his death); he was reported to have been the best violin pupil of Michael Christen Festing, a well-known London musician; and he was appointed one of His Majesty's Musicians in Ordinary in 1760 (for which he received an annual salary of £40 plus £16 2s 6d for livery)[2]. He lived in Lewes from 1729 until his death in 1770.[3] He gave private dancing, music and deportment lessons, and in 1729 John Fuller of Brightling Park entered in his account book an agreement with 'Mr. Philpot to teach the children to dance once a week at twelve pence a week each child, without any entrance money' (at that time Fuller had six boys and one girl over 11 years of age).[4] In 1735 Fuller's account book[5] shows Philpot being paid £3 3s 'for teaching Stephen and Harry to Fiddle', and 7s 6d 'for Fiddlestrings'. In 1736 he was paid £2 3s 'for attending spinnet'; and in 1742 £1 1s 6d 'for coming from Lewes and Tuneing the spinnet'. The relationship between Philpot and the Fullers, which spanned at least 14 years, appears to have been close; in three years there were payments of 2s 6d for 'Philpotts Boy'/'Jack Philpott', and in 1743 Fuller subscribed £7 7s (five guineas on his own account, one guinea each on behalf of Jack and Harry) towards the 'Teaching his son John Philpot'. Henry Manning's account book (he was a surgeon-apothecary and landowner of Lewes) records payments to Philpot for teaching Manning children over a period of 20 years, beginning in 1734, when Philpot received £1 10s for giving Edward Manning dancing lessons for one half-year; payments for lessons, and his daughter Bet's and son Ned the younger's attendance at Philpot's 'dancing school' (from 1741; also £3 pa), continued at least until 1754 (when Manning's surviving account book ends).[6] Among Philpot's pupils were Lady Frances and Lady Charlotte, daughters of the Duchess of Somerset (of Petworth House), to whom he dedicated his short book, *An Essay on the Advantage of a Polite Education joined with a Learned One* (1747)[7] - Manning paid Philpot 10s 6d for a copy in January 1748. From this book it has been concluded that he taught at several boarding schools for young gentlemen,[8] but it was a girls' boarding school that he established with his wife, Elizabeth, certainly by 1757, when William Poole, by then securely entrenched among the gentry of mid-Sussex, sent his daughters aged 7 and 11 to

the Philpot school.[9]   In the book he stressed that 'Education is of great moment and importance... to the welfare and happiness of both sexes';[10] and he agreed with Mary Anstell, the 17th-century feminist, that women need to be educated so they will trust their own minds and not be deceived by the praises of others.[11]   When he quotes John Weaver, he significantly omitted certain phrases; for example, Weaver wrote 'they [ladies] are qualified to converse with advantage with men, for whom they were design'd' - Philpot omitted the last five words.[12]

Philpot achieved a high social status for a dancing master and musician. His appointment (1760) as one of His Majesty's Musicians in Ordinary was for life; c1767 he published *An Introduction to the Art of Playing on the Violin*.[13] In 1733 he rented, for £15 a year, the St Anne's parsonage, with a washhouse with a pigeon house over it, a draw-well, two stables, a garden and a courtyard.[14] By 1742 he had moved to a house in Southover High Street, where he lived until 1751, when he returned to the St Anne's parsonage (assessed rent for poor rates £7 pa), for which he paid the poor rates until his death; in 1759 he rented additionally (assessed rent for poor rates £3 pa) the house next door to the parsonage.[15] In 1753 he purchased a copyhold farm in Lindfield of 100 acres, with house, buildings and woodland;[16] in his will, he bequeathed his eldest daughter, Ann, £200 from the revenue of the property.[17] He is described in documents as 'Esquire' and 'gentleman'.[18]

Philpot's wife, Elizabeth, died in 1761; he continued to run the school until his death in 1770, when it was taken over by his eldest daughter, Ann.[19] In an advertisement in *SWA* in December 1770, announcing the continuation of the school, she noted: 'The same Music and Dancing-Master as in her late Father's Time.'[20] She paid the poor rates on both adjacent houses in April 1771; by October that year she had married Phillip Gasteneau, who paid the rates October 1771 to October 1772.[21] At the end of 1772 the school was taken over by Philadelphia and Charlotte Lund (see below).[22] Despite the long tradition of the school, and her inheritance from her father, Ann was probably the Mrs Ann Gastino/Gastinau for whose maintenance the St Anne's overseers paid £2 10s per quarter from the 1783-4 year to 1789;[23] and who was buried at All Saints, 1 July 1789, aged 57.
[*Stephen Philpot, Elizabeth Philpot, Ann Philpot* (later Gastineau)]

1. Cobau, J. 'Stephen Philpot: A Gentleman Dancing-Master', MS in private hands (*SP* hereafter), 1, citing Philpot's *An Essay on the Advantage of a Polite Education Joined with a Learned One* (1747) (*Essay* hereafter), vii.   2. Woolgar *Spicilegia*, II, 25; *SP*, 2, citing Straeten, E. Van der, *The History of the Violin* (1933), 403; *SP*, 5, citing PRO LC3/58, 66; *SP*, 6, citing PRO LC3/19, 46, 56, PRO LC 5/56, PRO LC2/30, 31, 32. 3. *SP*,2. 4. ibid. citing ESRO SAS/RF 15/26.   5. ESRO SAS/RF 15/28.   6. ESRO SAS/I 302.   7. *SP*, 10, citing *Essay*, iii, iv. 8. *SP*, 1, citing *Essay*, 47. 9. *SP*, 1; Brent, J., 'The Pooles of Chailey and Lewes... 1732-79', *SAC* **114**, 79. 10. *SP*, 4, citing *Essay*, ix. 11. *SP*, 4. 12. *SP*, 4. 13. *SP*, 5, citing PRO LC3/58, 66; *SP*,6. 14. *SP*, 7, citing ESRO LEW/C 5/3/5-13. 15. ESRO PAR 411/30/1; *SP*, 7, citing ESRO SAS/I 37; SP, 3. 16. Balneath Manor Court Book, ESRO AMS 4599. 17. *SP*, 9, citing ESRO SAS/WG 465. 18. *SP*, 9, 10. 19. Tibble, R. 'The Pattern of Schooling in Lewes...' (1981, revised MS 1987), 7; *SWA* 10.12.70 (both news item and ad). 20. *SWA* 10.12.70.   21. ESRO PAR 411/30/1.   22. *SWA* 21.12.72.   23. ESRO PAR 411/31/3.

Another charity school   (F: 1733)
John Head was master of the charity school set up originally by Henry Pelham [qv above]. In 1733 the correspondence of the Duke of Newcastle (Pelham) records the following items:

> August 1733:   Head would not promise his vote to the Pelhams
> October 1733:   Head had 'entered the enemies club' [ie. joined the Tories]
> November 1733: It is reported that Head is to have £20 pa to teach 20 poor children which Sergison & Garland [the Pelhams' political opponents] are to clothe and 'the school begins on Monday'.[1]

It is not known how long this politically inspired charity school survived. Head took private pupils, and in 1736-7 was teaching Henry Manning's son Harry for £1 4s pa before he went on to Steyning grammar school.[2]   [*John Head*]

1. Brent, C., pers. comm. citing BL Add MS 32,688 ff 75, 527 and 32,689, f 19.   2.   ESRO SAS/I 302.

Rand family boys' day and boarding school   (Rs: 1732- into 19c)
Cater Rand senior probably came from Colchester, Essex, where he owned property; he was in the excise, and was posted to Lewes in 1714. By November 1732 he was a schoolmaster at Lewes, being paid 18s by Thomas Pelham of Stanmer for Owden's boy's schooling; the following September he received from the same source £1 10s 6d for the same boy's schooling for ¾ year. He is described as schoolmaster in the 1734 poll book. He received further payments for schooling from the Newcastle estate from 1734 to 1740, and from at least 1737 he was being paid £20 a year, presumably for Newcastle's 'free school' (see below). He also had private pupils. In 1733-4 Henry Manning paid him 16s for schooling his son Edward (aged 7-8) before he was sent to Steyning grammar school; and later, when his son Harry was at Lewes grammar school, paid him, presumably as writing master, and also appears to have paid him for schooling his daughter Bet; such payments continued from c1742 to Cater Rand's death in 1748, after which there was a further payment to Rand's son, Charles. By 1744 Cater Rand had set up school at 159/160 High Street (originally one house), adjoining St Michael's church on the east, as a tenant of the Pelham family. He was buried at St Michael's, 20 May 1748.[1]

On his death the school was carried on by his son, Charles. Like his father, Charles was also writing master to the grammar school, and was paid by Henry Manning 1753-4 for teaching his youngest son then at the grammar school (Rand apparently taught the grammar school boys at his own school, since Manning also paid him for 'firing' and 'breaking up'). Charles married Lucy Verall, 15 January 1749. He died in 1763. His widow, Lucy Rand, continued to run the school, probably until Michaelmas 1772, when it was continued by Charles and Lucy's son, Cater Rand junior. In 1780 and 1781 Lucy Rand was living in another house in St Michael's; she died 5 December 1781, 'of a cancerous disorder'.[2]

Cater Rand junior was by inclination and achievement a surveyor and civil engineer, and he promoted the school with a strong scientific bias (see below). From at least 1773 his school was a boarding school.[3] In 1775, (a) he married Mary Scrace, daughter of the master of the *White Hart* inn[4] (his mother, Lucy Verrall, had also been daughter of the master of the *White Hart* inn[5]); (b) had fitted up a room in his house as a physics laboratory;[6] and (c) by December that year had 'taken the House adjoining his own, and by opening proper Communications, has fitted it up in a convenient Manner, for the Reception of Boarders'.[7] This house - 161 High Street - he bought in 1779. But on 7 July 1784, described as a bookseller, stationer, dealer and chapman, he was declared bankrupt;[8] his household goods had been put up for auction in June 1784, and his house was put up for auction in December that year[9] (though in the land tax returns to 1791, and in a survey of 1791, he is still shown as proprietor of the house[10]); a dividend was paid, at the *White Hart* inn, on 21 September 1789.[11] He continued as a tenant of the Pelham family, both for the 'school' (part of 159/160) and, from 1792, for 161 (though the rent for the latter was not collected).[12] In the poll book for the general election of 1790 he is described, not as a schoolmaster, but as 'surveyor of the forts on the coast of Sussex'. But he is listed as schoolmaster in *Univ. Directory* 1793 and 1794, he was still renting the school in St Michael's in 1800, and in fact the school continued until 1807 or 1808. He was still an undischarged bankrupt in 1808.[13] In 1809, when he was 60, he relinquished the High Street houses and retired to a small, newly-built house he bought in North Street. In 1812, 'Rand' was nominally writing master at the grammar school, but does not appear to have actually taught there at that time.[14]

The Rands' school was supported by the Newcastle estate for a considerable period.

As noted above, 1737-39 Cater Rand senior was receiving £20 pa (and had received other payments for schooling from 1732: one of £10 in November 1736 suggests that, in addition to payment for the schooling of particular boys, a round fee had by then been established). By 1764 Lucy Rand was receiving £12 pa, 'by his Grace's free gift towards educating 18 Boys at the writing School at Lewes'. And at 23 January 1765 there were 18 boys 'belonging to his Grace the Duke of Newcastle's Free School'.[15] Pelham estate account books from 1769 to 1795,[16] show both the rents paid by the Rand family and 'free gifts' made to them for (now) 'teaching 12 boys to read and write'. The latter payments consisted of the £12 pa and were paid continuously for this whole 26-year period (from Michaelmas 1789 to Michaelmas 1795 the £12 pa was paid as 'salary'). The Pelham support was probably a political gesture: a house occupier who paid the poor rate was a 'householder' and entitled to vote, and also the 12 free boys were possibly the sons of tradespeople who had a vote. Payments covering the period from Michaelmas 1768 to Michaelmas 1772 were made to 'Mrs. Rand'/'Lucy Rand', thereafter to Cater Rand. It is therefore likely that Cater Rand junior formally took over the school at Michaelmas 1772. At the time of Cater Rand's bankruptcy, the payments for 21 months (£21), from Michaelmas 1782 to midsummer 1784, were paid to 'Cater Rand's Assignees'; for the period from midsummer 1784 onwards payments were again made to Cater Rand direct. The rent paid by the Rands was, for most of the period, £12 pa - the same as their 'free gift' for teaching 12 boys. The rent of £12 paid by Lucy Rand for the year to Michaelmas 1769 was partly off-set by allowances for 12 months land tax, at £1 4s, and '2 years wall rent to the churchwardens, part of this house having been built on the church wall of St. Michael's, 1s 4d. Lucy Rand paid the rent to Michaelmas 1774 (although Cater Rand had received the 'free gift' of £12 pa from Michaelmas 1772); from 1775 to 1785 Cater Rand paid the £12 pa. For the year to Michaelmas 1786 the rent of the house was split, Cater Rand paying only £8; and from Michaelmas 1786 until Lady day 1789, when the relevant account book ends, he paid just £4 pa 'rent for the School' (ie. for a schoolroom).

  Cater Rand junior's first advertisement mentioning his school, in September 1773, stated that 'Youth are Boarded, Educated, and qualified for all Manner of Business'.[17] His longer advertisement for the school in December 1773, after stating that the boys were taught by himself and 'proper assistants', continued: 'MR. RAND, with an ardent Desire of opening the narrow, confined Ideas of Youth, (which is too much neglected) intends going through a COURSE of LECTURES in EXPERIMENTAL PHILOSOPHY [ie. science] Three Evenings a Week, which will at once blend genuine Erudition with the first Principles of Religion, Taste, and Learning, and elevate their Minds, as they advance in Years, above the low Pursuits of sensual and tasteless Amusements.'[18] In 1774 he noted that he 'taught the various Branches of Mathematics, with the Use and Construction of the latest improved Instruments, &c. to facilitate and expedite the Theory and Practice of the Mathematical Arts, which immediately concern us, and are indispensably necessary in the common Affairs of Life, by ocular Demonstration, in a Series of Lectures, and the Learners own Practice on the Globes, Orrery, Conic Sections, Hadley's Quadrant, Theodolite, Sector, Scale, Sliding-Rule, Charts, Maps, Diagrams, &c. &c. and on a large Philosophical Apparatus, consisting of Electrical Machines, Air Pump, the Mechanical Powers, Microscopes, Telescopes, Hydrostatic Balance, and many other Contrivances, to render the Mathematical Arts easily attainable.'[19] In 1775, 'Religion, Morality, Chronology, and History' were mentioned among the subjects taught, and he noted that he had 'A large private Playing Yard, walled round'.[20] In 1776, 'FRENCH is taught in the House, by Mons. DARCEL, a Native of France.'[21] During these years Rand was also giving series of public lectures on scientific subjects, and promoting evening classes on the same.[22] In 1779 he was styling his school 'Lewes Commercial and Mathematical School', where 'the Plan of which is to form the Man of

Business', and the subjects taught were 'the English Language grammatically, Writing, Arithmetic, Book-keeping, the practical Parts of the Mathematics, viz. Geometry, Trigonometry, Logarithms, Navigation, Dialling, Perspective, Mensuration, Fortification and Gunnery, Gauging, Surveying, &c.'; with in addition scientific lectures through the winter, open to 'any young Gentlemen in the town' at half a guinea for the course, on Astronomy, Geography, Mechanics, Hydrostatics, Hydraulics, Optics, Magnetism, Chemistry, Pneumatics, and Electricity. His terms for boarders were £18 pa, with 1 guinea entrance.[23]

For the Rand/Gwynne controversy in 1779 over the timing of the summer vacation, see Grammar school above. For Cater Rand as surveyor and engineer, see Schedule 2.

Advertised in *SWA*:
> School: Sep (4), Oct (4), Nov (2), Dec (3) 1773; Jan, Dec (2) 74; Jan (3), Jun (2), Sep (3), Dec 75; Jan (2), Sep (3) 76; May (3) 79.
> Publications: Sep (4), Oct (4), Nov (2) 1773; Dec (2) 74; Jan (3) 75; Aug (3), Sep (2) 96.
> Public lectures: Dec (3) 1773; Jan (3), Feb (3) 74; Sep (3), Dec 75; Jan (2), Sep (3) 76; May (2) 79.

[*Cater Rand senior, Charles Rand, Lucy Rand, Cater Rand junior, Mons. Darcel* (French master)]

1. Farrant, J.H., 'Civil Engineering in Sussex around 1800, and the Career of Cater Rand', *Sussex Industrial History* 6 (Winter 1973/4), 4; St Michael PR; Farrant, J.H., pers. comm. citing BL Add MS 33,161 (Accounts of Thomas Pelham of Stanmer, 1730-34), ff 118, 164, and BL Add MS 33,157 (Cash Account of Robert Burnet, agent to the Duke of Newcastle for his property in Sussex, 1734-41) f 4 & ff, ff 22, 35, 41, 50, 51, 60; ESRO SAS/I 302. 2. Lucas, P. 'The Verrall Family of Lewes', *SAC* **58**, 127; *SNQ* **1**, 213; ESRO SAS/I 302; ESRO AMS 2132; ESRO Land Tax, St Michael; *SWA* 10.12.81; St Michael PR. 3. *SWA* 6.9.73. 4. St Michael PR; Farrant, op. cit., 4. 5. Lucas, op. cit., 127. 6. *SWA* 12.6.75. 7. *SWA* 25.12.75. 8. ESRO SAS/LEW 34. 9. Farrant, J.H., pers. comm. citing *SWA* 21.6.84, 13.12.84. 10. ESRO Land Tax, St Michael; Woolgar *Spicilegia*, I, 525-44, MS at SAS. 11. *The Lewes and Brighthelmston Pacquet* 3.9.89. 12. ESRO AMS 2133; Farrant, J.H., pers. comm., citing ESRO ACC 4600/102. 13. ESRO SAS/LEW 33. 14. Farrant, op. cit.,5; *EP*1 (1819), 235. 15. Farrant, J.H., pers. comm. citing BL Add MS 33,338, ff 71-72, and BL Add MS 33,139, f 146. 16. ESRO AMS 2132, 2133; Farrant, J.H., pers. comm. citing ESRO ACC 4600/102, f 149. 17. *SWA* 6.9.73. 18. *SWA* 13.12.73. 19. *SWA* 12.12.74. 20. *SWA* 25.12.75. 21. *SWA* 12.9.76. 22. Eg. *SWA* 13.12.73, 17.1.74: see list of lectures in next sentence, ads for them in *SWA* below, and Farrant, op. cit., 5, for details of the number of lectures and their subjects. 23. *SWA* 10.5.79.

Beard's school (Rs: 1733, 1750, 1755)

George Beard (1690-1772) was a schoolmaster in the Cliff. In the Newcastle correspondence for August 1733, re the county elections, it is stated that if George Beard does not vote the Duke's line, he will not teach Dr Russell's children to write (Dr Russell, of Malling deanery, by advocating Brighton's healthiness, was 'founder' of its fashionable prosperity).[1] In 1750 Beard paid the Cliff churchwardens £1 10s for one year's rent for the Market House, where he kept a school. In 1755 he again paid them £1 10s, presumably for the same.[2] He was nominated parish clerk in 1740 by the then rector of St Thomas at Cliffe, Edward Lund. He died in 1772, aged 82. [*George Beard*]

1. Brent, C., pers. comm. citing BL Add MS 32,688, f 56. 2. 'Extracts from Cliff Churchwardens Accounts', in Woolgar, *Spicilegia*, II, 233 (MS at SAS).

Halstead's school (Rs: 1741-2)

Henry Manning paid him for 'schooling' his sons when they were at Lewes grammar school, and he was probably writing master there; he charged 1s at each 'breaking up' and probably kept his own school. Probably also taught Manning's daughter Bet (perhaps as writing master to Philpot's 'dancing school'?).[1] [*James Halstead*]

1. ESRO SAS/I 302.

Verrall's school   (Rs: 1750-2)
Thomas Verrall was paid by Henry Manning for schooling his son Ned (six in 1750): 27
December 1750, 8s; 25 January 1752, 'to Xmas last one Year', 13s; 25 January 1753, '¾ yr
to Michaelmas last', 9s (Ned then went on to Lewes grammar school).   [*Thomas Verrall*]
1. ESRO SAS/I 302.

Burton's school   (R: c1750)
Walter Gale, master of Mayfield school, noted in his diary for 26 April 1750: 'I set off for
Brighthelmstone, and came at noon to Malling-street [Lewes], and went to the Dolphin.
Kennard told me that Burton's successor had had a great many scholars, but that their
number began to decrease, by reason of his sottishness, and he offered, if their dislike of
him should increase, to let me know of it. The rain clearing off at three o'clock, I set out
for Brighthelmstone, passing through Southover...'[1] From this it appears that Burton had a
school, almost certainly in Lewes and perhaps in the Cliff, that by 1750 had been taken over
by a successor.   [*Burton*]
1. *SAC* 9, 196 (corrected date).

Mrs Relfe's girls' boarding school   (R: 1762)
In February 1762 Mrs Relfe, 'who hath for many Years kept a Boarding-School, for young
Ladies, with great Reputation, in Lewes,' advertised to deny a report that she was intending
to give up the school: '... she still carries on the Business, with the same Assistants, as usual;
where young Ladies may be genteely boarded, and instructed in every necessary
Accomplishment, upon moderate Terms.'[1] (Thomas Turner's sister, Sarah, born 17 August
1738, was sent to school at Lewes;[2] perhaps she attended Mrs Relfe's school.)
[*Mrs Relfe*]
1. *SWA* 22.2.62.   2. Jennings, G.H., ed. *Thomas Turner - The Diary of a Georgian Shopkeeper* (1979), 81.

Mrs Ridge's school   (R: 1768)
In January 1769 Elizabeth Ollive, announcing the opening of her own girls' boarding school,
described herself as 'late Teacher to Mrs. RIDGE, who lately declined the Business on
Account of her Health';[1] from which it can be gathered that Mrs Ridge had a school which
she gave up some time in 1768.   [*Mrs Ridge*]
1. *SWA* 30.1.69.

Hearnden's boys' boarding school   (Rs: 1769-71)
Benjamin Hearnden specifically promoted his school for qualifying boys for business, and
was the first schoolmaster in Sussex, so far traced, to have done so. An advertisement in
August 1769 began: 'YOUTH Boarded, and expeditiously qualified for Business / By BENJ.
HEARNDEN, Schoolmaster / In the CLIFFE, LEWES'. He taught 'WRITING in the
various Hands now in Use. ARITHMETIC, thro' all its Branches, both Practical and
Theoretical, viz. VULGAR, DECIMAL, &c. FRACTIONS, with the Extraction of the
Roots, DUODECIMALS, MERCHANTS ACCOMPTS according to the Italian Method.
GAUGING, any Branch of MENSURATIONS, &c. by concise and practical FORMS.'
Hearnden's business clients would be concerned with time and money, and he stressed - 'No
Pains will be spared, that they may make a speedy Progress'; and he added the usual
assurance - 'and a particular Attention will be paid, as well to their Morals as Manners.' He
also promised, 'Those who shall please to entrust him with the Tuition of their Children,
may depend on the greatest Care and Tenderness of them': this was conventionally included
in such advertisements, but Hearnden may have meant it more than most - when later master
of Mayfield school, with his own private boarding school also, he made the most forceful
apologia recorded in Sussex for the sympathetic approach to teaching [qv MAYFIELD].[1]
        In addition to his own school, Hearnden was also writing master to a girls' boarding

school. When appointed master of Mayfield school in 1771, he advertised his Lewes school as follows: '... there will be a Vacancy for a Schoolmaster, in the CLIFF, LEWES, at Christmas next, who will have the Opportunity of coming into a large School of Boys, on very reasonable Terms, besides the Advantage of being WRITING MASTER to a Young LADIES BOARDING-SCHOOL.' In the same advertisement he announced that, at Mayfield, 'he intends to continue taking in Boarders as usual.'[2]

He resigned Mayfield school at Christmas 1783, and returned to Lewes, opening the *Wheat-Sheaf* inn in Malling Street in January 1784.

Advertised in *SWA* Aug (2), Dec 1769; Jan 70; Nov 71; (inn) Jan 84.
[*Benjamin Hearnden*]
1. *SWA* 21.8.69.   2. *SWA* 25.11.71.

Elizabeth Ollive's girls' boarding school   (F: 1769)
In January 1769 Elizabeth Ollive, daughter of Samuel Ollive, tobacconist of Bull House, and then aged 19, opened a boarding school for young ladies 'at Mr. Feron's, two Doors above Verral's Coffee-House, in Lewes; where all those who shall please to favour her with their Children, may depend upon having the greatest Care taken of them...' She had formerly been a teacher to Mrs Ridge, who had lately given up her school on account of her health.[1]

In July 1769, Samuel Ollive died. In March 1771 Elizabeth married, as his second wife, Thomas Paine (of *The Rights of Man*, &c.), 12 years her senior. He had lodged with the Ollives on coming to Lewes as excise officer in February 1768; after Samuel's death, he had moved out of the house, but joined the widow in running the tobacco (and later grocery) business. By 1774 Paine's grocery and tobacco business failed, and on 14 and 15 April 1774 'all the household furniture, stock in trade and other effects of Thomas Paine, grocer and tobacconist near the West Gate, in Lewes' were sold by auction. In June of that year, Thomas and Elizabeth formally separated. It is not known how long Elizabeth continued as schoolmistress; in 1793 she was a mantua-maker, near London; she eventually lived with her brother, Thomas, a watchmaker at Cranbrook, Kent. (See Schedule 2 for biographical details.)   [*Elizabeth Ollive*]
1. *SWA* 30.1.69.

The Miss Lunds' girls' boarding schools   (Rs: 1772-85)
In December 1772 Philadelphia and Charlotte Lund, daughters of Rev Edward Lund, then aged 46 and 39 respectively, announced that they were moving their boarding school for young ladies into the Philpot school premises in St Anne's (so the Lunds' school had been in existence before then). After Stephen Philpot's death in 1770, the latter had been run by his daughter, Ann, who had now married and given up the school. By then the school occupied two neighbouring houses, one being the St Anne's parsonage. The Lunds' advertisement noted that it was 'a very airy and healthy Situation'. They offered careful instruction in religion, morality, and polite behaviour, with 'The English Grammar and Reading in the best and newest Method, French, Tambour-Work, and all Sorts of Useful and Ornamental Needle-Work'. Music, dancing, drawing, writing, arithmetic and geography were 'by proper MASTERS'.[1]

At the end of 1776 the partnership between the two sisters was dissolved.[2] Philadelphia apparently continued with the school in St Anne's for a time. In January 1777 Charlotte announced that 'she has taken a commodious House on SCHOOL-HILL, LEWES, for the EDUCATION of YOUNG LADIES. Proper Masters are engaged for every genteel Accomplishment, and the strictest regard will be paid to the Morals of her Pupils'. She had 'Genteel Accomodations for Parlour Boarders', and the school opened on 20 January. It was at 25 School Hill.[3]

However, there is no record of her paying land tax on the property after 1780 (when the surviving records begin), and it seems as if Charlotte may have moved back to St Anne's in 1778 and taken over Philadelphia's school there. Philadelphia was charged poor rates on the St Anne's property - that is, for the two adjoining houses - from April 1773 to April 1777; from May 1778 to March 1784 the poor rates were paid by Charlotte. From June 1784 to August 1785 Charlotte was charged for just one house (the parsonage). Land tax assessments show Charlotte as charged for just the one house from 1780 (when the surviving assessments begin) to 1785, when the school was taken over by Miss Ryall (who, according to the poor rates, took on both the adjoining houses from 1791). The Lunds' school had apparently shrunk by the last years of their tenure.[4]

[*Philadelphia Lund, Charlotte Lund*]

1. *SWA* 21.12.72.   2. *SWA* 13.1.77.   3. ibid.; *SAC* **93**, 4.   4. ESRO Land Tax, All Saints, St Anne; ESRO PAR 411/30/1.

Boys' and girls' day school   (F: 1770)
In June 1770 the following advertisement appeared: 'AT Mr. Nutley's near the White-Hart Back-Gate in St. Mary's-Lane, Lewes, is a Gentleman that was educated in London, who intends opening a Boys' day SCHOOL, as a MASTER, to teach Youth to READ and WRITE the ENGLISH TONGUE, to give the true Spelling and right Pronunciation, correct, with Ease and Propriety; Also ARITHMETIC, according to the best approved Methods now used in the Academies in London, &c. Young LADIES are likewise taught as above either at their own Houses, or at the School. He proposes opening School on Monday next, the second of July.'[1] [Possibly Mr Tasker's school (see below), though his was a boys' boarding school by 1773.]

1. *SWA* 25.6.70

Tasker's boys' boarding school   (R:1773)
In May 1773, 'At Mr. TASKER's SCHOOL, at Lewes, Young Gentlemen are Boarded, and instructed in ENGLISH, WRITING, and ACCOMPTS, on moderate Terms.'[1]

[*Tasker*]

1. *SWA* 31.5.73.

Grooms' (day) school   (Rs: 1774-82).
Thomas Grooms was a schoolmaster at Lewes in 1774 and 1780 (poll books). In 1782, John Grooms was paying £3 3s pa to the Shelley estate for a schoolroom that had been made, after Christmas 1781, out of the loft of a warehouse in West Gate Lane. The schoolroom is recorded in a survey of 1790: 'Old building late Malthouse now Stables & a School Room'.[1] In 1780 and 1781 Thomas Grooms was occupying a house in St Michael's; from 1782 to 1789 this house was occupied by John Grooms.[2]

[*Thomas Grooms, John Grooms*]

1. ESRO SAS/DN 184 (property no. 27); Woolgar *Spicilegia*, I, 525-44, MS at SAS.   2. ESRO Land Tax, St Michael.

The Miss Adams's girls' boarding school   (F: c1774.   Rs: 1781- into 19c)
The sisters Mary and Hannah Adams had kept a school from c1774;[1] from at least 1781 the school was in the Cliffe, Lewes; in November 1782 the sisters denied a report that they were giving up their school, where they offered board, English, plain and fine needlework, 'with many other Branches of useful and polite Learning', for £15 pa; writing, use of the globes, dancing, music and French were extras, taught by visiting masters.[2] In July 1789 they had moved from their house in the Cliffe to School Hill, at 208, on the north side, which had 'a good Garden and Play Ground', where the school flourished until c1817.[3] In a 1790 survey of Lewes the house is shown as owned by Mary Adams, with 20 inhabitants.[4] In addition to the house used as a school (assessed for land tax at a rent value of £6 15s, reduced to £5 in 1794 and to £3 15s in 1796), Mary Adams also owned the house next door,

which she rented out.[5]

In 1790 the 'Young Ladies at Miss Adam's Boarding School' subscribed £2 2s to the public appeal for the three Michell orphans left destitute at the death of their father, Richard Michell, curate of Eastdean and schoolmaster.[6]

At the end of 1792 Hannah Adams went to Paris to study French, but was caught there by the war, and was not able to return until the end of 1795. In December 1795, their advertisement appeared in both English and French, and the school offered English, French, geography, ancient and modern history, plain and fine needle and fancy work. Hannah Adams had 'passed three years at Paris devoted to the study of the French language, and lately returned to her native country' - and traumatic years they must have been for her, prevented from returning by the war, held in Paris through the worst excesses of the Revolution and the Terror. In the 1790s one of the sisters held 'enlightened' views, and one was reactionary; the 'enlightened' sister was almost certainly Hannah, who had gone to Paris when the Revolution was well under way and may have been inspired to go at that time by sympathy with the early ideals of the Revolution (see ADAMS, Hannah, in Schedule 2).[7]

The school suffered nuisance and danger from bonfires and fireworks on School Hill at the 5 November celebrations. Mary Adams and her neighbour John Spilsbury actively campaigned against such nuisance, and in consequence in 1797 squibs with stones tied to them, fireworks and combustibles were thrown into their houses, setting Spilsbury's house and part of Miss Adams's furniture on fire. In 1798 they petitioned the magistrates for protection, and as a result nearly 100 special constables were sworn in to preserve the peace on 5 November - they were unable to prevent a bonfire on School Hill, but did deter the use of fireworks there (apart from a few squibs thrown surreptitiously into the fire).[8]

In 1800 William Austin was drawing master at the school.[9]

The school took day pupils as well as boarders. A bill of 1804 has survived, for a half-year's education for a Miss Grover, daughter of Simon Grover, a Lewes vetinerary surgeon; the annual fee for day girls was then £2 2s, but there were a number of extras:[10]

	£	s	d
Miss Grover half a year's Edu'n to Chmas	1.	1.	-
A french Gram'r		3.	6
A Copy-Book			8
Fables Vo. french		2.	6
A Spellg. Book		1.	3
Dancing	2.	2.	-
Entrance to Do.		10.	6
French	1.	1.	-
Entrance to Do.		10.	6
Use of Books & News p'r.		2.	-
Breaking up & Fine		3.	6
	£5.	18.	5
Dancing deducted	2.	2.	-
	3.	16.	5

Advertised in *SWA* Nov, Dec 1782; Jul 89; Jun 93; Jan 94; Dec 95; Jan 96. In *Univ. Directory* 1793, 94; *Baxter's Directory* 1805.

[*Mary Adams, Hannah Adams, William Austin* (drawing master)]

1. Letter from Elizabeth Hitchener to Shelley, 23 October 1811, in Jones, F.L. *The Letters of Percy Bysshe Shelley*, v.1 (1964), 160. 2. ESRO Land Tax, St Thomas; *SWA* 25.11.82. 3. *SWA* 20.7.89; ESRO Land Tax, All Saints; Davey, L.S. *The Street Names of Lewes* (1970), 50. 4. Woolgar *Spicilegia*, I, 525-44, MS at SAS. 5. ESRO Land Tax, All Saints. 6. *SWA* 1.3.90. 7. *SWA* 28.12.95. 8. *SWA* 5.11.98, 12.11.98. 9. *SWA* 24.3.1800 (Austin ad). 10. ESRO AMS 634.

Parish schooling   (Rs: 1775, 1787-9)

In 1775 the St Michael overseers paid small sums for John Glazebrook's (Grizbrook's) schooling, at 2d a week (8d in April; 1s 6d in June; 4d 'for 2 Weeks Schooling' in July). But such support for a pauper child appears to have been rare. (In 1776 they paid £5 'towards apprenticing Will'm Grizbrook', perhaps John's elder brother.)[1]

The St Anne's overseers' accounts[2] show the following payments:

		£	s	d
1787 June 23	Paid for Eliz'h Gates Scooling	0.	1.	4
1788 March 15	Paid for a Book for Ann Jenner	0.	0.	6
	Paid for Scooling of Feering & Gates	0.	3.	0
March 29	Paid for Eleven weeks Scooling for E'h Gates	0.	1.	10
1789 Jan'y 13	Paid Mrs Goldsmith for Little Gates School as P Bill	0.	8.	0
1789-90 year	Mrs Goldsmith's Bill for Gates Schooling	0.	11.	9

These payments indicate that the parish did pay, at least on occasion, for the schooling of individual pauper children (at 2d or 3d a week). Mrs Goldsmith was probably the wife of William Goldsmith, a shoemaker in the parish, who was paid by the overseers for supplying shoes (eg. 19s 7d in 1781; 8s 10d in 1782) and larger amounts in some years (eg. £4 13s 11d in 1790; £4 4s 5d in 1791) in settlement of his bills, for which the services/goods were not specified but may possibly have included some charges for his wife's teaching.
[*Mrs Goldsmith*]

1. ESRO PAR 414/31/1/2.   2. ESRO PAR 411/31/3.

Jones, private tutor   (R: 1775)

In January 1775 H. Jones advertised to 'all Gentlemen and Ladies in and near LEWES, That he proposes to instruct Young Gentlemen, at their own Houses, in Book-keeping, Algebra, Trigonometry, the Projection of the Sphere, Gauging, Surveying, Dialling, Navigation, and the Use of the Globes in Geography, Navigation, and Astronomy.' His advertisement is notable for promoting the fascination of geography and astronomy, for both sexes, and for seeking encouragement from gentlemen 'who are Lovers of the Arts and Sciences'. He also advertised surveying services.

> He humbly conceives, that he shall meet with the Approbation of those Gentlemen who are conversant in Geography and Astronomy, when he recommends the Use of the Globes, as a very useful and entertaining Science, to those Gentlemen and Ladies who desire to improve their Knowledge of our Planet, and of the glorious, though most amazing Works of the Creator, visible around us, a competent Knowledge of which may be soon obtained.
> ☞ Estates accurately surveyed, and neatly planned, Timber, &c. measured, Levels taken for the conducting of Water, &c.
> N.B. As he can be well recommended by Gentlemen of Fortune and Character, he humbly hopes he shall meet with Encouragement from those Gentlemen who are Lovers of the Arts and Sciences.
> A Line, left for him at the STAR, will be duly attended to.

[*H. Jones*]

1. *SWA* 2.1.75.

<u>Mrs Symonds' girls' day and boarding school</u>   (Rs: 1782-3)
<u>Mr Symonds' boys' day, evening and boarding school</u>   (F: 1783.   Rs: 1783-92)
In November 1782 Mrs Symonds advertised her girls' boarding school, 'opposite Mr. Woodgates, in the Cliffe'. The girls were 'taught the English Language grammatically; and instructed in every Branch of useful and ornamental Needle-work, Embroidery, &c.' for 14 guineas pa. 'Every other Branch of Female Education is taught by approved Masters in the Town.' No entrance money was required. She also kept a day school: 'Constant Attendance will be paid to a Day-School, and the next Christmas Vacation will be omitted.'[1]
A year later, her advertisement for the girls' school included the following:
>   Mr. SYMONDS intends opening a Boys' school after the Holidays, where he will teach English, Writing, and Arithmetic, and also an Evening School.
>   N.B. No Entrance Money will be required.[2]
In July 1788, acknowledging the encouragement he had received, William Symonds announced that he had engaged 'a proper Assistant' in his school, and that 'He limits the number of his Boarders to Six, on reasonable Terms.'[3] Symonds also had separate stationery and bookselling businesses, which he advertised in 1789 and 1792 (in the latter advertisement, he advertised a sale of musical instruments and books).[4] In January 1793 the school was taken over by Edward Pugh, and run as a day school (see below).[5] Symonds was clearly getting into financial difficulties. In May that year, in addition to his bookselling and stationery businesses, he added those of auctioneer and paperhanger,' in which he hopes for the encouragement of the public';[6] but in December 1793 he assigned all his estate and effects to trustees, to be sold for the benefit of his creditors; in November 1795, his creditors were called to submit their accounts, and in December 1795 all his effects were sold by auction.[7]
Mrs Symonds was almost certainly the Mrs Elizabeth Symonds admitted into the East Gate Baptist church in the Cliffe in May 1786; William Symonds had been admitted in September 1785. The church records show that Elizabeth Symonds died in July 1787, and that William was excluded from the church in January 1791, following a report 'prejudicial to the moral character of Brother Symonds'.[8]
[Mrs (Elizabeth?) Symonds, William Symonds]
1. *SWA* 11.11.82.   2. *SWA* 22.12.83.   3. *SWA* 14.7.88   4. *SWA* 23.3.89, 30.4.92.   5. *SWA* 7.1.93.
6. *SWA* 13.5.93.   7. *SWA* 23.6.94, 16.11.95, 14.12.95.   8. ESRO NB 1/1/1A.

<u>Bartlett's school</u>   (Rs: 1785- into 19c)
John Bartlett, schoolmaster of Lewes, rented a 'school' or 'school house' in All Saints parish from 1785 to 1790 (assessed for land tax at 'rentals' from £1 10s to £2 5s).[1] In 1790 his house was in Fish Street, on the west side, rented from Serjt. Kemp, and there were six inhabitants.[2] From 1791 to 1794 he continued at this house (land tax 'rental' £3 pa), and additionally rented a schoolhouse in St John sub Castro, owned by Henry Shelley (land tax 'rental' £1 10s pa). In 1795 the schoolhouse passed to Thomas Mantell, and Bartlett continued to rent it (though he appears to have moved to a cheaper house, land tax 'rental' £1 pa, and the next year into a different house, land tax 'rental' £1 10s pa). In 1796 the schoolhouse was occupied by a Mr Cruttenden; but in 1798 John Bartlett is shown as the owner of 'Land Garden Schoole', almost certainly the same schoolhouse, occupied that year by a Mrs Stokes (land tax 'rental' £1 10s pa). That year and the following John Bartlett was one of the land tax assessors for the parish. In 1799 and 1800 (and 1801) he is shown as both owning and occupying the 'Garden and School Room', while continuing to occupy the house he rented in the parish.[3] Described as 'schoolmaster' in a 1790 survey of Lewes, and in poll books of 1790, 1796 and 1802.[4]   *[John Bartlett]*

1. ESRO Land Tax, All Saints. 2. Woolgar, *Spicilegia*, I, 525-44, MS at SAS. 3. ESRO Land Tax, St John sub Castro. 4. Woolgar, op. cit.; *SWA* 28.6.90; poll books 1796, 1802 at ESRO.

<u>Miss Ryall's girls' boarding school</u> (originally <u>Brooksbank and Ryall's</u>)   (Rs: 1786-93)
In December 1787 the school was advertised as 'Brooksbank's and Ryall's'.[1] In October 1788 they announced that their partnership was dissolved, by mutual consent, and that the school would in future be carried on by Miss Ryall.[2] In fact, Susan Ryall paid the land tax, 1786-93, on the premises in St Anne's that had previously housed the Lunds' school (and before that the Philpots' school). From April 1786, from the poor rates assessments, she occupied just the one house there, the parsonage (the Lunds appear to have given up in the 1780s the adjacent house that they, and the Philpots before them, had earlier occupied).[3] In a survey of 1790, Miss Ryall's boarding school was occupying only one of these two houses, with 19 people living in the house; but from May 1791 she was assessed for poor rates on both the houses.[4]

Ryall's Christmas holidays seem to have been a little longer than most, ending on 26 January in 1789, 25 January in 1790, 24 January in 1791.[5]

In February 1790 the young ladies of Miss Ryall's boarding school gave £1 1s to the public subscription for the three Michell children left destitute orphans at the death in January of Richard Michell, schoolmaster, and curate of Eastdean.[6]

At Christmas 1793 Miss Ryall resigned the school to the Miss Dodsons (see below), taking a courteous advertisement to announce this: 'MISS RYALL returns her grateful acknowledgements to her friends, for the encouragement she has received; takes the liberty of soliciting the continuance of their favors to the MISS DODSONS, to whom she has resigned her School, at Lewes.'[7] That month, December 1793, she married William Rose, curate of Little Horsted, who the next month opened his boys' boarding school at the parsonage there (later moved to Uckfield).

Advertised in *SWA* Dec 1787; Oct 88; Jan 89; Jan, Dec 90; Jun, Dec 91; Jun, Dec 92; Jun, Dec 93.
[*Miss S. Brooksbank, Susannah Ryall*]

1. *SWA* 24.12.87. 2. *SWA* 6.10.88. 3. ESRO Land Tax, St Anne; ESRO PAR 411/30/2.
4. Woolgar *Spicilegia*, I, 528, MS at SAS; ESRO PAR 411/30/2. 5. *SWA* 5.1.89, 4.1.90, 27.12.90.
6. *SWA* 22.2.90. 7. *SWA* 23.12.93.

<u>Mrs Hook's school</u>   (R: 1787)
Mrs Hook had a school 'near the Market-House'. In April 1787 she announced that she had given up the school and 'is just returned from LONDON, with a fresh and fashionable Assortment of MILLENARY GOODS.'[1] Probably the Mrs Hannah Hook admitted into the East Gate Baptist church in the Cliffe in May 1786.[2]   [*Mrs (Hannah?) Hook*]
1. *SWA* 30.4.87. 2. ESRO NB 1/1/1A.

<u>Raymond's boys' French boarding school</u>   (Rs: 1787- into 19c)
By 1787, Victor Amedée Raymond, a Swiss, had established his academy in Lewes, where 'YOUNG GENTLEMEN are genteelly boarded, and carefully taught FRENCH, LATIN, ENGLISH, WRITING, ARITHMETIC, GEOGRAPHY, and the Use of the GLOBES...
The Terms are moderate, and no Entrance Money required. Dancing, Music, Drawing, &c. are extra Charges.' The distinguishing feature of the school was -
French is the only Language allowed to be spoken among the Scholars...[1]
More specifically, as noted in 1793:
French, is the only Language allowed to be spoken among the Scholars, in and out of school hours; Sundays only excepted.[2]
Raymond first described his school in advertisements as a 'French Academy' in 1788, when he advertised for an assistant 'properly qualified to teach WRITING, ARITHMETIC, and

ENGLISH... N.B. The Preference, and a due Encouragement will be given to a Person versed in Navigation, or in any other Part of the Mathematics.[13]

In August 1788 John Byng, later Viscount Torrington, and his wife took their son Henry to the school: 'He, poor little Fellow, to be placed here at School for the 1st time... After Dinner we took our Son Henry to the School, seemingly very fit for little Fellows, (kept by Mr. Raymond - a Swiss, and his wife, - who are very Careful People, and competent of such Charge) where I hope he will improve in Strength by the goodness of the Air.' The Sussex air was presumably efficacious - later in life Henry became a Vice-Admiral.[4]

From 1783 to 1785 Raymond had rented 135 High Street, and from 1786 to 1788 174 High Street;[5] at Easter 1789 he announced that 'he has purchased that large, most commodious, and very airy Mansion House of Dr. FREWEN, situated on the Middle of SCHOOL HILL [on the north side], which he will enter upon immediately, for the Reception of the young Gentlemen, after the short Recess of Easter.'[6] An Easter recess, as well as the longer holidays at midsummer and Christmas, is seldom mentioned by the schools, and it is helpful to have this evidence of it. (Raymond's midsummer and Christmas holidays were at that time 4½ weeks each, starting on a Thursday, with school reopening on a Monday.[7]) In 1790 there were 42 people living in the house,[8] which suggests a substantial boarding school for the time - it was considerably larger than the grammar school. The house, previously that of Dr Frewen, the pioneer of inoculation against the smallpox, had once been the *Turk's Head* inn; in 1789 it was reported to have had 31 windows; it was owned and occupied by Raymond from 1789 into the 19th century; in 1821 it was demolished to make room for Albion Street.[9]

In July and August 1791 Raymond's long advertisements were in French. They began:

> Comme il est à présumer qu'en conséquence du traité de commerce qui subsiste entre la FRANCE & la GRANDE BRETAGNE, quantité de personnes engagées dans les affaires ou autres, seront bien aises de faire instruire leurs enfans dans la Langue Françoise, Monsieur RAYMOND qui tient une pension accréditée à LEWES, dans le Comté de SUSSEX, prend la liberté de leur offrir ses services...

> [As it is to be assumed that, as a result of the commercial treaty which exists between FRANCE and GREAT BRITAIN, a number of people engaged in business activities or otherwise, would be well advised to have their children taught in the French Language, Mr. RAYMOND, who has an accredited boarding school in LEWES, in the County of SUSSEX, takes the liberty of offering them his services...]

Raymond continued: 'He will neglect nothing in order to satisfy the parents or guardians of the young people that they entrust into his care, and the successes which have already crowned his work in this field, allow him to speak with confidence. French is taught grammatically in his school and the constant contact of the boarders with Mr. Raymond allows them to make rapid and solid progress. Also taught are the scholarly Languages, Writing, Arithmetic, English, the Globes & Geography. The price for boarders is 18 Guineas a year. Drawing, Music & other accompanying Arts are paid for separately...' He gave the names and addresses of four people who could be applied to in London.[10]

In December 1791 he announced that 'for the better accomodation of his Scholars, he has built, adjoining to his Dwelling-house, a large and commodious School-room, 40 feet by 20, and 13 feet high. The Play-ground is extensive and contiguous to the School-room.'[11]

In January 1795 he offered references 'to respectable families, whose sons have now completed their education.'[12] By July 1795 the curriculum was 'English, Greek, Latin,

French, Writing, Arithmetic in its various branches, Merchants Accompts, Mensuration, and Geography,' taught by Raymond and 'able assistants'.[13] In 1796 Nicholson was music and dancing master at the school, being sponsored by Raymond (as Nicholson noted in an advertisement) to the extent that 'Mr. RAYMOND gives Mr. NICHOLSON the free use of his large Dining-room, to teach any Scholars that may offer, till he can meet with another every way suitable to his wishes.'[14] In 1800 William Austin was drawing master at the school, attending part of Mondays.[15]

In *Univ. Directory* 1793 and 1794, 'J. Raymond' is listed as schoolmaster (V.A.Raymond is not mentioned), but Victor Amedée was still thanking the public for their patronage in 1819.[16] The academy was listed in *Baxter's Directory* 1805.

It is notable that Raymond's French Academy was successful through the time of the French Revolution and the Terror, and the long war with France, when Sussex was substantially garrisoned by the military.

Raymond was a protestant dissenter, and his daughters Marie Petroline and Victoire Justine were baptised at the Westgate meeting house.

Advertised in *SWA* Jul 1787; Jun (2), Jul, Dec 88; Apr (2), May, Jun, Jul, Dec (2) 89; Jun, Jul, Dec (2) 90; Jul (2), Aug, Dec 91; Jan (2), Jul (2) 92; Jan (2), Jul (2), Dec (2) 93; Jun, Jul 94; Jan (2), Jul (2) 95; Jan (2), Jul (2) 96; Jan (2) 97.

[*Victor Amedée Raymond, (J.Raymond?), Nicholson* (music and dancing master), *William Austin* (drawing master)]

1. *SWA* 16.7.87. 2. *SWA* 8.7.93. 3. *SWA* 28.7.88. 4. Andrews, F., ed. *The Torrington Diaries* (1954 edn), 9-28; *SCM* v.7, 300, 302. 5. ESRO Land Tax, St Michael and St Anne; house nos. from Brent, C., pers. comm. 6. *SWA* 13.4.89. 7. *SWA* 15.12.88, 28.6.90, 13.12.90. 8. Woolgar *Spicilegia*, I, 525-44, MS at SAS. 9. Davey, L.S. *The Street Names of Lewes* (1970), 14-15; ESRO Land Tax, All Saints; Tibble, op cit, 5. 10. *SWA* 25.7.91. 11. *SWA* 26.12.91. 12. *SWA* 5.1.95. 13. *SWA* 6.7.95. 14. *SWA* 19.9.96. 15. *SWA* 24.3.1800 (Austin ad). 16. Brent, C., pers. comm. citing *SWA*.

Sarah Harman's school   (R: 1788)
Referred to in *SWA* 28 January 1788: '... Sarah Harman... who keeps a little school here...'
[*Sarah Harman*]

Sunday schools   (F: c1788.   Rs: 1789-91)
By February 1788 the inhabitants of Southover had already entered into a subscription for a Sunday school in that parish;[1] and in Lewes a public meeting was called for 13 February, at six o'clock in the evening, at the *Star* inn, 'to consult on a proper Plan' for the establishment of a Sunday school 'in Lewes, the Cliffe, and adjacent Places'.[2] That meeting, chaired by Sir Henry Blackman, was well attended; it agreed 'that the Institution of SUNDAY SCHOOLS is highly laudable and ought to be encouraged'; but 'no well-digested plan being produced, nothing conclusive, as to the mode of its establishment, was resolved on'; and a further meeting was called for 28 February, at the *White Hart*.[3] Lewes, containing a number of parishes, was faced with a problem that had not arisen at Brighton, where a large Sunday school had been established earlier that month, namely '... whether one general School, under the direction of a Committee of Subscribers at large, or distinct parochial Schools, were the most eligible... '[4] At the second February meeting 'of the GENTLEMEN, CLERGY, and principal INHABITANTS of the Town of *Lewes*, and its Neighbourhood', a society was established for the support and encouragement of Sunday schools in Lewes and its environs, and a subscription was opened for the purpose (and 'a very liberal subscription was entered into'). Sir Henry Blackman was appointed treasurer, and 14 gentlemen, being of the committee (for which a minimum annual subscription of 1 guinea was required), were nominated to receive subscriptions.[5] At a further meeting on 14 March, at the *Bridge Coffee-House*, officers were appointed and procedures agreed, and it was resolved:

That it be recommended, (and it is herein accordingly recommended) to all Ministers, Churchwardens, Overseers, and other Inhabitants of the Town of Lewes, the Cliffe, and Neighbourhood thereof, to open and establish SUNDAY-SCHOOLS, within their respective Parishes, for the Instruction of poor Children, of all Denominations.

That parochial Schools opened as above recommended, on proper Application being made to the Secretary, be entitled to the Benefit of the general Fund, raised for the support of this Institution, in such Proportion as their Exigences may require, or as a Committee at their meeting shall judge proper.[6]

Lewes, then, adopted central funding for the support of individual parish Sunday schools. No doubt such were established, but it is not known how many, or when. On 21 December 1789, on the last day of its season, the theatre at Lewes gave a performance of the *Merchant of Venice* and the *Apprentice* 'for the benefit of the Sunday Schools'; '... the Manager and his company have generously agreed, that the WHOLE amount of this night's performance, shall go to the above laudable institutions. The idea of playing for the Sunday Schools, both here and at Brighton, originated with Lord Eardley, whose contributions have been very liberal on the occasion.'[7] Lewes, however, does not seem to have been as effective as Brighton at fund-raising, and the following week the *SWA* reported on the theatre's charity performance: '... the receipt of the house fell much short of what we could have expected, from an amusement that had charity for its object. An address on the occasion was delivered by a gentleman of the town, and by whom we are told it was written; but he spoke it in a tone of voice too low for us to hear him distinctly, or to catch enough of it's connection to decide on its merit. We can therefore only say, that he made his exit with applause.'[8]

In March 1790 Southover parish advertised for a properly qualified person, 'to instruct the CHILDREN of the SUNDAY SCHOOL, belonging to the above parish, in PLAIN PSALMODY.'[9]

In her will dated 8 December 1791, Elizabeth Langton of Battle, endowing a charity school, referred to 'Sunday School as now practised at Brighthelmston or Lewes.'[10]

In October 1792, at the Quarter Sessions held at Lewes, the chairman in his charge to the grand jury 'observed and lamented, that of late felonies had much increased in this division of our County; and as a means of preventing them in future, he recommended attention to *Sunday* Schools.'[11]

1. *SWA* 4.2.88 (editorial).   2. ibid. (ad).   3. *SWA* 18.2.88 (editorial and ad).   4. ibid. (editorial).
5. *SWA* 3.3.88 (editorial and ad).   6. *SWA* 17.3.88 (ad).   7. *SWA* 21.12.89 (editorial and ad).
8. *SWA* 28.12.89.   9. *SWA* 22.3.90.   10. ESRO PAR 236/1/1/5, f 5r.   11. *SWA* 8.10.92.

Bedding's school   (Rs: 1790, 1791)
John Bedding was 'schoolmaster' at the general election of 1790.[1] In 1791 he rented ('Mr. Biding') the schoolhouse in All Saints parish previously used by John Bartlett for his school (see above).[2]   [*John Bedding*]
1. *SWA* 28.6.90   2. ESRO Land Tax, All Saints

Button's boys' day and later boarding school   (F: 1791.   Rs: 1791- into 19c)
John Button, a Baptist, then aged 29, opened in the High Street his 'English Grammar School' on 11 July 1791, 'Where particular attention will be paid to teach the English Language grammatically: likewise Writing and Arithmetic, by the most approved methods. N.B. The strictest attention will be paid to the various tempers and dispositions of the Pupils, and that mode of instruction adopted to suit their several capacities, and which will tend to conciliate their esteem both for their Tutor and their Learning.' His terms were:

Reading, Writing, and Arithmetic,   10s. 6d. per quarter.

Reading --- --- ---   6s. 0d. per quarter.[1]

Button's school is distinguished by his strong advocacy of teaching English grammatically, and his denigration of classical schooling. In July 1792 he pronounced:

> The knowledge of the English language must be allowed on all hands to be of the greatest importance to an Englishman; yet upon examination it will be found, that the study of it is less attended to than any other. Dead and foreign languages are constantly taught grammatically, but that mode is scarcely ever pursued respecting our own; and it is rare to find a man that has any grammatical knowledge of English, except what he has obtained by a Latin Grammar.

> M. SHERIDAN, in his treatise on British Education, asks the following question:- "Would it be credited, were it not warranted by fact, "that a polished and rational people should be at a great expence of labour, "time, and money, to have their children instructed in languages which can "never be of any use to them in life, and seldom contribute to their "pleasure; whilst they neglect entirely to have them instructed in one which "would be of perpetual use to them in whatsoever rank or station they were "placed, upon matters of the highest importance, as well as the common "occurences of life; and which might be a principal mean of procuring them "profit and promotion?"[2]

He had by then, a year after opening his school, 'proper assistants', and had 'opened a spacious and commodious House opposite St. Michael's Church, in Lewes, lately occupied by Mr. Chatfield Turner, Attorney at Law; where he intends to teach all the branches of English education' - namely, reading, writing and arithmetic. But by the end of that year, '... At the request of many of his friends he has added to the advantages of an *English Classical School*, which was his original plan, those of *Greek, Latin*, and *French...*'[3] By July 1793 his terms were, for boarders 18 guineas pa, for parlour boarders 30 guineas, for day scholars 1 guinea per quarter (double the cost at opening two years previously). Greek, Latin or French were 2 guineas a year extra. Despite including these languages in his curriculum, Button was unrepentant of his promotion of English, styling his school 'BUTTON'S ENGLISH CLASSICAL ACADEMY':

> It is now generally allowed that Children may attain a perfect knowledge of the ENGLISH without the aid of any *dead* or *foreign* language; yet an absurd attachment to the old method of instruction, has hitherto prevented many practical illustrations of a theorem, so interesting to the parents of youth in the middle orders of society.

> To the notice of such in particular, J. BUTTON begs leave to submit the outlines of a plan, which has already been crowned with the most flattering success and approbation.

> While the lower classes of his School are engaged in Reading, Writing, Spelling and Recitation, the higher learn English Grammar and Rhetoric, and parse and explain our best English Poets and Historians, as others do the Greek and Latin. They are also regularly exercised in Recitation, Spelling, Penmanship, Arithmetic, Letter-writing, Geography, the Histories of Greece, Rome, and their native country. - Vulgar or provincial phraseology and accent, are likewise carefully corrected.[4]

In 1794 Button set out to build his own new school on ¾ acre of land in St Anne's parish (on which he paid 6s land tax in 1795). The venture was fraught, as the following extracts from *SWA* show:

6 October 1794:

> Last night the skeleton of a building erecting for Mr. Button's Academy in this town, was blown entirely down by the high wind.

13 October 1794:

> The builders of Mr. Button's Academy, 'tis thought will sustain a loss of about forty pounds by the accident that happened to it, and was mentioned in our last.

29 December 1794:

> Last Wednesday, at about ten minutes past one in the afternoon, a fire broke out in the premises lately erected in a field near St. Anne's Church, in this town, and designed for Mr. Button's Academy. The flames spread and raged with such fury, owing to a strong north-easterly wind, that the building was nearly consumed in the short space of fifty minutes, two of its chimnies and a small portion of the brick walls, only, being left standing at two o'clock. The damage is estimated at nine hundred pounds, but luckily for the builders, who must otherwise have suffered the loss, the premises were insured about ten days or a fortnight before. The fire took place in the absence of the carpenters, who had left on the hearth of the school-room some embers that the wind, blowing hard down the chimney, re-kindled and carried out among the shavings, which instantly burst into a blaze, and communicated their flame so rapidly to the floors and timbers, that in a few minutes after, when the fire was discovered, it had gained so much the ascendancy that no attempts were made to extinguish it, though an engine was upon the spot.

On 28 April 1795 Button put the land up for sale by auction.[5] In the meantime he was suffering from lack of space. In 1794 and 1795 he rented the schoolhouse in All Saints where John Bartlett previously had kept school (assessed for land tax at a 'rental' of £2 pa).[6] In December 1794 he 'begs leave to inform those Ladies and Gentlemen whose children he could not receive into his Academy last half-year, for want of room, that FIVE of his young Gentlemen having just completed their education, there are now SO MANY vacancies, which shall be impartially filled according to priority of application from this day.'[7]

By January 1796 (in which year he moved to the Cliffe - see below) his terms for boarders were up to 20 guineas a year. He was still vigorously promoting an English classical education:

> His novel system of instruction being now fully vindicated from doubt or cavil, by the most flattering circumstances of practical success, he confidently engages that, under his care, any Boy of common abilities, will speedily attain a graceful delivery, and classical correctness in the English Language without the least acquaintance with any other, ancient or modern. But for the convenience of those who are designed for any of the learned professions or foreign trade, the Greek, Latin, and French are taught with diligence and accuracy in his School, together with Writing, Arithmetic, and the Mathematics. - The Gentleman who teaches Navigation, has had the same department, with the advantages of practical illustration, on board a Man of War.
>
> The health, morals, and cleanliness of the Pupils are inspected with unremitting attention.[8]

And again, in 1799:

> Emboldened by a successful probation of nearly ten years, J. BUTTON respectfully lays before a candid Public the outlines of his

System of Education - A System not less beneficial in its effects than novel in its institution. Experimentally disgusted with the tedious and almost unprofitable drudgery of learning the rudiments of the *Greek* and *Latin* languages, exacted from so many boys not in preparation for any of the learned professions, he has effectually contrived to lead his pupils to a *Classical knowledge of their Native Tongue*, by means of rational grammar, a critical acquaintance with the best English Authors, both in prose and verse, Ancient and Modern History, Geography, correctness of style, and graceful recitation; together with Writing, Arithmetic, Book-keeping, and a general or partial course of the Mathematics, according to the taste or professional designation of each pupil. - And in order to combine with the above recited advantages those of a *Preparatory School*, Greek, Latin, and French, are accurately taught to such as need them.[9]

In 1797 Button advertised the 'Public Examination' of his pupils at the *Star Assembly Room*, when at least 29 different boys were billed to give recitations.[10] Among them was Gideon Mantell, who later became a celebrated surgeon and geologist; his father was a dissenter, and we find the surnames of other boys in the list occurring in the records of the Eastgate (Baptist) and Westgate meeting houses;[11] Button's school maintained a strong nonconformist connection. In 1800 a similar 'Public Examination' was noticed by *SWA*:

> ... the young gentlemen, of Mr. Button's academy... recited, at the Star Inn, a well-chosen Selection of Pieces from the works of our most esteemed authors, in a manner extremely gratifying to a very numerous and respectable auditory, and with a degree of ease and emphatic propriety which manifested the ability and indefatigable assiduity of Mr. Button and his assistants.[12]

In 1800 William Austin was drawing master at the school, attending on Mondays.[13]

From 1796 to the end of the century Button was occupying a house in the Cliffe owned by Robert Ashdown, where Mrs Chaffin (probably a dissenter, as Button was) had previously had her girls' boarding school [qv below]. In the 1796 land tax assessment the 'rental' was shown as £9 10s; it fell to £8 11s 3d in 1798 and 1799, and rose to £10 10s in 1800.[14] Formerly - until 1778 - this had been the *Swan* inn; by 1800 it had been rebuilt with bay windows and a smart doorway, and Button bought it in 1802. From his death in 1825 the school was run by his son William, also a Baptist and a Radical, until 1865.[15]

Advertised in *SWA* Jul (2) 1791; Jan, Jul (2), Dec 92; Jan (2), Jul (3) 93; Jan (3), Jul (2), Dec (2) 94; Jul 95; Jan (2), Jul (3) 96; Jun, Jul 97; Jan (3), Jul (3) 98; Jan (3), Jul (2) 99; Jan, Jul 1800. In *Univ. Directory* 1793, 1794.
[*John Button, William Austin* (drawing master)]

1. *SWA* 11.7.91.   2. *SWA* 2.7.92.   3. *SWA* 31.12.92.   4. *SWA* 1.7.93.   5. ESRO Land Tax, St Anne; *SWA* dates cited and 20.4.95.   6. ESRO Land Tax, All Saints.   7. *SWA* 22.12.94.   8. *SWA* 4.1.96, 4.7.96.
9. *SWA* 7.1.99.   10. *SWA* 19.6.97.   11. For example, Button (2 boys), Fuller (2 boys), Johnston, Brown, Lee, Smith, Read, Bull (ESRO NB 1/1/1A, NU 1/1/2). 12. *SWA* 23.6.1800.   13. *SWA* 24.3.1800.   14. ESRO Land Tax, St Thomas.   15. Brent, C. *Historic Lewes & Its Buildings* (1985), 50-1, and *Georgian Lewes* (1993), 98.

Langdon's boys' boarding school   (R: 1792)

In December 1792 Rev J. Langdon of Lewes advertised that he intended 'after the Christmas Recess, to take under his care a few young Gentlemen, who will be boarded, and instructed in the various branches of useful and polite Literature. The greatest attention will be paid to the improvement, health, and morals of the pupils.'[1] In 1792 he occupied a house in St John sub Castro (land tax 'rental' £7); he is not shown there before 1792, and in 1793 this house was occupied by another; perhaps the school did not develop.[2]   [*J. Langdon*]

1. *SWA* 17.12.92.   2. ESRO Land Tax, St John sub Castro.

Meane and Davey's girls' boarding school   (Rs: 1792-4)
P. Meane and M. Davey had, by 1792, a girls' boarding school near St Michael's church.
They had a very short Christmas holiday, reopening after the Christmas recess on 7 January
1793.[1] At the school, 'the English language is taught grammatically, all kinds of useful and
ornamental Needle-work; the French language; and every other branch of polite, and useful
female education.'[2]
    From 1792 to 1794 (not before) a Mary Davey, probably the M. Davey above,
occupied a house in St Michael's owned by Lord Hampden (land tax 'rental' £2 10s). In
1793 and 1794 a much larger house (land tax 'rental' £12 10s), also owned by Lord
Hampden, was occupied by 'Miss Mean & Davey', and would have housed their girls'
boarding school. They appear to have moved or closed their school in 1794, and the larger
house was then taken over by Edward Pugh (see his school below).[3] Mary Davey may have
been related to Thomas Davey, an apothecary and deacon of the Baptist Eastgate church in
1786; Edward Pugh's wife was formerly Mary Symonds Davey, and almost certainly the
same as the M. Davey above - both Edward and his wife were Baptists.
[*P.Meane, M. (Mary) Davey*]
1. *SWA* 31.12.92.   2. *SWA* 7.7.94.   3. ESRO Land Tax, St Michael.

Hewitt's evening school   (R: 1792)
In October 1792 Thomas Hewitt, 'Inspector of the New Goal [sic], Lewes', advertised the
opening of an evening school 'for the instruction of Persons in Architecture, Landscapes, &c.
on reasonable terms'. His advertisement was headed 'EDUCATION', and the school was
presumably intended for young ladies and gentlemen.[1]   [*Thomas Hewitt*]
1. *SWA* 15.10.92.

Mrs Chaffin's girls' boarding school   (Rs: 1793-4)
By January 1793 Mrs Chaffin had a girls' boarding school in the Cliffe. Her terms were 16
guineas pa, washing included, no entrance.[1] In 1793 and 1794 she rented a house in the
Cliffe from Robert Ashdown (land tax 'rental' £10 7s 6d, so it was quite a large house); in
1795 the occupier is shown as 'Late Chaffin' and from 1796 it was rented by John Button
for his school [qv above].[2] Mrs Chaffin was the widow of James Chaffin, Collector of
Excise at Lewes; he married Ann Holford, as his second wife, in 1761, and he died in 1787;
they were dissenters, three of their children being baptised at Westgate chapel (1762-6); Ann
Chaffin was admitted to Eastgate Baptist chapel in 1787, and left it, for London, in 1797.
[*Ann Chaffin*]
1. *SWA* 7.1.93, 8.7.93.   2. ESRO Land Tax, St Thomas.

Mr and Mrs Edward Pugh's day schools for boys and girls, and later boys' boarding school
(Boys: F:1793.   Rs: 1793- into 19c.   Girls: Rs: 1795-1800?)
In January 1793 Edward Pugh opened his boys' day school in the Cliffe, taking over
William Symonds' school [qv above], 'where he intends to instruct the youth committed to
his care in every branch of English education.' He had been, for seven years, a teacher 'in
one of the most respectable Academies near the Metropolis.'[1] (His wife's second christian
name was 'Symonds', so there was probably a family connection with the Symonds.)
    By July 1795 Mr and Mrs Pugh were advertising their schools jointly, thanking
'their Friends and the Public, for the encouragement they have met with in their respective
schools.' 'E. PUGH, for the better accomodation of his Pupils, has taken a commodious
room near the NEW MARKET, LEWES, and will open School on MONDAY, the 13th
INSTANT. MRS. PUGH's School opens the MONDAY following.'[2] From 1795 to 1798
Edward Pugh was renting a substantial house in St Michael's from Lord Hampden (land tax

'rental' £12 10s; in 1798, £10), that had previously housed Meane and Davey's boarding school [qv above].[3] By January 1799 they were in North Street, with a joint school, and were taking both day scholars and boarders.[4]

In November 1800 Mrs Pugh died, aged 26. Edward married again, and in January 1802 'Mr. & Mrs. Pugh' advertised the reopening, after the Christmas recess, of their school for day scholars and boarders.[5] Edward Pugh was a Baptist, being admitted into the Eastgate Baptist church in the Cliffe in May 1793; his first wife, Mary Symonds Pugh (née Davey, and probably related to Thomas Davey, an apothecary and deacon of the church in 1786) had been admitted in July 1792. William Symonds, whose school he took over in 1793, had also been a Baptist.

Advertised in *SWA* Jan (2), Jul 1793; Jul 95; Jan (2) 99; [Jan 1801]. Edward Pugh, schoolmaster, was in the poll books for 1796 and 1802 (though he did not poll at the latter election); and 'Pugh, schoolmaster', in Star Lane, probably Edward, was in *Baxter's Directory* 1805.

[*Edward Pugh, Mary Symonds Pugh*]

1. *SWA* 7.1.93.   2. *SWA* 6.7.95.   3. ESRO Land Tax, St Michael.   4. *SWA* 7.1.99.
5. *SWA* 4.1.1802.

Day school   (R: 1794)
In January 1794 there was a day school (not identified) 'where from 30 to 40 other little Children had been constantly at School and at play' with a child of William Hoather infected with smallpox.[1]

1. *Town Book of Lewes, SRS* 69, 94f.

The Miss Dodsons' girls' boarding school   (F: 1794.   Rs: 1794-6)
The Miss Dodsons took over Susan Ryall's school in St Anne's from January 1794, 'where young Ladies will be boarded and educated, at £16 16s. per annum, entrance £1 1s. The greatest attention will be paid to their health, morals, and general improvement. French, Dancing, Music, Drawing, Geography, and Writing, by the most approved Masters.'[1]

The school continued until the end of 1796. In January 1797 all the effects of the Miss Dodsons' boarding school were sold by auction. These included 'twelve very neat beds', which gives some idea of the limited number of girls that would have been boarded at the school (though pupils at boarding schools usually slept more than one to a bed: in 1796 Mrs Norton at Preston school charged 2 guineas a year extra for a single bed).[2]

The 1795 land tax return shows the house (which was owned by Rev William Gwynne) as being occupied by Phillip Dodson; that for 1796, by Miss Dodson. From January 1794 to November 1796, Miss Dodson paid the poor rates on 'her two houses' (ie. the parsonage house and the adjacent house, that together comprised Ryall's and then the Dodsons' school).[3]

Advertised in *SWA* Dec (2) 1793; Jan, Jun, Jul, Dec 94; Jun, Jul 95; Jan (2), Jul 96.

[*Miss Dodson senior, Miss Dodson junior*]

1. *SWA* 23.12.93.   2. *SWA* 16.1.97.   3. ESRO Land Tax, St Anne; ESRO PAR 411/30/2.

John Pugh's school   (Rs: 1796-1800)
Land tax returns show John Pugh as occupier, from 1796 to 1800, of the schoolhouse/ school in All Saints parish that had previously been John Bartlett's school [qv] and for two years before Pugh had been occupied by John Button [qv].[1] He presumably kept a school there, but no other references to John Pugh, schoolmaster, have yet been traced. *Baxter's Directory* 1805 has 'Pugh, schoolmaster' in Star Lane, but this was perhaps Edward (see his school above).   [*John Pugh*]

1. ESRO Land Tax, All Saints.

<u>Dunn's boys' (boarding) school</u>   (F: 1796.   Rs: into 19c)
In 1802 James Charles Tracy Dunn advertised his Friars Walk Academy, where he took not more than 30 pupils,[1] which had been established in 1796[2] (presumably by him). By 1823 and probably earlier it was a boarding school.[3]   He sponsored lectures in stenography, encouraged 'scenic entertainment', and set up 'a very handy turning lathe'. When he died in 1837 the school was continued by his son (of the same names), who resigned as master of Cuckfield grammar school.[4] In 1799 he was engaged by Mrs Gell to teach the girls of her boarding school 'Writing and Accomptmanship' [qv].   He was a member of Lewes Tabernacle from 1817.   [*James Charles Tracy Dunn*]

1. Brent, C., pers. comm., citing *SWA* 10.1.1802.   2. ibid, citing *SWA* 11.7.1836.   3. *Pigot's Directory* 1823-4.
4. Brent, C. *Geo. Lewes* (1993), 99.

<u>Mrs Gell's girls' day and boarding school</u>   (F: 1798.   Rs: 1798- into 19c)
Mrs Gell opened her girls' boarding school in Star Lane on 1 February 1798.[1] She had formerly been for some years a milliner, haberdasher and perfumer, on School Hill. She gave up the making of Millinery at the beginning of 1797, the rest of her business then being carried on 'under the firm of John Gell' - though she herself was advertising the sale of gloves, ribbons, muslins, gauzes, hats, &c. in December 1797, just before she opened her school. John Gell was probably her husband, or perhaps brother: from 1797 to at least 1800, All Saints land tax assessments show him occupying a house there (land tax 'rental' £3 15s); it was presumably this house to which Mrs Gell moved her school, to Friars Walk, in 1799 (see below) - no other house there is shown in the occupancy of either a Mr or Mrs Gell.[2]

At her school, 'The Young Ladies will be boarded and taught the French and English languages, gramatically; Writing, Arithmetic, Geography, Astronomy, History, &c. and also the fashionable Needle Works, and a Knowledge of Domestic Œconomy, for Twenty Guineas per Annum. - Parlour Boarders, Thirty Guineas per Annum. - Day Scholars, Fifteen Shillings per Quarter. Music, Dancing, and Drawing, on the usual Terms, by well qualified Masters.'[3] 'The House is large, airy, and commodious, well calculated for a Seminary, being in a recluse part of the town, and affording a free access to the salubrious air of the South Downs. Coaches to and from London to Brighthelmston, every day. Distance eight miles from Brighton, and fifty from London.'[4]

Gell was entrepreneurial. She started her school near the top of the market. Hers is the only girls' school in Sussex known to have included 'Domestic Œconomy' in the curriculum. She promoted, in 1799, 'her new system of useful and polite literature... In this course of instruction the lessons of theory are regularly applied to practical improvement.'[5] The 'Principal Studies' were then listed as 'French and English Grammar, Philosophical Grammar, Natural History, Prosody, Composition, Elocution, Arithmetic, and Geography.' Although no doubt taught elsewhere, natural history and elocution are rare in such a subject list, as are philosophical grammar and prosody for girls. Eighteen months after starting her school, she took a house in Friars Walk, All Saints, opposite the Priory ('The approach is extremely convenient, and to the advantages arising from retirement, it unites that of a South aspect.'); and from July 1799 she styled the school 'Priory-House Boarding School' (later 'Friar's Walk Ladies' School').[6] Her advertisement became more extended:

As "the principles of knowledge become the most intelligible to young "minds when they are explained and inculcated by practical illustration and "direction," the Pupils will be instructed by a regular course of exercise in the prosody, analysis and synthesis of the French and English Languages; they will also be taught Geography, and the use of the globes; and as their progress or abilities may suggest, the study of Astronomy will be added, and the method for instructing them in this elegant science, having been adopted for the improvement of the Pupils of this School only, and is so far from requiring any intense application, that it affords them an agreeable relaxation, in lieu of those frivolous pursuits which too often occupy the time and attention of young Ladies, and not infrequently, to the total exclusion of all solid and useful learning.[7]

While running the school, she seems to have kept an interest in the haberdashery business. John Gell does not seem to have prospered with it: in August 1798 he announced that he would 'commence selling off his stock of Goods, as he is going into another line of business';[8] but in October that year it was the stock in trade of Mrs Gell, milliner and haberdasher, School Hill, that was sold by auction.[9] Rather confusingly, in March 1799, John Gell, of School Hill, announced that he was 'now selling the remaining part of his Haberdashery Stock of Goods', adding: 'N.B. The Hosiery and Law Stationery Businesses will be continued in future at his other House, therefore these premises are to be lett...'[10] John Gell is probably the same as the Mr Gell, referred to in Mrs Gell's advertisement for her 'Academy' in January 1800: 'Mr. GELL's DRAWING ACADEMY, for young Gentlemen, will open on Wednesday, the 24th of January instant, and continue every Wednesday and Friday afternoon...' [qv below].[11]

When she started her school, French was taught 'by a Teacher who has been educated in a Convent of Benedictines in France',[12] but this teacher had apparently left by September 1799, when Gell advertised that 'in addition to domestic well qualified Assistants, she has engaged the most eminent Masters to attend and instruct her Pupils, in the various branches of useful and polite learning; particularly, Mr. DUNN, Writing and Accomptmanship. - Mons. BERTHOLET, late Prebendary of Peronne, French. - Mr. PRINCE, Organist of the Chapel Royal, Brighton, Music; and others of equal celebrity in Dancing, Drawing, &c. &c.'[13]

In July 1800 she announced that 'she has been in London, and engaged with a Lady, whose abilities and accomplishments have been found fully adequate to the important task of education, in some of the first Schools in England'; this lady would, inter alia, 'superintend Drawing, at One Guinea per quarter.' Italian was now added to the curriculum, and the basic fee was up to 22 guineas pa. The confident advertisement makes it hard to appreciate that two and a half years previously, Mrs Gell had been a milliner and haberdasher:

> Mrs GELL feels herself fully authorized in assuring the Public, that every branch of useful and elegant education will be brought forward in her School, on the most tried and approved plans: - The English, French, and Italian Languages, grammatically, (the idioms of the latter Languages will be particularly attended to); Geography and History, on plans lately adopted, which render them amusing and interesting studies to young persons: those, together with Writing, Arithmetic, and all the fashionable works, will be included under one head, at Twenty-two Guineas per annum.[14]

The promotional touches here - the reference to the new assistant being engaged by Mrs Gell *in London*; the emphasis given to the teaching of French and Italian idioms - suggest she was good at public relations. Mr Corbyn, the Brighton dancing master, taught her girls, and the following report (stimulated by Mrs Gell?) appeared in *SWA* 15 December 1800:

> Mr. Corbyn's Public night, at the Star Inn, on Tueday evening, for Mrs. Gell's scholars, was numerously attended by most of the principal families in Lewes, and its neighbourhood. - Mr. Corbyn must have been highly gratified by the applauses of so numerous and so genteel a company.

> The graceful movement and polite deportment of Mr. Corbyn's scholars, exhibited ample proofs of the master's ability and attention; and the minds of the young Ladies' parents must have felt a lively interest in that which so visibly excited the approbation of all present.

The following week *SWA* published a protest, from 'A Friend to Truth, and the old-established Schools in Lewes', who had been at the event and begged leave 'to correct the Puff which appeared in your last paper, by observing, that it would have been nearer the truth had you inserted that the PUBLIC (or BALL) was for the Ladies of a School near Brighton; it being evident that the Scholars of the School therein mentioned, formed but a very INCONSIDERABLE part of the groupe.'

One other original Gell touch was to refer to the quality (and quantity) of the food provided at her school:

> The morals and health of the young Ladies committed to her Care, will ever be minutely attended to. Her table is supplied with the best of provisions, and always a sufficiency.[15]

In January 1802 Mrs Gell advertised that her school would be opened on the 20th (that is, after the Christmas vacation) 'under the direction of a Person of great experience in the School business'.[16] But on 1 March that year, an 'Advertiser', who had 'presided for some time in a Seminary of consequence in the Metropolis', announced 'that in the course of a few months she intends OPENING A SCHOOL, in Lewes, for the Reception of YOUNG LADIES' and parents and guardians who were interested in the proposed undertaking were 'respectfully requested to convey their communications on the subject, to Mrs. GELL, Lewes.'[17] Perhaps Mrs Gell had not been as acceptable, or her school had not been as successful, as her advertisements and promotion may have suggested.

Advertised in *SWA* Jan (2), Jun, Jul 1798; Jan, Mar, Jul (2), Sep 99; Jan, Jul 1800; [Jan 1801].

[*Mrs S. Gell, Mr Gell?* (drawing master), *James Charles Tracy Dunn* (writing and accounts master), *Mons. Bertholet* (French master), *William Prince* (music master), *Mr Corbyn* (dancing master)]

1. *SWA* 8.1.98, 15.7.99. 2. ESRO Land Tax, All Saints. 3. *SWA* 8.1.98. 4. *SWA* 25.6.98.
5. *SWA* 11.3.99. 6. *SWA* 1.7.99, 15.7.99, 12.1.1801. 7. *SWA* 15.7.99. 8. *SWA* 20.8.98.
9. *SWA* 1.10.98. 10. *SWA* 25.3.99. 11. *SWA* 13.1.1800. 12. *SWA* 29.1.98. 13. *SWA* 30.9.99.
14. *SWA* 14.7.1800. 15. *SWA* 30.9.99. 16. *SWA* 11.1.1802. 17. *SWA* 1.3.1802.

Gell's boys' drawing academy   (F: 1800)

In January 1800, in Mrs Gell's advertisement for her girls' boarding school in Friars Walk, the following paragraph was added:

> Mr. GELL's DRAWING ACADEMY, for young Gentlemen, will open on Wednesday, the 24th of January instant [the 24th was a Friday; the 22nd was presumably meant; Mrs Gell made a similar mistake with the reopening of her school after the Christmas holiday], and continue every Wednesday and Friday afternoon. - An exceeding valuable collection of original Drawings and Paintings, in landscapes, heads, whole length figures, animals, flowers, &c. &c. is provided for the improvement of the Pupils.[1]

He was probably John Gell, formerly haberdasher and in 1799 having hosiery and law stationery businesses [qv <u>Mrs Gell's school</u> above].   [*(John?) Gell*]

1. *SWA* 13.1.1800.

<u>Wallis and Shadgett's girls' boarding school</u>   (F: before July 1801)
In July 1801 Miss Wallis and Miss Shadgett announced the reopening, 'after the present vacation', of their boarding school for young ladies in the Cliffe.[1] In January 1802 they announced that 'they have taken a large, commodious House... in the Cliff...'[2]
      The land tax assessment for 1801 shows Miss Wallis occupying a house in the Cliffe at a 'rental' of £3 12s 6d. (In the assessment for 1800, this house was occupied by another.) The 1802 assessment shows her occupying a different house there at a 'rental' of £5 5s; but she was not there in the 1803 assessment.[3] The school thus appears to have started in the Cliffe in the latter part of 1800, or the beginning of 1801, and to have failed or been moved by 1803.
[*Miss Wallis, Miss Shadgett*]
1. *SWA* 13.7.1801.   2. *SWA* 11.1.1802.   3. ESRO Land Tax, St Thomas.

<u>Other schoolmasters/mistresses</u>

      <u>James Kent</u>, 'schoolmaster of Lewes' in his will dated 15 December 1708 (ESRO W/A 47.173).

      <u>Stephen Keeler</u>, writing master at the grammar school 1716, 1717, when he was paid £1 pa for teaching a private pupil there, Nicholas Gilbert, to write.[1] Buried as 'wrighting mastar' 1731.[2]
      1. ESRO ACC 2462/1.   2. St John sub Castro PR.

      <u>Richard Button</u>, schoolmaster, in 1719 helped to buy the freehold of Westgate meeting house (Brent, C. *Geo. Lewes* (1993), 152).

      <u>Mr Silk</u>, an itinerant lecturer on science subjects; in an advertisement in 1761 for a series of lectures at Lewes, he offered tuition for boys and girls:
            N.B. Young Ladies and Gentlemen are with Ease and Readiness taught
            Geography and Astronomy in the Description and Use of the Globes.[1]
      1. *SWA* 5.10.61.

      <u>G. Picknell</u>, schoolmaster, of All Saints parish, in March 1768 (poll book, in Woolgar *Spicilegia*, II, 26, MS at SAS).

      [Cruttenden] In 1796 Mr Cruttenden occupied a schoolhouse in the parish of St John sub Castro, (land tax 'rental' £1 10s). He also occupied a house there (land tax 'rental' £1) and a garden (land tax 'rental' £1). The schoolhouse had previously been occupied by John Bartlett, schoolmaster, and from 1798 was owned by Bartlett and from 1799 again occupied by him.[1] Cruttenden probably kept a school there in 1796.
      1. ESRO Land Tax, St John sub Castro.

      [Mrs Stokes] In 1798 Mrs Stokes occupied 'Land Garden Schoole' in St John sub Castro, owned by John Bartlett, schoolmaster. He occupied the 'Garden & School room' himself from 1799. Mrs Stokes possibly kept a school there in 1798.[1]
      1. ESRO Land Tax, St John sub Castro.

      <u>Mary Cornwell</u> (1753-1807) Schoolmistress of Lewes in her will of 17 November 1800 (see Schedule 2).

      [John Burtenshaw] Schoolmaster in Lewes in 1802, when he voted but his vote was 'adjudged to be bad' (poll book 1802). He may well have been a schoolmaster there in 1800.

      [John Smith], assistant schoolmaster in 1803, in St Thomas in the Cliff (*Sussex Militia List 1803, Pevensey Rape, Southern Division* (1988)).

The following were schoolmasters/mistresses at Lewes by 1805 (*Baxter's Directory*) and may have been there by 1800:

[Mrs Brown] In 1805 had a school in North Street. [In 1823 Mary and Lucy Brown had a girls' boarding school in the High Street, and Benjamin Brown had a boys' day school in Lancaster Street (*Pigot's Directory* 1823-4).]

[Carter] In 1805 had a 'Preparatory Academy'.

[John Inskip] In 1805 was a schoolmaster in Botany Bay.

[Henry Roscorla] In 1805, schoolmaster (*Baxter's Directory*, under 'Names omitted in Directory').

Dancing and music masters

(James?) Lun Dancing master to the grammar school 1717, 1718, when on two occasions he was paid 10s for instructing Nicholas Gilbert, then aged 11 and a private boarder at the school.[1] He also began to teach dancing at Kester's (Hurstpierpoint or near?), May 1718.[2] Perhaps the James Lunn of Lewes, gent, of a marriage licence, May 1718.[3]
1. ESRO ACC 2462/1.   2. *SAC* 25, 183.   3. *SRS* 6, 220.

Stephen Philpot   (Rs: 1729-70?) - see his school above.

James Lambert (1725-88) Taught both music and painting at Lewes. He was organist at St Thomas's from 1745 until his death in 1788.[1]
1. *SAC* 90, 137-41.

Thomas Hadleston In 1772 had a school in North-street, Chichester, for teaching French, dancing, and fencing with the small sword [qv under CHICHESTER]. He attended at Lewes every Monday: 'Gentlemen and Ladies, who chuse to be taught at Home, will be waited upon, by directing a Line for him at the STAR INN, in Lewes'. He offered 'Dancing, in a graceful and polite Manner, at Half a Guinea per Quarter, and Half a Guinea Entrance. In three Weeks Time he teaches the Minuet, upon moderate Terms, to any Person from Twelve to Thirty Years of Age and upwards, fit to appear in any Company.' He 'composes and teaches all Sorts of French, Allemande, and English Dances.'   (*SWA* 20.7.72)

Charles Mathews A London dancing master, he advertised in *SWA* in 1774 as follows:

MR. CHARLES MATHEWS, many Years FIRST DANCER at the THEATRE ROYAL, in DRURY-LANE, and the THEATRE ROYAL COVENT-GARDEN; the OPERAS at PARIS, and at BRUSSELS; also DANCING-MASTER to his late Royal Highness the DUKE of YORK, and PRINCE CHARLES and PRINCE ERNEST of MECKLENBURG STRELITZ, her MAJESTY's two BROTHERS, intends doing himself the Honour of coming to LEWES, &c. &c. &c. every Week constant, in order to teach BOARDING-SCHOOLS and private SCHOLARS.   Any Gentlemen or Ladies belonging to the Boarding-Schools, wanting a private Dancing-Master, will be faithfully attended on, by directing a Line to Mr. CHARLES MATHEWS, No. 7, MARTLET-COURT, BOW-STREET, COVENT-GARDEN; or at the THEATRE ROYAL, COVENT-GARDEN, LONDON.   (*SWA* 21.2.74)

Note: Whether or not Mathews (see above) established a practice in Lewes, there was clearly a demand in the town, as the following advertisement indicates. It appeared in *SWA*, 2 November 1778:

WANTED

At LEWES.

A PERSON or Persons qualified to teach MUSIC and DANCING; and as there are many Schools, and [illegible] Families in and about the Town, that may make it very advantageous.

Such Person or Persons that come well recommended, and properly qualified, by applying to the SCHOOLS and GENTRY of Lewes, will not fail meeting with all due Encouragement.

N.B. For further Information apply to the PRINTER.

Mr. Peoly   (Rs: 1778, 1779) He took several advertisements in 1778 to thank friends for their encouragement since he had been at Lewes, and announced that 'having engaged himself in a Business in London' which would take him away from Lewes at some times of the year, he had 'taken Mr. THRING into Partnership'.[1] He took an advertisement in December 1778 to announce that he had no intention of leaving Lewes.[2] In January 1779 Peoly and Thring announced that 'they shall open School on Monday the 25th January instant, and will constantly attend as follows: at HERSTMONCEUX every Monday; at LEWES, Tuesdays, Fridays, and Saturdays; and at BRIGHTHELMSTON every Wednesday and Thursday.'[3] Although not specifically described as such, they were clearly dancing and music masters. (See John Thring below.)

1. *SWA* 9.11.78.   2. *SWA* 14.12.78.   3. *SWA* 11.1.79.

John Thring   (Rs: 1778-1800) Born at Cambridge and living there until he was taken into partnership by Mr Peoly at Lewes in 1778,[1] John Thring became the doyen of the dancing masters based at Lewes. Peoly described him as 'a Gentleman of Character and Abilities'.[2] In January 1779 they were attending at Herstmonceux every Monday (almost certainly at the Allfrees' school), at Lewes on Tuesdays, Fridays and Saturdays, and at Brighton every Wednesday and Thursday.[3] Since Peoly had taken Thring into partnership because he had 'engaged himself in a Business in London' which would take him away from Lewes at some times of the year, Thring was probably the active partner in Sussex. After 1779 there are no further references to Peoly.

The first of very many concerts 'for the benefit of Mr. Thring' was advertised in March 1780: Thring was First Violin; tickets, to be had of Mr Thring and at the Coffee-House, were 3s each.[4] In April, Thring thanked those who had attended, and 'those whose Children are under his Tuition in MUSIC and DANCING'.[5] In June 1780, and again in December 1780, he promoted balls at the *Star Assembly Room*, New Shoreham, 'where Minuets, Cotillons, &c. will be danced by his Scholars'; 'To begin at Six o'Clock', and 'the Dancing for the Company to become general' at Nine o'Clock in June, Eight o'Clock in December; tickets were 2s 6d each.[6] In January 1783 he promoted, for his benefit, a concert and ball at the *White Hart* in Lewes ('Assisted by the Band belonging to the SUSSEX REGIMENT').[7] He promoted another concert and ball there a year later; and in December 1786 'his Annual Public CONCERT and BALL', again at the *White Hart*.[8] In 1787 it was held at the *Star Room*.[9] His concerts and balls at Lewes were advertised in 1789 ('Mr. THRING has provided a POST-CHAISE for the use of his friends, in Lewes, on the above evening'); 1790 ('A CHAISE will be provided as usual'); 1791, and each year to 1795; 1796 (for the joint benefit of

Thring and Beckett); 1797, and another that year in October, which was postponed to November 'on account of the movements now taking place among his Military Patrons' - and was reported afterwards by *SWA* as 'more numerously and respectfully attended than any he had ever before the honour of conducting'; 1798; 1799 ('Mr. Thring's Concert at the Star, on Thursday, was very fashionably attended, and proved a rich treat to the Lovers of Harmony. The excellent band belonging to the Sussex Regiment, assisted by Reinagle, and a few amateurs, were the performers.'); 1800, in March, and another in October.[10]

Apart from Lewes, and New Shoreham (mentioned above), he promoted concerts and balls at Battle (1789, 1790); and Herstmonceux (1793; advertised by Mr and Mrs Allfree, at whose boys' and girls' boarding school he presumably taught); and Seaford (1798).[11]

In 1796 Thring's monopoly of being dancing master to all the Lewes schools came under attack. In September, as 'DANCING and MUSIC-MASTER, LEWES' he advertised: 'Reports having been maliciously circulated, asserting that it was the intention of J. THRING to decline business, and that he did not teach the Scotch and other fashion-Steps, he has found it necessary thus publicly to deny them; and to invite the Parents and Guardians of the rising generation to attend the PUBLIC DANCING EVENING of his Pupils, at the Star Inn, on Friday next, when they may have ocular demonstration of the progress of the young Ladies and Gentlemen under his tuition, and of his ability in his long-experienced profession of a Dancing- and Music Master.'[12] Nicholson (see below) was then being sponsored by Victor Amedée Raymond, with his substantial French academy; and Holloway (see below), who in February had opened a dancing and music academy at Brighton, opened another in St Mary's Street, Lewes, in September, majoring on 'NEW DANCES'. *SWA* of 19 September 1796 featured three consecutive advertisements, by Thring, Nicholson and Holloway. That month Thring advertised 'his thanks for the numerous and respectable attendance of his Friends, at the Public Dancing Evening of his Scholars, on Friday last; and for the many marks of approval with which he was then honoured. Mr. THRING has had the honor of being entrusted with the education of all the young Ladies and Gentlemen in Lewes and its neighbourhood for the last 18 years past, and has been happy enough to give universal satisfaction; encouraged by which, notwithstanding the attempts which are now making to injure him in his profession, (by an interested foreign Schoolmaster,) he presumes with confidence to solicit a continuance of public patronage and support...'[13] In January 1797 he referred to his 'constant and assiduous attendance at Schools, and at his Dancing Room in Lewes, which is conveniently and genteely fitted up for the purpose' (perhaps Nicholson was still using Raymond's dining-room, made available to him until he could find suitable premises) and stressed that 'Mr. THRING's Pupils will be taught every new and fashionable step, Scotch reels, Cotillons, and Country Dances', and noted that he had as assistant 'one of the first Violin Players, in the dancing line, in the country... who has an opportunity of procuring the most fashionable tunes and dances, even before they are published in the world' (a riposte to Holloway).[14] But with Nicholson and Holloway set up in Lewes (in June 1797 the latter gave 'his ANNUAL BALL... when he hopes for the short time the young Ladies and Gentlemen have been under his tuition, their exertions will merit the approbation of their Friends... '[15]), Thring's monopoly was broken. By 1793, Rawlins, from Brighton, was teaching at the *Pelham Arms* every Saturday; by 1797, if not before, Mr Richard had replaced Thring as the Allfrees' dancing master at Herstmonceux;

Nicholson was backed by Raymond's school; in 1800 Mrs Gell at her school was using Mr Corbyn from Brighton.[16] But Thring carried on: in November 1797 - 'To his Patrons in Lewes, who continue to support him, in his profession of DANCING-MASTER, despiting the illiberality with which he has been treated by the Heads of some of the Schools... His abilities, as a Master, he wishes to be judged by his long experience, and by the progress of his present Pupils.'[17]

Despite Thring's controversy with Nicholson, at Mr Reinagle's concert in 1799, they performed together with Reinagle.[18]

He was described as dancing master in the Lewes survey of 1790, when he occupied a house in the High Street (between St Swithin's Lane and Bull Lane) with six living in the house. He continued to rent this house (land tax 'rental' assessments from £9 15s down to £9) from 1791 to at least 1800.[19] In *Univ. Directory* 1793 and 1794 as as dancing master. In the 1796 poll book as music master; and in 1798, with Beckett (probably his assistant, mentioned above), he had a 'Music Shop' in the town.[20] He was in the 1802 poll book, but did not vote.

Thring was a dissenter, and his daughter Sarah was baptised at the Westgate meeting house in 1786. (For an account of his being plunged into the river, with his horse, and rescued, see Schedule 2.)

1. *SWA* 9.11.78.   2. ibid.   3. *SWA* 11.1.79.   4. *SWA* 27.3.80.   5. *SWA* 10.4.80.
6. *SWA* 19.6.80, 18.12.80.   7. *SWA* 27.1.83.   8. *SWA* 5.1.84, 18.12.86.   9. *SWA* 19.11.87.
10. *SWA* 7.12.89, 1.11.90, 21.11.91, 3.12.92, 11.11.93, 29.12.94, 7.12.95, 11.4.96, 9.1.97, 16.10.97, 23.10.97, 30.10.97, 10.12.98, 8.7.99, 15.7.99, 10.3.1800, 27.10.1800.   11. *SWA* 25.5.89, 2.8.90, 20.5.93, 14.5.98.   12. *SWA* 19.9.96.   13. *SWA* 26.9.96.   14. *SWA* 23.1.97.   15. *SWA* 22.5.97.
16. *SWA* 15.12.1800.   17. *SWA* 13.11.97.   18. *SWA* 25.2.99.   19. Woolgar *Spicilegia*, I, 527; ESRO Land Tax, St Michael.   20. *SWA* 14.5.98 (Dibdin ad).

James Henry Rawlins Opened his 'Academy of Dancing' in Brighton in November 1783 [qv]; he attended boarding schools, taught privately at home, also taught music, provided musicians for balls, let and tuned harpsicords, pianofortes and spinnets. Notably, he claimed to attend London masters twice a year, 'in order to be able to teach every Thing that is, or may be new and fashionable.'[1] In January 1793 he advertised, under the heading 'DANCING', that 'he has engaged the Room at the Pelham Arms, Lewes, where he intends to teach every Saturday after the present vacation.' His terms were 15s per quarter, with no entrance. He added: 'N.B. Proper allowance to Governors and Governesses of Schools.'[2]
1. *SWA* 14.7.88.   2. *SWA* 7.1.93.

Nicholson Advertised in September 1796 as music and dancing master, offering his services 'to the Inhabitants of LEWES and its vicinity'. 'He proposes to teach the most fashionable Dances...'; and offered private lessons on the harpsichord or pianoforte, at a guinea and a half per quarter, and a guinea entrance. 'N.B. SCHOOLS attended upon the established terms of the country; and private Families attended upon terms according to their respective distances.' He was sponsored by V.A.Raymond, who had a successful academy on School Hill and gave him 'the free use of his large Dining-room, to teach any Scholars that may offer, till he can meet with another every way suitable to his wishes.'[1] For John Thring's attack on Raymond for backing Nicholson, see Thring above: but despite this controversy, at Mr Reinagle's concert and ball at the *Star* inn on 26 February 1799, when Nicholson was 'Leader of the Band', he, Thring and Reinagle were billed to perform one piece together.[2] In June 1799 Nicholson advertised his 'SCHOLARS' BALL', at the *Star* inn: 'The Minuets and Cotillons will commence at seven o'clock, and the Country Dances for the Company immediately after the Scholars' performances are finished.' Tickets were 3s each.[3] In June 1801 he again advertised his 'SCHOLARS' BALL'.[4]

1. *SWA* 19.9.96.　2. *SWA* 25.2.99.　3. *SWA* 3.6.99.　4. *SWA* 1.6.1801.

Holloway　In 1794 Holloway, then a music and dancing master of Newington, taught at Mr and Mrs Dubbins' girls' boarding school at Horsham. By the beginning of 1796 he had moved to Brighton and in February opened his academy there in North Street. In September 1796 he additionally opened an academy at Lewes, 'for instruction in the polite accomplishments of DANCING and MUSIC. For which occasion he has engaged an elegant Room in ST. MARY'S STREET, where Ladies and Gentlemen may be instructed, as *private* or *quarterly* Scholars, in the most elegant stile.' He included a paragraph headed 'NEW DANCES', and ended: 'N.B. Schools punctually attended. Bands procured for private and public Balls; and Piano Fortes tuned at the shortest notice.'[1] In May 1797 he advertised his 'ANNUAL BALL... when he hopes for the short time the young Ladies and Gentlemen have been under his tuition, their exertions will merit the approbation of their Friends'. He then had an assistant, who 'will perform several select Pieces on the Grand Piano Forte'. Tickets, at 3s each, could be had at the *Star* inn, Lewes, or of Mr Holloway at Brighton.[2] In September 1797, 'Mr. Holloway's Music and Dancing Academy' was at 'the Great Room, in St. Mary's-street, Lewes'.[3]

1. *SWA* 19.9.96.　2. *SWA* 22.5.97.　3. *SWA* 11.9.97 (Austin ad).

[Beckett]　In April 1796 there was a concert and ball at the *Star Room*, Lewes, for the benefit of Messrs Thring and Beckett (for which there was 'a very numerous and fashionable attendance');[1] in 1797 tickets for a concert by Beckett and Page were to be had 'Of Mr. BECKETT, at Mr. THRING's';[2] and in 1798 Messrs Thring and Beckett had a music shop in Lewes.[3] Beckett was almost certainly the assistant at Thring's dancing and music school, described by Thring in 1797 as 'one of the first Violin Players, in the dancing line, in the country, who has been 15 years under the instruction of Mr. THRING, and who has an opportunity of procuring the most fashionable tunes and dances, even before they are published to the world'.[4]

1. *SWA* 11.4.96, 2.5.96.　2. *SWA* 13.2.97.　3. *SWA* 14.5.97 (Dibdin ad).　4. *SWA* 23.1.97.

William Prince　Organist of the Chapel Royal, Brighton, and music master there into the 19th century, was in September 1799 music master to Mrs Gell's girls' boarding school at Lewes (*SWA* 30.9.99). (Also a composer - see Schedule 2.)

Corbyn　A dancing master at Brighton [qv: Rs 1798-1800], he taught the girls at Mrs Gell's boarding school at Lewes [qv]. In December 1800 *SWA* carried a favourable report of his 'public night, at the Star Inn... for Mrs. Gell's scholars... numerously attended by most of the principal families in Lewes, and its neighbourhood', when 'The graceful movement and polite deportment of Mr. Corbyn's scholars, exhibited ample proofs of the master's ability and attention.'[1] The following week, a correspondent pointed out that Mrs Gell's scholars 'formed but a very INCONSIDERABLE part of the groupe', and that it would have been nearer the truth to have said 'that the PUBLIC (or BALL) was for the Ladies of a School near Brighton' (probably Mrs Norton's school at Preston).[2]

1. *SWA* 15.12.1800.　2. *SWA* 22.12.1800.

[Peckham]　Music master at Lewes in 1805 (*Baxter's Directory*), he may have been teaching there in 1800.

Drawing and art masters

James Lambert (1725-88) Taught both music and painting at Lewes. Youngest child of a flaxdresser, he was a self-taught painter. His work was exhibited at the Royal Academy in 1775 and 1776; in the 1780s he was commissioned, with Samuel Grimm, by Sir William Burrell to make drawings of all the notable antiquities and important houses in Sussex (now in the British Museum). In an advertisement for the sale of his goods and paintings, after his death in 1788, he was described as 'bookseller, stationer, print seller, & landscape painter'. (*SAC* **90**, 137-41; *SAS Newsletter*, no. 64, August 1991).

Thomas Hewitt (architecture, landscapes, &c.)   R: 1792 - see his evening school above.

William Austin An established drawing master in London, moved to Brighton in 1797, and in January 1798 offered his services to 'the Masters and Governesses of Schools, and Parents and Guardians of Youth, of both Sexes, in the neighbourhood.'[1] By March 1800 he was teaching at Gwynne's grammar school, Raymond's academy, Button's academy and Miss Adams' girls' school, attending at Lewes on Mondays.[2] He offered instruction in drawing, painting, and etching; figures, heads, landscapes, ruins, caricatures, birds, fruit, flowers, either in oil, water colours, chalks, tints, or body colours, 'all of which he studied under the best Italian, French, Flemish, and English Masters; and since has had the honour, during his residence in London, of being patronized by near a thousand Noblemen, Gentlemen, and Ladies, as Pupils, including the younger branches from Westminster, Eton, Harrow, and other great Schools, and private Families at their Country Seats.'[3]

In June 1798 there was a violent storm at Lewes, with hail in the form of sheets of ice, which caused great damage and much broken glass: 'Mr. Austin... was observed very busy here, in taking sketches from the picturesque scraps of broken glass, occasioned by the above storm, which furnished a great variety of very curious figures, and amongst them were such as might challenge the pencil of the most skilful caricaturist.'[4]

1. *SWA* 29.1.98.   2. *SWA* 24.3.1800.   3. ibid.   4. *SWA* 18.6.98.

Gell (R: 1800) - see his boys' 'drawing academy' above.

Fencing master

Thomas Hadleston (R: 1772 - see under dancing masters above) He taught, inter alia, fencing with the small sword, at 1 guinea per quarter, and a guinea entrance. Based at Chichester, he attended at Lewes on Mondays. (*SWA* 20.7.72)

French masters

Thomas Hadleston (R: 1772 - see under dancing masters above) He had resided in Paris several years, and taught French 'by concise Grammar Rules, at a Guinea per Quarter, and Half a Guinea Entrance. Ladies at the same Time have an Opportunity of learning or improving in the Italian Writing Hand.' Based at Chichester, he attended at Lewes on Mondays. (*SWA* 20.7.72)

Darcel, a 'Native of France', was French master to Cater Rand's boys' school in 1776. (*SWA* 12.9.76)

Bertholet, 'Late Prebendary of Peronne', was French master to Mrs Gell's girls' school in 1799. (*SWA* 30.9.99)

LINCH (WOODMANS GREEN)   1724: 11 families   1801: pop. 78

School   (R: 1742)
At the 1742 visitation there was no free or charity school, but there was apparently a schoolmaster in the parish, of 'good Life' and 'diligent', who came to church and caused his scholars to come, and taught them the catechism.[1]
1. WSRO Ep.I/22/1.

LINCHMERE (LINCHMORE)   1724: about 30 families   1801: pop. 249

Dame school   (R: 1762)
At the 1762 visitation, 'there is a poor Woman that teaches School'.[1]
1. WSRO Ep.I/22/1.

LINDFIELD   1717: about 164 families 1801: pop. 1,077

Baker's grammar school   (R: 1731)
On 24 February 1731 Charles Baker subscribed 'before his being admitted to teach a Grammar Schoole att Lindfield.'[1]   There is no other record of a grammar school at Lindfield; presumably Baker kept a small private school. He was perhaps the Charles Baker formerly master of the Lightmaker school at Horsted Keynes [qv], and probably the C.Baker, master of Steyning grammar school, 1736-53 [qv].   [*Charles Baker*]
1. WSRO Ep.I/39/21, reverse ff 139-138.

Wood's boys' day school   (R: 1735)
The Stapley family account book records, for 20 May 1735: 'I did carry my son John to Mr Browne at Lindfield, to board att 3s per week and the 23rd day he is to goe to schole to John Wood to read and writ for 6d. per week.'[1] (John was then about 9 years old.)   [*John Wood*]
1. ESRO HIC 472.

Mrs Smith's girls' boarding school   (F: Christmas 1790)
In November 1790 Mrs Smith advertised her girls' boarding school at Lindfield, 'To open at CHRISTMAS next'. 'Board, washing and lodging, with education, viz. English, French, and every branch of needle-work, at FIFTEEN POUNDS and FIFTEEN SHILLINGS, per annum. - The use of the Globes, TWO POUNDS and TWO SHILLINGS per annum.' There was no entrance fee required; music, dancing, drawing and writing were extras, 'at the usual rate'.[1] (In 1793 at the house 'late Occupied by Mrs Smith, Schoolmistress', 6 French gentlemen & officers were resident.[2])   [*Mrs Smith*]
1. *SWA* 15.11.90.   2. *SAC* **35**, 176.

Barwick's boys' boarding school   (F: 1793)
At the beginning of 1793 Rev Henry Barwick opened a boys' boarding school at Lindfield:
> His plan is to take twelve young Gentlemen, only, and to qualify them for Business, the Public Schools, or University.
> His terms for English, TAUGHT GRAMMATICALLY, Writing, Accounts, Short-hand, Book-keeping, History, Geography, and Philosophy, Sixteen Guineas a year; the Classics, French, and Mathematics, Eighteen Guineas, and One Guinea entrance.

When earlier, in 1779, he had opened a similar school at Hastings, his fees were 20 guineas pa, with 2 guineas entrance: perhaps they had proved too expensive. It is interesting that 'Short-hand' was included in the basic curriculum. Barwick added:
> Lindfield is a very healthy, pleasant Village, situate in a genteel and respectable neighbourhood, 38 miles (on the public road) from London, 15

from Brighton, 12 from Lewes, and 3 from Cuckfield.
    N.B. Mr. BARWICK, has had the honour (and he flatters himself
with credit) of educating several of the Nobility, Gentry, &c. of this
Kingdom, during a period of upwards of twenty years.[1]
    Advertised in SWA Jan (2), Jul (2) 1793.
[*Henry Barwick*]
1. *SWA* 14.1.93.

Other schoolmasters

        Stephen Vine, schoolmaster of Lindfield, 1779. Discovered Roman road at St
        John's Common, and wrote account of this in *Gent. Mag.* (1781). (*SAC* **77**, 27)

        [March Pierce], a cripple, schoolmaster at Lindfield in 1803 (*Sussex Militia List
        1803, Pevensey Rape Northern Division* (1988), 64).

LITLINGTON   1724: 19 families   1801: pop. 101
No 18th-century schooling traced.

LITTLEHAMPTON (HAMPTON PARVA) 1724: 30 families 1801: pop. 584
Chaloner's school   (R: pre-1741)
Thomas Chaloner, 'exciseman and schoolmaster at Shoreham and Littlehampton', was
imprisoned for debt in Horsham gaol. (He was also a poet, and called himself 'The Merriest
Poet in Christendom'.) He was released, probably c1741, through the intervention of
Charles Eversfield, MP for Horsham.[1]   [*Thomas Chaloner*]
1. Albery, W., 'The Sussex County Gaol at Horsham (1540-1845)', *SCM* v.6, 742-4; *SAC* **18**, 106.

Dame or petty schools, charity school   (Rs: 1742, 1758, 1769- into 19c)
The visitation return for 1742 reported (against 'any unlicensed teachers?') 'few small Colers'
[ie. scholars], and that there was a schoolmaster in the parish, who was of 'good Life' and
'diligent', came to church, and taught his scholars the catechism. There was no free or
charity school. There was a similar report in 1758. In 1769 and 1772 the churchwardens
reported a free charity school, and a schoolmaster in the parish (as in 1742). In 1769 they
noted that the charity children were put out to service. The apparent references to a
schoolmaster in these returns may have related to a schooldame; the charity school
mentioned derived from the will of Jane Downer, dated 8 June 1763, who gave a rent-
charge of £1 5s pa issuing out of her farm at Barnham, for teaching two girls of
Littlehampton reading and needlework. This annuity continued to be received, at least to
1819, when it was paid to a schoolmistress to teach two poor girls.[1]
1. WSRO Ep.I/22/1; *EP2* (1819), 166.

Neale's school   (R: 1779)
Rev Neale advertised his school at Littlehampton in 1779 'For children whose cases require
sea water', noting that 'Much company resort to it [Littlehampton] to improve their health'.
The classics and 'mercantile knowledge' were taught; the basic fee was 16 guineas pa.
Music, drawing, dancing and bathing were extras, each at 13s. per qr.[1] (Neale later had a
grammar school at Arundel [qv].)   [*Robert Neale*]
1. *Hampshire Chronicle* 18.1.79, 31.5.79.

Newport's school   (R: c1780-90)
In the High St, c1780-90.[1] (A brewery on the site from 1816.)   [*Newport*]
1. Bristow, R., in *Sussex Industrial Arch Soc Newsletter* no.17 (Jan 1978), 10.

LITTLE HORSTED (HORSTED PARVA) 1724: about 20 families 1801: pop. 207

<u>Rose's boys' boarding school</u>   (F: 1794.   Rs: 1794-1800)

William Rose, curate of Little Horsted, then aged 28, opened his school at the beginning of 1794 in the parsonage there, 'for the reception of Twelve young Gentlemen, who will be boarded and instructed in the Greek, Latin and French Languages; the Mathematics; in Writing, Arithmetic, and every other branch of useful and polite literature.' He noted that: 'The above House is in a very healthy situation, being built on a rising ground, and commanding a delightful prospect of the adjacent country. It is 44 miles from London, and 14 from Brighthelmston. - Stage Coaches pass by it, to and from both those places, every day.'[1]

One of Rose's pupils was Henry Gage, eldest son of the 3rd Viscount Gage of Firle and later (in 1808, at the age of 17) the 4th Viscount. He came to the school when he was six, and his schooling bills totalled £65 5s 9½d for the year 1798; £72 7s 5d for 1799; £71 5s 1d for 1800; and £39 10s 2d for the first half of 1801.[2]

In 1800 Rose became master of Saunders' charity school at Uckfield [qv], moving his private school there and grafting it onto the charity school. He spent nearly £1,000 improving the premises, and built up a substantial private school.[3]

[*William Rose*]

1. *SWA* 30.12.93; Lewes, St Michael PR (marr. reg.); CI.   2. ESRO SAS/G/ACC 741; *Burke's Peerage* (1953).   3. Lower, *Worthies*; *EP2* (1819), 185.

LODSWORTH   1724: 108 families   1801: pop. 443

No 18th-century schooling traced, but see EASEBOURNE, where there was a small charity school throughout the 18th century (Lodsworth Liberty (chapel) was treated as part of Easebourne parish: the population shown relates to the Liberty).

LULLINGTON   1724: 4 families   1801: pop. 32

No 18th-century schooling traced.

LURGASHALL (LURGASALE) 1724: 64 families   1801: pop. 521

No 18th-century schooling traced.

LYMINSTER (LEOMINSTER) 1724: 58 families   1801: pop. 357

Warningcamp tithing: <u>121</u>
478

No 18th-century schooling traced.

MADEHURST   1724: 20 families   1801: pop. 133

No 18th-century schooling traced.

MARESFIELD (MARRISFIELD) 1724: about 70 families 1801: pop. 960

<u>Bonner's charity school</u>   (F: c1693. Rs: through 18c)

Richard Bonner, rector of Maresfield, and schoolmaster there in 1683, who was buried 18 January 1693, by will dated 20 January 1690 left a schoolhouse and a field in Maresfield, and rent-charges of £2 10s pa issuing out of a house and land in Ringmer, in trust, for appointing a competent schoolmaster to teach two poor children, under 14, the English tongue, and the principles of the Christian religion. The total income amounted to about

£4 pa, of which Bonner directed that 10s should be expended in the entertainment of his trustees at their yearly meeting; and that a bible, of value not exceeding 8s, should be given each year to some poor child of the parish, under 14, who should best deserve it, in the discretion of the rector. Although only two poor children were covered by this bequest, Bonner required that the school be called 'Bonner's School'. The residual amount due to the schoolmaster was generous for teaching just two poor children (about 7½d a week, against the usual 2d); the schoolmaster also had the use of the schoolhouse, and no doubt kept a private petty school there as well. This may have been Bonner's intention, and may account for his naming the school. In 1695 Richard Turner subscribed, to teach at the free school of Maresfield. By 1819 the charity had been incorporated with a national school; Bonner's cottage was occupied by a schoolmistress, who received £25 pa, made up by voluntary subscriptions; two boys were taught free, under the Bonner charity, the others paid 1d a week.[1] [*Richard Turner?*]

1. WSRO Ep.I/26/3, 66-7; *EP2* (1819), 171-2; *SAC* **106**, 6; WSRO Ep.I/3/4.

[Mrs Maynard's girls' boarding school]   (R: 1801)
Mrs Maynard had a girls' boarding school at Maresfield in 1801. In January 1802 she advertised for an assistant.[1] [*Mrs Maynard*]

1. *SWA* 11.1.1802.

MAYFIELD   c1760: 179 houses   1801: pop. 1,849

Charity schooling   (Rs: 1707(-18?), 1716, 1725-6?, 1729?, 1730-1, 1745-8, 1763-4)
A letter to the SPCK, dated 21 September 1708, refers to 'Mr. Sawyer of Mayfield who had been a very helpful Man in those parts, by teaching Children their Catechism and to read and write gratis.'[1] The SPCK annual *Account* for the previous year recorded a charity school at Mayfield in 1707, and this continued in their lists until 1718; but it is unlikely that a charity school was formally established at that time, and the number of children taught had fallen away by 1716, when Edward Sawyer wrote to the SPCK on 12 December, 'That whereas in the Charity School there [ie. at Mayfield], above 20. Children have been taught to read and write &c. they are now reduced to 3. or 4.'[2]

Despite being dropped from the SPCK lists, there are references to a schoolhouse at the church in 1725, 1726 and 1729. The churchwardens paid Joseph Beale 4s 6d 'for Cleneing ye Scoulehouse Leds & pasages & Spouts' in 1725, and 4s for the same task in 1726. In 1729 Simon Wilmshurst was paid 1s 'for a hook for ye Scoolehouse door'.[3] This schoolhouse was situated at the north end of the south aisle of the church but was boarded off from the nave.[4] It was almost certainly here that by 1730 one of the earliest Sunday schools in Sussex was operating - long before the Sunday school movement of the 1780s. James Oldfield wrote to the SPCK on 25 October 1730, 'That he is endeavouring to introduce Catechising there [ie. at Mayfield] & last Sunday had about 30. Children for whose Use he desires some Books to be paid for.'[5] In April the following year he ordered some further 'small practical Tracts' from the SPCK, and noted 'That he has made a good Collection at Mayfield for the poor Children to the number of abt 40 and hopes it will become a regular Charity School as soon as their Workhouse is set up wch ye Parish is now consulting abt.'[6] Later in 1731, on 12 July, he acknowledged receipt of tracts sent to him, and noted 'That he has several Child'n at School but cannot yet form it into a regular Charity One but hopes to do it wn their Workhouse is finish'd.'[7]

In January 1733 the churchwardens paid 9d for 'Mending a look [ie lock] for the Scoolhouse door & a Staple'[8]; but no further mentions of a school have been traced until the 'regular' charity school was established in 1749 (see below).

From 1745 to 1748 the overseers paid four sums of 2s 6d each to John Marchant 'for Scooling Richd Hesmar',[9] but this appears to have been an isolated example of such support for a pauper child. By at least 1764, and probably for some years before, there was a school at the workhouse [qv below]. However, in 1763 and 64 the overseers again paid small sums for the schooling of an individual child: in October/November 1763 Thomas Roads was paid 2s 'for Schooling Matt'w Richardson'; in December 1763/January 1764 he was paid 1s 'for Scoul'g of Thos Richardson's Son', presumably the same boy; and in March/April 1764, 1s 4d, and in April/May 1764, 8d. In January/February 1764 he was paid 10d for teaching 'the poor Children', so presumably more than one boy.[10]

[*Edward Sawyer, John Marchant, Thomas Roads*]

1. SPCK ALB v.1, 1400. 2. SPCK ALB v.7, 5057. 3. ESRO PAR 422/31/1/2. 4. Burchall, M. J., 'Educating the Poor, Mayfield School 1750-1771', BA dissertation, West Sussex Institute of Higher Education (1982), 15. 5. SPCK ALB v.15, 10973. 6. SPCK ALB v.16, 11213. 7. SPCK ALB v.16, 11302. 8. ESRO PAR 422/31/1/3. 9. ibid. 10. ESRO PAR 422/31/1/4.

Sunday school?   (R: 1730)
See under Charity schooling above.

Charity school   (F: 1749. Rs: 1749- into 19c)
In 1749 the inhabitants of Mayfield raised a subscription to establish a charity school in the parish. By December that year donations totalling £371 had been promised; the final total was £480 18s, from 41 donors who gave sums ranging from 5s to 150 guineas. Michael Baker (1716-50), squire and patron of the church, son of a former vicar, and head of a gentry family long settled in the town, gave £157 10s; John Kent (-1764), a wealthy yeoman farmer, £150; Henry Pelham (1695?-1754), MP, Chancellor of the Exchequer, £50 (in fact he gave £100, but only £50 is shown in the original list); Richard Trevor, Bishop of St David's, who in 1743 had inherited the Glynde estates, including Bivelham manor in Mayfield, £21; John Edwards of Mayfield, who had been sheriff of Sussex, £20; and John Apsley of Lewes (who held Gatehouse in Mayfield by marriage), John Godman (-1751) the vicar of Mayfield, Samuel Baker, gentleman of Mayfield, and Marthanna Baker, also of Mayfield, all gave 10 guineas. These nine provided 92% of the total subscription. Of the 32 lesser subscribers, who between them accounted for 8% of the total, nine were gentlemen (one was Edward Sawyer, whose enthusiasm for charity schools has been recorded above; another was a surgeon), 13 were yeomen, four were widows and one a spinster, and five were tradesmen (a mercer, a plumber, a butcher, an innholder and a peruke maker).[1] Later, in August 1751, it was agreed that the names of these subscribers should be enshrined on boards to be erected in the parish church; and this was done, the names being painted by Walter Gale, the schoolmaster (for £1 14s 3d). The cost to the charity of making and erecting the boards was £9 11s 7d (including 1s for drink for the workmen who put them up).[2]

    Six trustees were elected; and by indenture dated 17 May 1750, Michael Baker in consideration of £450, granted to the trustees an annual rent-charge of £18 out of his manors of Bungehurst and Isenhurst in Mayfield and Heathfield. The deed specified that the managers (the trustees together with the vicar of the time) were to appoint a schoolmaster and 24 poor children of the parish, to be taught gratis, reading English, writing and arithmetic. 10s pa was to be laid out in books, £1 pa for fuel, 10s for the expenses of the trustees, and the residual £16 was to go to the schoolmaster. The managers were required to maintain a register, recording their acts, their accounts, and the appointments of schoolmaster and scholars. This register or minute book provides the most complete record that we have of any 18th-century Sussex school.[3]

    Although the charity school was thus formally set up in May 1750, it was in fact operating from Michaelmas 1749. The first master, Walter Gale, had been then appointed, and the managers' accounts for October 1750 record the following payment:

> Paid the Schoolmaster for 3 Quarters teaching School before the Schoole was regularly founded due at Midsum'r 1750 pursuant to a Prior Agreement with him at £12 P Ann -   9. 0. 0[4]

The managers drew up a list of rules for the school on 29 June 1750, at which date Gale's appointment was formally confirmed; these rules closely followed guidelines recommended by the SPCK (Edward Sawyer, whose earlier involvement with the SPCK has been noted above under Charity schooling, was one of the trustees). The master was to be a member of the Church of England, 'of sober life and Conversation'; must well understand 'the Grounds and principles of the Christian Religion' and must be approved by the Minister; must be 'of a meek and humble Behaviour', and 'have a good Government of himself and Passions'; must 'frequent the Holy Communion'; must 'have a Genius for Teaching'; and must 'write a good Hand and Understand well Arithmetic.' His duties were defined by seven rules:

> 1st   That He attend the School in the Summer Half year from the hours of seven to Eleven in the Morning and from One to five in the Evening And in the Winter from Eight to Eleven in the Morning and from One to Four in the Evening.
>
> 2nd   That He teach the Children the true spelling of Words and make them mind their Stops and read distinctly.
>
> 3rd   That He make it his chief Business to instruct the Children in the Principles of the Christian Religion as professed by the Church of England, and laid down in the Church Catechism which He first teach them to pronounce distinctly And then Use an Exposition to be approved of by the Minister.
>
> 4th   That He take particular Care of the Manners and Behaviour of the Poor Children And by all proper Methods discourage and Correct the Beginnings of Vice such as lyeing swearing cursing stealing &c.
>
> 5th   That He bring the Children to Church and sitt with them there every Lords day and at other times when there shall be Divine Service And do take Care that they have their Bibles and Common Prayer Books.
>
> 6th   That He use in the School a Form of Prayer Morning and Evening such as shall be approved of by the Minister.
>
> 7th   That the Childrens names be called over Morning and Evening And if absent their names taken notice of, And for greater Faults such as lyeing stealing swearing Truancy, such to be noted in Monthly or Weekly Bills and be laid before the Managers every Time they meet in Order for Correction or Expulsion.

Later that year, on 5 October, the managers agreed that the school holidays should be 'a Fortnight at Christmas a Fortnight at Whitsuntide and Four Weeks at Bartholomewtide', and 'such Saints days as by the Rubrick of the Church of England are appointed to be observed But nevertheless That they attend Divine Service at Church those days if any be.'[5]

There was thus a clear Christian purpose to the school. The school was in fact kept in the church (see below); and the managers tried to ensure that the master met his religious obligations - Gale's diary records that on Sunday, 17 September 1758, 'The old man [Kent - one of the trustees] met the children and heard some of them say the Lord's prayer'; and on 14 December that year, 'The two old men, Kent and Edwards, came to school, and attended while the boys went through the Exposition and Catechism, and also reading the prayers.'[6] In 1757, Gale - perhaps as a defensive move against Kent, who was continually attacking him - obtained a licence from the diocese, whereby 'Walter Gale, in whose fidelity we greatly confide', was licensed by the Church 'to teach and instruct the youth of the parish of Mayfield...'[7]

When the school was formally set up on 29 June 1750, 16 children were appointed - nine boys and seven girls. These children had undoubtedly been at the school earlier, probably from its start at Michaelmas 1749: at October 1750 five were moved into a class of 'writers', having learnt to read. The number 16 was probably related to the master's salary, which, before the subscription had been completed, had been £12 pa: from June 1750 the salary was £16 pa, and the number of children to be taught was specified as 24. A further eight (five boys and three girls) were appointed on 5 October 1750, bringing the total at the school to 24.[8] (In February 1750 Gale had been in discussion with the managers as to the number of scholars he would teach for £16 pa; John Kent had proposed 24 but, according to Gale, 'after much debate the number was fixed at 21, the third part of which are supposed to be writers.'[9] However, by October that year there were 24 in the school, though only five were writers.)

Michael Baker, the prime mover in setting up the school, died in July 1750, and by his will dated 28 May 1750, bequeathed a house and garden for the residence of the schoolmaster, 'in consideration of which the trustees were to add to the school such additional number of children as they should think proper.'[10] As a consequence, three more children, 'on the house', were added to the establishment from 29 March 1751.[11] In fact, Gale continued to live with his mother at Calkins Mill, and the house was let. The rent, from two tenants, totalled £6 5s, and after tax, the balance was paid to Gale; for example, for the year to Lady day 1752, and also in the following year, he received £5 19s. From Lady day 1754 the rents were £7 pa, but repairs were often necessary: for the three-year period to Lady day 1757, taxes totalled 16s, repairs £12 5s 8d, and Gale received £7 18s 4d; for the next two-year period, after taxes of 16s and repairs of £4 18s 0¼d, he received £8 5s 11¾d.[12]

The number of children at the school remained at 27 until April 1773, except for a period from January 1762 to September 1767, when the managers, in receipt of a gift of £10 10s from Richard Porter, vicar of Mayfield (who died in February 1762, aged 46), used this to send two more children to the school (Gale, the master, being paid 7s 6d a quarter for them for a time) and also to send some very young children to a dame school, 'Widow Dukes'; during this period the number put to school by the charity ranged from 27 to 35. After about a year at the dame school, most of the children sent there moved into the charity school proper. (£2 4s 8d of Porter's gift was used in 1761 to pay for work 'abt the School'.) Another Michael Baker, nephew of the Michael Baker mentioned above, by will dated 2 March 1771 left £100 to the school, and on 9 April 1773 the managers recorded that, as a result, five more children would be appointed, over and above the 27; but they then only appointed three, and one further in July; and from 7 January 1774 there were no children 'on the House, on Account of the Necessary Repairs wanting to be done thereto': from that date until January 1783 the number at the school remained constant at 28. (It fell to 27 for the first half of 1783). In July 1783 the trustees received a further bequest of £100, under the will of Thomas Baker dated January 1781; this was consolidated with Michael Baker's £100 (on which Thomas Baker had hitherto paid the interest) and invested in bank stock annuities: the total number of charity children at the school was increased to 39, and this number was maintained from this date into the 19th century.[13]

The school was kept in the old schoolroom in the church. This does not appear to have been entirely satisfactory. Within a month or two of beginning to teach there, Walter Gale noted in his diary, 14 December 1749, 'I found the greatest part of the school in a flow, by reason of the snow and rain coming through the leads.'[14] Ten years later, in 1759, he wrote 'a paper' for the managers - 'Whereas the deplorable situation of the schollers of the free school, arising from their being confined in a close room with a charcoal fire, hath been made to appear, it is thought absolutely necessary to do something whereby the pernicious vapour which arises may be vented and carryed off, for which purpose a cupola has been proposed; it appears by an estimate that the charge will amount to £3 3s.; it is proposed to raise that sum by subscription.'[15] His proposal does not appear to have been taken up. When he was dismissed in 1771, Gale wrote an an angry letter to *SWA*, which included: 'The room where the school is kept is small, and wants light greatly; the teacher, between Martinmas and Christmas, is constantly obliged to finish his afternoon's duty by candle-light. It has a chimney, which oftentimes smokes so abhominably, that 'tis not only an annoyance, but great hindrance, both to teacher and scholars.' And Gale referred to his 'twenty-two years of uncomfortable servitude'[16] The schoolroom was maintained by the parish, as well as, to a small extent, by the charity. In 1750 the churchwardens paid John Parfitt £6 17s 9d 'For Woork don a Bou't the Scoolhouse and Over the porch'.[17] In 1753 the school managers paid £2 10s 3d towards 'Flooring the Schoolroom' and in 1761 £2 4s 8d for 'work abo't the School'.[18] In 1760 the overseers paid John Perfett [Parfitt] £2 9s 1d 'For woork don att the Free School', and also Thomas Dan £3 6s 10d 'For 1550 Brecks to the Free School & 1125 to the Woorkhouse'.'[19] In 1763 the churchwardens paid Edward Bushnell 11s 6d 'For Glazing att the Church & scoolhouse'.[20] In 1772 the churchwardens paid for considerable repairs: £3 18s 8d to William Weston Jun., 'for work at the School Room'; £2 13s 3d to Thomas Dann, 'for Bricks for the School Room'; £2 10s to John Bushmal, 'for Glassing at the School'; £8 18s 2d to John Parfitt, 'for Work at the Church and the School Room'.[21]

The managers' quarterly register shows, from December 1750 to July 1780, the numbers of children who were writers. For three quarters this information is not available, and omitting the first three quarters when the school was building up, and the period from January 1765 to September 1767, when the position was distorted by additional young children put into a dame school under Porter's gift, the average proportion of writers was as follows:

March 1751 to October 1764	(55 quarters)	33%
October 1767 to July 1780	(51 quarters)	30%

The peak incidence of writers occurred during the second period: for the two years January 1773 to October 1774 (eight quarters), the average proportion of writers was 46%.[22] As Burchall has noted, the children were taught to write on paper, not slates. In the March 1751 accounts the managers paid 3s 7d 'for Paper for Writing Books', in October 1751 11s 'for a Rheam of Paper'; and there are many such entries in the accounts.[23] In July 1752 the managers paid a considerable sum - £4 10s 6½d - for 'Books for the use of the School'. (Under the trust deed, the trustees were required to lay out 10s pa on buying books for the school.)[24]

Of the 574 appointments to the school (excluding re-appointments) made by the managers from 1750 to 1800 inclusive, 391, or 68%, were boys, and 183, or 32%, were girls. On average, children joined the school when they were 8 or 9, and left when they were 11 or 12, staying at the school for about 3 years; but there were many variations from this pattern. Girls were, on average, about a year older than boys on joining, and stayed at the school half-a-year less than boys. For 525 children we know the reasons why they were 'removed' from the school: very remarkably, only one appears to have been dismissed for misbehaviour.[25]

In addition to the children on the charity foundation, the masters also took private pupils. In April 1759 Gale recorded in his diary: 'I was called upon by Bassett, who came to quarrel with me on account of my correcting his boy for some enormous crimes he had been guilty of, all which he foolishly denied at first, and insisted upon it that his boy was unjustly corrected; yet in the end he confessed everything that the boy was beat for.' There was no Bassett boy on the charity foundation at that time, and he was clearly a private pupil.[26] When, in 1759, Kent brought two children to the school to 'be taught free', Gale asked him 'how many I was to teach free' - which suggests that he taught others for payment.[27] (The two children - George Wilmshurst and Elizabeth Hook - were appointed to the charity school in October that year.[28]) The managers' accounts show small sums being received from 'foreign scholars' for heating in the school (eg. April 1754, 'for Coal', 1s 3d; October 1754, 'for Fire', 1s 9d; January 1758, 'Fire money', 3s 5d):[29] it is suggested that 'foreign scholars' were private pupils at the school. On 10 January 1755 Ed. Weston was removed from the charity foundation (having been at the school 1¾ years) because 'his father able to pay'; on 2 May 1766 Joseph Bassett was removed (having been at the school six months) because the managers 'think him not intitled to ye Charity'.[30] The Weston reference in particular suggests that parents could pay to have their children at the school. Both removals, and that of John Eastwood in 1777, 'To make room for others more worthy of Charity',[31] and of several others removed, more ambiguously, simply to make room for others 'more worthy',[32] show that the managers were trying to provide schooling for poor children who could benefit from it. But, at the other end of the social scale, Burchall has suggested that the 'poor' children offered schooling were not pauper children but children of the 'deserving poor' who were not in receipt of parish relief. In the 50 years following its foundation, 13 children were removed from the school because they had 'gone to the workhouse' (and one other was temporarily suspended for this reason). But the surnames of many children at the school also appear amongst those receiving relief from the parish; and the action was not quite as harsh as it may appear, since there was also a school at the workhouse [qv below]. Of those removed because they had 'gone to the workhouse', ten left before 1780, and so we know if they were a reader or a writer when they left: not one was a writer. Ann Ashby was removed for this reason in January 1768, after 2¼ years as a reader; but her younger sister Susanna, who was also then at the school, was not removed (she stayed at the school for four years, for 1¼ as a writer). Katherine Gatland was removed for this reason in July 1768 (after 1¼ years at the school as a reader) but her younger sister Sarah, who was also then at the school, was not removed (she stayed until 1769). Transfer to the workhouse school when a child or his or her parents was put into the workhouse does not appear to have been automatic.[33]

The evidence that Gale took private pupils while master of the charity school is inferred from indirect references, but his successor, Benjamin Hearnden, publicly advertised the fact. He had previously had his own school at Lewes, and on his appointment to Mayfield he advertised 'that he is appointed Master of MAYFIELD FREE SCHOOL, where he intends to continue taking in Boarders as usual...'[34] Prior to his appointment, the trustees had advertised the position in November 1771: 'WANTED, at Old Christmas-Day next, for the CHARITY-SCHOOL, at MAYFIELD, in Sussex, a SCHOOL-MASTER, well qualified to teach WRITING and ARITHMETIC. The present Salary Sixteen Pounds per Annum, with a very good dwelling House for the Master, for which twenty-seven poor Children go free.'[35] In an advertisement in April 1772 the connection between the charity school and the private boarding school is explicit. This advertisement by Hearnden is notable for its advocacy of the gentle approach to education - which would have applied to the charity children as well as the private pupils:

This is to give NOTICE
THAT the FREE-SCHOOL-HOUSE, at MAYFIELD, on a dry healthy
Situation, is opened for the Reception of YOUTH, who are Boarded and
Educated in the different Branches of useful Learning, by BENJAMIN

HEARNDEN, Master of the Free-School, late Schoolmaster at LEWES.

Parents may divest themselves of the Apprehensions often attendant on sending their Children to Boarding-Schools, "that proper care is not taken of them," as they may be assured to the contrary; and that the greatest Tenderness and Endearments are used instead of Severity and unnecessary Constraint; and the utmost Pains taken to improve them, as the imaginary Difficulties young Minds are apt to think will attend their Progress in Learning are removed, all Perplexities and Obscurities extirpated, and the old rugged and tremendous Road (by many trod with Fear and trembling) is disused, and a new one perfectly smooth and easy substituted, wherein the Duty of the School from being irksome and laborious is rendered pleasant and recreative.

His Terms are THIRTEEN GUINEAS per Annum, washing, and mending Linnen and Stockings included.[36]

The combined school was apparently successful and in 1774 Hearnden was advertising for an assistant (he described himself as 'Master of the Free School at Mayfield; by whom Youth are boarded, and qualified for Business, with the utmost Expedition.').[37]

When Hearnden resigned, at the end of 1783, the trustees advertised the position again - 'Salary, 24 1. per Ann. and a convenient Dwelling house; for which Thirty-nine poor Children are to be instructed in Reading, Writing, and Arithmetic.' Private day pupils were presumably acceptable, but the advertisement ended: 'N.B. The Master will not be allowed to take any Boys as Boarders.'[38]

At Christmas 1783 Thomas Weller, who had had his own boys' boarding school at Heathfield [qv], was appointed master, and continued as such until his death in 1807.[39] In 1819 the charity commissioners noted that there were 116 children in a national school, which had been built by subscription within the last three years, of whom 39 were considered as on the foundation and were taught free: 'The master is allowed to take pay scholars, as his salary is so small, and there are no subscriptions to assist the charity.'[40]

Further details of the masters (particularly Walter Gale, part of whose diary has survived) are given in Schedule 2. Here are noted some of their other occupations, which may have affected their teaching at the school. Walter Gale, who had been dismissed from the excise, was artistic, in that he designed patterns for handkerchiefs, shoes and quilts, painted the commandments for East Hoathly and Mayfield churches, and for the latter a picture of Moses and Aaron; he painted a shop sign, and probably others; he designed and inscribed gravestones; he sold books and stationery, and bound books. He was also a surveyor, being absent from the school on occasion for this business; he measured roads for the parish; a farm map of his which has survived is marked 'No.18', indicating that he made at least 17 others. For the parish, he on occasion acted as clerk, kept the workhouse accounts, and mended the prayer book. His diary reveals a deep interest in religion, and (not uncommon at the time) a fascination with superstitions. He was dismissed from the school - after 22 years - 'for neglecting the duties thereof':[41] in a letter to *SWA* at that time he noted that, while he had increased his circumstances, 'what I have accumulated, have not arisen from the School, but from the more gainful Employments I have from Time to Time engaged in.'[42] Benjamin Hearnden's attitude to teaching methods, arguing for gentleness rather than severity, has already been noted. When he resigned from the school, he opened an inn in Lewes. Thomas Weller was a surveyor and accomplished draughtsman, and drew maps for local gentry.

[*Walter Gale, Benjamin Hearnden, Thomas Weller*]

1. Walter Gale's diary, *SAC* **9**, 189 (date references in this source have been corrected, where applicable, from

calendars for the years in question and by cross-reference with the school managers' register); ESRO AMS 5601/1 (the trustees and managers' register) hereafter MSB [Mayfield School Book], which opens with the full subscription list; biog. details from Burchall, op. cit., 17-19; Farrant, J., pers. comm. citing ESRO SAS/FB 113 (Henry Pelham's subscriptions).   2. MSB 30.8.51, 3.7.52.   3. Copies of the deeds are included at the beginning of MSB. 4. MSB 5.10.50.   5. MSB 29.6.50, 5.10.50.   6. *SAC* 9, 201.   7. ibid, 204.   8. MSB passim.   9. *SAC* 9, 193.   10. MSB 5.10.50.   11. MSB 29.3.51.   12. MSB 14.11.52, 12.10.53, 8.7.57, 6.7.59.   13. MSB 16.10.61 & ff, 9.4.73 & ff, 11.7.83 & ff.   14. *SAC* 9, 188.   15. ibid, 204-5.   16. *SWA* 2.12.71.   17. ESRO PAR 422/31/1/4.   18. MSB 6.4.53, 16.10.61.   19. ESRO PAR 422/31/1/4.   20. ibid.   21. ESRO PAR 422/31/1/5.   22. MSB passim.   23. MSB 29.3.51, 4.10.51, & passim.   24. MSB 3.7.52, 28.12.50. 25. Analyses of MSB; PRs &c (see Schedule 3).   26. *SAC* 9, 204.   27. ibid.   28. MSB 26.10.59. 29. MSB 12.4.54, 18.10.54, 20.1.58.   30. MSB 10.1.55, 2.5.66.   31. MSB 11.4.77.   32. MSB, eg. 9.7.72, 10.10.77, 8.1.79.   33. Burchall, op. cit., 27; MSB passim; Mayfield PR.   34. *SWA* 25.11.71.   35. *SWA* 4.11.71.   36. *SWA* 20.4.72.   37. *SWA* 21.11.74.   38. *SWA* 17.11.83.   39. MSB 5.12.83, -.8.1807. 40. *EP*2 (1819), 172-3.   41. MSB 18.10.71.   42. *SWA* 16.12.71.

Workhouse school   (R: 1764)
When Thomas Ashby was removed from the charity school in July 1764, the managers noted: 'taken into the workhouse and taught there'.[1] Thirteen children were removed from the charity school because they had 'gone to the workhouse', but transfer to the workhouse school when a child of his or her family was put into the workhouse does not appear to have been automatic [qv Charity school above].
1. MSB -.7.64.

Widow Duke's dame school   (Rs: 1765-7)
Between January 1765 and September 1767 the managers of Mayfield charity school sent 4-8 small children to 'Widow Dukes', for about a year, before they joined the charity school proper [qv Charity school]. She almost certainly kept a dame school. (Her literacy is evidenced by the parish paying her, in 1748, 10s for 'a'making the Poor Book.')[1]
1. MSB; ESRO PAR 422/31/1/3.

Gale's boys' school   (R: 1771)
When he was dismissed as master of the charity school at the end of 1771, Walter Gale immediately advertised his own school, as follows:
> THE abovesaid WALTER GALE, in another Part of the Town of MAYFIELD, will continue a School, by whom Youth will be carefully instructed and expeditiously taught,
> WRITING in all its useful Hands.
> ARITHMETIC in its different Branches.
> MENSURATION of every Kind, and the
> ITALIAN Method of ACCOMPTS,
> By whom Gentlemen may have true and accurate Surveys and Maps of their Estates made; Inscriptions neatly cut in Stone; be supplied with and Grave Stones well wrote, and have Books in plain Binding bound. At his House he sells all Sorts of Books and Stationary Ware; and by whom Clerks are assisted.[1]

Gale died in November 1772, less than a year later. [*Walter Gale*]
1 *SWA* 2.12.71.

MERSTON   1724: 8 families   1801: pop. 77
No 18th-century schooling traced.

MIDDLETON   1724: 4 families   1801: pop. 40
No 18th-century schooling traced.

MIDHURST   1724: 200 families   1801: pop. 1,073

Grammar school   (F: 1672. Rs: through 18c, though the free school failed in the 1760s and 1770s)

The school was founded 15 November 1672 in his lifetime by Gilbert Hannam, coverlet maker of Midhurst, who provided £20 pa for a schoolmaster to teach, free, 12 boys in Midhurst Latin, Greek, writing and arithmetic, the town undertaking to fit up the loft of the Market-house as a schoolroom. Hannam died 17 March 1678, and by will dated 11 April 1674 made provision for continuing the funding of the school. Admission was confined to 'such as can, at their first coming to school, well read the Bible or Testament', and preference was to be given to boys whose parents 'declare that theire desire and designe is to continue them soe longe at schoole till they understand the Latine and Greeke tongue and bee fitt for the university'. As for the master, 'no man who is a professed Papist, or popishly inclined, or a dissenter from the Protestant faith by law established, shall be capable of teaching at the school.'[1]

As with other Sussex grammar schools, the charity was abused by trustees and masters during the 18th century, becoming moribund, with no scholars at all, by 1769. In 1786 an information against the master and trustees was laid before the Lord Chancellor. By the early 19th century the school had recovered with again 12 boys on the foundation, though the school was then primarily a private grammar school. By 1819, the free boys were down to six, partly because an assistant master at the grammar school had set up his own school in competition (teaching reading, writing and Latin) and partly because a national school had been established in the town by then, where poor children were taught free. The foundation scholars at the grammar school were, in 1819, given a classical education on the same footing as the private pupils; their parents had to furnish them with books, and were 'respectable inhabitants and tradesmen of the town'.[2]

Rev Richard Oliver, master c1698-1710, was minister (perpetual curate) of Midhurst from before 1700 (but apparently not instituted until 1709). In 1706 a petition to the trustees, signed by 48 inhabitants, complained that he neglected his school duties. He promised to provide an assistant, but did so only for a short time, and there were further complaints. He resigned in 1710.[3]

Henry Levitt, master 1710-16, licensed in 1714, was 'a young man of 21', curate of Bepton and vicar of Heckfield, Hants, in 1715. He appears to have given up the school in 1716, when Everard Levitt, perhaps an older brother, took over.[4] Master 1717-35, he was in fact licensed to teach at Midhurst in 1716; he was minister of Easebourne in 1716, curate of Bepton from 1716, rector of Up Waltham from 1731. He was petitioned against by the inhabitants, and was dismissed by the trustees in 1735.[5]

Serenus Barrett, master 1735-57, was at his appointment also rector of Fishbourne, and incumbent of West Dean and Easebourne, and minister of Midhurst (all appointments held till his death), and was aged 58. After about 15 years he became infirm and unable to teach, and the school was given up for a time. In 1751 the buildings were out of repair, and the school was in financial difficulties. Barrett died in 1757.[6]

Francis Atkins, who had been appointed usher in 1751 to assist the infirm Serenus Barrett, was appointed master in January 1758. He was master for 30 years. He was also minister of Midhurst, and also vicar of Horsham from 1769, which he held until his death; also vicar of Climping from 1772 to 1788, and also rector of Poynings from 1786 until his death. In 1769 the Midhurst churchwardens reported that there was a free-school in the parish, but 'there are no scholars'. C1780 John Pratt complained to the trustees that 'the Revd. Schoolmaster pocketted the money and had kept no School for 16 years' ; his applications to the trustees were without effect, and after a three-year struggle he filed a Bill in Chancery, 'and compelled them to their own disgrace to re-establish the School.' In January 1786 an information against Atkins and the trustees was laid before the Lord Chancellor, and in 1788 Atkins resigned.[7]

Atkins was succeeded by his usher, Charles Parson. From 1784 to 1786 Parson had also been curate of Chiddingfold with Haslemere; he was minister (perpetual curate) of Fernhurst from 1787 until his death in 1795. The (private) school flourished in his time, with boarding accommodation for 60 boys. He was followed as master by Rev Robert Pargeter, who resigned in 1799.[8]

Rev John Wooll was appointed master on 5 November 1799, but had presumably taken office earlier as on that same day he presided at a public exhibition of composition and oratory by the boys. *SWA*, reporting this, noted that 'four months have not passed since the introduction of public speaking into the school' - presumably by Wooll, who had probably taken over at least by midsummer. Wooll left in 1807 to become headmaster of Rugby.[9]

The performance on 5 November 1799 was attended by 'a considerable company of the principal Nobility and Gentry of the County of Sussex' - including two earls and a lord. 'Nothing could go off with greater eclat than did the first performance'; it took place 'at the School-house'; prizes were awarded for English poetry composition and for oratory; 14 boys performed (five of whom had younger brothers at the school). There is no evidence that any of these boys were charity scholars, and the school was clearly almost entirely a private grammar school, and successful as such. A similar performance was given the following year, on 27 May, also well attended by 'the Noblemen and Gentlemen of the County', and well reviewed in *SWA*. The size of the school in the 18th century is not known - apart from there being no free scholars at all c1765-80, and boarding accommodation for 60 in the 1790s. In 1810 there were about 70 boys, all but a few of them private pupils. In 1819 there were six charity boys, 70 private boarders and a few private day boys.[10]

Some details of the school at the end of the century have been given by William Holloway, who went there in 1792, aged 8, and rose to become head boy. It was 'a good Classical School' with 'a Meadow for the Boys playground in Summer & a large gravelled one for Winter: one extensive lofty Room for School & Meals with suitable Bedrooms for the accommodation of sixty boys... The Revd. Charles Parson was the Master, while the household department was presided over by his widowed Mother, a very worthy old Lady, who anxious to make gentlemen of us all never failed, when we chanced to go into the Dwelling house, to point out to us the Portrait of William of Wykeham which hung in the Dining room, repeating at the same time the following Distich

  Manners make the Man

  Says William of Wykeham.'

He was later there under Dr John Wooll, who increased the charges, built a separate room for meals, banished the cane and introduced 'the more Classical birch', all of which Holloway approved.[11]

[*Richard Oliver, Henry Levitt, Everard Levitt, Serenus Barrett, George Pigett, Francis Atkins, Walter Islip, Charles Parson, Robert Pargeter, John Wooll*]

1. Row, E.F. *History of Midhurst Grammar School* (1913) ['Row' hereafter], passim; *VCH* ii, 428; *EP2* (1819), 174. 2. WSRO Ep.I/22/1; Row, 53; *EP2* (1819), 176. 3. Row, passim; Cowdray Arch. 4485. 4. Row, passim; WSRO Ep.I/3/5, Ep.I/1/10. 5. Row, passim; *SAC* **106**, 18; WSRO Ep.I/3/5, Ep.I/1/10, E138/3/1. 6. Row, passim; CI; WSRO E138/3/1. 7. Row, passim; WSRO Ep.I/22/1, E138/3/1; CI. 8. Row, passim; WSRO E138/3/1; *SAC* **100**, 25. 9. Row, passim; WSRO E138/3/1; *SWA* 11.11.99. 10. *SWA* 11.11.99, 2.6.1800; Row, 69; *EP2* (1819), 176. 11. Bagley, G.S., in *SAC* **100**, 24-6.

Charity schools   (Rs: 1769, 1798, 1799)
In 1769 the churchwardens reported that, apart from the free grammar school at which there were no scholars, 'There are some private charity schools which are supported by accidental Contributions'. They did not know how many children were taught at these schools, but added: 'They are taught to read, & generally put to Service.'[1]
By 1798 there was a large girls' charity school in the parish. A vestry minute records the following:

> July 25=1798   At a Meeting of the Inhabitants of Midhurst held at the
> Spread Eagle at the Request of Lady Montague Mrs Pointy & the Revd Mr
> Loyd [minister of Midhurst] - to give them leave to take a seat from the
> Gallery for Seventy Girls belonging to the Charity School from this and
> Neighbouring parishes or to erect a Gallery over the present One - neither
> of which proposals was consented to by the Inhabitants whose names are
> undersigned they being of the Opinion that no Alteration whatsoever should
> be made in the Church on that Account there being no Room to spare the
> Church being Crowded with people from different parishes.   [Ten
> signatures]

It is interesting that the request - by Lady Montague of Cowdray and Mrs Pointy, correctly Mrs Poyntz, sister to the 8th Viscount Montague, with the support of the minister - should be so aggressively rejected. However, this decision was overturned just over six months later. A minute for 1 February 1799 (the document is slightly damaged) recorded:

> At a Meeting of the Inhabitants of Midhurst held at the Angel Inn   It is
> agreed by the said Meet[ing] that Mrs Poynty may make any alteration She
> please in the back Gallery for the Accomodat[ion] of the Charity Children
> not Incommod[ing] the Lattin Boys.
> [Nine signatures - four of whom signed at 25 July 1798 above.][2]

1. WSRO Ep.I/22/1.   2. WSRO Par 138/12/1.

Miss Stevens' girls' boarding school   (Rs: 1789, 1794)
Miss M.A.Stevens, 'Governess of the Ladies' Boarding-School, at *Midhurst*', advertised in June 1789, acknowledging 'the Success she has experienced in the Establishment of her School'. Her terms were 1 guinea entrance, and 14 guineas pa for board, English and needle-work. 'The other Branches of Education to be paid for exclusively.' She noted that 'the Health, Morals, and Improvement of the Young Ladies intrusted to her Care, shall be particularly attended to and promoted'; and added: 'MIDHURST is deservedly distinguished for the Salubrity of its Air, and delightfully pleasant Walks; it is also remarkable for Mineral Waters of a most excellent Quality; and there is a regular Communication with London, by the Post and Public Carriages, every Day in the Week.'[1] In May 1794 she announced that she would be moving her school to Petworth at midsummer [qv].[2]   [*Miss M.A.Stevens*]

1. *SWA* 22.6.89. 2. *SWA* 12.5.89.

Other schoolmasters/schoolmistresses

Mary Brown, schoolmistress 1793 (*Univ. Directory*)

Jane Dudman, schoolmistress 1793 (*Univ. Directory*)

John Randal, schoolmaster 1793 (*Univ. Directory*)

[Flambard], French master at Midhurst, R: c1806 ('Somers Clarke's Recollections', ESRO ACC 3733/6, 11)

MID LAVANT   1801: pop. 198

No 18th-century schooling traced.

MOUNTFIELD   1724: 45 families   1801: pop. 564

No 18th-century schooling traced. (For details of the Cooper charity, with provision for teaching poor children of this parish, which did not however come into effect, see SALEHURST.)

NEW FISHBOURNE   1801: pop. 309

No 18th-century schooling traced.

NEWHAVEN (MEECHING)   1724: 49 families   1801: pop. 584

Charity school   (Rs: 1707-10)

The SPCK annual *Account* for 1707 recorded a charity school at Newhaven: 'Eight Boys and 12 Girls taught to Read, Write, and the Catechism; to which Purpose 20 l. *per Annum* is subscribed, and the Children wear Caps and Bands.'   The school was listed to 1710 but dropped in 1711: Anthony Springett had written to the SPCK in May 1711, that the school at Newhaven 'is sunk because the contributor could not agree about a Master'.[1] This was confirmed by Joseph Grave in 1713: '... ye School at Newhaven is dropt Occasioned by ye Division in the Town.'[2]

1. SPCK ALB v.2, 2576.   2. SPCK ALB v.4, 3716.

Parish schooling   (Rs: 1799- into 19c)

In the year Easter 1800 to Easter 1801 the parish paid Naomi Sage £2 8s 6d 'for Schooling'. They also paid Samuel Sage 10s 6d as vestry clerk. The previous year they had paid 'Mrs Sage Bill' of £1, almost certainly for schooling; Samuel Sage had received his clerk's salary of 10s 6d from the 1796-7 year. In the 1801-2 year Samuel Sage received £1 8s 4d 'for Schooling and Clark'. In the 1802-3 year Mrs Lee was paid £3 6s 'for Schooling for Parish Children'; in 1803-4 Susannah Lee was paid £1 16s 6d 'for Schooling &c.'; and payments to her continued to 1807. In appears, therefore, that from 1799 the parish was paying small sums each year for schooling the 'Parish Children'. These may have been children in the workhouse.[1] [*Naomi Sage*]

1. ESRO PAR 426/1/1.

NEWICK   1724: 63 families   1801: pop. 393

Boys' schools   (Rs: 1705-10, (1714?))

William Hay of Glyndebourne, later MP, poet and author, was sent to school at Newick in 1705. He was then aged 9/10. In 1710 he was removed to a larger school at Lewes, probably the grammar school, before going to Oxford in 1711/2.[1] The school at Newick was almost certainly kept by the rector, Joseph Hoyle, who was buried there 14 September 1711.[2] In 1714 there is a reference to a schoolhouse as part of the church/parsonage premises, when the then rector, Vincent Cooper, tried to lease the great and small tithes of Newick, except the parsonage and schoolhouse. (The parsonage was the substantial property now known as the 'Old Rectory'.)   It is probable that Cooper, like Hoyle before him,

augmented his income by teaching sons of local gentry.[3] [*Joseph Hoyle, Vincent Cooper*]
1. Horsfield *Lewes* II, 178.   2. Newick PR.   3. Lindsey, J. *The Story of a Sussex Village* (1983), 15.

<u>Lady Vernon's girls' charity school</u>   (F: 1771. Rs: 1771- into 19c)
Lady Vernon's school was founded by deed dated 1 January 1771, executed jointly by
George Venables Vernon, 2nd Baron of Kinderton, and Louisa Barbara his wife, who
granted to trustees a rent-charge of £50, arising out of the manors of Warningore and
Newick, the advowson of Newick, and Newick Place [now Newick Park: Lady Vernon was
the only child and heir of Lord Bussy Mansell, of Newick Place, a wealthy and substantial
landowner]. Of the £50 pa, £15 pa was to be paid to a schoolmistress, who was to live in
a house lately built for that purpose, to instruct 12 poor girls of Newick in reading, writing
and needlework, and such other work as the owners of Newick Place for the time being
should think proper, to make them useful servants. £15 pa, or so much as should be
necessary, was to be spent on clothing the children, at the rate of £1 5s for each child. A
further interesting provision was that an additional £10 pa was to be paid to the mistress for
maintaining, washing, lodging, boarding and instructing one other poor girl, to live in the
schoolhouse to assist the mistress, and a further £5 pa, or so much thereof as should be
needful, was for clothing this girl. The residual £5 pa, and any savings that might be made
out of the charity, were to be used for fuel in the schoolhouse and repairs. No child was
to be admitted under six, or continue beyond 14 years of age. The trustees, together with
the owner of Newick Place, were the managers, and had the appointment of the
schoolmistress and children.
        The deed provided for the appointment of new trustees when only two survived,
but when the original trustees died no others were appointed and by 1819 the management
of the school was by the owners of Newick Place. At that time, 1819, the school was
flourishing, with its premises, schoolmistress, pupil-assistant, and 12 girls. Again in 1867
there were 13 girls in the school; and about that time Lady Vernon's school became the state
school for girls. The original schoolhouse survives, as a private residence (1990); and over
200 years after its foundation, the charity's now substantial assets continue to benefit girls
in the parish.[1]
1. *EP2* (1819), 176-7; Lindsey, op. cit., 14, 15, 34.

<u>Wood's school</u>   (R: 1780s)
William Kenward (1767-1828) wrote in his journal: 'After having received a suitable
Education for a Tradesman from Mr Wood schoolmaster at Newick whom I attended some
Years by my Uncles generosity I was Apprenticed in 1784 to Mr Izard Breeches maker and
Glover at E Grinstead...'   (His uncle was William Kenward, maltster and farmer of
Fletching.)[1] [*Wood*]
1. 'The Journal of William Kenward', in the possession of D.Kenward of Piltdown; Kenward, D., pers. comm..

<u>Parish schooling</u> (R: 1800)

In November 1800 the overseers 'paid Master Roser for Mackerels Girls schooling 0.2.0'.
They paid a further 2s for her schooling in April 1801, for 6 weeks (ie. at 4d a week), and
4s in May 1802. However, there are no other payments for schooling recorded in the
overseers' accounts 1775-1801.[1]   [*William? Roser*]
1. ESRO AMS 5554 (1775-80), PAR 428/30/1 (1781-).

NEWTIMBER   1724: 14 families   1801: pop. 148
No 18th-century schooling traced.

NINFIELD (NENFIELD, NINVIL) 1724: about 40 families 1801: pop. 492

School (F: 1671. R: 1702)
In 1674 the vicar, John Bowyer, entered in the parish register:
> May 15th 1671 Mr. John Sone A.B. Aula Catherine Cant. did then begin
> to teach or instruct youth in the chancell of the parish church of Ninfield,
> upon my Leave & Request & hath continued so doing till the date hereof
> being the 22 of july 1674, & Long may he continue:
> J:B

On the preceding page opposite is an undated (apart from 'May 20') list of parishioners, which includes: 'Mr. Nathaniel Mills Schoolmaster, formerly Mr. John Sone'.[1] John Sone had died in 1681 (buried at Waldron 25.2.1681). In 1698 Nathaniel Mills, probably by then at Ninfield, was taking boarders - George Luxford was sent to him, at £12 pa 'for his bord and scoulling'.[2] Nathaniel Mills married at Ninfield in 1702, so that the school almost certainly continued into the 18th century.
[*Nathaniel Mills*]
1. ESRO PAR 430/1/1/1.   2. *SNQ* **12**, 170.

Mercer's boys' boarding school   (R: 1792)
In June 1792 William Mercer Jun. advertised his boys' boarding school at Ninfield, 'In which are taught, the English Grammar, Arithmetic, with all the Hands of Writing now in use' . His terms were 12 guineas pa 'to the age of nine years; above nine to twelve, fourteen ditto; and twelve to sixteen years, sixteen guineas.' He noted that 'Great attention will be paid to preserve good morals'; and that 'The School stands upon a very dry, healthy spot, about four miles from the Sea; and commands a beautiful, extensive, prospect of the County round about.'[1]   [*William Mercer jun.*]
1. *SWA* 25.6.92.

NORTH AMBERSHAM   1801: pop. 106
[Part of the Hampshire parish of Steep until 1844.]

No 18th-century schooling traced

NORTHCHAPEL   1724: 78 families   1801: pop. 621

Schools   (Rs: 1742, 1758, 1769, 1775)
Visitation returns give the following:[1]
> 1742:   No free or charity school, but 'There is a Woman Teacheth little children. She doth [teach them the catechism]'
> 1758:   A schoolmaster who came to church and taught his scholars the catechism.
> 1769:   One or more unlicensed teachers, including a schoolmaster of 'good Life' and 'diligent', who came to church and caused his scholars to come, and taught them the catechism. The children were generally put out to service (this against the question relating to any charity school, which might possibly suggest a charity school there - there is a 'Yes' opposite the question asking if there was any hospital, alms-house or free-school in the parish).
> 1775:   No free or charity school, but a schoolmaster, as in 1769.

1. WSRO Ep.I/22/1.

[Private tuition] (R: 1801)
In July 1801 'Rev. Renolds' advertised, under the heading 'PRIVATE TUITION', for two pupils, to be received into his family, 'to improve them in the CLASSICS, WRITING and

ARITHMETIC. Terms for Education, Board, Washing, and Lodging, 50 Guineas per year each.'[1] [*Morgan Reynolds*]

1. *SWA* 6.7.1801.

NORTHIAM   1724: about 70 families   1801: pop. 997

Charity school   (F: 1614. Rs: through 18c)

In 1614 Robert Iden, 'for the goodwill I bear to the educacon of yought', conveyed a house and two acres of land in Northiam to trustees, the rents and profits of which, after keeping the premises in repair, were to be paid to a schoolmaster, resident in Northiam, to teach the children of the parish. By will dated 7 September 1723, George Barnsley, one time rector of Northiam, left £500 for the education of poor children in three parishes, one of which was Northiam, to whom his executors gave £100. In 1727 this was invested in a rent-charge, to yield £3 10s pa. That same year, by deed dated 10 August 1727, Thomas Frewen the elder, in whom the rent-charge of £3 10s was vested, and Thomas Frewen the younger, in whom a rent-charge of £3 was vested, covenanted to apply this income for the education of poor children of Northiam, in spelling, reading, writing, accounts, and in the church catechism and the grounds and principles of the Christian religion, as professed by the Church of England; and that a schoolmaster should be provided for that purpose, who should teach as many children as the charity would allow at the rate of 10s per head. The £6 10s from the two rent-charges was paid to the master, and this meagre salary continued into the 19th century.[1] However, the school was further supported by the Frewen family. They re-built the schoolhouse in 1729: Richard Wide received £15 10s 6d for workmen's time, 'for two Rebild ye Schoolhouse and For Taking Down ye Owld House Diging Sand Makeing Allteration', and there were bills for materials and services such as £6 6s for bricks, £3 16s for glazing, £5 17s 9d for nails, bolts and hooks, £4 15s 10d for legal costs - the tradesmen were paid by instalments, and a number of the bills were not settled until October 1737.[2] (The school was rebuilt again early in the 19th century, on the land given by Robert Iden, at the expense of about £800, defrayed by John Frewen Turner, Esq.[3])   Stephen Hatch's bill 'For the use of the Schoolhouse' included, at 26 May 1730,

12 Dych's Spelling books	0.10. 6
1 doz ABCs	0. 0. 9[4]

By 1739 the then master, Fox, was very old and too infirm to discharge his duties properly; the number of scholars fell away and the credit of the school declined. This led to controversy between the parish and the trustees, and among the trustees - one of whom, 'Cozen Frewen', had his children educated at the school and wanted a better master, while another, Thomas Frewen of Brickwall, was insistent that justice be done to 'old Fox'. The trustees did appoint another master, but Fox also continued in office until at least 1742.[5] (The Fox family apparently remained in possession of the schoolhouse - though after old Fox, they did not teach - until at least 1798.[6]) There was another disagreement between the trustees in 1784, when one withheld payment of the £3 10s annuity on grounds of the 'insufficiency of that schoolmaster for his office', while another, John Frewen Turner, paid the schoolmaster out of his own pocket.[7]

In 1800 the then schoolmaster, George Lord, "receives the profits of the House and Garden and Orchard, but there are no Children taught" (from a letter by George Springett, trustee). 'Apparently he had declined to teach, because he had not received "what was just and right" for what he had done.'[8] The problem seems to have been sorted out - Lord was paid at the full salary rate 'for Teaching School' prior to his resignation in 1805: on 21 November 1805 he received £35 15s, or 5½ years' salary.[9]

The master's salary being so small, he was almost certainly allowed to take

additional private pupils. This is indicated by the fact that in 1770 John Rootes jun. was assistant to his father at the 'Free-school', which suggests that there were reasonable numbers at the school; moreover, John Rootes jun. also kept a boys' boarding school, offering writing and arithmetic (see below) - the boys were probably taught in the free-school.[10]
[*Fox, Martin, John Rootes sen., John Rootes jun., George Lord*]

1. *EP*1 (1819), 237-8; ESRO FRE 8182 (2); Frewen, A.L. *History of Brickwall in Sussex and of the Parishes of Northiam and Brede* (1909), 18.   2. ESRO FRE 8181.   3. ESRO FRE 8182.   4. ESRO FRE 8181 (3).   5. ESRO FRE 1284-7, 1294.   6. Davis, W.L. *O Rare Norgam* (1965), 66.   7. *EP*1 (1819), 238.   8. Davis, op. cit., 66.   9. ESRO FRE 8182 (31).   10. *SWA* 17.12.70.

Thankful Frewen's boys' boarding school   (Rs: 1710-22)
Thankful Frewen (1669-1749), rector of Northiam, boarded and taught the classics to boys of his family and sons of local gentry. A notebook of his has survived in which he recorded his pupils, the fees they had paid, and the Latin and Greek texts they studied, from January 1710 to September 1722. Among his limited number of scholars were his own sons John (later rector of Guestling), Thomas (later surgeon at Rye) and Edward (later DD of Robertsbridge), and his nephews Charles Frewen and George Bishop. His fees were £16 pa for board and schooling, or £2 pa for schooling only; and he frequently received gratuities from parents of a guinea or half a guinea. Excluding his own sons, of his 11 recorded pupils 1710-22, three stayed with him 1/1¼ years, four 2/3 years, two 4/4½ years, and two as long as 7½/7¾ years. He subscribed as schoolmaster October 1714, and presumably continued to teach beyond the date given above.[1]   [*Thankful Frewen*]

1. ESRO FRE 533; WSRO Ep.II/1/1.

Parish schooling (R: 1729)
In 1729 Elizabeth Soane was paid 6s 8d by Thankful Frewen, rector, 'for 20 weeks Schooling for goodman pankhurst boys' (ie. 4d a week, presumably 2d a week for each of two boys). Her bill, which included this item, also covered payments for making clothes, presumably for the poor of the parish. She signed the receipt.[1]   [*Elizabeth Soane*]

1. ESRO FRE 8181 (3).

Rootes' boys' boarding school   (R: 1770)
In December 1770 John Rootes jun. advertised his school, 'Where Youth are boarded, and carefully instructed in writing in the most useful Hands of England, Arithmetic both vulgar and decimal, by the best and most approved Methods.' The boys were probably taught at the free-school, where John Rootes jun. was assistant to his father. He also advertised that he 'Binds and sells all sorts of Books, and Stationary Wares, as neat and as cheap as in London; also, hires out several Sorts of Books, consisting of Histories, Voyages, Travels, Lives, Memoirs, Poetry, &c. at Half a Guinea a Year, or Three Shillings per Quarter.'[1]
[*John Rootes jun.*]

1. *SWA* 17.12.70.

Mrs Thornton's (later Johnson and Bishop's) girls' boarding school   (Rs: 1772, 1773)
Mrs Thornton had a girls' boarding school at Northiam prior to January 1773, when Mrs Johnson and Miss Bishop announced that the school would be continued by them, and opened on 19th April next.[1]   [*Mrs Thornton, Susan Johnson, Mary Bishop*]

1. *SWA* 18.1.73.

NORTH MARDEN   1724: 5 families   1801: pop. 20

No 18th-century schooling traced. (In 1755, 'No School at all'; in 1762, no scholars in the parish.[1])

1. WSRO Ep.I/22/1.

NORTH MUNDHAM   1724: 38 families   1801: pop. 324

<u>Charity school</u>   (Rs: 1733, 1737)
In 1733 the churchwardens noted that 'Mr Covert hath set up a Charity School for ten
Children of this parish who are taught at his charge' ; and in 1737, that there was a free-
school, 'chiefly maintained by the minister'.[1] (By 1755 there was no free-school in the
parish.)   Rev Charles Ranulph Covert was instituted in 1709; he died in 1759, aged 75.[2]

1. WSRO Ep.I/22/1 (1733 visitation return dated from churchwardens' names).   2. CI.

NORTH STOKE   1724: 14 families   1801: pop. 48

No 18th-century schooling traced.

NUTHURST   1724: about 60 families   1801: pop. 465

<u>Dame schools</u>   (Rs: 1733, 1737, 1742)
Visitation returns give the following:
        1733: 'We have School[s] but for small Children to learn to read.'
        1737: 'no one but a woman yt teaches children'.
        1742: 'A woman teaches to read.'
(There was no free or charity school in the parish at these dates; and in 1762 and 1779 there
was reportedly no school in the parish.)[1]

1. WSRO Ep.I/22/1 (1733 visitation return dated from churchwardens' names).

ORE   1724: about 25 families   1801: pop. 243

No 18th-century schooling traced.

OVING   1724: 57 families   1801: pop. 464

<u>Charity school/schooling</u>   (Rs: 1732- into 19c)
Stephen Challen of Shopwick, yeoman, by will dated 1730, left property in Chichester, half
the rents of which were to be used by the minister and churchwardens of Oving 'for the
schooling and teaching of ten poor children... to read.'[1] In 1733 the churchwardens reported:
'We Have one [charity school], about one Year since by inDowment', where 'a Bought Six
to Read'. In 1758 they reported the free-school but noted: 'We have no School Master' - so
the children were taught by a dame. In 1765: 'We have a small Endowment for a Charity
School, and we send as many Children as the Endowment will admit, & a proper care is
taken of the children... The Person that teacheth School has no Licence, but is very orderly,
and diligent. The Endowment will not admit of a Licence.' In 1775 they noted that the
revenue was 'A very small one of 40sh.'[2] The income remained at £2 pa into the 19th
century, and in 1819 the churchwardens were paying this to a schoolmaster for teaching five
very young children to read, who were afterwards sent on to the Chichester national
schools.[3]

1. *EP2* (1819), 159.   2. WSRO Ep.I/22/1 (1733 visitation return dated from churchwardens names).
3. *EP2* (1819), 177.

OVINGDEAN (OVINGTON)   1724: 4 families   1801: pop. 85

No 18th-century schooling traced.

PAGHAM   1717: 83 families   1801: pop. 652

No 18th-century schooling traced.

PARHAM   1724: 8 families   1801: pop. 51

[School?]
At the 1729 visitation the churchwardens answered 'Yes' to the question asking if their
schoolmaster was of a sober life &c, possibly indicating a schoolmaster there, although they
did not answer any of the other questions relating to schools or teachers.[1]
1. WSRO Ep.I/22/1.

PATCHAM (PETCHAM)   1724: 30 families   1801: pop. 286

No 18th-century schooling traced.

PATCHING   1717: about 20 families   1801: pop. 192

No 18th-century schooling traced.

PEASMARSH   1724: about 70 families   1801: pop. 611

No 18th-century schooling traced. (In 1724, the churchwardens noted '... 20s p an. given
by Dr Johnson to buy Books for the poor...', which suggests that some of the poor at least
could read.[1])
1. WSRO Ep.I/26/3, 28-9.

PENHURST   1724: 14 families   1801: pop. 81

No 18th-century schooling traced.

PETT   1724: about 17 families   1801: pop. 185

No 18th-century schooling traced.

PETWORTH   1724: about 370 families 1801: pop. 2,264

Duke of Somerset's free grammar school   (F: c1691. R: 1705)
A surviving document in Petworth House is headed: 'Orders to be observed in the Government of the free School of Petworth endowed by his Grace Charles Duke of Somerset A.D.
1691'. (Charles was then 29, and had been Chancellor of Cambridge University for two
years.)   The school was for not more than 30 poor scholars of Petworth, 'whose Parents
shall be judged unable to pay for their Education in Grammar, &c.'   It was a grammar
school: boys had to be able to read a chapter of the bible before being admitted; the school
was divided into five classes; before leaving the first class, a boy had to be able to read,
pronounce and write English well; detailed syllabuses for each of the other four classes were
specified, to the extent of listing the classic authors to be studied on the different days of
the week in every class. Latin was begun in the second class, Greek in the fourth. The
master's salary was £20 pa, with a house (the schoolhouse was in North Street).   To be
admitted to the school, boys had to be 'ready and willing to be instructed and examined in
the Catechism of the Church of England', and within three months after admission be able
to give 'a ready and rationall Account' of it 'upon Examination in the Church'. There were
to be prayers and bible readings every morning and afternoon at the school, and the master
and scholars were to attend the parish church every Saturday evening, and at both morning
and evening prayer every Sunday and Holy-day.   An interesting provision was for the role

of monitors: for each of the five classes, 'the Head-Scholar of each class Shall be a Monitor to every boy in his Class and shall every Morning and afternoon within half an hour after their meeting in the School give an account in writing to the Master of such as are absent from his Class.' The monitors were also on duty when the school attended church, being required to give a written account 'of the Absense and Misdemeanours of every Boy in his Class... to the intent that such as have absented or misbehaved themselves may be punished.' School hours were from 7 to 11 and 1 to 5 in the summer, 8 to 11 and 1 to 5 in the winter.[1]

The Duke of Somerset's accounts for 1693 show George Goodwin, schoolmaster, being paid £5 a quarter for teaching poor children;[2] he was presumably master of the grammar school. It is not known whether Goodwin continued there into the 18th century, nor indeed for how long the school continued. It had probably ceased by 1726, if not before, when at the visitation the churchwardens recorded 'Two private schoolmasters' but made no mention of any free-school.[3] In December 1705 Henry Wright, AB, was licensed to instruct boys in the grammar school of Petworth (perhaps succeeding Goodwin; he was probably the HW, rector of Upwaltham (near Petworth) 1706-18, and rector of Bodegton [Burton] cum Coots [Coates] (adjacent to Petworth) 1713); he (or another of the same name, which seems unlikely) was also licensed in November 1715 to instruct boys in the parish[4] - perhaps the grammar school had then ceased.
[*George Goodwin?, Henry Wright*]

1. *SNQ* **15**, 85-91.   2. *SAC* **96**, 74.   3. WSRO Ep.I/22/1.   4. WSRO Ep.I/1/10, 24.12.05, 16.11.15; CI.

Wright's school? (R: 1715?)
In 1705 Henry Wright was licensed to teach boys in the grammar school of Petworth (see above); in November 1715 he was again licensed (or another of the same name, which seems unlikely) this time to teach boys in the parish.[1] It is speculated that by 1715 the grammar school had ceased (it had apparently ceased at some time before 1726 - see above) and that Wright then had his own school.   [*Henry Wright*]
1. WSRO Ep.I/1/10.

Sayer's school   (R: 1725)
The probate inventory of James Sayer, 'schoolmaster Deceased', was taken on 19 January 1726.[1] Sayer was relatively well off: his inventory totalled £165, with £120 under 'Money at interest'. Among the items listed were 'Books, paper, penknives, Ink-glass & quills' (valued at £1 1s); 'one spy glass & copper plate' (2s 6d); 'two maps & two pictures' (10s); 'One Binicircle 10th   : chain & other Instrum'ts : for land surveying, wth rules & drawing instruments' (£3). That he had his own school is indicated by the entry, 'forms in the School' (10s).   [*James Sayer*]
1. WSRO Ep.I/29/149/289.

School   (R: c1720-90?)
In 1794 a 'venerable woman' was buried at Petworth, aged 92, who 'had kept a school in one house in the above parish upwards of 70 years.'[1] She would appear to have been the longest-serving schoolmistress in Sussex in the 18th century. [*Elizabeth Wickcliffe or Elizabeth Houneymond* - see Schedule 2]
1. *Portsmouth Gazette* 30.6.94.

Schoolmasters and schools   (Rs: 1726, 1758, 1762, 1765, 1769, 1775)
Visitation returns give the following:[1]

1726: 'Two private schoolmasters' [one probably Wright].

1758: A schoolmaster of 'good Life' and 'diligent', who taught his scholars the catechism.

1762: 'There is a man in ye Parish who teaches Children to read & write. We apprehend he is not licenced; but he is a man of very sober life, & very diligent in his business. He is not a constant comer to Church But instructs his Scholars very carefully in ye Church Catechism.'

1765: 'We have two [schoolmasters] that teach school, we know not that they are licenced, they are sober men and diligent.'

1769: A schoolmaster of 'good Life' and 'diligent', who came to church and caused his scholars to come, and taught them the catechism.

1775: [Any unlicensed teachers?] 'they teach, we know nothing of a Licence'. A schoolmaster, 'very Diligent for what we know', who taught his scholars the catechism.

1. WSRO Ep.I/22/1.

Taylor's boys' and girls' charity school   (F: not before 1775. Rs: 1783- into 19c)
Rev John Taylor, a fellow of Winchester College, by will dated 20 March 1753, gave £2,400, the interest of which was to be applied by the rectors for the time being of Petworth, Tillington and Duncton in establishing a school in Petworth for the education of 10 poor boys and 10 poor girls. The master's salary was to be £35 pa and, in addition to teaching reading, writing and arithmetic, he was to instruct the children in 'the grounds of Christianity'. The warden of Winchester college (or if he was incapacitated, the sub-warden) and two other fellows of the college, to be nominated by the warden and fellows, were to be the visitors, guardians and supervisors of the school, and were personally to inspect it once in four years, on 1 July, or within 16 days after. By a codicil dated 10 April 1775, Taylor gave a further £800, the interest of which was to be used to provide clothing for the 10 boys and 10 girls.[1]

In 1783 James Goldring was master, and was also operating his own private boys' boarding school from the premises (see below): 'The School is spacious, and has been long established, (being also a Free School).'[2] In 1796 Goldring was advertising for an usher - 'A young man, who can write a good hand, and understands Arithmetic.'[3]

An untitled notebook records pupils at the school c1799, showing joining dates from 1796, and other lists, one headed 'A list of Mr. Taylor's School, July 12th : 1803'.[4]
[*James Goldring*]

1. *SAC* **14**, 21; *VCH* ii, 439; *EP2* (1819), 177.   2. *SWA* 29.12.83.   3. *SWA* 18.1.96.   4. WSRO Petworth Ho. Arch. 1763.

Parrott's boys' boarding school   (F: c1780. Rs: 1782-93)
Advertising his school in July 1790, Benjamin Parrott referred to the civilities 'he has more than ten years experienced', suggesting that he started his school about 1780.[1] In 1782 he was advertising for an assistant ('A YOUNG MAN... he must write a good Hand, and understand Accounts well.').[2] In a long advertisement in January 1784, he observed that -

> ... the following most useful and necessary Branches of Literature are taught with Care, Humanity, and Expedition; namely, Spelling correctly, Reading according to Points, Cadence, and Emphasis; the Art of Writing all the different Hands with Ease and Elegance; Arithmetic in all its various Parts, both Vulgar and Decimal; Mensuration of all Manner of Superficies and Solids; Logarithms, Trigonometry, and Navigation; also, Algebra, and Geometry; the Art of investigating and regulating Accompts of Merchants, &c. according to the modern Mode, which is agreeable to that practised by the Italians.

His terms for instruction in the above, with board, lodging, washing, &c., were 12 guineas pa, and half-a-guinea entrance. 'Those who wish their Children to be instructed in the Latin and English Languages grammatically, will be charged Two Guineas more per Annum, and One Guinea Entrance.' The advertisement also noted:

> The most essential Part of Education is not neglected here, viz. giving Boys Rules and Maxims of Oeconomy, which enable them to enact their Part on the Stage of Life with Prudence and Circumspection, and consequently make their Characters truly amiable.

Parrott had an assistant, and fiercely proclaimed the professionalism of both himself and his assistant:

> He and his Assistant (who has taught at some of the most reputable Academies in England) are not broken Tradesmen, but regular-bred Schoolmasters from their Infancy, whose Characters may be learnt from Persons of undoubted Veracity.[3]

In a short advertisement later that year, in June, his approach was summarised: 'Young Gentlemen are genteely boarded, carefully taught, and most tenderly treated...' And there is the earliest mention so far traced of a school prize:

> N.B. This Tide, the SILVER PEN was won (by Writing) in the above School, by Master JONES, of Horsham.[4]

By 1790 Parrott was also advertising 'Books, Stationary, and Musical Instruments, as cheap as in London: and Instruments let out to hire.'[5]

At the beginning of 1791 he announced that 'he has purchased and entered on a very large and convenient dwelling house, with a delightful garden, a pleasant and extensive play-ground, situate in a healthy part of the town, and entirely private.'[6] He also advertised for 'an articled Assistant, of good family... a premium will be expected.' In this advertisement he first describes his school as an academy, and in an advertisement later that year the school is referred to as 'Petworth Academy.'[7]

In addition to his own school, Parrott also taught writing and accounts at Mrs Hews girls' boarding school (see below).

Despite the apparent success of his school, in 1793 Benjamin Parrott was the beneficiary of a charity - one of two 'Poor Tradesmen' of Petworth that year, each given £6 5s.[8]

Advertised in *SWA* Jan (2), Jun 1784; Jul (2) 90; Jan (2), Jul 91; Jan (2) 92. In *Univ. Directory* 1793.

[*Benjamin G. Parrott*]

1. *SWA* 12.7.90.   2. *SWA* 15.7.82.   3. *SWA* 12.1.84.   4. *SWA* 7.6.84.   5. *SWA* 12.7.90.
6. *SWA* 10.1.91.   7. *SWA* 11.7.91.   8. WSRO Petworth Ho. Arch. 1763.

Goldring's boys' boarding school   (Rs: 1783-96)

James Goldring was master of Taylor's charity school (see above), onto which he grafted his own boys' boarding school. From 1781 to 1822 Goldring owned a house, on the north side of Church St, that had until the mid-18th century been *The Blue Lion* (the site later became part of the churchyard)[1]. In an advertisement in December 1783,[2] he offered instruction 'in Writing all the Hands now in use; Vulgar and Decimal Arithmetic; Extraction of the Roots; Logarithms; Mensuration of all Manner of Planes and Solids; Land Surveying; Algebra; Geometry; Conic Sections; Trigonometry; Navigation, and Book keeping; with every other Denomination of Learning necessary to form a useful Member of Society.' His terms were £12 a year, 'and with Tea, One Guinea more.' He noted that Petworth was 'A Town pleasantly situate in the western Part of the County of Sussex, on a dry soil, and very healthy Spot; and distant from LONDON about Fifty Miles, being on the Road from

LONDON to ARUNDEL; to and from which Places a Diligence passes three Times a Week. The School house is large and convenient, and is situate in an agreeable Part of the Town. The School is spacious, and has been long established, (being also a Free School.)' Goldring's advertisement is notable for its reference to books and newspapers, taking up an idea promoted by Thornton of Horsham earlier that year:

> It is too obvious, that Scholars educated in the Country are in general confined in their reading to very few Books; and thus when they are put the least out of their Track, they are totally at a Stand. To obviate every Objection of this Kind, the best Authors, as well as the Newspapers, will be introduced...

In January 1796 Goldring advertised for an usher ('A YOUNG MAN, who can write a good hand, and understands Arithmetic'), so his school was continuing then.[3] [*James Goldring*]

1. *SAC* **99**, 143.   2. *SWA* 29.12.83.   3. *SWA* 18.1.96.

Mrs Hews' girls' day and boarding school   (Rs: 1790, 1793)
Mrs Hews advertised her boarding school in July 1790,[1] where 'young Ladies are genteelly accomodated, and expeditiously taught, all kinds of plain and ornamental Needle-Work, the English and French Languages grammatically, Writing and Accounts, at Fourteen Guineas a year, and One Guinea Entrance: Music and Dancing, Fifteen Shillings per quarter: Day-Scholars (French and Needle-Work) Ten Shillings and Sixpence per quarter.' Writing and accounts were taught by Mr Parrott, 'Master of the Gentleman's Boarding-School, in Petworth.' There is a reference to the 'Happiness' of the girls - 'their Health, Happiness, and Morals invariably and faithfully regarded.' In *Univ. Directory* 1793. [*Mrs Hews*]

1. *SWA* 12.7.90.

Miss Stevens' girls' boarding school   (F: (at Petworth) 1794)
Miss M.A.Stevens, governess of a girls' boarding school at Midhurst [qv], announced in May 1794 that, 'by the recommendation of many respectable people, she intends, at Midsummer next, to remove to Petworth, where she will open a SCHOOL, for the reception of young Ladies, to be carefully instructed in every branch of Female Education: - Board, English, and Needle-Work, Sixteen Guineas per Annum; Entrance, One Guinea. - French, Writing, and Arithmetic, to be paid for exclusively.'[1] (The basic fee was up 2 guineas on her Midhurst school in 1789.)   [*Miss M.A.Stevens*]

1. *SWA* 12.5.94.

PEVENSEY (PEMSEY)   1724: 26 families   1801: pop. 192

Charity school/schooling   (Rs: (1736-41, 1743), 1775-1800)
From at least 1736 a small charity school at Westham was supported by the Cavendish family, the Compton Place accounts showing payments of £5 pa to a schoolmaster for teaching 8 or 9 children. In 1784 the payment was made by Lady Cavendish to the schoolmaster, Richard Thompson. It appears that Pevensey children attended this school, for the Compton Place accounts include a memorandum dated 23 September 1785 (the day of Richard Thompson's funeral) signed by John Preston, minister, and eight others, giving their opinion that 'John Christian is a person well Qualified to succeed the late Mr. Thompson in the instruction of the Poor children in Pevensey and Westham in reading, writing & accounts.'[1] (At the same time, the churchwardens and overseers of Westham, with other inhabitants, put forward their approval of Edward Barnard 'as a proper person to teach school, in the Vestry room of the Parish Church of Westham'.[2])

From at least Lady day 1775, Matthias D'Oyly, vicar of Pevensey, had paid £2 2s pa to Richard Thompson for teaching three poor children of Pevensey. For the year from

Lady day 1786, Richard's widow, Mary Thompson, was paid £2 2s for teaching three children; and she continued to receive this sum for teaching three poor children until at least Lady day 1800. However, from Lady day 1787, D'Oyly also paid £2 2s pa to John Christian for teaching three poor children of Pevensey. So by 1787 the number of children taught had increased to six, and this continued to at least Lady day 1800.[3] D'Oyly was vicar of Pevensey from December 1767 until his death cJanuary 1816, so his support for the charity school there may have extended before and beyond the dates shown above.
[*Richard Thompson, Mary Thompson, John Christian, Charles Christian?*]
1. Budgen MS at SAS, v.117, f 6. 2. ibid. 3. ESRO SAS/GT 1/2/1, 1/2/2, 1/2/3: these account books of the lawyer, Charles Gilbert of Lewes, record 'Account with Revd Mr D'Oyly' from 1776 to 1800 only.

Girls' school   (R: 1799)
SWA 17 June 1799 included the following report:
> Tuesday a very large snake crept into a schoolroom for young ladies, in the street of Pevensey. The governess and her fair pupils, (perhaps mindful of the misfortune of our first parent) screamed aloud, and fled from the speckled reptile in every direction; their cries brought a neighbouring gentleman into the schoolroom, who ridded the little fair ones of their alarm, by instantly killing the unwelcome intruder.

PIDDINGHOE   1724: 23 families   1801: pop. 194

No 18th-century schooling traced.

PLAYDEN (PLOYDEN, SALTCOTT) 1724: 12 families 1801: pop. 179

Parish schooling   (Rs: 1731-2, 1743-4, 1781-6)
A number of loose overseers receipts have survived relating to the schooling of pauper children in the 18th century.[1] From 20 November 1731 to 5 April 1732 (the period covered by a surviving receipt) they paid William Wybourn 6d a week for schooling Joseph Comber: Wybourn was then master of Saunders' boys' charity school in the neighbouring parish of Rye; he also kept his own private school, to which the Playden overseers sent the boy; Joseph Comber was then 11. Another receipt shows that in 1743 and into 1744 they paid Mary Colens (who signed the receipt by mark) 2d a week for seven weeks and 3d a week for 31 weeks for schooling Martha Neal; Martha became 7 during this period. From May 1781 they paid for the schooling of four Head children - two older girls, Hannah and Ann (Ann was then just 9) and two younger boys, John and James (James was only 3½ at that time). Until April 1782 all four were taught by Sara Stevens (a very neat writer, who may well have kept her own school), the girls at 3d a week, the boys at 2d. Receipts covering the period from the beginning of 1783 to 13 October 1783 show the boys only being taught, by Jane Dawes, at 3d a week; from then until April 1784 the boys were taught by Sarah Roun (who signed by mark), at 2d a week. Another receipt shows that James, the youngest, was taught by W.King, at 2d a week, for 12 weeks of 1785 and nine weeks of 1786: James would then have been 8. (W.King may have been the William King, later in 1793 a schoolmaster at Battle.)   [*William Wybourn, Mary Colens, Sara Stevens, Jane Dawes, Sarah Roun, W.King*]
1. ESRO PAR 445/31/1/14.

PLUMPTON   1724: 40 families   1801: pop. 1,710

Charity school   (F: 1715. Rs: 1715-22, c1735- into 19c)
Anthony Springett, writing to the SPCK in April 1716, informed them that 'there are 3.

Parish's where the Children are all taught to read & their Catechism Viz . Westmeston cum Chiltington, Plumpton & Street.[1] Writing from Plumpton in May 1722, he noted: 'That the Schools in that Neighbourhood still continue in a flourishing Condition tho' there are grievous Complaints against them as the Occasion of the want of Servants in those parts'.[2] In the SPCK annual *Account of the Charity-Schools* for 1724, the foundation date of the school at Plumpton is given as 1715. (The *Accounts* for 1725-40 give county totals only: these imply that the school continued throughout this period - as it almost certainly did - but as there is no change at all in the county total 1730-40, these later lists must be regarded as suspect.)

Anthony Springett, who died in 1735, gave by will an exchequer annuity of £13 to the Plumpton, Westmeston and Chiltington schools. The annuity expired in 1806.[3] John Martin of Chiltington, by will dated 1 October 1797, left £4 6s 8d pa 'to support a school in the hamlet of Chiltington' when Springett's charity to the hamlet of Chiltington 'shall cease to be paid': in 1819 this bequest was being received by the rector of Westmeston who paid 4 guineas annually to a schoolmistress in neighbouring Plumpton for teaching 8 children (boys or girls) reading and needlework, the residue being laid out in books.[4]

1. SPCK ALB v.6, 4772.   2. SPCK ALB v.11, 7053.   3. *SAC* **122**, 143; a confirmatory receipt, made c1752 but relating to the receipt in January 1737 of two years' annuities (£26), signed by Edward Wilson, is included in 'The free-school Book of Brighthelmston', at Brighton Library, SB 279 FRE.   4. *EP1* (1819), 225-6.

Dame school   (R: c1787)
John Dudeney, born in 1782, whose father and grandfather were shepherds, wrote: 'I was sent to school to an old woman who lived at Plumpton Place, of the name of Mascall, whose husband was bailiff over a few fields for Lord Pelham. I learnt nothing there but to drive the ducks into the moat, and my mother, fearing I might fall in, took me away after I had been there only a few weeks.'[1] (Dudeney's account gives a record of rural home teaching, and self-instruction - see Schedule 3.)   [*Mrs Mascall*]
1. *SAC* **2**, 253.

POLING   1724: 21 families   1801: pop. 170
Charity schooling   (F: c1782. Rs: c1782- into 19c)
John Tilly, by will dated 12 December 1775 (he was buried at Poling 12 December 1781), left a rent-charge of £3 pa, to be paid to a schoolmaster or mistress living in Poling to instruct poor children of the parish in reading. The children were to be appointed by Thomas Amore and his heirs (to whom the land yielding the rent-charge had been devised) and the churchwardens and overseers. In 1819 the rent-charge was being paid to a schoolmaster for teaching eight children of both sexes to read and say the catechism.[1]
1. *EP2* (1819), 177; Poling PR.

PORTSLADE   1724: 24 families   1801: pop. 284
No 18th-century schooling traced.

POYNINGS   1724: 18 families   1801: pop. 173
Charity schooling   (F: c1786. Rs: c1786- into 19c)
George Beard (1749-86), curate and rector of Poynings for 54 years, at his death in June 1786 left the interest of £100 in the Funds for the education of poor children of the parish. This gift was not mentioned in his will, but was administered by the succeeding rector, whose executor after his death in 1796, transferred to the next rector £100 3% reduced stock upon this trust. The latter paid £3 pa to a schoolmistress for teaching 8 children of the

parish, boys and girls, to read (he also paid for the instruction of an additional number of children of the parish).   [He used the £100 to redeem land tax, and in 1819 the charity commissioner considered the charity to be entitled to £4 13s pa from the rector.][1]

1. *SAC* **15**, 231; *EP2* (1819), 177.

PRESTON   1724: 20 families   1801: pop. 222

Mrs Norton's girls' boarding school   (F: 1796. Rs: 1796-1800)
On 18 July 1796 Mrs Norton, widow of John Bridger Norton, late excise officer of New Shoreham, opened her girls' boarding school at Preston House (then in the ownership of William Stanford[1]). Her terms were:

> Education, (including French and Geography) Board and Washing for young Ladies, above ten years of age, Twenty-two Guineas per Annum.
> For young Ladies under that age, Eighteen Guineas per Annum.
> For half Boarders, Twelve Guineas per Annum.
> For Parlour Boarders, Forty Guineas per Annum.
> Day Scholars, for Education, French, &c. and Dinners, Three Guineas per Quarter.
> Music, One Pound One Shilling per Quarter.
> Entrance, One Pound One Shilling.
> Dancing, One Pound One Shilling per Quarter.
> Writing, Fifteen Shillings per Quarter.
> The washing of clear muslin frocks, caps, and tippets, will be an extra charge.
> Tea, twice in the day, will be an additional charge of Two Guineas per Annum.
> A Single Bed will be an extra charge of Two Guineas per Annum.
> Each Lady is requested to bring a knife, fork, table-spoon, and four towels.

She noted that:

> Preston Place [sic] is situated within a mile and a quarter of Brighton, in a vale skirted with wood and meadow, and surrounded by the South Downs. The Mansion-House stands in the centre of a lawn, which consists of about six acres; and the Village of Preston is celebrated as well for the salubrity of its air, as for the beauty of its situation.[2]

In 1797 she advertised for a housekeeper.[3] In 1799 she noted that: 'The best Masters are engaged, on the usual terms; and no extra charges made, but with the approbation of the Parents.'[4]   William Austin of Brighton was the drawing master;[5] and Mr Corbyn was probably the dancing master - when *SWA* reported Mr Corbyn's ball at Lewes in December 1800 as being 'for Mrs. Gell's scholars' (she had a school in Lewes), a correspondent complained that it would have been nearer the truth to say it was 'for the Ladies of a School near Brighton' - presumably Mrs Norton's at Preston. This ball 'was numerously attended by most of the principal families in Lewes, and its neighbourhood...   The graceful movement and polite deportment of Mr. Corbyn's scholars, exhibited ample proofs of the master's ability and attention.'[6]

Advertised in *SWA* May (4), Jun (2), Jul (2) 1796; Jan, Sep 97; Jul, Dec 98; Jan, Jul (2) 99.

[*Mrs Norton, William Austin (drawing master), William Corbyn (dancing master)*]

1. Beevers, D., Keeper of Preston Manor, pers. comm.   2. *SWA* 9.5.96.   3. *SWA* 4.9.97.
4. *SWA* 15.7.99.   5. *SWA* 23.6.1800 (Austin ad).   6. *SWA* 15.12.1800, 22.12.1800.

PULBOROUGH   1724: about 80 families   1801: pop. 1,334

Schools   (Rs: 1729, 1733, 1758, 1775, 1779)
Visitation returns give the following:[1]
    1729:   A schoolmaster in the parish, described by the churchwardens as 'pretty good'.
    1733:   No free-school, but: 'We have a writing master not Licensed', who came to church and caused his scholars to come, and instructed them in the catechism.
    1758:   A schoolmaster, whose way of life and diligence were 'As well as any in Country in general'; 'He is sometimes at Church; his Scholars also, as oftener as far as we know, and we believe he may [teach them the catechism].'
    1775:   No free or charity school. In response to the question asking if any person taught who was unlicensed, 'no Schoolmaster doth' - which suggests that there might have been one or more school dames. There was also a schoolmaster (presumably licensed), of 'good Life' and 'diligent', who came to church and caused his scholars to come, and taught them the catechism.
    1779:   A schoolmaster, of 'good Life' and 'diligent'.
1. WSRO Ep.I/22/1.

Sunday school   (Rs: 1786-99)
Churchwardens' and overseers' accounts show that there was a Sunday school in the parish from at least January 1786: on 5 March that year Dame Sheppard was paid 3s 6d (she received 6d a week for teaching Sunday school - on 16 July she was paid 2s 6d for five Sundays). She was paid through to July. On 4 June 1786 Nicholas Warner was paid 14s for 14 weeks schooling; later payments make it clear that he received 1s a week for teaching Sunday school, and he continued to be paid until November 1799. Warner may have been the parish clerk - in 1798 there is a payment of £6 13s 6d to him for 'salary &c.'.[1] [*Dame Sheppard, Nicholas Warner, Wilmer*]
1. WSRO Par 153/31/1.

PYECOMBE   1724: 14 families   1801: pop. 134
No 18th-century schooling traced.

RACTON   1801: pop. 111
No 18th-century schooling traced.

RINGMER   1717: about 90 families   1801: pop. 897

Charity school   (F: c1698. Rs: through 18c)
In 1695 Dame Barbara Thomas, wife of Sir William Thomas, and Sybilla Stapley, daughter of Sir John Stapley, gave £100 each for the purchase of lands and hereditaments, the rents whereof were to be used for teaching the poor of Ringmer to read and work, 'thereby as well to ground them in the principles of the Christian religion and doctrines of the church of England, as to excite them to industry'. On 7 October 1698 (the two benefactresses having died shortly before this date) Sir William Thomas, in respect of these two sums, created an annuity of £10, charged on his manor of Folkington. The annuity was to be employed in teaching 16 poor children of Ringmer and providing them with bibles.[1]
    Anthony Springett, writing to the SPCK from Lewes in 1727, reported that 12 boys

and 6 girls were being taught at the school.[2] Henry Snooke, vicar of Ringmer, who died aged 70 in 1727, left £1 10s to the school to buy such books as his successor should think fit; and his son, also Henry, in his will of 1762, requested that the two charity school dames and all the children should 'attend him to church' , and each child was to be given a small common prayer book.[3] The manor court roll in 1759 describes a cottage, stable and garden by the churchyard as having also a schoolhouse, lately erected, which may have been where the charity school was then kept. In 1778 the Duke of Dorset, lord of the manor, gave land on Ringmer Green, and a schoolhouse was erected there, paid for by public subscription. The annuity continued to be paid into the 19th century. By 1819 the schoolhouse had been enlarged, and the charity school united with a national school, over 100 children then being taught.[4]

The endowment was small - £8 15s pa for teaching and £1 5s pa for buying bibles[5] - and it is likely that the children were taught by dames throughout the 18th century. In January 1749 Widow Taylor was buried, 'who had been School Dame for several Years & had thereby gain'd a good Name'.[6] In 1762 Henry Snooke's will (see above) referred to the two charity school dames. In February 1770 the parish advertised for a governor for the workhouse, adding: 'Note, If the Man has a Wife who is capable of teaching a School, there is one that can be tacked to it, which will make it more advantageous to them.'[7] In 1802 the overseers' rate-book lists the free school, with William Peckham as occupier:[8] he was presumably the schoolmaster, and, in view of the small annuity for the charity school, would probably have had his own paying pupils as well.
[*Widow Taylor, William Peckham?*]

1. Kay, J., 'The Ringmer Charity School', *Ringmer History Newsletter*, no.42, 2-3; *EP*1 (1819), 238-9. 2. SPCK ALB v.2, 2576. 3. Kay, op. cit., 3; Ringmer PR. 4. Kay, op. cit., 4; *EP*1 (1819), 238-9. 5. *EP*1 (1819), 238-9. 6. Ringmer PR. 7. *SWA* 5.2.70. 8. Kay, op. cit., 4.

RIPE (ECKINGTON, HEYINGTON) 1724: 34 families 1801: pop. 296

No 18th-century schooling traced.

ROBERTSBRIDGE (ROTHERBRIDGE) - see also SALEHURST

Robertsbridge was part of the parish of Salehurst, but those schools specifically identified as being in Robertsbridge are here described.

Pike's boys' boarding school (Rs: 1771-91)
George Pike, presumably helped by his wife Mary, had 'a high-class boarding school' in Robertsbridge; it stood nearly opposite the entrance of the *George Hotel* yard. The Pikes were Methodists, and when John Wesley visited the area, he stayed with them at the 'Old Grange House Academy'. Five such visits were recorded, one in 1771, two in 1778, one each in 1779 and 1784 (when Wesley was 81). Wesley conducted preaching services in a large schoolroom attached to Pike's house, which would accommodate a congregation of 150 persons. Pike was leader of the Methodist Society Class of Robertsbridge from 1774 until within a short period of his death, at 62, in 1792. His usher, John Mitchell, was also a Methodist, and a member of the same Class from 1774 to 1791.[1]

Pike died 4 July 1792, and it was almost certainly his school that was advertised in *SWA* in May of that year for sale by auction:

> A BOARDING SCHOOL... A CAPITAL MANSION, with gardens, orchards, large and convenient stabling, barn, lodge, and other out-buildings, and several pieces of exceeding rich meadow and arable land adjoining, containing in the whole twenty acres, more or less, which have for several years past been occupied by the Proprietor (who is going to

retire from business) as a Boarding-School for young Gentlemen, with great reputation and success... if taken for a School, [may be] entered upon at Midsummer next, and a purchaser of good character and reputation may have a recommendation from the Proprietor to very extensive connections.

The Premises are situate at the upper-end of the town of Robertsbridge aforesaid, in a dry and healthy place adjoining the turnpike road leading from London to Hastings...[2]

[*George Pike, John Mitchell, Henry Goodsens?*]

1. Austen, E., 'John Wesley, the 'Pikes' and early Methodism in Robertsbridge...', *The Proceedings of the Wesley Historical Society*, v.15, part 5 (1926), with many MS annotations by Austen, ESRO AMS 6361/2.   2. *SWA* 28.5.92.

Mrs Goodsens' girls' boarding school   (Rs: 1777-8)
In May 1777 Mary Goodsens advertised her school as follows:[1]

A BOARDING SCHOOL for YOUNG LADIES,
At ROBERTSBRIDGE, in SUSSEX,
WHERE will be taught all Sorts of Needle Work, Tambour, &c.   The greatest Attention will be paid to forward every Scholar in the most eligible and polite Accomplishments, and strict Regard had to their Morals,
By their most obedient Servant,
MARY GOODSENS.
. Entrance Half a Guinea, Board and Schooling Twelve Guineas per Year, and Breakings-up Five Shillings per Year.
N.B. Dancing and Writing Masters will attend on reasonable Terms.

A year later she announced that she had now taken for her school, 'a handsome, commodious House and Gardens, late in the Occupation of JOHN NICHOLS, Esq. situated at the Entrance of the TOWN, upon the High-road from London to Hasting.'[2]

Mary Goodsens was a Methodist in 1780, as was Henry Goodsens, schoolmaster, who was probably her husband and may have been a master at Pike's school [qv above]. They are not included in a Robertsbridge Methodist list of members in 1791, and may have left the district by then.[3]

[*Mary Goodsens*]
1. *SWA* 12.5.77.   2. *SWA* 4.5.78.   3. Austen, op. cit.

Dame school   (R: c1785)
William Catt, born 1780, whose father farmed at Robertsbridge, was sent to a dame school there.[1]

1. Lower *Worthies*, 217.

Vinall's school?   (Rs: 1788?-?)
George Vinall was appointed the first master of Robertsbridge charity school when it opened in April 1796 [qv below]. In September 1828, a school committee, negotiating union with the National Society, referred to Vinall 'who has so faithfully & honourably performed his duty for a period of 40 years.'[1] It is inferred that Vinall was teaching from c1788, some eight years before the charity school began, and it seems probable that he had his own school in Robertsbridge. He and his wife Mary were established in the parish (of Salehurst) at that time, their son James being baptised there in 1785, and their daughter Penelope in 1787.[2] [*George Vinall*]
1. ESRO PAR 477/25/1/1.   2. Salehurst PR.

Charity schools   (F: 1796. Rs: 1796- into 19c)
A subscription charity school was opened in Robertsbridge on 5 April 1796.[1] Subscribers

could nominate one child for each guinea subscribed, 'Such Children to be only poor persons, and not a Subscribers' (though one or two subscribers appear to have nominated relatives, presumably poor - Charles Woods nominated Harriet Woods, daughter of John; John Haiselden nominated Joseph Haiselden, son of Joseph). The boys were to be taught 'to Spell and to Read and also Writing and Arithmetic; provided the Subscriber of a Child shall think proper to find Books and Slates for that purpose.' The girls were to be taught the same, 'and also knitting and plain needle work'. No child was to be admitted under 5 or over 12. Every child was to be sent to school 'perfectly free from Vermin, their Hands and Face washed clean; and as neat in apparel as the Circumstances of their parents will admit.' The children, attended by the teacher, were to 'go in procession to attend Divine Service every Sunday Morning and Afternoon, and at other times when Divine Service shall be performed in Salehurst Church.' A charity sermon was to be preached annually in May in the parish church of Salehurst, for the benefit of the charity.

The rules refer to 'the schools', and clearly two were envisaged, for boys and girls respectively. There were initially 28 subscribers who nominated 38 children (and presumably subscribed 38 guineas, though one subscriber is marked 'Gratis'). Twenty-six of the children nominated were boys, 11 girls, with one nomination unfilled. Their ages ranged from 5 to 11, with one boy of 4 (despite the rules): the mean age was 8.[2]

School hours were from 8 to 11 and 1 to 4.30 in the summer (Lady day to Michaelmas) and from 9 to 11 and 1 to 3.30 in the winter. Holidays appear to have been short: later, in 1824, the 'Winter holiday' began on Christmas day and the school reopened on the third Monday after Christmas; the Easter holiday began on Good Friday, the school reopening on the following Wednesday; the midsummer holiday began on the Monday before Midsummer day, the school reopening that day fortnight.

The first teachers to be appointed were George Vinall and his wife Mary. They received in total £21 pa, though at the end of the first year, in March 1797, they were given 'as a present' over and above the yearly salary, two guineas 'in Consideration of the very great attention' paid by them. The charity also paid 8 guineas pa for the rent of the house and premises.

In 1802 the schoolroom was given up and Vinall was allowed 8 guineas rent (presumably finding his own school room); by 1822 he was receiving this rent and a salary of only £18 pa. In 1828 the schools became formally united to the National Society, though the implementation was delayed, the committee negotiating this reporting that: 'The infirmities of your respected master, Mr. Vinall, have not allowed him to devote his time to the acquirement of the National System; & your Committee did not feel themselves justified in recommending the removal of an officer who has so faithfully & honourably performed his duty for a period of 40 years.' (The charity school had been going for 32 years, so perhaps Vinall was a teacher there before.) In 1829 the school was remodelled, reopening in May with a new master and mistress (who were paid 9s and 4s a week respectively). A year later, in May 1830, there were 79 children at the school, 37 boys and 42 girls, 'receiving instruction every day in the Week except Saturday - on Sunday in addition to the above there are 20 Boys & 5 Girls.'

[*George Vinall, Mary Vinall*]

1. School book, ESRO PAR 477/25/1/1.   2. Based on 33 children (1 child not nominated, 4 boys age not known), from ages given in list, supplemented and corrected from PR data.

Other schoolmaster

Henry Goodsens, 'Schoolmaster' in Robertsbridge Methodist members list 1780. Probably husband of Mary Goodsens, who had a girls' boarding school [qv above]. He probably either had his own school, or was a master at Pike's school [qv above]. (Austen, op. cit.)

Dancing master

> Stephen Devas Late of Robertsbridge, dancing master, he had died by July 1780, when an advertisement called for any who had demands on his estate. (*SWA* 24.7.80)

RODMELL   1724: about 30 families   1801: pop. 256

No 18th-century schooling traced.

ROGATE   1724: 60 families   1801: pop. 518

School   (R: 1769)
The visitation return for 1769 gives a schoolmaster, of 'good Life' and 'diligent', who came to church and caused his scholars to come, and taught them the catechism. (But apparently no schoolmaster in 1762 or 1775.)[1]
1. WSRO Ep.I/22/1.

ROTHERFIELD   1801: pop. 1,963

Fermor's charity school   (F: 1744. Rs: 1744- into 19c)
Sir Henry Fermor, by will dated 21 January 1733, provided for up to £1,500 to be used by his trustees to build a chapel or a church and a charity school in or near Crowborough, for the benefit of the parishes and parishioners of Rotherfield and Buxted. A further £4,000 was to be laid out in the purchase of lands, one quarter of the rents being used to maintain a schoolmaster at the school (the other three-quarters to provide for a minister of the church of England to officiate at the church). A further £500 was to be laid out in the purchase of lands, the rents being used to repair the church and schoolhouse. And a further £3,000, similarly invested, was to be used to buy wool, hemp and books for the benefit of the poor children to be taught at the school. The schoolmaster and children were to be nominated by John Boorder, alias Fermor (his illegitimate nephew) and the heirs male of his body, or should he die without male issue, by the minister and majority of freeholders of Rotherfield. No child was to be admitted under 7, nor continue for more than 4 years; they were to be taught to read, write and cast accounts, and were not to exceed 40 in number.[1]
> Sir Henry Fermor died in 1734, and his charities were in Chancery from the time of his death until 1796.[2] However, the school was built by 1744, which date is above the door of the school building (later the vicarage), and in 1746 Charity Farm was purchased, apparently with the £500 (to keep the church and school in repair).[3] But the trustees did not invest the £4,000 and £3,000 in land, as Fermor's will directed, but in South Sea Annuities and 3% Reduced Annuities; in 1891 B.Firmin calculated that this mismanagement had cost the charity between £37,000 and £101,000 (depending on the land-values used in the calculation). Throughout the 18th century the charity's accounts were not properly kept.[4] Trouble between the parish and the school's trustees is evidenced in minutes of Rotherfield vestry meetings. In 1747 they agreed to petition the court of Chancery for their rights; in 1748 they empowered Rev Tatton to take counsel's opinion in the matter; there are other such references in 1748 and 1751, and in 1753 they agreed to petition the court of Chancery to appoint new trustees to Sir Henry Fermor's will and charity; it was not until 1759 that this was settled and the court appointed 8 trustees, 4 put forward by the heir of the last of the original trustees, who had inherited the trusteeship, and 4 by the rector of Rotherfield. (In 1755 the parish overseers paid Anthony Cole £2 5s'for Whiteing the Cloath for the Scollers at the Charity School'.) Distrust of the trustees continued in the 1770s: on 15

December 1771 the churchwardens were empowered 'to put out to any undertaker to manufacture and prepare: 180: Ells of flaxen Linnen cloath for Shirting and 30 paire of woollen yarn Stockins for the use of the Children in the Charity Scoole'; and the vestry agreed to indemnify the churchwardens for the cost of the work, as ordered by the 'Trustees to Sr Henry Farmers Charitys', should the trustees fail to pay. A similar indemnity was given in November 1772, for the same quantities. From June 1792 appointments of children to the school are recorded in the vestry minutes (presumably because the last male issue of John Boorder, alias Fermor, who had the right to appoint master and scholars, had died in 1791[5]). From 1792 to the end of the century 73 boys were appointed, 11 girls; the children were aged about 7½ on joining.[6]

In 1819 the charity commissioners reported: 'Thirty children, boys or girls, are sent to the school from the parish of Rotherfield, and ten from Buxted. This proportion is said to have been settled many years since between the two parishes. Buxted is at a greater distance from the school than Rotherfield; and that part of Buxted next to the school is not so populous as the adjoining part of Rotherfield. Some of the Buxted children come near four miles to school, and some of the Rotherfield three miles.' The children were 'taught reading, writing, and arithmetic, free of expense, and are wholly clothed once a-year, and supplied with books. The school is always full, and there are many applications for every vacancy.' From 1797, following the order of the court of Chancery of 1796, the investments of the charity were settled, yielding (in 1819) £32 8s 9d pa for the schoolmaster, £105 pa for clothing the children, and about £12 pa for books and stationery. The school was also kept in repair, and the schoolmaster had a house, garden, and land, in all about 4½ acres.[7]

William Okill, the first master, was appointed under Sir Henry Fermor's will, who left him - apart from his salary as schoolmaster - the sum of £20 and £2 pa during his life. He was followed as master by his son-in-law, David Dadswell, and the latter's son, Edward Okill Dadswell.

[*William Okill, David Dadswell, Edward Okill Dadswell*]

1. *EP3* (1820), 440. For Sir Henry Fermor and John Boorder, see Hackworth, J. *Sir Henry Fermor C of E School 1744-1994* (1994). John Boorder was the illegitimate son of Sir Henry's youngest brother, John, by Ann Jonson, who later married John Boorder. 2. *EP3* (1820), 440. 3. Hackworth, op. cit. 23, photo insert 108-9. 4. *EP3* (1820), 440-1; ESRO AMS 5818, Firmin, B., 'An Account of Sir Henry Fermor's Endowment at Crowborough' (1891), 34, 39. 5. See Hackworth, op. cit., 23. 6. ESRO PAR 465/4/1; Hackworth, op. cit., 31; ESRO PAR 465/6/6 (ages of children from Schedule 3). 7. *EP3* (1820), 440-2.

Parish schooling/workhouse school   (Rs: 1759, 1761-3, 1772, 1773, 1779)

In November 1731 the churchwardens and overseers put before the parishioners their proposal 'To Buy or Build a Charity Schoole and Alms House for the Poor', and this was agreed. There do not appear to be any further references to this charity school, the plan for which was probably superseded by Sir Henry Fermor's will of 1733 [qv above], but work on a workhouse was put in hand. In August 1733 a vestry agreed that this 'should be Finished as soon as Possible it can be done.' In February 1742 a meeting was called 'Concerning the Work house wither it shall be put Downe or whither it shall not' (no decision is recorded). In February 1756 it was agreed 'that the Workhouse Shall be Set up againe and that the Workhouse shall be Repaired in the best and Cheapest manner it can be.' In April 1760 it was agreed that the workhouse should be taken down and rebuilt. From 1761 the governing of the workhouse was 'put out' under annual agreements. The Workhouse inventories taken in February 1761, April 1762 and March 1763 identify a room in the workhouse as the 'School Room'. The agreement of 6 January 1772, when the workhouse was put out to William Cole senior and his son Robert Cole, included the following:

And the sd William Cole and his son Robert Cole Doth hereby Promise and
agree to teach and Instruck or caus to be taught And Instrucked all the poor
Children in the Workhouse During the term of this Agreement [one year]
to Learn to read there Books and to be taught the Church Catechism and
to Oblige them to Attend the Church every Sunday Dureing Divine Servis:
and the three Chilldren which used to be paid for out are to come into there
care that is El'z. Piddles Mary Boanjes and the Wid. Pentcurstes

It would appear from this that the parish may have previously been paying for the schooling
of these three poor children, unless the reference is for their maintenance. (On 2 April 1759
the overseers paid Daniel Manser 9d for a boy's schooling.)   The same provision for a
school at the workhouse is included in the agreements of 29 January 1773, with William
Wickins of Greenhedges and James Damper junior, and 16 February 1779, with Henry
Hallet.[1]

[*Daniel Manser*]

1. ESRO PAR 465/4/1, PAR 465/6/7.

Rice's boys' boarding school   (R: 1780)

In December 1780 the following advertisement appeared under the heading 'PRIVATE
EDUCATION':

MR. RICE, of ROTHERFIELD, having undertaken the Care of three young
Gentlemen, for Education, would be glad to accomodate three more; which
Number he proposes not to exceed.[1]

Rice was curate of Rotherfield, conducting marriages there from September 1776 to January
1786 (he inducted Rev Richard Crawley into the church and rectory in April 1782).[2]

[*Edward Rice*]

1. *SWA* 18.12.80.   2. Rotherfield PR.

Other schoolmaster

[William Hider], schoolmaster at Rotherfield 1803 (*Sussex Militia List, Pevensey
Rape Northern Division* (1988), 87).

ROTTINGDEAN   1724: 28 families   1801: pop. 543

[Mrs Beard's girls' boarding school?]   (R: 1774?)

When, in June 1774, Mrs Jane Beard announced that she was opening a girls' boarding
school at Hailsham, she described herself in the heading as 'from ROTTINGDEAN'. The
implication is that she had previously kept a school at Rottingdean.[1]   [*Jane Beard*]

1. *SWA* 13.6.74.

Hooker's boys' boarding school   (F: 1792. Rs: 1792- into 19c)

Thomas Redman Hooker[1] was appointed vicar of Rottingdean in 1792, after a year as rector
of Whatlington; before that he had been curate at Beddington, Surrey, and Greenford,
Middlesex. At both the latter places he had also been a schoolmaster. In a survey of
Rottingdean made in 1832, it is noted that Hooker had conducted his school at the Vicarage
House for the last forty years - that is, from his appointment in 1792, when he was 30 - 'in
which more of the sons of the nobility have been educated than in any other similar school
in the kingdom.'[2] His pupils were prepared, almost exclusively, for entry into Eton.

Much that is known of Hooker's school relates to the early 19th century, but it
would have been dominated throughout by his strong personality. Amongst his pupils were
Cardinal Manning, Sir Edward Bulwer-Lytton the novelist, the three sons of Lord
Faversham (who presented him with a silver inkstand, and a picture at one time in Hove
Town Hall), the son of Jerome Bonaparte, brother of Emperor Napoleon. As a young man,

Hooker was described as 'excelling at cricket, swimming and skating; a fine rider'.[3] His favourite sport was hunting (he often took boys from his school with him) and for 20 years he was master of the Lewes and Brookside Harriers. He had travelled on the continent for more than two years and had studied both French and Italian. He was a talented amateur artist, and 'skilled in vocal and instrumental music'.[4] He played the cello; when he injured his right arm in a riding accident, he had his cello restrung and taught himself to play with the bow in his left hand.

Hooker was not only popular with his gentry pupils, but with his parishioners also. He on occasion acted as look-out man for the local smugglers. He sang with the village children. He showed great benevolence towards any shipwrecked sailors (when his languages could often prove helpful). He encouraged the self-taught shepherd, John Dudeney, then on a Rottingdean farm, who opened his own school in Lewes in 1804. He established a free school for the children of the poor, and a Sunday school [qv below]. (For a fuller account of Hooker, see Schedule 2.)
[*Thomas Redman Hooker*]

1. Tibble, R., 'Rev. Thomas Redman Hooker DD (1762-1838)', *SFH* v.8, no.4 (December 1988), 149-53 (Tibble hereafter), from which the information here is taken. 2. Tibble, citing Moens, S.M. *Rottingdean...* (1953), 43, citing Parlby, S.C.B., from his survey of 1832. 3. Tibble, citing Beckett, A., in *SCM* v.17 (1943), 10. 4. ibid.

Charity school   (F: c1797?)
Hooker (see his school above) founded a free school for the children of the poor, probably before the end of the 18th century.[1]

1. Tibble, 151.

Sunday school   (Rs: c1797- into 19c)
Hooker (see his school above) established a Sunday school and superintended it for over 40 years. He died in April 1838, so the Sunday school would have been founded towards the end of the 18th century.[1]

1. Tibble, 151, citing Beckett, op. cit., 10.

RUDGWICK   1724: about 100 families 1801: pop. 760

[Reith's school?]
George Reith was licensed to teach children in Sussex, 16 March 1691; he was vicar of Rudgwick 3 February 1675 to 1716, and probably kept school there into the 18th century.[1]
[*George Reith*]

1. WSRO Ep.I/3/4; CI.

School   (Rs: 1758, 1762)
Visitation returns show that there was a schoolmaster in the parish in 1758 and 1762. (There was no free or charity school.)[1]

1. WSRO Ep.I/22/1.

RUMBOLDSWYKE   1801: pop. 224

School/charity school   (R: 1760)
Joseph Lambert (flaxdresser in 1729, later a yeoman), who was baptised at Ditchling in 1701 and buried at Rumboldswyke in 1764, in his will dated 11 May 1760, proved 23 April 1766, directed that 'my benefaction of 40s. a year to the school at Ditchling nr. Lewes for teaching poor boys to read only and my like benefaction of 40s. a year to a like school in the parish of Rumboldswyke to be continued for seven years from my decease.'[1] So, prior to 1760, there was a school a Rumboldswyke, where poor boys were taught to read. It probably also had paying pupils.

1. *SAC* **90**, 115.

RUSPER   1724: 65 families   1801: pop. 399

Dame schools   (Rs: 1758, 1762)
In 1758, there was no schoolmaster in the parish, 'only two Old Women' who taught school. There was a small dame school there in 1762, and the school dame taught her scholars the catechism.[1]

1. WSRO Ep.I/22/1.

Dissenter's school   (R: 1762)
In 1762 there were two small schools in the parish, one of which was kept by a school-master who did not come to the parish church - 'he goes to ye Meeting'.[1] He was probably a General Baptist, or possibly a Quaker (in 1724 there were reportedly 5 'Anabaptist' and 3 Quaker families in the parish[2]).

1. WSRO Ep.I/22/1.   2. WSRO Ep.I/26/3, 16-17.

RUSTINGTON (RUSTON)   1724: 38 families   1801: pop. 261

Dame school   (R: 1758)
In 1758 'an old woman' kept a school.[1]

1. WSRO Ep.I/22/1.

RYE   1724: about 200 families 1801: pop. 2,187

Grammar school   (F: c1640. Rs: through 18c)
By will dated 10 September 1638 Thomas Peacock of Rye, gentleman, left a house in the Longer-street, that he had built for the purpose, to house a free grammar school; and he left £910 to be laid out in lands to yield a rent-charge of £32, together with a rent-charge of £4 arising out of the *Mermaid* tenement, which were to be used to pay the schoolmaster and maintain the premises. The mayor and jurats of Rye were to appoint the schoolmaster and the scholars, and to govern the school. Peacock intended to found a grammar school, and by orders made by the mayor and jurats (and their counsel, as provided for in the will) no boy was to be admitted till they could read the Old and New Testament, and when admitted they should be instructed in the grammar and good Latin and Greek authors. Through the 18th century and into the 19th no boys were appointed unless they required a classical education. Previous to 1791, the master took private scholars, and from at least 1771 to 1791 there were no free boys at all on the foundation. For those 20 years the free grammar school had failed.[1]

In 1791 the school was united with Saunders' charity school (see below), under one master and using Peacock's schoolhouse. The master received the income from both charities, but there was little demand for a free classical education; there were 'very rarely' any scholars on the Peacock foundation, and never more than two or three. In 1803 there were only 16 boys in the combined school. In 1809 Peacock's school was brought before the court of Chancery, and under the master of the rolls' report the nature of the grammar school was changed: the number of children on the foundation was to be limited to 50, and they were to be taught reading, writing, arithmetic and mathematics, and the art of navigation. The master was to continue to teach both schools, and was to be 'skilful in the Latin tongue'. However, by a later judgment, in 1820, the two schools were to be separated (which occurred in 1828); the master of Peacock's school was required to educate 50 boys, and could no longer take private pupils.[2]

Nicholas Mannooch, ordained deacon in 1680 and master 1680-1724, was mayor of Rye on several occasions between 1690 and 1704, and was thereby also a trustee of the school. On his death in December 1724, Rev Lewis Jones was appointed, then aged 28. He became also curate of Rye, and from 1741 rector of Little Horsted, which would have augmented his salary. For further income he rented off the schoolhouse - perhaps he had no scholars. In 1746 the governors found that he had let the school buildings fall into disrepair, renting them to an innkeeper: the garden was used to keep hogs and fowls in, and part of it used as a skittle alley; the schoolroom was filled with lumber and the upper room with corn. His salary was withheld until repairs had been paid for, so he received only £1 0s 10½d in 1747, 12s 1d in 1748, £2 17s 4¼d in 1749. Thereafter he received the full salary of £34 10s. He was master for 25 years, dying in December 1759, aged 63.[3]

He was succeeded, both as master and curate of Rye, by Peter Collett,[4] who was master for 30 years. He was additionally incumbent of Udimore from 1761 until his death,[5] and rector of Denton from 1777.[6] At his death in September 1790, aged 55, *SWA* reported that he 'has left a widow and six children, totally destitute, to bewail his loss'; at the instigation of Lord Eardley, a public subscription was raised, which by May 1791 had totalled £439 7s[7]. In January 1792 there was published a pamphlet, price 6d, *A Sixpenny Christmas Box*, the profits from which 'will be given to the Michell and Collett orphans'.[8] (The Michell orphans were the children of Richard Michell, curate and schoolmaster of East Dean.) Collett's widow, his second wife, lived in Rye until 1841, when she died aged 95.

When, in 1791, Peacock's and Saunders' schools were combined, Rev William Jackson was appointed joint master. Jackson had had his own school at Stone, in Kent, and as the combined Peacock and Saunders salary, totalling about £52 10s, did not seem sufficient to induce him to give up his school at Stone, he was allowed to take his own private pupils (as his predecessors had done).[9] In 1795 he was also appointed curate of Playden and East Guldeford.[10] In 1820, as a result of the Chancery case, he could no longer take private pupils;[11] but by 1819 his salary was £34 10s from Peacock's charity, plus £4 pa he received from letting the school garden, and £105 from the Saunders' charity, or in total about £144 pa, less charges for repairs of the farm at Udimore from the rent of which most of the Saunders' income derived.[12] He died in August 1828, aged 72.

[*Nicholas Mannooch, Lewis Jones, Peter Collett, William Jackson*]

1. *EP*3 (1820), 442-4.   2. ibid; *VCH* ii, 425; Vidler, L.A. *History of Rye Grammar School, 1639-1939* (1939), 22.   3. Vidler, op. cit., 14-15; ESRO RYE 112/49-61.   4. ESRO RYE 114/1; WSRO Ep.I/1/11.   5. WSRO Ep.I/1/11; CI.   6. *SWA* 17.2.77; CI.   7. *SWA* 4.10.90, 18.10.90, 2.5.91.   8. *SWA* 2.1.92.   9. Vidler, op. cit., 20; ESRO RYE 114/1.   10. Vidler, op. cit., 21.   11. ibid.   12. *EP*3 (1820), 444, 446-7.

Charity school   (F: c1708. Rs: 1709-24?)

The SPCK annual *Account of the Charity-Schools* for 1709 records a charity school at Rye for 'Twelve poor Boys and Girls maintained at School by Moneys collected at the Holy Sacrament.' The school had been set up since the previous published *Account*, of 1707. By 1711 the sacrament money was being supported by 'some private Charities', and the children were maintained at school 'with an Addition of some Work'. In February 1713, George Barnsley, from Sedlescombe, advised the SPCK that the number of children at Rye was 30 'supported by Subscriptions but ye contributions are not sufficient to Cloath ym.'[1] In the *Account* for 1713 the number of children was accordingly increased to 30, though in February 1714 George Barnsley advised the SPCK 'That the Towns of Rye and Battel are not so Zealous in promoting so good a work, but that he hopes the Schools there will be settled on a better foundation for ye future.'[2] The *Account* for 1716 mentions additionally the Saunders' bequest (see below). The school was still listed in 1724, and by implication from the county totals (the only data included from 1725), until at least 1740; but as there is no change at all in the Sussex totals of schools or scholars from 1730 to 1740, these later lists must be treated as suspect.

1. SPCK ALB v.4, 3453.   2. SPCK ALB v.5, 3905.

<u>Saunders' boys' charity school</u>   (F: 1721. Rs: 1721- into 19c)
James Saunders, of Winchelsea at his death, yeoman, with lands at Wittersham in Kent, a Baptist, born at Hastings and buried there 27 January 1709, by will dated 7 January 1709 left all his estate to set up educational charities in Rye and Hastings. His was one of the largest educational endowments made in Sussex in the 18th century. The income from his estate was to be accumulated for ten years from his death and the resulting sum laid out in lands, in the name of and settled upon the mayor, jurats and town council of Rye for the time being, and their successors, who were immediately to rent a school and pay the remainder of the income from the lands to a schoolmaster, who should teach the poor children of Rye reading English, writing, casting accounts, and the art of navigation. After the ten years accumulation of the income from his estate, noted above, the estate was to pass to the corporation of Hastings, for the purpose of establishing charity schools there [qv]. Accordingly, in 1719 the accumulated sum was used to purchase a farm at Udimore for £720, which was conveyed in trust to the mayor, jurats and town council of Rye, for the purpose of establishing the charity school. In the early years of the trust the income averaged about £22 - £20 being paid to the schoolmaster and £2 for the rent of a schoolroom. (By 1771, the master only got £16 pa, out of which he had to provide a schoolhouse: see below.) The school opened on 19 April 1721, with 23 scholars and William Hawney as master. The mayor, jurats and town council were, by Saunders' will, responsible for appointing the master (appointments were made for three-year terms) and the children, who were not to exceed 70 in number. As noted above, Saunders was a Baptist, and the second order drawn up by the governors at the establishment of the school was as follows:

> That the founder of the said school being a dissenter, and no persons either of the Church of England or of the Protestant dissenters being excluded by the founder's will from the same privilege with those of his own persuasion, no schooler or schoolers shall be required by the master to goe to any place of worship or to learn any catechism without the consent and approbation of his or their parents or guardians, soe as they goe to some place of worship on every Lord's Day.

School hours were, from 20 October to 20 March, 8 a.m. to 4 p.m., with 1½ hours break in the middle of the day; from 20 March to 20 October, 7 a.m. to 5 p.m., with a 2 hour break. Holy days were holidays; as were Saturday afternoons and Thursdays from 3 p.m. Vacations were 20 days at Christmas, 10 each at Easter and Whitsuntide, and 3 at Bartholomewtide.[1]

A large number of loose school lists have survived,[2] running from the early days of the school to June 1785 (with others for the 19th century). The lists, signed by the master, are headed 'A Register of the Schollars belonging To my School On the Foundation', suggesting that from the beginning the master also took private pupils, as could be expected from the small salary available for the free pupils. William Wybourn certainly did - a loose receipt has survived showing that he was paid 6d a week between 27 November 1731 and 5 April 1732 by the Playden overseers for schooling Joseph Comber (who was then aged 11).[3] All the scholars appointed were boys. Numbers ranged from 28 (cSeptember 1722) down to 10 at Lady day 1769: from September 1722 to January 1728 (19 lists) the average was 21; from April 1728 to March 1731 (11 lists), 14; from July 1731 to Lady day 1757 (92 lists), 21; from midsummer 1757 to Michaelmas 1763 (17 lists), 15. From 1764, the governors ordered that the number should be reduced to 12,[4] and from Christmas 1764 to June 1785 (44 lists), the average number was indeed 12. On average, boys started at the school when they were 9 and left when they were 13. Half the boys had brothers who also went to the school.[5]

Prior to 1791, the masters were: First, William Hawney. Then William Wybourn, 1727-44, on whose death in November 1744, his widow, Sarah, was directed by the governors to continue the school until Lady day 1745, when John Hogben was appointed. John Hogben, 1745-69, was elected a Freeman of Rye, 20 August 1760, a clause preventing a freeman being the master being cancelled on the same date. Then came George Jewhurst, April 1769 to December 1771, who had been a scholar at the school 1760-2. Then John Hill, January 1772 until his death in July 1786; Rev Edward Leece Fleming, July 1786 to May 1788; John Sturley, May 1788 to Easter 1791, when his three-year appointment expired.[6] In 1791 the school was united with Peacock's school [qv above], using Peacock's schoolhouse, under the mastership of Rev William Jackson, who had previously had his own school at Stone, in Kent. He was additionally appointed curate of Playden and East Guldeford in 1795, and continued as master until his death in 1828, aged 72.[7]

In October 1771 the trustees placed the following advertisement for a master, which identifies both the low salary - £16 pa, out of which he had to find a schoolhouse - and the fact that the school was substantially a private school:

> WANTED for the WRITING-SCHOOL at RYE in SUSSEX, a MASTER, well qualified to teach Writing and Arithmetic. The Foundation is 16 l. per Annum, for which twelve Scholars go free. There are many other Scholars besides these on the Foundation whose Parents pay for their Education; therefore if the Master is diligent and capable there is a Certainty of his having a good School.
>
> N.B. There is no School-House, but the Master must provide one at his own Expence.[8]

The rent from the farm at Udimore was, in 1791, £32. It was afterwards raised to £50, and in 1809 to £89 5s 6d. In 1809 the charity was taken to the court of Chancery, accused amongst other things of letting the farm at too low a rent, as a consequence of which it was afterwards let for £110. The charity also had an income of £7 10s pa, less £1 land tax, from 'drowned lands' (purchased by James Saunders in 1708); the matter of the 'drowned lands', by then reclaimed, was still before the courts in the 19th century. In 1811, as a consequence of the Chancery case, Jackson was no longer allowed to take private pupils; his salary then, from the two foundations, was about £144, less charges for repairs of the farm at Udimore. By a Chancery judgement in 1820, the two schools were again to be separate, and this was effected in 1828, on Jackson's death. By 1820 there were about 40 boys on Saunders' foundation. They were taught reading, writing, and accounts, 'and the master is ready and competent to instruct them in mathematics, and the art of navigation, but the latter have seldom been required.' At the separation in 1828, there were 68 boys in the school - very close to the limit of 70 that Saunders had set in his will.[9]

[*William Hawney, William Wybourn, Sarah Wybourn, John Hogben, George Jewhurst, John Hill, Edward Leece Fleming, John Sturley, William Jackson*]

1. Vidler, op. cit., 16-18; WSRO Ep.I/26/3, 22-3; *EP*3 (1820),445; *VCH* ii, 426.   2. ESRO RYE 114/10 (183 18c lists have survived, 9 of them undated; there are several gaps in the sequence).   3. ESRO PAR 445/31/1/14; Playden PR.   4. Vidler, op. cit., 20.   5. Analyses of data in Schedule 3.   6. See Schedule 2.   7. Vidler, op. cit., 20, 22.   8. *SWA* 21.10.71.   9. *EP*3 (1820), 445-6; Vidler, op. cit., 21, 23.

Jarretts' school   (Rs: 1775, 1777, 1780, 1788)

Richard Jarrett of Rye was identified as a schoolmaster in wills of 1775[1] and 1777.[2] As trustee and executor of the former, he was party to an assignment of property in 1780.[3] In 1776 he purchased, for £110, a house on the south side of Middle Street, from the executor of the will of Sarah, wife of John Usher, late wife of William Wybourn of Rye.[4] In 1788, then described as 'gent', he sold this house, for £140, to Henry Jarrett junior, of Rye, schoolmaster; it was then described as 'House and carpenter's shop, now used as a schoolhouse, formerly occupied by... Sarah Wybourne and John Hogben, now and for some time past Henry Jarrett and Henry Jarrett his father...'[5] William Wybourn was master of Saunders' school, 1727-44; his widow, Sarah, then ran the school for six months, when John Hogben became master, 1745-69. The Saunders' charity did not own a schoolhouse and the master had to provide one; it seems likely that, during Wybourn's and Hogben's time as master, the school was kept at the house later purchased by Richard Jarrett, and that he also kept school there; and that his school was carried on within the family when Richard sold the house to Henry Jarrett. Richard was probably the Richard Jarrett buried at Rye in 1806, aged 87. Henry, the schoolmaster (born 1766), was probably the Henry Jarrett who was declared bankrupt in 1830.[6] [*Richard Jarrett, Henry Jarrett junior*]

1. ESRO AMS 4635.   2. ESRO WMD Box 18.   3. ESRO AMS 4636.   4. ESRO WMD Box 14.   5. ibid.
6. ibid.

Pape's school   (F: 1794)
In December 1793 Rev Pape advertised, under the heading 'PRIVATE EDUCATION', his small and expensive school, as follows:

> THE REV. MR. PAPE, of RYE, (a pleasant, healthy situation, near the SEA-COAST, in the county of SUSSEX, distant from LONDON 60 miles, between which places a Coach passes three times a week) purposes to BOARD and EDUCATE in the different branches of learning preparatory to the University or Business, FOUR young Gentlemen: they will enjoy all the advantages of private TUITION, immediately under his own care, and be treated in every respect as his own sons.
>
> Mr. PAPE has been HEAD-MASTER of a PUBLIC SCHOOL several years in the North of England, and is happy to observe that he can give, what he trusts will be deemed the most satisfactory references, on being addressed at RYE.
>
> One Gentleman is already engaged; - Terms, 50 Guineas per annum.[1]

He was almost certainly Daniel Pape, curate of Rye.[2] [*Daniel Pape*]

1. *SWA* 9.12.93.   2. Rye PR (marr. reg.).

SALEHURST   1724: about 157 families 1801: pop. 1,611
See also ROBERTSBRIDGE, which was in Salehurst parish but had a distinct identity. The following Robertsbridge schools are described thereunder:
Pike's boys' boarding school   (Rs: 1771-91)
Mrs Goodsen's girls' boarding school   (Rs: 1777-8)
Dame school   (R: c.1785)
Vinall's school?   (1788?- ?)
Robertsbridge charity school   (F: 1796. Rs: 1796- into 19c)
    Other master: Henry Goodsens   (R: 1780)
    Dancing master: Stephen Devas   (R: before 1780)

Bulloch's school   (R: 1700)
On 3 December 1700 James Bulloch was paid 10s by Elizabeth Cowper, widow of John, yeoman of Salehurst, 'for ten weeks skooling for Sarah and Elizabeth Cowper to teach them to write'.[1] Bulloch probably kept a petty school, charging 6d a week for 'writing' pupils, and was almost certainly there at the beginning of the 18th century. [*James Bulloch*]

1. *SAC* **61**, 63.

Mrs Hammond's school   (R: 1700)
On 20 January 1701 Mrs Hammond was paid 8s by Elizabeth Cowper, widow of John, yeoman of Salehurst, 'for teaching hanna to read for five and forty weeks'.[1] She almost certainly kept a dame school, probably charging 2d a week for 'readers', and would have been there at the beginning of the 18th century.   [*Mrs Hammond*]
1. *SAC* **61**, 63.

Jenkin's boys' boarding school   (F: 1783)
In December 1782 Stephen Jenkin, vicar of Salehurst, advertised, under the heading 'PRIVATE TUITION', that, 'being fixed on a very airy and healthy Situation at SALEHURST, within Half a Mile of the great Turnpike Road between HASTINGS and LONDON', he wished 'to be intrusted with the Care and Tuition of a few young Gentlemen'. The number would be limited to 12 only. He offered 'to instruct them in the English Language, Classical Learning, Writing, and Accompts, as well as their Morals, Exercise, Diet, &c.', for 25 guineas pa, with 2 guineas entrance. 'French, Music, Dancing, &c. if required, to be paid extra.'[1] Jenkin ran his advertisement for eight consecutive weeks. [*Stephen Jenkin*]
1. *SWA* 28.12.82, and each week to 10.2.83.

Note: John Cooper, by will dated 27 July 1691, directed that if his children died without lawful issue then all his estates, after his wife's death, were to be let or disposed of to pay £20 a year to an honest, faithful and industrious woman, in the town of Robertsbridge, to teach the children of poor men, women, and widows that should be sent to her from the parishes of Salehurst, Etchingham, Ewhurst, Mountfield, or Brightling. (Horsfield noted that, by the returns made to parliament in 1786, the annual value of the endowment appeared to have been £45.[1]) However, in 1819 the charity commissioners reported that 'no school has ever been established or money paid for that purpose and we doubt whether the charitable uses, contemplated by the testator, can ever take effect under this will.'[2]
1. Horsfield *Sussex* (1835), I, 585.   2. *VCH* ix, 224; *EP1* (1819), 239-40.

SEAFORD   1724: 70 families   1801: pop. 847
Charity schools   (F: 1706. Rs: 1706-53, 1765, 1776-80)
There are several references to charity schools at Seaford through the 18th century, but there was not an endowed charity school, and it is not known whether the references are to one school that continued from 1706 to at least 1780, or whether they refer to different ventures.
       The SPCK annual *Account of the Charity-Schools* records the founding of a charity school in 1706. In the 1707 *Account*: 'Here is a school, which is much encouraged. A Gentleman hath lately given 5 1. for buying Bibles for the Children.' The 1715 *Account* recorded 12 children at the school (they are entered under 'boys' but when the SPCK was not advised of a specific sex split, all children were entered under 'boys'.) In April 1716 Anthony Springett, writing to the SPCK from Lewes, reported that the school at Seaford 'began in 1706, out of wch 36 are gone Some to Trades others to Sea, & Service'.[1] The school continues in the SPCK lists to 1718, and in 1724; from 1719 (except for 1724) individual schools are not listed and only county totals are given; by implication, the school continued to at least 1740, but since there are no changes at all in the Sussex totals of schools or scholars from 1730 to 1740, the later lists must be regarded as suspect. Thomas Cox in *Magna Britannia*, published in 1730 but perhaps citing earlier information, repeats the SPCK description, but adds: '... and others pay for their Schooling'; so from early days private scholars were taught alongside the charity children.[2] Richard Ellis was schoolmaster at Seaford in 1710, almost certainly of the charity school as he was in 1737, suggesting

continuity of the charity school during this period (see his school below). The Duke of Newcastle supported the charity school at Seaford, subscribing £17 pa, at least from 1736 to 1739, and Henry Pelham subscribed £3 pa from at least 1734 to 1753.[3] The school is referred to in Newcastle papers in 1753, and a 1765 list survives of 'the Charity Children in the School of Seaford given by his Grace the Duke of Newcastle and the members of Parliament'.[4] Benjamin Stevens was then schoolmaster, and there were 25 charity children at the school, 20 boys and 5 girls. The Duke of Newcastle had been paying £17 pa for the education of 24 children, but his agent, Abraham Baley, noted that he was to cease to pay this after Lady day 1765.[5]

Another supporter of the school was George Medley. Account books kept by his solicitor, Charles Gilbert, have survived for the period 24 January 1776 to 14 January 1796, showing payments made on Medley's behalf.[6] On 28 March, 18 July, 11 October, 30 December 1776, Sarah Osbon was paid £1 5s, '1 Quarters Salary for teaching 12 Children of Seaford'. She thus received £6 pa, or 10s per child. These payments to her continued until Michaelmas 1780. (She was the widow of John Osbon, a husbandman, who died in 1765.) At the same time Medley was also paying Rev Williams £15 pa 'for instructing a certain Number of poor Boys at Seaford', the payments to him covering the period from January 1776 to Michaelmas 1780. Williams was curate of Seaford from 1772 (and previously curate of Tarring Neville), and also had his private boys' boarding school at Seaford from 1770 (see below).

[*Richard Ellis, Benjamin Stevens, Sarah Osbon, Thomas Williams*]

1. SPCK ALB v.6, 4772. 2. Cox, T., pub. *Magna Britannia* (1730), 566. 3. Farrant, J., pers. comm., citing BL Add MS 33,157; ESRO SAS/FB 112 and 113. 4. Doff, E., pers. comm., citing BL Add MS 33,058, f 487, and BL Add MS 33,059. 5. Kelch, R.A., *Newcastle: A duke without money: Thomas Pelham-Holles 1693-1768* (1974), 180. 6. ESRO SAS/GT 1/3/3.

Ellis's school (Rs: 1710, 1735, 1737, 1756)

Richard Ellis was a schoolmaster at Seaford in 1710, almost certainly of the charity school [qv above] as he was in 1735 and 1737. Since the charity children numbered only 12, he would probably also have kept his own private school. Around 1730 at least, there were both charity and private pupils at the school.[1] Under a bill of detection presented at Easter 1711:

> Sarah Wood of ye sd: parish [Seaford] widdow was delivered of a Bastard child & that Rd: Ellis of the sd parish Schoolmaster was ye Reputed Father, That for several years past the sd Rd: was & is a married man, & that the sd. Rd: & Sarah (as they have heard & believe) at diverse times in the year 1710 did commit the Crime of Adultery together at several places, & even in the parish Church of Seaford.[2]

However, Ellis continued as the schoolmaster at Seaford. He was there in 1735 when he was paid £3 by Henry Pelham ('Mr. Ellis's school at Seaford'), and in November 1737, when he was paid the £17 that the Newcastle estate gave to the charity school for the year to Lady day 1737.[3] He was still teaching school in his schoolhouse in 1756, and probably to his death in 1759.[4] [*Richard Ellis*]

1. Cox, T., op. cit., 566. 2. WSRO Ep.II/15/10, f 23. 3. Farrant, J., pers. comm., citing ESRO SAS/FB 112, and BL Add MS 33,157. 4. ESRO W/A 60.28.

[Girls' boarding school?] (R: c.1756)

In August 1757 John Hubbesty, curate of Seaford, wrote to his brother Zachary at Kendal recommending a boarding school 'lately set up at Chelsea': 'the Mistress of it is a particular acquaintance of mine... she went from this place, and is look'd upon by all in this Neighbourhood as extremely well qualified for the Undertaking... The Rates [which he enclosed] may seem high, but they are the common Rates of every genteel Boarding

School.'[1] It seems from this likely that the mistress kept a school at Seaford, before moving to Chelsea.

1. ESRO AMS 6126/17.

[Steven's school]   (R: 1765)
Benjamin Stevens was master of the charity school in 1765 [qv above]. A school list of 25 names is headed 'charity Children in the School of Seaford', which suggests that Stevens also kept a private school (as Richard Ellis had done some 30 years before - see his school above).[1]   [*Benjamin Stevens*]

1. Doff, E., pers. comm., citing BL Add MS 33,059.

Williams' boys' boarding school   (R: 1771)
On 14 January 1771 Thomas Williams, then curate of Tarring Neville, opened a boarding school at Seaford, offering 'Grammar, Arithmetic vulgar and decimal, Geometry, Navigation, and the Italian Method of Book-keeping: Prices as in the neighbouring Schools'. He noted that: 'If any infirm Children should want the Benefit of bathing in the Sea, as well as to be forwarded in their Education, proper Assistants will be procured at a moderate Price.'[1] Williams was curate at Seaford from November 1772 to May 1785. From at least January 1776 until Michaelmas 1780, he was additionally paid £15 pa by George Medley 'for instructing a certain Number of poor Boys at Seaford.'[2]   [*Thomas Williams*]

1. *SWA* 17.12.70.   2. ESRO SAS/GT 1/3/3.

Mrs Beard's girls' boarding school   (R: 1784)
Mrs Jane Beard, who had a girls' boarding school in Brighton from 1775, moved her school to Seaford at Michaelmas 1784, 'at the Desire of her Friends' [that is, the parents of her girls]. In an advertisement addressed to 'the Nobility and Gentry', she noted: 'The salutary Air of Seaford, the Conveniences and Accomodations for bathing, and its Retirement, give it a decided Superiority in Point of Situation, to almost every other Spot in Sussex; many insuperable Objections having been made to a Place of public Resort and Amusement for Female Tuition.'   Her terms were 18 guineas pa 'for common Boarders that bathe', and 15 guineas 'for them that do not bathe', and 26 guineas for parlour boarders, 'and to find their Washing and Tea'.   There was no entrance fee. 'Proper Masters for Dancing and Music, Writing and Accompts will be provided, to be paid for extraordinarily.'   'Seaford is situated ten Miles from Lewes and twelve Miles from Brighthelmston, to which there are constant and daily Conveyances from London.'   [*Jane Beard*]

1. *SWA* 31.5.84.

Jenkins' boys' boarding school   (F: 1790)
In October 1790 Rev George Jenkins announced that he had taken 'the house called the WEST-HOUSE for the purpose of boarding and educating a few Young Gentlemen'. He offered to instruct them 'in Classical Learning, and in those branches of education which the Profession they are intended for more particularly requires. The Elements of Chemistry and Geometry, and of Natural History and Philosophy [ie. science] will be carefully taught and explained.'   The inclusion of chemistry in the list of subjects is unusual. 'The Health and Morals of his Pupils he will most industriously consult; he will study their several dispositions, and treat them with tenderness and humanity; and he will devote his whole time to their improvement in every thing that may render them, at a future period, useful members of society.'   He noted that: 'The situation of Seaford is exceedingly healthy and pleasant; it adjoins the South Downs on the North, and on the South the Sea.'[1]   Advertised in *SWA* Oct, Nov (2), Dec 1790.   [*George Jenkins*]

1. *SWA* 18.10.90.

Dancing master

> John Thring, dancing master of Lewes from 1778 to at least 1800 [qv], gave a concert, for his benefit, at the *New Inn*, Seaford, in May 1798, followed by a ball. As with other concerts and balls that he arranged in other places, it almost certainly featured performances by his scholars at Seaford. (*SWA* 14.5.98)

SEDLESCOMBE (SELSCOMB) 1724: about 50 families   1801: pop. 510

Charity school   (F: by 1729. Rs: 1729- into 19c)

George Barnsley, rector of Sedlescombe for 49 years, who died in 1723, left by will dated 7 September 1723, £500 for the education of poor children in three parishes, of which Sedlescombe was one, the others being Northiam and Burwash, where Barnsley had sometime also been rector. The children were to be those 'whose parents are not of ability to pay for their learning', and they were to be instructed 'in the knowledge and practice of the Christian religion as professed and taught in the Church of England in the best manner of the Charity Schools now in use in the Kingdome'. On 8 February 1729 Robert Payne, of Saltwood, Kent, advised the SPCK of three schools 'lately open'd and supported by a Legacy from Mr. Barnsley and other Contributions', at Burwash, 'Selscomb' and Saltwood, with a fourth 'design'd at Northiam'. The Sedlescombe school was 'for about 20 or 24 Children'. The distribution of Barnsley's legacy was at the discretion of his executors, who allocated £150 to Sedlescombe. In 1729 an estate of nine acres, with premises, in Westfield, called Darbyes, was conveyed to trustees for the support of a charity school in Sedlescombe; the cost of £184 was met by Barnsley's legacy and subscriptions. On 27 December 1731 a lease for waste land in Sedlescombe Street, at a rent of 6d pa, was assigned to Rev Thornton and others, in trust, 'to build a Charity School thereon'; and the following day the Duke of Newcastle renewed the term of the lease (due to expire in 1752) for 99 years from its expiration, at a rent of 1d pa. The assignment provided that the rector should be a trustee ex-officio, and that at the school the poor children of the parish should be taught to read and write.[1]

> A 'Sedlescomb School' book, begun in June 1748, has survived.[2] It opens with the general rules agreed on 23 June 1748 by the three trustees, John Ingram, rector, Henry Bishop, gentleman of Sedlescombe, and John Plumer, gentleman of Battle; these include:-

> Parents of the children admitted in the said School not to detain them from ye School unless by consent of one or more of the trustees, and this consent to be granted only at such times of the year when the children may earn something towards the maintenance of the rest of the family.

> Parents to keep their children admitted to the said School sweet & clean, that they not be a Nusance to rest of the School, if they do not & upon admonition therof do not amend such child or children to be discharg'd by any one of the trustees upon complaint made to him by the Master.

> The Number of the Scholars not to exceed twenty, & every writer to be reckon'd as two.

> The master to be carefull to instruct the Children in the principles of the Christian Religion as profess'd in the Church of England.

> When the school debts are paid the money remaining from a Legacy of the late Revd Mr Francis Brown Wright to the free School be applyed to buying of Testaments & Bibles for the use of the Scholars in the said School only.

At that date (23 June 1748) there were 11 children at the school, six boys and five girls; on the following day two more were added, a boy aged 7 and a girl aged 12.

In 1755 the mastership became vacant 'through incapacity, by reason of age of Isaac Gostling Late master', and Thomas Colbran Junr, of Ninfield, was appointed master, to teach the poor children 'Reading Writing accounts & the Church Catechism'. He was then aged 18. On page 9 of the school book is the following:

I Thos Colbran was appointed Master of the
Free School at Sedlescomb at Ladytide 1755

$$\begin{array}{r} 1812 \\ \underline{1755} \\ 57 \text{ Years} \end{array}$$

aged $\underline{18}$ when appoint'd
75 my age at
Ladytide 1812

Colbran continued as master until his death in 1816, aged 79, having held the appointment for 61 years - the longest tenure of any schoolmaster in Sussex in the 18th century.

At his appointment the trustees allowed him 'the use of the house called the School House, in order to teach therein the poor Children committed to his Care & others who may come to him for Instruction '.[3] This provision was important, as the master's salary from the charity comprised just the rent from the Westfield property, less repairs necessary to it. By 1805 the full salary appears to have been £21 pa, with frequent deductions for repairs at Westfield;[4] by 1819, the rent was £24, from which the master was paid £20 pa.[5] Colbran would have taken private day pupils from his appointment; he also undertook land surveying, and made many maps of local estates, to augment his income. He was successful enough to spend £40 on making an addition to the schoolhouse, in consideration of which the trustees agreed in 1771 to pay him £2 pa in the event of his being prevented by sickness or accident from managing the school, or should he die, the term of this 'insurance' being for 20 years (ie. running to 1791): in such an event, the payments would be made out of the salary due to his successor.[6] Colbran's extension of the schoolhouse was almost certainly made for him to accommodate boarders, for from 1770 he grafted a boys' boarding school onto the free school (see below). In 1776 he announced that he had declined land-surveying, in order to devote 'his whole Time and Attention to the Management and Instruction of his Scholars'.[7] His methods, promoted for his private school, would presumably have applied also to his free pupils - 'Instead of Severity, he uses the most gentle and attractive Methods to excite his Scholars to a Love of Learning, and takes the greatest Care that they may early imbibe the Principles of Religion and Morality.'[8] At the appointment of his successor, the trustees recorded that Colbran had been demanding entrance money on the admittance of free scholars, and declared that 'no entrance money shall be in future demanded of such free scholars.'[9]

The school book contains occasional school lists, which distinguish between the readers and writers. In May 1755, just after Colbran had taken over, there were 10 readers and one writer. By 1758 and 1759 (two lists) he had increased the proportion of writers to over a third of the school (38%). In the 1770s (two lists) the proportion was again 38%; in the 1780s (three lists), 41%. In the 1790s and at 1800 (five lists), almost two-thirds of the school (61%) were writers. Numbers in the school varied from 8 to 13, averaging 11; the notional totals, for which writers counted as 2, ranged from 12 to 18, and (by 1800 at least) was meant to be 20, for the 1800 list is annotated as follows:

Readers [there were in fact 3]   3
Writers [there were in fact 5] $\underline{10}$
13

$$\begin{array}{r} 20 \\ \underline{13} \\ 7 \text{ Vacancies} \end{array}$$

Some lists, excluded from the above analyses, were clearly running lists, covering a period of time. One, headed 1761, did not identify writers, but showed for most of the children their date of entrance; for 12, their baptisms are in the Sedlescombe register; 9 of these 12 joined the school when they were 6 or 7; one at 4 (almost 5), one at about 8, and one at 12. The list includes 3 or 4 appointments made later, in 1762, and covers 21 children: 11 were boys, 10 were girls.

[Isaac Gostling, Thomas Colbran]

1. *EP*1 (1819), 240; Lucey, B. *Twenty Centuries in Sedlescombe* (1978), 282; SPCK ALB v.14, 10083; Wadey, J.E., 'The School at Sedlescombe', *SNQ* **15**, 186; ESRO AMS 1582.   2. ESRO ESC 148/1/1.   3. ibid.
4. Wadey, op. cit., 188.   5. *EP*1 (1819), 240-1.   6. Wadey, op. cit., 188-9.   7. *SWA* 3.6.76.   8. ibid.
9. Wadey, op. cit., 189.

Colbran's day school and boys' boarding school   (F: 1755 (boarding school, by 1770). Rs: 1755- into 19c)

Thomas Colbran was master of the charity school from 1755 [qv above]. From his appointment, the trustees allowed him 'the use of the house called the School House' and he was able to take his own private pupils in addition to the charity children.[1] About 1770 he spent £40 extending the schoolhouse (in consideration of which the trustees granted him a modest form of insurance against sickness or accident preventing him from working: see Charity school above); in February 1770 he advertised his boarding school for boys 'not above fourteen Years of Age', offering reading, writing, arithmetic, &c., and board, for £12 pa and 5s entrance; he could then accommodate 10 boarders.[2] At midsummer 1774 the fees were increased to £13 pa ('including washing, mending of Stockings, Copy-books, Pens and Ink') 'which he hopes they [his 'Friends'] will not think more than equivalent to the exorbitant Price, that all kinds of Provision are now advanced to.'[3] A dancing master was then in attendance. Colbran also undertook surveying, and taught it at his school, but in 1776 he announced that 'he has declined Land-Surveying, (except measuring a few Pieces near Home, for the Benefit of any of his Scholars, who may be desirous of attaining the Art of Surveying,) and devotes his whole Time and Attention to the Management and Instruction of his Scholars'.[4] His purpose was 'to qualify his Pupils for Trade and Business',[5] and he promised to take 'the greatest care of their Morals, both in School, and at Play.'[6] His approach to teaching has been cited above ('Instead of Severity, he uses the most gentle and attractive Methods to excite his Scholars to a Love of Learning...'[7]). His curriculum was set out in more detail in 1778: 'English, Writing, Arithmetic, both in Whole Numbers and Fractions, Vulgar and Decimal, the Extraction of the Square and Cube Roots, with their Uses, Duodecimals, Practical Geometry, Timber Measure, Guaging, the Rudiments of Algebra, and Book-keeping, both by Single and Double Entry.'[8] The annual fee stayed the same until 1787, when it increased to £14 pa;[9] but from 1776 he had also charged 3s 6d at each vacation (Christmas and Summer) 'for Breaking-up, and Servants'; and 15s for each vacation (of a month each) for boarders who did not go home (increased to 1 guinea a time in 1787).[10] From 1787 1s a quarter was charged for pens and ink (previously included under the basic fee); and 'If Tea (for Breakfast) be required', this was 1 guinea a year extra.[11] There was 'A convenient airy Field, near the School for the young Gentlemens Exercise'.[12] Colbran's charity pupils, and presumably his private day pupils, comprised both boys and girls, but he found it expedient to announce: 'Mr. Colbran does not board both sexes.'[13] The school apparently continued until Colbran's death in 1816, aged 79.[14]

   Advertised in *SWA* Feb 1770; May (2) 74; Jun, Dec 76; May (2), Jun 77; Jun, Dec 78; Jun 79; Jan, Jun 80; Dec 82; Jun 87.

[Thomas Colbran]

1. ESRO ESC 148/1/1, 8.   2. *SWA* 26.2.70.   3. *SWA* 23.5.74.   4. *SWA* 3.6.76.   5. *SWA* 30.12.76.
6. *SWA* 5.5.77.   7. *SWA* 3.6.76.   8. *SWA* 8.6.78.   9. *SWA* 25.6.87.   10. *SWA* 3.6.76, 30.12.76, 25.6.87.

11. *SWA* 25.6.87.   12. *SWA* 14.6.79.   13. *SWA* 14.6.79.   14. Wadey, op. cit., 189.

SELHAM   1724: 7 families   1801: pop. 78
No 18th-century schooling traced.

SELMESTON (SYMSON)   1724: 17 families   1801: pop. 130
No 18th-century schooling traced.

SELSEY   1724: about 100 families 1801: pop. 564
School   (Rs: 1755, and later in 18c?)
At the 1775 visitation there was no free or charity school in the parish, but there was a
schoolmaster, of 'good Life' and 'diligent', who came to church and taught his scholars the
catechism.[1] Horsfield, in 1835, recorded that Rev William Walker of Chichester erected a
schoolhouse for the children of the parish,[2] but this could have been any time between 1774
and 1807.
1. WSRO Ep.I/22/1.   2. Horsfield *Sussex* II, 36; CI.

Sunday school   (R: 1788)
A Sunday school was opened in October 1788, 'under the patronage of the Minister'
(William Webber; he died in 1790).[1]
1. *SWA* 6.10.88; CI.

SHERMANBURY   1724: 29 families   1801: pop. 274
[Ward's school?]   (R: 1691)
In 1691 Richard Ward, rector, recorded in his tithe book, 'Then Rec'd of him [Mr Thomas]
all his dues for his Sons Schooling';[1] so he was then keeping a small private school. Ward
was rector until his death in 1706, so it is possible his school continued into the 18th
century.   [*Richard Ward*]
1. WSRO Par 167/6/1.

Bear's boys' boarding school   (Rs: 1736-44)
John Bear, rector from 1711 to his death in 1762, aged 88, kept a small boarding school for
the sons of local gentry, at least between 1736 and 1744. He never took more than two
boys at a time. His fees were a minimum of 50 guineas a year (with washing and mending
'out of the House' an extra, at about £3 pa). A writing master and a dancing master could
be provided. Amongst his pupils were Sir Edward Frewen's grandson and Sir Thomas
Webster's son; one of Admiral Haddock's sons was there in 1743. Another pupil was John
Inskip, whose father was a poor currier at Uckfield, but who was the heir of Sir John Lade
(who died in 1740, when Inskip was about 10); he was the ward of John Fuller of Brightling
Park; he had been sent by his uncle, Sir John Lade, to Tonbridge school, but in 1743 John
Fuller removed him, as after three years he could scarcely read, and sent him to John Bear,
where, in less than a year, he was 'very much improved in his reading' and had begun
studying Latin.[1]   [*John Bear*]
1. *SAC* **114**, 338; *SAC* **22**, 165; ESRO SAS/RF 15/25, FRE 1153, 1294; *SAC* **104**, 84-5.

SHIPLEY   1724: 130 families   1801: pop. 997
Schools (Rs: 1729, 1733, 1737, 1758, 1779)
No free or charity school is recorded in the parish, but visitation returns give the following:[1]
        1729: 'We have one who teaches school who is of a sober life.'

1733: 'Our clerk teaches School. He is diligent in the business. He and his Scholars come to Church. He Instructs ym in the Church Catechism.'

1737: 'There is only a Petty School Taught by ye Clarke' [described in similar terms to 1733].

1758: 'Our parish Clark teaches a little School' - he was of 'good Life' and 'diligent', came to church and caused his scholars to come, and taught them the catechism.

1779: A schoolmaster of 'good Life' and 'diligent', who taught his scholars the catechism.

1. WSRO Ep.I/22/1.

SHOREHAM	1724: families	1801: pop.
New Shoreham	160	799
Old Shoreham	22	188
	182	987

Nye's school   (Rs: 1695-1704?)

The New Shoreham parish register, bought in 1695, was 'keept by Edmund Nye Schoole-Master'. Nye was the parish clerk, and (from the handwriting) entered up the register to 1703. He was buried 31 May 1704. His son Elias was born in April 1696 and Edmund was probably not old; he almost certainly kept his school to 1703, and probably until his death in 1704.[1] [*Edmund Nye*]

1. WSRO Par 170/1/1/3, f 1 and passim.

Charity school   (Rs: 1714, 1722)

There was a schoolhouse in New Shoreham by June 1714, when a vestry held there drew up a code of rules 'for the government of the Charity School maintained by the parish'. It would appear that subscribers had undertaken to pay for a schoolmaster to teach 20 or 30 children of the parish 'upon condition the whole Parishioners of the said parish wch payeth taxes to Church & Poor shall subscribe to stand to & keep the rules and orders hereunder written.'

The schoolmaster was to be 'of a sober life' and 'well grou'ded in ye principles and Discipline of the establish'd Church of England'; he was to teach his scholars 'the true spelling of words and distinction of syllables with the points and stops and to write a legible hand with the grounds of Arithmetick'; he was to bring the children to church 'twice every Lords day and as often in the week days as there shall be divine service performed', to see they behaved properly at church and joined in the public service, and 'to have their Bibles and Common Prayer books bound together; for their better instruction...' (so each child apparently had their own bible and prayer book). On Thursday afternoons and Saturday mornings he was to teach and explain the catechism to the children 'when capable', and bring them to church every Sunday to be catechised by the minister. There were to be prayers at the school every morning and evening, and the master was to 'teach his Schollers to pray att home when they go to bed and when they rise up, and to use graces before and after meat, which prayers and graces are to be approved of by the Minister of the place.' It was very much a church school. The then vicar, Rice Williams, agreed to teach the school. The minister, constable, churchwardens and overseers for the time being, together with 'twelve others of the chief inhabitants, that payeth the most Taxes to the Church and poor' were to govern the school, determine the number of children, and appoint them.[1]

In February 1722 there was a confrontation between the parish and the minister, and Rice Williams was prosecuted by the churchwardens for various misdemeanours, including 'For keeping ye Parishioners out of ye School house being ye place of their usual

assembling about parish business.'[2] Rice Williams died in 1727.
[*Rice Williams*]

1. *SAC* **51**, 179-80, citing WSRO Par 170/12/1.   2. ibid, 172.

Chaloner's school   (R: pre-1741)
Thomas Chaloner, 'exciseman and schoolmaster at Shoreham and Littlehampton', was imprisoned for debt in Horsham gaol; but it is not clear if he carried out both occupations at both places. (He was also a poet, 'called the merriest poet in Christendom'.) He was released c.1741 through the intervention of Charles Eversfield, MP for Horsham.[1] [*Thomas Chaloner*]

1. Albery, W., 'The Sussex County Gaol at Horsham (1540-1845)', *SCM* v.6, 742-4.

Rodez' school   (R: 1755)
Henry Rodez was a schoolmaster of New Shoreham in 1755, when his son James was apprenticed to Robert Dixon of Rochester, mariner.[1] [*Henry Rodez*]

1. Guildhall Museum, Rochester, RCA/02/19: MS Register of apprentices, 12 July 1755 (indenture dated 1 May 1755).

Clement's boys' school   (R: 1792)
In September 1792 Simon Clement, who had taught school some time at Shoreham, advertised 'that he will teach any young Gentleman Navigation, together with the Lunar Observations for THREE GUINEAS, or Navigation without the Lunar Observations for TWO GUINEAS.' He claimed to be 'a perfect Master of Navigation; being acquainted with every part of the Mathematics upon which Navigation depends', and also taught 'Latin, Mensuration, Algebra, Geometry, Trigonometry, Fluxions, &c. &c.'[1] Previously a schoolmaster at Arundel (R: 1787/8). Also a surveyor. In *Univ. Directory* 1793. [*Simon Clement*]

1. *SWA* 10.9.92.

Other schoolmistress

Deborah Geer, schoolmistress at Shoreham, *Univ. Directory* 1793.

Dancing master

John Thring, dancing master of Lewes from 1778 to at least 1800 [qv], held a ball at the *Star*, New Shoreham, on 26 June 1780, 'where Minuets, Cotillons, &c. will be danced by his Scholars.' The ball began at 6 o'clock, 'the Dancing for the Company to become general at Nine o'Clock'. Tickets were 2s 6d each. He held another similar ball at the *Star* Assembly Rooms in December that year (on this occasion the dancing became general at 8 o'clock). (*SWA* 19.6.80, 18.12.80)

Note: John Gray, rector of Southwick, who died in 1751, by will dated 15 October 1750, left £40 towards setting up a charity school for the instruction of poor children of Old Shoreham and Southwick, in reading, writing and working, and the church catechism; if the attempt at setting up the charity school should fail, 'for want of better encouragement, or any other cause', the £40 was to go to the SPCK. But the money was never paid out of Gray's estate; no such charity school appears to have been set up in either parish, nor was any such sum paid to the SPCK. (*EP3* (1820), 448; *VCH* vi, I, 172)

SIDLESHAM   1724: 88 families   1801: pop. 805

Dame schools   (Rs: 1733, 1737)
At the 1733 visitation: 'There are women that teach to read. There is no school-master.' There was no free or charity school. In 1737, opposite the questions 'Doth any one in your

Parish teach School... without Licence...?' and 'Is your School-master of good Life and... diligent...?', the churchwardens answered, 'Yea we believe Pretty well': so perhaps there was a schoolmaster then, though they were probably referring to the school dames (see 1733 above). The 'schoolmaster' came to church 'often', and taught 'his' scholars the catechism.[1]

1. WSRO Ep.I/22/1 (1733 return dated from churchwardens' names).

SINGLETON   1724: 45 families   1801: pop. 445

Petty school/dame schools   (Rs: 1758, 1762, 1775)
At the 1758 visitation: 'There is a poor man teaches school, but says He is not, as yet, able to pay for a Licence'. The churchwardens believed him to be of 'good Life' and 'diligent'; he came to church and caused his scholars to come, and taught them the catechism.
        At 1762: 'There is a poor woman that teaches School'. The churchwardens (misunderstanding a question about the charity school, if such existed) noted that the children were generally put out 'to Husbandry'.
        At 1775: 'There is a little School for teaching young children to read - kept by a woman of good character. She comes to Church, but further cannot say [ie. whether she caused her scholars to come]. We believe she does [teach her scholars the catechism]'.[1]

1. WSRO Ep.I/22/1.

[See also WESTHAMPNETT for possible Goodwood estate schooling.]

SLAUGHAM   1724: 80 families   1801: pop. 560

No 18th-century schooling traced.

SLINDON   1747: 65 families (no. of Protestants, 199; Papists, 109)
                     1766: 65 families (no. of Protestants, 240; Papists, 86)
                     (*Secker*, 218)   1801: pop. 374

Dame school   (R: 1788)
In 1788 there was a 'little school kept by a protestant mistress.'[1]

1. Kinoulty, M.A., 'A Social Study of Roman Catholicism in West Sussex in the Eighteenth Century', MA thesis, University of Wales (1982), WSRO Add MS 34,673, 182, citing Moore's visitation, 1788, return of Rev J. Smelt, vicar of Slindon, 14 January 1788, Lambeth Palace Library VP II/2/1, f 468.

Catholic school   (R: 1788)
In 1788 there was 'a Popish School very lately erected'. This school was probably supported by Lord Newburgh.[1]

1. Kinoulty, op. cit., ibid.

SLINFOLD   1724: about 65 families   1801: pop. 550

Petty school/dame schools   (Rs: 1762, 1779)
Answers to visitation questions in 1762 and 1779 indicate one or more unlicensed teachers, including a schoolmaster of 'good Life' and 'diligent', who 'generally' came to church and caused his scholars to come, and who taught them the catechism.[1]

1. WSRO Ep.I/22/1.

SOMPTING (SOUMTING)   1724: near 40 families   1801: pop. 405

Dame schools/petty school   (Rs: 1733, 1775)
At the 1733 visitation: 'we have no School Master only Dames', who taught their scholars the catechism. At the 1775 visitation, answers indicate a schoolmaster (though the churchwardens may have been thinking of a school dame or dames), of 'good Life' and

'diligent', who came to church and caused his scholars to come, and taught them the catechism .[1]

1. WSRO Ep.I/22/1 (1733 return dated from churchwardens' names).

SOUTH AMBERSHAM   1801: pop. 157
[Part of the Hampshire parish of Steep until 1844.]

No 18th-century schooling traced.

SOUTH BERSTED   1717: about 70 families   1801: pop. 737

Mrs Hitchcock's school   (R: 1776)
John Baker, a solicitor of the Inner Temple who had retired to Horsham and in 1776 was 64, wrote in his diary for Sunday, 1 September 1776:

> Dined con Farmer Grey... [Grey was a farmer whose farmhouse was in South Bersted: he was a tenant in North Bersted of John Baker, as trustee for his brother Thomas Baker's estate]. Little Betsy went to eat Fromenty at her school-mistress's, Mrs. Hitchcock, as did all her scholars (about 8 who give 3d a week), which has been a matter of great expectation for some days (little Betsy showed away with her new sombrero and boca).[1]

Baker had recorded earlier, on 22 August, that little Betsy was just over three years old; she was baptised 15 July 1773, and is the youngest 18th-century scholar so far recorded in Sussex. [*Mrs Hitchcock*]

1. Yorke, P.C. *The Diary of John Baker* (1931), 50, 365.   2. ibid, 363; South Bersted PR.

SOUTHEASE   1724: 14 families   1801: pop. 108
No 18th-century schooling traced.

SOUTH HEIGHTON   1801: pop. 90
No 18th-century schooling traced.

SOUTH MALLING - see LEWES

SOUTH STOKE   1724: 13 families   1801: pop. 106
No 18th-century schooling traced.

SOUTHWICK   1724: 22 families   1801: pop. 271
No 18th-century schooling traced.

Note: John Gray, rector of Southwick, who died in 1751, by will dated 15 October 1750, left £40 towards setting up a charity school for the instruction of poor children of Old Shoreham and Southwick, in reading, writing and working, and the church catechism; if the attempt at setting up the charity school should fail, 'for want of better encouragement, or any other cause', the £40 was to go to the SPCK. But the money was never paid out of Gray's estate; no such charity school appears to have been set up in either parish, nor was any such sum paid to the SPCK. (*EP3* (1820), 448; *VCH* vi, I, 172)

STANMER   c1760: 9 houses & 1 farm 1801: pop. 105
No 18th-century schooling traced.

STEDHAM   1724: 44 families   1801: pop. 258

No 18th-century schooling traced.

STEYNING   1724: about 140 families   1801: pop. 1,174

<u>Grammar school</u>   (F: 1614. Rs: through 18c)
The grammar school was founded by William Holland by deed dated 16 June 1614, who gave a house and garden for the schoolhouse and 25 acres of land, the income from which was to keep the house in repair and pay the schoolmaster £20 pa. The master was not to be away from the school more than 28 school days in a year, and was to provide 'in some good sort' for the teaching of the scholars in his absence. The number of scholars was limited to 50, none to be admitted who could not read English distinctly. No able child dwelling in the town might be turned away. Every scholar on his first admittance was to pay 1s to the schoolmaster, or 2s if a 'foreigner' (this was for the master's examination of them, to see if they could read English distinctly); and every scholar was to pay 8d a year - 1d each quarter for brooms and rods [ie. canes], and 4d at the Feast of St Michael for wax candles for use in the winter. Interestingly, the scholars of the four chief forms had to speak in Latin at all times; only the schoolmaster could give permission for English to be spoken.[1]

Bernard Chatfield of Steyning, apothecary, by will dated 15 April 1717 and proved 14 November 1718, gave the schoolmaster land that in 1724 augmented his salary by £3 pa.[2]

Although described as a free grammar school, the free scholars were not restricted to children of the poor - the word 'poor' does not occur in the statutes - and no able child or youth dwelling in the town could be turned away. Private pupils were envisaged from the start, Holland ruling that the master could not take more than six boarders in his house. In the 18th century some boarders - such as Edward Hards in 1734 - lodged with families in the town.[3] From 1735 to 1740 Henry Manning of Lewes was paying for his sons £2 pa each for their schooling and £12-15 pa each to the master for their board (there were extras for books &c. and also payments to local tradesmen for shoes, mending clothes, powdering and cutting their hair, &c. - see Schedule 3, MANNING, Edward (1725-44)).[4]

As with other Sussex grammar schools, the charity was abused in the 18th century, to the point when there were no free scholars at all. In 1733 the churchwardens reported the free grammar school with a revenue 'of thirty Pounds a year or there about... paid to the schoolmaster', but added: 'Much neglected, the School master is Vicar of Shoreham by which there are No Boys at School the Inhabitants being deeply concern'd at the great abuse of the Charity - The School being hired out to A writing master Contrary to the Intent of the donor & the Inhabitants Oblig'd to send out their Children to other Schools for Better Improvement so that it is Intirely become A Sinecure.'[5] In 1804 the *Gentleman's Magazine* referred to John Morgan who had been master since 1778: 'He enjoys the stipend and emoluments as master, but why the duty is not performed I am not acquainted. This contumacious master who neglects to teach holds possession of the School House and refuses to admit the Trustees' servants.'[6] A public petition in 1816, complaining of breaches of trust in the management of the charity, led to a Chancery case: Morgan resigned in 1817.[7] The commissioners on the education of the poor, reporting in 1819, noted: 'This school does not appear to have been of much advantage to the town and neighbourhood of Steyning during the late master's time [ie. from 1778]. The average number of scholars is stated not to have exceeded two.'[8] So much for William Holland's limit of 50 free scholars. One reason for there being few scholars, as a former trustee alleged, was 'the disinclination of the inhabitants of Steyning to a classical education for their children'; and another trustee

8. Steyning Grammar School. Watercolour by W.H. Brooke, 1820. (SAS Library Acc. No. 3663. By courtesy of the Sussex Archaeological Society.)

gave as a reason 'the severity of the late master towards the boys'. The commissioners were sceptical of the latter: in the public petition of 1816 one witness swore that he had been obliged to leave around 1780 because of harsh treatment, but this was the only such allegation and was committed 36 years before; and in 40 years of Morgan's mastership, no complaint had been made at any time to the Bishop of Chichester (the channel provided for in Holland's original deed), or to the trustees (until just before Morgan's resignation).[9]

John Mathew was licensed in 1692 to teach boys in the rudiments of grammar and arithmetic within the borough of Steyning; he was appointed vicar of Steyning in 1702 (when nominated, he described himself in the register as 'ye schoolmaster of Steyning'). He appears to have been an active and caring parish priest (see <u>Sunday school?</u> below). He was master in a list of feoffees of 1717 and probably master until about 1723 (though he continued as vicar of Steyning until 1745). In June 1723 William Prescott was licensed to instruct children in 'ye Free School of Steyning'. He was not long at the school: by April 1728 Edward Martin was master (Mr Lamb acting as his locum for a time). Martin was licensed in September 1729, then aged 30. The year before he had been instituted to the vicarage of New Shoreham (when he died in 1766, he was also rector of Southwick and vicar of Lancing). Martin was master in 1733 (from the churchwardens' reference to the master that year being vicar of Shoreham - see above), when there were 'No Boys at School' and the school was being hired out to a writing master. John Hart, who was instituted as rector of Wiston in 1731, was the next master; he was 'rector of this church [Wiston] and Master of Steyning School' when he died in July 1736, aged 45. C. Baker (probably the Charles Baker who had subscribed in February 1731, 'before being admitted to teach a grammar school at Lindfield') took over as master when Hart died in 1736, though Mrs Hart continued to be paid for boarding private pupils at least until the end of 1737; and another Baker, Charles Vaughan, was master from 1753 to 1778; he was at the same time rector of Edburton, and from 1776 also the vicar of Lyminster. John Morgan was master from 1778 until he resigned (following public complaints - see above) in 1817; he was also curate of Old Shoreham from 1770 to 1818.[10]

In Charles Vaughan Baker's time, some of the private pupils appear to have been very young boys for a grammar school - in April 1775 Master Purdy, six years old, was sent to the school (he had never been out to school before).[11]

[John Mathew, Thomas Pooly (writing master)?, William Prescott, Edward Martin, Mr Lamb (locum), John Hart, C. Baker, Stephen Philpot (dancing master), Charles Vaughan Baker, John Morgan]

1. Sleight, J.M. *A Very Exceptional Instance* (1981), passim; *VCH* ii, 424. 2. Wadey index at SAS; WSRO Ep.I/26/3, 16-17. 3. Sleight, op. cit., 23, 32, 69. 4. ESRO SAS/I 302. 5. WSRO Ep.I/22/1. 6. Sleight, op. cit., 40. 7. ibid, 43-53; *EP2* (1819), 180. 8. *EP2* (1819), 181. 9. ibid, 181-2; Sleight, op. cit., 32. 10. Sleight, op. cit., passim; CI; WSRO Ep.I/22/1; WSRO Ep.I/1/11; *SAC* **25**, 197; ESRO SAS/I 302; and see Schedule 2. 11. *SAC* **52**, 72.

Pooly's school?   (R: 1702)

Thomas Pooly was 'writing master' at his burial 14 June 1702.[1] He had probably kept his own school, and may also have taught at the grammar school. *[Thomas Pooly]*

1. Steyning PR.

Dendy's school   (Rs: 1715, 1716)

The 'school of Richard Dendy', on the north side of the High St, is referred to in a property deed of 1716. He is 'of Steyning, Schoolmaster' in other deeds of 1715, 1716.[1] He died in 1723.   *[Richard Dendy]*

1. Wiston Archives, 6227-9, 6455-8.

[Sunday school?]   (R: 1724)
At the 1724 visitation the churchwardens reported that the incumbent, John Mathew, catechised every Sunday afternoon from Michaelmas to Lady day; and after recording the number of dissenting families in the parish ('5 Quakers, 4 Anabaptists, 2 Presbyterians') they added: 'Note Many of the Children of these come to Church'.[1] Mathew appears to have been an unusually active and caring incumbent for his times, and the fact that children of dissenters came to church suggests that he gave them some schooling. He was vicar of Steyning from 1702 until his death in 1749.

1. WSRO Ep.I/26/3, 16-17.

Schools   (R: 1733)
At the 1733 visitation the churchwardens, recording the complete failure of the free grammar school (see above), noted: 'the Inhabitants Oblig'd to Send out their Children to Other Schools'. So there were other schools in the town at that time, one of them being kept by a writing master at the grammar schoolhouse, which he rented.[1]

1. WSRO EP.I/22/1

Workhouse school/parish schooling   (Rs: 1737, 1782-5)
At the 1737 visitation the churchwardens reported that 'the children [in] the work house... are taught to read spin &c.'[1] The earliest record of the workhouse is in 1729,[2] but it is not known how long a school was kept there for the pauper children.

　　　Every week from 21 December 1782 to 14 May 1785, the parish paid 2s to 'Dame Drewett for the school'. (She was also paid in this period 1s 6d 'for toping 2 Gowns' and 10d 'for altering Kit Patchen's Gown'.) This parish school was very possibly also kept in the workhouse.[3]

[*Dame Drewett*]

1. WSRO Ep.I/22/1.   2. Cox, E.W., and Duke, F. *In and around Steyning* (1954), 75-6.   3. WSRO Par 183/31/2.

Evershed's boys' day and boarding school   (R: 1790s)
William Evershed (1751-1808), schoolmaster at Steyning, was formerly a potter. He was a Baptist, and an occasional preacher. He was referred to as a schoolmaster in a will of 1788, but may then have been at Billingshurst. From the pottery he moved to Steyning where he set up a small day school with a few boarders. He also probably did some land-surveying - one of his boarders (William Evershed, 1784-1865) went with him sometimes to draw the chain. In 1797 he was occupying a house in Steyning with a land tax 'rental' assessment of £4.

[*William Evershed*]

1. Evershed, P.B., pers. comm., citing Frank Evershed's Notebooks, recording conversations with Mrs Carter in 1876 and 1877, the will of John Dean of Shipley dated 26 June 1788, and Steyning Land Tax; Caffyn, J.M., *Sussex Believers* (1988), 273.

STOPHAM   1724: 21 families   1801: pop. 164

No 18th-century schooling traced. (Specifically, in 1769, 'No one teaches School'.[1])
1. WSRO Ep.I/22/1.

STORRINGTON   1724: about 80 families   1801: pop. 846

Petty/dame schools   (Rs: 1737, 1742, 1758)
At the 1737 visitation, there was a schoolmaster in the parish, of 'good Life' and 'diligent', who came to church and caused his scholars to come, and taught them the catechism. In 1742, there was apparently a schoolmaster who taught his scholars the catechism. In 1758: 'There are who teach School', one of them being a schoolmaster -'His Scholars come [to

church]' and 'We believe, He does instruct 'em [in the catechism]'.[1]
1. WSRO Ep.I/22/1.

<u>Charity school</u>   (F: c.1763. Rs: c.1763- into 19c)
Mrs Jane Downer, by will dated 8 July 1763, left £500, on trust, the interest of which was to be paid to a schoolmaster for teaching 20 poor children of Storrington, girls as well as boys, to read, write and cast accounts. The trustees were to appoint the schoolmaster and the children, and if there were not 20 such children from Storrington, the number was to be made up from adjoining parishes. No child was to be admitted younger than six, nor to continue after 13.[1] In 1779 the income from the endowment was £20 pa,[2] in 1819, £15 pa.[3] From 1806, a further gift yielded (in 1819) a further £15 pa, for teaching 10 more poor boys and girls. In 1819 the master was also taking private pupils, and the total school numbered about 70.[4]

The original 'Rules of the Free School in Storrington' have survived (being given the accredited date of 1763).[5] These included:

School hours: Lady day to Michaelmas, 7 to 12 and 1 to 5; Michaelmas to Lady day, 8 to 12 and 1 to 4. So the children had an early start, with nine hours schooling each day in the summer, seven hours in the winter. A pencilled superscription implies that the summer starting time was later changed to 8 o'clock.

Church and catechism: 'The Master and Children to attend Divine Service at Church all Wednesdays and Fridays in the Year and every Day in Passion Week.' [They also attended on Sundays, as the rule on truancy makes clear - see below.] 'The Master to instruct the Children not only in Reading, Writing and Arithmetick but very carefully also in the Church Catechism, at least twice a Week.'

Daily prayers: Prayers were to be said at the beginning and ending of school each day: the prayers to be used were specified (in the morning, for example, the confession, the Lord's prayer, the collect of the week, the second and third collects for morning prayer, the thanksgiving, St Chrysotom's prayer and the grace); the number of prayers appears to have been later reduced.

Holidays: The Christmas vacation was from the eve of St Thomas to the Monday after Epiphany (18 to 24 days); Easter, from the Thursday before Easter to the Monday after Easter week (11 days); Whitsun, from the Saturday before Whitsunday to the Monday fortnight (16 days). The Whitsun vacation appears to have been later reduced to 9 days. 'The Festivals, and Solemn Days appointed to be observed in the Church of England' were holidays, as were Saturday afternoons, and Mrs Downer's birthday, 18 January, 'and whenever the Trustees shall think proper to indulge with leave of absence some or all the Children in Wheat-harvest.'

Discipline: 'If any Child after Admittance shall be absent from School through Idleness or resentment of the ordinary correction, or the Parent knowing and consenting thereto, or be missing at Church on a Sunday, except in Cases unavoidable, and shewed to be such by the Parents, He or She to be Struck off the List for ever.'

'If any Child shall be found to have a Scald Head, or Vermin therein more than Common, or to be infected with the Itch, Such Child to be forbidden the School, till clear and well of those Nuisances.'

'If any Child shall be guilty of Notorious Swearing or Lying after repeated

Admonitions, such Child to be discharged from the School.'

From 1771 to 1785 William Phillips was master of the free school.[6]   In 1785 he moved to Henfield and opened his own successful boys' boarding school. James Coates was a schoolmaster in Storrington in 1799, and probably master of the free school. [*William Phillips, James Coates*]

1. *EP*2 (1819), 182.   2. WSRO Ep.I/22/1.   3. *EP*2 (1819), 182.   4. ibid.   5. WSRO Par 188/25/1.
6. From his ads for his Henfield school, *SWA* 11.12.86, 27.8.87.

Eason's boys' boarding school   (R: 1794)

In May 1794 Robert Eason advertised his boarding school for young gentlemen at Storrington, announcing that he had 'taken a house in an airy and pleasant part of the town, where youth are educated in the English Language, Writing, Arithmetic, Geometry, the Use of the Globes, Merchants Accounts, &c.'   His terms were 12 guineas pa, and half a guinea entrance. Tea was 1 guinea extra.[1]   [*Robert Eason*]

1. *SWA* 5.5.94.

STOUGHTON   1724: 60 families   1801: pop. 502

School   (R: 1733)

At the 1733 visitation there was a schoolmaster in the parish 'yt teaches to read & write'. 'He is [of 'good Life' and 'diligent']. He doth [come to church and cause his scholars to come]. He doth [teach them the catechism].'[1]

1. WSRO Ep.I/22/1.

STREAT   1724: 25 families   1801: pop. 112

Charity school   (Rs: 1709 or 1710?, 1716-22)

The account book of William Dobell Esq., of Streat Place, shows a payment on 3 December 1709 or 1710 of £3 to 'Goody Balcombe, for 1 year's teaching school due at Mich's'.[1] This may well have been for a small charity school in the parish: the payment would have covered at least 360 child/weeks, or about 8-10 poor children for the year.

In April 1716 Anthony Springett advised the SPCK that there was a charity school at Streat, where 'the Children are all taught to read & their Catechism'.[2]   Writing again in May 1722, from Plumpton, next to Streat, he reported that 'the Schools in that Neighbourhood still continue in a flourishing Condition tho' there are grievous Complaints against them as the Occasion of the want of Servants in those parts.'[3] The school was listed in the SPCK annual *Account of the Charity-Schools* in 1724 and, by implication from the summary county totals, to at least 1740; but as there was no change at all in the county totals of schools or scholars from 1730 to 1740, these later lists must be regarded as suspect.

1. *SAC* **4**, 99.   2. SPCK ALB v.6, 4772.   3. SPCK ALB v.11, 7053.

SULLINGTON   1724: about 24 or 25 families 1801: pop. 256

No 18th-century schooling traced.

SUTTON   1724: 53 families   1801: pop. 303

School   (Rs: 1762, 1769)

At the visitations in 1762 and 1769 there was a schoolmaster in the parish who came to church and caused his scholars to come.[1]

1. WSRO Ep.I/22/1.

Workhouse school   (R: 1793)

In 1793 a paid teacher was appointed to teach the pauper children in the workhouse to read, and to give them religious instruction. 25 copies of *Reading Made Easy* were obtained that year (11 were still in stock in 1804).[1] (NB This was a united workhouse, serving (in 1791) eight parishes, and later 11.[2])

1. *W. Sussex History* 32 (1985), 17.   2. Rev A. Young, *General View of the Agriculture of the County of Sussex* (for the Board of Agriculture, 1813), 453.

[Sunday school?]

Nicholas Turner, rector of Sutton, was advertised to preach the charity sermon at Brighton church on 27 September 1789, on behalf of the Brighton Sunday school and school of industry. He did not, apparently, preach in the event, but it seems unlikely that he would have been asked to do so unless he had a Sunday school in his own parish. Turner had been instituted to the rectory of Sutton in June of that year.[1]

1. *SWA* 21.9.89; CI.

TANGMERE   1717: 16 families   1801: pop. 136

Charity schooling   (F: 1741. Rs: 1741- into 19c)

The parish was entitled to send two poor children, boys or girls, to the charity school in Boxgrove, founded and endowed by the Countess Dowager of Derby [qv BOXGROVE]. The school was set up in 1741. The children were clothed, and taught reading, writing and arithmetic. In 1787 the trustees agreed to educate, but not to clothe, an additional six boys, one of whom would have come from Tangmere.

TARRING NEVILLE (TERRING) 1724: 11 families   1801: pop. 74

No 18th-century schooling traced.

TELSCOMBE (TEDDISCOMB) 1724: 6 families   1801: pop. 89

Charity schooling   (Rs: c.1727- into 19c)

Josiah Povey, rector of Telscombe, who died in 1727, left by will dated 30 March 1727 a house, lands and premises at St John's Common, in trust, the rents thereof to be paid to a fit person to teach the children of Telscombe to read, write and sew. He stipulated that neither the rector of Telscombe for the time being, nor the vicar of Piddinghoe, should teach any of the children or receive any of the rents. He also left his stable in Telscombe to be used as the schoolroom. The stable, 25 feet by 18, was in a ruinous state by 1779, and appears never to have been used as a schoolroom. The rents were almost certainly used by the churchwardens and overseers, as they were in the early 19th century, to send children to different school dames. From 1796 the rent of the property was £9, which, after land tax, left £6 6s for the children's schooling. In 1819 there was no school in Telscombe, and the children were sent into the neighbouring parishes, at a distance of 3 or 4 miles, 7 or 8 to a dame school at Rottingdean, and 2 to one at Piddinghoe. Because of the distance the children had to go, there were not sufficient applications to absorb the whole of the income received.[1]

1. ESRO SAS/DN 36; *EP*2 (1819), 183-4.

TERWICK (TURWICK)   1724: 9 families   1801: pop. 91

No 18th-century schooling traced.

THAKEHAM (THAKAM)   1724: about 40 families   1801: pop. 539*
            *Population 1801 includes inmates of a workhouse serving seven united parishes.
No 18th-century schooling traced.

TICEHURST   1724: 150 families   1801: pop. 1,436

Adam's school   (Rs: 1754, 1756)
John Adam, schoolmaster, with his wife and daughter, moved from Rolvenden, Kent, to
Ticehurst in 1754.[1] He was a schoolmaster at Ticehurst in 1756, when his daughter died.
[*John Adam*]
1. Burchall, M.J., ed. *Eastern Sussex Settlement Certificates 1670-1832* (1979), 44.

Workhouse school/parish schooling   (Rs: c.1761, 1764, 1794)
At a vestry meeting in November 1757 it was unanimously agreed that it was very necessary
'to have ye Children of the poor within this parish Instructed in the Duties of Religion &
fed & Cloathed in a Decent Manner.'   The churchwardens and overseers were desired to
take subscriptions for providing a schoolhouse; but the project failed. In May 1760 a vestry
agreed 'to build a poor house in Newark's platt which belongs to the Parish, not exceeding
the sum of three Hundred pounds, with a proper Room in it for a School'. Nothing happened
immediately, but after the matter was raised again in May 1761, John Noakes undertook to
give £100 towards the cost if the remainder was raised by a voluntary subscription obviating
recourse to the poor rates. This appears to have been done. In January 1794 the parish paid
John Wickham 2s 6d 'for teaching the Children in the house their books &c.' (John
Wickham was a cobbler, paid by the parish from at least 1782 for mending the shoes of the
poor; they also paid for his 'quarters' at 6d a week, from at least 1782 to 1793, and in 1800
he received 1s 3d relief, 'being ill.'[1]) It is possible that there was some schooling for pauper
children from the erection of the combined workhouse and schoolhouse to the end of the
century.[2]
        On 23 March 1764 the parish agreed to put out Mary Oliver for 1s a week from
Lady day 1764 to Lady day 1765, and to find her 'Necessary Clothing', 'and to give her 4
Shillings Over, on Acct of sending her to School'.[3] So the parish was then, at least on
occasion, prepared to pay for the schooling of a poor child.
[*John Wickham*]
1. ESRO PAR 492/31/1/4.   2. Hodson, L.J. *Ticehurst* (1925), 157-8.   3. ESRO PAR 492/31/1/3.

Tandy's school   (R: 1778)
Richard Tandy was identified as 'the Schoolmaster' at the burials of his daughter Sarah and
son Richard in 1778. His children were baptised at Ticehurst between 1762 and 1776. He
was constable in 1782, and vestry clerk from at least 1782 to 1799; in September 1799 he
gave up as vestry clerk, being 'through Indisposition not capable of Paying Attention to that
Business any Longer.' He died in 1803.[1]   [*Richard Tandy*]
1. Ticehurst PR; ESRO PAR 492/31/1/4.

Boorman's school   (R: 1792)

In 1792 Arthur Boorman, schoolmaster, was renting a house in Ticehurst for £2 10s, and
it seems probable that he was keeping a school there.[1] He rented accommodation in the
parish from 1773 to 1796, but at his burial in 1800 it was noted that he 'had been servant
to the Revd Ossory Medlicott Vicar here'.[2]   [*Arthur Boorman*]
1. Wadey's index at SAS, citing Rev Andrew Kentman's *Parochialia* (1794).   2. ESRO PAR 492/30/3; Ticehurst
PR.

[Boarding and day school?]   (R: 1800?)
In March 1801 the following advertisement appeared:[1]

BOARDING and DAY SCHOOL WANTED
TO BE LETT
And entered upon at Lady-day next
A Large commodious HOUSE, conveniently Situated
for the above purpose, in the village of Ticehurst, where
such an undertaking will meet with liberal en-
couragement by the inhabitants and neighbourhood.
For further particulars, apply to WM. NOAKES, of
Ticehurst aforesaid.

This advertisement suggests that the house was probably used for a school previously, and
that possibly William Noakes was master of it.   [*William Noakes?*]
1. *SWA* 23.3.1801

TILLINGTON (TOLITON)   1724: about 100 families 1801: pop. 614

School (R: 1758)
At the 1758 visitation there was a schoolmaster in the parish, of 'good Life' and 'diligent',
who 'commonly' came to church and caused his scholars to come, and who taught them the
catechism.[1]
1. WSRO Ep.I/22/1.

[The rector of Tillington for the time being was one of the trustees of Taylor's charity
school, Petworth, under the will of John Taylor (a codicil to which was dated 1775);
perhaps children of Tillington were eligible for this school. (See PETWORTH)]

TORTINGTON (TORTON)   1724: 9 families   1801: pop. 68

No 18th-century schooling traced.

TREYFORD   1724: 14 families   1801: pop. 95

No 18th-century schooling traced. (Specifically, in 1775, 'No children taught'.[1])
1. WSRO Ep.I/22/1.

TROTTON   1724: 40 families   1801: pop. 329
                     (1724 and 1801 figures include Tuxlith)

School (R: 1742)
At the 1742 visitation there was a schoolmaster in the parish, of 'good Life' and 'diligent',
who came to church and caused his scholars to come.[1]
1. WSRO Ep.I/22/1.

Dame schools   (R: 1758)
At the 1758 visitation: 'Some Poor Women teach to read'.[1]
1. WSRO Ep.I/22/1.

TUXLITH   (1724 and 1801: pop. included under Trotton)

No 18th-century schooling traced.

TWINEHAM   1724: 26 families   1801: pop. 238

Dame Bellchamber's school?   (R: 1734)

On 20 August 1734 Jane, John and Samuel Stapley went to Dame Bellchamber's, 'the boys at 2d. and Jane at 4d. per week'.[1] It is probable that the dame school was in or very near Twineham.   [*Dame Bellchamber*]

1. ESRO HIC 472

UCKFIELD   1717: about 40 families   1801: pop. 811

Saunders' boys' charity school   (F: before 1718? Rs: 1718- into 19c)

In his will dated 31 October 1718, Anthony Saunders, rector of Buxted (DD, and chancellor of the cathedral church of St Paul, London, and rector of Acton, Middlesex), who never married, and died in January 1720, among other bequests left a schoolhouse in Uckfield, together with the means of supporting a charity school there - which suggests that the school was in existence when he made the will.[1] The first master of the school, John Lloyd, who was probably curate at Uckfield, was certainly taking private pupils there as early as midsummer 1718,[2] and was possibly teaching a charity school as well.

Saunders' school was for the education of 12 poor boys, six from Buxted and six from Uckfield, in reading and writing the English tongue, and learning the church catechism. To support the school, he left a house, a schoolhouse (in Church Street; it continued in use into the 19th century and is commemorated by a plaque in the 20th) and some 14 acres of land in Uckfield, and additionally £10 pa to be paid to the schoolmaster, clear of all taxes, arising from premises with 16 acres called 'the Rocks' in Buxted, and two houses and 120 acres of land, also in Buxted (the residue of the rents from Buxted was to be used to put out as apprentices poor boys of that parish). Writing to the SPCK in September 1729, William Clarke of Buxted reported the income of the school as about £30 pa. Saunders also bequeathed his library of about 200 volumes to the school, for the use of the master and scholars.[3]

John Lloyd, the first master, was a clerk of Buxted when he married there in 1710. As noted above, he took private pupils, certainly from 1718 to 1721. Curate of Uckfield; perhaps inducted as rector of Maresfield in 1728 (there were two Rev John Lloyds in Sussex at that time), he subscribed in 1730, 'to teach school in Uckfield'. He was buried at Uckfield in 1738. He was followed by Robert Gerison, curate of Uckfield, who also took private pupils. He was also rector of Nuthurst from 1773 until his death in 1799, aged 87; and vicar of South Malling 1779 to 1793. His successor, William Rose, was curate of Little Horsted, and from January 1794 kept a boarding school there for 12 young gentlemen, offering Greek, Latin, French, mathematics, writing, arithmetic, 'and every other branch of useful and polite literature'.[4] In 1799 he followed Gerison as curate of Uckfield, and in 1800 he moved his private school to Uckfield, grafting it onto Saunders' school. By 1819 he had spent nearly £1,000 improving the school premises, and the school had become essentially a private school for the sons of Sussex gentry and clergy, achieving a high reputation as such. For a time the 12 charity boys were taught by an assistant in a room adjoining the schoolhouse, but by c.1817 an arrangement was made, with the approval of the Saunders' trustees, whereby the schoolmaster (who had the use of the Saunders' premises, and the £10 pa) paid £20 pa to the master of the National School where the 12 charity boys were educated free.[5]

[*John Lloyd, Robert Gerison, William Rose*]

1. *EP*2 (1819), 184; Buxted PR; Lower, *Worthies*, 63.   2. ESRO ACC 2462/1: Uckfield was a separate parish annexed to Buxted and served by a curate responsible to the rector of Buxted (Gilbert, H.D. 'Education Yesterday: The Saunders' Foundation and the Uckfield National Schools' (1963), MS at ESRO, 2.)   3. *EP*2 (1819), 184-5;

Lower, *Worthies*, 8; SPCK ALB v.15, 10384.   4. *SWA* 30.12.93.   5. *EP*2 (1819), 185. For fuller references re the masters, see Schedule 2.

<u>The Ellis's charity school</u>   (F: c.1718. Rs: 1718- into 19c)
The memorial inscription at Uckfield for Mary Ellis, who died in 1718, aged 61, records that she 'gave 4 l a-year, to be paid yearly to some woman in this parish, who shall be well qualified to teach to spell and read English, ten poor children of this parish.' Dorothy Ellis, who died in 1731, aged 73, by will dated 12 June 1728 confirmed and augmented her sister's charity, leaving £300 on trust, to be invested in land, the rents therefrom to provide £5 pa for the teaching of the ten poor children, and £5 pa to provide bread for 12 poor families, the residue going to other charitable purposes. The legacy was not laid out in lands, however, but 'improvidently applied in the purchase of a rent-charge of ten guineas per annum'. The provision of the bread required more than its share, and by 1819 £4 10s pa was being applied to the education of poor children. However, ten such children were then still being taught spelling and reading by a schoolmistress: 'The children are very young and are placed under the care of the schoolmistress for three years, before admission into the national school at Uckfield.' In 1827 the school was kept 'in a small building, at a short distance from the London road, and leading to the church'.[1]
1. Horsfield *Lewes* II, 236; *EP*2 (1819), 184.

<u>Markland, private tutor</u>   (Rs: c.1744-52)
Jeremiah Markland, noted classical scholar and editor of classical authors, was for the greater part of his life a tutor. He lived at Uckfield from 1744 to 1752, where he was tutor to Edward Clarke (later a fellow of St John's, Cambridge) and presumably others.[1] [*Jeremiah Markland*]
1. Lower, *Worthies*, 345; Horsfield, *Sussex* I, 367.

<u>Other schoolmasters</u>

> <u>John Curteis (Curtis)</u> was a schoolmaster of Uckfield at his death in 1799, either having his own school or possibly being assistant at the Saunders' school (see above). He kept the parish accounts, and 'was a very useful man in his neighbourhood, and much respected'. (He was swept away by a violent flood in September 1799, being rescued still alive, but dying an hour and a half later.) (*SWA* 30.9.99, 7.10.99)

> [William King], schoolmaster at Uckfield 1803 (*Sussex Militia List 1803, Pevensey Rape Northern Division* (1988)). Probably same as WK whose children, by Catherine, baptised Uckfield 1783, 84 (& by Philadelphia, 1785, 87, 90), so probably teaching then (Uckfield PR).

> [George King], assistant schoolmaster at Uckfield 1803. Probably baptised 1 August 1784, son of William (see above) & assistant to father, in which case only 15-16 in 1800. (ibid).

> [John Packnell], schoolmaster at Uckfield 1803. Perhaps John Pocknell whose children were baptised Uckfield 1784-93, in which case probably teaching then (but if so, militia list age classification incorrect). (ibid)

UDIMORE (ODDIMORE)   1724: 36 families   1801: pop. 321
No 18th-century schooling traced.

UP MARDEN   1724: 46 families   1801: pop. 255

Schools (Rs: c.1710?, 1728, 1733, 1755, 1762, 1765, 1775- into 19c)
There are references to schoolmasters in the parish throughout the century, and from c.1742 there was some provision for charity schooling (see below). The latter was almost certainly met by sending a few poor children to private petty or dame schools.

> 1710?: A map of Upmarden Farm, c.1710, shows 'School House Meadow'.[1]
> 1728:   Charles Martin was a schoolmaster 'of Westmarden in Upmarden' in his marriage licence.[2] He was probably the Charles Martin appointed schoolmaster in Walberton in 1733, at the start of the free school there.

At the visitations:[3]

> 1733:   'We have one that teacheth scool but hath No Liecence as I Now of. he is [of 'good Life' and 'diligent']   he Doth [come to church and cause his scholars to come]   he Doth [instruct his scholars in the catechism]'
> 1755, 1762, 1765, 1775: in each of these years there was a schoolmaster in the parish (of 'good Life' and 'diligent', who came to church and caused his scholars to come, and taught them the catechism).

[*Charles Martin*]

1. *SRS* **61**, 27.   2. *SRS* **9**, 300.   3. WSRO Ep.I/22/1.

Charity schooling   (R: c.1742?- into 19c)
In the return to parliament concerning charities, 1786, it was stated that Rev Dr Cox gave £100 by will for teaching poor children of Compton and Up Marden, the sum being vested in George Farrell and yielding £3 10s pa. Dr Cox was formerly rector of the parishes of Compton and Up Marden, and died c.1741. Neither the will nor any relevant document relating to the charity has been traced, but in the 1790s, and into the 19th century, £3 10s pa was being paid by the heirs of George Farrel or Farhill to a schoolmaster at Up Marden.[1]

At the Up Marden visitation of 1755 the churchwardens noted 'No particular Charity School', suggesting some provision for charity schooling (ie. the Cox bequest) but not sufficient to establish a charity school as such. In 1762 they recorded a free school, with a revenue 'none certain', run according to the will of the donor; and similarly in 1765, a free school with a revenue of £4 from endowment, and they noted that the children were 'Putt to Husbandry bisiness'. In 1755, however, the churchwardens reported that there was no free or charity school (which would have been technically correct) but recorded their schoolmaster, as noted above.[2]

1. *EP2* (1819), 160.   2. WSRO Ep.I/22/1.

UPPER BEEDING (BEDING, SEAL, SELA) 1724: about 40 families 1801: pop. 689*
              * Population 1801 includes Lower Beeding, not a separate parish in the 18c.

No 18th-century schooling traced.

UP WALTHAM   1801: pop. 65

No 18th-century schooling traced.

WADHURST   c1760: near 200 houses   1801: pop. 1,677

Charity school   (F: c.1716. Rs: c.1716- into 19c)
In 1716 Lucy Barham left £5 pa for teaching poor children to read.[1] In 1730 John Barham left £5 pa for the education of 12 poor children of Wadhurst, charged on his estate called Shoesmiths; his will has never been traced, but he was presumably regularising Lucy Barham's earlier bequest. The rent-charge continued to be paid by the owner of Shoesmiths

into the 19th century, when (in 1819) it was supplemented by £5 pa from the parish, to enable 12 children to be taught reading and writing by a schoolmaster.[2]

The school was referred to in the 18th century as 'the Charity-School at Wadhurst',[3] but with such a small endowment the schoolmasters would also have taken private pupils. In 1747 Thomas Hunt was charged 2s window tax for the 'Scool House' (it had nine windows)[4]; he was previously (and perhaps still) a barber, and probably kept the charity school as well as a private school. His second son, Stephen, was also schoolmaster at Wadhurst, being buried there in 1791, aged 59; and his third son, Samuel, was in 1795 'late a teacher at the Charity-School at Wadhurst'.[5] Samuel was in the poorhouse when he died in 1801, aged 65. [*Thomas Hunt?, Stephen Hunt?, Samuel Hunt*]

1. Wace, A.A., ed. *The Story of Wadhurst* (by Mrs Rhys Davids, 1894) (1924), 52.   2. *EP2* (1819), 185; Horsfield *Sussex* I, 415.   3. *SWA* 27.4.95.   4. ESRO ACC 472 (Land Tax Misc.). 5. *SWA* 27.4.95.

Hunts' school   (Rs: 1747, 1791, 1795?)
For details of Thomas Hunt's school, and those of his sons Stephen and Samuel, see Charity school above.   [*Thomas Hunt, Stephen Hunt, Samuel Hunt?*]

Mrs Baker's school   (R: 1791)
Jane Baker, schoolmistress, died in 1791, aged 55. She was the wife of John Baker, linen weaver, and probably kept a dame school.[1]   [*Jane Baker*]
1. Wadhurst PR.

Jeffery's boys' school   (F: 1791. Rs: 1791, 1793)
Richard Jeffery advertised the opening of his boys' school on 3 October 1791, offering 'writing in all the various hands, and every branch of polite literature, Arithmetic both vulgar and decimal, the Extraction of Roots, Mensuration of Superficies and Solids, Geography, Geometry, plain and oblique Trigonometry, Algebra, and every part of the Mathematics. The English Grammar, also the Rudiments of the Greek and Latin Tongues, will be taught upon easy terms.'[1]

In 1793, under the heading 'DEFAMATION', he offered a reward of 10 guineas for bringing to justice 'he, she, or they, the authors, abettors, or propagators, of the... vile, malicious, and diabolical scandal' that had slandered his character 'to the prejudice of his reputation, as an instructor of youth, and injury of his business.'[2]
[*Richard Jeffery*]
1. *SWA* 26.9.91.   2. *SWA* 9.9.93.

Mrs Dan's school   (R: 1796)
Mary Dan, schoolmistress, died in 1796. She was the wife of John Dan (perhaps the John Dann, schoolmaster of Bexhill free school from 1776 to 1789) and she probably kept a dame school.[1]   [*Mary Dan*]
1. Wadhurst PR.

WALBERTON   1724: 49 families   1801: pop. 502

Charity school   (F: 1733. Rs: 1733- into 19c)
John Nash, by will dated 24 May 1732, left to the churchwardens and overseers and their successors, a newly-built house with garden in Walberton, and the means to keep it in repair, for the use of a schoolmaster, and also an annuity of £12 arising from his estates in Walberton, for the education of poor children of the parish.[1] The school was operating in 1733, when at the visitation the churchwardens reported a free school with a revenue of £12 pa 'with a very good House & Garden', though 'It is not as yet Governed and ye Revenue imployed According to the will of ye Donor'. Charles Martin and Ann Rewell were teachers, and the schoolmaster 'comes to Church Himself and Causes his Schoolers also.

He sometimes Doth Instruct His Scholers in ye Church Catechism.'[2]   The school and schoolmaster (of 'good Life' and 'diligent') were recorded at the visitations in 1742, 1758, 1765, 1769 and 1772. At the last, it was noted that there were 12 children.[3] About 1780, the house was pulled down and another was appropriated to the school. By 1819 there were 18 children at the school, 7 boys and 11 girls, taught reading, writing and arithmetic by the schoolmaster and his wife, with the vicar catechising the children, with others, during Lent.[4]
[Charles Martin, Ann Rewell]

1. *EP2* (1819), 185.   2. WSRO Ep.I/22/1.   3. ibid.   4. *EP2* (1819), 185-6.

WALDRON   1724: 87 families   1801: pop. 752

Charity school   (R: 1713)

In November 1713 Edward Sawyer of Mayfield advised the SPCK that there was a charity school at Waldron.[1] The school was shown in the SPCK annual *Account of the Charity-Schools* from 1714 to 1724, and by implication (from 1725 only the county totals were given, with notes of any additional schools) to at least 1740; but as there is no change at all in the Sussex totals of schools and scholars from 1730 to 1740, the later lists must be regarded as suspect. (In 1730 Thomas Cox in *Magna Britannia* mentions the school, but he appears to be copying from the SPCK list.[2])

1. SPCK ALB v.4, 3756.   2. Cox, T., pub. *Magna Britannia* (1730), 566.

Sunday school   (F: 1786. R: 1788)

The Sunday school at Waldron, established about February 1786, was one of the first in the county. By February 1788 the school had 134 children, aged from 7 to 16, both boys and girls, of whom 100+ would be present on any one Sunday - a very large number for any school of the period, but especially for a village school. It was supported by public subscriptions, which not only covered the expense of a master, books for the children and other incidental charges, but also enabled 15 to 20 children to be sent to a day school throughout the year. This last extended use of the funds is of interest, since it goes far beyond any mere observance of 'the Lord's day'. A correspondent from Waldron, writing in 1788, made a number of shrewd points about the Sunday school. He countered criticism of the educational value of such a school:

> As to that specious objection which some have made, that young persons instructed but <u>one day</u> in seven are not likely even to learn to read, I am happy to have it in my power to lay a-side, as futile and fallacious; for I aver there are at this time several at our Sunday-school, that did not know so much as the letters when they first entered, who are now able to read decently, and <u>without any other assistance</u>.

The writer noted the positive interaction between children at the school and their parents:

> Besides, when children have books given to them, and have the <u>name</u> of going to school, their parents will do all in their power to instruct them, when at the same time, but for the Sunday-school, they would not, of themselves, have taken the trouble of teaching them a <u>single letter</u>.

The effects on the parents went further than this:

> Our Sunday-school has not only been a means of instructing the children to read, and giving <u>them</u> an idea of Morality and Religion, but even their <u>parents</u>, who before were too apt to spend the sabbath in sloth and idleness, and sometimes in riot and intemperance, have since the commencement of this laudable institution, been pretty regular in their attendance at public worship.

The writer saw the purpose of Sunday schools as 'to rescue the children of the poor from ignorance, idleness, and vice, and to instruct them in the duties of morality and religion... to lead them, by a pious and moral conduct, to happiness on earth, and to everlasting glory and felicity in the world to come'.[1]

1. *SWA* 11.2.88.

Day school/Waters' school   (Rs: 1788, 1790, 1792, 1795- into 19c)
The subscriptions to the Sunday school, which was started in 1786, were so liberal that it was found possible, in addition to the Sunday school, to send 15 to 20 children to a day school throughout the year. This report was given in February 1788, so there was a day school in the parish then.[1]

John Waters, 'Schoolmaster & Vestry Clerk many years', was buried in 1820. Summary churchwarden accounts[2] show very many payments to him from 1787, and he was referred to as 'schoolmaster' three times in 1790. It seems very likely that he kept the day school referred to above. Waters was also governor of the workhouse; he is referred to as 'Governor' in 1788, 1792 and 1796: large payments made to him (eg. one of £76 2s 8d in 1789, of £106 12s 9d in 1791, of £69 10s 9d in 1799) almost certainly relate to the work-house. (In this same capacity he made several small payments to the parish - for shirting, sheeting, tire, and a number 'for his son's board'.) In 1792 and 1795 he received payments specifically for schooling; these were probably for schooling pauper children at his school, rather than for any teaching at the Sunday school (see Parish schooling below).   [*John Waters*]

1. *SWA* 11.2.88.   2. ESRO PAR 499/9/1.

Parish schooling   (Rs: 1792, 1795, 1798)
Summary churchwarden accounts[1] occasionally identify payments for schooling, indicating that the parish, sometimes at least, paid for the schooling of pauper children (apart from the Sunday school - see above - and the children sent to a day school on the surplus of the Sunday school subscriptions).

On 9 April 1792 John Waters (see his school above) was paid 3s for 'School pr Bill', and on 1 October that year 6s 8d for the same; on 6 April 1795 he was paid 17s 10d for 'School'g'. From at least 1794 to 1799 John Russell (he was an overseer in 1797) was paid 2s 6d a week for keeping Sarah Elliott (eg. 1 September 1795, 'Mr Russell to keeping Sarah Elliott from Easter to Mich's 26 weeks at 2s 6d - £3.5.0.'); the payment to him on 2 October 1798 was 'for keeping Elliott's Girl 25 Weeks & Schooling - £3.11.8': ie. £3 2s 6d for keep, 9s 2d for schooling. A payment to him of £3 11s on 15 March 1799, 'for Elliotts Girl', likewise perhaps included some extra above keep, possibly for schooling.

1. ESRO PAR 499/9/1.

[Russell's school?]   (R: 1798?)
In 1798 John Russell received payment from the parish for a child's schooling (see Parish schooling above); he may have kept a school. [*John Russell?*]

WARBLETON   1724: about 120 families 1801: pop. 908

Charity school   (Rs: 1799, 1800)
In February 1799 the following advertisement appeared:

FREE SCHOOL AT WARBLETON, IN
SUSSEX.
WANTED,
At Lady-day, 1799,
A MAN and his WIFE, who can produce good

> characters, and are properly qualified to instruct the
> scholars of both sexes in all the different branches of
> common and useful learning.
> Enquire of Mr. HAWES, at Warbleton aforesaid.[1]

Two years later there was another such vacancy: an advertisement by the parish in
December 1800 for a man and his wife to superintend the management of the poor in the
workhouse, 'At Lady-day next', included the following:

> And another MAN and his WIFE also wanted, at the
> same time, as Master and Mistress of the Free School,
> at Warbleton aforesaid, to instruct the youth of both
> sexes in common and useful learning, and needlework.
> Enquire of the Churchwardens and Overseers of
> Warbleton aforesaid.[2]

There was clearly a free school in the parish at that time, for both boys and girls; there does
not appear to be any record of any endowment for such a school and it was almost certainly
a subscription school, managed by the churchwardens and overseers.

1. *SWA* 11.2.99.   2. *SWA* 15.12.1800.

WARMINGHURST (WORMINGHURST)   1724: no. of families not entered
                                                                    1801: pop.112

No 18th-century schooling traced.

WARNHAM   1724: 70 or so families   1801: pop. 680

Dame schools   (R: 1758)
At the 1758 visitation the churchwardens reported: 'No School but Old Women'.[1] So more
than one dame school then. (See also other specific dame schools below.)
1. WSRO Ep.I/22/1.

Dame Willard's school   (Rs: 1773, 1777-88)
In the diary of John Baker, a solicitor of the Inner Temple who was then 61 and living in
Horsham, there is the following entry for 27 December 1773:

> Sat near half an hour on the bridge where usually go in summer. Coming
> by mill, man catching rats, which were driven out of the bank by a ferret
> with dogs who seized them in the water. Going to turnpike, met two boys,
> one carrying bag to mill - sensible but clownish boy - said he was ten years
> old, went to one Dame Willard's at Warnham, he living a mile further, to
> school. She had about thirty scholars, 2d a week the readers, did not know
> how much the writers, of which some few whom the widow taught herself,
> and had no maid, only a daughter Kitty.[1]

'Dame Willard' was Jane Willard, wife of John; she was not a widow - she died in 1798,
and John in 1801. The daughter, Kitty, was aged 15 in 1773. It is clear that this was a
substantial dame school, with its 30 children, and teaching writing as well as reading.

Dame Willard also received many payments from the parish for teaching poor
children from 1777 to 1788.[2] These were paid regularly (with some hiatuses) every two
months, and ranged from 5s 3d to 15s 5d. At the peak (January/February 1779, when she
received the 15s 5d 'for Scouling two months') she would have been teaching, at 2d a week,
about 12 parish children. The annual payments could be substantial, but their variability
across the years could have proved difficult if Willard had not also kept a private school:

				£ s d
Calendar year:	1778	(first full year)	Total payments:	3.16. 9½
	1779			4. 6. 8½
	1780			3.10. 2
	1781			2. 8. 7
	1782			1.17. 0
	1783	(no payments till September)		0.18. 5
	1784	(payments now made monthly)		3.17. 8
	1785			4. 8. 7½
	1786			2. 2.10½

(apparently no parish schooling paid for in the church
years 1786-7, 1787-8)
1788 (the parish schooling taken over by another
in midsummer; Willard then aged 65)   0.12. 7

[*Jane Willard*]
1. *SAC* **52**, 62.   2. WSRO Par 203/31/1.

Parish schooling   (Rs: 1777-89)

The parish paid for the schooling of pauper children ('the Children'/'the workhose Children'/'the parish Children') from April 1777 to June 1789, except for the church years 1786-7 and 1787-8.[1]   For the amounts paid, see Dame Willard's school above and Dame Botting's school below: for most of this period the parish appears to have been paying for about 10-12 children, the number falling to 7-8 in the later years. [*Jane Willard, Pollos (Molly) Botting*]
1. WSRO Par 203/31/1.

Dame Botting's school   (Rs: 1786-9)

'Pollos' (Molly) Botting was paid by the parish for schooling 'the Parish Children' in 1786 and from July 1788 to June 1789. She received 4s in April 1786 (perhaps when Jane Willard was ill: see her school above); the parish apparently did not pay for such schooling in the church years 1786-7 and 1787-8; in the summer of 1788 she took over the schooling of the parish children from Jane Willard, receiving c.5s a month, the last payment by the parish for this purpose being made in June 1789.[1] Botting might well have kept a private dame school, as Willard had done, besides teaching the parish children. [*Pollos (Molly) Botting*]
1. WSRO Par 203/31/1.

Harvey's school?   (Rs: 1798-1802)

Between the ages of six and ten, the poet Shelley, born at Warnham 4 August 1792, was sent to a day school run by the vicar of Warnham. Richard Holmes, his biographer, noted:

> He went each morning down the lane to the vicarage carrying a bundle of
> books under his arm, and he learnt the rudiments of Latin and Greek. His
> father liked him to learn passages of Latin poetry, and he would recite them
> by heart in the drawing-room after tea, acting out the meaning with his
> arms. His sisters Elizabeth and Mary watched Bysshe in silent admiration,
> amazed not only that he could remember so many words but that he could
> show by the expressions on his face and the waving of his arms that he
> knew what they meant. His mother liked him to recite the comic mock-
> melancholy of Gray's lines on The Cat and the Goldfish...[1]

Richard Harvey was vicar from May 1798 to May 1805, and was presumably Shelley's schoolmaster.[2]   [*Richard Harvey?*]

1. Holmes, R. *Shelley: the Pursuit* (1974: Penguin edn. 1987), 1987 edn., 2, 4. Holmes gives the vicar as Edwards, a Welshman; but Edwards was not instituted until July 1805. The 'home' description is from Hellen Shelley (Percy Bysshe's sister, born when he was seven) in Hogg, T.J. *The Life of Percy Bysshe Shelley* (1858), 1933 edn., Wolfe, H., ed., I, 23.   2. CI.

WARNINGCAMP - see LYMINSTER

WARTLING   1724: about 100 families 1801: pop. 858
No 18th-century schooling traced.

WASHINGTON   1724: about 70 families   1801: pop. 512
School   (R: 1737)
The visitation return for 1737 recorded one schoolmaster, of 'good Life' and 'diligent', who came to church and caused his scholars to come.[1]
1. WSRO Ep.I/22/1.

WEST BLATCHINGTON   1724: no. of families   1801: pop. 0
                                     not entered

Not surprisingly, no 18th-century schooling traced.

WESTBOURNE   1724: about 130 families 1801: pop. 1,549
Schools (Rs: 1733, 1755, 1758, 1765)
At the 1733 visitation: 'We have one that teacheth Scool. He is [of 'good Life' and 'diligent']   He doth [come to Church and cause his Scholars to come]   He doth [instruct his Scholars in the Church Catechism]' A schoolmaster, of 'good Life' and 'diligent', who came to church and caused his scholars to come, was also reported at the visitations in 1755, 1758 and 1765.[1]
1. WSRO Ep.I/22/1.

[Other schoolmaster?]

> [George Waliston] was a schoolmaster at Westbourne in 1689, but it is not known
> if he continued there into the 18th century. (WSRO Ep.I/17/33, f 152r)

WEST CHILTINGTON   1724: 80 families   1801: pop. 558
Charity school   (F: c.1634. Rs: through 18c)
William Smith, of Angmering, in 1634 by will bequeathed £250, to be laid out in the purchase of lands, £4 of the rents from which were to go to the poor people of Chiltington, and the remainder of the rents, of £5 or more, to maintain a licensed schoolmaster, 'for and towards the breeding, teaching and education of all youth, as well poor as rich, either male or female, then born or to be born in Chiltington.' The schoolhouse, used through the 18th century, carried the date of 1635, and was improved in 1798 by the schoolmaster at a cost of £90 (£20 was covered by subscriptions, the rest being paid by himself).[1] At the 1724 visitation, the benefaction of a school 'for the Use of the poor' was recorded, the sum paid to the master being £9.[2] By 1737 the revenue of the school had risen to £12 pa, and by the 1770s to £16 pa.[3] Schoolmasters are recorded in 1723 (Nathaniel Wilmer licensed), 1729, 1742, 1758, 1775, 1779, 1788 (Richard Lewry licensed).[4] In 1742 it was noted that there were nine children at the school; in 1819 there were about 50, chiefly children of poor parents, with about 20 other paying pupils from neighbouring parishes.[5] (In 1819 the income of the charity was up to £47, but only £20 went to the schoolmaster, £4 going to

the poor under Smith's will, and the rest towards the costs of a Chancery case a few years earlier.[6]) [*Nathaniel Wilmer, Richard Lewry*]

1. *EP2* (1819), 157; WSRO Ep.I/26/3, 18-19. 2. WSRO Ep.I/26/3, 18-19. 3. WSRO Ep.I/22/1. 4. ibid; WSRO Ep.I/1/11 (22.6.23); Wadey index at SAS, citing CCC Diary (for 1788). 5. WSRO Ep.I/22/1; *EP2* (1819), 159. 6. *EP2* (1819), 158.

WEST DEAN (East Sussex)   1724: 8 families ['4 in   1801: pop. 88
West Dean and 4 in Exceet
(formerly a distinct Parish
with a Church in it)']

No 18th-century schooling traced.

WEST DEAN (West Sussex)   1724: 55 families   1801: pop. 510

Village school   (R: 1733)
At the 1733 visitation there was no free or charity school, but: 'The Minister teaches School at ye request of ye Parish but is willing either to throw it up; or to take a Licence if Your Lordship insists upon it. He diligently instructs his Scholars in the Church Catechism.'[1] Thomas Leyland, the minister, was instituted to the vicarage in 1728 (he was also curate of Shipley and rector of Singleton); he was vicar for 36 years, dying in 1763.   [*Thomas Leyland*]

1. WSRO Ep.I/22/1.

Dame schools/petty schools   (Rs: 1758, 1762, 1775)
From the visitation returns:[1]
> 1758:   There were 'School Dames' in the parish, who taught their scholars the catechism.
> 1762:   'There is a Schoolmaster, a poor unfortunate man from Chichester but we believe He is pretty Sober & diligent & pretty well answers ye three following Enquiries [ie. Is he of 'good Life' and 'diligent'? Does he come to Church and cause his Scholars to come? Does he teach them the Catechism?]'
> 1775:   There was a schoolmaster in the parish, 'the Clerk of the parish': he was of 'good Life' and 'diligent', came to church and caused his scholars to come, and taught them the catechism. (This was John Humphrey.[2])

[*John Humphrey*]

1. WSRO Ep.I/22/1.   2. Peckham, W.D., intro. to transcript of PR, citing 'Clerk's waste book', WSRO Par 65/9/1.

WESTFIELD   1724: 78 families   1801: pop. 306

No 18th-century schooling traced.

WEST FIRLE (FIRLE)   1724: 34 families   1801: pop. 494

Charity schooling   (Rs: 1793- into 19c)
The 3rd Viscount Gage's account book[1] shows that he supported a charity school at West Firle from at least 1793 and into the 19th century. Originally for 10 boys, it seems from the sums he paid to have been enlarged towards the end of the century, and that possibly he also supported a Sunday school there (see below). The relevant entries are:
1793   Dec 31   Thomas Mockett Schooling Ten Boys   3.10.0
1794   Dec 24   Thos Mockett schooling 10 Boys   3.10.0

1796	Jul 25	Mocketts School Bill	1. 2.0
1797	Jul 12	Hasemans School Bill	1.15.3
	Nov 28	Haseman Schooling of Boys and Church attendance with them £3.18.0 a/c 3.7.3	7. 5.3
	Dec 28	The Church Children	10.0
	Dec 30	Pierces Bill for Childrens Schooling in 97	7. 5.0
1798	Dec 31	Haseman for Childrens Schooling 98	8.18.0
1799	October 8	Heaseman Schooling the Boys	8.18.0
	Dec 25	Haseman Schooling Boys due Xmas 99	8.18.0
1800	Apr 9/18/19	Haseman	3. 3.0
1802	Apr 19	School Boys	3. 3.0

[*Thomas Mockett, Haseman (Heaseman), (Samuel?) Pierce*]

1. ESRO SAS/G/ACC 741.

[Sunday school?]   (R: 1797?)

The reference to 'The Church Children' in the 3rd Viscount Gage's accounts, and the amounts paid by him for schooling in 1797 and later (see <u>Charity schooling</u> above), suggest that he may well have supported a Sunday school in the parish. It is possible that he also supported one in Alciston [qv] (and in 1793 he subscribed £2 2s to the East Meon Sunday school, in Hampshire).[1]

1. ESRO SAS/G/ACC 741.

WEST GRINSTEAD   1724: about 106 families 1801: pop. 939

<u>Charity schooling/dame schools/petty schools</u>   (Rs: through 18c)

About 1644, William Dowlin, curate of the parish, lodged £41 19s with friends, directing in his sickness and in his will that after the charges of his funeral and other dues were paid, they should keep the remainder for a year and a month; and if by then there were no lawful demands on it, they should dispose of it to some charitable use. In 1652 an annuity of £2 was purchased, payable out of certain lands called Cucklets in Thakeham, and was settled in trust for the payment of poor children's schooling in West Grinstead, by the appointment of the minister of the parish.[1] Accounts relating to this charity from 1698 to 1730 are included in the parish register.[2] Until Lady day 1713, the income is shown as a rent, and tax is deducted from it; from Lady day 1713, a full annuity of £2 was received and this continued into the 19th century. Although the sum disbursed in 'schooling ye poor Children' was small, the accounts are of interest in the large number of different people who were paid for teaching poor children: in some years, three or four were paid. Some or all of these probably kept dame or petty schools, to which the poor children were sent.

Dates of payments		
(Richard Penfold's wife)	(1698)	
Goody Somersol	1698-1704	
Goody Hews	1699, 1703, 1709	
Probably same as Widow Hews	1715-18	
(Goody Howard)	(1700)	
Henry Aylin	1700-3	
Goody Trower	1701-5	
Widow Slater	1701-2	(paid for 2 children at 2d a week for 71 weeks)
Goody Flote	1704-7	
Goody Hodges	1705	
Perhaps same as Goody Hodges	1725	

*Stiles	1706	
*West	1707	
*Moses Gratwick	1708	
Mrs Web	1709	(paid for schooling 6 poor children for 2 weeks, then 3 for 27 weeks)
Henry Vaus	1710-14	(received quarterly payments, and appears to have taught 7-8 children throughout)
Ann Moor	1717-18	
John Hews wife	1718-23	
Goody Stringer	1719	
Challoner's wife	1721-7	(probably wife of Richard: the wife of John Challoner also received payments at same time)
Burtenshaw	1724	(NB: payment for 'writing')
Goody Snashal	1724	
Buttinger	1724-5	
Goody Lineger	1725	
James Stile's wife	1725	
Herriot	1725-6	
Goody Challoner, wife of John	1727	
Bricknell	1727-9	(probably taught 4-5 poor children)
Sarah Whisky	1727	
Mary Botting	1728	
Goody Flint	1728-9	
Wife of W. Woolven	1730	
Widow Whitebread	1730	
[...] Lanaway	1730	

* Perhaps received by husbands on behalf of their wives.

At the 1742 visitation: 'We only have little schools... Our Minister has forty shillings a year to put out poor children wch he employs to Learn them to read.' In 1758 the churchwardens answered 'Yes' to the question asking if there were any unlicensed teachers in the parish.[3]

See also Roman Catholic dame schools below.

[For names of schoolmasters/mistresses, see list above]

1. *EP*2 (1819), 165-6; Horsfield, *Sussex*, II, 253.   2. WSRO Par 95/1/1/3.   3. WSRO Ep.I/22/1.

Roman catholic charity dame schools   (Rs: 1727-59)

From at least 1727 until her death in 1754, Elizabeth Hayes kept a school for Catholic children. (In 1727 there were 24 Catholic children in the parish, from 18 households.) She was financed - or was supposed to be - by the Caryll family.   John Baptist Caryll continually failed to pay her salary. Fr Henry Heighton wrote to him, urging him to help 'Madame Hayes, the pious schoolmistress, who spends her life teaching the poor children of West Grinstead and has always been with the Caryll family. Her needs are very great. For 2 years she has received nothing...' In 1754 Fr Francis Short reminded him that 'Mrs. Hayes salary becomes due on Lady Day. As she now depends entirely on your goodness and charity, she hopes you will be so good as to send her an order for the money, to prevent the many miseries she must otherwise necessarily fall into. The rent of the house she is in, & in which she continues to teach, is five and forty shillings a year, the Cheapest to be come at; and if not paid when due, Mrs. Hopkins will infallibly turn her out of Doors.' This

264 Schools

letter was unanswered after a month, and Elizabeth Hayes wrote to Caryll herself requesting the payment of her £10 pa. She died a few months later, and the school was carried on by 'her poor servant Kitty Flutter who had lived with her many years, on very small wages... & indeed latterly since she [Mrs Hayes] grew so infirm ye cheif support of the School.' In 1758 Kitty Flutter wrote to John Baptist Caryll (who had agreed to her keeping on the school on the same footing that Mrs Hayes had it before) to say that her salary was two years overdue and that she was 'in great Necessity'; and she wrote again in 1759 to claim her £10 salary. The school had probably closed before the last of the Carylls left England for France in 1767.[1] [*Elizabeth Hayes, Kitty Flutter*]

1. McCann, T.J., 'West Grinstead: a centre of Catholicism in Sussex 1671-1814', *SAC* **124**, 206-7; Caplan, N., 'The Sussex Catholics c.1660-1800', *SAC* **116**, 28.

Workhouse school   (R: 1794)
In an inventory of the workhouse, made on 4 April 1794, one of the rooms is identified as 'the Schooll Room', suggesting that there was probably some sort of school there for pauper children.[1]

1. WSRO Par 95/37/16.

WESTHAM   1724: 49 families   1751: pop. 293*
                                                          1801: pop. 560
* Includes 44 boys under 16 and 34 girls under 14 (John Nicholl's 'Exact list of the inhabitants of Westham, July 1751', in Budgen MS at SAS, v.117, f 43).

Charity school   (Rs: 1736-41, 1743, 1783-85)
The Cavendish family supported a charity school at Westham, paying a schoolmaster £5 pa for teaching (in 1736) nine poor children, and (in 1784) eight poor children. Such payments are recorded 1736-41, in 1743,, and in 1784 (for the year from 25 March 1783, 'on a/c of Charitable Gift of Lady Cavendish').[1] The school was kept in the vestry room of the parish church of Westham, and the poor children were taught reading, writing and accounts.[2] All the payments so far traced were made to schoolmasters, who probably kept private schools as well. (See also PEVENSEY.)   [*John Pike, John Serjeant, Joseph Grover, Richard Thompson.* When Thompson died in 1785 *Edward Barnard* was recommended as master by the churchwardens, overseers, bailiff and a number of parishioners of Westham, while *John Christian* was recommended by the minister (John Preston, curate) and other parishioners for teaching 'the Poor children in Pevensey and Westham'.[3]]

1. Budgen MS at SAS, v.129, 32, 33, 36, 39, 41; v.86, f 32; v.119, f 9.   2. ibid, v.117, f 6.   3. ibid.

WESTHAMPNETT   1801: pop. 400

At Goodwood House:

Schoolmasters / tutors

Jones. When Henriette Ann Le Clerc, reputed to be the 3rd Duke of Richmond's illegitimate daughter by Madame de Cambis, was brought over from France in 1778, then aged 5 or 6, to be brought up at Goodwood House, she was put into the charge of Mr Jones. He was presumably her tutor. (Reese, M.M. *Goodwood's Oak* (1987), 209)

Monsieur (Rev Mr) Tournay was paid £60 pa by the Duke of Richmond for teaching the Lennox boys at Goodwood House from 1797 to 1801. (WSRO Goodwood MS 247)

Rev W.J.A.Vincent was paid £200 pa by the Duke of Richmond in respect of the

Lennox boys being educated by the Duke at Goodwood House. The first quarterly payment (£83 9s) was made April-June 1800, and was followed by payments of £50 salary each quarter through to 1801. The boys also had another master (see Tournay above) and a writing master; Vincent's duties are not specified in the accounts but he was almost certainly tutor to them. (WSRO Goodwood MS 247)

[Writing, dancing, music, singing and Italian masters visiting Goodwood House are shown under CHICHESTER.]

Schoolmistresses

Mrs Shaw was paid £1 6s in 1797 by the Duke of Richmond for 'Children's Schooling'. The children were probably from the Goodwood estate. (WSRO Goodwood MS 247)

Mary Blesard was paid £2 18s 4d in 1798 and 9s 9d in 1799 by the Duke of Richmond 'for Schooling Children', almost certainly from the Goodwood estate. (WSRO Goodwood MS 247) After the death of the Duchess in 1796, she reputedly became the Duke's mistress and the mother of three daughters by him. From 1797, then aged 29 and described as a housekeeper, she received an annuity of £50; in his will of 1806, the Duke left her an annuity of £450. (See Schedule 2)

Miss Richardson was paid £1 3s 10d in 1799, as 'School Mistress', by the Duke of Richmond. This was perhaps for teaching children from the Goodwood estate, and (from her description as schoolmistress in the accounts) she probably kept a school in the locality. (WSRO Goodwood MS 247) [Richardson & Smart had a girls' boarding school in Chichester (Rs: 1793, 1797) and Richardson E.M. & F. had one there in 1811.]

Martha Tupper was paid by the Duke of Richmond for 'Schooling Mary Colbert', receiving three quarterly payments of 5s 5d and one of 3s 4d, the first being paid July-September 1799 and the last October-December 1800. (WSRO Goodwood MS 247)

WEST HOATHLY (HOADLY) 1724: 100 families   1801: pop. 794

Burjerys' boys' boarding school   (R: 1752)
In 1752 Bristow Burjery senior and junior, of West Hoathly, advertised that they taught '*Reading, Writing, Arithmetic* (both Vulgar and Decimal, in all its Varieties) *Mensuration* and *Algebra*', and boarded youth at reasonable rates.[1]   [*Bristow Burjery sen, Bristow Burjery jun*]
1. *SWA* 24.2.52.

WEST ITCHENOR   1724: 8 families   1801: pop. 161

No 18th-century schooling traced.

WESTMESTON (WESTMYNTON)   includes EAST CHILTINGTON

	1724		1801
Westmeston	31 families		pop. 205
East Chiltington	25		163
	56		368

Charity school/schooling   (Rs: 1716- into 19c)
In April 1716 Anthony Springett, at Lewes, advised the SPCK, 'There are 3 Parish's where
the Children are all taught to read & their Catechism Viz. Westmeston cum Chiltington.
Plumpton & Street'.[1]   In 1722 he reported, from Plumpton, 'That the Schools in that
Neighbourhood still continue in a flourishing Condition tho' there are grievous Complaints
against them as the Occasion of the want of Servants in those parts'.[2]   The school at
'Westmeston cum Chiltington' was in the SPCK annual charity school list of 1724, and by
implication from the county totals of schools (all that were published thereafter, unless new
schools were added, in which event they were detailed) at least until 1740; but as there was
no change at all in the county total 1730-40, the later lists must be regarded as suspect.
      Under the will of Anthony Springett, who had the living of Westmeston at his
death in 1735, he left an Exchequer annuity of £13 to the Plumpton, Westmeston and
Chiltington schools. The annuity expired in 1806.[3]   John Marten, by will dated 1 October
1797, left £4 6s 8d pa, arising from premises, to 'support a school in the hamlet of
Chiltington' when Mr Springett's charity to the hamlet of Chiltington 'shall cease to be paid'.
Of this sum, 6s 8d was to be laid out in books for the use of the school. By 1819 Marten's
bequest was being paid to the rector of Westmeston, who was paying £4 4s pa to a
schoolmistress in the adjoining parish of Plumpton for teaching eight children (boys or girls)
in reading and needlework.   The remainder, with some addition from a charity at
Westmeston, was laid out in books.   Thus, though there was provision for schooling poor
children, there was no school at East Chiltington by 1819; nor was there one then at
Westmeston.

1. SPCK ALB v.6, 4772.   2. SPCK ALB v.11, 7053.   3. *SAC* **122**, 143; a confirmatory receipt, made c.1752
but relating to the receipt in January 1737 of two years' annuities (£26), signed by Edward Wilson, is included in
'The free-School Book of Brighthelmston', at Brighton Library, SB 379 FRE.   4. *EP*1 (1819), 225, 240.

WEST STOKE   1724: 10 families   1801: pop. 76

No 18th-century schooling traced. At the 1762 visitation: [any unlicensed teachers?] -'not
one'. [Is your schoolmaster... &c?] - 'no schoolmaster in ye Parish'. [Any charity school?] -
'none. I wish we had a School to Instruct Children. Not one. nor never did.'[1]
1. WSRO Ep.I/22/1.

WEST TARRING   1717: about 100 houses   1801: pop. 487

Writing school   (Rs: 1700, 1703)
In January 1700 John Cole signed the subscription book, and in November 1703 William
Stiles did so, in both cases '... to Teach a Writing Schooll at West Tarring'.[1]   [*John Cole,
William Stiles*]
1. WSRO Ep.I/3/3.

Charity school   (Rs: 1712, 1714)
John Strype, rector of West Tarring 1711-37 (he was also rector of Low Leyton in Essex)
maintained at his expense a charity school there in 1712 for 12 boys;[1] in 1714 the school
was for 12 boys and girls.[2] This was continued by Dr Jeremiah Milles, rector 1746-79 (he
was succeeeded by his son Richard Milles, 1779-1823).[3] Such a school probably continued
through the century, for in the early 19th century there was a free school supported by
payments from rectors: in 1804 it was attended by 10 children.[4] [*Thomas Emery?* - see his
school below]
1. SPCK ALB v.3, 3156; *Secker*, 232.   2. SPCK ALB v.5, 4129.   3. *Secker*, 232; *Al. Oxon.*.
4. *VCH* vi, I, 279.

Emery's school   (R: 1735)
In his will dated 23 January 1735, Thomas Emery was a schoolmaster of West Tarring.[1]
Perhaps master of the charity school above [qv]: if so, he would almost certainly have had
his own school as well. He died in 1742.[2]
1. WSRO STA I/12 p. 115.   2. PR.

[Phillips' boys' boarding school]   (R: 1802)
In January 1802 N. Phillips advertised his school at West-Tarring, where 'Young Gentlemen
are boarded and educated in the ENGLISH LANGUAGE, WRITING and ARITHMETIC'.[1]
Perhaps this school was operating in 1800. (This was perhaps the 'Tarring Academy' -
though the curriculum seems modest for an 'academy' - the writing book of one of whose
pupils, dated December 1803, has survived.[2])   [*N. Phillips*]
1. *SWA* 11.1.1802.   2. WSRO Add MS 36,773.

WEST THORNEY   1801: pop. 71

No 18th-century schooling traced. (In 1775, specifically 'no School in the Parish' .[1])
1. WSRO Ep.I/22/1.

WEST WITTERING   1724: about 70 families   1801: pop. 396

Charity schooling   (F: 1712. Rs: 1712- into 19c)
By will dated 16 February 1702 Oliver Whitby bequeathed his properties in West Wittering
to a trust, to establish and maintain a school in Chichester for 12 boys, four of whom were
to be from West Wittering, and to pay for six poor children of West Wittering to be taught
to read and to buy them necessary books.
        See CHICHESTER for the Oliver Whitby school there. The boys, whose parents
were not to be dissenters and who were exempt from the poor tax, were boarded and clothed
(having blue gowns) and were taught writing, arithmetic and the mathematics. (In 1792,
the trustees, advertising for a master, stated that preference would be given to one who had
a practical knowledge of navigation, and was capable of teaching it.)   Oliver Whitby died
in February 1703, but the school was not opened until 1712, at 16 West Street, since the
trustees needed first to build up capital to finance it. The school continued into the 19th
century.
        In 1712 also was recorded the first payments for teaching the six poor children at
West Wittering: in the trust accounts with the parsonage, the vicar was given a credit of
£1 14s paid to Goody Light for the schooling of six children for the year, and also 7s 11d
for books. Payments to Goody Light continued until 1721, after which payment was made
to 'the School Dame', often named, at 1s per week. In fact, from at least 1741 until the end
of the century (there being just two half-years when no payment appears to have been
made), £1 3s was paid for the six months to midsummer and £1 6s for the six months to
Christmas - or 2d a week per child for a 49-week school year. On occasion, the accounts
mention that the number of children taught was six, and that they were taught to read.
Visitation returns reported this as a 'free school' in 1758, 1762 and 1775, and in 1775 noted:
'Six boys instructed by a poor woman at the above Salary [£2 8s pa]'. By 1819 the six
children were all poor girls, and they were taught reading and needlework.[1]
[For masters of the Oliver Whitby school, Chichester, see CHICHESTER. *Goody Light,
Martha Newell, Mary Young, Mary Voaks*]
1. WSRO E 35D/3/1; *SAC* **125**, 262; *EP2* (1819), 156, 186; WSRO Ep.I/22/1.

WHATLINGTON   1724: about 23 families   1801: pop. 211

Charity schooling   (Rs: (from c.1738?), c.1795- into 19c)
According to the returns made to parliament in 1786, Edward Theobald in 1738 left £20 for teaching poor children of the parish, vested in the minister and parish officers. And about 1795, the incumbent paid 'an aged woman' for schooling two or three charity children. By the 19th century an annual rent-charge of £1 10s was applied to sending as many children to dame schools as funds permitted. It would seem, therefore, that the small charity did survive, from about 1738 through the 18th century.[1]

1. *EP2* (1819), 186; *EP30* (1837), 680-1.

WIGGONHOLT   1724: 7 families   1801: pop. 42
No 18th-century schooling traced.

WILLINGDON   1724: 28 families   1801: pop. 347
No 18th-century schooling traced.

WILMINGTON   1724: 35 families   1801: pop. 236

Capper's boys' school   (Rs: 1790, 1795)
In a report on a journey he made from Lewes to Eastbourne in November 1790, Stebbing Shaw, referring to Wilmington Vicarage, noted: 'In this commodious situation Mr. Capper receives a few pupils upon a very genteel and liberal plan.'[1] The winter of 1794-5 was a time of great distress among the poor, when many parishes raised subscriptions to subsidise bread for the poor. In February 1795 *SWA* reported:

> We hear that the Rev. Mr. Capper, of Wilmington, and the young gentlemen under his care, have raised a contribution among themselves to supply every poor family in that parish with a certain quantity of butcher's meat, weekly, in proportion to their numbers, at two-pence the pound under the market-price, for several weeks to come, so that they have now the benefit of obtaining the two chief articles of life, BREAD and MEAT, at a reduced and moderate rate, during this inclement season.[2]

Capper was vicar of Wilmington from 1779 to his death in 1835. (For his character, see Schedule 2.)
[*James Capper*]

1. Shaw, S., 'Excursion from Lewes to Eastbourn', *The Topographer* v.3 (1791), 377.   2. *SWA* 23.2.95.

WINCHELSEA   1724: about 35 or 40 families   1801: pop. 627

Parish schooling/Hogsflesh's school?   (Rs: 1765-8)
On 30 May 1766 the Winchelsea overseers paid Mr Hogsflesh £1 10s 'for 1 Years School'g for young Bennet Sutus [= Suters?] & Sidger'. (Perhaps he was paid 2½d per week for a 48-week year for each child.) For each of the two following years (Easter 1767 to Easter 1768, and 1768-9) he was also paid £1 10s 'for a Years School'g'.[1] Hogsflesh probably kept a private school in the parish, to which the three poor boys were sent by the overseers.
[*Hogsflesh*]

1. ESRO PAR 511/31/1/1.

WISBOROUGH GREEN   1724: 120 families   1801: pop. 1,307

Petty schools/dame schools   (Rs: 1733, 1742, 1762, 1775, 1779)
Visitation returns give the following:[1]

1733: 'poor women teach the children and take what care they can in the instruction of those that are sent to them'.

1742: A schoolmaster in the parish: 'we know not' if he is of 'good Life' and 'diligent'; he came to church and caused his scholars to come, and taught them the catechism.

1762: Again a schoolmaster, who came to church and caused his scholars to come, and taught them the catechism.

1775: 'Small Schools for Reading and writing'.

1779: The churchwardens reported the curate's school (see below), 'And here are some small Schools'.

1. WSRO Ep.I/22/1.

Reynolds' school   (R: 1779)

At the 1779 visitation the churchwardens reported: 'The Curate of our Parish keeps a School for reading, writing and accompts.'[1] The curate was Morgan Reynolds, from September 1765 (when he first signed banns) to June 1781 (when he performed his last marriage there) and probably to 1784 (signed BTs 1782, 1784).[2] [*Morgan Reynolds*]

1. WSRO Ep.I/22/1.   2. Wisborough Green PR, BTs.

Parish schooling   (Rs: 1796-9)

Overseers' accounts (1784-1809)[1] show parish payments for schooling from January 1796 to March 1799. Jane Gravatt received payments totalling 16s 4d in 1796, £1 3s 3d in 1797, £1 10s 9d in 1798, and 3s in 1799. (In the last year she also received 1s for 'making a Gown'.) Dame Sherbourne was paid 1s 'for Schooling' in 1798. [*Jane Gravatt, Dame Sherbourne*]

1. WSRO Par 210/31/1.

WISTON   1724: about 20 families   1801: pop.258

School   (R: 1733)

At the 1733 visitation there was a schoolmaster in the parish, of 'good Life' and 'diligent', who came to church and caused his scholars to come, and taught them the catechism.[1]

1. WSRO Ep.I/22/1.

School   (R: c.1800)

A plan of the Old Parsonage House, dated 1801, shows a schoolhouse next to the old rectory south-east of the church.[1] This may have been a schoolhouse used by the rector for a private school (see Well's school below) but is more likely to have been the village school. An undated school list survives, giving village children at the school: from their baptisms, the date of the list is probably 1802 or 1803.[2] Since at least one of the children was born in 1789, the school was almost certainly operating by 1800. The list is interesting in that it shows equal numbers of boys and girls. There are four gaps in the list, perhaps indicating different dates of joining, or later additions. There are 21 names before the first gap, probably indicating the size of the school, 11 boys and 10 girls. The whole list comprises 29 names, 14 boys and 15 girls. The school was probably maintained by Charles Goring, who by 1819 was maintaining a school there for 50 children during the week and 58 on Sundays, the charity commissioners observing that this school admitted all the children of the poor who were capable of instruction .[3]

1. WSRO Wiston MS 5602; *VCH* vi, I, 268.   2. WSRO Par 211/25/1.   3. Sleight, J.M. *A Very Exceptional Instance* (1981), 39.

[Wells' boys' boarding school]   (R: c.1800?)

George Wells, rector of Wiston 1796-1839, at one time educated 'in his family four or six noblemen's sons of the highest rank, for which his learning and acquirements eminently qualified him.' This school had closed by 1814.[1] [*George Wells*]

1. Evans *Worthing* v.II (1814), 157.

WITHYHAM   1724: about 100 families 1801: pop. 1,074

Parish schooling   (Rs: 1744, 1746, 1747)
On 23 March 1744 the Withyham overseers paid 2s 'for schooling for Mary Mills' (for whose keep they paid). On 7 September 1746 they paid Isaac Bungard 4s 'for Instructing the Poor Boys in Singing Psalms'; and on 4 January 1747 they paid him a further 4s 'for 4 Boys Singing'.[1] [*Isaac Bungard (singing master)*]

1. ESRO PAR 512/31/1.

Boyce's school   (Rs: c.1755-66)
Thomas Burr, in *The History of Tunbridge-Wells*, published in 1766, noted that the curate of Withyham had opened a school there 'about ten or twelve years ago... which has met with great encouragement from the surrounding farmers'; Burr referred to 'the success he has met with', and recommended other curates to imitate him and add to their narrow stipends.[1] The curate was Edward Boyce, who conducted marriages at Withyham as curate from November 1754 to November 1771.[2] The schoolhouse was one of the cottages on School House Hill.[3]
  [*Edward Boyce*]

1. Burr, Thomas Benge *The History of Tunbridge-Wells* (1766), 265-6.   2. Withyham PR.   3. Sutton, C.N. *Historical Notes of Withyham, Hartfield and Ashdown Forest* (1902), 85.

WIVELSFIELD   1724: 70 families   1801: pop. 442

Charity schooling   (Rs: 1760 (or earlier)- into 19c)
Frances More of Wivelsfield, spinster, by will dated 12 December 1723, proved 3 August 1727, gave to trustees farms in Sussex and Surrey and five leasehold properties in Westminster, to be sold, and the first £100 to be raised from the sale to be laid out in the purchase of lands, and until such a purchase could be made to be placed out at interest, the interest and rents of the lands to be used to give at each Christmas £2 to poor persons of Wivelsfield, and the residue to provide a schoolmaster or dame for teaching so many poor children of Wivelsfield as they shall nominate to read well and say the Church catechism, and to buy books for the children if any surplus should remain. The lands were not purchased by the trustees until 1760 (for £95), but the schooling may well have started earlier on the basis of the interest on the £100. In 1787 the net income was £4 pa; it later rose to £5, and c.1815 to £7. In the 1790s the charity put six children to school, paying 2d a week for each and spending between £2 and £3 a year.[1]

1. *SAC* **36**, 43-4; *EP2* (1819), 187.

WOODMANCOTE   1724: about 30 families 1801: pop. 231

School (R: 1725)
Philip Shore, rector of Woodmancote from 1711 (and previously master of Cuckfield Grammar School), took private pupils. He died at Rayleigh, Essex, 6 May 1725, returning from Cambridge, where he had placed a pupil at Trinity (William Campion).[1] [*Philip Shore*]

1. Attree, F.W.T., in *SAC* **36**, 61.

[In 1804 there was a school for eight children.][1]

1. *VCH* vi, III, citing WSRO Ep.1/3/1, f 26.

WOOLAVINGTON   1724: 25 families   1801: pop. 192

No 18th-century schooling traced.

WOOLBEDING   1724: 23 families   1801: pop. 212

No 18th-century schooling traced.

WORTH   1724: about 120 families 1801: pop. 1,501

Charity school   (F: 1767. Rs: 1767- into 19c)
Timothy Shelley, by deed dated 12 February 1767, granted a rent-charge of £8 to the rector and parish officers of Worth, in trust, to pay the same to a schoolmaster (to be approved by the grantor and his heirs), to teach 16 of the poorest children of the parish to read. The charity continued into the 19th century.[1]

1. *EP2* (1819), 187.

Felbridge charity school   (F: 1783. Rs: 1783- into 19c)
In 1783 James Evelyn founded a charity school at Felbridge, at which three free places were for children from Worth, who lived within 2½ miles of the school - two boys, aged between 6 and 10, and one girl, aged between 6 and 13. They were to be taught reading, writing, arithmetic and to repeat the catechism. [For details of the school, see under EAST GRINSTEAD.]

YAPTON   1724: 48 families   1801: pop. 543

Petty/dame schools   (Rs: 1742, 1758)
At the 1742 visitation: 'Some Doe teach school without license', and there was a schoolmaster in the parish, of 'good Life' and 'diligent', who came to church and caused his scholars to come, and taught them the catechism. At the 1758 visitation, again a schoolmaster, as above. In 1762 the churchwardens reported: 'no school'.[1]

1. WSRO Ep.I/22/1.

Charity school   (F: 1767. Rs: 1767- into 19c)
Stephen Roe, of London but born in Yapton, by will dated 17 October 1766, left £1,200 3% South Sea annuities to the minister, churchwardens and overseers of the parish, on trust, that they should apply £20 pa of the interest towards educating so many poor boys and girls of the parish as they should choose (the remaining £16 of interest going to other charitable uses). The visitation return for 1769 reported that the free school had been set up in 1767, that the children were taught to read and write, and that there was a schoolmaster, of 'good Life' and 'diligent', who came to church and caused his scholars to come, and taught them the catechism. In 1772 there were 20 children in the school, as there were in 1819.[1]

1. *EP2* (1819), 188; Horsfield *Sussex* II, 115; WSRO Ep.I/22/1.

UNPLACED SCHOOLS

Harvy's boys' boarding school   (R: 1714)

In September 1714 Harvy was paid £4 5s 6d for a quarter's board and school for Nicholas Gilbert.[1] Gilbert was then eight, and his home was in Eastbourne; at Michaelmas that year he was sent to Lewes grammar school.   [*Harvy*]

1. ESRO ACC 2462/1.

Pointin's school   (R: 1731)

In May 1731 Anthony Stapley 'went to school' to Thomas Pointin 'by the week to write & read & cast account for sixpence a week',[1] which suggests Pointin kept a school. He was a visiting tutor in Hurstpierpoint in 1722 [qv under Other masters] and his school may well have been there in 1731. [See Thomas Pointin in Schedule 2]

1. ESRO HIC 472

Miss Leach's school   (R: 1734)

The Stapley family account book records:[1]

> 20 Aug 1734: 'Sarah Stapley went to Will Best to board at 3s 6d per week
> & to Miss Leach for 6d a week to schole'
> 2 Dec 1734: 'Sarah Stapley came from William Best and I payed him £2
> 9s for board & payed Miss [Leach] 7s for her schooling and 1s for firing
> in all £2 17s.'

Sarah Stapley was a daughter of John Stapley of Hickstead (Twineham).[2]   [*Miss Leach*]

1. ESRO HIC 472.   2. Comber *Sussex Gen.(Horsham Centre)*, 331.

Dame Bellchamber's school   (R: 1735)

The Stapley family account book records: 20 Aug 1734, '... and Jane, John, and Samuel to their dame Bellchamber the same day, the boys at 2d and Jane [at] 4d per week.'[1]

Jane, John (born 1726) and Samuel were children of John Stapley of Hickstead; the school was presumably in or very near Twineham.[2]   [*Dame Bellchamber*]

1. ESRO HIC 472.   2. Comber, op. cit., 331.

Miss Beard's school?   (R: 1735)

The Stapley family account book records:[1]

> 1735, June 16. Jane Stapley went to board att John Bodle att 3s 6d per
> week.
> 1735, Nov. 26th. Payed John Bodle £1 15s in full for 10 weeks board for
> Jane Stapley and payed Miss Beards bill, 3s 2d.

It is assumed from this that Miss Beard was a schoolmistress (cf. the diary entry under Miss Leach's school above). '3s.2d.' would cover 9½ weeks at 4d a week. Jane Stapley was a daughter of John Stapley of Hickstead (Twineham).[2]   [*Miss Beard*]

1. ESRO HIC 472.   2. Comber, op. cit., 331.

Burtenshaw's school   (R: 1736)

The Stapley family account book records:[1]

> 1736, July 10. Payed Tho. Burtenshaw his half-years salary for teaching
> the Girls & boy, £1 10s in full.

[*Thomas Burtenshaw*]

1. ESRO HIC 472.

French charity school   (Rs: 1775-85)

The Goodwood steward's account book, running from the Lady day quarter 1775, shows payments of £5 5s pa (ie. by the Duke of Richmond) for the 'French School', from 1775 to

1785. In 1779 it was described as the 'French charity school'. The payments were made to Pierre Meure from 1775 to 1782, and to E. Artand from 1782 to 1785, who were probably masters of the school. Such annual subscriptions may have been paid in earlier years than those covered by this account book. Regular subscriptions to two other charity schools are recorded in these Goodwood accounts, both in Chichester, but the French charity school may have been elsewhere, and perhaps outside Sussex.[1] [*Pierre Meure, E. Artand*]

1. WSRO Goodwood MSS 244, 245, 247.

A clergyman's boys' boarding school   (R: 1783)
In 1783 a clergyman 'who resides on a remarkably healthy and elevated Part of the South Downs of this County' and had 'two young Gentlemen as private Pupils', advertised under the heading 'PRIVATE TUITION' that he wished 'to increase the Number to Four only'. 'His Mode of Instruction is, to give them Lectures after the Manner of the Universities, in Greek, Latin, and English Classics, Astronomy, and Geography; and to assist them in Writing and Arithmetic. He endeavours also to make them his Friends and constant Companions, and introduces them into whatever Company his Family sees.'[1] Advertised in *SWA* Jun (4), Dec (2) 1783.

1. *SWA* 2.6.83

Martha Brown's girls' boarding school   (Rs: 1799-1800)
Martha Brown was paid by the Duke of Richmond, of Goodwood, as 'School Mistress for Mary Ann Larner'. The payments came to 16 guineas for a year, with 17s 6d extra in one quarter, and were for 'Board & Tuition'. The first payment was made January-March 1800 and the last October-December 1800.[1] [*Martha Brown*]

1. WSRO Goodwood MS 247.

SOME SCHOOLS OUTSIDE SUSSEX THAT ADVERTISED IN SUSSEX

GOUDHURST   Grammar school.   R: 1777. Douthwaite master. Boarding and the classics, at 20 guineas pa, 2 guineas entrance. French, dancing, writing, &c. extras. 'A CURACY is wanted at any convenient Distance from GOUDHURST.' (*SWA* 29.12.77)

GREENWICH   Boys' academy.   R: 1792.   Son of the late Rev Peter James announced continuation of the Greenwich Academy for young gentlemen. (*SWA* 27.2.92)

GROOMBRIDGE   Writing school. R: 1772. Charles Ley master. English grammar, writing, arithmetic both vulgar and decimal, book-keeping, mensuration, gauging, surveying, dialling, every part of practical astronomy, use of the globes, maps, &c. Now takes boarders. (*SWA* 20.4.72)

GUILDFORD   Girls' boarding school.   Rs: 1783, 1784. Mrs Shepheard mistress. Had been many years established. All the different branches of education, all kinds of the most fashionable fancy needlework. Proper assistants. In 1784 denied 'a malicious report' that she intended to decline her school at Christmas.   (*SWA* 6.1.83, 18.10.84)

Boys' boarding school.   R: 1799.   Thomas Mare master. School at the Holy Trinity Parsonage House.   Board and English, writing, arithmetic, merchants accounts, geography and mensuration, at 18 guineas pa. French, dancing, &c. extras. Stresses 'the most important parts of Commercial Education': '... in a small space of time, youth have been completely instructed for Trade at the Seminary, and are now filling up their stations in society with reputation to themselves, and advantage to their Friends and the Public...' (*SWA* 23.12.99)

HAVANT   French and English girls' boarding school. R: 1784. Mrs Lagrange mistress. Had been established for 11 years. Advertised her annual exhibition of pupils' work - embroidery, stoco, cloth-work, paper-work, muslin, &c. (*SWA* 7.6.84)

HAWKHURST   Girls' boarding school. Rs: 1798, 1799. Late Mrs Pawley mistress. In 1798 Mr Pawley announced that he would carry on the school with Mrs Barber and able assistants.   English and French taught grammatically, music, dancing, drawing, writing and arithmetic, by Mr Pawley 'and the most approved masters'. In 1799 Mesdms. Barber and Hall announced that they had taken over the school in partnership (Mr Pawley would continue to teach writing). 'Every young Lady to give three months notice previous to leaving the School, or pay the quarter.' (*SWA* 28.5.98, 16.12.99)

KENNINGTON-LANE
Surrey   Girls' boarding school.   R: 1793. Mrs Gregory mistress.   (*SWA* 14.1.93)

LONDON (near)   Boys' boarding school. R: 1787. A clergyman master, 'who has for some Time been engaged in the Tuition of Youth.'   For ' a few Young Gentlemen', combines 'the principal Advantages of a public and private Education'. 'The Preceptor is now at Brighthelmston, with some of his Pupils, in order to give them the Benefits of Sea Bathing during the present Vacation.' (*SWA* 16.7.87)

                      Boys' boarding school at Parsons Green.   R: 1791. Mr and Mrs Sketchley master and mistress. They 'are now at Brighton, where they propose spending every Midsummer Vacation in company with some of their little pupils, and may be spoken with every morning during their stay, at their house, No.14, Russell street.' (*SWA* 4.7.91; repeated 11.7.91, 18.7.91)

REIGATE   Boys' boarding school.   Rs: 1777, 1783. John Vevers master (had been assistant at Rev Dr Barwis's academy in Soho Square, London). School was at Woodhatch Place, a mile out of the town, and - in 1783 - had been established 'near Thirty Years, with great Success, (seldom having a less Number than Fifty Boarders, but mostly Seventy, or upwards).'   Board and Latin, Greek, French, writing, arithmetic, mathematics, book-keeping, geography, the rudiments of astronomy, the use of maps and globes, at 14 guineas pa, 1 guinea entrance. Later, French, dancing and drawing at 10s 6d per quarter, 10s 6d entrance. 'Lectures will be read weekly in Morality, Religion, and useful Literature.' (*SWA* 29.9.77, 17.2.83, 1.9.83)

                      Boys' boarding school.   R: 1779. Rev Withers master. Boys 'compleatly qualified for the University, 'Compting-House and Trade' at 15 guineas pa, no entrance. (*SWA* 10.5.79)

Boys' boarding school.   R: 1788. Rev Thomas Sissons master, Rev Haygarth assistant. Pupils not to exceed 24. Fees 16 guineas pa, 1 guinea entrance. (*SWA* 4.2.88)

ROUEN (France)   Boys' boarding school, in village near Rouen.   Rs: 1788, 1789. For 4 or 5 young gentlemen (two 'already engaged and preparing for the Voyage'). French, the learned languages, mathematics, merchants' accounts, 'and every other necessary Kind of Learning will be taught, that may be required.' Noted that the commercial treaty between the two kingdoms, rendered 'the Knowledge of the French Tongue of great Utility to those concerned in the Mercantile Line'. And that 'the greatest Attention will be paid to their Morals, WITHOUT AFFECTING THEIR RELIGION.' (*SWA* 29.12.88, 16.2.89)

Girls' boarding school.   R: 1792. The Miss Greens, mistresses. By 1792 they had 'near 30 young Ladies of the most reputable families in the neighbourhood' and now invited pupils from 'their own country'. They noted that: 'A perfect liberty of conscience is permitted.' Board and French and English grammatically, plain work and embroidery, history, writing, accounts, drawing, vocal music and the forte piano, inclusive (except clothes and washing) for £27 pa. They added that Rouen is 30 miles from Dieppe, 'at which town English Packet Boats arrive regularly twice a week from Brighton. There has not been the least riot in Rouen, since the commencement of the present disorders in France.' [But in less than a year France declared war on Britain.] (*SWA* 12.5.92)

TENTERDEN   Girls' boarding school.   R: 1782. Mrs Ellis mistress.   School established before 1782, when she moved to a new house. Board and French and English grammatically, geography, and all kinds of useful and fancy needlework, at £15 pa, 1 guinea entrance. French, writing, music and dancing by visiting masters. (*SWA* 4.11.82)

TONBRIDGE   Boys' boarding school.   R: 1778. 'Tunbridge School', Rev V. Knox master. 20 guineas pa. (*SWA* 13.7.78)

Boys' boarding school.   Rs: 1790, 1792, 1794, 1797. 'Tunbridge Academy', Rev T. Jefferson master.   Opening announced August 1790. In 1792, fees 18 to 30 guineas pa, no entrance.   In 1797, number limited to 22; fees - under 10, 21 guineas pa; above 10, 23 guineas; younger parlour boarders, 26 guineas; older parlour boarders, 30 guineas. (*SWA* 30.8.90, 9.1.92, 30.6.94, 3.7.97)

TUNBRIDGE WELLS

Girls' boarding school. On Mount Sion; opened 1771. Mrs Dunage mistress, who had received her education in France and 'is qualified to teach that polite Language, in its greatest Perfection'. Board and English and French grammatically, fine needlework, tambour-work, and arithmetic, at £15 pa, 10s 6d entrance. Writing, 6s per quarter. Dancing, 12s per quarter. (*SWA* 24.6.71)

WESTERHAM   Girls' boarding school.   R: 1787. Mrs Downman mistress. Had moved her school to Westerham from Islington. Board and English, French, needlework, at 15 guineas pa, no entrance.   'Mrs. DOWNMAN teaches her improved artificial Flower Work, Cloth Work, Fillagrees on Caddies, Fire Screens, &c. Paper and Wafer Work in Flowers, Landscapes, Birds, &c. either by the Lesson or Piece; and Ladies may be accomodated as Parlour Boarders by the Week, or Month, for the Learning of such Work.' She noted that 'Parents and Guardians, who favour Mrs. DOWNMAN with the Education of their Children, (and are in Trade) may depend on having a Return of the Money.'   (*SWA* 1.1.87)

SCHEDULE 2

SUSSEX SCHOOLMASTERS AND SCHOOLMISTRESSES OF THE 18th CENTURY

Includes any person paid to teach children.

Includes unpaid charity school teachers.

Includes tutors and specialist teachers (eg dancing, drawing, French).

Surnames in italics indicate schoolmistresses.

Names in box brackets indicate persons likely to have taught in the 18th century but for whom documentary evidence of the fact has not yet been traced.

Further information about the teachers and the schools where they taught is given in Schedule 1 (cross references are indicated in Schedule 2 by [qv]). Duplication has as far as possible been avoided between Schedules 1 and 2, and source-references given in Schedule 1 are not repeated in Schedule 2 unless additional material is here included.

ADAM, John: Schoolmaster at Ticehurst. Moved there from Rolvenden, Kent, 23 February 1754, with wife Elizabeth and daughter Grace. Described as 'Schoolmaster' in settlement certificate and at burial of daughter Grace, 25 May 1756. [Settlement certificate; PR]

ADAMS, Hannah: Schoolmistress from c1774. With elder sister Mary [qv] had a girls' boarding school in Lewes from at least 1781 to c1817, initially in the Cliffe and from 1789 on School Hill. Joint owner with Mary of the schoolhouse on School Hill and another house which they rented out. Towards the end of 1792, when the French Revolution was well under way, she went to Paris to study French; tried to leave in January 1793, but could not obtain the 'necessary assurances of protection' until March, by which time France and Great Britain were at war, and she was detained in Paris for 3 years. We know from Elizabeth Hitchener, one of their pupils, that in the 1790s one of the Miss Adams held radical views, while the other was reactionary; a strong bond grew up between Hitchener and the radical Miss Adams -'me alone of all her pupils did she love as her child.' That the latter was Hannah is indicated by the following - Hitchener wrote to Shelley in 1811 (when she was 29) that the radical Miss Adams was 'so circumstanc'd with a Sister, who is the opposite of her, that she is not more at liberty to me than I am to her' (Hitchener's parents condemned the friendship) and 'having too much virtue for the age has ever been an object of persecution.' It was Hitchener's intention to achieve financial independence by building up a successful school so that she 'could offer her an asylum'; this makes sense if her Miss Adams was the 'persecuted' younger sister, it is most unlikely if she was the headmistress of a long-established, well-respected and successful boarding school. Hannah, then, taught her 'to have an opinion' (unconventional instruction for girls at that time) and inculcated her with radical principles. For Adams to have gone to Paris in 1792 simply to have learnt French, would have been extremely foolhardy; she was probably motivated, in part at least, by strong sympathy with the early ideals of the French Revolution. After giving up the school in c1817 she apparently retired to Rosemundy House, St Agnes, Cornwall. [Jones, F. L. *The Letters of*

Percy Bysshe Shelley v 1 (1964); Land Tax Lewes All Saints; *SWA* 24.6.93, 28.12.95]

ADAMS, Mary (1757-1823): With her sister Hannah had a girls' boarding school in Lewes [qv] from at least 1781 to c1817, initially in the Cliffe and from 1789 on School Hill. For most years the Land Tax returns show the school premises as occupied, or owned and occupied, by Mary Adams, and she was undoubtedly the headmistress; joint owner with Hannah of the schoolhouse on School Hill and another house which they rented out. In the 1790s Mary Adams suffered damage from and campaigned against the 5 November celebrations on School Hill. She and Hannah were probably related to the Rev Charles Adams, curate of St Thomas in the Cliffe from 1782, who in 1783 and 1784 occupied the house on School Hill which later became the Adams' school. Mary died on 1 April 1823 (aged 66) at the residence of her sister, Rosemundy House, St Agnes, Cornwall. [Land Tax Lewes St Thomas, All Saints; Lewes St Thomas PR; St Agnes, Cornwall, PR; *SWA* 21.4.1823]

ADEANE, Mrs: With Mrs Townley, opened a girls' boarding school in Brighton January 1799 [qv].

AKERMAN, Samuel (-1813): Master of Angmering charity school. Appointed 1777. Died 10 April 1813, '36 Years Master of the free School in this place'. [Baker, L. A. in *Sussex Life* (Sep 1966); MI, Dunkin NB 6.13 in SAS Library]

AKHURST, John: Master of Eastbourne charity school [qv; see also Another (charity?) school]. Paid £15 a year by the Cavendish family to teach 15 poor boys (Rs 1734-47). When in 1734 a faction campaigned to remove him, he was supported by Thomas Worge, the Earl of Wilmington's agent, who reported that 'Old mas'r Akehurst was very much amended in his Writing and perfect in Accts to the Rule of three, the man is both diligent and sober.' He was still master in 1747.

[ALDERTON, Thomas]: In 1736 was paid 4s by the Burwash parish for schooling a poor boy for half a year. (Also paid 6d for shaving the boy's head twice.) The schooling perhaps undertaken by his wife? [qv Parish schooling]

ALEXANDER, Mr Serjeant-Major: Of Lord Heathfield's Light Dragoons, he instructed the boys of Mossop's school, Brighton, in military manoeuvres, 1788-89, and was commended in *Sussex Weekly Advertiser* 1 June 1789 following their public display.

[ALLEN, Samuel]: Had an academy in South Street, Chichester, c1804 and probably earlier. [*Chichester Guide* (c1804); *Holden's Directory* (1805)]

ALLFREE, Ann (-1780): From c1767 she and her husband Edward Alfree [qv] ran a boarding school 'for YOUTH of both SEX' at Herstmonceux offering a full education for both boys and girls [qv]. Ann was responsible for the girls 'Department'. Died 1780. [PR]

ALLFREE, Edward (1744-1808): From c1767, with wife Ann Alfree [qv] ran boarding school for 'YOUTH of both SEX' at Herstmonceux offering a full education for both boys and girls [qv]. Also advertised as surveyor [map of a Peasmarsh estate, surveyed by him in 1791, survives]. Ann died 1780 and he married secondly (aged 39) 20 April 1783, at Seaford, Elizabeth Simmons, aged 17 [qv], by whom he had 13 children (7 sons and 6 daughters). Son of first marriage, Edward Motte (baptised 1773) went to Oxford and became curate of Herstmonceux 1796-1804 (from marriage register), later Minor Canon of Rochester; 2 of his sons went to Cambridge. Of Edward and Elizabeth's children, Henry Francis went to Oxford (but died aged 24), John and Mary Ann had set up adjacent boarding schools in Brighton by 1822. Buried 4 August 1808, aged 64. [ESRO AMS 4595; *SRS* **25**; *Al. Oxon.*; *Al. Cant.*; PRs]

ALLFREE, Elizabeth (1766-1850): Daughter of Thomas Simmons of Seaford, blacksmith. She married 20 April 1783 (aged 17) Edward Allfree [qv] as his second wife, and with him ran a boarding school for both boys and girls [qv], she being responsible for the girls. Had 13 children by Edward (the first baptised 12 August 1784), none of whom appear to have died in infancy, although three died as children. After husband's death 1808, she continued to own the school at least to 1839; estate mapped by pupil 1823 ['Harlots, Chapmans and Chickmolt...The property of Mrs Alfree']. Died

at Iford, buried Herstmonceux 6 June 1850, aged 84. [*SRS* **25**; PRs; ESRO TD/E 89; ESRO AMS 5879/1]

AMON, Joseph (-1789): After wife Mary's death 1779, paid £4 a year by Icklesham parish to Michaelmas 1786 for schooling 10-14 poor children at the free school. A poor man, the parish paid for his wife's 'laying forth' and burial, and he received 'poor pay' on occasions 1780-87. Married 29 March 1741, Mary Sutors. Buried 1 December 1789. [ESRO PAR 401/30/2, 401/30/3; PR]

AMON, Mary (-1779): Paid £4 a year by Icklesham parish 'for Schooling for Free School' in church years 1776-77, 1777-78. Née Sutors, married Joseph Amon [qv] 29 March 1741 and buried 2 July 1779; the parish paid for her 'laying forth' and burial. Husband took over the school. [ESRO PAR 401/30/2; PR]

ANSTIE, Elizabeth (1746-1833): Schoolmistress at (probably) Eastbourne. Married 24 December 1774 at Eastbourne, writing master to the school, Thomas Palmer [qv]. They moved to East Grinstead c1775. Had 12 children. Born 28 February 1746, died 26 June 1833. [Leppard, M. J. pers. comm. citing family historians]

ARNOLD, Dr: Music master [qv under CHICHESTER]. Paid by the Duke of Richmond for music lessons for Henriette Le Clerc, 1786-90.

[ARTAND, E.]: Probably master of a French charity school supported by the Duke of Richmond who paid him £5 5s a year for same 1782-85 [qv UNPLACED SCHOOLS].

ATKINS, Francis (1719?-96): Master of Midhurst grammar school 1758-88 [qv]. Probably son of John of Renwick, Cumberland; Queen's College, Oxford, matriculated 27 March 1738, aged 18; BA 1742. Curate of Easebourne when, 6 November 1751, appointed usher, Midhurst grammar school, to teach the school in light of the master's infirmity (Barrett); appointed master 25 January 1758. Minister of Midhurst 14 January 1758 to death, vicar of Horsham 1769 to death, vicar of Climping 1772-88, rector of Poynings 1786 to death. Circa 1780 John Pratt complained to the school trustees, without effect, that 'the Rev'd Schoolmaster pocketted the money and had kept no School for 16 years'; in January 1786 information against Atkins and the trustees was laid before the Lord Chancellor. Atkins resigned 16 April 1788. Died 1796. [*Al. Oxon.*; *HMGS*; CI]

ATKINSON, John (1741-84): Master of Chichester grammar school 1776-84 [qv]. Prebendary of Chichester, rector of Bepton 1776 to death. In 1784 census at West Street, Chichester; also then owned property in North Street. Native of Kendal, Westmorland (in will) and probably the JA, son of John of Kendal in Westmorland, at Edmund Hall, Oxford, matriculated 18 May 1763, aged 22. Died at Brompton 26 June 1784, buried at Bepton on 2 July 1784. [*VCH* ii; WSRO MP 414, 417; CI; *Al. Oxon.*; *SWA* 5.7.84]

ATTREE, Dame: Paid by Cowfold parish for schooling poor children from 1785 into 19th century [qv Parish schooling]. Payments ranged from 1s or 2s a month (when schooling shared) to 4s, the normative rate; no payments April 1791 to June 1795, when the poor were 'put out'. Also received payments for weaving, making clothes. Wife of Richard Attree (paid by parish for weaving) who was buried 1797; thereafter she was 'Widow Attree'. [WSRO Par 59/31/3-4; PR]

AUSTEN, Robert (1708-86): Master of Lewes grammar school at 1753 and to resignation Michaelmas 1775 [qv]. In letter to Mr Shelley, 1775, gives salary of master as £57 16s 8d, plus the 'commodious house for the purpose of taking boarders with a Stable and Garden', for which he took 12 free scholars. Also took private day boys [qv MANNING, Edward (1744-) in Schedule 3; his father gave Austen 'perquisites' of £2 2s in 1753 and 1754 (as much again as the basic schooling fee)]. Son of Robert of Tenterden, Kent, esq; Merton College, Oxford, matriculated 11 December 1725, aged 17. Signed Hamsey bishop's transcripts 1752, 1756, 1770; curate of St Anne Lewes (conducted marriages as curate 9 June 1754 to 11 December 1770, and on 5 November 1772) and curate St Michael Lewes (conducted marriages as curate 3 June 1754 to 3 September 1771). After trying for various livings, 1752-65, instituted vicar of Laughton

1778, held to death. Leisure interest was tracing the antiquities of Lewes. Married at Heathfield 29 September 1748 Mary Burgess of Burwash; she died 18 January 1782; he died 20 October 1786, aged 78. [*Al. Oxon.*; CI; Brent, C., pers. comm. citing Newcastle correspondence; PRs; *SWA* 9.1.75, 23.10.86; Woolgar; Dunvan, P. *History of Lewes* (1795)]

AUSTIN, William (1732-1820): Drawing master at Brighton (from 1797) [qv] and to schools at Brighton, Lewes and Preston. A pupil of Bickham, exhibited Royal Academy 1776; claimed that in London he had been 'patronized by near a thousand Noblemen, Gentlemen, and Ladies, as Pupils, including the younger branches from Westminster, Eton, Harrow, and other great Schools, and private Families at their Country Seats.' Published original prints of his portraits of many famous people, including the Prince of Wales and Duke and Duchess of York. The *Sussex Weekly Advertiser* reported that, after a great storm at Lewes in 1798, he had been 'very busy here, in taking sketches from the picturesque scraps of broken glass...which furnished a great variety of very curious figures'. In December 1798 he subscribed one guinea to a fund for families of Brighton fishermen taken prisoner by a French privateer. But by 1817 he had lost his sight and was in financial distress; died in 1820 in extreme poverty, aged 88. [*SWA* 18.6.98, 10.12.98, 18.3.1800; Bishop, 8]

AXEL, Mary (1733-1811): Paid by Framfield parish very small sums in 1798 and 1799 'for Schooling', presumably the workhouse children. Buried 12 February 1811, aged 78, a singlewoman. [ESRO PAR 343/31/1/4; PR]

AYLING, Henry: Paid small sums by the Dowlin charity 1700-03 (10s 10d; £1 7s 2d (2 years); 16s 2d) for schooling poor children of West Grinstead. [WSRO Par 95/1/1/3]

[*BAILEY, Miss*]: Had a girls' boarding school in North Street, Chichester, by c1804. Probably the Miss B who rented a house in St Olave's parish from 1799. [*Chichester Guide* (c1804); Land Tax]

BAKER, Charles (-1753?): Master of Lightmaker's charity school, Horsted Keynes [qv] in the early 1730s. In January 1738 was paid 4¼ years arrears of salary (£85) plus £4 14s towards repairs he had made to the school house. Reputed to have married sister of Ralph Clutton, rector of Horsted Keynes 1738-61. His son John baptised at Horsted Keynes 1734. Probably the CB master of Steyning grammar school [*see below*]. [*Sussex History* **2**, no. 7; PR]

BAKER, Charles (-1753): Master of Steyning grammar school [qv] 1736-53. Probably the CB who subscribed 24 February 1731 'before his being admitted to teach a Grammar Schoole att Lindfield'; and probably the CB master of Horsted Keynes charity school [*see above*]. Buried 31 March 1753 ('Charles Baker, schoolmaster'). [SAS Wadey's index; WSRO Ep.I/39/21; PR]

BAKER, Charles Vaughan (1719-84): Master of Steyning grammar school [qv] 1753-78. Son of Charles, of Glasbury, Radnorshire. Brasenose College, Oxford, matriculated 2 April 1737, aged 17; BA 1740: MA from St John's College, Cambridge, 1774. Ordained deacon (Chichester) 1742, priest 1743; rector of Edburton 1754 to death and vicar of Lyminster 1776 to death; chaplain to George, Baron Cranley. Licensed February 1769 'to perform the Office of Schoolmaster in the Free Grammar School of Steyning'. Married Elizabeth Wilson, daughter of Edward, rector of Westmeston; she died 17 May 1802, aged 77. He died 2 August 1784, aged 65, buried at Edburton 6 August 1784. [Sleight, J. M. *A Very Exceptional Instance* (1981); *Al. Oxon.*; *Al. Cant.*; CI; WSRO Ep.I/3/7; PR; MI, SAS Dunkin NB 7.9]

BAKER, Jane (1736-91): Schoolmistress at Wadhurst. Buried 16 June 1791, 'Schoolmistress, wife of John Baker, Linen Weaver - Aged 55 years'. [PR]

BAKER, Miss M.: Had a girls' boarding school at Eastbourne 1798, 1799 [qv].

BAKER, Thomas (1660-1729): Master of Chichester grammar school [qv] 1701-29. Son of Richard, of London; St Paul's school; Trinity College, Cambridge, matriculated 1677, aged 17; BA 1682, MA 1696. Prebendary of Highleigh and master of the grammar school 17 April 1701. Licensed 'to teach in ye

Grammar-School in Chichester' 10 October 1701. Also had the livings of All Saints, Chichester 1704 to death, Sidlesham (most of which tithes went to the prebend of Highleigh) c1704 to death, St Olave Chichester c1714 to death, West Stoke 1721 to death. Buried at the cathedral 13 April 1729. [*SAC* **106**; WSRO Ep.I/1/10]

BALCOMBE Goody: In December 1709 or 1710, paid by William Dobell of Streat Place 'for 1 year's teaching school due at Michaelmas - £3'. [qv STREAT Charity school].

BALDOCK, Mrs: With daughter, had a girls' boarding school at East Grinstead 1792 [qv].

BALDOCK, Miss: With mother, had a girls' boarding school at East Grinstead 1792 [qv].

[BANESTER, Samuel]: In April 1762 paid £1 1s by Icklesham parish 'for Larning them to sing'; presumably included teaching the children. [*SAC* **32**]

BARBER, Thomas: A lay clerk paid by Walond [qv his singing school, CHICHESTER] out of his salary as organist of Chichester cathedral, to take over the duties of Master of the Choristers in 1794.

BARCLAY, William: Opened a boys' boarding school at Arundel 1787 [qv]. Previously had an academy at Southgate, Middlesex.

BARNARD, Edward: Recommended as schoolmaster for Westham 1785 [qv WESTHAM Charity school].

BARRETT, Serenus (1677-1757): Master of Midhurst grammar school [qv] 1735-57. Born 17 October 1677, son of the Rev Michael of Pyecombe. Lincoln College, Oxford, November 1693, aged 16 (where joined by twin Edward, March 1694: older brother Michael matriculated Brasenose College Oxford 1689). Vicar of Tortington 1703-09, vicar of Kirdford 1709-13, vicar (sequestrator) of Westdean 1715-19, rector of Fishbourne 1723 to death, minister of Midhurst 1725 to death. Appointed master at age 58; after c15 years became infirm and unable to teach. Died 24 December 1757. [*HMGS*; CI; *Al. Oxon.*; WSRO E138/3/1]

BARTLETT, John: Had a school at Lewes (Rs 1785 into 19th century) [qv]. On 24 December 1791 his wife died 'suddenly, and unperceived, by her husband's side'. [*SWA* 26.12.91]

BARWICK, Henry: Curate of St Clement, Hastings, January - September 1779, he opened a boys' boarding school at Hastings after the Easter holidays 1779 [qv]. Curate of Bexhill 1780-92, and still had a boys' boarding school [qv]. In 1793 opened a boys' boarding school at Lindfield [qv], when he claimed to have educated 'several of the Nobility, Gentry, &c. of this Kingdom, during a period of upwards of twenty years'. Perhaps the HB, vicar of South Malling 1797-98. [*SAC* **26**]

BASCHET, Nicholas: French master at Brighton (Rs 1788-93). Taught at schools and had his own French evening school [qv]. From the University of Orleans.

BEAR, John (1674-1762): Rector of Shermanbury 1711 to death, he kept a small boarding school for sons of local gentry in the 1730s and 1740s [qv]. Married Mary Burton, widow (mother of Dr John Burton, author of *Iter Sussexiensis*); she died 23 April 1755, aged 80. He died 9 March 1762, aged 88. [*SAC* **114**; CI]

BEARD, Miss: In 1735 paid for teaching Jane Stapley, daughter of John of Hickstead [qv under UNPLACED SCHOOLS].

BEARD, George (1690-1772): Had a school in the Cliffe, Lewes (Rs 1733, 1750, 1755) [qv]. Parish clerk of St Thomas at Cliffe, 1740 to death when succeeded by son John. Probably the GB baptised at Pyecombe 23 March 1690, son of Edward and Anne. Married at Pyecombe 20 June 1722, Jane Wickham, daughter of John and Jane (née Freind); she was buried at St Thomas's 1785, aged 94. Had 5 children (3 sons and 2 daughters). His will of 1767 (proved 1772) left a property with gardens, orchard and brookland, divided into 3 houses, and gave sums totalling £155 10s lent on bills to his sons and sons-in-law; mentions wife Jane, sons John and George, daughter Jane (married George Lambert), son-in-law Francis Hoey (married daughter Ann), grandson George Beard Hoey. Buried 27 March 1772, aged 82. [*SAC* **90**;

ESRO SM/D 9.82]

BEARD Jane: Opened a girls' boarding school at Hailsham June 1774 [qv], just after bankruptcy of husband Daniel, a merchant, dealer and chapman of Rottingdean; may previously have had a school at Rottingdean. In 1775 planned to move the school to Lewes but instead took over at Whitsun 1775 Miss Russell's girls' boarding school at Brighton [qv]. In February 1784, as 'Widow of Mr Daniel Beard, lately deceased', denied she intended to close the school; but at Michaelmas that year she moved her school to Seaford [qv], her announcement of the same being addressed to 'the Nobility and Gentry'. [*SWA* 13.6.74, 2.2.84]

BECKETT: Assistant to John Thring, Lewes dancing and music master [qv Beckett under LEWES Dancing and music masters]. Violinist, under Thring's instruction for 15 years. Joint beneficiary with Thring of concert and ball 1796; with Page of concert 1797; joint owner with Thring of music shop 1798.

BEDDING, John: Schoolmaster of Lewes (Rs 1790, 1791) [qv].

BELLCHAMBER, Dame: Schoolmistress in 1734, probably in or near Twineham. Taught John (then aged 8) and Samuel Stapley for 2d per week and Jane Stapley for 4d per week. [ESRO HIC 472; Comber *Sx. Gen.*]

[**BENNET**]: Music teacher and organist in West-Gate, Chichester, c1804 and probably earlier. [*Chichester Guide* (c1804)]

BERTHOLET, Monsieur: 'Late Prebendary of Peronne', taught French at Mrs Gell's girls' boarding school Lewes 1799. [*SWA* 30.9.99]

BEST, Henry (1701?-55): Schoolmaster at Fletching 1747 [qv]. Probably baptised 10 September 1701, son of George and Mary. Married Mary, their son Henry baptised 3 August 1750. Buried 20 December 1755. [PR]

BETTS, Mrs: see **GRIDLEY, Charlotte**

BIRD, Drury (1684-1734): Vicar of Bolney 1714-34, his tithe book records payments he received for schooling children in Cuckfield.

Son of John (-1709), rector of Knapwell, Cambridgeshire, and master of Knapwell School. (His elder brother John (-1728) became vicar of Reigate, Surrey.) School, King's College. Admitted Christ's College, Cambridge, 5 February 1701 (aged 17); BA 1705. Ordained deacon (Chichester) 1705, priest 1708. Curate of Playden 1708; curate of Udimore 1710-15; vicar of Bolney 1714 to death in 1734. Wife, Anne: their son Drury buried at Udimore 1714; at Bolney, son John born 18 May 1716, daughters Anne born 24 March 1718, Mary buried 17 May 1721, Grace baptised 30 May 1721. [WSRO Par 252/6/3; *Al. Cant.*; CI; *SRS* 15]

BISHOP, Miss Mary: With Mrs Susan Johnson, continued Mrs Thornton's girls' boarding school at Northiam 1773. [*SWA* 18.1.73]

BLAGDEN, Bragg (1715-81): Had a small school in Chichester (R 1761) [qv]. Son of George, alehouse-keeper, he was born and at school in Chichester; St John's College, Cambridge, 1735 (aged 20); BA 1739, MA 1752. Ordained deacon (Norwich) 1739, priest (Chichester) 1741. Curate of Binstead 1747, rector of Binstead 1764-81; perpetual curate of Mid-Lavant 1752-81; prebendary of Chichester 1753; rector of Singleton 1763-65; rector of Slindon 1764-81; chaplain to the Duke of Richmond. In 1761, then aged 46, he had a large and increasing family, and was described by Archbishop Secker as 'A worthy man'. He died 3 February 1781. [*Secker*, 214 (some errors in footnote concerning clerical appointments); *Al. Cant.* (some errors concerning clerical appointments); CI]

BLANCH, Miss Martha: With Miss Mary Blanch had a girls' boarding school at Arundel (Rs 1788, 1799) [qv].

BLANCH, Miss Mary: With Miss Martha Blanch had a girls' boarding school at Arundel (Rs 1788, 1799) [qv].

BLAND: Usher at Lewes grammar school 1718. (Given 10s by trustees of Nicholas Gilbert when latter left the school.) [ESRO ACC 2462/1]

BLESARD Mary (1768-): Paid £2 18s 4d in

1798 and 9s 9d in 1799 by the Duke of Richmond 'for Schooling Children' - presumably children from the Goodwood estate. She was first mentioned in steward's accounts 1788. After the death of the Duchess in 1796, Mary became the Duke's mistress. From 1797, then 29 and described as housekeeper, she received an annuity of £50. Later known as Mrs Bennet. In 1802 she contributed £1,000 to the £4,000 paid for a property at Earls Court in Middlesex. Under Richmond's will of 1806 she received an annuity of £450. She had 3 illegitimate daughters by the Duke - Elizabeth probably died young, Caroline and Mary were accepted by the family. Daughter Mary married William Light, a distinguished surveyor who founded the city of Adelaide, Australia; Caroline married Henry Napier, naval captain and historian of Florence, where they settled. Mary (Blesard) Bennet had a house in Florence, and was buried in the English cemetery there. [WSRO Goodwood MS 245, 247; Reese, M. M. *Goodwood's Oak* (1987); *DNB*]

BLUNT, Robert: Schoolmaster at Horsham 1772. From John Baker's diary, [Saturday] 30 May 1772: 'Afternoon Sir John, Mr Dyer and I out on common, saw boys play at cricket, among them oldest master, Robert Blunt.' [*SAC* 52]

BOOKER, Dame: Paid by Billingshurt parish 1777-79 for schooling parish children [qv Parish schooling].

BOORMAN, Arthur (1739-1800): Schoolmaster at Ticehurst in 1792 [qv]. Buried 9 May 1800, aged 61.

BOTTING, Mary: Paid 3s 6d in 1728 by the Dowlin charity for schooling poor children at West Grinstead. [WSRO Par 95/1/1/3]

BOTTING, Pollos (Molly): Paid by Warnham parish for schooling the parish children 1786, 1788 and 1789 [qv her school].

BOTTING, William: Paid a small sum from Horsted Keynes offertory collections for the poor for schooling a poor boy, 1744 [qv Parish schooling].

BOUCHIER, Mrs Anne: Mistress of the girls' Blue Coat charity school, Chichester. Received payments on behalf of the school 1724, 1732, 1736, 1739 and 1742-56. (Perhaps related to John B, 'minister of the Gospel' buried 23 September 1719 (bishop's transcript 15 October 1719) and Susan B, buried 26 October 1712, both at St Andrew, Chichester. A Richard Bouchier was Archdeacon of Lewes 1693 and canon of Chichester 1694.) [WSRO Cap.V/1/1; *Al. Oxon.*]

BOX, Mary (1761-95): Kept a school at Hailsham in the early 1790s [qv for details of her religion and marriage to Strict Baptist pastor Francis Brown]. Died December 1795, the year of her marriage, aged 34. During her last illness she wrote a hymn, which was sung at her funeral; it included the lines 'Most precious to my soul the thought/ Of being called while young.' [Chambers, R. F. *The Strict Baptist Chapels of England* II]

BOYCE, Edward: Curate of Withyham, 1754-71, he kept a school there from c1755 [qv].

BREEN, Willlam (-1807): Schoolmaster of Brighton (Rs 1788-1807). In January 1788, with Morling, reinstated J. Morling's (deceased) French and English boys' boarding school and evening school [qv]. By 1790 had his own day school [qv]. 'Schoolmaster' in will, dated 4 December 1807, which left personal estate (less than £200) to wife Sally, who survived him, and property in trust for maintenance and education of children - Mary, Elizabeth, Sarah and Judith (when youngest child 21, property to be sold and proceeds divided equally between them). The 'Misses Breen' had a girls' day school at Brighton in 1824. Also parish clerk; described as such at burial, 28 December 1807. [ESRO W/A 70.312; *Baxter's Directory* (1824); PR]

BRICKNELL: Paid by the Dowlin charity for schooling poor children at West Grinstead (in 1727, £1 7s 9d; in 1728, 18s 6d; in 1729, £1 5s 1d). [WSRO Par 95/1/1/3]

BRIGGS, R.: Assistant at Mossop's boys' boarding school, Brighton [qv], when the latter died 7 April 1794; he ran the school until June 1794, when he opened his own boarding school [qv]. Signed, as 'Minister', Brighton marriage banns April 1793 and on occasion to April

1794. [PR]

BRINKHURST, Dame (-1785): Paid by Buxted parish 2s or 2s 6d a month for teaching the workhouse children from November 1784 probably to April 1785 (in May the parish paid for her 'Laying'). [ESRO PAR 286/31/1]

BRISTED, John (1696-1783): Master of Lewes grammar school 1745-c50 [qv]. Baptised at Burwash 14 April 1696, son of Ezekiel, rector of Newhaven, and Elizabeth. In 1714 received £3 4s 11d from the Steere charity, Lewes (which was especially for sons of poor clergy) towards going to Clare College, Cambridge; so almost certainly was a scholar at Lewes grammar school. To Clare College 1713, BA 1717, MA 1735. Vicar of St Mary Nottingham, rector of Cotgrave, Nottinghamshire. Rector St Anne Lewes 1725 to death, rector St Michael Lewes 1731 to death, rector Slaugham 1749 to death. Died at Sherborne, Dorset 25 January 1783, aged 86. [PR; Horsfield *Lewes*; *Al. Cant.*; CI; *St Anne's history* (1990); *St Michael's history* (1979); *SWA* 3.2.83]

BROOK, William: Took over Mossop's boys' boarding school in Brighton following the latter's death in 1794 [qv Mossop's school and Brook's school]. Came to Brighton from Herstmonceux.

BROOKSBANK, Miss S.: With Susan Ryall, had a girls' boarding school in Lewes by 1787 [qv]. In 1788 the partnership was dissolved and the school continued by Ryall.

[BROOME, Thomas]: Schoolmaster at Eastbourne (Rs 1801, 1803). Acquired Myers' boarding school 1801 [qv] whilst curate of Eastbourne. Schoolmaster, aged 17-55, in 1803 militia list. [*SGLH* 6, no. 1]

[BROWN, Mrs]: Had school in Lewes 1805 and probably earlier [qv Other schoolmistresses].

BROWN, Martha: Had a girls' boarding school in 1800, to which the Duke of Richmond sent Mary Larner [qv under UNPLACED SCHOOLS].

BROWN, Mary (1715-1791): Buried at

Cuckfield 23 October 1791, 'schoolmistress', aged 76. [PR]

BROWN, Mary: Schoolmistress at Midhurst 1793. [*Universal British Directory* (1793)]

[**BROWNE, Mary (Molly)**] (1758-1845): Had a school in Ditchling, probably from late 1790s; a Baptist and a dedicated teacher [qv Other schoolmistresses].

BUCKOLL: Son of Stephen Buckoll, with whom he opened a boys' boarding school in Brighton in 1793 [qv]; from 1795 the school was advertised only under 'Stephen Buckoll'.

BUCKOLL: Another son of Stephen Buckoll who in 1794 apparently joined his father's and brother's boys' boarding school in Brighton, then advertised under 'Buckoll & Sons' [qv]; from 1795 the school was advertised only under 'Stephen Buckoll'.

BUCKOLL, Stephen (-1797): Master of a large day school for 40 years, then in 1793, with son, opened a boys' boarding school in Brighton [qv]. In 1785 owned and occupied house, schoolhouse and garden in West Street, Brighton (also owned and rented out 2 houses in North Street, at land tax 'rental' of £1 5s each). Buried 28 December 1797. [PR]

BULLIS, John (1680-1737): Vicar of Billingshurst 1706-1737, he had a school there in 1733 [qv] and probably earlier and later. Born at Ely, Cambridgeshire, son of Thomas, and at school there; Christ's College, Cambridge, 1696, aged 17; BA 1701, LLB 1725. Vicar of Billingshurst 1706 to death, rector of Sullington 1725 to death. Married 16 April 1711, at Selmeston, Katherine Green, only daughter of William, vicar of Selmeston. Their daughter Olive married Ishmael Kilwick, schoolmaster of Chichester [qv]. Died 19 December 1737, buried 22 December 1737, aged 56. His 'Library of Books' was valued at £30. [*Al. Cant.*; CI; MI Chichester Cathedral, SAS Dunkin NB 7.1; PR; WSRO Ep.I/29/21/233]

BULLOCH, James: Schoolmaster at Salehurst, December 1700 [qv].

BUNGARD, Isaac: Paid by Withyham parish

to teach poor boys to sing 1746-47 [qv Parish schooling].

BURCHFIELD, Dame: Paid by Buxted parish 2s or 2s 6d a month for schooling the workhouse children, 1789 and probably 1790 and beyond. Also paid for other services. [ESRO PAR 286/31/1]

BURGESS: 'Burges wife' paid 2d a week by Alciston parish for schooling a poor girl for 30 weeks, 1750-51. [ESRO PAR 227/31/1]

BURGESS, Dame: Schoolmistress at Glynde charity school, 1765 [qv].

BURGES, Maggs: Schoolmaster at Horsham 1793 [qv Other masters]. Was in South Street in 1787.

BURJERY, Bristow senior: Had a boys' boarding school at West Hoathly, with Bristow Burjery, junior, 1752 [qv]. Wife Elizabeth; their twin daughters Elizabeth and Hannah baptised 5 March 1738. [PR]

BURJERY, Bristow junior: With Bristow Burjery, senior had a boys' boarding school at West Hoathly 1752 [qv]

BURNET: Paid by Grey Coat charity school, Chichester, £1 1s, 1760-61, for teaching the boys to sing. [WSRO Cap.V/1/1]

BURT, Elizabeth (-1773): For 28 years paid by Icklesham parish for schooling poor children [qv], initially at 8s per quarter (1745) rising to £4 a year 1761-73. A poor woman, she received small sums from offertory collections for the poor, and 'poor pay' at least from 1764 to 1769. Also paid for boarding poor folk, knitting, mending clothes. Wife of Robert Burt, who died 1762. Buried 11 May 1773. [PR]

BURT, N.: Moved his naval academy from London to Henfield 1787 [qv]. Ex-Royal Navy.

BURTENSHAW: Paid 9s in 1724 by the Dowlin charity for teaching poor children of West Grinstead to write. [WSRO Par 95/1/1/3]

[**BURTENSHAW, John**]: Schoolmaster at Lewes 1802. [Poll book]

BURTENSHAW, Thomas: In 1736 paid £1 10s for teaching the Stapley 'girls and boy' for ½ a year. Location of school not known. [ESRO HIC 472]

BURTON: Had a school in Lewes a little before 1750 [qv].

BUTTINGER: Paid 14s in 1724 by the Dowlin charity for schooling poor children of West Grinstead. [WSRO Par 95/1/1/3]

BUTTON, John (1761-1825): Had a successful boys' day and boarding school at Lewes from 1791 into 19th century [qv]. Described as an 'English Classical School', it was distinguished by JB's strong advocacy of teaching English grammatically and his denigration of Latin and Greek (though these were available at the school). Born 26 December 1761 at Bishopsgate, London, son of John (perhaps the JB buried All Saints Lewes, 23 July 1784, aged 55). A Baptist, he had a classical education under Dr John Ryland, Baptist pastor, Northampton, and was probably, like his brother William, baptised in the river Nen by him whilst a schoolboy. Two of his sons gave recitations (one in both English and French) at a 'Public Examination' of JB's pupils at the *Star Assembly Room* in 1797. A Philosophical Radical, read the *Examiner*, admired Charles James Fox; allegedly listed in Pitt's own Black Book as a 'dangerous demagogue', but denied being a Leveller or Republican. After his death in 1825, the school was run by his son William, also a Baptist, until 1865. Buried All Saints Lewes, 2 June 1825, aged 63. [Brent, C. *Geo. Lewes* (1993); Lower *Worthies*; PR]

BUTTON, Richard: Schoolmaster, in 1719 helped to buy the freehold of Westgate meeting house, Lewes. [Brent, C. *Geo. Lewes* (1993)]

BYSSHE, Thomas (1659-1720): Master of Cuckfield grammar school 1682-1704 [qv]. Baptised 25 March 1659, son of Mr Christopher and Mary of Cuckfield (and grandson of John Bysshe, rector of Pyecombe); at Cuckfield grammar school; St John's College, Oxford, 1677, aged 17; BA Oriel College, Oxford 1681. Curate at Wivelsfield in 1684. Married Elizabeth, daughter of Thomas Woodyer of Lindfield. Rector of Tarring Neville and South Heighton 1698 to death,

vicar of Eastbourne 1704 (when he retired from the grammar school) to death. In 1704 also, MA from Christ's College, Cambridge. Buried at Eastbourne 15 February 1720. [PRs; *Al. Oxon.*; CI; *Al. Cant.*]

CAMBRIDGE, Mary: Opened a girls' boarding school at Eastbourne 1776, majoring on needlework [qv].

CANT, Samuel (-1759): Subscribed 14 November 1735 'before his admission to practice the Art of a Schoolmaster'. Master of Hastings grammar school 1738-59 [qv]. From Leicestershire. Also surveyor; references to his work include maps of Downash Farm in Hailsham for Edward Milward of Hastings, 1731; of estate at Winchelsea, 1747; of estate of John Collier of Hastings, 1750; and of estates at Pevensey 1748, Hastings 1753 and Westfield 1755. Churchwarden St Clement Hastings, 1745. Died 1759 after failing health for 4 years and buried 19 April 1759. His will left small sums to a sister and several nephews and nieces, and his estate to 'my dutifull Niece Sarah Cook' (she married Peter Holness) to use or sell - he noted, lest she be cheated if selling, that the house was shown as worth £160 in his account book but was now worth £200; his personal estate included 'Books, Instruments, Globes, School Furniture'. Described at probate as schoolmaster and surveyor. [WSRO Ep.II/1/1; *HHGS*; ESRO SAY 1415, PAB 212, AMS 2365, W/A 60.50; HM MA 62, 191; Hastings All Saints PR]

CAPPER, James (1755-1835): Had a boys' boarding school at Wilmington, where he was vicar for 55 years [qv]. Born 1755, son of William and Rebecca of Rugely, Staffordshire (father later a mercer and draper of Birmingham), who had a family of 10 sons and 4 daughters. His sister Mary later a Quaker minister in Birmingham. St John's College, Cambridge, 1775; scholar; BA 1779, MA 1782. Ordained (Rochester) 1779, vicar of Wilmington 1779 to death; appointed surrogate for granting marriage licences, Archdeaconry of Lewes, 1799; domestic chaplain to Duke of Dorset 1799; prebendary of Chichester, 1802 to death; rector of Ashurst, Kent, 1802 to death. Married January 1781 to Catharine Jane, daughter of Walter Biddulph, esq; children - Selina Sarah born 30 December 1781, James

9. Detail from a map of the estate in Hastings of John Collier, esq., surveyed by Samuel Cant, 'Schoolmaster and Surveyor', 1750. (ESRO SAY 1415.) Cant was master of Hastings Grammar School 1738-59; like many other schoolmasters he augmented his income by

Henry born 6 July 1782; Catharine buried 6 January 1787; married secondly on 4 October 1804, daughter of James Nicklin of Hackney, Middlesex, esq. In 1790 was one of the first subscribers (gave £2 2s) to public subscription for the relief of 3 orphan children of the Rev Richard Michell, schoolmaster of Eastdean. In February 1795, a time of great distress among the poor, he and 'the young gentlemen under his care' raised a contribution to supply every poor family in the parish with butcher's meat, weekly, in proportion to their numbers, at 2d the lb under market-price. Died in London 2 March 1835, aged 81, and buried at Wilmington 11 March 1835. His Quaker sister Mary wrote to a friend a few days after his death - 'Thy unfeigned sympathy is truly cordial to me; also thy kindness in sending the lovely harbingers of Spring, which now adorn my appartment and cheer me. I thought as I separated them, (and now think with a sigh of tender sadness) could my beloved brother James have entered my room, he would have admired their beauties, and said, with his usual courtesy, 'And how nicely sister Mary has arranged them!' Ah! how memory brings to mind his gentleness in early life, his patience with my untowardness; and in maturer days, his liberality in pleading my cause, as being of an age to judge for myself respecting the most acceptable way of worshipping God. I do not remember ever to have heard an unkind word from his lips, or a harsh censure, on any occasion.' [*Al. Cant.*; ESRO PAR 510/7/3; CI; PR; *SWA* 15.2.90, 23.2.95, 14.10.99, 28.10.99]

CARACCIOLI, Charles: 'Master of the Grammar School', Arundel, when in 1766 he published *Antiquities of Arundel*. [*SAC* **18**]

[**CARLETON, Bell** (-1746)]: Perhaps master of Amberly school, from which Thomas Halsey went to Peterhouse, Cambridge in 1740. Vicar of Amberley from 1721 (also vicar of Lyminster from 1721 and vicar of West Angmering from 1741). Wife Sarah died 20 May 1746, aged 56; he died next month and was buried 25 June 1746. [*Al. Cant.*; CI]

[**CARTER**]: Had a 'Preparatory Academy' at Lewes by 1805. [*Brighton and Lewes Guide* (1805)]

CARUSS, Thomas: Probably usher of Midhurst grammar school; in January 1736 signed receipt for £3 15s 'for the Schooling of Twelve Boys one Quart'r'. [*HMGS*]

CASTLEY, James (1745-): Master of Lewes grammar school 1775-78 [qv]. Son of John of Drybeck, Westmorland. Queen's College, Oxford, matriculated 14 June 1764, aged 19; BA 1770, MA 1773. Curate St Anne Lewes (conducted marriages as curate 15 September 1772 to 18 June 1778); curate St Michael Lewes (conducted marriages as curate 8 February 1773 to 4 March 1778); signed Hamsey bishop's transcripts 1773, 1779. Party to the formal agreement of separation between Thomas Paine and his wife Elizabeth (née Ollive) [qv], 4 June 1774. [*SWA* 11.9.75, 4.12.75, 31.8.78; PRs; CI; Williamson, A. *Thomas Paine* (1973)]

[*CATHERY, Mrs*]: Had a preparatory school for boys at Chichester by c1804 [qv Other schoolmistresses].

CHAFFIN, Ann: Had a girls' boarding school at Lewes (Rs 1793-94) [qv]. Née Holford, married James Chaffin, widower, at Lewes, 1 December 1761 (he was 'Collector of Excise for this County'). They were nonconformists: 3 children baptised at Westgate chapel, James in 1762, another James in 1764, Ann in 1766. Husband died 10 June 1787, aged 58. Ann was a Baptist; admitted 'as transient member' to Eastgate Chapel 5 April 1784 by letter of recommendation from the church at Greenwich, Kent; shown as admitted 1 April 1787 in list of members. On latter date also admitted were Mary Chaffin (excluded 24 September 1794 for holding unitarian beliefs) and Frances Chaffin. On 23 August 1784 Ann agreed to subscribe 10s 6d per quarter for support of the pastor (only one member subscribed more, £1 1s, 2 the same, 22 lesser amounts). On 22 February 1793 'A Letter from Ann Chaffin was read which declared her steadfastness in the faith, and her affection to the Church' (cf Mary Chaffin above). In February 1797 she left the church at Lewes for 'the Church in London under the Pastoral care of Brother John Rippon, DD'. From 1796 the house in the Cliffe she had rented for her school was rented by John Button, also a Baptist, for his boys' school. [St Michael PR; *SWA* 18.6.87; All Saints PR;

ESRO NU 1/1/2, NB 1/1/1A]

CHALLONER, wife of John: Paid 5s in 1727 by the Dowlin charity for schooling poor children of West Grinstead. Possibly the Goody Challoner paid for the same 1721-25 (see *CHALLONER*, wife of Richard). [WSRO Par 95/1/1/3]

CHALLONER, wife of Richard: Paid 13s 10d in 1727 by the Dowlin charity for schooling poor children of West Grinstead, and probably the Goody Challoner paid in total £6 10s 10d for the same 1721-25 (yearly range £1 2s 4d to £1 15s 8d). [WSRO Par 95/1/1/3]

CHALONER, Thomas: Exciseman and schoolmaster at Shoreham and Littlehampton. Gaoled at Horsham for debt as a young man; released c1741 through intervention of Charles Eversfield, MP. Also a poet, and flattering verses to Eversfield apparently obtained his release. As 'Schoolmaster at New Shoreham and Little Hampton', he published in 1732 *The Merriest Poet in Christendom, or Chaloner's Miscellany, being a salve for every sore, containing all his extempore flights, satyrs, songs, turns of fancy, and humours, &c.* [Albery, W., in *SCM* 6, 742-4; *SAC* 18, 106]

CHAPMAN, Thomas: In 1769 was authorised by Eastbourne vestry 'to take possession of the school house belonging to the parish and teach school therein' [qv Parish schooling].

CHRISTIAN, Charles: Paid £2 2s by the Rev Matthias D'Oyly of Pevensey for schooling 3 poor children of Pevensey from Lady Day 1793 to Lady Day 1794. Unless 'Charles' an error in lawyer Gilbert's 'Account with Rev'd Mr D'Oyly', he was probably standing in for John Christian [qv] who was paid as above 1787-1800 except for this one year. [ESRO SAS/GT 3, 210]

CHRISTIAN, John: Recommended as schoolmaster for teaching 'the Poor children in Pevensey and Westham in reading, writing & accounts', 23 September 1785 - the day Richard Thompson, schoolmaster of Westham charity school, was buried. Another faction recommended another master [qv PEVENSEY Charity school]. From Lady Day 1787 to at least Lady Day 1800 he was paid £2 2s per

annum by Matthias D'Oyly, vicar of Pevensey 1767-1816, for schooling 3 poor children of Pevensey. (For the year to Lady Day 1794, Charles Christian apparently received the payment.) Married a Mary, their infant son buried at Pevensey 8 October 1781. [CI; PR]

CLARK, Mrs: Sunday school mistress at Bishopstone 1793-1800, for which she was paid by the parish £2 12s a year (ie 1s a week) [qv].

CLARKE, Robert: Master of the Grey Coat boys' charity school, Chichester [qv] from its foundation, Lady Day 1710, to Christmas 1748. Also master of the Oliver Whitby boys' boarding charity school, Chichester [qv] from its opening in 1712 to Christmas 1748. (For salaries recieved, etc, see under the schools.) When he retired at Christmas 1748 the Oliver Whitby trustees awarded him an annuity of £10 'for his former Services and on Account of his great Age'.

CLEMENT, Simon: Schoolmaster at Arundel 1788, and later at Shoreham [qv]. By 1792 he had 'taught School some time' at Shoreham. Offered, specifically, navigation; also mathematics, Latin etc. Also a surveyor. [*DLS*]

CLOWES, Elizabeth: Née Elizabeth Harraden, of Chichester, married 21 April 1774 William Clowes, schoolmaster [qv]. On his death, she kept a small school [qv] in order to support 2 children. [St Olave PR]

CLOWES, William: Had a boys' boarding school at Chichester [qv]. Reputedly brought up and educated at Oxford. Married 21 April 1774 Elizabeth Harraden of Chichester (he first advertised his boarding school the following month). Their son William (later a successful London printer) baptised 18 January 1779. Died when son still an infant. [Willis, T. G. *Records of Chichester* (1928); St Olave PR; St Peter the Less PR]

COATES, James (1757?-1832?): Schoolmaster of Storrington (identified as such at baptism of daughter, 1799). Probably master of the charity school [qv], perhaps from 1785 when William Phillips left. Married there, 21 March 1780, Anne Greenfield; 10 children baptised 1780-1799 (the first baptised 7 May 1780). Anne buried 6 August 1809, aged 50. Probably the

JC buried 7 September 1832, 'of the Workhouse, 75 years'. [PR]

COHEN, Emmanuel Hyam (-1823): Kept a Jewish boys' school in Brighton, probably from the 1780s [qv]. A native of Nederwerrn in Northern Bavaria, came to Brighton in 1782. Credited as the real founder of the Jewish community there. Acted as Shochet (Ritual Slaughterer). Associate of Moses Mendelsshon, philosopher and grandfather of the composer. Married Hannah Benjamin. Left 4 sons and 6 daughters (eldest son, Levi Emanuel, founded the radical *Brighton Guardian* in 1827). Died 1823, when his estate was valued for probate as 'less than £20'. [Spector, D., in *SGLH* **3** no. 3 (1981)]

COLBRAN, Thomas (1737-1816): Born at Ninfield, baptised there 11 March 1737, son of Thomas and Rachel, he was appointed master of Sedlescombe charity school [qv] in 1755, aged 18, having assisted the previous master Isaac Gostling in his old age. Held the appointment for 61 years, until his death in 1816 - the longest tenure of any 18th-century Sussex schoolmaster. From the start he was allowed to take private pupils also, and from 1770 took up to 10 boys as boarders, having spent £40 extending the schoolhouse (in consideration of which the trustees agreed to pay £2 a year in the event of his being prevented by sickness or accident from managing the school, or in the event of his death, the term of this 'insurance' being 20 years). Also undertook land-surveying, but in 1776 gave this up in order to devote 'his whole Time and Attention to the Management and Instruction of his Scholars' (surviving estate maps: 1760 (Sedlescombe), 1769 (Ewhurst), 1774 (Guestling), 1774 (Brede and Udimore), 1790 (Sedlescombe)). At the appointment of his successor, the trustees recorded that he had wrongly been demanding entrance money on the admission of the free scholars. Married 24 November 1768 Elizabeth Birch of Battle; had issue -Thomas 1769 (died as infant), George 1771, Elizabeth 1773 (died as infant), Elizabeth 1774 (baptised 3 days after burial of the infant Elizabeth), William 1775. Wife died 1778; he died 1816 (buried 26 November). [PRs; ESRO SAS/ACC 375-376, SAS/AN 243; HM MA 111, 125]

COLE, John: Subscribed 19 January 1700 'to teach a writting Schooll att West Tarring' and was probably teaching there in 1701 (William Stiles subscribed for the same purpose in 1703). [WSRO Ep.I/3/3]

COLENS, Mary: A loose receipt dated 24 March 1744 shows Playden parish paid her 8s 11d for schooling Martha Neal (then aged 7) - 7 weeks at 2d per week and 31 weeks at 3d per week. She signed the receipt by mark. [ESRO PAR 445/31/1/14]

COLLETT, Peter (1735-1790): Master of Rye grammar school 1760-90 [qv]. Son of Richard, of London, gent; St John's College, Oxford, 1751; BA 1756. Licensed as schoolmaster 'in the Free School of Rye' 1 October 1760; curate of Rye 1760 to death; licensed as curate of Udimore 3 January 1761, held to death; rector of Denton 1777 to death. Married firstly Margaret, died 6 May 1770; secondly, 18 February 1773, at Udimore, Elizabeth Woodhams, daughter of Thomas, farmer of Udimore, 'a most amiable young lady, with a genteel fortune, and every other qualification to make the connubial state happy'. Died 14 September 1790, aged 55, leaving 'a widow and six children, totally destitute'. On Lord Eardley's recommendation, a public subscription was raised for their relief, which by May 1791 totalled £439 7s. In January 1792 *A Sixpenny Christmas Box* was published, price 6d, the profits being given 'to the Michell and Collett Orphans'. His widow, Elizabeth, died 11 February 1841, aged 95. [*Al. Oxon.*; WSRO Ep.I/1/11; CI; *SWA* 1.3.73, 17.2.77, 4.10.90, 2.6.91, 2.1.92; Rye PR; MI Rye church]

COLLINS, Richard (-1801): Usher at Horsham grammar school 1789-1801 [qv]. Also parish clerk (another RC, presumably his father, buried 16 June 1790, also parish clerk). Voted in Parliamentary election 19 June 1790 as 'of South Street, Horsham, Schoolmaster'. Buried 1 July 1801, as 'Clerk of this Parish'. [*HCS*; Albery, W. *Parliamentary History of Horsham* (1927); PR]

[COOKE]: Pianoforte master, at Russell Street, Brighton, 1805. [*Button's Directory*]

COOK, John (-1792): Schoolmaster of Cuckfield. Buried 20 May 1792 as 'schoolmaster and Vestry Clerk'. Will dated 19 December 1791 mentions late wife [Hannah, qv COOK, Richard, below] and son Richard, deceased. Principal beneficiary 'my natural Daughter Mary Green now an infant of a Year old and daughter of Ann Green my Servant', to whom he bequeathed in trust his copyhold premises, specified items, and residue of estate after legacies to sons John and William, grandson Richard Cook and natural grandson William Newington. [PR; ESRO W/A 66.383]

COOK, Richard (1757-89): Schoolmaster of Cuckfield, and governor of the workhouse. Buried as such, 3 November 1789. Baptised 25 May 1757, son of John and Hannah. [PR]

COOPER: Paid 12 sums, ranging from 2s 6d to £1 2s 6d between April 1768 and October 1771, by Alfriston parish for schooling (the money coming from sacrament collections) [qv Parish schooling]. Received 3d per week per boy. Referred to as 'Mr' in parish accounts; probably kept a petty school to which the parish sent a few poor boys. [ESRO PAR 230/1/1/1]

COOPER, Vincent (1681?-1734): Rector of Newick 1711-34. Reference to schoolhouse and parsonage 1714; previous incumbent kept a school there to 1710; VC probably also augmented his income by teaching sons of local gentry [qv Boys' schools]. Son of Nathan, of Chirton, Wiltshire, clerk. Chorister Magdalen College, Oxford; matriculated 16 April 1698, aged 17; demy 1701-09; BA 1705, MA 1708, fellow 1709-20, BD 1717; ordained deacon (Oxford) 1706, priest (Oxford) 1710. (Three brothers also at Oxford.) Also rector of Bramber and vicar of Buttolphs annexed 1720 to death. Wife Mary died 30 August 1732. He died 25 September 1734, buried at Newick 30 September 1734. [CI; *Al. Oxon.*; PR]

COOPER, William: Schoolmaster, St Andrew parish, Chichester 1791. [WSRO Add MS 2134]

CORBYN, William: Dancing master of Brighton (Rs 1798-1800) [qv]. At 35 New Street c1799; at 6 Nile Street 1800. Freemason; in register of Royal Clarence Lodge 1799 (first year registration required by law). [*SWA* 29.9.1800; ESRO QDS/1/EW1]

CORBYN, junior: One of the 'Messieurs Corbyn', dancing masters of Brighton 1799 [qv CORBYN, William].

CORNWELL, Mary (1753-1807): Schoolmistress at Lewes; so described in her will of 17 November 1800. Buried, St John sub Castro, 30 December 1807, aged 54. Unmarried; her only brother, Robert, yeoman of Mayfield, executor and residual legatee (her goods etc less than £200) after bequests to Mantell family - £50 to Gideon Mantell (later celebrated geologist: see Schedule 3), £5 each to his parents, Thomas, cordwainer, of Lewes, and Sarah, and £2 2s to each of their other children. In his journal for 13 July 1820 Gideon Mantell refers to her: 'my dear old lady Mrs C[ornwell] of Lewes, who fostered me when a child, and treated me with the greatest kindness while she lived'. [ESRO W/A 70.213; PR; Curwen, E. C. (ed) *The Journal of Gideon Mantell* (1940)]

COTTINGTON, (Samuel?) (1758?-1806?): Schoolmaster at Framfield. Paid, with Tyler, by parish, 1794-97, £4 a year for schooling 10 poor children, arising out of the Smith and Wharton charities [qv Charity schooling] (The payments for schooling continued to end of century but recipients not named after 1797.) Possibly Samuel C, buried 5 October 1806, aged 48, married. [ESRO PAR 343/11/2; PR]

CRIPPS, Elizabeth: In 1771, with Charlotte Gridley, opened a girls' boarding school at Battle [qv].

CROFT, Mrs: In 1793 opened a French and English girls' boarding school at Hooe [qv].

CROPLEY, William Heaton (1770-): In 1794 proposed to prepare 'a limited number of young gentlemen' for university, at 4 Golden Lion Lane, Brighton [qv]. Born at Chelmsford, Essex (baptised there 16 July 1770), son of William, clerk, of West Ham, Essex. Eton; Magdalene College, Cambridge, 1788; to Clare College 1789; BA 1792; deacon (London) 1792. Signed marriage banns, Brighton, April 1791 - March 1795. [*Al. Cant.*; PR]

CRUTTENDEN, Everenden (1741-1824): Master of Bexhill parish charity school, 1789-1800 and probably later [qv Parish free school].

Baptised at Bexhill 8 November 1741, son of John and Elizabeth; buried there 8 January 1824, aged 84. [PR]

CRUTTENDEN, Sarah: Mistress of Mary Herbert's charity school for girls, Brightling [qv] from its opening in 1733 to 1763. The school had 6 charity girls, and she was initially paid 3s a week excluding August (when the school was closed), or £7 4s a year. From May 1738 she was paid instead 1d per day's teaching per child, which reduced her income [for details, see Herbert's charity school]. She also kept her own school [qv], teaching both boys and girls at 2d a week. She also received payments from John Fuller for 'damasque for Caps' (16s 3d, 1735) and 'Holland' (linen cloth: £2 6s 3d, 1735; 10s, 1737). Referred to as 'Mrs' in the school accounts and probably wife of Thomas, who received the money due to her on occasion. [ESRO PAR 254/25/1, SAS/RF 15/28]

[CRUTTENDEN, (William?)]: Probably schoolmaster in St John sub Castro, Lewes, in 1796 [qv Other schoolmasters]. (Possibly William C, who occupied a house there in the following year.) [Land Tax]

CUNNINGHAM, Richard (1735-): Schoolmaster at Angmering 1767 (marriage licence 29 December 1767) [qv Charity school]. He married Judith Woods of Angmering (1740-) 5 January 1768. Their children, baptised at Angmering: James (1769), Sarah (1770), Charlotte (1774), Jeremiah (1776). [*SRS* 32; PR, from Baker, L., pers. comm.]

CURTEIS (CURTIS), John (-1799): Schoolmaster of Uckfield [qv Other schoolmasters]. In the last week of September 1799 there was a violent flash flood; at Uckfield bridge the water was reported to have risen 5 feet in the space of one minute; Curteis and a neighbour, vainly trying to dam the water from their houses, were swept away; they were discovered 3 hours later, about 300 yards downstream, lodged against a willow tree; a man, at the risk of his life, swam out and found Curteis still alive (the other was dead); by the help of ropes and a long ladder, he was got out and taken to a public house, 'where he appeared sensible and uttered several words, but expired about an hour and a half

afterwards...Curteis was a very useful man in his neighbourhood, and much respected. He kept the parish accounts, which, with a number of other accounts of consequence to individuals, were carried away by the flood; but the desk that contained most of them, was found a few days since, at the bottom of the river, and the parish poor-book was picked up yesterday. The above disastrous event was witnessed by Lord Gage, who gave the man that ventured into the water, two guineas, for his humane exertions.' Gage's accounts show that he also gave £2 2s each to the widows of the two men who drowned; so Curteis was married. Buried 3 October 1799. [*SWA* 7.10.99; ESRO SAS/G/ACC 741; PR]

DADSWELL, David (-1803): Master of Fermor's charity school, Rotherfield [qv], 1772-c93. Succeeded father-in-law, William Okill [qv]; was succeeded by son, Edward Okill [qv]. Of Rotherfield, married at Withyham 10 September 1747 Ann Okill of Rotherfield (baptised at Sevenoaks 31 March 1731, daughter of William and Jane). At Charity Farm, which he managed for the Fermor Trust. Baptisms of children: Jane (3 July 1748), Edward Okill (2 December 1750), David (24 December 1752), Hannah (6 April 1755), Robert (1 January 1757), James (16 August 1761), Ann (29 April 1764), Nicholas (29 April 1766), Elizabeth (15 February 1769). Wife Ann buried 30 June 1800 and he buried 5 April 1803. [Hackworth, J. *Sir Henry Fermor C of E School 1744-1994* (1994); Withyham, Rotherfield PRs]

DADSWELL, Edward Okill (1750-1832): Master of Fermor's charity school, Rotherfield [qv], c1793-c1822. Succeeded father, David [qv]. Baptised 2 December 1750, son of David and Anne. Married 18 July 1786 Elizabeth Taylor, 20, daughter of Elizabeth, widow. Had issue, including son David Taylor, baptised 2 February 1800, who succeeded him as master. Also churchwarden Rotherfield and farmer, Laurel Tree Farm, Boarshead. Buried 16 February 1832, 'The Schoolmaster of Crowboro' Charity, Yrs 82'. [Hackworth, J. *Sir Henry Fermor C of E School 1744-1994* (1994) and pers. comm.; PR; *SRS* 25]

DANN, John: Schoolmaster of Bexhill [qv Parish free school]. Paid by the parish £6 a year salary for the 'Free School' and about 10s a year 'for firing for the free Scholars', of which there were 10 (which suggests he also had private pupils), from Easter 1776 to Easter 1788. From 1782 also paid £1 a year for 'Book keeping for Overseers', and on 5 occasions 2s 'for writing the Militia List'. (Perhaps husband of Mary [qv]; if so, had moved to Wadhurst by 1796.)

DAN, Mary (-1796): Schoolmistress of Wadhurst. Buried 14 October 1796, 'Mary Wife of John Dan, School=Mistress'. (Perhaps wife of the JD above.) [PR]

DARCEL, Monsieur: French teacher; 'a Native of France'. Taught at Cater Rand's school, Lewes, 1776. [*SWA* 12.9.76]

DAVEY, M. (Mary Symonds?) (-1800?): With P. Meane, had a girls' boarding school at Lewes (Rs 1792-94) [qv]. Probably Mary Davey, of St Michael parish, and probably a Baptist [see Schedule 1]. Probably related to Thomas Davey, apothecary and deacon of Eastgate Baptist church. Very probably the Mary Symonds Davey [qv under PUGH] who married Edward Pugh, schoolmaster, 1794 (Thomas Davey was the witness); c1794 the Pughs took over, for their joint schools, the house previously occupied by Meane and Davey's girls' school.

DAVIES, Morgan (-1799): Had a boys' boarding school, Eastbourne (Rs 1775-93) [qv]. Also master of Eastbourne charity school from 1775 to Christmas 1783 [qv]. Rector of Litlington 1784 to death. Licensed as perpetual curate of Udimore 1792, but non-resident, and he authorised by bond the churchwardens and overseers to receive his salary of £20 and appoint and pay their own curate; resigned 1796. Also sometime curate of Brede, to 1795. Married 20 April 1784, at Eastbourne, Jane Auger. Died 1799. [SAS Budgen MS v.119; *SWA* 13.11.75; CI; PR]

DAVIS: Schoolmaster at Arundel: had joined Priest's boys' boarding school by January 1787, when the school was advertised under both their names [qv]. The curriculum was then extended to include Latin, also mensuration, merchants' accounts and geography (previously extras); so these probably taught by Davis. In

January 1789, Priest was on his own again.

DAVIS, David: Master of Chichester grammar school 1784-97 [qv, also for details of his private boarding school]. *The Victoria County History of Sussex* gives 'of Pembroke [College], Cambridge'. Vicar of Bury 1795 (then BD); resigned 1813. DD (Cambridge) 1797. Married in London (St Anne, Soho), 7 June 1796, Sarah Ives, of that parish. [*VCH* ii; CI; *Portsmouth Gazette* 24.7.97; *SNQ* 6]

DAVY, Thomas (1729-1801): Scholar (as adult) and friend of Thomas Turner, who kept East Hoathly school 1755-56; taught school for Turner on occasion. Shoemaker; married, July 1761, Mary Virgo, widow; parish clerk 1777. Died 1801, aged 72. [Worcester, D. K. *The Life and Times of Thomas Turner of East Hoathly* (1948); Vaisey, D. (ed) *The Diary of Thomas Turner* (1984)]

DAWES, Jane: Schoolmistress of Playden. Surviving loose receipt dated 21 April 1783 shows parish paid her 7s 6d for schooling John and James Head for 15 weeks (ie 3d per week per boy); for similar receipt for 7s for schooling the 2 boys, 28 April 1783 - 14 July 1783, payee not identfied but probably her; and third similar receipt shows Stephen Dawes was paid 7s (presumably on Jane's behalf) for 1 quarter's schooling of the boys, 14 July 1783 - 13 October 1783. During this time John Head was 7, James 5. [ESRO PAR 445/31/1/14]

[**DEBARDE, Alexander Hils**]: Schoolmaster at Eastbourne 1803. Then aged 17-30, unmarried and with no children under 10. [*SGLH* 6, no. 1]

DENDY, Richard (-1723): Schoolmaster of Steyning (reference to his school 1716: qv). Married 1713 Mary Beard of Steyning (marriage licence 28 July 1713). Daughter Mary baptised 30 May 1714 (parish register gives mother 'Dorothy'?). Churchwarden 1714. In 1716 with wife Mary sold property in Steyning for £80. In 1715, described as 'schoolmaster' bought a property in Steyning for £80 and in 1722, described as 'gent', another for £180, which two he bequeathed by will dated 3 May 1723 to wife Mary, with remainder to daughter Mary. Buried 12 November 1723. Widow married Richard Borman of Steyning, apothecary. Daughter

Mary married Richard Lawson of Bosham, clerk (both dead by 1772: their eldest son, James Lawson, then a sword cutler of St Clement Danes, Middlesex, married Helena). [Freeth, S. (ed) *The Wiston Archives* **II**; *SRS* **6**; PR]

DENNIS: Dancing master of Brighton [qv under <u>Dancing and music masters</u>]. In 1793 took over Rawlins' practice. Then at 31 West Street.

DEVAS, Stephen (-c1780): Dancing master of Robertsbridge. Dead by 24 July 1780. [*SWA* 24.7.80]

DICKENSON: Schoolmaster at Framfield. In 1792 and 1793, with Tyler, paid by parish £4 a year for schooling 10 poor children, arising out of the Smith and Wharton charities [qv <u>Charity</u> <u>schooling</u>] In 1794, part of the annual payment was made to 'Dickensons Creditors'. [ESRO PAR 343/11/2]

DINE, William (c1725-): Schoolmaster at Chiddingly. Published in 1771 *Poems on Several Occasions* (printed by William Lee, Lewes; 72 pages; price 1s). The preface, 'The PRINTER to the READER', stated that the author 'is between forty and fifty Years of Age, and has, for some Time past, kept a little School in the Parish of Chiddingly, in the County of Sussex, and was lately made Clerk of the said Parish. All his Time before was spent in husbandry Labour, excepting his being employed a few Seasons in the Hop Excise, previous to which he received some Instruction: All his other Learning, he acquired by his own Study and Application, having never been put to any School. He was always in low Circumstances, on account of a large Family which he had, and still has, partly to support; and could purchase but few Books, besides a Dictionary. Having a natural Taste for POETRY, he would borrow what Books he could, of that Sort, of his Friends, and read them by Night'. On page 15 Dine states that he was 'upwards of 40 Years of Age' when writing a poem dated September 1768. Married, 12 April 1748, Ann Turle of Chiddingly. Died before 15 December 1811, when his widow was buried, aged 84. [PR]

DIVALL, Nicholas: Paid monthly by Framfield

parish from November 1794 to June 1797 for schooling children, undoubtedly the workhouse children. Payments ranged from 11d to 2s 6d (his predecessor, Henry Pain, appears to have been paid a third of 1d per child per week). Total paid to him in 1795 was £1 2½d (in 1796 he would have received more, but the total cannot be ascertained as in one payment schooling is combined with 'the work Bill'). Back in April 1789 he had been 'Allow'd' 5s, presumably by way of relief in need. [ESRO PAR 343/31/1/4]

DIXON, John (1704-74): Schoolmaster at Chichester. Died 8 February 1774, aged 70; buried as 'schoolmaster', St Martin, 11 February 1774. Wife Ann died 29 March 1762, aged 67. [*SAC* **50**; PR]

DOD, Henry: Schoolmaster at Henfield (reference 1707 from a deed in the church chest). [de Candole, H. *The Story of Henfield* (1976)]

DODSON, Miss senior: With sister, had a girls' boarding school in Lewes, 1794-96 [qv], taking over Miss Ryall's school at Christmas 1793. In January 1797 all the school effects were sold by auction. (Perhaps the Mary Dodson of Lewes who married, 5 January 1797, John Baker of Lewes, grocer.) [*SWA* 9.1.97; Lewes St Anne PR]

DODSON, Miss junior: See DODSON, Miss, senior. (In 1798 Elizabeth Dodson, youngest daughter of the late Rev Christopher, rector of Hurstpierpoint, married there the Rev Marchant, but she has not been identified as one of the Lewes schoolmistresses.) [*SWA* 23.4.98]

DREWETT, Dame: Schoolmistress of Steyning. Paid 2s a week by the parish 'for the school', perhaps at the workhouse, from 21 December 1782 to 14 May 1785. (On 30 April 1785 the 2s was paid to 'Mr Drewet for school', presumably her husband.) Two other payments to her are recorded: 15 April 1783, 'for toping 2 Gowns' 1s 6d; 29 March 1783, 'for altering Kit Patchen's Gown' 10d. [WSRO Par 183/31/2]

DUBBINS: From December 1790, joined wife [qv] in advertisements for their girls' boarding school at Horsham. From January 1791 various

'Sciences' were taught to the girls - perhaps his contribution?

DUBBINS, Mrs: By October 1786 had a girls' day and boarding school at Horsham, in a large house, erected 'purposely for a School' [qv]. Her school was notable for its enlightened approach - for its emphasis on kindness and persuasion, as opposed to 'the cruel severity of harsh discipline', and its wide curriculum (various 'Sciences' were taught to the girls - unusual for this period).

DUDMAN, Jane: Schoolmistress at Midhurst 1793. [*Universal British Directory*]

DUKE, Widow: Had a dame school at Mayfield in the 1760s, and probably earlier. The managers of Mayfield charity school [qv] sent children to her, under 'Mr Porter's gift', from January 1765 to September 1767, when the gift had been expended; the number they sent rose from 4 at January 1765 to 8 at January 1767; all these children later went on to the charity school. Her literacy is evidenced by the parish paying her, in 1748, 10s for 'a'making the Poor Book'. Widowed by February 1748. (Perhaps Mary Duke, widow, buried 3 March 1780.) [ESRO PAR 422/31/1/3; PR]

DUNN, James Charles Tracy (1770-1837): Schoolmaster at Lewes. In January 1802 master of Friars Walk Academy (established 1796, probably by him). In 1799 also engaged by Mrs Gell, as a 'most eminent Master', to teach the girls of her boarding school 'Writing and Accomptmanship'. Eastgate Baptist church archives contain property deeds relating to him 1804 and 1806. On his death in 1837 the school was taken over by his son, Rev J C T (same names), who resigned as master of Cuckfield grammar school (where he had been scathingly criticised by the Charity Commissioners for charging 'free' scholars £8 8s a year in order to exclude poor children from his private school). Married 14 January 1804 Ann May (daughter of Edward and Jane). Children: James Charles Tracy born 27 October 1804; Rebecca born 3 December 1809; Edward born 3 December 1811; Sarah born 17 February 1814; Fanny born 19 February 1816. Member of Lewes Tabernacle from 1817. Buried All Saints, Lewes, 19 May 1837, aged 67. Survived by wife Ann. Will (dated 11 June 1814, proved 19 May 1851 by Ann) left properties in trust for benefit of wife and her children; on her death or re-marriage, estate to be divided amongst his child or children. (At delayed probate, goods etc valued at less than £20.) [ESRO NB 1/3-8; Brent, C. *Geo. Lewes* (1993) and pers. comm. citing *SWA* 10.1.1802, 11.7.1836; *EP* 30 (1837), 696; Lewes All Saints PR; ESRO NC 2/7/1, W/A 83.792]

DUNVAN, Paul: Usher at Lewes grammar school for 'some years'. Of French extraction. Author of Lee's *History of Lewes and Brighthelmston* (1795) (in which he gives an eulogistic account of Button's new school in St Anne's, implying that it was - on this site - operational; in fact the school was burnt down while building and Button sold the land). Befriended John Dudeney [qv Schedule 3] when the latter was a 10-year-old shepherd boy on the Downs; Dunvan wanted to see a wheatear's nest, which Dudeney found for him; Dunvan gave him 'a small History of England and Robinson Crusoe, and I read them both with great interest'. Was named as a 'riotous' Radical at a town meeting in 1792, and his anonymous *History* (above) was aggressively radical. [Lower *Worthies*; *SAC* 2; Brent, C. *Geo. Lewes* (1993)]

DURNFORD, Thomas (1717-92): Vicar of Harting, he tutored Harry Fetherstonhaugh, son of Sir Matthew of Uppark, prior to his being sent to Eton. Reputed to be 'learned and charming'. Son of Thomas, of Rockbourne, Hampshire, clerk. Wadham College, Oxford, matriculated 21 June 1733, aged 16; BA 1737, MA 1740, B and DD 1752. Instituted vicar of Harting 27 October 1744 (his father instituted 12 June 1744, but resigned); held to death in 1792. Married Ann Collins, younger sister of the poet; marriage unhappy and they separated; she died 1789 (buried 25 October 1789, St Andrew, Chichester). Son Stillingfleet to Wadham College, Oxford; vicar of Felpham 1778 to death in 1786. Daughter married Ulrick Fetherstonhaugh (brother of Sir Matthew) who became rector of Harting in 1757. [Meade-Fetherstonhaugh, M. and Warner, O. *Uppark and its People* (1964); Gordon, H. D. *History of Harting* (1877); CI; *Al. Oxon.*]

EASON, Robert: Opened a boys' boarding school at Storrington 1794 [qv].

EDWARDS, Rev E.: Had a boys' day and boarding school at Hurstpierpoint by 1796; advertised as 'Hurst Grammar School' [qv].

EDWARDS, Richard Swinfen (1732-72): Curate of Burwash, opened a boys' school 1761 (boarding available nearby) [qv]. Born in London, son of Grif[fith?], tailor. Westminster School, then St John's College, Cambridge, 27 October 1748, aged 16; BA 1753, MA 1756; ordained deacon (Ely) 1756, priest (Chichester) 1758. Buried 24 December 1772, at Burwash, 'Curate of this parish'. [*Al. Cant.*; PR]

ELLESS, Francis: Schoolmaster of East Hoathly, 1756-59 [qv Village school]. Took over school from friend Thomas Turner; they learnt surveying together [qv MASON, Christopher] and Turner taught him decimals and the use of the slide rule. Moved to Alfriston 1759, and later to Uckfield.

ELLIS: Schoolmistress at East Grinstead 1799, in *Palmer's Rhyming Directory* (reprinted in *East Grinstead Observer* 7 November 1896): 'Smith and Ellis each impart/ To misses young, the needles art'.

ELLIS, James: Subscribed 6 January 1705, 'to instruct Children in a School at Harting and to have a Lycence therefore'. [WSRO Ep.I/3/5]

ELLIS, Richard (-1759): Schoolmaster at Seaford (Rs 1710-56). Under a bill of detection, Easter 1711: that 'Sarah Wood of ye said parish [Seaford] widow was delivered of a Bastard child & that Richard Ellis of the said parish Schoolmaster was ye Reputed Father, That for several years past the said Richard was & is a married man, & that the said Richard & Sarah (as they have heard & believe) at diverse times in the year 1710 did commit the crime of Adultery together at several places, & even in the parish Church of Seaford.' However, he continued as schoolmaster there, receiving subscriptions for the charity school from Henry Pelham (1735) and the Duke of Newcastle (1737) [qv Charity schools and Ellis's school]; and in his will of 28 July 1756 left, amongst other property, the 'Schoolhouse wherein I now teach School'. His properties in Seaford and personal estate left to wife Elizabeth, his executrix (who survived him) and after her death, variously to his 3 daughters - Elizabeth

Attree, widow of Benjamin of Horsham; Mary Collings, widow of John of Seaford; Sarah Bollard, wife of Benjamin. Other beneficiaries were grandsons Richard Ellis Collings, John Collings, granddaughters Mary Collings, Elizabeth Bollard. Buried 10 March 1759. [ESRO W/A 60.28; PR]

EMERY, Thomas (-1742): Schoolmaster of West Tarring in his will dated 23 January 1735 (proved 13 April 1742). He left his estate to his brother Nicholas, basket-maker of Tiverton, Devon, with remainder to his friend and executor Lambert Henly of Broadwater, gent. Buried 27 March 1742. [WSRO STA I/12, p 115; PR]

ENGLISH: Schoolmistress at Brighton 1791, 1793. [*Universal British Directory*]

EVANS, Hugh (1668-1732): Vicar of Arundel 1720 to death. Licensed to teach boys in a school at Arundel, 5 September 1721. 'Mr Evans has a private school, & licensed, & every way regular' (visitation, 1726). Also vicar of Eartham 1714 to death. Son of Evan of Llanvihangel, Cardigan. New Hall, Oxford, matriculated 5 July 1686, aged 18; BA (Corpus Christi College) 1690, MA (King's College, Cambridge) 1720. Buried at Arundel 25 October 1732. [WSRO Ep.I/26/3, Ep.I/1/10, Ep.I/22/1; *SAC* **106**; *Al. Oxon.*; *Al. Cant.*]

EVEREST, R.: With S. Everest (probably wife) took Guestling charity school 1772, and advertised for boarders, both boys and girls [qv Everest's school]. Perhaps Robert, son of Stephen and Elizabeth, baptised 20 November 1724 at Guestling. [PR]

EVEREST, S.: See **EVEREST, R.**

EVERSHED, William (1751-1808): Schoolmaster at Steyning [qv] and perhaps previously at Billingshurst (referred to as 'of Billingshurst, Schoolmaster' in an uncle's will dated 1788). Had been a potter and brickmaker. Moved to Steyning where he kept a small day school with a few boarders (was renting a house there 1797); also probably did land-surveying. Baptist and occasional preacher, son of William, farmer, and Mary (née Dean) of Billingshurst, Baptists. Married 21 May 1776, at Frittenden, Kent, Elizabeth Bonniwell (1759-

1821; she married secondly, 1816, Philip Kensett, Baptist); one son, four daughters, two of whom died young. Buried 26 July 1808 (Waterside Chapel, Wandsworth). [References as for his school]

EXALL, John (-1777): Schoolmaster of Harting; Roman Catholic [qv Petty and dame schools and Charity schooling for details of his school, poverty, ill-health and local opposition to him running a proposed charity school]. Was 'between 60 and 70 years of age' in 1750. Probably the JE buried 7 October 1777, in which case he lived to 90 or more. [PR]

FEARON, Joseph Francis (1762-1816): Master of Cuckfield grammar school 1786-1800 [qv]. Born 8 March 1762, son of Joseph, vicar of Peasmarsh, and Sarah (née Fletcher). Took over the grammar school in same year he matriculated at St Alban's Hall, Oxford, aged 23. BA 1791, MA 1792. Rector of Clapham 1786-88; vicar of Fittleworth 1788-1801; sequestrator of Coldwaltham 1788-1801; sequestrator of Bury 1789-95; prebendary of Chichester; prebendary of Hove (Rs 1789, 1790); vicar of Preston cum Hove 1789-90; sequestrator of Stoughton 1790; rector of Selsey 1790 to death; joint registrar Archdeaconry of Lewes 1793; all these appointments while master of the grammar school, then vicar of Cuckfield 1801 to death. On 27 September 1789 preached charity sermon at Brighton on behalf of the Sunday school and school of industry, which resulted in a 'very considerable' collection. On Christmas day 1793, gave a good dinner to all the soldiers quartered in Cuckfield, about 40 in number. A freemason, in 1797 preached a sermon (later published) at the laying of the foundation stone of the new freemason hall at Lewes; member of the South Saxon Lodge (Lewes) 1799 (first year when such registration required by law). Married 6 June 1793, at St George Hanover Square, Middlesex, by the Bishop of Chichester, Jane Clutton, daughter of William of Cuckfield (she died 13 March 1841, aged 75). Died on Christmas Day 1816, aged 54. [Peasmarsh PR; *Al. Oxon.*; CI; *SWA* 28.9.89, 10.6.93, 6.1.94, 24.4.97; ESRO QDS/1/EW1]

FELDWICK, James (1728-96): Schoolmaster at Ditchling, c1770-96. Died 20 December 1796 (buried on Christmas Day), aged 68.

[*SWA* 26.12.96; PR]

FISHER: Dancing master of Chichester (Rs 1776-86) [qv CHICHESTER under Dancing masters for details].

[FLAMBARD]: French master at Midhurst (R c1806).

FLEMING, Edward Leece: Master of Saunders' charity school, Rye, 12 July 1786 - 23 May 1788 [qv]. Curate/assistant curate of Rye, 1786-1787. [PR (marriages)]

FLINT, Goody: Received from the Dowlin charity 5s 6d in 1728, 2s 10d in 1729, for schooling poor children of West Grinstead. [WSRO Par 95/1/1/3]

FLORANCE, James: A young lawyer, in 1793 he was a master at Hay's school, Chichester, [qv] and also tutored boys privately in the classics and mathematics [qv]. ('Schoolmaster' in 1793 poll book.) A Baptist, he married 12 July 1793, Charlotte Dally, of a Quaker family. Their daughter Eliza, born 1793 (eldest of 13 children), was baptised aged 6 at Baffins Lane Unitarian chapel, and married in 1820 William Johnson Fox, weaver boy, preacher, orator, politician, and minister at Baffins Lane for many years. In her memoir, she noted that a debating society (apparently mostly nonconformists and/or poets) met monthly, often at their house, as 'our large drawing room was convenient for the purpose'. JF had own library, and gave one of the rooms in his house for the use of the 'Library Society', which, with Dr Sanden as President, he inaugurated in 1792. [*Chichester Papers* no. 20; *A Memoir of Mrs Eliza Fox* (1869); Chichester Subdeanery PR; *Observer and West Sussex Recorder* 24.11.1909]

FLOTE, Goody: Received from the Dowlin charity 3s in 1704, 4s 2d in 1706, for schooling poor children of West Grinstead. [WSRO Par 95/1/1/3]

FLUTTER, Kitty: Mistress of Roman Catholic charity school at West Grinstead [qv]. In 1754 took over the school when predecessor, Elizabeth Hayes, died. Had been servant to Mrs Hayes 'for many years, on very small wages...and indeed latterly since she [Mrs

Hayes] grew so infirm ye cheif support of the School'. Due to receive £10 a year from John Baptist Caryll, but in 1758 this was 2 years overdue. School probably closed before 1767.

FOOCKS, John: Schoolmaster at Chichester in 1784, living in Little London, with one maidservant. [WSRO MP 414, 417]

FORD, Thomas: 'Teacher of the Mathematics' at Ditchling, 1733, from a map of Oldland Farm, Keymer, made by him. Also mapped Billingham Farm in Udimore and Brede in 1761, and estates in Bolney in 1775 and Barcombe in 1779. [WSRO Add MS 41,248; ESRO AMS 4854, 3424, SAS/WG 889]

FOX: Master of Northiam charity school [qv]. Controversy between parish and trustees, and among trustees, when by 1739 he was too old and infirm to carry out duties properly. Another master was appointed but Fox continued in office until at least 1742 (and the Fox family apparently remained in possession of the schoolhouse until at least 1798, though after 'old Fox' they did not teach).

FRENCH, Mrs: Paid by Alfriston parish, out of certain sacrament collections [qv], for schooling - 15s 3d in 1769, 15s 9d in 1770, 15s 3d in 1771 (probably received 3d per week per child). Probably had own dame school, to which the parish sent a few poor children.

FRENCH, Sarah: Schoolmistress of Brightling. Received 10 payments from John Fuller between 1732 and 1745 for schooling children (two paid to husband Edward; one to 'Widd French', perhaps her mother-in-law). Sometimes the children are named - never more than 2, but she probably had other pupils. Paid 3d a week for teaching 'Lusted's Girl', 2d a week each for 'Sander's boy' and 'Crouch's'. Née Laurence, married Edward French 29 February 1719. [ESRO SAS/RF 15/28; PR]

FREWEN, Thankful (1669-1749): Rector of Northiam for 56 years (15 March 1693 to death), he kept a day and boarding school for boys of his family and sons of local gentry (Rs 1710-22) [qv]. Baptised 2 February 1669, son of Thomas, rector of Northiam, and Mary (née Everenden). School at Northiam; St John's College, Cambridge, 1685; BA 1689; ordained

deacon (London) 7 June 1691, priest (Lincoln) 12 March 1693. Married Sarah Spencer, of Cranbrook, Kent, and had issue: Mary, John, Thomas, Winifred, Edward, Sarah, Selina. (The 3 boys all attended his school; John became vicar of Fairlight, rector of Guestling; Thomas a surgeon at Rye; Edward a DD, of Robertsbridge.) Wife died 1734. Died 2 September 1749, aged 81. [CI; Warne, H. (ed) *A Catalogue of the Frewen Archives* (1972); PR; *Al. Cant.*]

GALE, Walter (1716-72): Master of Mayfield charity school from its foundation for 22 years [qv for many details about him]. Baptised 20 February 1716, son of John of Framfield (- 1752) and Ann (Browning, née Easton; c1678-1756) who had married at Glynde 30 June 1715. Family of some social standing; father occupied one of the highest rented properties in Framfield; mother's 2 daughters by first marriage both married into local gentry families, and WG was god-father to their children. Apparently received some classical education, also understood mathematics. Joined the excise, but was dismissed after twice being fined for offences. Started at Mayfield charity school 1749. Augmented salary of £16 a year plus house by taking private pupils, and by undertaking a variety of artistic commissions, and surveying [see Mayfield school for details]. Licensed 1757 to teach at Mayfield, but unsettled enough to enquire after other jobs - a return to the excise, master of a proposed charity school at Ticehurst in 1758, and that same year he applied for a position as furnace clerk. Like many contemporaries, he was both religious and superstitious. Regularly attended church, and once dreamed of becoming a minister: 'I dreamt last night that I should be advantageously married, and be blessed with a fine offspring, and that I should live to the age of 81, of which time I should preach the gospel 41 years; this I conceived in my sleep was a prophetical dream, which GOD in his infinite mercy grant, together with ability to perform that holy function'. (But he did not marry, nor have children, nor become a preacher.) When his sister was very ill he noted: 'on Thursday last, the town clock was heard to strike 3 in the afternoon twice...The strikes at the 2d striking seemed to sound very dull and mournfully; this, together with the crickets coming to the house at Laughton just at our coming away, I look upon to be sure presages of my sister's death.' In the pages of his diary which survived (until 1857) there are many references to books he owned or borrowed - including several religious books, an *Introduction to Astrology*, the 4-volume novel *Pamela*, the 3-volume *Philander and Silvia*, Raleigh's *History of the World*, Camden's *Britannia*. He tried his hand at verse: 'at 6 o'clock I finished a poem on Mr Baker's journey [to Bristol], which I showed to Mr Keats, and it met with his approbation.' When in 1771, after 22 years at the school, he was dismissed 'for neglecting the duties thereof', he immediately set up his own school in the parish [qv], and also advertised as surveyor, supplier and inscriber of grave stones, book-binder, bookseller and stationer. But he died less than a year later (buried at Framfield 23 November 1772). When dismissed from the school, he wrote long, bitter and self-exculpatory letters to the *Sussex Weekly Advertiser*, in which he referred to the fact that he had 'increased my Circumstances', not from the school 'but from the more gainful Employments I have from Time to Time engaged in'; some evidence of his improved 'circumstances' is given by his will, dated 12 March 1767 - though we do not know to what extent his estate covered its provisions. 20 poor men of Mayfield were each to get 5s to carry his body to Framfield for burial, plus 24s more in common for their expenses on the way; he specified the stonemason who was to carve his gravestone; he left £100 to be laid out in land, the income from which was to pay for 9 loaves of bread each Sunday for 9 'Poor and ancient Persons' of Framfield (who did not receive public charity from the poor rate) 'as long as the World endureth'; Stephen Parker, the sexton, and his wife were to live rent-free for their lives in the cottage they then occupied, that Gale owned; he left an annuity of £2 12s to his uncle-in-law and aunt, and among other bequests sums ranging from £5 to £20 to nieces, nephews and godchildren; the residue of his estate was to be divided equally between his 4 nephews (except his books and instruments, which went to two of them who were his executors). [*SAC* 9; Burchall, M. J. 'Educating the Poor, Mayfield School 1750-1771', BA dissertation, West Sussex Institute of Higher Education (1982); PRs; ESRO W/D9.113]

GAMON, Margaret (-1729): Mistress of

Brighton girls' charity school from its opening, 30 September 1702 [qv]. Paid £6 10s a year initially, £8 a year from Michaelmas 1704; signed receipts. 'Mrs Gamon' at opening of school, and probably wife of Richard (buried 27 February 1720). Buried, widow, 23 October 1729. [BSB; PR]

GASTINEAU, Ann**:** see ***PHILPOT, Ann***

GEERE, Ann? (-1810?): On 3 occasions paid very small sums by Cowfold parish for schooling pauper children (30 April 1797, 3d 'for Schooling'; 28 April 1797, 6d; 7 July 1798, 6d 'for teaching the Children'). Perhaps acted as occasional stand-in for Dame Attree [qv]. Probably 'Ann Geer, widow' buried 20 October 1810, and perhaps wife of 'James Geers, Pauper' whose daughter Sarah was baptised 10 March 1788. [WSRO Par 59/31/4; PR]

GEER, Deborah (1766-95): Schoolmistress of Shoreham 1793. Baptised 27 November 1766, daughter of William and Deborah (née Boyce; buried 11 October 1818, aged 85), who married 26 May 1766. Buried 7 April 1795. [*Universal British Directory* (1793); New Shoreham PR]

GELL, (John?)**:** Had a 'drawing academy' for boys, Wednesday and Friday afternoons, in Lewes, January 1800 (probably at same house as Mrs Gell's girls' boarding school in Friars Walk) [qv]. Probably John Gell, formerly haberdasher and in 1799 having hosiery and law stationery businesses.

GELL, Mrs S.**:** Opened a girls' boarding school in Lewes 1798 [qv]. Previously a milliner, haberdasher and perfumer on School Hill. Probably wife of John, who took over her shop when she set up school, and rented a house in All Saints parish (where she kept her school) 1797 to end of century. [*SWA* 9.5.96, 2.1.97, 21.12.97, 29.1.98, for references to her previous business]

GERISON, Robert (formerly MARGERISON) (1710 or 11-99): Master of Saunders' charity school, Uckfield, probably from 1738 to death [qv]. Also tutored private pupils, eg sons of William Clarke, rector of Buxted, and Thomas Dicker [qv Schedule 3]. Of Yorkshire, at school at Bradford; Peterhouse, Cambridge, 8 July

1730, aged 18; scholar 1730; BA 1734, MA 1737. Ordained deacon (Lincoln) 1734. Curate of Uckfield, probably from 1738 to 1778; rector of Nuthurst 1773-79; vicar of South Malling 1779-93. Married, 1739, at Uckfield, Mary Fuller (buried 6 June1747); son John baptised 8 October 1741, daughter Mary baptised 24 December 1745. Early in April 1789, returning from London, he arrived at the inn there to find the stage coach had left; he decided to walk, and got home at night, having walked 40 to 50 miles - he was then aged 77. Died 26 April 1799, aged 87, 'after a few weeks illness, occasioned by a fall he received, on his return on foot from Isfield'; buried at Uckfield 4 May 1799. NB: 'Margerison' at marriage and baptism of son 1741, 'Gerison' at baptism of daughter 1745 and burial of wife 1747; conducted marriages as 'Margerison' to 1760, 'Gerison' thereafter. [*Al. Cant.*; PR; CI; *SAC* **26**; *SWA* 9.4.89, 29.4.99]

GILLHAM, Elizabeth: Received 6s 1½d from Fletching parish 17 March 1776 and 4s 11½d 23 March 1777 'for Eliz: Smith's Schooling'. Either the EG, widow, buried 14 August 1778, or the EG buried 26 December 1812, aged 74; perhaps the Elizabeth Botting who married George Gillham 16 April 1759. [ESRO SPK/P1; PR]

GIRLE, Elizabeth: Catholic schoolmistress of Arundel, 1714 [qv Catholic dame school].

GOATER, Mary (Mrs): Mistress of the Blue Coat girls' charity school, Chichester [qv]. Received payments on behalf of the school in years to Michaelmas 1723, 1724, 1731, 1733, 1734, 1735 (signed receipts 1723, 1724). [WSRO Cap.V/1/1]

GOLDRING, James: Master of Taylor's charity school, Petworth 1783 [qv], onto which he grafted his private boys' boarding school (Rs 1783-96) [qv]. Had a circulating library at Petworth, and accepted advertisements for the *Lewes and Brighthelmston Pacquet*, 1789. About 1800 was, at Petworth, one of the 7 owners of printing presses in Sussex registered under the Act of 1799. [*SAC* **130**; *Lewes and Brighthelmston Pacquet* 8.10.89]

GOLDSMITH, Mrs: In January 1789 received from the parish of St Anne Lewes, 8s 'for

Little Gates School' (ie 48 weeks at 2d) and in the 1789-90 year 11s 9d 'for Gates Schooling' (ie 47 weeks at 3d). Smaller payments had been made in 1787 and 1788 for Elizabeth Gates and Feering's schooling, perhaps also to her. Probably wife of William Goldsmith, shoemaker, whose bills were paid by the parish from 1781; some of the larger bills (eg £4 13s 11d in 1790, £4 4s 5d in 1791), which did not specify services or goods supplied, may perhaps have included charges for his wife's teaching. [ESRO PAR 411/31/3]

GOODSENS, Henry: Schoolmaster at Robertsbridge in 1780; married, then in Methodist list of members, as was Mary Goodsens, schoolmistress, married, almost certainly his wife. They are not in list of members, 1791, and may have left the district by then. [qv Pike's boys' boarding school, Mrs Goodsen's girls' boarding school]

GOODSENS, Mary: Had a girls' boarding school at Robertsbridge 1777, 1778 [qv]. In Methodist list of members, Robertsbridge, 1780, married, as was Henry Goodsens, schoolmaster, married, almost certainly her husband. They are not in list of members, 1791, and may have left the district by then.

[GOODWIN, George]: Schoolmaster at Petworth in 1693, when paid £5 per quarter for instructing poor children by the Duke of Somerset. Almost certainly master of the Duke's free grammar school, started c1691, at which the master's salary was £20 a year [qv]. Perhaps master there until December 1705, when Henry Wright was licensed to instruct boys in the grammar school of Petworth.

GOSNOLD: Dancing master of Chichester (R 1775). Published *Cotilion and Country Dance Book* (1775). [Qv CHICHESTER under Dancing masters for details].

GOSTLING, Isaac: Master of Sedlescombe charity school, probably from its foundation c1729 [qv]. Was replaced at Lady Day 1755, 'through incapacity, by reason of age'. Also did surveying (references to estate maps by him 1746, 1752). [ESRO AMS 1239, 4836]

[GOWER, Samuel (1772?-)]: Schoolmaster at Hellingly 1803. A cripple, then aged 17-55.

Probably baptised there 24 May 1772, son of Samuel and Phoebe (née Rolfe), who married at Hellingly 19 February 1772 (SG was of Hailsham, probably baptised there 26 September 1740, son of John and Anne). An SG buried Hellingly 31 October 1803 (aged '39', but age entry appears to have been amended). [*Sussex Militia List 1803, Pevensey Rape Southern Division* (1988); PRs]

GRATWICK, Moses: Received 9s in 1708 from the Dowlin charity for schooling poor children of West Grinstead.   [WSRO Par 95/1/1/3]

GRAVATT, Jane: Paid by Wisborough Green parish for schooling poor children, 1796-99, the payments totalling 16s 4d in 1796, £1 3s 3d in 1797, £1 10s 9d in 1798, and 3s in 1799. [WSRO Par 210/31/1]

GREEN, Thomas: Schoolmaster at Arundel. Licensed to teach boys there, 1 July 1730. [WSRO Ep.I/1/11]

[*GREGORY, Mrs*]: Had a boarding school at North Parade, Brighton, by 1805.   [*Button's Directory* (1805)]

GREGORY, John: Had a school at Bosham by 1775 [qv]. Was a curate there 1772-78.

GRIDLEY, Charlotte (later Mrs Betts): With Elizabeth Cripps, opened a girls' boarding school at Battle 1771 [qv]. In April 1781, as 'Mrs Betts, late Miss Gridley', opened her own girls' boarding school there [qv].

GROOMS, John: Schoolmaster at Lewes (R 1782) [qv Grooms' school].

GROOMS, Thomas: Schoolmaster at Lewes (Rs 1774, 1780) [qv Grooms' school].

GROVER, Elizabeth (1706-27): Daughter of John Grover (1677-1752), Quaker master of Brighton charity school. She kept a memorandum book entitled 'Chronology', which included 'I Elis. Grover dwelt at Rigate in the year 1721' (perhaps she was at school there; her sister Mary had been sent to school in London in 1715) and showed she enjoyed considerable travel: 'My mother and Selfe was in the West Country to visit our Relations in

the Year 1719'; 'This present year [1726?] I went to visit my Relations in Dorsetshire and went thence to London And into Yorkshire and Westmoreland'. She recorded: 'Began first to Teach in the new Schooll house in ye 11th mo. 1725/6' [presumably 1725, when the Springett brothers bought a house for the charity school]. Then aged 19, she probably taught the girls' charity school there. Born 20 November 1706, second daughter, sixth child, of John and Elizabeth. Died in 1727. [Clayton, C. E. in *SAC* **36**; Quaker Brighton register, transcript at SFHG]

GROVER, John (1677-1752): Master of Brighton charity school, 1702-50 [qv]. Born 1677, at Hurstpierpoint, into a Quaker family, and remained a Quaker all his life. A shepherd boy in youth, he was a maltster of Brighton when, aged about 20, he married, 29 July 1697, Elizabeth Harrison (daughter of William, deceased, shoemaker); they had 7 children, one or probably 2 dying in infancy. Self-taught, he was reputedly helped by the Rev Falkner (perhaps sometime vicar of Brighton) and the Scrase family (a John Scrase was his predecessor as master). Trustee of the Quaker meeting house in February 1701. Appointed master of the charity school September 1702. Acquired a high reputation for his mathematical skill, and taught navigation at the school. Meagre salary of £8 a year, so also took paying pupils, and acted as the local scrivener; he obtained a considerable knowledge of the law, and was among the appraisers (and was usually the scribe) of 76 out of the 118 surviving probate inventories of Brighton residents, 1710-50, and witness to, and probably draftsman of, many wills. For the church (though a Quaker), he prepared the bishop's transcripts for many years from 1702, and was appointed bishop's attorney in the lease of Brighton rectory in 1741. A notebook of his (surviving in the 19th century), probably written for the instruction and amusement of his children or pupils, was filled with arithmetical rules and problems, with fine penmanship 'supplemented by wonderful flourishes, emblematic devices of swans, fishes, and other objects, and gaily coloured borders and interlining'. His son John and daughter Mary had the smallpox in 1701, and he had it in 1702. Despite his small salary from the charity school, he was successful enough to send daughter Mary to school in London (1715) and his daughter Elizabeth to Reigate (1721), perhaps also to school (and to allow her extensive travel - qv above). Lived in North Street, moved to East Cliff 1702, then to Ship Street 1710. Died 29 September 1752, aged 75. 'Schoolmaster' in will of 27 September 1752 (proved 1 June 1753), which left legacies to grandchildren Simon Grover, Isaac Grover, John Horne, Elizabeth Horne, 'all my mathematical books' to son William [qv below], residue of estate equally to son William and daughter Mary Horne. [Farrant, J. in *SAC* **122**; Clayton, C. E. in *SAC* **36**; Quaker Brighton register, transcript at SFHG; ESRO SOF 9/1, W/A 58.727]

GROVER, Joseph: Master of Westham charity school from Michaelmas 1736 to 1738 [qv]. Taught 9 poor children for £5 a year. In July 1738 intended to go to Jamaica (but later, fearing war would break out with Spain, did not go); was to take a letter from John Fuller to his son Rose in Jamaica, in which JF cited Captain William Markwick's recommendation of Grover: 'I know him well...one that has taught School, writes a good hand, a very good Accomptant, and a very good Surveyor of Land, And indeed a very Ingenious man.' JF added that he was 'also a very sober person', and had some knowledge of surgery, having cured a boy of a compound fracture. [SAS Budgen MS v.129; ESRO SAS/RF 15/25]

GROVER, William (1704-68): Schoolmaster of Brighton (from deed of 1735, and at marriage 1738), perhaps at the charity school [qv]. Born 21 July 1704, son of John (1677-1752) [qv above] and Elizabeth. Quaker, trustee for meeting houses at Lewes (1737) and Brighton (1768) and for burial grounds at Brighton (1735), Chichester, Rottingdean (1735), Twineham (1735). Married 20 February 1738, Elizabeth Ellis, daughter of Elias, Quaker, grocer of Lewes. Also a surveyor (R 1749). Inherited father's mathematical books and half his estate (after legacies to grandchildren). [Quaker Brighton register, transcript at SFHG; *DLS*; ESRO SOF 9/1, W/A 58.727]

GURNETT, George (1696-1746): Master of East Grinstead school: in 1724 his pupil Robert Staples admitted Trinity College, Cambridge. Son of George, of Dorking, Surrey. School at

Kingston, Surrey (Mr Winde). Admitted sizar (age 20) Trinity College, Cambridge, 26 June 1716. Scholar 1719; BA 1720; MA 1723. Deacon (Chichester) 20 September 1719; priest (Chichester) 23 December 1722. Rector West Chiltington 1728, held to death; by 1732 domestic chaplain to Baron Abergavenny; vicar East Grinstead 1732, held to death. Died 2 October 1746. [*Al. Cant.*; CI; MI East Grinstead]

GWYNNE, William (c1745-1817): Master of Lewes grammar school, 1778-1807 [qv]. Son of Edward, of Neath, Glamorgan, matriculated Jesus College, Oxford, February 1765, aged 19; BA 1768, MA 1784. Curate St Anne Lewes, 1778 (marriage register), rector 1783 (marriage register) to death; curate Hamsey 1780 (bishop's transcript), rector 1784 to death; Earl of Abergavenny's domestic chaplain 1784. Acquired Steere exhibitions [qv Grammar school] for sons William and Frederick (son William curate under him St Anne 1797, rector of Denton 1800, rector St Michael, Lewes, 1815). Wife Elizabeth buried 20 April 1810. Buried 24 April 1817, aged 73. [*Al. Oxon.*; CI; *SWA* 10.5.84; St Anne PR]

HACKMAN, Thomas: Master of Oliver Whitby boys' boarding charity school, Chichester, 1797-1808 [qv], onto which he grafted his private boys' boarding school [qv]. The first charity school payment to him, £86 1s 3½d, was 'for half a year & 2 weeks Board and Teaching the Boys to Xmas 1797 & Bill of Incidents to that time'. Appears to have continued with his own school after leaving the charity school. [WSRO E35D/8/3, E35D/3/1; *Holden's Directory* (1811)]

HADLESTON, Thomas: In 1722 opened a school in Chichester where he taught French, dancing and fencing [qv]. Also taught at Lewes and Brighton.

HALL, Elizabeth: Schoolmistress at East Grinstead 1793. 'Schoolmistress' in draft census return 1811 (then in eastern half of Amherst House, High Street), and in 2 letters (John Hoath to William Hall) 26 January 1812 and 12 December 1814. In the last, referred to as 'Cousin Joseph Hall's mother', she 'has been so fortunate as to get a place in Sackville Colledge [almshouse] she teaches School as

Usual but sleeps in Colledge...I think she will find it a great Relief in her declining years.' [WSRO Par 348/26/2/6, Add MS 39,854]

HALL, Thomas (-1747): Schoolmaster of Fletching, from his will, 23 June 1747, which left to his wife Pleasant Hall otherwise Sharp (who survived him) property in Abingdon, Berkshire, for life, then in trust to brother Edward Sharp of Warborough, Oxfordshire, to be sold and the money divided equally between daughter Mary Hall otherwise Sharp and her brothers Richard and Jasper; rest of estate (effects less than £20) to wife, sole executrix. Buried 29 July 1747. [ESRO W/A 57.657; PR]

HALLETT, Mrs: In 1801 received 10s 9d from Ditchling parish 'for schooling', probably either the workhouse school or the Sunday school [qv].

HALSTEAD, James: Schoolmaster of Lewes. Writing master to the grammar school 1741-1742 [qv]. Probably had own school [qv]; perhaps also writing master to Philpot's girls' school. Voted 1734, 1741 (for Tories); rented 100 High Street. [Brent, C. pers. comm.]

HAMMOND, Mrs: Schoolmistress at Salehurst 1700 [qv].

HANNAY, Joseph (1754-1842): Master of the combined Parker's grammar school and Saunders' charity school, Hastings, 1800-1816 (Saunders' charity school was closed from 1812, as a result of a Chancery case) [qv]. Previously in the Excise, had served at Rye and Dover before being posted to Hastings, where in January 1788, with the help of a party of the 11th Light Dragoons stationed in the town, he seized 4 horses and 48 casks of smuggled brandy and geneva near Bo-peep. Following public controversy over the schools, he resigned in October 1816, and immediately opened his own school for private pupils only (but agreed to teach any of his former charity school boys free of charge until the new master for Parker's school had come). He was also immediately re-elected a jurat; and Mr Milward appointed him as his personal accountant at salary of £100 a year. Married Kitty Carswell, daughter of Joseph, mill-owner; their only son died 1816, aged 14. Lived at 34 All Saints Street. Died 1842, aged 88. [*HHGS*]

HARBEN, Miss: With Miss Wayte, had a girls' boarding school at Brighton 1791 into 19th century [qv under Wayte's and Widgett's girls' boarding school]. Had apparently left the school by 1804.

HARISON, Mary: Youngest daughter of Lancelot Harison of Folkington Place, esq, was in 1797, with sister, schooling all the poor children of the parish [qv]. Married 10 August 1797, at Folkington, Eardley Wilmot Lade Michell, of Brighton, at the same time as her sister Sally married William Michell. [*SWA* 14.8.97; PR]

HARISON, Sally: Daughter of Lancelot Harison of Folkington Place, esq, was in 1797, with sister, schooling all the poor children of the parish [qv]. Married 10 August 1797, at Folkington, William Michell of Brighton, esq, at the same time as her sister Mary married Eardley Michell. [*SWA* 14.8.97; PR]

HARMAN, Sarah: Had a small school at Lewes in 1788. [*SWA* 28.1.88]

HARRINGTON, Mrs: Schoolmistress and artist at Brighton, 1775 [qv]. Published an illustrated book on geography and use of maps. As an artist ('sole artist, by the King's special appointment') she 'has had the Honour of taking the Profiles of the first Personages, and most distinguished Nobility in this Kingdom. - That no person may be deprived of their own or their Friend's Likeness, the Price will be so moderate as 2s 6d. Nothing required unless the most perfect Likeness is obtained. - Specimens to be seen at Mrs SMITH's, in *West-Street*. - Time of sitting less than five minutes.' [*SWA* 24.7.75]

HART, John (1691-1736): Master of Hurstpierpoint charity school 1714-31 [qv]; master of Steyning grammar school c1733 to death in 1736 [qv]. Born in Staffordshire; Clare College, Cambridge, 28 July 1709; matriculated 1710, BA 1714. Preached at Hurst parish church 1719. Rector of Wiston 1731 to death. Died 21 July 1736, aged 45. After his death Mrs Hart continued to board the grammar school boys, at least to end of 1737. [*Al. Cant.*; *VCH* vi part 1; MI Wiston]

HARVEY, Richard (1766-1816): The poet

Shelley, born at Warnham 4 August 1792, was sent to a day school run by the vicar, from the age of 6 to 10. The vicar then was RH, and is assumed to have been Shelley's schoolmaster [qv]. Son of Richard of Eastry, Kent; Trinity College, Cambridge, 10 July 1783, aged 17; matriculated 1784, BA 1788, fellow of Clare College, Cambridge 1789, MA (from Clare) 1791. Ordained deacon 1788, priest 1790 (Canterbury). Curate of Swingfield and Acrise, Kent, 1788, of Littlebourne, 1791; vicar of Leatherhead, Surrey, 1798; vicar of Warnham 1798-1805; rector of Ham, Kent, 1809 to death. Died 1816. [*Al. Cant.*; CI]

HARVY: In September 1714 was paid £4 5s 6d for a quarter's board and schooling for Nicholas Gilbert (then 8; his home was in Eastbourne; he was sent to Lewes grammar school at Michaelmas that year). [ESRO ACC 2462/1]

HASEMAN (HEASMAN): Master of a charity school, almost certainly at West Firle, 1797-1800 [for details of payments received from third Viscount Gage, see Charity schooling].

HAWKINS, Mrs Mary (-1806): Paid by Billingshurst parish 6d a week for schooling, probably the workhouse children, May 1788 to June 1789 [qv Parish schooling]. Later received 'relief' from parish, and from 1796 weekly poor pay. Buried 19 February 1806. [WSRO Par 21/31/1; PR]

HAWNEY, William: First master of Saunders' charity school, Rye [qv]; appointed 24 March 1721 (the school opened 19 April 1721). Probably took private pupils as well. [*HRGS*]

HAY, Alexander (1658-1725): Master of Horsham grammar school, 1700-06 [qv]. A Scot, graduated at St Andrews University. Vicar of Itchingfield 1696 to death; suspected of Jacobite sympathies. Resigned grammar school 1706. Died 3 January 1725, aged 66. [*HCS*; CI]

HAY, Alexander (c1735-1806): Had a school at Chichester for many years [qv], which his 'circumstances' made it necessary for him to continue when almost 70 years old. Chaplain to St Mary's Hospital, Chichester, to death; non-residential vicar of Wisborough Green 1785 to

death. Author of *History of Chichester* (1804). Married firstly Mary (buried 9 May 1777), issue 3 sons; married secondly 3 February 1778, Elizabeth Rolfe, singlewoman (signed by mark), issue 2 sons, 4 daughters. At West Gate, Chapel Street, 1784 (rented house) with wife, 3 sons, one daughter, a maidservant and a male lodger. Died there 15 November 1806. [*Chichester Papers* no. 20; WSRO MP 414, 417]

HAYES, Elizabeth (Mrs) (-1745): Mistress of Catholic charity school at West Grinstead [qv]. Suffered acute financial difficulties as often not paid salary of £10 a year promised by John Baptist Caryll.

HEAD, John: Master of Pelham's Grey Coat boys' charity school, Lewes [qv] from at least 1721 to 1733. That year switched allegiance to the Tories, who set him up with another charity school [qv]. Also took private pupils, including girls (Rs 1726, 1728, 1736-37).

HEAL: Dancing master. In July 1703 began to teach (at one guinea entrance, and one guinea a quarter) 7 year-old Elizabeth Burrell, daughter of Timothy, of Ockenden House, Cuckfield. [*SAC 3*]

HEARNDEN, Benjamin (1744-): By 1769, then about 25, had a boys' boarding school in the Cliffe, Lewes [qv]. Also writing master to a girls' boarding school. Appointed master of Mayfield charity school at end of 1771 [qv], where he also kept a private boys' boarding school; promoted teaching through gentleness as opposed to fear. Resigned Christmas 1783, and in January 1784 opened the *Wheat-Sheaf* inn in Malling Street, Lewes. Baptised 27 December 1744, son of William, sawyer, of Lewes (died 1762) and Abigail (née Whiskey, daughter of Edward (died 1759) and Abigail (died 1756); she died 1770), who married 25 December 1736. Married 1 August 1769, Barbara Pack Gold, of St Anne, Lewes (both signed). In December 1770, following mother's death, he sold 119 High Street, Lewes (which had come into his possession through his mother) for £129. [*SWA* 5.1.84; St Anne PR; deeds of Ashdown House, 119 High Street, Lewes, in private possession]

HENRY, M.: Dancing master. In 1786 he was

paid £2 2s by the Duke of Richmond for teaching Henriette Le Clerc (then aged 13 or 14) at Goodwood House. [WSRO Goodwood MS 244]

HERRIOT: Received 4s 2d in 1725, 4s 6d in 1726, from the Dowlin charity for schooling a poor girl of West Grinstead. [WSRO Par 95/1/1/3]

HEWARD, Ann: Schoolmistress of Cocking, 1732-34. Taught 5 poor children to read and learn the catechism at 2d per week per child. Wife of William. [WSRO Par 53/12/1]

HEWITT, Thomas: Under the heading 'EDUCATION', advertised the opening of an evening school in Lewes on 22 October 1792, for instruction 'in Architecture, Landscapes, &c.' [qv]. He was 'Inspector of the New Goal, Lewes'.

HEWS, Goody: Received payments from the Dowlin charity for schooling poor children of West Grinstead, May 1699 (7s 6d), April 1703 (11s 9d), March 1709 (5s 4d). Probably same as the Widow Hews paid in December 1715 (7s 10d), December 1716 (13s 6d) and January 1718 (7s 11d); and possibly the Widow Hews paid in May 1725 (6s 11d). (See also HEWS, wife of John). [WSRO Par 95/1/1/3]

HEWS, wife of John: Received payments from the Dowlin charity for schooling poor children of West Grinstead, to Lady Day 1718 (17s 4d), April 1719 (£1 6s 10d), December 1721 (10s 5d), November 1722 (14s 6d), November 1723 (12s 3d). Perhaps the Widow Hews paid in May 1725 (6s 11d) (but not the same as the Widow Hews paid 1715-18: see HEWS, Goody above). [WSRO Par 95/1/1/3]

HEWS, Mrs: Had a girls' boarding school at Petworth (Rs 1790, 1793) [qv].

[HIDER, William]: Schoolmaster at Rotherfield 1803, then aged 17-55 (and ruptured). [*Sussex Militia List 1803, Pevensey Rape Northern Division* (1988)]

HILL, John (-1786): Master of Saunders' charity school, Rye, from January 1772 to death. Buried 5 July 1786. [*HRGS*]

HITCHCOCK, Mrs: Schoolmistress of South Bersted [qv]. In 1776 had about 8 scholars, at 3d a week, including little Betsy Grey, aged 3.

[HITCHENER, Elizabeth (1782-1822)]: After leaving the Miss Adams's school [qv her entry in Schedule 3], her ambition was to achieve financial independence by establishing a school so that she could offer 'an asylum' to her loved mentor, the radical and 'persecuted' Hannah Adams. She may well have started teaching by 1801; by 1811, then 29, she had a well respected school at Hurstpierpoint. She was tall, thin, black-haired and dark-eyed; self-possessed, earnest and articulate. By 1811 she had made contact with the radical Godwinian set in London; that year she met Shelley (then nearly 19, he was staying with his uncle, Captain Pilfold of Cuckfield, whose daughter was one of her pupils); an intellectual friendship developed, with long discussions on religion and philosophy, and intense correspondence, EH becoming Shelley's confidante and 'sister of my soul'. The interception of a box of subversive propaganda, sent by Shelley from Ireland and addressed to her, led to her being investigated by the authorities, and to a watch being kept on her. In July 1812 she was persuaded to join the Shelley establishment at Lynmouth (Shelley, his young wife Harriet, 17, and her older sister Eliza, 30); she went with them when they fled Lynmouth for Wales. Initially welcomed by Harriet, before the end of the year there was friction between EH and the 2 girls, and after the party had spent some weeks in London, in November EH was pushed out of the group, Shelley agreeing to pay her £100 a year (probably to work for the cause in Sussex); but only one such payment was ever made, and £100 which EH had lent the Shelleys in June was apparently never repaid. Back in Hurst, EH was the subject of laughter and scandal, and assumed to be Shelley's cast-off mistress. She went abroad, married an Austrian officer, later returned and kept a school at Edmonton. Died 1822 (the same year as Shelley). In 1818 she had published a book of verse, *The Fireside Bagatelle*, and in 1822 a long poem, *The Weald of Sussex*, under her maiden name. Introductory verses to the latter include a nostalgic reference to her time with Shelley, but now, 10 years later, though still an advocate for 'reason', she warns 'great reason's advocates', however 'sound and just' their theory, to consider whether 'the mass the many' are ready to adopt it; and before destroying any part of ordered society, they must be certain they can restore 'order's law', lest anarchy 'Again to savage life reduce mankind,/ And, in one common sea of ruin, wreck/ All, all the lovely charities of life'. [Holmes, R. *Shelley: the Pursuit* (1974); Jones, F. L. *The Letters of Percy Bysshe Shelley* (1964); Cameron, K. N. *The Young Shelley* (1951); Hitchener, E. *The Weald of Sussex* (1822)]

HODGES, Goody: Received 4s in 1705 from the Dowlin charity for schooling a poor girl and boy of West Grinstead, and (unless this is a different Goody Hodges) 4s 2d in 1725 and 6s 6d in 1726 for schooling a poor boy at 2d a week. [WSRO Par 95/1/1/3]

HOGBEN, John: Master of Saunders' charity school, Rye, from Lady Day 1745 to Lady Day 1769 [qv]. Elected freeman of Rye 20 August 1760, the clause preventing a freeman being the master being cancelled on the same date. [ESRO RYE 114/13; *HRGS*]

HOGSFLESH, Mr: Schoolmaster of Winchelsea (Rs 1765-68). Paid £1 10s by parish in 1766 for 1 year's schooling of 3 poor boys, and £1 10s 'for a Year's schooling' in the 2 following church years. Probably kept his own school to which the poor boys were sent. [ESRO PAR 511/31/1/1]

HOLFORD, Joan: Received from Horsted Keynes offertory collections [qv Parish schooling] small sums for schooling individual poor boys, 1744-46. Also probably taught the workhouse school, and in 1747 the parish paid 6s 'for half a Cord of Wood which Joan Holford had on ye acct of ye poor Children'; may have been paid for schooling out of the rent obtained by the parish for Lightmaker's schoolhouse. Wife of James, who received charity from the offertory money.

HOLLOWAY: Music and dancing master. In 1794, then of Newington, was teaching at the Dubbins' girls' boarding school, Horsham. By beginning of 1796 had moved to Brighton and opened an academy there [qv]. Also opened an academy at Lewes that same year [qv under Dancing masters].

HOLMAN, Ann (- by 1833): With husband James, kept a day school in the 1790s (and into 19th century) at Yew Tree Cottage, Quaybrook, East Grinstead [qv]. Had died by 1833 when her daughter, Martha Heasman, was admitted to the cottage. [Miss Molloy in *East Grinstead Observer* 25.9.1909]

HOLMAN, James (-c1840): With wife Ann, kept a day school in the 1790s (and into 19th century) at Yew Tree Cottage, Quaybrook, East Grinstead [qv]. Admitted to a copyhold cottage, with 3 acres, 1791, following death of father, also James (previous tenant; buried 19 April 1790). Died c1840. [Reference as for HOLMAN, Ann]

HOLNEY, (Eleanor?) (-1721?): Mistress of the Blue Coat girls' charity school, Chichester. Received payments on behalf of the school (as Mrs Holney) 1715-21. Probably Eleanor Holney, buried 11 March 1721. [WSRO Cap.V/1/1; All Saints PR]

HOOK, Mrs (Hannah?): Had a school near the Market-House, Lewes [qv], which she resigned April 1787, setting up as a milliner with 'a fresh and fashionable Assortment' of goods from London. Probably the Mrs Hannah Hook admitted Eastgate Baptist church 1786 after being baptised there, who later married Wood; she left the church 1 October 1801. [ESRO NB 1/1/1A]

HOOK, Thomas: Master of Eastbourne charity school from Christmas 1783 [qv]. Initially paid £10 a year for teaching 10 children, then (by 1785) £15 a year for teaching 15. Had left by Michaelmas 1794. [SAS Budgen MS v.119]

HOOKER, Thomas Redman (1762-1838): Schoolmaster of Rottingdean. Born 1762 at Tonbridge, Kent, son of Thomas of Tonbridge Castle, esq. Westminster School; Oriel College, Oxford, 1780, aged 17; BA 1784, MA 1786, BD and DD 1810. Ordained deacon 1784, priest 1786. When he left Oxford was described as 'a handsome and most accomplished man; skilled in vocal and instrumental music; a good draughtsman; excellent at cricket, swimming and skating; a fine rider.' Deciding to become a travelling tutor, first went to Blois, France, where he studied French and Italian; then travelled the continent for 2 years with 2 pupils, the Earl of Powiscourt and a friend of the earl. At some point, his father lost the family fortune when a gunpowder mill blew up. Curate at Greenford, Middlesex, and with a friend started a boys' boarding school at nearby Hanwell; then curate at Beddington, Surrey, taking some of his pupils with him. Rector of Whatlington 1791; resigned 1792 when, at 30, appointed vicar of Rottingdean. (The living was in the gift of the Duke of Dorset, who had employed Hooker as secretary; 2 livings becoming vacant at that time, Dorset let Hooker and another protégé throw dice for Rottingdean - Hooker won). From 1809 also had the living of Boxted, Essex, but lived at Rottingdean. Married firstly at Boxted, Essex, 28 July 1789, Mary Cook, daughter of the Rev Robert (and cousin of Jane Austen) who died at Boxted January 1798, aged 34; married secondly 1801, Emma Jane Greenland, who died at Brighton, shortly after husband. Of his children, Thomas (predeceased father) became a barrister and later judge, John became vicar of Thorp Acre, Leicestershire, Mary married a doctor, William King, Anna (predeceased father) married S. C. B. Parlby, who made a survey of Rottingdean in 1832. From the time he came to Rottingdean, Hooker kept a very successful school there for the sons of the nobility and gentry (he added a new wing to the vicarage, and a Georgian front) [qv for some of his notable pupils]. But he was not bedazzled by his close connections with the aristocracy: he befriended the young shepherd, John Dudeney, let him use his telescope and gave him free access to his library; soon after arriving at Rottingdean, he started a Sunday school which he superintended for over 40 years, and also a charity school for the poor children, who were allowed to use the vicarage meadows for their games; he was a constant benefactor to the poor; he helped and comforted shipwrecked sailors; he identified himself with the village to the extent of acting as lookout man for the local smugglers. He was both a dedicated sportsman (master of the Lewes and Brookside Harriers 20 years) and a lover of the arts (played the cello, and was a competent artist). Died 12 April 1838, aged 76. A memorial bust was erected in the parish church 'by his parishioners, pupils and friends'; the inscription included: 'His pupils and parishioners will long Revere his memory: the former for his unwearied attention and parental regard: the latter for his kindness to the poor, and faithful discharge of his parochial duties. By nature a man of talent; by education a man of learning; by grace a Man of God.' A few days after his death a rough verse was published in the local paper under the heading, 'From the Villagers of Rottingdean/ On the Sudden Death of Dr Hooker'; it included the lines: 'Our kind and much lov'd pastor! he is gone!.../Deep silence reigns where'er his voice before/ Was heard so kindly at each cottage door;/ "Ah! how d'ye do? can I do aught today?/ Send food or raiment? or remain to pray?"/ His daily rounds no more will comfort bring,/ No more will he with village children sing!' Tributes to a remarkable man. [Tibble, R. 'Rev Thomas Redman Hooker DD' *SFH* **8**, no. 4 (1988); *Al. Oxon.*; Rottingdean PR; *SWA* 22.1.98; *Gentleman's Magazine*, Oct 1838; *Lewes and Brighthelmston Pacquet* 6.8.89]

HOPKINS, William (1706-86): Master of Cuckfield grammar school 1756-86 [qv]. Son of John, of Monmouth, Monmouthshire; All Souls' College, Oxford, 19 November 1724, aged 18; BA 1728. Curate Waldron 1729; priest (Chichester) 15 March 1731; vicar of Bolney 1734 to death. Died 1786 (buried 28 April 1786). [Cooper, W. V. *History of the Parish of Cuckfield* (1912); *Al. Oxon.*; CI]

[HOUNEYMOND, Elizabeth (-1794)]: Perhaps the schoolmistress of Petworth who was probably the longest-serving schoolmistress in Sussex in the 18th century. [See note under WICKCLIFF, Elizabeth].

[HOWARD, Goody]: Received 12s 6d in May 1700 from the Dowlin charity for schooling poor children of West Grinstead. Possibly kept a dame school there. [WSRO Par 95/1/1/3]

HOWARD, Jonathan: Had a boys' boarding school at Ewhurst 1775 [qv].

HOWLETT, Francis (1751-1831): First parish schoolmaster of Hailsham [qv]. Parish advertised April 1777, having raised a subscription of £20 a year, so he probably became schoolmaster then. Came to Hailsham with a party of strolling players, settled there, married a local girl. Also postmaster, tax-collector, vestry clerk, printer, travelling librarian, musician ('showing great devotion but little ability'). Always wore a pig-tail. Buried 12 June 1831, aged 80. [Geering, T. *Our Sussex Parish* (1925 edition); MI]

HOYLE, Joseph (-1711): Almost certainly kept a school for sons of local gentry at Newick, of which rector 1690 to death [qv under Boys' schools]. Of Yorkshire: to Emmanuel College, Cambridge, 1680; BA 1684, MA 1687; ordained deacon (London) 1685. Wife Jane; daughter Jane born 1696; son Joseph born and died 1697; daughter Margaret born and died 1699; son John born 1701 (to Balliol College, Oxford, 1719). Will (20 September 1710) provided for wife Jane, sole executrix; £600 for daughter Jane when 21 or on marriage; estate to son John when 21; mentions nieces Margaret and Sarah Longbottom (conditional legatees) and brothers-in-law Matthew Marten and Thomas Lintott (overseers of the will). Buried at Newick 14 September 1711. Jane Hoyle (probably his widow) buried there 14 January 1722. [CI; *Al. Cant.*; PR; ESRO W/A 48.65; *Al. Oxon.*]

HUBBARD, Jane (-1784): Schoolmistress of Ditchling. Buried there 11 April 1784. [PR]

HUDSON, Thomas (1750-1819): Schoolmaster at Brighton, 1778-89. Of St John's College, Cambridge (*Gentleman's Magazine*), MA. With Hugh Owen, opened a boys' day and boarding school, 25 March 1778 [qv]; previously at William Gilpin's celebrated academy at Cheam. Curate of Brighton (signed marriage banns as such April 1779 to November 1789, when appointed vicar). Ordained priest (Chichester) 21 December 1780; vicar of Wisborough Green 1781-85. Partnership with Owen dissolved 24 June 1782. School taken over by John Mossop, January 1787. Prebendary of Chichester; vicar of Henfield 1785-89; vicar of Brighton 1789-1804; erected and owned the Chapel Royal, the first stone of which was laid by the Prince of Wales 25 November 1793; chaplain to Prince Regent; rector of Ditchling 1795 to death; vicar of Fittleworth 1804 to death. Married at Brighton, 18 September 1780, Elizabeth Widgett, spinster (probably the Miss E. Widgett who took over Woodgate's circulating library on the Steyne and published *A Description of Brighthelmston* in 1778; and established the Post Office there; she resigned the library to Bowen in July 1779 [qv *WIDGETT*, Miss]). On

committee of a patriotic society at Brighton, set up in 1792 in reaction to the French Revolution, 'for the Protection of Liberty, and Property against REPUBLICANS and Levellers'; there was a great procession and rally in December of that year. Died at Fittleworth 12 May 1819, aged 69. His widow died at home in Ship Street, Brighton, 13 October 1823. [Brighton PR; *Al. Cant.* (some entries dubious); CI; *Gentleman's Magazine* (1819); *SWA* 2.12.93; Bishop, 134]

HUMBER, Richard (-c1830): Schoolmaster at Brighton. With Hunter, opened a boys' boarding school at 38 Middle Street, 23 July 1792 [qv under Measor's and Hunter's school]. Nonconformists, they took the boys to worship at the Countess of Huntingdon's chapel (his wife, Mary, had as a girl been a member of the choir there). Had a school on his own by 1799 (when wife advertised care of weakly children who needed the benefit of sea-bathing). Also bookseller and bookbinder. Mathematical and scientific interests; a founder and first president of Brighton Scientific Society (1800). Wife Mary (née Jutten); their son John buried 10 January 1787; she had died by 1830. In his will, dated 4 August 1830, proved 1 June 1831, he was 'late Schoolmaster'; one of his executors and trustees was Eliza Golds, his housekeeper, who was left £100 'agreeably to a Wish expressed by my late Wife', plus an extra one year's wages and £10 'for a mourning'; another executor was Samuel Farncombe Sanders of Brighton, schoolmaster; among the beneficiaries were 'The poor belonging unto the Chapel of the late Countess of Huntingdon Brighton' (£10) and 'The Deacons belonging unto the Baptists Chapel Bond Street Brighton' (£10); another Brighton schoolmaster, John Measor, was left £100; £400 was left to the children of his wife's deceased brothers Thomas and John Jutten; apart from these children there were 20 named beneficiaries and the bequests totalled £1,190 (plus Golds' extra year's wages); any residue was to be given to his poor relations, whether legatees or not; at probate his goods etc were valued at not more than £1,500. [Bishop, 339; PR; ESRO W/A 77.415]

HUMPHREY, John (1722-1800): Schoolmaster of Westdean (West Sussex) 1775. Parish Clerk 1766 to death; churchwardens' accounts show many payments to him, one such (3 July 1778) was 18s 4d 'for Cleaning the Church=Windows, Communion Plates - Washing Surplices &c'. Baptised 28 September 1722, son of John (buried 13 June 1748) and Mary of Chilgrove. Married 29 December 1748, Mary Warner of Westdean (buried 13 February 1775). Buried 24 June 1800. [WSRO Ep.I/22/1; W. D. Peckham's introduction to transcript of PR citing 'Clerk's waste book'; PR; WSRO Par 65/9/1]

HUNT, Mrs: Had a school at Horsham 1773 [qv]. (Possibly wife of one of the 2 Charles Hunts [qv below]).

HUNT, Charles (-1782): Usher at Horsham grammar school [qv], 1743 to death in 1782 (buried 6 January 1782). Followed Richard Hunt as usher; succeeded by son Charles. [*HCS*; PR]

HUNT, Charles (1740-89): Usher at Horsham grammar school 1782-89 [qv]. Son of Charles, usher before him. Died 29 January 1789, aged 49 (buried 2 February 1789); described on memorial inscription as 'writing-master to the Free School in the Parish'. [*HCS*; PR; MI (SAS Slyfield MS)]

HUNT, Richard (-1743): Usher of Horsham grammar school 1697 to death in 1743, serving under 7 masters [qv]. In 1725 quarrelled with the master, Francis Osgood (Hunt 'was playing the old game of collaring the scholars' entrance money and encroaching on the master's living space'). Buried 15 June 1743. [*HCS*; PR]

HUNT, Samuel (1737-1801): Master of Wadhurst charity school (his father Thomas and brother Stephen also schoolmasters there) [qv]. Baptised 1 April 1737, third son of Thomas, barber, and Jane. In April 1795, returning to Wadhurst, a gate blew to as he was passing through and knocked him down, and he broke a leg. Died in the poorhouse; buried 23 June 1801, aged 65. [*SWA* 27.4.95; PR]

HUNT, Stephen (1731-91): Schoolmaster of Wadhurst, and probably of the charity school [qv]. Father Thomas and younger brother Samuel also schoolmasters there. Baptised 10 October 1731, second son of Thomas, barber, and Jane. Married 19 April 1756, Elizabeth

Wickham of Wadhurst. Buried as schoolmaster 25 August 1791, aged 59. [PR]

HUNT, Thomas: Schoolmaster of Wadhurst (had schoolhouse there 1747); probably master of the charity school [qv]. Previously a barber. Sons Stephen and Samuel also schoolmasters at Wadhurst. Wife Jane buried 12 May 1749. [PR]

HUNTER: With Measor, had a boys' day and evening school at Brighton by 1791, when they denied they were 'declining the School' [qv]. But in 1792, at the same address (38 Middle Street), with Richard Humber, Hunter opened a boys' boarding school. Nonconformists, they took the boys to worship at the Countess of Huntingdon's chapel. By 1799 Humber was on his own [qv].

[HUNTER, Mrs]: With Mrs Taylor, had a girls' school at Henfield sometime before January 1802. [*SWA* 11.1.1802]

HURDIS, James (1763-1801): After graduating at Oxford, was for some time tutor to George Pelham, youngest son of Lord Pelham (later Earl of Chichester). His pupil later became Bishop of Bristol, then Exeter, and finally of Lincoln. Poet. [For biographical details, see Schedule 3]

INGRAM, James (1692-1756): Master of Cuckfield grammar school 1719-42 [qv]. Baptised 4 August 1692, son of John, rector of Chipstead (buried 5 February 1718) and Elizabeth (née Pigeon). Merchant Taylors school; Jesus College, Cambridge, 22 March 1711; BA 1715, MA 1725. Ordained priest 1716; master of Cuckfield grammar school 10 March 1719, and shortly after curate of Cuckfield and chaplain to Richard, Viscount Irwin; vicar of Oving 1725-47; resigned grammar school by 12 May 1742; rector of Sedlescombe 1746 to death; in 1746 also chaplain to Henry, Viscount Irwin, and from that year also vicar of Westfield. Married firstly 22 March 1723, Mary Warden (1699-1726, daughter of Thomas of Cuckfield and Prudence); married secondly 5 April 1733, at Chailey, Mrs Ann Heesman, of Cuckfield. Died at Sedlescombe 3 September 1756 (buried 7 September 1756), aged 64; wife Ann died 12 June 1785, in 86th year (memorial inscription).

Will 17 July 1756, proved (Prerogative Court of Canterbury) 27 November 1756 by sons John and James, left rents of farm and lands in Ashurst, Sussex, to wife Ann for life, residue of estate equally divided between his 2 sons (John died 1803: Chailey memorial inscription). [*VCH* ii; *SAC* **49**, **72**; *Al. Cant.*; CI; PRs, MIs]

INGRAM, William Moon (1743-): Master of Grey Coat boys' charity school, Chichester, from Michaelmas 1778 to Lady Day 1794 [qv]. From 1797 to 1802 was writing master to the Lennox boys at Goodwood House [qv under Chichester Other schoolmasters, for sums paid to him; see LENNOX, Charles, Schedule 3, for their other tutors]. Married secondly, (marriage licence 15 January 1784), aged 41, Sarah Lake of Harting, aged 19 (daughter of Ann, widow). That year, 1784, living in West Street, with wife, son and daughter (in 1813, his son, purser of the *Pelican*, mentioned in despatches for good conduct and bravery at the capture of the *Argus*). Children baptised at St Martin: Charlotte (7 March 1791); Sarah (7 October 1793); Mary (23 August 1795); George (7 May 1800); Charles Frederic (4 November 1802); Eliza (11 November 1804); Octave Ann (16 December 1805). [*SRS* **35**; WSRO MP 414, 417; WSRO Goodwood MS 247; PR]

[INSKIP, John]: Schoolmaster at Botany Bay, Lewes, 1805, and probably earlier. (A John Inskip owned (from 1797) and occupied (from 1799) a house in St John sub Castro; possibly the JI, peruke maker, aged 22, who married there, 25 December 1775, Susannah Spilsbury, aged 21). [*Baxter's Directory* (1805); Land Tax; PR; *SRS* **25**]

ISLIP, Walter (1748-1813): Usher to Atkins at Midhurst grammar school [qv]. Born at Soulby, Westmorland, son of Robert, farmer. Pembroke College, Cambridge, 9 January 1765, aged 17; BA (6th Wrangler) 1769; MA 1780. Curate of Bepton 1775-78; rector of Elsted 1773-85 (presented by Robert Islip of Soulby, Westmorland, gent, who was of Stedham, Sussex, gent, by 1785). Between 1778 and 1785 held the livings of Lodsworth, Easebourne, and was vicar of Aldingbourne (last to death). Resigned from grammar school 31 March 1785. Rector of Stedham with Heyshott 1785 to death. Married Mary Bird, daughter of the Rev William, of Crosby-

Garrett, Westmorland. Son William Bird Islip, born 1782 at Midhurst, at St Pauls School (1792) and Eton, scholar, 1795, then Emmanuel College, Cambridge, 1799. Died at Stedham 28 February 1813, aged 65. Wife Mary predeceased him. [*HMGS*; *Al. Cant.*; CI]

JACKSON, William (1756-1828): Appointed master of the combined Peacock's (grammar school) and Saunders' (charity school) schools Rye in 1791 [qv]. Previously had his own school at Stone, Kent, and was (until 1811, following Chancery case) allowed to take his own pupils at Rye. Continued as master to death, aged 72. Curate of Playden (conducted marriages there as such 1794-1803 and 1814-28, and as 'Officiating Minister' 1792 and 1806-11) and curate of East Guldeford (conducted marriages as such 1798-1824). Married Ann Palmer (1762-1843), sister of Thomas, schoolmaster [qv]. Daughter married Thomas Palmer's son Thomas, also a schoolmaster. Died 19 August 1828. Wife Ann died 26 December 1843, aged 81. [*HRGS*; PRs; Playden MI; Leppard, M. J. pers. comm. citing family historians]

[JAMES]: In charge of Mayfield school [qv] when master Gale was away for a month surveying in 1759. On his return Gale found that George Richardson [one of the older boys] 'through James's too mild treatment was got to be master...the day before James had been so indiscreet as to suffer Richardson's boy George to bring beer into the school, and, old Kent [one of the managers] coming in before the mug was out, the boy asked him to drink; thereupon he fell into a great heat, and drove the boy out of the school'. [*SAC* **9**]

JAMESON, William (1743-1821): Master of Horsham grammar school 1773-1806 [qv]; when he resigned, the grammar school was reported as 'a school wholly without scholars'. Born 1743, son of John of Bolton, Yorkshire. Queen's College, Oxford, 1765; BA 1770; ordained deacon (Chester) 1769, priest (Chichester) 1770; MA (from St John's College, Cambridge) 1792. Curate of Horsham 1770; rector of Clapham 1788 to death; vicar of Horsham 1796 to death. Governor of the grammar school 1806 to death. Involved in politics, in Tory interest. Married at Horsham, 22 December 1772, Judith Vinall of Horsham (died 1784). Died 29 October 1821, aged 78 (monumental inscription erected by daughter). [*HCS*; *Al. Oxon.*; *Al. Cant.*; CI; PR; MI Horsham (SAS Slyfield MS)]

JARRETT, Henry (1766-): Schoolmaster of Rye [qv]. Baptised 9 July 1766, son of Henry and Margaret. Probably the HJ bankrupt in 1830. [PR]

JARRETT, Richard (1719-1806): Schoolmaster of Rye [qv]. Also surveyor (R 1752). Bought house in Middle Street for £110, 1776; sold it to Henry Jarrett junior, schoolmaster, for £140 in 1788 ('gent' in deed). Probably the RJ, son of RJ, at Saunders' charity school, Rye, 1732-36. Buried 11 March 1806, aged 87. [ESRO AMS 4831; PR]

JEFFERY, Richard: Opened a boys' school at Wadhurst 1791 [qv]. In 1793 offered 10 guineas reward for bringing to justice those who had defamed him by 'vile, malicious, and diabolical scandal', 'to the prejudice of his reputation, as an instructor of youth, and injury of his business'.

JENKIN, Stephen (1756-1827): Vicar of Salehurst, opened a boys' boarding school there at beginning of 1783 [qv]. Born 1756, son of John, ironmonger and brazier of Newgate Street, London. St Paul's school (exhibitioner); Corpus Christi College, Cambridge, 1775 (scholar); ordained deacon (Peterborough) 1778; BA 1779. Vicar of Salehurst 1779 to death; vicar of Selmeston 1801 to death. Married Ann Starr; daughter Elizabeth born 31 March 1787; daughter Palacia born 20 March 1789; son William born 1 January 1791. Died 3 April 1827, aged 72. Widow Ann died 15 November 1828. [*Al. Cant.* (some date errors); CI; PR; MI; SAS Cockayne I]

JENKINS, George: Opened a boys' boarding school at Seaford 1790 [qv].

JENNER, William: From Michaelmas 1784 to Easter 1788 received 6d a week from Billingshurst parish for schooling the children in the workhouse [qv under Parish schooling]. Also paid 5s a week for 'looking after the Workhouse'.

JEWHURST, George (1750-): Master of

Saunders' charity school, Rye [qv]. Appointed 10 April 1769; successor appointed 13 January 1772. Was himself a scholar at the school, 1760-62 [qv Schedule 3]. [*HRGS*]

JOEL, Thomas: Had a boys' boarding school at Chichester (Rs 1769, 1770) [qv]. Author of *An Easy Introduction to the English Grammar* (Chichester 1770), composed for the convenience of children under 7 and printed for use in his school. A General Baptist, came to Chichester in 1760 as assistant to Mr Preddon, General Baptist pastor 1730-61, and himself pastor 1761-62. Wife admitted to General Baptist chapel 1767. Published *A Letter to Occasional Conformists* (Chichester 1771). For his award of £20 against J White for slander in 1774, see his school. [McCann, T. J. in *SAC* 130]

JOHNSON, Mrs Susan: With Mary Bishop, continued Mrs Thornton's girls' boarding school at Northiam, reopening the school 19 April 1773 [qv].

JONES: Tutor to Henriette Ann Le Clerc at Goodwood House from 1778 [qv her entry in Schedule 3].

JONES, Mrs: Had a girls' boarding school at Horsham (Rs 1782-84) [qv]. Widow of Rev Jones, curate of Slinfold (buried there 24 April 1776). [PR]

JONES, H.: Tutor at Lewes 1775, specialising in mathematics, geography and astronomy [qv]. Also surveyor.

JONES, Jenkyn: First master of Lightmaker's charity school, Horsted Keynes [qv]. In 1708 was living at Mote Croft, a house Lightmaker had built near the church for his school. Married 6 January 1708, Mary Wood, cousin and heiress of the late rector, John Wood. [*SAC* **34**; WSRO Par 384/6/2; ESRO W/A 46.105]

JONES, John: Curate of Billingshurst, shared with John Lander £1 2s 6d paid by parish for schooling 6 charity children for 6 months from Michaelmas 1795. For the next 6 months he received the full £1 2s 6d for the 6 children, and for the year to Michaelmas 1797 £2 12s. In 1797 also received 10s 6d for conducting a pauper marriage. Signed burial register as curate 1796, 1797; had left by 1798, and Lander took over the schooling again from Michaelmas 1797. Perhaps took private pupils as well. [WSRO Par 21/31/2; PR]

JONES, Lewis (1696-1759): Master of Rye grammar school for 35 years, 1724-59 [qv]. In 1746 was found to have allowed the school buildings to fall into disrepair and to have let them to an innkeeper for storing timber and corn, and the garden for keeping hogs, fowls and a skittle-alley. Son of Hugh, of Pennal, Merioneth. Jesus College, Oxford, matriculated 12 March 1718, aged 20. Also curate of Rye, and rector of Little Horsted 1741 to death. Lived in Market Street, Rye. Wife Elizabeth buried 18 February 1747. Died 13 December 1759, aged 63. [*Al. Oxon.*; *SAC* **13** (MI); CI; PR; *HRGS*]

KEELER, Stephen (-1731): Writing master at Lewes, buried as such 17 August 1731. Was paid £1 a year for teaching Nicholas Gilbert to write when he was at Lewes grammar school, 1716, 1717. [St John sub Castro PR; ESRO ACC 2462/1]

KEITH, George (1638-1716): Rector of Edburton 1705 to death, he apparently taught most of the parish children to read and say their catechism [qv]. MA. Buried 25 March 1716. [CI; date of birth from Kirby, E. W. *George Keith*]

KELTON, John (-1777): Master of Hartfield charity school [qv]. Subscribed 13 July 1733, 'before his Admission to teach Scholl at Hartfield'. Died 26 May 1777, 'of Hartfield, many years master of the Charity School there'. Also surveyor (R 1747). [WSRO Ep.II/1/1; *SWA* 2.6.77; ESRO AMS 4084(3)]

KENNEDY, James: Schoolmaster, at 17 Duke Street, Brighton, 1799. [*Cobby's Directory*]

KENT, James (-1708 or 09): Schoolmaster of Lewes in his will dated 15 December 1708, proved 18 February 1709. Left £30 plus £60 owing to him, plus gold piece, silver cup, silver spoon, gold ring, specified furniture, etc to daughter Anne, residue of estate to wife Elizabeth, sole executrix, who survived him. [ESRO W/A 47.173]

KILWICK, Ishmael (1722-1802): Master of both the Grey Coat charity school and the Oliver Whitby boarding charity school, Chichester [qv] - of the Oliver Whitby school for 44 years, from Christmas 1748 to midsummer 1792 (when he was 70); of the Grey Coat school from Lady Day 1763 to Michaelmas 1778. Married Olive Bullis, daughter of John, vicar of Billingshurst and schoolmaster. In 1784 at the Oliver Whitby house in West Street, with wife, 2 daughters, a maidservant and 12 charity boys. Wife Olive died 27 November 1791, aged 68. Died in South Street, 28 August 1802, aged 80. [WSRO MP 414, 417; MI Chichester Cathedral (SAS, Dunkin 7.1)]

[KING, George (1784?-)]: Assistant schoolmaster at Uckfield 1803. Then aged 17-30, unmarried, and incapable of bearing arms. Probably son of William, schoolmaster, and Catherine, baptised 1 August 1784, and assistant to father. [*Sussex Militia List 1803, Pevensey Rape Northern Division* (1988); PR]

KING, W.: Received 2d a week from Playden parish for schooling an 8 year-old boy for 12 weeks in 1785 and 9 weeks in 1786 [qv Parish schooling]. Signed receipt. Probably same as William King next below.

KING, William: Schoolmaster at Battle 1793. (See KING, W., above) [*Universal British Directory*]

[KING, William]: Schoolmaster at Uckfield 1803. Then aged 17-55, lame. Children of WK and Catherine baptised 26 May 1783 (Philadelphia), 1 August 1784 (George); children of WK and Philadelphia baptised 18 December 1785 (Mary), 28 October 1787 (Elizabeth), 4 April 1790 (William). [*Sussex Militia List 1803, Pevensey Rape Northern Division* (1988); PR]

[KNIGHT, William (-1809)]: Master of Eastbourne charity school from at least midsummer 1801. Received £15 a year for teaching 15 poor children. Married firstly, 5 October 1785, Elizabeth Hodly (buried 19 June 1793); married secondly, 11 July 1799, Lydia Taylor. Schoolmaster of Eastbourne in will dated 5 April 1809 (proved 18 May 1810) which left properties (and goods valued at less than £300) and mentioned: wife Lydia; Thomas and Mary Rollison, their sons William, Henry, Thomas, John, James, and daughter Sarah; Joseph and Susanna Wilkins, their sons George, Joseph and his son Joseph, and daughters Mary, Jane. Buried 15 November 1809. [SAS Budgen MS v.119 and 117; PR; ESRO W/A 70.778]

LAMB: In 1728 Mr Lamb of Ditchling went to Steyning to take care of the grammar school while the master, Edward Martin, was away. [*SAC* **25**]

LAMBERT, James (1725-88): Taught both music and painting at Lewes. Baptised 29 December 1725 at Willingdon, youngest child of John (1690-1764), flaxdresser, and Susanna (née Bray). Attended a writing school, became musician and painter. (An illustration from an engraving of his painting *View of Brighthelmston* (1765) is included in Bishop's book.) Won 25 guinea premium from Society of Arts 1770; exhibited at Society of Artists 1761-64, Free Society of Artists 1768-73, Royal Accademy 1774-78. Sir William Burrell commissioned him (1775-80) and Samuel Hieronymus Grimm (1780-91) to make drawings of all the notable antiquities and important houses in Sussex. Organist at Cliffe church 1745 to death in 1788. Married 29 April 1760, at Stopham, Mary Winton; their only child died as infant. Nephew James Lambert (1741-99) also a landscape painter. Trustee and guardian to 3 daughters of George Smith of Chichester (1714-76), landscape painter. Died at Lewes 7 December 1788. When his goods and paintings sold, 1789, described as bookseller, stationer, printseller and landscape painter. [*SAC* **90**; Bishop facing p 112; *SAS Newsletter* 64 (1991)]

de LAMBILLY, Laurent Xavier Martin (1763-1836): Dancing and fencing master, and French teacher, Chichester [qv under Dancing masters for details of his teaching dancing to the Lennox boys at Goodwood House 1800-02, and an amusing account of him teaching Sarah Douglas]. At North Street c1804; owned house in St Bartholomew's 1807; paid tax on part of a house in the parish 1810-20. R. C. born 11 November 1763, younger son of Pierre Laurent Marie, 1st Marquess de Lambilly (1735-85). Married Mary Fifield (probably daughter of his

Chichester neighbour, Arthur, shoemaker); their children born in Chichester, Frances Mary (6 May 1805), Caroline (23 February 1807), Frederick (21 May 1809), Alfred (12 July 1810), Louisa (29 November 1812), George Ludovic (23 April 1814), Matilda Catharine (25 November 1815), Louisa Augusta (20 November 1817). [McCann, T. J. pers. comm.; *Registers of Brockhampton* (1949); *Chichester Guide* (c1804); Land Tax; WSRO Par 38/9/1]

LANAWAY: Received 12s 10d in 1730 from the Dowlin charity for schooling poor children of West Grinstead. [WSRO Par 95/1/1/3]

LANDER, John: Schoolmaster of Billingshurst (Rs 1794 - into 19th century) [qv Parish schooling and Lander's school].

LANGDON, J.: Cleric, opened a boys' boarding school in Lewes 1792 [qv].

LAWRENCE, John: Singing master at Burwash 1720 (subscribed 5s towards new gallery in the church). [Egerton, J. C. *Sussex Folk and Sussex Ways* (3rd edition 1924)]

LEACH, Miss: Schoolmistress 1734 [qv under UNPLACED SCHOOLS].

LEVITT, Everard (c1687-1747): Master of Midhurst grammar school 1717-35 (succeeded brother Henry) [qv]. Son of Everard, of Stanton, Gloucestershire. Pembroke College, Oxford, matriculated 28 March 1705; BA 1708, MA 1712. Licensed to teach boys at Midhurst, 5 June 1716; minister of Easebourne 1716; curate of Bepton 1716 to death; rector of Pett 1726, exchanged for rectory of Upwaltham, 1731 to death. Dismissed as master of grammar school 29 July 1735, following local petition. Died 14 December 1747, aged 60 (buried at Easebourne). [*HMGS*; *Al. Oxon.*; CI; WSRO Ep.I/1/10, E138/3/1; MI (SAS, Dunkin 6.8). NB: Sources do not agree on all dates]

LEVITT, Henry (c1689-): Master of Midhurst grammar school 1710-16 [qv]. Son of Everard, of London, gent. Chorister, Winchester, 1696-1700, scholar 1700; New College, Oxford, matriculated 30 May 1707, aged 18; BA 1711, MA 1716, proctor 1722. Licensed to teach boys in school of Midhurst, 25 August 1714. Curate of Bepton in 1715; vicar of Heckfield,

Hampshire, 1715; vicar of Hornchurch, Essex, 1722. [*HMGS*; *Al. Oxon.*; CI; WSRO Ep.I/1/10]

[**LEWIS, senior**]: One of the Messrs Lewis, schoolmasters in Westgate, Chichester, c1804. [*Chichester Guide* (c1804)]

[**LEWIS, junior**]: See LEWIS, senior.

LEWIS, William: Licensed to teach boys in the diocese of Chichester, 21 September 1721. Vicar of Donnington when son Charles died 12 August 1711; warden of Hospital of St James, Chichester, 4 February 1713. [WSRO Ep.I/1/10; CI]

LEWRY, Richard: Schoolmaster at West Chiltington. Married 1783, at Petworth, Mary Pennell, aged 18, and that year moved to West Chiltington. Licensed to teach an English school there, 19 January 1788. Son Charles also master of the school later (was such in 1851, then aged 65). [Neale, K. *Sussex History* **1**, no. 5; SAS Wadey card index, citing CCC Diary 1783-1797]

LEYLAND, Thomas (1699-1763): At 1733 visitation at Westdean (West Sussex): 'The Minister [Thomas Leyland] teaches School at ye request of ye Parish but is willing either to throw it up; or to take a Licence if Your Lordship insists upon it.' Born 1699 at Kellamergh, Lancashire (baptised at Kirkham 30 April 1699), son of John, husbandman. School, Kellamergh (Mr Taylor); St John's College, Cambridge, 21 June 1718, aged 19; BA 1722, MA 1723. Ordained priest (Ely, letters dimissory from Chichester) 20 February 1725. Vicar of Westdean 1728 to death; perpetual curate of Shipley 1741 to death; rector of Singleton 1743 to death. Died at Westdean 2 October 1763, aged 63. [WSRO Ep.I/22/1; *Al. Cant.*; CI]

LIGHT, Goody: Schoolmistress at West Wittering [qv Charity schooling]. In 1712 paid £1 14s by the Oliver Whitby trustees for schooling 6 children for a year, and payments to her continued until at least 1721. [*SAC* **125**, citing WSRO E35D/3/1]

LINEGER, Goody: Received from the Dowlin charity 8s 2d in 1725 for schooling poor

children of West Grinstead. [WSRO Par 95/1/1/3]

LLOYD, John (-1738): First master of Saunders' charity school, Uckfield [qv]; also had private pupils, including Nicholas Gilbert of Eastbourne, who had been at Lewes grammar school, for whom he received £9 10d in February 1719 for 'half a years Board & Schooling', £9 3s in August 1719 (and 3s given to 'Mr Lloyd's Servants'), £9 14s in February 1720, £8 5s 10d in July 1720, £8 10s in March 1721. At Buxted 1710, probably curate there. Later curate of Uckfield. Subscribed 13 June 1730 'before his admission to teach school at Uckfield'. There were two Rev JLs in Sussex at this time; the other (1691- ; son of James, rector of Clapham) was vicar of Chiddingly 1737-48. One of the two also rector of Maresfield, instituted 9 July 1728; *Alumni Cantabrigienses* attributed to JL (1691-) but perhaps the JL here listed, as the next rector, Henry Michell, instituted 10 October 1739 (ie after this JL's death). This JL perhaps BA Jesus College, Oxford, 21 April 1702, MA 16 March 1705. Married at Buxted, 23 November 1710, Lucy Shoebridge of Buxted. Buried at Uckfield 30 October 1738. [ESRO ACC 2462/1; WSRO Ep.II/1/1; *Al. Cant.*; *Al. Oxon.*; CI; PRs]

LONG, John (-1764): Schoolmaster at East Hoathly 1760-64 [qv]. Friend of Thomas Turner. Went into the excise 1764 but died of small-pox November 1764, having apparently contracted it from an innoculation. [Vaisey, D. (ed) *The Diary of Thomas Turner* (1984)]

LORD: Schoolmaster at Battle 1702. [*SNQ* **12**]

LORD, George (1762-): Master of Northiam charity school in 1800 [qv]. In 1800, George Springett, trustee, wrote: 'The school goes on as usual, that is to say Geo. Lord receives the profits of the House and Garden and Orchard, but there are no Children taught.' Apparently he had declined to teach because he had not received 'what was just and right'. On 21 November 1805 he was paid by Springett £35 15s 'for Teaching School'; the annual salary then and after was £6 10s a year, so the payment covered 5½ yrs. Resig ' 1805. Probably born 8 March 1762, son ' William, rector of Northiam (-1779) and Ma [ESRO FRE 8182 (31); Davis, W. L. *O Rare Norgam*

(1965); PR]

LOVER, Joshua (-1727): Schoolmaster at Chichester [qv]. Probably a Baptist. Also maltster (marriage licence 31 October 1724; will 6 July 1727). Married firstly 1 November 1709, Ann Whitman; married secondly 1 November 1724, Sarah Carver of Chichester. Daughter Mary married Benjamin Martin, schoolmaster [qv] (marriage licence 29 October 1729; their son named Joshua Lover Martin). James Spershott [qv Schedule 3] described his death: 'John Page Esq native of this City, coming from London to Stand Candidate here, a great number of voters went on Horseback to meet him. Among the rest Mr Joshua Lover a noted School Master, a sober man in the General, but of flighty Passions. As he was Seting out, one of his Scollers, Patty Smith (afterwards my Spouse) asked him for a Coppy, and in haste he wrote the following. "Extreames beget Extreams, Extreams avoid. Extreams, without Extreams, are not Enjoyed". He set off in High Carrier, and coming down Rook's Hill before the Sqr [square] rideing like a mad man To and fro, forward and back ward, Hallooing among the Company, The Horse at full Speed fell with him and kill'd him. A Caution to the flighty and unsteady: and a verification of his Coppy'. Buried 7 July 1727 (the day after making his will); probate to his widow, Sarah, 12 June 1729. [*SRS* 12; Chichester Palace Chapel PR; Subdeanery PR; St Pancras PR; Millburn, J. R. *Benjamin Martin* (1976); *SAC* 30; PRO PROB/11/630 section 170]

LUN (James?): Dancing master of Lewes. 1717, 1718, twice paid 10s for teaching Nicholas Gilbert when at Lewes grammar school. May 1718, 'began to teach at Kester's' (Hurstpierpoint, or near). Probably the James Lunn of marriage licence, 8 May 1718, 'James Lunn of Lewes, gent, and Elizabeth Chittenden of same, spinster'. [ESRO ACC 2462/1; *SAC* 25; *SRS* 6]

LUND, Charlotte (1733-): With sister Philadelphia, had a girls' boarding school at Lewes before December 1772, when they moved it to St Anne parish [qv]. Their partnership was dissolved 1777, when Charlotte set up her own school on School Hill (apparently moving back to St Anne the following year). Baptised 1 March 1733,

daughter of Edward, rector of St Thomas Lewes (-1776) and Mary (-1739). Had died by November 1798, when Philadelphia died. [St John Southover, PR; *SWA* 12.11.98]

LUND, Philadelphia (1726-98): With sister Charlotte, had a girls' boarding school at Lewes before December 1772, when they moved it to St Anne parish [qv]. Their partnership was dissolved 1777 [qv LUND, Charlotte]. Baptised 18 August 1726, daughter of Edward, rector of St Thomas Lewes (-1776) and Mary (-1739). Died 7 November 1798, unmarried. [St John Southover, PR; *SWA* 12.11.98]

McDONALD, James: Master of the Oliver Whitby charity school, Chichester, 1792-97 [qv].

MANNOOCH, Nicholas (-1724): Master of Rye grammar school 1680-1724 [qv]. Of Kent; Emmanuel College, Cambridge, 30 April 1674; BA 1678; ordained deacon (London) 6 June 1680. Mayor of Rye 1690, 1691, 1692, 1698, 1700, 1703, 1704. Died 24 December 1724 (buried 28 December 1724); survived by wife Mary who died 8 March 1735, aged 81 (buried 13 March 1735). [*Al. Cant.*; *HRGS*; Vidler, L. A. *New History of Rye* (1934); PR]

MANSER, Daniel: In 1759 Rotherfield parish paid him 9d for schooling a poor boy. (On 5 February 1764 they paid him 3d 'for Pulling the bucket out of the well'.) [ESRO PAR 465/6/7]

MARCHANT, John: Received from Mayfield parish 4 sums of 2s 6d, 1745-48, for schooling a poor boy. Was an overseer in the 1745-46 year. (In 1746 parish paid him 10s 6d 'for 62 lbs of led for waits for the Poor house'.) [ESRO PAR 422/31/1/3]

MARCHANT, John: Schoolmaster of Brighton. At 2 Brighton Place 1799, 1800 (Mary Marchant, mantua-maker, was at the same address), and 'writing master' there 1805. (Perhaps the JM, surveyor, of map of Homesdale in Fletching 1783.) [*Cobby's Directory* 1799, 1800; *Button's Directory* 1805; ESRO AMS 2834]

MARCHANT, Richard (-1785?): Opened a boys' boarding school at Brighton 1757 [qv].

Was 'late of Truley, in Edburton' (perhaps a son of 'Mr Richard Marchant and Charity his wife, of Truely'; of their children Charlotte was baptised 1720, John 1723, William 1728). Probably 'Mr Richard Marchant', buried at Brighton 18 July 1785. [PRs]

MARGERISON, Robert - see **GERISON, Robert**

MARKLAND, Jeremiah (1693-1776): Private tutor at Uckfield when living there 1744-52 [qv]. Born 18 October 1693, son of Ralph, vicar of Childwall, Lancashire. Christ's Hospital, London; Peterhouse, Cambridge, 1710, aged 17; BA 1713; MA 1717; fellow 1718. Noted classical scholar. Died 7 July 1776, aged 82. [*DNB*; *Al. Cant.*]

MARTIN: Schoolmaster of Northiam charity school [qv]. Appears to have been appointed in 1729, when the previous master 'old Fox', though continuing in office, was too old and infirm to carry out his duties. Probably left 1742 when (Fox still there) the trustees were considering another schoolmaster (John Rootes). [ESRO FRE 1285, 1294]

MARTIN, Benjamin (1705-82): Schoolmaster of Chichester [qv]. Baptised 1 March 1705 at Worpleston, Surrey, son of John, gent, farmer and landowner. Attended village school, otherwise self-educated. Married 1729 (marriage licence 29 October 1729), then described as 'merchant' of Guildford, Mary, daughter of Joshua Lover (-1727), of Chichester, schoolmaster, Baptist [qv]; their son named Joshua Lover Martin. The Martins were Baptists (the Baptist community at Chichester were strong subscribers for one of BM's books published 1737). Either a legacy or wife's dowry (she inherited £100 or half-share of her father's estate if more) enabled him to buy books, instruments etc. By 1734 he had a boys' boarding school at Chichester, with a strong mathematical and scientific bias. At South Street in 1737 (lease). Also had a shop where he probably sold microscopes (he had devised a new one) and other instruments. Published many books 1735-82, including *The Philosophical Grammar* (1735), a science textbook, dedicated to 'British youth of both sexes', which ran to 8 editions by 1778 and was translated into Dutch, French, Italian,

Greek and Russian; *The Young Trigonometer's Compleat Guide* (1736); and an English dictionary which preceded Dr Johnson's. By 1737, with 4 books published in 2 years, styled himself as author; by 1741 his main source of income was as a peripatetic lecturer on scientific subjects. Perhaps also land-surveyor. In 1742 moved to Reading and opened a boys' boarding school there (advertisement in *Reading Mercury* 4 January 1742); but probably not affluent as a month later his wife advertised as a milliner. In 1756 launched an instrument-making business in Fleet Street, London, where he also lectured, and which he ran for 26 years. Wife died 30 October 1781. In January 1782 he was declared bankrupt; tried to commit suicide - this unsuccessful, but he died 9 February 1782. Described in *Gentleman's Magazine* as 'One of the most eminent mathematicians of the age'. [Milburn, J. R. *Benjamin Martin* (1976) and *Benjamin Martin - Supplement* (1986); *SRS* **12**; *DLS*]

MARTIN, Charles: Schoolmaster at Upmarden 1728, and master of Walberton charity school in 1733, when it opened [qv]. Then described at visitation as 'a person of sober Conversation. He comes to Church Himself and Causes his Schoolers also. He sometimes Doth Instruct His Scholers in ye Church Catechism'. Married (marriage licence 3 October 1728) Joyce Forster of Upmarden. [*SRS* **9**; WSRO Ep.I/22/1]

MARTIN, Edward (1698-1766): Master of Steyning grammar school [qv]. Licensed 27 September 1729. In 1733 the churchwardens reported the school much neglected, with no scholars. Was replaced soon after. Born 30 June 1698, at Rothwell, Northamptonshire. School, Merchant Taylors; Clare College, Cambridge, 1717; BA 1721. Ordained deacon (Chichester) 1722; priest (Ely, letters dimissory from Chichester) 1724. Vicar of New Shoreham 1728, vicar of Lancing 1743, rector of Southwick 1756, all to death. Married at Pyecombe, 7 July 1737, Elizabeth Temple; their daughter Elizabeth baptised there 11 May 1738. Died 13 April 1766, aged 67 (buried in chancel, Lancing). Letters of administration 7 May 1766 to daughter, Elizabeth Lloyd. [*Al. Cant.*; CI]

10.   Benjamin Martin (1705-1782), kept a boarding school in Chichester 1734-41. Self-taught,
he became a celebrated mathematical author, lecturer, and maker of scientific instruments.
Portrait from *Encyclopaedia Londiniensis* (1816).

MARTIN, William: Schoolmaster at Chichester 1782. [Poll book, WSRO Add MS 2133]

MASCALL, (Mary?) (-1794?): Had a dame school at Plumpton in the 1780s [qv]. Lived at Plumpton Place; husband bailiff 'over a few fields' for Lord Pelham. An 'old woman' in the 1780s, probably Mary, wife of Thomas, buried 5 January 1794, aged 80. [*SAC* **2**; PR]

MASON, Christopher (-1770): In 1734 a faction petitioned the Earl of Wilmington to replace John Akhurst, the first master of Eastbourne charity school [qv], by 'one Mr Mason', who was qualified to teach mathematics and the measuring of land. When Akhurst was continued at the charity school, the faction set up Mason in another school [qv]. Also surveyor. In 1758 Thomas Turner of East Hoathly [qv] (fearing his trade of shopkeeper was failing) and his friend Elless arranged for CM to instruct them 'in the art of land-measuring', and they worked with him on some farm surveys. Married, son John baptised and buried 1738; wife Ann buried 28 February 1758. Buried 23 April 1770. [*DLS*; Vaisey, D. (ed) *The Diary of Thomas Turner* (1984); PR]

MATHEWS, Charles: Dancing master of London, who visited Lewes every week. Advertised 1714 [for his career and qualifications, see under Dancing and music masters].

MATHEW, John (1672-1745): Master of Steyning grammar school 1692-c1723 [qv]. Of Trinity College, Dublin. Licensed 21 September 1692 to teach boys grammar and arithmetic at Steyning. Vicar of Steyning 1702 to death. Probably also taught children in the church, Sunday afternoons, Michaelmas to Lady Day (in 1724 the churchwardens noted that many of the children of dissenters 'come to Church', this probably because JM gave them some schooling). Daughter Ann married Mordaunt Michael and had issue (Elizabeth and Ann). Died 16 November 1745, aged 73. Left £10 to poor of Steyning. Wife Elizabeth received £30 a year under his will; died 27 February 1748, aged 81. [Sleight, J. M. *A Very Exceptional Instance* (1981); CI; WSRO Ep.I/26/3; MI SAS Dunkin MS 8.4; WSRO STC I/38 pp 95-7]

[MAYNARD, Mrs]: In 1801 had a girls' boarding school at Maresfield. (Perhaps wife of John, who occupied a shop and house (land tax rental of £2), 1790-1800; in 1801 'Maynard, John, esq' occupied a mill there.) [*SWA* 11.1.1802; Land Tax]

MEANE, P.: With M. Davey [qv for Baptist connections] had a girls' boarding school at Lewes 1792-94 [qv].

MEASOR: With Hunter, had a boys' day and evening school at 38 Middle Street, Brighton, 1791 [qv]. In 1792, at the same address, Hunter, with Richard Humber, opened a boys' boarding school. (In 1805, a Measor was a schoolmaster in Ship Street). [*Button's Directory* 1805]

MERCER, William junior: Had a boys' boarding school at Ninfield 1792 [qv].

[MEURE, Pierre]: Probably master of the French charity school supported by the Duke of Richmond, who paid him £5 5s a year 1775-1782 for the 'French school'/'French charity school'. Location of school not known; perhaps outside Sussex. [WSRO Goodwood MS 244]

MICHELL - see also MITCHELL

MICHELL, Henry (1715-89): Vicar of Brighton 1744-89, took occasional pupils. One, for a short time, was Arthur Wellesley (later Duke of Wellington). Friends included Garrick, Foote, Dr Johnson. Baptised St Michael Lewes, 20 August 1715, son of John and Elizabeth. School, Lewes; Clare College, Cambridge; BA 1736; MA 1739; fellow 1738-1740. Rector of Maresfield 1739 to death; vicar of Brighton and rector of Blatchington 1744 to death. Wrote on classical antiquities. Died at Brighton 31 October 1789. [*SAC* **97**; *Al. Cant.*; *DNB*; Lewes St Michael PR]

MICHELL, Mark: Had a boys' boarding school in North Street, Chichester (Rs 1788 - into 19th century) [qv]. Had been 8 years assistant to Richard Figg at Churcher's College, Petersfield.

MICHELL, Richard (1738-90): Had a boys' boarding school at Eastdean (East Sussex) [qv]. Advertised 1777 that he proposed to teach 5 or

6 pupils the classics, etc (location then not known); was at Eastdean by 1778. Baptised 17 May 1738, son of John, butcher of Portslade, and Sarah. Lewes grammar school, Tonbridge school; St John's College, Cambridge (sizar) 1758; ordained deacon (Chichester) 1766, priest 1781; curate of Rotherfield 1769-76; curate of Eastdean with Friston 1778 to death. Regular contributor to the *Sussex Weekly Advertiser* under the names 'A Forester' and 'The Man of the Rocks'; a 2-volume collection of these pieces, *Fugitive Pieces*, printed in his lifetime but published 1790 shortly after his death. Married 16 May 1780, at Eastdean, Mercy Card; they were occupying the whole of the vicarage in 1783. Mercy died November 1786, following birth and death of daughter Marianne. Died 26 January 1790, leaving 3 destitute orphans, John, Sarah and Philadelphia. A public subscription for their relief (subscribers headed by Lord Eardley) raised £351. On 2 January 1792 a pamphlet was published, *A Sixpenny Christmas Box* (6d), the profits of which were to go to the Michell and Collett orphans. [PRs; *Al. Cant.*; Lower *Worthies*; *SWA* 1.2.90, 15.2.90, 25.10.90, 2.1.92]

MILES, William: Schoolmaster of Bosham, 1761-63 [qv under Dame and petty schools]

MILLER, Ann: Received 2 to 3s a month from Buxted parish for 'Teaching the Children in the workhouse their Books', from end of 1782 to April 1783, and again in May 1785. [ESRO PAR 286/31/1]

MILLS, Nathaniel: Schoolmaster at Ninfield, early 18th century [qv]. George Luxford, a distant relative, was a boarding pupil of his 1698, at £12 a year (probably at Ninfield). His sister Rachel married another George Luxford. Married 18 April 1702, at Ninfield, Sarah Spray of Burwash. Their daughter Mary residual beneficiary under will of his sister Rachel 1726. [PR; *SNQ* 12]

MINSHULL, Mrs: Mistress at the Blue Coat girls' charity school, Chichester [qv]. Received payments on behalf of the school 1713. [WSRO Cap.V/1/1]

MITCHELL - see also MICHELL

MITCHELL, Widow (-1781): A poor widow

paid £2 a year for schooling poor children by Horsted Keynes parish, which had taken over Lightmaker's charity school after the trustees had lost the endowed capital [qv]. In 1777 Mitchell was being paid the £2 for schooling 4 children. Died December 1781. [ESRO GLY 3466; Bird, R. *Sussex History* 2, no. 7 (1984)]

[**MITCHELL, Hugh**]: Schoolmaster at Fletching 1803, he married at Fletching 12 October 1786 Alice Bull of Fletching, spinster. Described in marriage licence as gardener, of Epsom, Surrey, aged 30 and upwards. [*Sussex Militia List 1803, Pevensey Rape Northern Division* (1988); PR; *SRS* 26]

MITCHELL, John: Usher at George Pike's school, Robertsbridge, 1774 or earlier to 1791 [qv]. A Methodist (like the Pikes), in lists of class members 1774-91 (when the Robertsbridge class ceased for 20 years).

MOCKETT, Thomas (1757?-1807?): Schoolmaster 1793-96, almost certainly at West Firle [qv]. On 31 December 1793 paid by 3rd Viscount Gage £3 10s for 'Schooling Ten Boys', the same on 24 December 1794, and on 25 July 1796 £1 2s for his 'School Bill'. Also appears to have been a collector of income tax. There were several Mockett families at West Firle and in 1791 at least two Thomases who rented land there. Perhaps baptised 21 January 1757, son of Alexander and Mary (née Pettit), who married 21 October 1754, and perhaps the TM buried 25 May 1807. Probably related to Alexander M (baptised 1794, son of John and Ann), schoolmaster at Firle in 1830. [ESRO SAS/G/ACC 741; PR]

MOLINI, P.: Italian master. Received £4 1s 9d in 1787, £7 12s in 1788, £3 8s 3d in 1789, and £4 4s for 1790 and 1791, from the Duke of Richmond for teaching Henriette Le Clerc [qv Schedule 3] at Goodwood House. (She was 14 or 15 in 1787, 18 or 19 in 1791). [WSRO Goodwood MS 244, 245]

MOOR: Spinet-master. Taught the Fuller children at Brightling Park (c1728?). [*SAC* 104]

MOOR, Ann: Received small sums from the Dowlin charity (6s 3d in 1717, 3s 9d in 1718) for schooling poor children of West Grinstead.

[WSRO Par 95/1/1/3]

MOOREY, William: Schoolmaster at Chichester (Rs 1782, 1784) [qv]. Married Jane, their son Henry baptised St Martin 12 December 1777. In 1784 at house in St Martin's, which he owned, with wife, 3 sons, 2 daughters. [PR]

MORFOOT, James: Barber/schoolmaster, near Horsham, 1778 [qv]. Children 'Edicated in Reading, Righting And Account'.

MORGAN, John: Master of Steyning grammar school 1778-1817 [qv]. Complained against in *Gentleman's Magazine* 1804 and public petition 1816. Only had average of 2 boys on the foundation. Resigned 1817. Curate of Old Shoreham 1770-1818.

MORLY, Richard (-1752 or 53): Schoolmaster of Cuckfield (so described in will). Also surveyor (Rs 1745-51). Under his will, dated 7 December 1752, proved 5 April 1753, his 'late wife's' clothes went to her sisters Ann and Elizabeth Huggett; his customary house and 2 acres to his mother Katherine for life, then to Samuel Baker of Pyecombe, husbandman, for life, then to nephew Richard Morly son of John for life, then 'to the next oldest son of my heirs whose name shall be Richard Morly'. Residue of estate to mother, his executrix. [ESRO W/A 58.707; *DLS*]

[MORLEY, William]: Singing master. In 1778 paid £1 11s 6d by Icklesham parish 'to teach the People of Icklesham to sing Psalms'. Probably also taught the children. [*SAC* **32**]

MORLEY, William (1762-1800): Schoolmaster of Cuckfield (Rs 1793, 1800) [qv]. Buried 17 September 1800, aged 38. Will dated 10 March 1800, proved 17 January 1801, left copyhold premises in Cuckfield and all personal estate in trust to wife Elizabeth for life or until her re-marriage, when to be sold and divided equally between his children, Elizabeth, William (baptised 23 December 1792), Jane, John (baptised 29 January 1798). [ESRO W/A 68.560; PR]

MORLING: With William Breen, in 1788 reinstated J. Morling's (deceased) French and English Academy (boarding school) at Brighton [qv].

MORLING, J. (-c1787): Had a French and English Academy at Brighton [qv Morling's and Breen's boys' boarding school]

MORPHEW, Robert: Schoolmaster at East Grinstead 1793. [*Universal British Directory* 1793]

MORPHEW, William: Schoolmaster at Hartfield 1797 and 1801; probably master of charity school. Had son William. [*SWA* 13.11.97, in advertisement by Militia Society; deeds of Fowlers cottages East Grinstead, in possession of Tamplins (reference to will of Richard Edwards of East Grinstead)]

MOSSOP, John (1756-94): Schoolmaster of Brighton. 'A north-countryman, of almost gigantic figure'; obituary in *Gentleman's Magazine* gives MA of St John's College, Cambridge (but academic references confused or missing). Came to Brighton as curate 1786, and took over the boys' boarding school run by fellow curate Thomas Hudson, styling it the 'Grammar School' [qv]. Published 1788 *Elegant Orations, ancient and modern, for the Use of Schools*, which featured modern English speeches and classical orations (done into English) from which he claimed 'youth will obtain a sufficient confidence for public speaking...without that hazard of their morals which accrues from the foolish custom of acting plays'. Published 1791, for the use of schools, *Mathurini Corderii Colloquia Selecta; or Select Colloquies of M. Cordery*, which included analysis of the principal colloquies, 'the DECLENSION and GOVERNMENT of the Declinable Parts of Speech, and a REFERENCE to the Rules of the ETON GRAMMAR' (it cost 2s and was 'well bound'). In 1792 wrote *A description of Brighthelmstone and the Adjacent Country* for Crawford's Library, repeated in 1793 (the guide then being printed for J. Gregory) and - several years after JM's death - with minor changes as Fisher's *Brighton New Guide* of 1800 and later. Contributed local archaeological notes to *Gentleman's Magazine*, and undertook (but as far as is known did not complete) a natural history of the county. For the last, in 1791 he appealed for help to 'the NOBILITY,

GENTRY, CLERGY, LITERATI, &c Of the COUNTY of SUSSEX', since 'my scholastic avocations will not permit me to pay the personal attention necessary to complete the work, in so accurate a manner as I could wish', and he proposed to send the clergy a printed questionnaire. For his cadet corps at the school, and his public support for Dr Knox when the latter was in acrimonious confrontation with officers of the Surrey Militia stationed in Brighton, see Schedule 1; he was on the committee of a patriotic society at Brighton, set up in 1792 in reaction to the French Revolution, 'for the Protection of Liberty and Property against REPUBLICANS and Levellers' - there was a great procession and rally in December of that year. Besides curate of Brighton, he was also curate of Rottingdean (signed the vestry minutes as such 1790-92). In 1793 contributed £1 1s for improvements on the Steine. Founder member of the Royal Clarence Lodge of freemasons 1789, and Master of the Lodge 1791, 1792; as chaplain of the Lodge preached at freemason services at Brighton and Arundel. Died, after a short illness, 7 April 1794, aged 38. Survived by wife, his executrix. [Tibble, R. 'Revd John Mossop MA (1756-1794)' *SFH* **8**, no. 8 (1989); *Gentleman's Magazine* Mar 1788, Apr 1794; Bishop, 134; St Nicholas PR; ESRO PAR 466/9/2; *SWA* 28.6.90, 14.10.90, 3.1.91, 18.4.91, 12.9.91, 9.12.93, 14.4.94, 21.4.94]

MUZZELL, Abraham: Schoolmaster at Hurstpierpoint. In 1719 was paid 7s 6d for schooling William Balcombe. Master of the charity school, 1732 to at least 1751 [qv]. (Ann Bull, baptised 28 January 1647, daughter of Richard of Albourne, married an AM of Hurstpierpoint, perhaps the schoolmaster's father?) [*SAC* **25**; Comber *Sx. Gen.*]

MYERS, John (1757-1834): Had a boys' boarding school at Eastbourne from 1791 [qv]; also master of the charity school by 1792 [qv], for which he received £15 a year for schooling 15 poor children from Lord Cavendish. St John's College, Cambridge; MA; curate of Willingdon by 1792; vicar of Rye 1793 to death; perpetual curate of Udimore 1799. Married Eleanor, their son John Simpson baptised at Eastbourne 16 June 1794, son William Thomas baptised 29 November 1795 (he became curate of Eltham, Kent, and died 23

December 1841, aged 46). Gave up Eastbourne schools 1801. Mayor of Rye 1823. Buried there 28 October 1834, aged 77. His widow died 21 February 1836, aged 77. [CI; PRs; Vidler, L. A. *New History of Rye* (1934)]

NEALE, Robert (1750-): Had a boys' boarding school at Littlehampton in 1779 [qv], and later (Rs 1790-93) in Arundel, styled 'Arundel Grammar School' [qv]. Born at Henley-on-Thames, son of the Rev James, master of the grammar school there. St John's College, Cambridge, 3 July 1770, aged 19; did not reside; admitted St Edmund Hall, Oxford, matriculated 26 April 1771, aged 19. Probably curate of Littlehampton 1776, when (aged 26) he married Rachel Osborne (aged 17), daughter of John, mariner (marriage licence 23 September 1776). [*Al. Cant.*; *SRS* **35**]

NEWELL, Martha: Received £2 9s a year, 1741-55, from the Oliver Whitby charity, to teach 6 poor children of West Wittering to read [qv Charity schooling]. [WSRO E35D/3/1]

NEWLAND, Mrs: Mistress of the Blue Coat girls' charity school, Chichester [qv]. Received payments on behalf of the school in 1793, and annual subscriptions of £2 2s from the Duke of Richmond 1798-1801. [WSRO Cap.V/1/1, Goodwood MS 247]

NEWNHAM, John: Master of Lightmaker's charity school, Horsted Keynes, c1777-80 [qv]. Received £8 a year to teach 8 poor children.

NEWPORT: 'Newport's school' was in the High Street, Littlehampton, c1780-90.

NICHOLS, Adrian: Schoolmaster of Angmering 1714 [qv Charity school]. He married firstly Elizabeth, their son Adrian baptised 1691. Elizabeth was buried 4 February 1711. He married secondly (marriage licence 1 April 1714) Margaret Darbey of Chichester, widow. [PR, from Baker, L., pers. comm.; *SRS* **12**]

NICHOLSON, James: Music and Dancing master, Lewes, from 1796 [qv under Music and dancing masters]. Freemason, South Saxon Lodge, Lewes, 1799 (first year registration required by law) as 'Professor of Musick'; also in register of Arundel Lodge 1799 as 'Honorary

Member from South Saxon Lodge' and as member 1800. (Thomas N, dancing master, probably his son [qv]). [ESRO QDS/1/EW1]

[**NICHOLSON, Thomas**]: Dancing master, Lewes, 1818, in register of South Saxon Lodge of freemasons. Probably son of James [qv] and perhaps referred to in *Baxter's Directory* 1805 under 'Nicholas & Son, dancing masters'. [ESRO QDS/1/EW1]

NOAKES, Thomas: Schoolmaster at Brede, 1794 [qv Charity school].

[**NOAKES, William**]: In 1801, under the heading 'BOARDING and DAY SCHOOL WANTED', a large house in Ticehurst was advertised to let, suggesting it had previously been used as a school, and that possibly William Noakes, to whom enquirers were directed, was master of it [qv].

NORTON, Mrs: Opened a girls' boarding school at Preston 1796 [qv]. Widow of John Bridger Norton, collector of customs at New Shoreham.

NYE, Edmund (-1704): Schoolmaster at New Shoreham. Identified as such on opening page of 1695 parish register which he kept to 1703. Parish clerk. Married Ruth, their son Elias born 4 April 1696. Buried 31 May 1704. [PR]

OAKSHOT, Widow: Received 7s 10d from the Nash charity for schooling poor children of Bosham between 16 March 1761 and 25 April 1763. [WSRO Par 25/9/1]

OKILL, William (-1785): First master of Fermor's charity school, Rotherfield [qv]; appointed under Fermor's will (he died 1734) though the school not built until 1744. Also received under the will, apart from master's salary, £20 and annuity of £2 for life. Then of Sevenoaks; married Jane, 4 of their children baptised there; youngest, Ann (baptised 31 March 1731) married at Withyham 10 September 1747 David Dadswell (both of Rotherfield) who succeeded WO as master in 1772 [qv]. WO buried at Rotherfield, 'Schoolmaster at Crowborrow', 11 February 1785. [Hackworth, J. *Sir Henry Fermor C of E School 1744-1994* (1994); Withyham, Rotherfield PRs]

OLIVER: Schoolmaster at Brighton (Rs 1791, 1793). [*Universal British Directory*]

OLIVER, Richard: Master of Midhurst grammar school c1698-1710 (referred to as 'the present schoolmaster of the Free School' in Midhurst in deed of 30 June 1698) [qv]. Inhabitants petitioned against him for neglecting the school, 1706. Resigned 1710. Curate of Midhurst by 1700; perpetual curate 1709. Wife Mary. [*HMGS*; Dibben, A. A. (ed) *The Cowdray Archives* 2 (1964), numbers 4485, 4684; *SAC* **18**, **20**; (entry in *Al. Oxon.* queried)]

OLIVIERS, Monsieur: Dancing master. Received £4 4s in 1786 and £2 12s 6d in 1787 from the Duke of Richmond for teaching Henriette Le Clerc (then aged about 14) at Goodwood House. [WSRO Goodwood MS 244]

OLLIVE, Elizabeth (1749-1808): Opened a girls' boarding school in Lewes January 1769 (when aged 19) [qv]; previously assistant to Mrs Ridge, who had given up her school on account of health. Born 16 December 1749 (baptised 27 December 1749 at Westgate chapel), daughter of Samuel, tobacconist. Father died July 1769. Married 26 March 1771, as his second wife, Thomas Paine, 12 years her senior (later to write the *Rights of Man*; he had married, 27 September 1759, at Sandwich, Mary Lambert, an orphan and servant maid; she died 1760). Paine had come to Lewes 1768 as excise officer (having at one time been a schoolmaster) and lodged with the Ollives. After Samuel's death, he moved out of the house but joined the widow in running the tobacco business, and appears to have taken this over: in April 1774 all the household furniture, stock in trade and other effects of Thomas Paine, grocer and tobacconist, were sold by auction. In June 1774 Elizabeth and Thomas formally separated. Paine left for America and did not return to England until 1787. Following the separation, Paine is reported to have assisted her financially on several occasions and 'always spoke tenderly and respectfully of his wife' (Rickman, Paine's friend and biographer); and Elizabeth got up and left the room if anyone criticised Paine. In 1793 the *Sussex Weekly Advertiser* denied a report that she was subsisting on her parish: she 'now follows the business of a mantua-maker, near London, by which she gets a good livelihood, independent of what she receives from her relations, who we believe are very kind to her'. She eventually went to live with her brother Thomas, watchmaker at Cranbrook, Kent. Died 27 July 1808. [ESRO NU l/1/2; St Michael PR; Williamson, A. *Thomas Paine* (1973); Godfrey, W. H. *At the Sign of the Bull* (1924); *SWA* 8.7.93]

OSBON, Sarah: Schoolmistress of Seaford. Received £5 a year from George Medley for schooling 12 children of Seaford from at least Christmas 1775 (when surviving Medley estate accounts begin) to Michaelmas 1780. Probably Sarah King who married, 19 August 1756, John Osbon of Seaford, husbandman, widower (she signed by mark); he was buried 29 July 1765. [ESRO SAS/GT 1/3/3; PR]

OSGOOD, Francis (1696-1773): Master of Horsham grammar school 1722-73 [qv]. Licensed 6 June 1723. In his time the grammar school failed, the number of boys falling from 50 to 0. Son of John, of Amesbury, Wiltshire; Oriel College, Oxford, matriculated 19 June 1713, aged 18; exhibitioner; BA 1717; ordained priest (Chichester) 1718; curate of Westmeston before coming to Horsham, of which curate for more than 50 years; also rector of Saltfleet St Peter, Lincolnshire, 1722-44. Married at Horsham, 6 January 1723, Katherine Reynell, daughter of late Canon John, vicar of Horsham and master of the grammar school; she died 1738, without issue. His Horsham interests included the county jail and the workhouse. His will forgave debts, gave £200 to one nephew, £700 to another (provided he returned from America within 20 years), left to sister-in-law Elizabeth Reynell farms at Nuthurst and Hurstpierpoint, lands at Twineham, shares in Dorking turnpike, etc. Died 1773. [*HCS*; WSRO Ep.I/1/11; *Al. Oxon.*; Horsham PR]

OWEN, Hugh: With Thomas Hudson, opened a boys' day and boarding school, Brighton, 1778 [qv]. They had previously been at William Gilpin's celebrated academy at Cheam. Their partnership was dissolved 24 June 1782. Owen later in partnership with John Dulot, with a circulating library on the Steine; this partnership dissolved 29 December 1791, Dulot carrying on the library, 'Mr Owen having entirely quitted that line of business'. (Dulot

was, by 1793 when he transferred the business to Gregory, also bookseller, stationer and bookbinder to the Prince of Wales and Duke of York.) [*SWA* 19.8.82, 16.4.92, 6.5.93]

[PACKNELL, John]: Schoolmaster at Uckfield 1803. Then aged 17-30, married, and enrolled in voluntary infantry. But perhaps same as John Pocknell, whose children were baptised at Uckfield 1784-93, in which case militia list age classification incorrect. [*Sussex Militia List 1803, Pevensey Rape Northern Division* (1988); PR]

PAGE, Widow: Had a dame school at Clapham, 1772 [qv].

PAGE, Mary: Probably mistress at the Blue Coat girls' charity school, Chichester; received payment of behalf of the school, and signed receipt, 1726. [WSRO Cap.V/1/1]

PAINE, Miss: Mistress of the Brighton Sunday school and school of industry 1789-91 [qv]. Given credit for the 'respectable appearance' of the children 'under whose care and tuition they are' at a charity service (1789), and for the children's singing of a hymn (1791). In April 1792 the Sunday school and school of industry advertised for a mistress, and in June Miss Paine opened her own day school [qv], and at the same time a 'CHILD BED WAREHOUSE, No. 9, Little East-street, where she will make and sell all manner of child-bed linen, Ladies morning caps, morning gowns, petticoats, and every article in muslin, dimity, callico, &c. in the newest fashion, and at the lowest prices'. [*SWA* 5.10.89, 3.10.91, 16.4.92, 21.5.92]

PAYNE, Charles (1773-1849): Shepherd to John Ellman (of the Great Farm, Glynde), he was accustomed to carry a book with him when tending his flock on the Downs, and was engaged as schoolmaster by Ellman to teach the unmarried men and maidservants in his house to read and write. Married, 4 November 1796, a dairymaid whom he had taught (but she signed by mark) Lucy Salvage (their son John died 24 September 1842, aged 31). At Lord Somerville's spring show, 1808, won the shepherd's first prize for having raised 799 lambs from 600 ewes, and only lost 21. Died 29 June 1849, aged 76. [Walesby, A. 'Memoir of John Ellman' *Library of Agricultural and*

Horticultural Knowledge (3rd edition, 1834 and 4th edition, Lewes); PR; *SAC* **20**]

PAINE, Cornelius: Opened a boys' boarding school at Brighton 1777 (Rs into 19th century) [qv]. On the committee of a patriotic society at Brighton set up in 1792 in reaction to the French Revolution, 'for the Protection of Liberty and Property against REPUBLICANS and Levellers'; there was a great procession and rally in December of that year. High Constable of Brighton 1800 and 'in the Chair' at a meeting of inhabitants that agreed an address to the King, congratulating him on his escape from an attempted assassination. Churchwarden St Nicholas 1803-12. [Bishop, 134; *SWA* 26.5.1800; PR]

PAIN (PAYNE), Henry (1723-94): Paid monthly by Framfield parish from July 1789 to August 1794 for schooling 16-30 children, probably the workhouse children [qv Parish schooling]. Buried as a pauper 29 August 1794, widower, aged 71. [PR]

PAINE, Richard: Drawing master of Brighton 1791, 1793 (*Universal British Directory*); drawing master and stationer 1799, 1800 (*Cobby's Directory*).

PALMER, Thomas (1751-1821): Appointed master of East Grinstead charity school c1775, to teach 10 boys [qv]. From January 1784 also had own boys' boarding school. Also opened stationer's shop - invented a pen and got royal warrant. Listed in *Universal British Directory* 1793 as 'Bookseller, Stationer, Printer, Postmaster, Master of the Free School & Agent to the Phoenix Fire Office'. Born Appledore, Kent, 17 November 1751 (father a plumber and glazier). Had a school at (probably) Eastbourne, also writing master to a girls' school where he met mistress Elizabeth Anstie (1746-1833) whom he married, 24 December 1774, at Eastbourne. Their son Thomas baptised 28 September 1775 (privately) and 22 October 1775 at Eastbourne. His sister Ann married William Jackson, master of Rye grammar school [qv], and their daughter married TP's son Thomas. Gave up the school 1816, which was then taken over by his son Thomas (1775-1844) who moved it to Sackville College (almshouse) of which he was warden from 1813. Died 13 December 1821. Left £1000 to each of his 12 children. [Leppard, M. J. pers. comm. citing PRs and family historians]

PAPE, Daniel: 'Rev Mr Pape' opened a small expensive school at Rye 1793 [qv]; had been headmaster of a public school in the north of England. Almost certainly Daniel Pape, curate of Rye 1793-99, where he occupied the vicarage. Also curate of Playden (Rs 1793-95); rector of Slaugham 1794, which he resigned 1800. [Rye, Playden, marriage registers; Vidler, L. A. *New History of Rye* (1934); CI]

PARGETER, Robert (1759-1803): Master of Midhurst grammar school 1795-99 [qv]. Son of the Rev Robert, of Buckingham; Brasenose College, Oxford, matriculated 8 April 1775, aged 16; demy Magdalen College, Oxford 1777; BA 1778, MA 1781. Executor to Charles Parson, previous master of the grammar school, 1795. Resigned the grammar school 1799. Died in London 20 February 1803. [*HMGS*; *Al. Oxon.*; WSRO STC 1/45, pp 62-3]

[PARRIS, John]: Schoolmaster at Hellingly in 1813. Married, 18 January 1802, Susanna Vine, both of Hellingly, so perhaps schoolmaster there in 1800. 'Schoolmaster' at baptism of daughter Rebecca, 5 March 1813. Also surveyor (R 1816). [PR; *DLS*]

PARROTT, Benjamin: Had a boys' boarding school at Petworth c1780-93 [qv]. Also taught writing and accounts to the girls of Mrs Hews' boarding school. By January 1791 had bought a 'very large' house and garden for his school, and styled it 'Petworth Academy'; but in 1793 was one of two 'Poor Tradesmen' of Petworth each given £6 5s by way of charity.

PARSON, Charles (1758-95): Assistant master Midhurst grammar school 31 March 1785, at £20 a year. Master 16 April 1788 (at same salary) to death in 1795. From 1789 took over management of the school accounts, collecting rents, etc. Son of John, of Chichester, gent; New College, Oxford, 1773 (aged 15); BA 1778, MA 1780. Curate Bepton 1780-82; ordained priest (Chichester) 21 December 1782; curate of Chiddingfold with Haslemere, Surrey, 1784-86; perpetual curate of Fernhurst 1787 to death (from which he had a house and £50 a year from the Cowdray estate, of which only £20 secure). Died 11 February 1795, aged 36 (memorial inscription Easebourne). Brother William a surgeon at Haslemere and Godalming. Sister Charlotte married the Rev Charles Alcock. [WSRO E138/3/1; *HMGS*; CI; *Al. Oxon.*; Tudor, A. M. *Fernhurst* (1934); WSRO STC 1/45, pp 62-63]

PARSONS, J.: Had a boys' boarding school at Beckley (Rs 1792, 1797) [qv]. Also surveyor (estate maps Beckley 1792 and Peasmarsh 1799 survive). [ESRO SAS/FB 420, AMS 4818]

PARSONS, Robert (-1794): Schoolmaster at Billingshurst (Rs 1787-94) [qv Parish schooling]. Received £2 5s a year from parish for schooling 6 poor children; probably had own pupils as well. Parish clerk. Buried 25 July 1794. [PR]

PARSONS, William: Singing master. Received £10 10s 9d in 1786, £8 9s 6d in 1787, £12 7s 3d in 1788, and £3 15s 6d in 1789, from the Duke of Richmond for singing lessons for Henriette Le Clerc at Goodwood House (she was 13 or 14 in 1786, 16 or 17 in 1789). [WSRO Goodwood MS 244, 245]

PATTERSON: In 1714 received £1 10s for schooling Nicholas Gilbert of Eastbourne, aged 7, for ¾ year. Probably had a petty school in the town. [ESRO ACC 2462/1]

[PECKHAM]: Music master of Lewes 1805. (Both George and Edwin Peckham, music masters of Lewes, were members of the South Saxon Lodge of Freemasons, Lewes, 1834.) [*Brighton and Lewes Guide* (1805); ESRO QDS/1/EW1]

PECKHAM, Mary (Mrs): Probably mistress of the Blue Coat girls' charity school, Chichester [qv]. Received payments of behalf of the school 1727 (signed receipt) and 1729. [WSRO Cap.V/1/1]

[PECKHAM, William]: Probably schoolmaster at Ringmer, 1802-07, when he occupied the charity school schoolhouse [qv].

PEIRCE, Thomas (-1725): Master of Lewes grammar school [qv]. King's College, Cambridge, BA 1701 (probably MA 1714). Licensed, Lewes grammar school, 12 June 1706. Subscribed as curate St Anne Lewes, 23

October 1706. Ordained (Chichester) 15 June 1711. Appointed corresponding member of The Society for Promoting Christian Knowledge c1713. Signed bishop's transcripts, Hamsey (probably as curate) 1715, 1717, 1718; rector St Thomas at Cliffe, Lewes, 1718 to death; rector St Anne, Lewes, 1720 to death. Wife Anne buried 15 March 1721. Buried 13 April 1725. [*Al. Cant.*; WSRO Ep.I/1/10, I/3/5; SPCK ALB v.14, 3716; CI; St Anne PR]

[*PENFOLD, wife of Richard*]: Received 13s in 1698 from the Dowlin charity for schooling poor children of West Grinstead; possibly kept a dame school, and may have taught in 18th century. [WSRO Par 95/1/1/3]

PEOLY: Dancing master of Lewes (Rs 1778, 1779) [qv]. Also had 'a Business in London'. In partnership with Thring [qv] January 1779; they also visited Herstmonceux and Brighton.

PERRY, Serjeant: Of Lord Harcourt's regiment of Light Dragoons. Instructed the boys of Mossop's school, Brighton [qv] in 'martial exercise', 1789-1790; commended in the *Sussex Weekly Advertiser*, following their 'annual review', 31 March 1790. [*SWA* 5.4.90]

[PHILLIPS]: Schoolmaster in the Pallants, Chichester, c1804. [*Chichester Guide* c1804]

PHILLIPS, Elizabeth (Mrs): Had a girls' boarding school, Arundel (Rs 1780-1793) [qv]. 'French is the general Language of her School'; Italian also taught.

PHILLIPS, James: Had a boys' boarding school at Horsham (Rs 1789, 1793) [qv]. In 1797 set up a joint surveying business with Matthew Phillips of Henfield [qv], James being based at Horsham. Probably the JP who, at Horsham, was one of the 7 owners of printing presses in Sussex registered under the Act of 1799. [*SAC* **130**]

PHILLIPS, Matthew (1794-): Assisted father William with his boys' boarding school at Henfield [qv]; by 1802 the school was kept by 'Messrs Phillips and Son'; that year father retired and MP ran the school till 1806. Also surveyor. In 1797, based at Henfield, set up a joint surveying business with James Phillips, based at Horsham. Taught surveying at the school. In advertisement for surveying, 1800, asked for early notice of orders, 'his scholastic employ preventing immediate attention to their favours'. Baptised at Storrington 4 September 1794, where father then schoolmaster, son of William and Sarah.

[PHILLIPS, N.]: Had a boys' boarding school at West Tarring by January 1802 [qv] (where Edward Phillips was vicar 1786-1803). [CI]

PHILLIPS, William: Master of Storrington charity school c1771-85 [qv]. Opened a boys' boarding school at Henfield 1785 [qv]; erected new school-room 1788; acquired extra 1½ acres for playground 1792. In 1788 claimed schoolmastering his only occupation, but later also did some surveying (estate map, Henfield, 1805). Married Sarah; their children baptised at Storrington, Mary (1771), Matthew (1774), Philadelphia (1777), Henry (1778), Charles (1783). Retired 1802, when son Matthew [qv] took over the school. Son Henry became a leading horticulturist and botanist. [PR; *DLS*; de Candole, H. *The Story of Henfield* (1976)]

[PHILPOTT]: In 1739 a Mr Philpott estimated that Chichester contained about 1,000 houses; William Cole, the antiquary, 'suspected him of being a schoolmaster'. [*VCH* iii]

PHILPOT, Ann (1732?-89?): Eldest daughter of Stephen Philpot, took over father's girls' boarding school, Lewes, when he died 1770 [qv]. Had married Phillip Gastineau and given up the school by December 1772 (school premises taken over by the Misses Lund). Perhaps the Mrs Ann Gastinau for whose maintenance St Anne parish paid £2 10s per quarter from 1783-84 year to 1789, and who was buried at All Saints 1 July 1789, aged 57.

PHILPOT, Elizabeth (-1761): With her husband Stephen Philpot, dancing and music master, had a girls' boarding school, Lewes, certainly by 1757 [qv]. Their son Charles baptised St Michael 1737. When she died 1761 (buried St Michael 19 November 1761) Stephen continued the school till his death in 1770, when it was continued by daughter Ann [qv]. [PR]

PHILPOT, Stephen (-1770): Dancing and music master of Lewes from 1729; had a

'dancing school' there, and with wife Elizabeth a girls' boarding school, which he continued after wife's death in 1761. [See Schedule 1 for his career, publications and achievements]. Was successful (referred to in deeds as 'esquire' and 'gentleman') and in 1753 purchased 100-acre copyhold farm in Lindfield. In 1760 appointed one of His Majesty's Musicians in Ordinary (with salary of £40 a year and £16 2s 6d for livery). Married Elizabeth. Eldest son, Stephen, became organist at Foundling Hospital Chapel, London (the greatest benefactor of which was George Frederick Handel). John Fuller contributed £7 7s to son John's schooling by 'Mr Festin' (probably Michael Festing, who had taught SP the violin). Youngest son, Charles, became a dancing master in Leicester, and inherited the copyhold farm in Lindfield. Daughter Ann continued the school after his death, and married Phillip Gastineau. Wife Elizabeth died 1761. Will dated 5 May 1762 left personal estate to daughter Ann, sole executrix; codicil dated 16 September 1768 left £10 each to sons George and Stephen and daughter Sarah, wife of Edward Trimby. Died 2 December 1770. [ESRO AMS 4599; Cobau, J. 'Stephen Philpot: A Gentleman Dancing-Master', manuscript in private hands; St Michael PR; ESRO W/A 62.325; *SWA* 10.12.70]

PICKERING, Miss, senior, PICKERING, Miss, junior: The Misses Pickering had a girls' boarding school at 41 West Street, Brighton (Rs 1791-1800) [qv].

PICKNELL, G.: Schoolmaster of All Saints, Lewes, 1768. Probably same as George Picknall, surveyor (Rs Rodmell 1759, Glynde and Ringmer 1768). [Poll book; *SRS* **61**; ESRO AMS 5693]

[PICKNELL, Samuel]: Schoolmaster and vestry clerk of Cuckfield in 1808 at burial of son Thomas, aged 2. Perhaps followed John Cook, buried 1792, also schoolmaster and vestry clerk. [PR]

[PIERCE, March]: Schoolmaster at Lindfield 1803, a cripple, then aged 17-55. [*Sussex Militia List 1803, Pevensey Rape Northern Division* (1988)]

PIERCE, (Samuel?) (-1807?): Schoolmaster,

almost certainly at West Firle; on 30 December 1797 received £7 5s from 3rd Viscount Gage 'for Childrens Schooling in 97'. Probably Samuel Pierce, buried 24 April 1807. [ESRO SAS/G/ACC 741; PR]

PIGGETT, George: Usher of Midhurst grammar school, appointed 3 September 1735. [WSRO E138/3/1]

PIKE, George (1730-92): For many years had a boys' boarding school at Robertsbridge [qv]. He and wife were Methodists, and John Wesley stayed with them on a number of occasions, 1771-84, and preached in the large school-room. Married Mary Raynor. Daughter Mary died 1769, aged 5; son Dean died 1769, aged 1. Died 4 July 1792, aged 62 (buried at Ewhurst). Wife Mary died 11 April 1803, aged 73. [Austin, see reference in Schedule 1]

PIKE, John: Schoolmaster of Westham (R 1736) [qv Charity school]. Taught 9 poor children for £5 a year. Also surveyor (estate map, Dallington, c1755?). [SAS Budgen MS v.129; ESRO ACC 2452/6]

PILBEAM, John (1724-91): Schoolmaster of Hurstpierpoint (references as such 1774 (bond) and 1779 (marriage licence: third marriage)); was at Hurstpierpoint from c1748 (previously at Cowfold). Baptised 7 April 1714 at Cowfold, son of John and Ann (née Michell). Married firstly at Edburton 16 September 1744, Ann Holden (-1748): issue Ann (1745- ; married Thomas Warner); William (1746-1746); Frances (1748-). Married secondly 13 October 1753 Mary Box (-1777): issue John (1753-1757); William (1755- : had illegitimate child by Mary May, c1774, married 1782 at Epsom Ann Barns); Thomas (-1757); John (1763-1763); Sarah (1766- : had illegitimate son, baptised 1787; married 1788 George Brayne). Married thirdly 30 December 1779 Sarah Weekes, widow (-1792). In 1737 inherited property in Cowfold from grandfather John Michell; also inherited property in Pulborough on mother's death. Buried 18 March 1791; will of 14 June 1790 ('gentleman' in will) left his estate to be sold and proceeds (under £1,000) to be divided equally between wife Sarah and his 4 surviving children. [WSRO Par 400/34/4/12, Add MSS 3258, 3264-3269; *SRS* **26**; ESRO W/A 66.146; PRs; Norma Pilbeam pers.

comm.]

PITTIS, Thomas (1669-1712): Master of Horsham grammar school, 1706-12. Son of Thomas, of Holyrood, Southampton, a chaplain to the King (later incumbent St Botolph's, Bishopsgate). New College, Oxford, matriculated 24 November 1687, aged 18; BA from Trinity College 1691, MA 1694. Rector of Warnham 1695 to death. Married 1695, at Nuthurst, Frances Pankhurst, daughter of John of Horsham, apothecary. Died 1712. (Letters of administration 10 May 1712 to Thomas Hunt, principal creditor, FP, relict, renouncing.) [*HCS*; *Al. Oxon.*; CI]

POINTIN, Thomas: Of Henfield, in 1722 taught arithmetic to son and daughter of Thomas Marchant, yeoman of Hurstpierpoint, 3 times a week for 2s 6d each per week. Apparently kept a school in 1731, perhaps at Hurstpierpoint [qv under UNPLACED SCHOOLS]. Also surveyor (estate maps, Clayton 1732 and 1746, Plumpton 1735? and c1750). Also excise officer 1740. Of Hurstpierpoint 1740. [*SAC* **25**; *DLS*; ESRO ACC 5179/13, ESRO DAN 2099, 2100]

POOLY, Thomas (-1702): Writing master of Steyning, buried as such 14 June 1702. Probably married Margaret and had daughter Margaret (Margaret Pooly, daughter of Margaret, widow, buried 29 July 1702). [PR]

PRESCOTT, William (1685-1739): Master of Steyning grammar school [qv]. Licensed 27 June 1723. Married Ann Davey, widow of John. Curate of Coombes at death, 17 August 1739, aged 54. Widow Ann married thirdly William Michael, and died 21 November 1762, aged 81. [WSRO Ep.I/1/11; CI (citing MI Bramber)]

[PRICE]: Schoolmaster at Burwash 1804, and probably earlier [qv].

PRIEST, Henry: Opened a boys' boarding school, Arundel, 1783 (Rs 1783-93) [qv].

PRINCE, William: Music master, and organist of the Chapel Royal, at 4 Princes Place, Brighton in 1799 (in East Street 1805) [qv]. Taught at Mrs Gell's girls' boarding school Lewes in 1799. Was also a composer; in 1797 his opera *The Disagreeable Surprise; or Saltinbanco* was put on at the Brighton theatre and performed many times; at a concert in the Promenade Grove in 1801 the special feature was an Ode in honour of the Prince of Wales' birthday composed by Prince. At a benefit concert for him, of Handel's sacred music, at the Chapel Royal in 1800, there were 21 principal performers, the choruses 'supported by upwards of eighty vocal and instrumental performers'. [Bishop, 59-60, 76, 346]

[**PRIOR (PRYER), James**]: Minister of Arundel Free Church c1797-1805, he opened a private day school to supplement his stipend.

PUGH, Edward: Opened a boys' day school, Lewes, 1793 [qv], taking over William Symonds' school. Had been for 7 years teacher in an academy near London. Son of David and Ann (his sister Ann buried 13 July 1796, aged 20, daughter of David and Ann). Baptist (see Schedule 1). Married 30 August 1794, at St Michael, Lewes, Mary Symonds Davey, Baptist (probably related to, perhaps daughter of, Thomas Davey, apothecary and Baptist deacon 1786, who was witness at the marriage). By 1795, he and Mary were advertising their schools jointly; by 1799 they were in North Street, with a day and boarding school. Mary died 12 November 1800, aged 26. He married again and in 1802 'Mr & Mrs Pugh' were advertising their day and boarding school in North Street. A radical, he supported William Green, an 'Advanced Radical', at the 1796 election. [*SWA* 11.7.96, 17.11.1800; St Michael PR; All Saints PR; ESRO NB 1/1/1A; Brent, C. *Geo. Lewes* (1993)]

PUGH, John: Occupied a schoolhouse/school in Lewes 1796-1800 and presumably kept a school there, as his predecessors there had done [qv].

PUGH, Mary Symonds (1773-1800): Schoolmistress at Lewes. Née Davey, Baptist (probably related to, perhaps daughter of, Thomas Davey, apothecary and Baptist deacon, who was witness at her marriage), probably the M. Davey [qv] who, with P. Meane, had a girls' boarding school at Lewes (Rs 1792-94). Married 30 August 1794 at St Michael, Lewes, Edward Pugh, schoolmaster and Baptist [qv]. About 1794 they took over for their joint

schools the house previously occupied by Meane and Davey's girls' school. By 1799 they had a day and boarding school in North Street. Died 12 November 1800, aged 26 (buried All Saints 15 November 1800). [ESRO NB 1/1/1A; St Michael PR; All Saints PR; *SWA* 17.11.1800]

PULLEN, Isabella: With Miss Widgett, opened a girls' boarding school in North Row, Brighton, Lady Day 1784 [qv]. Had been 'Governess of the Boarding School at CAMBERWELL'. Miss Widgett left in 1788, but Mrs Pullen continued with the school to at least 1800.

PUTTOCK, William (-1785): Schoolmaster of Billingshurst; described as such at burial of his wife 16 February 1773. From at least Michaelmas 1775 to death in 1786 (excluding the 1777-78 year) received £2 5s a year from the parish for schooling 6 poor children [qv Parish schooling]. Would also have kept his own school [qv]. Also vestry clerk, for which he received £2 2s (eg 1783) or £2 (eg 1785) a year; and received smaller sums for other clerical work. Buried 26 January 1785, 'schoolmaster'. [WSRO Par 21/31/1; PR]

RAND, Cater, senior (-1748): Schoolmaster at Lewes [qv Rand family school]. Probably from Colchester, Essex, where he owned property; was in the excise and posted to Lewes 1714. From 1732 to 1740 received payments from Thomas Pelham of Stanmer and the Duke of Newcastle for schooling individual boys, and from 1737 £20 a year for the Duke's charity school [qv]. From 1733 was schooling, for 16s a year, Edward Manning, son of Henry, surgeon-apothecary. Also writing master to the grammar school 1742 (when paid by Henry Manning for another son, then at the grammar school). By 1744 had established his school at 160 High Street. Married Anne; son Charles baptised 20 November 1719, daughter Elizabeth baptised 16 February 1733. Buried 20 May 1748. [Lewes St Michael PR]

RAND, Cater, junior (1749-1825): About 1773, when 23, took over the Rand family school from mother Lucy, who had run it from death of husband Charles Rand in 1763 [qv Rand family school]. Combined the Duke of Newcastle's 'Free School' with a boys' boarding school, with a strong mathematical/scientific bias; gave public lectures on scientific subjects. In 1782 his 'mathematical instruments' were insured for £350, his 'printed books' for £150 (cf the premises at £520). Declared bankrupt 1784 (inter alia had raised loans from 2 persons on insufficient security of the same land in Cranleigh, Surrey, and in one case at least had not paid the interest due); by then had added to his occupations those of bookseller, stationer, dealer, chapman and agent for the New Fire Office. But the school continued until c1808, and his status is perhaps indicated by the will of Lewes artist James Lambert (died 1799) who referred to him as 'my most respected friend Mr Cater Rand of Lewes, gentleman' (Lambert left him 'my pantagraft'). Had many interests: in 1773 published tables for valuing gold by weight; in 1775 published book of lectures on pneumatics, electricity and astronomy; in 1796 advertised proposal for publishing topographical map of Lewes; by 1799 had developed and patented 'an improved military telescope' and published a book on it (originally constructed for the private use of Thomas Pelham, it was favourably commented on by the Duke of York, and subsequently marketed). However, his main career was as a surveyor/civil engineer. In 1790 he was appointed 'Surveyor of the Forts, on the Coast of Sussex' (and was described as such, rather than 'schoolmaster', in list of voters that year). From c1773, when he took over the family school, he had (he claimed) been involved with drainage and water control surveys, producing then a plan for reorienting the harbour piers at Newhaven; in 1792 he was resident engineer for works to improve navigation of the Ouse below Lewes, and prepared plans for canals to improve Glynde reach (not implemented); in 1797 he reported on a dock scheme on the west side of the harbour; was commissioned to prepare plan for removing the shoal inside the piers; in 1810 revised the Admiralty survey of Seaford Bay. In 1792 prepared estimate for embanking the Cuckmere salts, in 1802 advised on improving drainage of Cuckmere Levels, in 1813 was surveyor for plans for improving navigability of the Cuckmere (which did not mature). In 1800 surveyed the Adur, including Shoreham harbour, with plan for improving the same; in 1807 surveyor to improve navigation of the river; from c1816 to c1820 involved with

works at Shoreham harbour. In 1812 advised on problems at Rye harbour, and c1816 surveyed the adjacent salt marshes. In 1808 produced plans for widening Lewes bridge (rejected as too expensive); in 1822 gave evidence to Commons' committee in support of a bill for a bridge over the Arun at Littlehampton. Involved with 'coal'; in 1801 reported favourably on discoveries of fibrous lignite at Heathfield and Waldron, and gave geologist Gideon Mantell details of borings at Newick and Bexhill. Conceived the original idea of the first railway in Sussex - the Offham inclined plane railway to link chalk quarries with lime kilns and a wharf on the Ouse; but the completed railway (opened 1809) was not to his design. Proposed canals or railways to connect Shoreham harbour with Brighton and Worthing, its main markets; calculated the 'Comparative Value of Horse and Mechanical Power of Steam for Rail or Tram Roads of Iron or Granite', and came down in favour of steam; kept specimen rails outside his house and envisaged a railway between London and Newhaven - then regarded as a visionary dream. Despite his surveying and engineering activities, continued his school until c1808, and even after that appears to have been, at least nominally, writing master to the grammar school (which carried the salary of £17 15s a year); but the *Sussex Weekly Advertiser*, reporting his death in 1825, described him not as schoolmaster but as a civil engineer. Baptised 29 January 1750, son of Charles and Lucy (née Verrall). Married 21 April 1775, Mary Scrase, daughter of master of the *White Hart*; she died 3 March 1783, aged 27, leaving 6 young children; their 2 sons later joined the East India Company (both predeceased father); of their 4 daughters, one went out to India, and 3 married army officers. Died 21 December 1825, aged 76 (buried St Michael 27 December 1825). [Farrant, J. H. in *Sussex Industrial History* no. 6 (1973/74); Farrant, J. H. pers. comm. citing Guildhall Library MSS 11936/291 (Sun Fire Insurance Office policy register), PRO B1/75 (Bankruptcy Order Book); *SWA* 4.10.73, 12.12.74, 10.3.83, 28.6.90, 15.8.96, 26.12.25; *SAC* **90**; *EP* 1 (1819); St Michael PR]

RAND, Charles (1719-63): Schoolmaster of Lewes. On death of father, Cater, 1748, took over the Rand family school [qv]. Writing master to grammar school. Baptised 20

November 1719. Married 15 January 1749 Lucy Verral [qv below]. Seat-holder at St Michael 1753 (probably as occupier of 159 High Street). Father of Cater junior [qv]. Witness to will of Stephen Philpot [qv], music and dancing master, 5 May 1762. Died 1763. [St Michael PR; Lucas, P. in *SAC* **58**; ESRO W/A 62.325]

RAND, Lucy (-1781): Schoolmistress of Lewes. On death of husband, Charles [qv], 1763, took over the Rand family school [qv], probably until Michaelmas 1772, when the school continued by son Cater [qv]. Daughter of Richard and Sarah Verrall, of the *White Hart*. Married 15 January 1749 Charles Rand. Died 5 December 1781, 'of a cancerous disorder' (buried St Michael 9 December 1781). [Lucas, P. in *SAC* **58**; *SWA* 10.12.81; St Michael PR]

RANDAL, John: Schoolmaster at Midhurst 1793. [*Universal British Directory*]

RAWLINS, James Henry: Opened an 'Academy of Dancing' at Brighton 1783 [qv]. (From January 1793 also taught at Lewes on Saturdays.) Also taught music 'on the most approved Methods', and: 'Music provided for Concerts, Balls, Assemblies. By giving Three Days Notice, any additional Number of Performers may be had from London. N.B. Harpsichords, Piano Fortes, and Spinets to let, tuned, and put in proper Order.' Mr Dennis appears to have taken over his practice from September 1793. [*SWA* 3.11.83, 7.1.93]

[**RAYMOND, J.**]: Schoolmaster at Lewes 1793, 1794 (*Universal British Directory*). Shown as occupier of house with 31 windows in All Saints 1789, owned by V. A. Raymond. (Perhaps confusion with RAYMOND, Victor Amedée, qv). [Land Tax]

RAYMOND, Victor Amedée (1749-1820): By 1787, with wife Ann, had a boys' French boarding school at Lewes [qv], where French was 'the only Language allowed to be spoken among the Scholars'. Swiss. A dissenter, his daughters were baptised at Westgate meeting house, Marie Petroline (born 30 January 1784, baptised 31 January 1784), Victoire Justine (born 31 January 1786, baptised 5 March 1786). Was still thanking the public for their

patronage in 1819. Buried 18 October 1820, aged 71. [ESRO NU 1/1/2; All Saints PR]

[**READING**]: Master of Lewes grammar school c1700. [*VCH* **ii**]

[**REITH, George** (-1716)]: Licensed to teach children in Sussex, 1691. University of Aberdeen; vicar of Rudgwick 3 February 1675 to death. Buried there 8 May 1716. [CI]

RELFE, Mrs: By 1762 had kept a girls' boarding school at Lewes for many years [qv].

RELFE, John (-1797): Schoolmaster of Fletching [qv]. Also parish clerk (in addition to salary - see Schedule 1 - received payments for burials, 2s 6d for an adult, 2s for a child). Married secondly, 4 February 1768, Frances Morris, widow; their son Thomas baptised 9 August 1768. Buried 27 April 1797. [ESRO SPK/P 1; PR]

[*RENDALL*]: Had a girls' school at Brighton 1805. [*Button's Directory*]

REWELL, Ann: Mistress of Walberton charity school at its opening 1733 [qv].

REYNELL, John (1661?-1722): Master of Horsham grammar school 1712-22 [qv]. Probably son of Richard of London, gent; if so, New College, Oxford, matriculated 31 July 1677, aged 16; BA 1681, MA 1685; vicar of Chesterton, Oxfordshire, 1684; rector of Huntingdon All Saints and St Mary 1690. Vicar of Horsham 1696 to death, canon of Chichester 1698. Married firstly Katherine Thomason, who died 1707 giving birth to her 21st child. Daughter Katherine married Francis Osgood, who assisted him as master and took over the grammar school at his death. Died 1722. [*Al. Oxon.*; *HCS*; CI]

REYNOLDS, Morgan: Curate of Wisborough Green 1765-81 (and probably to 1784), in 1779 kept a school there [qv]. Had been at Kirdford 1768, 1772, probably curate there; was at North Chapel 1791, and in 1801 advertised private tuition at 50 guineas a year [qv]. Vicar of Bury 1813-19. Married 12 June 1783, at Wisborough Green, Jane Hawkins. [*SRS* **32**, **35**; CI]

RICE, Edward: Had a boys' boarding school,

Rotherfield, 1780 [qv]. Curate there, 1776-86.

RICHARD: Had a school at Chichester in the 1790s [qv].

RICHARDS: Dancing master. Instructed the boys and girls of Allfrees' school, Herstmonceux [qv] and gave a ball for them 1797.

RICHARDSON, Miss: In 1799 received £1 3s 10d from the Duke of Richmond as 'School Mistress'. Perhaps taught children from the Goodwood estate and probably kept a school in the vicinity. (See also RICHARDSON, (E M?) below.) [WSRO Goodwood MS 247]

RICHARDSON (Ann?) (-1740?): Mistress of the Blue Coat girls' charity school, Chichester [qv]. Received payments (as Mrs Richardson) on behalf of the school in years ending Michaelmas 1737, 1738, 1740, 1741. Perhaps Ann Richardson buried 24 November 1740. [WSRO Cap.V/1/1; Subdeanery PR]

RICHARDSON, Elizabeth: Paid by Alciston parish for schooling poor children 1747-59 (perhaps to 1763) [qv Parish schooling]. Maximum received in year, £1 2s 5d; minimum 3s 4d. Wife of John. [ESRO PAR 227/31/1]

RICHARDSON, (E. M.?): With Miss Smart, took over Mrs Smart's girls' boarding school in Chichester 1785 [qv for details of the school]. Miss Richardson, 'a woman of superior education...very formal and precise', was the senior mistress. Presumably one of the Miss Richardsons who had a girls' boarding school in West Street c1804 (*Chichester Guide* c1804), identified as 'Richardson E. M. & F.' in 1811 (*Holden's Directory*).

[RICHARDSON, F.]: With sister, had a girls' boarding school in Chichester c1804, 1811. (See RICHARDSON, (E. M.?) above).

RICKWORD, Barbara: Had joined sister Mary [qv] with her girls' boarding school at Brighton by 1791. Schoolmistress there 1799 (*Cobby's Directory*: does not mention Mary).

RICKWORD, Mary: With Miss Russell, opened a girls' boarding school at Brighton 1769 [qv]. In 1775 Mrs Beard took over 'Miss

Russell's established Boarding School', while Miss Mary Rickword continued 'to take young Ladies at her Boarding-School' [qv]. By 1791 her sister Barbara had joined the school, which continued into 19th century.

RIDGE, Mrs: Had a girls' school in Lewes, which she gave up in 1768 on account of her health. [*SWA* 30.1.69 (Ollive advertisement)]

[RINGARD]: French master, Brighton, 1794 [qv under French masters]. Doctor of University of Paris; had been rector of the Royal Parish of St Germain L'Auxerrois.

ROADS, Thomas: Received 2s in 1763, 3s in 1764, from Mayfield parish for schooling Matthew Richardson, and 10d in latter year for teaching 'the poor Children'. [ESRO PAR 422/31/1/4]

ROCKETT, Miss: In 1793 opened a French and English girls' boarding school at Hastings [qv]. 'French is the only language that is allowed to be spoken among the scholars.'

RODEZ, Henry: Schoolmaster at New Shoreham 1755, when son James apprenticed for 7 years to Robert Dixon of Rochester, mariner, by indenture dated 1 May 1755. [Guildhall Museum, Rochester, RCA/02/19]

[ROFFE, Sarah]: Received payments, 1763-74, from Alciston parish in respect of poor children which may have been, in part at least, for schooling [qv Parish schooling].

ROOTS - see also BOOTS

ROOTES, John, senior: Master of Northiam charity school 1770 [qv], and probably much earlier - he was being considered for master by the trustees in 1742 and may have started then. Assisted by son John [qv]. [ESRO FRE 1294]

ROOTES, John, junior: Assisted father, John [qv], at Northiam charity school 1770. Also had own school there [qv]. Also bookbinder, bookseller and stationer, and hired books (for details, see Schedule 1).

[ROSCORLA, Henry]: Schoolmaster at Lewes 1805 (*Baxter's Directory*). One of 4 Lewes schoolmasters who formed a society of schoolmasters in 1811. Married firstly, at St Thomas at Cliffe, Lewes, 1809, Charlotte Hooey (1790-1813, daughter of George Beard Hooey and Hannah (née Collins) and great-granddaughter of George Beard [qv]); married secondly, at Bletchingly, Surrey, 1814, Ann Chapman. [*SWA* 4.2.1811; *SAC* **90**]

ROSE, William (1765-1844): Opened a boys' boarding school at Little Horsted 1794 [qv]; master of Saunders' charity school, Uckfield, and his own boys' boarding school there, c1800 [qv]. Born 2 December 1765. Curate of Glynde at 6 April 1793, and curate of Little Horsted at 15 May 1793 (from St Michael, Lewes, marriage register) and until 1798; curate of Uckfield from 1799; vicar of Glynde 1824 to death. Married 31 December 1793, at St Anne, Lewes, Susannah Ryall, schoolmistress of Lewes [qv]; their sons: Hugh James (born 9 June 1795, baptised Little Horsted, became Principal of King's College, London) and baptised at Uckfield, William Thomas (14 November 1796), Henry John (8 January 1800), William Charles (11 October 1802). Died 3 June 1844. [CI; PRs]

ROSER (William?): 'Master Roser' paid small sums by Newick parish for schooling 1800-02 [qv Parish schooling]. Perhaps William Roser, also paid £3 7s 6d for 'bill', 1802; for keeping Joseph Gasson 1804-05 year; 'for copper 1 load Wood' (£1 6s) 1803; 'for thaching the poor House' (4s 6d) 1804-05 year. Children of William and Mary Roser baptised to 1810. Another WR, of Barcombe, buried at Newick 16 April 1808, aged 67. [PR]

[ROTHWELL, John (-1705)]: Vicar of Henfield 1686 to death in 1705, licensed to teach boys there 1687 [qv]. Trinity College, Cambridge, 1659; scholar 1661; BA 1663, MA 1666; incorporated at Oxford 1671; ordained deacon (London) 1666, priest 1667; rector of Poynings 1679-87. Died 1705. [*Al. Cant.*; CI]

ROUN, Sarah: Paid by Playden parish for schooling 2 poor boys 1783-84 [qv Parish schooling]. Sarah Waller, widow, had married John Roun, widower, 27 May 1776 (he had married firstly, 12 April 1757, Sarah Stevens; he was buried 9 February 1788). [PR]

ROWE, Miss: With Mrs Watson, opened a day school at Brighton 1790 [qv].

RUSSELL, Miss: With Miss Rickword, opened a girls' boarding school at Brighton 1769 [qv]. Her school taken over by Mrs Jane Beard 1775 [qv], Mary Rickword continuing with her own school [qv].

RUSSELL, Bridget (1722-) or **Elizabeth** (1723-): One of whom, with half-sister Mary and sister Philadelphia, had a girls' boarding school in Chichester from c1750 [qv]. Bridget baptised 7 March 1722, Elizabeth baptised 17 September 1723, daughters of Henry and Anne. [Chichester St Olave PR]

RUSSELL, John: Received 8s 6d in 1798 from Waldron parish for schooling Sarah Elliott (also received 2s 6d a week for keeping her) [qv Parish schooling]. Overseer 1797.

RUSSELL Mary (1718-95): Eldest of 3 sisters, the others being half-sisters Bridget or Elizabeth, and Philadelphia, who had a girls' boarding school at Chichester from c1750 [qv]. Baptised 28 May 1718, daughter of Henry and Mary. Married 1754 (marriage licence 17 April 1754) Richard Shenton, Vicar Choral of Chichester Cathedral (he had been a chorister at Magdalen College, Oxford, 1740-45, matriculated there 15 May 1746, aged 16; he later had the livings of St Andrew, St Martin and St Bartholomew in Chichester, and Racton, Westdean, Singleton and Earnley). He was 12 years younger than Mary, and died 1785 aged 55 (buried in cathedral 2 November 1785). She died 1795, aged 78. [Chichester St Olave PR; McCann, A. *History of the Church and parish of St Andrew's Chicester* (1978); *SRS* **32**; *SAC* **78**; *Al. Oxon.*; WSRO Add MS 2758 ff 5v, 6r (Hayley's Epitaph Book)]

RUSSELL, Philadelphia (1726-1815): Youngest of 3 sisters, the others being half-sister Mary and sister Bridget or Elizabeth, who had a girls' boarding school at Chichester from c1750 [qv]. William Hayley, poet and critic, began his schooling there, and when 'a Child in Petticoats' received from her 'a bright silver Penny for reading well'; when he was 60-70, and she 80-90, he presented her with a copy of his major work, *The Triumphs of Temper*, and when she died in 1815 he wrote an epitaph for her. She was still keeping the school in 1811.

In 1784, owned a house in South Street, and also the playhouse in South Street; in 1791 she sold, for £300, to 5 Chichester bankers, a malthouse and granary which 'hath been lately taken down and is now rebuilding as and for a Theatre or Playhouse'. Baptised 14 February 1726, daughter of Henry. Died 13 May 1815, aged 90 (buried in the Paradise 20 May 1815). Monumental inscription at Chichester Cathedral includes, '...Was more than half a Century the kind and patient Instructress of Youth and her benevolent Heart ever the Orphans Refuge' (her niece, Lettice Heath (1761-1818) on same monumental inscription). [Osborne, N. in *Chichester Papers* no. 49; Subdeanery PR; MI Chichester Cathedral (SAS Dunkin 7.1)]

RYALL, Susannah W.: Had a girls' boarding school at Lewes, 1786-93 [qv]. At Christmas 1793 resigned the school to the Misses Dodson and that month married, 31 December 1793, William Rose, curate of Little Horsted, who the next month opened his boys' boarding school at the parsonage there (later moved to Uckfield). For her sons, see ROSE, William. [St Anne, Lewes, PR; *SWA* 6.10.88]

SAGE, Naomi (-1807): Received £2 8s 6d from Newhaven parish in 1800-01 year 'for Schooling', probably 'the Parish Children' (and was probably paid for same in 1799-1800 and 1801-02) [qv Parish schooling]. Almost certainly wife of Samuel, parish clerk. Buried 9 September 1807 (Samuel buried 25 August 1813). [PR]

SANDERS, Samuel (1768-): Had a day school from 1789 and a boys' boarding school from 1793 at Brighton [qv]. Almost certainly Samuel Farncombe Sanders (baptised at Brighton 31 January 1768, son of John and Ann) who married (marriage licence 7 October 1790) Elizabeth Smith of Newick, and as schoolmaster of Brighton was executor and trustee in will of Richard Humber, retired schoolmaster of Brighton, dated 4 August 1831. [PR; *SRS* **26**; ESRO W/A 77.415]

SAWYER, Edward (-1760): Gentleman of Mayfield; in 1708 The Society for Promoting Christian Knowledge was advised that he had taught children their catechism 'and to read and write gratis' [qv Charity schooling]. A Society for Promoting Christian Knowledge

correspondent. Founder manager of Mayfield charity school 1750 [qv]. Died 1 July 1760. [SPCK ALB v.1 1400, v.4 3756, v.7 5057; MSB]

SAYER, James (-1726): Schoolmaster of Petworth [qv]. Also surveyor. Buried 18 January 1726. Will left gold rings (of £1 value each) to sisters Elizabeth, wife of John May, and Sarah, wife of Edward Wood, 10s 6d to brother-in-law James Christmas and 5s to his son James Christmas, £50 to daughter-in-law Elizabeth Denyer, residue of estate to son-in-law William Denyer, sole executor. [PR; WSRO STC 1/34 f 19]

SCOTT, Edmund: 'Portrait Painter & Drawing Master' at Brighton 1805 (*Button's Directory*). Established there by 1799, when in register of freemasons (as 'Portrait Painter') of Royal Clarence Lodge, of which he was Master; also member of South Saxon Lodge, Lewes (1799 first year such registration required by law). [ESRO QDS/1/EW1]

SCRAS, John (-1702): Master of Brighton charity school when schoolbook opens, 1701 [qv]. Left on 30 August 1702; died the following November (buried 22 November 1702). (Perhaps baptised 14 March 1654, son of Richard and Elizabeth (née Cook, daughter of Richard); or baptised 1675 at Hove). [BSB; PR; Comber *Sx. Gen.*]

[*SCUTT, Mrs*]: Had a girls' (?boarding) school in Dorset Gardens, Brighton, in 1804. [*Fisher's New Brighton Guide*]

SERJEANT, John: Master of Westham charity school [qv] for 6 months from Lady Day 1736. [SAS Budgen MS v.129]

SHADGETT, Miss: With Miss Wallis, had a girls' boarding school, Lewes, c1800 [qv].

SHARPE (-1775): Dancing master at Chichester for many years who, after retirement, cut his throat in 1775 [qv].

SHAW, Mrs: In 1797 received from the Duke of Richmond £1 6s for 'Children's Schooling' (probably children from the Goodwood estate). [WSRO Goodwood MS 247]

SHEPPARD, Dame: Paid by Pulborough parish 6d a week for teaching Sunday school, 1786 [qv].

SHERBOURNE, Dame: Paid by Wisborough Green parish 1s 'for Schooling', 1798. [WSRO Par 210/31/1]

SHILLITO, George: Subscribed as schoolmaster at Horsted Keynes 26 July 1714. [WSRO Ep.II/1/1]

SHORE, Philip (1677-1725): Master of Cuckfield grammar school 1704-11 [qv]. Later schoolmaster at Woodmancote. Baptised 1 May 1677, son of John, rector of Hamsey (-1722; in his will, 'As to my worldly goods which are few and of little value...'; Philip was executor) and Bridgett. School, Westminster. Merton College, Oxford, 21 March 1694; BA 1697, MA 1701; also MA from Cambridge 1725. Vicar of Wartling 1705 to death; rector of Wivelsfield 1705-11; rector of Woodmancote 1711 to death; domestic chaplain to Elizabeth, Countess Dowager of Lindsay (R 1711). Died 6 May 1725 at Rayleigh, Essex, returning from placing a pupil (William Campion) at Cambridge. Left estate to wife Catherine, who survived him. [ESRO W/A 51.109, W/A 52.53; *Al. Oxon.*; *Al. Cant.*; CI; Hamsey PR; *SAC* **36**]

SHORTER, Elizabeth (1746-1819): Schoolmistress of East Dean (East Sussex). Received £5 a year from George Medley for schooling 12 children of East Dean, from Lady Day 1780 until at least Michaelmas 1795. Succeeded mother, Elizabeth Simpson [qv], who had received the same and died 1780. Baptised 2 January 1747, daughter of Joseph and Elizabeth Simpson. Married at East Dean, 23 September 1773, John Shorter, of Friston. Between 1774 and 1790 had 4 sons (one dying in infancy) and 4 daughters. Buried 5 March 1819, aged 72. Husband John buried 26 July 1829, aged 79. [ESRO SAS/GT 1/3/3-5; PR]

SHORTER, John (1728-81): Assistant master Hastings grammar school 1743-59; master 1759-81 [qv]. Licensed November 1758. Baptised 30 July 1728, son of John and Mary; married 23 September 1756, Elizabeth Hart; only one of 3 sons survived, John Goldsworthy, who succeeded father as master on his death in

1781. Also surveyor (Rs 1755 (Westfield), 1765 (Ore and Hollington), 1766 (estate of Edward Milward of Hastings), 1770 (Ore)). Chamberlain (ie borough treasurer) 1764; freedom of town 1772. Buried 16 February 1781, aged 52. [*HHGS*; All Saints, St Clement PRs; ESRO PAB 212, SAY 2747; HM MA 135, 137 and 146]

SHORTER, John Goldsworthy (1762-1835): Master of Hastings grammar school 1781-91 [qv]. Succeeded father. Baptised 28 February 1762, son of John and Elizabeth (née Hart). Freedom of Hastings 12 April 1783; elected jurat 1791, when he resigned as master; collector of customs, Hastings, 1801; 8 times mayor. In 1792 built a schoolroom on land adjoining Waterloo Passage, which remained in his possession until Joseph Hannay became master of the grammar school and Saunders' charity school. Buried 18 July 1835, aged 73. [*HHGS*; St Clement, All Saints PRs; *SWA* 21.4.83]

SILK: Lecturer and tutor (R 1761) [qv Lewes Other schoolmasters].

SIMPSON, Elizabeth (-1780): Schoolmistress of Eastdean (East Sussex). Received £5 a year from George Medley for schooling 12 children of East Dean and Friston from at least 21 August 1775 (when surviving accounts begin) to 21 August 1779. Wife of Joseph. Buried 16 February 1780. After her death the schooling continued by daughter Elizabeth Shorter. [ESRO SAS/GT 1/3/3; PR]

SKINNER, Mary (-1787): Paid by Buxted parish for schooling the workhouse children from May 1783 to October 1784, at 2s or 2s 6d a month. (Parish paid for keep of her boy 1783-89 and in December 1787 for her burial). [ESRO PAR 286/31/1]

SLATER, Widow: Received £1 3s 8d from the Dowlin charity for schooling 2 poor children of West Grinstead, 1701-02 (71 weeks at 2d a week each). [WSRO Par 95/1/1/3]

[SMALLFIELD]: Schoolmaster at Brede 1802. Occupied a house on Brede Hill. [ESRO AMS 6454/40]

SMART, Miss: With Miss Richardson, in 1785

took over mother's girls' boarding school at Chichester [qv] (Rs 1785-98). 'Miss Richardson's' school by 1800, and by 1804 the school was the 'Misses Richardson's'.

SMART, Mrs: Had a girls' boarding school at Chichester in 1783 [qv]. In 1785 resigned the school to her daughter and Miss Richardson.

SMITH, Mrs: Opened a girls' boarding school at Lindfield, Christmas 1790 [qv].

SMITH, Elizabeth: Schoolmistress at East Grinstead 1793, 1799 [qv]. (A Miss Smith had a boarding and day school there in 1832 and 1839.) [*Pigot's Directories*]

SMITH, George (1714-76): Drawing master at Chichester [qv]. One of 3 artist brothers. Son of William, cooper, later baker, Baptist minister Chichester, and Elizabeth (née Spencer). Trained as cooper but gave this up and joined elder brother William, who had a studio in London. They moved to Gloucester for a time, then back to London. GS also itinerant portrait painter, but with success of landscape paintings worked in London in a studio shared with brother John. About 1750 GS and JS returned to Chichester, living in North Street. GS won first premium Society of Arts 1760, 1761 and 1763; exhibited Society of Artists 1760, Free Society of Artists 1761-74 and Royal Academy 1774. *A Collection of 53 prints consisting of etchings and engravings by those ingenious artists Messrs George and John Smith of Chichester after their own paintings and other masters* was published 1770. In 1764 both William and John died. Married 1766 Ruth Southen (-1795); had 3 daughters. Died 7 September 1776, aged 62. James Lambert, artist of Lewes, and music and painting master, was trustee and guardian to his 3 daughters. [Pallant House Gallery *The Smith Brothers of Chichester*, exhibition catalogue (1986); Lower *Worthies*; Farrant, S. in *SAS Newsletter* Dec 1984; *SAC* **90**; *Portsmouth Gazette* 14.12.95]

[**SMITH, John**]: Assistant schoolmaster in St Thomas at Cliffe, Lewes, 1803. Then aged 17-30, unmarried. [*Sussex Militia List 1803, Pevensey Rape Southern Division* (1988)]

SMITH, William (-1782?): Schoolmaster of Bexhill [qv Parish free school], for which paid

£6 a year Easter 1754 to Easter 1756, Easter 1769 to Easter 1771, and almost certainly Easter 1772 to Easter 1776 (payments this last period not specifically identified as for schooling). Also parish clerk, for which paid £2 a year; also received £1 a year for keeping overseers accounts. Often paid 2s 6d 'for a Knell and Grave' at pauper burials, and received payments for clerical work (eg making indentures). Gave up parish duties April 1776. Perhaps the WS buried at Bexhill 3 April 1782 (other WSs buried there 27 March 1789 and 5 March 1795). [ESRO PAR 240/30/1; PR]

SMITHER, Mrs, SMITHER, Miss senior, SMITHER, Miss junior: Mrs and Misses Smither opened a preparatory boarding school at Goring 1800 [qv].

SNASHAL, Goody: Received 6s from the Dowlin charity 10 April 1724 for schooling poor children of West Grinstead. [WSRO Par 95/1/1/3]

SOANE, Elizabeth: In 1729 was paid 6s 8d by Rev Frewen, rector of Northiam, 'for 20 weeks Schooling for goodman pankhurst boys' (ie 4d a week - probably 2d a week for each of 2 boys). She signed the receipt with her name. The same receipt also covers payments to her for making clothes (probably for the poor). [ESRO FRE 8181 (4)]

SOMERSOL, Goody: Paid by Dowlin charity for schooling poor children of West Grinstead; received 10s, 1698; £1 5d, 1699; 18s 10d, 1700; 8s 4d, 1701; 7s 10d, 1702. [WSRO Par 95/1/1/3]

SPENCER, Thomas (1759?-): Master of Cuckfield grammar school, 1800-04. Perhaps son of Daniel, of St Mary's, Gloucester; Magdalen College, Oxford, matriculated 17 December 1776, aged 17; chorister 1772-77; clerk 1778. [Cooper, J. H. *History of the Parish of Cuckfield* (1912); *Al. Oxon.*]

STANFORD, Mrs: Schoolmistress at Horsham 1793. [*Universal British Directory*]

STEVENS, Benjamin (-1769): Master of Seaford charity school in 1765 [qv]. Buried, as 'Schoolmaster', 18 May 1769. Will dated 17 February 1764, proved 20 June 1769, left house and personal estate to wife Ann, sole executrix, who survived him. [PR; ESRO W/A 62.49]

STEVENS, John (1768-1837): Opened a boys' boarding school at Chichester 1796 [qv] and master of Chichester grammar school 1797-1802 [qv]. Son of John, of Bicester, Oxfordshire, gent; Winchester; New College, Oxford, matriculated 17 December 1787, aged 19; scholar 1787-89, fellow 1789, BA 1794, MA 1795. Curate of Eartham 1798-1800; rector of East Wittering 1802-13; rector of Birchanger, Essex, 1807; vicar of Swalcliffe with Epwell, Oxfordshire, 1808; rector of Great Poringland, Norfolk, 1813 to death. Died 25 January 1837. [*Al. Oxon.*; *VCH* **ii**; CI]

STEVENS, Miss M. A.: Had a girls' boarding school at Midhurst 1789 [qv]; moved her school to Petworth 1794 [qv].

STEVENS, Sara: Paid by Playden parish for schooling 4 poor children May 1781 to March 1782 (Hannah and Ann Head at 3d a week, and John and James Head at 2d a week). A neat writer; probably kept own school. [ESRO PAR 445/31/1/14]

STEVENSON, William: Dancing master. Received £4 4s 2d in 1787 and £2 12s 6d in 1788 from the Duke of Richmond for teaching Henriette Le Clerc (aged 14 or 15 in 1787) at Goodwood House. [WSRO Goodwood MS 244, 245]

STIFF, Mrs (Mary?) (1731?-1819?): Received £5 on 31 December 1793 from 3rd Viscount Gage for 'Schooling Children', almost certainly at Alciston. Perhaps the Mary Mockett, widow, who married Richard Stiff, widower, at Firle 29 August 1774, and was buried there 16 September 1819, aged 88 (in which case probably related to Thomas Mockett, schoolmaster at Firle in the 1790s, and Alexander Mockett, schoolmaster there 1830). [ESRO SAS/G/ACC 741; PR]

STILES: Received 10s 9d from the Dowlin charity, December 1706, for schooling poor children of West Grinstead (perhaps received on behalf of wife?). [WSRO Par 95/1/1/3]

STILES, wife of James: Received 7s 2d from the Dowlin charity, 1725, for schooling poor

children of West Grinstead. [WSRO Par 95/1/1/3]

STILES, William: Subscribed 4 November 1703, 'to Teach a writing Schooll at West Tarring'. [WSRO Ep.I/3/3]

STOCKAR, Peter (1688-): Master of Horsham grammar school briefly in 1712 [qv]; left the school after a few months being 'tempted from us by better preferments'. Baptised 19 October 1688, St Alphage Canterbury, son of James, rector of same. King's school, Canterbury; Trinity College, Cambridge, 1704; scholar 1705; BA 1708, MA 1714; ordained deacon (Norwich) 1711. [*HCS*; *Al. Cant.*]

[STOKES, Mrs]: Perhaps schoolmistress at Lewes 1798, when she occupied 'Land Garden Schoole' in St John sub Castro, owned by John Bartlett, schoolmaster (who occupied 'Garden & School room' himself from 1799). Also occupied 2 houses, 2 gardens and a stable in the parish. [Land Tax]

STONE, Widow: Paid by Icklesham parish 'for Scooling' (£1, 10 October 1773; £1 10s, 25 January 1774; 4s, 2 February 1774; 6s, 13 March 1774 - ie ¾ year at the then rate of £4 a year for the parish school) [qv Parish schooling and free school].

STONE, John: Master of Lightmaker's charity school, Horsted Keynes, c1780 to at least 1833 [qv]. His third wife, Philadelphia, taught the girls to work 'with their needle'.

STRETTON, Thomas: Dancing master at Chichester 1782. [WSRO Add MS 2133]

STRINGER, Goody: Received 7s 10d from the Dowlin charity, March 1719, for schooling poor children of West Grinstead. [WSRO Par 95/1/1/3]

STURLEY, John: Master of Saunders' charity school, Rye, 1788-91 [qv]. [*HRGS*]

SWAYSLAND, Stephen: Schoolmaster at East Grinstead 1793, 1799 [qv], and 1803, when unmarried, aged 31-50. Appointed master of Mayfield charity school from Michaelmas 1807. (A Swaysland had a day school at East

Grinstead in 1839). [*Sussex Militia List, 1803, Pevensey Rape, Northern Division* (1988); MSB; *Pigot's Directory* 1839]

SYMONDS, Elizabeth (-1787): Had a day school and girls' boarding school at Lewes 1782 [qv]. Wife of William [qv]; Baptist (baptised at Eastgate Baptist chapel and admitted 7 May 1786). Died 1 July 1787. [ESRO NB 1/1/1A]

SYMONDS, William: Opened a boys' day, evening and boarding school at Lewes, 1784 (wife Elizabeth had a day school and girls' boarding school - see above) [qv]. Also bookseller and stationer, and - after school taken over by Edward Pugh in 1793 - also auctioneer and paper-hanger. In December 1793 assigned his estate and effects to trustees to be sold for the benefit of his creditors. Baptist (baptised at East Gate Baptist chapel and admitted 4 September 1785); excluded from the church January 1791, following 'a report prejudicial to the moral character of Brother Symonds'. [ESRO NB 1/1/1A]

TANDY, Richard (-1803): Schoolmaster of Ticehurst. Identified as 'the Schoolmaster' at burials of daughter Sarah, 24 April 1778, and son Richard, 5 May 1778. Also vestry clerk 1782 (and probably earlier) to 1799: in September 1799 was replaced, being 'through Indisposition not capable of Paying Attention to that Business any Longer'. Constable in 1782. Paid by parish for providing quarters for poor persons (from 1782, or earlier, to 1793). Wife Mary; children baptised at Ticehurst: Ellen 1762, Julianna 1765, Richard 1769, Francis 1772, Sarah 1776. Rented house at £4 10s 1774-88. Buried 26 January 1803. [PR; ESRO PAR 492/31/1/4, 492/30/3]

TAPNER, John: Schoolmaster of Boxgrove 1761. Also surveyor (Rs 1761-79). [*DLS*]

TASKER: Had a boys' boarding school, Lewes, 1773 [qv].

TASKER, John (1688-1767): Schoolmaster at Horsham 1724 (from will of Elizabeth Furlonger). Born 1688, son of George (baptised at Balcombe 16 February 1689). Originally a blacksmith. Baptist; many years secretary to Horsham meeting; frequently 'scribe' to the

Baptist General Assembly between 1732 and 1757. In 1718 published *An examination of Mr Stokes arguments for Infant Sprinkling*, 87pp, published in London, 'Price 1s': "'Tis likely some will wonder', he wrote, 'that one of so mean a rank & so little skill should venture upon a work of this nature, but the most unlikely and despicable instruments are sometimes made able to bring to nought Things more honorable and excellent in man's account. Having therefore (as in my conscience I verily believe) Truth on my side I am not ashamed to own myself illiterate or unlearned.' Published in 1729 and 1751 pamphlets on separation from the Church of England. Died 15 December 1767. [Caffyn, J. M. *Sussex Believers* (1988); Maguire, L. J. *Records of the General Baptist Meeting House, Horsham, Sussex* 1 (published privately 1981); Kensett, E. *History of the Free Christian Church Horsham* (1921)]

TATTERSALL, John (1673-1740): Master of Cuckfield grammar school, probably from 1712 (when John Willis resigned) to 1718 [qv]. Licensed 3 July 1714. Baptised 15 October 1673, son of John, vicar of Waldron (-1707) and Miriam (-1695); St Paul's school; Jesus College, Cambridge, 1692; BA 1696; MA 1699. Rector of Hangleton 1709 to death; rector of Chipstead, Surrey, 1718 to death. Sons John (c1707-) and James (c1712-) both at Trinity College, Cambridge, and both later rectors. Died 3 September 1740. [*VCH* ii; Cooper, W. V. *History of the Parish of Cuckfield* (1912); Doff, E. pers. comm. citing BL Add MS 39449; *Al. Cant.*; CI; Waldron PR]

TAYLOR: Drawing master at Chichester, 1780 [qv].

TAYLOR, Widow (-1749): Schoolmistress at Ringmer. Buried 15 January 1749; parish register notes: 'had been School Dame for several Years & had thereby gain'd a good Name'. [PR]

[**TAYLOR, Mrs**]: With Mrs Hunter, had a girls' school at Henfield some time before January 1802. [*SWA* 11.1.1802]

TAYLOR, Sarah: Schoolmistress at Eastbourne 1792, 1793. [*Universal British Directory*]

THOMAS, William Humphrey (1761-82):

Very briefly, in 1782, assistant master at Paine's school, Brighton [qv]. From 'Cluuyn', Merioneth; Jesus College, Oxford, matriculated 10 June 1782, aged 21. 'Yesterday se'nnight a Welsh gentleman, who had lately left the University of Oxford, and came down to Brighthelmston, as an assistant to Mr Payne, a schoolmaster there, was seized with a violent fit of coughing, as he was coming out of church, and expired in about ten minutes afterwards.' Buried 30 July 1782. [*SWA* 5.8.82; *Al. Oxon.*; PR]

THOMPSON, Mary (1730-): Schoolmistress of Pevensey [qv Charity school]. After death of husband Richard (-1785), schoolmaster of Westham and Pevensey, continued to teach 3 poor children of Pevensey, as he had done, being paid by Rev Matthias D'Oyly, vicar of Pevensey 1767-1816, £2 2s a year from Lady Day 1786 to at least Lady Day 1800. Baptised 30 December 1730, daughter of Humphrey and Mary Palmer; married 12 May 1756, Richard Thompson. [CI; PR]

THOMPSON, Richard (-1785): Schoolmaster of Westham [qv Charity school] and Pevensey [qv Charity school]. On 25 March 1784 received from Lady Cavendish £5 for a year's teaching 8 poor children of Westham, and probably received £5 a year in other years. From at least as early as 1775 to death in 1785, also received £2 2s a year from Rev Matthias D'Oyly, vicar of Pevensey 1767-1816, for schooling 3 poor children of Pevensey (schooling continued by his widow, Mary, qv). Married at Pevensey, 12 May 1756, Mary Palmer; their son Thomas baptised 25 December 1756. Buried there 23 September 1785. [CI; PR]

THORNCOMB, Thomas: Master of a charity school at Arundel 1726. [WSRO Ep.I/22/1]

THORNTON, Mrs: Had a girls' boarding school at Northiam before 1773, when the school was continued by Mrs Johnson and Miss Bishop. [*SWA* 18.1.73]

THORNTON, James (1765-1817): Son of Richard [qv below] and partner with father in 'Horsham Academy' 1792 [qv Thornton's school]. In 1793 Lady Irwin conveyed to him 'Patchings', a burgage tenement. Appointed

usher of Horsham grammar school 1801, but as the grammar school was moribund, drew salary and taught at father's school. When in 1808 the Mercers Company and parish of Horsham revived the grammar school, JT refused to surrender his tenancy of the usher's house (which he let to his mother-in-law); this led to a Chancery case, and a new constitution for the grammar school in 1813, by which time JT had resigned his claims. In 1810 he had wife Anne and 6 children (of whom Richard William (died 15 January 1846, aged 58) married Mary (died 1 September 1877, aged 77); Catherine married Thomas Coppard, solicitor, and died 5 December 1832, aged 38)). Died 8 November 1817, gent, aged 52. [*HCS*; MIs Horsham (Bax MS at SAS)]

THORNTON, Richard: Had a boys' boarding school Horsham from c1765 into 19th century [qv]. Entrepreneurial and successful. Previously schoolmaster of Micklesham, Surrey; married at Horsham, 15 October 1763, Hannah Hewes (their daughter Elizabeth baptised 9 January 1777). Son James [qv above] taught at the school and became partner 1792. Involved in politics; in 1790 voted (on the basis of a scrap of burgage land near his schoolyard) for Lady Irwin's Tory candidates (he acquired from her part of the buildings of the old jail, which she had bought for the burgage vote); but in the 1806 General Election switched his allegiance to the Duke of Norfolk and the Whig interest; he was by then bailiff of the borough. [PR; *HCS*]

THORPE, Mrs: Kept a boys' and girls' boarding school at Battle; probably assisted by daughters. Between 1728 and c1750 the 7 children of John and Mary Collier of Hastings were sent to her, from 7 or 8 yrs old to 11 or 12; the boys went on to Westminster, the girls to Mrs Russell's school at Hampstead [qv Schedule 3]. The boys went out to a master, and their subjects included Latin and dancing.

THORP, E.: Master of Grimmett's charity school, Brighton [qv] and also of his own school there (R 1801) [qv].

THRING, John: Dancing and music master, Lewes (Rs 1778-1800) [qv Schedule 1 for his career and competition]. His work covered a wide area, and included at different times

Herstmonceux, Battle, Seaford, Brighton, Shoreham, Horsham. In March 1783 at Lewes, while he 'was washing his horse after a journey, at the edge of our river, between the bridge and the Bear Inn, the beast, by some accident, plunged head foremost, over the wharf, into the main channel, with his rider, who was thereby thrown from his seat, but fortunately, being able to swim a little, he kept his head above water till some person came to his assistance, and got him out. The horse, after being carried a little distance down the river, by the stream, turned himself, and swam under the bridge to Dr Poole's Yard, where he was saved, without suffering any material hurt, by Mr Robert Rice, of the Cliffe, to whose timely assistance Mr Thring also owes his preservation.' Came to Lewes from Cambridge. Married Frances, their daughter Sarah, born 10 February 1786, baptised at Westgate meeting house 25 February 1786. Witness of marriage, 22 August 1802, of Elizabeth Faithful Thring, aged 22, perhaps daughter, to Michael White, silversmith, widower, of Brighton. Freemason, South Saxon Lodge, Lewes, 1799 (first year registration required by law). [*SWA* 10.3.83; ESRO NU 1/1/2; Lewes St Michael PR; *SRS* 26; ESRO QDS/1/EWI]

TICEHURST (TYCEHURST), William: Schoolmaster, Battle, 1793, and agent for 'The New British Tontine'. Also land-surveyor (estate maps: Pett 1809, Whatlington and Sedlescombe 1826). Wife Ann; son Henry baptised 1813, Rowland James 1817, daughter Emily 1819. [*SWA* 7.1.93; ESRO SAS/B 717, SAS/AN 30; PR]

TIREMAN, Richard (1726-92): Master of Chichester grammar school 1768-76 [qv]. Son of Richard, of London; St John's College, Oxford, matriculated 30 June 1742, aged 16; fellow 1742-50; BA 1746, MA 1750. Priest-vicar Chichester cathedral 1763 (subdean and treasurer); sequestrator Sidlesham 1763-69; vicar of St Peter the Great, Chichester, 1767 to death; curate of Funtington 1767; vicar of East Marden 1767 to death; sequestrator St Peter the Less, Chichester, 1768 to death; vicar of Henfield 1779-84 (in succession to son, Richard Tireman, who was buried 11 March 1779); rector of Rodmell 1784 to death. Died 18 February 1792. [*Al. Oxon.*; CI]

TOMSETT, Thomas (-1755): Schoolmaster of East Hoathly [qv]. Died 5 March 1755.

TOPP (TUPP), Robert (1649-1701): Master of Chichester grammar school 1685-1701 [qv]. Son of Lingen, of Wotton, Shropshire, gent. Queen's College, Oxford, matriculated 10 May 1667, aged 18; perhaps BA from Jesus College; MA from King's College, Cambridge, 1681. Minor canon, Rochester, 1671-76; vicar of All Hallows, Hoo, Kent, 1672-75; vicar of All Saints, Rochester, 1673; rector of Addington, Kent, 1675-87; vicar of Donnington 1687 to death; curate of St Peter the Less, Chichester, 1688 and sequestrator 1690 to death. Son Edward (1677-) at Oxford. Died 1701. [*Al. Oxon.*; *Al. Cant.*; CI]

TOURNAY, Rev Mr (Monsieur): Received £60 a year from the Duke of Richmond for teaching the Lennox boys at Goodwood House 1797-1801. [WSRO Goodwood MS 247]

TOWNLEY, Mrs: With Mrs Adeane, opened a girls' boarding school at Brighton January 1799 [qv].

TROWER, Goody: Received payments from the Dowlin charity, 1701-05, for schooling poor children of West Grinstead (1701, 10s; 1703, 11s 4d; 1704, 8s; 1705, 4s). [WSRO Par 95/1/1/3]

TUPPER: Master of the Grey Coat boys' charity school, Chichester, from Christmas 1748 to 10 April 1763 [qv]. Received £15 a year for schooling 20 boys, plus extra when this number exceeded. [WSRO Cap.V/1/1]

TUPPER, Martha: Paid by the Duke of Richmond for schooling Mary Colbert, 1799-1800 (3 payments of 5s 5d and one of 3s 4d). [WSRO Goodwood MS 247]

[**TURNER, Richard**]: Subscribed 25 June 1695, to teach at the free school of Maresfield.

TURNER, Thomas (1729-93): Shopkeeper of East Hoathly, he kept the village school 1755-56 [qv]. Born 9 June 1729 at Groombridge, Speldhurst, Kent, son of John (1689-1752) and second wife Elizabeth (née Ovenden, of Rotherfield, 1697-1759); father moved to Framfield 1735, shopkeeper. Sister Sarah

(Sally) sent to school at Lewes. When 21, took over shop at East Hoathly (1750), which he bought in 1766. 'Draper' in memorial inscription, but also sold foods, flour, nails, salt, etc; weighed, packed and arranged transport of market produce - wheat, potatoes, cabbages, wool, hops; occasional barber; undertaker - made and distributed favours at funerals. Fearing his shop might fail, in 1758 took instruction in land-surveying, with friend Francis Elless (his successor as schoolmaster), from Christopher Mason [qv]. Churchwarden (in 3 years), overseer of the poor (in 4 years), surveyor of the highways (1 year), collector of taxes 1760-66; wrote up parish accounts; drafted and wrote simple wills. Married firstly, 15 October 1753, Margaret (Peggy) Slater (1733-61), daughter of Samuel and Ann of Hartfield, by whom a son, died in infancy; married secondly, 19 June 1765, Mary Hicks (1735-1807), daughter of Thomas and Mary, by whom one daughter and 6 sons (2 of whom died in infancy). Died 6 February 1793. [Vaisey, D. (ed) *The Diary of Thomas Turner* (1984)]

TYLER, (Benjamin?) (1755?-1807?): Schoolmaster of Framfield [qv Charity schooling]. In 1792 and 1793 with Dickenson, in 1794 with Dickenson's Creditors and Cottington, and from 1795 to 1797 with Cottington, paid by parish (from rent of Pound Farm, arising out of Smith and Wharton bequests) £4 a year for schooling 10 poor children. (Payments continued into 19th century but recipients not named after 1797.) Perhaps Benjamin Tyler, buried 8 July 1807, aged 52. [ESRO PAR 343/11/2; PR]

VAUS, Henry: Schoolmaster of West Grinstead. Received payments from the Dowlin charity for schooling poor children, probably 7-8, 1710-14 (£1 10s 5d for church year 1710-11; £2 11s 9d for 1711-12; £3 2s 4d for 1712-13; £3 3s 7d for 1713-14; £1 9s for 1714-15). [WSRO Par 95/1/1/3]

VENES, Elizabeth (-1791): Mistress of Mary Herbert's girls' charity school, Brightling, from Christmas 1763 [qv]. Wife of 'James Venes the Barber'. Son John buried 6 August 1747; daughter Constant baptised 24 July 1748. Buried 12 April 1791. (Husband James buried 6 May 1797.) [ESRO PAR 254/25/1; PR]

VERRALL, Thomas: Schoolmaster of Lewes (Rs 1750-52) [qv].

VIGORWAITE (VIGOR WAITE), John: Schoolmaster of Battle charity school (Rs 1735-45) [qv]. John Fuller of Brightling paid £2 a year from at least 1733 to 1745 to either John or Thomas 'Vigor Waite'/'Vigorwaite', both of whom were described as 'schoolmaster'; eg on 6 February 1735 'Paid John Vigorwate the Charity schoolmaster at Battel a year's salary due 2d February last £2'. (On 10 December 1737 he paid JV 12s 'for Bell Ropes'.) [ESRO SAS/RF 15/28]

VIGORWAITE (VIGOR WAITE), Thomas: Schoolmaster of Battle charity school (Rs 1733-40) [qv]. See VIGORWAITE, John for John Fuller payments: Thomas received the annual salary for years ending 2 February 1733, 1734, 1736, 1737 (described as 'schoolmaster'), 1738, 1740. (On 5 February 1740 he paid TV 13s 'for Bell Ropes and Clock Line'.) [ESRO SAS/RF 15/28]

VINAL, Ann: Paid by Cowfold parish for schooling from October 1796 to April 1798 [qv Parish schooling]. She received £1 1s 4d in 1796, £2 8s 4d in 1797 (including small sum for 'mending reels'), 15s 10d in 1798. Referred to as 'Mrs'/'Dame'; on 2 occasions schooling payments were made to John Vinal, presumably her husband. [WSRO Par 59/31/4]

VINALL, George: Master of Robertsbridge charity school [qv] from its opening in 1796 to 1829. Probably previously had own school there [qv]. Married Mary Noakes; their children baptised: 18 June 1783, Elizabeth; 4 March 1785, James; 10 September 1787, Penelope. Wife Mary mistress of the charity school. [Salehurst PR]

VINALL, Mary: Wife of George Vinall [qv above], they were appointed master and mistress of Robertsbridge charity school at its opening in 1796. Formerly Mary Noakes.

VINCENT, Rev W. J. A.: For c18 months, from early 1800 to mid 1801, was paid by the Duke of Richmond at the rate of £200 a year in respect of the Lennox boys, being educated by the Duke at Goodwood House. The boys also had another master and a writing master;

Vincent's duties not specified but probably tutor to them. [WSRO Goodwood MS 247]

VINE, John (-1770?): Master of Heathfield school (R 1750) [qv Village school]. Cousin of Walter Gale, master of Mayfield charity school. Perhaps the JV 'sen' buried 6 September 1770, whose wife Sarah was buried 30 October 1758 (other JVs buried 15 April 1766, 6 March 1774). [*SAC* **9**; PR]

VINE, Stephen: Schoolmaster of Lindfield (R 1779). Discovered Roman road at St John's Common, and wrote account of this in *Gentleman's Magazine* (1781). Also surveyor (R 1777). [*SAC* **77**; *DLS*]

VOAKS, Mary: Paid £1 6s by the Oliver Whitby charity for teaching 6 poor children of West Wittering to read, for the ½ yr to Christmas 1756 [qv Charity schooling]. [WSRO E35D/3/1]

[W., P.]: Advertised to schools, for a position, May 1800. Offered the classics, or writing, arithmetic, book-keeping, navigation and the use of the globes; and could assist in lower classes in French. Would attend any family in the vacation. [*SWA* 19.5.1800]

WADE, William (1704-68): Assistant master Chichester grammar school 1728; master 1729-68 [qv]. Licensed 4 August 1727. Born at Wakefield, Yorkshire; Clare College, Cambridge, 1721; BA 1725, MA 1731. Ordained priest (Chichester) 31 March 1728, and from that date rector of East Wittering cum Bracklesham to death; curate St Martin, Chichester, 1728 to death; curate St Bartholomew, Chichester, 1738 to death, and sequestrator from 1765; sequestrator St Peter the Less, Chichester, 1768 (year of death). Died 18 July 1768, aged 64 (buried St Martin 21 July 1768). [*SAC* **106**; WSRO Ep.I/1/11; *Al. Cant.*; CI]

WAITE, Vigor - see VIGORWAITE

[WALISTON, George]: Schoolmaster at Westbourne 1689. [WSRO Ep.I/17/33]

WALKER, Thomas (1761-1825): Curate of East Grinstead, opened a boys' boarding school July 1799 [qv]. (Signed banns and marriages as

curate 1789-1805). Seven daughters of TW and wife Mary baptised at East Grinstead 1793-1805. As librarian signed printed regulations of East Grinstead Book Club agreed 19 September 1804 (document in Town Museum). Vicar of West Hoathly 1805 to death. Died 10 January 1825, aged 63. Buried at Fletching 17 January 1825. [PRs; CI]

WALLER, Ann (1750-): Opened a girls' boarding school at Horsham 1781 (Rs 1781-95) [qv]. Almost certainly Ann Williamson, baptised 24 November 1750, daughter of Richard of Horsham and Elizabeth, who married 11 December 1770 George Waller of Horsham, innholder, son of Henry (probably the HW, innholder, buried 16 June 1763). GW, innholder, bankrupt April 1778. GW schoolmaster by 1793 [qv]. [PR]

WALLER, George (1742-1815): Schoolmaster at Horsham 1793 (*Universal British Directory*). Baptised 30 December 1742, son of Henry and Sarah; father probably the HW, innholder, buried 16 June 1763. Married, then an innholder, 11 December 1770, Ann Williamson of Horsham. Bankrupt (GW, innholder) April 1778. (Perhaps also the GW, mercer, bankrupt July 1784: the only other known GW in Horsham at that time was his uncle, baptised 1706, who was buried 1790, 'an ancient man'.) Wife was almost certainly the Mrs Waller who had a girls' boarding school at Horsham from 1781 [qv]. In January 1801, 'Charles Field was convicted of having stolen a quantity of wet linen, the property of George Waller, schoolmaster, of Horsham, and sentenced to transportation for seven years.' Buried 4 September 1815, aged 72. [PR; *SFH* **6**, no. 6, citing bankruptcies from *Gentleman's Magazine*; *SWA* 19.1.1801]

WALLIS, Miss: With Miss Shadgett, had a girls' boarding school at Lewes c1800 [qv].

WALLIS, Sarah: Schoolmistress of Cocking [qv Charity schools/schooling]. Received from the Challen bequest £1 16s 8d in 1731-32 year, £1 4s in 1732-33, £1 3s 7d in 1734 (and presumably some of the £4 12s 3d spent on schooling 1733-34), for teaching 7 or 8 poor children at 2d a week. Wife of John. [WSRO Par 53/12/1]

WALMSLEY, Henry (1689-1749): Master of Angmering charity school 1724 [qv]. Son of Henry, of Mellor, Lancashire, clerk. Brasenose College, Oxford; matriculated 20 February 1707, aged 18; BA 1710. Curate of Angmering, signed register as such 1714 to January 1748; licenced to serve the cure there February 1716, when instituted vicar of East Preston; rector of Coombs July 1749, but died very shortly afterwards. [WSRO Ep.I/26/3; *Al. Oxon.*; CI; Baker, L., pers. comm.]

WALOND, William (1755?-1836): In 1784 had a singing school in a house in the Close, Chichester, owned by himself [qv]. Perhaps son of William, composer (1725-70). Deputy organist of cathedral 1775, organist 1776-1801. Lived in poverty in Chichester after retirement, subsisting on an annuity raised by the sale of houses. [Plumley and Lees, see Schedule 1]

WALTER, Mrs: Mistress of the Blue Coat girls' charity school, Chichester [qv]. Received payments on behalf of the school for 24 years (years ending Michaelmas 1768 to 1792). [WSRO Cap.V/1/1]

[WARD, Richard (-1706)]: Rector of Shermanbury 1677-1706. In 1691 received from Mr Thomas 'all his dues for his Sons Schooling'. Perhaps taught into 18th century. [WSRO Par 167/6/1]

WARNER, Nicholas: Master of Pulborough Sunday school 1786-99 [qv]. Probably also parish clerk.

WATERS, John (1746-1820): Schoolmaster and vestry clerk, Waldron, for many years [qv Day school/Waters' school]. References as 'schoolmaster' 1790, in will dated 25 September 1820, and at burial. Received payments from parish for schooling pauper children 1792 (9s 8d) and 1795 (17s 10d). Also governor of workhouse. Will left copyhold estate in Waldron Street and personal estate to wife Mary for life or until re-marriage, when estate to be realised, £10 to grandson John Waters (son of William deceased), and rest to be divided equally between daughter Elizabeth wife of John Pain, daughter Sarah wife of Thomas Harmer, son Henry, daughter Charlotte wife of John Lulham, daughter Mary widow of Charles Randall, daughter Ann. Buried 1

December 1820, aged 74. [ESRO W/A 74.51; PR]

WATERS, Thomas: Schoolmaster of Houghton 1762 [qv School].

[WATKINS, John]: Schoolmaster at Frant 1803, when aged 17-55 and enrolled in voluntary infantry. Perhaps master of Frant school [qv] where 'military exercise' was an optional extra. [*Sussex Militia List 1803, Pevensey Rape Northern Division* (1988)]

WATSON, Mrs: With Miss Rowe, opened a day school in Brighton 1790 [qv].

WAYTE, Miss: Before July 1788, with Miss Widgett, had a girls' boarding school at Brighton [qv]. In 1791 had a girls' boarding school there with Miss Harben.

WEB, Mrs: Received 14s 6d from the Dowlin charity, 20 November 1709, for schooling poor children of West Grinstead. [WSRO Par 95/1/1/3]

[WEEKES, Mrs]: Had a girls' boarding school at Battle by 1801. [*SWA* 11.1.1802]

WELBY, Josiah (-1745): Master of Lewes grammar school 1725-45 [qv]. Previously (by 1719) had a boys school at Turnbull Street, London, where he never had more than 8-10 pupils, and was 'paid to be able to teach them Latin in a year and a half'; one pupil and later friend was Thomas Birch (1705-66, DD, historian and biographer, FRS, and secretary to Royal Society 1752-65). Licensed (for Lewes) 1 January 1726. Trustees obliged him not to take Orders, because his predecessor had neglected the school for his parish duties. In 1735, wanted to move because of political in-fighting (he supported the Duke of Newcastle and the Pelhams, but the Tories had set up 'a Parson in the neighbourhood' and were taking away his scholars); was thinking of taking Orders and finding a living elsewhere. However, continued at Lewes; was ordained deacon and priest (Chichester) 1743, but died 1745 (buried 25 January 1745, St Anne). His widow, Rachel, continued to look after the grammar school boarders after his successor, John Bristed, became master. [Knapp, E. F. pers. comm. citing *DNB* (Birch, Thomas) and

BL Add MS 4321; WSRO Ep.I/1/11; SAS Wadey index; PR]

WELLER, Thomas (1737-1807): Master of Heathfield village school [qv] and a boys' boarding school there [qv] (Rs 1775-82), and then master of Mayfield charity school [qv] from Christmas 1783 to death in 1807. Also surveyor: advertised as such 1775 and in later school advertisements; estate maps of 1784 (2), 1785, 1788 survive. Buried 25 August 1807, aged 70. [Map references: Lucas, P. *Heathfield Memorials* (1910), ESRO SAS/drawer A/4, AMS 4456, GLY 3118; PR]

[WELLS, George (1768-1839)]: Rector of Wiston 1796-1839, at one time (and perhaps in the 18th century) 'used to educate in his family four or six noblemen's sons'. His school had ceased by 1814. Son of Rev George, of Manningford, Wiltshire; New College, Oxford, matriculated 24 January 1787, aged 19; MA; BCL 1794. Rector of Albourne 1788-94 and 1826 to death; rector of Wiston 1796 to death; prebendary of Chichester 1822. Five of his sons went to Oxford - George, Charles, Henry, Francis, Edward. Died 24 May 1839, aged 71. [Evans *Worthing* 2 (1814); *Al. Oxon.*; CI; *Gentleman's Magazine* (1839)]

WENSLEY, James: In July 1797 was paid by Billingshurst parish 2s 'for Schooling', and from Michaelmas 1800 into 1801 1s a week for schooling the workhouse children [qv Parish schooling]. In 1798 was given by parish 10s 6d 'to help Burying his Son' and in 1799 7s 'for Cloaths for his Girl'. [WSRO Par 21/31/2]

WEST: In 1707 received 5s 8d from the Dowlin charity for schooling poor children of West Grinstead (possibly on behalf of his wife?). [WSRO Par 95/1/1/3]

WEST, John: Schoolmaster of Bolney (R 1791). With wife Susannah, owned 2 dwellings there, occupied one and rented out the other [qv].

WESTON, Nicholas (-1740): Schoolmaster at Heathfield [qv Village school]. Buried 14 May 1740.

[WHEELER]: Schoolmaster at Burwash 1804, and probably earlier [qv].

WHISKY, Sarah: In 1727 received 3s 2d from the Dowlin charity for schooling a poor boy of West Grinstead. [WSRO Par 95/1/1/3]

WHITEBREAD, Widow: In 1730 received 2s 4d from the Dowlin charity for schooling 2 poor children of West Grinstead. [WSRO Par 95/1/1/3]

WHITFIELD, Alexander: Schoolmaster of East Hoathly 1759-60 [qv Village school].

[WICKCLIFF, Elizabeth (-1794)]: Perhaps the schoolmistress of Petworth who was probably the longest-serving schoolmistress in Sussex in the 18th century. Under the byline 'Chichester, June 28' the *Portsmouth Gazette* (30 June 1794) reported: 'Last week two ladies were buried at Petworth, in this county, whose ages together amounted to 186 years, the one being 92, and the other 94. The former of these venerable women had kept a school in one house in the above parish upwards of 70 years.' Petworth parish registers and bishop's transcripts give 'Mrs Elizabeth Wickcliff', aged 92, buried 9 June 1794, and 'Elizabeth Houneymond', also aged 92, buried 15 June 1794.

[WICKENS, Widow]: Icklesham churchwardens' accounts for 1724 included payment of 10d 'for Worsted and a Hornebooke for Widdow Wickens Children'. (Possibly a school dame there?) [*SAC 32*]

WICKHAM, John: In 1794 paid 2s 6d by Ticehurst parish for schooling the workhouse children [qv]. A cobbler, he was paid by the parish from at least 1782 for mending the shoes of the poor; parish also paid for 'quarters' for himself and wife at 6d a week, from at least 1782 to 1793, and in 1800 he received 1s 3d relief, 'being ill'. [ESRO PAR 492/31/1/3]

WICKING, Stephen: Schoolmaster of Hastings 1721, probably of combined grammar school and Saunders' charity school [qv]. Subscribed 9 November 1721 'before his Admission to Teach School in Hasting'. Licensed 24 June 1726 to teach boys in Guestling (perhaps at a charity school maintained in his lifetime by rector Robert Bradshaw who by will endowed a charity school there [qv]). [WSRO Ep.II/1/1,

Ep.I/1/11]

WIDGETT, Miss: With Mrs Pullen, opened a girls' boarding school at Brighton at Lady Day 1784 [qv]. Before 1788, with Miss Wayte, had a girls' boarding school there [qv]. Probably sister of (or at least related to) the Miss E. Widgett, styled by Fanny Burney as 'the milliner and library-woman', who took over Woodgate's circulating library in Old Steine, and published *A Description of Brighthelmston* in 1778 (the Post Office was moved that year to her establishment; she was succeeded as librarian and postmaster by J. Bowen in July 1779); this Miss E. Widgett almost certainly the Elizabeth Widgett who married, 18 September 1780, Thomas Hudson [qv], then vicar of Brighton. In 1784 the Miss Widgett, schoolmistress, gave as her address 'the Rev Mr Hudson's, New Buildings'. [Bishop, 113; Harrison & North; *SWA* 16.11.78, 12.7.79]

WILBAR, Henry (-1792): Opened a boys' boarding school at Brighton 1787 [qv]. One Sunday morning in June 1791, a servant lad living at the school, William Stevens, who came from Sundridge, Kent, ran away having stolen 'one silver watch, one metal ditto, marked C. T. on the case, maker's name Stephen Beeching, Maidstone; one pair of round silver buckles; a quantity of shoes, and other articles'. Wilbar advertised a reward for his apprehension (2 guineas and all reasonable charges, on conviction); 'He is short in stature, dark complexion, dark strait hair; had on a thickset livery, and round hat, with a silver band.' A week later the boy was taken at the *Kings Head*, Chichester, 'with all the stolen effects (except a silver watch, a pair of silver buckles, and a silver hat-band, which he had sold to a Jew, in Arundel)' in his possession, together with other stolen goods from a house in Kent; he said he had been on the *Halswell*, East Indiaman, when she sank. At the Lewes assizes in August he was found guilty of stealing 'in the house of Mr Wilbar', 2 watches and sundry articles of wearing apparel, and was 'ordered to be transported for seven years'. At the same assizes Wilbar obtained a verdict, with £20 damages, against Mr Hargrave of Brighton, for defamation. Later that same year, in December, a man and a woman were committed to the house of correction in Lewes 'on a charge of having stolen and pledged with a pawnbroker, at Brighton, sundry articles of wearing apparel, the property of Mr Wilbar, of that place.' Wife Sarah; son Henry Coleman baptised 12 February 1792. Died 1792 (advertisement appealing for creditors 12 November 1792). [*SWA* 13.6.91, 20.6.91, 22.8.91, 12.12.91, 12.11.92; PR]

WILLARD, Jane (1723-98): Had a dame school at Warnham, with about 30 scholars [qv]; taught both reading and writing. Also paid by parish for teaching the poor children, from 1777 or earlier to 1788 (when 65: see Schedule 1 for details). Baptised at Horsham 28 April 1723, Jane Kewell, daughter of Henry and Jane; married there, 17 April 1750, John Willard. Daughter Kitty baptised at Warnham 26 December 1758. Buried at Warnham 11 May 1798. Husband John buried 22 May 1801. [PRs]

WILLIAMS, Miles (1719-86): In 1758, then curate of Ashurst, he kept a school there [qv]. Son of Rev Charles, of Llandough, Penarth, Glamorgan: matriculated Jesus College, Oxford, 3 November 1737, aged 18; BA 1741. In 1779, BA and MA, Jesus College, Cambridge. Rector of Shermanbury 1762-86, and vicar of Oving 1781-86. His will (dated 17 August 1785, proved 26 April 1786) mentions his wife Anne; eldest son Charles, rector of Woolbeding, and his wife Jane; son Miles, DD, and his wife Elizabeth; daughters Anne and Jane (both over 21 and unmarried) and Sarah (under 21). Specific bequests totaled £2,065, and interest on the residue of the estate went to his wife for her life (in addition to other bequests to her) and then the principal and interest to each of his 5 children equally. Bequests of £600 to each of his 3 daughters were to be subject to interest at the rate of £25 pa from the date of his death until they were paid (Sarah's when she was 21). He left £5 to the poor of Shermanbury (not in receipt of parish relief) and £5 likewise to the poor of Oving. His 'Books, papers and Manuscripts' went to his son Charles and 'My worthy & beloved Friend' Rev Edward Wilson, rector of Ashurst, were his executors, trustees, and guardians of his daughter Sarah. [*Al. Oxon.*; *Al. Cant.*; ESRO W/A 65.242; CI]

WILLIAMS, Rice (-1727): Vicar of New Shoreham 1713-27; master of charity school set

11.   John Wooll (1767-1833), headmaster of Midhurst grammar school 1799-1807 and subsequently headmaster of Rugby. From an engraving by Charles Turner after Sir Thomas Lawrence. (WSRO PD 1168)

up there in 1714 [qv]. Married at Rottingdean, 26 June 1722, Ann Littijohn of Portslade (perhaps widow of John, vicar of Portslade). Buried at New Shoreham 22 May 1727. [CI]

WILLIAMS, Thomas (1738-1821): Opened a boys' boarding school at Seaford January 1771 [qv]. Received £15 a year from George Medley from Christmas 1775, and perhaps earlier, to Michaelmas 1780, for schooling poor boys of Seaford [qv Charity schools]. Curate of Tarring Neville in 1770; curate of Seaford 1772-85; curate of East Blatchington 1784; vicar of Alfriston 1784 to death; sequestrator (rector) of Bishopstone 1802 to death. Died 8 August 1821, buried at Seaford 14 August 1821, aged 83. [CI; Seaford PR]

WILLIAMS, William: Schoolmaster at Burwash. Had a boys' boarding school there 1784 [qv], and probably a day school earlier. Also land-surveyor (advertised as such 1795). [*SWA* 20.4.95]

WILLIS, John (1676?-): Master of Cuckfield grammar school 1711-12 [qv]. In will of Robert Middleton, vicar of Cuckfield (died May 1713) as curate and schoolmaster, and was asked to preach his funeral sermon. Perhaps the JW, son of John of Hinxey, Berkshire, gent, who matriculated St Mary's Hall, Oxford, 17 December 1703, aged 27; BCL Oriel 1710 (but other JWs at Oxford matriculated 1697 aged 18, 1701 aged 16, 1708 aged 18). [*SAC* 50; *Al. Oxon.*]

WILMER: In 1786 paid by Pullborough parish 8s for teaching Sunday school for 8 weeks [qv].

WILMER, Nathaniel: Licensed 22 June 1723 to teach boys at school in West Chiltington [qv Charity school]. Also surveyor. [WSRO Ep.I/1/11; *DLS*]

WINTERBOTTOM, Thomas (c1652-1717): Licensed to instruct boys at East Grinstead 5 January 1711. Of Lancashire; admitted pensioner Jesus College, Cambridge, 19 April 1671, aged 19; matriculated 1675; BA 1676. Warden of Sackville College (almshouse) East Grinstead 1685-1716. Married (marriage licence 23 January 1686) Mary Fletcher, both 'of Lindfield'; 5 children baptised at East Grinstead 1687-1700. Rector of Ashurst, Kent, 1692-

1717; vicar of Birling, Kent, 1715-17. Died 7 July 1717. [WSRO Ep.I/1/10; *Al. Cant.*; Hills, W. H. *History of East Grinstead* (1906); *SRS* **6**; *Ashurst church guide*; PR]

WOOD: Schoolmaster at Newick c1780 [qv].

WOOD, Edward (-1794): Schoolmaster at Brede [qv Charity school]. Buried 11 June 1794. [PR]

WOOD, John (-1769): Schoolmaster at Lindfield in 1735 [qv]. Married there, 27 October 1723, Mary Osbourn (buried 12 January 1745); their children baptised: William (1725), Charles (1726), Elizabeth (1728), Thomas (1730), Robert (1732), Mary (1733), Ann (1735), Jasper (1738), Sarah (1739). Buried 1 November 1769. [PR]

WOOD, Mary (1716-99): Buried at Cuckfield 24 September 1799, 'schoolmistress', aged 83. [PR]

WOOLL, John (1767-1833): Master of Midhurst grammar school 1799-1807 [qv]. Left to become master of Rugby school (1807-28). Son of John of Westminster, esq. Balliol College, Oxford, matricultated 17 January 1785, aged 17; BA New College, Oxford 1790; MA 1794; BD and DD 1807; rector of Blackford, Somerset, 1796. Died 23 November 1833. [*Al. Oxon.*]

[WOOLLGAR, William]: Schoolmaster at Henfield. Licensed to teach boys there grammar, arithmetic etc, 9 November 1692. [WSRO Ep.I/1/10]

WOOLVEN: In 1730 received 2s from the Dowlin charity for schooling poor children of West Grinstead. Married. [WSRO Par 95/1/1/3]

WORGER, Sarah: In 1795 received £4 10s from the Cavendish estate for teaching 'one year', almost certainly at Eastbourne charity school [qv].

WRIGHT, Henry (1667?-1718?): Licensed to teach boys in the grammar school at Petworth 24 December 1705 [qv]. Licensed again, 16 November 1715, to teach boys in the parish of Petworth (perhaps the grammar school had

ceased by then). Perhaps son of George of
Paddington, Middlesex, gent; Christ Church,
Oxford, matriculated 15 July 1687, aged 20;
BA 1691, MA 1694. Almost certainly the
Henry Wright, BA, rector of Upwaltham (near
Petworth) 1706-18, and rector of Bodegton
[Burton] cum Coots [Coates] (adjacent parish to
Petworth) 1713. Died 1718 (another instituted
rector of Upwaltham 22 September 1718 by
death of HW). [WSRO Ep.I/1/10; *Al. Oxon.*;
CI]

WRIGHT, Phillip: Master of Grey coat boys'
charity school, Chichester, from April 1794 into
19th century [qv]. Received the Duke of
Richmond's annual subscription of £2 2s to the
charity school from 1790, so was probably the
master there under Ingram from that date.
(Identified as Phillip in Richmond's accounts).
[WSRO Cap.V/1/1, Cap.I/24/5, Goodwood MS
245, 247]

WYBOURN, Sarah: Wife of William, master
of Saunders' charity school, Rye [qv], on 21
November 1744 was directed by the governors
to continue the school following husband's
death, until Lady Day next (when Hogben
appointed master). She later married secondly
John Usher of Betherton, gent. [ESRO RYE
114/13, WMD box 14]

WYBOURN, William (-1744): Master of
Saunders' charity school, Rye, 1727-44 [qv].
Subscribed 10 June 1728. Also had own pupils.
Also surveyor (maps of Peasmarsh estates,
1736). Married Sarah, who survived him [qv].
Buried 20 November 1744, 'School Master'.
[RSB; WSRO Ep.II/1/1; ESRO AMS 4593;
HM MA 123; PR]

YOUNG, Mary (Mrs): Schoolmistress at West
Wittering 1755-75 [qv Charity schooling].
Received £2 9s pa from the Oliver Whitby
charity for teaching 6 poor children to read.
[WSRO E35D/3/1]

SCHEDULE 3

SUSSEX SCHOLARS OF THE 18TH CENTURY

Surnames in italics identify girls.

Names in box brackets identify school-children likely to have been at school in the 18th century but for whom documentary evidence of the fact has not yet been traced.

Surnames in round brackets indicate that the sex of the child is not known.

In most cases where a child's birth date is given beside their name, this has been inferred from their date of baptism, after allowing for the average birth/baptism interval.

The majority of children's names included here derive from charity school lists. In some cases the lists are not dated. This is particularly relevant to Saunders' charity school, Rye, where the surviving lists are on loose sheets. In almost all such cases it is possible to date the lists with reasonable accuracy from contextual or internal evidence, but in the schedule attributed dates are followed by a question mark in brackets - (?).

For each of the charity schools - that at Mayfield, from 1750, and Saunders' charity school at Rye, from 1722 - a very large number of 18th century school lists have survived. for a number of other charity schools there are occasional lists - Brightling girls' school, 1735-62; Brighton, at the begining of the century (with also lists of boys given coats or prayer books, and of leavers); Chichester Grey Coat school, 1710-14 (with names of many leavers later in the century from the school's accounts); Cocking, a few names 1731-33; Eastbourne, a few scattered lists; Lord Pelham's school at Lewes, 1784; Taylor's school at Petworth, children joining 1796-99; Robeertsbridge, at its opening in 1796; Seaford, 1765; Sedlescombe, a few lists 1748-61.

Many other scholars are recorded in parish records (eg appointments to Fermor's charity school, Rotherfield), parish, family and estate accounts, school histories (eg scholars at Midhurst grammar school), letters, diaries, biographies and newspaper reports.

The schedule only lists a minority of the children who would have attended school in the 18th century, but - dispite the preponderance of charity school children - it includes every type of scholar, from paupers to aristocracy.

ADAMS, Edward (1710-): Saunders' charity school, Rye. In lists from September 1722 (?) (first list) to January 1724 (?) (not in 8 April 1724). Baptised 21 June 1710 son of John and Anne. (Brother Isaac also at the school.) [RSB; PR]

ADAMS, James (1789-): Admitted to Robertsbridge charity school at its opening 5 April 1796, aged 7. Sponsored by Mr Pooke. Baptised 1 February 1789, son of George and Naomi (née Winder). [ESRO PAR 477/25/1/1; Salehurst PR]

ADAMS, Isaac (1714-): Saunders' charity school, Rye. In lists from 8 April 1724 (not in January 1724 (?)) to 10 January 1728; 17 April 1728 notes 'left the school'. Baptised 23 July 1714, son of John and Ann. (Brother Edward also at the school.) [RSB; PR]

ADAMS, Richard (1691-): Brighton charity school. In December 1705 list of 'writers'. Baptised 1 November 1691, son of Thomas and Mary. [BSB; PR]

ADAMS, Robert (1695-): Brighton charity school. In list of 'readers' of (probably) January 1702; still a 'reader' December 1705. Baptised 16 Aug 1695, Robart and Elizabeth twins of Robart. (Name of mother, Vertue, from baptism of brother Samuel, also at the school.) [BSB; PR]

ADAMS, Samuel (1700-): Brighton charity school. Added to December 1705 list of 'readers' (ie joined subsequently). Baptised 29 Aug 1700, son of Robert and Vertue. (Brother Robert also at the school.) [BSB; PR]

ADAMS, Stephen (1789-): Admitted Robertsbridge charity school at its opening 5 April 1796. Sponsored by Mr John Langford. Baptised 19 April 1789, son of Stephen and Philadelphia (née Fuller). [ESRO PAR 477/25/1/1; Salehurst PR]

ADAMS, Thomas: Brighton charity school. In December 1705 list of 'readers'. [BSB]

ADAMS, William (1713-): Saunders' charity school, Rye. In lists from September 1722 (?) (first list) to January 1726 (?) (not in 4 May 1726). Son of the widow of the late Ambrose

Adams. Born 5 April 1713, baptised 25 December 1713, son of Ambrose and Mary. [RSB; PR]

ADE, Joseph (1774-): Lord Pelham's charity school, Lewes [qv Rands' school]. Admitted Michaelmas 1784. There 10 October 1784, aged 10. Baptised 20 February 1774, son of Stapley and Ann. [ESRO AMS 6005; St Michael Lewes PR]

ADRIEN, Isaac (1719-): Saunders' charity school, Rye. In lists from 31 March 1731 (not in 6 January 1731) to 2 July 1735 (8 October 1735 notes 'left the school'). Baptised 28 June 1719, son of Daniel and Elizabeth. Father identified as a French refugee at baptism of John Baptist, 1 September 1706. (Brother Peter also at the school.) [RSB; PR]

ADRIEN, Peter: Saunders' charity school, Rye. In first school list September 1722 (?); 'Went to London' 6 February 1723. Son of Daniel. (Brother Isaac also at the school: qv.) [RSB]

[ALCOCK, John]: Perhaps at Midhurst grammar school. A native of Midhurst and elected to Winchester 1719. [*HMGS*]

[ALCOCK, Thomas]: Perhaps at Midhurst grammar school. A native of Midhurst and elected to Winchester 1721. [*HMGS*]

ALDRIDGE: Grey Coat charity school, Chichester. Left between Michaelmas 1769 and Michaelmas 1770. Given 10s 6d on leaving. [WSRO Cap.V/1/1]

ALLEN (ALLIN), Elizabeth (1744 or 45-): Brightling girls' charity school. Admitted between Michaelmas 1752 and Lady Day 1755, in which period she attended on 235 school days; left between Lady Day 1755 and 30 April 1757 in which period she attended on 317 school days. Baptised 14 January 1745, daughter of George and Grace. [ESRO PAR 254/25/1; PR]

ALLEN, George (1745-): Saunders' charity school, Rye. In lists from 9 April 1755 (not in 16 January 1754 - the only 1754 list) to midsummer 1757, where marked 'Left School'. Son of William, marked 'deceased' in midsummer 1757 list. Baptised 22 May 1745, son of William and Elizabeth. (Brothers Henry and Thomas also at the school.) [RSB; PR].

ALLEN, George: (1787-   ): Admitted Robertsbridge charity school at its opening 5 April 1796, aged 9. Sponsored by the Rev William Burrell Hayley. Baptised 15 April 1787, aged 3 weeks, son of George and Philadelphia.   [ESRO   PAR   477/25/1/1; Salehurst PR]

ALLEN, Henry (1728-): Saunders' charity school, Rye. In lists from 11 January 1738 (not in 5 October 1737) to 13 October 1742 (not in 5 January 1743). Baptised 27 October 1728, son of Justinian (Jesse) and Mary. [RSB; PR]

ALLEN, Henry (1735-): Saunders' charity school, Rye. In lists from 14 August 1745 (not in 10 April 1745); left school 2 June 1748. Baptised 28 March 1735, son of William and Elizabeth. (Brothers Thomas and George also at the school.) [RSB; PR]

ALLEN, John: Sedlescombe charity school. Admitted 19 April 1762. [SSB]

ALLEN, John (1769-): Saunders' charity school, Rye. Admitted 16 July 1777; in lists to Michaelmas 1781 (not in Lady Day 1782). Baptised 17 July 1769, son of Justinian and Hannah. [RSB; PR]

ALLEN, Justinian (1739-): Saunders' charity school, Rye. In lists from 3 October 1750 (not in 27 June 1750) to Michaelmas 1752, where marked 'July 10, 1752'. Baptised 1 July 1739, son of Justinian and Mercy. [RSB; PR]

ALLEN, Sarah: Brightling girls' charity school. Admitted between 31 July 1758 and 31 December 1761, in which period she attended on 125 school days. (No later records.) [ESRO PAR 254/25/1]

ALLEN, Thomas (1740-): Saunders' charity school, Rye. In lists from Michaelmas 1749 (not in 24 June 1749) to 15 January 1752, where marked 'left School'. Baptised 19 November 1740, son of William and Elizabeth. (Brothers Henry and George also at the school.) [RSB; PR]

ALLEN, William (1745-): Saunders' charity school, Rye. In lists from 16 January 1754 (not in Michaelmas 1753) to 14 January 1756 (not in 7 April 1756). Baptised 10 February 1745, son of John and Hannah. [RSB; PR]

ALLEN, William: Saunders' charity school, Rye. In lists from 9 April 1755 (not in 16 January 1754 - the only 1754 list) to midsummer 1756, where marked 'Left School'. Son of Thomas. [RSB]

ALSFORD: Grey Coat charity school, Chichester. Left between Michaelmas 1760 and Michaelmas 1761. Given 10s 6d on leaving. [WSRO Cap.V/1/1]

AMON (AMOND), John (1722-): Saunders' charity school, Rye. In lists from 7 July 1731 (not in 31 March 1731) to 28 March 1733 (4 July 1733 notes 'left the school'). Son of Thomas Amond, deceased. Baptised 6 January 1723, son of Thomas and Elizabeth Amon. (Brother Thomas also at the school.) [RSB; PR]

AMON, John (1763-): Saunders' charity school, Rye. Admitted 19 August 1772; in lists to Michaelmas 1775 (not in Christmas 1777 - the next surviving list). Baptised 1 July 1763, son of John and Mary. (Brother Thomas also at the school.) [RSB; PR]

AMOND, Thomas (1719-): Saunders' charity school, Rye. In lists from 7 July 1731 (not in 31 March 1731) to 28 March 1733 (4 July 1733 notes 'left the school'). Son of Thomas Amond, deceased. Baptised 6 November 1719, son of Thomas and Elizabeth Amond. (Brother John also at the school.) [RSB; PR]

AMON, Thomas (1766-): Saunders' charity school, Rye. Admitted 9 October 1776; in lists to Michaelmas 1781 (not in Lady Day 1782). Baptised 19 November 1766, son of John and Mary. (Brother John also at the school.) [RSB; PR]

AMPLEFORD: Brighton girls' charity school. Admitted when school opened 30 September 1702. 'John Ampleford's daughter'. Either Ann, baptised 19 April 1691, daughter of John and Elizabeth (née James), or Elizabeth, baptised 9 September 1694, daughter of John. (Brother at the boys' charity school.) [BSB; PR]

AMPLEFORD, Hulbert (1688-): Brighton charity school. In list of 'writers' 12 January 1702; had left by December 1705 and gone 'to a shipwright'. Baptised 6 May 1688, son of John and Elizabeth (née James). (Sister at the girls' charity school.) [BSB; PR]

ANCOCK, Thomas (1763-): Eastbourne charity school. Admitted 14 August 1769; still there January 1771. Baptised 24 May 1763, son of James and Elizabeth. [SAS Budgen MS v.105; PR]

ANNEL, Richard (c1700-): Grey Coat charity school, Chichester. Admitted at its foundation, Lady Day 1710. Aged 10 at Lady Day 1711. 'Discarded' between Lady Day 1713 and Lady Day 1714. [WSRO Cap.V/1/1]

ANSCOMB - see also AYNSCOMBE

ANSCOMB, Mary (1754-): A poor girl of Wivelsfield for whose schooling the parish paid 'Master Hart' £2 2s in 1770. Probably baptised 24 February 1754, daughter of Thomas and Elizabeth. [ESRO PAR 514/31/1; PR]

APPS, John (1745-): Saunders' charity school, Rye. In lists from 16 January 1754 (not in Michaelmas 1753); left school 31 January 1757. Baptised 2 January 1746, son of John and Lydia. (Brother William also at the school.) [RSB; PR]

APPS, William (1748-): Saunders' charity school, Rye. In lists from 11 January 1758 (not in Michaelmas 1757); left school 15 January 1759. Baptised 23 August 1748, son of John and Lydia. (Brother John also at the school.) [RSB; PR]

APPS, William (1771-): Saunders' charity school, Rye. Admitted 18 July 1781; in lists to 2 September 1782, which notes 'Left School'. Son of John Apps, deceased. Baptised 4 February 1771, son of John and Mary. [RSB; PR]

ARCHER, Thomas (1725-): Saunders' charity school, Rye. In lists from 10 January 1739 (not in 4 October 1738) to 29 April 1741 (8 July 1741 notes 'left the school'). Baptised 20

August 1725, son of John and Margaret. [RSB; PR]

ARCHPOOL: A poor girl of West Grinstead, who received schooling from Goody Trower, 1701-05, under the Dowlin charity. [WSRO Par 95/1/1/3]

ARCHPOOL: A poor boy of West Grinstead, who received schooling from Goody Trower, 1701-05, under the Dowlin charity. [WSRO Par 95/1/1/3]

(*ARCHPOOL*): 'W. Archpool's children' of West Grinstead received schooling 1730 under the Dowlin charity. [WSRO Par 95/1/1/3]

ARKCOLL: Button's school, Lewes. To recite at a 'Public Examination' at the *Star Assembly Room*, 22 June 1797. [*SWA* 19.6.97]

ARNOLD, John (c1700-): Grey Coat charity school, Chichester, from its foundation, Lady Day 1710. Aged 11 at Lady Day 1711. Left by Lady Day 1712. [WSRO Cap.V/1/1]

ARNOLD, Thomas (c1702-): Grey Coat charity school, Chichester, from its foundation, Lady Day 1710. Aged 9 at Lady Day 1711; there Lady Day 1714. [WSRO Cap.V/1/1]

ASHBY: Cater Rand's school, Lewes, January 1734 - September 1740. The Duke of Newcastle's accounts show payments of £2 per annum 'for schooling Ashby's son' (R: 1734, 1737, 1739, 1740). [BL Add MS 33,157]

ASHBY, Ann (1756-): Mayfield charity school. Admitted 11 July 1765; removed 15 January 1768, 'Taken into the workhouse', after 2 years as a 'reader'. Baptised 15 August 1756, daughter of Thomas and Susanna. (Brothers James, Richard, Thomas and sisters Mary, Susanna, also at the school.) [MSB; PR]

ASHBY, Ann (1789-): Mayfield charity school. Admitted 6 January 1797; removed 11 April 1800, taken out by parents. Baptised 17 October 1790, daughter of William and Hannah. (Sisters Hannah, Lydia, Philadelphia, also at the school.) [MSB; PR]

ASHBY, Elizabeth (1743-): Mayfield charity school. Admitted 14 November 1752; removed

10 January 1755, 'ill', taken home by parents. She had 2¼ years at the school, 1¾ years as a 'writer'. Baptised 10 April 1743, daughter of Reuben and Anne. (Brother John and sisters Lucy and Philadelphia, also at the school.) [MSB; PR]

ASHBY, Elizabeth (1769 or 70-): Mayfield charity school. Admitted 11 April 1777; removed 6 March 1781, 'Sufficiently Learned', after 4 years at the school, 2 years as a 'writer'. Baptised either (Betsy) 13 August 1769, daughter of Reuben and Omy, or 15 July 1770, daughter of Thomas and Sarah. (If baptised 1769, brothers James, John, Thomas, William and sister Hannah, also at the school.) [MSB; PR]

ASHBY, Hannah (1763-): Mayfield charity school. Admitted 19 January 1770; removed 5 April 1776, 'For Non-attendance, but pretty well Learned', after 6¼ years at the school, 3¼ years as a 'writer'. Baptised 22 May 1768, daughter of Ruben and Onie (Omy). (Brothers James, John, Thomas, William, and probably sister Elizabeth, also at the school.) [MSB; PR]

ASHBY, Hannah (1781-): Mayfield charity school. Admitted 15 October 1789; removed 11 October 1793. Baptised 11 November 1781, daughter of William and Hannah. (Sisters Ann, Lydia, Philadelphia, also at the school.) [MSB; PR]

ASHBY, James (1760-): Mayfield charity school. Admitted 16 October 1767; removed 15 January 1768, 'To make room for others'. Baptised 9 December 1760, son of Thomas and Susanna. (Brothers Richard, Thomas and sisters Ann, Mary, Susanna, also at the school.) [MSB; PR]

ASHBY, James (1776-): Mayfield charity school. Admitted 15 October 1784; removed 9 April 1790, taken out by parents but 'Sufficiently Learned'. Baptised 4 February 1776, son of Reuben and Ome. (Brothers John, Thomas, William, sister Hannah, probably sister Elizabeth, also at the school.) [MSB; PR]

ASHBY, John (1736-): Mayfield charity school. Admitted at foundation 29 June 1750; may have been at the school earlier, as master paid from Michaelmas 1749; removed 28 June 1751 'having Learn'd to read write & cast Accompt well'. Baptised 13 December 1736, son of Reuben and Anne. (Sisters Elizabeth, Lucy, Philadelphia, also at the school.) [MSB; PR]

ASHBY, John (1765-): Mayfield charity school. Admission not traced but probably 30 January 1772; in list for 8 April 1774 as having attended 2½ years but not in some previous lists (perhaps some confusion with brother William); removed 18 July 1777, 'taken away by his parents' after 5½ years at the school, 2 years as a 'writer'. Baptised 15 September 1765, son of Reuben and Ome. (Brothers James, Thomas, William, sister Hannah, probably sister Elizabeth, also at the school.) [MSB; PR]

ASHBY, Lucy (1746-): Mayfield charity school. Admitted 9 April 1755; removed 7 July 1758, taken out by parents after 3¼ years, 1¼ years as a 'writer'; but re-admitted 17 October 1760, removed 9 January 1761, 'sufficiently learned', having had 3½ years at the school in all, 1½ years as a 'writer'. Baptised 20 July 1746, daughter of Reuben and Anne. (Brother John, sisters Elizabeth, Philadelphia, also at the school.) [MSB; PR]

ASHBY, Lydia (1784-): Mayfield charity school. Admitted 6 July 1792; removed 11 July 1794, taken out by parents. Baptised 29 January 1784, daughter of William and Hannah. (Sisters Ann, Hannah, Philadelphia, also at the school.) [MSB; PR]

ASHBY, Mary (1754-): Mayfield charity school. Admitted 6 July 1764; removed 11 July 1765, 'sufficiently Learned' (but not a 'writer' at January 1765). Baptised 22 April 1754, daughter of Thomas and Susanna. (Brothers James, Richard, Thomas, sisters Ann, Susanna, also at the school.) [MSB; PR]

ASHBY, Mercy: Mayfield charity school. Admitted to 'Widow Dukes' dame school 11 January 1765; admitted to charity school 2 May 1766; removed 21 April 1769, for non-attendance, after 3 years at the school, 1¼ years as a 'writer'. [MSB]

ASHBY, Philadelphia (1750-): Mayfield charity school. Admitted 26 October 1764; removed 11 January 1765, 'Taken out by her Parents but Pretty well learn'd' after ¼ year as a 'writer'. Baptised 4 November 1750, daughter of Reuben and Anne, so 14 years old when joining the school briefly (NB Mary Hook also admitted at the same time, aged 13, and had just 1 year, all as a 'writer'. Brother John, sisters Elizabeth, Lucy, also at the school.) [MSB; PR]

ASHBY, Philadelphia (1786-): Mayfield charity school. Admitted 11 July 1794; removed 14 October 1796, taken out by parents. Baptised 5 November 1786, daughter of William and Hannah. (Sisters Ann, Hannah, Lydia, also at the school.) [MSB; PR]

ASHBY, Richard (1757-): Mayfield charity school. No formal admission but added to list of 7 January 1763; removed 8 April 1763, 'suspended to make room for older children', after just ¼ year (perhaps taken into the workhouse - see brother Thomas). Baptised 27 November 1757, son of Thomas and Susanna. (Brothers James, Thomas, sisters Ann, Mary, Susanna, also at the school.) [MSB; PR]

ASHBY, Susanna (1762-): Mayfield charity school. Admitted 16 October 1767; removed 18 October 1771, for non-attendance after 4 years at the school, 1¼ years as a 'writer'. Baptised 1 March 1762, daughter of Thomas and Susanna. (Brothers James, Richard, Thomas, sisters Ann, Mary, also at the school.) [MSB; PR]

ASHBY, Thomas (1755-): Mayfield charity school. Admitted 8 January 1762; removed 8 April 1763, 'suspended to make room for older children'; re-admitted 13 January 1764, but removed 6 July 1764, 'taken into the Workhouse and taught there', after 1¾ years at the school in total, as a 'reader'. Baptised 5 March 1755, son of Thomas and Susanna. (Brothers James, Richard, sisters Ann, Mary, Susanna, also at the school.) [MSB; PR]

ASHBY, Thomas (1772-): Mayfield charity school. Admitted 10 April 1778; removed 2 August 1782, for non-attendance. Baptised 12 June 1772, son of Reuben and Ome. (NB Another Thomas, son of Reuben and Ome baptised 1768 assumed dead; and another Thomas, son of Thomas and Sarah, baptised 13 February 1768, rather old at leaving for this school; also two other children of Reuben joined school at 6 years, and the 3 children admitted before Thomas and the one after were all aged 6. Brothers James, John, William, sister Hannah, probably sister Elizabeth, also at the school.) [MSB; PR]

ASHBY, William (1760-): Mayfield charity school. Admitted to 'Widow Dukes' dame school 17 October 1766 but apparently did not attend; admitted again 17 April 1767, and admitted to charity school 15 January 1768; removed 27 October 1769, for non-attendance, after 1¾ years at the school as a 'reader'; re-admitted 19 January 1770; apparently removed 7 January 1774, for non-attendance, after 4 further years as a 'reader'. Baptised 14 September 1760, son of Reuben and Ome. (Brothers James, John, Thomas, sister Hannah, probably sister Elizabeth, also at the school.) [MSB; PR]

ASTHY, John: Saunders' charity school, Rye. In lists from Christmas 1762 (not in 20 January 1762, previous surviving list) to Michaelmas 1763 (not in Christmas 1764, next surviving list). Son of John. [RSB]

ATKINS, Jemima: Mayfield charity school. Admitted 30 July 1779; removed 7 July 1780, taken out by parents after 1 year at the school, ¾ year as a 'writer'. [MSB]

ATKINSON, Robert: Brighton charity school. Joined as 'reader' after list of (probably) January 1702; given coat and hat July 1702; in 'writers' class by December 1705. [BSB]

ATKINSON, Thomas: Brighton charity school. Added at end of list of 'readers' December 1705 (ie joined subsequently). [BSB]

ATTREE, R.: Button's school, Lewes. To recite at a 'Public Examination' at the *Star Assembly Room*, 22 June 1797. [*SWA* 19.6.97]

AUSTEN (AUSTIN), John (1747-): Mayfield charity school. Admitted 14 October 1755; removed 11 January 1760, 'sufficiently Learned', after 4¼ years at the school, 1¼ as a 'writer'. Born 3 February 1747, baptised 12 February 1747, son of John and Martha. [MSB; PR]

AUSTEN, John Friend (1755-): At Seaford charity school 1765. Baptised 31 March 1755, son of John and Ann. [BL Add MS 33,059; PR]

AUSTEN (AUSTIN), Thomas (1753-): Mayfield charity school. Admitted 8 January 1762; removed 19 April 1765, for non-attendance after 3¼ years at the school, still a 'reader'. Baptised 21 August 1753, son of John and Mary. [MSB; PR]

AVERY, William (1710?-): Brighton charity school. Given prayer book 1718. Probably baptised 22 April 1710, son of John Avery. [BSB; PR]

AXEL, Anne: Brightling girls' charity school. Admitted 21 April 1738. There to year ending 30 April 1742 (in which year she attended on 210 school days). Probably daughter of Richard and Mary, whose daughter Mary started at the school the following year. [ESRO PAR 254/25/1]

AXEL, Mary: At Sarah Cruttenden's school, Brightling, 1739-42. On 17 October 1740 John Fuller paid Cruttenden for teaching her and Richard Axel for 71 weeks, at 2d a week for them both; and on 31 January 1743, £1 13s 8d for schooling her and Richard (probably for 101 weeks, now at 2d a week each). Probably same as Mary Axel (1736-) below, though would only have been 3-4 years when first at Cruttenden's. [ESRO SAS/RF 15/28]

AXEL, Mary (1736-): Brightling girls' charity school. Admitted between 1 May 1742 and 22 March 1744, in which period she attended on 57 school days; there to period 1 September 1745 to 31 July 1747, in which she attended on 285 school days; had 716 days at the school in total. Baptised 8 Aug 1736, daughter of Richard and Mary. (Probably same as Mary Axel above.) [ESRO PAR 254/25/1; PR]

AXEL, Richard: Sarah Cruttenden's school, Brightling. On 17 October 1740 John Fuller paid her for teaching Richard and Mary Axel for 71 weeks, at 2d a week for them both; and

on 31 January 1743, £1 13s 8d for schooling him and Mary (probably for 101 weeks, now at 2d a week each). Probably son of Richard and Mary. [ESRO SAS/RF 15/28]

AYERS (AYRES?), Henry: Brighton charity school. Joined 'writers' class after 12 January 1702; in list of 'writers' December 1705. [BSB]

AYRES, Jacob (1693-): Brighton charity school. Joined as a reader after list of (probably) January 1702; joined 'writers' class after 12 January 1702; left before December 1705 and went 'to Sea'. Baptised 23 July 1693, son of Jacob and Barbary. [BSB; PR]

AYERST, Thomas (1774-1855): Pike's school, Robertsbridge. George Pike, his wife and his usher were Methodists, as was Ayerst. Of Newenden, Kent, Thomas was for 60 years a Methodist leader and local preacher. Died 1855, aged 81. [*Proceedings of The Wesley Historical Society* **15** part 5 p130 (1926)]

AYLING: At Midhurst grammar school 1800. At a public performance of composition and oratory, 27 May 1800, took part with 3 others in a scene from Virgil's *Aeneid*. (At the first such performance by the school, 5 November 1799, a Mr Ayling was listed amongst the gentry attending.) [*SWA* 2.6.1800, 11.11.99]

AYNSCOMBE - see also ANSCOMB

AYNSCOMBE, Esther (1737-): Mayfield charity school. Admitted at foundation 29 June 1750; may have been at the school earlier, as master paid from Michaelmas 1749; removed 28 June 1751, for non-attendance; had ¾ year as a 'writer'. Baptised 17 September 1737, daughter of Nathaniel and Elizabeth. [MSB; PR]

AYNSCOMBE, Mary (1756-): Mayfield charity school. Admitted 17 October 1766; removed 16 October 1767 as a 'reader'. Baptised 25 January 1756, 'base born Child of Elizabeth Aynscombe'. [MSB; PR]

BACON, Thomas: Grey Coat charity school, Chichester. Left between Michaelmas 1767 and Michaelmas 1768. Given 10s 6s on leaving. [WSRO Cap.V/l/l]

BACON, William: Grey Coat charity school, Chichester. Left between Michaelmas 1762 and Michaelmas 1763. Given 10s 6d on leaving. [WSRO Cap.V/l/l]

BAILEY, Edward (1788-?): Admitted Robertsbridge charity school at its opening, 5 April 1796, aged 7. Sponsored by Mr John Catt. Son of Benjamin. [ESRO PAR 477/25/1/1]

BAILEY, Elizabeth (1768-): Mayfield charity school. Admitted 7 April 1775; removed 17 July 1778, taken out by parents but 'pretty well learned'. Baptised 30 January 1768, daughter of William and Elizabeth. (Five brothers, 2 sisters, also at the school.) [MSB; PR]

BAILEY, James (1776-): Mayfield charity school. Admitted 11 July 1783; removed 17 January 1788, for non-attendance. Baptised 21 June 1776, son of William and Elizabeth. (Four brothers, 3 sisters, also at the school.) [MSB; PR]

BAILEY, John (1778-): Mayfield charity school. Admitted 7 April 1786; removed 9 July 1790. Baptised 10 March 1778, son of William and Elizabeth. (Four brothers, 3 sisters, also at the school.) [MSB; PR]

BAILEY, Katherine (1781 or 82-): Mayfield charity school. Admitted 10 July 1789; removed 5 July 1793, for non-attendance. Baptised 11 January 1782, daughter of William and Elizabeth. (Five brothers, 2 sisters, also at the school.) [MSB; PR]

BAILEY, Mary (1770-): Mayfield charity school. Admitted 17 July 1778 (when sister Elizabeth left); in lists to 18 April 1783 (no removal notice but not in 11 July 1783, when brother James admitted). Had 4¾ years at the school, 4 years as a 'writer'. Baptised 24 February 1770, daughter of William and Elizabeth. (Five brothers, 2 sisters, also at the school.) [MSB; PR]

BAILEY, Richard: Mayfield charity school. Admitted 9 July 1756, as a 'writer'; removed 6 July 1759, 'sufficiently Learned'. [MSB]

BAILEY, Richard (1774-): Mayfield charity school. First appears in lists 12 April 1782;

removed 10 April 1789, taken out by parents, after 7 years at the school. Probably baptised 22 March 1774, son of William and Elizabeth. (Another Richard baptised 3 December 1775, son of Richard and Lydia. If son of William, 4 brothers, 3 sisters, also at the school; if son of Richard, 2 brothers also at the school.) [MSB; PR]

BAILEY, Thomas: Mayfield charity school. Admitted 29 March 1751; removed 28 June 1751, for non-attendance but re-admitted same date; removed 27 December 1751, for non-attendance, but re-admitted again 27 March 1752; removed 6 July 1753, 'well learn'd, gone to Service'; he had been a 'writer' for 2 years. [MSB]

BAILEY, Thomas (1772-): Mayfield charity school. Admitted 8 January 1779; removed 9 April 1784, 'Sufficiently Learned'. Baptised 19 June 1772, son of William and Elizabeth. (Four brothers, 3 sisters, also at the school.) [MSB; PR]

BAILEY, Thomas (1778-): Mayfield charity school. Admitted 12 October 1787; removed 9 July 1790, 'Sufficiently Learned'. Baptised 2 August 1778, son of Richard and Lydia. (Brother William, perhaps brother Richard, also at the school.) [MSB; PR]

BAILEY, Thomas (1790-): Admitted Robertsbridge charity school at its opening, 5 April 1796, aged 5. Sponsored by Messrs Munn and Peters. [ESRO PAR 477/25/1/1]

BAILEY, William (1765-): Mayfield charity school. Admitted 10 April 1772; removed 13 October 1775, 'Sufficiently Learned', after 3½ years at the school, all as a 'writer'. Baptised 25 November 1765, son of William and Elizabeth. (NB Joined at same time as John Ashby, also aged 6. Four brothers, 3 sisters, also at the school.) [MSB; PR]

BAILEY, William (1773-): Mayfield charity school. Admitted October 1781; removed 9 July 1784, for non-attendance. Baptised 9 May 1773, son of Richard and Lydia. (Brother Thomas, perhaps brother Richard, also at the school.) [MSB; PR]

BAILEY, William (1788-): Mayfield charity

school. Admitted 12 April 1799; removed 8 April 1803, taken out by parents. Baptised 2 March 1788, son of William and Edith. [MSB; PR]

BAKER, Benjamin: Mayfield charity school. Admitted 6 July 1753; removed 11 July 1755, taken out by parents, after 2 years at the school, 1½ years as a 'writer'. [MSB]

BAKER, Eunice (1751-): Mayfield charity school. Admitted 14 October 1763; removed 18 October 1765, for non-attendance. Baptised 14 March 1751, daughter of George and Elizabeth. (Brother George, sister Kezia, also at the school.) [MSB; PR]

BAKER, Fanny: Mayfield charity school. Admitted 11 July 1783; removed 7 July 1786, 'Sufficiently Learned'. (NB Fanny baptised 29 November 1778, daughter of Robert and Mary, assumed too young - would have been admitted at 4 years, 'sufficiently learned' at 7.) [MSB; PR]

BAKER, George (1753-): Mayfield charity school. Admitted 14 October 1763; removed 19 April 1765, for non-attendance; re-admitted 18 October 1765; removed 17 October 1766, for non-attendance after 2½ years in total at the school, ½ year as a 'writer'. Baptised 23 April 1753, son of George and Elizabeth. (Sisters Eunice, Kezia, also at the school.) [MSB; PR]

BAKER, Henrietta (1753-): At Seaford charity school 1765. Daughter of Thomas Baker, junior. Baptised 23 December 1753, daughter of Thomas and Sarah. [BL Add MS 33,059; PR]

BAKER, James: Midhurst charity school. Admitted as charity scholar, 1793. [*HMGS*]

BAKER, Job: Mayfield charity school. Admitted 7 July 1786; removed 10 April 1789, for non-attendance. [MSB]

BAKER, John: Saunders' charity school, Rye. In lists from 15 October 1740 (not in 9 July 1740) to June 1743 (?) (not in 26 October 1743). Son of William. [RSB]

BAKER, John (1758-): Saunders' charity school, Rye. Admitted 6 May 1767; left Lady

Day 1769. Baptised 15 May 1758, son of John and Mary. (Brother Thomas also at the school.) [RSB; PR]

BAKER, Kezia (1749-): Mayfield charity school. Admitted 14 October 1763; removed 2 May 1766, still a 'reader', taken out by parents. Baptised 30 April 1749, daughter of George and Elizabeth. (Brother George, sister Eunice, also at the school. NB Baptised 1 February 1772, Stephen a base-born son of Kezia Baker.) [MSB; PR]

BAKER, Samuel (1746-): Sedlescombe charity school. In lists 3 May 1755, 10 April 1758, (started 'writing' 8 May 1758), 22 February 1759. Baptised 28 November 1746, son of Samuel and Elizabeth. [SSB; PR]

BAKER, Thomas (1760-): Saunders' charity school, Rye. Admitted 3 May 1769; in lists to Christmas 1770 (not in midsummer 1773, next surviving list). Baptised 9 March 1760, son of John and Mary. (Brother John also at the school.) [RSB; PR]

BAKER, William (1750-): At Seaford charity school 1765. Baptised 9 November 1750, son of William and Mary. [BL Add MS 33,059; PR]

BAKER, William: Mayfield charity school. Admitted 11 July 1800; removed 14 October 1803, taken out by parents. [MSB]

BALCOMB, David (1791-): Mayfield charity school. Admitted 11 April 1800; removed 6 April 1804, taken out by parents. Baptised 31 July 1791, son of David and Elizabeth. (Sister Elizabeth also at the school.) [MSB; PR]

BALCOMB, Elizabeth (1789-): Mayfield charity school. Originally admitted 12 July 1799 but not in 18 October 1799 list, when admitted again (so probably did not join until October); removed 9 April 1802, taken out by parents. Baptised 4 May 1789, daughter of David and Elizabeth. (Brother David also at the school.) [MSB; PR]

(**BALCOMBE, M.**): Taught arithmetic by Mr Pointin, visiting tutor from Henfield, 1722. This arranged by Thomas Marchant, yeoman of Hurstpierpoint, when he arranged for his daughter Bett to be taught. [*SAC* **25**]

BALCOMBE, William: In 1719 Thomas Marchant of Hurstpierpoint paid Abraham Muzzell 7s 6d for his schooling. [*SAC* **25**]

BALDOCK, Benjamin (1771-): Mayfield charity school. Admitted 10 April 1778; removed 18 April 1783, taken out by parents 'and Sufficiently Learned', after 5 years at the school, 3 years as a 'writer'. Baptised 24 November 1771, son of Thomas and Elizabeth. (Brothers Oliver, Thomas, also at the school.) [MSB; PR]

BALDOCK, Oliver (1776-): Mayfield charity school. Admitted 7 April 1786; removed 8 April 1791, 'taken out some Time since by his parents' (he is in 7 January 1791 list). Baptised 14 July 1776, son of Thomas and Elizabeth. (Brothers Benjamin, Thomas, also at the school.) [MSB; PR]

BALDOCK, Thomas (1774-): Mayfield charity school. Admitted 18 April 1783 (also admitted 11 July 1783, probably assigned to different charity source on expansion of school); removed 7 April 1786. Baptised 8 January 1775, son of Thomas and Elizabeth. (Brothers Benjamin, Oliver, also at the school.) [MSB; PR]

BALDWIN: Grey Coat charity school, Chichester. Given 10s 6d on leaving, 3 May 1773. [WSRO Cap.V/1/1]

BALDWIN, William: Grey Coat charity school, Chichester. Left between Michaelmas 1766 and Michaelmas 1767. Given 10s 6d on leaving. [WSRO Cap.V/1/1]

BALDY: Brighton girls' charity school. Admitted when school opened, 30 September 1702. 'Widow Baldy's daughter'. (One of Mary, baptised 23 November 1690, daughter of Francis; Joanna, baptised 26 October 1693, daughter of Francis and Joanna; or Sarah, baptised 20 October 1695, daughter of Francis and Hannah. Brother Francis at the boys' charity school.) [BSB; PR]

BALDY, Francis (1688-): Brighton charity school. In 'writers' list 12 January 1702; had left by December 1705 and been 'apprenticed'

(trade not given). Baptised 9 December 1688, son of Francis and Hannah (née Grinsted). (A sister was at the girls' charity school.) [BSB; PR]

BALLARD, Ann: Eastbourne charity school. Admitted Lady Day 1778; there at Christmas 1779. [SAS Budgen MS v.117]

BANKS, Winefred (1742-94): A poor girl, Alciston parish paid for her to be schooled by dames 1749-54. Baptised 24 July 1742, daughter of Thomas and Ann, her father died January 1746, when she was 3½. She, her brother Thomas and her mother were supported by the parish. In 1750 the parish arranged and paid for Ann's second marriage, to Thomas Baker; the Bakers were removed to another parish, but Alciston continued to look after the 2 children. The parish paid for Winefred's keep, clothes and some schooling, laying out in total £15 4s 7d (£10 4s 4½d on keep, £3 16s 4½d on clothing, 14s 1½d on schooling, 9s 9d on a doctor); the last 'schooling' payment, in January 1760 (when Winefred was 17 years) was 4s 'for Six Pounds of Tier [ie flax] for to larne Wine Banks to spin'. She did not marry. When 45, she again appeared in the poor book; in 1788 and 1789 the parish paid for her keep and some clothes; in March 1794 they paid 11s 6d for a pair of sheets for her, and later that month for her burial (20 March 1794, aged 51). [ESRO PAR 227/31/1; PR]

(BANNISTER): Eastbourne charity school. Admitted Lady Day 1779; there at Christmas 1779. [SAS Budgen MS v.117]

BANNISTER, Ann (1758-): Eastbourne charity school. Admitted 11 April 1768; still there January 1771. Baptised 26 October 1758, daughter of John and Anne. [SAS Budgen MS v.105; PR]

BANNISTER, James (1726-): At Eastbourne charity school 1734. Baptised 12 August 1726, son of James and Ann. (Brother John also at the school.) [Chatsworth, Devonshire Collection, Compton Place, Box P; PR]

BANNISTER, John (1732-): At Eastbourne charity school April 1741. Baptised 10 April 1732, son of James and Ann. (Brother James also at the school.) [SAS Budgen MS v.129;

PR]

BARDEN, William (1789-): Admitted Fermor's charity school, Rotherfield, 14 May 1797. Baptised 19 July 1789, son of Thomas and Frances. [ESRO PAR 465/4/1; PR]

BARNARD: A poor girl of West Grinstead, daughter of John, who received schooling, 1724, under the Dowlin charity. [WSRO Par 95/l/1/3]

(BARNARD): One or more Barnard children of West Grinstead who received schooling, 1730, under the Dowlin charity. [WSRO Par 95/1/1/3]

BARNARD, John: At Eastbourne charity school 1734. [Chatsworth, Devonshire Collection, Compton Place, Box P]

BARNS, John: Saunders' charity school, Rye. In lists from 8 October 1735 (not in 2 July 1735) to 7 April 1736 (20 October 1736 notes 'left the school'). Son of William, deceased. [RSB]

BARNES, William (c1703-): Grey Coat charity school, Chichester. Admitted between Lady Day 1712 and Lady Day 1713, aged 9; there Lady Day 1714. [WSRO Cap.V/1/1]

BARNET: Brighton girls' charity school. Admitted when school opened, 30 September 1702. 'Widow Barnet's daughter'. [BSB]

BARRY, Willoughby (1707-): Lewes grammar school. Son of George, surgeon. To St John's College, Cambridge, 1719; MB 1725, MD 1728. [*Al. Cant.*]

BARTLETT, James: Saunders' charity school, Rye. In lists from 10 January 1739 (not in 4 October 1738) to 15 October 1740 (7 January 1741 notes 'left the school'). Son of Richard. (Brother John also at the school.) [RSB]

BARTLETT, John: Saunders' charity school, Rye. In lists from 20 October 1736 (not in 7 April 1736) to 5 October 1737 (11 January 1738 notes 'left the school'). Son of Richard. (Brother James also at the school.) [RSB]

BARTON, Thomas (1704-61): At Lewes

grammar school. Of Sussex. Admitted pensioner (age 17) Peterhouse, Cambridge, 15 January 1722. Scholar 1722; BA 1726; fellow 1726; MA 1729. Ordained deacon (Ely) 21 December 1729; priest (Chichester) 4 June 1732. Rector of Warbleton 1732 to death. Married Catherine (-1749); children: Thomas (1734-35), Thomas (1738-), Henry (1739-), John (1741-), Catherine (1742-), Frances (-1743), Frances (1744-45). Died 2 January 1761 (buried 6 January, aged 56). [*Al. Cant.*; CI; PR]

BARTTELOT, George (1788-1872): At Midhurst grammar school 1793 (NB very young for grammar school?). Later in life, of Stopham; father of Sir Walter, first baronet. [*HMGS*]

BASSETT: At Mayfield school in 1759. The master, Walter Gale, recorded in diary 14 April 1759: 'I was called upon by Bassett, who came to quarrel with me on account of my correcting his boy for some enormous crimes he had been guilty of, all which he foolishly denied at first, and insisted upon it that his boy was unjustly corrected; yet in the end he confessed everything that the boy was beat for.' There was no Bassett boy at the charity school at that time and he was clearly one of Gale's private pupils. [*SAC* 9, 204; MSB]

BASSETT, Elizabeth (1783-): Mayfield charity school. Admitted 15 October 1790; removed 10 April 1795, taken out by parents. Baptised 26 October 1783, daughter of Jane Bassett [sic]. [MSB; PR]

BASSETT, John (1756-): Mayfield charity school. Admitted 9 July 1762; removed 26 October 1764, 'Suspended to make room for others', after 2¼ years at the school and just become a 'writer'. Baptised 7 March 1756, son of John and Mary. (Brother Joseph also at the school.) [MSB; PR]

BASSETT, John (removed Mayfield charity school 1793) - see **MARTIN, John**

BASSETT, John (1783-): Admitted Fermor's charity school, Rotherfield, 3 May 1794. Baptised 20 October 1783, son of William and Mary. [ESRO PAR 465/4/1; PR]

BASSETT, Joseph (1757?-): Mayfield charity school. Admitted 18 October 1765; removed 2 May 1766, 'think him not intitled to ye Charity'; then a 'reader'. Baptised 10 January 1758, son of John and Mary. (Brother John also at the school.) [MSB; PR]

BASSETT, Joseph (1770-): Mayfield charity school. Admitted 6 March 1781; removed 15 October 1784, 'Sufficiently Learned'. Baptised 14 December 1770, son of Joseph and Ann. (Brother Thomas, probably sister Mary, also at the school.) [MSB; PR]

BASSETT, Mary (1775?-): Mayfield charity school. Admitted 7 July 1786; removed 8 January 1790, 'Sufficiently Learned'. Probably baptised 21 June 1775, daughter of Joseph and Ann. (Another Mary baptised 22 August 1774, daughter of Stephen and Abigail, but Mary baptised 1775 probably correct as brothers Joseph and Thomas also at the school.) [MSB; PR]

BASSETT, Stephen: Mayfield charity school. Admitted 10 April 1789; removed 15 October 1790, for non-attendance. [MSB]

BASSET, Thomas: Brighton charity school. Joined some time after 'readers' list of (probably) January 1702; in list of 'readers' December 1705. [BSB]

BASSETT, Thomas (1772-): Mayfield charity school. Admitted 6 July 1781; removed 14 January 1785, 'Sufficiently Learned'. Baptised 5 January 1773, son of Joseph and Ann. (Brother Joseph, probably sister Mary, also at the school.) [MSB; PR]

BASSETT, William (1782-): Admitted Fermor's charity school, Rotherfield, 3 May 1794. Baptised 27 October 1782, son of William and Sarah. [ESRO PAR 465/4/1; PR]

BATCHELOR, John (1725-): Saunders' charity school, Rye. In lists from 25 October 1732 (not in 5 July 1732) to 28 June 1738 (?) (4 October 1738 notes 'left the school'). Baptised 14 February 1725, son of John and Mary. (Brother William also at the school.) [RSB; PR]

BATCHELOR, William (1738-): Saunders'

charity school, Rye. In lists from Christmas 1747 (not in Michaelmas 1747) to 15 January 1752, when marked 'December 7'. Baptised 29 September 1738, son of John and Mary. (Brother John also at the school.) [RSB; PR]

BATES, Henry: Saunders' charity school, Rye. In lists from 25 March 1747 (not in Christmas 1746) to 3 April 1751, which notes 'Absent 14 weeks' (not in midsummer 1751). Son of Henry. [RSB]

BAYSHAW, Mary: At Cocking charity school 1733. [WSRO Par 53/12/l]

BAYSHAW, William: At Cocking charity school 1732. [WSRO Par 53/12/l]

BEACH, Henry (1698-): Brighton charity school. Added at end of 'readers' list December 1705 (ie joined subsequently). Probably baptised 28 July 1698, son of Richard. (Another Henry Beach born 21 March 1699, baptised 26 April 1699, son of Stone, but son of Richard more probable as Henry and Richard son of Richard (1700-) next to each other in list. Another Henry Beach baptised 14 June 1691, son of George and Mary probably too old for this school.) [BSB; PR]

BEACH, Michael (1688-): Brighton charity school. In list of 'writers' 12 January 1702; left before December 1705 and went 'to sea'. Baptised 30 September 1688, son of Thomas and Mary (née Glover). [BSB; PR]

BEACH, Richard (1693-): Brighton charity school. Admitted after 'readers' list of (probably) January 1702; in 'readers' list December 1705. Baptised 5 February 1693, son of Richard and Susanna (née Persi). (NB 'Readers' list of December 1705 includes another Richard Beach - see Richard Beach (1700-) - also son of Richard. Assumed the 2 fathers different Richards, the elder, father of Richard Beach (1693-), probably baptised 11 May 1656, son of Thomas junior and Ann, the younger, father of Richard Beach (1700-), probably baptised 8 September 1667, son of Henry and Joan.) [BSB; PR]

BEACH, Richard (1700-): Brighton charity school. Added at end of 'readers' list December 1705 (ie joined subsequently). Baptised 7

March 1700, son of Richard. (Brother Henry probably also at the school. NB 'Readers' list December 1705 included another Richard Beach: see Richard Beach (1693-).) [BSB; PR]

BEALE, Edward (1752-): Mayfield charity school. Admitted 6 July 1759; removed 14 October 1763, 'Sufficiently Learn'd'; re-admitted 6 July 1764 but removed 26 October 1764, 'Sufficiently Learned', after 4½ years in total at the school, 2¼ years as a 'writer'. Baptised 24 May 1752, son of Abraham and Mary. [MSB; PR]

BEALE, Elizabeth (1783-): Mayfield charity school. Admitted 9 April 1790; removed 11 April 1794. Baptised 23 March 1783, daughter of Joseph and Elizabeth. (Brother Joseph, sisters Isabella, Sarah, also at the school.) [MSB; PR]

BEALE, Isabella (1787-): Mayfield charity school. Admitted 7 July 1797; removed 11 April 1800. Baptised 25 December 1787, daughter of Joseph and Elizabeth. (Brother Joseph, sisters Elizabeth, Sarah, also at the school.) [MSB; PR]

BEALE, Joseph (1751-): Mayfield charity school. Admitted 17 October 1760; removed 8 January 1762, 'To make Room for those having more Occasion'; re-admitted 6 July 1764 but removed 26 October 1764, 'sufficiently Learned', after 1½ years in total at the school, 1 year as a 'writer'. Baptised either February 1751, son of John and Mary, or 27 September 1751, son of Joseph and Elizabeth. [MSB; PR]

BEALE, Joseph (1772-): Mayfield charity school. Admitted 11 July 1783; removed 7 July 1786, 'Sufficiently Learned'. Baptised 6 December 1772, son of John and Mary. (Brother Thomas also at the school.) [MSB; PR]

BEALE, Joseph (1781-): Mayfield charity school. Admitted 8 January 1790; removed 5 July 1793, for non-attendance. Baptised 15 July 1781, son of Joseph and Elizabeth. (Sisters Elizabeth, Isabella, Sarah, also at the school.) [MSB; PR]

BEALE, Sarah (1785-): Mayfield charity

school. Admitted 11 April 1794; removed 8 January 1796, 'Taken into the Workhouse'. Baptised 22 May 1785, daughter of Joseph and Elizabeth. (Brother Joseph, sisters Elizabeth, Isabella, also at the school.) [MSB; PR]

BEALE, Thomas (1775-): Mayfield charity school. Admitted 15 October 1784; removed 10 April 1789, for non-attendance. Baptised 19 March 1775, son of John and Mary. (Brother Joseph also at the school.) [MSB; PR]

BEAN - see also BENEY

BEAN, John (1744-): Saunders' charity school, Rye. In lists from 4 July 1753 (not in 28 March 1753); left school 28 February 1757. Baptised 15 September 1744, son of John and Elizabeth. [RSB; PR]

BEAUMONT, William: Brighton charity school. Given prayer book 1715. [BSB]

BEAVIS (BEVIS), Elizabeth (1773-): Sedlescombe charity school. There 29 September 1784 and 29 September 1786 (still a 'reader'). Baptised 5 September 1773, Elizabeth Reeve daughter of Mary Beavis. [SSB; PR]

BECKETT, Nicholas (1759-): Eastbourne charity school. Admitted 15 June 1770; there 1771. Baptised 31 January 1759, son of Samuel (-1770) and Susanna. [SAS Budgen MS v.105; PR]

BECKET (BACKAT), William (1726-): At Eastbourne charity school 1734. Baptised 7 August 1726, son of William and Mary. [Chatsworth, Devonshire Collection, Compton Place, Box P]

BEECHING, Henry (1759-): Saunders' charity school, Rye. Admitted 15 May 1771; in lists to Michaelmas 1774, which notes 'Left School'. Baptised 22 August 1759, son of Coleman and Mary. (Brothers John, Thomas, also at the school.) [RSB; PR]

BEECHING, John (1756-): Saunders' charity school, Rye. Admitted 29 June 1768; in lists to Christmas 1770 (not in midsummer 1773, next surviving list). Baptised 27 December 1756, son of Coleman and Mary. (Brothers Henry,

Thomas, also at the school.) [RSB; PR]

BEECHING, John Coleman (1760-): Saunders' charity school, Rye. Admitted 11 January 1769; in lists to Michaelmas 1773 (not in midsummer 1774, next list). Baptised 15 May 1760, son of John and Elizabeth. [RSB; PR]

BEECHING, Thomas (1750-): Saunders' charity school, Rye. In lists from midsummer 1759 (not in 4 April 1759) to Michaelmas 1763 (not in Christmas 1764, next surviving list). Baptised 14 November 1750, son of Coleman and Mary. (Brothers Henry, John, also at the school.) [RSB; PR]

BELTON, John (1692-): Brighton charity school. In 'writers' list 12 January 1702; left by December 1705 and went 'to husbandry'. Baptised 3 April 1692, son of John and Martha (née Greener). [BSB; PR]

BENEY/BENE/BEANY -see also BEAN

BENEY (BENE, BEANEY), Barbara (1778-): Mayfield charity school. Admitted 17 January 1788; removed 9 July 1790. Baptised 15 February 1778, daughter of William and Elle. (Five brothers also at the school.) [MSB; PR]

BENEY (BENE, BEANY), Benjamin (1775-): Mayfield charity school. Admitted 9 April 1784; removed 6 July 1787, taken out by parents. Baptised 26 December 1775, son of William and Elle. (Four brothers and a sister, also at the school.) [MSB; PR]

BENEY (BENE), Henry (1784-): Mayfield charity school. Admitted 5 July 1793; removed 11 July 1794, for non-attendance. Baptised 17 December 1784, son of Thomas and Sylvestra. [MSB; PR]

BENEY (BEANY), James (1765-): Mayfield charity school. Admitted 9 July 1773; removed 7 January 1774, 'By desire of parents, to work in shaving Hoppoles etc'; re-admitted 8 April 1774; removed 11 April 1777, for non-attendance, after 3½ years in total at the school, 1½ years as a 'writer'. Baptised 22 September 1765, son of William and Elle. (Four brothers and a sister, also at the school.) [MSB; PR]

BENEY (BEANY), John (1768-): Mayfield charity school. Admitted 5 July 1775; removed 17 July 1778, taken out by parents but 'pretty well learned', after 3 years at the school, ¾ year as a 'writer'. Baptised 5 June 1768, son of William and Elle. (Four brothers and a sister, also at the school.) [MSB; PR]

BENEY (BEANY), Thomas (1763-): Mayfield charity school. Admitted 21 July 1769; removed 9 July 1773, for non-attendance after 4 years at the school, 1¼ years as a 'writer'. Baptised 26 December 1763, son of William and Elle. (Four brothers and a sister, also at the school.) [MSB; PR]

BENEY (BEANY), William (1772-): Mayfield charity school. Admitted 17 July 1778; removed 6 July 1781, taken out by parents. Baptised 1 March 1772, son of William and Elle. (Four brothers and a sister, also at the school.) [MSB; PR]

BENEY, William: Admitted Robertsbridge charity school at its opening, 5 April 1796. Sponsored by William Boys, esq. [ESRO PAR 477/25/1/1]

BENNET: In May 1766 Winchelsea parish paid Mr Hogsflesh £1 10s 'for 1 Years School for young Bennet Sutus & Sidger'; for each of the church years 1767-68, 1768-69, they also paid him £1 10s, probably for the same 3 boys. [ESRO PAR 511/31/1/1]

BENNET, Elizabeth (1787-): Admitted Robertsbridge charity school at its opening, 5 April 1796, aged 8. Sponsored by Mr John Hilder. Baptised 15 July 1787, daughter of James and Biddy (née Bailey). [ESRO PAR 477/25/1/1; Salehurst PR]

BERRY, James (1782-): Mayfield charity school. Admitted 11 October 1793; removed 6 January 1797, taken out by parents. Baptised 3 November 1782, son of Richard and Elizabeth. (Sister Mary also at the school.) [MSB; PR]

BERRY, Mary (1784-): Mayfield charity school. Admitted 11 October 1793; in lists to 8 January 1796, omitted in list for 8 April 1796, no removal recorded but another takes her place. Baptised 24 October 1784, daughter of Richard and Elizabeth. (Brother James also at the school.) [MSB; PR]

BERRY, William: Mayfield charity school. No admission but in list of 9 January 1795 takes the place, in same position in list, of William Rose, for whom no removal [qv], perhaps same person; removed 8 April 1796, taken out by parents. [MSB]

BIGGS, William: Grey Coat charity school, Chichester, from its opening Lady Day 1710. Left between Lady Day 1711 and Lady Day 1712. [WSRO Cap.V/1/1]

BICKNELL -see BIGNAIL (BIGNAL)

BIGNAIL, John: Mayfield charity school. Admitted 9 April 1779; removed October 1781, taken out by parents. [MSB]

BIGNAIL (BICKNELL), Nicholas (1777 or 78-): Mayfield charity school. Admitted 7 July 1786; removed 9 April 1790, taken out by parents but 'Sufficiently Learned'. Baptised 11 January 1778, son of Thomas and Elizabeth Bicknell. (Sister Susanna also at the school.) [MSB; PR]

BIGNAL (BICKNELL), Susanna (1775-): Mayfield charity school. Admitted 9 April 1784; in lists to 11 July 1788; in list for 17 October 1788 her name is crossed through and another written in. Baptised 2 May 1775, daughter of Thomas and Elizabeth Bicknell. (Brother Nicholas also at the school.) [MSB; PR]

BINSTED: Grey Coat charity school, Chichester. Left between Michaelmas 1762 and Michaelmas 1763. Given 10s 6d on leaving. [WSRO Cap.V/1/1]

BIRDIT, John (1721-): Saunders' charity school, Rye. In lists from 31 March 1731 (not in 6 January 1731) to 4 July 1733 (not in 2 January 1734). Returned in lists 5 April 1738 (father now dead; not in 11 January 1738) to 3 October 1739 (6 February 1740 notes 'left the school'). Baptised 6 August 1721, son of John and Elizabeth Burdet. (Brothers Josiah, Thomas, also at the school.) [RSB; PR]

BIRDIT, Josiah (1719-30): Saunders' charity school, Rye. In lists from 25 June 1729 (not in

2 April 1729 (?)) to 1 April 1730; list of 22 July 1730 notes 'Josiah son of John Burdit is Dead'. Baptised 23 September 1719, son of John and Elizabeth Burdett. (Brothers John, Thomas, also at the school.) [RSB; PR]

BIRDIT, Thomas (1717-): Saunders' charity school, Rye. In lists from 19 May 1725 (not in January 1725 (?)) to 31 March 1731 (7 July 1731 notes 'Thomas Birdit at Service'). Baptised 23 August 1717, son of John and Elizabeth Burdett. (Brothers John, Josiah, also at the school.) [RSB; PR]

BISHOPP, George: son of George and Mary (née Frewen, born 1673), he attended uncle Rev Thankful Frewen's school at Northiam, 28 April 1712 to November 1716. A record of the classics he studied survives. His mother paid £2 per annum for his schooling, with ½ guinea gratuities at times. [ESRO FRE 533; Warne, H. M. *A Catalogue of the Frewen Archives* (1972)]

BISHOP, Henry (1789-): Admitted Fermor's charity school, Rotherfield, 14 May 1797. Baptised 11 October 1789, son of William and Martha. [ESRO PAR 465/4/1; Buxted PR]

BISHOP, J. (1708?-): Brighton charity school. Given prayer book 1718. Probably baptised 15 February 1708, John son of John and Joan (Joseph, son of John, baptised 28 January 1711, perhaps too young). [BSB; PR]

BISHOP, John (1779-): Mayfield charity school. Admitted 8 January 1790; removed 10 January 1794. Baptised 27 March 1779, son of William and Mary. (Brother Thomas also at the school.) [MSB; PR]

BISHOP, Thomas (1787-): Admitted Robertsbridge charity school at its opening, 5 April 1796, aged 9. Sponsored by William Boys, esq. Baptised 4 March 1787, son of James and Mary. [ESRO PAR 477/25/1/1; Salehurst PR]

BISHOP, Thomas (1790-): Mayfield charity school. Admitted 12 April 1799; removed 6 April 1804, taken out by parents. Baptised 15 August 1790, son of William and Mary. (Brother John also at the school.) [MSB; PR]

BLAGDEN, senior: Midhurst grammar school. At school's first public performance of composition and oratory, 5 November 1799, he took part with 2 others in a scene from Milton's *Paradise Lost*, speaking the role of Belial. [*SWA* 11.11.99]

BLAGDEN, junior: At Midhurst grammar school 1799. Inferred from reference to 'Blagden senior' [qv].

BLUNDELL, Henry (1786-): Admitted Robertsbridge charity school at its opening, 5 April 1796. Sponsored by Mr John Cruttenden. Baptised 27 October 1786, son of Stephen and Elizabeth (née Beeney). [ESRO PAR 477/25/1/1; Salehurst PR]

BLUNT, Ann (1785-): Admitted Robertsbridge charity school at its opening, 5 April 1796, aged 10. Sponsored by Mr Thomas Tyrrell. Baptised 7 August 1785, daughter of Thomas and Ann (née Oliver). [ESRO PAR 477/25/1/1; Salehurst PR]

BLUNT, Harry (1767-): Steyning grammar school. John Baker's diary gives: 14 October 1774, 'stopt and spoke with little Harry Blunt at door of school and Mrs Baker, the Master's wife, with him'; 14 February 1775, 'went to Steyning and dined at Chequers; sent for little Harry Blunt who came and dined with us'; 24 April 1775, 'came Mr Scawen and Mr Blunt, who had been to Steyning in Mr Blunt's chaise and two horses (Mr Scawen drove) to Mr Baker's school at Steyning in with little Harry Blunt and Master Purdy, six years old. Have never been out to school before.' Last reference is to Purdy; Harry Blunt was born 1767, son of Samuel by his second wife, and so 7 or 8 in 1775. Later married Mary Atkinson. [Yorke, P. C. *The Diary of John Baker* (1931); *SAC* **52**]

BOANJES, Mary: At Rotherfield workhouse school, 6 January 1772. [ESRO PAR 465/4/1]

BODLE, Abraham: Sedlescombe charity school. There 29 September 1784, 29 September 1786, 29 September 1787 (still a 'reader'). [SSB]

BONES, Ann (1768-): Mayfield charity school. Admitted 11 April 1777; removed 7 April 1780, for non-attendance after 3 years at the school, 1 year as a 'writer'. Baptised 20 October 1768, daughter of John and Sarah. (Brother Thomas also at the school.) [MSB; PR]

BONES, John: Mayfield charity school. Admitted 11 October 1793; removed 11 April 1794. [MSB]

BONES, (Stephen?) (1790?-): Admitted Fermor's charity school, Rotherfield, 5 June 1796, 'son of John Bones'. Probably Stephen, baptised 21 November 1790, son of John and Sarah ('poor'). [ESRO PAR 465/4/1; PR]

BONES, Thomas (1770-): Mayfield charity school. Admitted 11 April 1777 (with sister Ann); removed 30 July 1779, for non-attendance, still a 'reader'. Baptised 15 April 1770, son of John and Sarah. [MSB; PR]

BOON, Mary: Brighton girls' charity school. Admitted at some time after 25 March 1703 (probably before end of 1705). [BSB]

BOON, Richard (1694-): Brighton charity school. In list of 'readers' of (probably) January 1702; given coat and hat July 1702; in list of 'writers' December 1705. Baptised 12 April 1694, son of Richard and Elizabeth (née Cobby). Father, baptised 18 August 1767, son of William, was master of the *Thomas and Elizabeth* in 1726. [BSB; PR; Tibble, R., pers. comm.]

BOORE, Charles (1773-): Lord Pelham's charity school, Lewes [qv Rand's school]. Admitted Lady Day 1784. There 10 October 1784, 'aged 10' in list. Probably baptised 8 January 1773, son of Charles and Hannah. [ESRO AMS 6005; All Saints Lewes PR]

BOORE, George (1774-); Lord Pelham's charity school, Lewes [qv Rand's school]. Admitted Michaelmas 1783. There 10 October 1784 (but crossed through in list and probably left soon after); 'aged 11' in list. Probably born 9 October 1774, son of Charles and Hannah. [ESRO AMS 6005; All Saints Lewes PR]

BOOTS, John (c1700-): Grey Coat charity school, Chichester, from its opening, Lady Day 1710. Aged 10 at Lady Day 1711. Between Lady Day 1712 and Lady Day 1713 transferred

'Into ye other School' (ie the Oliver Whitby boarding charity school, then run by the same master). [WSRO Cap.V/1/1]

BOOTS (ROOTS?), Josias: Sedlescombe charity school. There 21 October 1793 (a 'writer') and 20 October 1794. (NB 'Roots' occur in Sedlescombe parish register.) [SSB]

BORRER, William (1781-1862): Born at Henfield 13 June 1781, eldest son of William Borrer, esq, who moved to Pakyn's Manor, Hurstpierpoint, and was in 1802 High Sheriff of Sussex. Received early education at a mixed school at Hurstpierpoint; at 13 or 14 moved to John Morphew at Carshalton, Surrey. Became noted botanist; elected to Linnaean Society 1805. At 29, married daughter of Nathaniel Hill, esq, banker of Brighton. Became resident of Henfield and died there, 10 January 1862, aged 80. [Lower *Worthies*]

BOURNE, Thomas (1747-): Saunders' charity school, Rye. In list of 7 April 1756 as an addendum, then in lists to Michaelmas 1760 (not in Christmas 1760). Baptised 29 October 1747, son of Edward and Tabitha. [RSB; PR]

BOWYER, Thomas (1747-): Mayfield charity school. Admitted 11 April 1760; removed 11 July 1760, 'suspended for Non Appearance', after ¼ year as a 'reader'. Baptised 5 November 1747, son of Joseph and Sarah. [MSB; PR]

BOXAL: Lord Pelham's charity school, Lewes [qv Rand's school]. Added to list of 10 October 1784. [ESRO AMS 6005]

BOXALL, James (1785-): Petworth charity school. Admitted 10 December 1797; had left by Michaelams 1801. Baptised 28 December 1785, son of John and Hannah. [WSRO Petworth House Archives 1763; PR]

BOYS, James: Brighton charity school. In list of 'readers' of (probably) January 1702; given coat and hat July 1702; joined 'writers' class sometime after 12 January 1702; had left by December 1705 and gone 'to sea'. [BSB]

BOYS, Ruth (1694-): Brighton girls' charity school. Admitted when school opened, 30 September 1702. 'Mary Boys' daughter'.

Baptised 8 January 1694, daughter of George and Mary. [BSB; PR]

BRAD, John (1714-): Saunders' charity school, Rye. In lists from 11 August 1725 (not in June 1725 (?)) to 5 October 1726 (11 January 1727 notes 'Absent from Scholl'). 'Son of Rob Brad, Doser Maker'. Baptised 28 February 1714, son of Robert and Ann. (Brother Robert also at the school.) [RSB; PR]

BRAD, John (1718-): Saunders' charity school, Rye. In lists from June 1725 (?) (not in 19 May 1725, in 11 August 1725) to 4 July 1733 (not in 2 January 1734). 'Son of the Deceased Robert Brad'. Baptised 22 March 1718, son of Robert Bradd, seaman, and Mary. Father buried 23 October 1720. [RSB; PR]

BRAD, Robert (1710-): Saunders' charity school, Rye. In lists from September 1722 (?) (first list) to January 1725 (?) (not in 19 May 1725). 'Son of Robert Brad Dosser Maker'. Baptised 1 October 1710, son of Robert and Anne. (Brother John also at the school.) [RSB; PR]

(BRADFORD): Eastbourne charity school. Admitted June 1772. [SAS Budgen MS v.105]

BRADFORD, Peter (1724-): At Eastbourne charity school 1734. Baptised 7 May 1724, son of Peter and Mary. [Chatsworth, Devonshire Collection, Compton Place, Box P; PR]

BRAN, Richard (1691-): Brighton charity school. In list of 'writers' 12 January 1702; had left by December 1705 and gone 'to sea'. Baptised 7 June 1691, son of Thomas and Elizabeth (née West). [BSB; PR]

BRAPPELL, William (1692 or 93-): Brighton charity school. Admitted as 'reader' after list of (probably) January 1702; had left by December 1705. Baptised either 11 September 1692, son of Thomas and Elizabeth (née Vezer), or 20 August 1693, son of William and Elizabeth. [BSB; PR]

BRAZIER, James (1751-): Saunders' charity school, Rye. In lists from Michaelmas 1761 (not in Lady Day 1761); left school 26 January 1765. Baptised 7 May 1751, son of James and Mary. [RSB; PR]

BREADEN, John: Eastbourne charity school. There December 1738 (?) and April 1741. [SAS Budgen MS v. 129]

BREADS, Edward: Saunders' charity school, Rye. In lists from 25 March 1752 (not in 15 January 1752) to midsummer 1756, in which marked 'Left School'. Son of John, deceased. (Probably brother James also at the school.) [RSB]

BREADS, James (1739-): Saunders' charity school, Rye. In lists from Michaelmas 1748 (not in midsummer 1748); left school 6 October 1752. Son of John, deceased. Baptised 1 August 1739, son of John and Elizabeth. (Probably brother Edward also at the school.) [RSB; PR]

BREADS, Joseph (1716-): Saunders' charity school, Rye. In lists from 19 April 1727 (not in 11 January 1727) to 6 January 1731 (not in 31 March 1731). Son of Thomas, who died between lists of 22 July 1730 and 14 October 1730. Baptised 19 February 1716, son of Thomas and Jude. (Brothers Mark, Thomas, also at the school.) [RSB; PR]

BREADS, Mark (1713-): Saunders' charity school, Rye. In lists from June 1725 (?) (not in 19 May 1725; in 11 August 1725) to 29 June 1726 (5 October 1726 notes 'left the school'). Baptised 11 November 1713, son of Thomas and Judith. (Father died 1730 - see BREADS, Joseph. Brothers Joseph, Thomas, also at the school.) [RSB; PR]

BREADS, Thomas (1711-): Saunders' charity school, Rye. In lists from September 1722 (?) (first list) to 8 April 1724 (not in January 1725 (?)). Baptised 2 August 1711, son of Thomas and Judith. (Father died 1730 - see BREADS, Joseph. Brothers Joseph, Mark, also at the school.) [RSB; PR]

BREADS, William (1714-): Saunders' charity school, Rye. In lists from 19 May 1725 (not in April 1725 (?)); 19 April 1727 notes 'gon to serve an aprentice-ship'; not in 12 July 1727 or 4 October 1727, but returned in 10 January 1728; 17 April 1728 notes 'left the School'. 'Son of John Breads, Butcher'. Baptised 14 April 1714, son of John and Mary. Probably brother of John Breads, butcher (baptised 2

June 1710, son of John (died 1726) and Mary) who married a Mary, and who was executed 8 June 1743 for murdering Allen Grebell at night on 16 March 1743. He had meant to kill James Lamb, the Mayor, who had fined Breads for giving short weight in his shop. Breads hung on his gibbet on the river bank for 50 years. (At 5 April 1756 his only surviving sons, then of age, were Joseph and Richard.) [RSB; PR; *SNQ* **9** and **5**]

BREEN, [Susan or Mary] (1689 or 93 -): Brighton girls' charity school. Admitted when school opened, 30 September 1702. 'Susan Brin's daughter'. Either Susan, baptised 13 January 1689, daughter of Henry and Susan (née Perssi), or Mary, baptised 17 June 1693, daughter of same. [BSB; PR]

BREEN, James: Brighton charity school. Joined 'writers' class at some time after January 1702; had left by December 1705 and gone as 'Apprentice to A marriner'. [BSB]

BREEN, William (1700-): Brighton charity school. Added at end of list of 'readers' December 1705 (ie joined subsequently). Baptised 7 March 1700, son of William junior and Elizabeth. [BSB; PR]

BRIDGER, Anne (1695-): Brighton girls' charity school. Admitted at some time after 25 March 1703 (probably before end of 1705). Baptised 1 September 1695, daughter of Thomas and Ann (née Buckrell). (Brother Thomas at the boys' charity school.) [BSB; PR]

BRIDGER, Isaac (1692-): Brighton charity school. In list of 'writers' 12 January 1702 and December 1705. Baptised 24 April 1692, son of Isaac and [blank] (first wife Joan (née Brapple) buried 8 March 1689). [BSB; PR]

BRIDGER, John: Mayfield charity school. Admitted 6 July 1764; removed 16 October 1767, 'Sufficiently Learned', after 3¼ years at the school, 1½ years as a 'writer'. (Perhaps nonconformist family; on 18 April 1809 a building occupied by John Bridger in Mayfield was registered for the worship of Baptists.) [MSB; WSRO Ep.V/17/14]

BRIDGER, Richard: Lewes grammar school.

Letter from John Bridger of Coombe Place, gent, to Molly Bridger, undated but probably c1763: 'surprised to find Dicky at home, Mr Austen [master of the grammar school] not having sent for him till yesterday.' [ESRO SHR 909]

BRIDGER, Thomas (1693-): Brighton charity school. Shown twice in record of those joining 'readers' after the (probably) January 1702 list; in list of 'writers' December 1705. Baptised 16 July 1693, son of Thomas 'and his wife' (Ann Buckrell; they married 19 January 1683). (Sister Anne at the girls' charity school.) [BSB; PR]

BRISSENDEN, Mary (1727-): Brightling girls' charity school. There at 21 April 1738, to year ending 1 May 1740, in which year she attended on 187 school days. Baptised 23 July 1727, daughter of John and Elizabeth. (Sister Susanna also at the school.) [ESRO PAR 254/25/1; PR]

BRISSENDEN, Susanna (1731-): Brightling girls' charity school. Admitted 7 April 1741; there to c2-year period ending 22 March 1744, in which 23 months she attended on 444 school days; had 722 days at the school in total. Baptised 26 September 1731, daughter of John and Elizabeth. (Sister Mary also at the school.) [ESRO PAR 254/25/1; PR]

BRISTED, John (1696-1783): Almost certainly at Lewes grammar school. When at Clare Hall, Cambridge, he received in 1714 £3 4s 11d from the Steere charity for sending Lewes boys to Cambridge or Oxford. Later master of Lewes grammar school [qv].

BRISTOW, Henry: Admitted Fermor's charity school, Rotherfield, 25 May 1794. [ESRO PAR 465/4/1]

BRITON, Samuel: Grey Coat charity school, Chichester. Left between Michaelmas 1762 and Michaelmas 1763. Given 10s 6d on leaving. [WSRO Cap.V/1/1]

BROOKE: Grey Coat charity school, Chichester. Left between Michaelmas 1759 and Michaelmas 1760. Given 10s 6d on leaving. [WSRO Cap.V/l/l]

BROOK, Elizabeth (1750?-): Brightling girls' charity school. Admitted between Lady Day 1755 and 30 April 1757, in which period she attended on 218 school days; there to period 30 April 1757 to 31 July 1758, in which period she attended on 275 school days; had 495 days at the school in total. Probably baptised 19 October 1750, daughter of Samuel and Mary, though rather young for the school. [ESRO PAR 254/25/1; PR]

BROOKE, John: Grey Coat charity school, Chichester. Left between Michaelmas 1762 and Michaelmas 1763. Given 10s 6d on leaving. [WSRO Cap.V/1/1]

BROOK, William (1748-): Saunders' charity school, Rye. In lists from 11 January 1758 (not in Michaelmas 1757) to 20 January 1762 (not in Christmas 1762, next list). Baptised 21 October 1748, son of Jeremiah and Dorothy. [RSB; PR]

BROOKER, Edward (1748-): Mayfield charity school. Admitted 11 April 1760; removed 11 July 1760, 'suspended for Non Attendance', after ¼ year as a 'reader'. Baptised 31 May 1748, son of Edward and Mary. Father was a husbandman and had died by 31 May 1762, when Edward, then 14, bound himself apprentice for 7 years to Samuel Baker of Heathfield, tanner; Mayfield parish paid the premium of £11 10s. [MSB; PR; ESRO PAR 422/33/129]

BROOKER, Hezekiah (1760-): Mayfield charity school. Admitted 19 January 1770; removed 9 July 1772, 'Sufficiently Learned', after 2½ years at the school, 1 year as a 'writer'. Baptised 2 November 1760, daughter of David and Susan. [MSB; PR]

BROOKER (BOOKER), Michael (1787-): Admitted Fermor's charity school, Rotherfield, 3 May 1794. Baptised 21 January 1787, son of John and Elizabeth. [ESRO PAR 465/4/1; PR]

BROOKER, Nathaniel: Brighton charity school. In list of 'writers' 12 January 1702; had left by December 1705 and gone 'to sea'. [BSB]

BROOKER, William (1688-): Brighton charity school. Admitted sometime after (probably) January 1702; joined 'writers' class; had left by December 1705 and gone 'to sea'. Baptised 11 November 1688, son of James and [*blank*]. [BSB; PR]

BROOKS - see also BROOK/BROOKE

BROOKS: Admitted Eastbourne charity school January 1780. Son of Thomas. [SAS Budgen MS v. 117]

BROOKS, William: Grey Coat charity school, Chichester. Left between Michaelmas 1767 and Michaelmas 1768. Given 10s 6d on leaving. [WSRO Cap.V/1/1]

BROOMAN, William (1726-): Saunders' charity school, Rye. In lists from 7 April 1736 (not in 28 January 1736) to 2 April 1740 (9 July 1740 notes 'left the school'). Son of William, deceased. Baptised 4 November 1726, son of William and Elizabeth. [RSB; PR]

BROOMAN, William (1754-): Saunders' charity school, Rye. In lists from Michaelmas 1763 (not in Christmas 1762, previous surviving list) to Lady Day 1767 (not in Christmas 1768, next surviving list). Baptised 30 December 1754, son of William and Elizabeth. [RSB; PR]

BROOMFIELD: Brighton girls' charity school. Admitted when school opened, 30 September 1702. 'Widow Broomefield's daughter'. One of the daughters of Thomas and Hannah: (Hannah, baptised 12 December 1686, and Jane, baptised 16 September 1688, probably too old) Susan, baptised 5 April 1691, Mary, baptised 14 February 1697. Thomas had died by baptism of his son Thomas, 18 March 1698. (Probably brother Thomas at the boys' school.) [BSB; PR]

BROOMFIELD, Thomas? (1698?-): Brighton charity school. In list of 'readers' December 1705. No Christian name given in school book but almost certainly Thomas as his the only male Broomfield baptised in parish register this period: baptised 18 March 1698, son of Thomas deceased. (Probably sister at the girls' school.) [BSB; PR]

BROWN - see also BROWNE

BROWN: Brighton girls' charity school. Admitted when school opened, 30 September 1702. 'Widow Brown's daughter'. Probably one of: Mary, baptised 13 January 1689, daughter of Henry and Joan; Judith, baptised 6 April 1690, daughter of William; Sarah, baptised 9 August 1691, daughter of John; Ann, baptised 19 April 1696, daughter of Henry - and most probably Ann. [BSB; PR]

BROWN: Brighton girls' charity school. Admitted when school opened, 30 September 1702. 'Susanna Brown's daughter'. [BSB]

BROWN: Button's school, Lewes. To recite at a 'Public Examination' at the *Star Assembly Room*, 22 June 1797. [*SWA* 19.6.97]

BROWN: Admitted Fermor's charity school, Rotherfield, 5 June 1796. 'Son of Rich'd Brown Hyegate'. [ESRO PAR 465/4/1]

BROWN, James: Sedlescombe charity school. There 3 May 1755, 10 April 1758, 22 February 1759 (still a 'reader'). [SSB]

BROWN, William (1734-): At Steyning grammar school. Of Sussex. Admitted sizar (age 18) at Peterhouse, Cambridge, 1 June 1752, scholar 1752. [*Al. Cant.*]

BROWN, William?: Admitted Fermor's charity school, Rotherfield, 5 June 1796. 'Son of Will'm Brown' with 'William' added in margin. [ESRO PAR 465/4/1]

BROWN, William: Admitted Fermor's charity school, Rotherfield, 3 June 1798. [ESRO PAR 465/4/1]

BROWNE, George Joseph: Midhurst grammar school. Admitted as charity scholar 1793. [*HMGS*]

BROWNE, John: Midhurst grammar school. Admitted as charity scholar 1790. [*HMGS*]

BRYANT: Grey Coat charity school, Chichester. Left between Michaelmas 1752 and Michaelmas 1753. Given 10s 6d on leaving. [WSRO Cap.V/1/1]

BRYANT: Grey Coat charity school, Chichester. Left between Michaelmas 1754 and

Michaelmas 1755. Given £1 1s, 'leaving the school without Cloths' (the usual gift at this time was 10s 6d). [WSRO Cap.V/1/1]

BRYANT, Elizabeth (1763-): Mayfield charity school. Admitted July 1771; removed 11 April 1777, 'Sufficiently Learned', after 5¾ years at the school, 4¼ years as a 'writer'. Baptised 20 November 1763, daughter of Thomas and Martha. (Three brothers also at the school.) [MSB; PR]

BRYANT, John (1761-): Mayfield charity school. Admitted 17 April 1767 to 'Widow Dukes' dame school, but not in next list (4 September 1767); admitted charity school 15 January 1768; removed 9 July 1772, 'Sufficiently Learned', after 4¾ years at the school, 2¼ years as a 'writer'. Baptised 10 December 1761, son of Thomas and Martha. (Two brothers, one sister, also at the school.) [MSB; PR]

BRYANT, Thomas (1760-): Mayfield charity school. Admitted 24 January 1766 to 'Widow Dukes' dame school; admitted charity school 2 May 1766; removed 19 May 1771, 'Sufficiently Learned', after 5 years at the school, 1½ years as a 'writer'. Baptised 6 April 1760, son of Thomas and Martha. (Two brothers, one sister, also at the school.) [MSB; PR]

BRYANT, William (1759-): Mayfield charity school. Listed as being at 'Widow Dukes' dame school 11 January 1765; admitted charity school 18 October 1765; removed 20 July 1770, 'Sufficiently Learned', after 5¼ years at the school, 2¼ years as a 'writer'. Baptised 14 February 1759, son of Thomas and Martha. (Two brothers, one sister, also at the school.) [MSB; PR]

BUCK, Thomas: Saunders' charity school, Rye. In lists from 29 April 1741 (not in 7 January 1741) to 7 July 1742 (13 October 1742 notes 'left the school'). Son of Robert. [RSB]

[**BUDD, Martha** (1794-)]: In Wiston school list, c1803, and perhaps at the school in 1800. Baptised 19 October 1794, daughter of Thomas and Mary. [WSRO Par 211/25/1; PR]

BUFFEY, Richard (1709?-): Brighton charity school. Given prayer book 1717. Perhaps

baptised 23 March 1709, son of Richard. [BSB; PR]

BULL: Button's school, Lewes. To recite at a 'Public Examination' at the *Star Assembly Room*, 22 June 1797. [*SWA* 19.6.97]

BULL, John (1791 -): Petworth charity school. Admitted 21 April 1800. Born 12 October 1791, baptised 20 November, son of Edward and Mary. [WSRO Petworth House Archives 1763; PR]

BUMSTED (BUMSTEAD), Ann (1752-): Sedlescombe charity school. In lists 10 April 1758, 22 February 1759, 1761. Baptised 19 April 1752, daughter of Edward and Lucy. (Brothers Edward, Thomas, sister Elizabeth, also at the school.) [SSB; PR]

BUMSTED (BUMSTEAD), Edward (1767-): Sedlescombe charity school. There 18 April 1772 and 8 May 1775 (still a 'reader'). Baptised 15 March 1767, son of John and Mary. (Brother John, sister Olly, also at the school.) [SSB; PR]

BUMSTED (BUMSTEAD), Edward (1768-): Sedlescombe charity school. There 8 May 1775, a 'reader'. Baptised 27 March 1768, son of Edward and Lucy. (Brother Thomas, sisters Ann, Elizabeth, also at the school.) [SSB; PR]

BUMSTED (BUMSTEAD), Elizabeth (1755-): Sedlescombe charity school. Admitted 23 July 1761. Baptised 6 July 1755, daughter of Edward and Lucy. (Brothers Edward, Thomas, sister Ann, also at the school.) [SSB; PR]

BUMSTED (BUMSTEAD), John (1761-): Sedlescombe charity school. There 18 April 1772, a 'writer'. Baptised 22 November 1761, son of John and Mary. (Brother Edward, sister Olly, also at the school.) [SSB; PR]

BUMSTEAD, Mary: Sedlescombe charity school. Admitted 10 April 1758; in lists 22 February 1759, 1761 (when cross marked over name). [SSB]

BUMSTED (BUMSTEAD), Olly (1754-): Sedlescombe charity school. Admitted 16 April 1761. Baptised 18 August 1754, daughter of John and Mary. (Brothers Edward, John, also at the school.) [SSB; PR]

BUMSTED (BUMSTEAD), Thomas (1762-): Sedlescombe charity school. There 18 April 1772. Baptised 17 October 1762, son of Edward and Lucy. (Brother Edward, sisters Ann, Elizabeth, also at the school.) [SSB; PR]

BURDETT - see BIRDIT

BURGIS, Ann (1736-): Sedlescombe charity school. Admitted 24 June 1748, aged 12. [SSB]

BURGIS, John: At Haslewood school, Buxted, 1738 (perhaps under Saunders' charity schooling for girls which, later at least, also covered small boys). [ESRO PAR 286/1/1/1]

BURGIS, Mary: At Haslewood school, Buxted, 1739 (perhaps under Saunders' charity schooling for girls). [ESRO PAR 286/1/1/1]

BURNETT, William (c1702-): Grey Coat charity school, Chichester, from its opening Lady Day 1710. Aged 8 at Lady Day 1711. Still there Lady Day 1714. [WSRO Cap.V/1/1]

BURNHAM, Charles (c1705-): Grey Coat charity school, Chichester. Admitted between Lady Day 1712 and Lady Day 1713, aged 7. There Lady Day 1714. [WSRO Cap.V/1/1]

BURRELL, Elizabeth (1696-): When just 7, 'began to learne to dance', being taught by 'Mr Heal, the dancing-master', at 1 guinea entrance and 1 guinea per quarter. Born 25 June 1696, daughter of Timothy Burrell of Ockenden House, Cuckfield. [*SAC 3*]

BURT, Thomas: Grey Coat charity school, Chichester. Admitted between Lady Day 1713 and Lady Day 1714. [WSRO Cap.V/1/1]

BUSHBY, William (c1703-): Grey Coat charity school, Chichester, from its opening Lady Day 1710. Aged 7 at Lady Day 1711. Expelled (as were 4 others) between Lady Day 1712 and Lady Day 1713. [WSRO Cap.V/1/1]

BUSS, Anne (c1725-): Brightling girls' charity school. Admitted 6 April 1735, aged 10. (Had left by 21 April 1738.) [ESRO PAR 245/25/1]

BUSS, Elizabeth (1748-): Brightling girls' charity school. Admitted between Lady Day 1755 and 30 April 1757, in which period she attended on 445 school days; there at least to period 31 July 1758 to 31 December 1761 (no later records) in which period she attended on 647 school days; had at least 1,416 days at the school in total. Baptised 7 August 1748, daughter of William and Mary. [ESRO PAR 254/25/1; PR]

BUSS, Hannah (1752-): Brightling girls' charity school. Admitted between 31 July 1758 and 31 December 1761, in which period she attended on 183 school days. (No later records.) Baptised 26 November 1752, daughter of Thomas and Mary. [ESRO PAR 254/25/1; PR]

BUTCHER, Francis: Saunders' charity school, Rye. In lists from 10 April 1745 (not in 4 July 1744); in Michaelmas 1746 and Christmas 1746, which notes '9 weeks [absent] - left the School'. Son of John, deceased. [RSB]

BUTLER, Edward (1748-): Sedlescombe charity school. There 3 May 1755, 10 April 1758, 22 February 1759; started 'writing' 22 May 1758. Baptised 4 April 1748, son of Edward and Mary. [SSB; PR]

BUTLER, Edward (1785-): Sedlescombe charity school. Admitted 5 July 1795 (a 'writer'); there 25 December 1797 and 20 August 1798. Baptised 8 August 1785, son of Edward and Elizabeth. (Brother Robert also at the school.) [SSB; PR]

BUTLER, Richard: Brighton charity school. In list of 'readers' December 1705. [BSB]

BUTLER, Robert (1783-): Sedlescombe charity school. There 21 October 1793 (a 'writer') and 20 October 1794 (not in December 1797 list). Baptised 21 February 1783, son of Edward and Elizabeth. (Brother Edward also at the school.) [SSB; PR]

BUTTENSHIRE, Susan (1692-): Brighton girls' charity school. Admitted sometime after 25 March 1703 (probably by end of 1705). Baptised 8 May 1692, daughter of Andrew and Elizabeth. [BSB; PR]

BUTTON: Grey Coat charity school,

Chichester. Left between Michaelmas 1757 and Michaelmas 1758. Given 10s 6d on leaving. [WSRO Cap.V/1/1]

BUTTON, John Viney (1785-1873): Button's school, Lewes. To recite at a 'Public Examination' at the *Star Assembly Room* 22 June 1797. Son of John, Baptist, master of the school. To Cambridge (with Steere charity exhibition, qv under Lewes grammar school); took Anglican orders. At 19 published *Lewes Library Society; A Poem* (1804), and at 20 *Exercises on Elocution* (1805). [*SWA* 19.6.97; Brent, C. *Geo. Lewes* (1993)]

BYNG, Henry Dilkes (-1860): fourth son (ninth of 13 children) of the Hon John Byng (later 5th Viscount Torrington, 1743-1813) and Bridget (née Forrest) (-1823), he was taken by his parents to school for the first time to Raymond's school, Lewes, on 22 August 1788: 'After Dinner we took our Son Henry to the School, seemingly very fit for little Fellows, (kept by Mr Raymond - a Swiss, and his wife, who are very carefull people, and competent of such Charge) where I hope he will improve in Strength, by the goodness of the Air.' Henry later became a Vice-Admiral. Married Maria Jane Clerke (-1874) and had issue. Died 24 September 1860. [*SCM* 7; Andrews, F. (ed) *The Torrington Diaries* (1954 edition); *Burke's Peerage*]

CAFFIN, John (c1700-): Grey Coat charity school, Chichester, from its opening Lady Day 1710. Aged 10 at Lady Day 1711. Expelled (as were 4 others) between Lady Day 1712 and Lady Day 1713. [WSRO Cap.V/1/1]

CAMPANY, Mary (1789-): Admitted Robertsbridge charity school at its opening 5 April 1796, aged 6. Sponsored by Charles Lamb, esq. Baptised 26 July 1789, daughter of John and Lucy (née Martin). [ESRO PAR 477/25/1/1; Salehurst PR]

CAMPBELL, Charlotte (1786-): Admitted Robertsbridge charity school at its opening 5 April 1796, aged 9. Sponsored by Mrs Jenkin, wife of Rev Stephen, vicar of Salehurst. Baptised 2 January 1787 (aged 23 days), daughter of Septimus and Sarah (née Chainey). [ESRO PAR 477/25/1/1; Salehurst PR]

CAMPION, William (1707-78): Pupil of Philip Shore, rector of Woodmancote. Born 1707, eldest son of Henry of Combwell Manor, Kent, and later Danny Place, Hurstpierpoint, MP. Admitted Fellow-Comoner at Trinity College, Cambridge, 29 November 1724; matriculated 1725. Married Elizabeth Partheriche, daughter of Edward of Ely, and had issue (3 surviving sons and a daughter). Died 1 Aug 1778, buried at Hurstpierpoint. [*SAC* 36; *Al. Cant.* (WC first not 4th son of HC); Wooldridge, J. (ed) *The Danny Archives, a catalogue* (1966)]

(CAPLIN): Eastbourne charity school. Admitted Michaelmas 1778; there Christmas 1779. [SAS Budgen MS v.117]

CARD, Charlotte (1787-): Admitted Fermor's charity school, Rotherfield, 3 May 1794. Baptised 24 June 1787, daughter of John and Elizabeth. [ESRO PAR 465/4/1; PR]

CARD, John: Admitted Fermor's charity school, Rotherfield, 29 April 1798. Son of Richard. [ESRO PAR 465/4/1]

CARD, Henry (1789-): Admitted Fermor's charity school, Rotherfield, 25 May 1794. Baptised 22 November 1789, son of Charles and Mary. [ESRO PAR 465/4/1; PR]

CARDEN - see CARDING

CARDING, Edward (1694-): Brighton charity school. In list of 'readers' of (probably) January 1702; given coat and hat July 1702; also shown as joining 'readers' class after January 1702 list, so perhaps left and re-admitted; in list of 'writers' December 1705. Baptised 20 May 1694, son of Robert Carden and [*blank*] (mother probably Mary, from 1691 baptism of daughter of Robert Carden and Mary). [BSB; PR]

CARDING, French: Brighton charity school. In list of 'readers' December 1705. [BSB]

CARDING, Jacob (1707-): Brighton charity school. Given prayer book 1718. Baptised 14 September 1707, son of Jacob and Mary Carden. [BSB; PR]

CARE: A poor boy of Horsted Keynes for

whose schooling the parish paid, at 2d a week, 1744-46. Son of Henry. [WSRO Par 384/12/1]

CAREY, Walter: Sedlescombe charity school. In lists for 20 August 1798 (no Christian name) and 13 January 1800, as 'reader'. [SSB]

CARPENTER, John (1756-): Saunders' charity school, Rye. In lists from Michaelmas 1765 (not in Lady Day 1765) to Lady Day 1767 (not in Christmas 1768, next surviving list). Baptised 29 December 1756, son of John and Mary. [RSB; PR]

CATT, William (1776-1853): At dame school, Robertsbridge, his only education; 'he hated his books - but liked cricket'. Baptised at Uckfield 31 December 1776, son of John, farmer, and Elizabeth; father moved to Abbey Farm, Robertsbridge, when he was an infant. Married, at 19, Hannah Dawes of Ewhurst (died 1823); had 11 children. Farmed 2 years at Buxted, moved to mill at Lamberhurst; then with a cousin at first, later on his own, owned the Tide Mills at Bishopstone for 50 years. Also had stake in the West Street Brewery, Brighton. Buried, Bishopstone, 10 March 1853, aged 76. [Uckfield PR; Bishopstone PR; *Lower Worthies*]

CHADS, junior: At Midhurst grammar school 1799. (Inferred from reference to Chads senior, assumed to be Henry Chads, qv) [*SWA* 11.11.99]

CHADS, Henry Ducie (1788-1868): Midhurst grammar school. In 1800 went to Royal Naval Academy, Portsmouth. Later Admiral Sir Henry. Probably the elder Chads who took part in the school's first public performance of composition and oratory, 5 November 1799, and in the second, 27 May 1800, when, with 3 others, he played a scene from Virgil's *Aeneid*. [*HMGS*; *SWA* 11.11.99, 2.6.1800]

CHALLEN: Thornton's school, Horsham. On Saturday 3 January 1795 played Prince Henry in *Henry IV, part 1*. At the request of the audience ('the Gentry and Inhabitants of the town of Horsham') the play was performed again the following Monday. [*SWA* 5.1.95]

CHALLEN, John: At Cocking charity school 1732. [WSRO Par 53/12/1]

(CHALLONER, W.): A poor child of West Grinstead who received schooling under the Dowlin charity 1727. [WSRO Par 95/1/1/3]

[CHAMBERS, James]: In Wiston school list, c1803, and perhaps at the school in 1800. [WSRO Par 211/25/1]

[CHAMBERS, Thomas]: In Wiston school list, c1803, and perhaps at the school in 1800. [WSRO Par 211/25/1]

CHANDLER, Henry (1718-): Saunders' charity school, Rye. In lists from 2 April 1729 (?) (perhaps in 8 January 1729 when 'Michael' entry probably mistake for 'Henry'; not in May 1728 (?)) to 7 January 1730 (1 April 1730 notes 'Gon to be an apprentice'). Son of Michael, died 1725. Baptised 4 May 1718, son of Michael and Mary (but 'Mary' probably error for 'Elizabeth'). (Brothers John, Michael, Phillip, also at the school.) [RSB; PR]

CHANDLER, James Boykett (1743-): Saunders' charity school, Rye. In lists from 9 April 1755 (not in 16 January 1754, only 1754 list); left school 2 April 1759. Baptised 20 December 1743, son of Michael and Susan. (Brother John also at the school.) [RSB; PR]

CHANDLER, John (1716-): Saunders' charity school, Rye. In lists from December 1724 (?) (not in 8 May 1724) to 3 January 1733 (28 March 1733 notes 'left the school'). Son of Michael, buried 14 November 1725. Baptised 2 February 1716, son of Michael and Elizabeth. (Brothers Henry, Michael, Phillip, also at the school.) [RSB; PR]

CHANDLER, John (1740-): Saunders' charity school, Rye. In lists from 2 October 1751 (not in midsummer 1751) to midsummer 1757, where marked 'Left School'. Son of John, deceased by 14 January 1756 (not deceased at Michaelmas 1755). Baptised 29 July 1740, son of John and Mary. (Brother Richard also at the school.) [RSB; PR]

CHANDLER, John (1740-): Saunders' charity school, Rye. In lists from 25 March 1752 (not in 15 January 1752) to 16 January 1754 (only 1754 list; not in 9 April 1755, next surviving list). Baptised 5 December 1740, son of Michael and Susan. (Brother James also at the school.) [RSB; PR]

CHANDLER, Michael (1712-): Saunders' charity school, Rye. In lists from September 1722 (?) (first list) to 8 April 1724 (in 4 November 1724 entry is 'Chandler', no Christian name, but this probably John (1716-) qv); apparently returned to school briefly - in list for 19 April 1727 (not in 12 July 1727). ('Michael C' also in list for 8 January 1729 but this probably error for 'Henry', qv.) Baptised 30 April 1712, son of Michael (died 1725) and Elizabeth. (Brothers Henry, John, Phillip, also at the school.) [RSB; PR]

CHANDLER, Phillip (1721-): Saunders' charity school, Rye. In lists from 5 July 1732 (not in 29 March 1732) to 28 June 1738 (?) (4 October 1738 notes 'left the school'). Baptised 7 January 1722, son of Michael (died 1725) and Elizabeth. (Brothers Henry, John, Michael, also at the school.) [RSB; PR]

CHANDLER, Richard (1748-): Saunders' charity school, Rye. In lists from midsummer 1759 (not in 4 April 1759) to 20 January 1762 (not in Christmas 1762). Son of John, deceased. Baptised 6 May 1748, son of John and Mary. (Brother John also at the school.) [RSB; PR]

CHANDLER, Richard (1773-): Saunders' charity school, Rye. Admitted 6 March 1782; in lists to 24 June 1785, which notes '9 Absent' (presumably weeks; this is last surviving 18th century list). Baptised 27 May 1773, son of Richard and Mary. [RSB; PR]

CHANDLER, William (1770-): Saunders' charity school, Rye. Admitted 24 January 1783; list for 29 September 1783 notes 'Left School'. Son of John, deceased. Baptised 18 April 1770, son of John and Anne. [RSB; PR]

CHAPMAN, William: Admitted Fermor's charity school, Rotherfield, 20 August 1797. Son of William. [ESRO PAR 465/4/1]

CHATFIELD, Edward: Mayfield charity school. Admitted 27 October 1769; removed 19 January 1770, for non-attendance. [MSB]

CHEAL: 'Mrs Cheale's son' started at Hart's school, Hurstpierpoint, 31 October 1720 [qv Charity school]. [*SAC* **25**]

CHEYNEY, Hannah (1790-): Admitted Robertsbridge charity school at its opening, 5 April 1796, aged 6. Sponsored by Mr Robert Willsher. Entered as daughter of Samuel, but either daughter's or father's name incorrect. Probably baptised 21 August 1790, daughter of William and Elizabeth (née Hook). (Elizabeth, daughter of Samuel and Mary, was baptised 16 June 1790.) [ESRO PAR 477/25/1/1; Salehurst PR]

CHILD(S), William (1774-): Lord Pelham's charity school, Lewes [qv Rand's school]. Admitted Christmas 1783. There 10 October 1784, aged 10. Baptised 1 November 1774, son of William and Sarah 'from St Anns'. [ESRO AMS 6005; St Michael, Lewes PR]

CHOPPINO, Frederick (1784-): Brook's school, Brighton. On 18 December 1799, then aged 15, spoke a verse prologue, which he had written, to the annual play; a favourable report in *Sussex Weekly Advertiser*, 23 December 1799, cited the prologue in full.

CHURCHMAN: At Horsham workhouse school in 1773 [qv].

CLAPSON, Benjamin (1786-): Mayfield charity school. Admitted 9 January 1795; removed 11 January 1799, taken out by parents. Baptised 9 July 1786, son of Benjamin and Mary. (Two brothers, 1 sister, also at the school.) [MSB; PR]

CLAPSON, John (1775-): Mayfield charity school. Admitted 14 January 1785; removed 6 April 1787, for non-attendance. Baptised 3 December 1775, son of Benjamin and Mary. (Two brothers, 1 sister, also at the school.) [MSB; PR]

CLAPSON, Martha (1781-): Mayfield charity school. Admitted 12 October 1792; removed 11 July 1794, taken out by parents. Baptised 6 January 1782, daughter of Benjamin and Mary. (Three brothers also at the school.) [MSB; PR]

CLAPSON, William (1784-): Mayfield charity school. Admitted 12 October 1792; removed 6 July 1798, for non-attendance. Baptised 30 May 1784, son of Benjamin and Mary. (Two brothers, 1 sister, also at the school.) [MSB; PR]

CLARE, Charles: Midhurst grammar school. Admitted as charity scholar 1785. (Brother Francis admitted same year.) [*HMGS*]

CLARE, Francis: Midhurst grammar school. Admitted as charity scholar 1785. (Brother Charles admitted same year.) [*HMGS*]

(CLARK): At Widow Page's school, Clapham, June 1772. [*SAC* **71**]

CLARK, Charles (1790-   ): Admitted Robertsbridge charity school at its opening 5 April 1796, aged 6. Sponsored by Charles Lamb, esq. Baptised 7 February 1790, son of John and Lilly. [ESRO PAR 477/25/1/1; Salehurst PR]

CLARK, Edward (1721-   ): Saunders' charity school, Rye. In lists from 7 July 1731 (not in 31 March 1731) to 7 April 1736 (not in 20 October 1736). Baptised 29 November 1721, son of John and Mary. (Brothers John, Philip, also at the school.) [RSB; PR]

CLARKE, Edward (1730-86): Born 1730, son of William, rector of Buxted. Early education supervised by father's curate, Robert Gerison [qv] and Jeremiah Markland [qv]; then to Winchester. St John's College, Cambridge, 1748; BA 1752; MA 1755; fellow 1753-64. Priest (Chichester) 1756; rector Pepperharrow, Surrey, 1758-68; 1760, chaplain to embassy, Madrid; 1763 to Minorca, chaplain and secretary to General Johnstone. 1768, on father's death, rector of Buxted, also vicar of Willingdon and Arlington 1768, all to death. Prebend Hova Villa 1771, Hova Ecclesia 1772. Author, historical, etc. Died 24 November 1786. [Horsfield *Sussex*; *Al. Cant.*; *SAC* **12**; CI]

CLARKE, Edward Daniel (1769-1822): Born 6 June 1769 at the vicarage, Willingdon, son of Edward (1730-86) [qv above], he 'received his early education at the hands of an Uckfield clergyman'; then Tonbridge grammar school; Jesus College, Cambridge; BA 1790, MA 1794. 'While at college he constructed a balloon which he sent up with a kitten as passenger.' Tutor, traveller, collector of vases, coins and other antiquities, and mineral specimens. 1798, fellow of Jesus and bursar; LLD 1803. Died at Cambridge 1822. [*SCM* **8** (1934)]

CLARKE, James Stainer (1767-1834): Born at Mahon, Minorca, 1767, son of Edward (1730-86) [qv above]. A pupil of Robert Gerison, Uckfield; then Tonbridge grammar school; St John's College, Cambridge, 1784, scholar. Deacon 1789; sometime curate of Uckfield; priest 1790; vicar of Preston-cum-Hove 1790 to death. Naval chaplain 1795-99; domestic chaplain to Prince of Wales 1799, librarian to HRH 1805. LLB (Jesus) 1805; LLD 1816. Rector of Coombes 1804-08; canon of Windsor 1808 to death; rector of Tillington 1816 to death. Historiographer to the king 1812; deputy clerk of the closet to the king 1816. FRS and KB. Started, with John McArthur, the *Naval Chronicle*, which ran for 20 years; author, *Life of Horatio, Viscount Nelson*; *Life of James II*; *Sermons*, etc. Died at Brighton 14 October 1834 aged 67. [*SAC* **12**: CI; *Al. Cant.*]

CLARK, John (1724 or 25-   ): Saunders' charity school, Rye. In lists from 2 January 1734 (not in 4 July 1733) to 6 February 1740 (2 April 1740 notes 'left the school'). Son of Edward, deceased. Baptised 18 January 1725, son of Edward and Elizabeth. [RSB; PR]

CLARK, John (1726-   ): Saunders' charity school, Rye. In lists from 20 October 1736 (not in 7 April 1736) to 2 April 1740 (9 July 1740 notes 'left the school'). Baptised 4 January 1727, son of John and Mary. (Brothers Edward, Philip, also at the school.) [RSB; PR]

CLARK, John: Saunders' charity school, Rye. In lists from Michaelmas 1763 (not in Christmas 1762, previous surviving list); left school 14 September 1765. Son of John. (Brother Thomas also at the school.) [RSB]

CLARK, Philip (1731-   ): Saunders' charity school, Rye. In lists from 7 July 1742 (not in 14 April 1742) to 4 July 1744 (not in 10 April 1745, next surviving list). Baptised 12 February 1731, son of John and Mary. (Brothers Edward, John, also at the school.) [RSB; PR]

CLARK, Philip (1765-   ): Saunders' charity school, Rye. Admitted 2 December 1776; in lists to midsummer 1781, which notes 'Left School'. Baptised 25 December 1765, son of Philip and Mercy. (Brother Thomas also at the school.) [RSB; PR]

CLARKE, Robert (1750-): Saunders' charity school, Rye. In list of Christmas 1762 only (not in 20 January 1762, previous surviving list). Baptised 30 April 1750, son of Robert and Mary. [RSB; PR]

CLARK, Samuel (1768 or 69-): Saunders' charity school, Rye. Admitted 13 January 1779; in lists to Michaelmas 1781 (not in Lady Day 1782). Baptised 14 January 1769, son of Samuel and Amy. (Brother Thomas also at the school.) [RSB; PR]

CLARKE, Thomas (1757-): Saunders' charity school, Rye. Admitted 5 October 1768; left school 10 September 1770. Son of John, deceased. Baptised 13 July 1757, son of John and Mary. (Brother John also at the school.) [RSB; PR]

CLARK, Thomas: Saunders' charity school, Rye. Admitted 6 March 1782; in lists to 29 September 1784, which notes 'Left School'. Son of Philip. (Brother Philip also at the school.) [RSB; PR]

CLARK, Thomas: Saunders' charity school, Rye. Admitted 6 March 1782; in list for 24 June 1785 (last surviving 18th century list). Son of Samuel. (Brother Samuel also at the school). [RSB]

CLEMENS (CLEMENT), Edward (1769-): Saunders' charity school, Rye. Admitted 6 May 1778; in lists to 24 June 1783, which notes 'left School'. Baptised 25 January 1769, son of George and Anne. [RSB; PR]

CLEMENTS, William: Saunders' charity school, Rye. Admitted 21 April 1768; left school 19 November 1768. Son of Ann Clements. [RSB]

CLIFTON, John (1750-): Mayfield charity school. Admitted 10 April 1758; removed 17 October 1760, for non-attendance, after 2½ years as a 'reader'. Baptised 28 February 1750, son of Thomas and Mary. (Brother Thomas also at the school.) [MSB; PR]

CLIFTON, Thomas (1751-): Mayfield charity school. Admitted 13 October 1758; removed 6 July 1759, 'suspended for Non Attendance', after ¾ year as a 'reader'; in list for 17 October

1760, shown as 'came in room of Walker who has not attended since last quarter', but in same list removed for non-attendance. Baptised 18 August 1751, son of Thomas and Mary. (Brother John also at the school.) [MSB; PR]

COBBY: Button's school, Lewes. To recite at a 'Public Examination' at the *Star Assembly Room*, 22 July 1797. [*SWA* 19.6.97]

COBBY, John (1697-): Brighton charity school. Admitted as 'reader' sometime after list of (probably) January 1702; in 'readers' list December 1705. Baptised 3 October 1697, son of Robert (mother probably Mary, qv baptism 25 August 1695, Robart son of Robart Cobby and Mary). [BSB; PR]

COBBY, Michael (1701-): Brighton charity school. Given prayer book 1715. Baptised 24 August 1701, son of Michael. [BSB; PR]

COBBY, Reuben (1687-): Brighton charity school. Admitted as 'reader' sometime after list of (probably) January 1702; joined 'writers' class sometime after 12 January 1702; had left by December 1705 and gone 'to sea'. Baptised 22 May 1687, son of Robart and Elizabeth. [BSB; PR]

COBBY, Richard: Brighton charity school. Given prayer book 1715. [BSB]

COBBY, Thomas (1710?-): Brighton charity school. Given prayer book 1718. Perhaps baptised 9 April 1710, son of Thomas. [BSB; PR]

COBBY, Thomas: Brighton charity school. In list of 'readers' of (probably) January 1702; had left by December 1705 and gone 'to sea'. (Perhaps son of Thomas and Ann (née Friend), who married 21 February 1682.) [BSB; PR]

COBDON, John (c1704-): Grey Coat charity school, Chichester. Admitted Lady Day 1712, aged 7 ; there Lady Day 1714. [WSRO Cap.V/1/1]

COLBERT, Mary: The Duke of Richmond, of Goodwood, paid Martha Tupper for schooling Mary Colbert in 1799 and 1800 (5s 5d, and probably also an earlier payment of 5s 5d, in 1799; 8s 9d in 1800). [WSRO Goodwood MS

247]

COLE, David: Brighton charity school. Admitted sometime after 'readers' list of (probably) January 1702; had left by December 1705. (Perhaps son of Daniel, whose son Daniel was baptised 1696.) [BSB; PR]

COLE, Thomas (1786-): Admitted Fermor's charity school, Rotherfield, 4 August 1793. Baptised 11 April 1786, son of John and Elizabeth ('poor'). [ESRO PAR 465/4/1; PR]

COLEGATE, Daniel (1765-): Sedlescombe charity school. There 18 April 1772 (a 'reader') and 8 May 1775 (a 'writer'). Baptised 18 August 1765, son of James and Mary. [SSB; PR]

COLEGATE, Robert (1752-): Sedlescombe charity school. Admitted 16 October 1758; in lists to 1761, in which name later crossed through. Baptised 5 November 1752, son of James and Mary. [SSB; PR]

COLEMAN, Charles: Grey Coat charity school, Chichester. Left between Michaelmas 1767 and Michaelmas 1768. Given 10s 6d on leaving. [WSRO Cap.V/1/1]

COLMAN, Daniel: Mayfield charity school. Admitted 11 April 1788; removed 15 October 1789, for non-attendance. [MSB]

COLEMAN, George (1775-): Saunders' charity school, Rye. Admitted 10 January 1784 (see COLEMAN, William Thomas) but not in lists for 25 March 1784 or 24 June 1784; later lists give admission as at 14 July 1784. In list of 24 June 1785 (last surviving 18th century list). Baptised 5 September 1775, son of Stephen and Elizabeth. (Brothers John, William, also at the school.) [RSB; PR]

COLEMAN, John: Saunders' charity school, Rye. Admitted 10 December 1776; in lists to Michaelmas 1781, which notes 'Left School'. Son of Stephen. (Brothers George, William, also at the school.) [RSB]

COLEMAN, William Thomas: Saunders' charity school, Rye. Admitted 4 September 1782; list for 25 December 1783 notes 'Left School' and adds: '10 January 1784 Admitted

George Son of Stephen Coleman in the room of his Brother William Thomas Coleman, by an Order from the Rt Worp the Mayor.' Son of Stephen. On 31 March 1795, WTC married Margaret Dickson of St Botolph, Bishopsgate, London. (Brothers George, John, also at the school.) [RSB; St Botolph London, PR]

COLLICK, Abraham (c1700-): Grey Coat charity school, Chichester, from its opening Lady Day 1710. Aged 10 at Lady Day 1711; there Lady Day 1714. [WSRO Cap.V/1/1]

COLLIER: Brighton girls' charity school. Admitted when school opened, 30 September 1702. 'Widow Collier's daughter'. (Perhaps daughter of John and Elizabeth (née Knight), who married 20 April 1682.) [BSB; PR]

COLLIER, Cordelia (1722-79): Born 1722, daughter of John and Mary of Hastings [qv COLLIER, John]. Sent, probably when 8, to Mrs Thorpe's boys' and girls' boarding school, Battle, (2 brothers, 4 sisters, also at the school), then to Mrs Russell's school at Hampstead. Married 1748 Captain James Murray, fifth son of Lord Elibank; he served in America (but she suffered poor health and did not join him) including siege of Quebec, and was Major-General, Governor-General of Quebec 1760; returned to England 1766, lived at Battle until appointed Governor of Minorca 1774. Despite ill-health, Cordelia tried to join him there, but had to be sent home and died 1779, a few hours after returning to Battle. Died without issue. [Sources, see COLLIER, John]

COLLIER, Henrietta (1741-94): Born 1741: parents and schooling as COLLIER, Cordelia [qv]. Married 1771 Henry Jackson, of Middle Temple, and lived at Hastings. Died without issue 1794, aged 53. [Sources, see COLLIER, John]

COLLIER, James (Jemmy) (1721-47): Born 1721, son of John and Mary of Hastings [qv COLLIER, John]. By 1729, aged 8, had been sent to join older brother Jacky at Mrs Thorpe's boys' and girls' boarding school, Battle. By then could read and write, but was a reluctant letter-writer. That year his father wrote to his brother, 'tell him [Jemmy] I think him very extravagent in his paper to write but two lines in a whole sheet and desire his next may be longer when I will be sure to answer it.' Again, in June1729 - Jemmy's first year at the school - his father wrote to Jacky: 'I think he [Jemmy] should have wrote a letter and begg'd pardon for being Soe Naughty a boy a Market day as drinking & getting out of the George Balcony if you expect my favour you must both keep from any dangerous places or plays and never drink any thing of strong liquor but what I give you.' His father wrote a gentle reproof to Jemmy the following year: 'I also received your letter but think you are not greatly improv'd in your writing I a little Imagine that Since you are Turn'd Politician you mind little else I will buy you Whittingtons history but I observe you dont say one Word about his Cat.' Jemmy's interest in history and politics was persistent; when he was 7, still at home, he wrote to his brother at the Battle school: 'I want very much to come again to Battell to see the place where William the Conquerour Killed King Harold because I have read it in one of my pappas great books and also to see the bloody lake where the men were killed a fighting for their King and country.' In January 1731, when he was 9, he asked his mother to send him the King's Speech. When later at Cambridge, he was particularly interested in politics. The family letters bring Jemmy to life. His mother wrote to Jacky, 1729: 'I am sorry Jemmy has got a Cough tell him he should buy Sugar-Candy with his money w'c I hope will doe him good.' And in another: 'accordding to your request have Sent you some handkercheifs which I hope will please Jemmy because I think they are very gay.' By 1732, Jemmy, then 11, was at Westminster school with Jacky; he went to Clare College, Cambridge, 1738, and in 1742 entered Middle Temple; in 1745 he was mayor of Hastings. Died 1747, aged 26. [Sources, see COLLIER, John]

COLLIER, Jane (1727-1802): Born 1727: parents and schooling as COLLIER, Cordelia [qv]. In 1762, aged 35, she eloped with William Green, an engineer, and married in London. They lived in Lewes, paid frequent visits to Brighton and enjoyed a gay social life. WG (-1820) became a justice at Lewes, and stood for parliament 1796 as an Advanced Radical. She died without issue 1802. [Sources, see COLLIER, John; Brent, C. *Geo. Lewes* (1993)]

COLLIER, John (Jacky) (1720-32): Born 1720, elder son of John and Mary of Hastings. Father was a solicitor, in both London and Hastings; Hastings town clerk 1706-49, mayor five times between 1719 and 1741; assisted Duke of Newcastle politically and obtained appointments through his patronage; from 1733 agent for all the Pelham estates in Sussex. Mother, John Collier's second wife, was daughter of Rev James Cranston, vicar of both St Clement and All Saints, Hastings. Sent to Mrs Thorpe's boys' and girls' boarding school, Battle, probably in 1728 when he was 8; could then read and write well; taught by master, including Latin. Also learnt dancing, but wrote to mother 1730, 'I do not go to dancing any Longer'; however, a little later wrote: 'I did not intend to goe to dancing any longer but since it is my pappa's desire I should Goe I will and learn as soon as I can'. His letters to parents, always answered with affection, included requests for his marbles, his 'Great Coat and Boots', pens and paper, a fairing [pocket money], 'hankerchiefs', and various books - his *Seven Champions*, volumes of the *Arabian Tales*, Kennet's *Roman Antiquities*, Erasmus' *Colloquies*, Duck's poems [Stephen Duck], and Pope's and Prior's poems. His parents' and sister Elizabeth's to him include references to sending him shoes, stockings, a hat, shirts, some 'Raisins of the Sun', religious books, *Robinson Crusoe*, *The Seven Wise Masters* and from his father in London 'the dying Confessions of the 5 persons hang'd at Tyburn last week' and 'the Tryalls of all the Robbers and Theives this last Session'. His father once admonished him for gaming 'at soe high a rate' - he had borrowed money to stake but 'We have had very ill Fortune at our Cocks'. Went on to Westminster school 1732, when he was 12, but died there from smallpox that same year, to the great distress of his parents. [ESRO SAY (Matthews, H. M. 'The Papers of John Collier of Hastings. A Catalogue' (1966); Collier family correspondence), passim]

COLLIER, Mary (1725-83): Born 1725: parents and schooling as COLLIER, Cordelia [qv]. Married 1754, aged 28, Edward Milward of Hastings, gent (who had previously approached her younger sister Jane but had been refused: he was mayor of Hastings 1750, and then alternate years from 1753 to 1801; died 1811). Had issue. Died 1783. [Sources,

Dear Jacky   June 14th 1729

I received your letter by Dame Palmer & have sent your knife and fork and Jemmys Common Prayer Book I think he should have wrote a letter and begg'd pardon for being Soe Naughty a boy a Market Day as drinking & getting out of the George Balcony if you expect my favour you must both keep from any dangerous places or plays and never drink any thing of strong liquor but what I give you Your Grandma is pretty well but Molly had her ague again yesterday I desire Docto. Boting will take care of your finger My Blessing to you & Jemmy & you must be Sure to be good boys and then God Almighty will blefse you both I am

                              Your affectionate
                              Father John Collier

12. Letter, 1729, from John Collier of Hastings to his elder son Jacky (John), aged 9, at Mrs Thorpe's preparatory school in Battle. With his younger brother Jemmy (James) he went on from Battle to Westminster School when he was 12, but died of smallpox there. (ESRO SAY 1529)

see COLLIER, John]

COLLIER, Sarah (1739-1822): Born 1739: parents and schooling as COLLIER, Cordelia [qv]. Married 1763 Henry Sayer, attorney of Lincoln's Inn. Had issue. Died 1822, aged 83. [Sources, see COLLIER, John]

[**COLLINS, Charles**]: Perhaps at Midhurst grammar school. A native of Midhurst and elected to Winchester 1758. [*HMGS*]

COLLINS, John (1732-): At Eastbourne charity school April 1741. Baptised 30 September 1732, son of Edward and Elizabeth. [SAS Budgen MS v.129; PR]

COLLINS, John (1745-): Saunders' charity school, Rye. In lists from 9 April 1755 (not in 16 January 1754, the only 1754 list) to 4 April 1759 (not in midsummer 1759). Son of Nicholas, deceased. Baptised 24 October 1745, son of Nicholas and Ann. (Brother William also at the school.) [RSB; PR]

COLLINS, William (1721-1759): Poet. Born at Chichester on Christmas day 1721, son of William (hatter, mayor 1714, 1721; died 1734) and Elizabeth (née Martin, daughter of Edmund and Magdalen of West Wittering; died 1744), who married 12 February 1704. Probably at Chichester grammar school. To Winchester 1733; Queens' College, Oxford, 1740; demy [scholar] Magdalene College 1741; BA 1743. Published *Persian Eclogues* (1742) while undergraduate. To London 1744, little money, many literary plans but did not complete them. *Odes* (1747). Inherited c£2,000 from uncle, Lieutenant-Colonel Martin. Suffered from depression; for some time confined in an asylum; looked after by his sister at Chichester, and died there 12 June 1759. [Chichester Subdeanery PR, St Andrew PR; Johnson, *Lives* (1781); Hay, A. *History of Chichester* (1804); Willis, T. G. *Records of Chichester* (1928); *DNB*]

COLLINS, William (1739-): Saunders' charity school, Rye. In lists from 25 March 1749 (name written in - not in Christmas 1748 - in list for 24 June 1749 marked 'April 22') to 16 January 1754 (not in 9 April 1755, next surviving list). Son of Nicholas, deceased. Baptised 19 August 1739, son of Nicholas and

Anne. (Brother John also at the school.) [RSB; PR]

COMBER, Joseph (1720-38?): A poor boy of Playden for whose schooling the parish paid William Wybourn 6d a week at least from 27 November 1731 to 5 April 1732 (the period covered by a surviving loose receipt). Wybourn was master of Saunders' charity school in neighbouring Rye. JC then aged 11. 18 May 1720: 'Joseph Comber was baptiz'd'. 28 June 1738: 'Joseph Comber was buried' - perhaps the same. [ESRO PAR 445/31/1/14; PR]

COMBER, William (1774-): Lord Pelham's charity school, Lewes [qv Rand's school]. Admitted Lady Day 1781. There 10 October 1784, aged 10. Baptised 19 September 1774, son of Richard and Mary. [ESRO AMS 6005; All Saints PR]

COMBS: Grey Coat charity school, Chichester. Left between Michaelmas 1780 and Michaelmas 1781. Given 10s 6d on leaving. [WSRO Cap.V/1/1]

COOK, Beaumont (1708-): Brighton charity school. Given prayer book 1718. Baptised 29 October 1708, son of John and Jane. [BSB; PR]

COOKE, Daniel: Brighton charity school. In list of 'readers' December 1705. [BSB]

COOK, Francis (1696-): Brighton charity school. Admitted sometime after 'readers' list of (probably) January 1702; in 'readers' list December 1705. Was 'taken off from the free school', 'his parents now being able to continue him at schoole at their own charge'. Baptised 12 April 1696, son of Frances and [*blank*] (mother probably Ann - married 6 November 1687, Frances Cooke and Ann Whiting. Brother John also at the school.) [BSB; PR]

COOK, John (1694-): Brighton charity school. In list of 'readers' of (probably) January 1702; joined 'writers' class sometime after 12 January 1702; had left by December 1705 and gone 'to sea'. Baptised 9 September 1694, son of John and Jane (née Buman). [BSB; PR]

COOK, John (1698-): Brighton charity school. Added at end of list of 'readers'

December 1705 (ie joined subsequently). Baptised 13 November 1698, son of Francis (mother probably Ann - married 6 November 1687, Frances Cook and Ann Whiting. Brother Francis also at the school). [BSB; PR]

COOK, Matthew (1692-): Brighton charity school. Joined 'writers' class sometime after 12 January 1702; in 'writers' list December 1705. Baptised 26 September 1692, son of James and Sara. [BSB; PR]

COOK, Thomas: Brighton charity school. Given prayer book 1716 or 17. [BSB]

COOPER: Grey Coat charity school, Chichester. Given 10s 6d on leaving, 27 October 1772. [WSRO Cap.V/1/1]

COOPER, John (1732-): Saunders' charity school, Rye. In lists from 7 January 1741 (not in 15 October 1740) to Michaelmas 1745 (not in Christmas 1745). Son of Thomas, deceased. Baptised 5 November 1732, son of Thomas and Ann. [RSB; PR]

COOPER, William (c1700-): Grey Coat charity school, Chichester, from its opening Lady Day 1710. Aged 10 at Lady Day 1711. Between Lady Day 1713 and Lady Day 1714 was 'put out Apprentice'. [WSRO Cap.V/1/1]

COOTE, Richard Holmes (1786-1862): Midhurst grammar school. On leaving, became a clerk in the Customs. [HMGS]

COPPER, William (1725-): At Eastbourne charity school 1734. Baptised 4 February 1725, son of Thomas and Elizabeth. [Chatsworth, Devonshire Collection, Compton Place, Box P; PR]

CORBYN: Daughter of Corbyn, dancing master of Brighton; at a ball there, 5 September 1798, she 'displayed abilities which surprised every beholder'. [SWA 10.9.98]

CORK, Richard: Mayfield charity school. Admitted at formal opening, 29 June 1750, but may have been at school up to ¾ year earlier, as master paid from Michaelmas 1749; removed 28 June 1751, 'having Learn'd to read write & cast Accompt well'. [MSB]

CORNELYS: Thornton's school, Horsham. On Saturday 3 January 1795, played Falstaff in *Henry IV, part I*. At the request of the audience ('the Gentry and Inhabitants of the town of Horsham') it was performed again the following Monday. [SWA 5.1.95]

COURT, Charles: Midhurst grammar school. Admitted as charity scholar 1789. (Brother James also at the school.) [HMGS]

COURT, James: Midhurst grammar school. Admitted as charity scholar 1790. (Brother Charles also at the school.) [HMGS]

COURT, William: Midhurst grammar school. Admitted as charity scholar 1789. [HMGS]

[COWPER, Elizabeth]: Daughter of John, of Salehurst, yeoman (buried 31 October 1699) and Elizabeth, on 3 December 1700 her widowed mother paid James Bulloch 10s for 10 weeks teaching her and sister Sarah to write. [SAC **61**]

COWPER, Hannah: Daughter of John, of Salehurst, yeoman (buried 31 October 1699) and Elizabeth, on 20 January 1701 her widowed mother paid Mrs Hammond 8s for 45 weeks teaching her to read. [SAC **61**]

[COWPER, Sarah]: Daughter of John, of Salehurst, yeoman (buried 31 October 1699) and Elizabeth, on 3 December 1700 her widowed mother paid James Bulloch 10s for 10 weeks teaching her and sister Elizabeth to write. [SAC **61**]

CRAFT, Anne (1738-): Brightling girls' charity school. Admitted between 31 July 1747 and 10 June 1749, in which period she attended on 401 school days; there to period 10 June 1749 to 29 September 1752, in which she attended on 503 school days; had 904 days at school in total. Baptised 6 May 1738, daughter of Thomas and Hannah. (Four sisters also at the school.) [ESRO PAR 254/25/1; PR]

CRAFT, Elizabeth (1737-): Brightling girls' charity school. Admitted between 31 July 1747 and 10 June 1749, in which period she attended on 316 school days; there to period 10 June 1749 to 29 September 1752, in which she attended on 364 school days; had 680 days at school in total. Baptised 21 August 1737 (parents not given in parish register). [ESRO PAR 254/25/1; PR]

CRAFT, Elizabeth (1744 or 45-): Brightling girls' charity school. Admitted and left between 30 April 1757 and 31 July 1758, in which period she attended on 301 school days. Baptised 20 January 1745, daughter of Thomas. (Four sisters also at the school.) [ESRO PAR 254/25/1; PR]

CRAFT, Hannah (1741-): Brightling girls' charity school. Admitted between 29 September 1752 and Lady Day 1755, in which period she attended on 439 school days; there to period Lady Day 1755 to 30 April 1757, in which she attended on 465 school days; had 904 days at school in total. Baptised 3 October 1741, daughter of Thomas and Hannah. (Four sisters also at the school.) [ESRO PAR 254/25/1; PR]

CRAFT, Mary (1739 or 40-): Brightling girls' charity school. Admitted between 10 June 1749 and 29 September 1752, in which period she attended on 310 school days; there to period 29 September 1752 to Lady Day 1755, in which she attended on 184 school days; had 494 days at school in total. Baptised 20 January 1740, daughter of Thomas and Hannah. (Four sisters also at the school.) [ESRO PAR 254/25/1; PR]

CRAFT, Sarah (1748-): Brightling girls' charity school. Admitted between 31 July 1758 and 31 December 1761, in which period she attended on 132 school days. (No later records.) Baptised 3 July 1748, daughter of Thomas. (Four sisters also at the school.) [ESRO PAR 254/25/1; PR]

[CRESSWELL, James (1793-1803):] Midhurst grammar school, perhaps in 18th century. Memorial inscription at Midhurst: 'James Cresswell Scholar of Midhurst School and fourth son of Richard Cresswell Esq of Doctors Commons London who died on Sept the 20th in the year of our Lord 1803 Aged 10 years'. [*HMGS*]

CRISS, John (1728-): At Eastbourne charity school December 1738 (?). Baptised 24 February 1728, son of James and Catharine. [SAS Budgen MS v.129; PR]

CRITTALL, Ann (1790-): Mayfield charity school. Admitted 11 July 1800; removed 9 April 1802, taken out by parents. Baptised 26 September 1790, daughter of David and Hannah. (Two brothers, 1 sister, also at the school.) [MSB; PR]

CRITTALL, David (1788-): Mayfield charity school. Admitted 11 January 1799; removed 12 July 1799, taken out by parents. Baptised 1 June 1788, son of David and Hannah. (One brother, 2 sisters, also at the school.) [MSB; PR]

CRITTAL, David (1792-): Admitted Fermor's charity school, Rotherfield, 1 June 1800. Son of Ann Allen by her first husband. Baptised 4 November 1792, son of Thomas and Ann. [ESRO PAR 465/4/1; PR]

CRITTALL, Hannah (1789-): Mayfield charity school. Admitted 12 April 1799; removed 11 June 1800, taken out by parents. Baptised 28 September 1789, daughter of David and Hannah. (Two brothers, 1 sister, also at the school.) [MSB; PR]

CRITALL, William (1791-): Mayfield charity school. Admitted 12 July 1799; removed 9 July 1802, 'Gone from the parish'. Baptised 4 December 1791, son of David and Hannah. (One brother, 2 sisters, also at the school.) [MSB; PR]

CROFT, John (1787-): Admitted Robertsbridge charity school at its opening, 5 April 1796, aged 8. Sponsored by Mr Pooke. Baptised 17 March 1787, son of Edward and Mary (née Taylor). (Brother William also at the school.) [ESRO PAR 477/25/1/1; Salehurst PR]

CROFT, William (1788-): Admitted Robertsbridge charity school at its opening, 5 April 1796. Sponsored by John Micklethwaite, esq. Baptised 5 July 1788, son of Edward and Mary (née Taylor). (Brother John also at the school.) [ESRO PAR 477/25/1/1; Salehurst PR]

CROUCH: Taught by Sarah French at Brightling, who was paid by John Fuller for schooling 'Crouch Boy' - on 16 April 1733, for 38 weeks at 2d a week, on 18 May 1736, for

35 weeks at 2d a week, and probably for the period between, when other undetailed payments were made to her for schooling. (A John Crouch was John Fuller's mole catcher: eg paid 6 January 1735 19s 6d 'for catching 13 Dozen of Moles att 1s 6d per Dozen'.) [ESRO SAS/RF 15/28]

CROUCH, Elizabeth (1725-): Brightling girls' charity school. Admitted 6 April 1735, aged 10; discharged 21 November 1735, 'being absent above Twenty dayes in a quarter and very often not being att School above an hour in a day'; re-admitted 21 April 1738; had left by end April 1740; only at school 84 days in year 1 May 1738 to 1 May 1739, and 28 days in the following year. Baptised 15 August 1725, daughter of John and Elle (for note on John, see CROUCH above). [ESRO PAR 254/25/1; PR]

CROUCH, Elizabeth (1774-): Mayfield charity school. Admitted 11 July 1783; removed 7 July 1786, for non-attendance. Baptised 12 August 1774, 'a base-born Daughter of Amy Crouch'. [MSB; PR]

CROUCH, Susan: Mayfield charity school. Admitted 4 October 1751; removed 27 March 1752, for non-attendance, still a 'reader'. [MSB]

CROUCH, Tabitha (Tabath) (1747-): Brightling girls' charity school. Admitted between 31 July 1758 and 31 December 1761, in which period she attended on 18 school days. (No later records.) Baptised 9 October 1747, daughter of William and Mary. [ESRO PAR 254/25/1; PR]

CROUCH, Thomas (1787-): Admitted Robertsbridge charity school at its opening, 5 April 1796, aged 8. Sponsored by Mr Charles Verrall. Baptised 23 September 1787, son of William and Sarah (née Pettitt). [ESRO PAR 477/25/1/1; Salehurst PR]

CROUCHER: A poor boy of West Grinstead who received schooling 1725, under the Dowlin charity. [WSRO Par 95/1/1/3]

CRUTTENDEN, Elizabeth (1739-): Brightling girls' charity school. Admitted between 31 July 1747 and 10 June 1749, in which period she attended on 490 school days; there to period 10 June 1749 to 26 September 1752, in which she attended on 826 school days; had 1,316 days at school in total. Baptised 9 April 1739, daughter of Joseph and Mary. [ESRO PAR 254/25/1; PR]

CRUTTENDEN, Sarah (1747-): Brightling girls' charity school. Admitted between Lady Day 1755 and 30 April 1757, in which period she attended on 236 school days; there at least to period 31 July 1758 to 31 December 1761, in which she attended on 408 school days (no later records); had at least 981 days at school. Baptised 9 June 1747, daughter of John and Mary. [ESRO PAR 254/25/1; PR]

CULLEY, Thomas: Brighton charity school. Added to end of list of 'readers' December 1705 (ie joined subsequently). [BSB]

CURD, John: Admitted Fermor's charity school, Rotherfield, 14 September 1800. Son of Benjamin. [ESRO PAR 465/4/1]

CURD, Richard (1747-): Saunders' charity school, Rye. In lists from midsummer 1756 (? shown as 'James' as addendum to 7 April 1756 list, but another suspect name error same list) to Michaelmas 1761 (not in 20 January 1762). Baptised 17 September 1747, son of Richard and Martha. [RSB; PR]

CURTIS: Button's school, Lewes. To recite, in French, at a 'Public Examination' at the *Star Assembly Room* on 22 June 1797. [*SWA* 19.6.97]

CURTIS, Joseph: Steyning grammar school. Alleged, in a petition to Chancery (1816), that he had been obliged to leave the school c1780 because of harsh treatment by the master, John Morgan. [Sleight, J. M. *A Very Exceptional Instance* (1981)]

CUTTS, John (1742-): Saunders' charity school, Rye. In list of 16 January 1754 (not in Michaelmas 1753); in this list only (not in 9 April 1755, next surviving list). Baptised 5 January 1743, son of John and Anne. [RSB; PR]

DADD: Button's school, Lewes. To recite at a 'Public Examination' at the *Star Assembly*

Room, 22 June 1797. [*SWA* 19.6.97]

DADD, George (1722-): Saunders' charity school, Rye. In lists from 14 October 1730 (not in 22 July 1730) to 19 January 1732 (29 March 1732 notes 'left the school'); re-admitted, in 25 October 1732 (not in 5 July 1732) to 9 October 1734 (January 1735 missing; 9 April 1735 notes 'left the school'). Baptised 6 April 1722, son of John and Susan (father was sexton. Brother John also at the school). [RSB; PR]

DADD, John (1710-): Saunders' charity school, Rye. In lists from September 1722 (?) (first list) to 11 August 1725 (not in January 1726 (?) or 4 May 1726). Son of John, sexton. Baptised 10 November 1710, son of John and Susan. (Brother George also at the school.) [RSB; PR]

DADD, John (1736-): Saunders' charity school, Rye. In lists from 26 October 1743 (not in June 1743 (?)) to Michaelmas 1749 (not in Christmas 1749). Baptised 26 November 1736, son of John Dadd junior and Elizabeth. [RSB; PR]

DADSWELL (DIDSWELL), David (1788-): Admitted Fermor's charity school, Rotherfield, 3 May 1794. Baptised 9 March 1788, son of James and Mary. (Brother William also at the school.) [ESRO PAR 465/4/1; PR]

DADSWELL (DADIWELLS), William (1791-): Admitted Fermor's charity school, Rotherfield, 3 February 1799. Baptised 3 April 1791, son of James and Mary. (Brother David also at the school.) [ESRO PAR 465/4/1; PR]

DALLY: Grey Coat charity school, Chichester. Left between Michaelmas 1752 and Michaelmas 1753. Given 10s 6d on leaving. [WSRO Cap.V/1/1]

DALLY: Grey Coat charity school, Chichester. Left between Michaelmas 1755 and Michaelmas 1756. Given 10s 6d on leaving. [WSRO Cap.V/1/1]

DALLY: Grey Coat charity school, Chichester. Left between Michaelmas 1757 and Michaelmas 1758. Given 10s 6d on leaving. [WSRO Cap.V/1/1]

DANIEL, Ann (1775-): Mayfield charity school. Admitted 15 October 1789; removed 13 July 1791, taken out by parents. Baptised 10 September 1775, daughter of George and Rebecca. (Brother George also at the school.) [MSB; PR]

DANIEL, Fanny: Mayfield charity school. Admitted 13 May 1798; removed 10 April 1800. [MSB]

DANIEL, George (1783-): Mayfield charity school. Admitted 13 July 1791; removed 11 July 1794, for non-attendance. Baptised 18 May 1783, son of George and Rebecca. (Sister Ann also at the school.) [MSB; PR]

DANIEL, William: Saunders' charity school, Rye. In lists 8 October 1735 (not in 2 July 1735) to 2 April 1740 (9 July 1740 notes 'left the school'). Son of William. [RSB]

DANN, John (1721-): Saunders' charity school, Rye. In lists from 25 October 1732 (not in 5 July 1732) to 9 April 1735 (2 July 1735 notes 'left the school'). In school book, son of William or John ('William' to start with; becomes 'John' from 28 March 1733 until 'William' again 9 October 1734 to note on leaving school when again 'John'). Baptised 5 May 1721, son of William and Mary. [RSB; PR]

DANN, John (1771-): Mayfield charity school. Admitted 15 October 1779; removed 2 August 1782, for non-attendance. Baptised 30 June 1771, son of John and Mary. (Brother Thomas probably also at the school.) [MSB; PR]

DANN, Thomas (1772 or 73-): Mayfield charity school. Admitted January 1780; removed 9 April 1784, 'Sufficiently Learned'. Baptised either 18 October 1772, son of Thomas and Mary, or 20 May 1773, son of John and Mary - probably latter, as brother John admitted 3 months before. [MSB; PR]

DAVID, Henry (1771 -): Lord Pelham's charity school, Lewes [qv Rand's school]. Probably admitted Lady Day 1779. There 10 October 1784, aged 13. Baptised 28 October 1771, son of Henry and Susannah. [ESRO AMS 6005; St Anne PR]

DAVIES: Button's school, Lewes. To recite, in French, at a 'Public Examination' at the *Star Assembly Room*, 22 June 1797. [*SWA* 19.6.97]

DAVIS, Elias (1741-): Sedlescombe charity school. Admitted 24 June 1748, aged 7. Baptised 9 October 1741, son of Elias and Martha. [SSB; PR]

DAVIS, John: At Rev Thankful Frewen's school at Northiam, as a boarder, from 28 July 1715 to 28 July 1719. A record of the classics he studied survives. Son of John, who paid the fees of £16 per annum, with some 'gratuities'. [ESRO FRE 533]

DAVIS, John (1692-): Brighton charity school. Admitted as 'reader' sometime after 'readers' list of (probably) January 1702; joined 'writers' class sometime after 12 January 1702; had left by December 1705 and gone 'to a turner'. Baptised 26 June 1692, son of Stephen and Elizabeth. [BSB; PR]

DAVIS, Thomas: Son of Mary Davis of St Michael, Lewes, on 9 September 1784 he was apprenticed for 7 years to William Gwynne (master of the grammar school) 'to learn the art of reading and writing'. He was to receive meat, drink, clothing, lodging, &c. (Possibly the TD baptised at St Michael, Lewes, 27 January 1774, son of John and Mary.) [ESRO PAR 414/33/71]

DAVIS, William: Saunders' charity school, Rye. Admitted 11 December 1776; in lists to Lady Day 1782 (not in 2 September 1782). Son of Elias. [RSB]

DAVY, Thomas (1729-1801): At East Hoathly school 1755. Scholar (adult) and friend of Thomas Turner, master, and the same age. Taught school for TT on occasion. Shoemaker; married 1761 Mary Virgo, widow; parish clerk 1777. Died 1801, aged 72. [Worcester, D. K. *The Life and Times of Thomas Turner of East Hoathly* (1948); Vaisey, D. (ed) *The Diary of Thomas Turner* (1984)]

DAWES, Stephen: Saunders' charity school, Rye. Admitted 26 March 1766; in lists to Christmas 1770 (not in midsummer 1773, next surviving list). Son of Stephen. [RSB]

DAWES, Thomas (1771-): Saunders' charity school, Rye. Admitted 6 December 1780; in lists to Michaelmas 1781 (not in Lady Day 1782) but 29 September 1783 list notes 'Thomas son of Stephen Dawes to be readmitted the first Vacancy'; re-admitted 14 January 1784; 24 June 1784 notes 'left School'. Born 16 July 1771, son of Steven and Jane, Particular Baptists. [RSB; PRO RG 4/3365]

DEADMAN: Grey Coat charity school, Chichester. Left between Michaelmas 1761 and Michaelmas 1762. Given 10s 6d on leaving. [WSRO Cap.V/1/1]

DEAN, Joseph (1689-): Brighton charity school. In list of 'readers' of (probably) January 1702; given coat and hat July 1702; joined 'writers' class sometime after 12 January 1702; in 'writers' list December 1705. Baptised 24 November 1689, son of Joseph and Joan. [BSB; PR]

DENNET, Barbara (1696-): Brighton girls' charity school. Admitted after 25 March 1703, probably by end of 1705. Baptised 18 October 1696, daughter of Thomas and Jane (née Wood). (Brother Thomas at the boys' charity school.) [BSB; PR]

DENNET (DONNAT), Thomas junior (1700-): Brighton charity school. Given prayer book 1715. Baptised 17 November 1700, son of Thomas and Jane. (Sister Barbara at the girls' charity school.) [BSB; PR]

DIBBINS, John: Saunders' charity school, Rye. In lists December 1724 (?) (not in 8 April 1724) to June 1725 (?) (not in 11 August 1725). [RSB]

DIBBLE, Jeremiah (1751-): Saunders' charity school, Rye. In lists from Michaelmas 1761 (not in Lady Day 1761) to Lady Day 1767 (not in Christmas 1768, next surviving list). Baptised 18 March 1751, son of Jeremiah and Hannah. [RSB; PR]

DICKER, Thomas: Private pupil of Robert Gerison, master of Saunders' school, Uckfield. Became manager of Lewes Old Bank in 1795. [Gilbert, H. D. *Education Yesterday: The Saunders' foundation and the Uckfield National Schools* citing Dicker's autobiography]

DIGGENS, John: Midhurst grammar school. Admitted as charity scholar 1792. [*HMGS*]

DIVALL, Thomas: Admitted Fermor's charity school, Rotherfield, 3 May 1794. Son of William. [ESRO PAR 465/4/1]

DOLMAN, Edward (c1701-): Grey Coat charity school, Chichester. Admitted at opening Lady Day 1710. Aged 9 at Lady Day 1711. Expelled (as were 4 others) between Lady Day 1712 and Lady Day 1713. [WSRO Cap.V/1/1]

DONNAT - see DENNET

DOUCH, Robert (1724-): Saunders' charity school, Rye. In lists from 27 October 1731 (not in 7 July 1731) to 31 July 1734 (9 October 1734 notes 'left the school'). Father shown as 'Deceased' in list for 31 July 1734 (last entry for son). Baptised 12 March 1724, son of Robert and Elizabeth. [RSB; PR]

DOUST, Isaac (1760-): Sedlescombe charity school. There 18 April 1772, a 'writer'. Baptised 18 May 1760, son of Stephen and Susanna. [SSB; PR]

DOUST, Stephen: Sedlescombe charity school. Admitted 5 March 1760; in list for 1761. [SSB]

DOUST, Susanna: Sedlescombe charity school. Admitted 5 March 1760; in list for 1761. [SSB]

DOWNER (DONNER), Thomas (1687-): Brighton charity school. In list of 'readers' of (probably) January 1702; had left by December 1705 and gone 'to sea'. Baptised 7 August 1687, son of France Douner and [*blank*] (married 17 January 1682, Frances Doner and Susan Addums, 'Douner' at 1694 baptism of daughter). Younger brother of Francis, baptised 28 December 1684, who was probably master of the *Swan* boat in 1726 and father of Swan (1735-1816) founder of the Swan Downer charity school. [BSB; PR; Tibble, R., pers. comm.]

DOWNER, Thomas (1695-): Brighton charity school. In list of 'readers' December 1705. Baptised 16 June 1695, son of Thomas and [*blank*] (mother probably Martha: married 14

January 1683, Thomas Douner and Martha Jesper. Another T D, baptised 19 Aug 1688, son of Thomas and Martha, presumably died). [RSB; PR]

DRURY, William (1790-): Admitted Robertsbridge charity school at its opening 5 April 1796, aged 6. Sponsored by Rev Stephen Jenkin, vicar of Salehurst. Baptised 2 May 1790, son of Edward and Mary (née Bunce). [ESRO PAR 477/25/1/1; Salehurst PR]

DUDENEY, Henry (1753-): His son, John, wrote that his father was 'sent...to school for a while at Ditchling but I believe it was not for long. He was sent to tend the sheep as soon as he was old enough.' He was able later to teach his son to write a little and to do addition and subtraction. Baptised 21 November 1753, son of John (1720-1803, shepherd) and Alice (née Farncombe, 1721-95), who married 27 September 1747. [*SAC* **2**; *SFH* **7** No. 3]

DUDENEY, John (1782-1852): Son of Henry (1753-) [qv] and Sarah (née Geering) (1754-), was sent as a young child to Dame Mascall at Plumpton: 'I learnt nothing there but to drive the ducks into the moat and my mother, fearing I might fall in, took me away after I had been there only a few weeks. This was all the day schooling I ever had. My mother taught me to read and my father taught me to write a little in the winter evenings and to do addition and subtraction (all he knew of arithmetic).' Thereafter taught himself from books bought at Lewes, fairs, etc. Shepherd boy at 8; about 10, found wheatears' nests for Paul Dunvan (historian, usher at Lewes grammar school) who gave him a history of England and *Robinson Crusoe*; under shepherd at 16; moved to Kingston, near Lewes, 1799 at wage of £6 per annum; bought books on history, geography, astronomy, French, geometry, Hebrew; head shepherd 1802 at Rottingdean, where befriended by Dr Hooker, the vicar, who kept a school for the gentry [qv] and let him use his telescope and globes 'and gave me free access to his library'. In 1804, at 22, successfully opened a school at Lewes. [*SAC* **2**; *SFH* **7** No. 3]

DUDMAN, William: Midhurst grammar school. Admitted as charity scholar 1785. [*HMGS*]

DUELY, Henry: Mayfield charity school. Admitted 9 April 1790; removed 6 July1792, taken out by parents but 'Sufficiently Learned'. [MSB]

DUELY, Samuel: Mayfield charity school. Admitted 11 January 1793; in list for 11 October 1793 his place taken by Sarah Duely (no removal for Samuel, no admission for Sarah; she was probably his sister). [MSB]

DUELY, Sarah: Mayfield charity school. No formal admission but in list for 11 October 1793 took the place of Samuel Duely, probably her brother; removed 11 April 1794. [MSB]

DUKE, David (1773-): Mayfield charity school. Admitted 13 January 1786; removed 6 April 1787, 'sufficiently learned'. Baptised 31 October 1773, son of Thomas and Mary. (Sister Sarah also at the school.) [MSB; PR]

DUKE, Sarah (1763-): Mayfield charity school. Admitted 9 July1773; removed 7 April 1775, 'withdrawn by her parents' after 1¾ years as a 'reader'. Baptised 24 April 1763, daughter of Thomas and Mary. (Brother David also at the school.) [MSB; PR]

DUMBRELL, Abraham (1733-): At Eastbourne charity school April 1741. Baptised 16 June 1733, son of Abraham and Elizabeth. [SAS Budgen MS v.129; PR]

DUNFORD, William (c1701-): Grey Coat charity school, Chichester, from its opening Lady Day 1710. Aged 9 at Lady Day 1711. 'Discarded' between Lady Day 1713 and Lady Day 1714 (shown then as 'John', probably in error). [WSRO Cap.V/1/1]

DUNK, John (1725-): Saunders' charity school, Rye. In lists from 20 October 1736 (not in 7 April 1736) to 28 June 1738 (?) (4 October 1738 notes 'left the school'). Baptised 26 March 1725, son of Andrew and Elizabeth. (Brother William also at the school.) [RSB; PR]

DUNK, Sarah (1744 or 45-): Brightling girls' charity school. Admitted and left between 29 September 1752 and Lady Day 1755, and had 400 teaching days at the school. Baptised 27 January 1745, daughter of John. [ESRO PAR 254/25/1; PR]

DUNK, William (1722-): Saunders' charity school, Rye. In lists from 7 July 1731 (not in 31 March 1731) to 2 July 1735 (8 October 1735 notes 'left the school'); but not in lists for 27 October 1731, 19 January 1732, 29 March 1732 (in 25 October 1732) so probably absent for a time. Baptised 16 March 1722, son of Andrew and Elizabeth. (Brother John also at the school.) [RSB; PR]

DUNN, James: Eastbourne charity school. Admitted Michaelmas 1779; there Christmas 1779. [SAS Budgen MS v.117]

DUNN, Samuel (1762 or 63-): Eastbourne charity school. Admitted 3 August 1770. Baptised 23 January 1763, son of George and Mary. [SAS Budgen MS v.105; PR]

DUNSTONE: Button's school, Lewes. To recite at a 'Public Examination' at the *Star Assembly Room*, 22 June 1797. [*SWA* 19.6.97]

DUNSTONE, Mary (1750-): At Seaford charity school 1765. Baptised 12 July 1750, daughter of Samuel and Ann. [BL Add MS 33,059; PR]

DUPLOCK, Jeremiah (1764-): Mayfield charity school. Admitted 9 July 1773; removed 7 January 1774, 'being withdrawn by his parent' after ½ year as a 'reader'. Baptised 27 April 1764, son of John and Sarah. [MSB; PR]

DUPLOCK, John (1751-): Mayfield charity school. Admitted 11 July 1755; removed 26 October 1759, 'sufficiently Learned', after 4¼ years at the school, 1¾ years as a 'writer'. Baptised 24 April 1751, son of John and Elizabeth. (NB Very young when admitted, but joined at same time as older brother Joseph, and both left at same time.) [MSB; PR]

DUPLOCK, John (1755-): Mayfield charity school. Admitted 11 January 1765; removed 16 October 1767, 'Sufficiently Learned', after 2¾ years at the school (but probably not a 'writer': details missing from previous list). Baptised 30 April 1755, son of William and Ann. (Brother Thomas also at the school.) [MSB; PR]

DUPLOCK, Joseph (1747-): Mayfield charity

school. Admitted 11 July 1755; removed 26 October 1759, 'sufficiently Learned', after 4¼ years at the school, 2¾ as a 'writer'. Baptised 4 January 1748, son of John and Sarah. (Younger brother John admitted and removed same dates.) [MSB; PR]

DUPLOCK, Joseph: Mayfield charity school. Admitted 8 January 1762; removed 8 July 1763, taken away by parents, after 1½ years as a 'reader'. [MSB]

DUPLOCK, Susan: Mayfield charity school. Admitted 8 April 1763; removed 13 April 1764, taken out by parents, after 1 year as a 'reader'. [MSB]

DUPLOCK, Thomas (1757-): Mayfield charity school. Admitted 8 July 1763; removed 11 July 1766, 'taken out by his Father', after 3 years as a 'reader'. Baptised 28 April 1757, son of William and Anne. (Brother John also at the school.) [MSB; PR]

DUPLOCK, Thomas: Mayfield charity school. Admitted 7 April 1786; removed 17 January 1788, for non-attendance. [MSB]

DUPLOCK, William (1759-): Mayfield charity school. Admitted 2 May 1766 to 'Widow Dukes' dame school; admitted charity school 17 April 1767; removed 19 October 1770, 'Sufficiently Learned', after 3½ years at the school, ¾ year as a 'writer'. Baptised March 1759, son of Thomas and Mary. [MSB; PR]

DUPLOCK, William (1782-): Mayfield charity school. Admitted 13 July 1791; removed 11 January 1793, for non-attendance. Baptised 3 March 1782, son of Joseph and Ann. [MSB; PR]

[DURNFORD, Frances]: In Wiston school list, c1803, and perhaps at the school in 1800. [WSRO Par 211/25/1]

[DURNFORD, Jane]: In Wiston school list, c1803, and perhaps at the school in 1800. [WSRO Par 211/25/1]

[DURNFORD, Thomas]: In Wiston school list, c1803, and perhaps at the school in 1800. [WSRO Par 211/25/1]

DURRANT, Sarah: Mayfield charity school. Admitted 12 October 1753; removed 10 January 1755, for non-attendance, after 1¼ years as a 'reader'. [MSB]

DURRANT, Thomas (c1737-1800): Of East Hoathly, son of Joseph (-1777, blacksmith) and Sarah, taught by Thomas Turner, master of the school there, to read and write when he was in his teens. TT taught him at home in the evenings. Though 8 years his junior, a close friend of TT; a sportsman, good at cricket and a fast runner. Married 1776. Died 1800. [Vaisey, D. (ed) *The Diary of Thomas Turner* (1984)]

DYETT, Thomas Chariton (1762-): - see **ROBBINSON, Thomas Chatterton**

DYNE (DINE), John (1691-): Brighton charity school. In 'writers' list 12 January 1702; had left by December 1705. Born 26 November 1691, baptised 1 January 1692, son of Samuel Dine otherwise Wood. (Father probably Samuel baptised 19 June 1642, son of Thomas Wood otherwise Dine, and married, as Wood, Ann Tree, 1 July 1679, and was a mason.) [BSB; PR]

EARL, Martha: Eastbourne charity school. Admitted 13 June 1768; still there January 1771. Daughter of James. [SAS Budgen MS v.105]

EASON, John: A poor boy of Laughton for whose schooling the parish paid 7s in the year Easter 1738 to Easter 1739. (They also paid for his keep, at 6s a month, and for clothes for him to 1741.) [ESRO PAR 409/31/1/2]

EASTON, John (c1704-): Grey Coat charity school, Chichester. Admitted Lady Day 1712, aged 7; there Lady Day 1714. [WSRO Cap.V/1/1]

EASTWOOD, Anne (1740-): Mayfield charity school. Admitted 5 October 1750; removed 14 November 1752, for non-attendance (at 3 July 1752 she had been a 'writer' for 1 year). Baptised either 1 January 1745, daughter of John and Elizabeth, or (more probably) 27 January 1740, daughter of John and Katherine. [MSB; PR, BT]

EASTWOOD, George (1785-): Mayfield charity school. Admitted 10 January 1794; removed 6 July 1798, for non-attendance. Baptised 27 March 1785, son of John and Elizabeth. (Brother John also at the school.) [MSB; PR]

EASTWOOD, John (1764-): Mayfield charity school. Admitted 7 January 1774; removed 11 April 1777, 'To make room for others more worthy of Charity', after 3¼ years at the school, 1¼ years as a 'writer'. Baptised 28 October 1764, son of John and Mary. [MSB; PR]

EASTWOOD, John (1787-): Mayfield charity school. Admitted 8 April 1796; removed 12 October 1798, for non-attendance. Baptised 2 March 1787, son of John and Elizabeth. (Brother George also at the school.) [MSB; PR]

EDNEY: Grey Coat charity school, Chichester. Left between Michaelmas 1769 and Michaelmas 1770. Given 10s 6d on leaving. [WSRO Cap.V/1/1]

EDSALL, Thomas: Grey Coat charity school, Chichester. Left between Michaelmas 1767 and Michaelmas 1768. Given 10s 6d on leaving. [WSRO Cap.V/1/1]

EDWARDS, Ann (1758 or 59-): Mayfield charity school. Admitted 24 January 1766; removed 27 October 1769, 'Sufficiently Learned', after 3¾ years at the school, 1¾ years as a 'writer'. Baptised 16 January 1759, daughter of Thomas and Anne. (Brothers Thomas, William, also at the school.) [MSB; PR]

EDWARDS, Henry (1711-): Saunders' charity school, Rye. In lists from September 1722 (?) (first list) to January 1725 (?); June 1725 (?) notes 'Gon on the Mackaril Season'; 11 August 1725 notes 'Gon to Catch Mackril and are not yet Returned to the School'. Baptised 6 January 1712, son of John and Mary. [RSB; PR]

EDWARDS, Henry Lilburne (1763-): Saunders' charity school, Rye. Admitted 14 October 1772; in lists to Michaelmas 1775 (not in Christmas 1777, next surviving list). Baptised 17 February 1763, son of Henry and

Mercy. [RSB; PR]

EDWARDS, John: Saunders' charity school, Rye. In lists from 10 January 1739 (not in 4 October 1738) to 2 April 1740 (not in 9 July 1740 - replaced by brother Thomas). Son of William, barber. (Brothers Thomas, William, also at the school.) [RSB]

EDWARDS, Thomas (1731-): Saunders' charity school, Rye. In lists from 9 July 1740 (not in 2 April 1740) to Christmas 1745, which notes 'Absent 4 months' (not in 2 July 1746). Baptised 11 November 1731, son of William and Elizabeth. (Brothers John, William, also at the school.) [RSB; PR]

EDWARDS, Thomas (1763-): Mayfield charity school. Admitted 19 January 1770; removed 7 July 1775, 'Sufficiently Learned', after 5½ years at the school, 3 years as a 'writer'. Baptised 8 January 1764. Son of Thomas and Ann. (Brother William, sister Ann, also at the school.) [MSB; PR]

EDWARDS, William (1735-): Saunders' charity school, Rye. In lists from 2 July 1746 (not in Christmas 1745); 'Left School March 24 1750'. Baptised 11 June 1735, son of William and Elizabeth. (Brothers John, Thomas, also at the school.) [RSB; PR]

EDWARDS, William (1770-1779): Mayfield charity school. Admitted 10 October 1777; removed 15 October 1779, 'Dead', after 2 years at the school, 1 year as a 'writer'. Baptised 27 September 1770, son of Thomas and Ann. (Brother Thomas, sister Ann, also at the school.) [MSB; PR]

ELDRIDGE: Midhurst grammar school. At a public performance of composition and oratory, 27 May 1800, took part, with 3 others, in a scene from Virgil's *Aeneid*. [*SWA* 2.6.1800]

ELDRIDGE, Ann (1747-): Sedlescombe charity school. There 3 May 1755. Baptised 24 May 1747, daughter of William and Mary. (Brother William, sister Mary, also at the school.) [SSB; PR]

ELDRIDGE, Edward (1738-): Sedlescombe charity school. There 23 June 1748. Baptised 11 May 1738, son of William and Sarah.

(Sister Sarah also at the school.) [SSB; PR]

ELDRIDGE, John (1776-): Sedlescombe charity school. There 29 September 1784 (a 'writer'), 29 September 1786 and 29 September 1787. Baptised April 1776, son of Thomas and Elizabeth. [SSB; PR]

ELDRIDGE, John (1788-): Mayfield charity school. Admitted 8 April 1796; removed 11 April 1800, 'Sufficiently Learned'. Baptised 21 December 1788, son of John and Catherine. (Brother William, sister Sarah, also at the school.) [MSB; PR]

ELDRIDGE, Mary (1753-): Sedlescombe charity school. Admitted 15 May 1759; there 1761. Baptised 8 April 1753, daughter of William and Mary. (Brother William, sister Ann, also at the school.) [SSB; PR]

ELDRIDGE, Richard (1749-): Sedlescombe charity school. Admitted 6 April 1761. Baptised 23 January 1749, son of Richard and Ann. [SSB; PR]

ELDRIDGE, Sarah (1734 or 35-): Sedlescombe charity school. There 23 June 1748. Baptised 19 January 1735, daughter of William and Sarah. (Brother Edward also at the school.) [SSB; PR]

ELDRIDGE, Sarah (1786-): Mayfield charity school. Admitted 8 July 1796; removed 12 April 1799, taken out by parents. Baptised 31 December 1786, daughter of John and Catharine. (Brothers John, William, also at the school.) [MSB; PR]

ELDRIDGE, William (1764 or 65-): Sedlescombe charity school. There 18 April 1772 (a 'reader') and 8 May 1775 (a 'writer'). Baptised 13 January 1765, son of William and Mary. (Sisters Ann, Mary, also at the school.) [SSB; PR]

ELDRIDGE, William (1791-): Mayfield charity school. Admitted 12 April 1799; removed 9 July 1802, taken out by parents. Baptised 10 April 1791, son of John and Catharine. (Brother John, sister Sarah, also at the school.) [MSB; PR]

ELLIOT, John (1725-82): Lewes grammar school. Born 1725, in parish of St John-sub-Castro, son of Obadiah, proprietor of brewery in Fisher Street. After grammar school, articled to an attorney; became a lawyer, but was notable as an antiquary. Died 28 February 1782, aged 57. [Lower *Worthies*]

ELLIOTT, Sarah: A poor girl of Waldron for whom the parish paid for some schooling 1798. (Her keep was paid for by the parish, at 2s 6d a week, from at least 1794 to 1799.) [ESRO PAR 499/9/1]

ELLIOTT, William: Mayfield charity school. Entered in 24 January 1757 list; removed 10 April 1758, 'sufficiently learned', after 1¼ years at the school, 1 year as a 'writer'. [MSB]

ELLIS, Richard (1761-): Eastbourne charity school. Admitted 20 June 1768; still there January 1771. Baptised 4 December 1761, son of Richard, deceased (buried 7 October 1761) and Elizabeth. [SAS Budgen MS v.105; PR]

ELLIS, William (1734-): At Eastbourne charity school 1741. Baptised 20 November 1734, son of John and Ann. [SAS Budgen MS v.129; PR]

ELLMAN, John (1753-1832): Born at Hartfield 17 October 1753, son of Richard, farmer (who moved to Glynde in 1761) and Elizabeth, he was at school (presumably at Hartfield) for just 2 winter quarters. Later, he took tuition from Rev Thomas Davies, vicar of Glynde, whose daughter Constantia he married as his second wife. Father died 1780. JE was tenant of the Great Farm at Glynde, became a prosperous sheep breeder and agricultural improver. An advocate for education, he was a trustee and benefactor of Glynde charity school and Sunday school; he engaged a literate shepherd, Charles Payne, to teach the men and maid servants in his house to read and write; and sent his son, John, to Winchester. Married firstly 27 January 1783 at Hartfield, Elizabeth Spencer (died 1790); married secondly 15 December 1794, Constantia Davies. Died at Lewes 21 November 1832. [Walesby, A. 'Memoir of John Ellman', *The Library of Agricultural and Horticultural Knowledge* (3rd edition, 1834); *Ringmer History* No. 3 (1984); *SGLH* **2** No. 2 (1980)]

ELOY, Benjamin (1730-): Eastbourne charity school. There December 1738 (?), April 1741. Baptised 25 March 1730, son of Thomas and Sarah. [SAS Budgen MS v.129; PR]

ELPHICK, James: A maths exercise book of his survives, dated 1779. Probably the JE baptised at Herstmonceux 1766, son of Richard and Sarah. (Perhaps at Allfree's school?) [*SNQ* 16]

ERRIDGE: Eastbourne charity school. In Christmas 1779 list, marked 'to continue sometime Longer as he is small (for his age) they wish to put him apprentice to a Trade'. [SAS Budgen MS v.117]

ESPENET (ESPINET), Francis: Saunders' charity school, Rye. In lists from 11 January 1727 (not in 5 October 1726); 19 April 1727 notes 'gon to sea with his father'; 12 July 1727 notes 'Returned to the School June the 20th 1727, went away again July ye 7th day'. Son of David. Father was son of David senior, a French refugee who came to Rye in 1685; father married Elizabeth Dansays, of another French refugee family who came over at the same time, the 2 families being first cousins; Elizabeth was born at Soubissa, on the river Charente. Another David, probably Francis' brother, who was a peruke maker at Rye and deacon and for some time minister (though not universally approved) of the Particular Baptist chapel, Rye, died 28 October 1774, aged 56. [RSB; Holloway, W. *History of the Town and Port of Rye* (1847); PRO RG 4/2968]

EVANS: Button's school, Lewes. To recite at a 'Public Examination' at the *Star Assembly Room*, 22 June 1797. [*SWA* 19.6.97]

EVANS, George (1789-): Sedlescombe charity school. Admitted 9 March 1795; there 25 December 1797 (marked as changing from 'reader' to 'writer') and 20 August 1798 (a 'writer'). Baptised 5 April 1789, son of William and Jane. (Brother James, probably brother William, also at the school). [SSB; PR]

EVANS, James (1786-): Sedlescombe charity school. There 21 October 1793 (a 'reader') and 20 October 1794 (still a 'reader', and name crossed through). Baptised 25 June 1782, son of William and Jane. (Brother George, probably brother William, also at the school.) [SSB; PR]

EVANS, William: Sedlescombe charity school. There 21 October 1793 (a 'writer') and 20 October 1794 (name crossed through). (Probably brother to George and James above.) [SSB]

EVE (EAVE), John (1730-): Saunders' charity school, Rye. In lists from 15 October 1740 (not in 9 July 1740) to 11 January 1744 (4 July 1744 notes 'left the school'). Baptised 25 February 1730, son of William and Mary. [RSB; PR]

EVERSHED, William (1784-1865): A boarder at William Evershed's school at Steyning. [Evershed, P., pers. comm., citing Frank Evershed's notebooks, Mrs Carter's recollections]

FAITHFULL, Philadelphia (1751-): Brightling girls' charity school. Admitted between 30 April 1757 and 31 July 1758, in which period she attended on 154 school days; there to period 31 July 1758 to 31 December 1761, in which she attended on 535 school days (no later records); had at least 689 days at the school. Baptised 5 April 1751, daughter of John and Ann. [ESRO PAR 254/25/1; PR]

FARMER, Jesse (1788-): Admitted Fermor's charity school, Rotherfield, 29 April 1798. Baptised 17 August 1788, son of Henry and Sarah. (Brother William also at the school.) [ESRO PAR 465/4/1; PR]

FARMER, William (1769-): Saunders' charity school, Rye. Admitted 6 March 1782; in lists to 29 September 1784 (not in 24 June 1785). Probably baptised 28 April 1769, William [Atnoke?] son of William and Anne. [RSB; PR]

FARMER, William (1783-): Admitted Fermor's charity school, Rotherfield, 1 June 1792. Baptised 4 May 1783, son of Henry and Ann. [ESRO PAR 465/4/1; PR]

FARMER (FERMOR), William (1786-): Admitted Fermor's charity school, Rotherfield, 3 May 1794. Baptised 25 June 1786, son of Henry and Sarah. (Brother Jesse also at the school). [ESRO PAR 465/4/1; PR]

FARNCOMBE: Button's school, Lewes. To recite at a 'Public Examination' at the *Star Assembly Room*, 22 June 1797. [*SWA* 19.6.97]

FARNCOMBE, Lettice: Henry Farncombe was billed by John Head of Lewes for teaching writing to 2 daughters, 'entered' 18 April 1726, for ½ year at 6s 3d per quarter each, with pens at 4s and 6 books plus 'pens carried home', 3s 6d. And 'two Daughters againe', entered 6 May 1728, were billed for 1 quarter, with one, Lettice, continuing for a further quarter; extras were 3s for pens, 2s for 'both their breaking up at Whitsuntide' and 1s 6d for '3 Books more'. [*SAC* **40**, 275]

FARR, George (1766-): Saunders' charity school, Rye. Admitted 11 January 1775; left 22 May 1779. Baptised 15 February 1766, son of George and Mary. [RSB; PR]

FATHERS, Matthew (c1702-): Grey Coat charity school, Chichester, from its opening Lady Day 1710. Aged 8 at Lady Day 1711 There Lady Day 1714. [WSRO Cap.V/1/1]

FAULKNER, Ann: Mayfield charity school. Admitted 7 January 1791; removed 11 October 1793. [MSB]

(**FEERING**): A poor child of Lewes, for whose schooling the parish of St Anne Lewes paid a small sum, 15 March 1788. [ESRO PAR 411/31/3]

FELT, Michael: Saunders' charity school, Rye. In lists from 19 April 1727 (not in 11 January 1727) to midsummer 1728 (?) (in 17 April 1728, not in 8 January 1729). Son of David, deceased. Probably a Dutch family: David, son of Felt, a Dutchman, and Sarah baptised 20 May 1707 - Michael probably same parents. [RSB; PR]

FENNER, Andrew (1768-): Mayfield charity school. Admitted 7 July 1775; removed 30 July 1779, 'Sufficiently Learned', after 4 years at the school, 3 years as a 'writer'. Baptised 6 April 1768, son of Andrew and Mary. (Four brothers, 2 sisters, also at the school.) [MSB; PR]

FENNER, Andrew (1773-): Mayfield charity school. Admitted 12 April 1782; removed 7 April 1786, 'Sufficiently Learned'. Born 6 March 1773, baptised 9 May 1773 at Mayfield, Burwash Independent Calvinist Chapel. [MSB; PRO RG 4/2219]

FENNER, Andrew (1774-): Mayfield charity school. Admitted 7 July 1786; removed 11 April 1788 'Sufficiently learned'. Born 21 May 1774, baptised 10 July 1774 at Mayfield, Burwash Independent Calvinist Chapel. [MSB; PRO RG 4/2219]

FENNER, Elizabeth (1775-): Mayfield charity school. Admitted 8 April 1785; removed 6 July 1787, taken out by parents. Baptised 11 June 1775, daughter of Thomas and Esther. (Brothers John, Thomas, also at the school.) [MSB; PR]

FENNER, Elizabeth (1776-): Mayfield charity school. Admitted 5 January 1787; removed 9 April 1790, taken out by parents but 'Sufficiently Learned'. Born 18 June 1776, baptised 11 July 1776 at Mayfield, Burwash Independent Calvinist Chapel. [MSB; PRO RG 4/2219]

FENNER, Fanny: Mayfield charity school. Admitted 9 April 1790; removed 11 October 1793. (Perhaps nonconformist family: house of Andrew Fenner registered for worship of Presbyterians, 1707; house of John Fenner for worship of Independents, 1789.) [MSB; WSRO Ep.V/8/4, Ep.V/17/9]

FENNER, Hannah (1776-): Mayfield charity school. Admitted 7 April 1786; removed 11 April 1788, 'Sufficiently learned'. Baptised 16 July 1776, daughter of Andrew and Mary. (Five brothers, 1 sister, also at the school.) [MSB; PR]

FENNER, Henry (1755-): Mayfield charity school. Admitted 8 April 1763; removed 2 May 1766, 'well learned', after 3 years at the school, 1¾ years as a 'writer'. Baptised 19 November 1755, son of Andrew and Mary. (Four brothers, 2 sisters, also at the school.) [MSB; PR]

FENNER, James (1770-): Mayfield charity school. Admitted 17 July 1778; removed 6 July 1781, 'Sufficiently Learned'. Baptised 16 September 1770, son of Andrew and Mary. (Four brothers, 2 sisters, also at the school.)

[MSB; PR]

FENNER, John (1765-): Mayfield charity school. Admitted 13 October 1775 (incorrectly identified as 'Thomas' on admission; 'shoemaker' used in lists to distinguish him from JF 'carpenter'); removed 10 April 1778, 'Sufficiently Learned', after 2½ years at the school, all as a 'writer'. Probably baptised 14 May 1765, son of Thomas and Esther. (Brother Thomas, sister Elizabeth, also at the school). [MSB; PR]

FENNER, John (1768-): Mayfield charity school. Admitted 5 April 1776 ('carpenter' used in lists to distinguish him from JF 'shoemaker'); removed 9 April 1779, 'Sufficiently Learned', after 3 years at the school, all as a 'writer'. Probably born 4 November 1768, baptised 7 January 1769 at Mayfield, Burwash Independent Calvinist Chapel. [MSB; PRO RG 4/2219]

FENNER, John (1791-): Mayfield charity school. Admitted 10 January 1800; removed 9 April 1802, taken out by parents. Baptised 8 May 1791, son of John and Ann. [MSB; PR]

FENNER, Joseph (1773-): Mayfield charity school. Admitted 12 April 1782; removed 14 January 1785, 'Sufficiently Learned'. Baptised 29 April 1773, son of Andrew and Mary. (Four brothers, 2 sisters, also at the school.) [MSB; PR]

FENNER, Mary (1763-): Mayfield charity school. Admitted 20 July 1770; removed 9 July 1772, 'To make room for a more worthy object', after 2 years at the school as a 'reader'. Baptised 6 April 1763, daughter of Andrew and Mary. (Five brothers, 1 sister, also at the school.) [MSB; PR]

FENNER, Mary (1768-): Mayfield charity school. Admitted 8 January 1779; removed October 1781, 'Sufficiently Learned'. Born 5 February 1768, baptised 13 February 1768 at Mayfield, Burwash Independent Calvinist Chapel. [MSB; PRO RG 4/2219]

FENNER, Peter (1784-): Mayfield charity school. Admitted 6 January 1792; removed 14 October 1796, 'Sufficiently Learned'. Born 16 July 1784, son of William, tailor, baptised 12

August 1784 at Mayfield, Burwash Independent Calvinist Chapel. [MSB; PRO RG 4/2219]

FENNER, Sarah: Mayfield charity school. Admitted 21 April 1769; removed 7 April 1775, 'Sufficiently Learned', after 6 years at the school, 3 years as a 'writer'. (Perhaps nonconformist family; see note under FENNER, Fanny.) [MSB]

FENNER, Thomas (1767-): Mayfield charity school. Admitted 18 July 1777; removed 17 October 1778, for non-attendance, after 1¼ years as a 'reader'. Baptised 17 October 1767, son of Thomas and Esther. (Brother John, sister Elizabeth, also at the school.) [MSB; PR]

FENNER, Thomas: Mayfield charity school. Admitted 11 July 1788; removed 10 July 1789, taken out by parents. (Perhaps nonconformist family; see note under FENNER, Fanny.) [MSB]

FENNER, William (1760-): Mayfield charity school. Admitted 11 July 1766; removed 19 October 1770, 'Sufficiently Learned', after 4¼ years at the school, 2½ as a 'writer'. Baptised 11 October 1760, son of Andrew and Mary. (Four brothers, 2 sisters, also at the school.) [MSB; PR]

FENNER, William (1769-): Mayfield charity school. Admitted 11 October 1776; removed 6 March 1781, 'Sufficiently Learned', after 4½ years at the school, 1¾ years as a 'writer'. Born 12 April 1769, baptised 6 June 1769 at Mayfield, Burwash Independent Calvinist Chapel. [MSB; PRO RG 4/2219]

FENNER, William (1794-): Mayfield charity school. Admitted 11 April 1800; removed 13 July 1804, taken out by parents. Baptised 25 May 1794, son of William and Agnes. [MSB; PR]

FETHERSTONHAUGH, Sir Harry (1754-1846): Born at Uppark 25 December 1754, son and only child of Sir Matthew (died 1774) and Sarah. £1 1s paid to a writing master 1761. Tutored by Dr Durnford, vicar of Harting; then to Eton, and University College, Oxford (matriculated 1772, aged 17). On 12 September 1825, aged 71, married (in the saloon at Uppark) his head dairymaid, Mary

Ann Bullock, aged 20. (He took Mary Ann's sister, Frances, to Uppark to be educated by Miss Sutherland, his illegitimate daughter; the two were friends for life.) Died at Uppark 24 October 1846, aged 91; left everything he possessed to his wife (who died 1875). [Meade-Fetherstonhaugh, M. and Warner, O. *Uppark and its People* (1964); *Al. Oxon.*]

FIELD, Ansley (1786-): Mayfield charity school. Admitted 11 July 1794; removed 13 October 1797, taken out by parents. Baptised 19 March 1786, daughter of Richard and Sarah. (Three brothers also at the school.) [MSB; PR]

FIELD, Benjamin (1783-): Mayfield charity school. Admitted 13 July 1791; removed 11 July 1794, taken out by parents; re-admitted 8 April 1796; removed 6 January 1797, taken out by parents. Baptised 28 December 1783, son of Richard and Sarah. (Two brothers, 1 sister, also at the school.) [MSB; PR]

FIELD, Edward: Mayfield charity school. Admitted 13 October 1797; removed 15 October 1802, 'Sufficiently Learned'. [MSB]

FIELD, John (1741-): Saunders' charity school, Rye. In lists from 8 July 1752 (not in 25 March 1752); left the school 5 March 1756. Baptised 25 July 1741, son of Arthur and Sarah. [RSB; PR]

FIELD, Joseph (1791-): Mayfield charity school. Admitted 12 July 1799; removed 13 January 1803, taken out by parents. Baptised 26 June 1791, son of Richard and Sarah. (Two brothers, 1 sister, also at the school.) [MSB; PR]

FIELD, Richard (1788-): Mayfield charity school. Admitted 8 April 1796; removed 12 April 1799, taken out by parents. Baptised 27 January 1788, son of Richard and Sarah. (Two brothers, 1 sister, also at the school.) [MSB; PR]

FIELD, William: Mayfield charity school. Admitted 10 July 1789; removed 11 April 1794. [MSB]

FIEST: A poor girl of West Grinstead who received schooling, 1725-26, under the Dowlin charity. [WSRO Par 95/1/1/3]

FILMER, William (1727-): Saunders' charity school, Rye. In lists from 4 April 1739 (not in 10 January 1739) to 3 October 1739 (6 February 1740 notes 'left the school'). Baptised 2 July 1727, son of William and Mary. [RSB; PR]

FILMER, Charles (1763-): Saunders' charity school, Rye. Admitted 22 June 1774; in lists to Michaelmas 1775 (not in Christmas 1777, next surviving list). Baptised 11 July 1763, son of Jacob and Elizabeth. [RSB; PR]

FINCH, Ambrose (-dead by 1705): Brighton charity school. In 'writers' list 12 January 1702. Died while still at school, some time before December 1705. [BSB]

[FINLEY, Elizabeth (1794-)] In Wiston school list, c1803, and perhaps at the school in 1800. Baptised 11 January 1795, daughter of George and Ann. [WSRO Par 211/25/1; PR]

[FINLEY, Frances (1792-)] In Wiston school list, c1803, and probably at the school in 1800. Baptised 7 October 1792, Fanny, daughter of George and Ann. [WSRO Par 211/25/1; PR]

FLEEMING, Jasper: Brighton charity school. In list of 'readers' of (probably) January 1702. [BSB]

FLEMAN (FLEMING), Joseph (1693-): Brighton charity school. In list of 'readers' December 1705; added to 'writers' list after December 1705. Probably baptised 28 May 1693, son of John Fleming and Mary (née Banester). (Another Joseph baptised 11 May 1691, son of John Fleming, presumably died.) [BSB; PR]

FLETCHER, John (1694-): Brighton charity school. In list of 'writers' December 1705. Baptised 21 January 1694, son of John and Ann (née Percy). (Another JF, baptised 14 August 1689, son of John, presumably died.) [BSB; PR]

FLORANCE, Eliza (1793-): Briefly at Miss Richardson's school and about 9 years at Miss Russell's school in Chichester [qv for her accounts of these schools]. Born 1793 (baptised aged 6 at Baffin's Lane Unitarian Chapel) eldest of 13 children of James, schoolmaster and later barrister of Chichester, dissenter; her mother a Quaker, and as a child EF regularly attended the Quaker meeting with her grandmother. When about 7, went as day-girl to nearby Miss Richardson's in West Street, but had trouble with the school's insistence on learning the C of E catechism, and was quickly moved to Miss Russell's school in South Street as a day-boarder. She was often allowed an evening at the theatre; she regularly invested a penny a week on story books - such as *Cinderella and the glass slipper*, *Beauty and the Beast*. Had dancing lessons all her time at the school (at one point asked father for French lessons instead, but "you can teach yourself by the aid of French dictionary and grammar, but dancing is only to be acquired by exercising in the presence of a master"). Had harpsichord lessons 2 evenings a week from the young organist of Baffin's Lane Chapel (at 4d a lesson), and making progress, begged for a piano; with war-time inflation, money was tight - a quartern loaf cost 1s 8d to 2s, and the family required 6-8 loaves a day - and her father told her: 'as soon as bread is a shilling a loaf you shall have a piano': she had to wait a good many years, but got her piano in 1814 or 1815, when for 18 months she had the benefit of a London master. At 16 she was 'young and untamed as a colt', went birds-nesting with her brothers before breakfast, out in the fields miles from home, a 'high-spirited laughing girl'. In 1809, aged 16, she was sent to Miss Russell's small, select school in London (no connection with the Chichester Russells); she found herself behind the other girls in 'school-girl lore', especially arithmetic, but with the help of her teacher (author of many school manuals) soon caught up, and led the classes in history, chronology and geography. Was allowed to spend the weekends with two Unitarian families, and was 'launched into society', attending balls and concerts. After 18 months she returned home to relieve her mother - received and returned morning calls, did housework, some cooking, looked after the children, and taught 3 sisters from 9 till noon and again an hour after dinner. She helped with the Library Society, which earlier her father had co-founded and had given a room in his house for it; she read many books - eg Russell's *Modern Europe*, Milford's *Greece*, and the poets; with her brother James read the *Edinburgh Review* - they invested 5s a quarter

of their pocket money to possess it; she tried to learn what her brothers were taught at their more academic schools (Joyce's *Scientific Dialogues* was a favourite book). In 1820 she married William Johnson Fox (1786-1864) who had been Unitarian minister at Baffin's Lane Chapel and was then a minister in London; his father had been a peasant farmer; he became a famous preacher, orator and politician, and MP for Oldham (1847), espousing working-class causes. They had issue, but separated in 1834 on account of 'incompatibility of temper'. Eliza Fox's *Memoir* (comprising 'selections from the Journals, correspondence, and papers of Mrs Eliza Fox and her husband William Johnson Fox') was published in 1869 by her children 'in accordance with her wish' and dedicated to her. [*A Memoir of Mrs Eliza Fox* (1869); *DNB*]

FOOTE, Daniel (1754-77): Born c1754, son of a Chichester tradesman; went to grammar school, presumably at Chichester; after which taught himself science. At urging of friends, published *Poems on Various Occasions...three letters on moral subjects, &c*, which appeared 1777. On a country walk with friends, ate too many 'hedge-picks'; suffered an intestinal stoppage and died a few days later, 20 October 1777, aged 23. [Hay, A. *History of Chichester* (1804); *SAC* **130**]

FORD, Fanny (1781-): Mayfield charity school. Admitted 11 April 1794; removed 8 July 1796, for non-attendance. Baptised (Frances) 18 November 1781, daughter of Thomas and Ann. [MSB; PR]

FOORD (FORD), Jessy (1783-): Mayfield charity school. Admitted 6 July 1792; removed 10 April 1795, for non-attendance. Baptised 26 October 1783, son of William and Ann. (Brothers John, Robert, also at the school.) [MSB; PR]

FOORD, John (1771-): Mayfield charity school. Admitted 9 April 1779; removed 7 April 1780, after 1 year as a 'reader'. Baptised 14 June 1771, son of William and Ann. (Brothers Jessy, Robert, also at the school.) [MSB; PR]

FORD (FOORD), John: Mayfield charity school. Admitted 6 April 1787; removed 6 July 1787, 'having the Hooping-Cough'; re-admitted

17 January 1788; removed 9 April 1790, for non-attendance; re-admitted 9 July 1790; removed 6 April 1792. [MSB]

FORD, Robert (1791-): Mayfield charity school. Admitted 12 July 1799; removed 9 July 1802, taken out by parents. Baptised 17 July 1791, son of William and Ann. (Brothers Jessy, John, also at the school.) [MSB; PR]

FOSTER, Ann: Mayfield charity school. Admitted 10 October 1777; removed 17 July 1778, 'sufficiently learned', after ¾ year at the school, all as a 'writer'. Baptised either 9 May 1765, daughter of John and Elizabeth, or 26 March 1766, daughter of Thomas and Ann. [MSB; PR]

[*FOSTER, Elizabeth*]: Perhaps at Mayfield charity school. Admitted 17 July 1778; in list for October 1778; in 8 January 1779 her name changed to 'Thomas Foster'. The number of quarters recorded against Thomas continues as if he had joined in July 1778; either he replaced Elizabeth January 1779 without formal admission or her removal, or had taken her place at 17 July 1778. Baptised either 29 August 1767, daughter of John and Elizabeth, or 18 July 1773, daughter of John and Martha. Although the latter young to join school, she was sister to the Thomas who took her place. [MSB; PR]

FOSTER, George: Grey Coat charity school, Chichester. Left between Michaelmas 1767 and Michaelmas 1768. Given 10s 6d on leaving. [WSRO Cap.V/1/1]

FOSTER, John (1740-): Mayfield charity school. Admitted at formal opening of school 29 June 1750, but may have been at the school up to ¾ year earlier, as master paid from Michaelmas 1749; removed 6 April 1753, 'well learn'd'; had 1¾ years as a 'writer'. Baptised 2 March 1740, son of John and Ann. [MSB; PR]

FOSTER, John: Grey Coat charity school, Chichester. Left between Michaelmas 1762 and Michaelmas 1763. Given 10s 6d on leaving. [WSRO Cap.V/1/1]

FOSTER, Joseph (1772 or 73-): Mayfield charity school. Admitted 6 July 1781; removed 8 April 1785, for non-attendance. Baptised 12

January 1773, son of John and Elizabeth. [MSB; PR]

FOSTER, Thomas (1771-): Mayfield charity school. No formal admission but probably joined 8 January 1779, when his name replaces 'Elizabeth Foster' [qv], probably his sister; however, the record of quarters he attended is shown, probably in error, as if he had joined 17 July 1778 instead of Elizabeth. Removed 15 October 1784, 'Sufficiently Learned', after at least 5½ years at the school. Baptised 28 May 1771, son of John and Martha. [MSB; PR]

FORSTER (FOSTER), William (1789-): Admitted Fermor's charity school, Rotherfield, 8 January 1797. Baptised 12 May 1789, son of John and Martha ('poor'). [ESRO PAR 465/4/1; PR]

FOSHIER, John: Saunders' charity school, Rye. In lists from 20 April 1737 (not in 29 December 1736) to 2 April 1740 (9 July 1740 notes 'left the school'). Son of Michael. ('Fosshier' was a French refugee family.) [RSB; Holloway, W. *History of the Town & Port of Rye* (1847)]

FOWL, Bartholomew (1718-): Saunders' charity school, Rye. In lists from 2 April 1729 (?) (not in 8 January 1729) to 3 January 1733 (28 March 1733 notes 'Richard Fowll Left ye Schooll' - ie father's name, recorded in lists, entered instead of boy's). Baptised 3 August 1718, son of Richard and Elizabeth. (Brother William also at the school.) [RSB; PR]

FOWL, Edward (1712-): Saunders' charity school, Rye. In lists from September 1722 (?) (first list); June 1725 (?) notes 'Gon on the Mackaril Season'; 11 August 1725 notes 'Gon to Catch Mackril and are not yet Returned to the School'; in list late 1725 or early 1726; 4 May 1726 notes 'Left the Schooll'. Baptised 15 February 1712, son of William and Mary. [RSB; PR]

FOWL, William (1711-): Saunders' charity school, Rye. In lists from September 1722 (?) (first list) to December 1724 (?) (not in 19 May 1725). Baptised 7 September 1711, son of Richard and Elizabeth. (Brother Bartholomew also at the school.) [RSB; PR]

FOWLE, William: Saunders' charity school, Rye. Admitted 5 June 1765; left 15 December 1769. Son of William. [RSB]

FREEMAN, Elizabeth (1728-): Brightling girls' charity school. Admitted 18 July 1737, aged 10; there to year ending 1 May 1741, in which she attended on 175 school days. Baptised 10 May 1728, daughter of John and Sarah. (Sister Sarah also at the school.) [ESRO PAR 254/25/1; PR]

FREEMAN, Sarah (1730 or 31-): Brightling girls' charity school. Admitted during year ending 1 May 1741, in which she attended on 87 school days; there to 23-month period ending 22 March 1744, in which she attended on 279 school days; had 628 days at the school in total. Baptised 21 January 1731, daughter of John and Sarah. (Sister Elizabeth also at the school.) [ESRO PAR 254/25/1; PR]

FRENCH, Alexander (1705-): Brighton charity school. Given prayer book 1716 or 1717. Baptised 18 March 1705, son of Alexander and Elizabeth. [BSB; PR]

FRENCH, Robert (1757-): At Seaford charity school 1765. Baptised 17 April 1757, son of Robert and Mary. [BL Add MS 33,059; PR]

FRENCH, (Simon?) (1691?-): Brighton charity school. Admitted sometime after 'readers' list of (probably) January 1702 (listed only as 'French Boy'); had left by December 1705. Perhaps Simon, baptised 11 January 1691, son of John and Elizabeth (only male French baptism in parish register this period). [BSB; PR]

FREWEN, Charles (1701-62): Son of Thomas (1666-1731) and Sarah (née Stevens), attended his uncle Rev Thankful Frewen's school at Northiam from midsummer 1710 to Christmas 1717. A record of the classics he studied survives. His mother paid £2 pa (and 2 half-guinea gratuities pa) for his schooling. Later, Deputy Clerk of the Crown; married Alice Severne of Claines, Worcestershire. [ESRO FRE 533, and pedigree in Warne, H. *Catalogue of the Frewen Archives* (1972)]

FREWEN, Edward (1709-87): Son of Rev Thankful Frewen and Sarah (née Spencer), attended his father's school at Northiam from 26 April 1715. A record of the classics he studied survives. Later, DD, of Robertsbridge; married firstly Mary Stevens of Culham, Berkshire; married secondly Pallatia Jenkin (née Ash), widow of Rev William Jenkin of Herstmonceux. Died without issue. [ESRO FRE 533, and pedigree in Warne, H. *Catalogue of the Frewen Archives* (1972)]

FREWEN, John (1702-43): Son of Rev Thankful Frewen and Sarah (née Spencer), attended his father's school at Northiam from 23 January 1710. A record of the classics he studied survives. Later, vicar of Fairlight, rector of Guestling; married Margaret Atkins. Died without issue, 1743. [ESRO FRE 533, and pedigree in Warne, H. *Catalogue of the Frewen Archives* (1972)]

FREWEN, Thomas (1704-90): Son of Rev Thankful Frewen and Sarah (née Spencer), attended his father's school at Northiam from 28 April 1712 to October 1718, when he went to 'Mr Robinsons' for a year. A record of the classics he studied at Northiam survives. Later, surgeon at Rye; married Philadelphia Tucker. [ESRO FRE 533, and pedigree in Warne, H. *Catalogue of the Frewen Archives* (1972)]

FREWEN, Thomas (1716-66): At John Bear's small boarding school at Shermanbury, 1733. In a letter of 1741, he mentioned receiving a visit by his former tutor, John Bear. Born at Northiam 19 September 1716, son of Thomas of Brickwall (1687-1738) and Martha (née Turner: 1695-1752), and grandson of Sir Edward Frewen. At Oriel College, Oxford. Died unmarried, and buried at Norhiam 14 August 1766. [ESRO FRE 1153, 1294, 832-836; Warne, H. *Catalogue of the Frewen Archives* (1972); *Al. Oxon.*]

FRIST, Thomas: A poor boy of West Grinstead who received schooling, probably ending in 1712, under the Dowlin charity. [WSRO Par 95/1/1/3]

FROST, John (c1700-): Grey Coat charity school, Chichester. Admitted at its opening Lady Day 1710. Aged 10 at Lady Day 1711. There Lady Day 1714. [WSRO Cap.V/1/1]

FROST, Judith (1739-): Mayfield charity school. Admitted at formal opening of school 29 June 1750 but may have been at the school up to ¾ year earlier, as master paid from Michaelmas 1749; removed 29 March 1751, for non-attendance; re-admitted 28 June 1751; removed 4 October 1751, for non-attendance. Baptised 18 February 1739, daughter of Richard and Ruth. (Brother Richard also at the school.) [MSB; PR]

FROST, Richard (1745-): Mayfield charity school. Admitted 18 October 1754; removed 9 January 1756, for non-attendance, after 1¼ years at the school (still a 'reader'). Baptised 26 May 1745, son of Richard and Ruth. (Sister Judith also at the school.) [MSB; PR]

FRY, Edward (1735-): Mayfield charity school. Admitted 4 October 1751; removed 27 March 1752, 'well learned'; he had been a 'writer' for ½ year. (NB Thomas Smith, same age (ie 15 on admission), joined and left at same time as EF; both 'well learned' after 6 months.) Baptised 27 December 1735, son of Thomas and Hester. [MSB; PR]

FRYER, John (1729-): At Eastbourne charity school December 1738 (?). Baptised 20 July 1729, son of Edward and Sarah. [SAS Budgen MS v.129; PR]

FULLER: Grey Coat charity school, Chichester. Left between Michaelmas 1752 and Michaelmas 1753. Given 10s 6d on leaving. [WSRO Cap.V/1/1]

FULLER, Elizabeth (1730-): Brightling girls' charity school. Admitted 7 April 1741; there to 23-month period ending 22 March 1744, in which she attended on 159 school days; had 436 days at the school in total. Baptised 16 November 1730, daughter of Richard. [ESRO PAR 254/25/1; PR]

FULLER, Hans (-1737): fifth son of John and Elizabeth (née Rose) of Brightling Park, was taught dancing (from April 1729) by Stephen Philpot [qv]. Went to Tonbridge school; apprenticed to merchants in Lisbon 1736; died there of smallpox 18 March 1737. [SAC **104**; ESRO SAS/RF 15/26]

FULLER, J.: Button's school, Lewes. To recite at a 'Public Examination' at the *Star Assembly Room*, 22 June 1797. [*SWA* 19.6.97]

FULLER, Henry (1711-): third son of John and Elizabeth (née Rose) of Brightling Park, was instructed in the fiddle (1735) and probably taught dancing (from April 1729) by Stephen Philpot [qv]. At Charterhouse 1726-30; to Cambridge 1731; rector of North Stoneham, Hampshire; married Frances, daughter of Thomas Fuller of Catsfield. [*SAC* **104**; ESRO SAS/RF 15/26, 28]

FULLER, Richard (1721-): Saunders' charity school, Rye. In lists from 2 January 1734 (not in 4 July 1733) to 9 April 1735 (2 July 1735 notes 'Left the school'). Baptised 28 February 1721, son of Richard and Frances. [RSB; PR]

FULLER, Stephen: sixth son of John and Elizabeth (née Rose) of Brightling Park, was instructed in the fiddle (1735) and dancing (from April 1729) by Stephen Philpot [qv]. Went to Tonbridge school, then to Cambridge; fellow of Trinity, Cambridge, 1741; married 1744, Betsy Noakes; settled at Brightling Place. [*SAC* **104**; ESRO SAS/RF 15/26, 28]

FULLER, Thomas: fourth son of John and Elizabeth (née Rose) of Brightling Park, was taught dancing (from April 1729) by Stephen Philpot [qv]. Went to Tonbridge school, and then into business. [*SAC* **104**; ESRO SAS/RF 15/26]

FULLER, W.: Button's school, Lewes. To recite at a 'Public Examination' at the *Star Assembly Room*, 22 June 1797. [*SWA* 19.6.97]

FUNNELL, John: Admitted Fermor's charity school, Rotherfield, 29 July 1792. Son of John and Sarah. [ESRO PAR 465/4/1]

FUNNELL, Samuel: Admitted Fermor's charity school, Rotherfield, 29 April 1798. Son of Samuel. [ESRO PAR 465/4/1]

FURNER, John (1785-): Mayfield charity school. Admitted 11 October 1793; removed 11 April 1794. Baptised 8 January 1786, 'John Furner Son of Rose Hazleden Widow'. [MSB; PR]

FUZ, Thomas (c1704-): Grey Coat charity

school, Chichester. Admitted Lady Day 1712, aged 7. Expelled (as were 4 others) between Lady Day 1713 and Lady Day 1714. [WSRO Cap.V/1/1]

GAGE, Henry Hall (1791-1877): Rose's school, Little Horsted. Eldest son of Henry, 3rd Viscount Gage, of West Firle, born 14 December 1791; was sent to William Rose's boarding school early in 1798 (when he was 6); for this schooling father paid £65 5s 9½d in 1798, £72 7s 5d in 1799, £71 5s 1d in 1800 (when Rose became master of Saunders' charity school, Uckfield, and moved his private school there) and £39 10s 2d for the first half of 1801. Succeeded father (died 29 January 1808) as 4th Viscount, aged 16. Married 8 March 1813, Edith Maria (died 1857), eldest daughter of Hon Edward Foley, of Stoke Edith, Herefordshire, and had issue. Died 20 January 1877. [ESRO SAS/G/ACC 741; *Burke's Peerage*]

GALPING, Thomas: Grey Coat charity school, Chichester. Admitted between Lady Day 1713 and Lady Day 1714. [WSRO Cap.V/1/1]

GAMBLIN, John Manitt (1774-): Saunders' charity school, Rye. Admitted 16 July 1783; in list for 24 June 1785 (last surviving 18th century list). Baptised 5 April 1774, son of John and Sarah. [RSB; PR]

GARDINER: Grey Coat charity school, Chichester. Left between Michaelmas 1765 and Michaelmas 1766. Given 10s 6d on leaving. [WSRO Cap.V/1/1]

GARDENER, James (1772-): Sedlescombe charity school. There 29 September 1784 and 29 September 1786 (still a 'reader'). Baptised 14 February 1772, son of Daniel and Love. (Brother Shadrach also at the school.) [SSB; PR]

GARDNER, John (c1705-): Grey Coat charity school, Chichester. Admitted between Lady Day 1712 and Lady Day 1713, aged 7. There Lady Day 1714. [WSRO Cap.V/1/1]

GARDENER, Shadrach (1775-): Sedlescombe charity school. There 29 September 1784, 29 September 1786, 29 September 1787 (still a

'reader'). Baptised 9 July 1775, son of Daniel and Love. (Brother James also at the school.) [SSB; PR]

GASSON - see GASTON

GASTON (GASSON), Benjamin (1776-): Mayfield charity school. Admitted 8 April 1785; removed 11 July 1788, for non-attendance. Baptised [10-13] October 1776, son of James and Anne. (Five brothers also at the school.) [MSB; PR]

GASTON, Esther (1767-): Mayfield charity school. Admitted 11 October 1776; removed 8 January 1779, taken away by parents, after 2¼ years at the school as a 'reader'. Baptised 30 August 1767, daughter of Thomas and Susanna. (Brother John also at the school.) [MSB; PR]

GASTON (GASSON), James (1775-): Mayfield charity school. Admitted 9 April 1784; removed 6 April 1787, 'sufficiently learned'. Baptised 4 April 1775, son of James and Anne. (Five brothers also at the school.) [MSB; PR]

GASTON, John (1766-): Mayfield charity school. Admitted 5 April 1776; removed 8 January 1779, 'for Incapacity', after 2¾ years at the school as a 'reader'. Baptised 16 March 1766, son of Thomas and Susanna. (Sister Esther also at the school.) [MSB; PR]

GASTON (GASSON), John (1780-): Mayfield charity school. Admitted 9 July 1790; removed 5 July 1793, taken out by parents. Baptised 3 May 1780, son of James and Anne. (Five brothers also at the school.) [MSB; PR]

GASTON, Richard: Mayfield charity school. Admitted 9 July 1762; removed 13 January 1764, 'suspended for Non-Attendance'; re-admitted 13 April 1764; removed 24 January 1766, 'sufficiently learned', after 3¼ years at the school in total, 2¼ years as a 'writer'. [MSB]

GASTON (GASSON), Richard (1778-): Mayfield charity school. Admitted 6 July 1787; removed 13 July 1791, taken out by parents. Baptised 30 August 1778, son of James and Anne. (Five brothers also at the school.) [MSB; PR]

GASTON, Thomas: Mayfield charity school. Admitted 17 October 1766; removed 4 September 1767, taken out by parents but 'pretty well learn'd', after ¾ year, all as a 'writer'. [MSB]

GASTON (GASSON), Thomas (1782-): Mayfield charity school. Admitted 6 April 1792; removed 8 January 1796, for non-attendance. Baptised 28 April 1782, son of James and Ann. (Five brothers also at the school.) [MSB; PR]

GASTON (GASSON), William (1784-): Mayfield charity school. Admitted 11 July 1794; removed 8 January 1796, for non-attendance; re-admitted 14 October 1796; removed 13 April 1798, taken out by parents. Baptised 2 May 1784, son of James and Ann. (Five brothers also at the school.) [MSB; PR]

GATELAND - see also GATLAND

GATELAND, John (1760-): Saunders' charity school, Rye. Admitted 13 July 1769; in lists to Christmas 1770 (not in midsummer 1773, next surviving list). Baptised 1 January 1760, son of Isaac and Elizabeth. [RSB; PR]

GATES, Charles: Midhurst grammar school. Admitted as charity scholar 1789. Son of Thomas, carpenter. (Brother William admitted same year.) [*HMGS*]

GATES, Elizabeth: A poor girl of Lewes for whose schooling parish of St Anne Lewes paid 1s 4d, 23 June 1787; 1s 6d, 15 March 1788; 1s 10d for 11 weeks (= 2d a week), 29 March 1788; 8s (= 48 weeks at 2d), 13 January 1789; 11s 9d (= 47 weeks at 3d), in year 1789-90. [ESRO PAR 411/31/3]

GATES, Thomas: Midhurst grammar school. Admitted as charity scholar 1760. Son of Thomas, weaver. [*HMGS*]

GATES, William: Midhurst grammar school. Admitted as charity scholar 1789. Son of Thomas, carpenter. (Brother Charles admitted same year.) [*HMGS*]

GATLAND (GALLAND), Ann (1752-): Mayfield charity school. Admitted 6 July 1759; removed 11 July 1760, suspended for non-attendance, after 1 year as a 'reader'. Baptised 24 May 1752, daughter of William and Anne. (Three sisters also at the school.) [MSB; PR]

GATLAND, Hannah (1760-): Mayfield charity school. Admitted 16 October 1767; removed 22 April 1768, 'To make room for others', after ½ year as a 'reader'. Baptised 19 October 1760, daughter of William and Ann. (Three sisters also at the school.) [MSB; PR]

GATLAND, Katherine (1757-): Mayfield charity school. Admitted 'Widow Dukes' dame school 2 May 1766; admitted charity school 17 April 1767; removed 15 July 1768, 'Taken into the Workhouse', after 1¼ years at the school as a 'reader'. Baptised 6 March 1757, daughter of William and Anne. (Three sisters also at the school.) [MSB; PR]

GATLAND, Sarah (1755-): Mayfield charity school. Admitted 'Widow Dukes' dame school 2 May 1766; admitted charity school 17 April 1767; removed 21 April 1769, for non-attendance, after 2 years at the school as a 'reader'. Baptised 25 December 1755, daughter of William and Anne. (Three sisters also at the school.) [MSB; PR]

GAUSBY, Henry: Saunders' charity school, Rye. Admitted 14 October 1761; in lists to Michaelmas 1765, which notes 'Absent 6 weeks' (not in Lady Day 1767, next list). Son of Henry. [RSB]

(GAUSDEN): Eastbourne charity school. Admitted midsummer 1778; there Christmas 1779. [SAS Budgen MS v.117]

GAUSDEN, John: Saunders' charity school, Rye. Admitted 30 March 1772; in lists to Lady Day 1780, which notes 'Left School'; had 8¼ years there. Son of Thomas. [RSB]

GAUSDEN, Lucy (1761-): Eastbourne charity school. Admitted 12 January 1770. Baptised 1 November 1761, daughter of William and Grace. [SAS Budgen MS v.105; PR]

GAWN, James (1734-): Saunders' charity school, Rye. In lists from Christmas 1746 (not in Michaelmas 1746); 'Left School' 9 April 1750. Baptised 4 February 1734, son of James and Mary. (Father dead by 1749. Brothers John, William, also at the school.) [RSB; PR]

GAWN, John (1732-): Saunders' charity school, Rye. In lists from 9 July 1740 (not in 2 April 1740) to 10 April 1745 (not in 14 August 1745). Baptised 10 May 1732, son of James and Mary. (Father dead by 1749. Brothers James, William, also at the school.) [RSB; PR]

GAWN, William (1739-): Saunders' charity school, Rye. In lists from 25 March 1749 (not in Christmas 1748); 'Left School' 24 August 1752. 'Son of James Gawn, deceased'. Baptised 18 August 1739, son of James and Mary. (Brothers James, John, also at the school.) [RSB; PR]

GEALE - see JEAL

GEORGE, Robert: Grey Coat charity school, Chichester. Left 1774: '9 April To Rob't George on Leaving ye School and boat & waistcoat 15s 6d.' [WSRO Cap.V/1/1]

GEORGE, Robert: Grey Coat charity school, Chichester. Left between Michaelmas 1779 and Michaelmas 1780. Given 10s 6d 'on leaving the school Apprentice'. [WSRO Cap.V/1/1]

GIBBONS, Thomas (1757-): Saunders' charity school, Rye. Admitted 3 May 1769; in lists to Christmas 1770 (not in midsummer 1773, next surviving list). Born at Rye 19 December 1757, son of William and Mary Gybbon, Particular Baptists. (Brother William also at the school.) [RSB; PRO RG 4/3365]

GIBBON (GIBBINS), William: Saunders' charity school, Rye. In lists from 5 January 1743 (not in 13 October 1742) to 25 March 1749 (not in 24 June 1749). Son of William or Edward - William initially but changed to Edward 4 July 1744 (same position in list). [RSB]

GIBBON, William (1759-): Saunders' charity school, Rye. Admitted 20 April 1771; in lists to Michaelmas 1773 (not in midsummer 1774, next surviving list). Born at Rye 16 December 1759, son of William and Mary Gybbon, Particular Baptists. (Brother Thomas also at the school.) [RSB; PRO RG 4/3365]

GIBBS: At East Hoathly school 1756, under Thomas Turner. Son of Samuel (-1784), yeoman, and Elizabeth (née Fuller). [Vaisey, D. (ed) *The Diary of Thomas Turner* (1984)]

GIBSON, Thomas (1750-): Saunders' charity school, Rye. In lists from Michaelmas 1761 (not in Lady Day 1761) to 20 January 1762 (not in Christmas 1762, next surviving list). Baptised 10 October 1750, son of John and Elizabeth. (Brother William also at the school.) [RSB; PR]

GIBSON, William (1748-): Saunders' charity school, Rye. In lists from Michaelmas 1756 (not in midsummer 1756) to Lady Day 1761 (not in Michaelmas 1761). Baptised 12 October 1748, son of John and Elizabeth. (Brother Thomas also at the school.) [RSB; PR]

GILBERT, John (1752-): Mayfield charity school. Admitted 16 October 1761; removed 9 July 1762, 'not belonging to the Parish', after ½ year as a 'reader' (probably left during previous quarter). Baptised 4 July 1752, son of John and Anne. [MSB; PR]

GILBERT, Nicholas (1706-74): Baptised 20 November 1706, son of Nicholas, gent of Eastbourne (1673-1713: he had inherited Blatchington manor and lands from father Thomas; through wife, was one of the Lords of the Manor of Eastbourne; churchwarden there 1699-1701, 1712) and Mary (née Eversfield: 1677-1722). Father died 22 May 1713, when he was 6; his schooling thereafter paid for by trustees, whose accounts to March 1721 survive. They paid Mr Patterson £1 10s for ¾ year schooling (October 1712 - June 1713), probably a petty school at Eastbourne; Mr Harvey ¼ year board and schooling, £4 5s 6d (July - September 1713). He was then sent to Mr Peirce, Lewes grammar school, as a private pupil, from Michaelmas 1713 to midsummer 1718: entrance £1 1s 6d and annual payments of c£18-24; additionally £1 to a writing master and 2 payments of 10s to a dancing master; from 1714, when he was 8, he had his head shaved and wore a wig. Then went to John Lloyd (Uckfield), midsummer 1718 - December 1720; payments c£18 pa. Married 1732 Susannah Acton, of Ripe (1711-67). Died 29 July 1774, buried 4 August 1774, aged 67. [ESRO ACC 2462/1; Budgen, W. *Old*

Eastbourne (1912)]

GILBERT (GUILBERT), Thomas (1711-): Saunders' charity school, Rye. In lists from September 1722 (?) (first list) to January 1724 (?) (not in 8 April 1724). Baptised 2 March 1711, son of Thomas and Martha. [RSB; PR]

GILBERT, William (1687-): Brighton charity school. In list of 'readers' of (probably) January 1702; given coat and hat July 1702; joined 'writers' class sometime after 12 January 1702; had left by December 1705 and been 'apprenticed to mariner'. Baptised 27 November 1687, son of William and Elizabeth (née Grantum); mother buried 20 June 1689; father married secondly, 15 October 1689, Susan Tettersell. [BSB; PR]

GILBERT, (William?) (1790?-): Admitted Fermor's charity school, Rotherfield, 20 August 1797. Son of Robert. Probably baptised 12 December 1790, William, son of Robert and Catherine. [ESRO PAR 465/4/1; PR]

GILHAM, Ann (1762-71): Mayfield charity school. Admitted 19 April 1771; removed July 1771, 'Dead'. Baptised 10 November 1762, daughter of William and Ann. (Brother William, sister Elizabeth, also at the school.) [MSB; PR]

GILHAM, Elizabeth (1764-): Mayfield charity school. Admitted 19 April 1771; removed 5 April 1776, for non-attendance 'but pretty well Learned', after 5 years at the school, 3½ years as a 'writer'. Baptised 13 December 1764, daughter of William and Ann. (Brother William, sister Ann, also at the school.) [MSB; PR]

GILLHAM (GILLIAM), John (1694-): Brighton charity school. Admitted as 'reader' sometime after list of (probably) January 1702; joined 'writers' class sometime after 12 January 1702; had left by December 1705. Baptised 26 August 1694, son of John and Ales (née Avery). (Brothers Thomas, William, also at the school.) [BSB; PR]

GILLHAM (GILLIAM), Thomas (1696-): Brighton charity school. Joined 'writers' class sometime after 12 January 1702; in list of 'writers' December 1705. Baptised 11 October

1696, son of John and Ales (née Avery). (Brothers John, William, also at the school.) [BSB; PR]

GILLAM, William (1699-): Brighton charity school. Given prayer book 1715. Baptised 2 January 1699, son of John. (Brothers John, Thomas, also at the school.) [BSB; PR]

GILHAM, William (1761-1769): Mayfield charity school. Admitted 21 April 1769; removed 19 January 1770, 'Dead', after ½ year as a 'reader'. Baptised 24 March 1761, son of William and Ann; buried 22 December 1769. (Sisters Ann, Elizabeth, also at the school.) [MSB; PR]

GILL, William: Cocking charity school. There 1732, 1733. [WSRO Par 53/12/1]

GINMAN, Richard: Midhurst grammar school. Admitted as charity scholar 1790. [*HMGS*]

GLAZEBROOK, John: A poor boy of Lewes, for whom parish of St Michael's paid schooling bills: 17 April 1775, 8d (3 June 1775 they paid £1 4s 6d for his keep for 7 weeks, at 3s 6d a week); 24 June 1775, 1s 6d; 15 July 1775, 4d (for 2 weeks schooling). (NB In 1774-75 year, 'Widow Glazbrook Senior' and 'Widow Glazbrook Junior' both received poor pay. 17 June 1775, Widow Grizbrook moved to workhouse; July 1775 Widow Grizbrook died.) [ESRO PAR 414/31/1/2]

GODDEN, George Edwards (1782-): Mayfield charity school. Admitted 13 July 1791; removed 8 April 1796, taken out by parents. Baptised 2 February 1782, son of James and Mary. (Brother Matthew Lower also at the school.) [MSB; PR]

GODDEN, John (1712-): Saunders' charity school, Rye. In lists from 19 May 1725 (not in December 1724) to 10 January 1728 (17 April 1728 notes 'left the school'). Baptised 29 September 1712, son of Thomas and Elizabeth. (Brother William also at the school.) [RSB; PR]

GODDEN, Matthew Lower (1779-): Mayfield charity school. Admitted 5 January 1787; removed 13 July 1791, 'Sufficiently Learned'. Baptised 14 February 1779, son of

James and Mary. (Brother George Edwards also at the school.) [MSB; PR]

GODDEN, William (1710 or 11-): Saunders' charity school, Rye. In lists from September 1722 (?) (first list) to December 1724 (not in 19 May 1725). Baptised 12 January 1711, son of Thomas and Elizabeth. (Brother John also at the school.) [RSB; PR]

GODLY, Thomas: At Rev Thankful Frewen's school at Northiam, as a boarder, from 20 May 1715 to 6 June 1717. A record of the classics he studied survives. His fees (£16 pa) paid by a Mr Goring. [ESRO FRE 533]

GODMAN: Grey Coat charity school, Chichester. Left between Michaelmas 1757 and Michaelmas 1758. Given 10s 6d on leaving. [WSRO Cap.V/1/1]

GODMAN, Henry: Grey Coat charity school, Chichester. Admitted between Lady Day 1713 and Lady Day 1714. [WSRO Cap.V/1/1]

GODMAN, John (c1701-): Grey Coat charity school, Chichester. Admitted between Lady Day 1712 and Lady Day 1713, aged 11. There Lady Day 1714. [WSRO Cap.V/1/1]

[GODMAN, Joseph (1791-1874)]: At Midhurst grammar school, probably in 18th century. Subsequently at school at York. Son of Joseph, of Chichester and Merston, and Mary (née Hasler) of Bury. Later, JP for Surrey and High Sheriff 1862. [*HMGS*]

GODMAN, Thomas (c1704-): Grey Coat charity school, Chichester. Admitted Lady Day 1712, aged 7. There Lady Day 1714. [WSRO Cap.V/1/1]

(GODSMARK): A poor child of West Grinstead who received schooling (for at least 71 weeks, at 2d a week) from Widow Slater, 1701, 1702, under the Dowlin charity. (Brother or sister received the same.) [WSRO Par 95/1/1/3]

(GODSMARK): Another poor child of West Grinstead, as above.

GODSMARK: A poor girl of West Grinstead who received schooling from Goody Flote,

1706 (and probably 1707), under the Dowlin charity. [WSRO Par 95/1/1/3]

[GOLDING, Christopher]: Perhaps at Midhurst grammar school. A native of Midhurst and elected to Winchester 1723. [*HMGS*]

GOLDSMITH, James (1785-): Admitted Fermor's charity school, Rotherfield, 3 May 1794. Baptised 24 July 1785, son of Joseph and Jane ('poor'). [ESRO PAR 465/4/1; PR]

GOLDSMITH, John (1773-): Mayfield charity school. Admitted 2 August 1782 (apparently also admitted 11 July 1783; perhaps assigned to different charity source on expansion of the school); removed 5 January 1787, for non-attendance. Baptised 26 December 1773, son of John and Anne. (Brother William, sister Philadelphia, also at the school.) [MSB; PR]

GOLDSMITH, Philadelphia (1780-): Mayfield charity school. Admitted 12 October 1792; removed 11 April 1794. Baptised 26 November 1780, daughter of John and Anne. (Brothers John, William, also at the school.) [MSB; PR]

GOLDSMITH, Thomas: Admitted Fermor's charity school, Rotherfield, 25 May 1794. [ESRO PAR 465/4/1]

GOLDSMITH, William (1775-87): Mayfield charity school. Admitted 7 April 1786; removed 12 October 1787, 'Dead'. Baptised 21 December 1775, son of John and Anne; buried 26 August 1787, aged 12. (Brother John, sister Philadelphia, also at the school.) [MSB; PR]

GOODBEHERE: Button's school, Lewes. To recite, in both English and French, at a 'Public Examination' at the *Star Assembly Room*, 22 June 1797. [*SWA* 19.6.97]

GOOSE (GESSE?), Mary: Brighton girls' charity school. Admitted sometime after 25 March 1703 (probably by end of 1705). (Perhaps baptised 7 April 1789, daughter of John Gess and Mary, but this Mary rather old for school; no 'Goose' references in parish register.) [BSB; PR]

GORRINGE, Hannah (1791-): Mayfield

charity school. Admitted 11 April 1800; removed 8 January 1802, for non-attendance. Baptised 20 February 1791, daughter of Charles and Mary. [MSB; PR]

GORRINGE, William (1760?-): At school at Sedlescombe, almost certainly at Colbran's private boarding school. Exercise books of his, dated 1773-76, have survived; he was taught to write in at least 3 different hands, arithmetic, mercantile measures and documents (receipts, promises to pay, bills of exchange, bills, expense accounts, bonds, letters, wills and leases), mathematics (including compound interest, square and cube roots, geometry, trigonometry, mensuration of solids, eg prisms. tetrahedrons, timber, bricklayer's and plasterer's work, paving, flooring, tiling and thatching, casks, use of 'sliding-rule', land-surveying). One exercise, 'A Penal Bill', features 'William Gorringe of the Parish of Heathfield, Yeoman' and WG was probably the WG baptised at Heathfield 13 February 1760, son of Pennington and Sarah. [WSRO MP 2972, Add MS 39,850-853; Heathfield PR]

GOSLEY (GOSLYE), George (1732-): Saunders' charity school, Rye. In lists from 10 April 1745 (not in 4 July 1744) to 6 April 1748 (in list and crossed out; not in midsummer 1748). Baptised 6 September 1732, son of George and Elizabeth. (An earlier son George of theirs, baptised 28 November 1729, presumably died.) [RSB; PR]

GOSLEY, James (1749-): Saunders' charity school, Rye. In lists from midsummer 1756 (shown as 'Thomas' as addendum to 7 April 1756, probably name error) to Michaelmas 1763 (not in Christmas 1764, next surviving list). Baptised 19 July 1749, son of William and Mary. (Brother John also at the school.) [RSB; PR]

GOSLEY, John (1739-): Saunders' charity school, Rye. In lists from Christmas 1748 (not in Michaelmas 1748) to 4 July 1753, in which marked 'Left School'. Baptised 7 October 1739, son of William and Mary. (Brother James also at the school.) [RSB; PR]

GOSLEY, William (1717-): Saunders' charity school, Rye. In lists from 19 May 1725 (not in December 1724) to 14 October 1730 (not in 6

January 1731). Baptised 26 July 1717, son of John and Mary. [RSB; PR]

GOSTRIL, Abraham (1721-): Saunders' charity school, Rye. In lists 12 July 1727 (not in 19 April 1727) to 4 July 1733 (not in 2 January 1734). Baptised 7 May 1721, son of Michael and Mary. (Brother Michael also at the school.) [RSB; PR]

GOSTRIL, Henry (1726-): Saunders' charity school, Rye. In lists from 29 December 1736 (not in 20 October 1736) to 5 January 1743 (not in June 1743(?)). Baptised 19 March 1726, son of Edward and Rachel. [RSB; PR]

GOSTRIL, Michael: Saunders' charity school, Rye. In lists from 11 January 1727 (not in 5 October 1726) to 4 July 1733 (not in 2 January 1734). Son of Michael. (Brother Abraham also at the school.) [RSB]

GRACE, James (1702-): Brighton charity school. Given prayer book 1715. Born 24 December 1702, son of William. (Birth not baptism given in the parish register, so family probably dissenters.) [BSB; PR]

GRANT, Ann (1748-): At Sedlescombe charity school 3 May 1755. Baptised 11 March 1748, daughter of John and Mary. [SSB; PR]

GRAVELY, Richard (-1780): Midhurst grammar school. Admitted as charity scholar 1735. Son of Thomas (c1707-). Later, RG described as of Midhurst and Woolavington; also had estate at Chithurst. Died 1780, leaving 2 sons. [*HMGS*]

GRAVETT, Richard (1755-): Saunders' charity school, Rye. In lists from Michaelmas 1763 (not in Christmas 1762, previous surviving list); left school Lady Day 1769. Baptised 4 May 1755, son of Richard and Susannah. [RSB; PR]

GRAY - see also GREY

GRAY, John (c1703-): Grey Coat charity school, Chichester. Admitted between Lady Day 1712 and Lady Day 1713, aged 9. There Lady Day 1714. [WSRO Cap.V/1/1]

GRAY, Mary (1696-): Brighton girls' charity

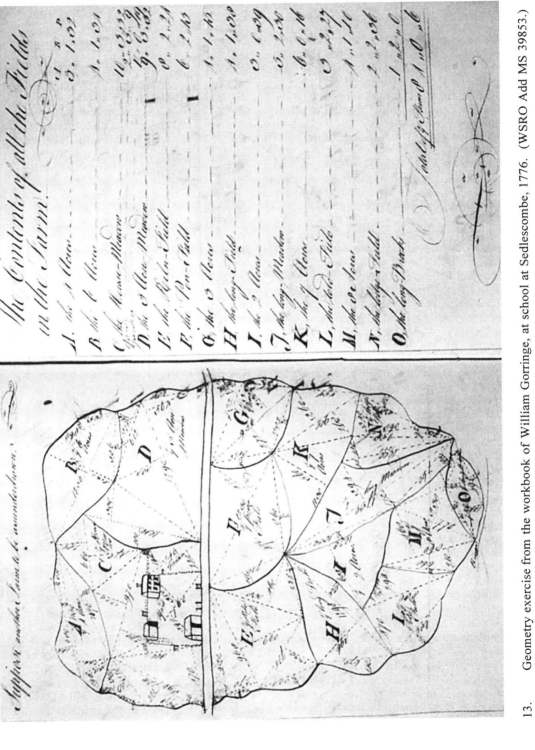

13. Geometry exercise from the workbook of William Gorringe, at school at Sedlescombe, 1776. (WSRO Add MS 39853.)

school. Admitted when school opened, 30 September 1702. Baptised 20 September 1696, daughter of Thomas and Mary (née Barton). [BSB; PR]

GRAY, Thomas (c1705-): Grey Coat charity school, Chichester. Admitted between Lady Day 1712 and Lady Day 1713, aged 7. There Lady Day 1714. [WSRO Cap.V/1/1]

GREEN, Thomas (1704-): Brighton charity school. Given prayer book 1715. Baptised 26 June 1704, son of John and Susan. [BSB; PR]

GREENAWAY, William (1728-): At Eastbourne charity school, December 1738 (?). Baptised 3 December 1728, son of Edward and Jane. [SAS Budgen MS v.129; PR]

GREENWOOD, Adam (1690-): Brighton charity school. In list of 'readers' of (probably) January 1702; had left by December 1705 and been 'apprenticed to Husbandry'. Baptised 20 April 1690, son of Clement and Elizabeth. [BSB; PR]

GREGSON (GRIGSON), Ann (1751-): Brightling girls' charity school. Admitted between 31 July 1758 and 31 December 1761, in which period she attended on 88 school days. (No later records.) Baptised 28 July 1751, daughter of William and Sarah. (Two sisters also at the school.) [ESRO PAR 254/25/1; PR]

GREGSON (GRIGSON), Elizabeth (1747-): Brightling girls' charity school. Admitted between Lady Day 1755 and 30 April 1757, in which period she attended on 407 school days; there to period 30 April 1757 to 31 July 1758, in which she attended on 115 school days; had 522 days at the school in total. Baptised 23 August 1747, daughter of William and Sarah. (Two sisters also at the school.) [ESRO PAR 254/25/1; PR]

GREGSON (GRIGSON), Sarah (1749 or 50-): Brightling girls' charity school. Admitted between Lady Day 1755 and 30 April 1757, in which period she attended on 458 school days; there at least to period 31 July 1758 to 31 December 1761 (no later records) in which she attended on 280 school days; probably left during this period and had 868 days at the school in total. Baptised 18 January 1750,

daughter of William and Sarah. (Two sisters also at the school.) [ESRO PAR 254/25/1; PR]

GREVATT, John (c1793-): Petworth charity school. Admitted 13 December 1800; there July 1803, aged 'about 10'. [WSRO Petworth House Archives 1763]

GREY - see also GRAY

GREY, Betsy (1773-): Daughter of 'Farmer Grey' of South Bersted; Grey was a tenant of John Baker, as trustee for his brother Thomas's estate. Baker stayed with Grey in the summer of 1776, and recorded in his diary for Sunday, 1 September 1776: 'Dined con Farmer Grey... Little Betsy went to eat Fromenty at her school-mistress's, Mrs Hitchcock, as did all her scholars (about 8 who give 3d a week), which has been a matter of great expectation for some days (little Betsy showed away with her new sombrero and boca)'. On 22 August 1776 Baker noted: 'Farmer Grey and little Betsy (3 years old last of last month)'; but he appears to have been a month out, as she was baptised 15 July 1773, Elizabeth, daughter of Thomas Gray and Elizabeth. Either way, Betsy, at just over 3, was the youngest 18th century Sussex scholar so far traced. [Yorke, P. C. (ed) *The Diary of John Baker* (1931); PR]

GRIFFITHS, John (1773-1852): Son of the late Rev John, of Rodmell, he received in 1791 £60 (ie 4 years at £15) from the Steere charity for assisting in sending Lewes boys to Cambridge or Oxford, and was probably a scholar of Lewes grammar school. Wadham College, Oxford, matriculated 15 April 1791, aged 18; BA 1794; Queen's College, MA 1797, BD and DD 1821. Many years master of King's school, Rochester; rector of Hinxhill, Kent, 1801, and vicar of St Margaret's, Rochester, 1803, to death 27 January 1852. [Horsfield *Lewes*; *Al. Oxon.*]

GRIMMETT, William: Brighton charity school. Later became a mariner, and a London merchant. By will, 14 March 1749, left bequests for clothing and educating 20 poor boys of Brighton. His school was founded in 1768, with an endowment worth £70 pa [qv].

GRINGOE, Charles (c1701-): Grey Coat charity school, Chichester, from its opening,

Lady Day 1710. Aged 9 at Lady Day 1711. Still there Lady Day 1714. [WSRO Cap.V/1/1]

GRINSTED: Brighton girls' charity school. Admitted when school opened, 30 September 1702. 'Elizabeth Grinsted's daughter'. One of: Elizabeth, baptised 30 March 1690, daughter of Robart and Elizabeth; Mary, baptised 19 August 1694, same parents; Susanna, baptised 3 January 1697, daughter of Robert. [BSB; PR]

GROUT, Abigail (1697-): Brighton girls' charity school. Admitted sometime after 25 March 1703 (probably by end of 1705). Baptised 6 June 1697, daughter of Andrew (mother Abigail, from other baptisms). (Brother Andrew at the boys' charity school.) [BSB; PR]

GROUTT, Andrew (1693-): Brighton charity school. In list of 'writers' 12 January 1702 and December 1705. Baptised 25 June 1693, son of Andrew and Abigail. (Sister Abigail at the girls' charity school.) [BSB; PR]

GROVER, G.: Button's school, Lewes. To recite at a 'Public Examination' at the *Star Assembly Room*, 22 June 1797. [*SWA* 19.6.97]

GRUGGEN, Thomas (c1700-): Grey Coat charity school, Chichester, from its opening, Lady Day 1710. Aged 10 at Lady Day 1711. Between Lady Day 1712 and Lady Day 1713 transferred 'Into the other School' (ie the Oliver Whitby charity school, which provided boarding, and was then run by the same master). [WSRO Cap.V/I/1]

GUNSTON, Edward (1713 or 14-): Saunders' charity school, Rye. In lists from September 1722 (?) (first list) to June 1725 (?) (not in 11 August 1725). Son of Edward, deceased. Baptised 18 January 1714, son of Edward and Alice. [RSB; PR]

GURLEY, John (1763-): Saunders' charity school, Rye. Admitted 15 May 1771; in lists to Michaelmas 1775 (not in Christmas 1777, next surviving list). Baptised 4 April 1763, son of Robert and Mary. [RSB; PR]

GURLEY, Robert (1750-): Saunders' charity school, Rye. In lists from 16 April 1760 (not in midsummer 1759, previous surviving list) to Michaelmas 1763 (not in Christmas 1764, next surviving list). Baptised 8 August 1750, son of Robert and Sarah. (Brother William also at the school.) [RSB; PR]

GURLEY, William (1755-): Saunders' charity school, Rye. In lists from Christmas 1764 (not in Michaelmas 1763, previous surviving list) to Lady Day 1767 (not in Christmas 1768, next surviving list). Baptised 23 June 1755, son of Robert and Sarah. (Brother Robert also at the school.) [RSB; PR]

GWYNNE, Frederick (1783-): Baptised 30 January 1783, son of Rev William, master of Lewes grammar school, and Elizabeth; was elected, 27 June 1800, to the Steere exhibition for assisting in sending Lewes boys to Cambridge or Oxford; to run for 4 years; received in total £72 4s. Presumably a scholar at father's grammar school. Then Hertford College, Oxford, matriculated 27 March 1801, aged 18. [Horsfield *Lewes*; *SRS* **69**; *Al. Oxon.*; Lewes St Anne PR]

GWYNNE, William (c1774-1825): Son of Rev William, master of Lewes grammar school, received £60 in 1795 (ie 4 years at £15 pa) from the Steere charity for assisting in sending Lewes boys to Cambridge or Oxford. Presumably a scholar at father's grammar school. Then Hertford College, Oxford, matriculated 14 May 1793, aged 19; BA 1799, MA 1812. Rector of Denton 1800 to death; rector of St Michael's, Lewes, 1815. Married at Exeter 21 June 1808, Henrietta Augusta Gordon, daughter of W. A. Gordon, esq, of Bowhill House. Died 1825. [Horsfield *Lewes*; *Al. Oxon.*; CI]

HADDOCK: A son of Admiral Haddock was at Bear's school, Shermanbury, in 1743 [qv].

HAINES, William (1778-1848): Midhurst grammar school. Painter and engraver. Born 21 June 1778 at Bedhampton, Hampshire; taken in infancy to Chichester. After Midhurst grammar school, apprenticed to Threw, engraver. Travelled abroad, back to England 1805; in Chichester, then studio in London; painted portrait miniatures; exhibited at Royal Academy etc. Died 24 July 1848. [Stewart, B. and Cutten, M. *Chichester Artists* (1987)]

HAISLEDEN - see HASELDEN

HALL: Grey Coat charity school, Chichester. Left between Michaelmas 1752 and Michaelmas 1753. Given 10s 6d on leaving. [WSRO Cap.V/1/1]

HALL, Elizabeth (1758-): Mayfield charity school. Admitted 21 April 1769; removed 16 October 1772, for non-attendance after 3½ years at the school, ¾ year as a 'writer'. Baptised 17 December 1758, daughter of William and Anne. (Two brothers, 3 sisters, also at the school.) [MSB; PR]

HALL, Henry: Mayfield charity school. Admitted 12 October 1798; removed 10 July 1801, taken out by parents. [MSB]

HALL, James (1744-): Saunders' charity school, Rye. In lists from 28 March 1753 (not in 3 January 1753) to midsummer 1757, in which marked 'Left School' (not in Michaelmas 1757). 'Son of Mary Hall' in Saunders' charity school lists. Baptised 6 August 1744, son of ['Thomas &' inserted] Mary Hall. (Brother John also at the school.) [RSB; PR]

HALL, James (1785-): Mayfield charity school. Admitted 11 October 1793; removed 17 October 1794, taken out by parents. Baptised 11 September 1785, son of Joseph and Ann. (Brothers Joseph, William, also at the school.) [MSB; PR]

HALL, John: Saunders' charity school, Rye. In lists from September 1722 (?) (first list) to 4 May 1726 (not in 29 June 1726). Son of widow Taylar. [RSB]

HALL, John (1729-): Saunders' charity school, Rye. In lists from 11 January 1738 (not in 5 October 1737) to 5 January 1743 (not in June 1743 (?)). Son of Thomas, deceased. Baptised 4 May 1729, son of Thomas and Mary. (Brother James also at the school.) [RSB; PR]

HALL, John (1766-): Mayfield charity school. Admitted 8 April 1774; removed 9 January 1778, for non-attendance after 3¾ years as a 'reader'. Baptised 9 February 1766, son of William and Ann. (One brother, 4 sisters, also

at the school.) [MSB; PR]

HALL, Joseph (1782-): Mayfield charity school. Admitted 5 July 1793; removed 8 April 1796, taken out by parents. Baptised 19 May 1782, son of Joseph and Ann. (Brothers James, William, also at the school.) [MSB; PR]

HALL, Mary (1761-): Mayfield charity school. Admitted 8 April 1774; removed 5 April 1776, 'Sufficiently Learned' [?], after 2 years as a 'reader'. Baptised 2 August 1761, daughter of William and Ann. (Two brothers, 3 sisters, also at the school.) [MSB; PR]

HALL, Rebecca (1752-): Mayfield charity school. Admitted 13 April 1764; removed 17 October 1766, for non-attendance after 2¼ years at the school, ¾ year as a 'writer'. Baptised 22 October[?] 1752, daughter of William and Anne. (Two brothers, 3 sisters, also at the school.) [MSB; PR]

HALL, Sarah (1745-): Mayfield charity school. Admitted 8 April 1757; removed 7 July 1758, taken out by parents, after 1¼ years at the school as a 'reader'. Baptised 14 April 1745, daughter of William and Anne. (Two brothers, 3 sisters, also at the school.) [MSB; PR]

HALL, William (1747-): Mayfield charity school. Admitted 15 October 1756; removed 10 April 1761, 'sufficiently learn'd', after 4½ years at the school, 1½ years as a 'writer'. Born 11 February 1747, baptised 3 March 1747, son of William and Ann. (One brother, 4 sisters, also at the school.) [MSB; PR]

HALL, William (1780-): Mayfield charity school. Admitted 11 April 1788; removed 6 January 1792, taken out by parents. Baptised 26 March 1780, son of Joseph and Anne. (Brothers James, Joseph, also at the school.) [MSB; PR]

HALSEY, Thomas (1721 or 22-): At Amberley School. Of Sussex. Admitted pensioner (aged 18) at Peterhouse, Cambridge 27 March 1740. Scholar 1740; BA 1744; Ordained deacon (Norwich) 1746. [*Al. Cant.*]

HAMMON, John (1733-): Saunders' charity school, Rye. In lists from 26 October 1743 (not in June 1743 (?)) to 4 July 1744 (not in 10

April 1745, next surviving list). Son of John, deceased. Baptised 11 September 1733, son of John and Ann. [RSB; PR]

HAMMOND, Thomas (c1703-): Grey Coat charity school, Chichester. Admitted between Lady Day 1712 and Lady Day 1713, aged 9. There Lady Day 1714. [WSRO Cap.V/1/1]

HARCOURT, Lee: At Rev Thankful Frewen's school at Northiam, as a boarder, from 26 June 1713 to 11 October 1714. A record of the classics he studied survives. His fees (£16 pa) paid by 'Lady Harcourt's Executrix'. [ESRO FRE 533]

HARDS, Edward (c1720-): At school in Steyning in 1734, aged 14, probably at the grammar school. Boarded with John Peyte, malster. (He was living c1792, aged 72.) [Sleight, J. M. *A Very Exceptional Instance* (1981)]

HARLING, William: Grey Coat charity school, Chichester. Left between Michaelmas 1767 and Michaelmas 1768. Given 10s 6d on leaving. [WSRO Cap.V/1/1]

HARMAN, George (1772-): Lord Pelham's charity school, Lewes [qv Rand's school]. Admitted Christmas 1781. There 10 October 1784, aged 12. Baptised 6 October 1772, son of Thomas and Sarah. [ESRO AMS 6005; All Saints Lewes PR]

HARMER, Thomas: Sedlescombe charity school. There 3 May 1755 (a 'writer'), 10 April 1758, 22 February 1759. [SSB]

HARNES, William: Lewes grammar school; then Queen's College, Cambridge. Paid £13 in 1765 by Steere's charity which assisted in sending Lewes boys to Cambridge or Oxford. [Horsfield *Lewes*]

HARRISON, Mary: Brighton girls' charity school. Admitted when school opened, 30 September 1702. 'Harrison's daughter Mary'. (Probably daughter of Quakers William and Susanna (née Nelson), who married 27 February 1694; birth, not baptism, of their son in parish register, October 1698.) [BSB; Quaker register, Lewes/Blatchington; PR]

(HART): Eastbourne charity school. Admitted Christmas 1777; there Christmas 1779. [SAS Budgen MS v.117]

HART, William (1727-): Eastbourne charity school. There December 1738 (?), April 1741. Baptised 22 November 1727, son of John and Mary. [SAS Budgen MS v.129; PR]

HARTLEY: Lord Pelham's charity school, Lewes [qv Rand's school]. Added to list of 10 October 1784. [ESRO AMS 6005]

HARTLY (HEARTLY), John (1690-): Brighton charity school. In 'writers' list 12 January 1702; had left by December 1705 and gone 'to sea'. Baptised 3 July 1690, son of John and Elizabeth (née Thomas). (Brother Robert also at the school.) [BSB; PR]

HARTLY, Robert: (1690-): Brighton charity school. In 'writers' list 12 January 1702; given coat and hat July 1702; had left by December 1705 and gone 'to sea'. Baptised 31 August 1690, son of Robart and [*blank*] (married 22 October 1689, Robart Hartely and Mary Snooke). [BSB; PR]

HARTLY, Robert (1695-): Brighton charity school. Admitted as 'reader' sometime after list of (probably) January 1702; in 'readers' list December 1705. Baptised 10 November 1695, son of John and Elizabeth (née Thomas). (Brother John also at the school). [BSB; PR]

HARTLY (HARTELY), Susanna (1693-): Brighton girls' charity school. Admitted sometime after 25 March 1703 (probably by end of 1705). Baptised 19 February 1693, daughter of Edward and Susanna. [BSB; PR]

HARVEY, George (1759-): Saunders' charity school, Rye. Admitted 24 August 1768; left 14 August 1773. Son of Nicholas, deceased. Baptised 18 August 1759, son of Nicholas and Elizabeth. (Brothers Nicholas, Robert, also at the school.) [RSB; PR]

HARVEY, James: Admitted Robertsbridge charity school in its first year (it opened 5 April 1796). Sponsored by Mrs L. Noakes (Laurence Noakes also subscribed). Son of Hz (probably son of Hezekiah, a daughter of whom was baptised 1794.) [ESRO PAR 477/25/1/1;

Salehurst PR]

HARVEY, John (1766-): Saunders' charity school, Rye. Admitted 19 April 1777; left 11 July 1778. Baptised 22 August 1766, son of John and Martha. [RSB; PR]

HARVEY, Nicholas (1752-): Saunders' charity school, Rye. In lists from Michaelmas 1761 (not in Lady Day 1761); left 23 March 1765. Baptised 21 November 1752, son of Nicholas and Elizabeth. (Brothers George, Robert, also at the school.) [RSB; PR]

HARVEY, Robert (1756-): Saunders' charity school, Rye. In lists from Michaelmas 1765 (not in Lady Day 1765) to Lady Day 1767 (not in Christmas 1768, next surviving list). Son of Nicholas, deceased in Lady Day 1767 list (next list after Michaelmas 1765). Baptised 3 September 1756, son of Nicholas and Elizabeth. (Brothers George, Nicholas, also at the school.) [RSB; PR]

HASELDEN, Benjamin (1758-): Mayfield charity school. Admitted 2 May 1766; removed 21 July 1769, for non-attendance after 3¼ years at the school, 1¼ years as a 'writer'. Baptised 24 March 1758, son of John and [*blank*]. [MSB; PR]

HASELDEN (HAISELDEN), Fanny: Mayfield charity school. Admitted 13 April 1798; removed 10 July 1801, for non-attendance. [MSB]

HASELDEN (HAISELDEN), George: Mayfield charity school. First entered in lists 12 April 1793, replacing 'John Haiselden' [qv]; removed 11 July 1794, for non-attendance. (Probably son of William and Ann; if so, brother John, sisters Mary, Sarah, also at the school.) [MSB]

HASSELDEN, John (1769-): Sedlescombe charity school. There 8 May 1775, a 'reader'. Baptised 5 November 1769, son of Thomas and Ann. (Brothers Thomas, William, also at the school.) [SSB; PR]

HASELDEN (HAISELDEN, HAZELDEN), John (1782-): Mayfield charity school. Admitted 7 October 1791; in lists to 11 January 1793; in list for 12 April 1793 'John' crossed

through and 'George' written in. Baptised 25 December 1782, son of William and Ann. (Probably brother George, sisters Mary, Sarah, also at the school.) [MSB; PR]

HASELDEN, Joseph (1747-): Mayfield charity school. Admitted 9 April 1756; removed 13 October 1758, for non-attendance after 2¼ years at the school as a 'reader'; brother Richard admitted in his place; but Joseph appears in next list (15 February 1759) and Richard does not; Joseph continues in lists to 11 April 1760, when removed for non-attendance, after 3¾ years at the school, ¾ year as a 'writer'. Baptised 10 May 1747, son of William and Sarah. (Three brothers also at the school.) [MSB; PR]

HAISELDEN, Joseph (1786-): Admitted Robertsbridge charity school at its opening, 5 April 1796. Sponsored by Mr John Haisleden. Baptised 27 August 1786, aged 3 weeks, son of Joseph and Elizabeth (née Hall). [ESRO PAR 477/25/1/1; Salehurst PR]

HASELDEN, Mary (1761-): Mayfield charity school. Admitted 17 April 1767 to 'Widow Dukes' dame school (but not in next list, 4 September 1767, after which Duke's ceased to be used); admitted to charity school 22 April 1768; removed 15 July 1774, 'Gone to Service', after 6¼ years at the school, 1½ years as a 'writer'. Baptised 19 October 1761, daughter of William and Ann. (Probably brother George, brother John, sister Sarah, also at the school.) [MSB; PR]

HASELDEN, Richard (1750-): Mayfield charity school. Admitted 17 October 1760 (but apparently joined during previous quarter); removed 6 July 1764, taken out by parents, after 4 years at the school, 1 year as a 'writer'. Brother of Stephen, whose place at the school he took over. Was originally admitted 13 October 1758, 'in room of his brother Joseph' [qv] but Joseph stayed there until April 1760. Baptised 17 November 1750, son of William and Sarah. (Three brothers also at the school.) [MSB; PR]

HASELDEN, Samuel, senior (1743-): Mayfield charity school. Admitted 29 March 1751; started 'writing' 19 January 1753; removed 6 July 1753, taken out by parents;

re-admitted 12 October 1753; removed 11 January 1754, 'To go to service', but appears in list for 12 April 1754 (no re-admission recorded - presumably did not go to service after all); removed 10 January 1755, 'To work', taken home by parent, after 3¾ years in total at the school, 1¾ years as a 'writer'. Baptised 20 March 1743, son of Richard and Mary. (Sister Sarah also at the school.) [MSB; PR]

HASELDEN, Samuel, junior (1745-): Mayfield charity school. No admission recorded but first appears in list for 12 October 1753, annotated 'F. Oak' (in which list Samuel senior was re-admitted); removed 1 January 1757, taken away by parents, after 3¾ years at the school, 1 year as a 'writer'. Baptised 22 September 1745, son of William and Sarah. (Three brothers also at the school.) [MSB; PR]

HASELDEN, Sarah (1740-): Mayfield charity school. Admitted at formal opening of school, 29 June 1750, but may have been there up to ¾ year earlier, as master paid from Michaelmas 1749; removed 19 January 1753, 'well learned'; had been a 'writer' for 2¼ years. Baptised 10 August 1740, daughter of Richard and Mary. (Brother Samuel also at the school.) [MSB; PR]

HASELDEN, Sarah (1763 or 64-): Mayfield charity school. Admitted 15 October 1773; removed 7 July 1775, for non-attendance after 1¾ years at the school as a 'reader'. Baptised 19 January 1764, daughter of William and Ann. (Probably brother George, brother John, sister Mary, also at the school.) [MSB; PR]

HASELDEN, Stephen (1749-): Mayfield charity school. Admitted 24 January 1757; removed 17 October 1760, 'his Brother Richard came in his room', after 3½ years at the school, still a 'reader'. Baptised 20 February 1749, son of William and Sarah. (Three brothers also at the school.) [MSB; PR]

HASELDEN (HAISELDEN), Susannah: Mayfield charity school. Admitted 11 July 1794; in list of 17 October 1794 her position is taken by John Underhill (no removal for SH, no admission for JU); re-admitted 8 April 1796; removed 12 October 1798, for non-attendance. [MSB]

HASELDEN, Thomas: Mayfield charity school. Admitted at formal opening of school, 29 June 1750, but may have been there up to ¾ year earlier, as master paid from Michaelmas 1749; no removal, but re-admitted 12 October 1753, identified as a 'writer' for 1¾ years; list of 11 January 1754 shows a TH but not as a 'writer', so perhaps another TH; no TH in list for 12 April 1754. [MSB]

HASSELDEN, Thomas (1766-): Sedlescombe charity school. There 8 May 1775, a 'reader'. Baptised 12 January 1766, son of Thomas and Ann. (Brothers John, William, also at the school.) [SSB; PR]

HASELDEN, William (1737-): Mayfield charity school. Admitted 5 October 1750; removed 3 July 1752, for non-attendance; at 27 March 1752 had been a 'writer' for 1 year. Baptised 1 April 1737, son of Thomas and Mary. [MSB; PR]

HASSELDEN, William (1764-): Sedlescombe charity school. There 18 April 1772 and 8 May 1775 (still a 'reader'). Baptised 13 May 1764, son of Thomas and Ann. (Brothers John, Thomas, also at the school.) [SSB; PR]

HASEMAN - see HEASMAN

HASTINGS, William (1751-): At Seaford charity school 1765. Grandson of John. Baptised 14 July 1751, son of Richard and Mary. [BL Add MS 33,059; PR]

HAWES, John (1698-1751): At Lewes grammar school. Born 13 November 1698, son of John, rector of Berwick and vicar of Alciston, and Frances (née Hay, of Westham: they married at Berwick 28 November 1695). Admitted pensioner (aged 17) Peterhouse, Cambridge, 2 March 1716; scholar 1716; BA 1720; MA 1723. Ordained deacon (London) 5 March 1721. Rector All Saints, Lewes, 1724-34; vicar of Glynde 1725 to death; rector of Berwick 1743 (succeeded father) to death. Buried at Glynde 27 January 1751. Bachelor; letters of administration granted 9 March 1751 to brother Edward, next of kin. [*Al. Cant.*; Berwick PR; Clarke, A. D. C. *Some Notes on the History of All Saints Parish* (1910); CI]

HAY, William (1695-1755): In 1705 sent to

school in Newick and in 1710 to a larger school in Lewes (probably the grammar school); to Oxford 1712; then studied law, till sight impaired by smallpox. MP for Seaford 1734. Wrote poetry and books, including *Remarks on the Laws relating to the Poor* (1735). Born 21 August 1695 at Glyndebourne; died there 22 June 1755. [Horsfield *Lewes*]

HAYS (HAYES), John (1734-): Saunders' charity school, Rye. In lists from 14 August 1745 (not in 10 April 1745); left 5 August 1748. Baptised 26 October 1734, son of Charles and Mary. (Brother William also at the school.) [RSB; PR]

HAYS, William (1729-): Saunders' charity school, Rye. In lists from 10 January 1739 (not in 4 October 1738) to 4 July 1744 (not in 10 April 1745). Baptised 4 July 1729, son of Charles and Mary. (Brother John also at the school.) [RSB; PR]

HAYLER, Henry (1774-): Sedlescombe charity school. There 29 September 1784 (a 'writer') and 29 September 1786. Baptised 10 March 1774, son of Edward and Ann. [SSB; PR]

HAYLEY, William (1745-1820): Poet and critic. Born at Chichester 9 November 1745, son of Thomas (son of Thomas, dean of Chichester; died when WH was very young) and Mary (daughter of Colonel Yates, MP for Chichester 1734-41). Sent to the Misses Russells' school and while 'a Child in Petticoats' was given 'a bright silver Penny for reading well' by the youngest sister, Philadelphia (with whom he kept in touch all her life, presenting her, when she was 63 - still a schoolmistress - with a copy of his master-work, *The Triumphs of Temper*). By 5, at Chichester a master had tried to teach him Latin, but when he was 5 his mother moved to London and he was sent to a boarding school at Kingston; then to Eton 1757, Trinity Hall, Cambridge, 1763. Lived on his patrimonial estate at Eartham until forced to let this, then moved to Felpham. A successful writer, in 1790 he was offered the laureateship, which he refused. Friend of William Cowper and William Blake, who illustrated his works. Among others, he helped the young poets William Hersee [qv] and Charlotte Smith [qv TURNER,

Charlotte]. Married firstly 1769, Eliza Ball (daughter of Thomas, dean of Chichester); she treated as own son WH's illegitimate son, Thomas Alphonso, born 5 October 1780, who died 1800, a young sculptor; they separated 1789; her mind was affected and she died 1797; married secondly 1809, Mary Welford; they separated after 3 years. Died at Felpham 12 November 1820. [Chichester All Saints PR; Hay, A. *History of Chichester* (1804); *Chichester Papers* **49**; *DNB*; *Encyclopedia Britanica*; see also Lucas, E. V. *Highways and Byways in Sussex* (2nd edition 1935)]

HAYLOR, Hannah: A poor girl of Alciston, the parish paid for her schooling by Dame Richardson, 1753-58. [ESRO PAR 227/31/1]

HEAD, Ann (1772-): A poor girl of Playden for whose schooling the parish paid from c1781. Surviving loose receipts show parish paid Sara Stevens (who could write neatly) 3d a week for schooling Ann from at least May 1781, when she was just 9, to April 1782. Baptised 17 May 1772, daughter of William (buried 23 September 1779) and Sarah (probably buried 31 March 1782). (Parish also paid for schooling brothers James, John, sister Hannah.) [ESRO PAR 445/31/1/14; PR]

HEAD, George: Eastbourne charity school. Admitted 15 June 1770. Son of John. [SAS Budgen MS v.105]

HEAD, Hannah: Eldest of 4 Head children of Playden for whose schooling the parish paid from c1781. Surviving loose receipts show parish paid Sara Stevens 3d a week for schooling Hannah from at least May 1781 to April 1782, when she was probably about 11. 10 years later, on 9 October 1791, her illegitimate daughter, Sarah, was baptised. Daughter of William (buried 23 September 1779) and Sarah (probably buried 31 March 1782). [ESRO PAR 445/31/1/14; PR]

HEAD, Henry (1728-): At Eastbourne charity school December 1738 (?). Baptised 18 February 1728, son of James and Elizabeth. [SAS Budgen MS v.129; PR]

HEAD, James (1777-): Youngest of 4 Head children of Playden for whose schooling the parish paid from c1781. Surviving loose receipts show parish paid Sara Stevens 2d a week for schooling James from at least May 1781, when he was only 3½, to April 1782; from January 1783 to 13 October 1783 Jane Dawes 3d a week for schooling him; from 20 October 1783 to 8 April 1784 Mrs Sarah Roun for schooling him and brother John, initially at 2d a week each plus 1s a quarter for 'Firing', and by April at 3d a week each; another receipt shows parish paid W. King 2s for schooling James for 12 weeks in 1785 at 2d a week, and 1s 6d for 9 weeks in 1786, James then 8. Baptised 14 December 1777, son of William (buried 23 September 1779) and Sarah (probably buried 31 March 1782). [ESRO PAR 445/31/1/14; PR]

HEAD, John (1725-): At Eastbourne charity school 1734. Baptised 18 September 1725, son of Jeremy and Elizabeth. [Chatsworth, Devonshire Collection, Compton Place, Box P; PR]

HEAD, John (1775-?91): One of 4 Head children of Playden for whose schooling the parish paid from c1781. Surviving loose receipts show parish paid Sara Stevens 2d a week for schooling him from at least May 1781, when he was 6, to April 1782; from January 1783 to 13 October 1783 Jane Dawes 3d a week for schooling him; from 20 October 1783 to 8 April 1784 Mrs Sarah Roun for schooling him and brother James initially at 2d a week each plus 1s a quarter for 'Firing', and by April at 3d a week each. Baptised 23 November 1775, son of William (buried 23 September 1779) and Sarah (probably buried 31 March 1782). Probably the JH buried 19 October 1791; if so, he would have died at 15. [ESRO PAR 445/31/1/14; PR]

HEASMAN, HESMAN, HASEMAN - see also HOSMAN/HOSMER/HOSMORE

HEASMAN, Ann (1767-): Mayfield charity school. Admitted 7 April 1775; removed 17 July 1778, taken out by parents but 'pretty well learned' after 3¼ years at the school, ¾ year as a 'writer'. Baptised 31 May 1767, 'a base-born' (no details of parent(s) but probably daughter of Richard Heasman and Anna Gorringe who married 22 October 1767, in which case 4 brothers, 3 sisters, also at the school). [MSB; PR]

HEASMAN, Benjamin (1784-): Mayfield charity school. Admitted 11 April 1794; removed 13 April 1798, taken out by parents. Baptised 19 December 1784, son of Richard and Ann. (Three brothers, 3, probably 4 sisters, also at the school.) [MSB; PR]

HEASMAN, Elizabeth (1776-): Mayfield charity school. Admitted 9 April 1784; removed 8 January 1790, taken out by parents. Baptised 15 December 1776, daughter of Richard and Anne. (Four brothers, 2, probably 3 sisters, also at the school.) [MSB; PR]

HEASMAN, John (1771-): Mayfield charity school. Admitted 10 April 1778; removed 18 April 1783, taken out by parents 'and Sufficiently Learned'. Baptised 30 June 1771, son of Richard and Anne. (Three brothers, 3, probably 4 sisters, also at the school.) [MSB; PR]

HEASMAN, Mary (1779-): Mayfield charity school. Admitted 6 April 1787; removed 15 October 1790, 'Suspended at the request of her parents'; re-admitted 13 July 1791; removed 6 April 1792. Baptised 31 January 1779, daughter of Richard and Anne. (Four brothers, 2, probably 3 sisters, also at the school.) [MSB; PR]

HEASMAN, Richard (1769-): Mayfield charity school. Admitted 5 April 1776; removed 10 April 1778, 'being Ill & Unable to Attend', after 2 years at the school as a 'reader'. Baptised 12 March 1769, son of Richard and Ann. (Three brothers, 3, probably 4 sisters, also at the school.) [MSB; PR]

HEASMAN, Sarah (1781-): Mayfield charity school. Admitted 5 July 1793; removed 10 July 1795, taken out by parents. Baptised 25 March 1781, daughter of Richard and Anne. (Four brothers, 2, probably 3 sisters, also at the school.) [MSB; PR]

HEASMAN, William (1774-): Mayfield charity school. Admitted 12 April 1782; removed 7 July 1786, 'Sufficiently Learned'. Baptised 22 May 1774, son of Richard and Anne. (Three brothers, 3, probably 4 sisters, also at the school.) [MSB; PR]

HEATHER: Grey Coat charity school,

Chichester. Left between Michaelmas 1752 and Michaelmas 1753. Given 10s 6d on leaving. [WSRO Cap.V/1/1]

HEATHER: Grey Coat charity school, Chichester. Left between Michaelmas 1755 and Michaelmas 1756. Given 10s 6d on leaving. [WSRO Cap.V/1/1]

HEMMINGS, James: Saunders' charity school, Rye. Admitted 14 July 1779; in lists to 29 September 1784 (not in 24 June 1785). Son of George, deceased. [RSB]

HEMSLEY, George (1773-): Mayfield charity school. Admitted 6 March 1781; removed 15 October 1784, 'Sufficiently Learned'. Baptised 14 February 1773, son of Abraham and Martha. [MSB; PR]

HEMSLEY, R[*blank*] (1706?-): Brighton charity school. Given prayer book 1718. Probably Richard, baptised 13 March 1706, son of George and Dorothy. [BSB; PR]

HERRINGTON, Charles (1792-): Petworth charity school. Admitted 5 August 1799; there Michaelmas 1801 (had left by 12 July 1803). Baptised 27 May 1792, son of Henry and Sarah. [WSRO Petworth House Archives 1763; PR]

HERSEE, William (1786-1854): The 'ploughboy poet'. At dame school in Coldwaltham. He later wrote: '...born in an humble cottage, and bred at the plough... debarred from every advantage of education, and instructed only by the village matron...' Described the school in poem, 'The Village Schoolmistress'. Baptised 12 February 1786, son of Richard and Elizabeth; father owned small farm at Coldwaltham, and was wheelwright. At 7, shepherd-boy on Downs; by 10 had learnt to plough. Went to Reigate 1798, perhaps apprenticed to printer there. About 1807 married Mary, orphan daughter of a miller; moved to Portsea, but back to Coldwaltham by 1808, where son born December 1808; had at least 10 children, most of whom died in infancy. Through printer, W. Mason, met William Hayley [qv], who encouraged and financed him; also obtained patronage of William Huskisson, MP, and probably through him appointed clerk in excise,

May 1809, at £84 pa, and moved to Pentonville. Published *Poems Rural and Domestic*, 1810 (but in debt and appealed to Hayley for loan of £400); third edition, with additional poems, 1829. From 1831 to 1852, edited the *Warwickshire Advertiser and Leamington Gazette*. Died 6 August 1854. [Tibble, R. 'William Hersee (1786-1854)' *West Sussex History* **42**; Hersee, W. *Poems Rural and Domestic* (1810)]

HEWETT, Thomas: At Cocking charity school 1732, 1733. [WSRO Par 53/12/1]

HEWETT, William: At Cocking charity school 1733. Son of John. [WSRO Par 53/12/1]

HEWIT: Grey Coat charity school, Chichester. Given 10s 6d on leaving, 3 November 1772. [WSRO Cap.V/1/1]

HIDER, Ann (1786-): Admitted Fermor's charity school, Rotherfield, 3 May 1794. Daughter of Widow Hider. Baptised 22 October 1786, daughter of Joseph and Elizabeth ('poor'). [ESRO PAR 465/4/1; PR]

HIDER, Henry (1788-): Admitted Fermor's charity school, Rotherfield, 29 April 1798. Son of Widow Hider. Baptised 3 August 1788, son of Joseph and Elizabeth. [ESRO PAR 465/4/1; PR]

(HILL): Child of John Hill at Widow Page's school, Clapham, June 1772. [*SAC* **71**]

HILTON, Joseph (1692-1756): Brighton charity school. Admitted as 'reader' sometime after list of (probably) January 1702; joined 'writers' class sometime after 12 January 1702; in 'writers' class December 1705. Baptised 16 October 1692, son of Andrew (blacksmith, deputy reeve 1708) and Mary. Became ropemaker; deputy reeve, beadle and bailiff of Brighton manor, 1723, 1730, 1747. Buried 2 January 1756, 'Town Poet and Cryer'. [BSB; PR; Harrison and North]

HITCHENER: Thornton's school, Horsham. On Saturday, 3 January 1795, played Hotspur in *Henry IV, part 1*. At the request of the audience ('the Gentry and Inhabitants of the town of Horsham') the play was performed again the following Monday. [*SWA* 5.1.95]

HITCHENER, Elizabeth (1782-1822): Daughter of Thomas Hitchener (formerly Yorke, a one-time Sussex smuggler, later innkeeper of the *Friars Oak* near Hurstpierpoint), was sent to the Miss Adams's boarding school at Lewes when 9, the school being chosen by her mother. There formed a strong bond with one of the Miss Adams's - almost certainly the younger sister, Hannah - who taught her 'to have an opinion' (unconventional instruction for girls at that time) and inculcated her with radical principles; 'me alone of all her pupils did she love as her child, she will say I first loved her'; Miss Adams was 'the Mother of my soul, the dear woman who educated me'. But this Miss Adams was 'so circumstanc'd with a Sister, who is the opposite of her that she is not more at liberty to me than I am to her' (as EH wrote later, when she was 29; the friendship was condemned by EH's parents) and 'having too much virtue for the age has ever been an object of persecution'. It was EH's intention to achieve financial independence by building up a successful school so that she 'could offer her an asylum'. [For her life after schooling see Schedule 2; see there also ADAMS, Hannah; Jones, F. L. *The Letters of Percy Bysshe Shelley* volume 1 (1964)]

HOAD, Joseph (1750-): Saunders' charity school, Rye. In lists from Christmas 1760 (not in Michaelmas 1760); left 16 March 1765. Baptised 4 April 1750, son of Thomas and Sarah. (Brother Thomas also at the school.) [RSB; PR]

HOAD, Thomas (1744-): Saunders' charity school, Rye. In lists from 25 March 1752 (not in 15 January 1752) to 16 April 1760, in which marked 'gone from School'. At the school 8¼ years. Baptised 23 November 1744, son of Thomas and Sarah. (Brother Joseph also at the school.) [RSB; PR]

HOADLEY, Joseph (1784-): Admitted Fermor's charity school, Rotherfield, 3 May 1794. Baptised 7 March 1784, son of Thomas and Jane. [ESRO PAR 465/4/1; PR]

(HOATHER): One of 3 children of William Hoather infected with smallpox in the winter of 1793-94, who recovered but had been sent 'during the whole Progress of the Disorder' to a day school in Lewes 'where from 30 to 40 other little Children...had been constantly at School and at play with the above mentioned infected Child.' [*SRS* **69**]

HOBBS, William (1791-): Admitted Fermor's charity school, Rotherfield, 29 April 1798. 'Son of William Habbs, Brittles'. Baptised 10 July 1791, son of William and Elizabeth. Later married and raised family in Rotherfield. [ESRO PAR 465/4/1; PR; McGill, C. pers. comm.]

HOBDEN, Samuel (1765-): Mayfield charity school. No record of admission but appears to have replaced elder brother Thomas in list for 15 October 1773; removed 5 July 1776, 'Taken out by his Father'. Baptised 27 October 1765, son of Thomas and Sarah. [MSB; PR]

HOBDEN, Thomas (1763-): Mayfield charity school. Admitted 20 July 1770; no record of removal but appears to have been replaced by younger brother Samuel in list for 15 October 1773. Baptised 6 November 1763, son of Thomas and Sarah. [MSB; PR]

HOLLOWAY: One of dancing master Rawlin's pupils, and principal dancer for figure dancing by his pupils at concert and ball at the *White Horse*, Brighton, 9 July 1793. [*SWA* 1.7.93]

HOLLOWAY, William (1785-1870): Midhurst grammar school [qv for his account of the school]. Admitted 28 July 1792. Became head boy. At school's first public performance of composition and oratory, 5 November 1799, he performed, in the role of Satan, with 2 other boys in a scene from Milton's *Paradise Lost*; the next year he won the prize for the best Latin poem, 'Medea suos filios trucidat', and spoke as Gabriel in another scene from Milton. Born 1 August 1785, at Emsworth, son of Joseph (-1785), corn-merchant. Married, 21 May 1809, Sarah Meryon of Rye (-1868), niece of Captain Amos, his mother's second husband. Farmed at Leigh until 1820; in brewery business at Rye for 18 years. Historian of Rye. Died at Rye 23 May 1870. [*SWA* 5.11.99, 27.5.1800; *SAC* **100**]

HOLMAN, Elizabeth (1751-): Brightling girls' charity school. Admitted between 31 July 1758 and 31 December 1761, in which period she attended on 315 school days. (No later records.) Baptised 24 October 1751, daughter of Isaac and Ann. [ESRO PAR 254/25/1; PR]

HOLMWOOD, Ansell: Admitted Fermor's charity school, Rotherfield, 29 April 1798. Son of Alexander. [ESRO PAR 465/4/1]

HOLT, Chadewick (1792-): Petworth charity school. Admitted 5 November 1800. Given a bible. Baptised 4 November 1792, Chidiwick, son of Thomas and Ann. [WSRO Petworth House Archives 1763; PR]

HOOD, Thomas (1749-): At Seaford charity school 1765. Baptised 20 August 1749, son of Edward and Sarah. [BL Add MS 33,059; PR]

HOOK, Ann: Mayfield charity school. Admitted 15 July 1774; removed 10 October 1777, for non-attendance, after 3¼ years as a 'reader'. [MSB]

HOOK, Edward (1745-): Mayfield charity school. Admitted 12 April 1754; removed 15 October 1756, taken away by parents, still a 'reader'. Baptised 3 November 1745, son of John and Jane. (Brother John also at the school.) [MSB; PR]

HOOK, Edward (1793 or 94-): Sedlescombe charity school. Admitted 1798; there 20 August 1798 and 13 January 1800 (still a 'reader'). Baptised 12 January 1794, son of Henry and Sarah. (Brother Henry also at the school.) [SSB; PR]

HOOK, Elizabeth (1747-): Mayfield charity school. Admitted 26 October 1759; removed 8 April 1763, 'sufficiently learned', after 3½ years at the school, 1¾ years as a 'writer'. Born 15 May 1747, baptised 1 June 1747, daughter of Charles and Elizabeth. (Brother John, sister Mary, also at the school.) [MSB; PR]

HOOKE, Elizabeth: Petworth charity school. Admitted 27 August 1800; there for 1 year. (Perhaps daughter of Henry, gardener, one of 2 'Poor Tradesmen' each given £6 5s in 1799.) [WSRO Petworth House Archives 1763]

HOOK, Hannah (1737-): At Sedlescombe charity school 23 June 1748. Baptised 6 February 1737, daughter of Richard and Ann. (Brother Henry also at the school.) [SSB; PR]

HOOK, Henry (1738-): At Sedlescombe charity school 23 June 1748. Baptised 13 November 1738, son of Richard and Ann. (Sister Hannah also at the school.) [SSB; PR]

HOOK, Henry (1766-): At Sedlescombe charity school 8 June 1775, a 'writer'. Baptised 27 April 1766, son of Henry and Mary. (Brother John also at the school.) [SSB; PR]

HOOK, Henry (1792-): Sedlescombe charity school. Admitted 1798 (a 'reader'); in 20 August 1798 list as 'reader' changed to 'now writer'; in 13 January 1800 list, and name crossed through. Baptised 13 May 1792, son of Henry and Sarah. (Brother Edward also at the school.) [SSB; PR]

HOOK, John (1742-): Mayfield charity school. Admitted 27 March 1752; removed 12 April 1754, 'well learned'; had been a 'writer' 1 year. Baptised 9 April 1742, son of Charles and Elizabeth. (Sisters Elizabeth, Mary, also at the school.) [MSB; PR]

HOOK, John (1747-): Mayfield charity school. Admitted 12 July 1754; removed 20 January 1758, 'to make room for others having made a good proficiency', after 3½ years at the school, 1 year as a 'writer'. Baptised 1 April 1747, son of John and Jane. (Brother Edward also at the school.) [MSB; PR]

HOOK, John: Mayfield charity school. Admitted 6 July 1759, as a 'writer'; removed 10 July 1761, 'sufficiently learned', after 2 years as a 'writer'. [MSB]

HOOK, John (1767-): At Sedlescombe charity school 8 May 1775, a 'writer'. Baptised 6 January 1768, son of Henry and Mary. (Brother Henry also at the school.) [SSB; PR]

HOOK, John: Mayfield charity school. Admitted 13 October 1775; removed 8 January 1779, 'for others more worthy', after 3¼ years as a 'reader'. [MSB]

HOOK, John (1769-): Mayfield charity

school. Admitted 7 April 1780; removed 6 March 1781, 'Sufficiently Learned', after 1 year at the school as a 'writer'. Probably baptised 5 November 1769, son of Edward and Ann. (Probably brother William also at the school.) [MSB; PR]

HOOK, Mary (1751-): Mayfield charity school. Admitted 26 October 1764; removed 11 July 1765, 'Taken out by her Parents but sufficiently learned', after ¾ year at the school, all as a 'writer'. Baptised 21 July 1751, daughter of Charles and Elizabeth. (NB Philadelphia Ashby also joined at the same time, aged 14, and had just ¼ year as a 'writer'.) (Brother John, sister Elizabeth, also at the school.) [MSB; PR]

HOOK, William (1773-): Mayfield charity school. Admitted 6 March 1781; removed 2 August 1782, for non-attendance. Baptised 24 January 1773, son of Edward and Anne. (Probably brother John also at the school.) [MSB; PR]

HOOPER, Odiarne: At Rev Thankful Frewen's school at Northiam, as a boarder, from 16 June 1712 to 4 March 1720. A record of the classics he studied survives. Son of Thomas, who paid £16 pa for his board and schooling (with some half-guinea gratuities eg at Easter, Whitsun, Christmas). [ESRO FRE 533]

HOPKINS, Joseph: Grey Coat charity school, Chichester. Left between Michaelmas 1767 and Michaelmas 1768. Given 10s 6d on leaving. [WSRO Cap.V/l/1]

HORE, Mary: At Cocking charity school 1733. [WSRO Par 53/12/1]

HORTON, Elizabeth: At Cocking charity school 1732, 1733. [WSRO Par 53/12/1]

HOSMAN/HOSMER/HOSMORE   - see also HEASMAN/HESMAN/HASEMAN

HOSMAN (HOSMORE), George (1759-): Mayfield charity school. Admitted 22 April 1768; removed July 1771, 'Sufficiently Learned', after 3¼ years at the school, 1¼ years as a 'writer'. Baptised 16 September 1759, son of Thomas and Mary. (Brother

Thomas also at the school.) [MSB; PR]

HOSMAN (HOSMER), Hannah (1788-): Mayfield charity school. Admitted 10 April 1795; removed 10 July 1795, for non-attendance. Baptised 3 February 1788, daughter of George and Sarah. (Sisters Mary, Sarah, also at the school.) [MSB; PR]

HOSMAN (HEASMAN), Mary (1780-): Mayfield charity school. Admitted 10 April 1789; removed 7 October 1791, taken out by parent but 'Sufficiently Learned'. Baptised 24 September 1780, daughter of George and Sarah. (Sisters Hannah, Sarah, also at the school.) [MSB; PR]

HOSMAN (HEASMAN), Sarah (1777-): Mayfield charity school. Admitted July 1785; removed 11 July 1788, taken out by parents; re-admitted 17 October 1788; removed 10 April 1789, taken out by parents. Baptised 23 February 1777, daughter of George and Sarah. (Sisters Hannah, Mary, also at the school.) [MSB; PR]

HOSMAN (HOSMORE), Thomas (1755-): Mayfield charity school. Admitted 8 April 1763; removed 16 October 1767, 'Sufficiently Learned', after 4½ years at the school, 1½ years as a 'writer'. Baptised 20 April 1755, son of Thomas and Mary. (Brother George also at the school.) [MSB; PR]

HOSMAN (HOSMER), Thomas (1787-): Mayfield charity school. Admitted 11 July 1794; removed 6 July 1798, taken out by parents. Baptised 22 April 1787, son of Thomas and Martha. [MSB; PR]

HOUNSILL (HUNSEL), John (1712-): Saunders' charity school, Rye. In lists from September 1722 (?) (first list) to January 1726 (4 May 1726 notes 'left the school'). Son of Mark, pipe-maker. Baptised 26 November 1712, son of Mark and Hannah. [RSB; PR]

HOUNSELL, Richard: Saunders' charity school, Rye. In lists from 4 July 1753 (not in 28 March 1753) to 9 April 1755 (not in midsummer 1755). Son of Alice. [RSB]

HOUSLEY, Elizabeth (1788-): Admitted Robertsbridge charity school at its opening, 5

April 1796, aged 7. Sponsored by John Alderton. Baptised 1 June 1788, daughter of Thomas and Anne (née Barham). [ESRO PAR 477/25/1/1; Salehurst PR]

HOVENDEN   - see also OVENDEN

HOVENDEN, John Hesimore (1716-): Saunders' charity school, Rye. In lists from January 1726 (?) (not in 11 August 1725) to 25 June 1729 (not in 7 January 1730). Son of Samuel, deceased. Baptised 30 September 1716, son of Samuel of Battle and Anne. [RSB; Rye PR]

HOVEND (OVENDEN), Thomas (1714-22): Saunders' charity school, Rye. In list of September 1722 (?) (first list), marked 'Deceased'. Baptised 21 April 1714, buried 9 December 1722, son of Thomas and Elizabeth. [RSB; PR]

[HOW]: Probably at Eastbourne charity school. List of 1771, after a 1772 addition, notes 'Hows Boy next vacancy'. [SAS Budgen MS v.105]

HOWEL, John: Brighton charity school. Given prayer book 1715. Either born 22 February 1700, son of Henry (brother at the school) or baptised 23 May 1703, son of John and Elizabeth (another JH, same parents, baptised 23 November 1701, presumably died). [BSB; PR; Union Street Independent Chapel register]

HOWELL, Thomas (1692-): Brighton charity school. In list of 'readers' of (probably) January 1702; given coat and hat July 1702; joined 'writers' class sometime after 12 January 1702; in list of 'writers' December 1705. Baptised 1 January 1693, son of Henry and Mary (née Long). (Brother John perhaps at the school.) [BSB; PR]

HOWELL, William (1755-): At Seaford charity school 1765. Baptised 20 September 1755, son of John and Mary. [BL Add MS 33,059; PR]

HUBBARD, Nicholas (1755-): At Seaford charity school 1765. Baptised 24 October 1755, son of Bartholomew and Jane. [BL Add MS 33,059; PR]

HUBBERSTY, Thomas: Probably at Lewes grammar school. Son of Rev John, rector of Folkington (dead by 1786) and Elizabeth, received 1786 £60 (probably 4 years at £15) from the Steere charity for assisting Lewes boys to go to Cambridge or Oxford. Queen's College, Cambridge, matriculated 1786; BA 1790; ordained deacon 1791; MA 1793. [Horsfield *Lewes*; *Al. Cant.*]

HUGGETT, John (1773-): Lord Pelham's charity school, Lewes [qv Rand's school]. Admitted Michaelmas 1780. There 10 October 1784, aged 11. [ESRO AMS 6005]

HUGHES, Richard (1757-): At Seaford charity school 1765. Baptised 10 December 1757, son of Thomas and Sarah. [BL Add MS 33,059; PR]

HULL, William (1694-): Brighton charity school. In list of 'readers' of (probably) January 1702; given coat and hat July 1702; still a 'reader' December 1705. Baptised 16 June 1694, son of William and Susan (née Silvester). [BSB; PR]

HULL, William: Saunders' charity school, Rye. In lists from 10 April 1745 (not in 4 July 1744); left 3 April 1746. Son of William, deceased. [RSB]

HUMPHREY, Samuel (1787-): Mayfield charity school. Admitted 19 January 1798; removed 11 July 1800, taken out by parents. Baptised 25 March 1787, son of Walter and Ann. [MSB; PR]

HUMPHERY (HUMPHRY), Thomas (1692-): Brighton charity school. In list of 'writers' 12 January 1702; left before December 1705 and went 'to sea'. Baptised 6 March 1692, son of Thomas and Mary (née Bartlatt). [BSB; PR]

HUMPHERY (HUMPHRY), William (1688-): Brighton charity school. In list of 'writers' 12 January 1702; left before December 1705 and went 'to sea'. Baptised 2 December 1688, son of Thomas and Joan. (Another WH, baptised 15 July 1694, son of Thomas and Mary, probably too young for record; the 2 fathers were different Thomases.) [BSB; PR]

HUNT,   Thomas   (1763-   ):   Admitted

Eastbourne charity school 27 April 1770. Baptised 31 July 1763, son of Thomas and Margaret. [SAS Budgen MS v.105; PR]

HUNTER, Elizabeth? (1688?-): Brighton girls' charity school. Admitted when school opened, 30 September 1702. 'John Hunter's daughter'. Perhaps Elizabeth, baptised 9 December 1688, daughter of John and Susan. [BSB; PR]

HUNTER, John (1757-): Saunders' charity school, Rye. In list for Lady Day 1767 (not in Michaelmas 1765, previous surviving list); not in Christmas 1768, next surviving list. Baptised 15 June 1757, son of William and Mary. (Brother William also at the school.) [RSB; PR]

HUNTER, Peter: Brighton charity school. Admitted as 'reader' sometime after list of (probably) January 1702; had left by December 1705 and gone 'to sea'. [BSB]

HUNTER, William (1750-): Saunders' charity school, Rye. In lists from Lady Day 1758 (not in 11 January 1758) to Michaelmas 1761 (not in 20 January 1762). Baptised 28 September 1750, son of William and Mary. (Brother John also at the school.) [RSB; PR]

HUNTLY, George (1784-): Mayfield charity school. Admitted 6 April 1792; removed 8 April 1796. Baptised 13 May 1784, son of Thomas and Ann. [MSB; PR]

HUNTLY, Mary (1744-): Mayfield charity school. Admitted 29 March 1751; removed 12 July 1754, 'Well learn'd', had been a 'writer' for 1¼ years. Baptised 25 February 1744, daughter of Anthony and Mary. [MSB; PR]

HURDIS, James (1763-1801): Chichester grammar school. Born 1763, son of James (1710-69), collector of customs, Newhaven, and second wife Jane (née Arlett, daughter of Richard of Durrington, married 17 January 1760). Father's first wife, Ann (née Humphrey, daughter of Cornelius, lawyer; she died 1755) had married against her father's wishes and forfeited dowry of £1,500, which went to her brother Henry, Lewes barrister; when James (1710-69) died, leaving wife Jane and 7 young children, of whom James aged 6, Henry

provided £40 pa to Jane for young James' welfare, and when 8 this used to send him to Chichester grammar school (there 1771-80), where encouraged to love of literature by master, John Atkinson (who at death, 1784, left him a legacy of books). 1780, matriculated St Mary's Hall, Oxford, aged 16; 1781-88, demy (scholar) Magdalen College, Oxford; 1782 awarded Steere exhibition (Lewes charity for assisting boys to Cambridge or Oxford) and received £60 over 4 years; BA 1783; 1784, tutor to George Pelham (later Bishop of Bristol, etc), son of Thomas, Earl of Chichester; MA 1787; fellow 1788-1800; BD 1794; DD 1797; professor of poetry 1793 to death, 1801. A keen musician, c1780 he owned and probably partly built a chamber organ. Curate of Burwash 1785-91, where he lived with 3 sisters; vicar of Bishopstone 1791 to death. Published 1788 a long poem, *The Village Curate* (which included a violent attack on girls' boarding schools: 'Are ye not apt/ To taint the infant mind, to point the way/ To fashionable folly, strew with flow'rs/ The path of vice, and teach the wayward child/ Extravagance and pride? Who learns in you/ To be the prudent wife, the pious mother?/ ...'Tis you untie/ The matrimonial knot; 'tis you divide/ The parent and his child.') Other poems followed, and works on biblical scholarship, Shakespeare, literary criticism. Friend of William Hayley and William Cowper. By 1793 had moved to Oxford; set up home there with 2 sisters. 1799 married Harriet, daughter of Hugh Minet, wealthy descendant of Huguenot family; sons born 1800, 1801, and posthumous daughter 1802. About 1800 was, at Bishopstone, one of the 7 owners of printing presses in Sussex registered under the Act of 1799. Died 23 December 1801, aged 38. [Tibble, R. 'Rev James Hurdis DD', *SFH* **7** (1986); *Al. Oxon.*; Horsfield *Lewes*; Plumley, N. and Lees, J. *The Organs and Organists of Chichester Cathedral* (1988); *SAC* **130**]

HUTCHINS, Edward Bumstead (1751-): Sedlescombe charity school. Admitted 4 April 1758; in lists 22 February 1759 and 1761, when crossed through. Baptised 8 December 1751, base born son of Ann Hutchins. [SSB; PR]

HUTSON, Joseph (c1745-64): At East Hoathly school 1755, pupil of Thomas Turner. Son of James, husbandman, and Mary (died 1756).

Died 1764, aged 19. [Vaisey, D., (ed) *The Diary of Thomas Turner* (1984)]

IDLE, Humphrey (1693-): Brighton charity school. In 'writers' list 12 January 1702; had left by December 1705 and gone 'to sea'. Baptised 15 October 1693, son of Jacob Idel otherwise Egel and Elizabeth (née Humphrys). [BSB; PR]

INSKIP, John (1731-): Pupil of John Bear, Shermanbury, 1743-44. Baptised 11 March 1731, son of Edward, a poor currier of Uckfield, and Philadelphia, daughter of Sir John Lade's eldest brother Vincent; when Sir John died, 3 June 1740, JI, then aged 9, inherited his estate, Lade having disinherited his heir, John Whithorne, who was to receive just £1 every Monday; became ward of John Fuller of Brightling Park and Rosehill. Lade had sent him to Tonbridge school but Fuller removed him, as after 3 years he could scarcely read, and sent him to Rev John Bear in 1743: 'I do not Expect he will make a great Scholler, but an honest sensible Gentleman he may, he being good Natured of a Tender disposition and very honest'. Later that year, Fuller to Bear: 'I doubt not but that you have found he is very apt to cry upon every Occasion, which I fear is Obstinacy, or rather a way which he has found out As he thinks to gett of, but this you will not mind, for I am very sure as we say of women he can cry when he will...I like not his Friends [ie family] coming to see him...I would therefore have you lett him know that he must go no where, without you go along with him...I shall take care of him in respect of his Relations, who are mostly mean people, I believe Counsell him not to Learn...As to the dancing Master it may create an Acquaintance among Country Girls, which may be as inconvenient to him as going amongst his relations...' After ¾ year with Bear, Fuller found him 'very much improved in his reading', and he had begun to study Latin. Fuller was only allowed to spend £50 pa from the estate on the boy's education; Bear's minimum basic fee was 50 guineas, and there were many extras for which Fuller paid, including a bureau and a 'scrutore', a dictionary and other books, a penny a day pocket money, and clothes: in April 1744, 'I...send him to you again with New Rigging, as much as we could gett ready in the time he has been here. We

shall send as soon as ready, Another Shirt a pair of Leather Britches, and a Canvass Wastcoate which he desired...I have told him when I hear from you of his Improvement in his Learning, that I would send for him hither for his diversion, And that he should not want any manner of Encouragement.' [Uckfield PR; ESRO SAS/RF 15/25, AMS 5718; *SAC* **104**]

IREDELL, Arthur (1758-1804): Lewes grammar school. Born 23 January 1758, son of Francis, of Bristol. Trinity College, Cambridge, 1778; scholar 1780; deacon 1781; BA 1782; MA 1786; priest 1788. Tutor to son of Mr (later Lord) Crewe, and friend of family throughout life. Curate of Guildford 1785; South Malling 1788; rector of Newhaven with Glynde and Southover 1791; chaplain to cousin, Earl Macartney. Married 1792 Ann Shrubb, daughter of James, of Guildford; had issue. Friend of Charles Fox, Sheridan, Burke, etc. Died 4 November 1804 on visit to Jamaica (had inherited, 1795, estates there from uncle Thomas). [*Al. Cant.*]

ISTED, Samuel: Admitted Fermor's charity school, Rotherfield, 3 June 1798. [ESRO PAR 465/4/1]

IZZARD, Jesse (1790-): Admitted Fermor's charity school, Rotherfield, 29 April 1798. Baptised 29 August 1790, son of William and Ann ('poor'). [ESRO PAR 465/4/1; PR]

IZZARD, Peter (1785-): Admitted Fermor's charity school, Rotherfield, 3 May 1794. Baptised 3 April 1785, son of William and Ann ('poor'). [ESRO PAR 465/4/1; PR]

JACKMAN, George (1703-): Brighton charity school. Given prayer book 1715. Baptised 5 December 1703, son of John. [BSB; PR]

JACOB: Grey Coat charity school, Chichester. Left between Michaelmas 1754 and Michaelmas 1755. Given 10s 6d on leaving. [WSRO Cap.V/1/1]

JACOB, Edward (1722-): Saunders' charity school, Rye. In lists from 31 March 1731 (not in 6 January 1731) to 28 March 1733 (4 July 1733 notes 'left the school'). Son of Thomas, deceased. Baptised 27 March 1722, son of Thomas and Mary. [RSB; PR]

JAMES, Robert (1723-): Saunders' charity school, Rye. In lists from 7 July 1731 (not in 31 March 1731) to 11 January 1738 (not in 5 April 1738). Baptised 13 September 1723, son of Robert and Mary. [RSB; PR]

JAMES, Thomas (1727-): Saunders' charity school, Rye. In lists from 8 October 1735 (not in 2 July 1735) to 4 July 1744 (not in 10 April 1745, next surviving list). Baptised 15 November 1727, son of Thomas and Susan. [RSB; PR]

JAMES, Thomas: Saunders' charity school, Rye. In list of 10 April 1745, marked with asterisk (not in 4 July 1744). Son of Thomas. [RSB; PR]

JAQUES, Dennett (1758-1837): Chichester grammar school. Baptised St Peter the Great, Chichester, 17 September 1758. Later printer and bookseller, Chichester. Married 1785, moved to London and set up press there. Died 26 October 1837. Sons Charles, John, William all became printers (and nephew Charles Austin Jaques a printer at Chichester). [McCann, T. J., in *SAC* **130**]

JARRATT/JARRETT

JARRATT (JARRETT), Charlotte (1786-): Mayfield charity school. Admitted 17 October 1794; removed 18 October 1799, taken out by parents, after 5 years at the school. Baptised 26 March 1786, daughter of Robert and Martha. (Brothers Jesse, William, sister Mille, also at the school.) [MSB; PR]

JARRATT, Jesse (1792-): Mayfield charity school. Admitted 11 April 1800; removed 13 January 1803, for non-attendance. Baptised 2 August 1792, son of Robert and Martha. (Brother William, sisters Charlotte, Mille, also at the school.) [MSB; PR]

JARRETT, John (-1732): Saunders' charity school, Rye. In lists from 31 March 1731 (not in 6 January 1731) to 19 January 1732 (29 March 1732 notes 'Dead'). Son of Richard. Buried 28 February 1732. (Brothers John, junior, Richard, also at the school.) [RSB; PR]

JARRETT, John: Saunders' charity school, Rye. In lists from 10 April 1745 (not in 4 July 1744) to Christmas 1748 (not in 25 March 1749). Son of Richard. (Brothers John, senior who died 1732, Richard, also at the school.) [RSB; PR]

JARRATT, John (1764-): Mayfield charity school. Admitted 15 October 1773; removed 12 January 1776, for non-attendance, still a 'reader'. Baptised 24 June 1764, son of Robert and Sarah. (Brother Robert also at the school.) [MSB; PR]

JARRATT, Mille (1790-): Mayfield charity school. Admitted 10 January 1800; removed 13 January 1803, for non-attendance. Baptised 4 April 1790, daughter of Robert and Martha. (Brothers Jesse, William, sister Charlotte, also at the school.) [MSB; PR]

JARRETT, Richard: Saunders' charity school, Rye. In lists from 25 October 1732 (not in 5 July 1732) to 28 January 1736 (7 April 1736 notes 'left the school'). Son of Richard. (Brothers John senior, died 1732, John, junior, also at the school.) [RSB]

JARRATT, Richard: Mayfield charity school. Admitted 15 July 1774; removed 11 April 1777, for non-attendance, still a 'reader'. [MSB]

JARRATT (JARRETT) Robert (1760-): Mayfield charity school. Admitted 20 January 1769; removed 21 July 1769, for non-attendance; re-admitted 19 October 1770; removed 19 April 1771, for non-attendance, still a 'reader'. Baptised 21 September 1760, son of Robert and Sarah. (Brother John also at the school.) [MSB; PR]

JARRETT, William (1788-): Mayfield charity school. Admitted 8 July 1796; removed 12 July 1799, 'sufficiently learned' (also entered as removed 18 October 1799). Baptised 5 February 1788, son of Robert and Martha. (Brother Jesse, sisters Charlotte, Mille, also at the school.) [MSB; PR]

JARVIS, Cripps: Admitted Fermor's charity school, Rotherfield, 21 December 1792. Son of James. [ESRO PAR 465/4/1]

JARVIS, James: Admitted Fermor's charity school, Rotherfield, 29 April 1798. Son of

James. [ESRO PAR 465/4/1]

JARVIS, Mary (1747-): Brightling girls' charity school. Admitted between Lady Day 1755 and 30 April 1757, in which period she attended on 207 school days; there to period 30 April 1757 to 31 July 1758, in which she attended on 324 school days; had 531 days at the school in total. Baptised 4 October 1747, daughter of Thomas and Elizabeth. [ESRO PAR 254/25/1; PR]

JEAL, Barnard (1752-): Saunders' charity school, Rye. In lists from Michaelmas 1763 (not in Christmas 1762, previous surviving list); left 23 March 1765. Son of Edward, deceased. Baptised 10 January 1752, son of Edward and Anne Geale. (Brother Edward also at the school.) [RSB; PR]

JEAL, Edward (1749-): Saunders' charity school, Rye. In lists from midsummer 1759 (not in 4 April 1759) to Christmas 1762 (not in Michaelmas 1763, next surviving list). Son of Edward, deceased. Baptised 6 January 1750, son of Edward and Anne. (Brother Barnard also at the school.) [RSB; PR]

JEFFERY, George (1695-): Brighton charity school. In list of 'readers' December 1705. Baptised 22 September 1695, son of John and Elizabeth. [BSB; PR]

JEFFERY, John (1690-): Brighton charity school. Admitted as 'reader' sometime after list of (probably) January 1702; in list of 'writers' December 1705. Baptised 6 April 1690, son of Thomas and Mary. [BSB; PR]

JEFFERY, Mary? (1697?-): Brighton girls' charity school. Admitted when school opened 30 September 1702. 'John Jefferey's daughter - the smith'. Probably Mary, baptised 18 July 1697, daughter of John (only JF daughter baptised in parish register). [BSB; PR]

JEFFERY, Richard (1784-1869): Probably boarder at Evershed's school at Steyning. Son of John of Washington and Ann (née Caffyn). [Evershed, P. B. pers. comm. citing Mrs Carter's recollections in F. Evershed's 'Notebooks']

JEFFERY (JEFFREYS), William (1786-):

Admitted Fermor's charity school, Rotherfield, 4 August 1793, son of James and Eliza of Buxted, but probably baptised 12 February 1786, son of James and Anne. [ESRO PAR 465/4/1; Buxted PR]

JEMMATT, Samuel: Midhurst grammar school. Admitted as charity scholar 1792. [*HMGS*]

JENKINS, senior: Midhurst grammar school. Recited his prize (English) poem, 'The Death of Agamemnon', at the school's first public performance of composition and oratory, 5 November 1799; also gave oration in Latin. Again won the prize for English composition 1800, for poem on 'The Beauties of Shakespeare and Milton'; also performed, as Agamemnon, with 2 others in scene from Homer. [*SWA* 11.11.99, 2.6.1800]

JENKINS, junior: Midhurst grammar school. At school's first public performance of composition and oratory, 5 November 1799, recited 'Description of Queen Mab' from Shakespeare; at the second 'literary performance', 27 May 1800, commended in the *Sussex Weekly Advertiser* for 'a very humorous and excellent performance of "The Progress of Discontent"'. [*SWA* 11.11.99, 2.6.1800]

JENNER, Richard: A poor boy of Burwash, the parish paid 4s for his schooling from 25 March 1736 to 29 September 1736 and, under the same bill, 6d for shaving his head twice. [ESRO PAR 284/31/1/1, loose receipt in ledger]

JENNER, William: At Seaford charity school 1765, but note in margin of list, 'Don't belong to Seaford'. Grandson of Thomas Verralls. [BL Add MS 33,059]

JENNINGS, Richard: Brighton charity school. Admitted as 'reader' sometime after list of (probably) January 1702; had left by December 1705. [BSB]

JEWHURST, Francis (1743-): Saunders' charity school, Rye. In lists from 8 July 1752 (not in 25 March 1752) to Michaelmas 1756, in which marked 'Left School' (not in 12 January 1757). Baptised 13 November 1743, son of Francis and Martha. (Brothers George, John, also at the school.) [RSB; PR]

JEWHURST, George (1750-): Saunders' charity school, Rye. In lists from midsummer 1760 (not in 16 April 1760) to 20 January 1762 (not in Christmas 1762, next surviving list). Later master of the school [qv Schedule 2]. Baptised 28 December 1750, son of Francis and Martha. (Brothers Francis, John, also at the school.) [RSB; PR]

JEWHURST, John (1737 or 38-): Saunders' charity school, Rye. In lists from Michaelmas 1748 (not in midsummer 1748) to 25 March 1752 (not in 8 July 1752). Baptised 6 January 1738, son of Francis and Martha. (Brothers Francis, George, also at the school.) [RSB; PR]

JOHNSTON: Button's school, Lewes. To recite, in French, at a 'Public Examination' at the *Star Assembly Room*, 22 June 1797. [*SWA* 19.6.97]

JONES: Master Jones of Horsham, won the Silver Pen, for writing, at Parrott's school, Petworth, June 1784. [*SWA* 7.6.84]

JONES, Jane (1784-): Admitted Robertsbridge charity school at its opening, 5 April 1796, aged 11. Sponsored by Mr Laurence Noakes. Baptised 26 April 1784, daughter of Thomas (buried 6 January 1789, aged 46) and Sarah (née Brockhurst). [ESRO PAR 477/25/1/1; PR]

JORDAN, John: Brighton charity school. Given prayer book 1718. [BSB]

JOSE, Henry (1735-): Saunders' charity school, Rye. In lists from 26 October 1743 (not in June 1743 (?)); left 11 April 1752 - had 8½ years at the school. Son of Henry, deceased. Baptised 2 January 1736, son of Henry and Ann. (Brother Stephen also at the school.) [RSB; PR]

JOSE, Stephen (1740-): Saunders' charity school, Rye. In lists from 8 July 1752 (not in 25 March 1752) to Michaelmas 1755 (not in 14 January 1756). Son of Henry, deceased. Baptised 7 November 1740, son of Henry and Anne. (NB Another SJ, same parents, baptised 27 April 1739, presumably died. Brother Henry

also at the school.) [RSB; PR]

JOY, Elizabeth (1696-): Brighton girls' charity school. Admitted when school opened, 30 September 1702. Baptised 29 November 1696, daughter of William and Gatred (Gartheg elsewhere). [BSB; PR]

[JUDEN, Henry]: In Wiston school list c1803, and perhaps at the school in 1800. [WSRO Par 211/25/1]

JUDEN, John (1793-): In Wiston school list c1803, and probably at the school in 1800. Baptised 1 December 1793, son of Harry and Frances. [WSRO Par 211/25/1; PR]

JUDENS: A poor girl of West Grinstead who received schooling 1705, under the Dowlin charity. [WSRO Par 95/1/1/3]

JUDENS: A poor boy of West Grinstead who received schooling 1705, under the Dowlin charity. [WSRO Par 95/1/1/3]

JUDGE, Benjamin: Mayfield charity school. Admitted 9 July 1784; removed 11 April 1788, taken out by parents. [MSB]

JUDGE, George: Mayfield charity school. Admitted 17 July 1778; removed 6 March 1781, taken out by parents. [MSB]

JUDGE, Thomas: Mayfield charity school. Admitted 14 October 1774; removed 5 July 1776, 'Sufficiently Learned'[?], after 1¾ years as a 'reader'. [MSB]

JUNIPER: A poor boy of West Grinstead, son of Widow Juniper, who received schooling from Henry Vaus, c1711, under the Dowlin charity. [WSRO Par 95/1/1/3]

JUPP, John (1696-): Brighton charity school. Admitted as 'reader' sometime after list of (probably) January 1702; in list of 'readers' December 1705. Baptised 1 November 1696, son of John and Elizabeth. (Brother Richard also at the school.) [BSB; PR]

JUPP, Richard (1701-): Brighton charity school. Given prayer book 1715. Baptised 12 October 1701, son of John and Elizabeth. (Brother John also at the school.) [BSB; PR]

JUPP, William (1698-): Brighton charity school. Admitted as 'reader' sometime after list of (probably) January 1702; in list of 'readers' December 1705. Baptised 27 February 1698, son of William and Sarah. (Father probably dead by 1700 - married 20 February 1700, John Briggs mariner and Sarah Jupp widow.) [BSB; PR]

KELSEY (KELSIE), James (1715-): Saunders' charity school, Rye. In lists from 29 June 1726 (not in 4 May 1726) to 10 January 1728 (17 April 1728 notes 'left the school'). Baptised 28 October 1715, son of Thomas and Jane. (Two brothers also at the school.) [RSB; PR]

KELSEY (KELSIE), Jeremiah (1722-34): Saunders' charity school, Rye. In lists from 7 July 1731 (not in 31 March 1731) to 31 July 1734; 9 October 1734 notes 'Deceased'. Baptised 20 February 1722, son of Thomas and Jane. (Two brothers also at the school.) [RSB; PR]

KELSEY (KELSIE), Thomas (1713-): Saunders' charity school, Rye. In lists from 8 April 1724 (not in January 1724 (?)) to 4 May 1726 (not in 29 June 1726, when brother James joined). Baptised 31 July 1713, son of Thomas and Jane. (Two brothers also at the school.) [RSB; PR]

KEMP, Henry: Mayfield charity school. No admission recorded; removed, for non-attendance, 11 July 1783 (not in previous list 18 April 1783, so only at school a short time). [MSB]

KENNETT, John (1741-): Saunders' charity school, Rye. In lists from Michaelmas 1753 (not in 4 July 1753) to 4 April 1759 (in which marked 'Jan 27'). Son of Thomas 'deceased' in list of 4 April 1759 (not deceased in Christmas 1758). Baptised 3 November 1741, son of Thomas and Elizabeth. (Three brothers also at the sch. Brother William also left school at 17.) [RSB; PR]

KENNETT, John (1750-): Saunders' charity school, Rye. In lists from 16 April 1760 (not in midsummer 1759, previous surviving list) to Michaelmas 1761 (not in 20 January 1762). Baptised 12 March 1750, son of John and Anne. [RSB; PR]

KENNETT, Thomas: Saunders' charity school, Rye. In lists from 3 October 1750 (not in 27 June 1750) to 28 March 1753 (not in 4 July 1753). Son of Thomas. (Three brothers also at the school.) [RSB]

KENNETT, Walter (1741-): Saunders' charity school, Rye. In lists from Michaelmas 1753 (not in 4 July 1753); left 4 July 1757. Baptised 3 November 1741, son of Thomas and Elizabeth. (Three brothers also at the school.) [RSB; PR]

KENNETT, William (1732-): Saunders' charity school, Rye. In lists from 14 August 1745 (not in 10 April 1745) to 24 June 1749 (not in Michaelmas 1749). Baptised 7 September 1732, son of Thomas and Elizabeth. (Three brothers also at the school. Brother John also left school at 17.) [RSB; PR]

KENT, Thomas (1704-): Brighton charity school. Given prayer book 1716 or 1717. Born 31 May 1704, baptised 4 April 1708, son of John and Elizabeth (perhaps dissenters at time of birth; two other Kent families were Presbyterians.) [BSB; Burchall, M. J. *Brighton Presbyterian Register, 1700-1837*]

KENWARD, Robert (1759?-): At Relfe's school, Fletching, Michaelmas 1763 to 1769. Surviving bill shows Relfe charged for him 3d a week for 'reading'; from June 1765, 6d a week for 'writing'; and from 24 October 1768, 1d a day (attendance was somewhat erratic). Probably baptised 13 April 1759, son of Robert and Mary (if so, went to Relfe at 4½); father probably Robert Kenward, junior, churchwarden 1763-65, 1770, and overseer 1768. [Loose bill in ESRO SPK/P1; PR]

KENWARD, William (1767-1828): Wood's school, Newick. From his journal: 'After having received a suitable Education for a Tradesman from Mr Wood schoolmaster at Newick whom I attended some Years by my Uncle's generosity I was Apprenticed in 1784 to Mr Izard Breeches maker and Glover at E Grinstead...' He ran away from his apprenticeship after 4 years, and some months later joined the army; served in India, Spain and Jersey; became a sergeant, and on retirement a Chelsea pensioner; his journal, well written and fluent, was written then. Probably son of John (1726-74), farmer, by his second marriage to Hannah Wood; his supportive uncle was William Kenward (1735-1815), malster and farmer of Fletching. [WK's journal; Kenward, D., pers. comm.]

KIDD, Isaac (1775-): Mayfield charity school. Admitted 11 July 1783; removed 6 April 1787, taken out by parents. Baptised 6 June 1775, 'a base-born Son of Mary Longly'. [MSB; PR]

KILLICK, Friend (1693-): Brighton charity school. Admitted as 'reader' sometime after list of (probably) January 1702; given coat and hat July 1702; had left by December 1705 and gone 'to sea'. Baptised 23 April 1693, son of John and Mary (née Friend). [BSB; PR]

KILLICK, Robert (1704-): Brighton charity school. Given prayer book 1718. Baptised 4 September 1704, son of Cornelius and Barbara. [BSB; PR]

KILLICK, William (1752-): An arithmetic exercise book of his, 1763, survives. Baptised at Shipley, 7 December 1752, son of Thomas and Mary. [WSRO MP 2671; PR]

KING, Anthony (1729-): Saunders' charity school, Rye. In lists from 9 July 1740 (not in 2 April 1740) to 8 July 1741 (28 October 1741 notes 'left the school'). Son of James, deceased. Baptised 13 May 1729, son of James and Ann. [RSB; PR]

KING, Daniel: Saunders' charity school, Rye. In lists from 8 April 1734 (not in January 1724 (?)) to December 1724 (?) (not in 19 May 1725). Son of Daniel, 'late deceased'. [RSB]

KING, John (1686-): Brighton charity school. In list of 'readers' of (probably) January 1702; given coat and hat July 1702; had left by December 1705 and gone 'to sea'. Baptised 8 August 1686, son of John and Sarah (née Harison). (Brother Simon also at the school.) [BSB; PR]

KING, Simon (1691-): Brighton charity school. Admitted as 'reader' sometime after list of (probably) January 1702; in list of 'readers' December 1705. Baptised 21 September 1691,

son of John and Sarah (née Harison). (Brother John also at the school.) [BSB; PR]

KING, Thomas (1688-): Brighton charity school. Admitted as 'reader' sometime after list of (probably) January 1702; had left by December 1705 and gone 'to sea'. Baptised 6 October 1688, son of Thomas and Sarah. [BSB; PR]

KING, Thomas: Admitted Robertsbridge charity school at its opening, 5 April 1796. Sponsored by John Micklethwaite, esq. Son of James. [ESRO PAR 477/25/1/1]

KNIFE: Button's school, Lewes. To recite at a 'Public Examination' at the *Star Assembly Room*, 22 June 1797. [*SWA* 19.6.97]

KNIGHT, Ann: Mayfield charity school. Admitted to 'Widow Dukes' dame school 23 January 1767 (not in 4 September 1767 list, when Duke's ceased to be used); admitted charity school 16 October 1767; removed 22 April 1768, taken out by parents, after 1 year at the school as a 'reader'. [MSB]

KNIGHT, Hannah (1761-): Mayfield charity school. Admitted to 'Widow Dukes' dame school 17 October 1766; admitted charity school 15 January 1768; removed 22 April 1768, taken out by parents, after 1½ years at the school as a 'reader'. Baptised 11 October 1761, daughter of William and Ann. [MSB; PR]

KNIGHT, John: Mayfield charity school. Admitted 12 October 1798; removed 11 April 1800. [MSB]

(**KNOWLE**): Child of Jacob Knowle at Widow Page's school, Clapham, June 1772. [*SAC* 71]

LADE, Simon (1770-): Mayfield charity school. Admitted 18 July 1777; removed 10 October 1777, 'to make room for others more worthy'; re-admitted 30 July 1779; removed 12 April 1782, 'Sufficiently Learned', after 3 years at the school, 2 years as a 'writer'. Baptised 6 May 1770, son of Simon and Sarah. [MSB; PR]

LANCASTER: Grey Coat charity school, Chichester. Left between Michaelmas 1758 and

Michaelmas 1759. Given 10s 6d on leaving. [WSRO Cap.V/1/1]

LANGRIDGE, Ann (1785-): Admitted Fermor's charity school, Rotherfield, 3 May 1794. Daughter of Widow Langridge. Baptised 3 July 1785, daughter of John (buried 6 April 1792) and Jane. (Brother James also at the school.) [ESRO PAR 465/4/1; PR]

LANGRDIGE, James: Admitted Fermor's charity school, Rotherfield, 29 April 1798. Son of Widow Langridge. (Sister Ann also at the school.) [ESRO PAR 465/4/1]

LANGTON: Button's school, Lewes. To recite at a 'Public Examination' at the *Star Assembly Room*, 22 June 1797. [*SWA* 19.6.97]

LARBY: Grey Coat charity school, Chichester. Left between Michaelmas 1765 and Michaelmas 1766. Given 10s 6d on leaving. [WSRO Cap.V/1/1]

LARNER, Mary Ann: The Duke of Richmond, of Goodwood House, paid £17 13s 6d between January and December 1800 for her to be boarded and taught for a year by Martha Brown, schoolmistress. (Also paid £1 10s for clothing for her.) [WSRO Goodwood MS 247]

LATHAM, John (1698-1754): Lewes grammar school, under Peirce. 1716, St John's College, Cambridge, aged 18; BA 1719-20; deacon (Ely) 1721, priest (Chichester) 1722; rector of Etchingham (succeeding father) 1724 to death; buried there 12 June 1754. Born at Etchingham, son of John, rector of Etchingham 1678 to death, 1724. [*Al. Cant.*]

LATTER, Charlotte: Admitted Fermor's charity school, Rotherfield, 29 April 1798. Daughter of Henry. [ESRO PAR 465/4/1]

LATTER (LETTER), Sarah? (1789?-): Admitted Fermor's charity school, Rotherfield, 29 April 1798. Daughter of William; christian name not given but probably Sarah, baptised 1 November 1789, daughter of William and Elizabeth. [ESRO PAR 465/4/1; PR]

LATTER, Sarah: Admitted Fermor's charity school, Rotherfield, 1 June 1800. Daughter of James. [ESRO PAR 465/4/1]

LAVENDER, Elizabeth: Mayfield charity school. Admitted 2 May 1766; removed 17 April 1767, taken out by parents, after 1 year at the school, ¼ year as a 'writer'. [MSB]

LAVENDER, Katherine: Mayfield charity school. Admitted to 'Widow Dukes' dame school 2 May 1766; admitted charity school 17 April 1767 (when Elizabeth Lavender left); removed 4 February 1771, 'sufficiently learned', after 4¾ years at the school, 1 year as a 'writer'. [MSB]

LAVENDER, John: Mayfield charity school. In list of those at 'Widow Dukes' dame school 17 October 1766 and presumably admitted then; admitted charity school 17 April 1767; removed 9 July 1772, 'Sufficiently Learned', after 5¾ years at the school, 2½ years as a 'writer'. [MSB]

LAVENDER, John (1787-): Mayfield charity school. Admitted 8 January 1796; removed 12 July 1799, 'having left the parish'. Baptised 15 July 1787, son of John and Mary. [MSB; PR]

LAVENDER, Thomas: Mayfield charity school. Admitted 9 July 1772 (when John Lavender left); removed 11 October 1776, 'for Incapacity' [?], after 4¼ years at the school, 1 year as a 'writer'. [MSB]

LEACH: Grey Coat charity school, Chichester. Left between Michaelmas 1759 and Michaelmas 1760. Given 10s 6d on leaving. [WSRO Cap.V/1/1]

LEACH: Button's school, Lewes. To recite at a 'Public Examination' at the *Star Assembly Room*, 22 June 1797. [*SWA* 19.6.97]

LEDBETTER, John (1767-): Sedlescombe charity school. There 8 May 1775, a 'reader'. Baptised 12 April 1767, son of Thomas and Elizabeth. (Brother William also at the school, and Thomas Ledbetter probably another brother.) [SSB; PR]

LEDBETTER, Thomas: Sedlescombe charity school. Admitted 12 May 1761; name crossed through in a 1761 list (which however contains entries to April 1762). (William Ledbetter admitted same time, probably brother.) [SSB]

LEADBETTER (LEADBEATER), William (1753-): Sedlescombe charity school. Admitted 12 May 1761. Baptised 27 December 1753, son of Thomas and Elizabeth. (Brother John also at the school, and Thomas Ledbetter probably another brother.) [SSB; PR]

LEAR: Midhurst grammar school. At the school's first public performance of composition and oratory, 5 November 1799, gave the speech of Norval, from Hume's *Douglas*; at the second, 27 May 1800, took part, with one other, in a scene of Wolsey and Cromwell. (Probably same as Francis Lear below.) [*SWA* 11.11.99, 2.6.1800]

LEAR, Francis (1789-1850): Midhurst grammar school. To Winchester 1801; Oriel College, Oxford, 1806; ordained priest. Son of Thomas (1746-1828) below. (Probably same as Lear above.) [*HMGS*]

LEAR, Thomas (1746-1828): Midhurst grammar school. Then to Winchester. Ordained priest. Born at Rustington; father of Francis above. [*HMGS*]

LE CLERC, Henriette Ann (c1774-): Reputed to be the 3rd Duke of Richmond's illegitimate daughter by Madame de Cambis. In 1778, when about 5 or 6, brought over from France by the Duke's sister, Louisa (she 'spued all the way' on the boat from Dieppe). Was put in charge of Mr Jones, presumably tutor, and brought up at Goodwood House, accepted within the family. Another of the Duke's sisters, Sarah, found her 'one of the most enchanting creatures I ever saw...a delightful companion for my Louisa, for she teaches her French and submission and humility - three very good lessons to learn.' Between 1785 and 1791 she was taught by 3 different dancing masters (qv Henry, Oliviers, Stevenson), a singing master (qv William Parsons), a music master (qv Dr Arnold), and an Italian master (qv Molini). From 1790, when 17 or 18, she received an allowance of 30 guineas a quarter. In 1793 also received £163 10s 9d, 'His Grace's allowance to replace Cloaths lost by the Fire'. The first official race meeting at Goodwood, a 2-day event, was held in April 1801: John Marsh, who was there, recorded in his diary for 27 April 1801, that 'the Duke had, to gratify Miss Le Clerc (as 'twas thought)

made a course and given a £50 prize'. Married, 1808, John Dorrien, who became a general. [Reese, M. M. *Goodwood's Oak* (1987); WSRO Goodwood MS 244, 245, 247. Hunn, D. *Goodwood* (1975); 'John Marsh Diary', Huntington Library, San Marino, California, USA, microfilm at WSRO]

LEE, G.: Button's school, Lewes. To recite at a 'Public Examination' at the *Star Assembly Room*, 22 June 1797. [*SWA* 19.6.97]

LEGAT, Robert (1702-): Brighton charity school. Given prayer book 1715. Baptised 10 May 1702, son of Robert. [BSB; PR]

LEIGHTON, Thomas (1773-): Lord Pelham's charity school, Lewes [qv Rand's school]. Admitted Christmas 1782. There 10 October 1784, aged 11. Baptised 28 December 1773, son of John and Fanny. [ESRO AMS 6005; Lewes St Michael PR]

LEMMAN, John (c1703-): Grey Coat charity school, Chichester. Admitted between Lady Day 1712 and Lady Day 1713, aged 9. There Lady Day 1714. [WSRO Cap.V/1/1]

LEMON: Grey Coat charity school, Chichester. Left between Michaelmas 1764 and Michaelmas 1765. Given 10s 6d on leaving. [WSRO Cap.V/1/1]

LEMPRIERE, Michael (1770-): Lord Pelham's charity school, Lewes [qv Rand's school]. Admitted Christmas 1778. There 10 October 1784, aged 14 (but crossed through in list and probably left soon after). [ESRO AMS 6005]

[LENNOX, Charles (1791-1860)]: Probably one of the 'Master Lennoxes' educated at Goodwood by the 3rd Duke of Richmond from 1797 to c1803, and tutored by the Rev Monsieur Tournay (1797-1801), William Ingram (writing master 1797-1802), Rev W. J. A. Vincent (1799-1801), Monsieur de Lambilly (dancing master, 1800-03) [for all of whom see Schedule 2]. (There were also payments for cricket balls for the Lennox boys - 6s 6d in 1800, 9s in 1801, 15s in 1802. There was a cricket team at Goodwood House at least as far back as 1725.) If attribution correct, born 3 August 1791, son of Charles (3rd Duke's nephew, an army officer in the West Indies 1794, and later - 1806 - 4th Duke of Richmond) and Charlotte (daughter of 4th Duke of Gordon); married 10 April 1817, Caroline (daughter of 1st Marquess of Anglesey; died 1874); later 5th Duke of Richmond; was Lieutenant-Colonel, served at Waterloo; Lord Lieutenant of Sussex; ADC to Queen Victoria; died 21 October 1860. [WSRO Goodwood MS 247; *Burke's Peerage*]

[**LENNOX, John George** (1793-1873)]: Probably one of the 'Master Lennoxes' educated at Goodwood by the 3rd Duke of Richmond from 1797 to c1803. (For parents and tutors, see LENNOX, Charles, above.) If attribution correct, born 3 October 1793; married 29 June 1818, Louisa Frederica Rodney, daughter of Hon John; later Lieutenant-Colonel and MP for Sussex; died 10 November 1873. [WSRO Goodwood MS 247; *Burke's Peerage*]

LETTY: Grey Coat charity school, Chichester. Left between Michaelmas 1764 and Michaelmas 1765. Given 10s 6d on leaving. [WSRO Cap.V/1/1]

LETTY: Grey Coat charity school, Chichester. Given 10s 6d on leaving, 25 March 1772. [WSRO Cap.V/1/1]

(**LEWIS**): Eastbourne charity school. Admitted Christmas 1778; there Christmas 1779. [SAS Budgen MS v.117]

LEWIS, John (1729-): Eastbourne charity school. There December 1738 (?), April 1741. Baptised 10 December 1729, son of Samuel and Elizabeth. [SAS Budgen MS v.129; PR]

LEWIS (LEWES), Mary (1735-): Brightling girls' charity school. Admitted between 2 April 1744 and 31 August 1745, in which period she attended on 220 school days; there to period 1 September 1745 to 31 July 1747, in which she attended on 310 school days; had 530 days at the school in total. Baptised 30 March 1735, daughter of Robert and Susanna. [ESRO PAR 254/25/1; PR]

LIN, Francis (Fran) (1706-): Brighton charity school. Given prayer book 1718. Baptised 29 September 1706, son of Francis and Anne.

[BSB; PR]

LIN, Leonard (1705-): Brighton charity school. Given prayer book 1716 or 1717. Baptised 22 January 1705, son of Leonard and Mary. [BSB; PR]

LINN, Masters (1688-): Brighton charity school. In list of 'writers' 12 January 1702; given coat and hat July 1702; had left by December 1705 and gone 'to sea'. Baptised 19 August 1688, son of Richard and Charity (née Masters). [BSB; PR]

LINFIELD, John (1738 or 39-): Saunders' charity school, Rye. In lists from Christmas 1747 (not in Michaelmas 1747); left 27 June 1751. Baptised 19 January 1739, son of William and Elizabeth. [RSB; PR]

LINTOTT: Button's school, Lewes. To recite at a 'Public Examination' at the *Star Assembly Room*, 22 June 1797. [*SWA* 19.6.97]

LLOYD, Thomas: Brighton charity school. Given prayer book 1715. [BSB]

LOCKYER, Thomas (1791-): Admitted Fermor's charity school, Rotherfield, 1 June 1800. Son of Thomas, Boarshead. Baptised 24 July 1791, son of Thomas and Mary (or see another TL baptised 22 January 1792, below). [ESRO PAR 465/4/1; PR]

LOCKYER, Thomas (1791 or 92-): Admitted Fermor's charity school, Rotherfield, 1 June 1800. Son of Thomas, of Tribden. Baptised 22 January 1792, son of Thomas and Catherine (or see another TL baptism 24 July 1791, above). [ESRO PAR 465/4/1; PR]

LONG, John: At Cocking charity school, 1733. [WSRO Par 53/12/1]

LONGLEY, John (1743-): Mayfield charity school. Admitted 4 October 1751; removed 6 July 1753, taken out by parents; had been a 'writer' for ¼ year. Baptised 9 October 1743, son of John and Mary. (Brother Robert also at the school.) [MSB; PR]

LONGLY, Lucy (1779-): Mayfield charity school. Admitted 17 January 1788; removed 6 July 1792, taken out by parents. Baptised 5

March 1779, daughter of Robert and Mary. (Three sisters also at the school.) [MSB; PR]

LONGLY (LONGLEY), Lydia (1784-): Mayfield charity school. Admitted 6 July 1792 (when sister Lucy removed); removed 8 April 1796, taken out by parents. Baptised 9 May 1784, daughter of Robert and Mary. (Three sisters also at the school.) [MSB; PR]

LONGLEY, Mary (1774-): Mayfield charity school. Admitted 14 January 1785; removed 13 January 1786, for non-attendance. Baptised 23 October 1774, daughter of Robert and Mary. (Three sisters also at the school.) [MSB; PR]

LONGLEY, Moses: Saunders' charity school, Rye. In lists from 28 March 1753 (not in 3 January 1753) to 11 January 1758, in which marked 'September 12 1757'. Son of Moses, deceased. [RSB]

LONGLEY, Robert (1747-): Mayfield charity school. Admitted 3 July 1752; removed 14 November 1752, for non-attendance. Born 10 February 1747, baptised 12 February 1747, son of John and Mary. (Brother John also at the school.) [MSB; PR]

LONGLEY, Sarah (1777-): Mayfield charity school. Admitted 5 January 1787; removed 9 April 1790, for non-attendance. Baptised 21 May 1777, daughter of Robert and Mary. (Three sisters also at the school.) [MSB; PR]

LORD, James (1767-81): At boarding school at Bexhill when drowned, 31 August 1781, 'having been permitted by his schoolmaster the Curate of Bexhill with several other less boys to bathe in the sea on a flowing tide, they escaped'; buried at Northiam 4 September 1781. Born 3 June 1767, baptised 10 July 1767, son of William, rector of Northiam (died 1779) and Mary (died 1801, aged 75). [Northiam PR; CI]

LOUCH, Sarah (1743-): Brightling girls' charity school. Admitted between 10 June 1749 and 29 September 1752, in which period she attended on 95 school days; there to period Lady Day 1755 to 30 April 1757, in which she attended on 292 school days; had 1,023 days at the school in total. Baptised 13 October 1743, 'a base born Child of Sarah Louch'. [ESRO

PAR 254/25/1; PR]

LUCAS: Thornton's school, Horsham. On Saturday 3 January 1795, played Douglas in *Henry IV, part I*; at the request of the audience ('the Gentry and Inhabitants of the town of Horsham') the play was performed again the following Monday. [*SWA* 5.1.95]

LUCAS, William (1692-): Brighton charity school. Added at end of list of 'writers' December 1705 (ie joined subsequently). Baptised 27 November 1692, son of John and Mary (née Gilliam). [BSB; PR]

LUCK, Abraham (1766 or 67-): Mayfield charity school. Admitted 9 April 1773; removed 10 April 1778, 'Sufficiently Learned'. Baptised 11 January 1767, son of Abraham and Elizabeth. (Brothers Richard, Thomas, also at the school.) [MSB; PR]

LUCK, Elizabeth: Mayfield charity school. Admitted 12 October 1798; removed 8 April 1803, taken out by parents. [MSB]

LUCK, John: Mayfield charity school. Admitted 27 October 1769; removed 15 October 1773, 'Sufficiently Learned', after 4 years at the school, 2¾ years as a 'writer'. [MSB]

LUCK, Richard (1762-): Mayfield charity school. Admitted 19 October 1770; removed 8 April 1774, after 3½ years at the school, 2¾ years as a 'writer'. Baptised 17 June 1762, son of John and Mary. [MSB; PR]

LUCK, Richard (1769-): Mayfield charity school. Admitted 17 January 1777; removed 7 July 1780, 'Sufficiently Learned', after 3½ years at the school, 2¼ years as a 'writer'. Baptised 23 April 1769, son of Abraham and Elizabeth. (Brothers Abraham, Thomas, also at the school.) [MSB; PR]

LUCK, Thomas: Mayfield charity school. Admitted 16 October 1772; removed 15 July 1774, for non-attendance. Re-admitted 14 October 1774; removed 13 October 1775, still a 'reader'. [MSB]

LUCK, Thomas (1773-): Mayfield charity school. Admitted October 1781; removed 15

October 1784, 'Sufficiently Learned'. Baptised 21 March 1773, son of Abraham and Elizabeth. (Brothers Abraham, Richard, also at the school.) [MSB; PR]

LUCK, Thomas: Mayfield charity school. Admitted 11 July 1794; removed 6 January 1797, for non-attendance. [MSB]

LUCKETT, Love (1771 or 72-): Saunders' charity school, Rye. In lists from 17 April 1728 (not in 10 January 1728) to 7 April 1736 (not in 20 October 1736); had 8¼ years at the school. Son of Love, deceased. Baptised 18 January 1722, son of Love and Ann. [RSB; PR]

LUCKETT, Richard: (1710-): Saunders' charity school, Rye. In lists from September 1722 (?) (first list); June 1725 (?) notes 'Gon on the Mackaril Season'; 11 August 1725 notes 'Gon to Catch Mackril and are not yet Returned to the School'; in list of late 1725 or early 1726, not in 4 May 1726. Baptised 2 December 1710, son of John and Mary. [RSB; PR]

LUSTED: 'Goody Lusteds Girl', taught by Sarah French at Brightling, 36 weeks to cApril 1732, 42 weeks to cApril 1733 (and perhaps further); schooling paid by John Fuller, at 3d a week. [ESRO SAS/RF 15/28]

LUSTED, Elizabeth (1787-): Admitted Robertsbridge charity school at its opening, 5 April 1796, aged 8. Sponsored by William Braban, esq. Baptised 19 May 1787, daughter of Isaac and Hester (née Forster). (Brother Jonathan also at the school.) [ESRO PAR 477/25/1/1; Salehurst PR]

LUSTED, Jonathan (1790-): Admitted Robertsbridge charity school at its opening, 5 April 1796, aged 6 or 7. Sponsored by William Braban, esq. Baptised 1 February 1790, son of Isaac and Hester. (Sister Elizabeth also at the school.) [ESRO PAR 477/25/1/1; Salehurst PR]

LUXFORD, George: At Lord's school, Battle, 1702. Previously, in 1698, he had been sent to board at Nathaniel Mills' school, probably at Ninfield, at £12 pa, Mills being distantly related. Son of Richard (father was son of Richard (-1674) and Catherine (née Henshaw);

Richard (-1674) was brother of George (-1712) who put GL to school). [*SNQ* 12]

MACKEREL, Elizabeth: A poor girl of Newick for whose schooling the parish paid: 2s to 'Master Roser', 3 November 1800; 2s for 6 weeks schooling 3 April 1801; 4s, 6 May 1802. [ESRO PAR 428/30/1]

MACKET: Grey Coat charity school, Chichester. Left between Michaelmas 1761 and Michaelmas 1762. Given 10s 6d on leaving. [WSRO Cap.V/1/1]

MANNING, Edward (1725-44): Baptised 17 August 1725, son of Henry, surgeon-apothecary and landowner of Lewes, and Ann (née Plumer), who married at Chailey 11 October 1724. At about 8 was sent to Cater Rand's school, at 16s pa; he was also taught dancing by Stephen Philpot, at £3 pa (father paid 5s 'entrance money' 23 June 1733). In 1735 sent to John Hart at Steyning grammar school, the costs of his first year there totalling £16 1s 11d; Hart died in July 1736 and the grammar school was taken over by Charles Baker (though Mrs Hart was paid for boarding him at least until the end of 1737). The cost of his schooling was £2 pa; the cost of boarding him £12-14 pa. There were also other expenses: it cost 4s each time for 'sending Ned to Stenning'; on 2 November 1736 his father gave 1s to Mrs Hart's maid, 1s pocket money to him, and paid 1s to a tailor, 3s to a shoemaker, 4s to a barber. In the summer of 1737 he was joined at the school by brother Henry. For schooling, books, board, costs came to £15-17 pa each; tradesmen's bills came to £1 12s 9d in 1738 (including 12s to 'ye Barber for powdering and Cutting ye Boys Hairs') and £1 18s 5d in January 1740; that month Manning paid Philpot £5 6s 6d for ¾ year teaching the boys dancing, presumably at the school. A year later he paid 16s for 'My Son Edw'd Pockets Exp &c for his Broth'r & Self'; and there were occasional payments of 2s 6d for Ned's or Harry's 'breaking up'. In 1741 the boys were moved to Lewes grammar school, under Josiah Welby: the fee was £2 2s pa for each boy; there were now no boarding costs, but James Halstead, writing master, was also paid (though his precise fees are not clear from Manning's accounts; his 'breaking up' charge was 1s each, Welby's 2s 6d). When paying Welby's bill of

£3 3s in January 1742, Manning 'gave him as a perquisite' £2 10s. Edward was not there long, leaving school at Christmas 1741, when he was 16. He died in the spring of 1744, aged 18. [St Michael Lewes PR; Chailey PR; ESRO SAS/I 302]

MANNING, Edward (1744-): Henry Manning's eldest son Edward [qv] died in the spring of 1744; a month or two later, on 24 July 1744, another son was baptised Edward. Father was surgeon-apothecary and landowner of Lewes; mother was Ann (née Plumer). Went to school when 4 (father's accounts, 16 November 1748: 'paid Ned's Schooling' 2s). From summer of 1750 was taught by Thomas Verrall, at 12s pa; with Verrall to Michaelmas 1752, when, aged 8, was sent to Lewes grammar school under Austen and Rand. On 10 October 1753 father paid Austen for 'a years Schooling with Entrance &c' £2 15s, and 'gave him perquisite' £2 2s, and 'gave Usher p do', 10s 6d (Manning gave the same perquisites to Austen and the usher in October 1754). Rand was presumably writing master to the grammar school, but that he taught the boys at his own school is indicated by the account entry, 6 November 1753, 'Ned for firing at Mr Rands 1s'. In January 1754 Manning paid 'Mr Rand's Bill 17s' and 'gave him 10s 6d'. In 1754 Ned was also attending Philpot's 'dancing school' - 14 November 1754, 'Firing for Ned at Rands & Philpots 2s'; 14 December 1754, 'Ned breaking up at Philpots 2s 6d'. His father's private account book ends 27 February 1755. [St Michael Lewes PR; ESRO SAS/I 302]

MANNING, Elizabeth (Bet) (1731-): Baptised 3 December 1731, daughter of Henry, surgeon-apothecary and landowner of Lewes, and Ann (née Plumer). From March 1741, when she was 9, attended Stephen Philpot's 'dancing school', at £3 pa; there to Christmas 1745. She also went to a writing school or was taught writing at Philpot's (in May 1742 father paid 2s 6d for her 'breaking up at ye dancing school' and 1s for her 'Breaking up at Writing'); her writing master was probably initially James Halstead and later Cater Rand; she appears to have continued with Rand after leaving Philpot's' dancing school. Rand's fees appear to have been £3 10s pa (and would probably have covered more than just writing) unless he was also still teaching brother Henry

[qv] in 1745-46, after he left the grammar school, when he was 17. Cater Rand died in May 1748, the school being carried on by his son Charles; in January 1749 Manning paid 'Mrs Rand's Bill £5 17s 10d' and 'Charles Rand's Bill 13s 6d'. Bet was then 17. Her father's accounts show expenditure on various items of clothing for her: the cost of her stays increased from 10s 6d in 1745 to £1 1s in 1747 to £1 8s in 1750; the biggest single item was £10 14s 3d in June 1750, when she was 18, paid to 'Mrs Mary Russell for Silk &c for Bet, as per Bill from Mr Partfield'. In 1753 Manning paid 13s 'for Bets Picture in miniature' (and a fortnight later £1 6s for 'Harry & Ned's pictures') and the following year he paid £2 7s for 'Bet's Picture in Colours'. [St Michael Lewes PR; ESRO SAS/I 302]

MANNING, Henry (1728-): Baptised 12 June 1728, son of Henry, surgeon-apothecary and landowner of Lewes, and Ann (née Plumer). When about 8, sent to John Head's school, at £1 4s pa (Head was then probably a master of a charity school sponsored by the Tories). After 1¾ years with Head, in the summer of 1737, then 9, joined brother Edward at Steyning grammar school, under Charles Baker (for fees and expenses, see MANNING, Edward (1725-44)). In the summer of 1741 the boys were moved to Lewes grammar school, under Josiah Welby and James Halstead, and later Cater Rand. Appears to have left the grammar school when about 15, but may have continued at Rand's school for some time [qv MANNING, Elizabeth]. Thereafter received many gifts from father of a guinea or ½ guinea, and in December 1751 (then 23) father paid £4 4s 'for a Watch for Harry' (and a few days later gave him £2 2s). Became an apothecary, like father; prospered, lived in a large house in Southover. In 1791 was Sheriff of Sussex. [St Michael Lewes PR; ESRO SAS/I 302; Horsfield *Sussex*; Brent, C., pers. comm.]

MANSER, Elizabeth: Mayfield charity school. Admitted 26 October 1764; removed 11 July 1765, taken out by parents 'but sufficiently learned', after ¾ year as a 'writer'. [MSB]

MANSER, Mary: Mayfield charity school. Admitted 8 April 1763; removed 11 January 1765, 'Well Learned', after 1¾ years, all as a 'writer'. (Possibly the MM baptised 15 June 1755, daughter of Thomas and Sarah, but 3 other Manser children this period not in parish register, 2 of whom, like MM, started as 'writers' - perhaps a nonconformist family.) [MSB; PR]

MANSIR (MANSER), Sarah: Mayfield charity school. Admitted 26 October 1759; removed 11 April 1760, taken away by parents after ½ year at the school as a 'writer'. [MSB]

MANSER (MANSIR), Thomas: Mayfield charity school. Admitted 26 October 1759; removed 9 July 1762, 'sufficiently Learned', after 2¾ years at the school, 2 years as a 'writer'. [MSB]

MANTELL, Gideon Algernon (1790-1852): Button's school, Lewes. Born 3 February 1790, son of Thomas (1750-1807; cordwainer of Lewes, said to have built the first Wesleyan chapel in the town) and Sarah (née Austin). Father's principles practically excluded son from the grammar school, and after a dame school he was sent to Button's school (Button was a Baptist). There, to recite at a 'Public Examination' at the *Star Assembly Room*, 22 June 1797. Later went to school in Wiltshire. Received £50 under will of Mary Cornwell (died 1807: see Schedule 2), schoolmistress of Lewes, who 'fostered me when a child, and treated me with the greatest kindness while she lived'. Became surgeon (specialised in midwifery) and celebrated geologist (discovered iguanodon fossil in Tilgate Forest): LLD, Yale. [Spokes, S. *Gideon Algernon Mantell* (1927); Curwen, E. C., (ed) *The Journal of Gideon Mantell* (1940); *SCM* **8**; *SWA* 19.6.97]

MARCH, Robert (1704-): Brighton charity school. Given prayer book 1715. Baptised 24 September 1704, son of Richard and Mary. [BSB; Union Street Independent Chapel (Presbyterian) Register]

MARCHANT, Ann (c1784-): Admitted Robertsbridge charity school at its opening 5 April 1796, aged 11. Sponsored by Mr Louis Pardieu. Daughter of Thomas. [ESRO PAR 477/25/1/1]

MARCHANT, Bett: Daughter of Thomas, yeoman of Hurstpierpoint. Taught arithmetic (at home presumably) by Mr Pointin of Henfield, 1722. [*SAC* **25**]

MARCHANT, John (1708-28): Son of Thomas, yeoman and gent of Hurstpierpoint, he 'began his accidence' 14 February 1715. Matriculated Pembroke College, Oxford, 23 November 1726, aged 18. Had smallpox at Oxford March 1728, and died from it 5 April 1728. [*SAC* **25**; *Al. Oxon.*]

MARCHANT, William (1701-): Son of Thomas, yeoman of Hurstpierpoint. When 21, taught arithmetic (at home presumably) 3 times a week, at 2s 6d a week, by Mr Pointin of Henfield, 1722. Baptised 3 November 1701, son of Thomas and Elizabeth. [*SAC* **25**; PR]

MARLEY, John (1771-): Saunders' charity school, Rye. Admitted 5 April 1780; in lists to 2 September 1782, which notes 'Left School'. (Probably left 12 August 1782 - see MARLEY, William.) Baptised 21 August 1771, son of Thomas and Elizabeth. (Brother William also at the school.) [RSB; PR]

MARLEY, William (1774-): Saunders' charity school, Rye. Admitted 12 August 1782 'in the room of his Brother'; in list for 24 June 1785, last surviving 18th century list. Baptised 29 September 1774, son of Thomas and Elizabeth. (Brother John also at the school.) [RSB; PR]

MARSH, John: At Richard's school, Chichester; left 4 June 1792. Later at school outside Sussex. Second son of John (1752-1828) and Elizabeth (-1818). Father trained as solicitor, but came into large inheritance 1782 and did not need to practise thereafter; moved to Chichester 1787; was a prominent composer (40 symphonies &c). John Marsh junior later a solicitor at Chichester. [Thomas, E., pers. comm. citing 'John Marsh Diary', Huntington Library, California, USA, microfilm at WSRO]

MARTEN/MARTIN

MARTEN: A poor girl of Laughton, daughter of Edward, for whom parish paid 4s for a book and schooling in year Easter 1751 to Easter 1752. (Parish also paid for altering her coat, 1s, and for her keep at 6s a month.) [ESRO PAR

409/31/1/2]

MARTIN, James: Mayfield charity school. Admitted 9 July 1762 (named as 'Jno', but this changed in next list and thereafter); removed 17 October 1766, for non-attendance, after 3¾ years at the school, 1½ years as a 'writer'. (Possibly the JM, son of John, farmer (dead by 3 June 1765), at which date the parish apprenticed him for 7 years to Charles Diggens, a tailor of Framfield - but the school lists shows JM at school till 1766; the JM who was apprenticed probably baptised 22 September 1749, son of John and Anne, and would have been old for the school in 1766.) [MSB; ESRO PAR 422/33/132; PR]

MARTIN, James (1781-): Mayfield charity school. Admitted 8 January 1790; removed 8 January 1796, for non-attendance. Probably baptised 7 October 1781, son of John and Mary (another JM baptised 8 March 1782 also son of John and Mary, but no burial of former in parish register and another JM also at the school - see below.) [MSB; PR]

MARTIN, James (1782-): Mayfield charity school. Admitted 6 April 1792; removed 5 July 1793, taken out by parents. Probably baptised 8 March 1782, son of John and Mary (see note under JM above). [MSB; PR]

MARTIN, John (1759-): Mayfield charity school. Admitted 'Widow Dukes' dame school 18 October 1765; admitted charity school 17 October 1766; removed 19 January 1770, for non-attendance, after 3¼ years as a 'reader'. Baptised 21 October 1759, son of James and Sarah. (Two brothers, 1 sister, also at the school.) [MSB; PR]

MARTIN, John [otherwise BASSETT, John?] (1779-): Mayfield charity school. Admitted 13 July 1791; in lists to January 1792; in 6 April 1792 his place in list is taken by 'John Bassett'; removed (as John Bassett) 11 October 1793. Baptised 18 November 1779, son of John and Mary. [MSB; PR]

MARTIN, Macey [ie Thomas] (c1785-): Admitted Robertsbridge charity school at its opening, 5 April 1796, aged 10. Sponsored by Messrs Munn and Peters. Son of Newland. [ESRO PAR 477/25/1/1]

MARTIN, Mary (1786-): Mayfield charity school. Admitted 10 July 1795; removed 18 October 1799, taken out by parents. Baptised 8 March 1786, daughter of John and Mary. [MSB; PR]

MARTIN, Miller (Millar) (1775-): Mayfield charity school. Admitted 7 July 1786; removed 10 July 1789, taken out by parents. Baptised 4 April 1775, son of John and Mary. [MSB; PR]

MARTEN, Samuel (1762-): Mayfield charity school. Admitted 'Widow Dukes' dame school 17 April 1767 (but not in next list, when Duke's ceased to be used); admitted charity school 15 July 1768; deleted in list for 7 January 1774, after 5¾ years at the school, 2½ years as a 'writer'. Baptised 30 January 1762, son of James and Sarah. (Two brothers, 1 sister, also at the school.) [MSB; PR]

MARTIN, Samuel (1788-): Mayfield charity school. Admitted 8 January 1796; removed 12 April 1799, taken out by parents. Baptised 20 July 1788, son of John and Mary. [MSB; PR]

MARTIN, Susanna (1758-): Mayfield charity school. Admitted 'Widow Dukes' dame school 11 January 1765; admitted charity school 11 July 1765; removed 17 April 1767, taken out by parents, after 2¼ years as a 'reader'. Baptised 15 May 1758, daughter of [James] and Sarah. (Three brothers also at the school.) [MSB; PR]

MARTIN, Thomas - see **MARTIN, Macey**

MARTIN, William (1774-): Mayfield charity school. Admitted 2 August 1782; removed 7 July 1786, for non-attendance. Baptised 15 May 1774, son of James and Sarah. (Two brothers, 1 sister, also at the school.) [MSB; PR]

MARTIN, William (1791-): Mayfield charity school. Admitted 19 January 1798; removed 10 April 1801 (incorrectly named as 'Samuel'). Probably baptised 20 March 1791, son of John and Mary (another WM baptised 18 March 1792, son of Thomas and Susan, very young for the school this period, and brothers and sisters of former probably also at the school). [MSB; PR]

MASCALL, John: At Rev Thankful Frewen's

school at Northiam, as a boarder, from 9 October 1717 to 27 September 1718. Fee of £16 pa paid by Robert Mascall. [ESRO FRE 533]

MASTERS, Thomas: Saunders' charity school, Rye. In lists from 29 April 1741 (not in 7 January 1741) to Christmas 1745, which notes 'Absent 3 Months' (not in 2 July 1746). Son of Thomas. Probably son of Thomas (1706-75) founder member of the Particular Baptist chapel, Rye, in 1750, and Mary (died 1777). (Brother William also at the school.) [RSB; PRO RG 4/2968]

MASTERS, William: Saunders' charity school, Rye. In lists from Christmas 1746 (not in Michaelmas 1746); left 14 December 1750. Son of Thomas. For probable parents, see brother MASTERS, Thomas. [RSB]

MATTHEWS: Grey Coat charity school, Chichester. Left between Michaelmas 1759 and Michaelmas 1760. Given 10s 6d on leaving. [WSRO Cap.V/1/1]

MAXWELL, senior: Midhurst grammar school. At school's first public performance of composition and oratory, 5 November 1799, spoke as Moloch in scene, with 2 others, from Milton's *Paradise Lost*; at second 'literary performance', 27 May 1800, won one of 2 prizes for oratory, for speaking the speech of Galgaens, translated from Tacitus. On both occasions a Mr Maxwell was listed among the gentry present. [*SWA* 11.11.99, 2.6.1800]

MAXWELL, junior: At Midhurst grammar school 1799, by inference from reference to 'Maxwell senior' - see above.

MAYHEW, Mary: At Cocking charity school 1732, 1733. [WSRO Par 53/12/1]

MAYNARD, Edward (1789-): Admitted Fermor's charity school, Rotherfield, 14 May 1797. Baptised 1 November 1789, son of Edward and Mary. [ESRO PAR 465/4/1; PR]

MAYNARD, Thomas (1784-): Admitted Fermor's charity school, Rotherfield, 1 June 1792. Son of Richard and Alice. Baptised 6 August 1784, 'Thomas Maynard Base Born Son of Alice Killick'; the same day Richard

Maynard and Alice Killick were married. [ESRO PAR 465/4/1;PR]

MEDHURST, Ann (1789-): Mayfield charity school. Admitted 13 April 1798; removed 11 July 1800, taken out by parents. Baptised 15 February 1789, daughter of John and Frances. [MSB; PR]

MEDHURST, Ann (1791-): Mayfield charity school. Admitted 6 July 1798; removed 15 October 1802, taken out by parents. Baptised 27 March 1791, daughter of Edward and Sarah. [MSB; PR]

MEDHURST (MIDHURST), Edward (1763-): Mayfield charity school. Admitted 27 October 1769; removed 19 January 1770, for non-attendance. Baptised 8 May 1763, son of William and Hannah. [MSB; PR]

MEDHURST, Edward: Mayfield charity school. Admitted 11 July 1800; removed 12 October 1804, taken out by parents. [MSB]

MEDHURST, Israel (1749-): At Seaford charity school 1765. Baptised 6 October 1749, son of Israel and Mary. [BL Add MS 33,059; PR]

MEDHURST, James (1792-): Mayfield charity school. Admitted 18 October 1799; removed 11 January 1805, 'sufficiently learned'. Baptised 17 June 1792, son of James and Ann. [MSB; PR]

MEDHURST, John (1755-): At Seaford charity school 1765. Baptised 1 February 1755, son of John and Catharine. [BL Add MS 33,059; PR]

MEDHURST (MIDHURST), John: Mayfield charity school. Admitted 26 October 1764; removed 2 May 1766, for non-attendance, after 1½ years as a 'reader'. [MSB]

MEDHURST, Thomas (1752-): At Seaford charity school 1765. Baptised 26 February 1752, son of William and Ann. [BL Add MS 33,059; PR]

MEDHURST, Thomas: Mayfield charity school. Admitted 11 July 1800; name apparently changes to 'Thomas Underhill' in list for 6 April 1804, then changes back again to TM in list for 12 April 1805 (perhaps TM away for a year); removed 11 April 1806, 'Sufficiently learned'. [MSB]

MEPHAM, Elizabeth (1744-): Mayfield charity school. Admitted 4 October 1751; removed 9 April 1756, 'suspended to make room for others where more Occasion is'; had been at the school 4½ years, ¾ year as a 'writer'. Baptised 9 June 1744, daughter of Richard and Elizabeth. (Probably brother Thomas, sister Martha, also at the school.) [MSB; PR]

MEPHAM, Esther: Mayfield charity school. Admitted 5 October 1750; removed 29 March 1751, for non-attendance. [MSB]

MEPHAM, Joseph (1746-): Mayfield charity school. Admitted 9 April 1755; removed 9 January 1756, for non-attendance, after ¾ year as a 'reader'. Baptised 13 April 1746, son of John and Sarah. [MSB; PR]

MEPHAM, Martha (1750-): Mayfield charity school. Admitted 8 July 1757 (named 'Mary' but this corrected in January 1758 and subsequent lists); removed 11 July 1760, taken out by parents, after 3 years as a 'reader'. Baptised 28 February 1750, daughter of Richard and Elizabeth. (Probably brother Thomas, sister Elizabeth, also at the school.) [MSB; PR]

MEPHAM, Thomas (1737-): Mayfield CS. Admitted at formal opening of school 29 June 1750, but may have been there up to ¾ year longer, as master paid from Michaelmas 1749; removed 3 June 1752, for non-attendance; at 27 March 1752 had had ½ year as a 'writer'. Probably baptised 24 July 1737, son of Richard. (Another TM baptised 22 February 1739, son of Joseph and Mary, but former more probable as 2 other children of Richard at the school, and others of his age admitted when school formally opened. If so, sisters Elizabeth, Martha, also at the school.) [MSB; PR]

MERCER, Thomas (1729-): Saunders' charity school, Rye. In lists from 5 April 1738 (not in 11 January 1738) to 11 January 1744 (4 July 1744 notes 'left the school'). Son of Thomas, deceased. Baptised 14 April 1729, son

of Thomas and Mary. (Brother William also at the school.) [RSB; PR]

MERCER, Thomas (1737-): At Sedlescombe charity school 23 June 1748. Baptised 15 July 1737, son of Joseph and Elizabeth. [SSB; PR]

MERCER, William (1731-): Saunders' charity school, Rye. In lists from 5 April 1738 (not in 11 January 1738) to June 1743 (?) (26 October 1743 notes 'left the school'). Son of Thomas, deceased. Baptised 24 January 1731, son of Thomas and Mary. (Brother Thomas also at the school.) [RSB; PR]

MERCHANT: A poor boy of Laughton, son of John, for whom the parish paid 2d 'for a horning Book', 31 December 1755. [ESRO PAR 409/31/1/2]

MERION, John (1716-): Saunders' charity school, Rye. In lists from June 1725 (?) (not in 19 May 1725, in 11 August 1725) to 7 July 1731 (27 October 1731 notes 'left the school'). Baptised 24 August 1716, son of Lewis and Margaret. (See note on family under MERION, Lewis, probably his brother and also at the school.) [RSB; PR]

MERION, Lewis [Louis?]: Saunders' charity school, Rye. In lists from September 1722 (?) (first list) to April 1723 (?) (January 1724 (?) notes 'an apprentice'). Almost certainly son of Lewis, whose son John at the school [qv]. Meryon: a French Protestant refugee family; came to Rye latter part of 17th century. Name variants: Merigan, Mirinian, Merian, and at John's baptism, Marriagne, at Thomas's, Miriam. [RSB; Holloway, W. *History of the Town and Port of Rye* (1847)]

MERYON, Lewis (1739-): Saunders' charity school, Rye. In lists from midsummer 1751 (not in 3 April 1751) to Michaelmas 1753 (not in 16 January 1754). Son of Lewis, deceased in list of 2 October 1751. Baptised 13 November 1739, son of Lewis and Mary. (See note on family under MERION, Lewis, above. Brother Thomas also at the school.) [RSB; PR]

MERION, Thomas (1733-): Saunders' charity school, Rye. In lists from 26 October 1743 (not in June 1743 (?)); 2 July 1746 notes 'Absent 11 weeks'; Michaelmas 1746 notes 'left the school

March 29th'. Baptised 1 August 1733, son of Lewis and Elizabeth. (See note on family under MERION, Lewis, above. Brother Lewis also at the school.) [RSB; PR]

MERRIOT, Nevill (c1701-): Grey Coat charity school, Chichester. Admitted at its opening, Lady Day 1710; aged 9 at Lady Day 1711; there Lady Day 1714. [WSRO Cap.V/1/1]

MERRIT, Amey (1792-): In Wiston school list c1803, and probably at the school in 1800. Baptised 9 September 1792, base born daughter of Mary Liliot. (Thomas Merreat and Mary Liliot married 19 January 1795. Sister Martha also at the school.) [WSRO Par 211/25/1; PR]

[MERRIT (MERRAT), Martha] (1795-): In Wiston school list c1803, and perhaps at the school in 1800. Baptised 2 August 1795, daughter of Thomas and Mary. (Sister Amey also at the school.) [WSRO Par 211/25/1; PR]

MESSAGE (MESSUAGE), John (1771-): Mayfield charity school. Admitted 11 April 1777; removed 6 July 1781, 'Sufficiently Learned', after 4¼ years at the school, 2¾ years as a 'writer'. Baptised 28 February 1771, son of John and Jane. [MSB; PR]

METCALFE: Midhurst grammar school. At the school's first public performance of composition and oratory, 5 November 1799, won the prize for oratory, with Oratio Annibalis, E. Livio. (A Captain Metcalfe was listed among the gentry attending.) At the second 'literary performance', 27 May 1800, again won a prize for oratory, with Scipio's speech from 21st book of Livy; also took part, with 2 others, in a scene from Homer. [*SWA* 11.11.99; 2.6.1800]

(MEWET): Eastbourne charity school. Admitted Christmas 1778; there Christmas 1779. [SAS Budgen MS v.117]

MICHELL - see also MITCHELL

MICHELL, Henry (1715-89): Educated at Lewes, presumably at grammar school. Baptised 20 August 1715, son of John and Elizabeth. Later vicar of Brighton; wrote on classical antiquities. (For career details, see

Schedule 2.) [*DNB*; Lewes St Michael PR]

MICHELL, Michael: A poor boy of Horsted Keynes for whom the parish bought a spelling book, 1s, in 1744. [WSRO Par 384/12/1]

MICHELL, Richard (1738-90): Lewes grammar school, under Robert Austen. Then Tonbridge school; sizar St John's College, Cambridge, 3 April 1758. Later schoolmaster, and curate of Eastdean. [Qv Schedule 2]. Baptised 17 May 1738, son of John, butcher of Portslade, and Sarah. [Portslade PR]

MILDRED: Grey Coat charity school, Chichester. Left between Michaelmas 1775 and Michaelmas 1776. Given 10s 6d on leaving. [WSRO Cap.V/1/1]

MILDRED, W.: Grey Coat charity school, Chichester. Left between Michaelmas 1768 and Michaelmas 1769. Given 10s 6d on leaving. [WSRO Cap.V/1/1]

MILHAM, John (1791 or 92-): Sedlescombe charity school. There 20 August 1798 and 13 January 1800 (still a 'reader'). Baptised 15 January 1792, son of John and Mary. [SSB; PR]

MILHAM, Richard: Sedlescombe charity school. There 25 December 1797 (a 'writer'), 20 August 1798, 13 January 1800. [SSB]

MILLER, Ann: At Haslewood school, Buxted, 1738 (perhaps under Saunders' charity schooling for girls). [ESRO PAR 286/1/1/1]

MILLER, Henry: At East Hoathly school 1755. From Thomas Turner's diary: '1755 Thursday 13 March. Mr Miller promised me his son should come to me to school. I received of him 18d due to Mr T. Tomsett [previous master] for six weeks schooling Henry.' [Vaisey, D. (ed) *The Diary of Thomas Turner* (1984)]

MILLS, John: Admitted Fermor's charity school, Rotherfield, 29 April 1798. Son of William. [ESRO PAR 465/4/1]

MILLS, Mary: Withyham parish paid 2s for schooling her, 23 March 1744. (The same day John Edwards was paid £1 13s 6d for keeping her till Lady Day 1744; the following year he was paid £1 10s for keeping her 1 year.) [ESRO PAR 512/31/1]

MILLS, Mary (1784-): Admitted Robertsbridge charity school at its opening, 5 April 1796, aged 11. Sponsored by Sir Godfrey Vassall Webster. Baptised 18 July 1784, daughter of John and Priscilla (née Sharpe). [ESRO PAR 477/25/1/1; PR]

MITCHELL - see also MICHELL

(MITCHELL): A poor child of Widow Mitchell's, of West Grinstead, who received schooling 1730, under the Dowlin charity. [WSRO Par 95/1/1/3]

MITCHELL?: 'Son of John Mitchel wife', admitted Fermor's charity school, Rotherfield, 3 May 1794. [ESRO PAR 465/4/1]

MITCHELL (MICHELL), George (1757-): Admitted Eastbourne charity school 11 January 1771. Baptised 15 May 1757, son of Thomas and Mary. [SAS Budgen MS v.105; PR]

MITCHEL, John: Admitted Fermor's charity school, Rotherfield, 14 May 1797. Of Buxted. [ESRO PAR 465/4/1]

MOCKFORD, Richard: Brighton charity school. Given prayer book 1718. Baptised either 7 July 1707, son of Richard, or 12 December 1708, son of Samuel. [BSB; PR]

MOON, John (1771-): Mayfield charity school. Admitted 11 July 1783; removed 7 April 1786. Baptised 18 October 1771, son of William and Anne. (Brothers Joseph, Sampson, also at the school.) [MSB; PR]

MOON, Joseph (1754-): Mayfield charity school. Admitted 10 July 1761 (as 'John', but shown as 'Joseph' in next list and thereafter); removed 8 January 1762, 'Suspended because young & can't well attend this Wintertime'; re-admitted 9 April 1762; removed 13 January 1764, 'Suspended for Non-Attendance Measles being in the Family'; re-admitted 13 April 1764; removed 6 July 1764, suspended for 'Non-Attendance' but re-admitted 26 October 1764 and had apparently attended during the interval; removed 10 October 1765, for

non-attendance, after 3½ years at the school in all, 1¼ years as a 'writer'. Baptised 14 July 1754, son of Joseph and Sarah. (Brother William, sister Mary, also at the school.) [MSB; PR]

MOON, Joseph (1776-): Mayfield charity school. Admitted 11 July 1783; removed 7 April 1786. Baptised 27 February 1776, son of William and Anne. (Brothers John, Sampson, also at the school.) [MSB; PR]

MOON, Joseph: Mayfield charity school. No formal admission, first appears in list for 17 October 1788; removed 7 January 1791, 'Sufficiently Learned'. [MSB]

MOON, Mary (1766-): Mayfield charity school. Admitted 5 July 1776; removed 17 July 1778, 'sufficiently learned', after 2 years at the school, ¾ year as a 'writer'. Baptised 28 September 1766, daughter of Joseph and Sarah. (Brothers Joseph, William, also at the school.) [MSB; PR]

MOON, Philadelphia (1784-): Mayfield charity school. Admitted 8 April 1796; removed 13 April 1798, taken out by parents. Baptised 5 September 1784, daughter of Thomas and Susanna. [MSB; PR]

MOON, Robert: Mayfield charity school. Admitted 22 April 1768; removed 19 April 1771, taken out by parents, after 3 years as a 'reader'. [MSB]

MOON, Sampson (1780-): Mayfield charity school. Admitted 9 July 1790; removed 11 July 1794, 'Sufficiently learned'. Baptised 1 November 1780, son of William and Anne. (Brothers John, Joseph, also at the school.) [MSB; PR]

MOON, Samuel: Mayfield charity school. Admitted 12 April 1799; removed 12 October 1804, for non-attendance, after 5½ years at the school. [MSB]

MOON, Thomas: Mayfield charity school. Admitted 30 July 1779; removed 7 April 1780, 'Gone to Service', after ¾ year as a 'reader'. (TM baptised 26 February 1764, son of Joseph and Sarah, and TM baptised 8 July 1764, son of John and Mary, probably too old for joining this school; no baptisms in the parish register for several other Moon children.) [MSB]

MOON, Thomas: Mayfield charity school. Admitted 13 April 1798; removed 10 January 1800, for non-attendance. [MSB]

MOON, William (1754-): Mayfield charity school. Admitted 10 April 1761; removed 26 October 1764, 'sufficiently learned', after 3½ years at the school, 1¼ years as a 'writer'. Baptised 15 March 1754, son of Sampson and Philadelphia. [MSB; PR]

MOON, William (1761 or 62-): Mayfield charity school. Admitted 19 April 1771; removed 14 October 1774, taken out by parents, after 3½ years at the school, 1¾ years as a 'writer'. Baptised [before 13] January 1762, son of Joseph and Sarah. (Brother Joseph, sister Mary, also at the school.) [MSB; PR]

MOOR, Arthur (1721-): Saunders' charity school, Rye. In lists from 29 March 1732 (not in 19 January 1732) to 31 July 1734 (9 October 1734 notes 'left the school'). Son of Thomas, deceased. Baptised 29 May 1721, son of Thomas and Mary. [RSB; PR]

MOORE, Frances (1787-): At Petworth charity school 5 August 1799. Baptised 28 January 1787, Fanny, daughter of John and Mary. [WSRO Petworth House Archives 1763; PR]

MOOR, John: Saunders' charity school, Rye. In lists from 11 July 1739 (not in 4 April 1739) to June 1743 (?) (not in 26 October 1743). Son of John, 'deceased' in list of June 1743 (?). [RSB]

MOOR, Nicholas (1722-): Saunders' charity school, Rye. In lists from 5 July 1732 (not in 29 March 1732) to 9 April 1735 (2 July 1735 notes 'left the school'). Son of Nicholas, deceased. Baptised 6 April 1722, son of Nicholas and Maudlin. [RSB; PR]

MOORE, Thomas: Saunders' charity school, Rye. In lists from midsummer 1748 (not in 6 April 1748) to 15 January 1752, in which marked 'Octr 26' (not in 25 March 1752). Son of Thomas. [RSB]

MOORE, William (1775-): Saunders' charity school, Rye. Admitted 8 June 1785; in list of 24 June 1785, last surviving 18th century list. Baptised 13 December 1775, son of Thomas and Mary. [RSB; PR]

MORFEY/MORPHEW

MORFEY (MORPHEW), Thomas (1752-): Sedlescombe charity school. Admitted 24 April 1759; there 1761. Baptised 15 October 1752, son of William and Elizabeth Morphew. (Brother William also at the school.) [SSB; PR]

MORFEY (MORFEE, MORPHEW), William (1744-): Sedlescombe charity school. There 3 May 1755, 10 April 1758 (a 'writer'), 22 February 1759. Baptised 13 May 1744, son of William and Elizabeth Morphew. (Brother Thomas also at the school.) [SSB; PR]

MORRIS: Daughter of James, was at school at Buxted, 1739 (perhaps under Saunders' charity schooling for girls). [ESRO PAR 286/1/1/1]

MORRIS: Daughter of Thomas, was at school at Buxted, 1739 (perhaps under Saunders' charity schooling for girls). [ESRO PAR 286/1/1/1]

MORRIS: Grey Coat charity school, Chichester. Given 10s 6d on leaving, 27 October 1772. [WSRO Cap.V/1/1]

MORICE: Grey Coat charity school, Chichester. Left between Michaelmas 1777 and Michaelmas 1778. Given 10s 6d on leaving. [WSRO Cap.V/1/1]

MORRIS, James (1703-): Brighton charity school. Given prayer book 1715. Baptised 6 October 1703, son of James and Anne. [BSB; PR]

MORRIS, John (1728-): Eastbourne charity school. There December 1738 (?), April 1741. Baptised 4 October 1728, son of William and Ann. (Brother William also at the school.) [SAS Budgen MS v.129; PR]

MORRIS, William (1725-): At Eastbourne charity school 1734. Baptised 16 April 1725, son of William and Anne. (Brother John also at the school.) [Chatsworth, Devonshire Collection, Compton Place, Box P; PR]

MORRIS, William: Admitted Fermor's charity school, Rotherfield, 27 October 1793. Son of Thomas. [ESRO PAR 465/4/1]

[MORRISON, John]: Perhaps at Midhurst grammar school. A native of Midhurst and elected to Winchester 1728. [*HMGS*]

[MORRISON, Thomas]: Perhaps at Midhurst charity school. A native of Midhurst and elected to Winchester 1718. [*HMGS*]

MORTIMER, Charles (1729?-): Eastbourne charity school. There December 1738 (?), April 1741. Perhaps baptised 24 November 1729, son of Roger and Sarah. [SAS Budgen MS v.129; PR]

MORTIMER, John Hamilton (1741-79): Was at school at Lewes (though Lower states that his early education 'had been much neglected'). Born 1741 at Eastbourne; father owned a mill there and was at some time collector of customs. Uncle a painter, and JHM showing some proficiency, he was sent to London under Thomas Hudson, master of Sir Joshua Reynolds and Joseph Wright (latter a fellow-pupil and friend). Studied under various masters, became a historical painter. Lived in London, noted for the freedom and extravagance of his life. 1775 married Jane Hurrell, a farmer's daughter; became a reformed character, retired to Aylesbury. Exhibited at Royal Academy 1778. Died 4 February 1779. [Sunderland, J. 'John Hamilton Mortimer, His Life and Works' *Walpole Society* **52** (1986, printed 1988); Lower *Worthies*; *DNB*]

MOSE, Thomas (c1706-): Grey Coat charity school, Chichester. Admitted between Lady Day 1713 and Lady Day 1714, aged 7. [WSRO Cap.V/1/1]

MUDDLE: Grey Coat charity school, Chichester. Left between Michaelmas 1765 and Michaelmas 1766. Given 10s 6d on leaving. [WSRO Cap.V/1/1]

MUDDLE, Sarah: Mayfield charity school. Admitted 29 March 1751; removed 28 June 1751, for non-attendance. [MSB]

MUGGERIDGE, Charles (1791-): Admitted Petworth charity school 20 October 1800. Baptised 6 November 1791, son of Edward and Martha. [WSRO Petworth House Archives 1763; PR]

MUGRAGE (MUGRIDGE), Thomas (1693-): Brighton charity school. In list of 'readers' of (probably) January 1702; given coat and hat July 1702; had left by December 1705. Baptised 23 July 1793, son of Thomas and Elizabeth. [BSB; PR]

MURRIL: One of 2 poor sisters of West Grinstead who received schooling 1724, under the Dowlin charity. [WSRO Par 95/1/1/3]

MURRIL - see **MURRIL**, above.

(MURRIL): A poor child of William Murril's, of West Grinstead, who received schooling 1730, under the Dowlin charity. [WSRO Par 95/1/1/3]

(MURRIL): Another poor child of William Murril's, of West Grinstead, who received schooling, 1730, under the Dowlin charity. [WSRO Par 95/1/1/3]

NABBS, James (1761-70): Saunders' charity school, Rye. Admitted 3 October 1770; only in Michaelmas 1770 list, which has added note, 'James the son of Thos Nabbs died'. Son of Thomas, deceased. Baptised 1 November 1761, son of Thomas and Elizabeth. (Brothers John, Thomas, also at the school.) [RSB; PR]

NABBS, John (1756-): Saunders' charity school, Rye. In list for Lady Day 1767 (not in Michaelmas 1765, previous surviving list); not in Christmas 1768, next surviving list. Son of Thomas, deceased. Baptised 18 April 1756, son of Thomas and Elizabeth. (Brothers James, Thomas, also at the school.) [RSB; PR]

NABS, Thomas (1754-): Saunders' charity school, Rye. In lists from Christmas 1762 (not in 20 January 1762, previous surviving list) to Michaelmas 1765 (not in Lady Day 1767, next surviving list). Son of Thomas (not then deceased). Baptised 25 September 1754, son of Thomas and Elizabeth. (Brothers James, John, also at the school.) [RSB; PR]

NAILER (NAILARD), Mary (1778-): Mayfield charity school. Admitted 13 July 1791; removed 6 April 1792. Baptised 4 February 1778, daughter of Richard and Susanna. (Sister Susanna also at the school.) [MSB; PR]

NAILER (NAILARD), Susanna (1780-): Mayfield charity school. Admitted 6 January 1792; removed 17 October 1794, taken out by parents. Baptised 4 August 1780, daughter of Richard and Susanna. (Sister Mary also at the school.) [MSB; PR]

NASH: Grey Coat charity school, Chichester. Left between Michaelmas 1776 and Michaelmas 1777. Given 10s 6d on leaving. [WSRO Cap.V/1/1]

NASH, Elizabeth (1739-): Brightling girls' charity school. Admitted between 31 July 1747 and 10 June 1749, in which period she attended on 430 school days; there to period 10 June 1749 to 29 September 1752, in which she attended on 643 school days; had 1,073 days at the school in total. Baptised 20 May 1739, daughter of Robert and Susan. (Sisters Mary, Susanna, also at the school.) [ESRO PAR 254/25/1; PR]

NASH, J.: Grey Coat charity school, Chichester. Left between Michaelmas 1768 and Michaelmas 1769. Given 10s 6d on leaving. [WSRO Cap.V/1/1]

NASH, Mary (1742-): Brightling girls' charity school. Admitted between 29 September 1752 and Lady Day 1755, in which period she attended on 434 school days; there to period Lady Day 1755 to 30 April 1757, in which she attended on 237 school days; had 671 days at the school in total. Baptised 11 June 1742, daughter of Robert and Susanna. (Sisters Elizabeth, Susanna, also at the school.) [ESRO PAR 254/25/1; PR]

NASH, Susanna (1740-): Brightling girls' charity school. Admitted and left between 10 June 1749 and 29 September 1752, in which period she attended on 53 school days. Baptised 14 November 1740, daughter of Robert and Susanna. (Sisters Elizabeth, Mary, also at the school.) [ESRO PAR 254/25/1; PR]

NEAL, Martha (1736-): A poor girl of Playden, the parish paid Mary Colens 8s 11d for schooling her - 7 weeks at 2d a week, 31 weeks at 3d a week (loose receipt dated 24 March 1744; Colens signed the receipt by mark). Baptised 26 December 1736, daughter of George (buried May 1740) and Mildred. [ESRO PAR 445/31/1/14; PR]

NEVATT (NEVET), James (1790-): Petworth charity school. Admitted 10 December 1797; there Michaelmas 1801 (had left by 12 July 1803). Baptised 14 April 1790, son of Bartholomew and Elizabeth. [WSRO Petworth House Archives 1763; PR]

NEW, Charles: At Tarring Academy 1803, and almost certainly earlier. A manuscript writing book of his, dated 1803, has survived; this features very fine pen embellishments and decorations. [WSRO Add MS 36,773]

NEWBERY (NEWBURY), William (1760-): Saunders' charity school, Rye. Admitted 28 June 1769; in lists to Michaelmas 1773 (not in midsummer 1774, next surviving list). Baptised 17 September 1760, son of William and Mary. [RSB; PR]

NEWMAN, Edward: A poor boy of Horsted Keynes for whom the parish bought a spelling book, 1s, in 1746. [WSRO Par 384/12/1]

NEWTON: Grey Coat charity school, Chichester. Left between Michaelmas 1758 and Michaelmas 1759. Given 10s 6d on leaving. [WSRO Cap.V/1/1]

NOBLE, George (1703-): Brighton charity school. Given prayer book 1716 or 1717. Baptised 10 September 1703, son of George and Sarah. [MSB; PR]

NORMAN, John (1779-): Mayfield charity school. Admitted 17 October 1788; removed 13 July 1791, for non-attendance. Baptised 25 July 1779, son of Thomas and Mary. [MSB; PR]

NORMAN, Robert (1780-): Mayfield charity school. Admitted 11 April 1788; removed 15 October 1789 for non-attendance. Baptised 9 July 1780, son of Robert and Mary. [MSB; PR]

NORMAN, Thomas (1783-): Admitted Fermor's charity school, Rotherfield, 1 June 1792. Baptised 23 February 1783, son of John, sexton, and Martha. [ESRO PAR 465/4/1; PR]

OAKE, Phillip (1712-): Saunders' charity school, Rye. In lists from September 1722 (?) (first list) to January 1724 (?) (not in 8 April 1724). Son of Phillip, deceased. Baptised 4 April 1712, son of Phillip and Jane. (Brother William also at the school.) [RSB; PR]

OAKE, William (1714-): Saunders' charity school, Rye. In lists from 8 April 1724 (not in January 1724(?)) to January 1726(?) (not in 4 May 1726). Son of Phillip, deceased. Baptised 4 December 1714, son of Phillip and Jane. (Brother Phillip also at the school.) [RSB; PR]

[**OCKENDEN, John**]: In Wiston school list c1803, and perhaps at the school in 1800. [WSRO Par 211/25/1]

ODIARNE, Richard: At Rev Thankful Frewen's school at Northiam from 28 March 1720 to 13 September 1722. [ESRO FRE 533]

ODIARNE, Thomas: At Rev Thankful Frewen's school at Northiam from 22 July 1717 to 26 March 1720. [ESRO FRE 533]

OFFARD, Nancy: At Horsham workhouse school in 1773 [qv].

OGLE, George: Saunders' charity school, Rye. In list for September 1722(?) (first list) only. (Probably brothers Michael, Miles, also at the school.) [RSB]

OGLE, Michael: Saunders' charity school, Rye. In lists from April 1723 (?) (not in September 1722 (?)) to January 1724 (?) (not in 8 April 1724). Son of George. (Brother Miles, probably brother George, also at the school.) [RSB]

OGLE, Miles: Saunders' charity school, Rye. In lists from 8 April 1724 (not in January 1724 (?)) to 8 January 1729 (not in 2 April 1729 (?)). Son of George. (Brother Michael, probably brother George, also at the school.) [RSB]

OLDEN, Jacob (-by 1705): Brighton charity school. In list of 'readers' of (probably) January

1702; given coat and hat July 1702; died before December 1705. [BSB]

OLDFIELD: At Joel's boarding school, Chichester, [qv] in 1773, when he took the lead in the school play, *The Tragedy of Cyrus*, (put on at the new theatre in the city), and 'gave such proof of a theatrical genius as was scarce ever known'.

OLIVER, Mary: A poor girl of Ticehurst for whom the parish paid 1s a week maintenance and provided 'Necessary Clothing', and gave 4s over 'on Acct of sending her to School', in the year Lady Day 1764 to Lady Day 1765. [ESRO PAR 492/31/1/3]

OLIVER, Richard (1693-): Brighton charity school. In list of 'readers' of (probably) January 1702; had left by December 1705 and been 'apprenticed to mariner'. Baptised 1 October 1693, son of Richard and Elizabeth (née Lucus). [BSB; PR]

ONGLEY, Anne: Mayfield charity school. Admitted at formal opening of school, 29 June 1750, but may have been there up to ¾ year earlier, as master paid from Michaelmas 1749; removed 28 June 1751, for non-attendance. [MSB]

OSBORNE, Mary: Petworth charity school. Admitted 9 September 1800; there for 2 years. [WSRO Petworth House Archives 1763]

OSBORNE, William (c1701-): Grey Coat charity school, Chichester, from its opening Lady Day 1710. Aged 9 at Lady Day 1711; still there Lady Day 1714. [WSRO Cap.V/1/1]

OTTAWAY, Gosley: Saunders' charity school, Rye. In lists from 24 June 1749 (not in 25 March 1749) to Michaelmas 1753 (not in 16 January 1754). Son of John. (Brother John also at the school). [RSB]

OTTAWAY, John (1733-): Saunders' charity school, Rye. Added to Michaelmas 1745 list and in Christmas 1745; Christmas 1746 notes 'Absent 4 weeks'; in 25 March 1747, but crossed out. Baptised 7 January 1734, son of John and Mary. (Brother Gosley also at the school.) [RSB; PR]

Scholars

OVENDEN - see also HOVENDEN

OVENDEN, Charles (1768-): Mayfield charity school. Admitted 5 July 1776; removed 7 July 1780, 'Sufficiently Learned,' after 4 years at the school, 1 year as a 'writer'. Baptised 30 October 1768, son of William and Mary. [MSB; PR]

OVENDEN (AVERDEN?), William (1790-): Admitted Fermor's charity school, Rotherfield, 29 April 1798. Baptised 14 February 1790, son of William and Hannah. [ESRO PAR 465/4/1; PR]

OVETT (OVAT): Brighton girls' charity school. Admitted when school opened, 30 September 1702. 'Alis Ovat's daughter'. Baptised either 26 January 1690, Ales, daughter of John and Ales; 2 October 1692, Jone, daughter of John; or 27 April 1695, Elizabeth, daughter of John and Ales. (William, master of the *Charity* in 1726, was her uncle.) [BSB; PR; Tibble, R., pers. comm.]

OWDEN: Rand's school, Lewes. Thomas Pelham of Stanmer paid Cater Rand 18s on 31 November 1732 'for Owden's boy's school', and £1 10s 6d on 29 September 1733 'for three quarters schooling for J. Owden's boy'. [BL Add MS 33,161]

[PACKHAM, George (1792-1872)]: At Lightmaker's charity school, Horsted Keynes. Born 1792, son of John of Shortbridge, Fletching, miller. Apprenticed to William Sudds of the Cliffe, Lewes, millwright. Married Sarah 1811; became miller; in 1823 went to France, designed watermill, had a biscuit factory and an oil mill, designed his own sawmill. Friend of the king, Louis Philippe. Returned to England; retired to Brighton. Died 1872. [Packham, G. *SFH* **8** No. 7]

PAGE: Grey Coat charity school, Chichester. Left between Michaelmas 1763 and Michaelmas 1764. Given 10s 6d on leaving. [WSRO Cap.V/1/1]

PAGE, John (1771-): Mayfield charity school. Admitted 6 July 1781; removed 11 January 1782, 'being Ill and Taken out by his parents'. Baptised 15 June 1771, son of Thomas and Elizabeth. [MSB; PR]

PAGE, Lucy: A poor girl of Laughton for whose schooling the parish paid 5s 7d in the year Easter 1751 to Easter 1752. (They also paid for her keep, at 6s a month, 1754/55, 1755/56, 1756/57; and £2 2s 1757/58, 1758/59; and £1 17s 6d 1759/60.) [ESRO PAR 409/31/1/2]

PAIN/PAINE/PAYNE

PAINE: Brighton girls' charity school. Admitted when school opened 30 September 1702. 'Widow Paine's daughter'. [BSB]

PAINE: Brighton charity school. In list of 'writers' December 1705. [BSB]

PAINE: Pupil of Corbyn, dancing master, Brighton. At a Ball there 5 September 1798, as 'a very little boy', he 'danced a hornpipe admirably'. [*SWA* 10.9.98]

PAINE, Cornelius (1691-): Brighton charity school. Admitted as 'reader' sometime after list of (probably) January 1702; joined 'writers' class sometime after 12 January 1702; in 'writers' class December 1705; when he left went 'to sea'. Baptised 9 August 1691, son of Cornelius and Anne. (Brother John also at the school.) [BSB; PR]

PAINE, Friend (1696-): Brighton charity school. Admitted as 'reader' sometime after list of (probably) January 1702; had left by December 1705 and been 'apprenticed to mariner'. Baptised 5 July 1696, son of Thomas and Ann. [BSB; PR]

PAYNE, George (1729-): Eastbourne charity school. There December 1738 (?), April 1741. Baptised 16 September 1729, son of John and Mary. [SAS Budgen MS v.129; PR]

PAIN, Hannah (1737-): At Sedlescombe charity school 23 June 1748. Baptised 30 January 1737, daughter of John and Hannah. [SSB; PR]

PAINE, John (1694-): Brighton charity school. Admitted as 'reader' sometime after list of (probably) January 1702; in list of 'readers' December 1705; added at end of list of 'writers' December 1705 (ie joined subsequently). Baptised 25 November 1694, son of Cornelius (mother was Ann, from baptisms of other children. Brother Cornelius also at the school.) [BSB; PR]

PAIN, Joseph Buckoll (1700-): Brighton charity school. Given prayer book 1715. Baptised 29 November 1700, Joseph Buckoll, son of John and Sarah (née Buckoll). [BSB; Union Street Independent Chapel (Presbyterian) register]

PAINE, Nathaniel (1757-): Mayfield charity school. Admitted 9 July 1762; removed 17 October 1766, for non-attendance, after 4¼ years at the school, ½ year as a 'writer'. Baptised 7 June 1757, son of William and Sarah. [MSB; PR]

PAIN, Robert: Grey Coat charity school, Chichester. Left between Michaelmas 1766 and Michaelmas 1767. Given 10s 6d on leaving. [WSRO Cap.V/1/1]

PAINE, Thomas (1687 or 88-): Brighton charity school. In list of 'writers' 12 January 1702; had left by December 1705 and gone 'to sea'. Baptised 15 January 1688, son of Thomas and Elizabeth. [BSB; PR]

PAINE, Thomas: Brighton charity school. Given prayer book 1716 or 17. [BSB]

[PAYNE, William]: Perhaps at Midhurst grammar school. A native of Midhurst and elected to Winchester 1722. [*HMGS*]

PAINE, William: Mayfield charity school. Admitted 9 January 1761; removed 8 April 1763, taken out by parents, after 2¼ years at the school, 1¼ years as a 'writer'. [MSB]

PAIN, William: Admitted Midhurst grammar school, as a charity scholar, 1789. [*HMGS*]

PALMER, Henry: Admitted Midhurst grammar school, as a charity scholar, 1792. [*HMGS*]

PANKHURST, Edmund: Mayfield charity school. Admitted 9 April 1790; removed 7 October 1791, taken out by parents. [MSB]

PANKHURST, Edward (1723-): In 1729 Elizabeth Soane was paid 6s 8d by Rev Thankful Frewen, rector of Northiam, 'for 20 weeks Schooling for goodman pankhurst boys' (ie 4d a week, or 2d a week for 2 boys). Baptised 26 March 1723, son of Edward and Joan (née Gower). (Brother William also schooled by her.) [ESRO FRE 8181 (4); PR]

PANKHURST, William (1718-): In 1729 Elizabeth Soane was paid 6s 8d by Rev Thankful Frewen, rector of Northiam, 'for 20 weeks Schooling for goodman pankhurst boys' (ie 4d a week, or 2d a week for 2 boys). Baptised 2 November 1718, son of Edward and Joan (née Gower). (Brother Edward also schooled by her.) [ESRO FRE 8181 (4); PR]

PANKHURST, William (1737-): At Sedlescombe charity school 23 June 1748. Baptised 27 February 1737, son of Thomas and Ann Pancost. [SSB; PR]

PARFITT, Mary: Mayfield charity school. Admitted 3 July 1752; removed 9 April 1755, taken away by parents, after 2¾ years, still a 'reader'. [MSB]

PARFITT, Ursula: Mayfield charity school. Admitted 10 July 1761; removed 8 January 1762, 'To make Room for those having more Occasion', after ½ year as a 'reader'. [MSB]

PARKER: Admitted Fermor's charity school, Rotherfield, 5 June 1796. Son of William. [ESRO PAR 465/4/1]

PARKER, Josiah (1715-): Saunders' charity school, Rye. In lists from 19 May 1725 (not in April 1725 (?)) as 'Joseph' or 'Jos:' to 11 January 1727 when name changes to 'Josiah'; in 10 January 1728 (only) as 'John'; then 'Josiah' to 25 June 1729 (not in 7 January 1730). (Probably called 'Jo' throughout.) Son of Nicholas, deceased. Baptised 2 November 1715, son of Nicholas and Martha. [RSB; PR]

PARKER, Nicholas Tettersall (1695-): Brighton charity school. In list of 'readers' of (probably) January 1702; joined 'writers' class sometime after 12 January 1702; in list of 'writers' December 1705. Baptised 22 September 1695, son of Cornelius. [BSB; PR]

PARKER, Sarah (1735-): Mayfield charity school. Admitted at formal opening of school

29 June 1750, but may have been there up to ¾ year earlier, as master paid from Michaelmas 1749; removed 29 March 1751, 'on account of her going to Service', but re-admitted 28 June 1751; removed 4 October 1751, for non-attendance. Baptised 26 May 1735, daughter of Stephen and Elizabeth. (Sister Ursula also at the school.) [MSB; PR]

PARKER, Stephen: Mayfield charity school. Admitted 19 January 1753, but not in list for 6 April 1753 or lists to 9 April 1755 when admitted again; removed 11 July 1755, 'for Non Attendance, never came'. [MSB]

PARKER, Ursula (1737-): Mayfield charity school. Admitted at formal opening of school 29 June 1750, but may have been there up to ¾ year earlier, as master paid from Michaelmas 1749; removed 3 July 1752, for non-attendance, still a 'reader'. Baptised 29 June 1737, daughter of Stephen and Elizabeth. (Sister Sarah also at the school.) [MSB; PR]

PARKHAM (PECKHAM), Richard (1757-): Mayfield charity school. Admitted 17 October 1766; removed 27 October 1769, 'Sufficiently Learned', after 3 years at the school, 1½ years as a 'writer'. Baptised 30 October 1757, son of William and Anne (father farmed 34 acres at Earls and 18 at Allcocks.) [MSB; PR; *SFH 9* No. 5 (1991)]

PARKS, Edward (1753-): Mayfield charity school. Admitted 11 January 1760; removed 13 April 1764, taken out by parents, after 4¼ years at the school, 1½ years as a 'writer'. Baptised 9 March 1753, son of John and Mary. (Brother John also at the school.) [MSB; PR]

PARKS, Elizabeth (1757-): Mayfield charity school. Admitted 16 October 1767; removed 21 April 1769, for non-attendance, after 1½ years as a 'reader'. Baptised 8 April 1757, daughter of Thomas and Mary. (Admitted and left same dates as older sister Mary.) [MSB; PR]

PARKS, John (1744-): Mayfield charity school. Admitted 6 April 1753; removed 12 July 1754, for non-attendance; probably re-admitted 10 January 1755 and removed 9 April 1755, for non-attendance. Baptised 29 July 1744, son of John and Mary. (Brother Edward also at the school.) [MSB; PR]

PARKS, Mary (1754-): Mayfield charity school. Admitted 16 October 1767; removed 21 April 1769, for non-attendance, after 1½ years as a 'reader'. Baptised 5 April 1754, daughter of Thomas and Mary. (Sister Elizabeth also at the school.) [MSB; PR]

PARKS, Thomas (1785-): Mayfield charity school. Admitted 11 April 1794; removed 8 April 1796. Baptised 12 June 1785, son of Thomas and Hannah. [MSB; PR]

PARSONS: A poor girl of West Grinstead who received schooling, 1707, under the Dowlin charity. [WSRO Par 95/1/1/3]

PEACOCK, Clara (1787-): Petworth charity school. Admitted 27 August 1800; there 2 years. Probably baptised 26 March 1787, daughter of Richard and Susanna. (Another CP baptised 2 September 1795, daughter of John and Elizabeth, but no children admitted as young as 5 years old 1796-1800 and no girl under 8; two girls of 12 admitted.) [WSRO Petworth House Archives 1763; PR]

PEADLE, John (1750-): Saunders' charity school, Rye. In lists from 11 January 1758 (not in Michaelmas 1757) to Michaelmas 1763 (not in Christmas 1764, next surviving list). Baptised 5 June 1750, son of John and Mary. [RSB; PR]

PEADLE, Mark (1721-): Saunders' charity school, Rye. In lists from 29 March 1732 (not in 19 January 1732) to 29 December 1736 (20 April 1737 notes 'left the school'). Baptised 17 March 1721, son of Moses and Margery. (A Moses Peadle admitted to freedom of Rye, by right of birth, 1708; his son, admitted 16 May 1739, by birth, became army officer; his portrait still existed 1847.) [RSB; PR; Holloway, W. *History of the Town and Port of Rye* (1847)]

PEARCE - see PEIRCE

PECK, Samuel (1790-): Admitted Robertsbridge charity school at its opening 5 April 1796. Sponsored by John Micklethwaite Esq. Baptised 11 June 1790, son of John and Elizabeth. [ESRO PAR 477/25/1/1; Salehurst PR]

PECKHAM - see PARKHAM

PEERLESS/ PERLESS / PURLESS

PURLESS (PEERLESS), Eliza (1786-):
Admitted Fermor's charity school, Rotherfield,
3 May 1794. Baptised 26 November 1786,
daughter of Thomas Peerless and Elizabeth,
'poor'. [ESRO PAR 465/4/1; PR]

PURLESS, George: Admitted Fermor's charity
school, Rotherfield, 3 May 1794. Son of
William. [ESRO PAR 465/4/1]

PERLESS, James: Admitted Fermor's charity
school, Rotherfield, 29 April 1798. Son of
Widow Perless. [ESRO PAR 465/4/1]

PEIRCE/PEARCE/PIERCE

PEIRCE (PIERCE), John (1716-): Saunders'
charity school, Rye. In lists from 5 October
1726 (not in 29 June 1726) to 7 July 1731 (27
October 1731 notes 'left the school'). Baptised
27 November 1716, son of Robert and Mary.
[RSB; PR]

PEARCE, Joseph (1745-): Saunders' charity
school, Rye. In lists from Christmas 1758 (not
in midsummer 1758) to midsummer 1759 (not
in 16 April 1760, next surviving list). Baptised
24 April 1745, son of Robert and Elizabeth.
[RSB; PR]

PELHAM, George (1766-1827): Youngest son
of Lord Pelham, later Earl of Chichester, he
was tutored 1784 by James Hurdis [qv] at the
family seat of Stanmer. Then Clare College,
Cambridge, BA 1787; briefly in army (Guards
officer), then the church; bishop of Bristol
1803, then Exeter 1807, then Lincoln 1820.
Married 14 December 1792, Mary, daughter of
Sir Richard Rycroft (she died 1837, without
issue). Died 7 February 1827. [*DNB*]

(PENCURSTES): Child of Widow Pencurstes,
at Rotherfield workhouse school, 6 January
1772. [ESRO PAR 465/4/1]

PENFOLD: A poor girl of West Grinstead,
daughter of William, who received schooling
1725-26, under the Dowlin charity. [WSRO
Par 95/1/1/3]

PENFOLD, Edward Greenfield (1787-1855):
Midhurst grammar school. Probably the
'Penfold, senior' who, at the school's first
public performance of composition and oratory,
5 November 1799, took part, with one other, in
a scene from Thomson's *Agamemnon*, playing
Melisander. At the second 'literary
performance', 27 May 1800, took part, with 2
others, in a scene from Homer. Later, Deputy
Lieutenant for Sussex. [*HMGS*; *SWA* 11.11.99,
2.6.1800]

PENFOLD, Hugh (1783-1864): Midhurst
grammar school. (Perhaps the 'Penfold, senior'
attributed to Edward above, qv.) Later, Deputy
Lieutenant for Sussex. Assumed surname
WYATT for Penfold in 1839. [*HMGS*]

PENFOLD, Hugh (1788-1850): Midhurst
grammar school. [*HMGS*]

PENTICOST, Dennis (1746-): Mayfield
charity school. Admitted 27 March 1752;
removed 20 January 1758, 'sufficiently
learned', after 5¾ years, 2½ years as a 'writer'.
Born 17 December 1746, baptised 1 February
1747, son of Thomas and Martha. (Joined at 5;
brothers John, Richard, probably brother
Edmund (Edward), also at the school.) [MSB;
PR]

PENTECOST, Edward (Edmund?) (1751?-
): Mayfield charity school. Admitted 13
October 1758; removed 17 October 1760, 'for
Non Attendance being taken into the
Workhouse', after 2 years as a 'reader'.
Probably same as Edmund, baptised 1 January
1752, son of Thomas and Martha; if so, joined
at 6, and brother to Dennis, Richard, both of
whom joined at 5, and brother John, all at the
school. [MSB; PR]

PENTICOST, Elizabeth: Mayfield charity
school. Admitted 27 March 1752; removed 19
January 1753, taken out by parents. Probably
same as the EP admitted 12 October 1753;
removed 9 April 1755 (but when latter left, her
time at school is taken from October 1753),
taken out by parents, still a 'reader'. [MSB]

[PENTICOST, Elizabeth]: Mayfield charity
school. Admitted 12 October 1753; removed 9
April 1755, taken out by parents, still a
'reader'. But probably same as EP admitted 27

March 1752 [qv above]. [MSB]

PENTECOST, John (1757-): Mayfield charity school. Admitted 6 July 1764; removed 20 January 1769, 'sufficiently learned', after 4½ years at the school, 1 year as a 'writer'. Baptised 7 April 1757, son of Thomas and Martha. (Brothers Dennis, Richard, and probably brother Edmund (Edward) also at the school.) [MSB; PR]

PENTICOST, Martha: Mayfield charity school. Admitted at formal opening of school 29 June 1750, but may have been at the school up to ¾ year earlier, as master paid from Michaelmas 1749; removed 27 March 1752, for non-attendance (still a 'reader'); re-admitted 19 January 1753, as a 'writer'; removed 12 October 1753, taken out by parents; re-admitted 14 October 1755; removed 9 January 1756, 'sufficiently learned', recorded as having had 1 year in total as a 'writer'. (NB In lists to March 1751 entered as 'Martha Pensherst', but evidence suggests 'Penshurst' an error for 'Penticost'.) [MSB]

PENTECOST, Richard (1754-): Mayfield charity school. Admitted 26 October 1759; removed 17 October 1760, 'for Non Attendance being taken into the Workhouse', after 1 year as a 'reader'. Baptised 22 April 1754, son of Thomas and Martha; so joined at 5 (brother Dennis also joined at 5, probably brother Edmund (Edward) at 6; brother John also at the school.) [MSB; PR]

PENTICOST, Thomas (1749?-): Mayfield charity school. Admitted 9 January 1756; removed 11 April 1760, for non-attendance, after 4¼ years, still a 'reader'; re-admitted 9 April 1762, as a 'writer'; removed 15 October 1762, for non-attendance, after 4¾ years at the school in total, ½ year as a 'writer'. (Cf PENTICOST, Martha, above.) Son of Thomas, labourer. Probably baptised 2 June 1749, son of Thomas and Martha Penckherst (NB same name confusion concerning Martha.) In June 1762, when 13, bound himself apprentice to John Corke of Rotherhithe, Surrey, cooper, for 7 years from 2 June 1763; the parish paid the premium of £11 10s. [MSB; PR; ESRO PAR 422/33/130]

PERRY, Anne (1721-): Brightling girls'

charity school. Admitted 21 November 1735, aged 15. Baptised 23 March 1721, daughter of Thomas and Anne. (Sisters Mary, Susannah, also at the school.) [ESRO PAR 254/25/1; PR]

PERRY, Elizabeth (1752-): Brightling girls' charity school. Admitted between 31 July 1758 and 31 December 1761, in which period she attended on 49 school days. (No later records.) Baptised 19 November 1752, daughter of William and Mary. [ESRO PAR 254/25/1; PR]

PERRY, Mary (1730-): Brightling girls' charity school. Admitted 7 April 1741; there to year ending 30 April 1742, in which year she attended on 74 school days; had 95 days at the school in total. Baptised 6 September 1730, daughter of Thomas and Anne. (Sisters Anne, Susannah, also at the school.) [ESRO PAR 254/25/1; PR]

PERRY, Susannah (1723-): Brightling girls' charity school. Admitted 6 April 1735; had left by 21 April 1738. Baptised 27 March 1723, daughter of Thomas and Anne. (Sisters Anne, Mary, also at the school.) [ESRO PAR 254/25/1; PR]

PERRY, William: At Sarah Cruttenden's school, Brightling, 1735 and 1736. On 1 June 1736 John Fuller paid her 6s 10d for teaching him '41 weeks ending the 5th May Last att 2d'. [ESRO SAS/RF 15/28]

PETTER, John (1736-): Saunders' charity school, Rye. In lists from 14 August 1745 (not in 10 April 1745); left 29 October 1750. Son of John, deceased. Baptised 16 June 1736, son of John and Mary. (Brother William also at the school.) [RSB; PR]

PETTER, William (1734-): Saunders' charity school, Rye. In lists from 8 July 1741 (not in 29 April 1741) to Michaelmas 1747 (not in Christmas 1747). Son of John, deceased. Baptised 27 February 1734, son of John and Mary. (Brother John also at the school.) [RSB; PR]

PETTET, James: A poor boy of Alciston, the parish paid bills for his schooling (at 2d a week) by Dame Richardson between 1757 and 1759 (and possibly later: payment to her for him, 16 February 1763, not specified as for schooling). [ESRO PAR 227/31/1]

PETTITT, John (1745-): Mayfield charity school. Admitted 11 January 1754; removed 20 January 1758, 'to make room for others having made a good proficiency', after 4 years at the school, 1¼ years as a 'writer'. Baptised 10 February 1745, son of John, sawyer, and Mary. Father buried 2 June 1757. On 6 July 1759, aged 14, bound himself apprentice for 7 years to Richard Collins of Rotherfield, forgeman; parish paid premium (£6 at time of indenture, plus £6 3½ years later, if JP still then living); Collins to instruct JP 'in the Art of a Forgeman...finding unto the said Apprentice sufficient Meat, Drink, Apparel, Washing and Lodging, and all other Necessaries during the said term'; JP's signature was clear and competent. (Brother Thomas, sister Mary, also at the school.) [MSB; PR; ESRO PAR 422/33/127]

PETTITT, Mary (1748-): Mayfield charity school. Admitted 11 July 1755; removed 8 July 1757, 'suspended only to make room for the Waters who hath more Occasion' after 2 years as a 'reader'. Baptised 11 December 1748, daughter of John and Mary. (Brothers John, Thomas, also at the school.) [MSB; PR]

PETTITT, Sarah: At Haslewood school, Buxted, 1739 (perhaps under Saunders' charity schooling for girls). [ESRO PAR 286/1/1/1]

PETTITT, Thomas (1746-): Mayfield charity school. Admitted 10 January 1755; removed 14 October 1757, 'suspended only to make room for Hannah Stevens having more Occasion'; re-admitted 11 July 1760; removed 17 October 1760, for non-attendance, 'being taken into the Workhouse', after 2¾ years in all at the school, about ¼ year as a 'writer'. Baptised 28 September 1746, son of John (sawyer, died 1757; qv PETTITT, John) and Mary. On 5 June 1761 apprenticed by parish for 7 years to James Avard of Mayfield, fellmonger, glover and breeches maker (premiums: £5 now, £5 on 6 October 1764). (Brother John, sister Mary, also at the school.) [MSB; PR; ESRO PAR 422/33/128]

PETTO, Charles (1786-): Petworth charity school. Admitted 19 September 1796 (had left by Michaelmas 1801). Baptised 3 September 1786, son of Thomas and Ann. [WSRO Petworth House Archives 1763; PR]

PHILCOX, James (1782-): Sedlescombe charity school. There 21 October 1793 (a 'reader'); not in list for 20 September 1794. Baptised 1 December 1782, son of Thomas and Mary. (Brother John also at the school.) [SSB; PR]

PHILCOX, John (1778-): Sedlescombe charity school. There 29 September 1786 (a 'reader') and 29 September 1787 (a 'writer'). Baptised 15 November 1778, son of Thomas and Mary. (Brother James also at the school.) [SSB; PR]

PHILCOX, William: Sedlescombe charity school. There 29 September 1784 (a 'writer'), 29 September 1786 and 29 September 1787. [SSB]

PHILIPS, Mary: At Cocking charity school, 1733. [WSRO Par 53/12/1]

PHILIPS, Mercy: At Cocking charity school, 1732. [WSRO Par 53/12/1]

PHILP, William: Midhurst grammar school. Admitted as charity scholar 1788. [*HMGS*]

PIDDLES, Elizabeth: At Rotherfield workhouse school, 6 January 1772. [ESRO PAR 465/4/1]

PIDDLESDEN, Edward (1786-): Admitted Fermor's charity school, Rotherfield, 10 May 1793. Baptised 17 June 1786 (with brothers Peter, William, sister Elizabeth) son of John and Elizabeth, 'poor'. [ESRO PAR 465/4/1; PR]

PILBEAM, Joseph (1729-): Eastbourne charity school. There December 1738 (?) and April 1741. Baptised 5 September 1729, son of Samuel and Elizabeth. [SAS Budgen MS v.129; PR]

PINK, Richard (1740-): Saunders' charity school, Rye. In lists from 3 January 1753 (not in Michaelmas 1752) to Michaelmas 1753 (not in 16 January 1754). Son of Robert, deceased. Baptised 8 April 1740, son of Robert and Elizabeth. [RSB; PR]

PIPER, Anne (1691-): Brighton girls' charity school. Admitted sometime after 25 March 1703 (probably before December 1705). Baptised 23 August 1691, daughter of Cornelius Pipper and Elizabeth (née Jacaket, ie Jackett). [BSB; PR]

PIPER (of Trodgers), George (1749-): Mayfield charity school. Admitted 17 October 1760, as a 'writer'; removed 8 January 1762, 'To make Room for those having more Occasion'. Baptised 16 November 1749, son of John and Elizabeth. (Brother John also at the school.) [MSB; PR]

PIPER, George (1753-): Mayfield charity school. Admitted 4 May 1759; removed 14 October 1763, 'sufficiently learned', after 4½ years at the school, 2 years as a 'writer'. Baptised 12 [September] 1753, son of Richard and Gift. [MSB; PR]

PIPER, Good Gift: Mayfield charity school. Apparently admitted 12 July 1754; removed 18 October 1754, for non-attendance. [MSB]

PIPER (of Trodgers), John (1751-): Mayfield charity school. Admitted 17 October 1760 (apparently started before); removed 9 July 1762, 'to make room for One that has more Occasion', after 2 years at the school, 1¼ as a 'writer'. Baptised 14 March 1751, son of John and Elizabeth. (Brother George also at the school.) [MSB; PR]

PIPER, John (1763-): Mayfield charity school. Admitted 9 July 1772; removed 13 October 1775, 'Sufficiently Learned', after 3¼ years at the school, all as a 'writer'. Baptised 13 November 1763, son of John and Sarah. [MSB; PR]

PIPER, Mary (1782-): Mayfield charity school. Admitted 11 April 1794; removed 8 April 1796. Probably baptised 9 May 1782, 'Mary Piper Daughter of Mary Arkquit, base-born'. [MSB; PR]

PIPER, Thomas (1737-): Mayfield charity school. Admitted 5 October 1750; removed 28 June 1751, for non-attendance, still a 'reader'. Probably baptised 6 November 1737, son of Richard and Goodgift (another TP baptised 3 January 1738, son of Thomas and Mary, but

former more probable as Goodgift Piper, also at the school, probably daughter of Richard and Goodgift; both this Thomas and Goodgift a very short time at the school). [MSB; PR]

PIPER, Thomas (1777-): Mayfield charity school. Admitted 11 July 1788; removed 9 April 1790, taken out by parents but 'Sufficiently Learned'. Baptised 6 January 1778, son of John and Sarah. [MSB; PR]

PIPER, William (1786-): Mayfield charity school. Admitted 8 April 1796; removed 13 April 1798, taken out by parents. Baptised 22 January 1786, son of John and Sarah. [MSB; PR]

PIPPIN: Grey Coat charity school, Chichester. Left between Michaelmas 1757 and Michaelmas 1758. Given 10s 6d on leaving. [WSRO Cap.V/1/1]

PLUMMER, John: At Rev Thankful Frewen's school, Northiam, from 25 June 1716 to 6 June 1717. [ESRO FRE 533]

POLCOCK (POCOK), Mary (1693-): Brighton girls' charity school. Admitted when school opened 30 September 1702. 'Mary Pokock's daughter'. Baptised 20 August 1693, daughter of William Pocok and Mary (née Wood). [BSB; PR]

POLCOCK (POCOK), Nicholas (1696-): Brighton charity school. In list of 'readers' of (probably) January 1702; given coat and hat July 1702; had left by December 1705. Baptised 14 June 1696, son of Nicholus Pocok and [*blank*] (mother was probably Ann (née Pocoke), from marriage and baptism of daughter Elizabeth 1693). [BSB; PR]

POLLARD, John: Mayfield charity school. Admitted 20 July 1770; removed 15 October 1773, 'Sufficiently Learned', after 3¼ years at the school, 2½ years as a 'writer'. [MSB]

POLLINGTON, Nicholas: At Eastbourne charity school April 1741. [SAS Budgen MS v.129]

POLLINGTON, Robert (1788-): Admitted Fermor's charity school, Rotherfield, 14 May 1797. Of Buxted. Baptised 19 May 1788, son of Robert and Mary. [ESRO PAR 465/4/1; Buxted PR]

POOLE, Grace (1749-): At Philpot's girls' boarding school, Lewes, 1757. Baptised 24 November 1749, daughter of William Poole Esq of the Hook, Chailey, and Dorothy. (WP's first wife, Grace, died 1743; he married secondly, 1744, Dorothea, daughter of Rev Daniel Walter of Cuckfield; she died 21 October 1750, and he married thirdly, 1753, Mary Lee.) [*SAC* **114**; Chailey PR]

POOLE, Henrietta (Harriet) (1746-): At Philpot's girls' boarding school, Lewes, 1757. Baptised 24 October 1746, daughter of William Poole Esq of the Hook, Chailey, and Dorothy (qv POOLE, Grace, above.) [*SAC* **114**; Chailey PR]

POWEL: Grey Coat charity school, Chichester. Left between Michaelmas 1755 and Michaelmas 1756. Given 10s 6d on leaving. [WSRO Cap.V/1/1]

POWELL, Isaac (1773-): Mayfield charity school. Admitted 11 October 1782, but not in next list and presumably never attended then; admitted again 11 July 1783; removed 8 April 1785, for non-attendance. Baptised 13 June 1773, son of John and Elizabeth. (Three brothers also at the school.) [MSB; PR]

POWELL, John (1757-): Mayfield charity school. Admitted 13 April 1764; removed 22 April 1768, for non-attendance, 'but pretty well Learned', after 4 years at the school, 1¾ years as a 'writer'. Baptised 13 March 1757, son of John and Elizabeth. (Three brothers also at the school.) [MSB; PR]

POWELL, James (1770 or 71-): Mayfield charity school. Admitted 7 July 1780; removed 9 April 1784, 'Sufficiently Learned'. Baptised 16 January 1771, son of John and Elizabeth. (Three brothers also at the school.) [MSB; PR]

POWELL, Thomas: Saunders' charity school, Rye. In lists from September 1722 (?) (first list) to 4 November 1724 (not in January 1725 (?)). Son of widow Powel. [RSB]

POWEL, Thomas (1738-): Saunders' charity school, Rye. In lists from Christmas 1749 (not in Michaelmas 1749) to 25 March 1752 (not in 8 July 1752). Baptised 9 December 1738, son of Thomas and Jane. [RSB; PR]

POWELL, William (1760-): Mayfield charity school. Admitted 21 April 1769; removed 10 April 1772, for non-attendance; re-admitted 9 July 1772; removed 7 January 1774, by desire of parents, 'to work in shaving Hoppoles etc', after 4½ years at the school, still a 'reader'. Baptised 19 October 1760, son of John and Elizabeth. (Three brothers also at the school.) [MSB; PR]

PRATT, Ansley (1789-): Admitted Fermor's charity school, Rotherfield, 29 April 1798. Baptised 28 June 1789, daughter of Richard and Hannah. (Brother George also at the school.) [ESRO PAR 465/4/1; PR]

PRATT, Elizabeth (1787-): Admitted Petworth charity school 10 December 1797. Baptised 3 August 1787, daughter of George and Elizabeth. (Brother George also at the school). [WSRO Petworth House Archives 1763; PR]

PRATT, George (1786-): Admitted Fermor's charity school, Rotherfield, 3 May 1794. Son of Richard, junior. Baptised 4 June 1786, son of Richard and Hannah. (Sister Ansley also at the school.) [ESRO PAR 465/4/1; PR]

PRATT, George (1794-): Admitted Petworth charity school 15 December 1800. Baptised 5 October 1794, son of George and Elizabeth. (Sister Elizabeth also at the school). [WSRO Petworth House Archives 1763; PR]

PRICE, John: Mayfield charity school. Admitted at formal opening of the school 29 June 1750, but may have been there up to ¾ year earlier, as master paid from Michaelmas 1749; removed 3 July 1752, taken out by parents; re-admitted 14 November 1752; removed 6 April 1753, 'well learned', but re-admitted 12 October 1753; removed 11 January 1754, for non-attendance; of his time at school, had ¼ year as a 'writer'. [MSB]

PURCHAS, George (c1700-): Grey Coat charity school, Chichester. Admitted at its opening, Lady Day 1710. Aged 10 at Lady Day 1711. 'Discarded' between Lady Day 1712 and Lady Day 1713. [WSRO Cap.V/1/1]

PURDY (c1769-): From the diary of John Baker of Horsham: '1775, April 24 -...came Mr Scawen and Mr Blunt, who had been to Steyning in Mr Blunt's chaise and two horses (Mr Scawen drove) to Mr Baker's school at Steyning in with little Harry Blunt and Master Purdy, six years old. Have never been out to school before.' [*SAC* **52**]

PURLESS - see PEERLESS

QUINEL, Michael: A poor boy of Rotherfield for whose schooling the parish paid 9d, 2 April 1759. [ESRO PAR 465/6/7]

RAINER, Derick (1689-): Brighton charity school. In list of 'readers' of (probably) January 1702; joined 'writers' class sometime after 12 January 1702; had left by December 1705 and gone 'to sea'. Baptised 21 July 1689, son of Derick Rayner. [BSB; PR]

RAMSDEN, Thomas (1744-): Saunders' charity school, Rye. In lists from Michaelmas 1753 (not in 4 July 1753); left 10 May 1758. Son of John, deceased. Baptised 3 April 1744, son of John and [*blank*]. [RSB; PR]

RANGER, Jemima (1793-): Mayfield charity school. Admitted 11 April 1800; removed 12 April 1805, 'sufficiently learned'. Baptised 1 April 1793, daughter of John and Jemima. [MSB; PR]

RANGER (RAINGER), Richard (1774-): Lord Pelham's charity school, Lewes [qv Rand's school]. Admitted Lady Day 1784. There 10 October 1784, aged 9. Born 5 November 1774, son of Richard and Elizabeth. [ESRO AMS 6005; All Saints PR]

READ: Button's school, Lewes. To recite at a 'Public Examination' at the *Star Assembly Room*, 22 June 1797. [*SWA* 19.6.97]

REDHEAD, Elizabeth (1736-): At Sedlescombe charity school 23 June 1748. Baptised 4 December 1736, daughter of William and Ann. [SSB; PR]

REED, John (1772-): Sedlescombe charity school. There 29 September 1784 (a 'writer') and 29 September 1786. Baptised 19 November 1772, son of William and Susanna. (Brother Thomas also at the school.) [SSB; PR]

REED, John: Eastbourne charity school. Admitted Michaelmas 1779; there Christmas 1779. [SAS Budgen MS v.117]

REED, Keziah (-1768): Admitted Sedlescombe charity school 6 April 1761. Buried 27 April 1768. [SSB; PR]

REED, Mary: Admitted Sedlescombe charity school 6 April 1761. [SSB]

REED, Samuel (1784 or 85-): Admitted Fermor's charity school, Rotherfield, 4 August 1793. Of Buxted. Baptised 16 January 1785, son of William and Mary. [ESRO PAR 465/4/1; Buxted PR]

REED, Thomas (1774-): Sedlescombe charity school. There 29 September 1784, 29 September 1786, 29 September 1787 (still a 'reader'). Baptised 4 September 1774, son of William and Susan. (Brother John also at the school.) [SSB; PR]

REEDS, Ann (1753-): At Seaford charity school 1765. Baptised 21 January 1753, daughter of Richard and Sarah. [BL Add MS 33,059; PR]

RELF, Elizabeth (1740-): Brightling girls' charity school. Admitted between 10 June 1749 and 29 September 1752, in which period she attended on 330 school days; there to period Lady Day 1755 to 30 April 1757, in which she attended on 455 school days; had 1,360 days at the school in total. Baptised 23 November 1740, daughter of William and Elizabeth. (Sister Sarah also at the school.) [ESRO PAR 254/25/1; PR]

RELF, Sarah (1748-): Brightling girls' charity school. Admitted between 30 April 1757 and 31 July 1758, in which period she attended on 322 school days; there at least to period 31 July 1758 to 31 December 1761 (no later records) in which she attended on 556 school days; had at least 878 days at the school. Baptised 28 January 1748, daughter of William and Elizabeth. (Sister Elizabeth also at the school.) [ESRO PAR 254/25/1; PR]

RELF, Richard: Taught by Sarah French at

Brightling, 1739-42. On 30 April 1740, John Fuller paid to her husband 11s 10d for teaching him and another boy to 26 April 1740; 15 May 1742, she was paid 15s 2d for schooling the same 2 boys. [ESRO SAS/RF 15/28]

RENOE, James (1730-): Saunders' charity school, Rye. In lists from 29 April 1741 (not in 7 January 1741) to June 1743 (?) (not in 26 October 1743). Baptised 29 May 1730, son of James and Ann Renow. [RSB; PR]

RENOE, William (1732-): Saunders' charity school, Rye. In lists from 5 January 1743 (not in 13 October 1742); 2 July 1746 notes 'Absent 5 weeks'; Michaelmas 1746 notes 'Absent 19 weeks' and name crossed out. Baptised 18 August 1732, son of William and Mary Reno. [RSB; PR]

REYNOLDS, Robert (1739-): Saunders' charity school, Rye. In lists from 25 March 1747 (not in Christmas 1746) to midsummer 1751, which notes 'Absent 10 weeks' (not in 2 October 1751). Baptised 25 May 1739, son of Robert and Mary. [RSB; PR]

RICE, Mary (1754-): At Seaford charity school 1765. Baptised 14 June 1754, daughter of Robert and Mary. [BL Add MS 33,059; PR]

RICH, George: Brighton charity school. Given prayer book 1715. [BSB]

RICH, Martha (1756-): Admitted Eastbourne charity school 27 April 1770. Baptised 29 August 1756, daughter of Richard and Elizabeth. [SAS Budgen MS v.105; PR]

RICHARDS, J. (-1770): Joel's school, Chichester. Died there 17 February 1770. The *Sussex Weekly Advertiser* published an elegy on his death written by a fellow scholar, D. F. junior. He had sung 2 pastoral duets, in the character of Damon, 18 December 1769. [*SWA* 26.2.70]

RICHARDS, James: Midhurst grammar school. Admitted as charity scholar 1790. [*HMGS*]

RICHARDSON, Ann (1757-): Mayfield charity school. Admitted 'Widow Dukes' dame school 11 July 1765; admitted charity school 2

May 1766; removed 20 July 1770, 'Sufficiently Learned', after 5 years at the school, ¾ year as a 'writer'. Baptised 12 May 1757, daughter of Nicholas and Anne. (Brother Nicholas also at the school.) [MSB; PR]

RICHARDSON, Constance (1739-): At Sedlescombe charity school 23 June 1748. Baptised 13 April 1739, daughter of Richard and Mary. (Brother Richard also at the school.) [SSB; PR]

RICHARDSON, Elizabeth (1745-): Mayfield charity school. Admitted 14 October 1755; removed 6 July 1759, 'sufficiently Learned', after 3¾ years at the school, 1¼ as a 'writer'. Baptised 7 April 1745, daughter of Thomas and Elizabeth. (Three brothers, 1 sister, also at the school.) [MSB; PR]

RICHARDSON, Elizabeth (1761-): Mayfield charity school. Admitted 9 April 1773; removed 9 July 1773, for non-attendance after ¼ year as a 'reader'. Baptised 25 October 1761, 'dau of Ann Richardson'. [MSB; PR]

RICHARDSON, George (1746-): Mayfield charity school. Admitted 9 April 1756; removed 26 October 1759, 'sufficiently learned', after 3½ years, 2 years as a 'writer'; re-admitted 10 July 1761, 'being lame with his arm by the small Pox'; removed 8 January 1762, 'For Misbehaviour after Admonition', having been at the school 4 years in total, 2½ years as a 'writer'. In his diary for 3 October 1759, Walter Gale, the master, who had been away for a month surveying, recorded: 'I came to Mayfield and found in the church-porch [the school was kept in the church] the two Wilmhursts and Geo. Richardson, who through James's too mild treatment was got to be master. I ordered him into the school, and took the management myself. I was told by Mr Downer that the day before James had been so indiscreet as to suffer Richardson's boy George to bring beer into the school, and, old Kent [one of the school managers] coming in before the mug was out, the boy asked him to drink; thereupon he fell into a great heat, and drove the boy out of the school.' Baptised 4 January 1747, son of Thomas and Lucy. (Six brothers, 2 sisters, also at the school.) [MSB; *SAC* **9**; PR]

RICHARDSON, George: Mayfield charity school. Admitted 11 April 1794; removed 13 April 1798, taken out by parents. [MSB]

[RICHARDSON, George]: In Wiston school list, c1803, and perhaps at the school in 1800. [WSRO Par 211/25/1]

RICHARDSON, Herbert (1757-): Mayfield charity school. In list for 11 January 1765, at the 'Widow Dukes' dame school; admitted charity school 19 April 1765; removed 21 April 1769, 'sufficiently Learned', after 4¼ years at the school, 1½ years as a 'writer'. Baptised 31 October 1757, son of Thomas and Lucy. (Six brothers, 2 sisters, also at the school.) [MSB; PR]

RICHARDSON, James (1761-): Mayfield charity school. Admitted 21 April 1769; removed 5 January 1775, 'Sufficiently Learned', after 5¾ years at the school, 2¾ years as a 'writer'. Baptised 21 October 1761, son of James and Goodgift. (Brother Thomas also at the school.) [MSB; PR]

RICHARDSON, John (1745-): Mayfield charity school. Admitted 27 March 1752; removed 9 April 1756, 'sufficiently learned', after 4 years at the school, 2¼ years as a 'writer'. Baptised 30 June 1745, son of Thomas and Lucy. (Six brothers, 2 sisters, also at the school.) [MSB; PR]

RICHARDSON, John (1753-): Mayfield charity school. Admitted 11 January 1760; removed 17 October 1760, 'for Non Attendance being taken into the Workhouse', after ¾ year as a 'reader'. Baptised 29 March 1753, son of Thomas and Elizabeth. (Two brothers, 2 sisters, also at the school.) [MSB; PR]

RICHARDSON, John (1778-): Mayfield charity school. Admitted 17 January 1788; removed 6 April 1792, 'Sufficiently Learned'. Baptised 22 November 1778, son of James and Anne. (Brother William also at the school.) [MSB; PR]

RICHARDSON, John: Mayfield charity school. Admitted 5 July 1793; removed 19 January 1798, taken out by parents. [MSB]

RICHARDSON, Lucy (1754-): Mayfield charity school. Admitted 6 July 1764; removed 2 May 1766, 'Sufficiently Learned', after 1¾ years at the school, all as a 'writer'. Baptised 29 April 1754, daughter of Thomas and Lucy. (Seven brothers, 1 sister, also at the school.) [MSB; PR]

RICHARDSON, Mary (1742-): Mayfield charity school. Admitted 10 January 1755, as a 'writer'; removed 9 April 1756, 'sufficiently learned', after 1¼ years at the school, all as a writer. Baptised 3 May 1742, daughter of Thomas and Lucy. (Seven brothers, 1 sister, also at the school.) [MSB; PR]

RICHARDSON, Mary (1750-): Mayfield charity school. Admitted 6 July 1759; removed 17 October 1760, 'for Non Attendance being taken into the Workhouse', after 1¼ years as a 'reader'. Baptised 25 February 1750, daughter of Thomas and Elizabeth. (Three brothers, 1 sister, also at the school.) [MSB; PR]

RICHARDSON, Matthew (1751-): Mayfield charity school. Admitted 17 October 1760; removed 6 July 1764, taken out by parents, after 3¾ years at the school, 1¾ years as a 'writer'. Baptised 2 December 1751, son of Thomas and Lucy. (Six brothers, 2 sisters, also at the school.) [MSB; PR]

RICHARDSON, Matthew: In October/November 1763 Mayfield parish paid Thomas Roads 2s 'for Schooling Matthew Richardson'; in December 1763/January 1764 he was paid 1s 'for Scouling of Thos Richardson's son'; and in March/April 1764, 1s 4d, April/May 1764, 8d. (In 1763 Ruth Levett was paid 1s 6d for 'making a pair of Bricks and Wastcoate for Mat'w Richardson'; and throughout the period Widow West was paid 1s 6d a week for keeping 'Thos Richardson's Child'.) Perhaps son of Thomas and Elizabeth, other children of whom were taken into the workhouse in 1760. [ESRO PAR 422/31/1/4; MSB]

RICHARDSON, Nicholas (1751-): Mayfield charity school. Admitted 2 May 1766; removed 17 April 1767, for non-attendance, after 1 year at the school, ¼ year as a 'writer'. Baptised 9 June 1751, son of Nicholas and Anne. (Sister Ann also at the school.) [MSB; PR]

RICHARDSON, Reuben: Mayfield charity school. Admitted 8 April 1796; removed 11 July 1800, taken out by parents. [MSB]

RICHARDSON, Richard (1750-): At Sedlescombe charity school 3 May 1755, 10 April 1758, 22 February 1759 (still a 'reader'), 1761. Baptised 16 July 1750, son of Richard and Mary. (Sister Constance also at the school.) [SSB; PR]

RICHARDSON, Robert (1747-): Mayfield charity school. Admitted 12 July 1754, but apparently did not attend then; also admitted 18 October 1754 (list of 10 January 1755 shows him with 1 quarter attendance only); removed 10 April 1758, 'sufficiently learned', but re-admitted 7 July 1758; removed 13 October 1758, 'sufficiently learned', after 3¾ years at the school in total, 2 years as a 'writer'. Baptised 30 January 1747, son of Thomas and Elizabeth. (Two brothers, 2 sisters, also at the school.) [MSB; PR]

RICHARDSON, Samuel (1755 or 56-): Mayfield charity school. Admitted 8 April 1763; removed 17 April 1767, taken out by parents, 'Well Learn'd', after 4 years at the school, 2 years as a 'writer'. Baptised 8 January 1756, son of Thomas and Lucy. (Six brothers, 2 sisters, also at the school.) [MSB; PR]

RICHARDSON, Thomas senior (1740-): Mayfield charity school. Admitted 5 October 1750; removed 18 October 1754, 'well learned', after 4 years at the school, 3½ years as a 'writer'. Baptised 28 September 1740, son of Thomas and Lucy. (Six brothers, 2 sisters, also at the school.) [MSB; PR]

RICHARDSON, Thomas junior (1743-): Mayfield charity school. Admitted 5 October 1750; removed 4 October 1751, for non-attendance; re-admitted 27 March 1752; removed 14 October 1755, 'well learned', after 3½ years at the school in total, 2¼ years as a 'writer'. Baptised 25 April 1743, son of Thomas and Elizabeth. (Two brothers, 2 sisters, also at the school.) [MSB; PR]

RICHARDSON, Thomas (1765-): Mayfield charity school. Admitted 7 April 1775; removed 17 January 1777, for non-attendance, after 1¾ years as a 'reader'. Baptised 21 July 1765, son

of James and Goodgift. (Brother James also at the school.) [MSB; PR]

RICHARDSON, William (1748-): Mayfield charity school. Admitted 9 April 1756; removed 11 January 1760, 'sufficiently Learned', after 3¾ years at the school, 1 year as a 'writer'. Baptised 31 May 1748, son of Thomas and Lucy. (Six brothers, 2 sisters also at the school.) [MSB; PR]

RICHARDSON, William (1775-): Mayfield charity school. Admitted 18 April 1783 (also admitted 11 July 1783, assigned to different charity source on expansion of school); removed 10 April 1789, for non-attendance, after 6 years at the school. Baptised 9 March 1775, son of James and Anne. (Brother John also at the school.) [MSB; PR]

RICHARDSON, William Westbrook (1788-1871): Midhurst grammar school. Later, of Findon Place; JP, and Deputy Lieutenant for Sussex. [*HMGS*]

RIPPINGTON, senior: At East Hoathly school 1755. In diary of Thomas Turner, master: 'Tues 1 July. Received of Rippington's boys 6d for 1 week's schooling due a-Saturday last.' [Vaisey, D., (ed) *The Diary of Thomas Turner*]

RIPPINGTON, junior: At East Hoathly school 1755. (See RIPPINGTON, senior, above.)

ROBBINS: Midhurst grammar school. At the school's first public performance of composition and oratory, 5 November 1799, took part, with one other, in a scene from Thomson's *Agamemnon*, playing Arcas. At the second 'literary performance', 27 May 1800, took part, with 3 others, in a scene from Virgil's *Aeneid*. [*SWA* 11.11.99, 2.6.1800]

ROBERTS, Abel: Admitted Fermor's charity school, Rotherfield, 25 May 1794 ('Feb'ry 2d' in margin). Son of William. [ESRO PAR 465/4/1]

ROBERTS, William (1753-): At Seaford charity school 1765. Baptised 4 November 1753, son of William and Susanna. [BL Add MS 33,059; PR]

ROBERTS, William (1782-): Admitted Fermor's charity school, Rotherfield, 1 June 1792. 'Son of John and Hannah Roberts'. Baptised 24 December 1782, son of John and Naomi (Naomi buried 30 July 1785; John, widower, and Hannah Dray married 24 April 1787). [ESRO PAR 465/4/1; PR]

ROBBINSON, George (1764-): Saunders' charity school, Rye. Admitted 22 June 1774; in lists to Christmas 1777, which notes 'Left School'. Baptised 23 May 1764, son of John and Mary. (Brother John also at the school.) [RSB; PR]

ROBINSON, John (1759-): Saunders' charity school, Rye. Admitted 29 June 1768; in lists to Christmas 1770 (not in midsummer 1773, next surviving list). Baptised 25 September 1759, son of John and Mary. (Brother George also at the school.) [RSB; PR]

ROBBINSON, Thomas Chatterton (1762-): Saunders' charity school, Rye. Admitted 19 August 1772, as 'Thomas Chariton son of Elizabeth Dyett'; in lists to Michaelmas 1773 under this name; in next list, Michaelmas 1774, becomes 'Thomas Chatterton Robbinson' (same admission date, same position in list); in lists under this name to Michaelmas 1775 (not in Christmas 1777, next surviving list). Baptised 1 December 1762, 'Thomas Chatterton Bastard Son of Elizabeth Robinson'. [RSB; PR]

ROBSON: Button's school, Lewes. To recite at a 'Public Examination' at the *Star Assembly Room*, 22 June 1797. [*SWA* 19.6.97]

ROGERS: Midhurst grammar school. At a public performance of composition and oratory, 27 May 1800, took part, with one other, in a scene of Wolsey and Cromwell. A Mr Rogers was listed among the gentry attending. [*SWA* 2.6.1800]

ROGERS, James: Admitted Fermor's charity school, Rotherfield, 5 June 1796. ('James' in marginal note.) Son of Henry. [ESRO PAR 465/4/1]

ROGERS, John: Saunders' charity school, Rye. In list for 8 April 1724 (not in January 1724 (?)); not in next list, 4 November 1724, to June 1725 (?); in lists from 11 August 1725 to 10 January 1728 (17 April 1728 notes 'left the school'). Son of John. [RSB]

ROGERS, John: Saunders' charity school, Rye. Admitted 22 June 1774; in lists to Lady Day 1779, which notes 'left School' (next list midsummer 1779). Baptised 7 July 1769, son of John and Ann; but sister, not identified as twin, baptised same day, and John probably born earlier - at this date would have been very young for this school. (Brother William also at the school.) [RSB; PR]

ROGERS, Richard (1703-): Brighton charity school. Given prayer book 1716 or 1717. Baptised 8 September 1703, son of Richard and Sarah (another RR baptised 2 December 1700, same parents, and another RR baptised 1 October 1702, buried 23 October 1702, same parents). [BSB; PR]

ROGERS, William Rabbett (1770-): Saunders' charity school, Rye. Admitted 12 January 1780; in lists to Lady Day 1782 (not in 2 September 1782). Baptised 28 September 1770, son of John and Anne. (Brother John also at the school.) [RSB; PR]

ROLLINS: Grey Coat charity school, Chichester. Left between Michaelmas 1759 and Michaelmas 1760. Given 10s 6d on leaving. [WSRO Cap.V/1/1]

[ROOK, Benjamin (1794-)]: In Wiston school list, c1803, and perhaps at the school in 1800. Baptised 26 June 1794, son of Henry and Sarah. [WSRO Par 211/25/1; PR]

ROOK, Fanny (1791-): In Wiston school list, c1803, and probably at the school in 1800. Baptised 31 January 1791, daughter of Henry and Sarah. [WSRO Par 211/25/1; PR]

ROOTS?, Josias - see **BOOTS, Josias**

ROSE, Elizabeth (1745-): Mayfield charity school. Admitted 9 April 1755; removed 14 October 1755, for non-attendance, after ½ year as a 'reader'; apparently re-admitted 9 July 1756; in list for 24 January 1757 her name is crossed out. Baptised 15 September 1745, daughter of Richard and Mary. (Four brothers also at the school.) [MSB; PR]

ROSE, Elizabeth (1778-): Mayfield charity school. Admitted 15 October 1784; removed 9 April 1790, taken out by parents but 'Sufficiently Learned', after 5½ years at the school. Baptised 29 March 1778, daughter of John and Anne. (Two brothers, 3 sisters, also at the school.) [MSB; PR]

ROSE, George (1749-): Mayfield charity school. Admitted 17 October 1760; removed 13 April 1764, for non-attendance after 3½ years at the school, still a 'reader'. Baptised 17 October 1749, son of Richard and Mary. (Three brothers, 1 sister, also at the school.) [MSB; PR]

ROSE, James (1787-): Mayfield charity school. Admitted 10 July 1795; removed 12 April 1799. Baptised 23 December 1787, son of John and Ann. (One brother, 4 sisters, also at the school.) [MSB; PR]

ROSE, Jenny (1782 or 83-): Mayfield charity school. Admitted 11 January 1793; removed 11 April 1794. Baptised (Jane) 18 January 1783, daughter of John and Ann. (Two brothers, 3 sisters, also at the school.) [MSB; PR]

ROSE, John (1744-): Mayfield charity school. Admitted 27 March 1752; removed 8 April 1757, taken away by parents, after 5 years at the school, 1¾ years as a 'writer'. Baptised 10 June 1744, son of Richard and Mary. (Three brothers, 1 sister, also at the school.) [MSB; PR]

ROSE, John (1779-): Mayfield charity school. Admitted 6 April 1787; removed 13 July 1791, taken out by parents. Baptised 31 October 1779, son of John and Anne. (One brother, 4 sisters, also at the school.) [MSB; PR]

ROSE, Mary (1782 or 83-): Mayfield charity school. Admitted 11 April 1794; removed 14 October 1796, taken out by parents. Baptised 18 January 1783, daughter of John and Ann. (Two brothers, 3 sisters, also at the school.) [MSB; PR]

ROSE, Philadelphia (1790-): Mayfield charity school. Admitted 6 January 1797; removed 14 October 1801, 'sufficiently learned'. Baptised 2 May 1790, daughter of John and Ann. (Two brothers, 3 sisters, also at the school.) [MSB; PR]

ROSE, Richard (1748-): Mayfield charity school. Admitted 17 October 1760; removed 10 July 1761, 'for Incapacity', after ¾ year as a 'writer'. Baptised 10 April 1748, son of Richard and Mary. (Three brothers, 1 sister, also at the school.) [MSB; PR]

ROSE, Thomas (1751-): Mayfield charity school. Admitted 17 October 1760; removed 19 April 1765, taken out by parents, after 4½ years at the school, still a 'reader'. Baptised 6 October 1751, son of Richard and Mary. (Three brothers, 1 sister, also at the school.) [MSB; PR]

ROSE, William: Mayfield charity school. Admitted 11 October 1793; no formal removal, but in list for 9 January 1795 he is replaced, in same position in list, by 'William Berry', for whom no formal admission [qv - perhaps same person; WB removed 8 April 1796, taken out by parents. [MSB]

RUSSELL, John (1726-): Saunders' charity school, Rye. In lists from 9 October 1734 (not in 31 July 1734) to 20 October 1736 (not in 29 December 1736). Son of John, deceased. Baptised 13 March 1726, son of John and Sarah. [RSB; PR]

[RUSSELL, Richard (1687-1759)]: At Lewes grammar school, perhaps early in 18th century. Baptised 26 November 1687, St Michael, Lewes, son of Nathaniel and Mary. Runaway marriage with only daughter and heiress of William Kempe of Malling Deanery (later reconciled with her family). Studied medicine at University of Leyden; Doctor of Medicine. Returned to Lewes 1729; occupied Malling Deanery soon after. 1750 published book (in Latin) advocating sea bathing for medical reasons; English version 1753, by which time he had so many patients at Brighton that he built Russell House there and moved in 1754. In 1755 published another book on diseases of the glands. Died in London 19 December 1759, aged 72 (buried at South Malling). Son William became serjeant at law; assumed mother's name of Kempe; died with out issue. Daughter Hannah married William Pepys. [Dale, A., in *SNQ* **14**]

RUTLEY, Alexander (1733-): Saunders' charity school, Rye. In lists from 2 July 1746 (not in Christmas 1745) to midsummer 1747, which notes 'Absent 11 weeks' and Michaelmas 1747, which notes 'Absent 23 weeks' (not in Christmas 1747). Baptised 28 November 1733, son of Alexander and Judith. [RSB; PR]

SAGE, Nicholas (1756-): At Seaford charity school 1765. 'Son of Sarah Sage'. Baptised 1 October 1756, son of Nicholas and Sarah. [BL Add MS 33,059; PR]

SALES, Joseph: Admitted Fermor's charity school, Rotherfield, 10 May 1793. Son of Samuel. [ESRO PAR 465/4/1]

SALES, Joseph: Admitted Fermor's charity school, Rotherfield, 29 April 1798. Son of Joseph. [ESRO PAR 465/4/1]

SALVAGE, Lucy: Dairymaid at John Ellman's farm, Glynde. Taught by Charles Payne, shepherd, engaged as schoolmaster by Ellman to teach the men and maidservants in his house to read and write. She married Charles Payne 4 November 1796 (but signed by mark). [Walesby, A., 'Memoir of John Ellman', *Library of Agricultural and Horticultural Knowledge* (4th edition); PR]

SANDERS - see SAUNDERS

SANDHAM: At Midhurst grammar school, 1793. Later a major in the Royal Artillery. [*HMGS*]

SARGENT: Admitted Eastbourne charity school January 1780. Daughter of George. [SAS Budgen MS v.117]

SARGENT, George: Eastbourne charity school. Admitted midsummer 1778; there 1779. [SAS Budgen MS v.117]

SARGENT, John (1722-): At Eastbourne charity school 1734. Baptised 11 November 1722, son of Mark and Katherine. [Chatsworth, Devonshire Collection, Compton Place, Box P; PR]

SANDERS: Taught by Sarah French at Brightling, 1735-36. On 18 May 1736, John

Fuller paid her for teaching 'Sanders Boy' 35 weeks at 2d a week. [ESRO SAS/RF 15/28]

SANDERS (SAUNDERS), Anne (1732-): Brightling girls' charity school. Admitted 7 April 1741; there to 23-month period ending 22 March 1744, in which she attended on 370 school days; had 660 days at the school in total. Baptised 26 March 1732, Anne and Lucy daughters of Samuel and [*blank*]. (Sister Lucy also at the school.) [ESRO PAR 254/25/1; PR]

SANDERS, George: Brighton charity school. Admitted as 'reader' sometime after list of (probably) January 1702; in list of 'writers' December 1705. Baptised either 28 October 1690, George and John twins of Robert (brother John also at the school (qv), perhaps brother Robert also) or 7 October 1695, son of William and Jane (née Vinson) (perhaps brother Robert also at the school). [BSB; PR]

SAUNDERS, James: Brighton charity school. Given prayer book 1715. (Perhaps baptised 13 January 1708, son of William, but would have been much younger than all others in list.) [BSB; PR]

SANDERS, John (1690-): Brighton charity school. Admitted as 'reader' sometime after list of (probably) January 1702; in list of 'writers' December 1705. Baptised 28 October 1690, George and John twins of Robert (mother probably Mary, from baptism of son Robert 1687). (Brother George probably also at the school, perhaps brother Robert also.) [BSB; PR]

SAUNDERS, John: Mayfield charity school. Admitted 11 April 1777; removed 12 April 1782, taken out by parents, after 5 years at the school, 2 years as a 'writer'. (No baptism in parish register; perhaps nonconformist family; house of Richard Sanders registered for worship of Anabaptists 1733.) [MSB; WSRO Ep.II/25/1]

SAUNDERS, John (1786 or 87-): Mayfield charity school. Admitted 17 October 1794; removed 12 October 1798, 'Sufficiently Learned'. Baptised 7 January 1787, son of Mary Saunders. [MSB; PR]

SAUNDERS (SANDERS), John (1791-):

Mayfield charity school. Admitted 18 October 1799; removed 8 April 1803, taken out by parents. Baptised 2 October 1791, son of John and Catharine. [MSB; PR]

SAUNDERS (SANDERS), Joseph (1778-): Mayfield charity school. Admitted 7 July 1786; removed 15 October 1789, for non-attendance. Baptised 26 April 1778, son of John and Susanna. (Three brothers, 1 sister also at the school.) [MSB; PR]

SANDERS (SAUNDERS), Lucy (1732-): Brightling girls' charity school. Admitted 31 January 1743; there to 23-month period ending 22 March 1744, in which she attended on 189 school days, all she had at the school. Baptised 26 March 1732, Anne and Lucy, daughters of Samuel and [*blank*]. (Sister Anne also at the school.) [ESRO PAR 254/25/1; PR]

SANDERS, Mary (c1724-): Brightling girls' charity school. Admitted 6 April 1735, aged 11; had left by 21 April 1738. [ESRO PAR 254/25/1]

SAUNDERS, Mary (1768-): Mayfield charity school. Admitted 10 October 1777; removed 11 July 1778, taken out by parents, after ¾ year as a 'reader'. Baptised 24 January 1768, daughter of John and Susanna. (Four brothers also at the school.) [MSB; PR]

SAUNDERS, Richard: Mayfield charity school. Admitted 5 April 1776; removed 9 April 1779, taken out by parents, after 3 years at the school, 1 year as a 'writer'. (No baptism in parish register; perhaps nonconformist family - see under SAUNDERS, John.) [MSB]

SANDERS, Robert: Brighton charity school. Given coat and hat July 1702. Baptised either 11 September 1687, son of Robert and Mary (brother John, perhaps brother George, also at the school) or 28 October 1688, son of William and Jane (née Vinson) (perhaps brother George also at the school). [BSB; PR]

SAUNDERS (SANDERS), Samuel (1780-): Mayfield charity school. Admitted 17 January 1788; removed 11 January 1793, for non-attendance. Baptised 18 June 1780, son of John and Susanna. (Three brothers, 1 sister, also at the school.) [MSB; PR]

SAUNDERS (SANDERS), Thomas (1706?-): Brighton charity school. Given prayer book 1716 or 1717. Perhaps baptised at Brighton 30 June 1706, son of Thomas and Elizabeth, of Chichester, Presbyterians (sister Elizabeth baptised same day). [BSB; Union Street Independent Chapel (Presbyterian) register]

SAUNDERS (SANDERS), Thomas (1772-): Mayfield charity school. Admitted 6 March 1781; removed 7 April 1786, 'Sufficiently Learned'. Baptised 30 August 1772, son of John and Susanna. (Three brothers, 1 sister, also at the school.) [MSB; PR]

SAUNDERS William: Brighton charity school. Given prayer book 1716 or 1717. [BSB]

SAUNDERS (SANDERS), William (1774-): Mayfield charity school. Admitted 2 August 1782; removed July 1785, for non-attendance. Baptised 18 June 1774, son of John and Susanna. (Three brothers, 1 sister, also at the school.) [MSB; PR]

(SAWYER): A poor child of Alfriston for whom the parish paid 8s for schooling, 1772. [ESRO PAR 230/1/1/1]

[*SAYERS, Elizabeth*]: In Wiston school list c1803, and perhaps at the school in 1800. [WSRO Par 211/25/1]

SCALE: Grey Coat charity school, Chichester. Left between Michaelmas 1757 and Michaelmas 1758. Given 10s 6d on leaving. [WSRO Cap.V/1/1]

SCALE, John: Grey Coat charity school, Chichester. Left between Michaelmas 1753 and Michaelmas 1754. Given 10s 6d on leaving. [WSRO Cap.V/1/l]

SCARDFIELD: Grey Coat charity school, Chichester. Left between Michaelmas 1754 and Michaelmas 1755. Given 10s 6d on leaving. [WSRO Cap.V/1/1]

SCOTT, James (1708-): Saunders' charity school, Rye. In lists from September 1722 (?) (first list) to January 1724 (?) (not in 8 April 1724). Son of John, mariner. Born 1 May 1708, baptised 8 August 1716, son of John and Lydia. [RSB; PR]

SCOTT, James (1749-): Saunders' charity school, Rye. Shown as addendum to list of 7 April 1756 but not in midsummer 1756; in lists from Michaelmas 1756 to 11 January 1758, where marked 'October 10 1757'. Baptised 15 February 1749, son of John and Mercy. [RSB; PR]

SEAL, Henry (1725-): Saunders' charity school, Rye. In lists from 5 July 1732 (not in 29 March 1732) to 3 October 1739 (6 January 1740 notes 'left the school'). Son of Henry, deceased. Baptised 5 February 1725, son of Henry and Ann. (Brother William also at the school.) [RSB; PR]

SEAL, Robert (1726-): Saunders' charity school, Rye. In lists from 9 July 1740 (not in 2 April 1740) to 15 October 1740 (7 January 1741 notes 'left the school'). Son of William, deceased. Baptised 3 June 1726, son of William and Mary. [RSB; PR]

SEAL, William (1726-): Saunders' charity school, Rye. In lists from 7 April 1736 (not in 28 January 1736) to 7 July 1742 (13 October 1742 notes 'left the school'); had 6½ years at the school. Son of Henry, deceased. Baptised 16 July 1726, son of Henry and Amy. (Brother Henry also at the school.) [RSB; PR]

(SEARLE): child of E. Searle at Widow Page's school, Clapham, June 1772. [*SAC* **71**]

SELLENS/SELLINS

SELLINS (SELLENS), James (1792-): Sedlescombe charity school. Admitted 1798; there 20 August 1798, a 'reader'; changed to 'now writer' in list of 13 January 1800. Baptised 13 May 1792, son of Robert and Mary. (Brothers John, Robert, also at the school.) [SSB; PR]

SELLINS (SELENS), John (1787-): Sedlescombe charity school. There 25 December 1797 (a 'writer') and in list for 20 August 1798 (crossed through). Baptised 23 December 1787, son of Robert and Mary. (Brothers James, Robert, also at the school.) [SSB; PR]

SELLINS (SELENS), Robert (1786-): Sedlescombe charity school. There 21 October

1793 (a 'writer') and 20 October 1794. Baptised 30 July 1786, son of Robert and Mary. (Brothers James, John, also at the school.) [SSB; PR]

SELLENS, Samuel (1776-): Mayfield charity school. Admitted 8 April 1785; removed 12 October 1787, for non-attendance (incorrectly shown as 'Thomas' - Thomas was removed 7 July 1786; Samuel in 6 July 1787 list, not in 12 October 1787). Baptised 28 March 1776, son of Thomas and Hannah. (Brother Thomas also at the school.) [MSB; PR]

SELLENS, Thomas (1774-): Mayfield charity school. Admitted 11 July 1783; removed 7 July 1786, for non-attendance. Baptised 25 August 1774, son of Thomas and Hannah. (Brother Samuel also at the school.) [MSB; PR]

SEYMOUR, Charlotte (-1805): Taught dancing by Stephen Philpot [qv]. Daughter of Charles, 6th Duke of Somerset, of Petworth House, and his second wife Charlotte (née Finch: they married 1726). Married 6 October 1750, Heneage, Earl of Aylesford. Died 15 February 1805. [*Burke's Peerage*]

SEYMOUR, Frances (-1761): Taught dancing by Stephen Philpot [qv]. Daughter of Charles, 6th Duke of Somerset, of Petworth House, and his second wife Charlotte (née Finch: they married 1726). Married 3 September 1750, John, Marquess of Granby. Died 25 January 1761. [*Burke's Peerage*]

SHARP, Elizabeth (1724-): Brightling girls' charity school. Admitted 3 May 1736; had left by 21 April 1738. Baptised 13 September 1724, daughter of Joseph and Sarah. [ESRO PAR 254/25/1; PR]

SHEATHER, Isaac (1729-): Eastbourne charity school. There December 1738 (?), April 1741. Baptised 13 December 1729, son of Daniel and Anne. (Brother William also at the school.) [SAS Budgen MS v.129; PR]

SHEATHER, William (1726-): At Eastbourne charity school 1734. Baptised 6 January 1727, son of Daniel and Ann. (Brother Isaac also at the school.) [Chatsworth, Devonshire Collection, Compton Place, Box P; PR]

SHELLEY, Percy Bysshe (1792-1822): Shelley, the poet, was born 4 August 1792 at Field Place, Warnham, eldest son of Timothy, MP, and Elizabeth (née Pilfold). At 6 he was sent to a day school in Warnham kept by the vicar (Richard Harvey), where he learnt the rudiments of Latin and Greek. At 10, sent to Syon House Academy, Isleworth; at 12, to Eton. (For an account of him reciting what he had learnt at the Warnham school, see Schedule 1, WARNHAM, Harvey's school; for his connection with Elizabeth Hitchener, schoolmistress of Hurstpierpoint, see her entry in Schedule 2.) [Holmes, R. *Shelley: The Pursuit* (1974); CI]

SHELTON, Charles: Eastbourne charity school. Admitted 3 April 1769; there January 1771. Son of William. [SAS Budgen MS v.105]

SHERGOLD, Samuel: Mossop's school, Brighton. Left a description of Mossop. Son of Mr Shergold of the Castle tavern. [Bishop]

SHOESMITH, Stephen (1757-): Mayfield charity school. Admitted 6 July 1764; removed 16 October 1767, 'Sufficiently Learned', after 3¼ years at the school, 1½ years as a 'writer'. Baptised 17 April 1757, son of Stephen and Martha. [MSB; PR]

SHORE, Jack: A boarder at John Hart's school, Hurstpierpoint, 1727-31, the fee of £14 pa being paid by Henry Campion of Danny. Probably son of Elizabeth Shore (who received the £14 for his board, 31 July 1731); in 1736 Campion received, on behalf of Mrs Shore and her children, £1,901 from Thomas Pelham for their share of Plumpton estate. [ESRO DAN 2198]

SIDGER: A poor boy of Winchelsea for whose schooling the parish paid. On 30 May 1766, Mr Hogsflesh received £1 10s 'for 1 Years Schooling for young Bennet Sutus & Sidger'. For each of the two following church years (1767-68, 1768-69) the parish paid him £1 10s, probably for the same 3 boys. [ESRO PAR 511/31/1/1]

SIMMONS, Matthew (1765-): Saunders' charity school, Rye. Admitted 14 October 1772; in lists to Michaelmas 1775 (not in Christmas 1777, next surviving list). No parents named in lists; baptised 5 March 1765, 'Matthew Bastard Son of Eliz: Simmonds'. [RSB; PR]

SIMMONS, William (1776-): Mayfield charity school. Admitted 15 October 1784; removed 5 January 1787, for non-attendance. Baptised 2 July 1776, son of Thomas and Sarah. [MSB; PR]

SINDEN, Thomas: Sedlescombe charity school. There 8 May 1775, a 'reader'. [SSB]

SISLEY, Thomas: Saunders' charity school, Rye. In lists from 29 March 1732 (not in 19 January 1732) to 7 April 1736 (20 October 1736 notes 'left the school'). Son of Thomas. [RSB]

SISLEY, William (1712-): Saunders' charity school, Rye. In lists from September 1722 (?) (first list) to 5 October 1726 (11 January 1727 notes 'Absent from Schooll'). Baptised 11 July 1712, son of Thomas and Mary. [RSB; PR]

SISLEY, Zilpah: Mayfield charity school. Admitted 10 April 1761; removed 14 October 1763, for non-attendance, after 2½ years as a 'reader'; re-admitted 17 October 1766; removed 17 April 1767, taken out by parents 'but pretty well learn'd'? (though apparently still a 'reader'). [MSB]

SKINNER, Anne (1728?-): Brightling girls' charity school. Had 183 days at the school in year ending 1 May 1741; on 7 April 1741 the trustees ordered: 'Anne Skinner daughter of William Skinner her mother not sending her to school be discharged'. But 'William' probably an error: in 1 May 1741 list there are two ASs, one marked 'JS' (ie John Skinner - see AS below), one marked 'TS' (ie probably Thomas Skinner); and this AS probably baptised 18 May 1728, daughter of Thomas and Dennys (if so, sister Eden also at the school). [ESRO PAR 254/25/1; PR]

SKINNER, Anne (1732-): Brightling girls' charity school. Had 98 days at the school in year ending 1 May 1741; on 7 April 1741 the trustees ordered: 'Whereas Anne Skinner daughter of John Skinner a Baseborne Child was borne in the parish of Ewhurst and belongeth to the said parish of Ewhurst be discharged'. Baptised 19 March 1732, 'Anne ye illegitimate daughter of Elizabeth Morris'. [ESRO PAR 254/25/1; Ewhurst PR]

SKINNER, David (1777-): Mayfield charity school. Admitted 9 April 1790; removed 13 July 1791, for non-attendance. Baptised 18 May 1777, son of William and Susanna. (Brothers Henry, Trayton, also at the school.) [MSB; PR]

SKINNER, Eden (Ede) (1735-): Brightling girls' charity school. Admitted between 2 April 1744 and 31 August 1745, in which period she attended on 274 school days; there to period 1 September 1745 to 31 July 1747, in which she attended on 232 school days; had 506 days at the school in total. Baptised 21 May 1735, daughter of Thomas and Dennes. (Sister Anne probably also at the school.) [ESRO PAR 254/25/1; PR]

SKINNER, Elizabeth: At Haslewood school, Buxted, 1738 (and perhaps 1739 also, when list of 3 included 'either Dray's or Skinner's Child'), perhaps under Saunders' charity schooling for girls. [ESRO PAR 286/1/1/1]

SKINNER, Fanny (1791-): Mayfield charity school. Admitted 12 July 1799; removed 8 April 1803, taken out by parents. Baptised 3 July 1791, daughter of William and Lucy. [MSB; PR]

SKINNER, George: Mayfield charity school. Admitted 7 October 1791; removed 11 October 1793. [MSB]

SKINNER, Henry (1779-): Mayfield charity school. Admitted 10 April 1789; removed 6 July 1792, taken out by parents but 'Sufficiently Learned'. Baptised 21 February 1779, son of William and Susanna. (Brothers David, Trayton, also at the school.) [MSB; PR]

SKINNER, James: Mayfield charity school. Admitted 6 July 1792; removed 11 October 1793. [MSB]

SKINNER, Mary (1744-): Brightling girls' charity school. Admitted between 10 June 1749 and 29 September 1752, in which period she attended on 317 school days; there to period 29 September 1752 to Lady Day 1755, in which

she attended on 650 school days; had 967 days at the school in total. Baptised 27 October 1744, daughter of Richard and [Mary]. [ESRO PAR 254/25/1; PR]

SKINNER, Ruth (1786-): Mayfield charity school. Admitted 11 July 1794; removed 7 July 1797, taken out by parents; apparently re-admitted 6 July 1798; removed 12 April 1799, taken out by parents. Baptised 21 May 1786, 'Ruth Daughter of Elizabeth Skinner'. [MSB; PR]

SKINNER, Trayton (1782-): Mayfield charity school. Admitted 10 April 1789; removed 11 July 1794, 'sufficiently learned'. Baptised 5 May 1782, son of William and Susanna. (Brothers David, Henry, also at the school.) [MSB; PR]

SMALE, James (1771-): Mayfield charity school. Admitted 7 April 1780; removed 9 April 1784, 'Sufficiently Learned'. Baptised 22 December 1771, son of Thomas and Anne. (Two brothers also at the school.) [MSB; PR]

SMALE, Samuel (1773-): Mayfield charity school. Admitted 6 July 1781; removed 14 January 1785, 'Sufficiently Learned'. Baptised 20 June 1773, son of Thomas and Anne. (Two brothers also at the school.) [MSB; PR]

SMALE, Stephen (1778-): Mayfield charity school. Admitted 11 April 1788; removed 12 October 1792, taken out by parents. Baptised 4 July 1778, son of Thomas and Anne. (Two brothers also at the school.) [MSB; PR]

SMART: Grey Coat charity school, Chichester. Left between Michaelmas 1777 and Michaelmas 1778. Given 10s 6d on leaving. [WSRO Cap.V/1/1]

SMART, Harriet: Admitted Petworth charity school 1 April 1799. [WSRO Petworth House Archives 1763]

SMELT: Midhurst grammar school. At the school's first public performance of composition and oratory, 5 November 1799, took part, with one other, in a scene from Shakespeare's *Julius Caesar*, in the role of Cassius. At the second 'literary performance', 27 May 1800, took part, with one other, in the scene of Edward and Warwick. [*SWA* 11.11.99, 2.6.1800]

SMITH: Grey Coat charity school, Chichester. Left between Michaelmas 1763 and Michaelmas 1764. Given 10s 6d on leaving. [WSRO Cap.V/1/1]

(SMITH): Child of Richard Smith at Widow Page's school, Clapham, June 1772. [*SAC* **71**]

SMITH: Button's school, Lewes. To recite at a 'Public Examination' at the *Star Assembly Room*, 22 June 1797. [*SWA* 19.6.97]

SMITH, Abigail (1771-): Mayfield charity school. Admitted 17 July 1778; removed 11 October 1782, 'Sufficiently Learned'. Baptised 17 March 1771, daughter of Thomas and Rachel. (Brother Thomas also at the school.) [MSB; PR]

SMITH, Charlotte (1749-1806)   -   see *TURNER, Charlotte*

SMITH, Elizabeth (1765-): A poor girl of Fletching for whose schooling the parish paid Elizabeth Gillham 6s 1½d (on 17 March 1776) and 4s 11½d (on 23 March 1777). Baptised 10 November 1765, daughter of Thomas and Jane. [ESRO SPK/P1; PR]

SMITH, Henry (1692-): Brighton charity charity school. Admitted as 'reader' sometime after list of (probably) January 1702; joined 'writers' class sometime after 12 January 1702; had left by December 1705, being 'removed to London'. Baptised 31 January 1692, son of Henry and Joan (née Bish). [BSB; PR]

SMITH, James (1765-): Saunders' charity school, Rye. Admitted 22 June 1774; in lists to Michaelmas 1775 (not in Christmas 1777, next surviving list). Baptised 13 September 1765, son of Thomas and Sarah. [RSB; PR]

SMITH, John: Grey Coat charity school, Chichester. Left between Michaelmas 1766 and Michaelmas 1767. Given 10s 6d on leaving. [WSRO Cap.V/1/1]

SMITH, Martha (Patty) (-1775): Lover's school, Chichester. In 1727 she was given a 'copy' by him, just before he galloped off and

was killed [qv Schedule 2, LOVER, Joshua]. Daughter of John Smith (brother of William, Baptist minister) and Sarah (née King). Married, 1734, at New Fishbourne, James Spershott, joiner, who in 1756 became joint Baptist minister. Buried 12 November 1775. [*SAC* **30**, **90**; *Chichester Papers* **30** 2, 18; Chichester St Pancras PR]

SMITH, R.: Grey Coat charity school, Chichester. Left between Michaelmas 1768 and Michaelmas 1769. Given 10s 6d on leaving. [WSRO Cap.V/1/1]

SMITH, Richard (1748-): Saunders' charity school, Rye. In lists from 16 April 1760 (not in midsummer 1759, previous surviving list) to Michaelmas 1761 (not in 20 January 1762). Son of William, deceased. Baptised 23 September 1748, son of William and Sarah. [RSB; PR]

SMITH, Sarah: Mayfield charity school. Admitted 7 January 1791; removed 6 January 1792. [MSB]

SMITHE (SMITH), Thomas (1729-): Saunders' charity school, Rye. In lists from 20 October 1736 (not in 7 April 1736) to 2 April 1740 (9 July 1740 notes 'left the school'). Son of John, deceased. Baptised 10 October 1729, son of John and Mary. [RSB; PR]

SMITH, Thomas (1735-): Mayfield charity school. Admitted 4 October 1751; removed 27 March 1752, 'well learned'; had been a 'writer' for the ½ year. (NB Edward Fry, same age, joined and left at same time, also 'well learned' after 6 months.) Baptised 1 January 1736, son of Thomas and Sarah. [MSB; PR]

SMITH, Thomas (1764-): Mayfield charity school. Admitted July 1771; suspended 7 July 1775 'on account of a Broken Leg'; re-admitted 13 October 1775; removed 11 October 1776, for non-attendance, after 5 years in total at the school, 2¼ years as a 'writer'. Baptised 8 April 1764, son of Thomas and Rachel. (Sister Abigail also at the school). [MSB; PR]

SMITH, William (1725-): Saunders' charity school, Rye. In lists from 29 March 1732 (not in 19 January 1732) to 27 March 1734 (31 July 1734 notes 'left the school'). Son of William, shown as 'deceased' in lists from 4 July 1733 (WS buried 17 June 1733). Probably baptised 17 March 1725, son of William and Eleanor (an earlier WS, same parents, baptised 1722, died 1722); but another WS, same parents, baptised 18 October 1732 (no burial of WS baptised 1725 in parish register). [RSB; PR]

SMITH, William: Saunders' charity school, Rye. In lists from 11 January 1738 (not in 5 October 1737) to 3 October 1739 (6 February 1740 notes 'left the school'). Son of William (not shown as 'deceased'). [RSB]

SMITH, William (1751-): Mayfield charity school. Admitted 11 July 1760; removed 17 October 1760, 'for Non Attendance being taken into the Workhouse', after ¼ year as a 'reader'. Baptised 25 August 1751, son of William and Mary. [MSB; PR]

SOMERS, Michael: Mayfield charity school. Admitted 29 March 1751; removed 28 June 1751, for non-attendance. [MSB]

SOUTER: Grey Coat charity school, Chichester. Left between Michaelmas 1751 and Michaelmas 1752. Given 10s 6d on leaving. [WSRO Cap.V/1/1]

SOUTHERTON / SUTHERTON

SUTHERTON: Grey Coat charity school, Chichester. Left between Michaelmas 1750 and Michaelmas 1751. On leaving, given 10s 6d 'towards clothing'. [WSRO Cap.V/1/1]

SOUTHERTON, Daniel (c1702-): Grey Coat charity school, Chichester. Admitted at opening of school Lady Day 1710. Aged 8 at Lady Day 1711. There Lady Day 1714. [WSRO Cap.V/1/1]

SPEARS, George (1786-): Sedlescombe charity school. There 21 October 1793, 20 October 1794, 25 December 1797 and 20 August 1798 (still a 'reader'). Baptised 19 March 1786, son of Robert and Elizabeth. [SSB; PR]

SPEARS, Robert: Sedlescombe charity school. There 21 October 1793 (a 'writer') and 20 October 1794. [SSB]

SPEED, John (1694-): Brighton charity school. In list of 'readers' of (probably) January 1702; given coat and hat July 1702; had left by December 1705. Baptised 18 November 1694, son of John and Susanna (née Howell). [BSB; PR]

SPEED, Matthew (1701?-): Brighton charity school. Given prayer book 1715. Probably baptised 20 April 1701, son of John. [BSB; PR]

SPEED, William (1695-): Brighton charity school. Admitted as 'reader' sometime after list of (probably) January 1702; joined 'writers' class sometime after 12 January 1702; in list of 'writers' December 1705. Baptised 13 October 1695, son of John and Elizabeth (née Speed). [BSB; PR]

SPERSHOTT, James (1710-89): 'Between the time of my Birth in 1710, and the year 1725, I was about 8 years at convenient times a School boy in Chichester, Sent by my Parents Living in the Manor Farm at Shopweek, since which time I have been a resident of the said City about 58 years.' Baptist; baptised as adult 6 September 1729; married 1734, at New Fishbourne, Martha (Patty) Smith [qv], daughter of John and Sarah, and niece of William Smith, Baptist minister (and father of the 3 Smith artist brothers); she died 1755. Joint Baptist minister 1756. Died 15 February 1789, aged 80, 'many years Preacher to the Anabaptist Meeting in the city of Chichester'. [*SAC* **29**, **90**; *SWA* 2.3.89]

SPICER, Inchen: Brighton charity school. In list of 'writers' 12 February 1702; had left by December 1705 and gone 'to sea'. [BSB]

SQUIRES (otherwise WELLS), Alexander (1782-): Mayfield charity school. Admitted 9 April 1790; in July 1791 list name changed to Alexander Wells (same position in list); removed (as Wells) 11 July 1794, 'sufficiently learned'. Baptised as Alexander Wells, 10 March 1782, son of James and Susanna. [MSB; PR]

STAFFELL, Abraham (1737-): Saunders' charity school, Rye. In lists from midsummer 1748 (not in 6 April 1748) to 16 January 1754 (not in 9 April 1755, next surviving list).

Baptised 7 December 1737, son of Henry and Mary. (Brother Richard also at the school.) [RSB; PR]

STAFFELL, Richard (1748-): Saunders' charity school, Rye. In lists from Lady Day 1758 (not in 11 January 1758) to Lady Day 1761 (not in Michaelmas 1761). Baptised 21 October 1748, son of Henry and Mary. (Brother Abraham also at the school.) [RSB; PR]

STAFFELL, Richard (1775-): Saunders' charity school, Rye. Admitted 6 October 1784; in list of 24 June 1785, last surviving 18th century list. Son of Richard, deceased. Baptised 1 November 1775, son of Richard and Mary. [RSB; PR]

STAINES (STANE), George (1701-): Brighton charity school. In list of those given prayer books 1716 or 1717 but his name crossed through. Baptised 1 January 1702, son of George Staines and [*blank*]. [BSB; PR]

STAINES (STANES), Job (1702-): Brighton charity school. Given prayer book 1716 or 1717. Baptised 24 May 1702, son of John and Joan (née Howell), who married 17 November 1700. [BSB; PR]

STAINES (STANES), John (1691-): Brighton charity school. In list of 'writers' 12 January 1702; had left by December 1705 and been 'apprenticed to shoemaker'. Baptised 5 July 1691, son of John and Ann. [BSB; PR]

STANDEN, Ambrose (1791-): Admitted Robertsbridge charity school at its opening, 5 April 1796. Sponsored by Mr James Bourne. Baptised 9 July 1791, son of Samuel and Susanna. [ESRO PAR 477/25/1/1; Salehurst PR]

STANDEN, John: Saunders' charity school, Rye. In lists from 2 January 1734 (not in 4 July 1733) to 5 October 1737 (11 January 1738 notes 'left the school'). Son of William. [RSB]

STANDEN, John (1786-): Admitted Robertsbridge charity school 29 August 1796 (the school opened 5 April 1796). Sponsored by Francis Hickes. Baptised 31 December 1786 (aged 3 weeks), son of James and Elizabeth. [ESRO PAR 477/25/1/1; Salehurst PR]

STANDEN, Louis (Lewis) (1786-): Admitted Robertsbridge charity school at its opening, 5 April 1796, 'aged 11' [10?]. Sponsored by Sir Godfrey Vassall Webster. Baptised 29 December 1786 (aged 5 weeks) son of Arthur and Anne (née Fuller). [ESRO PAR 477/25/1/1; Salehurst PR]

STANES - see STAINES

STANFORD, Sarah (1760-1835): The Miss Lunds' girls' boarding school, Lewes. Daughter of Richard, of Preston; her mother had died by 1762, when her father married, secondly, Mary Ockenden; father died 1769, when she was 9. Trustees' accounts show many purchases made for her, including £15 14s for a harpsichord in 1778, when she was 18, and £29 6s for a watch and chain in 1781, when she was 21. Died, unmarried, 19 December 1835, aged 75. [*SAC* **74**]

STANFORD, William (1764-1841): Steyning grammar school. Son of Richard, of Preston, and Mary; father died 1769, when he was 5. In 1772, when 7, sent to be educated by Mr Baker, almost certainly at Steyning grammar school (Mr Elgar of Steyning was paid 'for cloathes for Master Stanford'). Died 28 March 1841, aged 77. [*SAC* **74**]

STAPLES, Robert (1709-25): At East Grinstead school, under Gurnett. Son of John, vicar of East Grinstead 1690-1731. Admitted pensioner (aged 18) Trinity College, Cambridge, 6 June 1724; scholar 1725. Died in college; buried St Michael's, Cambridge, 19 December 1725. [*Al. Cant.*]

STAPLEY, Ann (1764-): Mayfield charity school. Admitted 19 April 1771; removed 11 April 1777, 'Sufficiently Learned', after 6 years at the school, 1½ years as a 'writer'. Baptised 18 July 1764, daughter of Edward and Susanna. (Brother Edward, sister Mary, also at the school.) [MSB; PR]

STAPLEY, Anthony (-1789): Son of John, of Hickstead, and Sarah (née Savage). The Stapley family account book, 1730-56, records for 8 October 1730 that he 'went to Board and Schole to Bridghelmstone [Brighton] to board att Thomas Browne for 4s 6d a week and he doth go to schole to John Grovers to read and write and cast account.' On 8 April 1731: 'payed Grover & Browne for Anthony board & scholling £7 6s 10d.' On 10 May 1731: 'Anthony Stapley went to school to Tho Pointer [Pointin] by the week to write & read & cast account.' On 3 February 1732: 'Anthony Stapley came away from Lindfield.' Died 1789. [Comber *Sx. Gen.*; ESRO HIC 472]

STAPLEY, Edmund (1784-): Sedlescombe charity school. There 21 October 1793 (a 'writer') and 2 October 1794. Baptised 17 October 1784, 'Edmund Weeks, son of Mary Stapley'. [SSB; PR]

STAPLEY, Edward (1772-): Mayfield charity school. Admitted 11 January 1782; removed 8 April 1785, for non-attendance. Baptised 14 June 1772, son of Edward and Susanna. (Sisters Ann, Mary, also at the school.) [MSB; PR]

STAPLEY, Henry (1758-): Sedlescombe charity school. There 18 April 1772, a 'writer'. Baptised 22 October 1758, son of Thomas and Mary. (Brother John, sister Mary, also at the school.) [SSB; PR]

STAPLEY, Jane (-1758): Daughter of John, of Hickstead, and Sarah (née Savage). The Stapley family account book, 1730-56, records for 26 August 1734 that 'Jane John and Samuel to their Dame Bellchambers the same day, the boys att 2d a week and Jane [at] 4d per week.' On 16 June 1735: 'Jane Stapley went to board att John Bodle att 3s 6d per week.' On 26 November 1735: 'Payed John Bodle £1 15s in full for 10 weeks board for Jane Stapley and payed Miss Beards bill 3s 2d.' Died 1758. [Comber *Sx. Gen.*; ESRO HIC 472]

STAPLEY, John (1726-48): Born 1726, son of John, of Hickstead, and Sarah (née Savage). The Stapley family account book, 1730-56, records for 26 August 1734 that, with sister Jane and brother Samuel, he went to Dame Bellchamber's, 'the boys att 2d a week and Jane 4d per week'. On 20 June 1735: 'I did carry my son John to Mr Browne at Lindfield to board att 3s per week and the 23rd day he is to go to schole to John Wood to read and write for 6d per week.' Buried at Twineham, 2 April 1748. [Comber *Sx Gen.*; ESRO HIC 472]

STAPLEY (STAPLER), John (1753-):

Sedlescombe charity school. Admitted between 23 July 1761 and 19 April 1762. Baptised 14 December 1753, son of Thomas and Mary. (Brother Henry, sister Mary, also at the school.) [SSB; PR]

STAPLEY (STAPELER), Mary (1749-): Sedlescombe charity school. There 3 May 1755. Baptised 16 July 1749, daughter of Thomas and Mary. (Brothers Henry, John, also at the school.) [SSB; PR]

STAPLEY, Mary (1767-): Mayfield charity school. Admitted 11 April 1777; removed 7 July 1780, 'Sufficiently Learned', after 3¼ years at the school, 1¾ years as a 'writer'. Baptised 22 March 1767, daughter of Edward and Susanna. (Brother Edward, sister Ann, also at the school.) [MSB; PR]

STAPLEY, Samuel: Son of John, of Hickstead, and Sarah (née Savage). The Stapley family account book, 1730-56, records for 26 August 1734 'Jane John and Samuel to their Dame Bellchambers the same day, the boys att 2d a week and Jane [at] 4d per week.' [Comber *Sx. Gen.*; ESRO HIC 472]

STAPLEY, Sarah (-1766?): Daughter of John, of Hickstead, and Sarah (née Savage). The Stapley family account book, 1730-56, records for 26 August 1734: 'Sarah Stapley went to Will Best to board at 3s 6d per week & to Miss Leach for 6d a week to schole.' On 2 December 1734: 'Sarah Stapley came from William Best and I payed him £2 9s for board & payed her Miss [Leach] 7s for her schooling and 1s for firing in all £2 17s.' Died 1766? [Comber *Sx. Gen.*; ESRO HIC 472]

STAPLEY, Thomas: Sedlescombe charity school. There 3 May 1755, 10 April 1758, 22 February 1759 (still a reader). [SSB]

STARR, George (1765-): Sedlescombe charity school. There 18 April 1772, a 'reader'. Baptised 24 February 1765, son of John and Mary. [SSB; PR]

STAR, John (1746-): Sedlescombe charity school. There 3 May 1755. Baptised 10 August 1746, son of John and Mary. [SSB; PR]

STEDMAN, John (1792-): Petworth charity

school. Admitted 31 March 1799; still there 12 July 1803. Given a prayer book. Born 25 April 1792, baptised 4 May 1792, son of John and Mary. [WSRO Petworth House Archives 1763; PR]

STEPHENS / STEVENS

STEPHENS: 'Robert Stephens's Girl' was a scholar at Buxted, 1739 (perhaps under Saunders' charity schooling for girls). [ESRO PAR 286/1/1/1]

STEVENS (STEPHENS), Ann (1755-): Mayfield charity school. Admitted 9 July 1762; removed 17 October 1766, for non-attendance, after 4¼ years at the school, ¾ year as a 'writer'. Baptised 28 September 1755, daughter of Joseph and Anne. (Brother Joseph, sisters Elizabeth, Mary, also at the school.) [MSB; PR]

STEVENS (STEPHENS), Elizabeth (1752-): Mayfield charity school. Admitted 17 October 1760; removed 6 July 1764, taken out by parents, after 3¾ years at the school, 1½ years as a 'writer'. Baptised 15 November 1752, daughter of Joseph and Ann. (Brother Joseph, sisters Ann, Mary, also at the school.) [MSB; PR]

STEVENS, Hannah: Mayfield charity school. Admitted 14 October 1757; removed 10 July 1761, 'sufficiently learned', after 3¾ years at the school, 1 year as a 'writer'. [MSB]

STEPHENS, John: Brighton charity school. Added to end of list of 'readers', December 1705 (ie joined subsequently). [BSB]

STEVENS, Joseph (1755-): At Seaford charity school 1765. Baptised 28 May 1755, son of Joseph and Elizabeth. (NB Master of the school in 1765 was Benjamin Stevens.) [BL Add MS 33,059; PR]

STEVENS (STEPHENS), Joseph (1764-): Mayfield charity school. Admitted 18 October 1771; removed 15 July 1774, for non-attendance, after 2¾ years as a 'reader'. Baptised 14 October 1764, son of Joseph and Ann. (Three sisters also at the school.) [MSB; PR]

STEVENS (STEPHENS), Mary (1758-): Mayfield charity school. Admitted 2 May 1766 to 'Widow Dukes' dame school; admitted charity school 16 October 1767; removed 15 January 1768, for 'incapacity'. Baptised 16 April 1758, daughter of Joseph and Anne. (Brother Joseph, sisters Ann, Elizabeth, also at the school.) [MSB; PR]

STEPHENS, Richard (1742-): Mayfield charity school. Admitted at formal opening of school 29 June 1750, but may have been there up to ¾ year earlier, as master paid from Michaelmas 1749; removed 10 January 1755, 'To work', taken home by parents, after at least 4¼ years at the school, 1½ years as a 'writer'. Baptised 5 November 1742, son of Richard and Sarah. (Sister Sarah also at the school.) [MSB; PR]

STEPHENS, Robert (1743-): Mayfield charity school. Admitted 6 April 1753; removed 14 October 1755, for non-attendance, after 2½ years at the school, 1¼ years as a 'writer'. Baptised 9 September 1743, son of Joseph and Martha. [MSB; PR]

STEVENS (STEPHENS), Sarah (1745-): Mayfield charity school. Admitted 20 January 1758; removed 6 July 1759, for non-attendance, after 1½ years as a 'reader'. Baptised 21 May 1745, daughter of Richard and Sarah. (Brother Richard also at the school.) [MSB; PR]

STEPHENS, Thomas: Eastbourne charity school. Admitted 11 April 1768; still there January 1771. Son of George. [SAS Budgen MS v.105]

STEVENSON (STEPHENSON), William (1789-): Admitted Fermor's charity school, Rotherfield, 29 April 1798. Baptised 29 November 1789, son of Joseph and Sarah. [ESRO PAR 465/4/1; PR]

STILES (STYLES), Edward (1790-): Mayfield charity school. Admitted 6 July 1798; removed 9 April 1802, taken out by parents. Baptised 21 March 1790, son of Robert and Ann. (Three brothers also at the school.) [MSB; PR]

STILES (STYLES), James (1786-): Mayfield charity school. Admitted 10 April 1795;

removed 7 July 1797, taken out by parents. Baptised 4 June 1786, son of Robert and Ann. (Three brothers also at the school.) [MSB; PR]

STILES (STYLES), John (1784-): Mayfield charity school. Admitted 6 January 1792; removed 10 July 1795, taken out by parents. Baptised 28 March 1784, son of Robert and Ann. (Three brothers also at the school.) [MSB; PR]

STILES, Thomas: Mayfield charity school. Admitted 9 April 1790; removed 5 July 1793, taken out by parents. [MSB]

STILES (STYLES), William (1788-): Mayfield charity school. Admitted 6 January 1797; removed 12 July 1799, for non-attendance. Baptised 8 June 1788, son of Robert and Ann. (Three brothers also at the school.) [MSB; PR]

STOCKS, Frank (1729-): Saunders' charity school, Rye. In lists from 4 April 1739 (not in 10 January 1739) to 4 July 1744 (not in 10 April 1745, next surviving list). Baptised 22 August 1729, son of Thomas and Ann. (Three brothers also at the school.) [RSB; PR]

STOCKS, George (1772-): Saunders' charity school, Rye. Admitted 16 July 1783; in list for 24 June 1785, last surviving 18th century list, which notes '3' (probably 3 weeks absent). Baptised 7 August 1772, son of John and Anne. (Brother James, possibly brother John, also at the school.) [RSB; PR]

STOCKS, James (1770-): Saunders' charity school, Rye. Admitted 6 March 1782; in lists to 24 June 1783 (not in 29 September 1783). Baptised 20 April 1770, son of John and Anne. (Brother George, possibly brother John, also at the school.) [RSB; PR]

STOCKS, John (1740-): Saunders' charity school, Rye. In lists from 2 October 1751 (not in midsummer 1751) to 4 July 1753, in which marked 'left School' (not in Michaelmas 1753). Son of Thomas, deceased. Baptised 15 February 1740, son of Thomas and Anne. (Three brothers also at the school.) [RSB; PR]

STOCKS, John (1755-): Saunders' charity school, Rye. In lists from Michaelmas 1763

(not in Christmas 1762, previous surviving list) to Lady Day 1767 (not in Christmas 1768, next surviving list). Baptised 30 January 1755, son of John and Anne. (Possible brothers George, James, also at the school.) [RSB; PR]

STOCKS, John (1776-): Saunders' charity school, Rye. Admitted 14 January 1784; in list of 24 June 1785, last surviving 18th century list. Son of John, junior. Baptised 26 April 1776, son of John and Mary. [RSB; PR]

STOCKS, Thomas (1733-): Saunders' charity school, Rye. In lists from 10 April 1745 (not in 4 July 1744, previous surviving list); list of 6 April 1748 notes 'Absent 14 weeks' (not in midsummer 1748). Baptised 2 February 1733, son of Thomas and Ann. (Three brothers also at the school.) [RSB; PR]

STOCKS, William: Saunders' charity school, Rye. In lists from midsummer 1748 (not in 6 April 1748) to 28 March 1753, in which marked 'left school' (not in 4 July 1753). Son of Thomas (deceased in list of Christmas 1749, not deceased in Michaelmas 1749). (Three brothers also at the school.) [RSB; PR]

STOCKS, William (1772-): Saunders' charity school, Rye. Admitted 6 March 1782; in list for 24 June 1785, last surviving 18th century list. Baptised 17 January 1772, son of William and Elizabeth. [RSB; PR]

STONE, Edward (1691-): Brighton charity school. In list of 'writers' 12 January 1702; had left by December 1705 and been 'apprenticed to shoemaker'. Baptised 29 November 1691, son of Thomas and Susan. (Perhaps brother Thomas also at the school.) [BSB; PR]

STONE, Peter (1693- by 1705): Brighton charity school. Admitted as 'reader' sometime after list of (probably) January 1702; joined 'writers' class sometime after 12 January 1702; died while still at school, sometime before December 1705, being 'drownded at sea'. Baptised 4 June 1793, son of Peter and Ann. (Brother Robert, perhaps brother Thomas, also at the school.) [BSB; PR]

STONE, Robert (1695-): Brighton charity school. Joined 'writers' class sometime after 12 January 1702; in list of 'writers' December

1705. Baptised 1 September 1695, son of Peter and Ann. (Brother Peter, perhaps brother Thomas, also at the school.) [BSB; PR]

STONE, Thomas: Brighton charity school. In list of 'writers' 12 January 1702; had left by December 1705 and gone 'to a Butcher'. Baptised either 20 October 1689, son of Thomas and Susan (brother Edward also at the school) or 15 June 1690, son of Peter and Ann (brothers Peter, Robert, also at the school). [BSB; PR]

STONE, Thomas (1764-): Saunders' charity school, Rye. Admitted 15 May 1771; in lists to Michaelmas 1773 (not in midsummer 1774, next surviving list). Baptised 30 June 1764, son of Isaac and Mary. (Brother William also at the school.) [RSB; PR]

STONE, William (1766-): Saunders' charity school, Rye. Admitted 22 June 1774; in lists to Lady Day 1780, which notes 'Left School' (not in Michaelmas 1780). Baptised 6 October 1766, son of Isaac and Mary. (Brother Thomas also at the school.) [RSB; PR]

STONER, Sarah (1791-): Admitted Petworth charity school 2 October 1799. Baptised 30 May 1791, daughter of William and Elizabeth. [WSRO Petworth House Archives 1763; PR]

STONER, Thomas: At Cocking charity school 1733. [WSRO Par 53/12/1]

STREETER, Edward (1761 or 62-): Mayfield charity school. Admitted 21 April 1769; removed 8 April 1774, after 5 years at the school, 2 years as a 'writer'. Baptised 13 January 1762, son of John and Sarah. (Two brothers also at the school.) [MSB; PR]

STREETER, Henry: Admitted Fermor's charity school, Rotherfield, 3 June 1798. [ESRO PAR 465/4/1]

STREETER, Joseph (1763 or 64-): Mayfield charity school. Admitted 5 January 1775; removed 11 April 1777, 'for Incapacity', after 2¼ years at the school, ¾ year as a 'writer'. Baptised 8 January 1764, son of John and Sarah. (Two brothers also at the school.) [MSB; PR]

STREETER, Richard (1766-): Mayfield charity school. Admitted 9 July 1772; removed 18 July 1777, 'Sufficiently Learned', after 5 years at the school, 2 years as a 'writer'. Baptised 7 September 1766, son of John and Sarah. (Two brothers also at the school.) [MSB; PR]

STRINGER: A poor girl of West Grinstead who received schooling 1724, under the Dowlin charity. [WSRO Par 95/1/1/3]

STRINGER, Samuel (c1701-): Grey Coat charity school, Chichester. Admitted at its opening Lady Day 1710. Aged 9 at Lady Day 1711. Expelled (as were 4 others) between Lady Day 1712 and Lady Day 1713. [WSRO Cap.V/1/1]

STRONG, James (1778-): Mayfield charity school. Admitted 6 July 1787; in list for 17 October 1788 his name overwritten to 'John' (no formal removal recorded). Baptised 8 June 1778, son of James and Anne. [MSB; PR]

STRONG, John: Mayfield charity school. In list for 17 October 1788, 'James' Strong is overwritten to 'John'; removed 9 April 1790, taken out by parents but 'Sufficiently Learned'. [MSB]

STRONG, William: Mayfield charity school. Admitted 9 April 1790; removed 13 July 1791, for non-attendance. [MSB]

STURT: Brighton girls' charity school. Admitted sometime after 25 March 1703 (probably by end of 1705). 'Thomas Sturts daughter'. [BSB]

SUMMERS, Edward: Saunders' charity school, Rye. In lists from 20 April 1737 (not in 29 December 1736) to 29 April 1741 (8 July 1741 notes 'left the school'). Son of William. (Older brother William, who left at same time, also at the school.) [RSB]

SUMMERS, William (1724-): Saunders' charity school, Rye. In lists from 8 October 1735 (not in 2 July 1735) to 29 April 1741 (8 July 1741 notes 'left the school'). Baptised 28 November 1724, son of William and Sarah. (Brother Edward also at the school.) [RSB; PR]

SUSANS, John (1741-): Saunders' charity school, Rye. In lists from 25 March 1752 (not in 15 January 1752) to 14 January 1756 (not in 7 April 1756). Baptised 25 April 1741, son of Thomas and Elizabeth. [RSB; PR]

SUSAN, John (1747-): Mayfield charity school. Admitted 12 April 1754; removed 13 October 1758, 'sufficiently learned', after 4½ years at the school, 1¾ years as a 'writer'. Baptised 18 December 1747, son of John and Elizabeth. (Brother William also at the school.) [MSB; PR]

SUSAN, William (1752-): Mayfield charity school. Admitted 10 April 1761; removed 8 July 1763, taken away by parents; re-admitted 13 January 1764; removed 26 October 1764, 'For Non Attendance, But Pretty well Learned'; re-admitted 19 April 1765; removed 18 October 1765, for non-attendance after 3½ years at the school in total, 2¼ years as a 'writer'. Baptised 31 May 1752, son of John and Elizabeth. (Brother John also at the school.) [MSB; PR]

SUTEHURST (SUTERS), John (1746-): Saunders' charity school, Rye. In lists from 9 April 1755 (not in 16 January 1754, previous surviving list); left 7 February 1757. Son of John, deceased. Baptised 18 December 1746, son of John and Mary. [RSB; PR]

SUTERS?, SUTUS: A poor boy of Winchelsea for whose schooling the parish paid. On 30 May 1766 Mr Hogsflesh received £1 10s 'for 1 Years Schooling for young Bennet Sutus & Sidger'. For each of the 2 following church years (1767-68, 1768-69) the parish paid him £1 10s, probably for the same 3 boys. [ESRO PAR 511/31/1/1]

SUTTON, Francis (1728-): Eastbourne charity school. There 1734 and December 1738. Baptised 2 April 1728, son of William and Elizabeth. (Brother William also at the school.) [Chatsworth, Devonshire Collection, Compton Place, Box P; SAS Budgen MS, v.129; PR]

SUTTON, William (1733-): At Eastbourne charity school April 1741. Baptised 22 July 1733, son of William and Elizabeth. (Brother Francis also at the school.) [SAS Budgen MS v.129; PR]

SWAIN, John (1713-): Saunders' charity school, Rye. In lists from September 1722 (?) (first list) to 10 January 1728 (17 April 1728 notes 'left the school'). Son of Edward, 'deceased' in lists from 8 April 1724. Baptised 1 July 1713, son of Edward and Mary. [RSB; PR]

SWAINE, John (1724-): Saunders' charity school, Rye. In lists from 20 October 1736 (not in 7 April 1736) to 5 October 1737 (11 January 1738 notes 'left the school'). Baptised 20 October 1724, son of John and Ann. [RSB; PR]

SWAINE, John Waters (1770-): Saunders' charity school, Rye. Admitted 14 April 1779; in lists to 2 September 1782, which notes 'Left School' (not in 29 September 1782). Baptised 26 November 1770, 'John Waters Bastard Son of Elizabeth Swaine'. [RSB; PR]

SWAIN, William: Saunders' charity school, Rye. In lists from 7 January 1730 (not in 25 June 1729) to 29 March 1732 (5 July 1732 notes 'left the school'); re-admitted, in lists from 28 March 1733 (not in 3 January 1733) to 9 April 1735 (2 July 1735 notes 'left the school'). Son of Mary Swain. [RSB]

SWEATMAN (SWEETMAN), Fanny (1788-): Mayfield charity school. Admitted 7 July 1797; removed 11 April 1800, taken out by parents. Baptised (Frances) 21 December 1788, daughter of Joseph and Elizabeth. [MSB; PR]

SWETMAN, Thomas: Mayfield charity school. Admitted 11 April 1760; removed 17 October 1760, 'for Non Attendance being taken into the Workhouse', after ½ year as a 'reader'. Probably same as Thomas Swetnam [sic], admitted 8 January 1762; removed 9 April 1762. [MSB]

SWIFT, John: Sedlescombe charity school. Admitted 26 October 1794; there 25 December 1797, 20 August 1798 (still a 'reader'). [SSB]

SYMONDS: 'William Symonds' Girl' was a scholar at Buxted 1739 (perhaps under Saunders' charity schooling for girls). [ESRO PAR 286/1/1/1]

TAMSETT, John: Saunders' charity school,

Rye. Admitted 10 January 1770; in lists to Christmas 1770 (not in midsummer 1773, next surviving list). Son of John. [RSB]

TAPLIN: Grey Coat charity school, Chichester. Given 10s 6d on leaving, Christmas 1772. [WSRO Cap.V/1/1]

TAPLIN: Grey Coat charity school, Chichester. Left between Michaelmas 1775 and Michaelmas 1776. Given 10s 6d on leaving. [WSRO Cap.V/1/1]

TASKER, Stephen (1788-): Admitted Fermor's charity school, Rotherfield, 29 April 1798. Baptised 5 October 1788, son of Philip and Hannah, 'poor'. [ESRO PAR 465/4/1]

TAYLER/TAYLOR

TAYLER (TAYLAR), America (1720-): Saunders' charity school, Rye. In lists from 29 June 1726 (not in 4 May 1726) to 22 July 1730 (not in 14 October 1730). Son of Moses, deceased. Baptised 18 November 1720, son of Moses and Joyce. [RSB; PR]

TAYLER, Ann: At Cocking charity school 1732. [WSRO Par 53/12/1]

TAYLOR, Elizabeth (1753-): Sedlescombe charity school. Admitted between 5 March 1760 and 6 April 1761. Baptised 23 November 1753, daughter of John and Mary. [SSB; PR]

TAYLOR, Hannah (1771-): Sedlescombe charity school. There 29 September 1784 (a 'writer'), 29 September 1786 and 29 September 1787. Baptised 1 May 1771, daughter of John and Mary. (Brother William also at the school.) [SSB; PR]

TAYLER, John: At Cocking charity school 1732, 1733. [WSRO Par 53/12/1]

TAYLOR, Mark (1785-): Admitted Fermor's charity school, Rotherfield, 3 May 1794. Baptised 11 November 1785, son of William and Sarah. [ESRO PAR 465/4/1; PR]

TAYLOR, Mary: At Cocking charity schoool 1733. [WSRO Par 53/12/1]

TAYLOR, Mary: Admitted Fermor's charity

school, Rotherfield, 29 April 1798. Daughter of Edward. [ESRO PAR 465/4/1]

TAYLOR, Nancy: At Mrs Hunt's school, Horsham, 1773. Daughter of governor of the workhouse. [*SAC* 52]

TAYLER (TAYLAR), Richard (1707-): Saunders' charity school, Rye. In lists from September 1722 (?) (first list) to January 1724 (?) (not in 8 April 1724). Baptised 28 June 1707, son of John and Eleanor. [RSB; PR]

TAYLOR, William (1696-): Brighton charity school. Admitted as 'reader' sometime after list of (probably) January 1702; in list of 'readers' December 1705. Baptised 21 June 1696, son of George and Dorothy. [BSB; PR]

TAYLOR, William (1701-): Brighton charity school. Given prayer book 1715. Baptised 3 October 1701, son of William and Ann, Presbyterians. [BSB; Union Street Indpendent Chapel (Presbyterian) register]

TAYLOR, William (senior) (1776-): Sedlescombe charity school. There 29 September 1784 and 29 September 1786 (still a 'reader'); name crossed through in latter list. Baptised 11 February 1776, son of John and Mary. (Sister Hannah also at the school.) [SSB; PR]

TAYLOR, William (junior): Sedlescombe charity school. There 29 September 1784, 29 September 1786 and 29 September 1787 (still a 'reader'). [SSB]

TEILING (TEELING, TEALING), John (1691-): Brighton charity school. In list of 'readers' of (probably) January 1702; in list of 'writers' December 1705; went he left he went 'to sea'. Baptised 1 February 1691, son of Francis and Elizabeth (née Lynn). [BSB; PR]

TEMPLEMAN, Thomas (1754-): At Seaford charity school 1765. Baptised 19 August 1754, son of William and Catharine. [BL Add MS 33,059; PR]

TETTERSELL, Nicholas (1694-): Brighton charity school. In list of 'readers' of (probably) January 1702; joined 'writers' class sometime after 12 January 1702; in list of 'writers'

December 1705. Baptised 10 June 1694, son of Jonas. [BSB; PR]

THOMAS, Ann (1749-): Mayfield charity school. Admitted 10 April 1758; removed 26 October 1759, for non-attendance, after 1½ years as a 'reader'. Baptised 7 February 1749, daughter of William and Jane. [MSB; PR]

THORP, Edward: Midhurst grammar school. Admitted as charity scholar 1793. [*HMGS*]

THORP, Stephen (1731-): Saunders' charity school, Rye. In lists from 26 October 1743 (not in June 1743 (?)); Michaelmas 1747 notes 'Absent 11 weeks'; Christmas 1747 notes 'Absent 22 weeks'; 6 April 1748 notes 'Absent 9 months' and name crossed out. Baptised 29 December 1731, son of William and Mary. (Brother William also at the school.) [RSB; PR]

THORPE, William (1747-): Saunders' charity school, Rye. In lists from Michaelmas 1755 (not in midsummer 1755) to midsummer 1759, where marked '22d April'. Son of William, 'deceased' in 14 January 1756 list. Baptised 12 June 1747, son of William and Mary. (Brother Stephen also at the school.) [RSB; PR]

TILDEN, George: At Rev Thankful Frewen's school, Northiam, as a boarder, from 29 July 1717 to 29 July 1720. A record of the classics he studied survives. Fees were £16 pa. Son of John. [ESRO FRE 533]

TILLSTONE: Button's school, Lewes. To recite, in both English and French, at a 'Public Examination' at the *Star Assembly Room*, 22 June 1797. [*SWA* 19.6.97]

TILT, William (1773-): Lewes grammar school, under Gwynne. Then Eton; Trinity College, Cambridge, 27 June 1791 (age 18); scholar 1794; BA 1795; won Middle Bachelor's prize 1796; won Senior Bachelor's prize for Latin Essays 1797; MA 1798. Signs Brighton marriage banns April, May 1796; priest (Norwich) 16 November 1817. Baptised 25 May 1773, at St Margaret, Westminster, son of William, auctioneer of London, and Mary; father later of Brighton, and presumably proprietor of the Public Subscription Rooms there (tea, promenade, balls). Married 4

February 1802, at Brighton, Mrs Newnham, widow of George Lewis Newnham, esq of Newtimber. [*SWA* 3.7.97, 10.7.97; St Nicholas, Brighton PR; *Al. Cant.*; *SWA* 15.2.1802]

TILTMAN, Richard (1749-): Saunders' charity school, Rye. In lists from Lady Day 1758 (not in 11 January 1758) to Lady Day 1761 (not in Michaelmas 1761). Baptised 14 March 1749, son of Richard and Mary. [RSB; PR]

TOBBOTT, Jesse (1774-): Lord Pelham's charity school, Lewes [qv Rands' school]. Admitted Lady Day 1784. There 10 October 1784, aged 10. [ESRO AMS 6005]

TOLER, Joseph: Grey Coat charity school, Chichester. Left between Michaelmas 1762 and Michaelmas 1763. Given 10s 6d on leaving. [WSRO Cap.V/1/1]

TOMPKINS, John Cole (1782-): At Midhurst grammar school when Cowdray House burnt down in 1797. Born 16 May 1782, son of John (1745-97) estate agent to the Shelleys of Michelgrove, mayor of Arundel, etc. [*SAC* **71**]

TOWNER, John (1692-): Brighton charity school. Admitted as 'reader' sometime after list of (probably) January 1702; joined 'writers' class sometime after 12 January 1702; had left by December 1705, being 'removed to Shoreham'. Baptised 10 April 1692, son of Thomas and Mary. [BSB; PR]

TOWNER, John: At Seaford charity school 1765. Son of Ann Towner. (Probably son of William and Ann; William was buried 1762.) [BL Add MS 33,059; PR]

TOWNSEND, J.: Grey Coat charity school, Chichester. Left between Michaelmas 1768 and Michaelmas 1769. Given 10s 6d on leaving. [WSRO Cap.V/1/1]

TRANGMER (TRANKMER), Rainer (1690-): Brighton charity school. In list of 'readers' of (probably) January 1702; had left by December 1705 and gone 'to husbandry'. Baptised 30 March 1690, son of William and Elizabeth (née Rainard). [BSB; PR]

TRIBE: Grey Coat charity school, Chichester.

Left between Michaelmas 1759 and Michaelmas 1760. Given 10s 6d on leaving. [WSRO Cap.V/1/1]

TRODD, Richard (c1700-): Grey Coat charity school, Chichester. Admitted at its opening, Lady Day 1710. Aged 10 at Lady Day 1711. Between Lady Day 1713 and Lady Day 1714 was 'put out Apprentice'. [WSRO Cap.V/1/1]

TRUNCHEON, Ann (1736-): Mayfield charity school. Admitted 5 October 1750; removed 27 March 1752, 'well learned'; had been a 'writer' for ¾ year. Baptised 10 March 1736, daughter of John and Sarah. (Brothers David, George, also at the school.) [MSB; PR]

TRUNCHEON, David (1745-): Mayfield charity school. Admitted 9 April 1755, as a 'writer'; removed 11 July 1755, for non-attendance, but re-admitted 14 October 1755; removed 24 January 1757, taken away by parents, after 1½ years at the school, all as a 'writer'. Baptised 21 February 1745, son of John and Sarah. (Brother George, sister Ann, also at the school.) [MSB; PR]

TRUNCHEON, George (1741-): Mayfield charity school. Admitted 14 November 1752; removed 6 July 1753, taken out by parents (still a 'reader'). Baptised 29 April 1741, son of John and Sarah. (Brother David, sister Ann, also at the school.) [MSB; PR]

TRUSLER, John (c1700-): Grey Coat charity school, Chichester. Admitted at its opening, Lady Day 1710. Aged 11 at Lady Day 1711. There Lady Day 1714. [WSRO Cap.V/1/1]

TUCKER: Grey Coat charity school, Chichester. Left between Michaelmas 1765 and Michaelmas 1766. Given 10s 6d on leaving. [WSRO Cap.V/1/1]

TUFFIN: Midhurst grammar school. At the school's first public performance of composition and oratory, 5 November 1799, took part, with one other, in a scene from Virgil, in the role of Dido. At the second 'literary performance', 27 May 1800, took part, with one other, in a scene from Milton, in the role of Satan. [*SWA* 11.11.99, 2.6.1800]

[*TUGNUT, Elizabeth*]: In Wiston school list c1803, and perhaps at the school in 1800. [WSRO Par 211/25/1]

[**TUGNUT, George**]: In Wiston school list c1803, and perhaps at the school in 1800. [WSRO Par 211/25/1]

[*TUGNUT, Jane*]: In Wiston school list c1803, and perhaps at the school in 1800. [WSRO Par 211/25/1]

[**TUGNUT, John** (1794-)]: In Wiston school list c1803, and perhaps at the school in 1800. Baptised 23 February 1794, son of James and Ann. [WSRO Par 211/25/1; PR]

[**TUGNUT, Thomas**]: In Wiston school list c1803, and perhaps at the school in 1800. [WSRO Par 211/25/1]

TUPPEN, Nicholas (1723-): Eastbourne charity school. There 1734 and December 1738 (?). Baptised 20 June 1723, son of William and Mary. [Chatsworth, Devonshire Collection, Compton Place, Box P; SAS Budgen MS v.129; PR]

TUPPEN, William: Brighton charity school. Given prayer book 1716 or 1717. [BSB; PR]

TURK, Joseph (1786 or 87-): Admitted Fermor's charity school, Rotherfield, 3 May 1794. Baptised 7 January 1787, son of Joseph and Lydia. [ESRO PAR 465/4/1; PR]

[*TURL, Elizabeth* (1794-)]: In Wiston school list c1803, and perhaps at the school in 1800. Baptised 4 May 1794, daughter of James and Mary. (Sisters Mary, Susan, also at the school.) [WSRO Par 211/25/1; PR]

[**TURLE, James**]: In Wiston school list c1803, and perhaps at the school in 1800. [WSRO Par 211/25/1]

TURLE, Mary (1789-): In Wiston school list c1803, and very probably at the school in 1800. Baptised 8 November 1789, daughter of James and Mary. (Sisters Elizabeth, Susan, also at the school.) [WSRO Par 211/25/1; PR]

[*TURLE, Susan* (1796-)]: In Wiston school list c1803, and possibly at the school in 1800 with sisters. Baptised 1 May 1796, Susanna, daughter of James and Mary. (Sisters Elizabeth, Mary, also at the school.) [WSRO Par 211/25/1; PR]

TURLE, Thomas: Eastbourne charity school. Admitted 11 January 1768; still there January 1771. Son of James. [SAS Budgen MS v.105]

TURNER: 'Widow Turner's Girl' was a scholar at Buxted, 1739 (perhaps under Saunders' charity schooling for girls). [ESRO PAR 286/1/1/1]

TURNER, Ann (1747-): Mayfield charity school. Admitted 9 January 1756; removed 9 July 1756, for non-attendance, after ½ year as a 'reader'. Baptised 16 August 1747, daughter of Thomas and Anne. (Four brothers also at the school.) [MSB; PR]

TURNER?, Charity: Admitted Fermor's charity school, Rotherfield, 3 May 1794. 'Daughter of Richard Turner's Wife'. [ESRO PAR 465/4/1]

TURNER, Charlotte (later Charlotte Smith) (1749-1806): Born in London 4 May 1749, daughter of Nicholas, of Bignor Park, and Anne (née Towers); when 3, mother died, and she was brought up by aunt. When 6, sent to school at Chichester, and while there, at father's desire, took drawing lessons from artist George Smith; after about 2 years, sent to a school at Kensington; schooling ended at 12. Married, 1765, Benjamin Smith, son of a director of the East India Company. In 1774, with 7 children, they moved to Lys Farm, Hampshire; but estate had to be sold and in 1782 Smith was imprisoned for debt; Charlotte shared his confinement, which lasted 7 months. She, with 12 children, lived for some months in a tumbledown chateau near Dieppe. On return, friendly separation from husband; helped him financially but refused to live with him. Lived for periods at Woolbeding House, near Midhurst, and at Brighton. Novelist and poet. Helped by William Hayley, and her first publication, *Elegiac Sonnets and other Essays* (1784), dedicated to him. Hymn by her sung by the children of Brighton Sunday school at a charity service 1789. 'Charlotte Smith is best remembered by her charming poems for children' (*The Encyclopaedia Britannica*). Died 28 October 1806. [DNB; *Enc. Brit.*; Lower *Worthies*; Lucas, E. V. *Highways and Byways*

in Sussex (second edition, 1935); *SWA* 21.9.89]

TURNER, George (1761-): Mayfield charity school. Admitted 22 April 1768; removed 8 April 1774, after 5¾ years at the school, 3 years as a 'writer'. Baptised 10 May 1761, son of Thomas and Ann. (Three brothers, 1 sister, also at the school.) [MSB; PR]

TURNER, George (1788-): Mayfield charity school. Admitted 10 July 1795; removed 11 April 1800, taken out by parents. Baptised 26 October 1788, son of George and Elizabeth. (Two brothers also at the school.) [MSB; PR]

TURNER, John: Mayfield charity school. Admitted 7 July 1775; removed 30 July 1779, 'Sufficiently Learned', after 4 years at the school, 1½ years as a 'writer'. [MSB]

TURNER, Nicholas (1741-): Mayfield charity school. Admitted at formal opening of the school 29 June 1750, but may have been there up to ¾ year earlier, as master paid from Michaelmas 1749; removed 11 January 1754, 'well learned'; had 3¼ years as a 'writer'. Baptised 4 March 1741, son of Thomas and Anne. (Three brothers, 1 sister, also at the school.) [MSB PR]

TURNER, Sarah (1738-): At school in Lewes mid-18th century. Born 17 August 1738, daughter of John, shopkeeper of Framfield (1689-1752) and second wife Elizabeth (née Ovenden, of Rotherfield, 1697-1759); sister of Thomas Turner of East Hoathly [qv Schedule 2]. [Jennings, G. H. (ed) *Thomas Turner, The Diary of a Georgian Shopkeeper* (1979); Vaisey, D. (ed) *The Diary of Thomas Turner* (1984)]

TURNER, Stephen (1751-): Mayfield charity school. Admitted 6 July 1759; removed 8 July 1763, taken away by parents, after 4 years at the school, 1 year as a 'writer'. Baptised 7 April 1751, son of Thomas and Anne. (Three brothers, 1 sister, also at the school.) [MSB; PR]

TURNER, Stephen (1791-): Mayfield charity school. Admitted 12 October 1798; removed 12 July 1805, 'sufficiently learned', after 6¾ years at the school. Baptised 24 April 1791, son of George and Elizabeth. (Two brothers also at the school.) [MSB; PR]

TURNER, Thomas: Mayfield charity school. Admitted 6 April 1753; removed 12 October 1753, taken out by parents, after ½ year, ¼ year as a 'writer'. [MSB]

TURNER, Thomas (1786-): Mayfield charity school. Admitted 11 July 1794; removed 6 July 1798, for non-attendance. Baptised 16 April 1786, son of George and Elizabeth. (Two brothers also at the school.) [MSB; PR]

TURNER, William (1754-): Mayfield charity school. Admitted 11 July 1765; removed 21 April 1769, 'sufficiently Learned', after 3¾ years at the school, 1¾ years as a 'writer'. On 27 April 1771, apprenticed by parish (from 30 March 1771) to Andrew Fenner of Mayfield, fellmonger, glover and breeches maker, for 4 years; total premium £4 4s, parish to provide his food, lodging and apparel. Baptised 17 November 1754, son of Thomas, husbandman, and Anne. (Three brothers, 1 sister, also at the school.) [MSB; ESRO PAR 422/33/133; PR]

TURNER, William (1766-): Saunders' charity school, Rye. Admitted 5 June 1776; in lists to Christmas 1779, which notes 'Left School' (not in Lady Day 1780). Baptised 19 September 1766, son of Francis and Sarah. [RSB; PR]

TUTT, Mary: At Eastbourne charity school 1734. [Chatsworth, Devonshire Collection, Compton Place, Box P]

TWYFORD, Samuel (c1787-1863): Midhurst grammar school. Son of Samuel, trustee of the school, and himself later trustee of the school for 37 years. Probably the 'Twyford, senior' who, at the school's first public performance of composition and oratory, 5 November 1799, took part, with one other, in a scene from Virgil, in the role of Aeneas. At the second 'literary performance', 27 May 1800, he spoke, 'most correctly', a Greek elegy on the late Dr Warton, composed by Dr Huntingford (Warden of Winchester, who was in the audience). On both occasions a Mr Twyford was listed amongst the gentry present. [*HMGS*; *SWA* 11.11.99, 2.6.1800]

TWYFORD, junior: Midhurst grammar school. By inference from reference to 'Twyford senior', [qv TWYFORD, Samuel, here assumed to have been 'Twyford, senior'].

TYERS: Grey Coat charity school, Chichester. Left between Michaelmas 1765 and Michaelmas 1766. Given 10s 6d on leaving. [WSRO Cap.V/1/1]

UNDERHILL, Elizabeth: Mayfield charity school. Admitted 17 October 1800; removed 9 April 1802, taken out by parents. [MSB]

UNDERHILL, Hannah (1787-): Mayfield charity school. Admitted 11 July 1794; removed 19 January 1798, taken out by parents. Baptised 14 October 1787, daughter of Daniel and Hannah. (Three brothers, 1 sister, also at the school.) [MSB; PR]

UNDERHILL, James (1790-): Mayfield charity school. Admitted 6 July 1798; removed 8 July 1803, for non-attendance. Baptised 11 April 1790, son of Daniel and Hannah. (Two brothers, 2 sisters, also at the school.) [MSB; PR]

UNDERHILL, John (1786-): Mayfield charity school. Admitted 11 October 1793; removed 8 July 1796, for non-attendance. Baptised 28 April 1786, son of Daniel and Hannah. (Two brothers, 2 sisters, also at the school. NB 2 John Underhills at the school between October 1794 and April 1796.) [MSB; PR]

UNDERHILL, John: Mayfield charity school. No formal admission, first appears in lists 17 October 1794; removed 19 January 1798, taken out by parents. (NB 2 John Underhills at the school between October 1794 and April 1796.) [MSB]

UNDERHILL, Philly (1792-): Mayfield charity school. Admitted 11 April 1800; in list for 11 January 1805, not in 12 April 1805 (no formal removal recorded). Baptised 22 April 1792, daughter of Daniel and Hannah. (Three brothers, 1 sister, also at the school.) [MSB; PR]

UNDERHILL, Sarah (1771-): Mayfield charity school. Admitted 5 January 1781; removed 18 April 1783, taken out by parents 'and Sufficiently Learned'. Baptised 26 May

1771, daughter of Thomas and Elizabeth. [MSB; PR]

UNDERHILL, Thomas (1777-): Mayfield charity school. Admitted 14 January 1785; removed 11 April 1788, taken out by parents. Baptised 11 May 1777, son of Daniel and Anne. (Mother died 1784 aged 38; father married secondly, 1785, Hannah Ashby. Two brothers, 2 sisters, also at the school.) [MSB; PR]

UPSTIL, Elizabeth: At Cocking charity school 1732. [WSRO Par 53/12/1]

UPSTIL, Sarah: At Cocking charity school 1733. [WSRO Par 53/12/1]

UPTON: A poor boy of Horsted Keynes, son of John, for whose schooling the parish paid 2s 6d in 1744. [WSRO Par 384/12/1]

UTTERSON: Midhurst grammar school. At the school's first public performance of composition and oratory, 5 November 1799, took part, with one other, in a scene from Shakespeare's *Julius Caesar*, in the role of Brutus. At the second 'literary performance', 27 May 1800, took part, with one other, in the scene of Edward and Warwick. [*SWA* 11.11.99, 2.6.1800]

VARNAM (VARNOM), John (1727-): At Eastbourne charity school 1734. Baptised 13 December 1727, son of Richard and Susannah. [Chatsworth, Devonshire Collection, Compton Place, Box P; PR]

VARNDEL: Grey Coat charity school, Chichester. Left between Michaelmas 1769 and Michaelmas 1770. Given 10s 6d on leaving. [WSRO Cap.V/1/1]

VASE, Nicholas: Midhurst grammar school. Admitted as charity scholar 1790. [*HMGS*]

VENAL: 'Thomas Venal's Girl' was a scholar at Buxted, 1739 (perhaps under Saunders' charity schooling for girls). [ESRO PAR 286/1/1/1]

VENICE, Elizabeth (1728-): Brightling girls' charity school. Admitted 21 April 1738; there to year ending 1 May 1741 (in which year she

attended on 103 school days). Baptised 29 September 1728, daughter of Isaac and Mary. (NB Another Elizabeth Venice baptised 29 March 1731, daughter of James and Elizabeth, but girls admitted aged about 10 this period; also another daughter of Isaac and Mary - Mary - at the school). [ESRO PAR 254/25/1; PR]

VENICE, Isaac: At Sarah French's school, Brightling, 1739-42. On 30 April 1740, John Fuller paid to her husband 11s 10d for schooling Isaac and another boy to 26 April 1740; and on 15 May 1742, paid her 15s 2d for schooling the same 2 boys. [ESRO SAS/RF 15/28]

VENICE, Mary (1736-): Brightling girls' charity school. Admitted between 2 April 1744 and 31 August 1745, in which 16-month period (no school in August) she attended on 318 school days; there to period 31 July 1747 to 10 June 1749, in which she attended on 329 school days; had 1,110 days at the school in total. Baptised 4 April 1736, daughter of Isaac and Mary. (Sister Elizabeth also at the school.) [ESRO PAR 254/25/1; PR]

(VERALL): Eastbourne charity school. Admitted Lady Day 1779; there Christmas 1779. [SAS Budgen MS v.117]

VERRALL, Charles (1745-): At his uncle, Charles Rand's school, Lewes, and Lewes grammar school, under Austen. Son of Charles, who was brother of Lucy, Charles Rand's wife. On 26 December 1760, father wrote to Duke of Newcastle, seeking position for him as clerk in a Government office: 'My Eldest Son Charles is 15 years old...he has been at the Latin School about 6 years, in which he is reckon'd a great Proficient, the same care has been taken to his Learning, Arithmetik, & to his Writing several good hands...the Character of my Son will bear the strictest examination, as to his learning & Morals his Schoolmasters at Lewes Messrs Austen & Rand, as well as the Gentlemen here and Neighbourhood will do him the same justice, equal to what I write of him...' [*SAC* **58**]

VERRAL, Edward: Eastbourne charity school. Admitted Christmas 1777; there Christmas 1779. [SAS Budgen MS v.117]

VICKERS, James (c1700-): Grey Coat charity school, Chichester. Admitted at its opening Lady Day 1710. Aged 10 at Lady Day 1711. 'Discarded' between Lady Day 1713 and Lady Day 1714. [WSRO Cap.V/1/1]

VIDLER, Thomas (1767 or 68-): Sedlescombe charity school. There 18 April 1772 and 8 May 1775 (still a 'reader'). Baptised 17 January 1768, son of Thomas and Mary. [SSB; PR]

VIGOR (VIGAR), James (1778 or 79-): Sedlescombe charity school. There 29 September 1786 (a 'reader') and 29 September 1787 (a 'writer'). Baptised 18 January 1779, son of James and Mercy (née Hayward). (Sisters Philly, Sarah, also at the school.) [SSB; PR]

VIGOR, Philly (1781-): Sedlescombe charity school. There 21 October 1793 (a 'writer'); not in 20 October 1794 list. Baptised 3 April 1781, daughter of James and Mercy (née Hayward). (Brother James, sister Sarah, also at the school.) [SSB; PR]

VIGOR, Samuel (1788-): Admitted Robertsbridge charity school at its opening 5 April 1796, aged 7. Sponsored by Messrs Munn and Peters. Son of Samuel. [ESRO PAR 477/25/1/1]

VIGOR (VIGAR), Sarah (1777-): Sedlescombe charity school. Admitted 13 May 1787 (as a 'writer'); there 29 September 1787. Baptised 24 March 1777, daughter of James and (Mary) Vigor ('Mary' an error for 'Mercy'; James married Mercy Hayward 19 August 1776). (Brother James, sister Philly, also at the school.) [SSB; PR]

VINALL (VINEALD), Edward (1753-): At Seaford charity school 1765. Baptised 1 January 1754, son of Edward and Mary. [BL Add MS 33,059; PR]

VINAL, William: Admitted Fermor's charity school, Rotherfield, 25 May 1794. [ESRO PAR 465/4/1]

VINE, John: At Seaford charity school 1765. Son of Widow Vine. [BL Add MS 33,059]

WADEY, Charlotte (1788-): Petworth charity school. Admitted 14 July 1800. There 2 years. Baptised 30 March 1788, daughter of Anthony and Margaret. [WSRO Petworth House Archives 1763; PR]

WAGNER, George (1764-1831): At school at Brighton (admission register St John's College, Cambridge); perhaps a pupil of Rev Henry Michell, vicar. Son of George (1722-96), the King's hatter, and Mary Wilhelmina (née Godde) (1731-1808). Born 1764; died 1831. [*SAC* **97**]

WAIT (WEIGHT), Henry: Saunders' charity school, Rye. In lists from September 1722 (?) (first list) to January 1724 (?) (not in 8 April 1724). Son of widow Weight. Perhaps a dissenting family (births of John Wait's children recorded as unbaptised, 1702-06, in parish register). [RSB]

WAIT (WEIGHT), John (1725-): Saunders' charity school, Rye. In lists from 2 July 1735 (not in 9 April 1735) to 14 April 1742 (7 July 1742 notes 'left the school'); had 7 years at the school. Son of John, 'deceased' in list of 14 April 1742. Baptised 2 January 1726, son of John and Mary. (Brother Richard also at the school.) [RSB; PR]

WAIT (WEIGHT), Richard (1733-): Saunders' charity school, Rye. In lists from 13 October 1742 (not in 7 July 1742); midsummer 1748 notes 'Absent 9 weeks' ; Michaelmas 1748 notes 'Absent 6 Months'; not in Christmas 1748. Son of John, deceased. Baptised 6 March 1733, son of John and Mary. (Brother John also at the school.) [RSB; PR]

WAKELIN, Elizabeth: Mayfield charity school. Admitted 29 March 1751; removed 28 June 1751, for non-attendance; probably same as the Elizabeth Wakelin admitted 11 January 1754, as a 'writer', removed 12 July 1754, for non-attendance. (Perhaps a nonconformist family; 4 other Wakelin boys at school, no baptisms in Mayfield parish register; a little later some Mayfield Wakelins members of Burwash Independent Calvinist Chapel.) [MSB]

WAKELIN, James (1754-): Mayfield charity school. Took the place of Norman Austen (admitted 11 July 1760 'but never came'); in list for 17 October 1760; removed 2 May 1766, 'sufficiently learned', after 5¾ years at the school, 1¾ years as a 'writer'. Baptised 9 June 1754, 'base born Child of Elizabeth Wakelin Widow'. [MSB; PR]

WAKELIN, Joseph: Mayfield charity school. Admitted 5 October 1750; removed 27 March 1752, 'well learned'; re-admitted 3 July 1752 (according to 'writer' records he never left); removed 19 January 1753, 'well learned', after 2¼ years at the school, 2 years as a 'writer'. (Perhaps nonconformist; qv WAKELIN, Elizabeth.) [MSB]

WAKELIN, Richard: Mayfield charity school. Admitted 19 January 1753; removed 9 July 1756, 'gone to Service', after 3½ years at the school, 1¼ years as a 'writer'. (Perhaps nonconformist; qv WAKELIN, Elizabeth.) [MSB]

WAKELIN, Robert: Mayfield charity school. Admitted 3 July 1752; removed 11 July 1755, 'well learned', after 3 years at the school, 2¾ years as a 'writer'. (Perhaps nonconformist; qv WAKELIN, Elizabeth.) [MSB]

WAKELIN, Thomas: Mayfield charity school. Admitted 12 July 1754; removed 8 April 1757, 'gone to Service' after 2¾ years at the school, 1 year as a 'writer'. (Perhaps nonconformist; qv WAKELIN, Elizabeth.) [MSB]

WAKELIN, William (1748-): Mayfield charity school. Admitted 24 January 1757; removed 10 April 1761, 'Gone to Service', after 4½ years at the school, 2½ years as a 'writer'. Baptised 13 March 1748, son of Joseph and Elizabeth. [MSB; PR]

WALKER, Edward: Mayfield charity school. Admitted 13 October 1758; removed 6 July 1759, 'suspended for Non Attendance'; re-admitted 11 July 1760; removed 17 October 1760, 'has not attended since last quarter', after ¾ year in all as a 'reader'. [MSB]

WALKER, Edward (1776-): Mayfield charity school. Admitted 9 April 1784; removed 17 January 1788, 'In the Workhouse', after 3¾ years at the school. Baptised 23 June 1776, 'Edward Walker a base-born Son of Sarah

Rose'. [MSB; PR]

WALKER, George: Mayfield charity school. Admitted 9 April 1756; removed 26 October 1759, for non-attendance, after 3½ years at the school, ¼ year as a 'writer'. [MSB]

WALKER, John (1770-): Mayfield charity school. Admitted 17 October 1778; removed 11 July 1783, taken out by parents. Baptised 23 September 1770, son of John and Mary. [MSB; PR]

WALKER, Joseph Webster (1778-): Mayfield charity school. Admitted 7 July 1786; removed 17 January 1788, 'In the Workhouse'. Baptised 25 December 1778, son of Edward and Elizabeth. (Brother William also at the school.) [MSB; PR]

WALKER, William (1776-): Mayfield charity school. Admitted 10 October 1783; removed 17 January 1788, 'In the Workhouse', after 4¼ years at the school. Baptised 28 July 1776, son of Edward and Elizabeth. (Brother Joseph also at the school.) [MSB; PR]

WALLIS (WALLACE), James: Brighton charity school. In 'writers' list of 12 January 1702; had left by December 1705 and gone 'to sea'. [BSB]

WALLS, Andrew (1702-): Brighton charity school. Given prayer book 1716 or 1717. Baptised 20 September 1702, son of William and Anne. [BSB; PR]

WALTER, Ann (1775-): Mayfield charity school. Admitted 6 April 1787; removed 11 July 1788, for non-attendance. Baptised 26 March 1775, daughter of Joseph and Ursula. (Brother Joseph also at the school.) [MSB; PR]

WALTER, Joseph (1767-): Mayfield charity school. Admitted 15 July 1774; taken out by parents after just 1 quarter as a 'reader' (14 October 1774 list). Baptised 22 February 1767, son of Joseph and Ursula. (Sister Ann also at the school.) [MSB: PR]

WARD, Charlotte (1789 or 90-): Admitted Petworth charity school 29 September 1799. Baptised 20 January 1790, daughter of William and Mary. [WSRO Petworth House Archives

1763; PR]

WARD, Edward (1738-): Saunders' charity school, Rye. In lists from Christmas 1746 (not in Michaelmas 1746) to 28 March 1753 (not in 4 July 1753). Baptised 21 February 1738, son of Thomas and Jane. (Brother Thomas also at the school.) [RSB; PR]

[**WARD, James**]: In Wiston school list c1803, and perhaps at the school in 1800. [WSRO Par 211/25/1]

WARD, Thomas (1736-): Saunders' charity school, Rye. In lists from Christmas 1746 (not in Michaelmas 1746) to 14 July 1753, in which marked 'Left Schooll'. Baptised 30 September 1736, son of Thomas and Jane. (Brother Edward also at the school. NB Not the same as Thomas Ward, son of Thomas, below; both of them appear in some lists.) [RSB; PR]

WARD, Thomas: Saunders' charity school, Rye. In lists from midsummer 1751 (not in 3 April 1751) to 16 January 1754 (not in 9 April 1755, next surviving list). Son of Thomas. (NB Not same as Thomas Ward above, also son of Thomas; both of them appear in some lists.) [RSB]

WARNER, William: Grey Coat charity school, Chichester. Left between Michaelmas 1753 and Michaelmas 1754. Given 10s 6d on leaving. [WSRO Cap.V/1/1]

WARNER, William: Midhurst grammar school. Admitted as charity scholar 1793. [*HMGS*]

WARREN: Grey Coat charity school, Chichester. Left between Michaelmas 1755 and Michaelmas 1756. Given 10s 6d on leaving. [WSRO Cap.V/1/1]

WARREN, Christopher: Grey Coat charity school, Chichester. Left between Michaelmas 1761 and Michaelmas 1762. Given 10s 6d on leaving. [WSRO Cap.V/1/1]

WASHER, Cornelius (1695-): Brighton charity school. Admitted as 'reader' sometime after list of (probably) January 1702; in list of 'readers' December 1705. Baptised 3 November 1795, son of Jacob. (Mother probably Sibyl:

married 22 November 1680, Jacob Washer and Sibyl Dudin; another son of theirs baptised 1693. Brother Israel also at the school.) [BSB; PR]

WASHER, Israel (1690-): Brighton charity school. In list of 'readers' of (probably) January 1702; given coat and hat July 1702; joined 'writers' class sometime after 12 January 1702; in list of 'writers' December 1705. Baptised 12 April 1690, son of Jacob and Sibyl (née Dudin). (Brother Cornelius also at the school.) [BSB; PR]

WASHER, Jane (1693-): Brighton girls' charity school. Admitted when school opened 30 September 1702. 'William Washer's daughter'. Probably Jane, baptised 27 August 1693, daughter of William and Joan (only William Washer's daughter in parish registers). [BSB; PR]

WATERS, Edward (1708?-): Saunders' charity school, Rye. In list of September 1722 (?) (first list); 'Went to be an apprentice' 12 February 1723. Probably baptised 1 July 1708, son of John and Susan. [RSB; PR]

WATERS, Edward (1735-): Saunders' charity school, Rye. In lists from 26 October 1743 (not in June 1743 (?)); 2 July 1746 notes 'Absent 9 weeks'; Michaelmas 1746 notes 'Absent 23 weeks' and name crossed out. Son of Samuel, deceased. Baptised 16 March 1735, son of Samuel and Susan. [RSB; PR]

WATERS, Elizabeth (1777-): Mayfield charity school. Admitted 6 July 1787; removed 9 April 1790, taken out by parents but 'Sufficiently Learned'. Baptised 9 February 1777, daughter of Nicholas and Elizabeth. (Brothers Nicholas, Thomas, also at the school.) [MSB; PR]

WATERS, John (1723-): At Eastbourne charity school 1734. Baptised 25 November 1723, son of Samuel. [Chatsworth, Devonshire Collection, Compton Place, Box P; PR]

WATERS, John (1739-): Mayfield charity school. Admitted 28 June 1751; taken out by parents 3 July 1752, after 1 year as a 'reader'. Baptised 2 December 1739, son of Thomas and Anne. (Brother Nicholas, sister Mary, also at the school.) [MSB; BT]

WATERS, Mary (1744-): Mayfield charity school. Admitted 28 June 1751 (with older brother John); removed 19 January 1753, taken out by parents. Baptised 22 July 1744, daughter of Thomas and Anne. (Brothers John, Nicholas, also at the school.) [MSB; PR]

WATERS, Nicholas (1745-): Mayfield charity school. Admitted 8 July 1757; removed 6 July 1759, 'sufficiently Learned', after 2 years at the school, 1¼ years as a 'writer'. Baptised 29 December 1745, son of Thomas and Anne. (Brother John, sister Mary, also at the school.) [MSB; PR]

WATERS, Nicholas: Mayfield charity school. Admitted 8 January 1779; suspended (with brother Thomas) January 1780, 'On acco't of the very ill behaviour of their Father To last during the pleasure of the Trustees'; re-admitted 7 July 1780; removed 9 April 1784, 'Sufficiently Learned'. Son of Nicholas and Elizabeth [qv WATERS, Thomas]. (Brother Thomas, sister Elizabeth, also at the school.) [MSB]

WATERS, Philadelphia (1786-): Admitted Fermor's charity school, Rotherfield, 3 May 1794. Baptised 26 November 1786, daughter of Thomas and Martha. [ESRO PAR 465/4/1; PR]

WATERS, Thomas (1768-): Mayfield charity school. Admitted 12 January 1776; removed 10 October 1777, 'to make room for others more worthy'; re-admitted 9 January 1778; suspended (with brother Nicholas) January 1780, 'On acco't of the very ill behaviour of their Father To last during the pleasure of the Trustees'; re-admitted 7 July 1780; suspended 5 January 1781, 'having a Broken Leg'; re-admitted 6 March 1781; removed October 1781, 'Sufficiently Learned'. Baptised 7 February 1768, son of Nicholas and Elizabeth. (Brother Nicholas, sister Elizabeth, also at the school.) [MSB; PR]

WATSON, John (1736-): Sedlescombe charity school. There 23 June 1748. Baptised 21 March 1736, son of John and Mary. [SSB; PR]

WATTER, William: Midhurst grammar school. Admitted as charity scholar 1795.

[HMGS]

WATTS, John: Brighton charity school. Admitted as a 'reader' sometime after list of (probably) January 1702; in list of 'readers' December 1705. [BSB]

(WEAKHAM): Child of Thomas Weakham at Widow Page's school, Clapham, June 1772. [SAC 71]

WEAVER, James (1763-): Sedlescombe charity school. There 18 April 1772, a 'writer'. Baptised 8 May 1763, son of John and Mary. (Brother William also at the school.) [SSB; PR]

WEAVER, John: Admitted Sedlescombe charity school 26 April 1762. (Sarah Weaver admitted same date.) [SSB]

WEAVER, Sarah: Admitted Sedlescombe charity school 26 April 1762. (John Weaver admitted same date.) [SSB]

WEAVER, William (1761-): Sedlescombe charity school. There 18 April 1772, a 'writer'. Baptised 6 December 1761, son of John and Mary. (Brother James also at the school.) [SSB; PR]

WEEVER, William: Admitted Fermor's charity school, Rotherfield, 3 June 1798. [ESRO PAR 465/4/1]

WEBB, Thomas (1695-): Brighton charity school. Admitted as a 'reader' sometime after list of (probably) January 1702; joined 'writers' class sometime after 12 January 1702; had left by December 1705 and been 'apprenticed to mariner'. Baptised 24 March 1695, son of Richard and Elizabeth (née Brappel). [BSB; PR]

WEBSTER: Son of Sir Thomas Webster, he was at Bear's school, Shermanbury [qv].

WEEKER - see WICKER

WEEKS - see WICKS

WEIGHT - see WAIT

WELLER, Joseph (1724-): At Eastbourne

charity school 1734. Baptised 10 March 1724, son of Thomas and Hannah. [Chatsworth, Devonshire Collection, Compton Place, Box P; PR]

WELLESLEY, Arthur (1769-1852): For a short time a pupil of Rev Henry Michell, vicar of Brighton. Later Duke of Wellington. [*SAC* 97]

WELLS, Alexander - see **SQUIRES, Alexander**

WELLS, James: Mayfield charity school. Admitted 16 October 1761, as a 'writer'; removed 9 April 1762. [MSB]

WELLS, James: Mayfield charity school. Admitted 11 July 1783; removed 17 October 1788, 'Sufficiently Learned'. [MSB]

WELLS, Mary (1779-): Mayfield charity school. Admitted 13 July 1791; removed 17 October 1794, taken out by parents. Baptised 7 March 1779, daughter of James and Susanna. [MSB; PR]

WELLS, William: Mayfield charity school. Admitted 10 July 1761; removed 6 July 1764, taken out by parents, after 3 years at the school, 1 year as a 'writer'. [MSB]

WELLS, William: Mayfield charity school. Admitted 18 April 1783 and again 11 July1783 (probably assigned to different charity source as school expanded); removed 17 October 1788, 'sufficiently Learned'. [MSB]

WENHAM, John: Sedlescombe charity school. There 20 August 1798, a 'reader'. In 13 January 1800 list, at top, as 'writer', but 'John' crossed out and 'William' entered [qv]. [SSB]

WENHAM, William: Sedlescombe charity school. There 25 December 1797, a 'writer', and 20 August 1798, where name crossed through, but also at top of 13 January 1800 list, 'John' Wenham crossed through and 'William' entered. [SSB]

WEST, Elizabeth (1787-): Mayfield charity school. Admitted 13 April 1798; removed 17 October 1800, taken out by parents (NB Incorrectly identified as 'Elizabeth Medhurst').

Baptised 15 May 1787, daughter of James and Elizabeth. (One brother, 2 sisters, also at the school.) [MSB; PR]

[WEST, Frances (1793-)]: In Wiston school list c1803, and perhaps at the school in 1800. Baptised 16 June 1793, Fanny, daughter of John and Mary. (Brother Richard also at the school.) [WSRO Par 211/25/1; PR]

WEST, Hannah (1777-): Mayfield charity school. Admitted 10 April 1789; removed 7 January 1791, taken out by parents. Baptised 18 May 1777, daughter of James and Elizabeth. (One brother, 2 sisters, also at the school.) [MSB; PR]

WEST, James (1781-): Mayfield charity school. Admitted 7 January 1791; removed 9 January 1795, taken out by parents. Baptised 18 February 1781, son of James and Elizabeth. (Three sisters also at the school.) [MSB; PR]

WEST, John (1754-): Saunders' charity school, Rye. Admitted 8 May 1765; in lists to Lady Day 1769 (not in Michaelmas 1769). Son of Jane West. Baptised 6 August 1754, son of Thomas and Jane. [RSB; PR]

WEST, Joseph (1765-): Mayfield charity school. Admitted 9 April 1773; removed 7 April 1775, withdrawn by parents. Baptised 1 January 1766, son of Jeffery and Mary (twin brother of Benjamin, who was buried 30 September 1772). [MSB; PR]

WEST, Mary (1784 or 85-): Mayfield charity school. Admitted 14 October 1796; removed 12 July 1799, taken out by parents. Baptised (Molly), 9 January 1785, daughter of James and Elizabeth. (One brother, 2 sisters, also at the school.) [MSB; PR]

[WEST, Richard (1795-)]: In Wiston school list c1803, and possibly at the school in 1800. Baptised 31 May 1795, son of John and Mary. (Sister Frances also at the school.) [WSRO Par 211/25/1; PR]

WESTON, Ann (1774-): Mayfield charity school. Admitted 11 July 1783; removed 5 January 1787, 'Sufficiently Learned'. Baptised 8 July 1774, daughter of William and Anne. [MSB; PR]

WESTON, Ann (1781-): Mayfield charity school. Admitted 15 October 1790; removed 6 January 1792, taken out by parents. Baptised either 9 September 1781, daughter of Robert and Ann (brothers Robert, William, also at the school) or 21 October 1781, daughter of Stephen and Ann. [MSB; PR]

WESTON, Ann: Mayfield charity school. Admitted 11 April 1800; removed 13 July 1804, taken out by parents. Probably baptised either 24 November 1793, daughter of John and Elizabeth, or 31 August 1794, daughter of Richard and Elizabeth. [MSB; PR]

WESTON, Edward (1744-): Mayfield charity school. No formal admission recorded; first appears in list for 6 April 1753; removed 10 January 1755, 'his father able to pay', after 1¾ years as a 'reader'. Baptised 13 September 1744, son of John and Katharine. [MSB; PR]

WESTON, Edward (1749-): Mayfield charity school. Admitted 8 April 1757; removed 10 April 1761, 'sufficiently learn'd', after 4 years at the school, ¾ year as a 'writer'. Baptised 9 November 1749, son of Edward and Margaret. (Sister Elizabeth, probably brother Richard, also at the school.) [MSB; PR]

WESTON, Elizabeth (1748-): Mayfield charity school. Admitted 9 April 1756; removed 11 January 1760, taken out by parents, after 3¾ years at the school, ½ year as a 'writer'. Baptised 1 May 1748, daughter of Edward and Margaret. (Brother Edward, probably brother Richard, also at the school.) [MSB; PR]

WESTON, Hannah (1779?-): Mayfield charity school. Admitted 12 October 1787; removed 6 January 1792, taken out by parents. Probably baptised 17 October 1779, daughter of Stephen and Sarah (another Hannah Weston baptised 3 November 1776, daughter of Richard, husbandman, and Sarah (died 1780), would have left late for this period). (Brother Stephen probably also at the school.) [MSB; PR]

WESTON, Henry (1787-): Admitted Robertsbridge charity school at its opening, 5 April 1796. Sponsored by Mr Richard Noakes. Baptised 1 June 1787 (aged 23 days), son of Thomas and Mary (née Bourne). [ESRO PAR 477/25/1/1; Salehurst PR]

WESTON, Jenny: Mayfield charity school. Admitted 19 January 1798; removed 14 October 1801, 'sufficiently learned'. (Probably sister to William admitted same date.) [MSB]

WESTON, John (1738-): Sedlescombe charity school. There 23 June 1748. Baptised 17 November 1738, son of William and Mary. [SSB; PR]

WESTON, John (1750 or 51-): Mayfield charity school. Admitted 8 January 1762; removed 15 October 1762, for non-attendance, after ¾ year as a 'reader'. Baptised 16 January 1751, son of Robert (buried 24 August 1755) and Mary (buried 20 June 1753). (Sisters Martha, Mary, also at the school.) [MSB; PR]

WESTON, John (1769-): Mayfield charity school. Admitted 7 April 1780; son of Edward and identified in lists as 'JW Carpenter' to distinguish him from 'JW Thatcher'; suspended 6 March 1781, 'on Acco't of his having the Itch'; re-admitted October 1781; suspended 12 April 1782, again 'on Acco't of his having the Itch'; apparently re-admitted 11 July 1783; removed 7 July 1786, 'Sufficiently Learned'. Baptised 27 December 1769, son of Edward and Sarah. (Brother Stephen, sister Margaret, also at the school.) [MSB; PR]

WESTON, John (1772-): Mayfield charity school. Admitted January 1780; son of John and identified in lists as 'JW Thatcher' to distinguish him from 'JW Carpenter'; removed 6 July 1781, taken out by parents. Baptised 1 March 1772, son of John and Susanna. (Mother buried 28 May 1779; father married secondly, 29 August 1780, Sarah Romery.) [MSB; PR]

WESTON, John (1789-): Mayfield charity school. Admitted 8 January 1796; removed 11 April 1800, taken out by parents. Baptised 13 September 1789, son of John and Sarah. [MSB; PR]

WESTON, Margaret (1759 or 60-): Mayfield charity school. Admitted 22 April 1768; removed 21 April 1769, for non-attendance after 1 year as a 'reader'. Baptised 13 January 1760, daughter of Edward and Sarah. (Brothers John, Stephen, also at the school.) [MSB; PR]

WESTON, Martha (1749-): Mayfield charity

school. Admitted 20 January 1758 (with older sister Mary); removed 4 May 1759, taken out by her uncle, Thomas Weston, after 1¼ years as a 'reader'. Baptised 5 May 1749, daughter of Robert (buried 24 August 1755) and Mary (buried 20 June 1753). (Brother John, sister Mary, also at the school.) [MSB; PR]

WESTON, Mary (1747-): Mayfield charity school. Admitted 20 January 1758 (with sister Martha); removed 4 May 1759, taken out by her uncle, Thomas Weston, after 1¼ years as a 'reader'. Born 30 January 1747, baptised 10 February 1747, daughter of Robert (buried 24 August 1755) and Mary (buried 20 June 1753). (Brother John, sister Martha, also at the school.) [MSB; PR]

WESTON, Mary: Mayfield charity school. Admitted 11 July 1783; removed 13 September 1786, for non-attendance. Baptised either 26 July 1774, daughter of John and Elizabeth, or 21 July 1775, daughter of Thomas and Martha (brother William also at the school). [MSB; PR]

WESTON, Richard (1751?-): Mayfield charity school. Admitted 26 October 1759; removed 9 July 1762, for non-attendance, after 2¾ years as a 'reader'. Baptised either 13 October 1749, son of William and Sarah (brother William also at the school) or 5 November 1751, son of Edward and Margaret (brother Edward, sister Elizabeth, also at the school); latter more probable as his brother Edward joined/left at similar ages. [MSB; PR]

WESTON, Robert (1772-): Mayfield charity school. Admitted 7 July 1780; removed 10 October 1783. Baptised 13 November 1772, son of Robert and Anne. (Brother William, perhaps sister Anne, also at the school.) [MSB; PR]

WESTON, Stephen (1756 or 57-): Mayfield charity school. Admitted 11 January 1765; removed 16 October 1767, for non-attendance, after 2½ years at the school, ¾ year as a 'writer'. Baptised 9 January 1757, son of Edward and Sarah. (Brother John, sister Margaret, also at the school.) [MSB; PR]

WESTON, Stephen (1787-): Mayfield charity school. Admitted 17 October 1794; removed 19

January 1798, taken out by parents. Baptised either 8 January 1783, son of John and Susan (brother John at the school), or 13 June 1787, son of Stephen and Sarah (sister Hannah probably at the school); latter more probable as former would have been rather old on leaving, and latter's joining age is compatible with the 10 adjacent joining scholars. [MSB; PR]

WESTON, Triphena: Mayfield charity school. Admitted 8 January 1796; removed 10 January 1800, taken out by parents. [MSB]

WESTON, William (1744 or 45-): Mayfield charity school. Admitted 28 June 1751; removed 4 October 1751, for non-attendance; admitted again 3 July 1752; removed 14 October 1755, 'well learned', after 3¼ years at the school, 2¼ years as a 'writer'. Baptised 11 January 1745, son of William and Sarah. (Brother Richard perhaps also at the school.) [MSB; PR]

WESTON, William (1778-): Mayfield charity school. Admitted 13 September 1786; removed 7 January 1791, 'Sufficiently Learned'. Baptised 3 June 1778, son of Thomas and Martha. (NB 5 other William Westons baptised in Mayfield this period, but either dead or too young for this period. Sister Mary perhaps also at the school.) [MSB; PR]

WESTON, William (1786-): Mayfield charity school. Admitted 14 October 1796; removed 12 October 1798; apparently re-admitted January 1799, when 'William Wilson' in list changed to 'William Weston'; removed 10 April 1801, taken out by parents. Baptised 19 June 1786, son of Robert and Ann. (Brother Robert, perhaps sister Ann, also at the school.) [MSB; PR]

WESTON, William: Mayfield charity school. Admitted 19 January 1798; removed 11 July 1800, taken out by parents. (Probably brother to Jenny admitted same date.) [MSB; PR]

WESTOVER, John (1744 or 45-): Mayfield charity school. Admitted 28 June 1751; removed 9 April 1755, 'sufficiently learn'd'; re-admitted 9 January 1756; removed 9 April 1756, 'sufficiently learned', after 4 years in total at the school, 1 year as a 'writer'. Baptised 20 January 1745, son of William and

Sarah. (Brother Thomas also at the school.) [MSB; PR]

WESTOVER, Thomas (1740-): Mayfield charity school. Admitted at formal opening of the school 29 June 1750, but may have been there up to ¾ year earlier, as master paid from Michaelmas 1749; removed 6 April 1753, 'well learn'd'; re-admitted 11 January 1754; removed 12 April 1754, 'well learned'; had 2¾ years as a 'writer'. Baptised 24 February 1740, son of William and Sarah. (Brother John also at the school.) [MSB; PR]

WEYMARK - see WIMARK

WHEELER: Button's school, Lewes. To recite at a 'Public Examination' at the *Star Assembly Room*, 22 June 1797. [*SWA* 19.6.97]

WHEELER, James (c1700-): Grey Coat charity school, Chichester. Admitted at its opening Lady Day 1710. Aged 11 at Lady Day 1711. There Lady Day 1714. [WSRO Cap.V/1/1]

WHISKEY: A poor girl of West Grinstead who received schooling 1717 (and probably 1718), under the Dowlin charity. [WSRO Par 95/1/1/3]

[WHITCOMBE, Francis]: Perhaps at Midhurst grammar school. A native of Midhurst and elected to Winchester 1768. [*HMGS*]

(WHITE): A poor child of West Grinstead who received schooling from Goody Trowers, 1703, under the Dowlin charity. [WSRO Par 95/1/1/3]

WHITE, Christopher (c1785-): Parsons' boarding school, Beckley. With brother Henry, aged 8, ran away from school on Thursday, 19 October 1797. Parsons advertised in the *Sussex Weekly Advertiser* on 13 November 1797, that they had gone to 'Benjamin Linghams, their Father-in-law, at Crowhurst', who on 23 October 1797 ordered them to return to school, but they 'have not been heard of since'. Described as 'aged twelve years, a short stout lad, has dark hair' and wearing a blue coat when they went away. Any person with information was asked to contact Parsons at Beckley, or two named persons at Icklesham, or

another at Ticehurst; they would be 'satisfied for their trouble and all reasonable expences paid.' The following week, 20 November 1797, the *Sussex Weekly Advertiser* reported that, 'The two run-away school-boys... have been discovered and returned to their friends.'

WHITE, Henry (c1789-): Parsons' boarding school, Beckley. Ran away from school, 19 October 1797, with 12-year-old older brother Christopher [qv]. Described in advertisement by school as 'eight years old, pale complexion, and light hair' and wearing a blue coat when they went away.

WHITEMAN, Thomas: Saunders' charity school, Rye. In lists from 10 April 1745 (not in 4 July 1744); left school 6 April 1748. Son of Thomas, 'deceased' in list of 14 August 1745. [RSB]

WICKENS, James: Admitted Fermor's charity school, Rotherfield, 29 April 1798. Son of William. [ESRO PAR 465/4/1]

WICKENS, Joseph (1785-): Admitted Fermor's charity school, Rotherfield, 3 May 1794. 'Son of Joseph Stephenson's wife'. Baptised 14 August 1785, son of John Wickens and Sarah. (John Wickens from Boarshead buried 7 June 1785; Joseph Stephenson and Sarah Wickens, widow, married 4 October 1789.) [ESRO PAR 465/4/1; PR]

WICKER (WEEKER) Ann: Mayfield charity school. Admitted 11 January 1760; removed 9 July 1762, for non-attendance; re-admitted 15 October 1762; removed 6 July 1764, taken out by parents, after 4¼ years at the school in total, 1¼ years as a 'writer'. [MSB]

WICKER, John (1744-): Mayfield charity school. Admitted 18 October 1754; removed 8 July 1757, taken home by parents, after 2½ years at the school, 1½ years as a 'writer'. Baptised 28 December 1744, son of Thomas and Sarah. (Brothers Thomas, William, also at the school.) [MSB; PR]

WICKER, John (1791-): Mayfield charity school. Admitted 11 July 1800; removed 6 April 1804, taken out by parents. Baptised 17 July 1791, son of John and Sarah. [MSB; PR]

WICKER (WEEKER), Thomas (1753-): Mayfield charity school. Admitted 6 July 1759; removed 13 April 1764, 'having been a sufficient time in the School', after 4¾ years there, 1¾ years as a 'writer'. Baptised 29 April 1753, son of Thomas and Sarah. (Brothers John, William, also at the school.) [MSB; PR]

WICKER, William (1757-): Mayfield charity school. Admitted 18 October 1765; removed 22 April 1768, for non-attendance, 'but pretty well Learn'd', after 2½ years at the school, ¾ year as a 'writer'. Baptised 26 June 1757, son of Thomas and Sarah. (Brothers John, Thomas, also at the school.) [MSB; PR]

WICKS / WEEKS

WEEKS: At school at Brightling 1739-41. On 9 June 1739, John Fuller paid Goody Weeks 3s 4d 'to pay for her Girls Schooling 22 weeks'; 19 January 1742, he paid 'Weeks his wife for her Girls schooling 48 weeks to Xmas last att 2d', 8s; 4 January 1743, again 48 weeks at 2d a week, 8s. [ESRO SAS/RF 15/28]

WICKS (WEEKS), Anne (1733-): Brightling girls' charity school. Admitted 9 January 1743; there to 23-month period ending 22 March 1744, in which she attended on 235 school days. Baptised 28 October 1733, daughter of Richard and Anne. [ESRO PAR 254/25/1; PR]

WICKS (WEEKS), Barbara (1725-): Brightling girls' charity school. Admitted 21 April 1738; there to year ending 1 May 1739, in which year she attended on 73 school days. Baptised 1 August 1725, daughter of Richard and Barbara (née Wimble). [ESRO PAR 254/25/1; PR]

WICKS (WIKES), Sarah (1738-): Brightling girls' charity school. Admitted between 2 April 1744 and 31 August 1745, in which period she attended on 238 school days; there to period 10 June 1749 to 29 September 1752, in which she attended on 145 school days; had 1,325 days at the school in total. Baptised 24 June 1738, daughter of Thomas and Mary. [ESRO PAR 254/25/1; PR]

WILKINS, Matthew (1694-): Brighton charity school. In list of 'readers' of (probably) January 1702; given coat and hat July 1702; joined 'writers' class sometime after 12 January 1702; in list of 'writers' December 1705; when he left was 'apprenticed to mariner'. Baptised 28 February 1694, son of Matthew and Elizabeth (née Prim). [BSB; PR]

WILLARD, Robert (1791-): Petworth charity school. Admitted 5 August 1799; had left by Michaelmas 1801. Baptised 20 February 1791, son of William and Elizabeth Janes Willard. [WSRO Petworth House Archives 1763; PR]

WILLARD, Robert (1787-): Admitted Robertsbridge charity school 29 August 1796 (school opened 5 April 1796). Sponsored by Mrs F. Hickes (Francis Hickes was another subscriber). Baptised 5 August 1787, son of Thomas and Ann (née Jarvis). [ESRO PAR 477/25/1/1; Salehurst PR]

WILLIAMS: Button's school, Lewes. To recite, in French, at a 'Public Examination' at the *Star Assembly Room*, 22 June 1797. [*SWA* 19.6.97]

WILLIAMS, Richard (1692-): Brighton charity school. In list of 'writers' 12 January 1702, and again December 1705. Baptised 24 January 1692, son of William and Debra (née Wingham). (Brother William also at the school.) [BSB; PR]

WILLIAMS, William (1697-): Brighton charity school. In list of 'readers' December 1705. Baptised 5 December 1697, son of William. (Mother probably Debrah: married 15 November 1786, William Williams and Debrah Wingham; and see baptism of Richard Williams above. Brother Richard also at the school.) [BSB; PR]

WILMSHURST, Elizabeth: Mayfield charity school. Admitted 19 January 1753; removed 9 April 1756, 'suspended to make room for others where more Occasion is', after 3¼ years at the school, still a 'reader'. [MSB]

WILMSHURST, George: Mayfield charity school. Admitted 26 October 1759; removed 8 April 1763, taken out by parents, after 3½ years at the school, 1 year as a 'writer'. [MSB]

WILMSHURST, Hannah: Mayfield charity school. Admitted 21 April 1769; removed, 'for this Quarter', 20 July 1770, after 1¼ years as a 'reader'; re-admitted 4 February 1771; removed 19 April 1771, 'Sufficiently Learned' [?], after 1½ years at the school. [MSB]

WILMSHURST, John (1713-): Saunders' charity school, Rye. In lists from September 1722 (?) (first list) to April 1725 (?); not in 19 May 1725 but in 11 August 1725 and January 1726 (?); not in 4 May 1726. Baptised 20 December 1713, son of Matthew and Elizabeth. [RSB; PR]

WILMSHURST, John: Mayfield charity school. Admitted 4 May 1759; removed 10 July 1761, 'sufficiently learned', after 2¼ years at the school, 1 year as a 'writer'. [MSB]

WILMSHURST, Mary: Mayfield charity school. Admitted 28 June 1751; removed 14 November 1752, for non-attendance (still a 'reader'). [MSB]

WILMSHURST, Simon (-1772): Mayfield charity school. Admitted 21 July 1769; removed 9 July 1772, 'Dead', after 3 years at the school, 1½ years as a 'writer'. Buried 9 June 1772. [MSB; PR]

WILMSHURST, Stephen: Mayfield charity school. Admitted 9 July 1772; removed 5 April 1776, 'Sufficiently Learned', after 3¾ years at the school, 2¼ years as a 'writer'. [MSB]

WILMSHURST, Susan: Mayfield charity school. Admitted 11 July 1755; removed 6 July 1759, 'Sufficiently Learned', after 4 years at the school, ¾ year as a 'writer'. [MSB]

WILSON, George: Mayfield charity school. Admitted 11 July 1788; removed 6 July 1792, taken out by parents but 'sufficiently Learned'. [MSB]

WILSON, Henry (1715-): Saunders' charity school, Rye. In lists from December 1724 (?) (not in 8 April 1724) to June 1725 (?) (not in 11 August 1725). Baptised 20 March 1715, son of Henry and Martha. [RSB; PR]

WILSON, John (1788-): Petworth charity school. Admitted 10 July 1796. (Had left by Michaelmas 1801.) Born 16 August 1788, baptised 16 November 1788, son of Thomas and Frances. [WSRO Petworth House Archives 1763; PR]

WILSON, Richard (1782-): Mayfield charity school. Admitted 9 April 1790; removed 11 July 1794, 'sufficiently learned'. Baptised 15 December 1782, son of Richard and Elizabeth. (Brother William also at the school.) [MSB; PR]

WILSON, William (1787-): Mayfield charity school. Admitted 11 July 1794; in list for 11 January 1799 name 'Wilson' crossed out and replaced by 'Weston' (as also in lists for April 1799 and July 1799). Baptised 6 May 1787, son of Richard and Elizabeth. (Brother Richard also at the school.) [MSB; PR]

WIMARK/WEYMARK

WEYMARK (WYMARKE), John (1691-): Brighton charity school. In 'writers' list of 12 January 1702; given coat and hat July 1702; had left by December 1705 and been 'apprenticed to a Barber & Tayler'. Baptised 22 February 1691, son of John and Elizabeth (née Gray). [BSB; PR]

WIMARK, Mary (1694-): Brighton girls' charity school. Admitted when school opened 30 September 1702. 'John Wimark's daughter'. Baptised 22 July 1694, Thomas and Mary, twins of John and Mary. (Only JW daughter in parish register this period. Brother Thomas - not the twin - at the boys' charity school.) [BSB; PR]

WIMARK, Thomas (1697-): Brighton charity school. Added at end of list of 'readers' December 1705 (ie joined subsequently). Baptised 21 March 1697, son of John and Mary. (Sister Mary at the girls' charity school.) [BSB; PR]

WINGHAM, Adam (1708-): Brighton charity school. Given prayer book 1718. Baptised 26 September 1708, son of Robert. [BSB; PR]

WINGHAM, Barak (1689-): Brighton charity school. In list of 'writers' of 12 January 1702; had left by December 1705 and been 'apprenticed'. Baptised 13 October 1689, son of Adam and Elizabeth (née Greenstid). [BSB; PR]

WISE, William (1786-): Sedlescombe charity school. There 21 October 1793, a 'reader'; moved to a 'writer' 21 October 1794; there 25 December 1797 and 20 August 1798. Baptised 21 November 1786, son of Henry and Lydia. [SSB; PR]

WITT: Grey Coat charity school, Chichester. Left between Michaelmas 1764 and Michaelmas 1765. Given 10s 6d on leaving. [WSRO Cap.V/1/1]

WOOD/WOODS

WOODS, Harriet (c1789-): Admitted Robertsbridge charity school at its opening, 5 April 1796, aged 6. Sponsored by Mr Charles Woods. Daughter of John. (Subscribers could nominate 1 child, who had to be a poor child and not their own; but perhaps could be a poor relative?) [ESRO PAR 477/25/1/1]

WOOD, Henry (1756-): At Seaford charity school 1765. Baptised 12 February 1756, son of William and Mary. [BL Add MS 33,059; PR]

WOOD, John: Brighton charity school. In list of 'readers' of (probably) January 1702; in list of 'writers' December 1705; when he left, went 'to husbandry'. (Too many JWs in parish register to identify.) [BSB]

WOOD, Robert (1784-): Admitted Fermor's charity school, Rotherfield, 3 May 1794. Baptised 24 October 1784, son of Robert and Elizabeth. [ESRO PAR 465/4/1; PR]

WOOD, William (1689-): Brighton charity school. In lists of 'writers' 12 January 1702 and December 1705; when he left, went 'to sea'. Baptised 20 October 1689, son of William and Elizabeth. [BSB; PR]

WOOD, William (1776-): Sedlescombe charity school. There 29 September 1784 and 29 September 1786; line through name in latter but in list for 29 September 1787 (still a 'reader'). Baptised 18 February 1776, son of William and Lucretia. [SSB; PR]

WOODGATE, Thomas (1787?-): Admitted Fermor's charity school, Rotherfield, 3 June 1798. Probably baptised 9 December 1787, son of Thomas and Philadelphia. [ESRO PAR 465/4/1; PR]

WOODHATCH, Francis: At 'Horsham Academy', ie Thornton's school [qv]. A sheet with printed illustrated frame and heading, 'The Five Senses', with a handwritten 4-line verse, subscribed 'Francis Woodhatch - 1794 - Horsham Academy', has survived.

WOODNUT, John (c1705-): Grey Coat charity school, Chichester. Admitted between Lady Day 1713 and Lady Day 1714, aged 8. [WSRO Cap.V/1/1]

WOODNOT, Matthew (c1702-): Grey Coat charity school, Chichester. Admitted at opening of school Lady Day 1710. Aged 8 at Lady Day 1711. There Lady Day 1714. [WSRO Cap.V/1/1]

WOODYER, Richard (c1701-): Grey Coat charity school, Chichester. Admitted at opening of school Lady Day 1710. Aged 9 at Lady Day 1711. There Lady Day 1714. [WSRO Cap.V/1/1]

WOOLGAR, Elizabeth (1755-): At Seaford charity school 1765. Baptised 10 February 1755, daughter of Richard and Susannah. [BL Add MS 33,059; PR]

WOOLLGAR, Thomas (1761-1821): Lewes grammar school. Born 1761 in Kent; when 2, family moved to Lewes; educated at grammar school, under Austen. Went into business; married, 1794, Anne Webb, and soon after retired from business, devoting himself to scientific research and public affairs. Died 1821, buried at Southover. [Lower *Worthies*]

WOOLLETT, John: Saunders' charity school, Rye. Admitted 28 June 1769; in lists to Christmas 1770 (not in midsummer 1773, next surviving list). Son of John, 'deceased' in list for Lady Day 1770. [RSB]

WOOLVIN, Henry: Eastbourne charity school. Admitted 10 April 1769; still there January 1771. Son of William. [SAS Budgen MS v.105]

WORGER, William (1723-): At Eastbourne charity school 1734. Baptised 27 November 1723, son of John and Susan. [Chatsworth,

Devonshire Collection, Compton Place, Box P; PR]

WORSELL, Richard (1774-): Saunders' charity school, Rye. Admitted 16 July 1783; in lists to 24 June 1785, last surviving 18th century list. Baptised 19 March 1774, son of Thomas and Jane. (Brother Thomas also at the school.) [RSB; PR]

WORSELL, Thomas (1769-): Saunders' charity school, Rye. Admitted 5 April 1780; in lists to 24 June 1783, which notes 'left School' (not in 29 September 1783). Baptised 29 April 1769, son of Thomas and Jane. (Brother Richard also at the school.) [RSB; PR]

WYATT, Hugh - see **PENFOLD, Hugh**

WYNDHAM, George (1787-1869): Midhurst grammar school. Then, at 12, entered the Navy. Later first Baron Leconfield. [*HMGS*]

YOUNG, Richard: Admitted Fermor's charity school, Rotherfield, 25 May 1794. [ESRO PAR 465/4/1]

INDEX OF PERSONAL NAMES

This index includes the names of all persons mentioned in the main text of the Introduction and the three Schedules (excluding footnotes and sources, but including captions to illustrations). Where the name of a school includes the name of a person, the name of the person in this context is not indexed (this arises when the name of the founder identifies the school; without exception, the founder is separately mentioned elsewhere, and is thus indexed).

No attempt has been made to distinguish between different individuals with the same name, or the same name spelt in different ways. Married women are indexed under both maiden and married surnames, when these are both given. Under a surname, first are given references to persons whose Christian name or style or status is unknown; then, under 'fam', any references to the general family; then to persons whose Christian name is not known but whose style or status is indicated in the sources - these are entered under designations such as 'child' [ch], Dame, Miss, Mr, Mrs, Rev, Widow [Wid], &c; then names are listed under first Christian names in alphabetical order. Second Christian names have been ignored. Certain common Christian names have been abbreviated, as follows:

Bart	Bartholomew	Hen	Henry	Rob	Robert
Ben	Benjamin	Jas	James	Sam	Samuel
Cath	Catherine	Jos	Joseph	Ste	Stephen
Chas	Charles	Kath	Katherine	Susan	Susannah
Dan	Daniel	Matt	Matthew	Thos	Thomas
Edw	Edward	Nat	Nathaniel	Wm	William
Eliz	Elizabeth	Nich	Nicholas		
Geo	George	Rd	Richard		

Alphabetization is word-by-word. Abbreviations have been indexed according to the abbreviated spelling (thus 'Jas' comes after 'Jane', 'Rd' comes before 'Reuben').

Because the index is comprehensive, repetition of information will necessarily occur when a person is mentioned in connection with an item that is referred to in different parts of the volume - all mentions of the person's name are indexed. (It is noted that the documentary sources of such information will normally only be given at one point in the volume.)

   * An asterisk after a page number indicates that there are on that page references to two or more different persons of that name.

   A page number in bold type indicates that there is on that page a biographical entry (ie in Schedule 2 or 3). When a biographical entry runs over onto another page the subject of the entry is only indexed once (the number of the page where the entry begins is given).

Ino

A SELECTIVE SUBJECT INDEX

This index does not include subjects frequently mentioned throughout the volume, such as charity schools, SPCK, the subjects taught at schools, place names, and the like, for which there are too many references to make indexing practical or helpful. The index covers a limited number of subjects for which there are scattered references through the volume, and which may be of interest to readers.

For the subjects listed, the index is comprehensive (covering the main text of the Introduction and the three Schedules, excluding footnotes and sources but including captions to illustrations); there will therefore be some duplication when the same item is referred to in different parts of the volume. (It is noted that the documentary source of such an item will normally only be given at one point in the volume.)

* An asterisk after a page number indicates that the indexed subject or description applies to or is associated with more than one named person on that page.